TRANSPORTATION PLANNING
HANDBOOK

Second Edition

John D. Edwards, Jr., P.E.

Editor

Institute of Transportation Engineers

Library of Congress Cataloging-in-Publication Data

Transportation planning handbook / John D. Edwards, editor — 2nd ed.
    p.   cm.
    "Institute of Transportation Engineers."
    Companion volume to: Traffic engineering handbook. 5th ed.
    Includes bibiographical reference and index.
    ISBN 0–935403–33–7
    1. Transportation—Planning—Handbooks, manuals, etc.
  I. Edwards, John D., 1933–   .   II. Institute of Transportation
Engineers.   III. Traffic engineering handbook.
HE152.5.T73   1999
388' .068—dc21   99-41567
                                                  CIP

The Institute of Transportation Engineers (ITE) is an international educational and scientific association of transportation and traffic engineers and other professionals who are responsible for meeting mobility and safety needs. The Institute facilitates the application of technology and scientific principles to research, planning, functional design, implementation, operation, policy development and management for any mode of transportation by promoting professional development of members, supporting and encouraging education, stimulating research, developing public awareness, and exchanging professional information; and by maintaining a central point of reference and action.

Founded in 1930, the Institute serves as a gateway to knowledge and advancement through meetings, seminars, and publications; and through our network of more than 15,000 members working in some 80 countries. The Institute also has more than 70 local and regional chapters and more than 90 student chapters that provide additional opportunities for information exchange, participation and networking.

Institute of Transportation Engineers
525 School St., S.W., Suite 410
Washington, DC 20024-2797 USA
Telephone: +1 (202) 554-8050
Fax: +1 (202) 863-5486
ITE on the Web: http://www.ite.org

ISBN: 0-935403-33-7
Publication No. TB-011A
1000/TA/300

This book was previously published by Prentice-Hall, Inc.

Contents

Preface

When the Institute of Traffic Engineers was created in 1930, one of the key roles the leadership identified for this new organization was to develop and disseminate technical information. Professionals and lay persons alike needed material to provide an objective understanding of transportation issues.

Consequently, in 1939, when ITE had fewer than 200 members, the Institute accepted a proposal from the National Conservation Bureau to prepare the first traffic engineering handbook. This publication became a reality in 1941. It was truly a milestone accomplishment, representing the first book dedicated to the subject of traffic engineering.

The Institute has taken seriously the need to provide objective information pertaining to the state-of-the-art in transportation engineering. The 1941 *Traffic Engineering Handbook* was subsequently updated in 1950 and 1965. In 1976 and again in 1982, the first and second editions of the *Transportation and Traffic Engineering Handbook* were prepared. The revised title was a reflection of the broadening perspective being given to traffic engineering by the profession.

In updating the 1982 edition of the *Transportation and Traffic Engineering Handbook,* the editorial committee realized that the amount of relevant information that warranted inclusion had become extensive. Justification existed to prepare both a *Traffic Engineering Handbook* and a *Transportation Planning Handbook.* The initial publication of these two separate *Handbooks* occurred in 1992.

The editorial committee working on the 1999 update of the *Handbooks* determined that the practice of preparing two separate handbooks should be continued. Each *Handbook* was carefully reviewed for state-of-the-art content and completeness. At the same time, both *Handbooks* are designed to be stand-alone publications. As a result, some duplication of material is necessary to assure that each *Handbook* adequately covers the necessary subject matter.

The primary purpose of the *Handbooks* is to provide practicing professionals and other interested parties with a basic day-to-day source of reference on the proven techniques of the practice. The *Handbooks* provide guidelines, and are not a documentation of standard practices. Although not intended to be used as textbooks, the Handbooks should serve as a valuable reference source. Each *Handbook* chapter contains a listing of key references.

The transportation engineering profession continues to broaden in scope. This is reflected by the new chapters in the 1999 editions that were not part of the 1992 editions. The world remains a dynamic place, and transportation continues to be key to economic competitiveness and quality of life. New issues—such as sustainable transportation, smart growth, seamless intermodal systems, innovative financing, and a recognition of the importance of better operating the transportation system—increasingly are becoming a part of what the profession must address. Many of these issues are touched upon in these *Handbooks.* No doubt the editors of future editions of the Handbooks will have the opportunity to significantly expand on the current knowledge base.

Dennis L. Christiansen, *P.E.*
Senior Editor

Wolfgang S. Homburger, *P.E.*
Associate Senior Editor

Acknowledgments

The planning and execution of the *Transportation Planning Handbook* was a team effort between the authors, editors, copywriters and ITE staff. This book was the result of many hours of cooperative efforts between persons located in many parts of the continent. It is a tribute to our modern communications systems that the work was completed so quickly and successfully.

Work began on the Second Edition in 1997 with the appointment of the Editorial Board and the Editors, and the selection of Authors and Chapter Reviewers. The Handbook Editors (there are two) along with the content review panel established the format and content of the books in early 1997. The Editors and Authors provided an outline of the chapter contents and the Authors did the rest. Each chapter was reviewed by a panel with that particular field of expertise. Comments and suggestions by the chapter reviewers were incorporated in the text where appropriate. The organization and planning for the 2nd Edition went very smoothly as compared to the first edition.

I am appreciative of the cooperative efforts of the authors and reviewers. My role as the editor was greatly assisted by those chapter authors who expeditiously provided their manuscript on schedule and addressed review comments meticulously. My special thanks to them. Thomas W. Brahms, Shannon Gore Peters, Ann O'Neill and Agneta Melén-Wilmot of the ITE Headquarters Staff contributed significantly to the mechanics of getting this book published and I am forever grateful to them.

And finally, I must say I have never worked with a more cooperative and energetic editorial board—Dennis Christiansen, Jim Pline and Wolf Homburger—who "hung in there" with me until the project was finished.

John D. Edwards, Jr.
Editor

Handbook Editorial Committee

Chair: Dennis L. Christiansen

Editors: John D. Edwards, Jr.
James L. Pline

Associate Editor: Wolfgang S. Homburger

Panel of Chapter Reviewers

Eugene D. Arnold

Richard F. Beaubien

Brian S. Bochner

Daniel Brand

Andrew Clark

Susanne Cook

Allan Davis

Frederick C. Dock

Richard D. Dowling

Wendell Fletcher

Allan T. Gonseth

Wulf Grote

Joseph W. Guyton

James R. Hanks

Robert C. Hazlett

Anthony Heppelman

Lester A. Hoel

Kevin Hooper

Walter H. Kraft

Thomas F. Larwin

Eva Lerner-Lam

Herbert S. Levinson

Win Lindeman

Stephen C. Lockwood

William J. Martin

Douglas McLeod

John Mason

Jeffrey S. Olsen

Thomas Parkinson

Norbert J. Pointner

Edward Papazian

Richard H. Pratt

Elizabeth Randall

Carlton C. Robinson

Christopher Sinclair

Gordon A. Shunk

Joel F. Stone, Jr.

David Swierenga

Gardner A. Taft

Ronald Tweedie

Robert A. Weant

Edward Weiner

George V. Wickstrom

William Wilkinson

CHAPTER 1
Introduction to Planning

John D. Edwards, Jr.
Transportation Consultant

Introduction

The interaction of transportation and society is best characterized by this quote from H. G. Wells: "The way people and goods get from one place to another is a trivial matter, but that *process* involves other matters that have an almost fundamental relationship to the social order."[1] These matters are what transportation planners are increasingly concerned with, from economic effects to environmental concerns. Transportation planning and transportation planners and engineers find themselves involved in an evermore complex environment of travel demands, land use patterns and urban form, and air quality issues.

Transportation planning is the functional area within transportation engineering that deals with the relationship of land use to travel patterns and travel demands; and the planning, evaluation, and programming of transportation facilities, including roadways, transit, terminals, parking, pedestrian facilities, bikeways, and goods movement. The policies of the Institute of Transportation Engineers (ITE) define transportation planning practice as:

> improving coordination between land use and transportation system planning; providing cooperative interaction between planning, design, and operation of transportation services; maintaining a balance between transportation-related energy use and clean air and water, and encouraging alternative modes of transportation that will enhance energy efficiency while providing high levels of mobility and safety.

While transportation planning is a functional area of transportation engineering, it frequently transcends the strict interpretation of "engineering" in that planning deals with broader areas, such as energy conservation and the environment. Transportation planning is but one of several functional areas of transportation engineering that include the following:

Traffic operations—the analysis, review, and application of traffic data systems to the operation of transportation facilities.

Traffic design—the determination of travel patterns and parking characteristics of transportation users in the planning and design of transportation facilities. Also included within this functional area is the application of land use and economic data in the development of policies for financing transportation improvement.

Traffic research—the conduct of theoretical and applied research to understand and develop new applications of technology that improve mobility, enhance the environment, and conserve energy resources.

Transportation planning was recognized as a separate discipline within ITE in the 1960s—about thirty years after ITE's formation. While planning of transportation facilities had gone on for decades before 1960, especially in the private sector, the 1962 Highway Act, which mandated and provided financing for the National System of Interstate and Defense Highways, provided the impetus for large scale transportation planning in the public sector on a national level.

---

[1] Wilfred Owen, *Transportation Planning Handbook*. (Prentice Hall, 1992).

ITE and Transportation Planning

ITE evolved from the Institute of Traffic Engineers, which was founded in 1930 in Pittsburgh, Pennsylvania. ITE is an international engineering and scientific organization composed of engineers, planners, educators, economists, and other professionals who, by their work or background, are involved in the planning, designing, training, or administration of transportation facilities and programs. ITE's International Board further defined the role of the organization in their 1997 vision statement: "To be the organization of choice for individual transportation professionals responsible for meeting society's needs for efficient and safer surface transportation systems."[2] An organization of 15,000 transportation professionals, ITE has members in 80 countries with 10 Districts, 64 local sections, and 90 student chapters. ITE—through annual meetings, networking, training programs, applied research, and public awareness—facilitates the application of technology and scientific knowledge to transportation problems and solutions. Through ITE programs and activities, members contribute individually and collectively toward the professional advancement of its members, to improving mobility for our constituents, to the stimulation of applied research, and to public awareness of the advantages of good transportation.

Toward this goal, ITE's programs include professional development seminars; guidelines and standards development; and technical committee research, reports, and meetings to allow members to network among their peers. The purpose of ITE's *Transportation Planning Handbook* is to further the knowledge of its members, professionals in related fields, and organizations as a part of its continuing effort to advance the profession.

About the *Handbook*

The traffic and transportation engineering handbooks—a series of publications that began in 1941 with the *Traffic Engineering Handbook*—have provided a repository of traffic information that has been used by transportation engineers and transportation planners in designing and operating our transportation system. This series of publications had subsequent updates in 1950 and 1965. These updates included an effort to broaden the content from purely highway topics to broader transportation subjects in the *Traffic and Transportation Planning Handbook* editions of 1976 and 1982—responding to the ever expanding role of transportation engineering in our society. With the 1976 and 1982 editions, additional transportation planning topics were introduced, and consequently the book became even larger.

In 1985, work began on a new edition of the *Traffic and Transportation Planning Handbook* with the appointment of a Content Advisory Committee chaired by Harold Michael. After considerable deliberation, the committee recommended publishing the *Traffic Engineering Handbook* and the *Transportation Planning Handbook* as separate documents. This decision simply reflects the growing body of technical knowledge and the expanding interest and involvement of our profession in the broader implications of transportation, such as environmental, economic, and land use issues. Therefore, fifty years after the first handbook was published, the first edition of the *Transportation Planning Handbook* was produced in 1992. Now the two handbooks serve as a basic set of reference documents.

The purpose of the *Transportation Planning Handbook* is to summarize the typical practices and characteristics of transportation use and to serve as a basic day-to-day reference on proven techniques and study procedures in the practice of transportation planning. The *Handbook* is not intended to represent a statement of a standard of practice for the profession or ITE, but it is a guide for the practicing transportation professional. The *Handbook* is also not intended to be used as a textbook, since no exercises are included; however, the *Handbook* serves as a reference source for educators and students. As such, every chapter contains a list of publications for further reading in each specific subject area. Because of the extensive body of knowledge of selected subject areas, such as transportation capacity, the coverage of many subjects in the *Handbook* is more in the nature of a summary, leaving the detailed discussion and examples to the more comprehensive documents. In these cases, liberal references to these works are included in the tables, figures, and text of this book.

---

[2] Institute of Transportation Engineers Vision Statement (Washington, D.C.: ITE, 1997).

While the first edition of the *Transportation Planning Handbook,* published in 1992, contained fifteen chapters, this edition contains twenty chapters representing the growing subject areas of involvement and concern to transportation planners. New chapters on "Goods Movement," "Transportation Models," "Traffic Calming," and "Bicycle and Pedestrian Facilities" have been incorporated to provide needed information on these subject areas. In addition to these new chapters, several chapters have been significantly expanded, such as "Planning Approach to Capacity" and "Transportation Operations and Management," including ITS and Urban Transit. These additions represent the transportation planner's concern for all modes of transportation, as well as for the emerging new technologies that will affect urban transportation.

As with the previous edition of the *Handbook,* world events are creating one of the most exciting periods in recent history. As predicted by Michael Walton in the preface to the first edition: "We are indeed becoming a global village, both economically and environmentally." The economic unification of Europe, the emerging Asian markets for transportation technology, and the environmental effects of events occurring around the world will have direct consequences, opportunities, and challenges for transportation professionals worldwide. The challenges of international competition, environmental issues, and the development of alternative energy sources are at the forefront of national policy initiatives as transportation plays a central role in each of these areas.

The Relationship Between the Handbooks

Concurrent with the preparation of the *Transportation Planning Handbook,* Second Edition, the preparation of the *Traffic Engineering Handbook,* Fifth Edition, is underway. As stated in the Introduction to the *Traffic Engineering Handbook:* "The purpose of the publication is to collate, in one volume, basic traffic engineering information as a guide to the best practice in the field."

The *Traffic Engineering Handbook* primarily includes information on the operations, design, and administration of transportation facilities, as opposed to the planning and administration of transportation facilities and systems discussed in the *Transportation Planning Handbook.* There is a certain amount of redundancy between the handbooks, as is necessary and desirable; but the editors have made a concerted effort to remove any contradictory information. The *Transportation Planning Handbook* includes a broader range of subject matter because of the nature of the discipline, but it has less detail on the specifics of each subject area. Some subject areas, such as traffic signals, signs, and street and roadway design are not addressed in the *Transportation Planning Handbook*—the transportation professional is directed to the *Traffic Engineering Handbook* for information on these subjects.

While the *Transportation Planning Handbook* covers a great many subject areas, additional detail will always be found in separate texts on a particular subject. For instance, Chapter 5, "Transportation Planning Studies," contains a summary of many different types of traffic and transportation studies, but it does not contain the level of details on particular studies as is included in the *Manual of Traffic Engineering Studies.* Likewise, the *Trip Generation Handbook* or *Traffic Calming in Practice* will always contain greater detail than the *Transportation Planning Handbook.* As stated previously in this chapter, the objective of the *Handbook* is to summarize the typical practices and characteristics of transportation use.

CHAPTER 2
Transportation and Society

Damian J. Kulash
President and CEO
Eno Transportation Foundation

Introduction

Vital Role of Transportation

When talking about transportation we commonly use words like "circulation," "congestion," "flow," or "artery"—words we also use to describe how blood moves through the body. This usage is not surprising, since these are practical terms for describing flows in networks. But they also suggest a far more profound similarity: transportation is a vital function of human society, just as blood is essential to human life. Both blood and transportation move essential material. Blood carries vital oxygen to all the body's critical organs, and it moves waste material out. Transportation moves people and goods to different neighborhoods, cities, states, and countries; and it allows people in those various places to trade and do business together. Just as life depends on a healthy circulatory system—along with the other bodily functions—society depends on good transportation—along with other social systems.

The relationships between transportation and society are numerous, deep, varied, ancient, and complex. Any summary of them sounds trite. Everyone has had extensive personal experiences using transportation. Transportation has influenced each of our choices about where to live, spend vacations, shop, or work. So inescapable is the tie between transportation and society that, like gravity, we take it for granted and cannot imagine a world without it.

The very hugeness of the transportation system hides its interdependence with society. The transportation system is the product of many decades'—indeed, of many centuries'—prior investment decisions and location choices. At any point, the transportation decisions being made by governments, companies, and individuals—even those that are pivotal, watershed decisions—affect only the fringes of the overall system. The cumulative value of facilities and vehicles that already exist is far greater than the amounts dealt with in periodic transportation legislation or corporate investments in transportation. For example, recent estimates of the value of U.S. highway infrastructure are in the $700 billion to $900 billion range. The value of the associated vehicle stock, which in 1996 included some 136 million automobiles, 65 million light trucks, and 6 million heavy trucks and buses, is in the range of $1,200 billion to $1,800 billion. Taken together, highways and their vehicles are worth more than the entire federal budget. When the value of railroad, aviation, public transportation, pipeline, port, ocean shipping, and other modes of transportation are added in, the value of transportation facilities is probably two to three times the size of the federal budget, or around half of the gross national product (GNP). In contrast, total government spending on transportation in 1996, by all levels of government and on all modes of transportation, was about one-twentieth of this cumulative investment. The vast array of transportation facilities now in place is the product of investments made over the centuries. Like culture itself, the transportation resources available to any one age are not just a contemporary creation, but a legacy from many previous generations.

A System of Disparate Parts

Transportation is also very decentralized, under the control of many independent companies, government agencies, and individuals. In the United States, most roads are owned and maintained by governments—cities, counties, states, or in some cases the federal government. Rail and pipeline rights of way are usually privately owned and maintained. Airports and ports are usually owned by public or quasi-public organizations, but they usually contain facilities that are owned by individual carriers. Both public and private organizations own terminals, stations, and other loading and interchange facilities. Vehicles and rolling stock are mostly owned by private interests—shippers, carriers, other companies, or individuals. The vast bulk of the costs of operating transportation systems are borne by these same private interests. Overall, the resultant character of the transportation system reflects all of these public and private interests, operating at different times and different places. Within this overall complex, most decisions are not aimed at changing the system per se. Rather, many local, regional, corporate, and individual actions end up shaping the system unintentionally as decisions are made to ship supplies, deliver products, boost profits, spur the economic development of a region, enlarge a port, eliminate a bottleneck, and the like. The resultant national transportation system is the product of countless separate decisions, most of which are made for other purposes. Government plans, programs, and regulations add a measure of structure and uniformity to this system; but a sea of unplanned, independent decisions continue to be major determinants.

The organizations and individuals who make transportation decisions naturally view the system with an eye to their own requirements. A major shipper may be preoccupied with getting better access to the nearest interstate route. A coastal city may place top priority on improving its port. A commuter in an urban area may care most about clearing up congested intersections on the route to work. A national provider of intermodal freight services may place terminal access issues high on the list. Such interests compete with each other: mode against mode, company against company, city against city, state against state, and so forth. Governments compete for public funds for system investments, and they compete to attract economic growth and jobs. Carriers and shippers compete for customers, for market share, for advantageous routes and fee structures, and for profits. All have a general interest in national transportation improvement, but their individual priorities are diverse and often conflicting.

As we look at transportation and society, it is important to remember that transportation is not a homogenous, fully planned system, but a resultant of diverse and competing forces. It is a huge system that is only partly planned and controlled by governments. It looks different when viewed from the perspective of each of the different public or private organizations whose decisions influence its shape. The discussion in this chapter cannot present all of these perspectives. Brevity necessitates several limitations. First, this discussion of transportation and society will be based predominantly on the United States. Second, while large regional and sectoral variations in transportation exist, this introductory chapter speaks mostly in terms of national averages. Third, to reduce a topic of this scale to a manageable set of themes and issues, omissions are unavoidable. I have tried to pick a few themes that affect both freight and passenger transportation in many regions of the country and that illustrate key connections between transportation and society. No two authors would necessarily agree on which key developments to select. My only hope is that the topics I have selected serve to illustrate how thoroughly transportation is embedded in the fabric of society.

Social and Economic Consequences

Virtually everything we do relies on transportation. Whenever we live through a transportation shutdown like a paralyzing snowstorm, carrier strike, or automotive breakdown, it forms a memorable hardship. We think back on it as an abnormal interruption of our interaction with the many activities, people, and places around which our lives revolve. We can cope with such disruptions for short periods, knowing we can repair the damage when things return to normal. Difficult as these outages may be, we see them as temporary abnormalities. But they are not. They are actually the normal, undeveloped state of things, absent the availability of transportation. Over the span of centuries, society and transportation have evolved, hand in hand, from periods when such hardships were permanent and unavoidable. Now we have come to expect a high level of transportation consistent with our advanced civilization.

Various writers have observed that transportation is a mirror of civilization. Centuries ago, the Abbe Reynal noted:

> Let us travel over all the countries of the earth, and whenever we shall find no facility of traveling from a city to a town, or from a village to a hamlet, we may pronounce the people to be barbarians.[1]

Many air travelers today, flying over remote regions of the globe where there are no roads, railroads, or other traces of transportation to be seen on the ground, have probably made similar observations. Civilized society depends upon

---

[1] Henry Parnell, *A Treatise on Roads* (London: Longman, Green, Orme, Brown, Green, and Longman, 1833), p. 2.

communication, organization, trade, surplus and specialization, security, and protection of personal freedoms. Transportation is intertwined with many of these components.

History offers numerous instances where transportation was essential in creating or preserving the social and economic order. The Roman road system is celebrated for consolidating administrative control over conquered territories, British naval power supported the growth of the empire, and building the transcontinental railway opened the U.S. west and helped create a union of states. Throughout the developmental years of the United States, transportation investments and their effects have spurred economic development and political integration. Albert Gallatin, Secretary of the Treasury, proposed the first national set of transportation projects just 31 years after the nation began. In 1807, when describing how his planned improvements would affect the newly formed nation, he wrote:

> No other single operation, within the power of government, can more effectively tend to strengthen and perpetuate that union, which secures external independence, domestic peace, and internal liberty.[2]

Trade between different regions is vital to economic development and directly dependent on transportation. Adam Smith, the father of economics, wrote in *The Wealth of Nations:*

> Good roads, canals, and navigable rivers, by diminishing the expense of carriage, put the remote parts of a country nearly on a level with those in the neighborhood of a town, and they are, upon that account, the greatest of improvements.[3]

From the ancient world to modern times, the fortunes of nations hinged on their access to resources and markets. Natural resources had little use until freed by transportation; crops in remote areas had little value until nonlocal markets for them opened up. Economic comparative advantages, which lie at the heart of modern advanced economies, could not be realized until transportation systems opened the door to regional trade, then national trade, and now global trade. A surge in transportation development made the industrial revolution possible. The development of waterways, canals, roads, and railroads opened up the vast interior and western parts of the United States. Countless local histories provide dramatic illustrations of the sudden rise in the value of crops, resources, and land as transportation access improved.

The British economist A.J. Youngston observes that the vital significance of improved transportation to economic development is "one of the few general truths which it is possible to derive from economic history."[4] In developed nations today, it is easy to overlook this rare "general truth." Yet the vital linkages between transportation and economic development are just as strong today in the global economy as they were when trading with a neighboring village was at the cutting edge of economic growth.

The U.S. Transportation System in the 1990s

Passenger Transportation

Much of our personal travel now occurs in trip chains—trips in which we string together a series of different, possibly unrelated purposes. For example, on the way home from work, a driver may begin the commute home, stop at the day care center and pick up the kids, continue on to the grocery store and dry cleaners, and then drive home. While it is not always possible to separate travel for one purpose from travel for others, recent statistics do show that we make more than half of our trips for personal business of various kinds. About one trip in five is made to go shopping, and about one in four is made for other family and personal business. (Table 2–1.) One in six trips is made for social and recreational purposes, about half of

---

[2] Albert Gallatin, *Report of the Secretary of the Treasury on the Subject of Public Roads and Canals,* 1808 (Reprints of Economic Classics, Augustus M. Kelly, 1968), p. 8.

[3] Adam Smith, *The Wealth of Nations* (1776).

[4] A. J. Youngston, *Overhead Capital: A Study in the Development of Economics* (Edinburgh: Edinburgh University Press, 1967).

which are to visit family and friends. Work trips also account for about one trip in six. Travel to church and school accounts for about nine percent of all trips.

The average American household spent more than $12,000 on transportation in 1996. About $8,000 of this was spent directly on fares and automobile-related expenses. Another $4,000 was spent indirectly for freight bills embedded in the price of purchased products.

Not surprisingly, the largest category of expenditures trace from our heavy use of automobiles. Cars and trucks cost the average household about $2,600. (Figure 2–1.) Gasoline and oil cost the average household a little under $1,400 per year; and repairs, parking, and storage cost a little more than $1,400 per year per household. Altogether, auto-related items cost the average U.S. household $6,693 in 1996.

The average U.S. household spent an additional $1,300 per year for airfares, bus and transit fares, and other forms of for-hire transportation. About $600 of this was spent on airfares, and about $200 was spent on local bus and transit fares. (Figure 2–2.)

Table 2–1 Personal Travel by Purpose of Trip: 1995

Purpose of Trip	Percent of Person Trips	Percent of Person Miles
Work	17.7	22.5
Work-related	2.6	5.8
Shopping	20.2	13.5
Doctor/Dentist	1.5	1.5
Other Family and Personal Business	24.2	19.9
Church and School	8.8	5.7
Visiting	8.2	11.2
Other Social and Recreational Business	16.7	19.5
Other	0.2	0.4
Total	100.0	100.0

Source: *Our Nation's Travel: 1995 Nationwide Transportation Survey, Early Results Report,* U.S. Department of Transportation, Washington, D.C.: Federal Highway Administration, September 1997, p. 11.

Over and above these direct expenditures on transportation, the average household spent an additional $4,700 per year for freight transportation. Many of these freight expenditures are hidden from consumers because they are built into the cost of final goods and services, but by any measure transportation is a key item in family budgets. Transportation expenditures, both direct costs and those passed along in the cost of goods purchased, account for more than one-third of median household income in the United States. For comparison, the average household spent about one-third of its budget on housing, about one-seventh on food (at home), and about one-twentieth on entertainment.

Freight Transportation

When it comes to moving goods, trucking is the dominant mode from an economic standpoint. More than three out of every four dollars spent moving goods go to pay for trucking. This massive industry employs nearly 2,300,000 truckers and truck

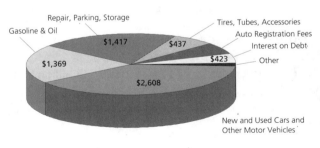

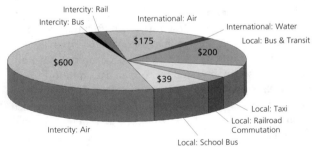

Figure 2–1 U.S. Total Expenditures per Household Related to Automobiles and Other Motor Vehicles, 1996.

(Total auto-related expense per household: $6,693.)

Source: *Transportation in America: 1997,* Lansdowne, Va.: Eno Transportation Foundation, 1997, p. 42.

Figure 2–2 U.S. Total Expenditures per Household on For-Hire Transportation, 1996

(Total expenditure on for-hire transportation: $1,255 per household.)

Source: *Transportation in America: 1997,* Lansdowne, Va.: Eno Transportation Foundation, 1997, p. 42.

terminal workers—a workforce twice as large as that of the airline, bus and subway, and taxi industries combined. The second largest freight mode, from a revenue perspective, is the railroad, which generates only about one-tenth the revenues of the trucking industry. Out of the $467 billion that the United States spent on freight transportation in 1996, 7.5 percent went into rail freight, 5 percent into water transportation, and 4 percent into air transportation of goods. (Figure 2–3.)

Financial statistics do not do justice to the massive physical quantities of material carried by pipeline, rail, and water transportation. These modes carry more than half of all freight ton-miles. They haul heavier commodities than trucks, as well as move them greater distances. Nationwide, rail carries 40 percent of all freight ton-miles, trucks carry 27 percent, and water carries 14 percent. Nowhere is the contrast between physical volume and transport revenue more striking than in the case of pipelines. Oil pipelines received only about $8.6 billion of revenue in 1996, less than one-fortieth the revenues of the trucking industry, yet they carried more than half as many ton-miles as trucks. (Figure 2–4.)

Economic Stakes in Transportation

Large investments have created a massive physical plant and vehicle fleet. Americans now own more than 200 million cars and light trucks—roughly one for each person sixteen years and older. There are nearly four million miles of roads in the United States, about half of which are paved. There are 136,542 miles of railroad track, 25,777 miles of navigable waterways, and more than 200,000 miles of petroleum pipelines.

This extensive system is financed by a combination of private and public investments. The transportation carriers invested $21 billion in new plant and equipment in 1994—$4 billion of this in air transportation, $7 billion in rail, and $10 billion in truck and other transportation. The manufacturing industries invested another $23 billion in transportation—$16 billion of this in motor vehicles and $3 billion for aircraft. Overall, the private sector invested more than $65 billion in new transportation plant and equipment in 1994. These numbers reflect only a subset of total transportation investments, since much of this investment is embodied in warehousing and plant improvements; and the transportation component cannot be isolated.

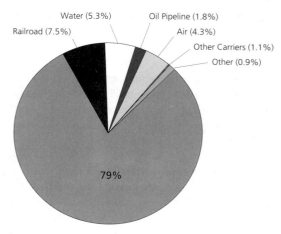

Figure 2–3   Percent of Freight Transportation Expenditures in the United States by Mode, 1996
(Total expenditures by all freight modes was $467 billion.)

Source: *Transportation in America: 1997*, Lansdowne, Va.: Eno Transportation Foundation, 1997, p. 40.

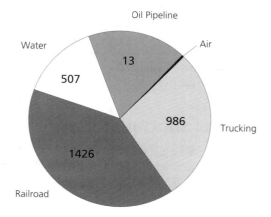

Figure 2–4   Ton-miles Transported by U.S. Freight Carriers, 1996.
(Total ton-miles by all modes was 3,563 billion.)

Source: *Transportation in America: 1997*, Lansdowne, Va.: Eno Transportation Foundation, 1997, p. 44.

Governments at all levels also make major expenditures for transportation. The federal government spent $35 billion on transportation in 1996, of which $20 billion was for highways and $8.5 billion for airports and airways. State and local governments spent an additional $111 billion on transportation, of which $93 billion was for highways. These massive expenditures represent both investment in new facilities and operation and maintenance of existing facilities. (Table 2–2.)

Transportation and Economic Growth

Many industries are vitally dependent on transportation. Better information on these dependencies became available in 1998 with the introduction of the transportation satellite accounts, which extended the U.S. input-output accounts to reflect transportation more accurately. These accounts show that the largest users of transportation in the United States in 1992 were manufacturing ($102 billion, 19 percent), services ($64 billion, 12 percent), construction ($52 billion, 10 percent), and wholesale and retail trade ($52 billion, 10 percent). These accounts show that transportation contributes 5 percent of the total value added to the U.S. economy.[5]

Transportation is used by all sectors of the economy, and the nation's gross expenditures on transportation are huge. Altogether Americans spent $1,263 billion on transportation in 1996, which represents nearly one-sixth of the GNP. As apparent from the similar growth patterns of the GNP and transportation spending since 1970, growth in transportation has generally paralleled growth in the GNP, although transportation expenditures trailed off a little in recent decades, relative to the GNP. (Figure 2–5.) Improvements in transportation productivity and logistics have helped to reduce this fraction, and such improvements are vitally important to economic growth. Over the years transportation expenditures and the GNP have grown side by side.

There are obvious ties between transportation spending and measures of overall economic activity, such as the GNP. Freight volumes are a rough but useful barometer of production. Every unit of economic output embodies transportation inputs that were made to get raw materials into production and to deliver finished products to consumers. When more goods are produced, transportation volumes are higher.

Table 2–2 Government Expenditures for Transportation Services and Facilities, 1996
(Millions of Dollars)

Mode	Federal	State and Local	Total
Airways	$ 6,935	-0-	$ 6,935
Airports	1,597	$ 7,251	8,848
Highways	20,186	93,255	113,441
Rivers and Harbors	1,032	1,925	2,957
Railroads	2,266	120	2,386
Transit	2,643	8,440	11,082
Total	$34,659	$110,990	$145,649

Source: *Transportation in America: 1997*, Lansdowne, Va.: Eno Transportation Foundation, 1997, p. 73.

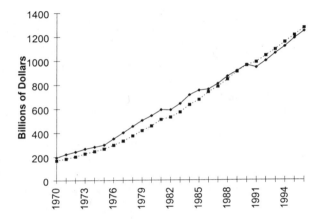

Figure 2–5 Total Transportation Bill Compared to the GNP

Legend: Solid line represents the nation's transportation bill

Dotted line represents one-sixth of the GNP

Source: *Transportation in America: 1997*, Lansdowne, Va.: Eno Transportation Foundation, p. 38, 1997.

Passenger transportation volumes are also tied to overall economic activity. Business trips and travel to work are directly tied to economic well being. Personal consumption of transportation for recreation, family visits, shopping, and many other purposes is also influenced by economic conditions. Thus both passenger transportation expenditures and freight transportation expenditures grow and shrink with the overall economy.

But transportation does not simply mirror the economy: transportation investments can also cause economic growth. A recent analysis of the nation's investment in highways and its economic performance found that the net social rate of return from transportation investment ran as high as 30 to 40 percent each year, well above the average return on private capital investments.[6] During the 1950s and the 1960s, the years when the nation began constructing the interstate highway system, the economic return from highway investment ran about 35 percent—more than double the rate of return that private capital produced during this period. At this rate, transportation investments paid for themselves in

---

[5] Bingsong Fang, Xiaoli Han, Ann M. Lawson, and Sherlene K.S. Lum, "U.S. Transportation Satellite Accounts for 1992," *Survey of Current Business* (Washington, D.C.: April 1998), pp. 16–27.

[6] M. Ishaq Nadiri and Theofanis P. Mamuneas, "Highway Capital and Productivity Growth," *Economic Returns from Transportation Investment* (Lansdowne, Va.: Eno Transportation Foundation, 1996).

three years in terms of overall economic growth. In recent years this return has fallen to around 10 percent, which is about the same as the return on private capital. Investments in facilities of national significance—ones that increase the capability of the overall network—show a return around 16 percent, still above the rate of return on private capital.

The transportation investments with the highest returns appear to be those that can produce what are called "network" effects. Network effects, as opposed to local improvements, raise the potential of the system as a whole. Increases in network capability benefit everyone linked to the network, even those located at points far removed from the point where improvements are made. For example, a strawberry grower in California and a restaurant diner in New York may benefit from highway improvements in Nevada. Unfortunately, network effects tend to be eclipsed by the site-specific, local benefits of new projects when alternative policies are weighed and when political decisions are made about new programs. Elected officials are keenly aware that building a transportation facility in a region brings very tangible, immediate benefits in terms of jobs, access, and land values. These site-specific benefits are an important consideration to the communities involved, but it is their expansion of the transportation network that brings most of the economic benefit.

Possible Changes in the Future

Transportation is thoroughly integrated into society, and its priorities and goals shift as the needs of society change. While history suggests that there has never been a civilization nor an age that did not rely on transportation, it also shows that the nature of that reliance has been very different from age to age and place to place. Even in the relatively short span of the automotive age, transportation priorities and concerns have changed repeatedly, echoing society's evolving concerns. "Getting the farmer out of the mud" was a rallying cry for surface transportation earlier in the century; then came construction of a coast-to-coast system of high-speed, limited-access highways; and recently demands have been increasing to integrate transportation more effectively with environmental, safety, and developmental goals. As transportation professionals plan and build for tomorrow, their work will be most valuable if it is able to anticipate how society's expectations will shift. With continued growth in population, affluence, and technological progress, tomorrow's opportunities and problems may well be different than today's. The continued emergence of the global economy, the aging of the baby boom, and many other foreseeable and unforeseen factors will shape the future of transportation.

More than ever, the private sector will influence this future, as transportation incorporates more communications and computational capabilities, as transportation operators provide overall logistics capabilities, as industries become more dependent on just-in-time distribution systems, and as deregulation of transportation moves from the national to the international sphere. No one can predict how these issues will play out, nor how the private sector will address them. Everyone engaged in transportation faces many unresolved issues and uncertainties, and each has developed working assumptions to draw upon in the face of speculative matters.

In the remainder of this chapter, I discuss several emerging developments that could redefine the linkages between transportation and society, especially as this affects issues faced by transportation planners working for public agencies. Fundamental shifts in technology, competitive structure, and regulatory frameworks may also greatly shift the complexion of transportation industries in future years, and planners in private companies may face a different set of issues as well. No one can confidently predict the public attitudes, laws, regulations, and methodological resources that will attach to them in the future. As unpredictable events unfold in the decades ahead, many areas will pose special challenges for planners. Eight of these are singled out for consideration here:

- development of intelligent transportation systems (ITS) and automated highways,

- continued worsening of traffic congestion,

- a growing focus on operational efficiency and potentially on congestion pricing,

- the explosion in information technology and its implications on where and how we work and travel,

- mounting concerns about global warming,

- growth in intermodal transportation,

- the severity of traffic safety problems,

- changing public expectations of transportation.

Intelligent Transportation Systems

Technological Potential

The dramatic strides that have been made in computing and communications capabilities are just beginning to find their way into the automobile and driver markets. We are occasionally reminded that there is more computer capacity on a new car than there was on early spacecraft, yet much of this remains invisible to drivers as it regulates a variety of engine, braking, and emissions control functions. Automation also has the potential to revolutionize features of automobiles and highways in ways that directly affect drivers. Navigation, crash avoidance, data on road and route conditions, information on roadside businesses and attractions, automation of driver functions, and many other potential applications are still in their infancy.

Today, many of the component capabilities are available off-the-shelf for other uses. For a nominal price, you can buy a CD-ROM with every street in the country at your neighborhood computer store. Spend a little more and you can buy a cellular telephone for your car or a global positioning system (GPS) unit that triangulates its location by beaming signals to satellites for use on your boat. Adaptive cruise control, which sets your car's accelerator based on the speed of the car in front of you, is now an option on some new cars. Field demonstrations of the automated highway system have shown that fully automated longitudinal control, obstacle detection, overtaking, and platooning are now possible. The capabilities of the Internet continue to surprise us week after week; and as communications and computing continue their rapid strides, the day is coming when every car will have Internet access supporting a wide array of services.

Picture yourself in the year 2050 (or could it be as soon as 2020?) as you are driving on the interstate from Atlanta to Miami, when you decide to make a local detour for food and scenery. You push a button on your on-board computer. Based on your exact location on the map, which is sensed using on-board GPS devices, the computer determines your location. It combines this information with its Internet listing of area restaurants and attractions, and on your on-board display it suggests two or three routes with good restaurants. You click on the one you want and the vehicle drives you there automatically on the shortest, least congested route. This is not far-flung science fiction: every feature of this is technologically possible today, much of it is now economical, and the costs of the more exotic features are dropping rapidly. Not only might you, as a future driver, be willing to pay for such capabilities, but every business that has ever paid for a billboard, a listing in the yellow pages, an Internet site, or a tourist magazine will have an interest in seeing these capabilities developed as well. With more than 200 million vehicles in the fleet, any device that can penetrate this market faces immense potential, so that device manufacturers will be driven to do the research needed to perfect new capabilities and make them economically competitive.

Organizational Implications

Realizing the potential for increased automation in the highway system will take many years. The vehicle/highway system is immense, involving roads, signals, vehicles, signs, markings, and communications systems under the control of many thousands of separate government units, private manufacturers, and other interests. There are immense problems of coordination, standardization, liability, and privacy that remain to be resolved. Just as it took the automobile itself many years to progress from being an expensive luxury to an everyday necessity, so too will it take decades before advances in communications, computing, and sensing become standard features in vehicles.

Government programs are helping to spur developments and channel individual advances to fit into a coordinated whole. The Joint Program Office for Intelligent Transportation Systems at the U.S. Department of Transportation and Federal Highway Administration is developing a system architecture that balances the needs for interoperability and standards with the need for incentives that stimulate private investment.

The business interests in introducing new sensing, communications, computing, and navigational capabilities to the auto fleet are so huge that these developments are likely to occur sooner or later. No one can predict with confidence which devices and capabilities will catch on and when they will catch on, just as an observer of the fledgling automobile industry in 1895 could never have predicted what the nation's highway system would look like in 1920 and beyond. But can anyone doubt that the leap in technological potential that is evident today in communications, computing, and sensing is at least as great as the invention of the automobile, or that its consequences on the interaction between society and transportation will be any less profound?

As highways become more technologically advanced in their interaction with vehicles, this could transform the private and organizational roles in surface transportation. If we ever reach the stage when drivers are not needed on portions of an automated highway system, will there be any distinction between public transportation and taxi service? Between taxis and rental cars? If these distinctions blur, so too will the organizational lines between many existing public agencies and private companies.

Amidst this rapidly growing technological potential, the role of public agencies could shift from being primarily providers of infrastructure or providers of specific services to being operators of the system. This trend is already emerging. In the case of highways, for example, back in the 1960s and 1970s public agencies concentrated on providing new capacity—interstate highways and other system expansion. In the last decade more and more attention has been focused on maintenance and preservation, as well as on improved traffic management. With the advent of automated highway capabilities, public agencies will increasingly be engaged in information flows, operational management, correcting system malfunctions in real time, and planning for operational improvements. The disciplinary skills needed for these roles, as well as the operational mentality, are different from those needed to plan and build new facilities. One of the biggest challenges to today's professionals in transportation agencies is to augment their own strengths to anticipate tomorrow's operational needs.

Congestion

History

Just as new transportation capabilities have made modern lifestyles possible and have contributed to economic growth, the erosion of transportation capabilities through congestion could undo those advantages. Everyone complains that congestion is bad; but behind this apparent common complaint there is little agreement about what congestion is, how it can most appropriately be measured, how much is tolerable, how to value its cost, which averages to use, and how to characterize the duration and extent of the problem. The severity of congestion depends on definitions, statistics, behavioral tolerances, personal values, social expectations, and comparisons; and these elements are poorly understood and not systematically accounted for.

Congestion is not a creation of the automobile age, but it has been a feature of urban living for as long as there have been cities. The poet Juvenal gives us a vivid description of what it felt like to be a common citizen on the streets of Ancient Rome, crowded with people and freight:

> One needs to have a lot of money to sleep in this town ...The vehicles moving down the narrow, winding streets, the quarrelsome crowd refusing to move on ...The rich man, when called away on business, will have himself borne through the crowd, which opens to make way for him; he will make swift progress over everyone's head in his vast Liburnian litter. As he goes, he will read, write, sleep within...And for all that he will arrive before us. In my case, the human tide in front of me prevents me from hurrying; the hastening throng behind me is thrusting into my back. Someone shoves an elbow into me; another man gives me a nasty jolt with a long beam. Here's a fellow also set on giving my head a whack with his joist and yet another with his mighty cask...A wagon is coming forward with a great bulk of timber swaying about on it; a second is loaded with a pine trunk. These are threatening the crowd as they swing in the air...[7]

---

[7] Raymond Chevallier, *Roman Roads* (University of California Press, 1976), pp. 67–70.

The discomfort and dangers experienced on Rome's crowded streets led Julius Caesar to issue a traffic ban in an attempt to tame the streets. Caesar's edict ordered unnecessary vehicles off the streets during daylight hours:

> ...no one shall drive a wagon along the streets...where there is continuous housing after sunrise or before the tenth hour of the day, except whatever will be proper for the transportation...of material for...public works, or for removing from the city rubbish...[8]

Apparently, Caesar's ban was but one of many such edicts, which suggests that this type of instrument was not very effective or not able to accommodate the many exemptions that were essential for public health and safety and for religious reasons. It appears that congestion continued in Rome, as it did in many other European cities, as population grew and particularly after private horse-drawn vehicles came into fashion centuries later. Traffic jams are reported in Renaissance Paris, and Victorian novelists describe hordes of workers crowding bridges into European cities following the industrial revolution. Photographs of New York City and other major metropolitan areas in 1900 show streets clogged with horse-drawn vehicles, pedestrians, and parked and loading vehicles. Throughout history, the size of the city, the location of activities within cities, and the regulation of public space have all been driven in part by congestion.

Measurements

At present, highway traffic congestion imposes severe costs in the form of traffic delays, schedule slippage, in-transit inventory costs, production interruptions when inventories fail to arrive when needed, wasted time for deliverymen and salesmen, wasted time to schedule in allowances for traffic uncertainties, wasted fuel, and environmental damage. Such costs are difficult to estimate, but rough estimates place them at several hundreds of billions of dollars per year in the United States.

The yardsticks used to measure congestion are varied and the ones that are most applicable to one situation are inadequate for addressing others. One recent review recommended that congestion should be measured by various yardsticks for different purposes. For example, travel time is a good measure for analyzing short roadway sections, total delay is appropriate for long sections, and the delay ratio is a good tool for corridor analysis. Depending upon the purpose, useful yardsticks also include differences in travel time, travel rate, delay rate, relative delay rate, and various other indices and measures.[9]

Traffic engineers have traditionally used a ranking system called the "level of service" to characterize flow conditions along a route segment.[10] Under this system, level of service A is defined as free flow, where the speed of an individual vehicle is controlled solely by the desires of the driver and the prevailing conditions. Progressively worse conditions are defined by levels B, C, and D. The worst is level of service F—breakdown conditions—where uniform moving flow cannot be maintained, causing a temporary reduction in capacity as queues build. The level of service definition has been very useful over the years, but there is growing recognition that it is not able to make the distinctions necessary to help set priorities for today's congested facilities. The worst condition, level F, might refer to a temporary snarl or a major standstill. It might refer to a five-minute jam when a shift is over at a big plant, or it might be a four-hour tie up on the regional beltway. Level F is a broad label that encompasses conditions that are disparate in severity and duration, and a more refined yardstick is needed to distinguish the levels of severity now experienced in long-term tie ups. Such disruptions are increasingly common, and their alleviation is a key concern in developing transportation and land use policies suited to crowded metropolitan areas. As will be discussed in Chapter 7, planning practices are now changing to address the duration of severe congestion.

[8] Dora Jane Hamblin and Mary Jane Grunsfeld, *The Appian Way: A Journey* (New York, N.Y.: Random House, 1974), p. 170.

[9] Tim Lomax, Shawn Turner, and Gordon Shunk, *Quantifying Congestion, National Cooperative Research Program Report 398*, Vol. 1, Final Report (Washington, D.C.: Transportation Research Board, National Research Council, 1997), p. 5.

[10] *Highway Capacity Manual—Special Report 209* (Washington, D.C.: Transportation Research Board, National Research Council, 1994).

Trends

Overall, most Americans probably sense that congestion is getting worse, but this is difficult to prove with statistics. Data on average commute times suggest possible worsening. The average commuting time rose by 40 sec. during the 1980s, according to data from the 1990 federal census, and from 21.7 min. in 1980 to 22.3 min. in 1990.[11] Similar results are reported by the "Nationwide Personal Transportation Survey." This survey found that the average commute time increased from 18.2 min. in 1983 to 19.7 min. in 1990 to 20.7 minutes in 1995. But do these longer commute times show that congestion is getting worse? Not necessarily. This same survey also found that because of a trend toward longer commutes, the speed of work trips actually increased from 28.0 to 33.6 miles per hour between 1983 and 1995.[12] The commuters surveyed were traveling greater distances at higher speeds—hardly proof of worsening congestion! Homes and workplaces are increasingly located further and further from urban central business districts, so that the trip time data for 1983 and 1995 partly compare trips in different parts of the metropolitan area. That is, the speedier trips at the later date include more travel at the distant fringe of the area, where streets are often less heavily used. Such a comparison does not really say anything one way or the other about the change in travel time for trips along the same routes.

From one year to another, traffic increases, more lanes and roads are added, and people and businesses move. Roads that are clogged with traffic are often prime candidates for improvement, and relocation decisions are often based on ease of access. An increase, or a reduction, in average commuting times in a region might reflect changes in congestion along specific highway segments; or it might reflect growth of population or jobs in less congested parts of the region, with no improvement at all in the trips that were used to compute the base year number.

For making year-to-year comparisons of congestion, one ongoing longitudinal study developed a useful index for comparing conditions over time in fifty urbanized areas in the United States.[13] This index compares actual traffic density to congested traffic density on a combination of freeways and principal arterial streets, computed at various intervals since 1982. Based on this index, traffic congestion appears to be getting much worse in most of the fifty areas studied. Between 1988 and 1994, the greatest increases occurred in Salt Lake City, Utah, where the congestion index increased by 31 percent; Columbus, Ohio; Cincinnati, Ohio; Charlotte, North Carolina; Detroit, Michigan; Minneapolis-Saint Paul, Minnesota; and Baltimore, Maryland, where the congestion index increased by 15 to 20 percent. Only five of the fifty urban areas studied showed decreases in the congestion index between 1988 and 1994, and none of these decreases was greater than 5 percent.

Tolerance

Surrounding all the ambiguity involved in the measurement of congestion there lies an even vaguer set of issues in depicting society's tolerance of congestion. There is no standard or uniform expectation of how much congestion is acceptable. Public tolerance for congestion varies from place to place and time to time. People from large metropolitan areas are often amused when they visit smaller communities and hear the locals complaining about congestion. Residents of small areas look with disbelief at the traffic snarls suffered by their big-city friends, and they ask why anyone would suffer such inconvenience. Incidents of "road rage" and aggressive driving could be interpreted as a sign that more drivers have reached their boiling point with congestion, but such behaviors could just as well be attributed to many other causes.

Congestion that was unacceptable in one era may be tolerated in another. Changes in technology have been accompanied by shifting expectations. Widespread development of limited-access highways has increased our familiarity with, and expectation of, free-flowing traffic. Air conditioning, stereo systems, and cellular telephones have added to motorist comfort and productivity; and in the process they may have tempered the irritation of congestion. For example, calls from car phones can greatly reduce the anxiety and disruption of plans caused by traffic delays. Car phones and faxes allow work and personal business to proceed in spite of congestion. As auto-based communications and information-processing capabilities increase to embrace more of what is now possible via the Internet, auto occupants may have many ways to use their time fruitfully; and this could diminish their sensitivity to congestion.

[11] Alan E. Pisarski, *Commuting in America II* (Lansdowne, Va.: Eno Transportation Foundation, 1996), p. 91.

[12] *Our Nation's Travel: 1995 Nationwide Transportation Survey, Early Results Report* (Washington, D.C.: U.S. Department of Transportation, Federal Highway Administration, September 1997), p. 11.

[13] Tim Lomax and Gordon Shunk, *Urban Roadway Congestion—1982 to 1994* (College Station, Texas: Texas Transportation Institute, 1997).

The transportation of goods, and all the economic interests associated with having timely delivery of inputs and efficient distribution of products, are also being threatened by congestion. At a minimum, congestion adds to shipping cost by requiring more driver time, by increasing in-transit inventory costs, and by reducing the efficiency of vehicle use. The delays and uncertainties associated with shipping over congested routes also add to the cost of production, and they erode the advantages of just-in-time delivery systems. Many companies attempt to escape the problem by rescheduling trips outside peak hours, by using nighttime pickup and delivery, or by shifting to less congested modes of transportation. Such shifts also add to the cost. Just as the construction of the interstate highway system made a substantial contribution to national economic growth, growing congestion on that system and other important routes could undo the network benefits that have been achieved and adversely affect national economic performance.

All in all, highway congestion is bad and likely to get worse. History offers few if any useful remedies for congestion. New technology, demand restrictions, pricing, and increased telecommuting could help. The search for solutions that are attuned to society's priorities will be a major thrust of transportation policy in the coming years; yet any attempt to support this debate with systematic data runs into statistical variations, inadequate definitions, and behavioral uncertainties. Congestion varies by time of day and from neighborhood to neighborhood; and broad averages cannot capture these differences. It varies in duration and severity, and no index or average can fully characterize its effects. Our tolerance for congestion is tempered by our individual day-to-day experiences and expectations. Our sensitivity to congestion depends partly on how comfortably and productively we can pass the time while stuck in traffic.

In future years, planners will find that congestion, which has always been an important concern, takes on added urgency and forces consideration of a broader range of policies and attitudes. This will require planners to develop more systematic characterizations of congestion and its costs. It will force increased planning attention to focus on the management and use of existing systems.

Operational Efficiency and Congestion Pricing

Economic Rationale

Introduction of ITS, lanes for the exclusive use of high-occupancy vehicles, rush-hour use of shoulders, ramp metering, intersection improvements, and other innovative techniques will make ever greater contributions as communities struggle to make efficient use of resources. In the face of growing congestion and a diminishing physical and political ability to add new system capacity, public policy will increasingly focus on improving the efficiency of system operations.

Operational efficiency has always been a concern of transportation agencies, but current constraints are increasingly leading to consideration of operational policies whose public acceptance is uncertain. Measures that physically or economically restrict travel have been notoriously slow to gain public acceptance, and most of the limited use of traffic demand management has come only when conditions were drastic and construction remedies were not feasible.

Economists have argued that the efficiency of highways could be much improved by setting prices to cover the marginal costs of a trip. Similar peak period pricing has been used effectively by airlines, transit systems, electric companies, and many other industries. A similar concept might be useful for roads. Prices could be set in such a way as to reckon in the time costs of the trip—both those borne by the traveler and those imposed on other travelers. Such "congestion pricing" goes beyond peak-period pricing (which simply refers to any peak premium) by calculating the peak premium at a level high enough to deter traffic and maximize system efficiency. This pricing policy would set high charges for road use on congested roads during rush hours and lower charges at other times and places. While the prospect of very high road-user fees may have been prominent when policies of this sort have been considered, recent variations of the concept such as "value pricing" place more stress on positive aspects like reduced off-peak fees or availability of revenues for other transportation purposes.

Societal Concerns

In spite of the economic arguments in support of congestion pricing, no U.S. cities have tried it. This lack of application probably stems from many causes, among them concerns about the associated administrative costs and difficulties, the possibility of adverse effects on poor persons, the apparent inequity of charging a fee for use of roads in addition to collection of fees for road construction within the Highway Trust Fund, and adverse public reactions to what might be seen as an unpopular tax or restriction on personal freedom. To many, the ability to move, like the ability to breathe, is so fundamental that it should not be made available to people with means and denied to those without. They see the road as more than a physical facility: it represents freedom of mobility and equality of access to modern society. It is seen as a basic right.

Throughout much of history, this distinction was very real:

> To the citizen of the twelfth, the fifteenth, or even the eighteenth century, the King's Highway was a more abstract conception. It was not a strip of land, or any corporeal thing, but a legal and customary right…What existed, in fact, was not a road, but what we might almost term an easement—a right of way, enjoyed by the public at large from village to village, along a certain customary course, which if much frequented, became a beaten track.[14]

This concept of a road has an egalitarian ring—an entitlement independent of economic class or social station. Any road user fee tends to run against this sense of entitlement. Congestion pricing, which is explicitly designed to be an economic barrier, poses a greater threat than gas taxes and conventional tolls, which merely recoup direct construction and maintenance costs.

Recent Changes

Nevertheless, a few cities around the world have turned to policies akin to congestion pricing, notably Singapore, Kuala Lumpur, Oslo, Bergen, and Trondheim. Will such policies become acceptable elsewhere? While much of the emphasis of public support for surface transportation in the past has been on adding new capacity, recent decades have seen more attention being given to nonconstruction measures that will improve system efficiency, such as traffic signal synchronization, incident management systems, traveler information systems, and ramp metering. As these capabilities are applied and congestion remains, consideration may move on to pricing measures.

Over and above philosophical arguments about the fairness and appropriateness of congestion pricing, one of the difficulties in advancing this concept has been the high administrative cost and difficulty of collecting the tolls. This obstacle is fading fast as the capacity to collect tolls in less burdensome ways has made huge advances in recent years via electronic toll collection.

The vast majority of U.S. roads are free of toll, supported by fuel taxes and other user fees paid to states and the Federal Highway Trust Fund. These fees are then returned to road users through various highway programs. In this financing environment, congestion pricing has appeared alien and threatening. But this resistance could fade with the introduction of HOT lanes—lanes reserved for high-occupancy or toll-paying vehicles, which are now being introduced in a few U.S. cities. The operators of HOT lanes impose substantial tolls for peak-hour travel. Experience along SR 91 in California, the earliest of the HOT lanes, shows that drivers are willing to pay rather than drive on congested alternate routes. Experiences like this could erode the resistance to congestion pricing that has been evident in recent years.

The ability to add new highway capacity is already severely restricted by budgetary constraints and public concerns about the environment, visual blight, and the quality of life. It will become evermore restricted as open space becomes scarcer and scarcer, and as esthetic, developmental, and environmental priorities continue to gain added force. This will lead to increased priority on achieving maximum system efficiency, forcing greater consideration—in concept at least—of measures such as congestion pricing, which have not been feasible in the past.

---

[14] Sidney and Beatrice Webb, *English Local Government: The Story of the King's Highway* (London: Longmans, Green and Co., 1913), p. 5.

Several parallel developments make reconsideration of pricing timely. As the technologies of ITS continue to advance, electronic identification of vehicles is becoming much more widespread, making congestion pricing more feasible administratively. As HOT lanes are built and operated, this form of economic demand management appears to be gaining public acceptance. Such developments suggest that congestion pricing, which has long been the very benchmark of political impossibility, is becoming less impractical, alien, and threatening than it was in the past.

Actual applications of congestion pricing will probably continue to be scarce, but planning consideration of demand restrictions, modest peak-period price premiums, and other pricing measures will be increasingly common. Consideration of such alternatives involves far more than technical issues: it raises the specter of consequences that clash with deep-set cultural attitudes, notions of fairness, and expectations of basic rights. Resolution of these matters will require new levels of public and political participation in planning.

Communications as a Substitute for Transportation

Communications Changes

The explosion in communications and computing capabilities has fueled a series of forecasts that these technologies will replace the need for travel. These predictions have been prompted by communications improvements in long-distance services, conference calling, videoconferencing, email, the Internet, file sharing, and facsimile transmission; but the anticipated substitution of communications for transportation has not materialized...yet. Certainly, more and more workers are finding that they can telecommute effectively. The business press and technical experts alike foresee continued expansion in computing and communications capabilities, and further sharp reductions in their costs. As a result, the substitution of communications for transportation, which has thus far mostly eluded us, finally appears to be on the brink of making substantial changes in how people work, leading to shifts in where they live and work, and when and where they travel. Already, one report indicates that about eight percent of all workers—or about 11 million people—now telecommute in one form or another.[15]

Transportation Implications

These shifts could have profound consequences on transportation. If significant numbers of workers are able to perform part or all of their jobs from their homes or other remote locations, this could reduce the number of commuting trips and business-related trips, as well as shift the times and places where such trips occur. It could allow small towns and distant suburbs to become viable places for telecommuting workers to live. Residents in all parts of the country, rural and urban alike, increasingly enjoy the same shopping opportunities, stock-market information and access, current news in electronic format, access to technical literature, and other benefits of the Internet. This ability frees self-employed and retired persons to choose their residence without regard to these amenities.

To the extent that people actually do shift location in response to these new communications capabilities, this could create radically different patterns of land use and transportation. Other forces, like proximity to schools, hospitals, churches, cultural attractions and the like will continue to weigh heavily in location decisions; but the rise of telecommuting could shift the balance by eliminating the importance of burdensome commutes, at least for those who can rearrange where work occurs. What might this do to the suburban boom of the past thirty or forty years? Census data show that although total population grew by 64 percent between 1950 and 1990, the number of people living in nonmetropolitan areas fell by 6.5 million; and the population of metropolitan areas increased by 33.8 million. Within metropolitan areas, the population of central cities grew modestly, by 45 percent between 1950 and 1990. The bulk of metropolitan growth—indeed of national growth—was in suburbs, which grew by 232 percent during these four decades. Freed from commuting constraints, this suggests that the newfound freedom offered by telecommuting might be to push the boundaries of suburbia still further out and to encourage satellite communities beyond the suburban fringes. These areas may now lie outside the reach of today's metropolitan planning.

---

[15] *Urban Transportation Monitor*, vol. 11, no. 14 (Fairfax Station, Va.: Lawley Publications, July 18, 1997), pp. 1–2.

Global Climate Change

Scientific Basis

Societal concern about the environment has become far more pronounced. All sectors of the economy—whether agriculture, manufacturing, mining, or transportation—and all aspects of environmental quality—noise, wetland preservation, hazardous materials, and air quality—are being reassessed in terms of these heightened environmental expectations, both in the United States and around the world. Increasingly, as with trans-national migration of acid rain, the issues are recognized to be regional or global in scope, giving rise to discussion of more broadly based environmental control strategies. Nowhere is this broadened concern more pronounced than in the case of emissions of gases that build up in the atmosphere and have the potential to alter climate around the world.

Huge uncertainties abound surrounding questions of when, where, and how much climate change will actually occur. There are many open disagreements about the climate models used to answer these questions. Experts' divergent predictions have spawned complex technical arguments and additional research. It is not always clear which is a balanced assessment, an alarmist exaggeration, or baseless optimism. But several key facts about global warming are well established. Anthropogenic emissions from mobile and stationary sources represent a small fraction—about 5 percent—of overall carbon dioxide emissions, the remaining 95 percent stemming from natural biogenic processes such as oceans, plant decay, and animal respiration. Various natural process absorb carbon dioxide at a somewhat greater rate than biogenic sources produce it, so that nature has a considerable capacity to accommodate human-generated creation of this gas. But the scale of human-generated emissions has exceeded this natural buffer in the last 150 years. The amount of carbon dioxide in the air has risen, as witnessed by measurements of cores from the Antarctic ice cap. This build up appears to be a result of the burning of wood, coal, and petroleum following the industrial revolution.

Transportation is a major contributor to greenhouse gasses. Vehicles emit large amounts of carbon dioxide, which is of particular concern to global climate change. In the United States about one-third of all anthropogenic carbon dioxide emissions are from transportation vehicles, and transportation emissions have been increasing more rapidly than those of most other sectors of the economy. Transportation also produces methane, nitrous oxide, and other greenhouse gases. Transportation emissions are troublesome not only because of their large scale and rapid increase, but also because of the difficulty of controlling them. If international treaties to control greenhouse gasses are ever enacted, the U.S. transportation sector, which accounts for seven percent of carbon dioxide emissions from all sources in all countries, will certainly be a primary focus of attention.

There are scientifically sound reasons why increased amounts of carbon dioxide, methane, and other greenhouse gases, in conjunction with increases in other atmospheric constituents, can cause earth's temperature to rise. Actual temperatures have in fact risen during in the last 150 years, but they have not done so in a regular, steady way. There was a sharp drop in temperature in the 1900s, a steady increase from 1910 to 1940, a cooling trend during the 1950s and 1960s, and a rising trend from 1970 on. On average, the temperature on the planet has increased between 0.5 and 1.0 degrees Fahrenheit over the last century. Whether or not the build up of greenhouse gasses has contributed to this pattern is uncertain, as is the extent and timing of their effect on future climate conditions.

Because carbon dioxide lasts for 50 to 100 years once it is formed, the long-term cumulative effects are worrisome. But their effect on global climate is hotly debated. The actual temperature increases of the last century are less than those predicted by most mathematical climate models. A variety of natural and anthropogenic causes make predictions difficult. Human-caused depletion of stratospheric ozone and increases in smog may retard global warming. Shifts in ocean currents, the jet stream, precipitation levels, snow cover and cloud cover, and volcanic eruptions affect the link between increased carbon dioxide levels and earth's average temperature; and temperature effects vary widely from one region to another.

As a result, predictions of future global warming and its effects stir up divergent reactions, ranging from alarmist to defensive. The Environmental Protection Agency predicts temperature increases of two to six degrees Fahrenheit by the year 2100. If this occurs, it could increase global precipitation, cause intense rainstorms, and increase the sea level along most of the U.S. coast by two feet. Global effects of this scale would bring severe economic and social consequences, especially in places like Bangladesh, with much low-lying land and limited economic resources. The amount of attention given to global warming by nations around the world is increasing, and these must deal with vast disparities in responsibility for current emissions of greenhouse gases, as well as the potential for development in other countries to exacerbate the problem. The United States now emits more than one-fifth of total global greenhouse gases. Per capita, China, Brazil, Mexico, and India emit far less, but as these countries adopt the automobile on a large scale it will add materially to global totals. International deliberations on global warming struggle to balance the disproportionate responsibility that industrial nations have for current emissions and the key role that developing nations will play in future emissions. Negotiations on international agreements to control emissions of greenhouse gasses reflect this divide, and the associated political sensitivities drive the responses of both industrial and developing nations.

Transportation Implications

As of this writing, the United States has not ratified an international treaty that would limit its overall emission of greenhouse gases, nor does it appear that it is likely to do so in the next several years. As alternative international arrangements have been discussed, these have led to the consideration, in concept at least, of policies to control greenhouse gases, including across-the-board measures such as carbon taxes, sector-specific regulations similar to the corporate average fuel economy standards applied to U.S. automobiles, and voluntary measures such as ride-sharing. Domestic and international policies might also entail emissions trading arrangements, whereby sectors or nations that cannot economically achieve their own targets are able to buy credits from others who have surpassed their targets. Within the transportation sector, decreases in greenhouse gasses might come from improvements in vehicular efficiency, substitution of fuels, reductions in travel, shifts of mode, changes in location of activities, and many other changes. Major reductions would require substantial changes in these areas.

No one can foretell how scientific understanding of this issue will advance, how international policies will evolve to address the problem, or whether natural phenomena will occur to alter the picture. Nor can one predict the pace with which technological developments will yield highway vehicles with greatly reduced emissions of greenhouse gases. The transportation sector has already made huge gains in vehicular fuel efficiency and operational coordination. Recent automotive news has highlighted new cars now being produced and ones that will be available within a few years that have dramatically improved fuel economy—60 to 100 miles per gallon—with concomitant reductions in emissions. Widespread introduction of these vehicles could transform the complexion of the entire set of issues surrounding global warming. In spite of major uncertainties like future technological capability and the many difficulties of quantitative prediction, there is nonetheless widespread scientific conviction that there is a serious problem associated with carbon dioxide levels, and that it may be self-defeating to wait and see how bad it is. As best we know, the carbon dioxide produced today will be here 50 to 100 years from now. Reversing a pattern of high emissions will take many years as new vehicles, travel restrictions, or land use patterns are phased in. The complexion of the issue is sharply different from one country to another, and global solutions will require negotiation of new forms of cooperation such as emissions-trading agreements.

The difficult process of crafting a solution to this problem is only beginning. The stakes are immense. The problem is growing. Solutions are slow and may be distasteful. For example, efficiency improvements might impose a cost in terms of vehicular performance; fuel substitution might involve reductions in convenience, range, or performance; and demand management could impinge on personal mobility. Yet public concern around the world is growing and intensifying the pressures for a coordinated international approach to the issue. Political responses are limited by public awareness. Society's assumptions about unrestricted mobility appear to be on a collision course with global warming. If future events unfold in a way that forces governments to enact global protective policies to combat human-caused alteration of climate, this could lead to consideration of measures that are viewed as unacceptable today. Planning for this contingency will require new tools to evaluate a wide range of governmental policies relative to transportation, land use, and vehicular technology.

Growth in Intermodal Transportation

One of the fastest growing sectors of transportation has been intermodal freight transportation, which provides origin-to-destination services using a mixture of two or more modes but allows the shipper to contract for this on a single freight bill. All of us are familiar with the convenience of overnight package delivery services and know from experience how this service, which might have seemed exotic at first, has become an everyday business necessity. Much of our office paperwork moves this way, as do many of the ever-growing volume of items that consumers purchase from catalogs or over the Internet. In 1960, the United Parcel Service reported that it carried $5 million in revenues for its trucking operations alone. By 1970 this figure had risen to $420 million and by 1980 to $3,963 million. In 1996, the United Parcel Service reported revenues of $16 billion on these operations.

Businesses making large shipments also stand to realize substantial benefits from intermodal freight transportation. Containerization of cargo has made it possible to move material rapidly and economically among ship, rail, and truck. Intermodal services have grown rapidly in recent years, and further growth is expected.

Intermodal Policy

Government policy has long recognized the need to adopt a comprehensive, multimodal vision. This was the driving force for the creation of the U.S. Department of Transportation in 1966 and for many state departments of transportation since then. At the national level, one administration after another has issued policy statements calling for an integrated national transportation policy, not just a funding strategy for highways and transit but a set of laws and institutions that would move us from a world of mode-specific policies and plans into one where transportation by all modes was treated methodically in its entirety. As logical as this sounds, it has proven to be impossible to design a national transportation system or to delineate a clear set of multimodal priorities for the nation. The task has been illusive because of the massive scale and complexity of a national transportation system. There are so many competing objectives—economic, social, regional, modal, corporate, and programmatic—that the task defies central planning and administration. Historically, the parts of this system have been difficult enough to coordinate one mode at a time. The prospect of governments creating "command and control" structures to achieve modal coordination and balance has threatened all involved—all modal interests, private as well as public agencies, and shippers as well as carriers. As a result, the goal of an integrated national transportation policy has remained more rhetorical than real.

The last two authorizing bills for surface transportation—in 1991 and 1998—introduced a new approach to intermodalism. Rather than attempt to design and implement command and control plans for the entire transportation sector, these acts instead created financial flexibility for using highway funding to address interconnections to the surrounding transportation networks. They allow resources to be focused strategically on bottlenecks in the overall multimodal transportation system.

This strategy is far less ambitious than planning, building, and maintaining a national transportation system. It extends traditional highway program funding to make it eligible for use on "intermodal connectors" that allow these resources to be used on other nonhighway transportation system improvements, and it takes one step toward expanding the program focus to address the needs of the system as a whole.

Recent legislation has also increased the attention given to major transportation corridors, which will also lead to more multimodal and intermodal projects. Such incremental steps appear to be workable devices for growing out of the traditional mode-specific planning framework into one where multimodal issues receive greater consideration. This means that the work of transportation planners, which has mostly been for governments and largely focused on highway and transit matters, will increasingly have to address how the regional economy is affected by improved rail or port access links or by access to international airline services. It means that more attention will be given to freight transportation within metropolitan areas, that new ways will be found for public agencies to collaborate with private shippers and private carriers, and that public agencies will be called upon to go beyond facility planning and to devote increased attention to operational management.

Safety

Cost of Crashes

Societal concern about transportation is heavily centered around safety. Around the world, 500,000 people are killed annually in motor vehicle crashes and 15 million are injured.[16] In the United States, more than 40,000 lives are lost in highway crashes each year, more than 5 million people are injured, and 27 million vehicles damaged. The National Highway Traffic Safety Administration estimates that these crashes cost the country $150 billion per year in lost productivity, medical costs, legal and court costs, emergency service costs, insurance administration costs, travel delay, property damage, and workplace losses. Airline disasters anywhere in the world are lead stories in the news. Train derailments and multicar pileups make the national news. Every one of the people who die on U.S. highways each year are covered in the local news, as are numerous truck jackknife incidents and hazardous materials spills. Few, if any, citizens get through life without experiencing a crash firsthand or without knowing someone killed in a traffic crash.

Much has been done to improve highway safety. Cars have safety belts, air bags, and many other safety features. Roads are being built and retrofit to higher geometric specifications, to have safer guardrails, energy-absorbing crash attenuators, and many other safety-enhancing features. The effect of all these improvements is evident. The number of traffic fatalities per mile driven has been dropping continuously year after year. In 1975, there were 2.95 fatalities for every hundred million miles traveled. By 1995, that rate had fallen to 1.98 fatalities. But much remains to be done. More than one-third of all crashes are caused in part by alcohol impairment, and more than two-thirds of highway crash victims were not wearing safety belts.[17] Our driving behaviors do not appear to match our expressions of concern about highway safety.

If visitors from another century were to arrive suddenly in contemporary U.S. society, they would probably be astounded by our progress in reducing fatalities from warfare and sickness. They would probably also be stupefied at the death caused by transportation. But having grown up in the auto age, we have become numb to its grim statistics. We have heard over and over that highway deaths are the leading cause of accidental death in the United States and the leading cause of death—accidental or otherwise—for persons between 15 and 24 years of age. We have heard that the United States has had more people die driving on its highways than fighting in its wars. Six out of every ten children born today will be injured in a highway crash during their lifetime. Through repetition, statistics like this have become dull; but the awful reality they represent is known to each of us through personal tragedies.

Future Challenges

Safety will continue to be a paramount issue in transportation planning. The advances that have been made in driver behavior, vehicle features, and road design form a strong basis for further progress. The future will also bring new problems. For example, the baby boom starts turning 65 in the year 2011. In their retirement years they are apt to remain auto dependent. They will face health and medical conditions that make driving risky for them and others. These risks can be reduced with ample anticipation and planning. Automobiles can be designed to make controls more compatible with the needs of older persons, new crash-avoidance technologies can help, and crashworthiness can be adjusted to reflect the changing demographics. Highway, transit, and pedestrian facilities can be improved to make them safer for older people. Better training and medical assessment programs can be made available and affordable to post-stroke patients and other rehabilitating drivers. Alternative transportation services can be improved to make them more accessible to retirees. Crashes involving older drivers will become an increasing priority on the highway safety agenda.

Improving safety while enhancing mobility, personal freedom, efficiency, esthetic, and other transportation concerns is a continuous and ever-changing balance. Speed limits, safety belt laws, regulations requiring air bags, crackdowns on drinking and driving, and other steps to control this balance stir considerable public attention. As technology has advanced and public concern has mounted, public policies have continued to encourage further improvements in transportation safety. The American Association of State Highway and Transportation Officials recently prepared the

---

[16] Christopher J.L. Murray and Alan D. Lopez, *The Global Burden of Disease* (Cambridge, Mass.: Harvard School of Public Health, Harvard University Press, 1997).

[17] *Traffic Engineering Handbook,* 4th ed. (Washington, D.C.: Institute of Transportation Engineers, Chapter 2, 1992).

Strategic Highway Safety Plan, designed to reduce highway deaths by 5,000 to 7,000 by 2004, using cost-effective measures that are acceptable to the general public. It includes initiatives to improve driver behavior, such as graduated licensing for younger drivers. It also addresses special users, specifically bicyclists; vehicles, particularly trucks; highways (minimizing the consequences of leaving the road, better intersection design, and safer work zones); emergency medical services; and improved safety management systems.[18] The substantial improvements that are possible through improved sensing and greater automation of functions can accelerate the pace of safety gains; but they will also raise difficult new issues of technological dependence, liability, governmental roles, and privacy. Striking a new balance between transportation safety and other societal concerns will continue to be a top priority of transportation planning in the years ahead.

Public Expectation of Transportation

Accomplishment and Disillusionment

Because transportation and society go hand-in-hand, the aspirations of society become the aims of transportation. These aims appear to have been less clearly drawn in recent years than they were in earlier eras. Articulating those aims at this juncture poses a special challenge. In earlier eras, one or another social goal has been matched by an exciting development in transportation; and this has stirred public interest and support. At the turn of the century, crowded, noisy, and polluted cities made urban dwellers long for escape, just as streetcars and the automobile made their deliverance possible. In the 1920s, the backwardness and isolation of rural areas made "getting the farmer out of the mud" a priority; and this led to a policy that saw highways not just as a tie to nearby cities, but as a truly interconnected network that tied cities and regions together. The 1939 Worlds Fair portrayed an exciting vision of coast-to-coast, high-speed highways that would dramatically increase the range of places Americans could visit, live, and work. In the 1950s, the United States set out to begin construction of the National System of Interstate and Defense Highways, a project that dominated transportation policy through the 1980s.

Today, transportation rarely ranks at the top of the list of hot issues in public opinion polls. The facilities in place appear to be largely taken for granted. Many local projects stir considerable public interest, but a larger share of national attention focuses on social concerns like environmental problems, noise, and safety. No radically different new locomotion technologies are known to be hovering just around the corner. The transportation sector, which is more crucial than ever, seems to be perceived to be a mature industry with an unexciting future.

The creation of the interstate system during the past forty years left strong imprints on the U.S. economy and development patterns. It reshaped where we live, work, shop, and spend spare time. It ushered in a new era in the marketing of roadside services—fast-food, motel chains, and major merchandisers. It triggered substantial gains in economic growth and it facilitated population expansion and metropolitan growth that might not have been achievable without it. But in spite of such benefits, it is seen by many as a mixed blessing. Critics perceive that it did not solve congestion problems in urban areas nor make driving more pleasant. They feel it exacerbated air pollution problems, split apart cities, and disfigured countrysides.

Such criticisms may be valid for some parts of the system and not for others. Everyone living in the United States today has his or her own opinion about the value of the system. Much has been written about it. As major new road systems are planned in Brazil, China, India, and elsewhere in the world, the U.S. interstate experience is being mined for useful inferences. It is a big chapter in economic and social history that will be analyzed and debated for years to come. One recent book describes it in these words:

> 'O public road,' wrote Walt Whitman in oft-quoted lines, 'You express me better than I can express myself.' In building the Interstate Highway System, the American people expressed themselves in all of their glory, all of their virtue, and not a few of their vices. The highways show our grace and our vision, but they also reveal, at times, our

---

[18] *Strategic Highway Safety Plan* (Washington, D.C.: American Association of State Highway and Transportation Officials, 1997).

impetuousness and our shortsightedness. They represent the height of American technology. They suggest all our dreams for what America might become—one nation, indivisible, bound for all time by concrete and asphalt strands. As so often happens, the dream played out differently over the four decades it took to build the Interstates, and we learned that the very roads we thought would unite us have sometimes actually divided us. Over the decades, the Interstates have reflected our shifting attitudes about technology, landscape, community, race relations, and the quality of our lives. Indeed, as our image of ourselves has changed from the one we had in 1956, so have our highways. In this way the Interstates have revealed our dreams and realities better than any of us could have predicted.[19]

There may never be a final verdict about whether there were better ways to deal with rising population, a growing economy, and the auto age. Nor will we ever be sure whether or not the shortcomings of the interstate system might have been better anticipated. Certainly the accomplishment was an unprecedented one, and one that produced immense economic benefits. It also taught us about limitations and unexpected consequences. In cycle after cycle, culminating with the building of the interstate system, we have found that a new road is not a permanent solution to congestion problems. We have learned that limited-access, high-speed highways may be efficient; but some scar the landscape and make bad neighbors for many.

Today our dependence on transportation is greater than ever. This dependence is growing daily, as metropolitan growth continues to push homes, jobs, and stores outward, and as we become reliant on catalog shopping, just-in-time production, increased recreational opportunities, international air access, and all the other social and economic changes that have accompanied the development of modern transportation.

Transportation programs reflect the growing diversity of society's needs and the desire to fit transportation more harmoniously into communities. The growing number of local-interest highway projects that have found their way into national legislation in several recent reauthorization cycles reflects the lack of a single, unifying vision behind the national highway program. This fragmentation, coupled with post-interstate understanding, could mark the beginning of a new era. The benefits that transportation can bring to society remain important, but public attention appears to focus increasingly on alleviating the costs imposed by the current system and extensions to it. Programs have been introduced to offset the negative effects of new transportation facilities and services and to pay for features that make projects more amenable to communities. An increasing share of funds goes into programs that improve how we integrate transportation with society's other goals.

Future Planning Challenges

For planners and other professionals working amidst these changing expectations, the shift in public expectations has sometimes been sudden and disillusioning. Seen only recently as the deliverers of mobility, speed, and efficiency that society wanted, the professionals who designed and built the interstate system are occasionally stunned to find themselves vilified for creating current environmental and urban problems.

Transportation plans, like any other plans, do not always end up as anticipated. But their unanticipated outcomes may point the way to future improvements. As public expectations about beautification, environmental quality, and safety have grown, planning has become more comprehensive. We now focus far beyond facility provision, increasingly addressing the challenge of system operation. We find ourselves increasingly challenged to work with new partners, new modes, new policies, and new social concerns, and to reconcile far-reaching public expectations. We know that no fixed set of disciplinary methods or professional tools can keep up with the challenge.

Planning will continue to be an evermore dynamic, pluralistic activity, responsive to the public and its elected representatives. It will be the voice for an ever-wider array of concerns, reflecting many complex links between transportation and society. We must continue to develop better ways to portray the full range of consequences of transportation actions and to describe how they affect each set of interests. We must work with more and more industries, companies, agencies, neighborhoods, and other groups with a stake in transportation matters. We must continue to

---

[19] Tom Lewis, *Divided Highways* (New York, N.Y.: Viking, 1997), p. 294.

synthesize all this effectively to support elected leaders in their search for solutions. As we look for a better match between the aspirations of society and the goals of transportation, we must reflect a seasoned understanding that political resolution of conflicts is the appropriate planning process, not an intruder into the realm of professionals. Our vision and our tools must continue to evolve to serve society's changing expectations.

CHAPTER 3
Commodity Flows and Freight Transportation

Russell B. Capelle, Jr.
Manager of Freight Data Programs
Bureau of Transportation Statistics and the
Bureau of Transportation Statistics staff[1]

Introduction and Important Changes Since the First Edition

Since the first issue of the *Handbook* was published in 1992, many changes have occurred in the world of freight transportation data. Transportation Research Board (TRB) Report 234, *Data for Decisions,* paved the way for the Intermodal Surface Transportation Efficiency Act of 1991 (ISTEA) to create the Bureau of Transportation Statistics (BTS). In 1994, the Interstate Commerce Commission (ICC), which had been around for more than a hundred years, was eliminated, with most remaining functions transferred to the Surface Transportation Board (STB) and the motor carrier financial data collection program managed by BTS.

Transportation planners and transportation engineers need to understand the importance of freight within the urban system, including global commodity flow issues that directly or indirectly affect their city. In a world of just-in-time (JIT), growing air freight movements, larger and larger vessels (over 6,000 TEUs [20-foot equivalent container units] and "FastShip" technology), and supply chains that extend around the globe, metropolitan planning organization (MPO) freight transportation planning cannot be viewed as just counting trucks in the traffic stream anymore, regardless of whether you are a transportation engineer in Boise, Botswana, Bremen, Bali, Bratislava, Beijing, Buenos Aires, or Brisbane.

Freight is moved to, within, and through urban areas not just in trucks; many package movements, retail deliveries, and other time-sensitive movements occur in commercial automobiles, including "virtual trucks" (sports utility vehicles, also known as SUVs). With JIT movements so critical to manufacturers, offices, and other businesses, counting "heavy trucks" and perhaps designing restrictive policies to exclude "trucks" from certain city streets may be counterproductive. Those in the business of trucking prevented from moving their freight on city streets in vehicles over 10,000 tons gross vehicle weight rating may react understandably to move their freight in cars, SUVs, motorcycles or bicycles—a response that *increases, not decreases* the total number of trips on the streets in the traffic analysis zones of the MPO's regional model! Even more importantly, nearly all passenger vehicle movements in cities *are the cause of or are in response to* freight activities. Ken Ogden said it best:

> . . . [F]rom the viewpoint of transport planning and policy . . . urban freight is important . . . . It is very significant in economic terms. The total resource costs of urban goods movement are comparable to those of urban person movement . . . In other words, about half of total urban transport costs, in economic terms, are related to freight.[2]

---

[1] Sections 3.3 and 3.4. of this chapter are closely adapted from the following sources: *Transportation Statistics Annual Report* (TSAR) (Washington, D.C.: Bureau of Transportation Statistics, 1997); section 3.3 is closely adapted from Chapter 10 by Lisa Randall; and section 3.4 is closely adapted from Chapter 9 by Felix Ammah-Tagoe, Wendell Fletcher (TSAR Project Director), and other BTS publications and data bases.

[2] Ogden, Kenneth Wade, "Urban Goods Movement and Its Relation to Planning" in *Proceedings of the Urban Goods and Freight Forecasting Conference* (Washington, D.C.: FHWA and TMIP, forthcoming, 1998, 2-1 to 2-14). Full text available on the Internet: http://www.bts.gov/ntl/

Passengers going to shop, going to work, coming from work, going to a restaurant for lunch or dinner, going to a movie, or just going for a drive are indeed making freight-related trips. If the trucks from the food and department store warehouses, from suppliers to manufacturers, from restaurant and entertainment supply houses, and from highway paving and construction companies had not made their trips, passengers would not be making theirs. Freight must be viewed by transportation planners and transportation engineers in proper perspective. While a traffic classification count might show "heavy trucks" to be a relatively small proportion of the traffic stream in an urban area, freight movement and commodity flows in, within, and from that metropolis are the *raison d'etre* for passenger movements.

Current State of Statistical Programs

After a lapse of twenty years since commodity flow data were available for the nation from the U.S. Bureau of Census' (Census) 1977 Commodity Transportation Survey, the 1993 Commodity Flow Survey (CFS) is a vast improvement and provides meaningful national commodity flow results. The 1993 CFS results are being used at not only the national level, but also at the state[3] and MPO[4] levels.

The 1997 CFS data collection was completed during 1998 at the Census, with whom BTS works closely. BTS makes CFS results accessible to users in print, on CD-ROM, and on the Internet. Publication and dissemination of 1997 CFS data will for the first time include tables of results for the metropolitan area (for the top fifty cities) and for the rest-of-state regions. BTS is actively encouraging MPOs and state departments of transportation (DOTs) to integrate CFS data in their regional modeling, statewide planning, and policy and impact analyses.

The Vehicle Inventory and Use Survey (VIUS), formerly Census' quinquennial Truck Inventory and Use Survey, has been used to provide truck trip table input for regional modeling. Based on work in 1997 at the Boston MPO, BTS has an active project to develop a Truck Trip Estimation Procedure (TTEP) using the VIUS data base. The 1997 VIUS data collection was completed by Census in 1998; and, with funds from the Transportation Equity Act for the 21st Century (TEA-21), BTS and Census hope to redesign VIUS in the future to include commercial cars and buses. The 1997 VIUS results are truck-only results, including pickups, SUVs, and vans.

Traditional freight data bases used for many years continue. The Federal Railroad Administration's (FRA) Rail Waybill statistics, Census' Trucking Annual Survey (formerly the Trucking and Warehousing Annual Survey), Census' County Business Patterns, and other major freight data bases are reviewed later in this chapter.

Management Systems and Freight Advisory Councils

To better plan for an intermodal world, ISTEA mandated the development of six management systems and one monitoring system. Some of the systems were later made voluntary, not mandatory. MPOs were asked to continue or create these six management systems: Congestion, Safety, Bridge, Pavement, Public Transit, and Intermodal Management Systems (IMS). The IMS is the one management system that explicitly deals with freight issues. The one monitoring system is the Highway Transportation Monitoring System.

An IMS in practice is a *structured process* for information and data collection and analysis, synthesis, and evaluation of alternative strategies to provide transportation professionals with the foundation for making strategic policy decisions.[5] Many freight data elements needed for IMSs are in the private sector. Planners and transportation companies need to work together to develop appropriate data bases.

As a result of ISTEA-stimulated activities, many MPOs formed Freight Advisory Councils to encourage interchange among MPO planners and transportation engineers, state and MPO decision makers and policymakers, freight trade organizations and associations, and the whole spectrum of transportation businesses (e.g., shippers, carriers, consignees).

---

[3] Black, 1997 and 1998; Erlbaum, 1998; Krishnan and Hancock, 1998.

[4] Biddle, Siaurusaitis, Matherly, and Perincherry, 1998.

[5] See Capelle, 1995b.

The Freight Advisory Council is not just a formality, but a necessity. It is *the* most important *networking resource*. Agencies can find out what issues are important to private sector users, define data needs on that basis, and initiate mechanisms for sharing private sector freight intermodal information.

The Need for Understanding the Bigger Freight Picture

MPO and state agencies need to better understand the global or national freight picture. Even within their jurisdictions, many agencies have state or metropolitan freight data but do not analyze it to gain greater understanding of regional freight movements. Some freight data bases may be archived once completed for specific projects and may not be made available to other projects, divisions, or agencies (e.g., truck classification counts). MPOs may not have geocoded the locations of trucking companies of different types to understand, for regional modeling purposes, the truck trip production and attraction nodes in their region, when commercial trucking industry directories of such locations are readily available.

Understanding freight commodity and traffic movements in the MPO region and beyond is the foundation upon which good regional freight modeling stands. The following sections cover commodity flows and freight transportation information and issues at the global, hemispheric, national, state, and MPO levels.

The United States and Global Freight Transportation[6]

International Trade: Freight Shipments To and From the United States

International trade has become an increasingly important component of the U.S. economy. The ratio of the sum of U.S. exports and imports to U.S. gross domestic product (GDP) (1) over time shows this trend clearly. GDP measures the value added by all goods and services in the economy, while the sum of exports and imports measures the size of the international trade component of an economy.)

This section briefly describes trends in international freight shipments to and from U.S. seaports and airports, as well as transborder land shipments by truck and railroad between the United States and Canada or Mexico. (Figure 3–1.)

Factors Affecting International Freight Flows

Growth and changes in the national and regional economies, business production and distribution changes, and regional and global trade agreements are key factors in international freight movements. GDP nearly doubled between 1970 and 1995.

Today's businesses often require higher priced, higher quality transportation to assure quicker product deliveries, on time, and with little product loss of damage. These requirements are one reason for the growth of trucking.

As business practices have changed, so too have the modal competitors, with, for example, rail carriers turning to intermodal arrangements or seeking technological improvements that cut costs. Business uses of more expensive transportation modes fit a pattern of a dynamic, globalized economy moving toward lower overall cost of production and product distribution.

In part because of improved and pervasive transportation infrastructure, businesses have more choice in siting new facilities than they did a few decades ago. Manufacturing companies may have branch plants, distribution centers, and supplier networks in far-flung locations, with raw materials, parts, and employees often in transit between facilities. It is often said that trucks today, with JIT transportation being so important, are warehouses on wheels. Efficient and reliable transportation permits interaction between these locations and extends the area over which industries can market their goods and services, thus increasing options for consumers.

---

[6] This section (3.3, "The United States and Global Freight Transportation") does not use footnotes. Instead, please see section 3.9, "Selected References, Partially Annotated," under BTS/TSAR, for the sources to which the numerical notes in parentheses in section 3.3 refer.

(Percentage of total metric ton-kilometers)

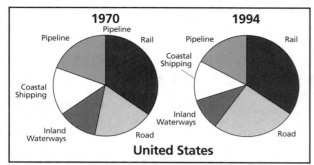

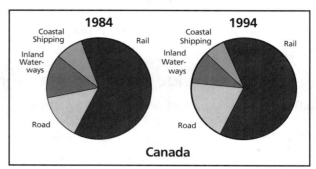

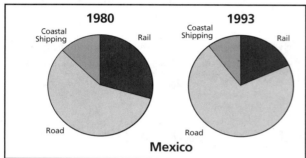

Figure 3–1   Domestic Freight Activity by Mode in Selected Countries and Regions

Note: Excludes domestic air freight, includes domestic coastal shipping where applicable and when available.

Source: Bureau of Transportation Statistics, U.S. Department of Transportation. *Transportation Statistics Annual Report 1997*, Washington, D.C.: BTS, U.S. DOT, 1997.

Waterborne Freight

Between 1970 and 1995, U.S. international waterborne freight nearly doubled, while domestic freight only grew by 15 percent. The total tonnage of all U.S. waterborne freight, including internal domestic commerce as well as international trade to and from U.S. ports, increased by 46 percent to 2.2 billion tons.

International waterborne traffic involves exports and imports through coastal and Great Lakes ports. The tonnage of imports and exports increased through coastal ports, but it declined for Great Lakes ports from 1970 to 1995 (2). In 1994, U.S. oceanborne imports and exports amounted to $517 billion (current dollars), an enormous increase from $49 billion in 1970 (3). Although both imports and exports grew, exports' share of the total value of waterborne trade fell from 50 percent in 1970 to 34 percent in 1994, indicating the negative U.S. trade balance. In 1970, east coast ports had over 50 percent of the total value of trade, with the west coast taking the third place at 20 percent. By 1993, the west coast was the leading region with 45 percent while the east had fallen to second place with 38 percent (4).

Air Freight

Air freight moves via all-cargo air carriers as well as by air carriers that transport primarily passengers. Between 1980 and 1995, freight revenue ton-miles by passenger carriers grew much faster in the international market (173 percent) than in the domestic market (88 percent). Revenue ton-miles produced by the all-cargo air carriers grew even faster. In 1995, the seven major all-cargo air carriers (5) flew 9.3 billion revenue ton-miles (international movements), up 405 percent from 1980.

Imports and exports shipped by air grew rapidly—from 11 percent of the value of all international trade in 1970 to 25 percent in 1994 (6). Air, however, only accounts for a small portion of exports and imports by weight.

BTS' *Transportation Statistical Annual Report, 1997* (see section 3.9 of this chapter) lists the nation's major international air freight gateway cities and the tonnage passing through them in 1994. U.S. flag carriers moved 41 percent of the international air freight tonnage. Among the nation's top 15 domestic gateways for international air shipments, the share of freight carried by U.S. flag carriers ranged from nearly 100 percent in Memphis, Tennessee, to 7 percent in Fairbanks, Alaska. Between January and May 1995, the period with the most recent information, the major country markets for U.S. products ranked by tons of air freight shipped were: Japan, the United Kingdom, Germany, Colombia, and South Korea (7).

Surface Freight

Surface trade is a key component of U.S. international trade, primarily because Canada and Mexico are the first and third largest trading partners of the United States, respectively. Surface trade between the United States and Canada increased eight percent to $295 billion in 1996. Trucks dominated surface freight movement accounting for approximately 68 percent or $200 billion of all U.S.-Canadian surface trade. Neighboring border states were the top five U.S. destinations for surface imports from Canada and include Michigan, New York, Ohio, Illinois, and Minnesota. These five states accounted for over half of the value of imports by all surface modes. The top five U.S. states for surface exports to Canada in 1996 were Michigan, Washington, Ohio, New York, and Illinois, accounting for 43 percent of value.

Several key land ports are critical conduits for this trade. Detroit, Buffalo, and Port Huron were the leading U.S.–Canadian gateways for trade by all surface modes, and for trade by truck, in particular. The port of Detroit, alone, accounts for 38 percent of all the surface trade between Canada and the United States. On an average day in 1996, 3,649 trucks crossed the border at the port of Detroit. Trade by rail remained relatively stable in 1996 at $56 billion or 19 percent of all traffic between the United States and Canada. An average of ten trains per day crossed each of those ports in 1996. The primary commodities traded by surface modes between the United States and Canada include motor vehicles and parts, fabricated material, heavy equipment and machinery, and food and related products.

U.S.-Mexican surface trade increased 19 percent to $115 billion in 1996. Trucks dominate U.S.–Mexican trade to an even greater extent than U.S.-Canadian. In 1996, trucks accounted for 80 percent of all surface trade, or $92 billion. This represented a 17 percent increase over 1995. By value, the major destination states for imports from Mexico in 1996 were Texas, Michigan, California, Arizona, and Tennessee.

The dominant gateway port on the southern border is Laredo, Texas. In terms of value, 34 percent of all U.S.–Mexican trade passed through Laredo. An average of 2,783 trucks and nine trains crossed the border at Laredo each day in 1996. El Paso, Texas, and Otay Mesa, California, followed Laredo with $23 and $11 billion in overall surface trade activity, respectively. Rail trade increased slightly between 1995 and 1996 to $17 billion, representing 15 percent of all surface transborder activity. Following Laredo, the top rail port was Eagle Pass, Texas, which experienced an average of four train crossings per day, totaling $4 billion worth of rail trade in 1996. Recent alliances between Kansas City Southern and Union Pacific-Southern Pacific and recently privatized Mexican rail lines have the potential to increase overall rail trade between the United States and Mexico and at Laredo and Eagle Pass, Texas in particular. The primary commodities traded by surface modes between the United States and Mexico include electrical machinery, motor vehicles and parts, plastics, optical and medical equipment and nuclear reactors, boilers and related machinery.

There is an east–west orientation evident in the nation's major highways and railways, linking Pacific Coast cities to the nation's interior and to Atlantic and Gulf Coast cities. In the western United States, highway and rail routes that run north to south tend to be relatively circuitous. There is little inland commercial waterway traffic west of the Mississippi River Basin, other than on the Columbia-Snake River System in the Pacific Northwest, and that traffic is east-west oriented.

A key freight access and infrastructure question in the coming years is how this pattern of supply will affect, and be affected by, new transportation demands arising from recently liberalized trade policies, notably the 1993 North American Free Trade Agreement with Canada and Mexico and the 1994 agreement resulting in the creation of the World Trade Organization (WTO), the successor to the General Agreement on Tariffs and Trade. The WTO was established on January 1, 1995.

Freight Transportation Trends in Other Countries

While the pace and extent of change vary, common trends are underway worldwide. In freight transportation, trucking is increasing its modal share at the expense of other modes. At the same time, many countries are also experiencing rapid growth in air freight transportation, although it accounts for a relatively small modal share. In general, these changes are occurring faster in countries with rapidly developing economies than they are in already industrialized countries.

Global competition and technological advances are changing the way in which many goods are manufactured and distributed within the United States and elsewhere in the world. Manufacturers often obtain raw materials and inputs, conduct operations, and rely on suppliers all around the world. Transportation innovations, coupled with the information technologies, have enabled close coordination between producers, transporters, and distributors of goods and materials at every stage of production.

As in the United States, sectoral economic changes influence freight activity in other countries. In most western European countries, manufacturing and services, rather than agriculture or mining, are the dominant economic sectors. Consequently, manufactured goods, often lower in weight and higher in value than traditional primary commodities, account for an increasing proportion of goods transported, stimulating a shift from rail to road and air transportation.

Many companies use information technology to quickly compare their stock levels (inventory) with existing and anticipated orders, and then to analyze resupply options. They can rely on readily available transportation services (including in some cases their own truck fleets) to deliver goods as they are needed, called JIT delivery.

Changes in the transportation industry itself affect how businesses transport goods. Growth in containerization and associated developments, such as doublestack rail and increased trade at certain ports, have contributed to growth in intermodal transportation. Recent railroad company realignments caused by consolidations and mergers are expected to improve efficiency and profits and reduce the costs for long-haul traffic.

Trends in Canada

Several factors, including recent economic performance, government policies, and geography, help to explain Canadian freight activity. Slow economic growth in the late 1980s and early 1990s constrained domestic freight activity during this period. Canada also saw a limited shift in output and employment away from resource-based industries toward manufacturing, knowledge-based, and service industries, affecting the level of freight activity and relative importance of modes. As the world's second largest country in land area, Canada's physiographic configuration and extent play an important role in Canada's freight transportation. For trans-Canadian freight transportation, rail has obvious competitive advantages, while road transportation has been an important mode in the manufacturing centers and large cities in the eastern provinces. Canadian national statistics show rail accounting for a little more than two-fifths and road transport one-fifth of domestic freight activity.

Trends in Mexico

Road dominates freight transportation in Mexico to a greater degree than in many other countries. Rail and, for geographical reasons, coastal shipping account for most of the rest of Mexico's domestic freight market. Air freight is growing rapidly.

Government policies and structural economic changes have influenced Mexican freight transportation. Reform of freight transportation began in the 1980s. The trucking sector, which had been organized into regional cartels with government-regulated tariffs, was deregulated in 1989. The World Bank estimated that efficiency gains (lower rates, higher quality service, and increased flexibility) from deregulation will amount to more than U.S. $500 million annually (8). Privatization and restructuring of domestic air transportation began in 1988, followed by deregulation of domestic airfares in 1991. Extensive privatization of Mexico's ports started in 1992; and privatization of the national railroad, Ferrocariles Nacionales de Mexico (FNM), officially began in 1996.

As part of privatization, FNM's rail lines were divided into five regional sections, with private firms allowed to bid on rights to the lines. Foreign companies have been allowed to bid for up to a 49-percent interest, and U.S. railroad companies are involved through alliances with Mexican investors and companies. In December 1996, an alliance between Transportacion Maritimia Mexicana, Latin America's largest integrated transportation company, and Kansas City Southern Railway, a regional U.S. railroad, won the first operating concession under the FNM privatization. The alliance, known as Transportacion Ferroviaria Mexicana, will operate Mexico's Ferrocarril del Noreste for fifty years, with the option of an additional fifty-year extension.

While rail infrastructure development has been limited until very recently, Mexico has engaged in intensive roadway development since the mid-1980s. Between 1989 and 1994, approximately 4,100 kilometers (2,548 miles) of new four-lane highways were constructed in Mexico. Because the government could not afford this level of investment alone, several public-private financing strategies were employed. State-owned banks and private construction companies financed and built the majority of new highways, which are primarily access-controlled toll roads. Construction costs have been estimated at $10 billion to $15 billion (9). Private sector consortia bid on concessions to finance, build, and operate toll roads. Generally, the government awarded concessions to companies that offered the shortest concession period; and many periods were quite short, some under ten years. As a result, some of the private sector consortia charged relatively high tolls to recoup their initial investment in construction. Consequently, Mexico had some of the highest tolls in the world—an average of 18 cents per kilometer, second only to Japan at 20.5 cents per kilometer (10). High tolls led to lower than expected traffic volumes, particularly among truckers who continued to use the older, more direct roadways connecting population and manufacturing centers. Beginning in 1993, the Mexican government increased the concession periods for several of the country's major tollways, with mixed results so far.

National and State Freight Transportation: State-to-State U.S. Commodity Flows[7]

More than six million business establishments in the United States rely on the nation's interconnected network of transportation services as they engage in local and interstate commerce and international trade. Because of the widespread availability of transportation and advances in information technology, U.S. businesses are able to transport raw materials, finished goods, services, and people effectively, often across great distances.

On a typical day in 1993, about 33 million tons of commodities, valued at about $17 billion, moved an average distance of nearly 300 miles on the U.S. transportation network (11). In 1993, nearly 13 percent of CFS shipments of office, computing, and accounting machines moved by air (including truck and air combination). In addition, about 27 percent of these shipments moved by parcel, postal, and courier services—with some proportion of this moved by air.

Freight transportation has become part of a complex logistical system that links the production and consumption processes of an economy that is becoming more globalized. Today, numerous establishments in the United States and around the world may be involved as a product is manufactured, assembled, and delivered to the consumer. To ensure that needed services are provided and delivery dates met, transportation providers often coordinate information about shipments, and can inform customers of progress during the course of a shipment. Firms may use several transportation modes to meet customer requirements that are as diverse as shipping several tons of chilled beef from Iowa to Tokyo by truck, rail, and sea in two weeks, or ensuring the next-day delivery of a birthday gift.

Commodity Movement in the United States as Measured by the 1993 CFS

Most freight movement is associated with the production, manufacture, and distribution of commodities. In addition, large quantities of materials are transported in activities as diverse as the relocation of households and businesses, the

---

[7] This section (3.4, "National and state freight transportation: state-to-state U.S. commodity flows") does not use footnotes. Instead, please see section 3.9, "Selected References, Partially Annotated," under BTS/TSAR, for the sources to which the numerical notes in parentheses in section 3.4 refer.

Table 3–1   Major Categories of Freight Shipments

Groups	Major components	Value or ton-miles	Comments
Raw materials			
Energy products (1994)	Crude oil[1]	582 billion ton-miles	Over 99 percent moved by pipeline and water
	Refined petroleum products[1]	465 billion ton-miles	About 91 percent moved by pipeline and water
	Natural gas[1]	20 trillion cubic feet by pipeline	A small portion moved by truck
	Coal[2] (1993)	$23 billion, 488 billion ton-miles	By value: about 52 percent moved by rail
Lumber, forest, and pulp or paper products (1993)[2]	Lumber or wood products	$127 billion, 121 billion ton-miles	By value: 86 percent moved by truck, 7 percent by rail
	Pulp or paper products	$195 billion, 101 billion ton-miles	By value: 82 percent moved by private or for-hire truck, 10 percent by rail
	Other forest products (e.g. bark)	$1.7 billion, 3.6 billion ton-miles	By value: 44 percent moved by for-hire truck
Mining products (1993)[2]	Metal ores (e.g. iron, copper, lead)	$20 billion, 37 billion ton-miles	By value: 64 percent moved by for-hire truck, 14 percent by rail
	Nonmetallic minerals (e.g. quarry stone, crushed stone, sand)	$21 billion, 155 billion ton-miles	By value: 76 percent moved by private and for-hire truck, 16 percent by rail
Farm and food products (1993)[2]			
Farm products	Grains, vegetables, fruit, livestock, and poultry	$142 billion, 276 billion ton-miles	By value: 68 percent moved by private and for-hire truck, 15 percent by rail, 7 percent by water
Food products	Processed meat or poultry, canned or preserved fruit, vegetables, dairy products, and beverages	$857 billion, 271 billion ton-miles	By value: 94 percent moved by private and for-hire truck
Fish products	Fresh fish and other marine products, fish hatcheries and farms products	$11 billion, 1.7 billion ton-miles	By value: 79 percent moved by truck, about 3 percent by truck and air combination
Manufactured, industrial and consumer products (1993)[2]			
Equipment, machinery, and instruments	Transportation equipment, electrical machinery, computers, and instruments	$1.7 trillion, 93 billion ton-miles	By value: 63 percent moved by truck, 17 percent by parcel, postal, and courier services
Industrial products	Chemicals, metals, rubber products, clay, concrete, glass, and stone products	$1.3 trillion, 474 billion ton-miles by rail	By value: 77 percent moved by truck, 6 percent
Consumer products	Apparel, furniture, leather products, tobacco, and textile mill products	$574 billion, 34 trillion ton-miles	By value: 75 percent moved by truck, 11 percent percent by parcel, postal, and courier services
Miscellaneous	Miscellaneous products of manufacturing, ordnance, and unknown	$322 billion, 19 billion ton-miles	By value: 73 percent moved by truck, 18 percent by parcel, postal, and courier services
Household and business moving (1994)[3]			
Household goods	Personal effects and general household goods	About 49 percent of moving industry shipments, 75 percent of its revenues	This sector's share of shipments has declined since 1987
Office moves	Furniture, equipment, and property of offices, stores, hospitals, museums, etc.	About 0.8 percent of moving industry shipments, 1.1 percent of its revenues	This sector has remained steady since 1987
Electronic and trade exhibits	Goods including objects of art, displays, and exhibits	About 50 percent of moving industry shipments, 24 percent of its revenues	Since 1987, this sector has grown the fastest in shipments
Municipal solid waste (MSW) and other waste materials			
	Municipal solid waste (1994)[4]	209 million tons; value and ton-miles information are not available	Trucks account for most movement. Rail shipments, while a small part of the total, are growing rapidly
	Waste and scrap (1993)[2]	$18 billion, 28 billion ton-miles	By value, 79 percent moved by truck, 17 percent by rail
	Waste hazardous materials/ substances (1993)[2]	$558 million, 314 million ton-miles	

Note: The data presented in this table exclude most imports shipments crossing the United states en route between foreign origins and destinations and shipments by service and retail industries and governments.

Sources:

[1] U.S. Department of Transportation, Bureau of Transportation Statistics, 1996: *National Transportation Statistics 199*, Washington, DC, December.

[2] U.S. Department of Commerce, Bureau of the Census 1996: *Commodity Flow Survey* data.

[3] American Movers Conference, 1995: *Moving Industry Financial Annual*, Alexandria, VA.

[4] U.S. Environmental Protection Agency, 1966: *Characterization of Municipal Solid Waste in the United States, 1995 Update*, Washington, DC, March.

Table 3–2   The 1993 Commodity Flow Survey

The Commodity Flow Survey (CFS) was undertaken by the Bureau of Transportation Statistics (BTS) and the Bureau of the Census, with the support of the Federal Highway Administration. It provides information on the value, weight, mode, and distance that commodities were shipped by industries in manufacturing, mining, wholesale trade, and selected retail and service industries during 1993.* The most comprehensive prior survey, the 1977 Commodity Transportation Survey, limited shipment measurements to manufactured commodities shipped beyond local areas of production.

The 1993 survey has major advantages over other sources of transportation data. For example, it:

- covers local freight movement, not just intercity shipments

- identifies parcel, postal, and courier as a separate mode of transportation

- includes freight movement between coastal ports, which has been ignored in other estimates; and

- estimates for the first time freight carried by intermodal combinations of carriers.

The 1993 CFS also gathered additional new information about shipments, determining whether commodities were shipped in containers, were hazardous materials, and were exports.

For the CFS, the Bureau of the Census collected data from approximately 200.000 business establishments, selected by geographic location and industry including all 50 states plus the District of Columbia. Each business surveyed reported on a sample of individual shipments made during a two-week period in each quarter of 1993. This produced a total sample of about 12 million shipments. From this sample of establishments and shipments, commodity flows were estimated for a universe of approximately 800.000 businesses.

Despite the extensive nature of the CFS, some freight flows were not sampled. The 1993 CFS covered export shipments, but obtained information about imports only in cases where a U.S. establishment took over a shipment after it reached a U.S. port of entry. Also, the survey excluded establishments classified in the Standard Industrial Classification as farms, forestry, fisheries, governments, construction, transportation, households, foreign establishments, and most retail and service businesses (except warehouses and catalog or mail-order houses). These sectors were excluded from the survey in order to achieve a cost-effective and manageable sample size. The CFS also did not cover shipments of crude oil. Most crude oil is moved by pipeline and water transportation, and Oak Ridge National Laboratory has estimated commodity flows for these two modes. (Where specified in this chapter, BTS has drawn on the Oak Ridge estimates to supplement the CFS findings. Otherwise, the CFS data alone are used.) Finally, the CFS obtained information about the major commodity shipped by the sampled establishment, but not about any secondary commodities included in the shipment, thus underestimating some commodity movements.

*Note: The selected retail and service industries were motion picture and videotape distributors, catalog mail-order houses, and auxiliaries such as warehouses.

Source: Bureau of Transportation Statistics, U.S. Department of Transportation. *Transportation Statistics Annual Report 1997*. Washington, D.C.: BTS, U.S. DOT, 1997.

delivery of mail and parcels, and the collection and disposal of solid waste. Table 3–1 shows estimates of the transportation of various commodity groups, measured by value and ton-miles (12).

Given this breadth of activity, no single source of information fully covers the movement of all goods in the economy. The broadest picture of domestic commodity movement is the 1993 CFS. (Table 3–2.) The CFS, conducted by the BTS and Census in 1993, is the most important single source of data about the domestic movement of goods, although some gaps still exist (e.g., it does not cover movement of farm products from the farm or government shipments).

The CFS sampled shipments by all modes of transportation from U.S. manufacturing, mining, wholesale trade, and selected retail trade and service establishments in 1993. It covered a far broader spectrum of the economy than the largest previous survey of freight movement, conducted in 1977. In 1993, domestic establishments in the sectors covered by CFS shipped materials and finished goods weighing 12.2 billion tons and generating 3.6 trillion ton-miles of transportation output. The goods shipped were valued at more than $6.1 trillion. These figures include an adjustment by Oak Ridge National Laboratory to estimate crude oil shipments by pipeline and water, which were not adequately covered in the CFS.

Table 3–3 presents the value, weight, value per ton, and ton-miles of major commodities shipped by establishments sampled by the CFS. The commodities are specified by two-digit Standard Transportation Commodity Classification (STCC) codes. Food and kindred products accounted for the highest dollar amount of shipments identified in 1993, followed by transportation equipment. The major commodities by weight were petroleum and coal products, nonmetallic minerals, and coal. Food and kindred products ranked fourth.

The transportation demands of more than 380,000 manufacturing establishments in the United States (13) reflect great diversity in products, geographic location, and customer needs. The major commodities vary greatly when ranked by the value per ton of different shipments. In 1993, ordnance, ammunition, and related accessories ranked highest,

Table 3–3 Shipments Identified in the Commodity Flow Survey: 1993

STCC Code	Commodity Description	Value (million dollars)	Tons (thousands)	Value per ton (dollars)	Ton-miles (millions)
	Petroleum and coal	382,920	3,015,778	127	774,872
29	Petroleum or coal products	359,471	1,885,833	191	287,081
11	Coal	23,449	1,129,945	21	487,791
	Timber and forest products	323,364	911,104	355	225,025
26	Pulp, paper, or allied products	195,002	217,233	898	100,721
24	Lumber or wood products, excluding furniture	126,662	663,351	191	120,669
08	Forest products	1,700	30,520	56	3,635
	Mining	40,973	1,935,943	21	192,312
10	Metallic ores	20,278	149,562	136	36,895
14	Nonmetallic minerals	20,695	1,786,381	12	155,417
	Farm and food products	1,010,388	1,499,389	674	548,990
20	Food or kindred products	856,884	859,764	997	270,984
01	Farm products	142,442	636,630	224	276,260
09	Fresh fish or other marine products	11,062	2,995	3,693	1,746
	Equipment, machinery, and instruments	1,704,766	160,553	10,618	93,191
37	Transportation equipment	652,474	87,617	7,447	49,098
35	Machinery, excluding electrical	442,770	34,180	12, 954	19,112
36	Electrical machinery, equipment, or supplies	411,030	30,156	13,630	19,591
38	Instruments, photographic goods, optical goods, watches, or clocks	198,492	8,600	23,080	5,390
	Industrial products	1,265,465	1,748,539	724	474,171
28	Chemicals or allied products	532,907	545,405	977	236,856
34	Fabricated metal products	237,316	84,895	2,795	30,489
33	Primary metal products	228,610	266,409	858	97,266
30	Rubber or miscellaneous plastics products	175,267	52,349	3,348	25,528
32	Clay, concrete, glass, or stone products	91,365	799,481	114	84,032
	Consumer goods	574,148	62,079	9,249	34,210
23	Apparel or other finished textile products	291,203	15,128	19,249	9,967
22	Textile mill products	102,189	24,757	4,128	11,341
25	Furniture or fixtures	69,471	16,568	4,193	9,789
21	Tobacco products, excluding insecticides	60,640	3,225	18,803	931
31	Leather or leather products	50,645	2,401	21,093	2,182
	Waste materials[1]	18,816	131,707	143	27,905
40	Waste or scrap materials	18,258	130,894	139	27,591
48	Waste hazardous materials or waste hazardous substances	558	813	686	314
	Miscellaneous and unknown	322,359	50,730	6,354	19,411
39	Miscellaneous products of manufacturing	200,803	20,731	9,686	10,992
41	Miscellaneous freight shipments	81,297	20,830	3,903	5,038
19	Ordnance or accessories	17,174	663	25,903	629
42	Containers, carriers or devices, shipping, returned empty	1,144	702	1,630	230
	Commodity unknown	21,941	7,804	2,812	2,522

[1] Excludes data on municipal solid wastes. Key: STCC = Standard Transportation Commodity Classification.

Note: The commodity groups cited above sum to the follow totals: for value, $5.8 trillion; for tons, 9.7 billion; and for ton-miles, 2.4 trillion. These totals differ from the larger totals specified in the text and in table 9–5 because they do not include additions to account for waterborne and pipeline shipments not fully covered in the Commodity Flow Survey.

Source: U.S. Department of Commerce, Bureau of the Census, 1996. *1993 Commodity Flow Survey, United States*, TC92-CF-52, Washington, D.C.

U.S. Commodity Shipment by Value per Ton: 1993 (in percent)

Categories	Value	Tons	Ton-miles
Less than $1,000	46.4	95.7	91.4
$1,000 to $5,000	12.4	2.2	3.6
More than $5,000	41.2	2.1	4.9

Note: The total used to calculate the percentages in this table excludes estimates of waterborne and pipeline shipment made by Oak Ridge National Laboratory, whereas table 9–5 includes these estimates.

Source: *1993 Commodity Flow Survey: United States*, TC92-CF-52, Washington, D.C.: U.S. Department of Commerce, Bureau of the Census, 1996.

averaging nearly $26,000 per ton. The second and third highest categories by value were (a) instruments and photographic and optical goods, and (b) leather products, averaging over $20,000 per ton. Nonmetallic mineral shipments ranked the lowest, at $12 per ton, followed by coal at $21 per ton. (Table 3–3.)

Manufacturing Equipment, Industrial Products, and Consumer Goods

In 1993, over $1.7 trillion worth of equipment, machinery, and instruments; $1.3 trillion in industrial products; and $574 billion of non-food consumer goods were shipped in the United States. (Table 3–3.)

Trucks and intermodal combinations carry a large proportion of manufactured goods. Trucks moved 63 percent of equipment and machinery, 77 percent of industrial products, and 75 percent of consumer goods in 1993. More specifically, 95 percent of the shipments within the United States of computing and office machines (valued at $153 billion) were carried by truck; parcel, postal, and courier services; or truck and air intermodal combinations.

Packages, Parcels, and Mail

Movement of letters, documents, and small packages and parcels containing products for service providers, other business, and households is a major freight activity, which is usually intermodal in nature. In 1993, U.S. businesses relied on parcel, postal, or courier services to transport goods valued at over $560 billion, producing 13 billion ton-miles in the process.

Municipal Solid Waste and Other Waste Materials

In 1994, Americans generated 209 million tons of municipal solid waste (14). Of this, 61 percent was sent to landfills, 15 percent went to incineration facilities, and 24 percent was shipped to recycling and composting facilities. Once picked up from a source, such as a household or store, municipal solid waste may be transported just a few miles or as much as 2,000 miles before reaching its final destination (15). Local decision makers choose how and where municipal solid waste is transported. Garbage trucks may transport refuse to a final disposal site or to a transfer station. In communities with curbside recycling, a portion of municipal solid waste is picked up and transported by truck directly to local recycling facilities. After some processing, separated materials (e.g., plastics, newspaper, and aluminum) are baled and hauled to processing facilities by truck and rail. In many rural areas, residents and businesses transport their trash themselves to a nearby landfill. The municipal solid waste that goes to transfer stations is compacted and then transported to a landfill or incinerator via trailer trucks, rail, or barge. Complete national data are not available on the shares held by different modes, but trucks seem to carry most municipal solid waste; barges transport the least. Railroads handle a small but growing share. In 1993, railroads shipped about 3.5 million tons of municipal solid waste, a 40-percent increase over 1992 (16). Landfill regulations in the 1986 amendments to the Resource Conservation and Recovery Act encouraged closing older, local landfills and developing large, regional landfills. While the goal of regionalization may be environmental protection or the capture of economies of scale in landfill operation, the change has tended to increase the hauling distances for municipal solid waste, thereby enhancing transportation's role.

An estimated nine percent of municipal solid waste is shipped interstate. These shipments are increasing, driven by regionalization of landfills and consolidation in the waste handling industry. Most interstate shipments are between adjacent states, but in some cases much longer distances are involved. New York, for example, shipped municipal solid waste to ten states in 1995. California shipped wastes 2,000 miles to Ohio in 1992. Some states dispose of municipal solid waste transported from Canada and Mexico. In 1992, Mexico shipped wastes to New Mexico, British Columbia shipped wastes to the state of Washington, and Ontario shipped wastes to several eastern states (17). Industrial scrap (consisting mostly of iron, steel, or other metal scrap commodities) and industrial waste are usually not part of the municipal solid waste stream, and they have their own collection and distribution network. There are markets for industrial scrap and for some kinds of industrial wastes. CFS data show that about 131 million tons of scrap materials and industrial waste were moved in 1993. By value, about 79 percent moved by truck and 17 percent moved by rail.

Household and Business Moving

The moving industry serves three markets: households (49 percent of total shipments in 1994, down from 61 percent in 1987), trade shows (50 percent in 1994, up from 38 percent in 1987), and offices (0.1 percent in 1994). In 1994, Census reported that about 43 million U. S. residents moved to a different location, 59 percent within the same county and the rest split about equally between intrastate and interstate moves (18).

Intrastate and Interstate Freight Movement

Origination of Shipments

Many factors affect the magnitude of shipments originating in a state, including the size of the state's population and economy, its resource base, and its land area. Not surprisingly, over one third of the shipments by value originate in states with large manufacturing bases, such as California, New York, Michigan, Texas, and Illinois. (Figure 3–2). These states were also the destination for a large portion of shipments. Nationally, about 62 percent of shipments by value and 35 percent by weight were sent out of state in 1993.

Destination of Shipments

The movement of manufactured products between states has a pattern of concentrated destinations: California, Texas, New York, and the historic industrial belt stretching from Illinois to Pennsylvania. Figure 3–3 shows the state of origin and the state of destination of the largest fifty interstate flows by value of shipment for manufactured goods. For example, California is the destination of six of the top fifty major interstate flows by value.

The concentration of shipments to and from California, Texas, New York, and Illinois arises in part from their large populations, manufacturing bases, and importance in assembling parts manufactured in other states. Another explanation for the concentration is that California, Texas, and New York have major ports; thus, shipments destined for those states include manufactured goods for export.

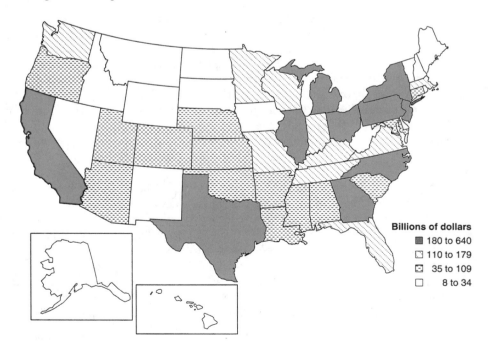

Billions of dollars

- ■ 180 to 640
- ▨ 110 to 179
- ▧ 35 to 109
- ☐ 8 to 34

Figure 3–2   Value of Commodity Shipments by State of Origin: 1993

Source: Commodity Flow Survey data, Washington, D.C.: U.S. Department of Commerce, Bureau of the Census, 1996.

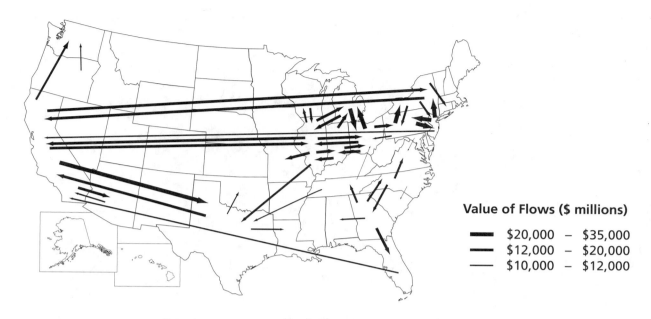

**Figure 3–3   Origins and Destinations of the Top Fifty
Interstate Commodity Flows by Value: 1993**

Source: Commodity Flow Survey data, Washington, D.C.: U.S. Department of Commerce, Bureau of the Census, 1996.

Highlights of Truck Shipments by State

The wealth of information to be gleaned from the CFS is well illustrated by Figures 3–4 and 3–5, which show interstate truck shipments by states. The pie charts show total shipments by truck that, in each case, moved within the state, passed through the state, or had either an origin or a destination within the state. The size of each pie chart indicates the size of all the truck shipments associated with the state, measured by value in the case of Figure 3–4 or by ton-miles for Figure 3–5.

Nationally, shipments crossing state boundaries accounted for 73 percent of the ton-miles and 55 percent of the value of commodity movements by truck. In 25 states, shipments passing through the state accounted for more than half of the value of commodity movements by truck; and in 19 states, through shipments were more than half of the state's ton-miles by truck.

Shipment Characteristics

Local transportation is important to businesses throughout the nation. In 1993, nearly 40 percent of the value and 67 percent of the weight of all shipments moved between places under 100 miles apart. More than 55 percent of the value and 79 percent of the weight traveled less than 250 miles.

High-value shipments on average were moved greater distances than low-value shipments. Low-valued goods are often ubiquitous (such as sand and gravel) and move only short distances. People and businesses are often willing to pay the extra cost of shipping high-value, often low-weight commodities long distances by air in exchange for speedy on-time delivery. Over 80 percent of shipments by parcel, postal, or courier services were under 100 pounds.

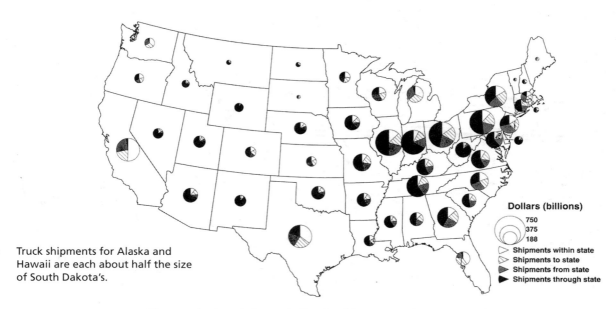

Truck shipments for Alaska and Hawaii are each about half the size of South Dakota's.

Figure 3–4   Value of Truck Shipments by State: 1993

Note: The size of each circle represents shipments by truck from manufacturing, mining, farming, and wholesale establishments. It does not reflect imports, shipments crossing the United States en route between foreign origins and destinations, and shipments by service industries, governments, and households. Shipments from, to, and within each state are compiled from the 1993 Commodity Flow Survey, supplemented by data compiled by Oak Ridge National Laboratory to include farm-based shipments in the 1992 Census of Agriculture. Oak Ridge estimated throughshipments by assigning flows to the most likely routes on the National Highway Planning Network.

Source: U.S. Department of Transportation, Washington, D.C.: Bureau of Transportation Statistics, May 1997.

Truck shipments for Alaska are about the same size as New Hampshire's and shipments for Hawaii are about the same size as Rhode Island's.

Figure 3–5   Ton-Miles of Truck Shipments by State: 1993

Note: The size of each circle represents shipments by truck from manufacturing, mining, farming, and wholesale establishments. It does not reflect imports, shipments crossing the United States en route between foreign origins and destinations, and shipments by service industries, governments, and households. Shipments from, to, and within each state are compiled from the 1993 Commodity Flow Survey, supplemented by data compiled by Oak Ridge National Laboratory to include farm-based shipments in the 1992 Census of Agriculture. Oak Ridge estimated throughshipments by assigning flows to the most likely routes on the National Highway Planning Network.

Source: U.S. Department of Transportation, Washington, D.C.: Bureau of Transportation Statistics, May 1997.

Freight Movement by Mode

Various factors influence the choice of mode, including type of commodity, transportation costs, modal service characteristics, and accessibility of shipper and receiver to the mode. Bulk commodities typically are transported slowly at a low unit cost. High-value, time-sensitive commodities often move by truck, air-truck, and rail-truck intermodal combinations.

From 1970 to 1995, ton-miles of domestic freight movement for all modes increased by 65 percent. Air carriers' ton-miles grew the most rapidly, more than quintupling over the period (19). Intercity truck ton-miles also grew rapidly, more than doubling. Trucking, including for-hire and own-use, was the most frequently used mode, measured both by shipment value (71.9 percent) and by weight (52.5 percent) for freight moved in 1993. (Table 3–4). Trucks were even more dominant for shipment distances of less than 500 miles.

Railroads produce slightly more ton-miles (26 percent in 1993) than any other mode. Freight train-miles increased only 7 percent between 1970 and 1995, the average length of haul rose 64 percent to 843 miles (20). Over 17 percent of all tons moved within the United States (some 24 percent of ton-miles) involved some form of waterborne transport in 1993, along the coasts, on the Great Lakes, and on inland waterways.

Intermodal Freight Shipments

In 1993, intermodal shipments exceeded 200 million tons of goods valued at about $660 billion. These figures are for shipments moved by two or more modes, as well as by parcel, postal, and courier services, but not including truck-air intermodal (21). These shipments accounted for about 11 percent by value, but just under 2 percent by weight. Truck and rail intermodal accounted, for 13 percent by value.

Intermodal shipments are higher in value per pound on average than typical single-mode shipments. The average value of goods shipped by air, including truck and air, was $22.15 per pound, followed by parcel, postal, and courier services at $14.91 per pound and by truck and rail combination at $1.02 per pound. Goods shipped only by truck averaged $0.34 per pound.

Table 3–4   U.S. Freight Shipments by Transportation Mode: 1993

	Value (billions)	Tons (millions)	Ton-miles (millions)	Value (percent)	Tons (percent)	Ton-miles (percent)
Total CFS plus ORNL estimates	$6,124	12,157	3,627,919	100.0	100.0	100.0
Truck (for-hire and private)	4,403	6,386	869,536	71.9	52.5	24.0
Water	251	2,128	886,085	4.1	17.5	24.4
Rail	247	1,544	942,561	4.0	12.7	26.0
Pipeline	180	1,343	592,900	2.9	11.0	16.3
Air (including truck and air)	139	3	4,009	2.3	0.03	0.1
Intermodal[1] total	660	208	235,856	10.8	1.7	6.5
Parcel, postal, and courier services	563	19	13,151	9.2	0.2	0.4
Truck and rail	83	41	37,675	1.4	0.3	1.0
Other intermodal combinations[2]	13	149	185,030	0.2	1.2	5.1
Unknown	243	544	96,972	4.0	4.5	2.7

[1] Intermodal is a combination of parcel, postal and courier services; truck and rail and other intermodal combinations including truck and water and rail and water. It excludes truck and air which is added to air transportation.

[2] Includes truck and water, rail and water, and other combinations.

Key: CFS = Commodity Flow Survey. ORNL = Oak Ridge National Laboratory

Note: The figures for water shipments in this table include the following rounded ORNL estimates: $187 billion, 1.6 million tons, and 614 billion ton-miles. The figures for pipeline shipments include these ORNL estimates: $90 billion, 859 million tons, 593 billion ton-miles.

Sources: Bureau of Transportation Statistics, U.S. Department of Transportation. *Transportation Statistics Annual Report 1997*. Washington, D.C.: BTS, U.S. DOT, 1997; 1993 Commodity Flow Survey data, Oak Ridge, Tenn.: Oak Ridge National Laboratory, 1993.

Goods shipped by rail, water, and pipeline averaged less than $0.10 per pound (22). Generally speaking, states producing goods with a high value per unit of weight moved a greater part of their shipments by intermodal transportation, while states producing goods with low value per unit of weight relied more on rail, water, and pipeline.

Freight Transportation at the Metropolitan Level

Below are descriptions of important sources of data and information for state and MPO freight transportation planners and engineers. There have been so many excellent sources in state and MPO freight planning since ISTEA began activating the discipline in 1992, that only a brief review is possible here. The reader is encouraged to consult the original sources.

Sources of Freight Data

At the state and metropolitan planning organization levels, use of national and macroregional data bases for state and MPO purposes is an important topic. Primary and secondary freight data collection can consume large amounts of budgetary, time, and person-power resources of state, MPO, and local jurisdictions.

Freight data collection is a major component of several recent projects, including some by the Federal Highway Administration (FHWA).[8,9] Some included a survey of freight issue leaders at MPOs. Cambridge Systematics, Inc., as part of National Cooperative Highway Research Project (NCHRP) 8–30, did a survey of state DOTs (38 responses or 60 percent) and MPOs (33 responses or 52 percent) in 1994–95. Their overall conclusion was that "[m]ost states and MPOs have little experience in freight forecasting" but "data availability is a critical consideration." One hurdle to overcome is that there are "significant differences between the needs of planners and policy analysts" at MPOs and states.

MPOs and states need a hands-on manual that shows them what freight data exist, where they may be obtained, and how they can be used. A *Freight Data Handbook for States and MPOs* is an active project at BTS and FHWA that will emphasize processes of ongoing freight data collection (rather than creating new "data cemeteries" from which information is seldom exhumed), what kinds of freight data are already available (decreasing the need for expensive commercial truck surveys in certain cases), and use of national freight data bases (the 1997 CFS data will be available for metropolitan-area and rest-of-state regions), and data analysis techniques used by states and MPOs.

Travel Model Improvement Program (TMIP) Freight Track Projects

TMIP is a DOT and Environmental Protection Agency (EPA) research program to respond to requirements of the Clean Air Act Amendments of 1990 and ISTEA 1991. This program addresses the linkage of transportation to air quality, energy, economic growth, land use, and the overall quality of life. TMIP addresses analytic tools and the integration of those tools into the planning process to better support decision makers. TMIP has the following objectives: increase the ability of existing travel forecasting procedures to respond to emerging issues; redesign the travel forecasting process to reflect changes in behavior, to respond to greater information needs placed on the forecasting process, and to take advantage of changes in data collection technology; and integrate the forecasting techniques into the decision-making process to provide better understanding of the effects of transportation improvements and allow decision makers the capability of making improved transportation decisions. For further information on TMIP and on the other "tracks" (the "Freight Track" is briefly described below), contact:

---

[8] Particularly recommended are the following: (1) Cambridge Systematics, Inc., NCHRP Report 388, *...Freight Transportation Demand*, 1997; (2) Capelle, *Planning and Managing Intermodal Management Systems....*, 1995b; (3) TMIP/Cambridge Systematics, Inc., *et al., Quick Response Freight Manual*, 1996/released 1997; and (4) Wegmann *et al., Characteristics of Urban Freight Systems*, 1996. Section 3 in Capelle's *Planning and Managing Intermodal Management Systems....*, "Answers to State and MPO Questions About IMS Data and Data Analysis Issues," provides a brief overview of primary and secondary freight transportation data bases and techniques.

[9] Capelle (1995b) summarizes data sources and data bases under the following (alphabetically listed) headings: associations, atlases, Census, companies, consulting firms, Corps of Engineers [U.S. Army], directories, highway department [state], [formerly] ICC [now STB] rail waybill statistics, Institute of Transportation Engineers, Port Import/Export Reporting Service (PIERS) data, studies [in your region] completed previously for other purposes, trade journals, trucking industry sources, and universities and research institutes. Capelle (1995b) has a review of the literature on freight forecasting and urban goods movement methods and models (pages 37–39) and an annotated bibliography (pages 65–100).

TMIP Information Request, Metropolitan Planning (HEP-20), Federal Highway Administration, U.S. Department of Transportation, 400 Seventh Street, SW, Washington, D.C. 20590.

BTS and FHWA staff are working together with the TMIP staff and the TMIP program review panel to develop MPO-useful freight planning and transportation engineering projects as part of the TMIP Freight Track. Projects include developing a TTEP for MPO regional modelers to use; a Small Business Innovation Research (SBIR) project to develop destination, mode, and routing choice models for freight; a *Freight Data Handbook for States and MPOs*; and several others.

Truck Trip Estimation Procedure

The TTEP is a technique for extracting representative data from Census' Vehicle Inventory and Use Survey, using the Statistical Analysis System (SAS), the Statistical Package for the Social Sciences (SPSS), or other analytical tools for large data bases. Each row of the VIUS matrix is a truck whose data were provided by one survey respondent. The category "truck" includes pickups and vans. Each column of the matrix is an attribute of that truck, including an expansion factor so results are applicable to the general U.S. truck population.

TTEP allows cross-tabulations of VIUS data and calculation of averages, such as average number of tours (a set of trips between stops) per day per truck trip-making behavior category. Tours-per-day averages and frequency distributions generated from the data base are used in MPO regional modeling to update truck trip tables and calculate data by transportation analysis zone for a region. See Capelle (1995c) for details of the estimating procedure. MPO regional modelers need to geocode trucking company locations and attributes from trucking industry directories so the locations of the production and of some attraction nodes in the region are known. Locating most attraction nodes is also dependent upon the MPO modelers' work site employment file, which usually contains employment and other data on businesses in the region categorized by standard industrial classification (SIC) code.

The calibration step is performed through videotaping truck movements at several locations where traditional automatic traffic recorders or truck classification counts are taken, and creating a conversion table to allow translation of data classified by traditional FHWA classes to the ten or more TTEP truck trip-making behavior categories (e.g., food/warehouse delivery, heavy haulers/garbage/dump, household goods, intermodal drayage, less-than-truckload, package/expedited/courier/air cargo, pickups/vans for business use, retail delivery, tankers, truckload, and not elsewhere classified/personal use). The project, using BTS funds from TEA-21, will develop software usable by any MPO region. The software would extract by the same procedure the averages needed for most larger MPOs. For example, Boston, Boise, and Baton Rouge would use the same procedure to get average tours per day and other data; the procedure would be the same but the output would be different for each region.

Freight Data Handbook for States and MPOs

BTS staff are writing, in coordination with what is now the FHWA Office of Metropolitan Planning and Programs staff, the publication *Freight Data Handbook for States and MPOs*. Available in 2000, it will identify freight data sources, where to find them, how to use them, and who is using them in statewide planning and MPO regional modeling. Several case studies will show how freight data are being used (e.g., Boston, Mass. and Portland, Oregon). The handbook complements the 1996 BTS *Directory of Transportation Data Sources* (which provides data base descriptions and contact information), by identifying users, data sources, uses, and user locations around the country.

Significant Freight Data Bases and Studies of Use to MPOs[10]

States DOTs and MPOs do not have to "reinvent the wheel" in data collection. There are several excellent federal and other freight data bases that can be used by state DOTs and MPOs. The Census and BTS, working in partnership, have

---

[10] See section 3.9, "Selected References, Partially Annotated," for complete references to section 3.6, "Significant freight data bases and studies of use to MPOs."

provided several excellent sources, reviewed below. Following these sources, research applying the federal data bases, private sector (industry/consulting) data sources, trade and professional journals, and other sources are described.

Census and BTS Data Bases and Data Sources

Under this heading nine data bases or data sources are highlighted. Potential users can consult BTS' *Directory of Transportation Data Sources* for information on public and private sector freight data bases; and they can visit the National Transportation Library (NTL) on the Internet to find full-text articles, reports, and studies done by MPOs, state agencies, consulting firms, and others.

Commodity flow data bases, such as Census' and BTS' CFS and the FRA's Rail Waybill Statistics provide valuable commodity-group-specific, modally-categorized freight flow information, which can be depicted in a geographic information system (GIS) or on maps using the data from BTS' and Oak Ridge National Laboratory's (ORNL) National Transportation Atlas Database. Census' County Business Patterns, used in conjunction with CFS and other data bases, provides valuable county-level weights and indexes for use in freight forecasting, rail-truck diversion, and other models. The operating equipment inventory for trucks is found in Census' VIUS. FHWA's Motor Carrier Management Information System (MCMIS) can provide additional recent data for the hundreds of thousands of trucks required to be part of MCMIS as they register for their DOT Number listed on the side of the truck cab.

BTS' *Directory of Transportation Data Sources*, 1996

This publication provides users with a comprehensive inventory of transportation freight and passenger data sources. A data source is defined as a computerized data base, a regularly scheduled or special hardcopy statistical report, or other data-access medium. Internet sites and home pages are not included. The *Directory* covers government sources as well as private sector and trade association materials. Each data source profile lists the following attributes of that data source: title, mode, brief abstract, source of data, geographic area of coverage, time span of data, development date, update frequency, number of records, file size, file format, media, significant features and limitations, corresponding printed source, sponsoring and performing organizations, availability, and contact for additional information.

Use this *Directory* as a reference tool to identify transportation and transportation-related information existent in North America.

U.S. DOT's and BTS' National Transportation Library

Begun in 1994 as the State and Metropolitan Area Regional Transportation System, the BTS has now developed, with the help and advice of other modal administrations in the U.S. DOT and the Special Libraries Association, the NTL. The NTL serves as a state and MPO publication clearinghouse, providing access to reports, publications, research summaries, and other descriptions of use to state and MPO planners. Data from other regions' studies may be usable as surrogate data in your regional modeling. (For more information visit NTL on the Internet at www.bts.gov/ntl.)

Census' and BTS' Commodity Flow Survey: 1993 and Plans for 1997

The CFS is the most comprehensive effort to identify where and how goods are shipped in the United States since 1977. It measures the value and weight of commodities shipped by manufacturing, mining, wholesale trade, and selected retail and service industries. Prior surveys only measured shipments by manufacturing firms. The CFS is undertaken through a partnership between the U.S. DOT's BTS and the U.S. Department of Commerce's Bureau of the Census. Census collected quarterly data in 1993, as part of its Economic Censuses, under the technical guidance of BTS. From a sample of 200,000 establishments, commodity flows were estimated for the universe of approximately 800,000 businesses. The 1997 CFS is underway now, and subsequent surveys are scheduled for every five years thereafter.

Data from the CFS for each state of origin include: mode of transportation, distance shipped, shipment size, commodities shipped, and state of destination. Origin and destination data for 89 National Transportation Analysis Regions provides commodity flow information below the state level in many regions.

FRA's and BTS' Rail Waybill Data: 1988–1992

The Rail Waybill Data CD-ROM contains the Carload Waybill Sample public-use files, which are proprietary samples of freight waybills submitted by Class I railroads to the Interstate Commerce Commission, an agency that no longer exists but whose statistical data programs, like this one, are now administered within STB or BTS.

The CD-ROM contains five years of data from 1988–1992 providing national coverage of railroads that terminate over 4,500 cars per year or five percent or more of a state's traffic. Public-use, aggregated, nonconfidential rail shipment data such as origin and destination points, type of commodity, number of cars, tons, revenue, length of haul, participating railroads, and interchange locations—reported as required by law to the former ICC—are included. Movements are reported by BEA (Bureau of Economic Analysis) area level and by STCC level. Origin and destination BEA areas are not included unless there are at least three freight stations and there are at least two more freight stations than railroads.

BTS' and ORNL's National Transportation Atlas Databases (NTAD), 1997

NTAD '97 is a set of national geographic data bases of transportation facilities that provide the framework to support research, analysis, and decision making across all modes of transportation. The data base includes geospatial information for transportation modal networks, intermodal terminals, and political and statistical areas with related attribute information. The data bases were compiled from many parts of the U.S. DOT, ORNL, the U.S. Army Corps of Engineers, and the National Park Service. Transportation terminals are represented as point data bases; transportation networks and services are represented as line data bases. The geographic reference files are represented as either point or polygon data bases.

NTAD '97 is available in both MS-DOS and UNIX compatible CD-ROM format. Although designed for use within a GIS, the files are in ASCII format so they can be used in any data base, spreadsheet, or other software package.

Census' County Business Patterns

This source of statistics on businesses within each of the over 3,500 counties in the country is done each year by Census. It is valuable information, including number of establishments within certain business categories in each county, which has been used in combination with other statistics ("data fusion") to create logistics cost models used by certain consulting firms—models that generate tons-by-truck and tons-by-rail multiplicands that are very useful in economic impact and other regional economic studies.

Census' and BTS' Vehicle [formerly "Truck"] Inventory and Use Survey

The BTS' Transportation Data Sampler 3 contains the 1992 VIUS [then TIUS], or one may obtain the microdata file for the VIUS on CD-ROM directly from Census.

VIUS has been the nation's trucking equipment inventory for three decades. Each record in the data base is a truck whose owner has responded to Census' VIUS survey instrument. Each column in the data base is an attribute of that truck. Attributes include: miles traveled, fuel consumed, commodities carried, and vehicle operator characteristics.

VIUS data have most often been used for national analyses (evaluating the importance of the federal-aid highway program, the impact of federal actions on motor carrier productivity, highway cost allocation analyses, and FHWA vehicle size and weight studies that Congress can use to develop appropriate highway investment levels and highway user charges). However, MPO-level truck trip data for use in regional modeling are possible and are explained more fully in section 3.5.3 on TTEP.

FHWA's Motor Carrier Management Information System

The Office of Motor Carriers of the FHWA maintains the Motor Carrier Management Information System (MCMIS). MCMIS contains information on the safety fitness of commercial motor carriers and hazardous material (HM) shippers subject to Federal Motor Carrier Safety Regulations and the Hazardous Materials Regulations. This information is available to the general public through the MCMIS Data Dissemination Program (contact: COmputing TechnologieS, Inc., 3028 Javier Road, Suite 101, Fairfax, Virginia 22031-4622; 703/280-4001).

Available reports include: Carrier File Extracts (drawing data from the MCMIS Carrier File, which contains demographic and safety information on about 375,000 active commercial motor carriers and HM shippers), Accident File Extracts, Carrier Safety Profiles, Personalized Carrier Reports, Personalized Accident Reports, Carrier Count Reports, and Accident Count Reports. MPOs and states can use the data to better understand identifying characteristics, location, and operation of motor carriers within their region.

BTS' State Freight Profiles

"What freight data sources can I use to get statistics for my state or my MPO within a state?" you might ask. BTS has the answer(s). The *State Freight Profile* series is a set of publications, one on each state. Each state's publication lists actual statistics for that state from the following selection of freight data sources:

- Transportation facilities (from the National Transportation Atlas Databases, 1997)

- Commodity movements (from the CFS, 1993)

- Exports to and imports from Canada and Mexico (from the Surface Transborder Freight Dataset)

- Rail shipments (from the Rail Waybill Data, 1988–1992)

- Waterborne commerce (from the United States Waterway Data)

- Transportation establishments (from the 1992 Census of Transportation, Geographic Area Series, TC92-A-1)

- Truck registration and vehicle-miles traveled (from the VIUS and FHWA's annual *Highway Statistics* publications)

- Motor carrier statistics (from the former ICC financial reports, the *Motor Carrier Financial and Operating Statistics*)

- Fatal truck crashes (from FHWA's *Truck and Bus Accident Factbook*)

- Rail accidents and fatalities (from the Railroad Accident/Incident Reporting System)

- Hazardous materials incidents (from the Research and Special Programs Administration's (RSPA) Hazardous Materials Incident Reporting System)

Examples: Applications of CFS Data in State and MPO Planning

CFS data have great potential, but the reader may ask: "Who's using them and how?" Several recent articles or presentations are summarized below. They focus on the ways in which CFS data are usable at state and MPO levels, and they reveal that a national data base is usable for purposes other than federal nationwide studies (e.g., truck size and weight studies, highway cost allocations studies, and so on).

Biddle, Siaurusaitis, Matherly and Perincherry, 1997

The authors of this study show how CFS 1993 data can be used for MPO planning in at the Hampton Roads MPO in Virginia. This is one of the first studies to apply CFS results at the MPO level.

Using as their primary data sources the 1993 CFS and the 1993 County Business Patterns, the project objective was as follows: "Develop a model that is both spatially and temporally transferable that will translate nationally available yearly commodity movements into daily truck trips." The authors propose a model formulation using methods that follow established procedures in the transportation modeling software MINUTP, which is a library of programs that provides the capability to perform the usual functions of traditional transportation planning with regard to trip generation, distribution, and network assignment. The model is tested by forecasting truck traffic for Hampton Roads, Virginia. The authors provide a table of "Model Results and Validation of Trucks by Facility Type" and propose future work needed to refine the model and reduce the differences between the validation truck percentage and the base-year model result by facility type.

Black, 1997 and 1998

From Black (1997):

> Using data primarily from the 1993 Commodity Flow Survey (CFS) this report develops a series of models for estimating the production and attraction of 19 different commodity groups as well as two types of mail for 145 geographic units in the United States; 92 of these are the counties in Indiana. This is followed by the calibration of fully-constrained gravity models for the flow of these commodities. Using modal share data from the CFS, the generated traffic is divided between the various modes. This project looked primarily at the highway and rail sectors and used digital representations of these networks for traffic assignment purposes. A very detailed Indiana digital road network was merged with a U.S. DOT digital highway planning network. New cost metrics were developed for each modal assignment. Productions and attractions were forecasted and the models and assignments were rerun for 2005 and 2015. A chapter on implementation suggests how the results of the project can be used for planning and policy development. Appendices include computer program code for the major software developed as well as parameters to run the gravity models.

Erlbaum, 1998

From Erlbaum's (1998) "Overview" section:

> The purpose of this report is to provide an overview of commodity flow in New York State. It does this by combining information from three diverse, but major sources of national freight data: the 1993 Commodity Flow Survey, the 1993 U.S. Waterway Data, and the Transborder Surface Freight Transportation Data (for Canadian trade). When combined, these sources attempt to present a picture of commerce in New York State relative to domestic and foreign trade. Background information is also provided to allow the reader to understand the differences in objective, collection methodology, coverage, time period and potential inconsistencies among the data sources.

> This report attempts to compare commodity flows in New York State with the nation, identify key shipment characteristics by mode of transport, examine flows to-from-within and through the state, and delineate Canadian from other foreign trade. The report indicates when possible, data deficiencies that may exist in the three major sources and assuages the impact of these deficiencies on rendering a correct picture of freight flow in New York State.

Krishnan and Hancock, 1998

An example of applying national data base results (CFS, 1993) for use at lower levels—state and MPO levels—is the work of Krishnan and Hancock. Not only do they use CFS results, but they also include results of another national and state data base, the Highway Performance Monitoring System. Below is part of the abstract of their paper:

> A methodology for calculating the truck flows on the various highways in Massachusetts from interstate commodity flow data has been presented here. Freight tons originating and ending in Massachusetts from neighboring New England states, New York, and New Jersey, have been converted to truck numbers using a quantitative procedure and distributed to different areas in the state using employment as an economic indicator variable. The truck flow is assigned to the important highways and validated against existing survey counts. On comparison, a large percentage of the roads show the estimated truck counts are within a tolerable error margin. The research also shows that statewide analyses need to be refined near urban areas due to a variety of complexities involved.

Other State and MPO Studies

Several articles and booklets in the mid-1990s have directly addressed state and MPO freight planners' challenges such as designing intermodal management systems (Capelle, 1995b); costs, design, and results of commercial vehicle surveys in North America (Lau, 1995; Chow, 1998); defining and obtaining data for statewide freight performance measures (Czerniak, 1996); freight forecasting sources and methods (Cambridge Systematics, Inc., 1996; CSI, 1997); surrogate data from other studies and other places than can be used in MPO regional modeling (Quick Response Freight Manual, 1997; Characteristics of Urban Freight Systems, 1997); county-to-county commodity flow data bases (Small Business Innovation Research, 1998); and information from major national FHWA-sponsored "national freight conferences" held in 1995, 1996, and 1997.

Section 3.9 of this chapter provides more information on sources listed above and on two SBIR "visual freight database" projects.

Conclusion

Knowledge about the "big picture" is critical in transportation planning today. Knowing about global freight issues, national commodity flows, and a wide variety of freight data bases is critical to good transportation planning.

So many transportation planners think freight is an unimportant subject that does not matter much to the metropolitan area. Trucks are a small percentage of the traffic stream and that's it. They fail to grasp the dynamic effect of freight on the regional economy, and the links to job creation, reasons for passenger movements, and shipment of freight in a wide variety of vehicles, including many that do not fit under the usual category of "trucks." As Ken Ogden (1995, 2–3) said: "about half of total urban transport costs, in economic terms, are related to freight."

This chapter has provided a broad view of commodity flows and freight transportation so readers will become interested in many issues and yet-unanswered questions in freight planning. With the initiatives under ISTEA and TEA-21 there are many opportunities and many challenges

The broad family of intelligent transportation system technologies hold great promise. There are many possible uses of GPS and locational data bases produced from them. There are methods of data fusion, data mining, and data sharing that will aid us in the future. As we move into the new millennium, we can look forward to using our growing knowledge of commodity flow and freight issues and many types of technology to help provide answers to the challenging freight planning questions on the horizon.

Selected References, Partially Annotated[11]

American Trucking Associations Foundation for the Baltimore Metropolitan Council. "Motor Carrier and Freight Movement Operational Characteristics in the Baltimore Region." April 1997 Draft. Baltimore, Md.: Baltimore Metropolitan Council, 1997.

Anderson, Marsha. "Goods Movement Studies," *Manual of Transportation Engineering Studies.* Washington, D.C.: Institute of Transportation Engineers, 1994.

Baltimore Metropolitan Council. *Freight Mobility Issues and Recommendations for the 1997 Baltimore Regional Transportation Plan: Report of the Transportation Steering Committee's Freight Movement Task Force.* Report BRTP-97-2d. Outlook 2020. Baltimore, Md.: Baltimore Metropolitan Council, September 1997.

Battelle Transportation Division. "Using GPS for Truck Activity Surveys." Technical Working Group Meeting, November 13–14, 1997, Arlington, Va., with Battelle staff (David Wagner and colleagues) presenting results of the surveys to date to an expert review panel assembled by FHWA (Elaine Murakami) and moderated by BTS' Russell B. Capelle, Jr.

Biddle, Brian, Victor Siaurusaitis, Deborah Matherly, and Vijay Perincherry. "Practical Methods for Freight Transportation Planning in Metropolitan Areas." CD-ROM of the *Proceedings* of the Transportation Planning Methods Applications Conference. Washington, D.C.: Transportation Research Board, 1997.

Black, William R. "Indiana Commodity Database Development and Traffic Assignment." Presentation at Transportation Research Board annual meeting. Washington, D.C.: TRB, January 1998.

Black, William R. *Transport Flows in the State of Indiana: Commodity Database Development and Traffic Assignment.* Phase 2. Bloomington, Ind.: Transportation Research Center and Department of Geography, Indiana University, July 15, 1997.

Brich, Stephen C. and G. Michael Fitch. "Opportunities for Collecting Highway Inventory Data With the Global Positioning System," *Transportation Research Record No. 1593.* Washington, D.C.: Transportation Research Board, 1997, pp. 64–71.

Bureau of Transportation Statistics, U.S. Department of Transportation. "National Transportation Library" (http://www.bts.gov/ntl/); "Home Page" (http://www.bts.gov/); and "Geographic Information Services" (http://www.bts.gov/gis/).

Bureau of Transportation Statistics, U.S. Department of *Transportation. Transportation Statistics Beyond ISTEA: Critical Gaps and Strategic Responses.* Washington, D.C.: BTS, U.S. DOT, 1998.

Bureau of Transportation Statistics, U.S. Department of Transportation. *Directory of Transportation Data Sources.* Washington, D.C.: BTS, U.S. DOT, 1996.

Bureau of Transportation Statistics, U.S. Department of Transportation. *Transportation Statistics Annual Report 1997.* Washington, D.C.: BTS, U.S. DOT, 1997. Footnote numbers (1) through (27) under sections 3.3 and 3.4 of this chapter are cross-referenced below to the original footnotes in TSAR 1997: footnote (1): The ratio of the sum of U.S. exports and imports to GDP should not be confused with the share of international trade as a component of GDP. The latter measures the net value of exports minus imports as a component of GDP; footnote (2): (U.S. Army Corps of Engineers, 1997, 1-4); footnote (3): (USDOC Census 1996b, table 1058); footnote (4): (USDOC Census 1990 and 1996b); footnote (5): All-cargo air carriers in 1995 were Challenge Air Cargo, DHL Airways, Emery Worldwide, Federal Express, Northern Air Cargo, Polar Air Cargo, and United Parcel Service; footnote (6): (USDOC Census 1990 and 1996b); footnote (7): (USDOT OIA 1996); footnote (8): (World Bank 1995b, 57); footnote (9): (World Bank 1995b and LBJ 1995); footnote (10): (LBJ 1995); footnote (11): TSAR 1997—USDOT BTS 1996b); footnote (12): Ton-miles are calculated by summing the product of the weight of shipment by the distance shipped. A ton-mile is the equivalent of moving one ton of goods one mile; footnote (13): (USDOC Census 1996b, table 839); footnote (14) Municipal solid waste includes discarded durable goods, nondurable goods, containers and packaging, food wastes and yard trimmings, and miscellaneous inorganic wastes. MSW comes from residential, commercial, institutional, and industrial sources. Industrial MSW is limited to packaging and office wastes, however, and does not include wastes generated by industrial processes. Most MSW was not covered by the CFS; footnote (15): (USEPA 1996); footnote (16): (Freeman 1996); footnote (17): (Repa 1993); footnote (18): (USDOC Census 1995, table 66; and 1996b, table 33); footnote (19): (USDOT BTS 1996a, 20); footnote (20): (AAR 1996, 33, 36); footnote (21): In table 9-5, shipments by intermodal truck and air were aggregated with shipments moved by air only; footnote (22): Calculated by BTS from 1993 Commodity Flow Survey data, plus additional data on pipeline and water provided by Oak Ridge National Laboratory.

Cambridge Systematics, Inc., et al. *A Guidebook for Forecasting Freight Transportation Demand.* NCHRP Report 388. Prepared by Cambridge Systematics, Inc.; Leeper, Cambridge & Campbell, Inc.; SYDEC, Inc.; and Thomas M. Corsi/Curtis M. Grimm. Washington, D.C.: Transportation Research Board, National Academy Press, 1997.

---

[11] An extensive recent annotated bibliography is included on pages 64–100 of Capelle's 1995b *Planning and Managing Intermodal Transportation Systems: A Guide to ISTEA Requirements.* An entry for this publication is included in the reference section of this chapter (section 3.9).

Beginning in 1992, NCHRP 8–30 aimed at creating guidance material on freight transportation demand forecasting. The contractors included the following: Cambridge Systematics, Inc. (Washington, D.C. office); Leeper, Cambridge & Campbell, Inc. (McLean, Va.); SYDEC, Inc. (Reston, Va.); and Thomas M. Corsi/Curtis M. Grimm (College Park, Md.).

Report 388 is "intended to be used as a reference document by transportation planners who require forecasts of freight transportation demand for facility planning, corridor planning, or strategic planning; or by those who wish to gain a greater understanding of influences on private decision making related to freight shipments. Transportation modelers, who may wish to incorporate some of the forecasting techniques presented into their models, also should find [the] *Guidebook* useful, as should educators, policy analysts, and corporate planners."

Particularly of interest to state and MPO freight intermodal planners is Report 388's Appendix C, "Freight Activity Data Sources," some of which are reviewed here but many of which are more appropriate for national freight demand forecasting studies and policy investigations. Report 388 is definitely required reading for state and MPO freight planners and transportation engineers; the following are the major Chapter and Appendix (*) headings:

- Freight Transportation System and Public Sector Planning
- Demand Forecasting for Existing Facilities
- Demand Forecasting for New Facilities
- Policy Analysis
  * Factors Influencing Freight Demand
  * Reviews of Freight Demand Forecasting Studies
  * Freight Activity Data Sources
  * Freight Transportation Survey Procedures and Methods
  * Statistical Forecasting Techniques
  * Estimating Transport Costs
  * Rail/Truck Modal Diversion
  * Three Modal-Diversion Models
  * Case Studies
  * Informative Needs Perceived by Public Agencies

The last appendix provides results of a survey of MPOs and other agencies done by the contractor, highlighting their *perceived* needs.

California Department of Transportation. 1998 California Transportation Plan, Statewide Goods Movement Strategy, Draft Issue Papers, August 4, 1997, unless otherwise indicated. (#1 "Goods Movement Transportation System Issues"; #2 "Goals, Objectives and Policies," October 30, 1997; #3 and #4 "Goods Movement Transportation Network Inventory, Constraints and Demands" ; #5 "Goods Movement Transportation System Recommendations"; #6 "Existing Roles and Responsibilities"; #7 "Alternatives Actions Inventory," November 3, 1997; #8 "Goods Movement Action Evaluation Methodology," October 30, 1997; #9 "Goods Movement Funding Sources and Criteria," October 30, 1997.)

Capelle, Russell B., Jr. "Available Data Sources for Truck Data Modeling at the State and MPO Levels." Paper presented at the Transportation Planning Methods Applications Conference, April 18, 1995, Seattle, Wash. Included a handout listing about 50 "Trucking/Intermodal Data Sources for Planners." (1995a)

Capelle, Russell B., Jr. "The 'I' Decade: Transportation in the 1990s," *Proceedings* of the International Symposium on Motor Carrier Transportation (Williamsburg, Va.: 5/31/93–6/4/93), 1994, pp. 61–62. (1994)

Capelle, Russell B., Jr. *Planning and Managing Intermodal Transportation Systems: A Guide to ISTEA Requirements.* DOT-T-95-03. Washington, D.C.: FHWA Office of Environment and Planning, Intermodal Division, 1995. (An annotated bibliography of recent freight-related sources is included on pages 64 to 100.) (1995b)

The following subjects of interest to freight planners and transportation engineers were covered:
- Organizing a freight advisory council/getting private sector companies involved
- What kinds of data? Where do I get data? What organizations, groups, directory publishers, and other sources can I use?
- Important state and regional data sources
- Developing data for truck facilities, and designing a truck company survey
- Freight forecasting and urban goods movement methods and models in the literature
- Maps of intermodal freight corridors
- Performance measure selection process and performance measure examples

Pages 24 through 29 list and briefly describe about 50 freight/freight intermodal data sources. An extensive annotated bibliography was included (pages 64 through 100).

Capelle, Russell B., Jr. "Regional Model Truck Trip Updating: Boston MPO Case Study," *Proceedings* of the National Freight Planning Applications Conference, San Antonio, Texas, October 14–16, 1996, forthcoming 1998 (article now available on BTS' NTL—www.bts.gov/ntl/—under "national freight conferences"). (1996)

Capelle, Russell B., Jr. "State/MPO-Level Freight Data and Data Modeling Research Projects: A 1995 Status Report on ISTEA-Stimulated Initiatives." Paper presented at the Transportation Research Forum annual forum, Chicago, Ill., October 20, 1995. October 20, 1995 Version. (An earlier version appeared in the *Proceedings* of the Transportation Research Forum [1995], handed out at the Chicago meeting.) (1995c)

"1997 CATS External Travel Study." One-page description. Chicago, Ill.: Chicago Area Transportation Study (CATS), January 24, 1997.

Chin, Shih-Miao; Janet Hopson; and Ho-Ling Hwang. "Estimating State-Level Truck Activities in America," *Journal of Transportation and Statistics,* Vol. 1, No. 1, January 1998, pp. 63–74.

Chow, Garland [University of British Columbia/University of Sydney]. "Review of North American Commercial Transport Data Collection and Modelling Experience." Report prepared for the Transport Data Centre, New South Wales [Australia] Department of Transport, 21 March 1997.

> Garland Chow, known internationally for his research and writings on the trucking industry, prepared a report for the Transport Data Center of the New South Wales (Australia) Department of Transport, printed 21 March 1997, entitled *Review of North American Commercial Transport Data Collection and Modelling Experience.* It is an excellent review and comparison of commercial vehicle survey (CVS) activity and the modeling efforts involved in them.
>
> On truck forecasting models, Chow notes that "[o]nly a fraction of the MPOs who have completed a CVS have gone on to develop a truck forecasting model, e.g., identify some form of trip generation or attraction relationships, but several MPOs with recently completed CVS state that they intend to do so. Many of the CVS in the U.S. are limited by sample sizes in developing a reasonable trip forecasting model." The booklet has an excellent and very recent bibliography of CVS reports by MPOs, consultant surveys of MPOs (e.g., Matherly, 1996), and analyses of truck survey results.

Christiansen, Dennis. *Urban Transportation Planning for Goods and Services—A Reference Guide.* Washington, D.C.: U.S. DOT, FHWA, 1979.

Commodity Flow Survey of 1993: BTS or Census publications and data sources available:
> CD-ROMs available: CD-CFS-93-1 (December 1996); CD-CFS-93-2 (March 1997); and CD-CFS-93-3 (1998).
> "State Summaries [of the CFS 1993]." Washington, D.C.: BTS, U.S. DOT, September 1996.
> "Truck Movements in America: Shipments From, To, Within, and Through States," *TranStats,* BTS/97-TS/1. Washington, D.C.: BTS, U.S. DOT, May 1997.
> "United States Highlights [of the CFS 1993]." Washington, D.C.: BTS, U.S. DOT, February 1997.

Czerniak, Robert. *The Use of Intermodal Performance Measures by State Departments of Transportation.* DOT-T-96-18. Washington, D.C.: U.S. Department of Transportation Technology Sharing Program, June 1996.

> Czerniak's *Use of Intermodal Performance Measures by State DOTs* offers a state-by-state review of freight and intermodal performance measures used and suggested for use in intermodal management systems and for other statewide freight planning and MPO freight planning purposes. The author reviews the literature on the subject, including papers presented at recent freight and intermodal planning conferences.

Donnelly, Rick [Parsons Brinckerhoff/Albuquerque office]. "The (First Generation) Michigan Statewide Truck Travel Forecasting Model," presentation at the National Freight Planning Applications Conference. San Antonio, Texas: October 14-16, 1996 (article now available on BTS' NTL—www.bts.gov/ntl/—under "national freight conferences).

DRI/McGraw-Hill. [study in 1994 for Oregon DOT—commodity flow study; get whole citation; study at home].

Earlbaum, Nathan. "An Overview of Commodity Flow in New York State. Presentation at the Transportation Research Board annual meeting, January 1998. Washington, D.C.

Federal Highway Administration. "Highway Performance Monitoring System—Strategic Reassessment," *Federal Register.* December 23, 1996 (Vol. 61, No. 247), pp. 67590–67592.

Fleet, Christopher R. *Selected Data-Related Resources & References for Transportation Planning* (since January 1992). Prepared for the TRB Conference on Information Needs to Support State and Local Transportation Decisionmaking into the 21st Century, March 2–5, 1997, Irvine, CA. Washington, D.C.: Transportation Research Board, February 14, 1997.

For-Hire Trucking Industry Study. Volumes I and II. FHWA-PL-95-037B. Prepared for FHWA by Trucking Research Institute of the American Trucking Associations Foundation in association with Martin Labbe Associates (FL) and Alan Pisarski (VA). Washington, D.C.: FHWA, 1992.

Hajek, Jerry J.; Gerhard Kennpohl; and John R. Billing. "Applications of Weigh-in-Motion Data in Transportation Planning." *Transportation Research Record No. 1364,* Washington, D.C.: Transportation Research Board, 1992, pp. 169–178.

"Identifying User Needs; Outreach to States and MPOs," *The Bureau of Transportation Statistics: Priorities for the Future.* Constance F. Citro and Janet L. Norwood, Editors. Washington, D.C.: National Research Council, National Academy Press, 1997, pp. 79–82.

Industry Directories (Trucking, Intermodal, Rail Industries).

> Business intelligence is for sale. Several major companies provide trucking industry directories, financial and operating statistics on trucking and rail companies, port import and export data, and so on.
>
> A rich vein of point-locatable trucking, rail, and other modal data are available in industry directories. Industry directories are moderately priced sources of locational and size information for private and for-hire trucking companies. MPOs planning truck exclusion routes would use these to find out where major concentrations of trucks are; directories typically list the address of the company or truck terminal and the number of power units (trucks) that are based there. For less-than-truckload carriers that have fleets based at a home office location, one needs to consult such directories as the MCD or NH&AC that list the LTL carriers' terminals by town or what towns are served by which carriers.

Indeed a very important use of these directories is in MPO regional modeling to locate the production nodes for truck trips (for truck trip table data) and the amount of trip "generators" located there (the number of trucks based there).

For attraction node locations (the destination point of the truck trip), many MPOs have employment data by SIC code purchased from a data supplier like Dun and Bradstreet, Wharton Economic Forecasting Associates, and others. Or you can easily get lists of whatever attraction nodes you want for your region. For example, did you know that you can get on disk locational information on any kind of business you want for anywhere in the country (see American Business Publishers, which is just one of many companies that provide yellow-pages-like information for companies sorted by SIC-code-like categories). Indeed ABP publishes business directories for each state summarizing that information, if you wish to order hard-copy information for your Library or Information Center. (For full contact information, see Capelle, 1995a)

- *American Motor Carrier Directory* (MCD) (K-III Information Co., Inc. in N.Y.: 212/714-3100)
- *Blue Book Quarterlies* (see TTS listing here)
- *Blue Book of Trucking Companies* (Transportation Technical Services in N.Y. and Va.: 800/666-4TTS)
- *[State] Business Directory* (American Business Publishers in Neb.: 402/593-4600)
- *Contract Carrier Directory and Routing Directory* (see TTS listing here)
- *Motor Carrier Annual Report* (see ATA listing here)
- *Motor Carrier Quarterly Report* (see ATA listing here)
- *National Highway and Air Carriers and Routes* (National Highway Carriers Dir., Inc.: 708/634-0606)
- *National Motor Carrier Directory* (see TTS listing here)
- *North American Truck Fleet Directory* (ATA in Va.: 800/ATA-LINE)
- *Official Intermodal Directory* (see K-III listing here)
- *Offical Motor Carrier Directory* (Official Motor Carrier Dir., Inc.: 312/939-1434)
- Owner-Operator Preferred Targets (OPT) (see TTS listing here)
- *Private Fleet Directory* (see TTS listing here)
- Regional Industrial Buying Guide for [your region] (Thomas Regional Dir. Co./Thomas Publishing Co., Inc. in N.Y.: 212/629-1560)
- Trucking Activity Report; The ATA (see ATA listing here)

Information Needs to Support State and Local Transportation Decision Making into the 21st Century. Conference Proceedings 14. Washington, D.C.: Transportation Research Board, National Research Council, 1997.

Intercity Modal Forecasts and Interactions: A report summarizing the intercity multimodal forecasts used in *Translinks 21: A Multimodal Transportation Plan for Wisconsin's 21st Century.* Madison, Wis.: Wisconsin Department of Transportation, no date [ca. 1996].

Intermodal Freight Transportation. Volume 1: Overview of Impediments, Data Sources for Intermodal Transportation Planning, and Annotated Bibliography. DOT-T-96-04. *Volume 2: Fact Sheet and Federal Aid Eligibility.* DOT-T-96-05. Final Report, December 1995. Prepared by Cambridge Systematics, Inc., with Apogee Research, Inc., Jack Faucett Associates, SYDEC, Inc. Washington, D.C.: Technology Sharing Program, U.S. Department of Transportation, 1996.

> This is a two volume 1996 FHWA publication of the December 1995 Final Report prepared by Cambridge Systematics, Inc., Apogee Research, Inc., Jack Faucett Associates, and SYDEC, Inc. for the FHWA. Many data sources are described in paragraph summaries and Figures 2–1 ("Scope and Coverage of Data Sources for Intermodal Planning"), 2–2 ("Type of Information by Modal System of Data Sources for Intermodal Planning"), and 2–3 ("Collection, Distribution, and Utilization of Data Sources for Intermodal Planning") are valuable cross-referencing displays. There is a seven-page annotated bibliography, which includes citations to trade journal articles valuable for freight planners and transportation engineers to read.

Intermodal Freight Transportation, Volume 2: Fact Sheet and Federal Aid Eligibility. DOT-T-96-05. Final Report, December 1995. Prepared by Cambridge Systematics, Inc., with Apogee Research, Inc., Jack Faucett Associates, Sydec, Inc. Washington, D.C.: Technology Sharing Program, U.S. Department of Transportation, 1996.

Intermodal Technical Assistance for Transportation Planners and Policymakers. Washington, D.C.: U.S. Department of Transportation Technology Sharing Program, December 1994.

Krishnan, Venkatesh and Kathleen L. Hancock. "Highway Freight Flow Assignment in Massachusetts Using Geographic Information Systems." Presentation at Transportation Research Board annual meeting, January 1998, Washington, D.C.

Lane, J. Scott and David T. Hartgen. "Diffusion of Transportation Planning Applications in Metropolitan Planning Organizations: Results of National Survey," *Transportation Research Record No. 1364.* Washington, D.C.: Transportation Research Board, 1992, pp. 45–52.

Lau, Samuel W. *Truck Travel Surveys: A Review of the Literature and State-of-the-Art.* Oakland, CA: Metropolitan Transportation Commission Library, 1995.

> Samuel W. Lau performed a valuable service for freight planners and transportation engineers when he, as an intern at San Francisco-Oakland, California's, Metropolitan Transportation Commission, wrote the January 1995 *Truck Travel Surveys: A Review of the Literature and State-of-the-Art.* Over 80 pages with appendices, this booklet (available around the time of its publication from the MTC Library, 101 Eighth Street, Oakland, Calif. 94607-4700; 510/464-7736; Fax 510/464-7848) has an excellent comparison chart of commercial vehicle surveys done throughout North America (costs of, number of responses, etc.). The booklet has the following chapters: national truck travel surveys; truck surveys and truck travel demand forecasting experiences in metropolitan areas (including Chicago Area Transportation Study [CATS],

Phoenix, Port Authority of New York and New Jersey, El Paso, North Carolina, Houston-Galveston, Calgary, Ontario, and Vancouver); California experiences; other research and studies of truck travel characteristics; computerized data collection of truck travel information; and conclusions and recommendations. This is a valuable overview of what has been done and what procedures and methodologies are "out there."

List, George F., and Mark Turnquist. "Goods Movement: Regional Analysis and Database." Final Report. Ithaca, N.Y.: University Transportation Research Center/Cornell University, June 15, 1993.

Matherly, Deborah. "MPO Freight Studies: Where, When, and How." (Tabular results of an MPO survey by COMSIS Corporation [COMSIS has now been dissolved; author is with TEMS, a consulting firm in Frederick, MD]. Silver Spring, Md.: COMSIS Corporation, 1996.

Matherly, Deborah. See "Biddle...."

Motor Carrier Management Information System (MCMIS) Data Dissemination Program Catalog. Publication No. FHWA-MC-96-032. Washington, D.C.: Office of Motor Carriers, FHWA, Fall 1996. (MCMIS is administered by Computing Technologies, Inc., 3028 Javier Road, Suite 101, Fairfax, Va. 22031-4622; 703/280-4001.)

Multimodal Freight Forecasts for Wisconsin: A technical report detailing the development of forecasts used in *Translinks 21: A Multimodal Transportation Plan for Wisconsin's 21st Century*. Prepared for WisDOT by Wilbur Smith Associates in association with Reebie Associates. Madison, Wis.: Wisconsin Department of Transportation, July 1996.

Muller, Gerhardt. *Intermodal Freight Transportation*. Third Edition. Washington, D.C. and Greenbelt, Md.: Eno Transportation Foundation and the Intermodal Association of North America, respectively, 1995.

National Conference on Setting an Intermodal Transportation Research Framework. Conference Proceedings 12. Washington, D.C.: Transportation Research Board, 1997. Papers and presentations at the National Conference... held in Washington, D.C., March 4–5, 1996 and sponsored by Defense Advanced Research Projects Agency, U.S. Department of Defense and Office of Intermodalism, U.S. Department of Transportation.

National Cooperative Highway Research Program, National Academy of Sciences (see also: Transportation Research Board). Several NCHRP projects of interest are listed:

NCHRP Project 2-20: Economic Trends and Multimodal Transportation Requirements. Phase 2 Draft Report prepared by Louis Berger International, Inc. reviewed by NCHRP Panel Members, late 1997.

The contractor is Louis Berger International, Inc. and the objective of the project is to develop guidance material to improve the ability of transportation professionals and decision makers to respond to the changing requirements of American business, in their planning efforts at the national, State, Metropolitan, and local levels. The research has been and will be carried out in a three-phased effort. The objective of the first phase is to identify and consider the *economic trends* affecting multimodal transportation, particularly to identify the most relevant trends that significantly influence changing transportation demand and service requirements. The main objective of the second phase is to identify and assess multimodal *transportation requirements* of American Business, in view of the previously identified economic trends. This second phase will then assess what are the implications of the economic trends on transportation infrastructure and services. Finally, the objective of the third phase is to identify and assess various *strategies* to address the changing requirements of American Business, while demonstrating methodologies and procedures so that planning practitioners can use the research findings.

- NCHRP Project 2-21 (now in progress): Economic Implications of Congestion.
- NCHRP Project 2-22: Needs in Communicating the Economic Impacts of Transportation Investment.
- NCHRP Project 3-55(4): Performance Measures and Levels of Service in the Year 2000 Highway Capacity Manual.
- NCHRP 8-30. See "Cambridge Systematics, Inc." above.
- NCHRP 8-32(5): Multimodal Transportation Planning Data. Jack Faucett Associates.
- (in progress). To develop guidelines on the availability and use of data to support statewide and metropolitan multimodal transportation planning pursuant to ISTEA and subsequent regulations.
- NCHRP Project 8-34: Major Investment Studies: Development of a Practitioner's Guidebook for Effective Study Design, Management, and Implementation.
- NCHRP Project 15-15: Collection and Presentation of Roadway Inventory Data.

National Freight Planning Conferences—sponsored by and supported by Intermodal Division, Office of Environment and Planning, FHWA, U.S. DOT. (Urban Goods Movement and Freight Forecasting Conference, Albuquerque, N.M., Sept. 1995 [*Proceedings* published 1996 and available on BTS web National Transportation Library site]; National Freight Planning Applications Conference, San Antonio, Texas, Oct. 1996 [*Proceedings* available on BTS, NTL Web site] [Note: Publication of both of these *Proceedings* together in one volume is planned for early 1998.]; National Freight Summit, Philadelphia, Pa., Nov. 1997 [*Proceedings* planned for publication in 1998]; the fourth conference in this series is planned for Seattle in late 1998 or in 1999.

There have been three national freight conferences to date and a fourth is planned for 1999 in Seattle. FHWA's Intermodal Division funded three conferences to date:

Urban Goods and Freight Forecasting Conference, Albuquerque, New Mexico, September 1995

National Freight Planning Applications Conference, San Antonio, Texas, October 1996

National Freight Summit, Philadelphia, Pennsylvania, November 1997

At each of these conferences freight planning and forecasting experts provided their thoughts and an invited list of participants discussed major issues in working groups and breakout sessions.

The Albuquerque conference in 1995 had the following speakers, invited papers (I), and discussion group leaders (D) (alphabetically):

- Joe Bryan (Reebie Associates)
  "Directions in Freight Data"
- Russell B. Capelle, Jr. (D) (then of Boston MPO's Central Transp'n. Planning Staff [CTPS])
- Arun Chatterjee (I) (University of Tennessee)
  "Urban Goods Movement Planning in USA: A Historical Perspective"
- Harry Cohen (then of Cambridge Systematics, Inc.)
  "Future Directions for Freight Modeling"
- Robert J. Czerniak (Conference Organizer) (New Mexico State University)
- Rick Donnelly (D) (Parsons Brinckerhoff)
- Monica I. Francois (D) (then of FHWA)
- Alan J. Horowitz (University of Wisconsin-Milwaukee)
  "Freight Forecasting: The Context"
- Dane Ismart (funding agency rep.) (then of FHWA, Intermodal Division)
  "FHWA Interests and Activities in Urban Goods and Freight Modeling"
- Thomas H. Maze (I) (Iowa State University)
  "An Iowa Approach to Statewide Freight Demand Models or the Onion Approach to Freight Demand Forecasting"
- Kenneth Wade Ogden (then of Monash University, Australia)
- Keynote address: "Urban Goods Movement and Its Relation to Planning"
- Randall Wade (Wisconsin Department of Transportation)
  "TRANSLINKS 21 Transportation Plan: Intercity Modal Forecasts and Interactions"

The National Freight Planning Applications Conference, held in conjunction with the Transportation Research Forum annual forum in San Antonio in 1996, focused around the following presentations and speakers (alphabetically):

- Felix Ammah-Tagoe and Bob Zarnetske (BTS/USDOT)
  "The Commodity Flow Survey and Other Public Freight Data Sources"
- Marsha Dale Anderson (StreetSmarts, Duluth, GA)
  "Handheld Computer Technology for Freight Data Collection"
- Frank Brogan and Rick Maldonado (Port of Corpus Christi Authority)
  "Northside Highway and Rail Corridor: Creating a Seamless Intermodal Network for the Customer"
- Joe Bryan (Reebie Associates)
  "Status Update of the Intermodal Freight Visual Database"
- Russell B. Capelle, Jr. (then of Boston MPO's Central Transp'n. Planning Staff [CTPS])
  "Regional Model Truck Trip Updating: Boston MPO Case Study"
- Elena K. Constantine (then of Mid-Ohio Regional Planning Council)
  "MORPC: An Equal Partner in the Greater Columbus Inland Port Program"
- Ted Dahlburg (Delaware Valley Regional Planning Commission)
  "Delaware Area Freight Plan"
- Fred S. Friedman (New Mexico Highway and transportation Department)
  "Freight Planning Obstacles and Resources in New Mexico"
- Eric Irelan (Skagit Council of Governments)
  "Skagit Countywide Air, Rail, Water, and Port Transportation System Study"
- Sara LaBelle (KANLACON Urban Area MPO [NC])
  "Suburban Truck Activity: A GIS Approach"
- Keith Mattson (then of Denver Regional Council of Governments)
  "Integrating Freight into Metropolitan Transportation Planning"
- Rebecca Meyer (American Trucking Associations, Inc.)
  "Freight Stakeholders National Network"
- Stefan Natzke (FHWA, Intermodal Division)
  "Public-Private Freight Planning Partnerships"
- Paul Nowicki (Burlington Northern Santa Fe Corporation)
  "Freight Transportation Planning: Bridging the Chasm Between Public and Private Sectors"
- Marc Roddin (Metropolitan Transportation Commission [Oakland, CA])
  "San Francisco Bay Area Seaport Planning"
- Reginald Victor (OKI Regional Planning Association [OH, KY, IN])
  "Freight Transport Planning for the Greater Cincinnati Area"
- Fred Wegmann (University of Tennessee)
  "Characteristics of Urban Freight: A New Manual"

Proceedings of the first two national freight conferences are available on the Internet and will soon be available in printed form. The *Proceedings* of the September 1995 Albuquerque, N.M., Urban Goods Movement and Freight Forecasting Conference and the *Proceedings* of the October 1996 San Antonio, Texas, National Freight Planning Applications Conference are available together on the BTS' National Transportation Library Web page (http://www.bts.gov/NTL/ or http://www.dot.gov/NTL). Both conference proceedings are being published together, and that booklet is due out in 1998.

The *Proceedings* of the third conference in the series, the November 1997 Philadelphia National Freight Summit is being edited and is due for separate publication in 1998.

New York Metropolitan Transportation Council. *Compendium of Freight Information*. New York, N.Y.: NYMTC, November 1997. Eleven pages of tables, charts and graphs of New York Metro area freight data.

"Northeast Freight Transportation Forecast . . . to 2004; DRI/McGraw Hill." Baltimore, Md.: Baltimore Metropolitan Council, 1997.

"Northeast Transportation Institute Conference; Report of the 1996 Annual/and DRI/McGraw Hill Northeast Freight Transportation Forecast . . . to 2004." Alexandria, Va.: American Trucking Associations, Inc., April 1997.

Ogden, Kenneth Wade. "Modelling Urban Freight Generation." *Traffic Engineering + Control*. London, England: March 1977, Vol. 18, No. 3, 106–109.

Ogden, Kenneth Wade. *Urban Goods Movement: A Guide to Policy and Planning*. Aldershot, UK: Wildwood Distribution Service, and Brookfield, Vt.: Ashgate Publishing Co. [Gower Publishing Co.], 1992.

Ogden, Kenneth Wade. "Urban Goods Movement and Its Relation to Planning" in *Proceedings of the Urban Goods and Freight Forecasting Conference*. Washington, D.C.: FHWA and TMIP, forthcoming, 1998, 2-1 to 2-14. (Full text available on the Internet: http://www.bts.gov/ntl/)

Perincherry, Vijay. See "Biddle...."

Phoenix Urban Truck Travel Model Project; Final Report. Prepared by Cambridge Systematics, Inc. Phoenix, Ariz.: Arizona Department of Transportation, 1991.

Pisarski, Alan E. *Metropolitan Goods Movement: Needed Changes to Foster Economic Growth*. Prepared for the Goods Movement Task Force of the Business Transportation Council. Washington, D.C.: BTC, ca. 1993.

"Pooled Fund Study." "Southeastern U.S. Transportation Infrastructure Development to Accommodate International Trade and Economic Growth with Special Emphasis on Latin America." Now in progress. Southeast Association of State Highway and Transportation Officials and Federal Highway Administration.

"Pooled Fund Study." Now in progress. Western Transportation and Trade Network.

Prem, Clyde E. , and Ping Yu. "Applying Urban Transportation Modeling Techniques to Model Regional Freight and Vehicle Movement," *Transportation Research Record No. 1518*. Washington, D.C.: Transportation Research Board, 1996, pp. 22–24.

Puget Sound Regional Council. *Analysis of Freight Movements in the Puget Sound Region*. Seattle, Wash.: PSRC, October 1994.

Quick Response Freight Manual. See "Travel Model Improvement Program."

Rawling, F. Gerald. *Statistical Summary and Value of the Intermodal Freight Industry in Northeast Illinois*. Working Paper 97-03. Chicago, Ill.: Chicago Area Transportation Study, July 1997.

Ruiter, Earl. *Development of an Urban Truck Travel Model for the Phoenix Metropolitan Area*. Final Report. Cambridge, Mass.: Prepared by Cambridge Systematics, Inc. for Arizona Department of Transportation, February 1992.

Ruiter, Earl R. "Phoenix Commercial Vehicle Survey and Travel Models." *Transportation Research Record No. 1364*. Washington, D.C.: Transportation Research Board, 1992, pp. 144–151.

"SBIR Projects." (Small Business Innovation Research Projects now underway, with FHWA funding.) Two teams: (1) Reebie Associates, Inc., Greenwich, Conn.; Standard and Poor's DRI/McGraw-Hill, Lexington, Mass.; and GISTrans, Boston, Mass.; and (2) Colography Group, Inc., Marietta, Ga.; and Caliper Corporation, Newton, Mass. The teams are developing a commodity flow data base product for eventual sale to customers.

To some extent each of the projects started out originally to produce a "county-to-county visual data base," and each is now oriented more toward a commodity flow data base, to some extent enhanced by the now-available results of the Census data products from the 1993 Commodity Flow Survey. Members of the two teams have changed over time, with Reebie being the only one of the original contractors which began the project in the early 1990s.

Siaurusaitis, Victor. See "Biddle...."

Southworth, Frank. "An Urban Goods Movement Model: Framework and Some Results," *Papers of the Regional Science Association*. Urbana, Ill.: Vol. 50, 1982, 165-184.

"Statewide Transportation Planning," *Transportation Research Circular No. 471*. Washington, D.C.: Transportation Research Board, May 1997. (Papers and presentations at the June 1996 TRB Committee on Statewide Multimodal Transportation Planning's national conference on statewide transportation planning at Coeur d'Alene, Idaho, in conjunction with the mid-year meeting of the Standing Committee on Planning (SCoP) of the American Association of State Highway and Transportation Officials.

TRANSLINKS 21: A Multimodal Transportation Plan for Wisconsin's 21st Century. Madison, Wis.: Wisconsin Department of Transportation, February 1995.

Transportation Research Board. *Data for Decisions*. Report 234. Washington, D.C.: National Academy Press, 1992.

Travel Model Improvement Program (TMIP). *Activity-Based Travel Forecasting Conference*. (Conference held in New Orleans, La., June 2–5, 1996.) Washington, D.C.: Technology Sharing Program, RSPA/USDOT, February 1997.

Travel Model Improvement Program. *Data Collection in the Portland, Oregon Metropolitan Area Case Study* (DOT-T-97-09). Washington, D.C.: FHWA, September 1996.

Travel Model Improvement Program. *Identification of Transportation Planning Data Requirements in Federal Legislation*. DOT-T-94-21. b (Prepared by Karla H. Karash and Carol Schweiger, EG&G Dynatrend, Burlington, Mass. for John A. Volpe National Transportation Systems Center.) Washington, D.C.: Technology Sharing Program, RSPA, U.S. DOT, July 1994.

Travel Model Improvement Program (Cambridge Systematics, Inc., COMSIS Corp., and University of Wisconsin-Milwaukee). *Quick Response Freight Manual*. Washington, D.C.: Technology Sharing Program, RSPA, U.S. DOT, September 1996 (but released to the public in late 1997).

> The reader is encouraged to study Chapter 6 of the QRF Manual, "Data Collection to Support More Accurate Freight Analysis," which discusses surveys, truck counts, and freight advisory committees as primary data sources and has a brief discussion of several secondary sources. Appendix K provides detailed information on many "Freight Transportation Data Sources," the source of most of which is the latest annual edition of the Bureau of Transportation Statistics' *Directory of Transportation Data Sources*. The QRF Manual's value for regional modelers at the MPO level may be the data in many of the tables that can be used as surrogate data for other regions. Notably Table 4–1, "Trip Generation Rates," p. 4–4, and detailed tables in Appendix D can be used for that purpose. Based on data from the Commercial Vehicle Survey in Phoenix (*Phoenix . . . .*, 1991; Ruiter, 1992), the data can serve as surrogate trip generation rates for other cities.

Travel Model Improvement Program. *Scan of Recent Data Research* (DOT-T-97-07). Washington, D.C.: FHWA, September 1996.

Institute of Transportation Engineers. *Transportation Planning Handbook*. Englewood Cliffs, N.J.: Prentice-Hall, 1992.

Trip Generation. Washington, D.C.: Institute of Transportation Engineers, 1991.

Turnquist, Mark A. See "List, George F."

U. S. Department of Transportation. *Progress Report on The National Transportation System Initiative*. Washington, DC: U.S. DOT, December 1996.

U. S. Department of Transportation, Office of the Secretary. *National Transportation Network Analysis Workshop, Proceedings* (September 6–7, 1995, Arlington, Va.). DOT-T-97-05. Washington, D.C.: U.S. DOT, OST, December 1996.

U. S. Department of Transportation, Office of the Secretary. *National Transportation System Performance Measures*. Final Report. DOT-T-97-04. Washington, D.C.: U.S. DOT, OST, April 1996.

Wegmann, Frederick J.; Arun Chatterjee; Martin E. Lipinski; Barton E. Jennings; and R. Eugene McGinnis. *Characteristics of Urban Freight Systems (CUFS)*. Final Report December 1995. DOT-T-96-22. Washington, D.C.: Intermodal Division, Office of Environment and Planning, FHWA and Technology Sharing Program, RSPA, 1996.

> The USDOT/FHWA booklet, *Characteristics of Urban Freight Systems* (CUFS) "has been designed to be a compilation of current data that pertain to urban freight movements" and the authors hope that CUFS "will become a staring point for the collection and integration of urban freight data for local planners."
>
> The following chapter headings provide the reader with an idea of the topics covered in CUFS:
> * Urban Commodity Movements—The Importance of Trucks
> * Characteristics of the National Commercial Truck Fleet
> * Urban Truck Travel Relationships
> * Truck Percentages on Roadways
> * Loading Zone Use Characteristics
> * Urban Truck Accidents and Incidents
> * Trip Rates
> * Truck Terminals
> * Design of Loading Dock and Loading Zone for Trucks
> * Rail-Truck Intermodal Transportation and Terminals
> * Air Cargo
> * Ports of the United States
> * References
>
> The authors note that "[a]ll data were obtained from survey studies and were not synthesized from analytical modeling efforts," with some cited studies dating from the 1970s "where more current data were not available."

Weiner, Edward. *Urban Transportation Planning in the United States: An Historical Overview*. Fifth Edition. DOT-T-97-24. Washington, D.C.: USDOT, OST, September 1997.

Professional and Trade Journals and Associations

Transportation Research Board Publications, Committees, Conferences, and Annual, and Mid-Year Meetings

The annual meeting of the Transportation Research Board (TRB) in Washington, D.C., during the third week in January each year provides a wealth of opportunity for state and MPO freight planners to learn about the latest research and data analyses in freight and intermodal transportation arenas. The TRB has 187 official committees, composed of about 25 members each, and from one to several hundred "friends of the committee." TRB committees that deal particularly with freight issues are the following; interested freight planners should contact the Chair of the appropriate committee (contact information is provided).

Many of the freight-related committees are in Division A, Group 1, "Multimodal Freight Transportation Section," including the following:

- A1B01 Inland Water Transportation

- A1B02 Freight Transportation Planning and Marketing (Ed Morlok, 215/898-8346)

- (There is not an A1B03 committee)

- A1B04 Motor Vehicle Size and Weight

- A1B05 Intermodal Freight Transport

- A1B06 Freight Transport Regulation

- A1B07 Urban Goods Movement (Noreen Roberts, 916/391-8526)

- A1B08 Ports and Channels

- A1B09 Freight Transportation Data (Russell B. Capelle, Jr., 202/366-5685)

- A1B10 Local and Regional Rail Transport

The "Transportation Forecasting, Data, and Economics Section of Division A, Group 1 includes the following TRB committees dealing with freight and other issues:

- A1C01 Transportation Economics

- A1C02 Passenger Travel Demand Forecasting

- [There is no A1C03 Committee]

- A1C04 Traveler Behavior and Values

- A1C05 Transportation Supply Analysis

- A1C06 Social and Economic Factors of Transportation

- A1C07 Transportation Planning Applications

- A1C08 Telecommunications and Travel Behavior

The "Transportation Systems Planning Section" of Division A, Group 1 includes:

- A1D01 Statewide Multimodal Transportation Planning

- A1D02 Transportation and Land Development

- A1D04 Public Involvement in Transportation

- A1D05 Transportation Planning Needs and Requirements of Small and Medium-Sized Communities

- A1D06 Transportation Programming, Planning, and Systems Evaluation

- A1D07 Access Management

- A1D08 Urban Transportation Data and Information Systems

- A1D09 Statewide Transportation Data and Information Systems (Ron Tweedie, 518/457-1965)

- A1D52 (Task Force) Travel Survey Methods

Other TRB committees and task forces of interest include:

- A1T51 Task Force on Intermodal Transportation

- A5T52 Task Force on Geographic Information Systems for Transportation (Wende O'Neill, 202/366-8876)

- A5T53 Task Force on National Data Needs and Requirements (Alan Pisarski, 703/941-4257)

In addition there are panels set up for particular issues and research projects under the National Cooperative Highway Research Program (NCHRP) and the Transit Cooperative Research Program (TCRP). Consult the latest TRB Directory or call or otherwise contact TRB at 202/334-3214; Fax 202/334-2519.

Professional Journals

Articles on the latest freight transportation research can be found in these and other professional and scholarly journals:

- *Journal of the Transportation Research Forum* (Reston, Va.: Transportation Research Forum)

- *Journal of Transport Geography* (UK: Royal Geographical Society/Institute of British Geographers)

- *Journal of Transportation and Statistics* (Washington, D.C.: U.S. DOT, Bureau of Transportation Statistics)

- *Journal of Transportation Management* (Nashville, Tenn.: Delta Nu Alpha)

- *Proceedings of the Council of Logistics Management* (Oak Brook, Ill.: Council of Logistics Management)

- *Transportation Journal* (Lock Haven, Pa.: American Society of Transportation and Logistics)

- *Transportation Quarterly* (Washington, D.C.: Eno Transportation Foundation)

- *Transportation Research* (Lund, Sweden: A, B & C)

- *Transportation Research Record* (Washington, D.C.: Transportation Research Board)

Trade Associations

Almost anything you can think of has a trade association that represents it, collects and analyzes information and statistics about it, and provides at reasonable prices a wealth of information on the subject of interest. Definitely that is true in freight transportation. Trade associations listed below have annual "trends" publications, annual compendia of statistics on their industry, quarterly or more frequent newsletters and updates on data, and other valuable sources for the state or MPO freight planner and transportation engineers.

For example, the American Trucking Association (ATA) through its ATA Foundation puts out such handy sources as fact books for each state and many large cities (e.g., "Trucking in Boston"); and they have "Trucking in the USA," which has information on each state, including histograms, other graphs, and statistics to show amount of goods moving by truck compared to other modes. Indeed, through its regional offices, ATA has done and is doing special commercial trucking surveys of ATA member trucking companies to provide certain MPOs with results they can use in freight planning. Central Massachusetts Regional Planning Association (Worcester, Mass., early 1990s) and the Baltimore Metropolitan Council (Baltimore, Md., in progress) are two locations where such surveys have been carried out.

- American Trucking Associations, Inc., Alexandria, Va. (703/838-1700; ATA Information Center Cathe Mahe/Susanne Hess 703/838-1880)

- Association of American Railroads, Washington, D.C. (Craig Rockey, 202/639-2319)

- National Private Truck Council, Alexandria, Va. (John McQuaid, 703/638-1300)

- Intermodal Association of North America, Greenbelt, Md. (Joanne Casey, 301/982-3400)

Trade Journals

To get the "flavor" of an industry and learn quickly about the "hot button" issues and the "thought leaders" in the industry, consult one of the many trade journals. The articles in the journals are instructive to the state and MPO freight planners and transportation engineers:

- *Atlantic Journal of Transportation* (Boston, Mass.: 617/328-5005)

- *Commercial Carrier Journal* (Radnor, Pa.:, 800/695-1214; 610/964-4000)

- *Fleet Owner* (White Plains, N.Y.: 914/949-8500)

- *Heavy Duty Trucking* (Irvine, Calif.: 714/261-1636)

- *Journal of Commerce* (New York, N.Y.: 212/208-0224)

- *Refrigerated Transporter* (Houston, Texas: 713/523-8124)

- *Traffic World* (New York, N.Y.: 800/245-8723)

- *Transport Topics* (Alexandria, Va.: The Newspaper of the Trucking Industry, 703/548-3662)

- *World Wide Shipping* (Odessa, Fla.: 904/358-3813)

CHAPTER 4
Urban Travel Characteristics

Marsha Dale Anderson
President, Street Smarts

Mobility and accessibility have become key operative words in examining travel. This has expanded the view of multiple modes of transportation to meet the needs and demands of society for efficient movement of people and goods. This chapter presents the current information on the travel characteristics in urban areas around the world.

Changes in decision-making demand a more complete understanding of how things are happening today and what the character of travel is for the coming new millennium. Historically we have focused on shortest distance or minimum time travel path, but an emphasis on quality of life has altered the choices and the decisions for much of the population. However, there are still those who do not have ready access to transportation opportunities; and for these groups, movement to jobs, health care, or other places is often a struggle. According to the most recent U.S. National Personal Transportation Survey[1] (NPTS), these groups primarily include low-income, elderly, and physically handicapped persons and recent immigrants.

The land use patterns that shaped many metropolitan areas and cities included a significant amount of high-density development and shorter travel distances. As these places expand geographically and densities decrease, the emphasis on auto use has grown. This is true both in the United States and in Europe. With the availability of autos and the acceptance or dependence on their use, travel patterns have also changed. Radial trips from suburb to downtown only represent a portion of daily travel. Suburb-to-suburb, or circumferential, travel has increased and represents a more scattered set of places and purposes to be served.

Fourteen countries around the world responded to a survey[2] about their transportation issues. These countries, ranked by population, represent a range from the 8th (Japan) to the 169th (Luxembourg) largest in the world. They indicated that good infrastructure and a good mass transit system were among the best features of their transportation systems. Management, enforcement, and congestion were among their worst features. Technology, transit, enforcement, and information sharing were suggested as the most promising solutions to the mobility and access needs for the future.

Travel Characteristics and Land Use Relationships

There has always been a relationship between land use patterns and trip-making characteristics. From the beginning of time, cities were first located near bodies of water where travel and commerce were feasible. This included coastal locations as well as places along inland waterways. The movement from the immediate vicinity of these places was a function of the availability of transportation. When walking was the mode of travel, cities were small and close to the water-based activities. With horses and wagons, streetcars, railroads, and then automobiles becoming additional choices, the distances that could easily be traveled increased; and this subsequently allowed cities to spread. With the expansion of developed land area came the need for roads to connect places.

Highway development allowed for the suburban and rural parts of nations to experience growth. Interstates and other high-speed facilities encouraged longer distance travel with more development occurring further from the traditional

---

[1] *Our Nation's Travel: 1995 NPTS Early Results Report* (Washington, D.C.: U.S. Department of Transportation, September 1997), p. 30.

[2] *The Urban Transportation Monitor* (Fairfax Station, Va.: Lawley Publications, January 16, 1998; and January 30, 1998), Jan. 16 issue, pp. 2–8; Jan. 30 issue, pp. 9–10.

city centers. Many trips today, however, are made quite regularly between what have been labeled as suburban and rural areas to the urbanized areas. This travel over longer distances for same day and often regular travel has shaped the geographical and temporal patterns, as well as the congestion issues, faced today.

The study of travel demand forecasting has shown that these associations can be quite complex. Trip rates vary both by land use and physical proximity to other land uses. Mode choices for passenger and freight transportation are a function of many factors including availability, convenience, length of trip, household income, level of education, commodity type and value, and number of people or quantity of goods to be moved.

When using analytical tools, it is important to understand how your study area compares to those that were the basis for deriving the findings. For example, if a trip generation rate is developed using data only from suburban communities, the application to an urban situation would certainly be suspect. Similarly, if the data were collected only in small cities, application to large urban areas would probably not be appropriate.

Population Trends[3]

It is valuable to look at population growth trends and changes in households to assess the volume and traffic pattern observations made in a particular area. For example, the city of Atlanta had a twelve-year population decrease of about 7 percent between 1980 and 1990; however, the Atlanta metro area saw an increase of 32 percent. This is consistent with the move to suburban and more rural areas historically observed with increases in mobility such as improved highways. The population shift changes the nature of travel, with more vehicle dependence and longer trips.

In the United States, metropolitan areas are defined by the Census Bureau by population. Originally referred to as "standard metropolitan areas," they were later called "standard metropolitan statistical areas," until 1983 when they became "metropolitan statistical areas" (MSAs). MSAs must include at least one city with 50,000 or more residents or a Census Bureau-defined urbanized area of at least 50,000 and a total population of at least 100,000 (75,000 in New England).

According to the U.S. Bureau of Census's population and household figures, which include more than 280 metropolitan areas, some metro populations are experiencing positive growth while others are experiencing negative growth. Overwhelmingly, the growth in metropolitan areas outweighs the declines, moving more population into urban areas as we approach the 21st century.

The relationship between population and number of households has changed quite significantly in recent years. In general, where there were even small increases in population, there were larger increases in the number of households. Where there is a decrease in population, the reduction in households is generally smaller than the population change. One interpretation is that there are more single-person and divorced households in these communities.

In the United States, Naples, Florida, had the greatest growth between 1980 and 1990, with almost a 77 percent increase in population. Casper, Wyoming, experienced the greatest decline, with almost a 15 percent decrease in population. The increase in the number of households in Naples was approximately the same as the population increase. However, in Casper the decrease in households was only 0.5 percent. Decatur, Alabama, had the largest decrease in number of households with a 5.5 percent reduction.

Table 4–1 lists the metropolitan area population, household, and density data for 1980 and 1990 for metropolitan areas with populations over 200,000.

In the United States, approximately 3 percent of the land area, 106,000 square miles, is considered urban; yet more than 70 percent of the population lives in urban areas. Annually, more than 1.5 trillion vehicle miles of travel (VMT) occur in the urban areas, of which approximately 6 percent is truck traffic. These trips are made on 1.9 million lane miles. The relationship of urban population and VMT to total area and travel is shown in Table 4–2.

---

[3] Much of the information in this chapter is from the 1990 U.S. Census. At this time, this is the most current information available. The Census will be updated in 2000, and the data collected should be available around 2002.

Table 4–1   Metro Area Rankings—Population and Households[4]

Metropolitan Area	Resident Population (April 1) 1990 Number	Rank	1980 Number	Rank	Percent change, 1980–1990 Percent	Rank	Per square mile of land area, 1990 Number	Rank	Households 1989 1,000	Rank	Percent change, 1980–1989 Percent	Rank
New York-Northern New Jersey-Long Island, NY-NJ-CT CMSA/NECMA	17953372	1	17412203	1	3.1	192	2353.8	1	6887.5	1	9.8	200
Los Angeles-Anaheim-Riverside, CA CMSA	14531529	2	11497549	2	26.4	42	427.8	46	5113.1	2	23.5	70
Chicago-Gary-Lake County, IL-IN-WI CMSA	8065633	3	7937290	3	1.6	206	1435.5	3	3017.3	3	9.1	209
San Francisco-Oakland-San Jose, CA CMSA	6253311	4	5367900	5	16.5	77	848.6	15	2374.1	4	16.2	130
Philadelphia-Wilmington-Trenton, PA-NJ-DE-MD CMSA	5899345	5	5680509	4	3.9	184	1103.6	6	2221.4	5	12.8	167
Detroit-Ann Arbor, MI CMSA	4665236	6	4752764	6	-1.8	234	901.4	13	1732.4	6	5.3	245
Washington, DC-MD-VA MSA	3923574	7	3250921	8	20.7	60	989.1	8	1424.1	8	21.4	84
Dallas-Fort Worth, TX CMSA	3885415	8	2930568	10	32.6	23	557.7	28	1431	7	35	32
Boston-Lawrence-Salem-Lowell-Brockton, MA NECMA	3783817	9	3662888	7	3.3	190	1550.5	2	1413.9	9	9	211
Houston-Galveston-Brazoria, TX CMSA	3711043	10	3099942	9	19.7	65	522.1	33	1348.6	10	23	75
Miami-Fort Lauderdale, FL CMSA	3192582	11	2643766	12	20.8	59	1012.4	7	1272.2	11	23.8	68
Atlanta, GA MSA	2833511	12	2138136	16	32.5	25	553.3	29	1058.3	13	39.9	18
Cleveland-Akron-Lorain, OH CMSA	2759823	13	2834062	11	-2.6	240	948.4	10	1068.7	12	4.8	248
Seattle-Tacoma, WA CMSA	2559164	14	2093285	18	22.3	53	434.4	45	973.7	14	22.9	76
San Diego, CA MSA	2498016	15	1861846	19	34.2	21	594.1	24	906.7	17	35.3	28
Minneapolis-St. Paul, MN-WI MSA	2464124	16	2137133	17	15.3	86	487.8	35	918.7	15	19.3	97
St. Louis, MO-IL MSA	2444099	17	2376968	14	2.8	196	458.5	42	918.5	16	8.7	214
Baltimore, MD MSA	2382172	18	2199497	15	8.3	132	913	11	874.7	20	14.2	151
Pittsburgh-Beaver Valley, PA CMSA	2242798	19	2423311	13	-7.4	271	584.8	25	904.9	18	2.2	263
Phoenix, AZ MSA	2122101	20	1509175	24	40.6	13	230.6	123	833.1	21	52.9	10
Tampa-St. Petersburg-Clearwater, FL MSA	2067959	21	1613600	22	28.2	37	809.5	17	887	19	35.1	30
Denver-Boulder, CO CMSA	1848319	22	1618461	21	14.2	90	410.4	54	760.6	22	25	63
Cincinnati-Hamilton, OH-KY-IN CMSA	1744124	23	1660257	20	5.1	177	672.8	21	656	23	11.8	179
Milwaukee-Racine, WI CMSA	1607183	24	1570152	23	2.4	202	896.3	14	608.9	24	8.7	215
Kansas City, MO-KS MSA	1566280	25	1433464	25	9.3	125	314	79	607.7	25	14.9	146
Sacramento, CA MSA	1481102	26	1099814	32	34.7	19	290.8	91	561.3	26	34.8	33
Portland-Vancouver, OR-WA CMSA	1477895	27	1297977	26	13.9	92	338.1	72	560.5	27	12.8	166
Norfolk-Virginia Beach-Newport News, VA MSA	1396107	28	1160311	31	20.3	61	828.4	16	476.2	30	23.4	71
Columbus, OH MSA	1377419	29	1243827	28	10.7	109	384.9	61	526.7	28	17.2	124
San Antonio, TX MSA	1302099	30	1072125	33	21.5	55	516.6	34	454.6	32	30.1	46
Indianapolis, IN MSA	1249822	31	1166575	30	7.1	151	407	55	473	31	13	164
New Orleans, LA MSA	1238816	32	1256668	27	-1.4	232	536.6	31	488.9	29	11.3	186
Buffalo-Niagara Falls, NY CMSA	1189288	33	1242826	29	-4.3	252	758.7	18	444.2	33	-0.3	271
Charlotte-Gastonia-Rock Hill, NC-SC MSA	1162093	34	971447	35	19.6	66	344	67	430.6	34	25.8	61
Hartford-New Britain-Middletown-Bristol, CT NECMA	1123678	35	1051606	34	6.9	160	741.8	19	421.2	35	13.3	162
Orlando, FL MSA	1072748	36	699904	52	53.3	6	422.7	49	401	36	58.7	7
Salt Lake City-Ogden, UT MSA	1072227	37	910222	40	17.8	72	662.9	22	349	47	20.6	90
Rochester, NY MSA	1002410	38	971230	36	3.2	191	341.9	71	370.7	40	8.3	221
Nashville, TN MSA	985026	39	850505	45	15.8	81	241.8	117	376	38	24.5	65
Memphis, TN-AR-MS MSA	981747	40	913472	39	7.5	146	426.3	47	360.7	44	15.6	134

[Based on 281 metropolitan areas (17 CMSAs, 249 MSAs, and 15 NECMAs) unless otherwise noted. All metro areas defined as of June 30, 1989. When metro areas share the same rank, the next lower rank is omitted. Due to rounding, metro areas may have same values and different ranks.]

[4] *State and Metropolitan Area Data Book 1991* (Washington, D.C.: U.S. Department of Commerce, August 1991), pp. XX–XXIII.

Table 4–1 Metro Area Rankings—Population and Households (continued)[4]

| Metropolitan Area | Resident Population (April 1) | | | | | | | | Households | | | |
| | 1990 | | 1980 | | Percent change, 1980–1990 | | Per square mile of land area, 1990 | | 1989 | | Percent change, 1980–1989 | |
	Number	Rank	Number	Rank	Percent	Rank	Number	Rank	1,000	Rank	Percent	Rank
Oklahoma City, OK MSA	958839	41	860969	43	11.4	103	225.7	127	378.5	37	17.7	117
Louisville, KY-IN MSA	952662	42	956426	37	-0.4	226	420.4	50	365.1	43	7.1	230
Dayton-Springfield, OH MSA	951270	43	942083	38	1	213	565	27	369.5	41	8.6	218
Greensboro-Winston-Salem-High Point, NC MSA	942091	44	851444	44	10.6	110	272.9	99	366.7	42	19.4	96
Providence-Pawtucket-Woonsocket, RI NECMA	916270	45	865771	42	5.8	167	973.8	9	339.6	48	9.4	203
Birmingham, AL MSA	907810	46	883993	41	2.7	200	228	125	360.7	44	14	152
Jacksonville, FL MSA	906727	47	722252	51	25.5	45	344	67	357.6	46	37.8	19
Albany-Schenectady-Troy, NY MSA	874304	48	835880	46	4.6	182	269.1	100	326.8	49	8.1	222
Richmond-Petersburg, VA MSA	865640	49	761311	49	13.7	94	294	87	312.7	50	16.1	131
West Palm Beach-Boca Raton-Delray Beach, FL MSA	863518	50	576758	61	49.7	7	424.5	48	373.4	39	59.3	6
Honolulu, HI MSA	836231	51	762565	47	9.7	120	1393.3	4	273.6	55	18.8	106
New Haven-Waterbury-Meriden, CT NECMA	804219	52	761325	48	5.6	174	1327.6	5	299.7	51	10.4	193
Austin, TX MSA	781572	53	536688	66	45.6	9	280	96	291	52	46.5	13
Las Vegas, NV MSA	741459	54	463087	74	60.1	4	93.7	244	271	57	55.8	8
Raleigh-Durham, NC MSA	735480	55	560774	64	31.2	27	364.8	65	272.8	56	37	23
Scranton-Wilkes-Barre, PA MSA	734175	56	728796	50	0.7	216	258.5	107	286.1	54	8.7	216
Worcester-Fitchburg-Leominster, MA NECMA	709705	57	646352	54	9.8	115	469	41	254.5	60	12.9	165
Tulsa, OK MSA	708954	58	657173	53	7.9	141	141.4	205	289.5	53	17.5	119
Grand Rapids, MI MSA	688399	59	601680	58	14.4	88	484.1	37	245	61	18.9	105
Allentown-Bethlehem, PA-NJ MSA	686688	60	635481	56	8.1	138	470	40	265.7	58	15.3	140
Fresno, CA MSA	667490	61	514621	69	29.7	33	111.9	225	225.6	68	26.4	58
Tucson, AZ MSA	666880	62	531443	67	25.5	46	72.6	253	265.2	59	35.7	26
Syracuse, NY MSA	659864	63	642971	55	2.6	201	276.1	98	239.5	64	7.1	231
Greenville-Spartanburg, SC MSA	640861	64	570210	62	12.4	100	305.2	83	240	63	21.5	81
Omaha, NE-IA MSA	618262	65	585122	59	5.7	173	322.6	78	232.2	66	11.4	185
Toledo, OH MSA	614128	66	616864	57	-0.4	227	450	43	237.4	65	7.8	224
Knoxville, TN MSA	604816	67	565970	63	6.9	159	218	135	240.1	62	16.7	127
Springfield, MA NECMA	602878	68	581831	60	3.6	188	525.4	32	221.1	69	9.3	204
El Paso, TX MSA	591610	69	479899	71	23.3	50	584	26	179.6	77	27.6	53
Harrisburg-Lebanon-Carlisle, PA MSA	587986	70	556242	65	5.7	171	295.3	86	231.2	67	14.9	145
Bakersfield, CA MSA	543477	71	403089	86	34.8	18	66.8	256	188.9	74	35.1	29
Baton Rouge, LA MSA	528264	72	494151	70	6.9	157	333	75	189.2	73	15.3	141
Little Rock-North Little Rock, AR MSA	513117	73	474463	73	8.1	134	176.4	173	192	71	13.6	156
Charleston, SC MSA	506875	74	430346	79	17.8	73	195.6	153	178.3	78	29.3	49
New Bedford-Fall River-Attleboro, MA NECMA	506325	75	474641	72	6.7	162	910.6	12	184.6	75	10.6	189
Youngstown-Warren, OH MSA	492619	76	531350	68	-7.3	269	477.8	39	191.8	72	2.7	257
Wichita, KS MSA	485270	77	442401	77	9.7	119	163.5	186	175.9	79	6.7	234
Stockton, CA MSA	480628	78	347342	95	38.4	15	343.4	70	164.1	84	31.7	44
Albuquerque, NM MSA	480577	79	420261	82	14.4	89	412.1	53	194.5	70	28.8	51

[Based on 281 metropolitan areas (17 CMSAs, 249 MSAs, and 15 NECMAs) unless otherwise noted. All metro areas defined as of June 30, 1989. When metro areas share the same rank, the next lower rank is omitted. Due to rounding, metro areas may have same values and different ranks.]

[4] *State and Metropolitan Area Data Book 1991* (Washington, D.C.: U.S. Department of Commerce, August 1991), pp. XX–XXIII.

Table 4–1   Metro Area Rankings—Population and Households (continued)[4]

Metropolitan Area	Resident Population (April 1)								Households			
	1990		1980		Percent change, 1980-1990		Per square mile of land area, 1990		1989		Percent change, 1980-1989	
	Number	Rank	Number	Rank	Percent	Rank	Number	Rank	1,000	Rank	Percent	Rank
Mobile, AL MSA	476923	80	443536	76	7.5	144	168.5	178	181	76	20.6	89
Columbia, SC MSA	453331	81	409953	84	10.6	111	311.1	81	169.3	82	27.2	55
Johnson City-Kingsport-Bristol, TN-VA MSA	436047	82	433638	78	0.6	218	152.2	195	172.1	80	11.6	181
Chattanooga, TN-GA MSA	433210	83	426443	80	1.6	208	207.2	141	169.5	81	12.4	170
Lansing-East Lansing, MI MSA	432674	84	419750	83	3.1	194	253.4	110	157.2	88	9.9	199
Flint, MI MSA	430459	85	450449	75	-4.4	253	672.9	20	160.1	86	3.5	252
Lancaster, PA MSA	422822	86	362346	92	16.7	76	445.5	44	153.3	91	23.8	69
York, PA MSA	417848	87	381255	88	9.6	121	293.3	88	157.8	87	16.7	126
Lakeland-Winter Haven, FL MSA	405382	88	321652	102	26	43	216.2	136	155.1	89	35.6	27
Saginaw-Bay City-Midland, MI MSA	399320	89	421518	81	-5.3	256	225	129	147	93	3.5	251
Melbourne-Titusville-Palm Bay, FL MSA	398978	90	272959	119	46.2	8	391.7	58	168	83	65.1	5
Colorado Springs, CO MSA	397014	91	309424	106	28.3	36	186.7	167	146.8	94	36.2	25
Augusta, GA-SC MSA	396809	92	345923	96	14.7	87	203.8	146	146.3	95	27.1	56
Jackson, MS MSA	395396	93	362038	93	9.2	127	167.3	182	143.2	97	19	103
Canton, OH MSA	394106	94	404421	85	-2.6	239	405.9	56	151.1	92	5.9	239
Des Moines, IA MSA	392928	95	367561	90	6.9	157	227.4	126	161.5	85	17.9	116
McAllen-Edinburg-Mission, TX MSA	383545	96	283323	111	35.4	17	244.4	116	107.3	123	41.5	15
Daytona Beach, FL MSA	370712	97	258762	127	43.3	10	335.2	74	153.9	90	45.5	14
Modesto, CA MSA	370522	98	265900	123	39.3	14	247.9	113	125	111	32	43
Santa Barbara-Santa Maria-Lompoc, CA MSA	369608	99	298694	107	23.7	49	135	210	131.4	107	20.2	93
Madison, WI MSA	367085	100	323545	101	13.5	95	305.3	82	143.9	96	19.3	98
Fort Wayne, IN MSA	363811	101	354156	94	2.7	199	268.4	101	135.4	101	8.4	219
Spokane, WA MSA	361364	102	341835	97	5.7	171	204.9	145	142.7	98	11.1	187
Beaumont-Port Arthur, TX MSA	361226	103	373211	89	-3.2	246	167.7	179	133.3	104	1.1	267
Salinas-Seaside-Monterey, CA MSA	355660	104	290444	109	22.5	52	107.1	231	116.3	117	21.5	83
Davenport-Rock Island-Moline, IA-IL MSA	350861	105	384749	87	-8.8	274	205.4	143	142	99	2.7	258
Portsmouth-Dover-Rochester, NH NECMA	350078	106	275753	117	27	39	329	76	127.7	109	34.3	35
Corpus Christi, TX MSA	349894	107	326228	100	7.3	150	229	124	121	115	15.7	132
Lexington-Fayette, KY MSA	348428	108	317548	104	9.7	118	235.5	119	134.7	102	18.4	110
Pensacola, FL MSA	344406	109	289782	110	18.9	70	205.1	144	132.8	105	33.3	39
Peoria, IL MSA	339172	110	365864	91	-7.3	270	188.8	165	132.2	106	1.1	266
Reading, PA MSA	336523	111	312509	105	7.7	143	391.7	58	130.9	108	14.3	150
Manchester-Nashua, NH NECMA	336073	112	276608	114	21.5	54	383.4	62	124.2	113	29.6	47
Fort Myers-Cape Coral, FL MSA	335113	113	205266	144	63.3	3	417	52	138.4	100	67.7	4
Shreveport, LA MSA	334341	114	333158	99	0.4	221	194.3	157	133.8	103	14	153
Atlantic City, NJ MSA	319416	115	276385	115	15.6	84	391.3	60	126.2	110	21.2	86
Utica-Rome, NY MSA	316633	116	320180	103	-1.1	230	120.6	220	114.9	118	2.9	255
Appleton-Oshkosh-Neenah, WI MSA	315121	117	291369	108	8.2	134	225.3	128	117.9	116	18.7	109
Huntington-Ashland, WV-KY-OH MSA	312529	118	336410	98	-7.1	267	144.7	200	124.6	112	4.7	249
Visalia-Tulare-Porterville, CA MSA	311921	119	245738	130	26.9	40	64.7	257	100.4	129	24.5	66

[Based on 281 metropolitan areas (17 CMSAs, 249 MSAs, and 15 NECMAs) unless otherwise noted. All metro areas defined as of June 30, 1989. When metro areas share the same rank, the next lower rank is omitted. Due to rounding, metro areas may have same values and different ranks.]

[4] *State and Metropolitan Area Data Book 1991* (Washington, D.C.: U.S. Department of Commerce, August 1991), pp. XX-XXIII.

Table 4–1 Metro Area Rankings—Population and Households (continued)[4]

Metropolitan Area	Resident Population (April 1) 1990 Number	1990 Rank	1980 Number	1980 Rank	Percent change, 1980-1990 Percent	Percent change Rank	Per square mile of land area, 1990 Number	Per sq mile Rank	Households 1989 1,000	1989 Rank	Percent change, 1980-1989 Percent	Percent change Rank
Montgomery, AL MSA	292517	120	272687	120	7.3	149	145.7	199	112.8	119	21.7	80
Rockford, IL MSA	283719	121	279514	113	1.5	209	356.8	66	108.8	121	9.8	201
Eugene-Springfield, OR MSA	282912	122	275226	118	2.8	197	62.1	259	108.6	122	4.9	247
Macon-Warner Robins, GA MSA	281103	123	263591	125	6.6	163	239.9	118	106.3	124	18.7	108
Evansville, IN-KY MSA	278990	124	276252	116	1	212	190.1	163	110.3	120	8.6	217
Salem, OR MSA	278024	125	249895	128	11.3	104	144.3	201	102.8	128	13.4	160
Sarasota, FL MSA	277776	126	202251	146	37.3	16	485.8	36	121.5	114	36.9	24
Erie, PA MSA	275572	127	279780	112	-1.5	233	343.6	69	103.8	127	7.2	229
Fayetteville, NC MSA	274566	128	247160	129	11.1	105	420.4	50	86.5	144	15.4	138
Binghamton, NY MSA	264497	129	263460	126	0.4	220	215.8	138	98.4	131	5.4	244
Provo-Orem, UT MSA	263590	130	218106	137	20.9	58	131.9	216	69.1	167	18.1	115
Brownsville-Harlingen, TX MSA	260120	131	209727	142	24	48	287.2	93	77.8	156	33.2	40
Poughkeepsie, NY MSA	259462	132	245055	131	5.9	166	323.7	77	91.6	139	13.6	157
Killeen-Temple, TX MSA	255301	133	214587	139	19	68	120.9	219	83	149	24.3	67
New London-Norwich, CT NECMA	254957	134	238409	134	6.9	156	382.8	63	92	137	12.5	168
Reno, NV MSA	254667	135	193623	148	31.5	26	40.2	271	106.1	125	37.4	21
Fort Pierce, FL MSA	251071	136	151196	178	66.1	2	222.5	131	98.7	130	69.1	3
Charleston, WV MSA	250454	137	269595	121	-7.1	267	200.5	151	105.8	126	6.4	236
South Bend-Mishawaka, IN MSA	247052	138	241617	132	2.2	203	540.2	30	91.9	138	6.6	235
Portland, ME NECMA	243135	139	215789	138	12.7	99	291	90	93.6	134	18.9	104
Columbus, GA-AL MSA	243072	140	239196	133	1.6	206	219.7	134	90.5	141	15.5	137
Savannah, GA MSA	242622	141	220553	135	10	114	263.8	104	92.3	136	19.7	95
Johnstown, PA MSA	241247	142	264506	124	-8.8	273	136.9	209	93.3	135	1.5	265
Springfield, MO MSA	240593	143	207704	143	15.8	80	194.3	157	91.2	140	18.2	113
Duluth, MN-WI MSA	239971	144	266650	122	-10	277	31.8	276	94.3	133	-3.7	280
Huntsville, AL MSA	238912	145	196966	147	21.3	56	296.8	85	94.6	132	41	16
Tallahassee, FL MSA	233598	146	190329	150	22.7	51	197.5	152	88.7	143	34	37
Anchorage, AK MSA	226338	147	174431	157	29.8	31	133.3	214	82.9	150	37.1	22
Roanoke, VA MSA	224477	148	220393	138	1.9	205	263.8	104	89.2	142	8.9	212
Kalamazoo, MI MSA	223411	149	212378	140	5.2	175	397.6	57	83.1	148	10.2	196
Lubbock, TX MSA	222636	150	211651	141	5.2	175	247.5	114	81.4	151	12.1	176
Hickory, NC MSA	221700	151	202711	145	9.4	124	190	164	86.4	145	21.4	84
Lincoln, NE MSA	213641	152	192884	149	10.8	107	254.7	108	84.3	146	17.5	121
Bradenton, FL MSA	211707	153	148445	181	42.6	11	285.6	94	83.5	147	34.7	34
Lafayette, LA MSA	208740	154	190231	151	9.7	117	208.7	142	74.5	158	19.2	100
Boise City, ID MSA	205775	155	173125	159	18.9	69	195	155	78.8	154	24.8	64
Gainesville, FL MSA	204111	156	171392	161	19.1	67	174.8	175	80.8	153	32.7	41

[Based on 281 metropolitan areas (17 CMSAs, 249 MSAs, and 15 NECMAs) unless otherwise noted. All metro areas defined as of June 30, 1989. When metro areas share the same rank, the next lower rank is omitted. Due to rounding, metro areas may have same values and different ranks.]

Source: *State and Metropolitan Area Data Book 1991*, Washington, D.C.: U.S. Department of Commerce, August 1991.

[4] *State and Metropolitan Area Data Book 1991* (Washington, D.C.: U.S. Department of Commerce, August 1991), pp. XX–XXIII.

Table 4-2 Net Land Area, Population, VMT, and Estimated Lane Miles[5]

State	General Measures							Travel Measures						
	Net Land Area (Square Miles)			Population				Annual Vehicle-Miles of Travel (Millions)					Estimated Lane-Mileage	
	Rural	Urban	Percent Urban	Rural (1,000)	Urban (1,000)	Percent Urban	Total per Square Mile	Rural VMT	Rural Percent Trucks	Urban VMT	Urban Percent Trucks	Total per Capita	Rural	Urban
Alabama	47,562	3,187	6.3	1,886	2,387	55.9	84	25,865	9.0	25,568	5.7	12,037	149,546	43,699
Alaska	569,400	930	0.2	254	353	58.2	1	2,053	6.6	2,062	3.9	6,779	22,889	3,927
Arizona	110,931	2,711	2.4	825	3,603	81.4	39	14,921	18.2	27,202	10.4	9,513	80,026	37,979
Arkansas	51,096	979	1.9	1,319	1,190	47.4	48	18,507	17.2	9,333	8.2	11,096	141,246	16,781
California	146,692	9,281	6.0	2,727	29,882	91.6	209	52,976	11.5	225,067	6.7	8,527	181,742	199,675
Colorado	101,942	1,787	1.7	762	3,061	80.1	37	14,822	12.8	21,319	4.5	9,454	144,708	30,683
Connecticut	3,287	1,558	32.2	637	2,638	80.5	676	6,899	6.9	21,236	5.1	8,591	18,283	25,487
Delaware	1,677	278	14.2	190	535	73.8	371	2,921	9.0	4,745	6.2	10,574	7,830	4,539
Dist. of Col.	—	61	100.0	—	554	100.0	9,082	—	—	3,316	3.2	5,986	—	3,444
Florida	45,490	8,505	15.8	1,796	12,604	87.5	267	33,500	11.9	96,504	4.9	9,028	137,136	109,409
Georgia	54,389	3,667	6.3	2,670	4,538	63.0	124	36,887	14.9	52,245	5.2	12,366	174,610	59,682
Hawaii	6,159	266	4.1	187	997	84.2	184	2,158	2.4	5,872	2.1	6,782	4,588	4,339
Idaho	82,284	467	0.6	631	558	46.9	14	8,676	13.9	4,285	7.1	10,901	113,361	8,139
Illinois	51,484	4,109	7.4	2,013	9,834	83.0	213	28,215	12.8	68,515	6.9	8,165	207,681	79,594
Indiana	34,004	2,094	5.8	2,096	3,707	63.9	161	34,140	12.5	32,080	8.8	11,411	149,966	41,777
Iowa	54,762	1,106	2.0	1,314	1,538	53.9	51	17,101	17.0	9,779	5.6	9,425	209,493	21,342
Kansas	80,642	1,181	1.4	914	1,658	64.5	31	14,039	11.1	11,903	3.6	10,086	249,440	21,960
Kentucky	38,339	1,393	3.5	2,060	1,824	47.0	98	23,674	10.2	18,912	4.9	10,964	128,908	22,698
Louisiana	41,969	1,597	3.7	1,387	2,956	68.1	100	20,710	16.6	17,385	12.1	8,772	95,818	31,520
Maine	30,379	486	1.6	768	473	38.1	40	9,440	8.0	3,379	4.7	10,330	40,612	5,530
Maryland	8,114	1,719	17.5	1,131	3,928	77.6	514	13,711	10.4	32,476	5.3	9,130	33,112	32,050
Massachusetts	4,788	3,052	38.9	748	5,344	87.7	777	8,295	6.4	41,661	3.8	8,200	24,852	48,478
Michigan	53,250	3,529	6.2	2,723	6,778	71.3	167	34,402	8.6	55,813	6.6	9,495	182,262	64,933
Minnesota	77,778	1,839	2.3	1,625	3,033	65.1	59	21,150	7.4	23,315	3.0	9,546	233,751	34,100
Mississippi	45,856	1,058	2.3	1,429	1,287	47.4	58	20,657	12.3	9,905	7.4	11,253	133,958	17,321
Missouri	66,884	2,014	2.9	2,029	3,330	62.1	78	27,547	13.8	33,615	6.5	11,413	215,613	35,724
Montana	145,296	260	0.2	443	413	48.2	6	7,106	11.7	2,340	7.0	11,035	137,303	5,162
Nebraska	76,444	434	0.6	643	994	60.7	21	9,888	16.1	6,350	4.1	9,919	176,701	11,213
Nevada	108,943	863	0.8	166	1,522	90.2	15	5,310	18.4	8,848	6.5	8,387	80,755	12,868
New Hampshire	8,559	465	5.2	588	574	49.4	129	6,391	4.6	4,596	3.3	9,455	24,917	6,176
New Jersey	5,040	2,379	32.1	982	7,006	87.7	1,077	12,100	6.5	50,234	5.1	7,803	24,490	53,153
New Mexico	121,365	553	0.5	666	1,051	61.2	14	13,346	13.8	8,164	5.4	12,528	109,783	13,972
New York	41,761	5,463	11.6	3,165	15,020	82.6	385	31,723	8.0	86,918	4.0	6,524	146,661	91,413
North Carolina	45,468	3,229	6.6	3,662	3,661	50.0	150	39,282	15.0	39,653	7.9	10,779	154,626	49,506

Source: *Highway Statistics 1996*, Washington, D.C.: U.S. Department of Transportation, 1997.

[5] *Highway Statistics 1996* (Washington, D.C.: U.S. Department of Transportation, 1997), p. 5.

Table 4-2   Net Land Area, Population, VMT, and Estimated Lane Miles (continued)[5]

	General Measures							Travel Measures						
	Net Land Area (Square Miles)			Population				Annual Vehicle-Miles of Travel (Millions)					Estimated Lane-Mileage	
								Rural		Urban				
State	Rural	Urban	Percent Urban	Rural (1,000)	Urban (1,000)	Percent Urban	Total per Square Mile	VMT	Percent Trucks	VMT	Percent Trucks	Total per Capita	Rural	Urban
North Dakota	68,846	148	0.2	320	308	49.0	9	5,021	13.2	1,720	5.1	10,734	171,770	3,983
Ohio	36,474	4,479	10.9	3,217	7,926	71.1	272	39,424	14.2	63,666	7.8	9,252	167,966	74,085
Oklahoma	66,651	1,993	2.9	727	2,574	78.0	48	18,759	—	20,668	—	11,944	202,974	29,184
Oregon	95,056	941	1.0	1,043	2,138	67.2	33	15,256	13.6	15,063	5.4	9,531	148,096	21,859
Pennsylvania	40,869	3,951	8.8	3,723	8,329	69.1	269	41,830	11.7	54,816	6.5	8,019	175,987	71,839
Rhode Island	517	528	50.5	67	930	93.3	954	927	3.9	6,193	2.4	7,141	2,826	9,894
South Carolina	28,686	1,425	4.7	1,677	2,020	54.6	123	24,749	8.2	15,007	5.3	10,754	110,946	23,782
South Dakota	75,648	250	0.3	417	323	43.6	10	6,034	14.6	1,783	6.3	10,564	164,605	4,318
Tennessee	38,484	2,735	6.6	2,139	3,180	59.8	129	26,362	10.9	32,073	7.0	10,986	140,264	39,283
Texas	253,449	8,465	3.2	4,899	14,264	74.4	73	57,776	13.1	127,610	6.0	9,674	442,317	184,994
Utah	81,300	867	1.1	368	1,634	81.6	24	7,327	12.5	12,212	5.1	9,760	72,649	14,431
Vermont	9,020	229	2.5	370	219	37.2	64	4,541	8.4	1,836	7.1	10,827	26,389	2,810
Virginia	37,118	2,480	6.3	2,168	4,508	67.5	169	31,329	10.9	39,973	5.5	10,680	107,301	42,663
Washington	64,359	2,222	3.3	1,359	4,158	75.4	83	15,944	10.4	33,461	6.2	8,955	125,655	38,473
West Virginia	23,656	431	1.8	1,265	561	30.7	76	12,725	10.2	4,968	11.3	9,689	65,404	6,851
Wisconsin	53,064	1,466	2.7	1,917	3,243	62.8	95	28,300	10.1	24,482	7.5	10,229	193,673	35,264
Wyoming	96,625	480	0.5	196	285	59.3	5	5,347	19.2	2,013	5.3	15,301	65,266	5,082
U.S. Total	3,431,856	105,570	3.0	70,308	195,431	73.5	75	960,063	11.9	1,522,139	6.1	9,341	6,320,755	1,857,068
Puerto Rico	2,619	840	24.3	1,119	2,664	70.4	1,094	3,892	3.8	11,807	2.9	4,150	15,460	15,041
Grand Total	3,434,475	106,410	3.0	71,427	198,095	73.5	76	963,955	11.9	1,533,946	6.1	9,268	6,336,215	1,872,109

Source: *Highway Statistics 1996*. U.S. Department of Transportation, Washington, D.C.: 1997.

[5] *Highway Statistics 1996* (Washington, D.C.: U.S. Department of Transportation, 1997), p. 5.

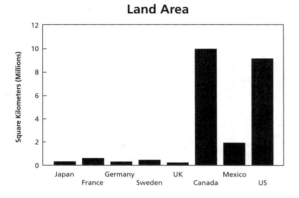

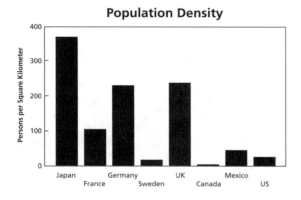

Figure 4–1   Population, Land Area, and Population Density for Selected Countries—1995[6]

Sources: *The World Factbook,* Washington, D.C.: Central Intelligence Agency, 1995 and 1996; *OECD in Figures,* 1997; *National Transportation Statistics,* Bureau of Transportation Statistics, 1997.

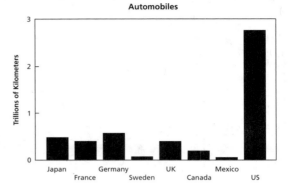

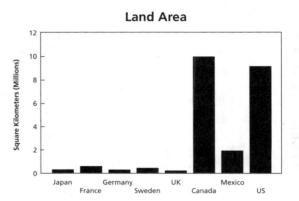

Figure 4–2   Total VKT and Average VKT for Selected Countries—1995[7]

Sources: *World Road Statistics,* International Road Federation, 1997; *OECD Environmental Data,* OECD; *1995 Highway Statistics,* Washington, D.C.: Federal Highway Administration.

Figure 4–1 shows the population, land area, and population density for select countries. Japan has the highest population density, while Canada has the lowest.

Figure 4–2 shows the total and average vehicle kilometers of travel (VKT) for select countries. By a factor of six, the United States has more total VKT than any of the countries shown in Figure 4–2. However, the United Kingdom and Canada have about 65 percent as many VKT per vehicle when comparing the average travel figures. When the VKT are compared to the population and land area of the countries, it is difficult to draw a direct relationship between these factors.

---

[6] *Highway Statistics 1996,* pp. VII–3.

[7] *Highway Statistics 1996,* pp. VII–6.

Demographics

In a recent U.S. Bureau of Transportation Statistics publication,[8] population characteristics were related to travel choices. The report indicates typical travel traits for different population groups. Figure 4–3 shows the miles of daily travel for various groups. There is a considerable difference in the amount of travel by group, with a range of 11 to 43 miles of daily travel per person.

A number of factors come into play when trip choices are made. It has been shown that some of these include auto ownership, level of education, and age of the traveler, as well as the availability of various modes, roadway conditions, and congestion.

Zero-vehicle households consistently make fewer trips than the general population. As average income and education increase, the amount of travel appears to increase as well. In the general population, as income increases from under $10,000 to over $40,000, daily trips increase from approximately 2.6 to almost 4. In the zero-vehicle households, the rates go from 2.0 to 2.5 trips per day. As level of education varies from "didn't finish high school" to "graduate school," the zero-vehicle population has a trip rate of 1.25 to 2.75 trips per day, as compared to 2.5 to 4.0 trips per day for the general population.[10]

In general, younger people make more trips than older people, ranging from about 3.5 trips per day for those under 19 years of age down to 0.5 for those over 75. A corollary to this is that 20 percent of the population under nineteen, up to 50 percent of the population over 75, made no trips.[11]

Employment

The location of employment centers, as well as residences, has changed in the last decade or so. More employment sites have moved from traditional "downtown" locations to more suburban sites. This has altered the travel for work volumes and patterns.

The U.S. average travel time to work ranges from 13 to 29 minutes,[12] with a mean of 21 minutes.[13] This figure

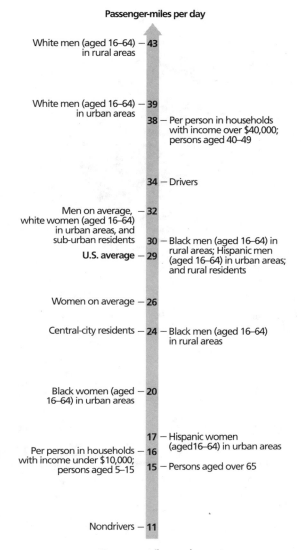

Passenger-miles per day

White men (aged 16–64) in rural areas — **43**

White men (aged 16–64) in urban areas — **39**

38 — Per person in households with income over $40,000; persons aged 40–49

34 — Drivers

Men on average, white women (aged 16–64) in urban areas, and sub-urban residents — **32**

U.S. average — **29**

30 — Black men (aged 16–64) in rural areas; Hispanic men (aged 16–64) in urban areas; and rural residents

Women on average — **26**

Central-city residents — **24** **24** — Black men (aged 16–64) in rural areas

Black women (aged 16–64) in urban areas — **20**

17 — Hispanic women (aged 16–64) in urban areas

Per person in households with income under $10,000; persons aged 5–15 — **16**

15 — Persons aged over 65

Nondrivers — **11**

Passenger-miles per day

Figure 4–3   Miles of Daily Travel—1990[9]

Sources: S. Rosenblum, "Travel by the Elderly," *1990 NPTS Report Series: Demographic Special Reports,* Washington, D.C.: U.S. Department of Transportation, Federal Highway Administration, 1995; S. Rosenblum, "Travel by Women," *1990 NPTS Report Series: Demographic Special Reports,* Washington, D.C.: U.S. Department of Transportation, Federal Highway Administration, 1995; *1990 Nationwide Personal Transportation Survey: 1990 NPTS Databook,* Vol. 1, Washington, D.C.: U.S. Department of Transportation, Federal Highway Administration, 1993.

---

[8] *Transportation Statistics Annual Report 1997* (Washington, D.C.: U.S. Department of Transportation, 1997).

[9] *Transportation Statistics Annual Report 1997,* p. 152.

[10] Richard Crepeau and Charles Lave, *The Access Almanac: Travel by Carless Households* (Berkeley, Calif.: Access, Fall 1996).

[11] Crepeau and Lave, *The Access Almanac: Travel by Carless Households,* pp. 29–31.

[12] *County and City Data Book 1994* (Washington, D.C.: U.S. Department of Commerce, August 1994), pp. 657, 693, 705, 717, 729, 741, 753, 765, 777, 789, 801, 813, 825, 837, 849.

[13] *Our Nation's Travel: 1995 NPTS Early Results Report,* p. 13.

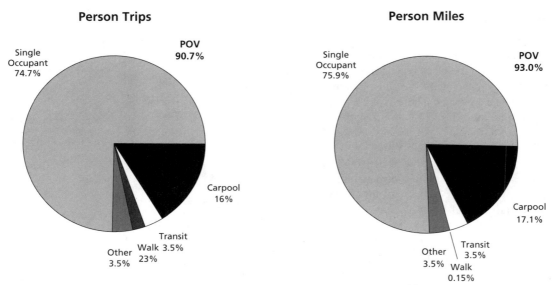

Person Trips

Single Occupant 74.7%

POV 90.7%

Carpool 16%

Transit Walk 3.5%
Other 23%
3.5%

Person Miles

Single Occupant 75.9%

POV 93.0%

Carpool 17.1%

Transit 3.5%
Other Walk
3.5% 0.15%

Figure 4–4   Work Travel by Mode[15]

Source: Our Nation's Travel: 1995 NPTS Early Results Report, p. 21.

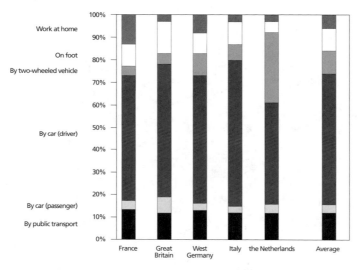

Figure 4–5   Modes of Transport Used by West Europeans To Go to Work[16]

Sources: U.R.F./Sofres Surveys, 1994.

does not include the almost 3.5 million people who work at home,[14] but it does include trips made by public transportation. Figure 4–4 shows the percentage of U.S. person trips and person miles by various modes of travel to work.

Figure 4–5 shows the modes of transport used in select western European countries to go to work. As can be seen from Figure 4–5, an average of 15 percent of Europeans use public transportation to get to work, as compared to an average of 3.5 percent of Americans.

In select western European countries, the average home-to-work trip takes 19 minutes by personal vehicle and 49 minutes by transit. Figure 4–6 shows the trip time comparisons for the countries.

---

[14] *Statistical Abstract of the United States 1997* (Washington, D.C.: U.S. Department of Commerce, October 1997), p. 629.

[15] *Our Nation's Travel: 1995 NPTS Early Results Report*, p. 21.

[16] Christian Gerondeau, *Transport in Europe* (Norwood, Mass.: Artech House, Inc., 1997), p. 322.

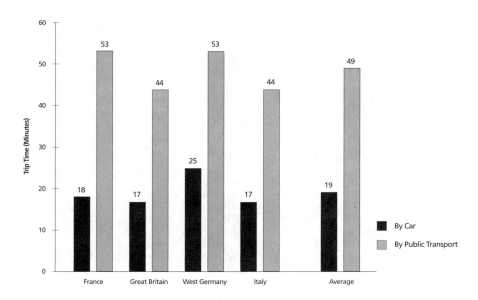

Figure 4–6 Trip Time Comparisons Between Home and Work[17]

Sources: U.R.F./Sofres Surveys, 1994.

Trip Generation

There are numerous ways to examine the amount of traffic generated in a given area. It can be done on a land use basis, on a population basis, or by a subset of the population. Trip generation is typically calculated for a specific time period, such as a peak period or a single day.

Depending on the questions to be answered by a particular analysis, one or more of these methods may yield meaningful results. It also needs to be determined if the measure will be in terms of vehicle trips or person trips. A trip is defined as a single, one-way movement from an origin to a destination. Each trip has two trip ends. Vehicle trips are measured in terms of vehicles generated by a unit of land use, while person trips are measured in terms of people generated by a unit of land use. If the vehicle occupancy for all vehicle types were 1.0, then the two measures would yield identical results. This is not usually the case, hence the need for the two measures. Figure 4–7 shows the percentage of vehicle trips with one or more than one occupant by trip purpose.

As can be seen from Figure 4–7, approximately 70 percent of all trips are made by a single-occupant vehicle, with a range from approximately 90 percent for work and work-related trips to 50 percent for social and recreational trips. One factor affecting vehicle trips is the availability of vehicles by household. Table 4–3 shows the top fifty MSAs ranked by total vehicles. It also shows the vehicles per household. With information available on trip rates by auto ownership, vehicle trips can be calculated. Or, if one were doing demand modeling, the number of vehicles per household could be used as a factor in the production equations, such as:

Home-Based Work Trips = 8 + 1.2 Auto Ownership (4–1)

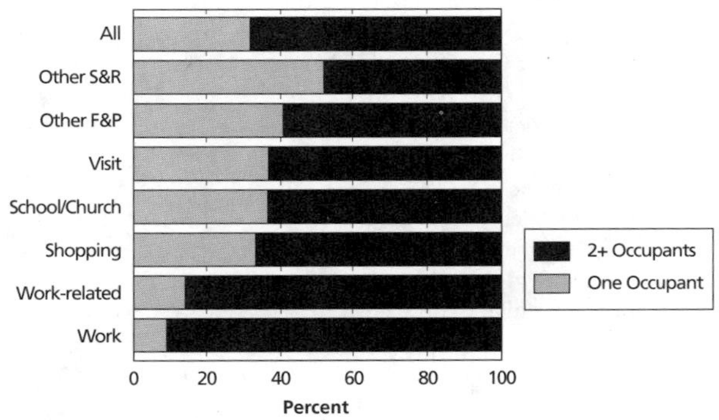

Figure 4–7 Percentage of Vehicle Trips by Vehicle Occupants and Trip Purpose[18]

Source: Our Nation's Travel: 1995 NPTS Early Results Report, p. 25.

[17] Gerondeau, *Transport in Europe*, p. 324.

[18] *Our Nation's Travel: 1995 NPTS Early Results Report*, p. 25.

Table 4–3   U.S. Metropolitan Areas Ranked by Total Household Vehicles—1990[19]

Total Household Vehicle Rank	Metropolitan Area (MSA/CMSA)	Total Household Vehicles	Total Households	Vehicles per Household	Population Rank	Vehicles per Household Rank
1	Los Angeles-Anaheim-Riverside, CA CMSA	8,683,297	4,909,218	1.769	2	10
2	New York-Northern New Jersey-Long Island, NY-NJ-CT CMSA	8,212,267	6,617,074	1.241	1	50
3	Chicago-Gary-Lake County, IL-IN-WI CMSA	4,348,736	2,903,236	1.498	3	44
4	San Francisco-Oakland-San Jose, CA CMSA	4,105,964	2,334,992	1.758	4	13
5	Philadelphia-Wilmington-Trenton, PA-NJ-DE-MD CMSA	3,223,870	2,151,624	1.498	5	44
6	Detroit-Ann Arbor, MI CMSA	2,884,944	1,724,767	1.673	6	28
7	Dallas-Fort Worth, TX CMSA	2,535,906	1,452,215	1.746	8	15
8	Washington, DC-MD-VA MSA	2,456,859	1,460,785	1.682	7	25
9	Boston-Lawrence-Salem, MA-NH CMSA	2,394,764	1,545,347	1.55	9	41
10	Houston-Galveston-Brazoria, TX CMSA	2,198,277	1,333,707	1.648	10	33
11	Atlanta, GA MSA	1,926,071	1,056,929	1.822	12	4
12	Seattle-Tacoma, WA CMSA	1,842,603	1,003,337	1.836	14	3
13	Miami-Fort Lauderdale, FL CMSA	1,824,275	1,220,097	1.495	11	46
14	Cleveland-Akron-Lorain, OH CMSA	1,734,601	1,058,648	1.639	13	35
15	Minneapolis-St. Paul, MN-WI MSA	1,637,796	935,760	1.75	16	14
16	San Diego, CA MSA	1,575,669	887,719	1.775	15	8
17	St. Louis, MO-IL MSA	1,541,254	923,639	1.669	17	29
18	Baltimore, MD MSA	1,386,652	879,968	1.576	18	40
19	Phoenix, AZ MSA	1,337,570	808,162	1.655	20	31
20	Tampa-St. Petersburg-Clearwater, FL MSA	1,324,492	870,999	1.521	21	43
21	Denver-Boulder, CO CMSA	1,319,114	739,001	1.785	22	7
22	Pittsburgh-Beaver Valley, PA CMSA	1,292,645	891,071	1.451	19	48
23	Cincinnati-Hamilton, OH-KY-IN CMSA	1,112,552	652,333	1.705	23	24
24	Kansas City, MO-KS MSA	1,042,823	602,514	1.731	25	19
25	Portland-Vancouver, OR-WA CMSA	1,020,217	576,083	1.771	27	9
26	Sacramento, CA MSA	1,003,202	557,811	1.798	26	6
27	Milwaukee-Racine, WI CMSA	962,920	601,967	1.6	24	37
28	Columbus, OH MSA	906,671	525,558	1.725	29	20
29	Norfolk-Virginia Beach-Newport News, VA MSA	831,017	494,145	1.682	28	25
30	Indianapolis, IN MSA	827,240	480,406	1.722	31	21
31	Charlotte-Gastonia-Rock Hill, NC-SC MSA	801,746	440,458	1.82	34	5
32	San Antonio, TX MSA	738,150	451,731	1.634	30	36
33	Hartford-New Britain-Middletown, CT CMSA	713,621	411,507	1.734	35	18
34	Providence-Pawtucket-Fall River, RI-MA CMSA	712,381	428,869	1.661	45	30
35	Orlando, FL MSA	689,522	402,519	1.713	36	23
36	Greensboro-Winston-Salem-High Point, NC MSA	688,062	372,191	1.849	44	2
37	Buffalo-Niagara Falls, NY CMSA	680,113	460,707	1.476	33	47
38	Nashville, TN MSA	664,577	375,849	1.768	39	12
39	Salt Lake City-Ogden, UT MSA	658,907	347,121	1.898	37	1
40	Oklahoma City, OK MSA	641,850	368,502	1.742	41	17
41	New Orleans, LA MSA	637,135	454,417	1.402	32	49
42	Dayton-Springfield, OH MSA	635,750	364,346	1.745	43	16
43	Rochester, NY MSA	618,665	374,856	1.65	38	32
44	Louisville, KY-IN MSA	616,488	367,421	1.678	42	27
45	Birmingham, AL MSA	609,983	344,912	1.769	46	10
46	Richmond-Petersburg, VA MSA	571,391	331,771	1.722	49	21
47	Jacksonville, FL MSA	565,113	343,043	1.647	47	34
48	Memphis, TN-AR-MS MSA	564,137	357,166	1.579	40	39
49	West Palm Beach-Boca Raton-Delray Beach, FL MSA	562,307	366,131	1.536	50	42
50	Albany-Schenectady-Troy, NY MSA	536,840	335,818	1.599	48	38

Sources: *1990 Census Transportation Planning Package*, Statewide Element, U.S. Census.

[19] U.S. Bureau of the Census (Internet resource: dragon.princeton.edu~dhb).

It is interesting to note that the top fifty MSAs by auto ownership are also the top fifty by population, and in most cases their positions in the two rankings vary only a little. However, there appears to be no relation between vehicles per household and population or total number of vehicles. Although the New York/New Jersey CMSA is second largest in the United States in terms of vehicle ownership and first in population, it has the smallest number of vehicles per household. In contrast, Atlanta ranks eleventh in total vehicles and twelfth in population but has the fourth highest ranking of vehicles per household.

For the countries cited in Figure 4–1, vehicle ownership is indicated in Table 4–4 below. The highest vehicle ownership rate is in the United States with Canada and Germany not far behind.

Table 4–4 Transportation Indicators for Selected Countries—1995[20]

	Asia	Europe				America		
	Japan	France	Germany	Sweden	United Kindom	Canada	Mexico	United States
Population	125,449,703	58,317,450	83,536,115	8,900,954	58,489,975	28,820,671	95,772,462	263,168,000
Land area (square kilometers)	337,835	547,030	356,910	449,964	244,820	9,976,140	1,972,550	9,166,600
Population density (persons per square kilometer)	371.3	106.6	234.1	19.8	238.9	2.9	48.6	28.7
GDP (billion $) (purchasing power equivalent)	$2,679.2	$1,173.0	$1,452.2	$177.3	$1,138.4	$694.0	$721.4	$7,247.7
GDP per Capita ($)	$21,357	$20,114	$17,384	$19,919	$19,463	$24,080	$7,532	$27,540
Percent of surface passenger[1] Kilometers by road transport	68.9%	92.7%	92.8%	94.2%	95.4%	99.7%	N/A	99.4%
Percent of surface freight[2] Ton kilometers by road transport	N/A	63.1%	57.5%	60.7%	88.5%	16.7%	N/A	28.2%
Total vehicle kilometers of travel Automobiles (in millions)	417,000	351,000	507,000	56,762	353,200	168,000	38,000	2,480,736
Total vehicle kilometers of travel Motorcycles (in millions)	N/A	6,000	11,500	612	4,110	N/A	1,074	15,767
Total vehicle kilometers of travel Buses (in millions)	6,870	2,500	3,600	2,034	4,700	N/A	537	10,272
Total vehicle kilometers of travel Trucks (in millions)	263,000	102,000	58,400	5,241	68,900	80,000	16,000	1,392,303
Average vehicle kilometers of travel per automobile	9,267	13,984	12,519	15,634	16,997	11,765	4,562	18,232
Average vehicle kilometers of travel per motorcycle	N/A	2,007	4,991	5,214	6,821	N/A	4,007	4,186
Average vehicle kilometers of travel per bus	28,041	31,646	42,138	139,535	43,925	N/A	4,099	14,985
Average vehicle kilometers of travel per truck	11,895	19,937	14,062	17,032	26,258	11,034	4,570	21,493
Number of Automobiles	45,000,000	25,100,000	40,499,442	3,630,760	20,780,000	14,280,000	8,330,000	136,066,045
Number of Motorcycles and Mopeds[5]	15,340,000	2,990,000	2,304,253	117,387	601,000	30,600	268,000	3,767,029
Number of Buses	245,000	79,000	85,434	14,577	107,000	65,600	131,000	685,504
Number of Trucks[6]	22,111,000	5,116,000	4,153,086	307,709	2,624,000	7,250,000	3,501,043	64,778,472
Automobiles per 1,000 persons	358.7	430.4	484.8	407.9	355.3	495.5	87.0	517.0
Motorcycles and Mopeds per 1,000 persons	122.3	51.3	27.6	13.2	10.3	1.1	2.8	14.3
Buses per 1,000 persons	2.0	1.4	1.0	1.6	1.8	2.3	1.4	2.6
Trucks per 1,000 persons[6]	176.3	87.7	49.7	34.6	44.9	251.6	36.6	246.1

[1] The data in this column for motorcycles are for 1993.
[2] The data in this column on trucks includes truck-tractors only.
[3] The data in this column are for 1993.
[4] The data in this column for automobiles and trucks are for 1993 and for motorcycles and buses are for 1991.
[5] The data for France are for 1993.
[6] The data for Sweden and Mexico exclude tractor trailers.
[7] Note change in the number of automobiles and trucks due to shift of two axle four tire light truck from automobile to truck category.

Sources: "World Road Statistics," International Road Federation, 1997; "1995 Highway Statistics," Federal Highway Administration.

---

[20] *Highway Statistics 1996*, pp. VII–5.

Again there appears to be no relationship between vehicles per person and population or total number of vehicles. It is important to explore some of the available sources for trip generation data, as well as some of the values. The preeminent source of information is the Institute of Transportation Engineers' (ITE) informational report *Trip Generation*, 6th Edition. Data collected over several decades have been analyzed, and both rates and equations for calculating trip generation by land use type are available. ITE's trip generation methodology produces trip end volumes by land use and by time of day. Table 4–5 contains some example rates and equations.

Note that these data give vehicle trip results. If one wanted person trips, a vehicle occupancy rate needs to be applied to adjust the findings. Trip generation rates in countries besides the United States can be quite different from those documented in *Trip Generation*. Table 4–6 shows trip generation rates for office and retail developments in Mexico City.

Other trip generation rates have been developed for more general measure. The latest NPTS indicated that the average daily person trip rate is 4.2. A study conducted in upstate New York showed daily trip rates by household ranging from 3.11 to 18.03 for household sizes as low as one person to those greater than six people. The average for all household sizes for all counties surveyed was 8.48 trips per household per day.

Table 4–7 shows a more detailed trip generation rate breakdown for the Philadelphia/Southern New Jersey area. The factors, in combination with the socioeconomic data, provide the traffic forecasts for the study area.

For certain land use types, it is also important to look specifically at truck trip generation. A more limited array of data are available for this analysis, and they are relatively dated. For urban analysis, however, they provide reasonable estimates for planning purposes. Many small truck trips in urban areas have been replaced in the past ten years by bicycle-riding couriers and technology, such as e-mail and facsimile machines. Table 4–8 presents some sample truck trip generation rates.

Table 4–5   Select Trip Generation Rates[21]

Land Use	Unit of Measure	Daily Trip Ends	A.M. Peak	P.M. Peak
General Office	1,000 square feet	11.01	1.56	1.49
Single Family Residential	dwelling units	9.57	0.75	1.01
Apartment	dwelling units	6.63	0.51	0.62
Shopping Center	1,000 square feet	42.92	1.03	3.74
Light Industrial	1,000 square feet	6.97	0.92	0.98
Hotel	occupied rooms	8.92	0.67	0.71
High School	students	1.79	0.46	0.15

Table 4–6   Trip Generation Rates for Two Offices and a Retail Store in Mexico City[22]

	Peak Hour of the Adjacent Street (Vehicle Trips per 1,000 square feet)					
	Morning			Afternoon		
	Total	In	Out	Total	In	Out
Trip Generation Rate From						
ITE—Corporate Office	1.2	89%	11%	1.1	17%	83%
Location 1 in Mexico City	0.88	74%	26%	0.35	29%	71%
Location 2 in Mexico City	0.57	94%	6%	0.84	2%	98%
Trip Generation From						
ITE—Retail	0.9	63%	37%	3.9	50%	50%
Retail garage in Mexico	0.2–0.3	99%	1%	2.1–3.3	48%	52%

Source: Hart, Joseph et al., "Trip Generation Factors in Mexico City," *1995 Compendium of Technical Papers*, Washington: Institute of Transportation Engineers, 1995.

[21] *Trip Generation*, 6th Edition (Washington, D.C.: Institute of Transportation Engineers, 1997), pp. 99–101, 263–265, 300–302, 503–505, 847–849, 1052–1054, 1337–1339.

[22] Joseph A. Hart et al., "Trip Generation Factors in Mexico City," *1995 Compendium of Technical Papers* (Washington, D.C.: Institute of Transportation Engineers, 1995), pp. 434–435.

Table 4–7 Trip Generation Rates by Type of Trip and Area Type[23]

| Trip Category | Socioeconomic Variable | Factors by Area Type | | | | | |
		1 CBD	2 Fringe	3 Urban	4 Suburban	5 Rural	6 Open Rural
1 Home-based work Person-trip productions	Employed adult residents	0.813	0.831	1.530	1.574	1.537	1.537
2 Home-based work Person-trip attractions	Total employment	1.478	1.477	1.447	1.411	1.467	1.467
3 Home-based nonwork Person-trip productions	Households owning 0 cars	0.54	0.57	0.62	0.98	1.14	1.14
	Households owning 1 car	2.36	2.49	2.70	4.25	4.98	4.98
	Households owning 2 cars	3.74	3.94	4.25	6.64	7.78	7.78
	Households owning 3+ cars	4.24	4.46	4.87	7.73	9.02	9.02
4 Home-based nonwork Person-trip attractions	Occupied dwelling units	0.61	0.71	0.81	1.43	1.43	1.53
	Basic employment*	0.20	0.26	0.36	0.71	0.71	0.71
	Retail employment	2.04	2.55	3.05	7.38	11.71	13.74
	Other employment	0.61	0.81	1.02	3.46	3.46	4.58
5 Nonhome-based Person-trip origins or destinations	Occupied dwelling units	0.22	0.27	0.32	0.54	0.54	0.54
	Basic employment**	0.11	0.16	0.22	0.32	0.22	0.22
	Retail employment	0.65	1.30	1.95	4.00	4.65	4.65
	Other employment	0.32	0.43	0.65	1.08	1.30	1.30
6 Light truck Vehicle trip origins or destinations	Occupied dwelling units	0.05	0.11	0.16	0.26	0.32	0.37
	Retail employment	0.16	0.26	0.63	0.74	0.84	0.95
	Other employment	0.09	0.11	0.21	0.21	0.32	0.32
7 Heavy truck Vehicle trip origins or destinations	Occupied dwelling units	0.05	0.06	0.07	0.09	0.10	0.10
	Manufacturing and wholesale employment	0.07	0.09	0.12	0.14	0.12	0.10
	Retail employment	0.10	0.19	0.29	0.39	0.48	0.48
	Other employment	0.03	0.10	0.17	0.25	0.30	0.35
8 Taxi Vehicle trip origins or destinations	Occupied dwelling units	0.10	0.03	0.02	0.01	0.01	0.01
	Transportation employment	0.30	0.07	0.07	0.04	0.04	0.04
	Other employment	0.10	0.07	0.05	0.04	0.03	0.02

* For the calculations of HDNW, trip attractions basic employment includes agricultural transportation/communications and finance.
** For NHB trips, basic is the same as above except that mining is redesignated as "Other."

Source: *Urban Travel Characteristics Database,* Washington: Institute of Transportation Engineers, April 1995.

Another perspective for examining trip generation is based on individual activity, not land use. According to the 1995 NPTS, the daily person trip rate is 4.2 for all trips for all persons over five years of age. With population information, an estimate of total person trips in an area can be estimated. Again, in a demand model, such a figure could be a factor or at least a means of checking the results for order of magnitude reasonableness.

Table 4–9 shows trip generation regression models developed for a housing estate in Nigeria based on population, auto ownership, and number of workers.

Figure 4–8 shows the number of trips per person by mode for select European countries.

It may also be useful to look at trip rates by subcategories. For example, African-Americans make, on average, 95 transit trips per year out of a total of 1,421 trips; while

Table 4–8 Select Daily Truck Trip Generation Rates (per 10,000 sq ft)[24]

Land Use	Mean Rate
Office	2.0
Retail	7.0
Hotel	0.9
Manufacturing	5.2
Warehousing	4.6

Sources: Alan M. Voorhees and Associates, Inc., *Summary Report of Preliminary Goods Movement Data,* Prepared for North Central Texas Council of Governments, December 1972; William Marconi, "Commercial Trucking and Freight Handling in the San Francisco Central Business District," *Proceedings of the Engineering Foundation Conference on Goods Transportation in Urban Areas,* September 1975, p. 305; Wilbur Smith and Associates, *Center City Transportation Study, Dallas, Texas, Phase II,* Prepared for Urban Mass Transportation Administration, December 1970; M.V. Bates, Ottawa: *Goods Movement by Truck in the Central Area of Selected Canadian Cities,* Canadian Trucking Association, 1970; "Traffic Considerations in Planning of Central Business Districts," *Traffic Engineering Magazine,* Washington, D.C.: Institute of Transportation Engineers, June 1964; Cather DeLeuw and Company, *Long-Range Transportation Plan for the Central Business District,* Dallas, Texas: July 1965.

[23] *Urban Travel Characteristics Database* (Washington, D.C.: Institute of Transportation Engineers, April 1995), p. 70.

[24] *Urban Transportation Planning for Goods and Services* (Washington, D.C.: U.S. Department of Transportation, June 1979), pp. III-15–III-17.

Caucasians make 15 out of 1,602 by transit. Hispanics make 48 trips (out of 1,535), vs. 25 trips (out of 1,572) made by non-Hispanics. Children make, on average, more than 1,300 trips per year. Between 900 and 1,000 of those trips are made by privately owned vehicles.

Trip Purpose

Trip-making occurs in particular patterns generally based on trip purpose. Overall travel patterns, even for given activities, will follow a profile on a given day, with a given week, during a given month of the year. Overall travel on the roads reflects the variation in the individual components. For example, there are more recreational trips at certain times of the year that influence the volumes measured on different types of facilities. The typical trip purposes that are examined and modeled include those for work, shopping, recreation, school, and other personal business.

Table 4–9   Trip Generation Regression Models for the Trans-Ekulu Housing Estate[25]

Zone	Regression Models	Correlation Coefficient (R)
1	$Y_1 = 109.54 + 2.38X_1 + 2.28X_3$	0.978
	$[Y_2 = 11.00 + 0.098X_1 + 2.00X_2]$	0.991
2	$[Y_1 = 11.05 + 0.22X_1 + 4.31X_3]$	0.994
	$[Y_2 = -3.64 - 0.34X_1 + 3.01X_2]$	0.985
3	$Y_1 = 336.45 + 1.47X_1 + 2.39X_3$	0.977
	$[Y_2 = 23.22 + 0.11X_1 + 1.53X_2]$	0.999

Y_1 = total daily trips in zone; Y_2 = total daily work trips in zone; X_1 = car ownership in zone; X_2 = number of workers in zone; and X_3 = number of dwellers in zone.

Note: The regression models in brackets are significant at the 5 percent level.

Source: "Development of Trip Generation Models for Land Uses in Nigeria," *ITE Journal*, Washington, D.C.: Institute of Transportation Engineers, p. 30.

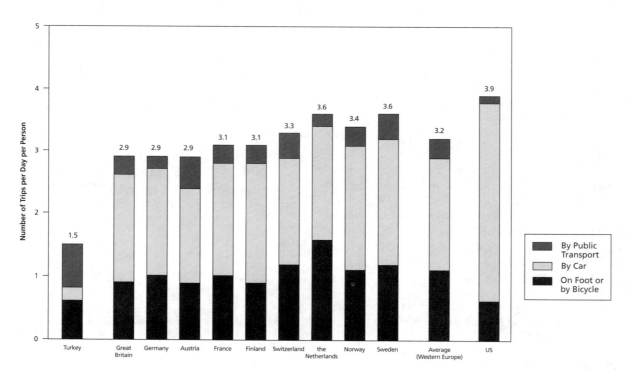

Figure 4–8   Number of Trips per Day per Person[26]

Sources: *A Billion Trips a Day and Updates; Nationwide Personal Transportation Survey (U.S.)*

[25] Douglas O.A. Osula, "Development of Trip Generation Models for Land Uses in Nigeria," *ITE Journal* (Washington, D.C.: Institute of Transportation Engineers, January 1991), p. 30.

[26] Gerondeau, *Transport in Europe*, p. 318.

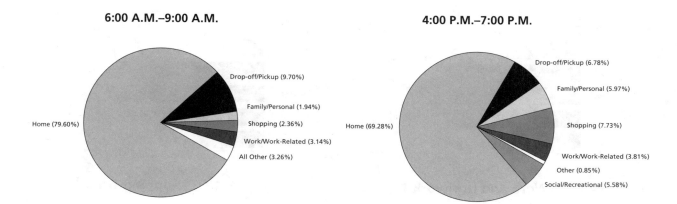

6:00 A.M.–9:00 A.M.

Drop-off/Pickup (9.70%)
Family/Personal (1.94%)
Shopping (2.36%)
Work/Work-Related (3.14%)
All Other (3.26%)
Home (79.60%)

4:00 P.M.–7:00 P.M.

Drop-off/Pickup (6.78%)
Family/Personal (5.97%)
Shopping (7.73%)
Work/Work-Related (3.81%)
Other (0.85%)
Social/Recreational (5.58%)
Home (69.28%)

Figure 4–9   1995 NPTS—Work as Destination Trip and Work as Origin Trips[27]

Source: *1995 Nationwide Personal Transportation Survey*, Federal Highway Administration, November 24, 1997.

The time of day when trips are made can be influenced by the activity itself and by the roadway characteristics. According to the latest NPTS, work trips accounted for almost 80 percent of the morning peak trip destinations and almost 70 percent of the afternoon peak trip origins. The majority of work trips are single purpose; however, in the mornings approximately 20 percent and in the evenings approximately 30 percent involve stops for other purposes, such as drop-off/pickup, shopping, personal business, and social or recreational events. Figure 4–9 shows the proportion of trips to work that originate at some place other than home and the proportion of trips leaving work that go to some place other than home. More than 90 percent of those trips and miles are accomplished in privately owned vehicles.

On a daily basis, however, commuting to and from work only accounts for approximately 20 percent of person trips and miles. The activities that generate both the greatest number of person trips and person miles are nonwork-related. Figure 4–10 shows the distribution of all purposes of travel, with shopping, family/personal and social/recreational travel accounting for the majority of trips.

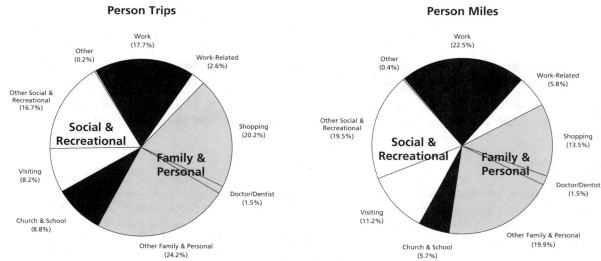

Person Trips

Work (17.7%)
Other (0.2%)
Work-Related (2.6%)
Other Social & Recreational (16.7%)
Shopping (20.2%)
Social & Recreational
Family & Personal
Visiting (8.2%)
Doctor/Dentist (1.5%)
Church & School (8.8%)
Other Family & Personal (24.2%)

Person Miles

Work (22.5%)
Other (0.4%)
Work-Related (5.8%)
Other Social & Recreational (19.5%)
Shopping (13.5%)
Social & Recreational
Family & Personal
Visiting (11.2%)
Doctor/Dentist (1.5%)
Church & School (5.7%)
Other Family & Personal (19.9%)

Figure 4–10   Purpose of Travel by Percent[28]

Source: Our Nation's Travel: 1995 NPTS Early Results Report, Washington, D.C.: U.S. DOT, Sept. 1997, p. 11.

---

[27] *Highway Information Update* (Washington, D.C.: Federal Highway Administration, November 24, 1997), p. 1.

[28] *Our Nation's Travel: 1995 NPTS Early Results Report*, p. 11.

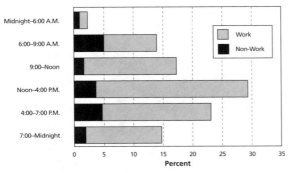

Figure 4–11   Work and Nonwork Trips by Time of Day[29]

Source: Our Nation's Travel: 1995 NPTS Early Results Report, Washington, D.C.: U.S. DOT, Sept. 1997, p. 14.

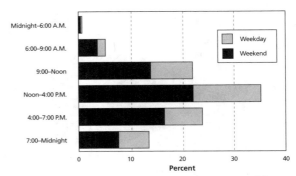

Figure 4–12   Shopping Trips[30]

Source: Our Nation's Travel: 1995 NPTS Early Results Report, Washington, D.C.: U.S. DOT, Sept. 1997, p. 15.

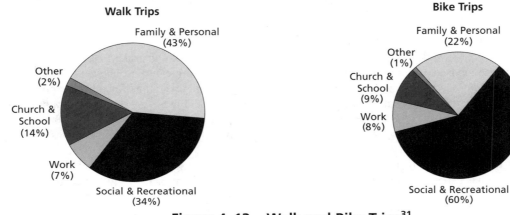

Figure 4–13   Walk and Bike Trips[31]

Source: Our Nation's Travel: 1995 NPTS Early Results Report, Washington, D.C.: DOT, Sept. 1997, p. 18.

Figure 4–11 presents the time of day patterns for work and nonwork trips, with the work trips most heavily concentrated in the 6 A.M. to 9 A.M. and 4 P.M. to 7 P.M. time periods. Nonwork trips peak in the noon to 4 P.M. period.

By time of day and day of week, shopping trips occur evenly throughout the week. Weekend and weekend shopping trips peak in the noon to 4 P.M. time period, as shown in Figure 4–12.

The NPTS showed that 65 million walk and bike trips are made every day. Seven percent of walk trips and 8 percent of bike trips are made for work. Figure 4–13 shows the breakdown of walk and bike trips by trip purpose.

Trip Length

Historically, people have tended to live in places where their travel to work and other frequently visited places was minimized. With many changes in demographics, the expansion of the road network, multiple career families, and the increasing focus on quality of life, this is now not always the case. The traditional road network strongly influences the geographic execution of travel. Radial roads tend to encourage travel from suburbs to city centers, but in many urbanized areas one now finds a significant amount of travel occurring suburb to suburb. The distances that people travel, or are willing to travel, is directly related to the trip purpose. For example, one is more likely to travel 20 or 30 minutes to reach a place of employment than to go to the store for a container of milk.

---

[29] *Our Nation's Travel: 1995 NPTS Early Results Report*, p. 14.

[30] *Our Nation's Travel: 1995 NPTS Early Results Report,* p. 15.

[31] *Our Nation's Travel: 1995 NPTS Early Results Report*, p. 18.

	1983	1990	1995	'83–'95 % Change
Average Work Trip Length (Miles)	8.5	10.6	11.6	36.5
Average Work Travel Time (Minutes)	18.2	19.7	20.7	13.7
Average Work Trip Speed (MPH)	28	32.3	33.6	20

Figure 4–14   Commute Profile[32]

Source: *Our Nation's Travel: 1995 NPTS Early Results Report*, p. 13.

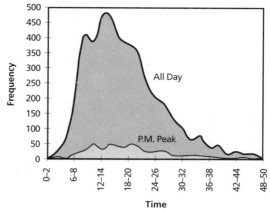

Figure 4–15   Trip Length Distribution[33]

Source: *1999 Household Survey*, Poughkeepsie, N.Y.

In the most recent NPTS, travel time and distance for work trips have both increased since 1983. Figure 4–14 shows historic work trip length, travel time, and speed. In the case of the commute trip in the United States, the average distance traveled is almost twelve miles, with an average travel time of almost 21 minutes. Both of these measures have increased since the early 1980s as a result of more growth in the suburban spread.

Trip lengths are important in the application of transportation models. See Chapter 5 for more details on these relationships. The length of travel varies by trip purpose and, to some extent, by time of day. In Poughkeepsie, New York, the vehicle trip distribution varied from 2 to 50 minutes, with the peak activities occurring between 8 and 20 minutes. Figure 4–15 details the trip length distribution.

In Houston, Texas, the calculated person trip lengths by trip purpose were found to be 22 minutes for home-based work trips and 11 minutes for home-based nonwork trips. The nonhome-based trips averaged 13 minutes, while trucks and taxis averaged 13.1 minutes.

If one chooses to, or is limited to, transit travel, the time and distance for many trip types is greater than comparable trips made by privately owned vehicles. Table 4–10 shows the travel time by trip purpose for those trips made by transit. In all categories, the majority of trips took between 30 and 59 minutes, with an average travel time of 43 minutes.

Figure 4–16 shows the trip length in minutes for various European localities from 1967 to 1992. Since the distances for the trips has increased, but the time has remained the relatively stable, it can be deduced that the speed and road network have improved. This can be seen in the Figure 4–14 as well.

Modal Trends

Modal choice by trip purpose or time of day affects the urban transportation system. Privately owned automobiles and light trucks offer the greatest flexibility and mobility. Yet for many who do not own vehicles, transit is the primary means of accessing jobs, shopping, medical services, and re creational activities.

Table 4–10   Average Transit Travel Time by Trip Purpose[34]

Travel Time (Minutes)	Expressed as Percent of Total by Trip Purpose				
	Work	School	Shopping	Other	All Purposes
10–29	20.3	27.5	31.9	22.1	24.5
30–59	56.2	49.6	41.6	48.3	51.1
60–89	20.1	18.1	18.0	21.0	19.2
Over 90	3.5	4.9	8.5	8.6	5.2
Average Travel Time (Minutes)	43.0	41.0	42.0	46.0	43.0

Source: "Transit Development Program for the City of Albuquerque's Transit System, July 1, 1983 to July 30, 1988," Middle Rio Grande COG of New Mexico, June 1983.

---

[32] *Our Nation's Travel: 1995 NPTS Early Results Report*, p. 13.

[33] *Urban Travel Characteristics Database*, pp. 138–139.

[34] *Urban Travel Characteristics Database*, p. 44.

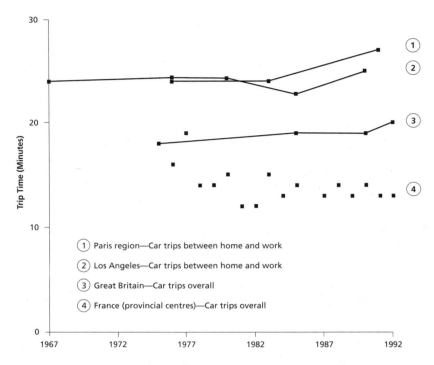

Figure 4–16 Stability of Trip Times by Car Over Time[35]

Sources: General Transport Surveys, Paris region; National Censuses and other surveys (United States); National Travel Surveys (Great Britain); *Transport Urbains* (French urban transport periodical).

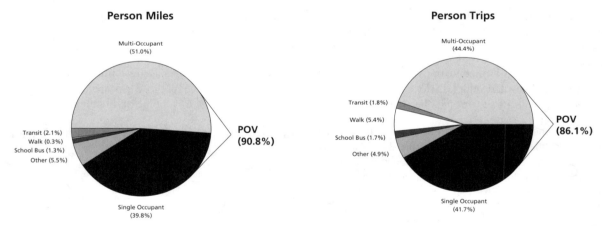

Figure 4–17 Means of Travel[36]

Source: Our Nation's Travel: 1995 NPTS Early Results Report, p. 17.

The volume of traffic using the road network is impacted by the split among modes. A full standard transit bus, for example, can accommodate up to seventy people. In a location where vehicle occupancy is 1.2 persons per vehicle, that would equate to 58 vehicles. The NPTS shows that 90 percent of person miles are by personal vehicle. Figure 4–17 shows the means of travel for total person trips and total person miles in the United States.

According to the Bureau of the Census, in 1994 119 million vehicles were urban household-based and generated 1,360 billion vehicle miles of urban travel. The data showed almost 68 percent passenger cars, 5 percent minivans, 6 percent

[35] Gerondeau, *Transport in Europe,* p. 328.

[36] *Our Nation's Travel: 1995 NPTS Early Results Report,* p. 17.

sport utility vehicles, 2 percent large vans, 18 percent pickup trucks, and 1 percent other. Almost 61 percent of the vehicles were used for commuting to and from work. For those using privately owned vehicles, a significant change in vehicle type has occurred between 1980 and 1995. Table 4–11 details the change.

Table 4–11   Period Sales and Market Share of Automobiles and Light Trucks[37]

	1980	1985	1990	1991[r]	1992[r]	1993[r]	1994[r]	1995
Minicompact								
Total sales, units	428,346	52,295	76,698	96,290	107,634	84,345	57,198	44,752
Market share, %	4.7	0.5	0.8	1.1	1.3	1.0	0.6	0.5
Subcompact								
Total sales, units	3,441,480	2,382,339	2,030,226	225,623	2,074,351	1,944,892	2,015,280	1,518,209
Market share, %	37.8	21.7	22.0	26.9	25.6	23.2	22.6	17.4
Compact								
Total sales, units	599,423	3,526,118	3,156,481	2,425,398	2,451,498	2,655,378	3,077,203	3,289,735
Market share, %	6.6	32.1	34.2	28.9	30.2	31.7	34.5	37.7
Midsize								
Total sales, units	3,073,103	3,117,817	2,511,503	2,305,773	2,249,553	2,445,842	2,359,898	2,498,521
Market share, %	33.8	28.4	27.2	27.5	27.7	29.2	26.5	28.6
Large								
Total sales, units	1,336,190	1,516,249	1,279,092	1,161,319	1,140,775	1,186,991	1,339,863	1,320,608
Market share, %	14.7	13.8	13.9	13.9	14.1	14.2	15.0	15.1
Two-seater								
Total sales, units	215,964	373,697	170,465	134,890	83,192	70,480	67,020	53,045
Market share, %	2.4	3.4	1.8	1.6	1.0	0.8	0.8	0.6
Fleet								
Total sales, units	9,094,506	10,968,515	9,224,465	8,379,963	8,107,003	8,387,928	8,916,462	8,724,870
Market share, %	100.0	100.0	100.0	100.0	100.0	100.0	100.0	100.0
Fuel economy, mpg	23.2	27.0	27.6	27.7	27.7	27.8	27.8	28.0
Small Pickup								
Total sales, units	516,412	863,584	678,488	628,098	586,752	332,470	365,322	356,856
Market share, %	23.3	20.4	15.0	15.5	13.4	6.6	6.4	6.0
Large Pickup								
Total sales, units	1,115,248	1,690,931	1,573,729	1,309,283	1,452,192	1,877,806	2,199,224	2,183,793
Market share, %	50.3	39.9	34.9	32.3	33.1	37.1	38.4	36.8
Small Van								
Total sales, units	13,649	437,660	932,693	888,165	968,361	1,129,459	1,263,933	1,257,116
Market share, %	0.6	10.3	20.7	21.9	22.0	22.3	22.1	21.2
Large Van								
Total sales, units	328,065	536,242	398,877	308,317	350,013	388,435	407,737	401,056
Market share, %	14.8	12.7	8.8	7.6	8.0	7.7	7.1	6.8
Small Utility								
Total sales, units	75,875	477,706	738,294	782,588	867,934	948,797	1,042,584	1,225,131
Market share, %	3.4	11.3	16.4	19.3	19.8	18.8	18.2	20.6
Large Utility								
Total sales, units	167,288[r]	229,242	192,544	131,740	167,199	378,710	445,601	509,914
Market share, %	7.5	5.4	4.3	3.3	3.8	7.5	7.8	8.6
Fleet								
Total sales, units	2,216,537	4,235,365	4,514,625	4,043,191	4,392,451	5,055,677	5,724,401	5,933,866
Market share, %	100.0	100.0	100.0	100.0	100.0	100.0	100.0	100.0
Fuel economy, mpg	18.1	20.4	20.5	20.6	20.4	20.5	20.4	20.2

[r] Revised.

* These figures represent only those sales that could be matched to corresponding EPA fuel economy values.

Source: *Light-Duty Vehicle MPG and Market Shares Systems*, Oak Ridge National Laboratory, 1996.

---

[37] *National Transportation Statistics 1997* (Washington, D.C.: U.S. Department of Transportation, December 1996), pp. 40–41.

Based on the 1990 Census, the fifty largest metro areas by population were identified and their travel to work characteristics summarized. Interestingly, carpooling is reportedly running 10 to 15 percent of the means of transportation to work, with a nationwide average of 12.9 percent. Historically work trips have the lowest carpooling rates of all trip purposes. The 1995 work carpooling rate is the same as it was in 1990 and remains the lowest in the 26-year history of the NPTS.

Public transit ranges from 0 to 47 percent. The usage in New York is exceptional due to the extent of the transit opportunity. Nationwide, the public transit usage averages 6.5 percent. Historically, work trips have had a higher rate of transit usage as a mode of transportation to work. That rate has been decreasing as employment sites relocate from the central city to suburban areas.

Table 4–12 Accessibility of Transit Service to Households in U.S. Urban Areas[38]

Distance to Nearest Transit Route	Percentage of Household
Subtotal: 1 mile or less	71
Less than 1/4 mile	50
1/4 to 1/2 mile	15
1/2 to 1 mile	6
More than 1 mile[1]	29

[1] Includes households reporting no service available.

Source: Volpe National Transportation Systems, Center calculations based on *1990 Nationwide Personal Transportation Survey,* microdata files, Washington, D.C.: U.S. Department of Transportation, Federal Highway Administration, 1990.

The most recent NPTS shows that work trips are primarily accomplished by three modes: approximately 2.3 percent by walking, 3.5 percent by transit, and 91 percent by private vehicle. The accessibility of transit is certainly a factor in the usage within a particular community. Based on a variety of sources, Table 4–12 summarizes the urban area accessibility to transit service, and Table 4–13 shows the growth in U.S. urban transit service for all transit modes. See Chapter 13 for a detailed discussion of transit use and planning issues.

In Australia, there is a significant amount of transit service, which varies from buses and trams, to ferry boats and trains. In 1994 in Brisbane, more than 48 million passengers traveled using the bus and ferry service, marking an average increase of 16 percent in one year. Throughout southeast Queensland, approximately one-fourth of the commuters use the rail network, a 6 percent increase from the previous year. In Sydney, sustained growth is being experienced with more than 850,000 passengers daily.[40]

In Canada, there were 89 transit systems operating in 1995, servicing more than 1.3 billion passengers trips annually.[41] Nonmotorized travel in the United States now represents a substantial amount of activity, with 56 million walk trips and 9 million bicycle trips. In other countries, there is often more dependence on transit and nonmotorized transportation. Table 4–14 shows the percentage of person trips by mode for selected cities. Table 4–15 presents similar data by trip purpose, again for selected cities.

Table 4–13 Growth in U.S. Urban Transit Service[39]

Transit Mode	Vehicles in Rush-Hour Service			Vehicle-Miles Operated (millions)			Route-Miles Serviced		
	1985	1995	Change	1985	1995	Change	1985	1995	Change
All modes	54,437	57,183	5%	2,101	2,377	13%	143,606	163,941	14%
All rail modes	11,832	13,120	11%	626	773	23%	5,251	6,185	18%
Heavy rail	7,673	7,973	4%	445	522	17%	1,322	1,458	10%
Light rail	534	734	37%	16	34	113%	384	568	48%
Commuter rail	3,625	4,413	22%	165	217	32%	3,545	4,159	17%
Bus	42,605	44,063	3%	1,475	1,604	9%	138,355	157,756	14%

Sources: *National Urban Mass Transportation Statistics, 1985*, Washington, D.C.: U.S. Department of Transportation, Federal Transit Administration, 1986; *1995 National Transit Database*, Washington, D.C.: U.S. Department of Transportation, Federal Transit Administration, 1997.

---

[38] *Transportation Statistics Annual Report 1997*, p. 183.

[39] *Transportation Statistics Annual Report 1997*, p. 18.

[40] Peter Moore, "The Changing Face of Urban Public Transit in Australia" (Internet resource: www.apta.com/intratl/intfocus/austral.htm).

[41] "Quick Facts on the Canadian Urban Transit Industry" (Canadian Urban Transit Association, Internet resource).

Table 4–14
Share of Total Person Trips by Various Modes for Selected Cities[42]

City	Year	Walk	Bicycle & NMV	Bus & Rail	Motorcycle	Automobile	Other	Total
Kanpur, India	1977	72	24	0	3	1	0	100
Tianjin, China	1987	60	41	9	0	0	0	100
Shenyang, China	1984	10	65	25	0	0	0	100
Shanghai, China	1986	38	33	26	—	3	**	100
Kathmandu, Nepal	1987	56	8	16	14	6	100	
Ahmedabad, India	1981	43	20	29	6	1	1	100
Bangalore, India	1984	44	12	36	6	2	0	100
Bandung, Indonesia	1976	—	—	—	40	16	46	100
Surabaya, Indonesia	1984	20	25	13	26	9	7	100
Delhi, India	1981	29	18	40	13	100		
Tokyo, Japan[1]	1988	—	45	28	**	27	0	100
Okayama, Japan[2]	1982	23	30	7	**	39	1	100
Matsuyama, Japan[2]	1982	27	23	12	**	34	4	100
Jakarta, Indonesia	1984	23	17	25	13	8	14	100
Bombay, India	1981	15	11	58	1	8	7	100
Melbourne, Australia[3]	1979	19	2	13	**	64	2	100

[1] *Movement of People in the Tokyo Urban Region,* Tokyo Urban Regional Traffic Planning Board (in Japanese), cited in Kazuo Uchida, "Current Issues in Tokyo Regional Transport Planning," *The Wheel Extended,* No. 77, Toyota Motor Corporation, Tokyo, Japan, p. 4.

[2] The Research Report on *Strengthening the Bicycle Network Function* (in Japanese), Japan Bicycle Road Association, 1988, Tokyo, p. 2.

[3] *Traffic in Melbourne Study: State of the System,* Vic Roads, Melbourne, Australia, November 1990, p. 2.

Note: ** Small amount included with bike/NMV category; data not available or included in other categories.

Sources: Michael Replogle, Non-Motorized Vehicles in Asian Cities, World Bank, 1991; *Movement of People in the Tokyo Urban Region,* Tokyo Urban Regional Traffic Planning Board (in Japanese), cited in Kazuo Uchida, "Current Issues in Tokyo Regional Transport Planning," *The Wheel Extended,* No. 77, Tokyo, Japan: Toyota Motor Corporation, p. 4; The Research Report on *Strengthening the Bicycle Network Function* (in Japanese), Tokyo: Japan Bicycle Road Association, 1988, p. 2; *Traffic in Melbourne Study: State of the System,* Melbourne, Australia: Vic Roads, November 1990, p. 2.

Classified Networks and Usage

A number of ways to describe road networks are commonly used. In the modeling framework, links and nodes are the basic units, representing roads, intersections, and interchanges. Attributes are assigned to each link or node, defining the type of facility and specific characteristics.

Another approach is to start with the broad picture of the network layout and then detail the roadway classifications. Using this method, one would generally define the types of roads by purpose. A grid network is very often found in an urban area, with roads parallel and intersecting at right angles to each other. Generally, if the terrain is level and if there can be relatively uniform spacing of roadways, such a network provides a high level of accessibility to the land area (though other types of networks can provide this also).

A radial network serves a very different purpose. Most often it is the configuration that links outlying areas to city centers. Traditionally, the pattern was "bedroom communities" in the suburbs and employment centers in the downtown areas with radial roadways and railroads connecting the two. Although there is some variation from that pattern now, it is still one of the dominant models. One result of this configuration is the heavily directional traffic by time of day on the roads that comprise the "spokes" of the radial system.

With the increase in urban congestion, circumferential roads were developed with the primary purpose of providing a bypass. Ring roads generally allow traffic that has neither an origin nor a destination in the central business district (CBD) to travel around it instead of through it. In some cities, such as Atlanta, Georgia, trucks *must* use the circumferential highway unless they have a pickup or delivery location inside the "ring."

Yet another way to describe the road network is to define a set of limited access roads, arterials, collectors, and residential streets that provide for mobility and access. From the higher order whose primary purpose is to move traffic to lower classifications, the volumes and speeds accommodated decrease, as the access to adjacent properties typically increases.

[42] "National Bicycling and Walking Study Final Report," *Travel Demand Forecasting,* CD-ROM (Washington, D.C.: Bureau of Transportation Statistics, April 20, 1992).

Table 4–15　Person Trip Mode Shares for Selected Cities and Trip Purposes[43]

City/Country	Purpose	Year	Walk	Bike/NMV	Bus	Rail	Motorcycle	Automobile	Other	Total
Australia[1]	Work Trips	1986	6.0	1.6	••	••	••	••	98.4	100
Adelaide[1]	Work Trips	1986	3.0	2.2	••	••	••	••	97.8	100
Canberra[1]	Work Trips	1986	3.6	2.0	••	••	••	••	98.0	100
Melbourne[1]	Work Trips	1950	••	10.0	••	••	••	••	90.0	100
		1976	••	1.0	••	••	••	••	99.0	100
		1981	5.8	1.8	4.1	12.0	1.0	74.7	0.6	100
		1986	5.3	1.7	3.5	11.2	0.9	76.1	0.5	100
Japan[2]	Commuting	1980	••	15.0	••	••	••	••	85.0	100
Tokyo[3]	Commuting	1968	—	25.8	9.4	51.9	*	12.9	0.0	100
		1978	—	23.1	4.7	47.2	*	25.0	0.0	100
		1988	—	21.7	2.9	46.0	*	29.4	0.0	100
	Personal Activity	1968	—	69.0	6.9	12.9	*	11.1	0.1	100
		1978	—	62.3	4.8	13.3	*	19.6	0.0	100
		1988	—	57.9	3.4	13.3	*	25.4	0.0	100
	Business Travel	1968	—	25.8	3.3	13.7	*	56.0	1.2	100
		1978	—	19.8	1.3	13.3	*	65.1	0.5	100
		1988	—	16.8	1.1	17.9	*	63.9	0.3	100
—Okayama[4]	Commuting	1982	6.1	28.4	6.4	4.7	*	53.9**	0.5	100
—Matsuyama[4]	Commuting	1979	12.7	28.6	10.1	6.1	*	41.5**	1.0	100

Sources: *Traffic in Melbourne: State of the System,* Melbourne, Australia: Vic Roads, November 1990, p. 2; Alan A. Parker, "The Future of Non-motorized Passenger Transport in Australian Capital Cities," Melbourne, Australia: National Transport Conference, May 23, 1989; "Current Issues and Problems of Bicycle Transport in Japan," Transportation Research Record No. 1294, Washington, D.C.: Japan National Census of 1980, cited in H. Koike, 1991, p. 40; Tokyo Urban Region Traffic Planning Commission, *Human Movement in the Tokyo Urban Region: From the Third Person-Trip Survey* (in Japanese), p. 11, cited in Tadashi Murao, "Reforming Transportation in the Megalopolis: Focus on Japanese Cities," *The Wheel Extended,* No. 78, Tokyo: Toyota Motor Corporation, December 1991, p. 14; The research report on *Strengthening the Bicycle Network Function* (in Japanese), Japan Bicycle Road Association, 1988, Tokyo, p. 2.

Roadway Usage

The opportunity for mobility is a function of many factors, including the availability of roadways on which travel can occur. In the United States, approximately one-fifth of all roadways are considered urban. With the majority of trips still occurring in privately owned vehicles, vehicle ownership is another measure of opportunity to make trips, as is the number of licensed drivers. In the United States, there are more than 200 million vehicles registered and approximately 180 million licensed drivers. There are a number of reasons why the number of vehicles exceeds the number of drivers, including back-up vehicles for personal use, rental fleets, and commercial fleets. By comparison, in Canada in 1996, there were a total of more than 17 million vehicles and almost 20 million licensed drivers.

VMT by Roadway Type

In the urban areas of the United States, the decade of the mid-1980s to mid-1990s saw an almost 50 percent increase in VMT with only an 18 percent increase in lane miles (the resulting congestion will be discussed later). Table 4–16 shows historic data on the highway miles traveled and lane miles by functional classification.

The physical condition of roadways can be an influencing factor on travel patterns as well as a result of travel choices. Table 4–17 shows data on roadway condition by functional classification for 1995. On the U.S. urban systems in 1995, only 39 percent of roads were reported to be in good or very good condition. The trend since 1990 has been toward fewer miles of roads in these categories.

Roadway usage varies by day of the week, as well as seasonally. Depending on location, the differences can sometimes be very large. For example, in recreational areas such as beaches, significant peaking occurs in the summer months and during other vacation periods. Many departments of transportation (DOTs) develop factors for day of week, week of month, and month of year, which are area-specific. The Florida DOT, for example, produces a weekly volume factor report. Based on 1994 data, in the Panama City area weekly recreational traffic varied from 0.77 to 1.4 in a typical week. The nonrecreational traffic variation was smaller, ranging from 0.82 to 1.25.

---

[43] "National Bicycling and Walking Study Final Report," *Travel Demand Forecasting.*

Table 4–16 Highway VMT vs. Lane Miles by Functional Class (Urban)[44]

Year	Arterial Interstate Urban VMT (millions)	Lane Miles	Other Arterial Urban VMT (millions)	Lane Miles	Collector Urban VMT (millions)	Lane Miles	Total Arterial & Collector VMT (millions)	Lane Miles
1985	216,160	57,327	578,170	371,802ʳ	89,552	162,203	883,882	591,332
1990	278,901	62,306	699,233	397,192ʳ	106,297	167,218	1,084,431	626,716
1991	285,325	62,936	707,518	401,076ʳ	107,281	164,752	1,100,124	628,764
1992	303,265	67,135	745,618	415,660ʳ	116,065	175,602	1,164,948	658,397
1993	317,399	69,135	774,049	432,473	117,950	181,035	1,209,398	682,643
1994	330,577ʳ	70,847	797,899ʳ	442,555	120,088ʳ	183,394	1,248,644ʳ	696,796
1995	341,528	71,392	815,164	445,662	126,891	185,059	1,283,583	702,113

ʳ Revised.

Note: Local VMT (vehicle-miles traveled) and local lane miles are not included.

Source: *Highway Statistics,* annual issues, Washington, D.C.: U.S. Department of Transportation, Federal Highway Administration, Tables HM-60, VM-2, and VM-2A.

Table 4–18 presents some general monthly vehicle travel trends on urban facilities.

Table 4–19 presents the Georgia DOT's daily and monthly factors by roadway classification.

As can be seen from Tables 4–18 and 4–19, VMT are generally highest during the summer months.

Congestion

Urban roadway congestion is a growing part of the travel experience. The latest estimates for fifty urban areas around the United States are summarized in Table 4–20, which clearly shows an increase in annual person hours of delay. More than 25 of the thirty largest urban areas experience congestion areawide. Most of the others are very close to that condition. Since the early 1980s drivers have been subjected to more and more delay, with increases of 15 percent in Philadelphia, Pennsylvania, to 260 percent in Cleveland, Ohio.

Annual person hours of delay ranged from 16 to 75 hours in 1994, compared to a range of 9 to 51 hours in 1982. The data presented earlier on rapidly increasing VMT with slowly increasing lane miles demonstrates one of the reasons for such a change in congestion. The roadway congestion index developed by the Texas Transportation Institute (TTI) indicates that for the top fifty urban areas, the values ranged from 0.76 to 1.52, with the western areas having the highest average of 1.21. The Los Angeles area ranked first with more than 180,000 VKT (112,000 VMT) daily on freeways and more than 134,000 VKT (83,000 VMT) on principal arterial streets. Table 4–21 lists TTI's roadway congestion indices for 1994.

It is also interesting to look at how much of the congestion is recurring and how much is incident-related. Delay hours for fifty urban areas are summarized in Table 4–22.

In contrast, Figure 4–18 shows the percentage of Europeans who do not encounter severe congestion on the way to work. On the average, only 10 percent of those surveyed said that they encountered traffic jams on the way to work.

At the same time peak hour congestion is increasing, there are noteworthy trends in speed characteristics on urban roadways. Between 1985 and 1992, average daily speeds in urban areas increased in all categories, for all road types. Table 4–23 summarizes the speed trends by urban roads.

Speeds on limited access facilities in the United States have increased with the repeal of the federally mandated speed limit. Table 4–24 shows speed data for two cities before and after the speed limit was lifted.

Urban Freight Movement and Distribution

The elements of goods movement that are observed in the urban freight system include: terminal activities, stem driving, zone driving, and dwell time activities. The terminal activities take place typically at the beginning and end of a tour,

---

[44] *National Transportation Statistics 1997,* p. 25.

Table 4–17   Highway Condition by Functional System (Urban)[45]

Interstate

Year	Not Reported	Poor	%	Mediocre	%	Fair	%	Good	%	Very Good	%	Unpaved	%	Total Reported	%
1990	—	993	8.6	*	*	3,717	32.2	*	*	6,817	59.1	—	—	11,527	100.0
1991	—	881	7.6	*	*	3,744	32.3	*	*	6,978	60.1	—	—	11,603	100.0
1992	—	884	7.1	1,651	13.2	2,122	17.0	3,487	28.0	4,322	34.7	—	—	12,466	100.0
1993	1,454	1,228	10.7	2,830	24.8	2,315	20.3	3,000	26.3	2,051	18.0	—	—	11,424	100.0
1994	4136	1,562	12.3	3,598	28.3	3,024	23.8	3,341	26.3	1,185	9.3	—	—	12,710	100.0
1995	857	222	1.8	1,057	8.6	6,237	50.7	3,389	27.5	1,402	11.4	—	—	12,307	100.0

Other Freeways and Expressways

Year	Not Reported	Poor	%	Mediocre	%	Fair	%	Good	%	Very Good	%	Unpaved	%	Total Reported	%
1990	—	172	2.2	*	*	3,365	43.9	*	*	4,133	53.9	—	—	7,670	100.0
1991	—	176	2.3	*	*	3,412	44.2	*	*	4,126	53.5	—	—	7,714	100.0
1992	—	220	2.6	499	5.9	2,740	32.4	2,380	28.1	2,626	31.0	—	—	8,465	100.0
1993	1,406	770	10.3	2,409	32.3	1,608	21.6	1,560	20.9	1,104	14.8	—	—	7,451	100.0
1994	725	337	4.1	861	10.4	3,917	47.4	1,812	21.9	1,343	16.2	—	—	8,270	100.0
1995	1,166	372	4.8	767	9.8	4,269	54.7	1,594	20.4	802	10.3	—	—	7,804	100.0

Other Principal Arterial

Year	Not Reported	Poor	%	Mediocre	%	Fair	%	Good	%	Very Good	%	Unpaved	%	Total Reported	%
1990	—	3,063	5.9	*	*	25,462	49.0	*	*	23,451	45.1	11	0.0	51,987	100.0
1991	—	3,469	6.6	*	*	25,687	49.1	*	*	23,166	44.3	27	0.1	52,349	100.0
1992	—	3,535	6.8	6,003	11.5	18,171	34.8	11,188	21.4	13,218	25.3	50	0.1	52,165	100.0
1993	13,107	6,238	15.7	10,970	27.6	9,088	22.9	7,682	19.3	5,750	14.5	—	—	39,728	100.0
1994	5,887	5,125	10.9	5,883	12.5	19,297	40.9	9,349	19.8	7,549	16.0	—	—	47,203	100.0
1995	11,352	5,152	12.4	6,097	14.7	19,565	47.2	6,608	15.9	4,022	9.7	—	—	41,444	100.0

Minor Arterial

Year	Not Reported	Poor	%	Mediocre	%	Fair	%	Good	%	Very Good	%	Unpaved	%	Total Reported	%
1990	—	6,691	9.0	*	*	36,202	48.5	*	*	31,393	42.1	370	0.5	74,656	100.0
1991	—	5,565	7.4	*	*	37,398	49.9	*	*	31,553	42.1	463	0.6	74,979	100.0
1992	—	6,329	7.9	11,519	14.3	27,411	34.1	15,416	19.2	19,283	24.0	410	0.5	80,368	100.0
1993	—	6,944	8.1	12,204	14.2	33,153	38.6	16,207	18.9	17,001	19.8	313	0.4	85,822	100.0
1994	—	5,918	6.7	10,798	12.3	33,470	38.1	17,974	20.5	19,386	22.1	306	0.3	87,852	100.0
1995	—	5,948	6.7	12,040	13.6	32,634	36.9	18,087	20.4	19,517	22.1	284	0.3	88,510	100.0

Collector

Year	Not Reported	Poor	%	Mediocre	%	Fair	%	Good	%	Very Good	%	Unpaved	%	Total Reported	%
1990	—	12,938	16.5	*	*	39,427	50.4	*	*	24,838	31.7	1,045	1.3	78,248	100.0
1991	—	8,662	11.2	*	*	41,255	53.5	*	*	26,334	34.2	846	1.1	77,097	100.0
1992	—	8,653	10.5	13,934	16.9	29,077	35.2	14,323	17.3	15,747	19.1	923	1.1	82,657	100.0
1993	—	9,204	10.8	14,339	16.8	32,798	38.4	14,658	17.2	13,549	15.9	830	1.0	85,378	100.0
1994	—	8,416	9.8	13,959	16.2	34,460	40.0	14,668	17.0	13,802	16.0	793	0.9	86,098	100.0
1995	—	8,463	9.7	14,648	16.8	34,036	39.0	14,998	17.2	14,472	16.6	714	0.8	87,331	100.0

Total Urban

Year	Not Reported	Poor	%	Mediocre	%	Fair	%	Good	%	Very Good	%	Unpaved	%	Total Reported	%
1990	—	23,857	10.6	*	*	108,173	48.3	*	*	90,632	40.4	1,426	0.6	224,088	100.0
1991	—	18,753	8.4	*	*	111,496	49.8	*	*	92,157	41.2	1,336	0.6	223,742	100.0
1992	—	19,621	8.3	33,606	14.2	79,521	33.7	46,794	19.8	55,196	23.4	1,383	0.6	236,121	100.0
1993	15,967	24,384	10.6	42,752	18.6	78,962	34.4	43,107	18.8	39,455	17.2	1,143	0.5	229,803	100.0
1994	7,028	21,358	8.8	35,099	14.5	94,168	38.9	47,144	19.5	43,265	17.9	1,099	0.5	242,133	100.0
1995	13,375	20,157	8.5	34,609	14.6	96,741	40.8	44,676	18.8	40,215	16.9	998	0.4	237,396	100.0

Sources: *Highway Statistics*, annual issues, Washington, D.C.: U.S. Department of Transportation, Federal Highway Administration, 1990–1995, Table HM-63 and revisions; *Highway Statistics*, annual issues, Washington, D.C.: U.S. Department of Transportation, Federal Highway Administration, 1990–1994, Table HM-63 and revisions; *Highway Statistics*, annual issues, Washington, D.C.: U.S. Department of Transportation, Federal Highway Administration, 1995, Table HM-64.

[45] *National Transportation Statistics 1997*, pp. 47–48.

Table 4–18 Estimated Individual Monthly Motor Vehicle Travel in the United States[46]

| System | 1996 Individual Monthly Vehicle-Miles of Travel (in Billions) | | | | | | | | | | | |
	Jan.	Feb.	March	April	May	June	July	Aug.	Sept.	Oct.	Nov.	Dec.
Urban Interstate	26.4	25.4	29.4	28.9	31.0	30.0	30.8	31.3	29.0	30.2	28.3	28.5
Urban Other Arterial	64.6	60.6	68.9	69.2	72.6	70.1	73.3	74.0	68.7	71.7	67.0	67.8
Other Urban	26.0	24.7	28.4	28.3	30.3	29.1	30.0	30.2	27.7	29.0	27.3	27.3
All Systems	183.9	175.2	203.3	204.5	219.7	214.1	224.7	226.8	205.6	213.5	198.4	198.9

Source: Federal Highway Administration.

Table 4–19 GDOT Monthly and Daily ADT Factors[47]

| Factor Group Description | Month | | | | | | | | | | | |
	Jan.	Feb.	March	April	May	June	July	Aug.	Sept.	Oct.	Nov.	Dec.
Rural/Small Urban												
Interstate	1.18	1.08	0.97	0.95	1.01	0.95	0.91	0.94	1.06	1.04	1.00	0.96
Rural Arterials	1.14	1.08	1.02	0.98	0.97	0.96	0.97	0.98	0.98	0.94	0.97	1.04
Rural Collectors	1.20	1.05	1.00	0.95	0.95	0.98	0.97	0.95	0.98	0.94	1.03	1.05
Small Urban Arterials	1.10	1.03	1.00	0.98	0.97	0.97	0.99	0.99	1.00	0.99	1.00	1.00
Small Urban Collectors	1.06	1.04	0.99	0.98	0.98	0.97	0.99	0.96	1.00	0.99	1.01	1.03
Urbanized Interstate												
(Outside Atlanta)	1.11	1.05	0.99	0.99	0.99	0.94	0.97	0.95	1.01	1.00	1.01	1.03
Urbanized Arterials	1.06	1.01	0.99	1.01	0.96	0.99	1.02	1.00	0.99	0.96	1.00	1.03
Urbanized Collectors	1.05	0.99	0.95	0.95	0.96	1.00	1.01	1.04	1.03	0.92	1.06	1.08
Atlanta Interstate												
(Not I-285)	1.08	1.02	0.98	0.96	0.98	0.96	0.98	0.96	1.01	1.03	1.04	1.02
Just I-285	1.09	1.05	0.99	0.97	1.01	0.98	1.00	0.96	1.00	0.98	1.00	0.97
Atlanta Arterials												
(FC 14,16)	1.03	1.03	1.00	0.97	0.98	0.98	1.02	0.99	1.00	1.00	1.02	0.99

| Factor Group Description | Day | | | | | | |
	Sunday	Monday	Tuesday	Wednesday	Thursday	Friday	Saturday
Rural/Small Urban							
Interstate	0.99	1.07	1.12	1.08	1.02	0.85	0.93
Rural Arterials	1.29	0.99	0.99	0.98	0.95	0.85	1.04
Rural Collectors	1.14	1.04	1.05	1.04	1.01	0.87	0.99
Small Urban Arterials	1.30	1.01	1.00	1.00	0.96	0.85	0.99
Small Urban Collectors	1.52	0.96	0.93	0.92	0.91	0.86	1.15
Urbanized Interstate							
(Outside Atlanta)	1.39	0.98	0.94	0.92	0.91	0.86	1.18
Urbanized Arterials	1.55	0.94	0.92	0.92	0.92	0.84	1.17
Urbanized Collectors	1.57	0.95	0.94	0.93	0.88	0.84	1.18
Atlanta Interstate							
(Not I-285)	1.28	0.99	0.96	0.95	0.93	0.88	1.12
Just I-285	1.43	0.97	0.93	0.92	0.91	0.86	1.17
Atlanta Arterials							
(FC 14,16)	1.41	0.98	0.95	0.94	0.94	0.87	1.07

Notes: To convert a 24-hour count to an estimated AADT (Annual Average Daily Traffic), determine which factor group contains the road on which the 24-hour count was made. In the row of factors corresponding to this factor group, locate the factors for the month and day of the week on which the count was made. Multiply the 24-hour count by both these factors to obtain estimated AADT.

To obtain an estimated 24-hour count from a known (or estimated) AADT, find the monthly and daily factors for the day for which the estimated 24-hour count is desired. Divide the AADT by both these factors to obtain the estimated 24-hour count.

These factors were derived from data obtained from 74 continuous count stations located throughout the state.

Source: GDOT Information Services, Chamblee, GA.

---

[46] *Traffic Volume Trends July 1997* (Washington, D.C.: U.S. Department of Transportation, September 16, 1997).

[47] Georgia Department of Transportation Information Services, Chamblee, Ga., May 27, 1998.

Table 4–20   Annual Person Hours of Delay per Eligible Driver—1982 to 1994[48]

Urban Area	Annual Delay per Eligible Driver						Percent Change 1982–1994
	1982	1986	1990	1992	1993	1994	
Northeastern Cities							
Baltimore, MD	13	21	26	30	31	31	138
Boston, MA	26	40	43	45	44	46	77
Hartford, CT	9	15	23	25	30	31	244
New York, NY	25	31	36	38	39	40	60
Philadelphia, PA	20	25	24	23	23	23	15
Pittsburgh, PA	13	20	24	25	26	27	108
Washington, DC	42	56	66	70	70	71	69
Midwestern Cities							
Chicago, IL	19	28	29	34	34	35	84
Cincinnati, OH	7	9	15	18	20	21	200
Cleveland, OH	5	7	13	15	16	18	260
Columbus, OH	11	14	22	23	22	22	100
Detroit, MI	30	36	44	51	57	57	90
Indianapolis, IN	4	5	7	8	12	17	325
Kansas City, MO	6	8	9	14	15	16	167
Louisville, KY	8	9	10	13	16	19	138
Milwaukee, WI	9	13	16	17	17	18	100
Minneapolis-St. Paul, MN	9	15	20	22	24	25	178
Oklahoma City, OK	9	11	12	14	14	14	56
St. Louis, MO	20	24	26	26	29	30	50
Southern Cities							
Atlanta, GA	29	48	45	47	53	56	93
Charlotte, NC	17	22	26	27	27	27	59
Ft. Lauderdale, FL	13	17	21	23	24	26	100
Jacksonville, FL	22	24	32	32	35	37	68
Memphis, TN	7	8	10	12	13	15	114
Miami, FL	30	35	49	47	51	53	77
Nashville, TN	14	23	28	26	24	26	86
New Orleans, LA	14	25	26	25	25	28	100
Norfolk, VA	18	29	32	30	29	30	67
Orlando, FL	13	18	17	18	22	24	85
Tampa, FL	21	24	26	28	27	28	33
Southwestern Cities							
Albuquerque, NM	9	13	18	17	20	24	167
Austin, TX	26	37	35	34	41	45	73
Corpus Christi, TX	3	4	4	7	7	9	200
Dallas, TX	36	56	54	53	53	55	53
Denver, CO	24	28	33	37	41	40	67
El Paso, TX	5	8	7	11	11	11	120
Fort Worth, TX	22	35	34	36	40	43	95
Houston, TX	51	55	55	57	60	61	20
Phoenix, AZ	30	34	37	39	40	38	27
Salt Lake City, UT	5	6	8	10	12	14	180
San Antonio, TX	15	26	22	25	28	29	93
Western Cities							
Honolulu, HI	25	29	31	35	37	36	44
Los Angeles, CA	41	60	65	64	65	63	54
Portland, OR	16	18	27	32	34	35	119
Sacramento, CA	14	19	26	25	29	29	107
San Bernardino-Riverside, CA	42	68	74	76	76	75	79
San Diego, CA	12	19	29	28	26	26	117
San Francisco-Oakland, CA	39	61	68	65	66	65	67
San Jose, CA	33	50	55	54	52	51	55
Seattle-Everett, WA	26	41	56	59	59	59	127
Northeastern Average	21	30	35	37	38	38	81
Midwestern Average	12	15	19	21	23	24	100
Southern Average	18	25	28	29	30	32	78
Southwestern Average	21	27	28	30	32	34	62
Western Average	28	41	48	49	49	49	75
Texas Average	23	32	30	32	34	36	57
Total Average	19	27	30	32	33	34	79
Maximum Value	51	68	74	76	76	75	47
Minimum Value	3	4	4	7	7	9	200

Source: TTI Analysis.

[48] *Urban Roadway Congestion—1982 to 1994,* Texas Transportation Institute, August 1997.

Table 4–21 1994 Roadway Congestion Index Value[49]

Urban Area	Freeway/Expressway Daily VKT[1] (000)	Freeway/Expressway Daily VKT[2] (Lane–Kilometer)	Principal Arterial Street Daily VKT (000)	Principal Arterial Street Daily VKT[3] (Lane–Kilometer)	Roadway Congestion Index[3]	Rank
Los Angeles, CA	181,930	20,430	134,270	6,650	1.52	1
Washington, DC	49,310	18,230	29,790	7,770	1.43	2
San Francisco-Oakland, CA	68,960	17,480	23,670	6,230	1.33	3
Miami, FL	17,030	15,900	27,610	7,310	1.32	4
Chicago, IL	67,820	16,300	59,570	6,880	1.28	5
Seattle-Everett, WA	34,290	16,380	15,900	5,930	1.25	6
Detroit, MI	47,660	16,130	43,500	6,110	1.24	7
San Diego, CA	44,800	15,900	15,780	5,520	1.21	8
San Bernardino-Riverside, CA	24,960	16,060	17,950	5,250	1.20	9
Atlanta, GA	53,130	15,350	20,530	6,010	1.18	10
New York, NY	141,800	13,970	89,680	7,190	1.15	11
Honolulu, HI	9,020	14,000	3,120	7,610	1.13	12
Houston, TX	53,070	14,650	18,900	5,220	1.12	13
New Orleans, LA	8,870	13,280	8,090	6,790	1.11	14
Portland, OR	13,910	13,820	7,570	6,710	1.11	14
Dallas, TX	41,380	14,120	16,950	5,480	1.09	16
Phoenix, AZ	16,740	13,870	29,980	5,560	1.09	16
Boston, MA	35,020	14,310	22,940	4,900	1.08	18
Tampa, FL	7,250	12,860	8,080	6,280	1.07	19
Denver, CO	21,690	13,480	18,110	5,950	1.07	19
Baltimore, MD	30,270	13,570	16,180	5,830	1.06	21
Sacramento, CA	17,110	13,040	12,800	6,260	1.06	21
San Jose, CA	27,170	13,720	11,710	5,270	1.06	21
Philadelphia, PA	33,680	12,090	35,420	6,670	1.05	24
Cincinnati, OH	21,690	13,680	7,120	5,300	1.05	24
Minneapolis-St. Paul, MN	33,330	13,350	11,500	5,760	1.04	26
Cleveland, OH	24,810	12,840	10,100	5,390	1.00	27
Milwaukee, WI	12,560	12,890	9,820	5,170	1.00	27
Ft. Lauderdale, FL	14,970	12,830	10,380	5,120	0.99	29
St. Louis, MO	33,170	11,870	20,490	6,360	0.98	30
Albuquerque, NM	4,700	11,680	7,680	5,610	0.98	30
Jacksonville, FL	10,500	12,540	10,550	4,850	0.97	32
Austin, TX	10,590	12,180	4,700	5,670	0.97	32
Fort Worth, TX	22,280	12,300	9,050	5,430	0.97	32
Nashville, TN	12,480	11,570	9,500	6,050	0.96	35
Columbus, OH	16,380	12,110	5,800	5,540	0.95	36
Louisville, KY	12,240	11,780	5,880	5,790	0.95	36
Charlotte, NC	6,170	11,610	5,300	5,480	0.94	38
Memphis, TN	8,690	11,490	9,290	5,390	0.94	38
Salt Lake City, UT	10,350	11,800	4,590	5,760	0.94	38
Hartford, CT	11,370	11,490	6,150	5,700	0.93	41
Norfolk, VA	9,780	10,470	8,170	6,590	0.93	41
Indianapolis, IN	15,300	11,590	8,450	5,250	0.92	43
San Antonio, TX	18,560	11,640	9,760	5,340	0.92	43
Orlando, FL	10,830	10,350	10,140	5,250	0.86	45
Oklahoma City, OK	12,480	10,470	7,490	5,310	0.85	46
Pittsburgh, PA	15,170	8,050	18,930	6,270	0.83	47
Kansas City, MO	25,160	9,990	9,050	4,970	0.80	48
El Paso, TX	6,150	10,190	5,470	3,890	0.78	49
Corpus Christi, TX	3,470	9,370	2,750	4,500	0.76	50
Northeastern Average	45,230	13,100	31,300	6,330	1.08	
Midwestern Average	26,880	12,750	16,560	5,650	1.01	
Southern Average	14,520	12,570	11,600	5,920	1.02	
Southwestern Average	19,000	12,300	11,630	5,310	0.97	
Western Average	46,910	15,650	26,970	6,160	1.21	
Texas Average	22,210	12,060	9,660	5,080	0.94	
Total Average	28,600	13,180	18,320	5,820	1.05	
Maximum Value	181,930	20,430	134,270	7,770	1.52	
Minimum Value	3,470	8,050	2,750	3,890	0.76	

Notes: [1] Daily vehicle-kilometers of travel.
[2] Daily vehicle-kilometers of travel per lane-kilometer.
[3] See Equation 1.

$$\text{Roadway Congestion Index (RCI)} = \frac{\frac{Freeway\ VKT/Ln\text{–}Km \times Freeway\ VKT}{13,000} \times \frac{Prin\ Art\ St\ VKT/Ln\text{–}Km \times Prin\ Art\ Str\ KVT}{5,000}}{Freeway\ VKT + Prin\ Art\ Str\ VKT}} \quad \text{Eq. 1}$$

Source: TTI Analysis.

[49] *Urban Roadway Congestion—1982 to 1994*, Volume 1: Annual Report, p. 10.

Table 4–22　Recurring and Incident Delay Relationships for 1994[50]

Urban Area	Peak Period Congested Daily VKT[1] Freeway (000)	Prin. Art. St. (000)	Freeway & Prin. Art St.	Daily Recurring Vehicle[3] Hours of Delay Freeway	Prin. Art. St.	Total	Daily Incident Vehicle[3] Hours of Delay Freeway	Prin. Art. St.	Total
Northeastern Cities									
Baltimore, MD	4,090	2,910	7,000	36,790	22,790	59,580	84,610	25,070	109,680
Boston, MA	7,090	4,130	11,220	66,110	31,360	97,460	231,380	34,490	265,870
Hartford, CT	1,020	970	1,990	8,690	6,590	15,280	23,470	7,240	30,710
New York, NY	38,290	34,300	72,590	319,230	291,590	610,820	798,080	320,750	1,118,820
Philadelphia, PA	3,790	11,950	15,740	31,260	96,790	128,050	65,660	106,470	172,120
Pittsburgh, PA	1,360	5,540	6,900	11,910	42,150	54,060	34,530	46,370	80,900
Washington, DC	15,530	11,390	26,920	145,110	89,370	234,490	319,250	98,310	417,560
Midwestern Cities									
Chicago, IL	18,310	17,420	35,740	175,650	130,660	306,300	210,780	143,720	354,500
Cincinnati, OH	3,420	960	4,380	28,180	6,660	34,840	22,550	7,320	29,870
Cleveland, OH	3,910	1,590	5,500	32,770	10,790	43,560	22,940	11,870	34,810
Columbus, OH	2,210	1,300	3,520	20,940	9,590	30,530	14,660	10,550	25,200
Detroit, MI	10,720	12,720	23,450	99,290	106,430	205,730	218,440	117,080	335,520
Indianapolis, IN	1,380	1,140	2,520	10,120	7,700	17,820	15,170	8,470	23,650
Kansas City, MO	1,130	1,020	2,150	8,870	7,070	15,940	27,500	7,770	35,280
Louisville, KY	830	1,590	2,410	7,460	12,120	19,570	8,200	13,330	21,530
Milwaukee, WI	1,700	1,550	3,240	14,380	12,070	26,450	14,380	13,280	27,650
Minn.-St. Paul, MN	5,250	2,850	8,090	45,810	23,200	69,010	41,230	25,520	66,740
Oklahoma City, OK	560	1,350	1,910	4,010	9,870	13,880	4,410	10,860	15,270
St. Louis, MO	3,730	5,530	9,260	32,040	38,180	70,220	38,440	42,000	80,450
Southern Cities									
Atlanta, GA	11,950	6,000	17,960	113,280	48,240	161,530	124,610	53,070	177,680
Charlotte, NC	970	1,430	2,400	7,460	11,070	18,520	5,960	12,170	18,140
Ft. Lauderdale, FL	2,700	2,340	5,030	22,480	16,910	39,390	33,730	18,600	52,330
Jacksonville, FL	1,650	2,610	4,260	13,180	18,580	31,750	19,760	20,430	40,200
Memphis, TN	780	1,460	2,250	6,030	9,470	15,500	6,630	10,420	17,050
Miami, FL	4,600	8,700	13,290	43,470	71,660	115,130	65,210	78,830	144,030
Nashville, TN	1,120	1,500	2,620	8,920	10,160	19,070	9,810	11,170	20,980
New Orleans, LA	2,000	1,820	3,820	17,200	12,970	30,160	30,960	14,260	45,220
Norfolk, VA	1,760	1,470	3,230	14,450	12,360	26,810	36,130	13,590	49,720
Orlando, FL	1,710	1,370	3,070	14,580	11,280	25,860	21,870	12,410	34,270
Tampa, FL	650	2,360	3,020	6,390	18,620	25,010	9,590	20,490	30,070
Southwestern Cities									
Albuquerque, NM	530	1,560	2,080	5,040	10,260	15,300	5,550	11,280	16,830
Austin, TX	2,860	1,060	3,920	25,400	7,130	32,530	27,940	7,840	35,780
Corpus Christi, TX	230	190	420	1,800	1,060	2,860	1,980	1,170	3,150
Dallas, TX	10,240	3,430	13,670	90,970	23,940	114,910	163,740	26,340	190,080
Denver, CO	5,370	4,480	9,850	49,520	35,010	84,540	49,520	38,520	88,040
El Paso, TX	690	250	940	5,500	1,740	7,240	6,050	1,920	7,970
Fort Worth, TX	4,510	1,430	5,940	40,080	7,950	48,030	72,140	8,750	80,890
Houston, TX	16,720	4,250	20,970	154,570	31,190	185,750	216,390	34,300	250,700
Phoenix, AZ	4,900	9,440	14,340	43,750	64,190	107,940	17,500	70,610	88,110
Salt Lake City, UT	1,400	930	2,330	12,290	5,620	17,910	7,370	6,180	13,560
San Antonio, TX	3,340	1,320	4,660	31,060	9,340	40,390	34,160	10,270	44,430
Western Cities									
Honolulu, HI	2,030	1,050	3,080	18,490	8,090	26,570	33,280	8,890	42,170
Los Angeles, CA	61,400	33,230	94,630	613,530	257,850	871,380	736,240	283,640	1,019,870
Portland, OR	2,500	2,040	4,550	22,230	15,130	37,360	44,450	16,650	61,100
Sacramento, CA	2,700	3,170	5,860	21,810	25,140	46,940	13,080	27,650	40,730
San Bernardino-Riv., CA	7,860	4,850	12,710	74,270	32,800	107,060	89,120	36,080	125,200
San Diego, CA	10,080	2,490	12,560	81,920	18,060	99,990	49,150	19,870	69,020
San Fran.-Oakland, CA	24,830	6,920	31,750	234,840	58,400	293,230	305,290	64,240	369,520
San Jose, CA	7,340	2,900	10,230	67,810	21,190	89,000	81,370	23,310	104,680
Seattle-Everett, WA	10,800	3,930	14,740	102,890	29,950	132,830	144,040	32,940	176,980
Northeastern Average	10,170	10,170	20,340	88,440	82,950	171,390	222,420	91,240	313,670
Midwestern Average	4,430	4,090	8,510	39,960	31,190	71,150	53,230	34,310	87,540
Southern Average	2,720	2,820	5,540	24,310	21,940	46,250	33,110	24,130	57,240
Southwestern Average	4,620	2,580	7,190	41,820	17,950	59,760	54,760	19,740	74,500
Western Average	14,390	6,730	21,120	137,530	51,840	189,380	166,230	57,030	223,250
Texas Average	5,510	1,700	7,220	49,910	11,760	61,670	74,630	12,940	87,570
Total Average	6,690	4,800	11,490	61,280	37,210	98,480	93,170	40,930	134,090
Maximum Value	61,400	34,300	94,630	613,530	291,590	871,380	798,080	320,750	1,118,820
Minimum Value	230	190	420	1,800	1,060	2,860	1,980	1,170	3,150

Notes: [1] Daily vehicle-kilometers of travel. Represents the percentage of daily vehicle-kilometers of travel on each roadway system during the peak period operating in congested conditions.
[2] Percentage of incident delay related to recurring delay.
[3] Facility delays as calculated by type and urban area.

Source: TTI Analysis and local transportation agency references.

---

[50] *Urban Roadway Congestion—1982 to 1994*, Volume 2: Methodology and Urbanized Area Data, pp. 26–27.

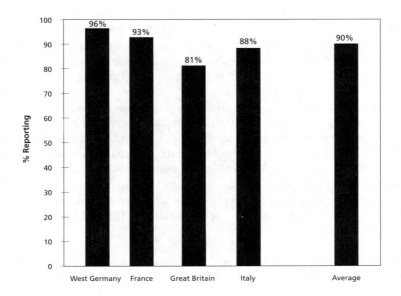

Figure 4–18   Proportion of Europeans Stating that They Do Not Usually Encounter Traffic Jams on the Way to Work[51]

Source: U.R.F./Sofres Surveys, 1994.

Table 4–23   Speed Trend Characteristics on Urban Roads[52]

	Interstate		Freeway		Principal & Minor Arterials	
	1985	1992	1985	1992	1985	1992
Average speed (mph)	57.3	57.7	56.9	51.7	53.5	54.1
Median speed (mph)	57.5	58.9	57.1	58.5	53.6	54.4
85th percentile (mph)	64.1	66.1	63.4	64.9	60.5	60.7
%> 55 mph[53]	64.7	70.1	60.8	67.5	43.0	42.5
%> 60 mph	32.3	41.5	29.4	35.5	16.7	18.4
%> 65 mph	11.3	17.5	9.5	13.4	4.9	5.9

Table 4–24   Car Speeds Before and After Speed Limit Changes[54]

Riverside, California						
Period	Number	Mean	Standard Deviation	85th Percentile	% Over 70 mph	% Over 75 mph
Before	3921	67	6.2	73	29	8
3 Months After	3674	69	6.1	75	40	13
6 Months After	3441	68	6.4	75	36	12
12 Months After	3786	69	6.5	75	41	14

Houston, Texas						
Period	Number	Mean	Standard Deviation	85th Percentile	% Over 70 mph	% Over 75 mph
Before	3097	65	5.9	71	15	4
3 Months After	3350	68	6.5	74	33	9
6 Months After	3611	69	6.4	75	41	12
12 Months After	3480	70	6.8	76	50	17

[51] Gerondeau, *Transport in Europe,* p. 326.

[52] *Highway Statistics 1996.*

[53] Data in this table are only for highways with a 55 mph speed limit.

[54] Richard Retting and Michael A. Greene, "Traffic Speeds Following Repeal of the National Maximum Speed Limit," *ITE Journal* (Washington, D.C.: Institute of Transportation Engineers, May 1997), pp. 43–45.

including paperwork, vehicle checks, and loading or unloading. Stem driving is the portion of the trip from the terminal to the first stop, or from the last stop back to the terminal. Most urban freight routes have concentrated areas where trucks service their customers. The movement from one location to another is the zone driving. Finally, the dwell-time activities are the actual pickups and deliveries within a facility. Occasionally, a driver may service several sites from an on-street space without moving his or her vehicle. All of that time would be considered dwell time.

The types of trucks performing most urban pickups and deliveries are usually in the lighter weight classes of vehicles. The light-weight trucks may account for as much as 70 to 90 percent of the total truck trips. In some locations where traffic congestion, geometric conditions, or local ordinances make the use of trucks difficult or impossible, freight activities are being made in automobiles, pickups, and taxicabs. Trucks represent approximately 10 to 30 percent of the total traffic in urban areas, with the higher percentages on the collectors and the lower percentages on urban interstates and freeways. Trucks represent a higher percentage of total traffic on surface streets than on interstates because many truck trips are local pickups and deliveries that never get on the interstate. Truck registrations in the United States have grown steadily since the 1960s, with the current volume at 76 million. See Chapter 3 for more detail on intercity truck and freight movement.

In 1993, in Japan there were more than eleven million commercial vehicles owned with approximately 11 percent registered as commercial trucks.[55] In Canada, the total vehicle registrations have increased from 16.6 million in 1992 to 17.2 million in 1996, with an increase in trucks from 3.35 to 3.58 million. Recent surveys have shown that light trucks consistently make more trips per day than any other class of trucks. They also have a higher trip frequency and shorter trip lengths. In Phoenix, for example, more than 96 percent of all commercial trips were made by trucks in the two lightest weight classes. The same survey indicated that light trucks average more than twelve trips per day compared to less than five for heavy trucks.

A number of studies have shown that between one-third and one-half of truck miles of travel are short haul trips of 200 miles or less. In the past ten years, there has been a noticeable change in the urban delivery system. Many shipments are transported by couriers using bicycle or other nonmotorized forms of travel. Urban congestion has been a factor in creating and encouraging this phenomenon. The trips that continue to be made by truck occur throughout the day, with the heaviest concentration in the midday period. A number of surveys have shown that long-distance or "through" trucks tend to avoid travel during the peak periods.

Figure 4–19 shows the hourly distribution of truck travel for Ottawa, Canada. The curves are similar for different truck types with variations in the peak percentage. Studies conducted as early as the 1970s in the United States show similar patterns, with a maximum 11 percent per hour between 8 A.M. and 10 A.M. The *1996 Quick Response Freight Manual*[56] indicates a median

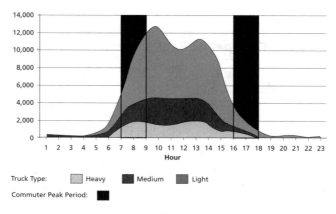

Figure 4–19   Twenty-Four–Hour Trip Distribution, Trucks, Ottawa, Canada[57]

Source: *National Capital Region Goods Movement Study, Technical Report*, Ottawa, Canada: Delcan Corporation and Goss, Gilroy and Associates, Ltd., TRANS—a joint technical committee on transportation systems planning, Figure 16, p. 37.

[55] "Analysis of Commercial Trucks" (Internet resource).

[56] *Quick Response Freight Manual* (Washington, D.C.: U.S. Department of Transportation, September 1996).

[57] *Characteristics of Urban Freight Systems* (Washington, D.C.: U.S. Department of Transportation, December 1995), p. 78.

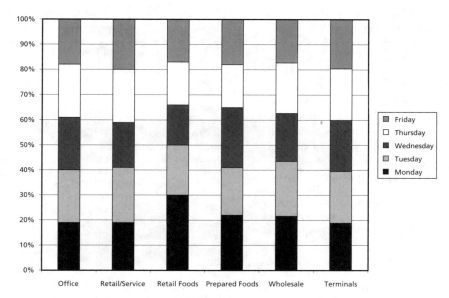

Figure 4–20   Daily Truck Distribution[58, 59]

Sources: Philip Habib, *Urban Goods Movement Planning*, Polytechnic Institute of New York; James Denis Brogan, *An Analysis of Truck Travel Demand Forecasting Techniques and Data Requirements,* unpublished doctoral dissertation, The University of Tennessee, Knoxville, Tenn.: June 1977.

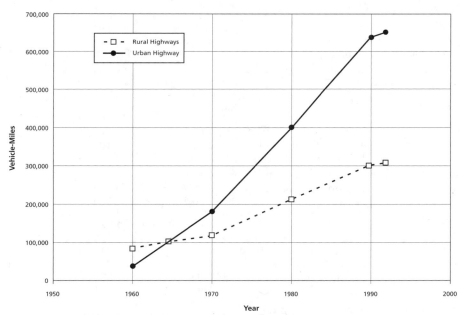

Figure 4–21   Relationship for Rural and Urban Truck Vehicle-Miles of Travel[60]

Source: *National Transportation Statistics, Annual Report*, Report No. DOT-VNTSC-BTS-93-1, Washington, D.C.: U.S. Department of Transportation, September 1993, Figure 7, p. 26.

---

[58] *Urban Transportation Planning for Goods and Services* (Washington, D.C.: U.S. Department of Transportation, June 1979), pp. 11–24.

[59] *Characteristics of Urban Freight Systems*, pp. 164, 173.

[60] *Characteristics of Urban Freight Systems*, p. 27.

Table 4–25(a) Example Daily Truck Trip Generation Equations[61]

Land Use	Daily Trip Generation	Variables
Office	$0.16 \times FA + 0.4$	FA = Floor Area (100 m²)
Residential	$0.032 \times DU + 0.45$	DU = Dwelling Units
Light Industry	$0.26 \times FA + 0.06 \times E + 2.4$	FA = Floor Area (100 m²) E = Employment
Retail	$0.06 \times E + 1.6$	E = Employment
Retail (food)	$0.33 \times FA + 242 \times E + 1.04$	FA = Floor Area (100 m²) E = Employment

Sources: Wilbur Smith Associates, Sylva Engineering Corp., and Epsilon Engineering, Inc., *Commercial Vehicle Survey*, prepared for Houston-Galveston Area Council, Houston, Texas: Wilbur Smith Associates, July 5, 1995; Philip A. Habib, *Curbside Pickup and Delivery Operations and Arterial Traffic Impacts*, Report No. FHWA/RD-80/020, Washington, D.C.: FHWA, February 1981.

hourly truck travel distribution of 11 percent of total daily truck trips occurring each hour between 9 A.M. and 1 P.M. The rest of the day tails off from these peak percentages. Comparing the various sources, the results are quite consistent.

Truck trips occur mostly during weekdays, with urban deliveries almost exclusively in that timeframe. Figure 4–20 shows the daily distribution of truck travel based on the compilation of pickup and delivery patterns by land use.

In the mid-1960s, the vehicle miles of truck travel for urban highways surpassed the rural miles. Figure 4–21 shows the growth in each through 1992. Urban travel is now significantly greater than rural, representing approximately twice as many vehicle miles. Of the larger vehicles, beginning with Class 3 (10,000 lbs/two axles/six tires), approximately 37 percent of all trips are made in urban areas.

Truck trip rates have been reported based on limited sampling. In one of the most significant urban goods movement studies completed in the 1970s, for select land uses, urban truck trip generation equations were developed for trucks in British Columbia. Table 4–25(a) presents some of these. Table 4–25(b) shows truck and truck-tractor registrations in the United States in 1996.

The most common trip ends for urban truck trips are illustrated in Table 4–26, which shows data from Phoenix, Arizona; Chicago, Illinois; Vancouver, British Columbia; and Houston, Texas. The typical land uses at the trip ends are: residential, retail, manufacturing, and warehousing.

Parking Characteristics

In urban areas, parking is provided on-street, in surface lots, in underground garages, and in elevated decks. Off-street

Table 4–25(b) Truck and Truck-Tractor Registrations, 1996[61]

	Total Trucks Registered in 1996	Truck-Tractors Registered in 1996
Alabama	1,553,872	64,883
Alaska	300,506	3,238
Arizona	1,212,276	10,761
Arkansas	765,273	8,451
California	9,771,261	151,600
Colorado	1,526,688	6,540
Connecticut	658,434	2,568
Delaware	192,760	4,870
Dist. of Columbia	35,021	191
Florida	3,561,872	59,604
Georgia	2,426,027	52,915
Hawaii	276,329	1,437
Idaho	572,857	8,392
Illinois	2,507,383	58,388
Indiana	2,023,886	49,904
Iowa	1,206,182	48,787
Kansas	947,909	20,312
Kentucky	1,077,620	20,372
Louisiana	1,394,443	25,502
Maine	377,873	4,987
Maryland	1,053,197	11,954
Massachusetts	1,147,344	11,877
Michigan	2,895,058	64,285
Minnesota	1,572,845	33,292
Mississippi	904,335	8,406
Missouri	1,762,022	42,607
Montana	533,205	13,367
Nebraska	665,057	27,743
Nevada	474,686	6,975
New Hampshire	373,530	5,127
New Jersey	1,403,947	17,002
New Mexico	768,981	3,326
New York	2,606,026	15,510
North Carolina	2,215,933	57,560
North Dakota	338,648	10,022
Ohio	3,127,633	74,209
Oklahoma	1,380,673	10,989
Oregon	1,310,438	18,181
Pennsylvania	2,669,913	62,475
Rhode Island	183,211	1,993
South Carolina	1,011,972	17,203
South Dakota	378,151	11,394
Tennessee	1,816,551	31,909
Texas	5,831,593	140,726
Utah	632,491	21,357
Vermont	200,281	1,964
Virginia	1,920,994	30,721
Washington	1,958,448	22,379
West Virginia	600,736	6,999
Wisconsin	1,485,803	35,500
Wyoming	328,032	3,377
Total	75,940,206	1,424,131

Sources: Wilbur Smith Associates, Sylva Engineering Corp., and Epsilon Engineering, Inc., *Commercial Vehicle Survey*, prepared for Houston-Galveston Area Council, Houston, Texas: Wilbur Smith Associates, July 5, 1995.

---

[61] *Characteristics of Urban Freight Systems*, pp. 121, 125, 130, 138, and 144.

Table 4–26   Land Uses at Truck Trip Ends[62]

Land Use	Maricopa Co., Arizona (Phoenix)	Chicago	Vancouver Light Trucks	Vancouver Heavy Trucks	Houston
Residential	22.9	18.1	—	—	20.3
Household	—	—	11	1	—
Retail	19.5	23.3	17	11	15.8
Garaging	11.5	—	—	—	—
Meal, Fuel, Base	—	—	12	17	—
Manufacturing, Warehousing	20.8	—	—	—	—
Manufacturing	—	14.3	—	—	—
Industrial	—	—	—	—	42.6
Factory	—	—	8	6	—
Terminal/Warehouse	—	21.0	—	—	—
Warehouse	—	—	20	23	—
Intermodal	—	—	4	14	—
Transportation, Utilities, Communications	2.2	—	—	—	—
Educational	—	—	—	—	1.9
School, Hospital	—	—	6	1	—
Medical	—	—	—	—	1.7
Medical, Government	3.4	—	—	—	—
Government	—	—	—	—	0.6
Public/Government	—	4.9	—	—	—
Office	—	—	—	—	7.7
Office/Services	9.0	12.0	—	—	—
Office, Medical, Rest	—	—	11	3	—
Construction	—	1.7	—	—	—
Construction Site	—	—	9	15	—
Landfill	—	0.6	—	—	—
Quarry, Pit	—	—	3	8	—
Agriculture	—	1.1	—	—	—
In Transit	—	1.2	—	—	—
Other	10.7	1.8	—	—	10.1

Sources: John P. Reilly, Arnold Rosenbluh, and F. Gerald Rawlings, "Factoring and Analysis of the Commercial Vehicle Survey Issues," *CATS Research News,* Chicago Area Transportation Study, 26(1), February 1987, pp. 29–46; Earl R. Ruiter, *Development of an Urban Truck Travel Model for the Phoenix Metropolitan Area,* Report No. FHWA-AZ-92-314, Phoenix, Ariz.: FHWA, February 1992, Table 3.12, pp. 3–12; *Truck Study,* Vancouver, B.C.: Vancouver City Engineering Department, August 1990, Figures 31 and 32; Wilbur Smith Associates, Sylva Engineering Corp., and Epsilon Engineering, Inc., *Commercial Vehicle Survey,* Houston, Texas: Houston-Galveston Area Council, July 5, 1995, Figure 13, pp. 4–19.

parking is generally provided to satisfy zoning or other governmental requirements. The required number of spaces can be based on many factors, not all of which are the result of a technical analysis of actual need. A study conducted in the state of Washington found that the average parking supply was 30 percent greater than the average parking demand.[63]

In a California study of office buildings conducted in 1995, average parking requirements were for 4.1 spaces per 1,000 sq ft. Peak occupancy at the same buildings showed less than 60 percent usage.[64] Chapter 14 provides more detail on parking generation rates and zoning requirements. ITE's informational report *Parking Generation* summarizes numerous case studies by land use and provides rates for peak demand.

A survey[65] of seventeen urban areas explored a variety of downtown parking issues. The areas varied in size from a population of 55,000 to 19 million, with a land area ranging from one-fourth square mile to 14 square miles. The number of jobs in the CBDs ranged from 2,500 to one million. Off-street parking spaces ranged in number from 250 to almost 170,000. On-street parking spaces ranged from 350 to more than 300,000 with most cities in the 1,000 to 4,000 range. Most spaces were available for a fee, ranging from $0.25 to $0.75 per hour. It is interesting to note that New York City

[62] *Characteristics of Urban Freight Systems,* p. 79.

[63] "1991 Parking Utilization Study," *The SMART Project,* CD-ROM (Washington, D.C.: Bureau of Transportation Statistics, June 1992).

[64] Donald Shoup, "The High Cost of Free Parking," *Parking Today* (Los Angeles, Calif.: Bricepac, Inc., April 1997), p. 20.

[65] *The Urban Transportation Monitor,* pp. 9–11 and pp. 8–11.

has the largest number of jobs and parking spaces, yet far exceeds all others in transit usage, with approximately 50 percent of work trips taking place by transit.

Commuting/Telecommuting

In an effort to use our infrastructure more efficiently, as well as respond to access issues of some members of the work force, nontraditional work arrangements are emerging. Telecommuting brings the work to the employee, as opposed to the employee going to the place of work. In 1995, the average worker who traveled to his workplace traversed more than 11 miles to work, taking more than 20 minutes, primarily by privately owned, single-occupant vehicles.

The number of federal employees telecommuting increased from 3,000 to 9,000 between 1995 and 1996, with fifty telework centers available nationwide. Efforts to promote telecommuting are underway in Europe through the European Commission's Advanced Communications Technologies and Services program. Additionally, international conferences are being held to share information and promote telecommuting.[66]

Many private telecommuting programs are underway. Examples include working at home, working at satellite or telework centers, hoteling, free addressing (where the employee works primarily at a client's office), and mobile or virtual offices (often based on a combination of home and vehicle). If mobile offices increase in popularity, it will be interesting to see what effect they have on overall urban travel.

The use of technology is significant for the success of each of these approaches. The employer benefits include reduced office space needs and costs; increased employee productivity, morale, and commitment; decreased sick leave; and increased ability to attract and retain employees and address special situations and needs. The employees benefit by a reduction in stress, time, and commuting costs; increased productivity, morale, job satisfaction, and responsibility; and ability to balance work and personal demands. The costs associated with telecommuting are shared by employer and employee in many cases, although there are examples of one or the other bearing the full cost. The community benefits from successful programs by travel reduction and the subsequent air quality improvements, a reduction in fuel consumption, and the development of resources in local communities to serve the needs of the telecommuters. In a report to the U.S. Congress on successful telecommuting programs,[67] some case studies revealed peak period travel reductions by telecommuters of 60 percent and an 80 to 90 percent reduction in daily miles traveled by telecommuters.

---

[66] *The Urban Transportation Monitor*, pp. 3 and 6.

[67] *Successful Telecommuting Programs in the Public and Private Sectors: A Report to Congress* (Washington, D.C.: U.S. Department of Transportation, August 1997).

CHAPTER 5
Transportation Planning Studies

Herbert S. Levinson, P.E.
Principal
Herbert S. Levinson Transportation Consultant
Robert P. Jurasin, P.E.
Senior Vice President
Wilbur Smith Associates

Introduction

Transportation planning studies are designed to collect and analyze information pertaining to present and future transportation needs. They are an integral part of the transportation planning process; and they provide the context and basis for establishing key transportation policy, investment, and design decisions. They include much of the information obtained in traffic operations studies, but they generally involve longer time horizons and larger geographic areas. They may be conditioned by, or designed to, assess transportation policy inputs. Thus, they may address alternate ways of meeting transportation needs, or show how a community's land-use and transportation policy can be better coordinated.

Scope

This chapter provides an overview of the principal transportation planning studies. It briefly reviews the major types of studies and gives guidelines for key study elements. It complements the information contained in Chapters 3, 4, 6, 9, 12, 14, 15, 16, 18, and 19 in this handbook. Further information on specific studies is contained in the *Manual of Transportation Engineering Studies*[1] and *Manual of Traffic Engineering Studies*.[2]

Statistical analyses are useful in collecting, analyzing, and interpreting transportation planning data. Therefore, the last part of the chapter summarizes basic statistical methods that have general applicability. A more detailed discussion of statistical methods is found in Chapter 5, "Statistical Analysis," in the *Traffic Engineering Handbook*.[3]

Approach

The common approach to most planning studies includes the following steps.

1. Establish the study scope, purpose, and goals.

2. Analyze existing conditions (including data collection, summaries, and analyses).

3. Identify existing problems and needs.

4. Assess future changes and needs (i.e., how will population increases, employment growth, and new developments influence travel magnitudes and patterns; and what needs emerge as a result of these changes?).

---

[1] Institute of Transportation Engineers, *Manual of Transportation Engineering Studies* (Englewood Cliffs, N.J.: Prentice Hall, 1994).

[2] *Manual of Traffic Engineering Studies*, 4th Edition (Washington, D.C.: Institute of Transportation Engineers, 1976).

[3] Institute of Transportation Engineers, *Traffic Engineering Handbook*, Fifth Edition (Washington, D.C.: ITE, 1999).

5. Develop and analyze options. The choice of options will depend on the study goals, existing and future needs, and community perceptions and preferences. This may be an iterative process in response to community concerns.

6. Select preferred options and prepare recommended plans. The recommended plans should be prepared in sufficient detail to ensure that their workability, costs, priorities, and implementation strategies are developed.

The amount and type of information that should be collected will depend on the nature of the overall study and its specific analysis needs, the accuracy required, and the costs involved. Careful planning in advance of an actual study, including the use of sampling procedures, can make the overall effort more effective.

Overview of Principal Planning Studies

This section provides a brief overview of the transportation planning studies that are commonly encountered in practice. These studies include: comprehensive urban transportation studies, major investment studies, corridor studies, central area and major activity center studies, traffic impact studies, and traffic system management studies. Table 5–1 gives the study scale and time span for these and other related studies and indicates where further discussions can be found in this handbook.

Comprehensive Urban Area Transportation Studies

The comprehensive, coordinated, and continuing transportation planning process was initiated in the 1950s as a prerequisite for federal funds in U.S. urban areas. It was designed to produce long-range (usually capital-intensive) transportation plans that are consistent with an area's future transportation and development needs. Over the years, the process has evolved to include both short- and long-range elements. The key steps in this iterative process are shown in Figure 5–1. Chapter 12 describes urban area transportation studies in greater detail.

Table 5–1   Typical Planning Studies

Study Type	Study Area	Time Span	Described in This Section	Further Description in Chapter
Long Range Transportation Plans (LRTP)	Region	20-year forecast	X	12
Transport. Improve. Program (TIP)	Region	5–10 years		12
Air Quality Conformity	Region, Corridor	5–20 years		8
Major Investment Study (MIS)	Corridors of Sub Areas	5–20 years	X	9
Intermodal Study (IS)/ Corridor Study	Corridors	5–20 years	X	18
Activity Center Analysis	Area	3–10 years	X	15
Site and Project Impact Analysis	Facility, Segment, Point	3–10 years	X	15
Transportation System Management Study	Facility, Segment, Area	3–10 years	(X)	19

(X) Brief Discussion only.

Source: Adapted from information furnished by R. Dowling.

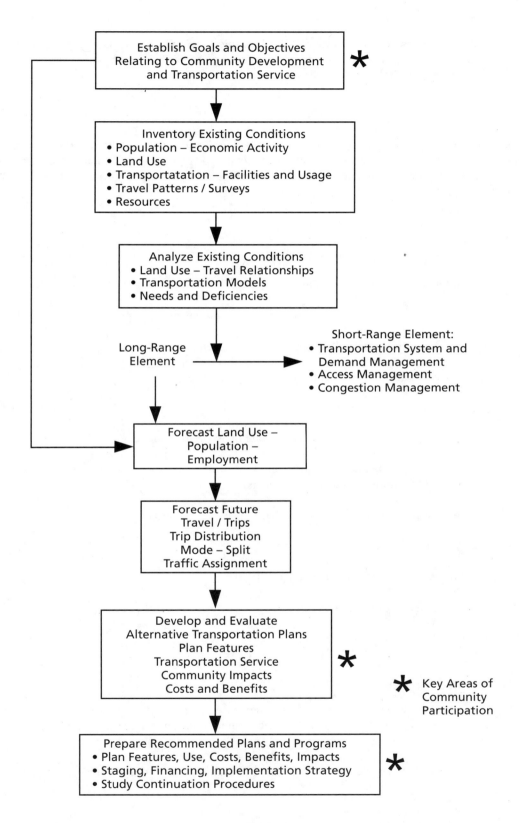

Establish Goals and Objectives
Relating to Community Development
and Transportation Service ✱

Inventory Existing Conditions
• Population – Economic Activity
• Land Use
• Transportatation – Facilities and Usage
• Travel Patterns / Surveys
• Resources

Analyze Existing Conditions
• Land Use – Travel Relationships
• Transportation Models
• Needs and Deficiencies

Long-Range
Element

Short-Range Element:
• Transportation System and
  Demand Management
• Access Management
• Congestion Management

Forecast Land Use –
Population –
Employment

Forecast Future
Travel / Trips
Trip Distribution
Mode – Split
Traffic Assignment

Develop and Evaluate
Alternative Transportation Plans
Plan Features
Transportation Service
Community Impacts
Costs and Benefits ✱

✱ Key Areas of
Community
Participation

Prepare Recommended Plans and Programs
• Plan Features, Use, Costs, Benefits, Impacts
• Staging, Financing, Implementation Strategy
• Study Continuation Procedures ✱

Figure 5–1   Comprehensive Urban Area Transportation Planning Process

Study Area

The study area should encompass the relevant political jurisdictions involved (i.e., towns and counties). It should also include any surrounding areas that are likely to become developed (or urbanized) by the design year, with population density generally exceeding 2,500 persons per square mile.

Goals

The process starts with a clear statement of the goals and objectives that should underlie plan development and evaluation. These goals should be developed by the communities involved, and they should incorporate public opinion. Goals should reflect mobility, economic, and environmental social objectives. Following are typical goals summarized by major perspective:

1. *Economic and environmental goals—*

    - Preserve and protect the environment.

    - Stimulate economic development.

    - Use transportation to enhance community development.

    - Coordinate land use and transportation investment.

    - Balance transport needs with community resources.

2. *Transportation service goals—*

    - Improve the quality of public and private transportation services.

    - Improve access to schools, jobs, and recreational and shopping areas for all residents (including transportation-disadvantaged individuals).

    - Reduce congestion at reasonable social and economic cost.

3. *Transportation impact goals—*

    - Minimize displacement of people and jobs.

    - Avoid land fragmentation.

    - Reduce air and noise pollution.

Inventories and Surveys

The next step involves inventories of existing land uses and transportation facilities. This includes travel surveys of people entering the study area and those living within it, traffic volume counts, transit coverage analysis, and special surveys of major activity centers.

- Roadside surveys provide travel information of nonresidents and are conducted around a cordon of the study area.

- "Household" surveys provide a census of daily travel by a sample of households.

- Truck and taxi surveys describe the amount and characteristics of commercial vehicle travel.

Existing Travel Patterns and Conditions

Origin-destination patterns are derived from the various travel surveys. "Trip generation" rates and models are obtained by relating trips to characteristics of activity centers and households. Screen-line checks are made to ensure the representative of the travel patterns data. Existing travel conditions and problems are identified to provide a clear picture of needs and deficiencies.

Population and Economic Projections

The next step involves making area-wide and analysis-unit projections of changes in population, employment, and land use. Future land-use plans are an important element in developing these forecasts.

Travel Demand Forecasts

Travel forecasts are made for the planning horizon years (i.e., ten or twenty years hence). These include: trip productions and attractions by analysis zone, distribution of trips between zones, estimation of person and vehicle-kilometers (VKT) of travel, allocation of travel between various transport modes, and assignment of trips to the committed transportation networks. See Chapter 6 for further details on travel forecasting methods.

Alternatives Analysis

Alternative transportation networks (including the no-build option) are then compared in terms of their usage and transportation service, community effects, costs, and benefits.

Recommended Plan and Program

The preceding analyses have traditionally resulted in a recommended and staged multimodal transportation plan and program. The features, uses, costs, benefits, and financing and staging of this plan are developed along with procedures to update and amend the plan.

This planning process is most appropriate for urban areas where considerable growth and change are anticipated. Since most areas now have overall plans, studies often focus on assessing the need for and environmental consequences of specific improvement projects.

Major Investment Studies

The major investment study (MIS) became an integral part of a metropolitan area's long-range planning process under the 1991 Intermodal Surface Transportation Efficiency Act (ISTEA). It is designed to provide decision makers with better and more complete information on available transportation options.

Context

MISs are called for in Section 450.318 of the joint Federal Highway Administration (FHWA)/Federal Transit Administration Final Rule on Statewide and Metropolitan Planning issued in the *Federal Register* on October 28, 1993 and effective November 29, 1993. This requirement was triggered by ISTEA, the 1990 Clean Air Act Amendments, and the National Environmental Policy Act of 1969.

An MIS for a corridor or subarea is undertaken when the need for a major metropolitan transportation investment has been identified in the metropolitan planning process and where federal funds are potentially involved. The MIS develops or refines the metropolitan transportation plan and leads to decisions by the metropolitan planning organization, in cooperation with participating agencies, on the design concept and scope of the investment officially described as a high-type highway or transit improvement of substantial cost that is expected to have a significant effect on capacity, traffic flow, level of service (LOS), or mode share at the transportation corridor or subarea scale.

The MIS provides a focused analysis and evaluation of the mobility needs and related problems of a corridor or subarea within the region. Depending on the scale of the issues and factors, it may identify a multimodal set of mobility investment and policy options to address those needs and problems; develop measures of benefits, costs, and impacts, as well as financial requirements; and allow comprehensive, multimodal analysis and evaluation of options. The MIS evaluation process leads to a decision on the design concept and scope for corridor and subarea major investments and policies that are then incorporated into a metropolitan area's transportation plan.

Scope and Steps

MISs normally include tasks for: problem definition (purpose and need statement); alternatives development; establishment of evaluation criteria and process for screening; a public involvement program; technical analyses including conceptual engineering, capital costs, operating and maintenance costs, and social and economic costs; and, as appropriate, environmental studies; financial analysis; and travel forecasting. Each work plan should reflect the status of planning in the study area, the kinds of alternatives to be considered, and other issues of importance to local decision makers. An environmental impact statement may be incorporated into the corridor analysis or form part of subsequent steps. See Chapter 9 for more detail on MIS studies.

Corridor Studies

Highway (and multimodal) corridor feasibility studies are similar in many aspects to MIS investigations. Although the focus is on highway improvements, good practice for the more complex larger scale corridor studies gives at least initial consideration to multimodal options. Economic growth and development are important considerations in assessing project feasibility.

FHWA study guidelines include the following:[4,5] (Table 5–2.)

- Studies should include advisory or steering committees to review, counsel, and assist the study as appropriate; and they should include members from concerned agencies when required by the scope.

- Typical study tasks are defined with each task leading to defined products, key decisions, and interim or final reports.

- Rational criteria should be used to determine whether more costly studies (i.e., over $400,000) and those involving potential high-level investments should be continued. Termination decisions should be made when appropriate data become available, and such a decision point should be defined in study work programs.

- Feasibility is defined to encompass criteria based on economic, environmental or social, and financial evaluations.

- A wide range of alternatives should be given at least initial consideration. These should include alternatives advocated by interested groups and governments. Consideration of all alternatives should involve appropriate documentation and public information.

- Economic evaluations should follow accepted good practice and guidelines published by the Office of Management and Budget.

---

[4] *Procedural Guidelines for Highway Feasibility Studies* (Washington, D.C.: Federal Highway Administration, July 1995).

[5] *Examples of Good Practice Highway Corridors Feasibility Studies Final Report* (Sydec, Inc., June 1996).

- Environmental and social evaluations should follow accepted good practice and all applicable federal law and regulations.

- Interim reports and other appropriate products should be prepared on a timely basis during studies, be clear to the nontechnical reader, and be made widely available through various mechanisms.

Another type of corridor study focuses on traffic operations and management. The studies look at existing and future problems and needs. Proposals include roadway widening, provision of turn lanes, better traffic signal coordination, access management, land use controls to facilitate corridor management, and possible new routes.

Table 5–2 Illustrative Examples of Tasks Within a Comprehensive Corridor Study

A. A study of the feasibility of improving an existing facility

Task 1.   Compilation of existing conditions, history of previous studies, determinations and commitments by elected officials, documentation of prior input from the public, business officials and public officials

Task 2.   Travel Forecast(s), design and environmental considerations, and preliminary cost estimates of reasonably practical alternative improvements

Task 3.   Economic study of the benefits of alternative improvements, preliminary determination of economic justification and financial feasibility

Task 4a. Determination to terminate the study. Documentation of considerations.

　　　　　or

Task 4b. Engineering and environmental feasibility and refinement of costs and mitigation

　　　　　and

Task 5b. Draft report (including Executive Summary)

　　　　　and

Task 6b. Final Report (including Executive Summary)

In this example, one of two possible study processes would be followed. In one case, Task 4a. would be completed, in which case the study would terminate with this task. Otherwise, the study would continue with Tasks 4b., 5b. and 6b., which would be the completion of the study.

B. A study of the feasibility of major improvements to and/or development of a multi-state transportation corridor

Task 1.   Compilation of existing conditions, history of previous studies, determinations and commitments by elected officials, relevant legislation, documentation of prior input from the public, business officials and public officials

Task 2.   Documentation of procedures to be used in analysis

Task 3.   Evaluation of alternative modes, management strategies, design levels (including various levels of technology) and locations

Task 4.   Travel Forecasts, modal, management design and environmental considerations, and cost estimates of reasonably practical alternative improvements

Task 5.   Economic study of the benefits of alternative improvements, preliminary determination of economic justification and financial feasibility

Task 6a. Determination to terminate the study. Documentation of considerations

　　　　　or

Task 6b. Engineering and environmental feasibility and refinement of costs and mitigation

　　　　　and

Task 7b. Draft report (including Executive Summary)

　　　　　and

Task 8b. Final Report (including Executive Summary)

In this example, one of two possible study processes would be followed. In one case, Task 6a. would be the final task. Otherwise, the study would continue with Task 6b. and be completed with Tasks 7b. and 8b.

Source: *Procedural Guidelines for Highway Feasibility Studies,* Washington, D.C.: Federal Highway Administration, July 1995.

Central Area and Major Activity Center Studies

Studies are frequently conducted of the CBD or other major activity centers to identify existing and future needs and opportunities. They are often done by multidisciplined teams that include urban designers and economists as well as transportation professionals. Sometimes the goal is to achieve particular urban design objectives (e.g., a street closure or pedestrian plaza). In other cases, major redevelopment projects provide an opportunity for changes in the street and public transport systems.

The studies should be multimodal. They should consider the needs of motorists, pedestrians, transit passengers, taxis, and goods delivery and emergency services. They should include analyses of:

- The capacity, continuity, and convenience of the street system.

- Public transport routes, stops, and interchange facilities.

- Pedestrian circulation patterns and needs.

- Access to and from major transportation terminals.

- Locations and patterns of goods delivery and service vehicle movements.

- On- and off-street parking and loading requirements.

It is desirable to conduct a cordon count of people entering, leaving, and accumulated within the study area by time of day and mode of travel. This count is useful to determine the role and reliance of public and private transport. Parking supply, usage, and accumulation studies are also useful.

Recommendations typically include:

- Changes in street routings, traffic controls, and parking regulations.

- Revised transit routes and stops, including transit lanes, streets, and exemption from turn restrictions.

- Physical changes to the street and transit system (e.g., extensions, widenings, narrowings, closures).

- Central area parking plan and policy.

- Pedestrian circulation plan.

- Means for implementing and enforcing key proposals.

Chapter 15 contains more detail on central business districts (CBDs) and major activity center studies.

Traffic Access and Traffic Impact Studies

Traffic impact studies assess the transportation needs and traffic impacts of a development on the surrounding road net. They assist public agencies and private developers in making development and transportation decisions. They respond to a wide range of issues that include preliminary site plan review; obtaining driveway (access) permits; determining necessary roadway improvements; preparing an overall access management plan; and performing a comprehensive study of roadway, transit, pedestrian and environmental issues.

Context

Traffic impact studies project future transportation demands, describe the impact of the increased demands, and suggest ways of alleviating the adverse effects of new developments. The transportation demands are defined as the need for the movement of people and goods by all forms of transportation including autos, carpools, transit, taxi, trucks, and bicycles or as pedestrians in and near a proposed development. The development may be residential, office, commercial, or a combination of these.

Thus, the studies evaluate the changes and effects that result from new land development; and they prepare off-site and on-site transportation improvements to accommodate the additional travel and traffic and to ameliorate impacts. The studies are an integral part of the site development review process. They are specifically concerned with the site traffic generation, its allocation between public and private transport, and its directional distribution and assignment onto existing or future roadways. They identify public safety requirements and determine the transportation needs of the site and the surrounding road system.

The traffic (or transportation) impact study may be part of an environmental impact report or environmental impact assessment. The environmental studies are required for all public and many private developments. Traffic impact studies are essential for many access management decisions. Wherever possible, it is desirable to evaluate the combined impacts not only of the proposed development but also of other likely nearby developments along the major roadways. Thus, the typical "traffic impact study" for an individual development should be broadened by simultaneously assessing the collective impacts of many related developments. In all cases, access plans for a parcel must be integrated with access to adjacent properties or developments on opposite sides of the road, or within the proposed improvement area.

It is difficult to anticipate future land development in the environs of a planned project. One approach is to consider the impacts of those developments that (1) are under construction, (2) have received land use approvals, or (3) have submitted applications.

Need

The minimum traffic and parking thresholds for when traffic impact studies should be conducted vary among public agencies. The Institute of Transportation Engineers (ITE) has suggested that a complete traffic impact analyses should be performed for each of the following situations:[6]

1. All developments that can be expected to generate more than 100 new peak hour vehicle trips on the adjacent street or for a lesser volume when a review of the site plan indicates the need.

2. In some cases, a development that generates less than 100 new peak hour trips should require a traffic impact study or assessment if it affects local "problem" areas. These would include high accident locations, currently congested areas, or areas of critical local concern.

3. All applications for rezoning.

4. All applications for annexation.

5. Any change in the land use or density that will change the site traffic generation by more than 15 percent, where at least 100 new peak hour trips are involved.

6. Any change in the land use that will cause the directional distribution of site traffic to change by more than twenty percent.

---

[6] *Traffic Access and Impact Studies for Site Development, Proposed Recommended Practice* (Washington D.C.: Institute of Transportation Engineers, 1988).

7. When the original impact study is more than two years old, access decisions are still outstanding, and changes in development have occurred in the site environs.

8. Necessary development agreements to determine "fair share" contributions to major roadway improvements.

The use of a lower threshold (i.e., less than 100 new peak hour trips) minimizes the chance that developments will be approved without a study. Agencies that require lower thresholds may reduce the scope of the study.

Scope

The scope of traffic impact studies depends on the type, location, and scale of development. In activity centers, where walk-in and transit trips are common (or have potential), both total person trips and vehicular trips should be analyzed. This involves estimates of mode split and vehicle occupancy. The adequacy of the site plan for transit riders and pedestrians should be assessed.

The types of information needed to reach appropriate traffic and development decisions normally include the following: (1) characteristics of the existing roadway and public transport systems, (2) characteristics of proposed developments, (3) future development traffic, (4) composite traffic on surrounding and approach roads, (5) road system adequacy and needs, and (6) access plans.

The study should accurately analyze the impact of specific developments, the adequacy of site access, and the suitability of on-site circulation and parking. It should provide the following information to accurately gauge impacts, needs, and opportunities for change: (1) projections of traffic volumes on individual roadway segments, (2) projections of turn movements at individual intersections or access drives, (3) the effects of numerous access points along an arterial as opposed to only a few consolidated access points, (4) the effects of modest changes in land use on the location of individual land uses, and (5) pedestrian and transit access requirements.

Basic Assumptions

At the start of a study it is desirable to establish basic terms of reference with public agencies. These include: (1) methods of capacity and LOS analyses, (2) planning horizon years, (3) extent of study area, (4) time periods to analyze, and (5) travel modes to consider.

1. *Planning horizon year*—the horizon year should be consistent with the size and build-out schedule of the development and anticipated major transportation system changes. Suggested horizon years are given in Table 5–3. A good guide is to set the planning year 3 to 5 years hence, when the proposed development would operate at its target productivity.

2. *Study area*—the study area limits should be based upon the type of land use, size of development, street system patterns, and terrain. A frequently used method is to carry the analysis to locations where site-generated traffic will represent five percent or more of the roadway's peak hour approach capacity.

3. *Time periods*—the analyses should focus on the periods of the day when a normal "background" highway traffic is at a peak and when site traffic peaks. Thus, the analyses time periods generally will vary for residential, office, industrial, retail, and recreational developments.

Steps

The study content will depend on the type and size of the development and the prevailing traffic conditions. Although the specific guidelines established by public agencies may vary, each study should contain the following information:

1. *Introduction*—a brief description of (a) the purpose of the study; (b) the type and size of the proposed development; and (c) the site location within the general area, including a site location map.

2. *Analyze existing conditions*—existing land uses in the site environs, including their zoning and availability should be identified. Transit services and roadway characteristics in the site environs should be described. Existing volume-to-capacity ratios and service levels should be indicated.

3. *Analyze future conditions*—anticipated future traffic in the site environs should be estimated.

   a. Background highway traffic should be projected to the design year.

   b. Anticipated site population on a daily basis and during design hours should be developed, including modes of arrival and vehicle occupancies. These should be translated into vehicle trips entering and leaving the site during each design hour. A common source for trip generation rates is *Trip Generation,* Sixth Edition.[7] In some cases, local rates for similar uses should be utilized.

Table 5–3 Suggested Traffic Impact Study Horizon Years

Development Size	Suggested Horizon(s)
Small (generating less than 500 peak hour trips)	Anticipated opening year, assuming full buildout and occupancy).
Moderate single phase (500–1,000 peak hour trips)	1. Anticipated opening year, assuming the buildout and occupancy. 2. Adopted transportation plan horizon year if the development is significantly larger than that included in the adopted plan or in forecasts for the area.
Large, single phase (over 1,000 peak hour trips)	1. Anticipated opening year, assuming full buildout and occupancy. 2. Adopted transportation plan horizon year.
Moderate or large, multiple phase	1. Anticipated opening years of each major phase, assuming buildout and full occupancy of each phase. 2. Anticipated year of complete buildout and occupancy. 3. Adopted transportation plan horizon year. 4. Additional years when a major area transportation improvement is completed.

Source: *Traffic Access Impact Studies for Site Development,* Washington, D.C.: Institute of Transportation Engineers, 1988.

   c. The proportion of pass-by trips should be deducted from the generated traffic volumes—especially for uses such as service stations, convenience stores, and drive-through restaurants. However, all trips must be included in assessing specific impacts and needs such as turn lanes.

   d. Approach directions of site development traffic should be estimated. Table 5–4 gives guidance for establishing influence areas and deriving approach directions.

   e. Site traffic on each direction of approach and in the site environs should be calculated by relating the approach directions to the site volumes.

   f. Composite traffic volumes should be obtained for each analysis period by superimposing the site volumes on the normal background traffic for the design years.

   g. The capacity and LOS implications of the combined volumes on the surrounding and approach road system should be determined.

4. *Prepare improvement plans*—recommended transit, roadway, and pedestrian improvements for the site environs should be carefully coordinated with the site traffic plan. The adequacy of these plans should be clearly identified in terms of both safety and service levels. Typical changes include adding turn lanes, revising traffic signal sequences, and adding new signals. Where signals are within 3,000 feet of each other, a signal coordination plan should be prepared.

---

[7] *Trip Generation,* Sixth Edition (Washington, D.C.: Institute of Transportation Engineers, 1997).

Table 5–4 Information Needed for Determining Influence Area and Site Traffic Distribution

Land Use Activity	Factors for Determining Areas of Influence	Data Base Within the Area of Influence
Regional Shopping Center	1. Competing similar commercial developments 2. Travel time—usually a maximum of 30 minutes	Population distribution* (sometimes weighted by projected spendable income in the proposed center)
Community Shopping Center	1. Competing similar commercial developments 2. Travel time—usually a maximum of 20 minutes	Population distribution* (sometimes weighted by projected spendable income in the proposed center)
Industrial Park and Office Park	Travel time—usually a maximum of 30 minutes or a distance of 10–15 miles is assumed	Population distribution*
Stadium	Travel time—usually a maximum of 40 minutes or more, dependent on the size and character of the stadium	Population distribution* (sometimes weighted by travel time; i.e., the longer travel time is weighted less)
Residential	Travel time—usually a maximum of 30 to 45 minutes or a distance of 10 to 15 miles is assumed	Employment-opportunity disbribution*

* Projections of population and employment-opportunity data should be used for the design year if possible.

Source: Evanston, Ill.: The Traffic Institute, Northwestern University.

The proposed development should be examined for the adequacy of its entrances and exits; internal circulation system; provisions for service vehicles, delivery trucks, and emergency circulation; pedestrian and transit access; and parking supply. Appropriate adjustments should be made to improve the site plan and to minimize the effects on surrounding neighborhoods.

Project Report

The traffic and transportation impact study report should clearly document findings, recommendations, and conclusions. Technical details such as detailed LOS computations should be placed in an appendix. Table 5–5 outlines the elements of a comprehensive traffic impact report. This outline should be modified to reflect specific needs. Basic elements can be reformatted for compatibility with environmental impact reports as appropriate.

The report should present a picture of existing and projected traffic conditions, including traffic volumes, service levels and capacity analysis, and improvement recommendations. It should provide a discussion of traffic safety and accident implications; present an illustrative site and roadway plan, including public transport and pedestrian components; and should demonstrate the adequacy of the plan. It must contain a clear and concise summary of findings, recommendations and developer responsibilities.

Transportation System Management Studies

Transportation system management (TSM) studies provide a complement or alternative to longer range, capital-intensive focused studies. They emerged in the mid-1970s as a way of making better use of existing transportation resources. The joint 1975 FHWA/ Urban Mass Transportation Administration "Urban Planning Regulations" defined TSM as operating, regulatory, and service policies so as to achieve maximum efficiency and productivity for the system as a whole.[8] The intent was to improve the efficiency of the existing system by better managing transportation demand and supply. Key components include traffic engineering, freeway management (including ramp metering, priority access and lanes for high-occupancy vehicles, transit service improvements, parking management, and demand management). Demand management, which includes ride sharing, pricing policies, employee incentive programs, and automobile restraint, is sometimes treated as a separate "management" program.

The key steps in the TSM planning process flow out of the problems and objectives for any given situation. They include defining goals, analyzing the problem, identifying likely solutions, screening candidate actions, assessing performance

---

[8] "Transportation Improvement Program," *Federal Register,* 23CPR Part 450, Subparts A and C (Washington, D.C.: U.S. Department of Transportation, Federal Highway Administration, and Urban Mass Transportation Administration, September 17, 1978).

Table 5-5 Sample Table of Contents—Site Traffic Access Impact Study Report

I. Introduction and Summary
  A. Purpose of Report and Study Objectives
  B. Executive Summary
    1. Site location and study area
    2. Development description
    3. Principal findings
    4. Conclusions
    5. Recommendations
II. Proposed Development (Site and Nearby)
  Summary of Development
    1. Land use and intensity
    2. Location
    3. Site plan
    4. Zoning
    5. Phasing and timing
III. Area Conditions
  A. Study Area
    1. Area of influence
    2. Area of significant traffic impact (may also be part of Chapter IV)
  B. Study Area Land Use
    1. Existing land uses
    2. Existing zoning
    3. Anticipated future development
  C. Site Accessibility
    1. Area roadway system
      a. existing
      b. future
    2. Traffic volumes and conditions
    3. Transit service
    4. Existing relevant transportation system management programs
    5 Other as applicable
IV. Projected Traffic
  A. Site Traffic (each horizon year)
    1. Trip generation
    2. Trip disiribulton
    3. Modal split
    4. Trip assignment
  B. Through Traffic (each horizon year)

    1. Method of projection
    2. Non-site traffic for in study area
      a. Method of projections
      b. Trip generation
      c. Trip distribution
      d. Modal split
      e. Trip assignment
    3. Through traffic
    4. Estimated volumes
  C. Total Traffic (each horizon year)
V. Traffic Analysis
  A. Site Access
  B. Capacity and Level of Service
  C. Traffic Safety
  D. Traffic Signals
  E. Site Circulation and Parking
VI. Improvement Analysis
  A. Improvements to Accommodate Base Traffic
  B. Additional Improvements to Accommodate Site Traffic
  C. Alternative Improvements
  D. Status of Improvements Already Funded, Programmed, or Planned
  E. Evalution
VII. Findings
  A. Site Accessibility
  B. Traffic Impacts
  C. Need for any Improvements
  D. Compliance with Applicable Local Codes
VIII. Recommendations
  A. Site Access/Circulation Plan
  B. Roadway Improvements
    1. On-site
    2. Off-site
    3. Phasing, if appropriate
  C. Transportation System Management Actions
    1. Off-site
    2. On-site operational
    3. On-site
  D. Other
IX. Conclusions

Source: *Traffic Access and Impact Studies for Site Development*, Washington, D.C.: Institute of Transportation Engineers, 1988.

(benefits and impacts), refining or combining actions, developing and implementing improvements, and monitoring the program once implemented. See Chapter 19 for more details on TSM.

Description of Specific Methods

This section describes specific planning study methods, including (1) inventories, (2) roadway classification studies, (3) traffic volumes, (4) travel times and speeds, (5) capacity, (6) travel pattern surveys, and (6) trip generation.

Inventories

Inventories are basic building blocks of the transportation planning process. They obtain information on roadways, traffic controls, parking, public transport, and land use that can be placed in manual or automated data bases and then presented in a meaningful manner. They are useful in classifying roads and streets, providing a data base for traffic operations and comprehensive studies, and in systematically describing existing conditions. From a transport planning perspective, inventories are usually keyed to links in the transport system or planning analysis zones.

The type of information included depends on the purpose planned for its use. Some inventories have long shelf lives (i.e., the data remain constant and require little updating), while others contain information that changes rapidly over time. The latter inventories require frequent updating to maintain their currency and usability.

Inventories must be accessible to be useful. They may be filed in paper form or on electronic media (e.g., computers), portrayed on maps of the study area (or portions of the study area), or displayed on aerial photos. Photo logging may be useful in some instances using either film or videotape. No matter how the information is stored, its accessibility is of utmost importance. It does no good to have vast amounts of data if the crucial element is not readily available.

The general types of inventories are described in the following paragraphs. Again, the specific information that is collected in any inventory depends on the use that is going to be made of the data.

Roadway Inventories

Roadway inventories include information on the street and highway network that is open to the public within a given area. In some cases, data collection may be extended to private streets as well. The data collected may be related to street segments (blocks or block faces), mile posts, or intersections.

A considerable amount of basic roadway data can be coded into a standard computer record. Table 5–6 illustrates possible coding systems for links and intersections. Inventory components include classification and administration, geometric features, physical conditions, and traffic control devices.

1. *Classification and administration*—the functional class of each roadway (e.g., freeway, expressway, arterial, collector, local), the jurisdiction where the road is located, and the agencies responsible for maintenance should be identified. Guidelines for classifying roadways are detailed in section 5.3.2.

2. *Geometric features*—the basic geometry of the street and highway segments is one of the most common inventories collected. It includes the physical design features that influence roadway operations and may include any or all of the following items relative to current conditions: right-of-way, street width (curb to curb or traveled way), shoulder width, sidewalk width, medians (raised or traversable), lane widths and configurations, intersection definition, locations of railroad and light rail transit crossings, and any other elements that affect roadway operations (e.g., bike lanes and midblock pedestrian crossings). It also may include physical conditions such as grades, curvature, sight distances, locations of roadside obstacles, and other hazards.

   Some inventories also collect data on street lights. Even curb-cut locations are recorded in a very complete inventory. The geometric inventory, once completed, is relatively stable since changes in road geometry or new street development are relatively few. The inventory can remain current for many years if changes are incorporated as they occur.

   Intersections are usually inventoried separately because of the different data that are assembled. Geometric data including intersection layout and dimensions, approach lane configurations, crosswalks, channelizing islands, and the like are collected with accuracies to the nearest foot. Traffic controls (signals, signs, and markings) are also located. (The detailed traffic control inventory is discussed briefly under "Traffic Control Devices.")

   Many of the data are initially compiled from agency files. As-built plans, plat books, construction drawings, striping or marking plans, and other such items provide a wealth of information. Because these data sources are not always current, a field check is essential to verify the accuracy of the file data, complete the inventory and ensure an accurate data base.

   Aerial photography can be used effectively to inventory the geometrics and pavement markings of streets and intersections. Care should be taken to ensure that the air photos are reasonably current, and field checks must be made to obtain changes that have occurred since the photos were taken. Flying between 10:00 A.M. and

2:00 P.M. minimizes lower shadows, and flying in winter misses leafy street trees. Photo or video logging of roadway characteristics and features is increasingly used to update or verify aerial photography.

Once assembled, data should be recorded in an easily retrievable manner. Some data may be portrayed on area maps (e.g., number of lanes on streets); on arterial strip maps (rights-of-way, geometric features, striping and markings, etc.); or in paper files organized by street, route, or other designation. However, it is more common to store the inventory in computer files. A good data base program file can incorporate all of the inventory data and permit easy access to the information. Retrieval can be done by any combination of the factors that are included in the data base.

Another method of storing data is the use of Computer-Aided Drafting and Design or Geographic Information System programs. These computer programs have become "a way of life" in design and operations offices. They are also used as the basis for many transportation planning computer programs. Thus, they can provide the data storage medium as well as the primary input to the advanced transportation planning programs.

3. *Physical conditions*—physical features of the road system are usually inventoried in concert with geometric data collection. They include pavement conditions; locations of structures such as bridges, overpasses, underpasses, tunnels, and major culverts; and overhead structure clearances.

Pavements are classified by type depending on the material and construction of the roadbed. Condition is usually categorized into classes such as excellent, good, average, poor, and badly deteriorated. The data can be summarized and used in determining paving expenditures and in planning for future needs. Comprehensive

Table 5–6   Sample Computer Coding Formats for Link and Intersection Inventories

Column	Item	Codes
A. Sample computer coding for link inventory		
1–4	Link number	Identified by node ends
6	Number of lanes of moving traffic	Number used directly as code
7–8	Approach width	Width in feet used as code
11	Parking condition	1–Full-time prohibition;
		2–Part-time prohibition during peak hours:
		3–Part-time prohibition during other times;
		4–Parking permitted at all times
12–13	Type of facility	First digit: 1–major, 2–minor
		Second digit: 1–freeway, 2–arterial, 3–collector, 4–local
14–15	Speed limit	Limit in mph used as code
20–26	Bus routes on link	Numeric codes or bus route numbers
27–28	Bus stops on link	1–beginning of link, 2–midblock, 3–end of link
30–59	Lightposts on link	Six poles can be coded with a 5-digit serial number for each
60–61/62–66	Sign type/location	Midblock signs; sign type code from state MUTCD; location coded by number
67–68/69–73		of nearest lightpole
74–75/76–80		
B. Sample computer coding for intersection inventory		
1–2	Intersertion number	Use node number
4–7	Approach link	Use approach link number
8	Number of lanes on approach	Use number of lanes as code.
10	Bus stop on approach	1–near side, 2–far side, 3–none
11	Type of control on approach	1–none, 2–STOP, 3–YIELD. 4–flashing yellow, 5–flashing red, 6–signal
12/13–14	Signal phase type/length	Phase type: 1–leading green, 2–lagging green, 3–through only, 4–exclusive left,
15/16–17		5–through plus lefts. Use seconds of green plus yellow for time.
18/19–20		
21–37	Signal phases for three other approaches	As above
38–54		
55–71		
72–79	Other regulations	1–RTOR, 2–No LT, 3–No RT, 4–other

Source: McShane, W.R. and Roess, R.P., *Traffic Engineering,* Englewood Cliffs, N.J.: Prentice Hall, 1990.

national survey manuals[9,10] outline needed data for pavement management studies. Representative state manuals are those of California,[11] Illinois,[12] and New York.[13]

4. *Traffic control devices*—"traffic control devices are all signs, signals, markings, and devices placed on, over, or adjacent to a street or highway by authority of a public body or official having jurisdiction to regulate, warn, or guide traffic."[14] Inventories normally include the type of device, size, legend, and color combinations; authority for and date of installation; dates of replacement, relocation, or revision; records of outages; and condition of equipment. See Chapter 12 of the *Traffic Engineering Handbook* for more detail on traffic control devices.

Parking Inventories

Parking space inventories are mainly conducted for central or outlying business districts and for major activity centers such as universities and medical centers. The inventories generally collect information on:

- Number of legal and illegal parking spaces by location and type of facility (e.g., on-street, lot, or garage).

- Ownership of spaces (i.e., public or private).

- Availability of spaces (i.e., open to public or restricted).

- Time limit and hours of operation.

- Rates, including meter locations.

- Special curb-use regulations (truck, taxi, and passenger loading zones).

Parking inventories typically should be conducted in total, although in some jurisdictions a previous study can serve as a starting point. The inventory data are usually recorded in a computerized data base, although some material may be portrayed on maps or summarized in tables. Maps are useful for reports and general presentations. A computerized data base is valuable, and it can be readily updated as conditions change.

Transit Inventories

Transit system inventories should cover all public systems, including those providing specialized services for elderly, handicapped, and school children. They may include information on private services such as long-distance carriers; charter services; commuter services (club buses); and services provided by individual office buildings, commercial centers, or residential developments.

Transit systems vary in governance, size, and type. Their service may be provided by a single agency or by several agencies. They may include bus systems or multimodal systems that operate buses, street cars, light rail, rapid transit, commuter railroads, inclines, and ferries. Larger systems generally maintain inventories that are periodically updated.

Transit inventories for planning purposes include:

---

[9] *Pavement Conditions Rating Guide* (Washington, D.C.: U.S. Department of Transportation, Federal Highway Administration, May 1985).

[10] *Pavement Surface Conditions Rating Systems* (Ottawa, Canada: Roads and Transportation Association of Canada, 1987).

[11] California State Department of Transportation, *California Pavement Management System Raters Manual* (Sacramento, Calif.: Caltrans, Division of Highway Maintenance, 1989).

[12] *Condition Rating Survey-Raters Guide* (Springfield, Ill.: Illinois State Department of Transportation, 1989).

[13] *Pavement Conditions Rating Manual* (Albany, N.Y.: New York State Department of Transportation, 1984).

[14] Federal Highway Administration, *Manual on Uniform Traffic Control Devices for Streets and Highways* (Washington, D.C.: U.S. Government Printing Office).

- A description of various providers, including the number of vehicles owned and service areas of each.

- A description of routes by service type (e.g., commuter rail, rapid transit, light rail transit, local and express bus, paratransit).

- Locations and types of stations and stops, transfer points, layover points, and terminals.

- Locations and characteristics of park-and-ride facilities, including parking capacities and rates.

- Service frequencies and hours of operation.

- Fleet size characteristics including age, type, size, and condition of vehicles; and seated, "schedule design," and "crush" capacities.

- Locations of transit priority lanes, streets, or ramps.

See Chapter 13 for more information on public transport.

Roadway Classification

All streets and highways within any given area should be classified in the early stages of a transportation study. *Jurisdictional* and *functional* classifications are often done in conjunction with a geometric inventory of streets. An *access* classification may be done where access management programs and plans are contemplated.

Jurisdictional Classification

Roadways can be grouped by political jurisdiction (i.e., by community or county) and by the agencies that have primary and secondary jurisdictional responsibility for their maintenance and operation (i.e., state, county, local).

Functional Classification

Transportation facilities in states, planning regions, and individual communities are normally classified according to the basic functions that they perform. The classification of roads and streets requires determining the degree to which land access functions should be (1) emphasized at the cost of the efficiency of movement or (2) discouraged to improve the movement function. Similarly, for transit networks, express routes primarily serve long-distance trips, while local routes provide more service to adjacent land uses.

The entire road system is traditionally classified by relating the proportion of through-movement to the proportion of access such as shown in Figure 5–2. In this hierarchy of highway facilities, the freeways, expressways, and major arterials constitute the major highway system; while collector and local streets comprise the local street system. Some organizations include collector streets in the major street category, leaving only local streets in the minor street system. Minor streets may be further subdivided into residential, commercial, and industrial streets. Public transport and pedestrian requirements may influence the roadway classification. Further details concerning concepts criteria and procedures can be found in *Highway Functional Classification*.[15]

Access Classification

An access classification system forms the basis for an access management policy. It defines (1) where access can be allowed between proposed developments and public highways and where access should be denied or discouraged; (2) where access should be limited to right turns into and out of the driveways leading to or from activity centers; and (3) where provisions, if any, should be made for left turns into and out of connecting driveways. It correlates the allowable access with a roadway's purpose and importance, functional characteristics, design features, and access spacing standards.[16]

---

[15] U.S. Department of Transportation, Federal Highway Administration, *Highway Functional Classification Concepts, Criteria, and Procedures* (Washington, D.C.: U.S. Government Printing Office, 1974).

[16] Koepke, F. J. and Levinson, H.S., *Access Management Guidelines for Activity Centers*, NCHRP Report 348 (Washington, D.C.: Transportation Research Board, National Research Council, 1992).

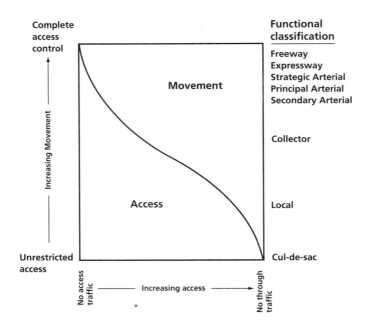

Figure 5–2 Relationship Between Access and Movement Functions of Streets and Highways

Source: Koepke, F.J. and Levinson, H.S., *Access Management Guidelines for Activity Centers*, NCHRP Report 348, Washington, D.C.: Transportation Research Board, National Research Council, 1992.

The classification is keyed to the functional classification system—but it takes into account existing and potential land developments. It can be done on a statewide, county, or municipal basis. It should be easy to understand and simple to apply.

Traffic and Travel Volumes

Traffic volume studies obtain information on the movement of vehicles on sections of the street or highway system. When vehicle occupants and public transport passengers are counted, information on the movement of people is obtained.

Information may be obtained for intervals of 5 minutes, 15 minutes, 30 minutes, one hour, one day, one week, or the entire year on the number of vehicles (or people) passing across a point or through an intersection. Counts may be classified by vehicle type, number of occupants, and direction of travel. They may include transit passengers and pedestrians. They may be performed by "automatic" (mechanical) or manual means.

Types of Traffic Volume Information

Traffic volume counts are expressed in relation to specific time periods. The base depends upon the type of information that is desired and its application. Transportation planning studies normally focus on longer time periods while traffic operations studies generally require peak hour or peak 15 minute periods. In a long-range planning context, traffic volume information is useful for validating travel patterns and demand models, as well as for providing inputs for capacity-restrained traffic assignments.

1. *Annual traffic*—the annual traffic represents the estimated or actual volume for an entire year. It is used to determine the annual traffic in a given geographic area; to establish trends in volume that can be related to future traffic growth; and to estimate highway user revenue—especially for toll roads, bridges, and tunnels. Annual traffic, when related to the distances involved, can be used to determine annual VKT or vehicle-miles of travel (VMT), which can be useful in computing accident rates and in assessing safety.

2. *Average daily traffic*—average daily traffic (ADT) or annual average daily traffic (AADT) volumes are used to measure the existing demand for service on the streets and highways in a study area. This permits an evaluation of the traffic flow with respect to the road system and the establishment of a major or arterial street network. These volumes are used to locate areas where new roads or improvements to existing roads are needed. ADT volumes are also used to prepare benefit-cost analyses to and to program capital improvements.

3. *Hourly traffic volumes*—hourly traffic flows in vehicles per hour are commonly used in traffic engineering studies. They are useful in planning studies to validate models. Information on vehicle types and turning movements help to assess existing (or future) traffic performance.

4. *Short-term counts*—short counts covering 5, 6, 10, 12, or 15 minute intervals are useful in determining peak flow rates, establishing flow variations within the peak hour, and identifying capacity limitations.

5. *Traffic density*—density (vehicles per lane per km or per mile) is obtained by dividing the hourly volume by the average speed. It is considered a better measure of street service than volume for uninterrupted flow along freeways, expressways, and major arterials. Density continues to increase as congestion increases, while volume reaches a maximum under moderate congestion and then decreases as congestion increases. Should a full stoppage occur, density is at its maximum while volume goes to zero.

Average Daily Traffic Counts

Average daily traffic and annual average daily traffic are usually obtained through machine counts. They count total volume without regard to direction or by direction. Two separate directional counts at the same location can be summed to obtain a total street count. Twenty-four hour counts are used to develop traffic flow maps, determine trends, and so on. Directional counts are used for capacity analyses, planning improvements, obtaining accumulations within a cordon, area, and other such purposes.

Counts are generally obtained by mechanical traffic counters. These counters use tubes and air switches or permanently located detector sensors (such as inductive loops or magnetometers) and appropriate detector electronic units. Nonreading counters may be used to obtain the 24-hour counts, although recording counters are frequently used. The *Manual of Transportation Engineering Studies*[17] contains further details on counting daily traffic.

Many states and cities have established generalized monthly and daily factors for various types of roads. Table 5–7 gives illustrative factors used by the Connecticut Department of Transportation for adjusting 24-hour traffic counts for a given day to annual average daily traffic. The 24-hour count given on a given day in a given month is multiplied by the appropriate factor in this table to obtain the AADT. Obviously, the appropriate "facility type" should be selected in applying such factors.

Many traffic counting programs can be developed depending on an agency's budget, personnel, and equipment available. All require the functional designation of the street system as a first step. Then, a series of major control stations are located to sample the traffic movement on the major street system. It is desirable to have at least one control station located on each freeway and major street. The minimum recommended duration and frequency of counting is a 24-hour directional machine count every second year.

Selected control stations, called key count stations, are used to obtain daily and seasonal variations in traffic volumes. At least one key count station should be selected from each class of street in both the major and minor systems. Key count stations are counted for one continuous week each year and for one 24-hour weekday each month. These counts provide adjustment factors to be used with coverage counts (below) to put volumes on a common basis.

Coverage counts are used to estimate ADTs throughout the street system. Major streets are divided into segments with uniform traffic conditions. A 24-hour, nondirectional count is made in each segment. The count is adjusted using the factors developed from the appropriate key count station to obtain the estimated ADT. Counts are normally repeated every four years, but changes in traffic may dictate more frequent recounts. In the minor street system, one 24-hour,

---

[17] Institute of Transportation Engineers, *Manual of Transportation Engineering Studies* (Englewood Cliffs, N.J.: Prentice Hall, 1994).

Table 5–7 Factors for Expanding 24-Hour Counts to Annual Average Daily Traffic Volumes — Connecticut (Based on 1994 and 1995 Continuous Count Station Data)

Group 1 — Urban
Station(s): 7, 12, 14, 24, 26, 30, 31, 32, 45, 49, 53, 54, 55 (13 Stations)

	Avg. Weekday	Friday	Saturday	Sunday
January	1.07	0.97	1.27	1.51
February	1.06	0.91	1.19	1.33
March	1.02	0.89	1.15	1.25
April	0.97	0.85	1.12	1.22
May	0.94	0.82	1.02	1.12
June	0.92	0.80	1.05	1.11
July	0.92	0.80	1.01	1.07
August	0.90	0.80	0.98	1.04
September	0.94	0.82	1.03	1.11
October	0.95	0.82	1.09	1.10
November	0.97	0.86	1.09	1.20
December	0.97	0.89	1.13	1.32

Group 2 — Rural
Station(s): 4, 10, 13, 16, 20, 50, 51 (7 Stations)

	Avg. Weekday	Friday	Saturday	Sunday
January	1.09	1.03	1.20	1.54
February	1.10	0.98	1.12	1.33
March	1.06	0.97	1.10	1.25
April	0.98	0.89	1.01	1.14
May	0.94	0.85	0.91	1.03
June	0.90	0.80	0.89	1.00
July	0.89	0.82	0.91	1.01
August	0.90	0.82	0.90	0.99
September	0.95	0.86	0.96	1.06
October	0.96	0.87	1.04	1.13
November	0.99	0.92	1.04	1.27
December	1.00	0.93	1.10	1.30

Group 3 — Interstate
Station(s): 27 (I-84 from Rte. 195 to Mass. State Line (1 Station)

	Avg. Weekday	Friday	Saturday	Sunday
January	1.53	1.11	1.42	1.34
February	1.54	1.01	1.19	1.01
March	1.36	0.93	1.20	0.92
April	1.26	0.89	1.09	0.85
May	1.18	0.77	0.86	0.75
June	1.08	0.72	0.89	0.71
July	1.02	0.68	0.78	0.67
August	0.94	0.64	0.70	0.63
September	1.17	0.77	0.92	0.73
October	1.18	0.76	1.00	0.72
November	1.29	0.87	1.02	0.84
December	1.34	0.99	1.23	1.12

Source: Connecticut Department of Transportation, Bureau of Policy and Planning—Planning Inventory and Data, Traffic Monitoring and Data Analysis Section.

nondirectional count should be taken for each 1.6 km (1 mile) of street. Counts are repeated when local circumstances indicate a need. Coverage counts can be made with nonrecording counters because only the 24-hour total volume is needed.

Traffic volume graphs are sometimes prepared to show the monthly, daily, and hourly traffic variations at a given location. Figure 5–3 (a), (b), and (c) each give an example of such a graph.

Table 5–7 Factors for Expanding 24-Hour Counts to Annual Average Daily Traffic Volumes — Connecticut (Based on 1994 and 1995 Continuous Count Station Data) *(continued)*

Group 4 — Urban
Station(s): 2, 5, 8, 9, 11, 15, 17 19, 22, 23, 25, 52 (12 Stations)

	Avg. Weekday	Friday	Saturday	Sunday
January	1.03	0.96	1.17	1.54
February	1.03	0.93	1.15	1.42
March	1.00	0.92	1.12	1.35
April	0.94	0.86	1.05	1.28
May	0.90	0.82	0.97	1.20
June	0.89	0.82	1.02	1.22
July	0.92	0.84	1.05	1.24
August	0.93	0.86	1.01	1.20
September	0.93	0.85	1.02	1.26
October	0.91	0.82	1.04	1.22
November	0.94	0.86	1.04	1.33
December	0.94	0.87	1.06	1.29

Group 5 — Recreational
Station(s): 1, 18 (2 Stations)

	Avg. Weekday	Friday	Saturday	Sunday
January	1.61	1.21	1.29	1.19
February	1.57	1.05	1.02	1.02
March	1.48	1.10	1.13	0.95
April	1.30	0.96	0.87	0.75
May	1.20	0.89	0.77	0.63
June	1.09	0.74	0.76	0.59
July	0.99	0.68	0.60	0.48
August	0.94	0.68	0.62	0.47
September	1.14	0.83	0.83	0.62
October	1.17	0.83	1.14	0.59
November	1.39	1.00	1.04	0.95
December	1.49	1.19	1.23	1.27

Group 6 — Interstate
Station(s): 33, 44 (I-95 from Rte. 9 to RI State Line (2 Stations)

	Avg. Weekday	Friday	Saturday	Sunday
January	1.25	1.11	1.28	1.48
February	1.25	1.01	1.19	1.31
March	1.18	0.99	1.12	1.14
April	1.09	0.89	1.07	1.02
May	1.05	0.83	0.92	0.99
June	0.96	0.78	0.87	0.86
July	0.88	0.71	0.74	0.77
August	0.84	0.68	0.70	0.73
September	1.03	0.82	0.91	0.91
October	1.06	0.85	1.06	0.97
November	1.11	0.93	1.05	1.12
December	1.12	0.98	1.18	1.30

Source: Connecticut Department of Transportation, Bureau of Policy and Planning—Planning Inventory and Data, Traffic Monitoring and Data Analysis Section.

Hourly Counts

Hour-by-hour traffic counts by direction of travel can be made for 12, 18, or 24-hour time periods by recording counters. Volumes are recorded in either 15-minute or hourly intervals by printing on paper tape, punching or encoding on machine-readable tape, or recording electronically for subsequent insertion in a personal computer. Machine-readable tapes are usually converted into computer input as well. The computer data can be summarized in many different forms depending on the ultimate use. See the *Manual of Transportation Engineering Studies*[18] for further details.

---

[18] Ibid.

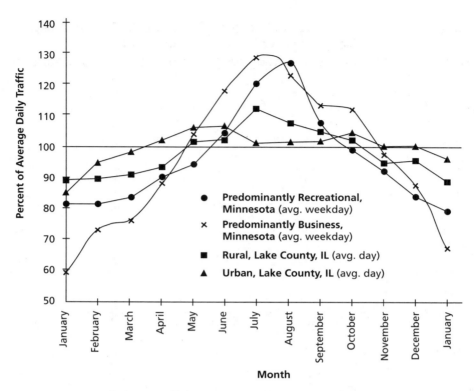

Figure 5–3(a) Monthly Traffic Variations

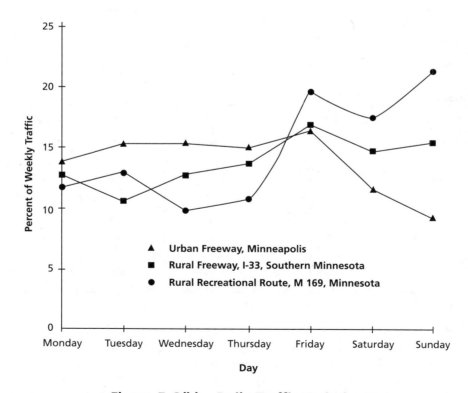

Figure 5–3(b) Daily Traffic Variations

Source: *Highway Capacity Manual*, Special Report 209, Third Edition, Transportation Research Board, National Research Council, Washington, D.C., 1997.

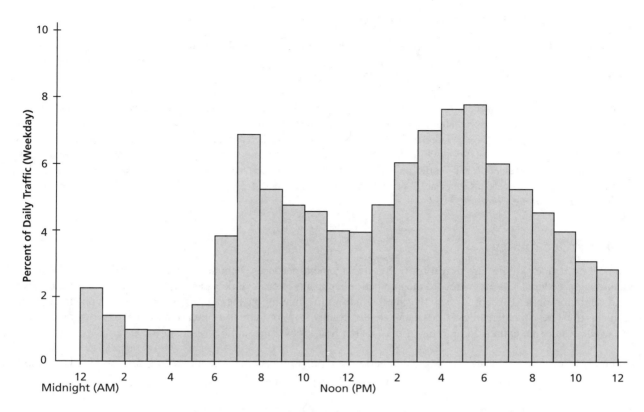

Figure 5–3(c)   Typical Weekday Hourly Traffic Variations (Typical Urban Freeway)

Source: Wilbur Smith Associates.

Manual traffic counts are widely used to obtain hour-by-hour variations in traffic flows, traffic composition, turning movements, and pedestrians. This information is used to define the duration and intensity of peak periods, to evaluate street capacity deficiencies, to assess the need for various traffic controls, to develop street designs, and to determine the effects of new developments on changed land uses. They also provide inputs for traffic model validation.

To avoid the high costs associated with turning movement counts, sample "short" counts are sometimes used. One method is to count each approach for a definite time period (e.g., 5 to 10 minutes per hour). Where intersections are close to each other, it is possible to sample count each intersection on a rotating basis. Counts should be done on a per signal cycle basis rather than for specified time periods. These methods should be used only when traffic conditions are relatively constant throughout the study period. Peak hour volumes of 800 or more vehicles per hour can be estimated within ±10 percent relative error with 68 percent confidence with short counts of 7 minutes per hour.[19]

Hourly variation patterns vary within and among communities. Values commonly found include:

Time	Percent of Daily Traffic
7:00 A.M. – 7:00 P.M.	65–70
8:00 A.M. – 6:00 P.M.	50
Peak hour (2 direction)	6–10
Peak hour (one-way)	4–7.5

---

[19] Adapted from Votaw, D. F. and Levinson, H.S., *Elementary Sampling for Traffic Engineers* (Saugatuck, Conn.: Eno Foundation for Traffic Control, 1962).

Vehicle-Kilometers (or Vehicle-Miles)

The amount of travel on a road system can be estimated by multiplying the daily (or annual) traffic volume on each section or link by its length. The estimates should be done separately for freeways and other roads. Where peak-hour traffic counts (or flow maps) are available, peak hour VKT (or VMT) can be estimated.

In urban areas, sampling procedures can be used to estimate daily VKT of travel. The road system should at minimum be classified by freeways, arterial streets, and local streets. Where possible, freeways should be further stratified by lanes or ADTs, and arterials should be grouped in 5,000-vehicle classes. Stratified random sampling procedures should be utilized taking into account the spatial, temporal, link length, and similar variations to obtain a composite variance for each class. Freeways and arterial street VKT should be estimated within ±5 percent relative error and local street VKT should be estimated within ±25 percent, both at 95 percent confidence. Procedures and parameters are detailed in the *Guide to Urban Traffic Volume Counting.*[20]

Vehicle Occupancy

Vehicle occupancy studies are useful for traffic management purposes. Vehicle occupancies are obtained by manual counting procedures. Observers record the number of occupants in each vehicle passing a given point. This is relatively easy for automobiles (except for heavily tinted windows in some limousines), vans, and trucks. Occupancy of transit vehicles must be estimated unless the transit vehicle actually stops or there is a concurrent transit passenger study under way. The results are expressed in terms of persons per hour or average number of persons per vehicle.

Vehicle occupancy at a location can be estimated by sampling procedures. The number of days of data collection for the time period under concern can be obtained by the following equation:

$$n = \frac{Z^2 \left(S_1^2 + S_2^2 + S_3^2 \right)}{E^2}$$

(5–1)

Where:

E	=	Allowable error or tolerance
S_1	=	Standard deviation of average occupancy across days in a single season
S_2	=	Standard deviation of average occupancy among seasons
S_3	=	Standard deviation of average occupancy across time periods during a day (time period of concern) at a location
n	=	Number of counts at a location
Z	=	Standard Normal Variate

Typical values of these standard deviations are as follows:

S_1	=	0.063
S_2	=	0.015
S_3	=	0.017

Further details on procedures and applications are contained in the *Guide for Estimating Urban Vehicle Classification and Occupancy.*[21]

---

[20] Ferlis, R. A., Bowman, L.A. and Cima, B. T., Peat Marwick Mitchell Company, *Guide to Urban Traffic Volume Counting Final Report* (Washington, D.C.: Federal Highway Administration, 1980).

[21] Ferlis R. A., Peat Marwick Mitchell Company, *Guide for Estimating Urban Vehicle Classification and Occupancy* (Washington, D.C.: Federal Highway Administration, March 1981).

Screenline Counts

A screenline is an imaginary line that bisects a planning area. The line is usually drawn along natural boundaries such as rivers, escarpments, or railroad rights-of-way to minimize the number of vehicular crossings and, therefore, the number of counting stations needed. Screenline counts are used in conjunction with origin-destination studies to expand volume data or to check the accuracy of origin-destination trip tables. Trip table crossings of the screenline are aggregated and compared to the actual ground counts at the screenline. The total trip tables are then adjusted to reconcile the differences.

Screenline counts are also used to help calibrate travel demand models and to detect trends or long-term changes in volume and direction of traffic due to significant changes in population land use, commercial and business activity, and travel patterns. In some situations, it is not necessary to count all crossings of the screenline as long as it is certain that traffic is not diverted to uncounted crossings. Counts may be made every year or every second year. They should be made on an hourly basis, to allow hour-by-hour comparisons with origin-destination data.

In some situations, especially where there may be considerable transit use, the number of people crossing the screenline can be counted.

Cordon Counts

Cordon counts are made by direction of travel around the perimeter of an enclosed "study area." The study area may be an entire urbanized area, a transportation study area, a city, a CBD, a neighborhood, an industrial area, or any other definable planning area.

The counts determine the number of vehicles and people entering, leaving, and accumulated within the cordon area by mode of travel and time of day (including pedestrians and bicyclists). Vehicles are classified by type—bicycles, automobiles, light trucks, heavy trucks, carpools, taxis, buses, light rail transit, rapid transit, and commuter rail trains. Vehicle occupancies are determined for each vehicle type and travel mode. Some agencies do not include truck drivers in their summaries of person movement. The counts may cover a full 24-hour period (particularly when recording counters are used), but more frequently they cover 16 hours (5:30 A.M. to 9:30 P.M. or 6:00 A.M. to 10:00 P.M.) or 12 hours (7:00 A.M. to 7:00 P.M.).

When counts are made around the city center or outlying activity center, it is desirable to estimate the number of people and vehicles that are already accumulated within the cordon area. This is especially important when the counts do not start before 7:00 A.M.

CBD cordon counts are often used to measure the transportation activity generated by the CBD. These counts are repeated on an annual or biennial basis to evaluate trends or changes in activity within the CBD. They are useful in identifying the roles and importance of various transport modes and in establishing transport policy. Results are summarized in graphic and tabular form to indicate daily and peak hour person movements, vehicle movements and occupancies by travel mode and vehicle occupancy, and accumulation of people by mode of travel throughout the day (an example is shown in Figure 5–4). An important planning use of the CBD cordon count is to compare public transport ridership projections with actual cordon crossings as part of a reasonableness check of ridership forecasts.

Future Traffic Volumes

Volumes are projected into the future by using past trends and extrapolating into the future; by using past growth rates; by detailed analyses of trip generation, trip distribution, modal split, and traffic assignment; or by a combination of these methods. In traffic impact studies, where the effect of a specific development on future volumes is the crucial issue, trip generation becomes a vital factor. Peak hour traffic is the important element since it defines the transportation requirements (i.e., demand) that are compared to the present and proposed transportation facilities (i.e., supply). This comparison determines the ability of the facilities to meet the demands imposed in the future.

Projections of future traffic on a new facility built to serve a specific new development (whether residential, industrial, or commercial) depend heavily on trips generated by the new development. New facilities that are built to augment the

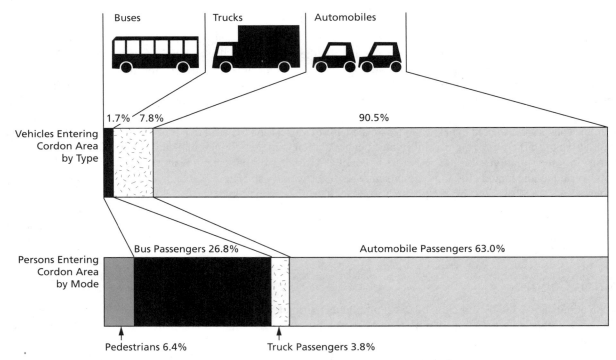

Figure 5–4(a)   Classification of Vehicles and Mode of Transportation Entering Cordon Area, May 1980, Los Angeles (Weekday)

Source: Los Angeles, Calif: Department of Transportation.

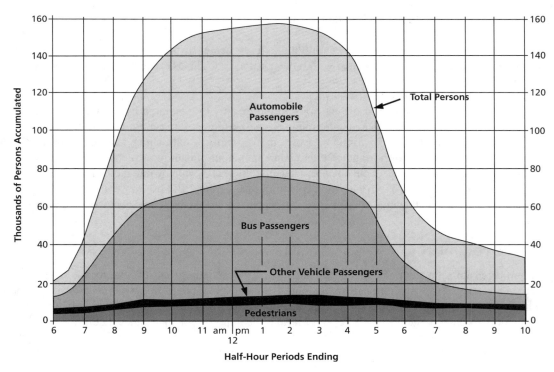

Figure 5–4(b)   Persons Accumulated in Cordon Area, May 1980, Los Angeles

Source: Los Angeles, Calif: Department of Transportation.

capacity in a corridor must be analyzed in a different manner; projections must include estimates of diverted traffic from existing facilities and induced traffic because of the increased capacity, as well as traffic generated by the land uses to be served. For freeways and major arterials, this may involve an iterative process that considers major developments that may locate near key interchanges.

In comprehensive planning studies, a travel forecasting model may be used. Such models are based on current travel behavior patterns and are validated by comparing current forecasts with actual traffic counts. Travel forecasting models involve complex mathematical formulations. They either estimate street traffic and transit use directly from the urban development forecasts or utilize the four-step process of trip generation, trip distribution, modal split, and traffic assignment. These models are discussed in greater detail in Chapters 6 and 12. Traffic volume forecasting techniques are also contained in most transportation planning texts; particularly valuable are *Urban Transportation Planning*,[22] Wright's *Highway Engineering*,[23] and *An Introduction to Urban Travel Demand Forecasting: A Self-instructional Text*.[24]

Capacity Studies

The capacity of a transportation facility reflects its ability to accommodate a moving stream of people or vehicles. It is a measure of the supply side of transportation. LOS is a measure of the quality of flow. The *Highway Capacity Manual* defines capacity as "the hourly rate at which persons or vehicles can reasonably be expected to traverse a point or section of a lane or roadway during given time period under prevailing conditions."[25]

Purpose

Capacity and LOS estimates are needed for most transportation planning and traffic engineering decisions. They address questions such as the following:

- What is the quality of service provided by an existing facility during peak periods, and how much traffic increase can be tolerated?

- What will be the future LOS on an existing or planning facility?

- What is the maximum number of people or vehicles that can be accommodated within a specified time period on a facility or within a corridor?

- What types of roadway or transit facilities are needed to accommodate a given level of person or vehicle flow?

- What lane configurations are needed for various levels of ADT on freeways or arterial roads?

- What highway or street designs (and hence capacities) are needed to serve a planned development?

- How many buses or railcars are needed to serve peak direction flow at a maximum load point; and can these transit vehicles be passed through the busiest station or other point of constriction, both now and in the future?

- How wide must the sidewalk on a street with high pedestrian activity be, and what holding space at street corners of a signalized intersection is needed?

Chapter 7 contains an overview of the 1994 *Highway Capacity Manual*.[26]

---

[22] Meyer, Michael D. and Miller, Eric J., *Urban Transportation Planning A Decision Oriented Approach* (New York: McGraw-Hill, 1984).

[23] Wright, Paul H., *Highway Engineering,* 5th Edition (New York: John Wiley & Sons, 1987).

[24] *An Introduction to Urban Travel Demand Forecasting—A Self Instructional Text* (Washington, D.C.: Federal Highway Administration and Urban Mass Transportation Administration, 1977).

[25] *Highway Capacity Manual Special Report 209* (Washington, D.C.: Transportation Research Board, National Research Council, 1994).

[26] Ibid.

Precision Considerations

The need for precision in determining capacity estimates depends upon the anticipated use of the data. Capacity estimates by link for demand modeling or air quality purposes generally require greater precision than estimates for establishing transport policy or lane requirements.

The results of capacity computations can only be as precise as the information or data used as inputs to the analyses. Actual traffic counts often have error rates of ±5 to 10 percent, while traffic projections twenty years in the future may have much larger errors. Most planning analyses use traffic projections that have a wide variance. Therefore, tabulated data should generally be rounded to the nearest fifty vehicles per hour, consistent with the guidelines in the *Highway Capacity Manual* (HCM).

In some situations, as in producing initial estimates of a regional road systems' adequacy or in setting lane requirements for a new development, simplified capacity procedures can provide initial inputs.

- The AADT per lane per day provides a broad-gauged guide to estimating roadway adequacy or lane requirements—when 25,000 AADT per freeway lane and 10,000 AADT per arterial lane are exceeded, additional capacity is usually needed.

- Critical lane analysis can be used to provide initial estimates of lane requirements for a new development. Conflict volumes that exceed 1,400 vehicles per hour (vph) generally exceed capacity; conflict volumes from 1,200-1,400 "approach capacity;" and those less than 1,200 vph are "under capacity." Shared through-and-left turn lanes can be assumed to be equivalent of 0.3 to 0.6 through-lanes. The basic data required for such an analysis include the number and use of lanes on each approach to the intersection and volumes (in vph) for each movement.

These and other alternatives to HCM procedures should be used only for initial planning. As more information is obtained, the HCM procedures should be utilized.

Travel Time Studies

Travel time and delay studies are among the most basic and important transportation analyses. The following sections describe their uses, nature, measurement, and application. More detailed procedures and guidelines can be found in the *Manual of Transportation Engineering Studies*[27] and in *Quantifying Congestion*.[28]

Uses

Travel time studies have a wide range of uses and application. Representative uses and applications in specific studies are shown in Table 5–8. They provide measures of a facility's or a system's performance and levels of service. They help to assess the adequacy of existing and proposed facilities, make traffic control and physical changes, and conduct economic assessments of proposals. They provide inputs to trip distribution, mode split, traffic assignment, and mode choice models. They also define markets for businesses, and when conducted on a periodic basis they quantify changes in mobility and congestion.

Basic Concepts

Travel time-related concepts include the following:

---

[27] Institute of Transportation Engineers, *Manual of Transportation Engineering Studies* (Englewood Cliffs, N.J.: Prentice Hall, 1994).

[28] Lomax T., Turner S., Shunk G., Levinson H.S., Pratt R. H., and Douglas G.B., *NCHRP Report 398 Quantifying Congestion* (Washington, D.C.: Transportation Research Board, National Research Council, 1997).

Table 5–8   Cross-Classification of Uses of Travel Time Congestion Measures

Uses	Monitoring & Needs Studies	Design & Operations Analyses	Evaluation of Alternatives	TDM, TSM, TCP, & Policy Studies	Development Impact Evaluations	Route & Travel Choice	Education
Identification of problems	X	X	X	X	X	X	X
Basis for government action/ investment/policies	X	X	X	X	X		X
Prioritization of improvements	X		X	X			X
Information for private sector decisions	X	X	X	X	X	X	X
Basis for national, state, regional policies and programs	X			X	X		X
Assessment of traffic controls, geometrics, regulations, improvements		X	X				X
Assessment of transit routing, scheduling, stop placement		X	X				X
Base case (for comparison with improvement alternatives)	X	X	X	X	X	X	X
Inputs for transportation models		X	X	X	X	X	X
Inputs for air quality and energy models		X	X	X	X		X
Measures of effectiveness for alternatives evaluation		X	X	X	X	X	X
Measures of land development impact				X	X		X
Input to zoning decisions					X		X
Basis for real-time choice decisions						X	X

Source: T. Lomax, S. Turner, G. Shunk, H.S. Levinson, R.H. Pratt, and G.B. Douglas. *Quantifying Congestion*, Vol. 1 Final Report and Vol. 2 User's Manual, Report 398, Washington, D.C.: Transportation Research Board, National Research Council, 1997.

- *Portal-to-portal travel time* is the total time spent in traveling from one place to another. It includes in-vehicle time (time actually spent traveling) and out-of-vehicle time (time spent waiting for transit ride transferring from one vehicle to another, and time spent walking between the vehicle and the origin and destination at both ends of the trip).

- *Travel time* is the time taken by a vehicle to traverse a given segment of street or highway. It includes running time, the time a vehicle is spent in motion and delay, and the time lost in traffic because of traffic control devices (fixed delay) and traffic frictions (operational delay). For public transport, dwell times at stops constitutes a major source of delay.

- *Congestion* is travel time or delay in excess of that normally incurred under light- to free-flow travel conditions. Unacceptable congestion is travel time or *delay* in excess of an agreed upon norm. This norm may vary by type of transportation facility, travel mode, geographic location, and time of day.

- *Mobility* is the ability of people and goods to move quickly, easily, and cheaply to where they are destined (e.g., how far one can travel in thirty minutes).

- *Accessibility* is the achievement of travel objectives within time limits regarded as acceptable.

Estimating Travel Times

Travel times (and delays) should be obtained by direct measurement wherever possible. Methods include test vehicles, license plate matching, aerial photography, interviews, probe vehicles, induction loops, and traffic reporting services. Surrogate prediction methods should be used to estimate future travel times (or changes resulting from improvements).

Where future speed and travel time estimates are required for existing roadways, surrogate travel speed estimates should be obtained for both the existing and future conditions. These estimates should then be combined with the directly collected travel speeds for existing conditions as follows:

Table 5–9 Summary of Selected Travel Time and Congestion Measures

Travel Rate	Travel Rate (minutes per km)	$= \dfrac{\text{Travel Time (minutes)}}{\text{Segment Length (km)}} = \dfrac{60}{\text{Average Speed (kph)}}$
Delay Rate	Delay Rate (minutes per km)	$= \dfrac{\text{Actual Travel Rate}}{\text{(minutes per km)}} - \dfrac{\text{Acceptable Travel Rate}}{\text{(minutes per km)}}$
Total Delay	Total Segment Delay (vehicle – minutes)	$= \left[\begin{array}{c} \text{Actual} \\ \text{Travel Time} \\ \text{(minutes)} \end{array} - \begin{array}{c} \text{Acceptable} \\ \text{Travel Time} \\ \text{(minutes)} \end{array} \right] \times \begin{array}{c} \text{Vehicle Volume} \\ \text{(vehicles)} \end{array}$
Corridor Mobility Index	Corridor Mobility Index	$= \dfrac{\text{Passenger Volume (persons)} \times \text{Average Travel Speed (kph)}}{\substack{\text{Normalizing Value} \\ \text{(e.g., 25,000 for streets, 125,000 for freeways)}}}$
Relative Delay Rate	Relative Delay Rate	$= \dfrac{\text{Delay Rate}}{\text{Acceptable Travel Rate}}$
Delay Ratio	Delay Ratio	$= \dfrac{\text{Delay Rate}}{\text{Actual Travel Rate}}$
Congested Travel	Congested Travel (vehicle – km)	$= \text{Sum of all} \left(\begin{array}{c} \text{Congested} \\ \text{Segment Length} \\ \text{(km)} \end{array} \times \begin{array}{c} \text{Traffic Volume} \\ \text{(vehicle)} \end{array} \right)$
Congested Roadway	Congested Roadway (km)	$= \dfrac{\text{Sum of all Congested Segment Lengths}}{\text{(km)}}$
Accessibility	Accessibility (opportunities)	$= \sum \begin{array}{c} \text{Objective fulfillment opportunities (e.g., jobs),} \\ \text{where Travel time} \leq \text{Acceptable travel time} \end{array}$

Source: Lomax T., S. Turner, G. Shunk, H.S. Levinson, R.H. Pratt, and G.B. Douglas. *Quantifying Congestion*, Vol. 1 Final Report and Vol. 2 User's Manual, Report 398, Washington, D.C.: Transportation Research Board, National Research Council, 1997.

$$\text{Future Estimate} = \text{Existing Measurement} \times \frac{\text{Future Surrogate}}{\text{Existing Surrogate}} \qquad (5\text{–}2)$$

Applications and Analysis

Table 5–9 gives some of the important measures (in addition to speed travel times per sec) that can be used in analyzing facility, corridor, or areawide performance.

Travel time and delay data can be depicted either graphically or tabulated. The information can be used to measure mobility and congestion, analyze facility or system performance, identify problems, and give inputs to demand models.

a. *Travel time contours*—travel time contour or isochronal maps show the distance that can be reached from a common origin (often the CBD) in a given time. They can compare peak and off-peak hours, thereby indicating the amount of congestion in each corridor. (Figure 5–5.) They also can compare travel times from year to year, thereby indicating the changes in mobility. Isochronal maps are also useful in defining the reach or market area for commercial outlets.

b. *Areas or corridors*—travel speeds along sections of roadways on a corridor or area can be presented as "speed flow maps," or delineated by legend. Alternatively, the distances traveled in five minute time intervals can be indicated.

c. *Routes*—travel times and delays along a route can be depicted by profiles of speeds and delays along a route (Figure 5–6), by graphic comparisons of peak and off-peak travel times, or by time-space trajectories. Travel time and delay information can be summarized by component such as shown in Figure 5–7; these data can also be aggregate by route.

Travel Surveys

Origin-destination (travel pattern) surveys are designed to obtain information on the number, type, and orientation of trips in an area; they include movements or passengers, vehicles, and cargo. The surveys estimate the nature and magnitude of existing travel and the characteristics of that travel, usually during an average weekday.

They define the total transportation behavior within an area during the survey period by time of day, mode of travel, and purpose of trip. The data collected provide answers to questions concerning an individual's or a household's travel patterns. They indicate when, where, how, and why people travel:

- *When*—time of day.

- *Where*—the beginning point and the end point of the trip.

- *How*—the mode used for the trip (e.g., auto driver, auto passenger, bus rider, taxi passenger, truck driver, bicyclist, or walker).

- *Why*—the purpose of the trip (e.g., work, shopping, business, appointment).

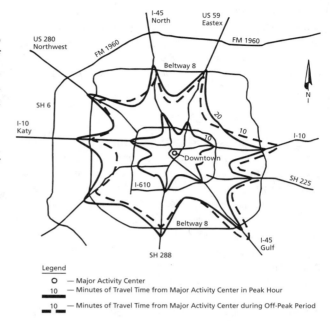

Figure 5–5   Example of Isochronal Travel Time Map

Source: Lomax T., S. Turner, G. Shunk, H.S. Levinson, R.H. Pratt, and G.B. Douglas. *Quantifying Congestion,* Vol. 1 Final Report and Vol. 2 User's Manual, Report 398, Washington, D.C.: Transportation Research Board, National Research Council, 1997.

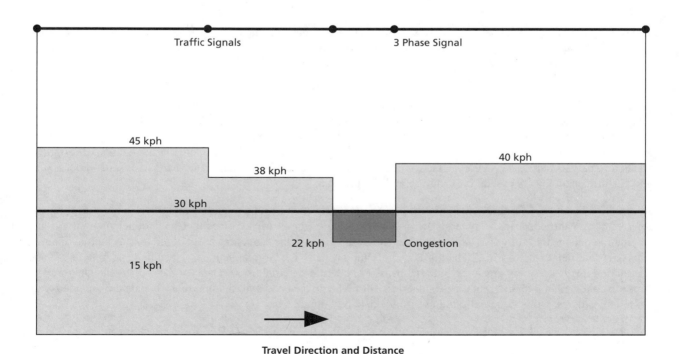

Figure 5–6   Illustrative Speed Profile

Many of the surveys are complex, and there are continual changes in survey designs and methods. For more detail, see *Methods for Household Travel Surveys*[29] in the *Travel Survey Manual*.[30] Also, a good overall discussion on survey methods is found in *Survey Methods for Transport Planning*.[31]

Uses and Applications

The surveys (household surveys, in particular) provide (1) information about how the existing transport system is used, (2) data that can be used to forecast future demands, and (3) attitudes or preferences of household members concerning possible policies or investments in transportation facilities. Existing travel demands are projected into the future to determine whether the current infrastructure is adequate to meet the future demands, to define the need for new facilities or improvements to present system, and to evaluate different growth rates and patterns.

Transportation planners utilize origin-destination (O-D) data to help plan and program major street systems, street improvements, new street locations, freeway location and design, interchange location, public transit networks and coverage, and terminal facilities (e.g., bus, truck, and off-street parking). Travel patterns are projected to a planning

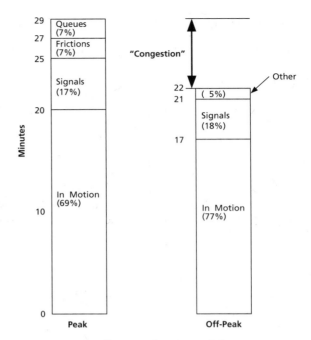

Figure 5–7 Illustrative Graphic Summary of Travel Times and Delays

horizon or design year (usually 15 to 25 years in the future) based on anticipated future economic and population growth, land use changes, vehicle ownership and usage, transit availability, costs and patronage, and other factors.

Overview

The scope and scale of travel pattern studies varies widely. They may encompass a single highway interchange or route or a series of routes as in a financial feasibility or corridor study. The survey area may contain a single neighborhood, a subdivision, or a commercial development; or it may encompass an entire metropolitan area, as in a comprehensive urban area transportation study.

Table 5–10 shows the common survey populations encountered and their use in the transportation planning and modeling process. These surveys generally form part of the comprehensive transportation studies that collect daily travel characteristics of a sample of travelers who are assumed to be representative of all travelers in the urban area. The studies also involve a collection of social, economic, land use, and population data. The principal steps include (a) establish zones for analysis purposes, (b) conduct external (or intercept) surveys, (c) conduct internal surveys, (d) process data and perform accuracy checks, and (e) analyze and expand data.

Information is required for three categories of person trips. Trips that travel completely and traverse the study area are referred to as "through-trips," "external trips," or "external–external trips." Trips that have either their origin and destination outside the study area while the other end of the trip is in the study area are referred to as "external–internal trips" or "internal–external trips." The third category (and usually the largest) includes trips that have both origin and destination inside the study area—as "internal trips" or "internal–internal trips." Data for these different categories of trips are collected in two different types of studies. Through-trip data and external–internal trip data are obtained from "external" studies, while "internal" studies provide data on internal trips.

[29] Stopher, P. R., and Metcalf H., *Methods of Household Travel Surveys,* Synthesis 236 (Washington, D.C.: Transportation Research Board, National Research Council, 1996).

[30] Cambridge Systematics, *Travel Survey Manual* (Washington, D.C.: U.S. Department of Transportation and U.S. Environmental Protection Agency, June 1996).

[31] Richardson A., Ampt, E.S., and Meyburg A.H., *Survey Methods for Transport Planning* (Melbourne, Australia: Eucalyptus Press, 1995).

Table 5–10   Common Travel Survey Populations and Modeling Uses of Different Travel Information

Survey Type	Common Survey Populations	Common Modeling Uses of Data
Household travel or activity surveys	Households within a pre-specified study area OR People within a pre-specified study area.	Trip generation, trip distribution, mode choice, time-of-day of travel, traveler behavior
Transit on-board surveys	Transit passenger trips on a pre-specified set of transit services.	Mode choice
Vehicle intercept or external station surveys	Vehicle-trips on one or more highway segments, perhaps by direction OR Person-trips by vehicle on those highway segments.	Trip distribution, model validation
Commercial vehicle surveys	Commercial vehicles garaged within a pre-specified study area. OR Commercial vehicle trips made by those vehicles.	Commercial vehicle travel (generation, distribution, time-of-day)
Workplace, establishment and special generator surveys	Employees of pre-specified establishments OR All trips to and/or from the establishment.	Trip attraction models, parking and transit cost/subsidy
Hotel and visitor surveys	Hotel guests at pre-specified establishments OR All trips to and/or from the hotel.	Visitor models (generation, distribution, time-of-day)
Parking surveys	All vehicles parked at pre-specified locations during a pre-specified time period OR All vehicle or person-trips to those parking locations.	Parking cost (for mode choice)

Source: Cambridge Systematics, *Travel Survey Manual*, Washington, D.C.: U.S. Department of Transportation and U.S. Environmental Protection Agency, June 1996.

The initial step is to define the study area. This area should encompass those parts of the urban region that will be urbanized in the planning horizon year. A cordon line is established around the study area that minimizes the number of roads (and hence survey stations) that are intercepted.

Traffic analysis zones, rings, and sectors should be discretely numbered. The size of the zones are governed by survey area size, population density, desired data items, and study purpose. Zones are smaller in the downtown area and larger in the sparsely populated outlying areas. The driving time across a zone should not exceed three to five minutes. Trips with both origin and destination within the zones should not compromise more than 15 percent of all trips.

External Surveys

The external (or intercept) surveys obtain travel information concerning external and external-internal trips made by motor vehicles. Separate surveys of rail, bus, and air travel may obtain additional travel information; these studies are specialized and depend on the particular information desired. Most are conducted by questionnaires distributed and filled out during individual trips.

Common types of studies include roadside surveys, postcard mail-back surveys, license plate surveys, vehicle intercept surveys, and lights-on surveys.

1. *Roadside interviews*—roadside interviews are the most common method of obtaining external travel information for comprehensive studies conducted in a large metropolitan area. Interview stations are established at all major roads and most other roads crossing the cordon line encompassing the study area (attempting to intercept at least 95 percent of the crossing traffic). Extreme care must be taken in locating and setting up the interview stations to ensure that vehicles can be safely stopped for interviews. A large sample of vehicles is stopped and the drivers are asked the origin and destination about the current trip. Some studies obtain additional information, such as trip purpose, where the car is garaged, routes followed, and

intermediate stops. A sample external survey interview form is shown in Chapter 5 of this handbook. The *Manual of Transportation Engineering Studies*[32] contains further details.

Roadside surveys are seldom used in large metropolitan areas today because of survey crew safety and the potential for traffic bottlenecks at interviewing locations. Other less intensive methods are used. A useful summary of their strengths and weaknesses is reported by Stokes and Chira-Chavala.[33]

2. *Postcard surveys*—where traffic is heavy, returnable postcards can be handed to the drivers at the intercept stations. This method is often used in conjunction with interview studies, especially during peak periods when it is not possible to delay vehicles long enough to complete an interview. (Other surveys rely on postcards entirely for their data.) The prepaid postcards are precoded with station identification and time, and they request the recipient to list the origin and destination of the trip and drop the card in any mailbox. A twenty to forty percent return is common from this type of survey. Data are expanded by hour and to a 24-hour total. Once again, through-trips must be halved because of the double interception of these trips.

3. *License plate surveys*—the license plate study can be used instead of the interview or postcard survey. Even with interviews or postcards, a license plate study may be necessary on freeway crossings of the cordon line. In this procedure, entire license plate numbers are recorded along with the time of observation. This is usually accomplished through the use of tape recorders. Usually, this type of study is conducted only during daylight hours, although where roadway lighting is of sufficient intensity, license numbers can be recorded during other periods.

Returns are stratified by time of day. A thirty percent return of the questionnaires is considered to be excellent. Returns as low as twenty percent will usually produce statistically valid data. The information received from the returned questionnaires is expanded by three factors. The first is to expand the percentage return to 100 percent of the plate numbers recorded. This factor equals 100 divided by the percentage return. The second factor expands the sample of license plates recorded to the total volume passing the station during each hour the plate numbers were recorded. This hourly factor equals the total volume in each hour divided by the number of plates recorded in that hour. The third factor expands the data to the full 24-hour total volume divided by the sum of the hourly volumes during which license plate numbers were recorded. Other adjustments factors (e.g., day of week, month of year) may also be applied. Finally, the through-trips must once again be halved because of the double exposure to intercept stations.

4. *Vehicle intercept surveys*—the vehicle intercept method can be used in small area studies. This procedure requires stations at all entrances and exits to the study area. Each entering vehicle is stopped and a precoded or colored card is handed to the driver with instructions to surrender the card as he or she exits the area. Exiting vehicles are stopped and the cards collected, or the notation that they had not received a card is made.

A variation of this procedure is to affix colored tape to the bumper of the entering vehicle or to tape the colored card to the windshield. This process eliminates the need for stopping vehicles at the exits from the area. It also permits the collection of data at intermediate locations within the study area. However, it poses problems in rainy weather.

5. *Lights-on studies*—the lights-on study is a variation of the vehicle intercept (or tag-on-vehicle study). This study traces individual vehicles from one entrance point to a maximum of two or three destination points, generally within one-half mile to one mile of each other. It is useful in tracing vehicles through a highway interchange or weaving area.

---

[32] Institute of Transportation Engineers, *Manual of Transportation Engineering Studies* (Englewood Cliffs, N.J.: Prentice Hall, 1994).

[33] Stokes, R.W. and Chira-Chavala, T., "Design and Implementation of Intercity Origin Destination Surveys," *Transportation Research Record 1936* (Washington, D.C.: Transportation Research Board, National Research Council, 1989, pp. 23–33).

Each entering vehicle is requested to turn its headlights on and to leave them on until it passes an exit station. This procedure only works during daylight hours. It is the least reliable of the surveys described, and it is only effective under very limited circumstances.

Internal Surveys

Internal surveys include household interviews, commercial vehicle surveys, surveys of workplaces and special generators, hotel and visitor surveys, and transit-on-board surveys.

1. *Household surveys*—household surveys began during the 1940s, and they became common during the 1950s as part of the comprehensive urbanized and transportation planning process. The initial studies involved home interviews in which respondents were asked to recall the trips made on the previous day. The samples ranged from about two percent in areas of over 5,000,000 to twenty percent in areas of less than 200,000 population.

    Within the past decade, the survey methods have changed dramatically. The surveys are done by telephone, involve small samples, and include trips made by walking and bicycling as well as by auto or transit. More than fifty such surveys have been completed in the past five years.

    The typical survey was conducted for a metropolitan planning organization on spring or fall days. The planned sample size was about 40,000 households; and about 9,000 households were contacted. Sampling of households was done using random digit dialing. The median cost of a completed household survey was less than $100. The interview time was 15 minutes per person and 33 minutes per household.[34]

    The key steps in conducting a household survey are shown in Figure 5–8. An often neglected but important part of the survey process is a pilot survey that should be used to test the survey instrument, sampling design, and interview process. The typical information collected is summarized in Table 5–11. The information shown in italics is used to obtain information on the allocation of household vehicles to different members of the population.

    Household surveys include (1) trip-based surveys that directly gather information on people's trips over some period using either diary or recall methods, (2) activity-based surveys that gather information on activities in which respondents need to travel during a set time period, or (3) time-use-based surveys that gather information on all activities in which respondents participate during a set time period. Surveys commonly use trip or activity diaries to minimize under-reporting of certain trips (i.e., short trips). They may also be designed to obtain stated response (i.e., stated preference) information. Figures 5–9 and 5–10 show illustrative survey forms for trip diaries.

    Reported response rates for various survey methods are: (1) face-to-face interviews, ninety percent; (2) telephone surveys, fifty percent; and (3) mailback, less than thirty percent.[35]

    Once the interviews have been completed, the travel data are coded by origin and destination. Each trip end (origin or destination) is coded to the zone where it occurred. The data are then expanded to the full sample (i.e., by a zonal factor that is calculated by dividing the total number dwelling units in the zone by the actual number of interviews successfully completed). Other factors are used to convert the data to an average weekday. Further adjustments are made by determining the total number of trips crossing screenlines established in the study area. The survey results are compared to the screenline counts, and correction factors are developed.

2. *Workplaces and major generators*—surveys of travel patterns and trip rates of major traffic generators can obtain targeted information about the nonhome end of the trip. The surveys involve (a) intercept or cordon counts of people entering, leaving, and accumulated within the city center by mode and time of day; and (b) interviews with a sample of the visitors and workers. Survey forms are distributed to employees at place of work and are usually administered as self-completed forms.

---

[34] Stopher, P. R., and Metcalf H., *Methods of Household Travel Surveys,* Synthesis 236 (Washington, D.C.: Transportation Research Board, National Research Council, 1996).

[35] Ibid.

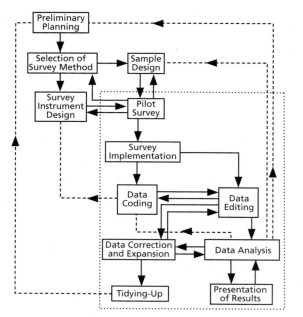

Figure 5–8   Flow Diagram of the Survey Process

Source: Stopher, P. R., and Metcalf H., *Methods of Household Travel Surveys,* Synthesis 236, Washington, D.C.: Transportation Research Board, National Research Council, 1996.

Table 5–11 Measures Included in Recent Travel Surveys

Category	Variable
Movement	Order of stages in a trip
	Trip purpose
	Main mode/modes of stages
	Start and end times of trip
	Number of passengers in the vehicle
	Location of trip ends
	Parking costs/transit fare
	Household vehicle used for trip
Person	Sex
	Age
	Participation in the labor market
	Profession
	Amount of work
	Driving license status
	Relationship of each person in the household
	Educational level
	Ethnic origin (race and Hispanic status)
Household	Number of persons
	Income
	Number of vehicles
	Dwelling-unit type
	Length of tenure of household
	Prior residence
	Number of workers in the household
Vehicles	Existence
	Make
	Model
	Year
	Odometer readings at beginning and end of diary period

Note: Items in italics reflect additions to traditional surveys.

Source: Stopher, P.R. and H. Metcalf, *Methods of Household Travel Surveys,* Synthesis 236, Washington, D.C.: Transportation Research Board, National Research Council, 1996.

3. *Transit surveys*—on-board transit surveys are usually distributed to passengers where boarding a bus or train. Forms are completed by passengers and deposited in a collection box or returned by mail. Response rates range from fifteen to forty percent and may vary by type of rider.

4. *Internal truck and taxi survey*—a separate survey collects information on the movements of trucks and taxis. Vehicles are grouped into classes for which separate analyses are desired (i.e., large trucks, small trucks, taxis). For each class, a sample is selected from a list of all vehicles garaged in the region where the data are collected only as part of a general urban travel study; the suggested sample size is 600 vehicles per class. However, for a detailed goods movement study, 2,000 vehicles should be sampled in each class of vehicles.[36]

    Information is obtained on garage address, description of vehicle, and trips made on a given day. Trip information includes origin and destination, time of start and end of trip, number of passengers (for taxis), and trip purpose (for trucks only). Commodity and goods carried may be included.

Data Analysis and Adjustments

Origin-destination studies produce vast amount of data that require analysis by computers. The coded data are entered into computer files; and the data are appropriately expanded, manipulated, and displayed in many forms. These include tables on trip characteristics, travel modes, and person travel. Origin-destination tables show person and vehicle trips between zones on an average weekday. In some studies, small sample sizes may preclude developing O-D tables; the data are used only to calibrate and validate travel models.

Survey accuracy is checked by comparing travel patterns across screen lines with actual ground counts on an hour-by-hour basis. Major barriers such as a river or railroad track provide logical screen lines. Other important considerations include:

---

[36] Homburger, W.S., Hall, J.W., Loutzenheiser, R.C., Reilly, W. R. *Fundamentals of Traffic Engineering,* 14th Edition (Berkeley, Calif.: Institute of Transportation Studies, University of California, Berkeley, May 1996).

9. WHERE DID YOU GO TO NEXT?

A) WHAT TIME OF DAY DID YOU BEGIN THIS TRIP? (Be exact, such as 4:32 a.m.)

_____ a.m. / p.m.

B) WHERE DID YOU GO?

( ) home
( ) work
( ) school
( ) shopping
( ) other (specify) _____

C) ADDRESS OR CROSS STREETS: _____

_____

CITY / TOWN: _____

NAME OF THAT PLACE: _____

D) HOW DID YOU GET THERE: _____
(Car, bus, train, airplane, walk, etc.)

E) WHAT TIME DID YOU GET THERE:

_____ a.m. / p.m.

. . . .

10. WHERE DID YOU GO TO NEXT?

A) WHAT TIME OF DAY DID YOU BEGIN THIS TRIP? (Be exact, such as 4:32 a.m.)

_____ a.m. / p.m.

B) WHERE DID YOU GO?

( ) home
( ) work
( ) school
( ) shopping
( ) other (specify) _____

C) ADDRESS OR CROSS STREETS: _____

_____

CITY / TOWN: _____

NAME OF THAT PLACE: _____

D) HOW DID YOU GET THERE: _____
(Car, bus, train, airplane, walk, etc.)

E) WHAT TIME DID YOU GET THERE:

_____ a.m. / p.m.

Figure 5–9   Sample Page from a Travel Diary

Source: Stopher, P. R., and Metcalf H., *Methods of Household Travel Surveys*, Synthesis 236, Washington, D.C.: Transportation Research Board, National Research Council, 1996.

6th Activity

1. What was the next thing you did? (Check ONE only)

At Home Activities (including sleeping, working at home)	☐
Pick Up or Drop Off a Person(s) — At Work	☐
Pick Up or Drop Off a Person(s) — At School / Child Care	☐
Pick Up or Drop Off a Person(s) — Other	☐
Work	☐
Work-Related	☐
School / College / University	☐
Child Care (Day Care / After-School Care)	☐
Shopping	☐
Social Activities / Recreation / Church / Eating Out	☐
Banking / Personal Business	☐
Bus Stop / Carypool / Vanpool / Park N Ride Activities	☐
Other (please specify) _____	☐

2. What time did you ARRIVE there? [:]
What time did you LEAVE there? [:]

3. WHERE were you?

Business / Store / Place Name

Address or Nearest Cross-streets

City / Town

4. How did you get there?   (Please check)

Walk (5 minutes or more)	☐	
Automobile / Minivan Driver	☐	Including yourself, how many persons were in the vehicle?
Passenger	☐	Including yourself, how many persons were in the vehicle?
Van / Light Truck Driver	☐	Including yourself, how many persons were in the vehicle?
Passenger	☐	
Carpool / Vanpool Driver	☐	Including yourself, how many persons were in the vehicle?
Passenger	☐	
Bus (SMART, DDOT, AATA)	☐	
Shuttle / Campus Bus	☐	
School Bus (K–12)	☐	
Taxi	☐	
Bicycle	☐	
Motorcycle / moped	☐	
Other	☐	

5. If you checked Automobile / Minivan / Van / Light Truck, or Carpool / Vanpool and you were the driver

Did you pay to park your vehicle? ☐ Yes   ☐ No

How much did you pay? Is this an

$ _____   ☐ Hourly Rate? ☐ Daily Rate?
☐ Weekly Rate? ☐ Monthly Rate?
☐ Other _____

6. If you checked bus or taxi

How much was your fare? $ _____

7. Was this the last activity you did today?

Yes ☐   STOP! Please turn to the inside back cover

No ☐   Please turn to the next page ➜

Figure 5–10   Sample Page from an Activity Diary

Source: Stopher, P. R., and Metcalf H., *Methods of Household Travel Surveys*, Synthesis 236, Washington, D.C.: Transportation Research Board, National Research Council, 1996.

a. Public transport riding derived from an internal survey can be compared with transit agency records and line ridership.

b. Work trips to and from major employment centers can be compared with estimates of the number of people employed in the zone. Allowance should be made for absenteeism.

c. Where discrepancies are sizeable, adjustments should be made to the survey data to correct them.

Presentation of Results

Survey results should be expressed clearly in graphic and tabular form. Summary tables should be presented in the body of the report, and the detailed tabulations (such as zone-to-zone origins and destinations) should be placed in, on, or near appendices.

Travel patterns are commonly displayed as desire line charts in which straight lines are drawn between O-D zones with the width of each line proportional to the number of trips made between the two zones on an average weekday. A different type of desire line chart summarizes the data further and shows the aggregated through-trips, internal–external trips, external–internal trips, and internal–internal trips. Desire line charts may also be prepared for special zones such as the CBD, a large industrial tract, a university, or a military installation. Contour maps (or isolines) showing the orientation and intensity of travel can also be prepared. Other data collected during the O-D study may be presented on maps of the area, sometimes keyed to analysis zones. Examples include population distribution or density, land use, and trip density.

Trip Generation

Trip generation analysis is an integral part of both regional and site-specific transportation studies. It provides a basis for systematically assessing the transportation demand impacts of changes in population, economic activity, and development.

Definitions

The number of trips generated by each unit of land or type of activity varies with social, economic, geographic, and land use factors. These relationships are defined as trip generation analysis. In *comprehensive* studies they include both trip productions and trip attractions. Trip productions relate to the "home" end of the trip, while trip attractions relate to employment or other nonhome end of the trip. Normally, trip productions serve as the control total to which aggregate trip attractions are adjusted. In *small* or *site-specific analysis,* the total trips beginning or ending in the area are estimated (i.e., person-destinations or vehicle destinations).

Sources

Guidelines for developing trip generation models are outlined in *An Introduction to Urban Travel Demand Forecasting— A Self Instructional Text.*[37] Information on trip rates are given in Chapter 4, "Urban Travel Characteristics;" and in *Characteristics of Urban Transportation Demand.*[38]

One of the most common sources of generation is *Trip Generation.*[39] This book compiles data from all over the country on many different types of land uses. Data points are grouped by land use and plotted. Best fit regression lines are also plotted where sufficient data exist. The document strives to present sufficient detail on the data points to provide the analyst with a reasonable basis for selecting appropriate rates to use in a specific study.

---

[37] *An Introduction to Urban Travel Demand Forecasting—A Self Instructional Text* (Washington, D.C.: Federal Highway Administration and Urban Mass Transportation Administration, 1977).

[38] Charles River Assoc. and Levinson, H.S., *Characteristics of Urban Transportation Demand—An Update,* (Urban Mass Transportation Administration, 1985).

[39] *Trip Generation,* Sixth Edition (Washington, D.C.: Institute of Transportation Engineers, 1997).

State, regional, and local transportation agencies often compile their own trip generation rates to be used in their regions. Some of these rates are based on local surveys of the different types of land use. Others may be arbitrarily decreed by the local authorities as conservative values to be used in planning or impact analyses for that area.

Most trip generation analyses have focused on trips in vehicles (i.e., vehicle driver, vehicle passenger, transit passenger). However, more recent analyses have also included pedestrian and bicycle trips. Thus, a clear definition of specific trips included in the trip generation analyses is essential.

Area-Wide Analysis

Trip generation relationships are established either by multiple regression techniques or through cross-classification (or category) analysis. Relations are developed on an individual unit (disaggregate) basis.

1. *Productions*—household trips are usually a function of median income per family, household size, and automobile ownership and availability. Other factors may include net residential density and distance from the city center. Rates (or relationships) are normally derived for total trips and for key trip purposes such as home-to-work. They are computed for a 24-hour period or for peak hours. A typical trip rate analysis such as shown in Table 5–12 gives daily person-trips per household as a function of auto ownership and family size. (Income could be used as an alternate to car ownership.)

2. *Attractions*—trip attractions are keyed to factors such as floor space, hospital beds, employees, and stadium seats. In comprehensive studies, various types of employment are commonly used to obtain trip attraction rates. An illustrative example is shown in Table 5–13.

3. *Future trips*—the number of future trips can be estimated by applying the trip generation relationships to future conditions. Estimates of future input parameters must be made. This may influence the factors used in establishing the initial relationships.

4. *Displaying results*—results can be presented as sets of equations and tables that are useful for computer operations. Families of curves may prove to be helpful in conveying results.

Table 5–12   Illustrative Example of Cross-Classification Analysis for Home-Based Trips

Persons per Dwelling Unit	Person Trips per Household per Day			
	Autos Per Dwelling Unit			
	0	1	2	3+
1	1.00	3.00	3.60	—
2	1.80	5.10	6.90	—
3	2.60	3.20	9.20	10.50
4	3.20	8.00	11.60	12.50

Note: Hypothetical Data (Excludes pedestrian and bicycle trips)

Table 5–13   Illustrative Trip Attraction Rate Analysis (Daily Attractions)

	Attractions per Household*	Attractions per Non-Retail Employee	Attractions per Retail Employee
Home-Based Work	Neg.	1.7	1.7
Home-Based Other	1.0	2.0	5.0–10.0[b]
Non-Home Based	1.0	1.0	3.0–5.0[b]

* These trips would be made to households other than the residence of the trip maker.

[b] Lower values for downtown retail employees.

Source: Meyer, Michael D. and Eric S. Miller, *Urban Transportation Planning, A Decision-Oriented Approach*, New York: McGraw-Hill, 1984.

Site-Specific Analysis

Person and vehicular trip rates for specific activities can be obtained by drawing a "cordon" around the activity under consideration and then counting the number of people entering and leaving by time of day by mode of travel. Counts of people are essential in urban settings, especially the city center. For free-standing suburban developments, vehicle trip rates will usually be sufficient.

The *Trip Generation* report[40] contains vehicular trip rates for a wide range of land uses. A summary of weekday, A.M. and P.M. peak hour vehicle trip rates for common land uses is presented in Table 5–14. The guide also contains rates for

---

[40] Ibid.

Table 5–14 Summary of ITE Trip Generation Rates and Average Number of Weekday Trip Ends

Code	Land Use	Unit	Daily Trip Ends Rate	S.D.	A.M. Peak Hour In	Out	S.D.*	P.M. Peak Hour In	Out	S.D.*
110	Light Industry	1,000 G.S.F	6.97	4.24	0.81	0.11	1.07	0.12	0.86	1.16
		Employees	3.02	1.86	0.37	0.17	0.69	0.09	0.33	0.67
130	Industrial Park	1,000 G.S.F.	6.96	5.64	0.73	0.16	1.05	0.19	0.73	1.10
		Employees	3.34	2.38	0.42	0.07	0.73	0.09	0.37	0.73
140	Manufacturing	1,000 G.S.F.	3.82	3.07	0.51	0.22	1.04	0.17	0.47	1.01
		Employees	2.10	1.65	0.29	0.11	0.65	0.17	0.20	0.62
150	Warehousing	1,000 G.S.F.	4.96	4.05	0.37	0.08	0.74	0.12	0.39	0.83
		Employees	3.89	3.08	0.37	0.14	0.74	0.21	0.38	0.80
151	Mini-Warehouse	1,000 G.S.F.	2.50	1.78	0.09	0.06	0.39	0.13	0.73	0.52
		G.F.A. Employees	56.28	46.89	4.50		3.99	2.96	2.74	5.05
210	Single Family Residential	D.U.	9.57	3.69	0.19	0.56	0.90	0.65	0.36	1.05
220	Apartment	D.U.	6.63	2.98	0.08	0.43	0.73	0.42	0.20	0.82
221	Low-Rise Apartment	Occupied D.U.	6.59	2.84	0.09	0.38	0.70	0.38	0.20	0.77
222	High-Rise Apartment	D.U.	4.20	2.32	0.08	0.22	0.55	0.21	0.14	0.59
223	Mid-Rise Apartment	D.U.	——N/A——		0.09	0.21	0.56	0.23	0.16	0.63
230	Residential Condo.	D.U.	5.86	3.09	0.07	0.37	0.69	0.36	0.18	0.76
240	Mobile Home Park	Occupied D.U.	4.81	2.60	0.08	0.32	0.66	0.35	0.21	0.76
270	Residential P.U.D.	D.U.	7.50	3.32	0.11	0.41	0.72	0.40	0.22	0.80
310	Hotel	Occupied Rooms	8.92	6.04	0.39	0.28	0.84	0.35	0.36	0.88
320	Motel	Occupied Rooms	9.11	4.39	0.23	0.41	0.84	0.31	0.27	0.78
330	Resort Hotel	Occupied Rooms	——N/A——		0.27	0.10	0.61	0.21	0.28	0.70
501	Military Base	Employees	1.98	1.64	0.39*	0.64		0.39*		0.63
520	Elementary School	Students	1.02	1.07	0.17	0.12	0.55	0.17	0.13	0.56
		Employees	13.13	6.10	3.71*	2.34		3.50*		2.73
522	Middle School Junior High School	Students	1.45	1.41	0.26	0.20	0.75	——N/A——		
530	High School	Students	1.79	1.54	0.32	0.14	0.71	0.06	0.09	0.39
		Employees	19.98	80.30	3.54		3.03	1.56		1.41
550	University/College	Students	2.38	1.57	0.17	0.04	0.46	0.06	0.15	0.46
560	Church	1,000 G.S.F.	9.11	7.20	0.39	0.33	1.88	0.36	0.30	1.01
565	Day Care Center	Employees	31.19	12.98	2.71	2.31	3.11	2.44	2.75	3.29
		1,000 S.F. G.F.A.	79.26	21.03	6.74	5.97	6.52	6.20	7.00	7.00
590	Library	Employees	48.85	17.00	——N/A——			2.18	2.57	2.70
		1,000 S.F.	54.00	22.16	——N/A——			3.40	3.69	3.87
610	Hospital	Employees Beds	5.77	2.90	0.23	0.08	0.57	0.08	0.21	0.54,
			11.77	7.14	0.77	0.30	1.18	0.06	0.28	1.17
620	Nursing Home	Occupied Beds	——N/A——		0.12	0.70	0.44	0.07	0.10	0.42
		Employees	4.03	2.51	——N/A——			——N/A——		
710	General Office Building	Employees	3.32	2.16	0.42	0.06	0.71	0.08	0.38	0.70
		1,000 G.S.F.	11.01	6.13	1.37	0.19	1.40	0.25	1.24	1.37
714	Corporate Headquarters	Employees	2.27	1.59	0.41	0.03	0.67	0.04	0.34	0.63
		1,000 S.F. G.F.A.	7.72	3.83	1.37	0.10	1.35	0.15	1.24	1.28
715	Single Tenant Office Building	Employees	3.62	2.41	0.46	0.16	0.74	0.08	0.42	0.72
		1,000 S.F. G.F.A.	11.57	8.30	1.58	0.20	1.51	0.26	1.46	1.49
729	Medical-Dental Office Building	Employees	——N/A——		0.42	0.11	0.76	0.36	0.70	1.08
		1,000 S.F. G.F.A.	36.13	10.18	1.94	0.49	1.92	0.99	2.67	2.46
731	State Motor Vehicle Department	Employees	44.54	11.02	2.64*	1.81		4.58*		2.43
		1,000 S.F. G.F.A.	166.02	49.39	9.84*	3.70		17.09*		7.58
732	United States Post Office	Employees	28.32	20.82	1.00	0.94	2.74	1.40	1.34	4.40
		1,000 S.F. G.F.A.	108.19	110.21	4.17	3.85	9.00	5.50	5.29	14.38
750	Office Park	1,000 S.F. G.F.A.	11.42	4.69	1.42	0.32	1.46	0.21	1.29	1.32
760	Research and Development Center	Employees	2.77	2.09	0.37	0.06	0.67	0.04	0.37	0.66
		1,000 S.F. G.S.F.	8.11	5.85	1.03	0.21	1.32	0.16	0.92	1.19
770	Business Park	Employees	4.04	2.20	0.38	0.31	0.69	0.09	0.30	0.64
		1,000 S.F. G.S.F.								

Notes: * = In and Out; D.U. = Dwelling Units; S.D. = Standard Deviation; G.F.A. = Gross Floor Area; G.S.F. = Gross Square Feet; G.L.A. = Gross Leasable Area; N/A = Not Available.

Source: *Trip Generation*, 6th Edition, Institute of Transportation Engineers, Washington, D.C., 1997.

Table 5–14 Summary of ITE Trip Generation Rates and Average Number of Weekday Trip Ends *(continued)*

Code	Land Use	Unit	Daily Trip Ends		A.M. Peak Hour			P.M. Peak Hour		
			Rate	S.D.	In	Out	S.D.*	In	Out	S.D.*
813	Free Standing Discount Superstore	1,000 S.F. G.F.A.	46.96	12.25	0.94	0.90	1.51	1.87	1.95	2.12
815	Free Standing Discount Store	1,000 S.F. G.F.A.	56.63	20.12	——N/A——			2.12	2.12	2.23
		Employees	28.84	7.28	——N/A——			——N/A——		
817	Nursery/Garden Center	Employees	22.13	10.56	0.89*		0.87	1.99		2.06
		1,000 S.F. G.F.A.	36.08	52.43	1.31*		2.41	3.80		5.32
818	Nursery (Wholesale)	Employees	——N/A——		0.34*		0.64	0.47		0.85
		1,000 S.F. G.F.A	——N/A——		2.40*		2.31	5.17		7.96
823	Factory Outlet	1,000 S.F. G.F.A.	26.59	12.02	——N/A——			1.54	0.75	1.69
820	Shopping Center	1,000 S.F. G.L.A.	42.92	21.39	0.63	0.40	1.40	1.80	1.94	2.73
831	Quality Restaurant	1,000 G.S.F.	89.95	36.81	0.81*		0.93	5.02	2.47	4.89
		Seats	2.86	1.96	0.03*		0.16	0.17	0.09	0.52
832	High Turnover (Sit-Down) Restaurant	1,000 S.F. G.F.A.	130.34	43.77	4.82	4.45	7.46	6.52	4.34	9.83
		Seats	——N/A——		0.24	0.23	0.70	0.24	0.18	0.75
834	Fast Food Restaurant with Drive-Through Window	1,000 S.F. G.F.A.	496.12	242.52	25.43	24.43	29.60	17.41	16.07	19.25
		Seats	19.52	9.97	0.70	0.52	1.41	0.50	0.43	1.16
841	New Car Sales	1,000 S.F. G.F.A.	37.50	24.92	1.61	0.60	1.92	1.12	1.68	2.02
844	Gasoline Service Station	Vehicle Fueling Positions	168.56	71.19	6.26	6.01	4.36	7.43	7.13	6.70
845	Gasoline Service Station with Convenience Market	Vehicle Fueling Positions	162.78	68.16	5.03	5.03	6.01	6.69	6.69	7.98
		1,000 S.F. G.F.A.	——N/A——		39.62	38.06	55.62	48.18	48.18	65.76
846	Gasoline Service Station with Convenience Market and Car Wash	Vehicle Fueling Positions	152.84	45.80	5.43	5.21	6.14	6.60	6.59	5.94
848	Tire Store	Service Bays	——N/A——		1.46	0.78	1.71	1.46	2.01	2.05
		1,000 S.F. G.F.A.	24.87	7.41	1.82	1.03	2.13	1.73	2.39	2.70
		Employees	——N/A——		2.11	1.13	2.10	2.11	2.92	2.23
849	Wholesale Tire Store	Service Bays	30.55	8.03	1.03	0.98	1.58	1.49	1.68	1.85
		1,000 S.F. G.F.A.	20.36	6.10	0.87	0.47	1.24	0.99	1.12	1.46
850	Supermarket	1,000 S.F. G.F.A.	——N/A——		1.98	1.27	3.11	5.87	5.64	4.76
851	Convenience Market (Open 24 Hours)	1,000 S.F. G.F.A.	737.99	336.24	32.70	32.69	28.37	26.86	26.87	18.60
852	Convenience Market (Open 15–16 Hours)	1,000 S.F. G.F.A.	——N/A——		15.51	15.51	24.36	16.94	17.63	17.61
853	Convenience Market with Gasoline Pumps	Fueling Positions	542.60	113.52	8.58	8.59	11.32	9.61	9.61	12.02
		1,000 S.F. G.F.A.	845.60	163.67	22.79	22.79	18.50	30.35	30.36	35.37
861	Discount Club	1,000 S.F. G.F.A.	41.80	14.35	——N/A——			1.86	2.00	2.47
		Employees	32.21	8.44	0.28	0.08	0.61	1.34	2.45	1.74
862	Home Improvement Superstore	1,000 S.F. G.F.A.	——N/A——		1.35	1.52	1.84	1.88	1.74	2.01
870	Apparel Store	1,000 S.F. G.F.A.	——N/A——		——N/A——			1.91	1.92	2.81
880	Pharmacy/Drug Store (Without Drive-Through Window)	1,000 S.F. G.F.A.	90.06	12.24	1.89	1.31	2.00	3.74	3.89	3.26
890	Furniture Store	1,000 S.F. G.F.A.	5.06	4.38	0.12	0.05	0.44	0.20	0.25	0.76
		Employees	12.19	7.22	0.48*		0.76	1.10*		1.25
896	Video Rental Store	1,000 S.F. G.L.A.	——N/A——		——N/A——			6.26*		6.13
912	Drive-In Bank	Employees	72.79	46.58	1.71	1.35	3.30	4.59	4.78	8.88
		1,000 S.F. G.L.A.	265.21	143.92	7.07	5.56	11.58	27.39	27.39	48.48

Notes: * = In and Out; D.U. = Dwelling Units; S.D. = Standard Deviation; G.F.A. = Gross Floor Area; G.S.F. = Gross Square Feet; G.L.A. = Gross Leasable Area; N/A = Not Available.

Source: *Trip Generation,* 6th Edition, Institute of Transportation Engineers, Washington, D.C., 1997.

evening and weekend conditions when travel to and from many activities peak. These rates reflect travel characteristics in suburban areas, and they do not apply in densely developed areas or in city centers with pedestrian and transit traffic.

Many of the data points are widely dispersed, as is apparent from the standard deviations shown in Table 5–14. Therefore, to establish local credibility, a survey of similar land uses in an area may be desired where an area of similar land use can be isolated (i.e., relatively few access points). Directional counts with mechanical counters can provide the desired information—not only the daily generation rate, but also the peak hour rates and the inbound-outbound directional split. However, it is often difficult to find an area of similar characteristics or one that can be sequestered for counting purposes. Also, many areas have mixed land uses where it is difficult to isolate the individual generation rates.

When an area has mixed uses now or in the future, individual rates can be applied to each use and aggregated for the area as a whole. Care must be taken to consider joint trips such as service trips that serve more than one land use (e.g., newspaper delivery, express mail). If some current uses are to be discontinued or changed in the future, the traffic currently being generated must be subtracted from the future traffic.

Modal Studies

This section contains guidelines for parking, transit, pedestrian, bicycle, and goods movement studies.

Parking Studies

Parking studies address various operational, planning, and policy concerns. They are instrumental in analyzing the use and capacity of existing facilities, the location and magnitude of existing and future demands, and the adequacy of access to off-street facilities; and they are helpful in establishing parking programs and setting parking policies. They address key questions such as:

- How much parking should be provided?

- Where should it be located?

- How should it be designed?

- What are its street traffic impacts?

- What will it cost?

- Who will pay for it?

- How will it be managed and operated?

Table 5–15 lists the various types of parking studies. Studies may be conducted to address a particular question, such as the feasibility of removing or installing parking meters or how to improve revenue control or accounting. They may quantify the parking space for a new development or an entire area. The traditional parking feasibility study usually includes analysis of parking supply and demand, alternative parking sites, and financial feasibility.

The scale of parking studies also varies. Some studies assess the adequacy of parking for a particular need, such as a shopping mall, office building, or a sports facility. Others evaluate the parking conditions in an area, such as the CBD, to establish time limits, parking rates, and the need for additional parking. Some provide a basis for modifying or removing

Table 5–15   Types of Parking Studies

Parking Supply/Demand Analysis—determines current and future parking supply and demand.

Market Study—determines how many users a facility on a particular site will capture, given the demand, competitive climate, and prevailing rates for parking.

Shared Parking Analysis—determines the need for parking in mixed-use/multi-use development areas, considering variations in the individual use needs by time of day, day of week, season, and the relationship of needs among land uses.

Site Alternatives Analysis—involves selection and comparison of sites for parking improvements reuqired to resolve documented parking shortages.

Schematic Design Study—involves developing the functional design for a proposed parking facility to a level of detail sufficient to obtain concurrence of the interested parties. These documents normally constitute the first phase of a design contract, but may be necessary in the study phase to provide the background information necessary to obtain consensus to proceed with design and funding.

Traffic Impact Analysis (TIA)—involves standardized traffic engineering analysis to determine the current and/or future traffic conditions and recommend improvements. Although the primary focus is generally to determine the effect of a proposed parking facility on traffic conditions, there may already be traffic problems that should be addressed simultaneously with parking problems.

Financial Feasibility Study—involves analysis of who is going to pay for the parking facility and how much they should pay. The financial analysis may include some or all of the following:

- development costs;
- revenue and operating expense projections;
- financing costs, interest rate, and term;
- stand-alone feasibility of a parking facility; and,
- feasibility of adding a new facility to an existing system.

Financing Method Analysis—involves a detailed study of various financing methods available, legal ram)fications thereof, and determination of the interest rate, term, insurance, debt reserves and other requirements. The options considered may include private/public partnerships, federal/state/local financing programs, private ownership and financing and/or "creative" sources of funding.

Parking Management and Policy Study—deals with the broad issues of where problems in parking conditions exist due to (or are correctable by changes in) management and operating strategies, decisions and/or policies.

Organization and Administration Review—involves detailed study of the administration and operation of the parking system as a whole. It considers such issues as allocation and utilization of resources, staffing needs, who should have responsibility for what functions, and the general organization chart for all parking functions. It is most often needed in order to establish a Parking Authority or other operating agency that will run an entire parking system.

Parking Revenue Controls and Operations Study—involves review of current revenue collection systems and other operational procedures and policies, to ensure that revenue is maximized and theft, fraud, and evasion are minimized.

Parking Equipment Acquisition—involves review of current and future operations and recommendations as to the appropriate type and number of access lanes and control equipment. Study phase ususally includes cost estimates and outline specifications; detailed construction documents would be provided in a later work effort.

Restoration and Maintenance—determines the extent of deterioration in a parking structure floor and frame, the appropriate repair and cost estimates of such repairs. Construction documents for repairs are not included in the study phase.

Source: *Parking Studies,* Parking Consultants Council and National Parking Association, June 1990.

---

curb parking, while others evaluate residential parking affected by outside parkers. Some provide a regional transit and carpool parking program as a complement or alternative to downtown parking studies.

Detailed descriptions of parking study techniques are described in several sources, such as *Conducting a Limited Parking Study,*[41] *Parking Principles,*[42] the *Manual of Transportation Engineering Studies,*[43] and *Parking Studies.*[44] Additional information on studies and analyses are contained in *Parking;*[45] *Parking Structures—Planning, Design, Construction, Maintenance and Repair;*[46] and the *Parking Handbook for Small Communities.*[47]

---

[41] National Committee on Urban Transportation, *Conducting a Limited Parking Study and Conducting a Comprehensive Parking Study* (Chicago, Ill.: Public Administration Service, 1958).

[42] *Parking Principles,* Special Report 125 (Washington, D.C.: Highway Research Board, 1971, pp. 75–88).

[43] Institute of Transportation Engineers, *Manual of Transportation Engineering Studies* (Englewood Cliffs, N.J.: Prentice Hall, 1994).

[44] *Parking Studies* (Parking Consultants Council and National Parking Association, June 1992).

[45] Weant, R. A. and Levinson, H. S., *Parking* (Saugatuck, Conn.: Eno Foundation for Transportation, 1990).

[46] Chrest, A. P. and Smith, M. S. and Bhuyan S., *Parking Structures—Planning Design Construction, Maintenance and Repair* (New York, N.Y.: Van Nostrand Reinhold, 1989).

[47] Edwards, J., *The Parking Handbook for Small Communities* (Washington, D.C.: National Main Street Center and Institute of Transportation Engineers, 1994).

Parking Needs Studies

The objective of most parking studies is to establish existing and future parking needs by comparing parking supply and demand. The studies obtain information on (1) parking supply characteristics, such as the number, location and cost of spaces, or who provides the spaces; (2) occupancy and use of spaces; (3) parker characteristics, including when, where, why and how long people park, and where they are going; and (4) parking space demands and needs for existing or new developments. A parking program, including facility locations, conceptual designs, costs, revenue, and financing often is a result of these studies. (See Chapter 14 for more information.)

The key study steps include (1) defining the study area, (2) conducting a parking space inventory, (3) determining parking occupancies (accumulations), (4) computing parker durations (length of stay) and parking space turnover (parkers per space per day), (5) obtaining basic characteristics of parkers (purpose, fee paid, destination), and (6) comparing parking supply and demands. Step 5 involves interviews with parkers and is normally done as part of a *comprehensive parking study*. Alternately, a *more limited parking study* can be performed in which parking demands are obtained by applying demand data for similar land uses, or by pro-rating the peak parking accumulation based upon the distribution of floor space or employment among areas.

1. *Study area definition*—the first step is to clearly define the study area. This area should include the traffic generators of concern and surrounding areas within a reasonable walking distance. It should include areas of current problems along with areas that might be affected by growth and change.

   Each block in the study area should be uniquely identified. Parking analysis zones may include these individual blocks (or groups of blocks) and then be aggregated to districts. Block faces can be numbered from 1 to 4 clockwise around the block, with the number 1 block face being on the north side of the block. Off-street facilities should be keyed to blocks and can be numbered from 5 up.

2. *Parking space inventory*—the existing on-street and off-street space supply should be inventoried by type of space. Curb spaces are usually classified by type of parking permitted: unrestricted spaces; truck, taxi, or bus loading zones; time-limit parking zones; and metered spaces by time limit. Off-street facilities and spaces are classified by type (lot or garage), availability (open to general public or restricted), and ownership (public or private). Capacities and rates are determined. Inventory data are tabulated and may be presented graphically. Curb space inventories can be presented graphically by superimposing the curb parking restrictions on maps of the area. (Figure 5–11.)

3. *Peak parking occupancies*—parking occupancy (or parking accumulation) studies determine the number of parking spaces occupied at various times of the day and identify the periods of peak use. Observations of curb and off-street space usage are made at regular intervals throughout the day. Curb space occupancy of parked vehicles should be done by block face. The number of occupied legal parking spaces, as well as commercial vehicles in loading zones and illegally parked or double-parked vehicles, should be counted. In small study areas, the observer may walk. In larger study areas, the observer may drive. Often there is both a driver and an observer present to count and record the information. Using two people in the car allows more area to be covered.

   Parking space occupancy data are presented in both tabular and graphic form. Spread sheet programs are useful in summarizing the data. The number of vehicle-occupied spaces and the percentage of spaces occupied are summarized by location and time of day. Data are aggregated for the area as a whole and are presented as an accumulation of parked vehicles in the area by time of day. The study should also provide information on the occupancy of loading zones as well as data on illegally parked and double-parked vehicles.

4. *Parking durations and turnover*—parking durations (the time parked at a given parking space) and turnover (the number of vehicle parked in that space throughout the study period) are useful in parking management activities. They provide a basis for changing time limits or rates, focusing on enforcement, and removing curb parking. Information is obtained by recording license numbers throughout the study period. (See the *Manual of Transportation Engineering Studies*[48] for further details.)

---

[48] Institute of Transportation Engineers, *Manual of Transportation Engineering Studies* (Englewood Cliffs, N.J.: Prentice Hall, 1994).

Parking duration and turnover are generally summarized in tables, by type of facility (e.g., curb-by different time limits, off-street-by retail lot, employee lot). Cumulative frequency distributions (ogives) are also useful in displaying the information.

5. *Parker characteristics*—characteristics of parkers are obtained from parkers at place of parking either by parker interviews or by postcard mailback surveys. The interviews are designed to obtain information on where people

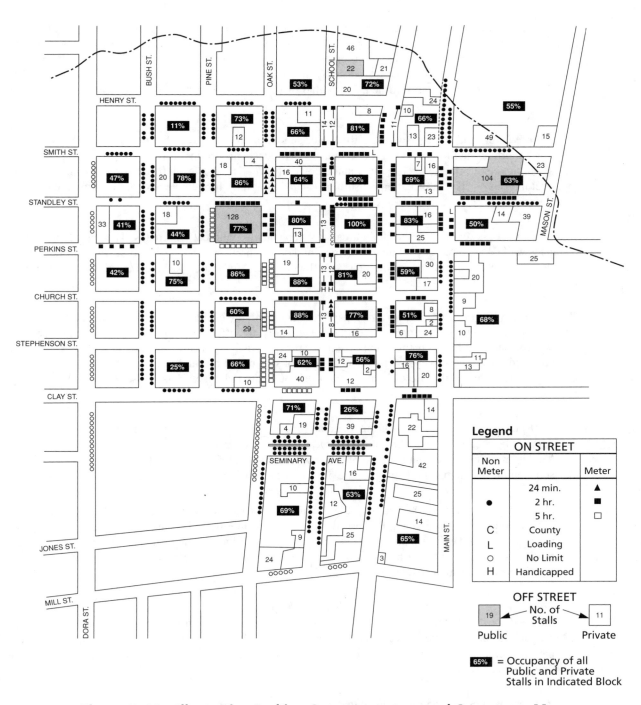

Figure 5–11   Illustrative Parking Space Inventory and Occupancy Map

Source: Institute of Transportation Engineers, *Traffic Engineering Handbook*, Fourth Edition, Englewood Cliffs, N.J.: Prentice Hall, 1992, Chapter 3.

park, trip purpose and frequency, trip origin, primary destination, length of time parked, parking fee paid, arrival and departure times, and distance walked from parking space to primary destination. The data are used to calculate the parking demand of an area, on a block-by-block basis. Occupancies, durations, and turnovers can also be obtained at the same time. Interviews are sometimes conducted at representative samples of curb and off-street parking facilities. Because of personnel limitations, an area may be subdivided and the interviews spread over several days.

A postcard survey requests the same information as an interview. Prepared return-address postcards are placed under the windshields of vehicles parked in the study area. In off-street facilities, attendants may distribute the cards to their customers. Each postcard is given an identifying number to indicate the location of the parking space where it was issued. Distribution is usually made during the peak hour, as rapidly as possible. About one-third of the postcards are returned. The value of this type of survey is limited because of possible response bias.

Surveys of visitors and employees at specific major generators such as office buildings and industrial plants provide important ancillary information about travel modes, trip origins, travel attitudes, and pedestrian flows. Employee information is usually obtained by employers, and visitor information is usually obtained by direct interviews. The information is useful in establishing rates for vehicle-and-person trips and parking generation.

Destinations of parkers within the study area are often shown graphically on maps. The trip purposes and distances walked are generally tabulated. Origins and destinations of vehicle trips to or from the study area are plotted on maps or on desire line charts. Influence areas for major parking facilities are sometimes illustrated.

6. *Parking supply and demand comparisons*—parking space needs are estimated on a block, district, or areawide basis by comparing parking supply and demand. Generally, the effective supply is estimated at 85 percent of the curb spaces and 90 percent of the off-street spaces. Existing parking demands in the city center can be estimated based on surveys of parkers' destinations or based on land-use type and intensity. Future parking demands generally are estimated based on anticipated changes in land use. Further descriptions follow.

   a. *Peak parking accumulation*—current demand may be estimated in areas where supply greatly exceeds demand by merely counting the accumulated vehicles at various times of the day. However, when the demand reaches 85 percent or more of the supply, it may not represent the true demand, as a result of some additional demand that may not be present because of the lack of adequate parking.

   b. *Demands based on parking surveys*—the traditional approach to estimating existing parking demands is based on surveys of parkers. Parkers along curb faces, in lots, and in garages are queried as to their times of entry and exit, trip purpose, and downtown destination. Demands then are aggregated for each block, zone, or district for each hour of the day. Peak demands then are compared with the effective supply area in each study area segment.

   c. *Land use based demands*—several land-use based approaches key demands to activities and eliminate the need for detailed parker interviews. The overall accumulations of parkers (adjusted as appropriate for parkers outside of the study area) are assumed to approximate the aggregated hour-by-hour downtown parking demand. This demand is allocated to the various subareas based on each area's relative share of downtown activity.

   Basic steps and data requirements include:

1. Inventory the location and number of existing parking spaces.

2. Observe the number of parked vehicles each hour from 6:00 A.M. through 5:00 P.M. on a typical weekday.

3. Obtain (or estimate) downtown employment and floor space for each analysis zone. Where there is a significant residential population in the downtown area, also estimate the number of dwelling units by analysis zone.

4. Estimate the approximate proportions of residential, long-term, and short-term parkers. The accumulated parked vehicles at 6:00 A.M. can be assumed to represent the residential parking demand. The accumulated vehicles at 10:00 A.M., less one-half the amount present at 6:00 A.M., can be assumed to represent the long-term parking demand. The accumulated vehicles during the hour of highest vehicle accumulation represents maximum parking demand in the study area. The accumulated vehicles at this time, less the accumulated vehicles present at 10:00 A.M. represent the short-term parking demand.

5. Each component of the peak accumulation is allocated on a block or analysis zone basis, in proportion to its relative share of parking demand generation as a function of the land-use intensity of each block. The number of employees in a block (or zone) is used to define that block's portion of total long-term demand. Commercial, retail, service, institutional, and restaurant square footage in each block (or zone) is used to define that zone's portion of total short-term demand. Likewise, the number of dwelling units in each block or zone is used to define that portion of total residential parking demand and represents the nighttime parking population.

   Where detailed land-use information is not available, zonal parking demand can be based on allocations keyed to employment. While less accurate, this represents a reasonable approximation since workers typically constitute about two-thirds of the peak accumulation.

The simplified three-zone example in Table 5–16 illustrates this approach.

d. *Demands based on parking generation rates*—parking demands can be estimated by using parking generation rates. This involves (1) tabulating the types and intensities of land uses throughout the study area; (2) estimating the amount of parking space needed per unit of land use, and applying these rates to the quantities involved; and (3) determining worker parking demand from questionnaires given to employees as appropriate.

Table 5–16   Illustrative Example for Allocating Peak-Parking Accumulation by CBD Analysis Zone

| | CBD Activity | | | | Parking Demand | | | | |
| | Employment | | Retail and Service Area | | Long-term Parkers | | Short-term Parkers | | |
Zone	No.	Percent	Floor Space (sq. ft)	Percent	Percent	No.	Percent	No.	Total
1	3,000	60	200,000	33	60	1,800	33	330	2,130
2	1,000	20	300,000	50	20	600	50	500	1,100
3	1,000	20	100,000	17	20	600	17	170	770
Total	5,000		600,000			3,000		1,000	4,000

Note: Peak accumulation = 4,000; long-term accumulation = 75 percent (or 3,000); and short-term accumulation = 25 percent (or 1,000).

Source: Levinson, H.S. and C.O. Pratt, "Estimating Downtown Parking Demands—A Land-Use Approach," *Transportation Research Record 957*, Washington, D.C.: Transportation Research Board, 1987.

This method is well suited for an individual development, existing or proposed, or for analyzing demands within the center of a small community. However, where there are shared uses or extensive public transport use, parking generation rates for free-standing suburban activities may overstate demand.

e. *An iterative approach*—this approach combines the two preceding methods. It applies parking generation rates for each land-use category to the activities in each analysis zone. Total demand is compared with the peak accumulation. The rates are then adjusted, and the process is repeated iteratively until the total calculated demand equals the observed peak parking accumulation. Demands for special activities can be identified and excluded from the iterative process.

f. *Future demand*—future parking demand is projected from existing demand. The amount of additional demand resulting from new office buildings, retail establishments, and other uses may be estimated by applying established parking generation factors, with appropriate adjustments for shared parking and transit use. Demand may be affected by changes in transit service and pricing policies.

Parking space supply, demand, and need are tabulated on a block-by-block or district basis. The information can be as displayed graphically. Deficiencies are generally concentrated in core areas with surplus spaces in surrounding areas.

7. *Parking program*—a program to improve parking conditions is often the final step in a parking study. The program recommendations should be based upon present and future needs and public policy decisions regarding how best to meet these needs (i.e., in the city center vs. at outlying express transit stations). This involves identifying alternate parking facility sites; preparing preliminary functional plans; estimating revenues, capital and operating costs, and financial feasibility; and developing a financing plan.

Parking Generation Studies

Parking generation rates are useful in assessing the adequacy of parking at existing developments and in estimating the spaces needed at new or expanded developments, the effects of changes in those developments, as well as the adequacy of existing developments. They also provide inputs for zoning regulations and bylaws—many jurisdictions have regulations that specify the amount of parking that must be provided for specific land uses. Chapter 14 contains detailed parking generation rates.

1. *Generation rate studies*—parking generation rates are obtained by observing the peak accumulations of vehicles throughout the day (and evening) and relating these accumulations to the floor space, employment, hospital beds, or other factors indicative of a land uses' parking activity. Ideally, a parking generation study is conducted at an isolated facility where the parking is used solely by the occupants of the buildings.

   It is difficult to observe parking occupancy at large parking areas with frequent evening operations—such as found around stadiums and regional shopping centers. In these cases, counts of vehicles entering and leavingby time period are necessary. These counts, however, include vehicles inmotion, resulting in some overstatement of actual parking demands.

2. *Shared parking*—mixed use developments typically have lower parking demands than those obtained by aggregating the demands based on individual uses. This is either because peak parking demands are separated by time of day or because people make multiple stops on a given trip (i.e., use sharing). Estimating shared parking requirements requires identifying both of these components.

   a. Parking demands for each time period can be estimated for each use and the composite demands computed. The largest combined parking demand should be used for estimating required spaces.

Table 5–17 Common Public Transportation Study Data Items, Uses, and Collection Methods

Data Item	Uses	Study Method
Load at peak point or other key point	Scheduling, planning	Point check, ride check
Running time and delay	Scheduling, planning	Ride check, trail car
Schedule adherence at specified points	Scheduling, evaluation, control	Point check, ride check, trail car
Boardings	Scheduling, evaluation, planning, reporting	Driver study, ride check
Distribution of boardings by fare category	Planning, marketing	Driver study, ride check
Boarding and alighting by stop	Planning	Automatic data collection equipment, ride check
Passenger kilometers	Evaluation, reporting	Automatic data collection equipment, ride check
Passenger characteristics and attitudes	Planning, marketing	Survey
Passenger origin and destination pattern along route	Planning, marketing	Special ride check, survey, inferred from automatic data collection equipment, point check, ride check

Source: *Transit Data Collection Design Manual, Final Report,* DOT-1-85-38, Urban Mass Transportation Administration, June 1985.

b. Where offices constitute most of the space in a mixed-use development (e.g., CBD), restaurant and retail shops may draw on workers for their patrons. Estimating the proportions of primary and secondary destinations requires direct interviews with patrons. The interviews should obtain information on trip purpose, travel mode, and whether the destination is primary or ancillary; they can be conducted at entrances to a generator.

Transit Studies

Transit studies obtain information on the quality of existing services and help establish the need for service improvements. They include operations planning for a given route, comprehensive operations analysis, short-range transit development programs, and major transit investment studies. They develop necessary information for analyzing the extent of usage, problems of traffic flow and safety, riding patterns, and traveler attitudes.

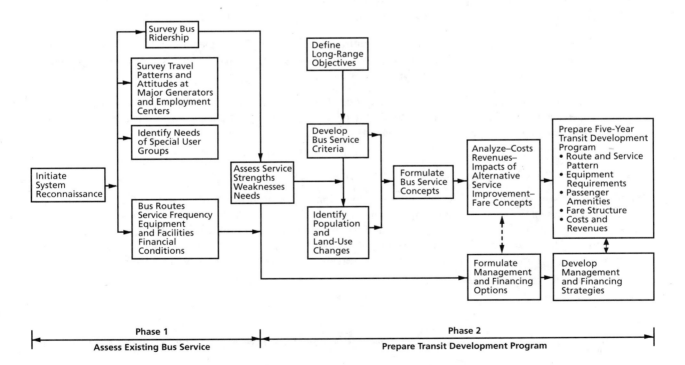

Figure 5–12 Typical Transit Study Design

Source: Wilbur Smith Associates.

Figure 5–12 gives a study design for a short-range transit development program. Table 5–17 lists some of the common public transit study data items and the methods used to collect the necessary information. Chapter 13 contains details on transit survey applications. Additional details on transit studies are described in *Urban Mass Transportation Travel Survey;*[49] the *Manual of Transportation Engineering Studies;*[50] *Transit Data Collection Design Manual;*[51] and *Transit Scheduling, Basic and Advanced Materials.*[52]

Transit Inventories

Inventories supply essential background information for other transit studies and for the evaluation of the service provided. Data gathered include transit network maps; schedules indicating frequency and hours of service on each route and travel times between various points in the network; a list of the rolling stock supplying the service showing its capacity, age, and condition; and the list of fares.

Service Coverage

Service coverage analysis indicates how well the existing (or planned) route network covers the population within the transit area. Typically areas within one-fourth to three-eigths of a mile of a bus route (or within one-half mile of a rail station) are delineated, and the population within these areas is estimated and aggregated. The percentage of the service area population within the specified walking distance is termed the "population coverage." This concept can be extended to include coverage of employment. The proportion of the service area population within a given distance of a transit stop *and* also within a specified distance of a work place represents the product of the two coverage values.

Passenger Count Studies

These studies provide information on boarding and aligning, vehicle loads, and adherence to schedules. They are useful in planning service studies, including the adjustment of routes and schedules; establishing bus stop locations; restricting turns along transit routes; adjusting street patterns and curb parking regulations; and developing transit priority measures, such as bus lanes and traffic signal priorities.

1. *Point checks*—point checks obtain information on passenger boardings and alightings and the loads on vehicles at one or more transit stops along the routes surveyed, usually the busiest stops. They may include studies of dwell times and passenger service times.

2. *Ride checks*—boarding and alighting checks can be performed along an entire transit route by direction of travel and time of day. This makes it possible to develop a profile of passenger loads by location and to compare these levels with the seats that are provided.

Passenger Surveys

Passenger surveys are useful for service planning and operation. These surveys determine trip origins and destinations; rider characteristics such as age, sex, trip purpose, and alternative modes available; traveler attitudes; and unmet travel needs. They are used to develop travel patterns and to correlate these patterns with land use, car ownership, and socioeconomic characteristics. Surveys may be conducted at transit stops; on transit vehicles; or at major travel generators, either as part of a comprehensive areawide travel study or as a special study of transit riders.

---

[49] Urban Transportation Systems Associates, *Urban Mass Transportation Travel Surveys* (Washington, D.C.: Federal Highway Administration, August 1972).

[50] Institute of Transportation Engineers, *Manual of Transportation Engineering Studies* (Englewood Cliffs, N.J.: Prentice Hall, 1994).

[51] *Transit Data Collection Design Manual, Final Report,* DOT-1-85-38 (Washington, D.C.: Urban Mass Transportation Administration, June 1985).

[52] Pine, R., Niemeyer, J., Chisholm, R. and Nelson/Nygaach, *TCRP Report 30 Transit Scheduling, or Basic and Advanced Manuals* (Washington, D.C.: Transportation Research Board, National Research Council, 1998).

Standard survey design should ensure that reliable, cost-effective results are obtained. Random selection of survey respondents is essential wherever sampling procedures are used. Reasonable sample sizes can be determined through standard statistical equations that consider level of confidence, allowable error, and the variability of the population. It may be necessary to increase initial sample sizes to account for possible nonresponse, although some survey bias may result, even in such cases.

Transit Speed and Delay Studies

These studies are similar to travel time studies for general traffic, but they also identify the delays caused at transit stops by passengers boarding and alighting, delays incurred where vehicles arrive ahead of schedule, and delays caused by crew changes or zone checks. The travel times and delays are obtained by observers riding on transit vehicles during various hours of the day. Table 5–18 gives an illustrative summary of bus travel times and delays.

Table 5–18 Bus Travel Times and Delays on Jamaica Avenue, Sutphin Boulevard to 168th Street, New York City, May 1989

Type of Delay	Seconds	Percent	Min/Km
Passenger Delay	56	11.7	0.67
Traffic Signals	89	18.5	1.06
Traffic Conflicts/Congestion	35	6.5	0.37
Subtotal	176	36.7	2.09
In Motion	304	63.3	3.62
Total Time	480	100.0	5.71

Average Speed (km/hr) 10.5 kpm (mph 16.5 mph)

Distance = 1.4 km (4,600 feet).

Source: Urbitran Associates, Inc. in association with H.S. Levinson, *Final Report Bus Priority Improvements Study, Analysis of Bus Priority Proposals*, N.Y.: New York City Department of Transportation, November 1986.

Pedestrian Studies

Pedestrian studies are used for a variety of purposes in transportation planning. They are used to establish safe route-to-school maps for elementary children, to establish the need for traffic controls, and to adapt controls to better serve pedestrian movement. The studies provide a basis for sidewalk improvements; and they help to justify pedestrian and transit malls, pedestrian skywalks, overpasses, tunnels, escalators, and moving belts. They are especially important in designing access to major pedestrian generators such as urban stadiums, convention centers, and downtown developments that generate large pedestrian movements. They are also useful in designing access to and within transit stations and terminals and in developing plans for sidewalk amenities and public open spaces.

An aging population requires more emphasis on providing pedestrian facilities and in changing some of the parameters (e.g., walking speed) traditionally used in pedestrian activities. The provision of special aids for handicapped persons (e.g., wheelchair ramps at intersections or to supplement stairs, audible traffic signals for the blind) has become an important aspect of the urban planning process.

Pedestrian studies include (1) studying pedestrian volumes, speeds, and capacities; (2) establishing needs for traffic controls; (3) surveying pedestrian trip origins, destinations, trip purposes, and walking distances; (4) developing pedestrian trip generation rates; (5) obtaining pedestrian attitudes and perceptions; and (6) analyzing pedestrian behavior and space use patterns. Detailed study procedures for obtaining and analyzing pedestrian volumes, walking speeds, needed gap sizes, and conflicts are contained in the *Manual on Transportation Engineering Studies*.[53] Descriptions of pedestrian behavior and street use studies are found in *Livable Streets*,[54] *The Social Life of Small Urban Spaces*,[55] and *City*.[56]

Volumes, Speeds, and Capacities

Pedestrian volume and flow studies may be expressed in terms of volume (persons per hour), flow rate (persons per minute per meter), spacing (square meter per person), or walking speed (meters per minute). Speed, flow rate, and density are interrelated. As flow rates on a sidewalk, crosswalk, passageway, ramp, or stairs increase, walking speed tends to

---

[53] Institute of Transportation Engineers, *Manual of Transportation Engineering Studies* (Englewood Cliffs, N.J.: Prentice Hall, 1994).

[54] Appleyard, D., *Livable Streets* (Berkeley, Calif.: University of California Press, 1981).

[55] Whyte, W. H., *The Social Life of Small Urban Spaces* (Washington, D.C.: Conservation Foundation, 1980).

[56] Whyte, W. H., *City* (New York, N.Y.: Doubleday, 1988).

decrease. After the flow rate reaches its maximum, density continues to increase toward a "jam density" or "crush density," and flow rate and walking speed approach zero.

Most pedestrian counts are made manually. Because they can be labor intensive, hours should be chosen carefully. Short-term sample counts may be used and then expanded to provide estimates for the period surveyed. Counts generally should be recorded by five minute intervals.

1. *Flow rates and capacities*—pedestrian capacity depends upon the effective walkway width. This effective width includes deductions of 0.15 meters (6 inches) or more to account for buildings, curbs, window displays, and other street furniture (e.g., poles, parking meters, planters, bicycle racks, newspaper racks, benches, bus shelters). Pedestrian capacity and LOS analyses are based on pedestrian spacing—the square meters of effective space per person. This is the reciprocal of density, the pedestrians per square meter. LOS standards express spacing in terms of square meters per person per minute. Chapter 7 contains data on pedestrian capacities and flow rates that reflect *Highway Capacity Manual* procedures.

2. *Walking speeds*—pedestrian walking speeds vary by LOS or density by area and by groups of people. Studies have shown walking speeds ranging from about 0.7 m (2.2 ft) per sec. to over 1.5 m (5 ft) per sec.[57, 58, 59] Many engineers have used 1.2 m (4.0 ft) per sec. in traffic engineering analyses. However, there is a growing tendency to use 1.1 m (3.3 ft) per sec. as a general value, and 0.9 m (3.0 ft) or 1.0 m (3.25 ft) per sec. for specific applications such as facilities utilized by elderly or handicapped people. Walking speeds below 0.9 m (3.0 ft) per sec. should not be used.

   A special pedestrian walking speed study is sometimes desirable to define an appropriate value to be used in an area under study. Such a study should have a defined distance delimited along the path traveled by the pedestrian population under consideration. Individual pedestrians are timed as they pass through the "trap." A sample of approximately 100 pedestrians should suffice. The sample should be collected during the time frame of interest (e.g., peak hour, noon, afternoon, or whatever). The data are plotted in a cumulative percentage curve. The fifth percentile value is usually the appropriate value to use for traffic control and safety purposes. Chapter 16 contains specific details on pedestrian facilities for similar planning techniques.

Traffic Control Studies

Pedestrian studies are conducted for traffic control purposes and include (a) determining adequate gaps for pedestrians crossing a street, and the proportion of time (in peak thirty minute periods) that these gaps are available; and (b) identifying minimum pedestrian volumes for installing traffic signals. Procedures for conducting these studies are found in the *Manual of Transportation Engineering Studies*.[60]

Door Counts

Counts of people entering and leaving buildings, stores, off-street parking facilities and transit terminals provide a basis for (1) establishing person-trip generation rates and (2) expanding sample interviews at the same locations. The counts should be made during the A.M., noon time, and P.M. peak periods for developing trip rates. When keyed to interviews, they should normally be conducted from 7:00 A.M. to 6:00 P.M. Trip rates are obtained by relating the pedestrian volumes to the characteristics of the activity surveyed such as floor space and employment. (If only exiting pedestrians are counted, the surveys could be done from 10:00 A.M. to 6:00 P.M.).

---

[57] Federal Highway Administration, *Manual on Uniform Traffic Control Devices for Streets and Highways* (Washington, D.C.: U.S. Government Printing Office).

[58] Sleight, R. B., "The Pedestrian," *Human Factors in Highway Safety Research* (N.Y.: John Wiley and Sons, 1972).

[59] Smith, P. T., *Safety and Locational Criteria for Bicycle Facilities*, FHWA Report RD 75-112 (Washington, D.C.: Federal Highway Administration, February 1976).

[60] Institute of Transportation Engineers, *Manual of Transportation Engineering Studies* (Englewood Cliffs, N.J.: Prentice Hall, 1994).

Pedestrian Interviews

Pedestrian interviews at major traffic generators provide information on destinations, trip purpose, arrival (or departure) mode, and distance walked. Interview data should be expanded to represent the total pedestrian movements for each time period based upon the actual ground counts. After expansion, duplicate trips (i.e., counted at buildings and at parking lots or transit terminals) should be eliminated. Data should then be aggregated by analysis zone, and interzonal origin-destination patterns (i.e., desire lines for walking trips) should be prepared. These trips can be compared with actual ground counts of pedestrians across screen lines and adjusted as needed.

Street and Plaza Analyses

Many pedestrian problems relate to the quality of the walking space. Qualitative factors such as sidewalk obstructions, blank walls, and ambiguous traffic controls can be observed. Use of public spaces—where people sit and stand, and the activities they engage in—can be obtained by aerial photography and by field observations. Results can be displayed graphically by location and time of day. Findings can be used to change the walking environment and the design of public space.

Bicycle Studies

Bicycle studies address the basic issues of (1) how well existing facilities operate and (2) where and how additional facilities should be provided. Answering these questions involves studies of existing and future demands; physical features of given facilities such as lane widths, average speeds, and stopping sight distances; observed effects of bike volumes on motor vehicle traffic (and conversely); and opportunities for providing improved bicycle facilities. Chapter 16 includes more detailed information on bicycle planning and surveys. Planning and design guidelines are contained in several studies.[61,62,63]

Goods Movement Studies

Goods movement involves the distribution of raw materials and finished products. It is handled by truck, train, ship, and pipeline with small amounts of high-value cargo going by air. The scale, types, and patterns of goods movement vary widely; studies should be keyed to specific needs. They generally involve obtaining information on (1) types and magnitudes of commodities shipped, (2) modes of conveyance utilized, (3) origins and destinations, (4) shipment and terminal travel times, (5) loading and berthing requirements, and (6) daily and hourly variations in shipments. Where trucks are involved, their number, type, weight, commodities carried, and use of roadways are important.

At the local level goods movement studies are usually undertaken in response to specific problems. Table 5–19 lists some of the operational safety economics, environmental problems, and the studies that are needed to address them.

Information Sources

There is a growing body of information on goods movement at the national, state, and local levels. A comprehensive listing of various commodity and freight transportation sources is given in Chapter 3. Principal sources include:

---

[61] Homburger, W.S., Hall, J.W., Loutzenheiser, R.C., Reilly, W. R. *Fundamentals of Traffic Engineering,* 14th Edition (Berkeley, Calif.: Institute of Transportation Studies, University of California, Berkeley, May 1996).

[62] Smith, P. T., *Safety and Locational Criteria for Bicycle Facilities,* FHWA Report RD 75-112 (Washington, D.C.: Federal Highway Administration, February 1976).

[63] Hope D., and Yachuk D., *Community Cycling Manual* (Ottawa, Canada: Canadian Institute of Planners, March 1990).

Table 5–19   Data Needs for Identifying Urban Goods Movement Problems

Downtown or High Density Distribution Centers	Interface/Terminals	System/Network

I. Operational
   A. Queuing counts at destination related to capacity of receiving and shipping facility
   B. Accident data
   C. Curbside usage
 	
   D. Inventory of loading zones
   E. Illegal stopping to load on streets
	I. Operational
	   A. Volume counts
	
	   B. Street use in area
	   C. Measures of total activity time, number of trucks, cargo hauled
	
	   D. Access route examined — time runs
	   E. Ease of access to loading docks
		I. Operational
		   A. Traffic counts with detailed vehicle classification
		   B. Speed and delay
		     1. System segments
		     2. Rail at grade crossings
		     3. Moveable bridges
		   C. Accident data
		   D. Access problems (low bridges, steep grades, load zoned roads, restricted acess by time of day.)

II. Economic
   Survey of shippers, receivers and operators
	II. Economic
	   Survey of terminal operators
		II. Economic
		   Survey of carriers operators
		   A. Truck
		   B. Rail
		   C. Water
		   D. Air

III. External Impacts
   A. Compute ranges of pollution using volume data
 	
   B. Monitoring
     1. Air
     2. Noise
	III. External Impacts
	   A. Aerial photos of terminal and surrounding area
	
	   B. Monitoring
		III. External Impact Monitoring
		   A. Air
		   B. Noise
		   C. Water

Source: Gendell, David S., et. al., *Urban Goods Movement Considerations in Urban Transportation Planning Studies*, Washington, D.C.: U.S. Department of Transportation, 1974.

1. *1977 Commodity Transportation Survey;*[64] *1993 Commodity Flow Survey;*[65] and *1997 Vehicle Inventory and Use Survey*, which is being completed.

2. *A Freight Data Handbook for States and MPOs* is being prepared by the Bureau of Transportation Statistics and the Federal Highway Administration.

3. Special surveys conducted by state departments of transportation (DOTs). These include, for example, Arizona's *Freight Movement Survey and Highway Carrier Attitude Survey.*[66] Truck volume and weight data are available from state DOT classification counts and from truck weight station records.

4. Information on urban goods movement is contained in *Characteristics of Urban Freight Systems*[67] and in many specific urban area studies.

A description of selected goods movement studies follows.

Truck Weight Studies

Information on truck weights are collected for many purposes, including pavement design, revenue estimates, motor carrier enforcement, highway cost allocation, and other planning and engineering activities. The vehicle weights are reported by motor freight companies as part of their reporting requirements. The recipient varies by state but is frequently the motor vehicle department through the registration process.

---

[64] *Commodity Transportation Survey* (Washington, D.C.: U.S. Bureau of Census, 1977).

[65] *Commodity Flow Survey* (Washington, D.C.: U.S. Bureau of Census, 1993).

[66] Radwan, A.E., M. Rahman, and S. Kalevela, "Freight Flow and Attitudinal Survey for Arizona," *Transportation Research Record 1179* (Washington, D.C.: Transportation Research Board, 1988, pp. 16–22).

[67] Wegmann, F. J., Chatterjee, Lipinski, M.E., Jennings, P. E., McGinnus, E. R., *Characteristics of Urban Freight Systems*, DOT-T-96-22 (Washington, D.C.: Federal Highway Administration, 1996).

Roadside weight checking is conducted with either permanent or portable scales, usually as part of an enforcement program. Following the changes in trucking regulations in the 1980s and the resulting changes to fleet mixes, truck size and weight studies are often conducted to evaluate the impact on types of trucks being used on pavement performance, geometric requirements, and changes in industry efficiencies. Choice of method should consider ADT volumes, percent trucks, percent trucks by type, percent trucks by commodity, interstate versus intrastate trips, site suitability, and nearby alternative routes.

- *Static scales* are required to certify truck weights and to establish a legal basis for identifying violators. This requires special truck access to avoid any spillback on the main travel lanes.

- *Weigh-in-motion* scales are used to determine if a truck is traveling within a reasonable range of legal weight limits. Information collected may include gross vehicle weight, axle weight, and tandem axle weight. Weigh-in-motion scales are often found at permanent truck weigh station sites, but they are used by some agencies in a roving mode.

Intercept Surveys

Truck operators can be interviewed at a cordon line around an urban area, often as part of a comprehensive transportation planning study. The surveys should identify the volume and types of commodities moving into and through an area, the destinations of these commodities, and the types of vehicles involved. The Port Authority of New York and New Jersey Authority, for example, conducts commodity surveys of vehicles crossing the Hudson River and Verrazano Narrows on a periodic basis. Intercept interviews can be conducted at truck weigh stations. Where these are located near the cordon line there is usually space for trucks to pull out for interviews.

Interviews

Interviews can provide detailed information of goods movement characteristics and problems. They can be conducted with shippers, carriers, and building owners, managers/tenants, with truck (or rail) owners and operators, and at terminals.[68]

1. *Building owner/manager/tenant* interviews should obtain information pertaining to:

    - *Building use*—floor space by use (e.g., office, retail), number of tenants, percentage occupied, number of employees, and the like.

    - *Delivery restrictions*—restrictions imposed by the building relating to hours of delivery and types of vehicles.

    - *Delivery reception*—location at which delivery and service vehicles park, off-street loading facility availability and utilization, location of freight elevators, and other factors.

    - *Delivery variations*—variations in deliveries by hour, day, or month.

    - *Enforcement*—building actions taken to assure proper usage of the available loading space.

    - *Size and type of shipments.*

    - *Origins and destinations of goods shipped or received.*

    - *Procedures for handling mail and trash.*

    - *Particular problems noted or experienced.*

    - *Reaction to various alternative solutions.*

2. *Truck owners and operators*—trip patterns can be obtained by interviewing the owners and operators of registered trucks. A sample should be selected from vehicle registration data; the percentage of total registered

---

[68] Christiansen, D., *Urban Transportation Planning for Goods and Services* (Washington, D.C.: Federal Highway Administration, 1979).

1. Company Name _____ address _____

2. Interviewee _____ title _____ phone # _____

3. Normal operation   hours: _____ ; days _____

4. Typical days activities (describe)

    _____

    _____

    _____

    _____

5. Trip generation peak hours: AM _____ Midday _____ PM _____

6. Load factors: average TL _____ average LTL _____

7. Capacity of terminal: Simultaneous   Daily

                          trucks   _____   _____

                          tonnage   _____

8. Commonly carried commodities   Annual Tons   Average Shipment Size

    _____   _____   _____

    _____   _____   _____

    _____   _____   _____

    _____   _____   _____

9. Percent tonnage within radius:

    0-25 miles _____   0-50 miles _____   0-300 miles

        0-1000 miles _____   _____

10. Cities served (list) _____

    _____

11. Relationship to other carriers: cross loading _____

        pickup/delivery to _____

12. Special facilities at terminal _____

    _____

13. Advantages of site _____

    _____

14. Disadvantages _____

    _____

15. Special street & traffic problems _____

    _____

Figure 5–13   In-Depth Terminal Interview Form Used in Dallas–Fort Worth Regional Goods Movement Study

Source: Christiansen, D., *Urban Transportation Planning for Goods and Services,* Washington, D.C.: U.S. Department of Transportation, Federal Highway Administration, 1979.

```
16. Ideal site description _____
    _____

17. Type of records available _____
    _____

18. Potential problems using records for data sample _____
    _____

19. Location of records _____ address
    _____ person responsible, _____ telephone

20. Records file according to:    ☐ date    ☐ consignee   ☐ commodity
       other (specify) _____

21. How complete are records (describe) _____
    _____

22. Record content (obtain typical record)
    a.  Commodity identification: (describe one)   ☐ not indicated
        ☐ indicated, not coded   ☐ coded*   *code used _____
    b.  Truck identification:
        ☐ not indicated              ☐ identified by classification
        ☐ identified by weight          other (specify) _____
    c.  Origins & destinations:      ☐ identified by address
        ☐ identified by customer        other _____
    d.  ☐ weight indicated           ☐ not indicated
    e.  ☐ number parcels indicated   ☐ not indicated
    f.  Other information (summarize) _____
        _____

23. Site description:
                    office        _____ sq. ft.
                    dock          _____ sq. ft.
                    warehouse     _____ sq. ft.
                    garage        _____ sq. ft.
                    site          _____ sq. ft.

24. Site diagram:
```

Figure 5–13   In-Depth Terminal Interview Form Used in Dallas–Fort Worth Regional Goods Movement Study (continued)

Source: Christiansen, D., *Urban Transportation Planning for Goods and Services,* Washington, D.C.: U.S. Department of Transportation, Federal Highway Administration, 1979.

truck owners interviewed should range from one to five percent depending upon the truck classification. Information should be obtained on (1) license owner and location where vehicle is based, (2) axle arrangement and body style, (3) cargo capacity, (4) commodities carried, (5) trips and stops made, and (6) related travel information.

3. *Terminals*—questionnaires can be distributed to for-hire truck terminals and followed by in-depth interviews. The same procedures can be followed for major rail marine or air carrier terminals. Interviews should obtain information such as the following:

- A detailed description of the routine operation of the terminal, including hours of operation, workflow, volume fluctuations, and types of commodities carried in the areas served.

- A description of operational characteristics of the terminal, including capacity, number and types of trucks and rail cars served, and special equipment used.

- The types of records maintained at the terminal that might be utilized in a comprehensive goods movement survey, including shipment patterns and commodity characteristics.

- Particular problems noted or experienced.

- Reaction to various alternative solutions.

Figure 5–13 shows the form used in the terminal interview process in Dallas, Texas.[69]

Mail-Out Surveys

A mail-out survey can be mailed to terminal operators. The *Yellow Pages* can be used to compile a basic mailing list. This list should be checked against Chamber of Commerce information and member lists of local terminal managers and cartage associations. Questionnaires should obtain information such as the following:

- Volume and types of freight carried.

- Size and design characteristics of the site.

- Peaking characteristics of demand.

- Age of facility and time of occupancy, by carrier.

- Operator's judgment relative to site location criteria.

- Historical and projected growth.

- Plans, if any, for new facilities.

Surveys in Dallas and Knoxville have reported response rates of about forty and sixty percent respectively.

On-Site Surveys

On-site surveys at office buildings, stores, and other land uses collect data on goods movement and relate this information to characteristics of the building or establishment. They collect information pertaining to operational characteristics (e.g., vehicle arrival time, time to complete a delivery, loading facility used, particular problems observed, owner and class of vehicle, previous origin, and next destination) and commodity flow characteristics (e.g., number of shipments, origin of delivery or destination of pickup, type of commodity, weight and number of parcels, and specific land use

---

[69] Christiansen, D., *Dallas CBD Goods and Services Distribution Project* (Dallas, Texas: Office of Transportation Programs, City of Dallas, 1980).

LOG DATE _____

Truck Mileage Reading at Start of First Trip _____ (miles)					
Truck Mileage Reading at End of Last Trip _____ (miles)					

Stop Number	Arrival and Departure Time at Each Stop		Location of Each Stop by Zone	Type of Business or Activity at Each Stop	Type and Quantity (units) of Freight Handled at Each Stop		Lead Factor for Truck or Trailer after Each Stop
Start of 1st Trip							
1st Stop							
2nd Stop							
3rd							
4th							
5th							
6th							
7th							
8th							
9th							
10th							
11th							
12th							

Figure 5–14   Urban Truck Daily Log Form

Source: *Street Smarts*, Transportation Consulting MDA, Inc., 1992.

generating the shipment). The number of personnel required at an individual site to perform the survey generally varies from one to five depending upon the type and layout of the building being surveyed.

On-Board Surveys

An individual is assigned to ride with a truck driver during the course of the route. The types of information collected are similar to those collected in on-site surveys. On-board surveys also yield information on:

- The problems encountered at a large number of locations covering a broad range of land activities in several different areas of the region.

- Point-to-point operating characteristics for various types of delivery vehicles. Data pertaining to how a vehicle's time is spent (e.g., traffic delay, running time, stop time for deliveries) can be obtained.

A sample trip log form is shown in Figure 5–14.

Loading and Unloading Studies

Studies of loading deck operations are used to determine space requirements and geometric design criteria. These studies investigate occupancy and dwell times—often by land use type. The information provides a basis for establishing desirable on-street and off-street loading space.

Statistical Considerations

Transportation planning studies involve the collection, analyses, and interpretation of data. This data may be qualitative or quantitative; it may be continuous or discrete. It may involve measuring traffic volumes, travel patterns, or traveler attitudes.

Statistical analysis methods are essential in this effort. They can address such questions as how to best characterize the distribution of travel times, speeds, or land uses; what sample sizes are needed at a specified level of accuracy to estimate shopper origins at a major activity center; or how to establish predictive relationships between land use and trip generation. This section provides some basic statistical concepts and general guidelines that underlie transportation planning studies. More detailed discussions can be found in Chapter 5 of ITE's *Traffic Engineering Handbook* and in standard statistics texts.

General Observations

Statistical considerations should permeate the entire transportation planning study process. It is essential to clarify the basic study objectives; plan investigations and collect information in appropriate ways; assess the structure and quality of data, including how to deal with errors, outliers, and missing observations; provide a thorough initial examination of the data to identify patterns and features; select and carry out appropriate statistical tests and analysis; compare findings with previous results; acquire further data if necessary; and interpret and communicate findings.[70]

Graphs and Tables

Graphs and tables should clearly and precisely communicate the information that should be conveyed. They should have clear, self-explanatory titles; and units of measurement should be stated. Axes of graphs should be labeled, and unnecessary information should be avoided; the ratio of data to ink should be kept high, and color should be used sparingly.[71] Tables should not be too complex.

Rounding Numbers

A major need is to convey the accuracy of the numerical data. Numbers should be rounded to the accuracy that is desired and that reflects the likely error in obtaining the data. The last significant figure in any answer should usually be of the same order of magnitude (in the same decimal position) as the uncertainty. For example, if the speed on a rural highway is recorded as 82.81 kph with an uncertainty of 0.5 mph, then it should be rounded to 82.8 ± 0.5. If the uncertainty is 3 kph, then it should be rounded to 83 ± 3. And if the uncertainty is 30 kph, then the answer should be 80 ± 30. However, numbers used in calculations should be kept to one more significant figure than is justified. Thus, recording an ADT of 18,236 implies an uncertainty of ± 1 vehicle per day; rounding to 18,240 implies an uncertainty of 10 vehicles per day; and rounding to 18,200 implies an uncertainty of 100 vph per day.

Forecasting future travel demand and other dimensions of change are based on current information and relationships, and assumption about how these might change. Since the validity of these assumptions cannot be tested, reporting forecast results to a high degree of precision is inappropriate.

---

[70] Chatfield, C., *Problem Solving, A Statisticians Guide,* 2nd Edition (London: Chapman & Hall, 1995).

[71] Tufte, E. R., *The Visual Display of Quantitative Information* (Cheshire, Conn.: Graphics Press, 1983).

Error Propagation

Errors tend to propagate as individual quantities are added, subtracted, multiplied or divided.

1. The maximum error in the sum or difference of two measurements is the equal to the sum of the possible errors in the individual measurements.

$$\text{Error in Sum} = \text{error}_1 + \text{error}_2 = e_1 + e_2 \tag{5-3}$$

2. The maximum possible error in the product of two measurements or observations is:

$$\text{Error} = ae_2 + be_1 + e_1e_2 \tag{5-4a}$$

Since the produce e_1e_2 is small relative to the other terms, the error is approximately $ae_2 + be_1$.

3. The relative maximum error in the product of two measurements is equal (approximately) to the sum of the relative error.

$$\text{Relative Error in Product} \cong \left(\frac{\text{error}_1}{a}\right) + \left(\frac{\text{error}_2}{b}\right) \tag{5-4b}$$

Where a and b are the base measurements 1 and 2, respectively.

However, if the individual uncertainties are independent and random, the likely uncertainties are computed as follows:

$$\text{Error in Sum} = \sqrt{e_1^2 + e_2^2} \tag{5-5}$$

$$\text{Relative Error in Product} = \sqrt{\frac{e_1^2}{a} + \frac{e_2^2}{b}} \tag{5-6}$$

These results can be extended to any number of observations or measurements. A simple example illustrates how these equations can be applied. Assume that the peak-hour trip generation for a shopping center can be estimated within ± 10 percent, and that the directions of approach can be estimated within 15 percent. Since the trip rates and approach directions are independent, Equation 5–6 should be used. The error in the approach traffic would be $\sqrt{10^2 + 15^2}$ or 18 percent. Thus, if the site traffic on approach A were 350 vph, the error in this traffic would be $(.18)(350)$ or ± 63 vehicles per hour.

Table 5–20 Examples of Populations and Samples in Transportation Planning Studies

Subject of Study	Population	Sample
Daily traffic at a given location	Set of all vehicle passages past the location in 24 hours	Set of all observed vehicle passages past the location in the 24-hour period
Mode of travel of people entering a store	Set of all people entering store	Set of people entering store who are interviewed
Spot speeds at a given location	Set of speeds of all vehicles passing the location	Set of speeds observed
Home interview origin-destination study (origins and destinations of trips in survey area)	Set of all dwelling units in survey area	Set of dwelling units where interviews are obtained
Trip origins of vehicles passing a given location	Set of trip origins of all vehicles passing the location	Set of recorded trip origins of vehicles passing the location

Source: Votaw, D.F. and H.S. Levinson, *Elementary Sampling for Traffic Engineers* (Saugatuck, Conn.: Eno Foundation for Highway Traffic Control, 1962.

Overview of Methods

The following sections provide an overview of descriptive and inferential statistics, present the common probability distributions that underline these methods, and give general guidelines for curve fitting and regression analysis.

- *Initial data analysis*—contemporary thinking has placed increased attention on exploratory or initial data analysis as a prerequisite to statistical inference and model formulation.

- *Inferential statistics (statistical inference)*—deals with ways to generalize results from a sample of observations to a larger group (or population). It includes areas estimating sample size, establishing confidence intervals, and conducting significance tests.

Statistical methods deal with both populations and samples. A *population* is the total class or set of elements (e.g., objects, people) under study. It may be *infinite* or *finite*. A *sample* is a subset of one or more elements of the population. The sampling may be done *without* replacement from a finite population. Where the population is infinite, the sampling is done *with* replacement. Table 5–20 provides illustrative examples of populations and samples that are normally encountered in transportation planning.[72]

Descriptive Statistics

Descriptive statistics organizes and characterizes the information contained in populations and samples. It deals with the various characteristics of frequency distributions, such as location and variation.

Location

Measures of location or central tendency are frequently used to describe and characterize data. The common measures include the arithmetic mean, median, mode, geometric mean, and harmonic mean.

1. The *arithmetic mean* is the most familiar and widely used measure. It is defined as μ for a population and $\bar{x}$ for a sample.

    The sample mean $\bar{x}$, is calculated as follows for samples of size n:

    $$\bar{x} = \frac{x_1 + x_2 + \dots x_n}{n} = \frac{\sum_{i=1}^{n} x_i}{n} \tag{5–7}$$

    For grouped data

    $$\bar{x} = \frac{x_1 f_1 + x_2 f_2 + \dots x_n f_n}{n} = \sum_{i=1}^{n} x_i f_i \tag{5–8}$$

    Where $f_1, f_2, \dots . f_n$ represent frequencies or weights for observations $x_1, x_2 \dots . x_n$, respectively.

    (Note: the population mean, μ, for a population of N elements is calculated similarly.)

2. The *median* represents the middle observation in a set of numbers that is ranked from lowest to highest. If the number of observations is odd, there is a single middle value; while if the number of observations is even, the median represents the average of the two middle values. (Interpolation may be necessary in dealing with frequency distributions.) The median is useful when there may be some extremely high or low values that would not result in a representative value of the sample mean. Household incomes, for example, are often better characterized by the median, since very high incomes would result in an unduly high average income.

---

[72] Adapted from Votaw, D. F. and Levinson, H.S., *Elementary Sampling for Traffic Engineers* (Saugatuck, Conn.: Eno Foundation for Highway Traffic Control, 1962).

3. The *mode* of a set of observations represents the observation that occurs most frequently. It is useful for counted data (e.g., the number of persons in a household) or as the *modal group* when measurement data has been grouped into ranges. Probabilistically, it is the most likely outcome in the sample.

Variation

The common measures of the variation (or spread) of data around its center include (1) the range, (2) the mean deviation, (3) the standard deviation, and (4) the interquartile range. Of these, the range and standard deviation are the most widely used.

1. *Range*—the range is defined as the difference between the largest and smallest elements of a sample (or population).

2. *Mean deviation*—the mean deviation is defined as the average of the absolute values of the deviations from the mean.

$$MD = \sum_{i=1}^{n} \frac{|x - \bar{x}|}{n} \qquad (5\text{--}9)$$

3. *Standard deviation*—the standard deviations of a set of observations is defined as the square root of the mean squared deviations about the mean. The equations for populations and samples are as follows:

$$\sigma = \sqrt{\sum_{i=1}^{N} \frac{(x_{i-}\mu)^2}{N}} \qquad (5\text{--}10)$$

$$s = \sqrt{\sum_{i=1}^{n} \frac{(x_{i-}\bar{x})^2}{n-1}} \qquad (5\text{--}11)$$

Where: μ =   mean of population

        $\bar{x}$ =   mean of sample

        N   =   elements in population

        n   =   elements in sample

For data grouped in frequency distributions, the corresponding equations are:

$$\sigma = \sqrt{\sum_{i=1}^{N} \frac{(x_{i-}\mu)^2}{N} f_i} \qquad (5\text{--}12)$$

$$s = \sqrt{\sum_{i=1}^{n} \frac{(x_{i-}\bar{x})^2}{n-1} j} \qquad (5\text{--}13)$$

4. *Variance*—the variance (V) is defined as the square of the standard deviation.

5. *Coefficient of variation*—The coefficient of variation defines the *relative* amount of variation. It equals the standard deviation divided by the mean, expressed as a percentage.

$$C.V. \ (in \ \%) = \frac{S}{\bar{x}} 100 \ or \ \frac{\sigma}{\mu} 100 \qquad (5–14)$$

6. *Percentiles* also express the spread or dispersion of data. Commonly used percentiles include the median (50 percentile) and the quartiles (25 and 75 percent percentiles). The 85 percentile is used as a base for setting speed limits.

7. *Interquartile range*—the interquartile range encompasses the observations in a cumulative frequency distribution that lie between the 25 and 75 percentiles.

8. *Box and whisker plot*—a "box and whisker" plot provides a quick way to characterize a distribution, identify "outlier" observations, and compare two or more distributions. This concept is shown in Figure 5–15. It includes a scale with a box beside it that extends from the lower quartile to the upper quartile. The whiskers reach to the lowest and highest values that lie within one (or 1.5) interquartile range, either above and below the box. Observations falling beyond this range are shown as "outliers".

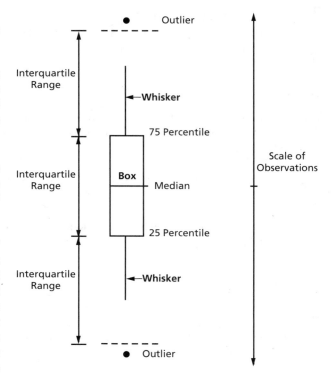

Figure 5–15   Box and Whisker Plot

Source: Adapted from Hutchinson, T.P., *Essentials of Statistical Methods in 41 Days*, Sydney, Australia: Ramsby Scientific Publishing, 1993.

Table 5–21 and Figure 5–16 show how the distribution of fifty spot speed observations can be summarized and characterized by these measures of location and spread.

The range can be used to provide a check or initial estimate of the standard deviation when the form of the distribution is known. Typical values for the standard deviation as a function of the range are:

Table 5–21   Illustrative Example Distribution of 50 Vehicle Speeds (Measured to the Nearest Kph)

Class (kph)	MidPoint (x)	Frequency (No. of Vehicles in each Class) (f)	x(f)	$x-\bar{x}$	$(x-\bar{x}^2)$	$(x-x^2)(f)$	Cumulative No. at or Below Upper Speed	Percentages Frequency	Percentages Cumulative
11.5 – 14.5	13	3	39	9.1	82.81	1248.43	3	6	6
14.5 – 17.5	16	7	112	6.1	37.21	260.47	10	14	20
17.5 – 20.5	19	9	171	3.1	9.61	86.49	19	18	38
20.5 – 23.5	22	14	308	0.1	0.01	0.14	33	28	66
23.5 – 26.5	25	8	200	2.9	8.41	67.28	41	16	82
26.5 – 29.5	28	4	112	5.9	34.81	139.24	45	8	90
29.5 – 32.5	31	3	93	8.9	79.21	237.63	48	6	96
32.5 – 35.5	34	2	68	11.9	141.61	283.22	50	4	100
		n = 50						100	

Notes: Mean = 22.1; Median 22.0 kph; Mode 22.0 mph (approx.); Lower Quartile = 17.5 kph; Upper Quartile = 25.0 kph; Interquartile Range = 75 kph; Standard Deviation = 5.2; Coeff. Of Variation = 23.5%.

$$\sum(x-\bar{x})f = 1,322.40$$

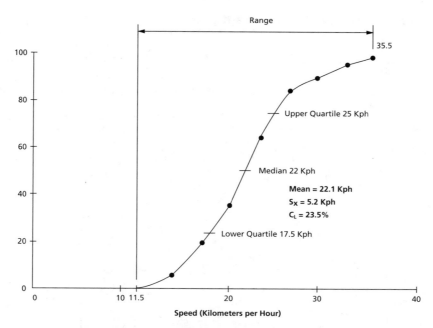

Figure 5–16   Cumulative Distributions of 50 Spot Speeds

- Uniform distribution, 0.29.

- Triangular distribution, 0.20.

- Normal (bell-shaped) distribution:

    $20 < n < 40$ 0.25

    $n = 100$ 0.20

    $n = 400$ 0.17

- Any distribution ≤ 0.50 range.

Thus, if the range was 200, the sample size 100, and the distribution normal, the standard deviation would be approximately (0.20) 200 or 40.

Probability Distributions

Various probability distributions are useful in characterizing data and in performing statistical tests. These distributions include a listing of all values of a random variable in graphic or tabular form or by equation. The individual probabilities range from 0 to 1. The total areas under each distribution (i.e., the cumulative probability distribution) equals unity.

Table 5–22 gives some important probability distributions, identifies each distribution's key parameters, and cites examples of applications. The distributions may be discrete (i.e., binomial and Poisson) or they may be continuous (i.e., exponential or normal).

Table 5–22   Some Important Frequency Functions

Name of Distribution	Frequency Function	Parameters	Examples of Applications
Binomial	$f(x) = C_x^n \, p^x(1-p)^{n-x}$ (C_x^n is a binomial coefficient)	p = probability of a given category	Populations having two categories† (e.g., "Successes" and "Failures," local vehicles and non-local vehicles, customer and traveler attitudes)
Poisson	$f(x) = \dfrac{e^{-m} m^x}{x!}$	m = expected value (mean)	Random arrival of cars in a parking garage entrance. Length of left turn storage lanes.
Hypergeometric	$f(x) = \dfrac{C_x^N 1 \, C_{n-x}^{N-N} 1}{C_n^N},$ N = Population size. N_1 = No. of "success" in population n = Sample size. x = No. of "Success" in sample. ($C_x^N 1, C_{n-x}^{N-N} 1, C_n^N$ are binomial coefficients)	N_1/N = Proportion of "successes" in population	Finite binomial population.
Multinomial	$f\left(n_1, n_2, ..., n_k\right) = \dfrac{n!}{n_1! \, n_2! ... n_k!} \, p_1^1 1 \, p_2^n 2 ... p_k^n k$ $(n_1+n_2+\,.\,.\,.+p_k=1)$. The parameters are $p_1, p_2, .\,.\,.,p_k$, where p_i = probability of drawing category i $(p_1+p_2+\,.\,.\,.+p_k=1)$.		Populations having k categories. $(k \geq 2)$.
Exponential	$\lambda e - \lambda x$	$x;\ \lambda > 0$	Distribution of headways.
Uniform	$f(x) = \dfrac{1}{b-a}$	a, b $a < x < b$	Distribution of Traffic Volumes within a given volume strata.
Normal	$f(x) = \dfrac{1}{\sigma \sqrt{2\pi}} e^{-(x-u)^2}$	u = expected value (mean) σ^2 = variance	Studies of spot speeds, reaction times, etc.
Standard Normal	$f(x) = \dfrac{1}{\sqrt{2\pi}} e^{-x^2/2}$	$u = 0$ $\sigma^2 = 1$	Calculations involving normal distributions. Useful in sampling analysis.

† In effect the populations are assumed to be infinite.

Source: Adapted from Votaw, D.F. and H.S. Levinson, *Elementary Sampling for Traffic Engineers*, Saugatuck, Conn.: Eno Foundation for Highway Traffic Control, 1962.

Normal Distribution

The normal distribution is the best known distribution and is widely used in statistical analyses. Many frequency distributions—such as speeds of motorists or heights of men—are normally distributed. The distribution is also used in making statistical inferences about samples. The standard normal distribution is used for this purpose. Any normal distribution can be transformed into a standard normal distribution as follows:

$$Z_a = \frac{X_a - \mu}{\sigma} \tag{5–15}$$

Where μ = population mean

X_a = observation

σ = standard deviation

Z_a = standard normal variate

Figure 5–17 shows a graph of the standard normal distribution: (1) the distribution is symmetric about the mean, (2) the x axis gives units of standard deviations from the mean, which are commonly defined as Z_a (or Z), and (3) almost the entire area under the curve lies within ± 3 standard deviations from the mean (i.e. $Z_a = \pm 3$).

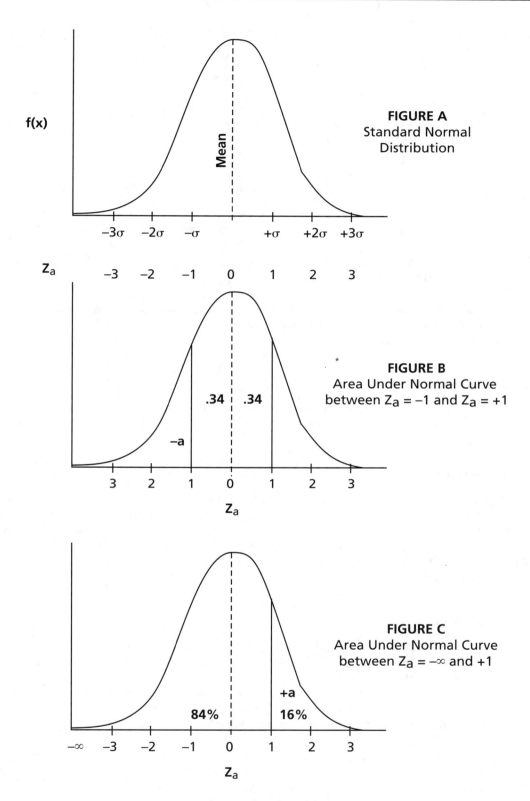

FIGURE A
Standard Normal Distribution

FIGURE B
Area Under Normal Curve between $Z_a = -1$ and $Z_a = +1$

FIGURE C
Area Under Normal Curve between $Z_a = -\infty$ and $+1$

Figure 5–17   Standard Normal Distribution

Representative confidence coefficients and the areas under the standard normal distribution that they encompass are as follows.

Confidence Coefficient (Z_a)	Area Encompassed	
	−a to +a	($-\infty$ to $+\infty$)
1.000	0.68	0.84
1.282	0.80	0.90
1.645	0.90	0.95
1.960	0.95	0.975
2.326	0.98	0.99
2.576	0.99	0.995

The application of these values is straightforward and is illustrated in Figure 5–17 (parts b and c).

- The Z_a value of ± 1.0 encompasses 68 percent of the area under the curve, while 16 percent on each tail of the curve would lie outside this range (Figure 5–17, part b.)

- If the goal is "not to exceed" a given value, then the area under the curve is read from $-\infty$ to Z_a. For $Z_a = +1.0$, about 84 percent of the area would be included, and 16 percent would fall outside. (Figure 5–17.) These are the values that are generally tabulated.

Other Distributions

Several other distributions are commonly used in sampling problems and analyses. These include the Students t, Chi-Square, and F Distributions. Their use is described in most statistics texts.

Sampling and Inference

Sampling procedures make it possible to draw inferences about a population. By sampling a small fraction of the entire population, it is possible to estimate characteristics that represent the population as a whole with enough accuracy to base decisions on the result with a reasonable level of confidence. Sampling procedures involve establishing confidence intervals, estimating sample sizes, and comparing various groups. They make it possible to address questions such as: How good are the results? What sample sizes are needed? Are the differences between two sample means or variances statistically significant?

Advantages and Uses

Sampling has several advantages. It is generally neither feasible nor possible to measure an entire population (e.g., 24-hour 365-day measurements of all travel in the Los Angeles Metropolitan area). In some types of inquiry, the choice lies between obtaining information by sampling or not at all. A main reason for sampling is economy, since sampling reduces the time and costs required to obtain vital information. A sample may actually produce more accurate results than a complete enumeration, since more careful supervision of the field work and data processing is possible. When an in-depth study of individuals is required, a small sample may permit comprehensive information to be collected.

Sample surveys are widely used in transportation and planning studies to obtain information on travel modes, patterns, frequencies, and attitudes; to determine population characteristics such as family income, car ownership, housing preferences, and mobility; and to quantify travel times, VKT of travel, and similar traffic parameters.

Principal Steps

The principal steps include the following:

1. Clearly state the objectives and reasons for the survey.

2. Define the population of interest to be sampled.

3. Identify the data to be collected.

4. Establish the desired degree of precision.

5. Determine the methods of measurement (e.g., household telephone survey versus home interview survey).

6. Construct the sampling frame for the population to be sampled. This frame should cover the entire population to be sampled, and each individual element must appear only once on the list.

7. Select the sample design and sampling plan. This includes initial estimates of sample size and precision, as well as time and cost implications.

8. Pre-test the survey instrument (e.g., questionnaire) and modify it as necessary.

9. Organize the field work, and collect the data.

10. Summarize, analyze, and interpret the data. Clearly indicate the amount of error that is expected in the most important elements.

11. Preserve the information assembled for future surveys. Quantifying key parameters, such as the variances, will prove useful in preparing future survey designs. Sampling theory plays an important role in steps 4, 6, 7, 8, and 10.[73]

Types of Samples

The samples drawn from a population may be probability or non-probability samples. The *probability* sample makes it possible to apply probability theory to estimate the extent to which a sample value differs from the population value. It is defined as a sample in which the probability of any individual member of the population being picked for the sample can be determined and has a nonzero chance of selection. When the population is finite, each element has an equal chance of being selected. *Non-probability* samples include judgement and quota samples. In judgement samples, personal judgement decides which individuals should be selected (for example, interviewing a "typical" group of households for their travel behavior). Quota samples attempt to obtain a representative sample of a specified number of individuals from a given subgroup of the population. Under the right conditions, these methods give useful results, but they are not amenable to sampling theory since no element of random selection is involved.

The common types of probability sampling include (1) simple random sampling, (2) stratified random sampling, (3) systematic sampling, and (4) cluster sampling.

1. *Simple random sampling*—this is the simplest and most widely used form of sampling. A simple random sample from an infinite population is selected in such a way that all observations chosen are statistically independent. A simple random sample from a finite population involves selecting n units out of the population, N, so that

---

[73] Cochran, W. G., *Sampling Techniques,* 3rd Edition (N.Y.: John Witey & Sons, 1977).

each individual element has an equal chance of being selected. In practice, a sample is drawn unit by unit. A table of random numbers may be utilized. For telephone surveys, random digit dealing procedures can be used.

2. *Stratified random sampling*—a stratified random sampling is obtained by dividing the population into classes or strata and then selecting a random sample from each strata. It is useful where there are wide variations among strata, and stratification would reduce overall sample size requirements for any given level of precision. It makes it possible to obtain data of known precision for certain subdivisions of the population. (For example, travel times on freeways and arterial streets.)

Table 5–23 Decisions, Outcomes, and Probabilities in Classical Tests of Hypotheses

Decision or Conclusion Reached	Possible Decisions and Outcomes True Condition	
	A. Ho is true HA is false	B. Ho is false HA is true
Reject Ho	Type I Error	Correct Decision
Do Not Reject HA	Correct Decision	Type II Error
Total Probability	1	1

Source: Adapted from Barber, G.M., *Elementary Statistics for Geographers*, New York, N.Y.: Guilford Press, 1988.

3. *Systematic sampling*—a systematic sample draws every Kth element of the sampling frame beginning with a randomly chosen point. (For example, if the first unit is 13, and every 15th unit is chosen, then units 28, 43, 58, and so on would be selected.) Systematic samples are easier to obtain than simple random samples in terms of time and cost. If spread more evenly over the population it may be more precise than simple random sampling. However, systematic samples may give poor precision where periodicity in the data exists.

4. *Cluster sampling*—cluster sampling divides the population into a series of mutually exclusive classes that are usually defined on the basis of convenience. Clusters are then selected for detailed study, usually by some random basis. Either a complete census or a random sample is obtained from each of the selected clusters. Results are then combined.

   Cluster sampling is useful where there are no reliable lists of elements in the population, or because of the ease of constructing lists of sampling units and time-and-cost efficiencies. However, cluster sampling usually results in higher sampling errors than other kinds of surveys.

For a given level of precision, stratified samples require the smallest sample, and cluster samples require the largest.

Errors in Sampling

When estimates are made from a sample, it is not likely that the sample estimate will be exactly the same as that obtained from a complete census. The difference between the two represents the sampling error, if both the sample data and population data are obtained by identical methods. When probability samples are used, the amount of this sampling error can be determined.

Nonsampling errors may exceed sampling errors, and they should be minimized by careful survey design and execution. They include errors associated with measuring a unit (i.e., standees on a crowded subway train); errors introduced in editing, coding, and tabulating surveys; and failure to measure some units in the sample (i.e., nonresponse).

The nonresponse errors include failure to survey particular units of the sample (i.e., people who refuse to be interviewed, are not at home, or are unable to answer). In these cases, there is no assurance that the nonrespondents would respond similarly to those sampled. Their nonresponse can be minimized by the method of survey (i.e., direct interview versus mailback) and by call back. In estimating sample sizes, it may be desirable to "oversample" various segments of the population surveyed to compensate for nonresponse; while this will address the sampling error, it may not necessarily compensate for nonresponse bias.

Table 5–23 shows the two types of errors that can occur in conducting significance tests and in estimating sample size.

(1) A *Type I* error occurs when the null hypothesis Ho is rejected incorrectly because of an extreme-looking sample. The probability of making a *Type I* error is α.

(2) A *Type II* error occurs when one incorrectly fails to reject the null hypothesis Ho because of a sample that looks consistent with Ho. The probability of a *Type II* error is denoted by β.

The *significance level* is equal to the probability of a *Type I* error (i.e., the probability of rejecting a true hypothesis). It is the value chosen for α.

Sampling Distributions

Several sampling distributions underlie confidence interval estimates and sample size computations.

1. *Central limit theorem*—when repeated, random samples of size n are drawn from a normal population with mean μ and standard deviation α, the distribution of the sample mean $\bar{x}$ will also possess a normal distribution with mean μ and standard deviation $\alpha/\sqrt{n}$.

   Where $\bar{x}$ possesses a distribution with mean μ and standard deviation s, then the sample mean $\bar{x}$, based upon a random sample of size n, will possess an *approximate* normal distribution with mean μ and standard deviation $\dfrac{S}{\sqrt{n}}$; the approximation becomes increasingly good as *n* increases.

   As a rule of thumb, this approximation is sufficiently close when the sample size exceeds 30.

2. *Standard error*—the standard error of the mean (i.e., the distribution of sample means) is obtained as follows:

$$\sigma\bar{x} = \frac{\sigma}{\sqrt{n}}$$

(5–16)

Where   =   standard deviation of population

   n   =   size of sample (number of obs)

$\sigma\bar{x}$ =   standard error

Since the standard deviation of the population is not usually known, it is estimated, -often from another sample. In such cases, the equation becomes:

$$S\bar{x} = \frac{S}{\sqrt{n}}$$

(5–17)

   S   =   standard deviation of sample

   $S\bar{x}$ =   standard error of the mean based on S

When the population is finite (and there is sampling without replacement), the equation for the standard error of the mean, $\sigma\bar{x}$ becomes:

$$\sigma\bar{x} = \frac{\sigma}{\sqrt{n}} \sqrt{\frac{N-n}{N-1}} \cong \frac{\sigma}{\sqrt{n}} \sqrt{1 - \frac{n}{N}}$$

(5–17)

The second term in this equation is called the *finite population correction factor*. It should be applied when the sample accounts for more than 15 to 20 percent of the population.

These sampling distribution theorems and relationships provide the basis for establishing confidence intervals and estimating sample sizes.

Confidence Intervals

A confidence interval describes the amount of error that can be associated with estimating the population mean from a sample. The size of this interval depends upon the amount of variation in the population (or sample) and the level of certainty desired. Confidence intervals can be established for either the normal distribution or the Student's *t*-Distribution. Table 5–24 gives areas under the standard normal curve, and Table 5–25 gives the various percentage points for the Student's *t*-Distribution.

Table 5–24 Areas Under the Standard Normal Curve

z	Prob (obs.>z) × 100	Prob (−z < obs. < z) × 100
0.0	50	0.0
0.5	30.9	38.2
1.0	15.9	67.2
1.28	10.0	80.0
1.5	6.7	86.6
1.64	5.0	90.0
1.96	2.5	95.0
2.33	1.0	98.0
2.57	0.5	97.5
3.0	0.14	99.7
3.5	0.02	100.0

Note: The tabulated values in the left column show the percentage of observations that exceed the given value, z, for a normal distribution, mean zero and standard deviation one; thus the values are one-tailed. The percentages of areas that lie within $\pm z$ are shown in the right column.

Source: Adapted from Fisher, R.A. and Yates, F., *Statistical Tables*, Fourth Edition, Edinburgh: Oliver and Boyd Ltd., 1953. Reprinted with permission.

In a wide variety of practical problems, it is reasonable to assume that the distribution of the sample mean minus the population mean when divided by the standard error [$(\bar{x} - \mu)/\sigma \bar{x}$] is approximately a standard normal distribution. This assumption is generally appropriate when the standard deviation is known and when the sample size, n, is large—usually at least 30 observations. The lower and upper confidence limits are as follows:

$$\mu^1 = \bar{x} - Z_a \frac{\sigma}{\sqrt{n}} \sqrt{\frac{N-n}{N-1}} \tag{5–18a}$$

$$\mu^{11} = \bar{x} + Z_a \frac{\sigma}{\sqrt{n}} \sqrt{\frac{N-n}{N-1}} \tag{5–18b}$$

Where

$\bar{x}$ = sample mean

Z_a = standard normal variate (i.e., 1.96 for 95 percent confidence level)

n = size of sample

N = size of population

σ = standard deviation of the population (known)

μ^1 and μ^{11} are the lower and upper confidence limits of the sample mean respectively

Table 5–25 Percentage Points of Student's *t*-Distribution

	Two-tailed probabilities			
	0.10	0.05	0.02	0.01
	One-tailed probabilities (α)			
ν	0.05	0.025	0.01	0.005
1	6.34	12.71	31.82	63.66
2	2.92	4.30	6.96	9.92
3	2.35	3.18	4.54	5.84
4	2.13	2.78	3.75	4.60
6	1.94	2.45	3.14	3.71
8	1.86	2.31	2.90	3.36
10	1.81	2.23	2.76	3.17
15	1.75	2.13	2.60	2.95
20	1.72	2.09	2.53	2.84
30	1.70	2.04	2.46	2.75
60	1.67	2.00	2.39	2.66
∞	1.64	1.96	2.33	2.58

Source: Adapted from Fisher, R.A. and Yates, F., *Statistical Tables*, Fourth Edition, Edinburgh: Oliver and Boyd Ltd., 1953. Reprinted with permission.

When n is small relative to N or the population is infinite, the finite population correction factor

$$\sqrt{\frac{N-n}{N-1}} \sim \sqrt{\frac{1-n}{N}}$$ can be omitted.

These equations also provide an approximate confidence limit for when the population standard deviation is not known and when the sample size, n, is at least 30.

When the value of σ cannot be regarded as known, especially when the sample size is less than 30, Student's t-Distribution should be used. The upper and lower confidence limit are computed as follows:

$$\mu^{1} = \bar{x} \frac{-t_a S}{\sqrt{n}} \sqrt{\frac{N-n}{N-1}} \tag{5–19a}$$

$$\mu^{1} = \bar{x} + \frac{t_a S}{\sqrt{n}} \sqrt{\frac{N-n}{N-1}} \tag{5–19b}$$

Where:

$\bar{x}$ = sample mean

S = sample standard deviation

n = sample size

N = population size

t_a = appropriate point of the Student's t-Distribution with n–1 degrees of freedom (i.e., for 10 degree of freedom, and 95 percent confidence, $t_a = 2.73$)

μ^{1} and μ^{11} are the lower and upper confidence limits respectively

Sample Size

Once the sampling method has been selected, the next step is to determine the appropriate sample size. In a practical sense, this size involves a balance between precision and costs. More specifically, it depends upon the variance of the population, the desired level of precision, and the allowable error. A large dispersion of the population and a small error augur toward large sample sizes and conversely.

Sample size equations are obtained by algebraically rearranging Equations 5–18 and 5–19 and by substituting E, the allowable error for $\bar{x} - \mu$.

When the standard deviation of the population is not known, the equation becomes

$$n_o = \frac{t_{n-1}^2 S^2}{E^2} = t_{n-1}^2 \frac{(CV)^2}{e^2} \tag{5–20}$$

Where

S = standard deviation (estimated)

E = absolute error (specified difference from mean of population)

t_{n-1} = t-value for Student's t-distribution with n–1 degrees of freedom based on desired confidence level (two-tailed test) where n is the sample size

CV = coefficient of variation (percent, actual or estimated)

e = specified relative error (percent)

n_o = sample size (infinite population)

This equation is difficult to use in practice since it requires estimates of the number of degrees of freedom in selecting the appropriate t value. But the degrees of freedom depends on the number of observations—the quantity to be estimated. Thus, an iterative procedure is required to obtain the sample size.

Therefore, the normal distribution is commonly used to estimate sample size.

$$\text{Sample Size, } n_o \cong \frac{Z^2 S^2}{E^2} \cong \frac{Z^2 (CV)^2}{e^2} \qquad (5\text{--}21)$$

Where Z = standard normal variate based on desired confidence level.

CV = coefficient of variation of sample

n_o = sample size

E = absolute error

e = relative error

This equation provides precise results when the standard deviation of the population is known. It provides reliable estimates when sample sizes exceed 30. It slightly understates the sample sizes (generally one or two observations) as compared with the Student's t-distribution when it is less. However, given the approximate nature of many variances and coefficients of variation that are used in transportation planning studies, it produces reasonable results—especially when the minimum sample size is specified (i.e., say at least five travel time runs). Where sample sizes of ten or less result from this equation, they should be recomputed using Equation 5–20.

When a population is finite, and the sample accounts for more than 15 percent of the population, the sample size should be reduced by the finite population correction factor.

$$n = \frac{n_o}{1 + \dfrac{n_o}{N}} \qquad (5\text{--}22)$$

Where n = finite population sample size

n_o = sample size, infinite population

N = size of population

Knowledge of the variability of the population is essential in estimating sample sizes. This might require a pilot (small scale) study to obtain an initial estimate of the variance or standard deviation. Table 5–26 gives some coefficients of variation that might prove useful in estimating sample sizes.

Once a sample is collected, its reliability should be determined by calculating confidence intervals based upon the sample's actual standard deviation. In some cases, additional samples may be needed.

A simple example illustrates the application of these equations. Assume that it is desired to estimate the mean dwell times at the maximum load point of a busy bus route. Bus volumes during the P.M. peak period average eighty vehicles. It is desired to estimate the mean dwell times with ±10 percent relative error at the 68 percent confidence level. The same size needed is estimated as follows:

$$n_o \cong \frac{Z^2 (CV)^2}{e^2}$$

where

Z = 1.00

CV = 60% (Table 5–26)

e = .10

n = $\dfrac{(1.00)^2 (0.60)^2}{(0.10)^2} = 36$

Table 5–26 Some Reported Coefficients of Variation (Percent)

1. Weekday Traffic Volumes (at a Location)

ADT	CV
5,000	16%
10,000	13%
20,000	10%
50,000	7.5%
100,000	6.0%
200,000	5.0%

2. Spatial Variation of Weekday Traffic Volumes (Among Locations)

Freeways	80–100%
Arterials	50–80%

3. Peak Hour Speeds (No. of Speed Runs)

Freeways	9–17%
Arterials	9–15%

4. Peak Hour Speeds—Spatial Variation (Among Locations)

Freeways	15–25%
Arterials	20–25%

5. Local Bus Speeds   25%

6. Bus Dwell Times at a Stop

Dwell Times < 20"	100%
Dwell Times > 20"	60%

7. Rail Transit Dwell Times at a Stop
   LRT 40% (range 30–100%)
   Rapid Transit 50% (range 30–60%)
   Rapid Transit 90% Grand Central Station

Source: Herbert S. Levinson.

Since 36 represents a sizable proportion of the total bus volume, the finite population correction factor should be applied.

$$n = \frac{n_o}{1 + \dfrac{n_o}{N}}$$

Where

n_o = 36

N = 80

n = $\dfrac{36}{1 + \dfrac{36}{80}} \cong 25$

If after collecting the survey data the coefficient of variation is found to be 0.75, then additional observations would be required. The computations are repeated by inserting CV = 0.75 in Equation 5–21. In this case, $n_o = 56$. Applying Equation 5–23 results in n = 33. Thus, 8 additional buses should be surveyed.

The following equation can be used to estimate sample sizes for categorized (binomial) data such as "yes-no" type responses. It assumes a simple random sample, a "large sample" approximation, and minimal nonsampling errors.

$$n_o = \frac{Z_2^2 p^2 q^2}{E^2} \qquad (5\text{–}23)$$

Where

Z = The number associated with the desired level of confidence.

p = Proportion of respondents responding yes (or proportion of attribute desired)

q = $1 - p$

E = Specified error in the estimates

n_o = Sample size for infinite population

To obtain the sample size, it is necessary to assign values to Z, p, q, and E.

Prior research may indicate the appropriate value of p to use for the critical questions under study. However, this is not always possible. Since the sample size is maximized when p = q = 0.5, this value is commonly used. Thus, the equation becomes:

$$n_o = \frac{Z^2 (0.25)}{E^2} \qquad (5\text{–}24)$$

Table 5–27 gives required sample sizes for various levels of confidence and margins of error based on this equation. Thus, to achieve an error of ±5 percent at 95 percent confidence, 384 observations are needed. Reducing the sample size to 96 would result in a ±10 error.

Table 5–27 Sample Sizes Required to Achieve Desired Levels of Confidence and Margins of Error

	Level of Confidence		
	90%	95%	99%
		Z Value	
Margin of Error	1.645	1.960	2.575
±1%	6765	9604	16590
±2%	1692	2401	4148
±3%	752	1068	1844
±4%	423	601	1037
±5%	271	384	664
±10%	68	96	166

Note: Assumes p = q = 0.50.

Source: Adapted from Rebecca Elmore-Valch, *A Handbook: Integrating Market Research into Transit Management*, TCRP Report 37, Washington, D.C.: Transportation Research Board, National Research Council, 1998.

Additional Applications

Sampling theory can be utilized to estimate standard errors of medians and standard deviations, establish confidence intervals, compute sample sizes for Poisson distributions, and conduct significance tests of differences between means and variances (i.e., before and after studies). Extensions of sampling theory are useful in developing experimental designs and in conducting analysis of variance tests. (Descriptions of these techniques and applications are found in Chapter 5 of the *Traffic Engineering Handbook*.[74])

---

[74] Institute of Transportation Engineers, *Traffic Engineering Handbook*, Fifth Edition (Washington, D.C.: ITE, 1999).

Regression Overview

Transportation planning studies and research investigations analyze relationships among a series of variables. In urban transportation planning studies, for example, trip rates of households have been related to household income and family size. The *Trip Generation* 95 report[75] relates trips generated by a shopping or employment center to factors such as employment and floor space; logit mode choice models relate mode choice to the relative "disutility" of a specific mode as measured by time and cost. See Chapter 6 of this handbook for a discussion of transportation models.

Regression analysis provides a systematic method for estimating relationships between the response (or respondent) variable and one or more explanatory variables. Regression may be simple (one explanatory variable) or it may be multiple (several explanatory or "input" variables). Relationships may be linear (i.e., a straight line) or nonlinear, and they may involve transforming variables to obtain linear patterns. Regression analysis makes it possible to establish confidence limits and prediction intervals.

Relationships are usually obtained by the "method of least squares" in which the sum of the squared deviations from a regression line are minimized. However, in some cases, such as calibrating a logit mode split model, the "method of maximum likelihood" is used.

Correlation analysis provides a measure of the strength of the linear association. Correlation coefficients range from −1 to +1, and the square of the correlation coefficient (i.e., r^2) indicates the amount of variation accounted for by the regression.

Modern computer programs permit analyses that were virtually impossible in the past. Consequently, regression analysis is widely used (and misused). Some application guidelines follow:[76]

1. At the outset, it is important to indicate *why* a regression analysis is desirable *and how* such an analysis will be used.

2. Scatter diagrams should be plotted to establish relationships among pairs of variables; to identify the correct form of a suitable model; to see if variables should be transformed to achieve linearity or reduce skewness; and to identify predictive variables that must be included or can be omitted.

3. Obvious "outliers" should be identified; they should be isolated, restudied, or even removed.

4. Multiple regression can be done either by *forward* selection or *backward* elimination. The number of variables should not exceed one-fourth to one-fifth of the number of observations.

5. It is important to check for independence and collinearity of variables. A simple correlation matrix among variables should be developed; where simple correlation coefficients are high, only one of the two highly correlated input variables should be used.

6. Sample size must be considered in assessing the significance of a correlation coefficient. A high r^2 from a small sample may not be meaningful.

7. High correlation coefficients do not necessarily imply cause and effect. Correlation is not causation. Therefore, the logic of any relationship should be clearly established.

8. The limitations of the fitted model should be recognized. Regression lines should only be used for prediction within the range of the actual data upon which the lines were based.

Statistical procedures for developing regression relationships and computing correlation coefficients, along with the basic underlying assumptions, are contained in many statistics text books, such as the *Statistics Manual*.[77]

---

[75] *Trip Generation,* Sixth Edition (Washington, D.C.: Institute of Transportation Engineers, 1997).

[76] Chatfield, C., Problem Solving, A Statisticians Guide, 2nd Edition (London: Chapman & Hall, 1995).

[77] Crow, E. L., Davis, F. A., Maxfield, M. W., *Statistics Manual* (N.Y.: Dover Publications, 1960).

Selected References

Appleyard, David. *Livable Streets*. Berkeley, Calif.: University of California Press, 1989.

Attanucci, J., Burns, I., Wilson, N. Data Collection Design Multi-Systems and ATE Management and Service Co. *Bus Transit Monitoring Manual*, Volume 1. Urban Mass Transportation Administration Report #UMTA-IT-09-9008-81-1. Washington, D.C.: UMTA and U.S. Department of Transportation, August 1981.

Barber, C. M. *Elementary Statistics for Geographers*, 2nd Edition. New York, N.Y.: The Guilford Press, 1997.

Box, P. and Oppenlander, S. *Manual of Traffic Engineering Studies,* 4th Edition. Washington, D.C.: Institute of Transportation Engineers, 1976.

Cambridge Systematics. *Travel Survey Manual*. Washington, D.C.: U.S. Department of Transportation and U.S. Environmental Protection Agency, June 1996.

Charles River Assoc. and Levinson, H.S. *Characteristics of Urban Transportation Demand—An Update*. Washington, D.C.: Urban Mass Transportation Administration, 1985.

Chatfield, C. *Problem Solving, A Statisticians Guide, 2nd Edition*. London: Chapman & Hall, 1995.

Chrest, A. P. and Smith, M.S. and Bhuyan S. *Parking Structures Planning Design Construction, Maintenance and Repair.* New York, N.Y.: Van Nostrand Reinhold, 1989.

Christiansen, D. *Urban Transportation Planning for Goods and Services*. Washington, D.C.: U.S. Department of Transportation, Federal Highway Administration, 1979.

Dowling, R., Kittelson, W., Zegeer, J., and Skabardonis A. *Planning Techniques to Estimate Speeds and Service Volumes for Planning Applications*. NCHRP Report 387. Washington, D.C.: Transportation Research Board, National Research Council, 1997.

Edwards, J. *The Parking Handbook for Small Communities*. Washington, D.C.: National Main Street Center and Institute of Transportation Engineers, 1994.

Federal Highway Administration. Site Impact Traffic Evaluation (SITE) Handbook. Springfield, Va.: U.S. Department of Transportation, NTIS, 1985.

Ferlis, R.A., Bowman, L.A. and Cima, B.T. Peat Marwick Mitchell & Company. Guide to Urban Traffic Volume Counting Final Report. Washington, D.C.: Federal Highway Administration, 1980.

Ferlis R.A. Peat Marwick Mitchell & Company. Guide for Estimating Urban Vehicle Classification and Occupancy. Washington, D.C.: Federal Highway Administration, March 1981.

Homburger, S. Wolfgang et al. Residential Street Design and Traffic Control, Washington, D.C.: Institute of Transportation Engineers, 1989.

Homburger, W.S., Hall, J.W., Loutzenneiser, R.C., Reilly, W.R. Fundamentals of Traffic Engineering, 14th Edition. Berkeley, Calif.: Institute of Transportation Studies, University of California, Berkeley, May 1996.

Institute of Transportation Engineers. Manual of Transportation Engineering Studies. Englewood Cliff, N.J.: Prentice Hall, 1994.

Institute of Transportation Engineers. *Parking Generation*, 2nd Edition. Washington, D.C.: ITE, 1987.

Institute of Transportation Engineers. *Traffic Access and Impact Studies for Site Development, Proposed Recommended Practice*. Washington, D.C.: ITE, 1988.

Institute of Transportation Engineers. *Traffic Engineering Handbook,* Fifth Edition. Washington, D.C.: ITE, 1999.

Institute of Transportation Engineers. *Trip Generation,* Sixth Edition. Washington, D.C.: ITE, 1997.

Koepke, F.J. and Levinson, H.S. *Access Management Guidelines for Activity Centers*, NCHRP Report 348. Washington, D.C.: Transportation Research Board, National Research Council, 1992.

Lomax T., Turner S., Shunk G., Levinson, H.S., Pratt R.H., and Douglas G. Bruce. *Report 398 Quantifying Congestion, Vol. 1 Final Report and Vol. 2 Users Manual*. Washington, D.C.: Transportation Research Board, National Research Council, 1997.

Meyer, M.D. *Urban Transportation Planning*. New York: McGraw-Hill, 1984.

Parking Consultants Council and National Parking Association. *Parking Studies*. Parking Consultants Council and National Parking Association, June 1992.

Richardson A., Ampt, E.S., and Meyburg A.H. *Survey Methods for Transport Planning*. Vienna, Austria: Eucalyptus Press, 1995.

Smith, P.T. *Safety and Locational Criteria for Bicycle Facilities*. Federal Highway Administration Report RD 75-112. Washington, D.C.: FHWA, February 1976.

Stopher, P.R., and Metcalf H. *Methods of Household Travel Surveys*. Synthesis 236. Washington, D.C.: Transportation Research Board, National Research Council, 1996.

Transportation Research Board, National Research Council. *Highway Capacity Manual*. Special Report 209. Washington, D.C.: TRB, National Research Council, 1997.

Urban Mass Transit Administration. *An Introduction to Urban Travel Demand Forecasting: A Self-instructional Text*. Washington, D.C.: U.S. Department of Transportation, 1977.

Urban Mass Transportation Administration. *Transit Data Collection Design Manual, Final Report*. DOT-1-85-38. Washington, D.C.: UMTA, June 1985.

Weant, R.A. and Levinson, H.S. *Parking*. Saugatuck, Conn.: Eno Foundation for Transportation, 1990.

Wegmann, F.J., Chatterjee, Lipinski, M.E., Jennings, P.E., and McGinnus, E.R. *Characteristics of Urban Freight Systems*. DOT-T-96-22. Washington, D.C.: Federal Highway Administration, 1996.

Wright, Paul H. *Highway Engineering*, 5th Edition. New York: John Wiley & Sons, 1987.

CHAPTER 6
Transportation Models

Cathy L. Chang, P.E., AICP
Senior Transportation Planner
Parsons Brinckerhoff Quade & Douglas, Inc., and
Daniel T. Meyers, AICP
Senior Transportation Planner
BRW, Inc.

Introduction

Transportation models are an integral part of the transportation planning process. Models serve as an analysis tool for transportation planners, and they aid decision-makers in evaluating alternative proposals. This chapter is intended to provide a broad, general overview of the various types of transportation models that are currently in use. A "model" can simply be defined as a mathematical representation of a process. Transportation models are developed for macroscale analysis (regional travel demand models), microscale analysis (discrete models), and postprocessing techniques. These models are used for a variety of purposes, including: developing regional transportation plans, analyzing the effects of major new developments, and estimating potential air quality impacts due to changes in the transportation system.

There are an abundance of transportation models in existence. However, they fall into two main categories: (1) those that consider the mass movement of individuals and (2) those that consider the movement of individuals within the group. For example, a regional travel demand model is concerned with the movements of large numbers of individuals in a regional system, while a traffic simulation model is concerned with the movements of individuals in a smaller subsystem. For this reason, these will be referred to as "regional travel demand models" and "discrete traffic models."

Other types of models are also used by planners and engineers in their analysis work. For example, most formulas in the *Highway Capacity Manual*[1] (HCM) may be considered as models (i.e., a model of the delay incurred at an intersection). In addition, land use models and demographic models are used to develop the inputs to travel demand models. Postprocessing models (such as those for intersection analyses and benefit/cost analyses) are applied to the outputs of travel demand models. Although these other types of models are also used by the profession, the focus of this chapter is on transportation models, specifically regional travel demand models, and discrete traffic simulation models.

This chapter is only meant to be a guide and is intended to give the reader an idea of what would be involved in developing various types of transportation models. The user will need to refer to other documents and reference materials (which are listed at the back of this chapter) to understand and implement the models. Other chapters of this *Handbook* provide more material on various related topics. These include:

- Chapter 3, "General Travel and Goods Movement."

- Chapter 4, "Urban Travel Characteristics."

- Chapter 5, "Transportation Planning Studies."

- Chapter 10, "Statewide Multimodal Transportation Planning."

- Chapter 11, "Intercity Passenger Travel."

---

[1] *Highway Capacity Manual*, Third Edition, *Special Report 209* (Washington, D.C.: Transportation Research Board, October 1994).

Transportation planning efforts are usually organized from large-scale to small-scale measures. Thus, this chapter is organized in a similar manner—from the regional travel demand models to the discrete traffic models. This introductory section is followed by a section on travel behavior surveys and other required input data. These surveys form the basis for most travel demand modeling work efforts. The traditional travel demand modeling process is described in some detail, with an overview of the software packages that could be used to implement the procedures. A later section discusses several improvements to the traditional travel demand modeling process.

The second portion of the chapter discusses discrete traffic models, including simulation models, as well as site traffic models. In addition, it also includes postprocessing models. This chapter concludes with a discussion of the inherent limitations in any type of models.

Background

Models are based on observations of actual travel behavior. Mathematical relationships are derived to describe the factors that determine travel. These models are calibrated and validated to match observed travel activity. Models provide a tool for professionals to analyze hypothetical scenarios, such as alternative land use development patterns, alternative demographic forecasts, major highway and transit investments, or even changes to the one-way street system in a downtown area. Models provide an estimate of the effects of potential changes on the transportation system. This allows the testing of several alternatives without actually making any physical changes to the roadways, transit system, and the like.

Model Consistency and Process

Model representation must be both accurate and consistent. That is, the mathematical model must accurately portray the activities being modeled. At the same time, the expression that is developed now must be applied under the same conditions in the future. Modeling can be considered an act of " rule-building." The " rules" that are incorporated in model development must be consistent with those used in model application.

In the modeling process, there are five primary components: model design, estimation, calibration, validation, and application. Model design (sometimes referred to as model specification) establishes the model structure and what submodels will be required, as well as their form. Model estimation involves determining the coefficients or relationships of the variables for each of the submodels. In model calibration, a set of parameters are usually iteratively adjusted so that the existing demographic data leads to the existing levels of trip making, traffic congestion, and other elements. In this manner, the model is "calibrated" to the existing conditions. Then, the model must be validated. In model validation, another set of existing data are used to verify that the model does indeed replicate existing conditions with reasonable accuracy. Only at this point is the model acceptable for use in future forecasting applications.

Models Versus Software

An important distinction needs to be made between "models" and "software." The model is the mathematical equations that are established by research and practical efforts that represent some aspect of traveler behavior. The software is the tool that is used to implement the model. A transportation model is composed of several submodels (e.g., trip generation, trip distribution, mode choice, trip assignment). Each of these submodels can be represented by a mathematical model. These mathematical models are then implemented in various transportation planning software packages (such as EMME/2, Minutp, TP+, TRANPLAN, Transcad, etc.).[2] Similarly, a site traffic study is a model of expected behavior that is implemented in a site traffic analysis software package. This chapter focuses on a general discussion of the actual models, with a secondary discussion of the software used for implementation.

---

[2] See later section and accompanying table for a detailed listing of transportation planning software packages.

Data Requirements for Regional Models

The transportation planning process and especially the regional modeling process are based on observed data. Data are required to develop, calibrate, and validate the models. Most of the information required describes existing conditions and characteristics of the study area. This section briefly covers the required data elements for the development of any regional travel demand model.

Inventory of Existing Conditions

One of the first steps in developing a transportation model is an inventory of existing conditions. This is crucial to establishing the base conditions from which the model is developed. Detailed inventory procedures can be found in the documentation available from federal, state, and local planning agencies.[3] Documentation and samples of available information should be carefully reviewed to assure their validity and accuracy for the uses intended. Particular concern should be paid to the age of the data, the procedures used in collecting the data, and its accuracy or reliability.

The data collected will be used to identify and quantify relationships among social, economic development, and transportation system factors that affect traveler decisions and create travel impacts on the system. Considerable reliance must be placed on research and previous travel analysis experience in order to obtain accurate information about the factors most influential for local travel.

Today, most planning data are maintained in a geographic information system (GIS). A GIS contains different layers representing the characteristics of the underlying landscape, as well as data that can be geographically linked to a specific location. Some examples of relevant data included in a GIS data base are: land use development, population and employment data, roadways and streets, traffic analysis zones, and the like. Maintaining the data in a GIS (rather than a spreadsheet or other tabular format) allows for easy geographic review of the data and simplifies map production. In addition, geographic analyses can be readily conducted. Furthermore, almost every travel demand model software developer is working to make GIS an integral part of their software package.

Land Use Data

Land use data in the form of a graphical map or some other representation form the basis for most demographic forecasts, which in turn serve as inputs to the regional model set. The land use plan or comprehensive development plan indicates the kind and intensity of activity for each land parcel in the region. Such a plan is usually based on guidelines put forth by the local government agency. The types of activities for the various land parcels could include: residential development, parks, office, retail, industrial, waste sites, and other kinds. Each type of development is listed along with a description of its characteristics. For instance, residential development might be described by the specific type of housing and the quantity (e.g., density measures, such as one dwelling unit per acre).

Demographic and Economic Data

Existing demographic and economic data are obtained from the census[4] data collection efforts every ten years. Additional information is also available through local counts and surveys of the general population in the area. These could include household interview surveys or workplace surveys that are discussed in the following sections.

Land use is inextricably linked to the distribution of population, households, and employment. These in turn, are primary inputs to the regional model set. Once a land use plan is established, a set of demographic and economic forecasts can be completed. Demographic forecasts are based on migration into and out of the study area, births, and deaths. Economic forecasts are developed to project future employment levels and their locations. Employment and population are directly related in that increases in population are accompanied by increases in employment. These forecasts are typically completed by the local planning agency or a state agency.

---

[3] See your local government agency for any inventories that may have been completed.

[4] In the United States, decennial data collection efforts are conducted by the U.S. Department of Commerce, Bureau of the Census. The Census Transportation Planning Package is a set of special tabulations of 1990 census data tailored to meet the needs of transportation planners.

Each of the existing data items as well as future forecasts are usually maintained as a separate layer in the local GIS system. Using the GIS system as an analysis tool, one could plot the population growth by zone. Alternatively, for market analysis work, one could measure the number of households within one mile of a new major retail mall. Both applications require the maintenance of data in some geographic manner, with appropriate display and analysis software. As with travel demand modeling software, there is an abundance of GIS software currently on the market.

Travel Behavior Inventories

Travel behavior inventories serve as the basis for most regional models. Several key questions must be answered to provide proper guidance for the travel survey design procedure:

- What is the purpose of the survey?

- What data are needed to accomplish that purpose?

- Where or from whom should the data be obtained?

- How should that source be contacted?

- What questions should be asked of the source?

- How can the questionnaire be formatted in order to achieve efficient processing and minimize potential ambiguities?

The survey design will determine the sample size, sampling plan, questionnaire design, and processing plan for data obtained in the survey. An organizational plan will be developed describing the management strategy for successfully completing the survey. Carefully designing the questionnaire is a crucial step. Figures 6–1 through 6–4 show various survey forms used in some recent data collection efforts.

These surveys form the basis for model calibration and validation as described above. Also, in model design, the format and nature of the data collected can limit the various models that can be tested. Thus, it is imperative that someone with extensive modeling experience review and comment on the survey forms.

Household Interview Survey

Each of these surveys serves a separate purpose and need. The household (or home) interview survey is intended to measure the travel (or activities) that take place by members of a specific household over one to three typical weekdays. The types of data collected fall into three broad categories: household characteristics, person characteristics, and trip (or activity) characteristics. Some example forms from a household interview survey are included as Figures 6–1A and 6–1B. The survey forms included in this chapter are meant as examples only, and they should not be used without review by knowledgeable modeling or experienced staff in both model development work and survey data collection efforts.

The household characteristics should include items, such as the actual street address (for geocoding purposes), the housing structure type, total persons in the household, number of visitors in the household on survey day, number of vehicles available or owned by the household, and the combined annual income of all household members. The person characteristics should include each person's relationship to the head of the household, his or her gender, age, license status, work status, as well as other descriptive information. The household and person descriptive information are collected through the household data form. An example is shown in Figure 6–1A.

The most significant data will come from the trip file. This should include information on each trip made by each household member for the survey period (i.e., one to three days). The types of trip information that should be collected include: person making trip, trip origin and destination, trip purpose, time of trip, mode used for trip, and number of occupants if using a private vehicle, as well as parking or transit costs involved in the trip. An example of the travel diary is shown

noaca

HOUSEHOLD DATA

Please answer the following questions about your household:

Is this your correct address?

2. How many people live in this household? _____

3. How many people are 5 years old or older? _____

4. How many visitors from outside of the area are staying with you on your travel day? _____

5. How many vehicles (cars, vans, light trucks, and motorcycles) are kept at home for use by members of your household? _____

6. Is your home:
   ☐ A 1-Family House Detached From Any Other House
   ☐ A Multi-Unit Building (Duplex/apartment/townhouse)

7. What was the combined income from all sources for all members of your household in 1993? (Please circle the appropriate letter.)

A. Under $5,000	F. $24,000 - $29,999
B. $ 5,000 - $9,999	G. $30,000 - $39,999
C. $10,000 - $14,999	H. $40,000 - $49,999
D. $15,000 - $19,999	I. $50,000 - $74,999
E. $20,000 - $24,999	J. $75,000 or more

Complete one line below for each member of your household. Each line of the table begins with a person number. Please be sure that the person number on this form matches the person number on each persons travel diary.

PERSON NUMBER	RELATIONSHIP				AGE	SEX	LICENSED TO DRIVE?	ARE YOU EMPLOYED: (Check only one box)					ARE YOU A STUDENT IN:			
	Spouse/ Partner	Child	Other Household Member	Out-of-Area Visitor				Full Time	Multiple Jobs	Part Time	Retired	No	Elem / Middle School	High School	Post-High School	Other
01	Head of Household					☐ M ☐ F	☐ YES ☐ NO	☐	☐	☐	☐	☐	☐	☐	☐	☐
02	☐	☐	☐	☐		☐ M ☐ F	☐ YES ☐ NO	☐	☐	☐	☐	☐	☐	☐	☐	☐
03	☐	☐	☐	☐		☐ M ☐ F	☐ YES ☐ NO	☐	☐	☐	☐	☐	☐	☐	☐	☐
04	☐	☐	☐	☐		☐ M ☐ F	☐ YES ☐ NO	☐	☐	☐	☐	☐	☐	☐	☐	☐
05	☐	☐	☐	☐		☐ M ☐ F	☐ YES ☐ NO	☐	☐	☐	☐	☐	☐	☐	☐	☐
06	☐	☐	☐	☐		☐ M ☐ F	☐ YES ☐ NO	☐	☐	☐	☐	☐	☐	☐	☐	☐
07	☐	☐	☐	☐		☐ M ☐ F	☐ YES ☐ NO	☐	☐	☐	☐	☐	☐	☐	☐	☐
08	☐	☐	☐	☐		☐ M ☐ F	☐ YES ☐ NO	☐	☐	☐	☐	☐	☐	☐	☐	☐
09	☐	☐	☐	☐		☐ M ☐ F	☐ YES ☐ NO	☐	☐	☐	☐	☐	☐	☐	☐	☐
10	☐	☐	☐	☐		☐ M ☐ F	☐ YES ☐ NO	☐	☐	☐	☐	☐	☐	☐	☐	☐

Please complete one line below for each vehicle available to your household (include cars you own or lease, company cars, rental cars, motorcycles, etc.). Please be sure that you use the correct vehicle number if one of the vehicles listed below is used for any trips made during your travel day.

VEHICLE NUMBER	MODEL YEAR	MAKE (Ford, Oldsmobile, Jeep, ...)	MODEL (Taurus, Ciera, Cherokee, ...)	TYPE OF FUEL (Check one)			ODOMETER READINGS ON TRAVEL DAY (Please record to nearest mile)	
				Gas	Diesel	Other	Beginning	Ending
1				☐	☐	☐		
2				☐	☐	☐		
3				☐	☐	☐		
4				☐	☐	☐		
5				☐	☐	☐		
6				☐	☐	☐		
7				☐	☐	☐		

This completes the household information needed. Please complete the attached travel diaries for all travel on your travel day. **Thank you for your cooperation!**

Figure 6–1A   Example of a Household Data Form from the Home Interview Survey

Source: Northeast Ohio Areawide Coordinating Agency. Printed with permission.

noaca

TRAVEL DIARY

INSTRUCTIONS:

- Record trips in the order you make them.
- Include the specific information requested for each trip.
- Record your trip even if it was made with another household member.
- Record walking and bicycle trips only if you leave the block you start the trip from (that is, if you cross a street).
- At the end of your travel day, leave all completed diaries in a convenient place at home so they will be available when the interviewer calls.
- Use the back of the form and an extra card, if necessary.
- If you have any questions about completing this travel diary, please call our toll-free number: **1-800-447-8287**

TRIPS FOR PERSON NUMBER: _____
(Use person number from household data form)

NAME: _____

TRAVEL DAY: _____

At 4:00 AM on the travel day, I was at:
☐ Home
☐ Other location as shown below (if not home)

Name of Place _____ Kind of Place _____

Address or Intersecting Streets _____

City, State, Zip Code _____

WHERE did you go?	KIND OF PLACE (home, bank, restaurant, ...)	PURPOSE of trip (Check one)	TIME of trip (Check AM, PM, Noon, Midnight)	MODE of travel (Check one)	IF IN CAR/VAN/-PICKUP		WHAT WAS THE TRANSIT FARE OR PARKING COST?
					Number in Vehicle (include yourself)	Vehicle Used	
① First I Went To: Name of Place / Address or Intersecting Streets / City, State, Zip Code		☐ Go Home ☐ Personal ☐ Go to Work ☐ Work Related ☐ School ☐ Drop off/Pick ☐ Shop up Passenger ☐ Eat Meal ☐ Change Mode ☐ Social ☐ Other ☐ Recreational	Start: ___:___ ☐ AM ☐ Noon ☐ PM ☐ Mdnt End: ___:___ ☐ AM ☐ Noon ☐ PM ☐ Mdnt	☐ Driver (Auto/Van/Pick-up) ☐ Passenger (Auto/Van/Pick-up) ☐ RTA Bus ☐ Motorcycle ☐ RTA Rapid Rail ☐ Bicycle ☐ School Bus ☐ Walk ☐ Other Public ☐ Other ___ Trans & Taxi			Cost: $ ___.___ ☐ Hourly ☐ Daily ☐ Weekly ☐ Monthly ☐ Other
② Then I Went To: Name of Place / Address or Intersecting Streets / City, State, Zip Code		☐ Go Home ☐ Personal ☐ Go to Work ☐ Work Related ☐ School ☐ Drop off/Pick ☐ Shop up Passenger ☐ Eat Meal ☐ Change Mode ☐ Social ☐ Other ☐ Recreational	Start: ___:___ ☐ AM ☐ Noon ☐ PM ☐ Mdnt End: ___:___ ☐ AM ☐ Noon ☐ PM ☐ Mdnt	☐ Driver (Auto/Van/Pick-up) ☐ Passenger (Auto/Van/Pick-up) ☐ RTA Bus ☐ Motorcycle ☐ RTA Rapid Rail ☐ Bicycle ☐ School Bus ☐ Walk ☐ Other Public ☐ Other ___ Trans & Taxi			Cost: $ ___.___ ☐ Hourly ☐ Daily ☐ Weekly ☐ Monthly ☐ Other
③ Then I Went To: Name of Place / Address or Intersecting Streets / City, State, Zip Code		☐ Go Home ☐ Personal ☐ Go to Work ☐ Work Related ☐ School ☐ Drop off/Pick ☐ Shop up Passenger ☐ Eat Meal ☐ Change Mode ☐ Social ☐ Other ☐ Recreational	Start: ___:___ ☐ AM ☐ Noon ☐ PM ☐ Mdnt End: ___:___ ☐ AM ☐ Noon ☐ PM ☐ Mdnt	☐ Driver (Auto/Van/Pick-up) ☐ Passenger (Auto/Van/Pick-up) ☐ RTA Bus ☐ Motorcycle ☐ RTA Rapid Rail ☐ Bicycle ☐ School Bus ☐ Walk ☐ Other Public ☐ Other ___ Trans & Taxi			Cost: $ ___.___ ☐ Hourly ☐ Daily ☐ Weekly ☐ Monthly ☐ Other

Figure 6–1B   Example of a Travel Diary Form from the Home Interview Survey

Source: Northeast Ohio Areawide Coordinating Agency. Printed with permission.

CORPUS CHRISTI *RTA* PASSENGER SURVEY

Dear Rider: *We need your help!* Please take a minute to complete this survey even if you filled one out before. This information will help RTA meet your current and future needs. When you have completed this questionnaire, please return it to the surveyor or place it in the specially marked box located near the exit door. THANK YOU!

1. **What is the street intersection nearest your home?** (neighborhood cross-street)

   _____ and _____ _____
   Street 1   Street 2   Zip Code

2. **Where did you get on this bus (nearest intersection)?**

   _____ and _____
   Street 1   Street 2

3. **How did you get to the bus stop?** (Circle only ONE)
   1 Transfer from another bus - route number and name: _____
   2 Walked   3 Drove auto   4 Passenger in auto   5 Other_____

4. **Where are you going to now?** (Circle only ONE)
   1 Work   4 Eating Place   7 Medical   10 Personal Business
   2 Home   5 College   8 Social/Recreation   11 Other_____
   3 Shopping   6 Other School   9 Visiting Friend

5. **Please tell us where that place is:** _____
                                              Place Name

   _____ _____   _____
   Street No. Street Name   Nearest Cross Street

6. **Where are you coming from on this trip?** (Circle only ONE)
   1 Work   4 Eating Place   7 Medical   10 Personal Business
   2 Home   5 College   8 Social/Recreation   11 Other_____
   3 Shopping   6 Other School   9 Visiting Friend

7. **Please tell us where that place is:** _____
                                              Place Name

   _____ _____   _____
   Street No. Street Name   Nearest Cross Street

8. **Where will you get off this bus?**

   _____ and _____
   Street 1   Street 2

9. **When you leave this bus, how will you get to your destination?** (Circle any that apply)
   1 Transfer to another bus - route number and name: _____
   2 Walked   3 Drove auto   4 Passenger in auto   5 Other_____

10. **Beginning with where you came from (Question 6) and ending with where you are going (Question 4), how many buses will you have ridden?** (Circle only ONE)
                        1   2   3   4 (or more)

11. **How many days a week do you make this trip?** (Circle only ONE)
        Less than 1   1   2   3   4   5   6   7

12. **How did you pay for your bus trip today?** (Circle only ONE)
        1 Cash   2 Pass   3 Transfer   4 Token

12A. **If you paid cash, what fare did you pay?** (Circle only ONE)
        1 $.10   2 $.25   3 $.50   4 $.75   5 $1.00   6 Free fare

12B. **If you paid with a pass, circle the appropriate type.**
        1 Regular   2 Discount (Senior)   3 Discount (Disabled)   4 Discount (Student)

Tell us about yourself:

13. **How many people, including you, live in your household?**_____

14. **How many people in your household, including you, are employed?**_____

15. **How many vehicles (cars, light trucks, vans, company cars, rental cars, motorcycles, etc.) in running condition are available for use by members of your household?**_____

16. **Was one of these vehicles available today for you to use for this trip?** (Circle only ONE)
                        1 Yes   2 No

17. **Which category below includes the combined annual income of all members of your household?** (Check only ONE)
    ☐ Less than $5,000   ☐ $20,000 to $24,999   ☐ $40,000 to $49,999   ☐ $100,000 to $124,999
    ☐ $5,000 to $9,999   ☐ $25,000 to $29,999   ☐ $50,000 to $59,999   ☐ $125,000 to $149,999
    ☐ $10,000 to $14,999   ☐ $30,000 to $34,999   ☐ $60,000 to $74,999   ☐ $150,000 or more
    ☐ $15,000 to $19,999   ☐ $35,000 to $39,999   ☐ $75,000 to $99,999

COMMENTS:_____

PLEASE PLACE THIS CARD IN THE RETURN BOX ON THE BUS.
THANK YOU FOR COMPLETING THIS SURVEY!

Figure 6–2   Example of a Transit On-Board Survey Form

Source: Texas Department of Transportation. Printed with permission.

in Figure 6–1B. Although the enclosed figure only shows three trips, the actual form used in the survey includes fifteen different trips.

Recent research in the field suggests that activity-based modeling may be more reflective of the actual travel behavior. For instance, travelers often create "journeys" out of multiple trips. Rather than analyzing each trip separately, the entire journey may be examined. Thus, recent surveys have turned to activity-based surveys, rather than trip-based. In this case, data are collected on the actual activities that persons are involved in. Thus, rather than having a person record his or her trips, they would record the location and duration of each of the activities that they were engaged in.

Transit On-Board Survey

Whether actual trips or activities are collected, the household interview surveys do not usually record many transit trips. This is because of the typically low transit trip-making in any region. Thus, a passenger survey of transit riders (referred to as an on-board survey) is often completed to supplement the household interview survey. In an on-board survey, data are collected on the train, bus, or other transit vehicle. Most of the same information that is collected in the household interview survey form is also included in the transit on-board survey form. An example of a transit on-board survey form is included as Figure 6–2.

Workplace Survey

A workplace or establishment survey is designed to work in conjunction with the household interview survey. The purpose of a workplace survey is to obtain data about the travel behavior of workers and visitors to workplaces within the region. These data include the modal characteristics of travel as well as the time and purpose of the travel. This survey seeks to obtain data for work trips and nonwork trips to a specific establishment during a typical day. The survey should collect travel data for a sample of the persons arriving at a sampled workplace. The arriving visitors and employees should both be surveyed in order to gather a complete picture of the trip activity at a specific workplace.

Figure 6–3A illustrates an example of the household information that might be collected from an employee as part of a workplace survey. Figure 6–3B shows the trip information that is collected. As with the household interview survey forms, all trips are collected—the figure shows an abbreviated example only. Also, as discussed earlier, in some recent surveys activities are collected rather than trips. This could also apply to a workplace survey.

External Survey

An external survey measures the traffic movements to, from, and through the area under study. Typically, these surveys are conducted at the periphery of the study area. A cordon is drawn on a map, representing the roads providing access to and from the region under study. At each roadway crossing, a count is made of the total number of vehicles crossing the cordon line. Simultaneously, a sample is taken of some of the vehicles to collect information on the traveler's origin and destination, as well as trip purpose. External surveys are typically collected during the morning and evening peak hours, and they are usually limited to a few questions in order to minimize the disruption of traffic.

Commercial Vehicle Survey

A commercial vehicle survey quantifies the truck movements within, into and out of, and through the region. The commercial vehicle survey could take place at designated screenlines, where high volumes of trucks are known to pass; or they could be conducted through the major trucking companies. Again, the same types of trip information would be collected, such as the truck trip origin, destination, and purpose. In addition, some information on the quantity of truck travel would also be collected. This information would be used to build a truck trip table, and to understand the implications of various traffic management schemes, particularly as they relate to trucking restrictions.

Figure 6–4A shows an example of the vehicle information that would be collected as part of a commercial vehicle (truck) survey. This information would be collected for each truck that is being surveyed. Then, for each truck, the driver would

Site #: _____
Sample #: _____
Survey Location: _____ Travel Day: _____
Month/Day

WORKPLACE EMPLOYEE TRAVEL SURVEY
PART 1: HOUSEHOLD INFORMATION
(if you have participated in prior surveys, please fill this form out anyway)

Employee's
Home Address: _____
Street Address

_____

_____
City   County   State   ZIP

How many people live at your home address? (Do not count guests) _____

How many people in your household (including yourself) are employed? _____
(Include full- and part-time.)
How many vehicles (cars, vans, light trucks, motorcycles) are available for use by members of your household? _____

Please list all vehicles available to your household (including company cars, rental cars, motorcycles, etc.) and complete the following:

Vehicle Number	Year	Make	Model	Circle One	Odometer Readings On Travel Day	
					Beginning	Ending
1				1)Diesel 2)Gas 3)Other____		
2				1)Diesel 2)Gas 3)Other____		
3				1)Diesel 2)Gas 3)Other____		
4				1)Diesel 2)Gas 3)Other____		
5				1)Diesel 2)Gas 3)Other____		
6				1)Diesel 2)Gas 3)Other____		
7				1)Diesel 2)Gas 3)Other____		

If you add up the <u>annual</u> incomes of <u>all</u> members of your household, into what range does it fall? (Check one)

1) ☐	Less than $5,000	6) ☐	$25,000 to $29,999	11) ☐	$60,000 to $74,999
2) ☐	$5,000 to $9,999	7) ☐	$30,000 to $34,999	12) ☐	$75,000 to $99,999
3) ☐	$10,000 to $14,999	8) ☐	$35,000 to $39,999	13) ☐	$100,000 to $124,999
4) ☐	$15,000 to $19,999	9) ☐	$40,000 to $49,999	14) ☐	$125,000 to $149,999
5) ☐	$20,000 to $24,999	10) ☐	$50,000 to $59,999	15) ☐	$150,000 or more

Figure 6–3A   Example of a Household Information Form from the Workplace Travel Survey

Source: Texas Department of Transportation. Printed with permission.

WORKPLACE EMPLOYEE TRAVEL SURVEY
PART 2: TRIP INFORMATION

SITE # _____

SAMPLE # _____

BEGIN: MY FIRST TRIP TODAY BEGAN AT   ☐ (1) Home   ☐ (2) Work   ☐ (99) Other Location

PLEASE ENTER YOUR:

_____

(Fill in address)

TRAVEL DAY: _____

DEPARTURE TIME: _____ am / pm

_____

(Place/address or nearest intersection, city, county, state, zip code)

Location Address	When did you get here/leave here?	Purpose of Trip (check one)	Mode of Transportation (check one)	Total number of people in car/truck/van (including self)	If Driver, what vehicle was used? (make/model)	If Bus, what was the fare? How did you get to the bus stop?
1. FIRST I WENT TO: _____ Name of Place _____ Address, or nearest intersection or landmark _____ City/State/Zip Do you normally work at ☐ Yes ☐ No or out of this location?	Arrive a.m. p.m. Depart a.m. p.m.	☐ (1) Return Home ☐ (2) Go to Work ☐ (3) Work Related ☐ (4) School ☐ (5) Social/Recreation ☐ (6) Eat Out ☐ (7) Shop ☐ (8) Pick up/Drop off Passenger ☐ (9) Change Travel Mode ☐ (10) Personal Business ☐ (11) Other _____	☐ (1) Driver (car/truck/van) ☐ (2) Passenger (car/truck/van) ☐ (3) Walk ☐ (4) Bicycle ☐ (5) Bus ☐ (6) School Bus ☐ (7) Taxi / Paid Limousine ☐ (8) Commercial Vehicle ☐ (9) Motorcycle ☐ (10) Other_____	number of people _____ If you paid parking, what was parking cost? ➔	Year Make Model $_____ per ☐ Hour ☐ Day ☐ Month	Fare: $ _____ ☐ (1) Drove and Parked ☐ (2) Dropped Off ☐ (3) Walked ☐ (4) Carpooled ☐ (5) Other_____
2. THEN I WENT TO: _____ Name of Place _____ Address, or nearest intersection or landmark _____ City/State/Zip Do you normally work at ☐ Yes ☐ No or out of this location?	Arrive a.m. p.m. Depart a.m. p.m.	☐ (1) Return Home ☐ (2) Go to Work ☐ (3) Work Related ☐ (4) School ☐ (5) Social/Recreation ☐ (6) Eat Out ☐ (7) Shop ☐ (8) Pick up/Drop off Passenger ☐ (9) Change Travel Mode ☐ (10) Personal Business ☐ (11) Other _____	☐ (1) Driver (car/truck/van) ☐ (2) Passenger (car/truck/van) ☐ (3) Walk ☐ (4) Bicycle ☐ (5) Bus ☐ (6) School Bus ☐ (7) Taxi / Paid Limousine ☐ (8) Commercial Vehicle ☐ (9) Motorcycle ☐ (10) Other_____	number of people _____ If you paid parking, what was parking cost? ➔	Year Make Model $_____ per ☐ Hour ☐ Day ☐ Month	Fare: $ _____ ☐ (1) Drove and Parked ☐ (2) Dropped Off ☐ (3) Walked ☐ (4) Carpooled ☐ (5) Other_____
3. THEN I WENT TO: _____ Name of Place _____ Address, or nearest intersection or landmark _____ City/State/Zip Do you normally work at ☐ Yes ☐ No or out of this location?	Arrive a.m. p.m. Depart a.m. p.m.	☐ (1) Return Home ☐ (2) Go to Work ☐ (3) Work Related ☐ (4) School ☐ (5) Social/Recreation ☐ (6) Eat Out ☐ (7) Shop ☐ (8) Pick up/Drop off Passenger ☐ (9) Change Travel Mode ☐ (10) Personal Business ☐ (11) Other _____	☐ (1) Driver (car/truck/van) ☐ (2) Passenger (car/truck/van) ☐ (3) Walk ☐ (4) Bicycle ☐ (5) Bus ☐ (6) School Bus ☐ (7) Taxi / Paid Limousine ☐ (8) Commercial Vehicle ☐ (9) Motorcycle ☐ (10) Other_____	number of people _____ If you paid parking, what was parking cost? ➔	Year Make Model $_____ per ☐ Hour ☐ Day ☐ Month	Fare: $ _____ ☐ (1) Drove and Parked ☐ (2) Dropped Off ☐ (3) Walked ☐ (4) Carpooled ☐ (5) Other_____

Figure 6–3B   Example of a Trip Information Form from a Workplace Travel Survey

Source: Texas Department of Transportation. Printed with permission.

be asked to record the information shown in Figure 6–4B. In this case, they would provide information about the time of the trip, the type of cargo transported, and the specific roadways being used.

Regional Travel Demand Models

Regional travel demand models examine the mass movements of persons within a study area. That is, the regional travel demand model is concerned with the movement of aggregated trips on an interchange, not the specific individuals that make up that movement. Regional models are an integral part of and input to transportation investment decisions. Following are some of the uses of travel forecasting analyses: in conceptual engineering and planning to size facilities and estimate capital costs, in transit operations planning to determine operating policies and estimate operating costs, in the financial analysis to forecast fares and toll revenues, and in the environmental analysis to examine the impacts from region-wide air quality to congestion on individual highway links.

COMMERCIAL VEHICLE (TRUCK) SURVEY

PART 1: VEHICLE INFORMATION
(If you have participated in prior surveys, please fill out this form anyway.)

SIC Code: _____   Vehicle License # : _____

Survey Location (zone): _____   Travel Day: _____
                                                              Month / Day

Company or Name of Owner (name on registration):

_____

Address of location where vehicle was based at beginning of travel day:

_____
                        (Street Address or Nearest Intersection)

_____
         City   State   ZIP

Vehicle Make: _____

Vehicle Model: _____

Vehicle Year: _____

Vehicle Fuel Type: 1) ☐ Leaded Gas   2) ☐ Unleaded Gas   3) ☐ Diesel
                       4) ☐ Propane   5) ☐ Other _____(Specify)

Vehicle Classification: 1) ☐ Single Unit 2-axle (6 wheels)
                            2) ☐ Single Unit 3-axle (10 wheels)
                            3) ☐ Single Unit 4-axle (14 wheels)
                            4) ☐ Semi (all Tractor-Trailer combinations)
                            5) ☐ Other _____

                       Gross Vehicle Weight: _____ pounds

                       Beginning Odometer Reading: _____

Figure 6–4A   Example of a Vehicle Information Form from the Commercial Vehicle Survey

Source: Texas Department of Transportation. Printed with permission.

Because of its wide use and its traditional implementation, this chapter focuses on the sequential "four-step modeling process." However, even within the traditional implementation, there are many variations, additions, and even deletions to this process. The flowchart in Figure 6–5 gives a brief overview and "map" of the various model components. The top three boxes represent input data to the entire modeling stream. The shaded boxes show the steps that are considered part of the traditional, sequential, four-step modeling process.

COMMERCIAL VEHICLE (TRUCK) SURVEY
PART 2: TRIP INFORMATION

PLEASE ENTER YOUR:

TRAVEL DAY: _____
Month / Day

TRUCK LICENSE #: _____

BEGINNING ODOMETER READING: _____

BEGIN: MY FIRST TRIP TODAY BEGAN AT:

_____
(Fill in address)

_____
(Place/address or nearest intersection, city, county, state, zip code)

Is this location your:

☐ (1) Base Location   ☐ (6) Home   ☐ (7) Other Location

What is your: a.m.
Departure Time_____ p.m.

a. Trip Number **1** WENT TO: _____ Name of Place _____ Address, nearest intersection, landmark _____ City/County/State/Zip Is this vehicle usually based at or out of this location? ☐ Yes ☐ No	b. Is this location in Travis, Hays, or Williamson County? ☐ Yes ☐ No If No, what road were you on when you entered / left the three county area? _____ Road / Highway	c. When did you get here/leave here? Arrive ___:___ a.m. p.m. Odometer Reading: Depart ___:___ a.m. p.m.	c. Type of Activity at This Location (check one) ☐ (1) Office building ☐ (2) Retail ☐ (3) Industrial site ☐ (4) Medical ☐ (5) Educational (12th grade or <) ☐ (6) Educational (College, trade, etc.) ☐ (7) Government ☐ (8) Residential ☐ (9) Other (Specify) _____
e. Purpose of Trip (check one) ☐ (1) Base Location / Return to Base Location ☐ (2) Delivery ☐ (3) Pick-up ☐ (4) Maintenance (fuel, oil, etc.) ☐ (5) Driver Needs (lunch, etc.) ☐ (6) To Home ☐ (7) Other _____	f. Type of Cargo (check one) ☐ (1) Farm Products ☐ (2) Forest Products ☐ (3) Marine Products ☐ (4) Metals & Minerals ☐ (5) Food, Health & Beauty Products ☐ (6) Tobacco Products ☐ (7) Textiles ☐ /8) Wood Products ☐ (9) Printed Matter ☐ (10) Chemical Products ☐ (11) Refined Petroleum or Coal Products ☐ (12)Rubber, Plastic or Styrofoam Products ☐ (13) Clay, Concrete, Glass or Stone ☐ (14) Manufactured Goods / Equipment	☐ (15) Wastes ☐ (16) Miscellaneous ☐ (17) Hazardous Materials Placard No.: _____ ☐ (18) Unclassified Cargo ☐ (19) Driver Refused to Answer ☐ (20) Unknown to Driver ☐ (21) Empty ☐ Other (specify) _____	d. Facilities Used (check all used for this trip) ☐ (1) I-35 N ☐ (15) RM 1869 ☐ (2) US 290 ☐ (16) SH 21 ☐ (3) US 183 ☐ (17) I-35 S ☐ (4) US 79 ☐ (99) None ☐ (5) SH 71 ☐ (6) SH 95 ☐ (7) SH 29 ☐ (8) Loop 1 ☐ (9) Loop 360 ☐ (10) SH 80 ☐ (11) SH 123 ☐ (12) FM 969 ☐ (13) FM 2720 ☐ (14) RM 32

Figure 6–4B   Example of a Trip Information Form from the Commercial Vehicle Survey

Source: Texas Department of Transportation. Printed with permission.

The actual model steps and mathematical formulations are dependent upon the application, time, and budget available. For instance, a model developed for a large regional population center is likely to be state-of-the-practice and would include all steps, as well as additional submodels. However, a much smaller rural area may not require the resources that are applied to the larger area. This does not diminish the ability of the model to assist decision-makers in making informed decisions. The model's needs and requirements (e.g., what is expected of the model) must be kept foremost in designing the model application.

A regional travel demand model has two major components. The first describes the transportation system and the accessibility it provides between subareas of the region. This component is commonly referred to as the "supply." It is composed of the "networks" that consist of mathematical representations of the highway and transit system in the area. The second component describes travelers, their travel patterns, and their sensitivities to changes in the transportation

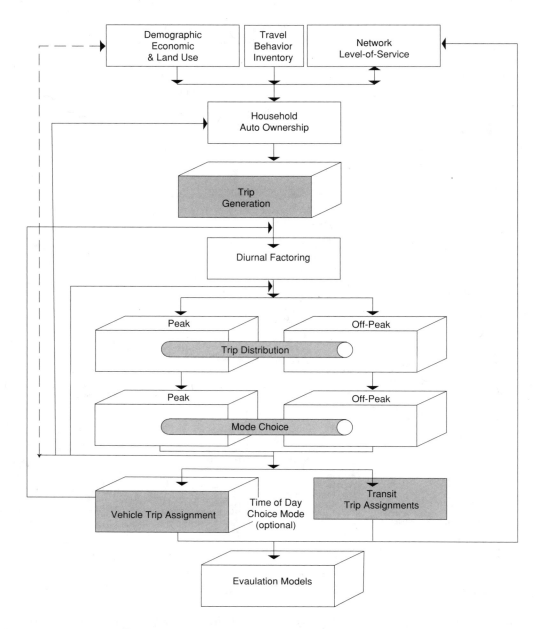

Figure 6–5   Travel Demand Model Flowchart

Source: Parsons Brinckerhoff Quade & Douglas, Inc. Printed with permission.

system. This component is generally termed the "demand," since these models generate the demand (or potential usage) of the supply system.

Networks

The highway and transit networks are computerized representations of the street system in the region. A network is composed of various nodes and links. Nodes are typically intersections or may simply be placed to give the network the proper "shape" when it is plotted; while links connect the various nodes together. Roads are entered in as links and transit lines are entered as a sequence of nodes. An example of a roadway network is depicted in Figure 6–6.

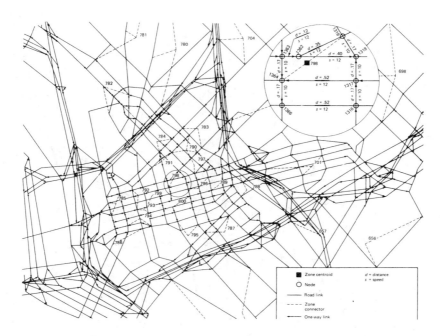

Figure 6–6   Example of a Roadway Network

Source: Institute of Transportation Engineers, *Transportation Planning Handbook,* First Edition, New Jersey: Prentice Hall, 1992, p. 104.

A special set of nodes represent zonal centroids. A zone is a small, homogeneous geographic area. Zones may be as small as a city block in a downtown area or as large as a few square miles in the outlying reaches of the network. The boundaries of a zone are typically defined by geographic barriers or by transportation features, such as rivers and roads. Zone boundaries should follow a census tract or block group boundaries where possible, to make it easier to correlate census demographic data to zones. Within a zone, the land use and spatial distribution of development should be fairly homogeneous. An area with widely varying development characteristics should be split into multiple zones. Figure 6–7 shows an example of a zone map.

Geographic information system (GIS) software provides a graphic environment for both storage and presentation of modeling data bases. For instance, demographic data can be stored at the zonal level within a GIS data base system. In this manner, both the modeling staff as well as those less accustomed to seeing demographic data associated with a zone number can review the data. Plots can be made of households and employment forecasts to see whether or not they make intuitive sense. In addition, a GIS can be used to display travel time and generalized cost contours for travel by specific modes. Finally, a GIS can serve as a tool to share this information with policymakers and the general public, who might not have the familiarity with reading transportation networks.

An example display of geographically related data is shown in Figure 6–8. This plot shows the change in daily parking costs. The various shading patterns correspond to the changes in the parking cost data. This is an example of the information that can be easily displayed in a geographic-based system. Some other items that are best displayed graphically include travel time contours, demographic data forecasts, and land use.

"Four-Step" Modeling Process

Models are continually adapting, changing, and improving with new research advances, as well as the demands placed upon them. The traditional, sequential "four-step process" is still used in a majority of locations. Thus, it is emphasized in this chapter. The steps that are generally considered part of the four-step sequential process include:

Figure 6–7   Example of a Zone Map

Source: Institute of Transportation Engineers, *Transportation Planning Handbook,* First Edition, New Jersey: Prentice Hall, 1992, p. 102.

- *Trip generation*—predicts the number of person trip ends that are generated by and attracted to each defined zone in a study area.

- *Trip distribution*—connects trip ends (productions and attractions) estimated in the trip generation model to determine trip interchanges between each zonal pair.

- *Mode choice*—determines the modes that will be used to travel on each zonal interchange.

- *Trip assignment*—assigns trips to specific highway or transit routes and determines the resulting highway volumes and transit ridership.

These steps are shown as the shaded boxes in Figure 6–5. There are other portions of the model that are only covered in a cursory manner in this chapter. The reader is referred to the multitude of textbooks, consultants, and other resources available and listed in this chapter's reference section.

Any model development work effort begins with the collection of relevant data and information, much of what was described in earlier sections of this chapter. At the same time, both highway and transit networks must be developed in order to represent the roadway system in place.

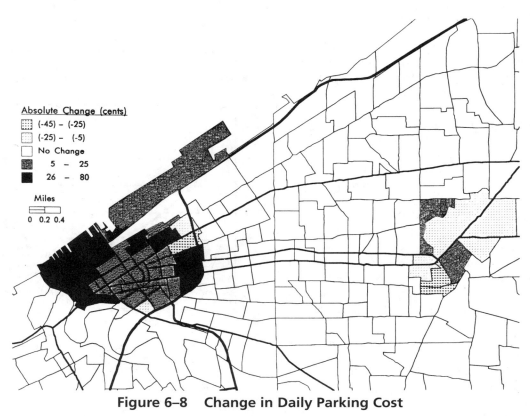

Figure 6–8 Change in Daily Parking Cost

Source: Barton-Aschman Associates, Inc. Printed with permission.

Trip Purposes

Each of the subsequent model components is based on some characteristics of the travelers involved, as well as their trip purpose. The establishment of trip purposes organizes travelers' trips into loosely defined classes where similar travel behavior is observed. This increases the accuracy of the model by using different trip purposes to account for variations in trip rates and trip length frequency distributions. In addition, the classification of trips into distinct trip purposes simplifies the evaluation of policy alternatives that may only affect a segment of the traveling population.

The total number of purposes depends on the analytical capabilities required of the model and the supporting data available. In defining trip purposes, all of the individual components in the modeling process need to be considered. The minimum set of trip purposes includes home-based work trips, home-based other trips, and nonhome-based trips. Home-based trips are based in the home, and they would include both trips to and from the home to an outside destination. Nonhome-based trips would include trips made while at work to a luncheon or to a meeting. However, it is recommended that the largest set of trip purposes that can be supported by the data be used. This will ensure that there is no loss of information in later submodels. Trip purposes can always be combined at a later stage in the modeling process, or they can even be eliminated if they are very small. The extended list of trip purposes may also include: home-based school, home-based shopping, home-based social and recreational activities, home-based entertainment, and home-based personal business. For nonhome-based trips, they can usually be further defined as nonhome-based work (i.e., a trip that somehow relates to work, such as a meeting or working in another office), and nonhome-based nonwork (e.g., going from the shopping center to dinner).

Trip Generation

A trip generation model predicts the total number of person trips that are produced by and attracted to each defined zone in a study area. This estimate of person trip ends is stratified by trip purpose. It is based on the characteristics of both the trip maker and the surrounding land uses. Trip maker characteristics are closely associated with the household attributes, such as household size, income, number of workers, and vehicles owned. Land use is functionally described in terms of its character, intensity, and the location of activities. It may also be described by the type and quantity of employment that it generates.

There are three subcomponents of the trip generation step: household submodels, production models, and attraction models. The household submodels are required to estimate the necessary distribution of households by category for input into the trip production model. Trip production rates are derived on a per household basis from household survey data. The application of such rates requires corresponding estimates of households by category. Households may need to be cross-classified by more than one scheme to satisfy the different trip purpose categories. Potential household classification variables include: number of persons per household, number of workers per household, number of vehicles owned or available to household, household income, and number of children in household. An example of a household size submodel is shown in Figure 6–9.

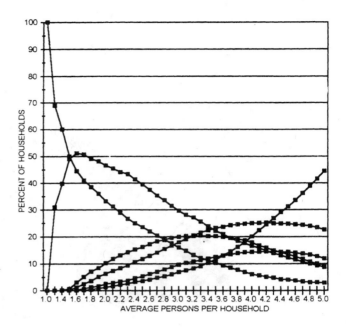

Figure 6–9 Example of a Household Size Submodel

Source: Parsons Brinckerhoff Quade & Douglas, Inc. Printed with permission.

Trip production models estimate the total number of trips by purpose, produced (or originating) in each zone. Production models are usually expressed using rates of the number of trips as a function of the characteristics of the household. Typically, the trip production model is developed using cross-classification by household size and some measure of wealth (e.g., household income or vehicle ownership level).

Trip attraction models predict the number of trips attracted to each zone. This is typically estimated with a regression model. The dependent variable is the number of trips attracted, while the independent variables are mostly related to land use activities. These activities might include employment by type and population, and school models and enrollment levels. If a workplace survey is conducted, disaggregate attraction models could be developed. In this case, the trip attraction rates are based on the employment type, as well as on some measure of household wealth.

Tables 6–1 and 6–2 show some example production and attraction models for various locations for different trip purposes. These are presented as an example only, and they should not be used without further consultation of the metropolitan planning organization (MPO) in the respective areas.

Trip Distribution

Trip distribution models connect trip ends (productions and attractions generated earlier) to one another to create a "flow" of trips in each interchange. Different trip distribution models are developed for each trip purpose. The typical distribution model is some form of the gravity model. The gravity model postulates that the number of trips from one analysis zone to another is directly related to the magnitude of activity within each zone (in terms of productions and attractions) as well as the accessibility between the zones. The interzonal accessibility is the inverse of the travel impedance, which may be measured by the automobile or transit travel time; or by a composite impedance, which could include times, parking fees, and other costs. The formulation of the gravity model is shown in Figure 6–10.

$$T_{ij} = P_i \frac{F(t_{ij})A_j}{\Sigma F(t_{ij})A_j}$$

where: T_{ij} = the number of trips produced by zone i and attracted to zone j

P_i = the total number of trip productions for zone i

$F()$ = the decay function; represents the rate at which a zone's atractiveness declines with increasing travel time

t_{ij} = the minimum zone-to-zone travel time, including terminal times

A_j = attractions estimated for zone j

Σ = the total number of zones

Figure 6–10   The Gravity Trip Distribution Model

Source: Institute of Transportation Engineers, *Transportation Planning Handbook,* First Edition, New Jersey: Prentice Hall, 1992, p. 113.

Table 6–1   Trip Production Models

Home-Based Work Sampled Trip Rate
1990 Twin Cities Travel Behavior Inventory (12/21/93)

Cars Owned	1	2	3	4	5	6+	Total
				HH Size			
0	0.296	0.500	1.154	1.154	1.154	1.154	0.372
1	0.693	0.826	1.497	1.497	1.776	1.776	0.859
2	1.182	1.677	2.231	2.231	1.962	1.962	1.923
3+	1.182	1.677	2.831	2.831	3.086	3.707	2.616
Total	0.707	1.453	2.386	2.411	2.416	2.546	1.786

Home-Based Work Sampled Trip Rate
1990 Twin Cities Travel Behavior Inventory (12/21/93)

Cars Owned	1	2	3	4	5	6+	Total
				HH Size			
0	0.031	0.031	0.031	0.031	0.031	0.031	0.031
1	0.102	0.102	0.102	0.102	0.102	0.102	0.102
2	0.221	0.279	0.279	0.279	0.415	0.415	0.288
3+	0.221	0.407	0.407	0.407	0.415	0.415	0.415
Total	0.109	0.240	0.320	0.328	0.404	0.386	0.266

Source: *Model Calibration Technical Memo #2: 1990 TBI Trip Production Model General Calibration,* Barton-Aschman Associates, Inc., January 1993. Printed with permission.

Alternatively, a logit-based model could be developed. The logit-based trip distribution model formulation is illustrated in Figure 6–11. In this case, the probability of selecting a particular destination zone is based on the number of trip attractions estimated for that destination zone, relative to the total attractions in all possible destination zones. The probability is applied to trip production estimates for the origin zones, making it conceptually similar to the gravity model. A substantial

Table 6–2   Trip Attraction Models

Home-Based Work Trips/Employee, All Areas
1990 TBI Established Survey (2/9/93)

Size	1	2	3	Total
		Establishment Type		
1	0.934	1.153	1.153	1.090
2	1.151	1.307	1.247	1.252
3	1.151	1.307	1.247	1.245
4	1.151	1.247	1.247	1.227
Total	1.145	1.263	1.245	1.232

Home-Based Work Trips/Employee, CBD Areas
1990 TBI Established Survey (2/9/93)

Size	1	2	3	Total
		Establishment Type		
1	1.129	1.129	1.129	1.129
2	1.003	1.252	1.252	1.171
3	1.003	1.151	1.151	1.071
4	0.853	1.151	1.151	1.094
Total	0.923	1.161	1.165	1.098

Home-Based Work Trips/Employee, 1st Ring
1990 TBI Established Survey (2/9/93)

Size	1	2	3	Total
		Establishment Type		
1	0.879	0.879	1.156	1.048
2	1.951	1.293	1.156	1.144
3	1.336	1.336	1.233	1.292
4	1.301	1.301	1.301	1.301
Total	1.254	1.305	1.248	1.275

Home-Based Work Trips/Employee, 2nd, 3rd Ring
1990 TBI Established Survey (2/9/93)

Size	1	2	3	Total
		Establishment Type		
1	0.857	1.227	1.227	1.108
2	1.391	1.391	1.391	1.391
3	1.291	1.332	1.332	1.328
4	1.291	1.245	1.332	1.271
Total	1.318	1.276	1.331	1.299

Source: *Model Calibration Technical Memo #4: 1990 TBI Trip Attraction Model General Calibration,* Barton-Aschman Associates, Inc., February 1993. Printed with permission.

strength of the logit-based model is the completely flexible opportunity to incorporate any type of explanatory variables. That is, any variable that is included in the utility expression is included in the logit model. These could include such variables as measures of urban form, density or area type measures, and size variables (e.g., quantity of office space).

$$P_{ij} = \frac{\exp(V_{ij})}{\sum\limits_{z} \exp(V_j)}$$

where:

P_{ij} = probability of trips from zone i choosing destination j

V_{ij} = natural logarithm of $A_j - \alpha t_{ij} + \beta t_{ij}^2$

A_j = trip attractions estimated for zone j

t_{ij} = highway travel time to zone j from zone i

$\exp(V_{ij})$ is e, the base of natural logarithms, raised to the V_{ij} power α and β are parameters to be estimated

Σ = the total number of zones

Figure 6–11   The Logit Trip Distribution Model Formulation

Source: Institute of Transportation Engineers, *Transportation Planning Handbook,* First Edition, New Jersey: Prentice Hall, 1992, p. 113.

Separate trip distribution models (whether of the gravity form or logit-based) should be estimated for each trip purpose or aggregation of trip purposes used in the trip generation model. For instance, the home-based shopping and home-based personal business purposes might be combined at the distribution stage of the modeling work. Each of the models should be calibrated by ensuring that the modeled trip length frequency distribution matches that from the observed data.

Mode Choice

Mode choice models are usually the most complex of the modeling chain. These models estimate the proportions of travelers that will use various modes of transportation, such as public transit, private automobile, bicycling, or walking. These primary modes are further subdivided into submodes. This could include various types of transit modes, such as commuter rail, light rail (where applicable), express buses, local buses, trolleys, and even monorails. The auto mode is further subdivided into two-person carpools, three-person carpools, and sometimes four+-person carpools. In addition, some mode choice models may include choices for toll facilities, as well as transit access mode (e.g., walk to transit, park-and-ride, or kiss-and-ride). The total person trips are allocated among the available travel modes according to the proportions developed from the mode choice models. These proportions, in turn, are dependent upon the relative levels of service offered by each mode, and the socioeconomic characteristics of the trip makers. As with generation and distribution models, different mode choice models are developed for each trip purpose.

The proportions of travelers that will use each transportation mode can be determined using different techniques—from the simplistic diversion curves to the more complex nested logit models. Some diversion curves are built into software programs. However, the most common mode choice models are based on a variation of the logit function. The logit function states that the probability of choosing a particular mode for a given trip is based on the relative values of the costs and levels of service on the competing modes for the trip interchange under consideration. Some of the cost and service variables that should be included are: in-vehicle travel times, transit waiting times, access and egress times, parking costs, auto travel times, transit fares, and any other cost that might affect a traveler's choice of mode. These variables are combined in a utility function, which is basically a weighted combination of the various cost and service variables. Figure 6–12 illustrates a utility function. By the mathematics of the logistic function,[5] the utilities are used to calculate the proportions of travelers using each alternative mode. Most mode choice models also reflect the economic status of the traveler through some measure of individual or household income or vehicle ownership.

[5] Available in any transportation modeling textbook, several of which are cited in the bibliography.

$$P_{g,i} = \frac{\exp\left[U_{g,i}\right]}{\sum\limits_{m} \exp\left[U_{g,i}\right]}$$

where:

$P_{g,i}$ = the probability of a traveler from group g choosing mode i for a particular trip

$\exp[U_{g,i}]$ = means "e," the base of natural logarithms, raised to the $U_{g,i}$ power

$\sum\limits_{m}$ = summation over all m available alternative modes

$U_{g,i}$ = the utility of a specific mode i for a particular socio-economic group g

The Utility relationship for the logit mode is defined as:

$$U_{g,i} = a_i\left[LOS_i\right] + b_{g,i}\left[SEC_{g,i}\right] + \varepsilon_i$$

where:

LOS_i = a set of variables describing the level-of-service provided by mode i for the particular trip

a_i = a set of coefficients corresponding to each LOS_i variable

$SEC_{g,i}$ = a set of variables describing the socio-economic characteristics of group g with respect to mode i

$b_{g,i}$ = a set of coefficients corresponding to each $SECg,i$ variable

ϵ_i = a specific constant for mode i that reflects unexplained variation for that mode

Figure 6–12   Example of a Logit Relationship for Mode Choice Models

Source: Institute of Transportation Engineers, *Transportation Planning Handbook,* First Edition, New Jersey: Prentice Hall, 1992, p. 114.

Figure 6–12 shows the logit formulation, including a mode choice logit-based model, and the utilities that feed into that model. The various parameters of the logit model (i.e., a and b in the equation) reflect the relative importance of the variables. These parameters must be estimated using statistical software packages to obtain accurate model coefficients. Mode choice model estimation is as much art as it is science. The practitioner must not only decide which variables to include in the model, but also how to include those variables.

In situations where there is a complex set of alternative modes available, the mode choice model may require another variation called the nested logit model. This form attempts to represent the choices in a more structured manner. Nesting is necessary when there are major competing alternatives within as well as between the principal modes. The same cost and level of service variables, as well as the traveler's economic status, are incorporated. In the nested model, a traveler is faced with primary choices, as well as secondary and sometimes even tertiary choices. Each choice must be modeled by some set of cost and level of service variables.

Time of Day Models

There are several methods to consider the effects of time of day activity. These are listed in increasing order of complexity:

1. no differentiation,

2. classical definition,

3. diurnal factoring,

4. time of day choice model.

These are each discussed briefly below. In the past, there was *no differentiation* between time periods. That is, a set of daily models were developed and assigned to a daily network. However, this method is unsuccessful in modeling any area with any significant level of congestion. In the *classical definition,* the home-based work (and possibly home-based university) trips are assigned to the peak network and all other purposes to the off-peak network in an hourly assignment. The peak and off-peak hourly assignments are then combined using another set of factors to create a daily assignment. This differentiation was selected because most home-based work and university trips occur during the peak period; while most nonwork trips occur during the off-peak period. However, this is not strictly true. Thus, *diurnal factoring* can be applied.

In *diurnal factoring,* a set of factors are developed from survey data to split each of the trip generation outputs into peak and off-peak periods. A set of parallel model development steps are carried though trip distribution and mode choice, with a final time of day choice model being implemented before assignment. This involves two sets of diurnal factors—one set applied to create the peak and off-peak periods for trip distribution and mode choice and a second set to create the peak and off-peak hours for assignment. This is illustrated in Figure 6–5. However, as noted before, not all areas need to follow all steps in the regional modeling process. The more simplistic *diurnal factoring* would apply the factors once, just before the assignment step.

The most complex analysis considers a full *time of day choice model.* These are typically logit-based and will estimate the share of trips occurring during the peak hour, shoulders, and off-peak. The actual number of time periods being analyzed depends on the area under study.

Of the four time of day methods described above, the simplest model that is acceptable would be the classical definition. If time and budget resources were available, consideration should be given to the more complex methods. Both the classical definition and diurnal factoring are illustrated in Figure 6–5, with an optional task for the *time of day choice model.*

Trip Assignment

In trip assignment, the mode specific trips are assigned to the appropriate network. The auto vehicle trips are assigned to the highway network, while the transit person trips are assigned to the transit network. The highway and transit assignments are completed mostly within the respective networks. However, in the case of park-and-ride to transit, the highway portion of the trip (i.e., drive access to transit) may be assigned on the highway network; while the actual transit portion of the trip is assigned to the transit network.

Historically, all trips between two zones were assigned to the minimum cost routes of the roadway network, regardless of the available capacity. This is termed an "all-or-nothing" assignment. However, it is unrealistic to expect that all trips would use the shortest path; thus, most transportation software packages use some version of the capacity-restraint equilibrium technique. In this approach part of the traffic is assigned to the roadway network. Then, the travel times are updated, speeds are recalculated, and additional traffic is assigned to the roadway network. The revised times on all links are determined by a volume-delay function. One example and widely used function is that from the Federal Highway Administration (FHWA).

$$T_c = T_f * \left[1 + \alpha * \left(\frac{v}{c} \right)^\beta \right]$$

where:

	T_c	=	congested time
	T_f	=	freeflow time
	v	=	volume
	c	=	capacity
	α, β	=	coefficients

However, this function has some shortcomings. For instance, on links with very high volume-to-capacity (v/c) ratios, there are large changes in the travel times. These large aberrations slow down convergence and can lead to overflow conditions and loss of precision. Secondly, for links with very low v/c ratios, the times are equivalent to the free flow travel time and basically reduces to an all-or-nothing assignment. Thus, more recent research[6] suggests that conical delay functions may be more appropriate.

$$T_c = T_f * \left[2 + \sqrt{\alpha^2 * \left(1 - \left(\frac{v}{c}\right)\right)^2 + \beta^2} - \alpha * \left(1 - \left(\frac{v}{c}\right)\right) - \beta \right]$$

where:

$$\beta = \frac{2\alpha - 1}{2\alpha - 2}$$

and other variables are as noted on page 194.

Most transportation planning software packages allow the user to enter the desired type of volume-delay function, whether it be the traditional FHWA curve, the conical curve, or some other user-defined curve. In any case, the assignment steps are iterated until all trips have been assigned and no traveler can improve their travel time by changing paths. After several iterations, equilibrium will have been reached and there will be very little change in speeds at subsequent assignment steps.

For a transit assignment, most software packages apply the all-or-nothing transit assignment, the rationale being that there are rarely closely competing transit routes in an efficiently designed system. However, some packages (notably EMME/2) allow for transit multipath assignments.[7] In this technique, transit trips on the same zonal interchange may use different paths to reach their final destination.

Model Calibration and Validation

As each of the model steps are developed, they must be calibrated to observed data. For instance, in calibrating a mode choice model, the various modal constants must be adjusted in order to match the observed shares. Each model step must also be validated against the observed data. In many instances, calibration and validation are iterative procedures. Once all models are able to accurately replicate observed behavior, they are applied in the full model stream—from trip generation through trip assignment.

Overall model validation is the final step in the model development process. The complete set of models described above are executed exactly as they would be applied in any future forecasting situation. This will result in a set of assigned volumes on both the highway network and the transit system. Comparisons are then made against the observed volumes to determine how accurately the model replicates existing conditions.

In a regional travel demand model there are many levels of validation a model must be subject to before it can be used in the analysis of transportation plans and projects. They can be further divided into those applied to highway models and those applied to transit models. There are very few calibration and validation standards that can be applied to a transit model. However, extensive work has been completed in designing highway calibration and validation target values. Some examples of the calibration criteria are presented in the following sections.

Land Use and Trip Generation

In the trip generation phase of the model development, the following evaluations should be completed.

- Review the network and zone system to determine the need for special generators or those land uses that have different trip characteristics and require their own trip generation rates (e.g., large airports, universities, automobile manufacturing plants).

- Compare production and attraction rates against standardized references and survey data from other areas.

---

[6] Heinz Spiess, *Conical Volume-Delay Functions, Publication No. 628* (Transportation Research Center, University of Montreal, 1989).

[7] INRO Consultants, Inc., *EMME/2 Users's Manual, Software Release 8.6b* (Montreal, Quebec, Canada, March 3, 1998).

- Check the ratio of total productions and attractions, as well as the percentage distribution of trip ends, by trip purpose to test the reasonableness of the trip generation model.

Network Development

The computerized network representation for the study area should be checked for reasonableness and validity. Any inconsistencies with the network should be corrected before any model assignments are completed.

Trip Distribution

In the trip distribution analysis the following comparisons should be completed.

- Review the average trip length from the distribution model with the average trip lengths from similarly sized cities or in reference materials. In most cases, the average trip lengths should be within fifteen percent of those typically found in reference materials and similarly sized cities.

- Review the percentage of intrazonal trip making and compare it to the typical percentages in reference materials.

Mode Choice

Mode choice calibration targets should be based on survey data that were collected as part of the development of the travel demand model. The modal bias constants that are part of the utility expressions should be adjusted until the modeled shares replicate the observed shares.

Vehicle Assignment Validation

Highway volumes are validated against a set of observed traffic counts. These counts may come from the state Department of Transportation (DOT), local government, or the MPO for the area. They will need to be organized and summarized at the link level that is used in the network. Then a series of cordon lines are drawn, and the cordon line assigned volumes are compared to the cordon line count data. These must be within certain tolerable limits in order for the model to be a useful tool.

At the link level, several types of comparisons should be made. The first type is an evaluation of the estimated to observed vehicle miles of travel by each of the geographical locations established for analysis in the trip distribution model comparisons (i.e., area aggregations of traffic analysis zones). This comparison would be made at the regional level as well as at the district level. A second type is the calculation of percent root mean square error by facility type, area type, and a range of volume categories. In the context of model validation, percent root mean square error is computed as follows:

$$\%RMSE = \frac{\sqrt{\frac{(V_o - V_e)^2}{N} * N}}{\sum V_o}$$

where: V_o = observed volume for link n

V_e = estimated volume for link n

N = number of observations or number of links

Aggregate validation targets for vehicle trips are measured primarily for the A.M. and P.M. peak hours. If 24-hour volumes are computed from the peak- and off-peak period volumes and are statistically fitted, they are of less value in determining model adequacy. The total A.M. and P.M. peak-hour volumes crossing each cordon or screenline should be within ten percent of the A.M. and P.M. peak-hour counts, respectively. On an individual link basis, the following tolerances should be applied:

- 75% of freeway link volumes within +/- 20%

- 50% of freeway link volumes within +/- 10%

- 75% of major arterial link volumes with 10,000 vehicles per day within +/- 30%

- 50% of major arterial link volumes with 10,000 vehicles per day within +/- 15%

Still another type of link level comparison is network plots in which differences between estimated and observed flows can be shown by color-coded bandwidths scaled to the difference or ratio. Most modeling packages have the graphic capabilities to produce such network plots.

It should be noted that when comparing forecasted volumes to ground counts, it is important to recognize that the ground counts probably contain a significant amount of error. Traffic volumes vary greatly by season and by day of week. Count discrepancies can also be attributed to variation in the mix of vehicles in the traffic stream, mechanical counter failure, field personnel mistakes, or improper counter location.

Transit Assignment Validation

A statistical analysis of 24-hour transit assignments on a route-by-route basis provides the basis for ascertaining the accuracy of the transit validation. Actual transit boardings for each route for an entire weekday can be obtained from on-board rider surveys or other available route level information. The observed and estimated boardings can be compared using regression analysis. Standards for validation of transit demand estimates depend heavily on the nature of model application expected and the related level of veracity embodied in the transit network. Often, detailed transit assignments to individual routes are not expected to be accurate; instead, corridor level flows are of primary interest. In such cases, corridor-screenline comparisons are more relevant and the model should reproduce flows at this level within ten percent for all major corridors.

The discussion of freight and truck issues are noticeably absent from this section. They are covered in detail in Chapter 3, "General Travel and Goods Movement."

Evaluation of Options

Travel demand models are used for input into the major investment study process, as well as for developing regional transportation plans. The purpose of most model development efforts is to produce a tool that is usable by the planning agency to measure the effects of various alternative development plans. Using the newly validated model, forecasts are run and the results presented to a governing board or a technical committee, or they are used for in-house analysis of various development options.

The analyst must ensure that the models are evaluated using the same set of "rules" that were used in the model development. That is, the consistent application of all model parameters and formulae are crucial to obtaining a usable set of forecasts.

Regional Modeling Software Packages

Virtually all regional transportation planning models are implemented via some set of software packages, statistical routines, and assorted external programs. In today's computing environment, the personal computer can run virtually all of the major software packages. The problem is deciding on which one. Tables 6–3A and 6–3B describe several of the popular transportation planning software packages. These vary widely in capability and cost, with each package having their own strengths and weaknesses. All of the packages have some graphical interface and some flexibility in implementing the various models that have been described above. The user should request a demonstration of each package from the individual vendors and compare the characteristics of each. The Institute of Transportation Engineers (ITE) has produced an informational report that can aid in this process.[8]

Improvements to Regional Models

The sequential four-step modeling practice has been in place for over forty years. The procedures were established in the early 1960s to address long-range planning and forecasting needs, especially for highways. However, the requirements that are placed on the forecasting procedures have grown. Where travel forecasting models once focused on the necessary capacity for new highway facilities, models are now expected to deal with a much broader set of issues. Some examples include: high-occupancy vehicle lanes, land use controls and incentives, and transportation demand management strategies.

Fortunately, the methods for travel forecasting have also advanced substantially over the last ten years. Whereas the typical model set of the 1980s may have consisted of a series of loosely related and mostly independent models, newer methods do a much better job of using and sharing information on the transportation system and with the travelers on the system.

In 1993, the U.S. DOT and the Environmental Protection Agency established the Travel Model Improvement Program (TMIP).[9] The purpose of the TMIP is to improve the quality of travel forecasting procedures for federal, state, and local agencies. The program pursues five tracks of activity:

Table 6–3A   Urban Transportation Planning Software Contacts

Software (Vendor)	Contact Person	Telephone No.	Facsimile No.	Email	Website
EMME/2 (INRO Consultants Inc.)	Michael Florian	514 369-2023	514 369-2026	sales@inro.ca	http://www.inro.ca
MINUTP (The Seiders Group)	Larry Seiders	510 583-7330	510 583-7340	General@uagworld.com	www.uagworld.com
QRS II (AJH Associates)	Shirley Horowitz	414 963-8686	414 963-0686	ajh@execpc.com	http://execpc.com/~ajh/
SYSTEM II (Science Applications International Corporation–Transportation Consulting Group)	Jim McBride	703 575-6734	703 820-7970	james.m.mcbride @cpmx.saic.com	www.saic.com
TMODEL2 (TMODEL Corp.)	Robert Shull	1-800-T2MODEL 206 463-3768	1-800-T2MODEL 206 463-5055	tmodel@tmodel.com	www.tmodel.com
TP+/VIPER (Urban Analysis Group)	Larry Seiders	510 583-7330	510 583-7340	Larry@uagworld.com	www.minutp.com
TRANSCAD (Caliper Corp.)	Howard Slavin	617 527-4700	617 527-5113	howard@caliper.com	www.caliper.com
TRIPS (MVA) or (Systemetica North America)	Tor Vorraa Or George Hoyt	+44 1483 728051 1-800-TRIPS10	+44 1483 755207 703 780-7874	trips@mva.co.uk tripsusa@erols.com	www.mva-group.com
URBAN/SYS, Including Tranplan (The Urban Analysis Group)	Victor Siu	650 321-2294	650 321-2294	trantp@uagworld.com	www.uagworld.com

---

[8] ITE Technical Council Committee 6F-47, *Selection and Use of Regional Transportation Microcomputer Planning Packages* (Washington, D.C.: ITE, February 1995).

[9] More detailed information on the Travel Model Improvement Program can be found on their website at http://bts.gov/tmip/wnew.htm.

Table 6–3B Urban Transportation Planning Software

Name of Software Program	Price, Price Options[1]	Formats Accommodated For Data Import and Export	Operating Systems Accommodated	CPU	RAM	Hard Disk Storage Space	Monitor	Digitizing Table	Other Requirements
EMME/2	$9,000 to $56,800 (Avg. price about $8,000 with multiple license discounts.)	Import: ASCII (Can accommodate input for any other package.) Export: ASCII	Windows 3.1/3.11, Windows 95, DOS, HP-UX, AIX, Digital Unix, Sun Solaris and Sun OS Windows NT 4.0	486/ Pentium; Unix work-stations or servers	8 Meg/ 32 Meg	200 Meg/ 2 Gig	Color (17" recom-mended)	Not necessary	High Resolution Graphic Adapter
MINUTP	Full system $6,000; 300 zone system $3,000	Import: ASCII, ArcView DXF Export: ASCII, DBF, ArcView, MapInfo.	DOS	386+	1 MB	5 MB	VGA	N/A	N/A
QRSII	300 zones with Advanced General Network Editor (Adv. GNE), $390; 600 zones with Adv. GNE, $585; 900 zones with Adv. GNE, $780; 2,400 zones with Adv. GNE, $975	Import: ASCII, CSV, HNET, custom variations on HNET Export: ASCII, CSV, WMF, EMF	Windows 95, 98 Windows NT 4.0	Pentium	16MB	3MB/ 40MB	VGA/ SVGA	Any table with windows driver supported; additional hardware not supported.	None
SYSTEM II (SAIC – Transporta-tion Consult-ing Group)	$6,000/site (U.S. and Canada) – $10,000/site (International); $9,000 for two sites, $12,000 for three or more sites (U.S. and Canada)	Import: TIGER, ArcView (shape), MapInfo (MIF), DXF, ASCII, and Btrieve Export: ASCII, dBase, ArcView, MapInfo, DXF, PCX, Btrieve	DOS, Windows 9X	486+	8+ MB	40+ MB	VGA+	N/A	HPGL, HPGL-2, Calcomp plotters supported
TMODEL (Tmodel Corporation)	$3,800 including NCAP and one year of main-tenance; educational $150; sample $125; 50% discount on multiple copies for same office.	Import: ASCII, TIGER, DXF, MapInfo, EMME/2, TRANPLAN, QRS, THE, MOTORs Export: ASCII, DXF, HPGL, TRANPLAN, PCX	DOS, Windows 95/98/NT.	Pentium	640 KB/ 16MB+	10 MB	VGA+	Optional-support Calcomp, HI, Kurta, Numonics, Summa Graphics	Mouse, plotter is optional – Supports HPGL, DesignJets, LaserJets
TP+/VIPER	$500 – $10,000 Update and multi-license discounts	Most common types: TP+, MINUTP, TRANPLAN, DBF, ASCII, ArcView, etc.	Windows 9X/NT DOS Unix (under development)	Pentium	OS Determines	10 MB +data	SVGA+	N/A	N/A
TransCAD	$2,995 – $9,995; multiple license discounts.	Import: ASCII, UTPS, TIGER, DBF, F.F. Binary, DXF, BTS, DGN, BNA, MapInfo, TRANPLAN, MINUTP, EMME/2, QRS, TRIPS, Excel, VPF, Ordinance Survey (Britain), ETAK, DLG, DEM, GIRAS, GEOTIFF, Digital Orthophotos, ODBC-compliant DBs, MAPTITUDE, ArcView, Shape, ArcInfo Export: ASCII, F.F. Binary, DBF, BNA, Shapefiles, DXF, BMP, JPEG.	Windows 3.1, 95, and NT	486, all Pentiums	16 MB/ 32 MB	50 MB/ 300 MB+	VGA/ SVGA	Any	CD-ROM
TRIPS	Sold on a modular basis. Price varies by computing environment model size and functionality. Starting price Basic Highways is $3,490. Licenses 2-5 70% off; license 6+, 90% off.	Import: ASCII, CSV Export: ASCII, CSV, HPGL, DXF.	Windows 3.11/95/98 /NT	386/ Pentium, UNIX	640 KB/ 32MB	10 MB depend-ing on problem	VGA/ SVGA/ XUGA	N/A	None
URBAN/ SYS (TRAN PLANN IS)	$8,000	Import: ASCII & ODBC compatible & dBase Export: ASCII & ODBC compatible & dBase	DOS, OS/2, UNIX (IBM, SUN, Hewlett Packard), Windows 3.1+, Windows 95, NT	386+ PC systems	16 MB	20 BM+ data	User option	N/A	Color plotter

Note: The information shown in the table is supplied by the vendor of each of the software packages listed.

[1] Educational discounts available for most packages. Multiple license discounts available for some packages. International surcharges apply to some packages.

Table 6–3B   Urban Transportation Planning Software (continued)

Name of Software Program	Trip Generation Options regression = a cross classification = b trip rates = c	Trip Distribution Options gravity model = a FRATAR = b other = c	Modal Split Options	Trip Assignment Options all or nothing = a capacity restraint = b stochastic/probalistic = c incremental = d equilibrium = e	Additional Options subarea focusing = a dynamic delay models for intersections = b select link assignment with capacity restraint = c
EMME/2	a, b, c; Any method may be implemented using matrix calculator. None for calibration	a, b, c; any method can be implemented using the balancing procedures (2-D and 3-D)	Logit and nested logit; any demand function may be used	a, c, d, e, versatile assignment procedure: fixed or variable demand, multiclass equilibrium assignment	a, b (interfaces with SATURN and NETSIM), c (select link analysis in equilibrium assignment); powerful features for path analysis
MINUTP	a, b, c	a, b, c, user	Logit and nested logit.	a, b, c, d, e, multiclass	a, b, c; network and matrix manipulation
QRSII	a, c, anything from a spread sheet	a, c, any distribution model from spreadsheet	Logit; multiple transit modes handled at network level	a, b, c (transit only), d (method of successive averages [MSA]), e	a (not automatic, instructions provided), b, c; select zone analysis, graphical skim trees, Window matrix creation
SYSTEM II (SAIC – Transportation Consulting Group)	Regression, cross classification, and trip rates supported	Gravity model and Fratar supported	Logit and nested logit	All-or-nothing, Capacity restrained, Stochastic, Incremental, Equilibrium Assignment Supported	Subarea focusing, Dynamic Delay Models for Inter-Sections, Select Link Assignments with Capacity restraint, Integration with Global Positioning Systems for Travel Time Runs, Multi-Modal Transit Assignment, Integrated Macro Language, Address Matching, Employee Commute Options, Growth Management Software, Extensive Set of Utilities. 146 programs in all
TMODEL (Tmodel Corporation)	a, b, c anything from a spreadsheet	a, b, c, O/D estimation from counts	Pre-distribution, post distribution with UMODEL, pivot point logit	a, b, d, HOV/multimodal, multi-point assignment (MPA), upstream queuing propagation (UQP)	a, b, c; select zone, select trip purpose turn movements, subarea trip table and network extraction, level of service, emissions
TP+/VIPER	a, b, c, user	a, b, user	User specified	a, b, d, e, user	a, b, c
TransCAD	a, b, c, logit, disaggregate models of trip frequency, ITE rates, any method can be implemented in macros, spread-sheet, FORTRAN, or C	a, b, c, estimation from counts; entropy calibration/ application; triproportional, distribution curves, simultaneous distribution-assign-ment, other methods from macros, spreadsheets, and user-written code	Logit and nested logit; Incremental logit, user specified equations and look-up tables; diversion curves	a, b, c, d, e. Stochastic user equilibrium, multimodal traffic assignment (cars, HOV, trucks, buses), generalized cost and toll road assignments, multiple user class, dynamic assignment; assignment with dynamic intersection delay. Several state-of-the-art transit assignment procedures including optimal strategies, generalized pathfinder (for overlapping routes), and stochastic user equilibrium for transit	A, B, a, b, c; preloading; comprehensive GIS functionality (thematic maps; geocoding; ground truth for transportation facilities and networks; geographic editing of TAZs, networks; buffering around roads, transit routes, and TAZs; contouring of terrain, travel time, and access-ibility data; beautiful map graphics with complete user control of graphic out-put; powerful database management); includes a vast array of transportation data (all U.S. streets, highways, railroads, airports, most transit property routes available); statistical analysis tools for model estimation (cross-tabs, multiple regression, multinominal logit); network conflation; tools for easy access to Census data; innovative batch mode with comprehen-sive scripting language intersection diagrams
TRIPS	a, b, c	a, b, c, partial gravity, logit O-D choice	Logit and nested logic; (both absolute and incremental)	a, b, c, d, e	a, b, c
URBAN/SYS (TRANPLAN, NIS)	a	a, b, c, spatial allocation	Logit, nested logic (both customized)	a, b, c, d, e	a, b (customized version), c

Table 6–3B   Urban Transportation Planning Software (continued)

Name of Sotfware Program	Integration With True GIS Packages	Enhanced Survey Expansion Methods	Geocoding of O-D Surveys	Software Analysis of Non-motorized Travel	Capabilities Compatibility With Land Use Allocation Models	Dynamic Assignment
EMME/2	Several users have developed ad hoc interfaces with their GIS. INRO has developed a set of utilities which facilitates the transfer between EMME/2 and ARCInfo	An incremental format for matrix input facilitates entering demand data from a survey	N/A	Walk trips, bicycle trips, etc., can be analyzed	Interface with land-use methods have been done (MEPLAN, EMPAL/DRAM)	N/A
MINUTP	Limited	None	None	User specifications	None	Special option
QRSII	Import or export CSV or ASCII format	No	No	No	Highway Land Use Forecasting Model II+ (HLFM II+)	No
SYSTEM II	Import/export – native ArcView & MapInfo – LAT/LNG conversions, shape files, network generation & reconciliation	N/A	Address matching, trip table generation from zone polygons/ boundaries, GPS data collection & map matching	Employee commute options analysis include walk, bicycle, car pool, vanpool, transit, and telecommute	Easily works with multiple network and zone structure systems	N/A
TMODEL (Tmodel Corporation)	Import and export of data with GIS. MapInfo and DXF files can be imported for use as graphic layers.	Normalizing, Frataring	N/A	User flexible network descriptions	ASCII import and export into trip generation/land use files	Upstream Queuing Propagation
TP+/VIPER	ArcView.shp.dbf	N/A	N/A	User specified	Non specific	No
TransCAD	Yes. TransCAD is a true topologically-structured GIS that, because of common data structures and import/export capabilities, has the best integration with other GIS packages such as ArcInfo, ArcView, MapInfo, GIS+, and Maptitude.	Yes	Yes	Yes, sample enumeration and sample scaling Agregation to zonal totals from survey records	Yes, walking can be treated explicitly and as part of the transit network for access, egress, and transfers	Yes
TRIPS	Linked to Arc Info/ArcView, MapInfo, and others	Includes basic survey package for survey expansion	Through links to GIS packages	Can be used for modeling walk and cycle routes	Interface to land use allocation models	Strong dynamic assignment capabilities
URBAN/SYS (TRANSPLAN, NIS)	Extensive development underway	No	No	No	Travel Time Interface (DRAM/EMPAL)	No

- *Track A: outreach*—receives information from users and disseminates the results through a review board, conferences, an information clearinghouse on the Internet, and a newly established training and technical assistance center.

- *Track B: near-term improvements*—focus on immediate improvements to the existing procedures and is producing manuals to assist practitioners. One such manual is *Short-Term Improvements to the Travel-Forecasting Process,* and a second is concerned with freight movement.

- *Track C: long-term improvements*—develop a regionwide microsimulation procedure, referred to as TRANSIMS. This project simulates the behavior of individuals and households, as well as the operation of vehicles on the transportation system.

- *Track D: data*—support the upgrading of current methods and develops new techniques. New manuals for data collection efforts are being developed, as well as a comprehensive manual of validation methods and the required data.

- *Track E: land use*—integrates the transportation and land use models.

Each of these tracks focuses on a different aspect of the travel forecasting model process. Numerous publications and documents have been produced detailing each of the tracks, as well as reporting on the progress of each track. Several of these are listed in the bibliography.

Introduction to Discrete Models

The development of a regional model is not always feasible nor practical. There are numerous factors that often play a significant role in determining if a regional transportation model should be developed or if another analysis tool should be used. Beyond the cost and time resources that a regional model development takes, there are other factors to consider. For instance, a discrete model may be preferred when attempting to model small changes to a transportation network, such as where best to locate parking ramps in a congested downtown area, simulating light rail transit operations along roadways, or making changes to a one-way street system. For these types of analyses, the discrete model is a more proper tool to use than a regional travel demand model.

Discrete modeling allows one to analyze the individual movements of traffic at the microscopic level, while the regional travel demand model allows analysis at a macroscopic level. The discrete model analyzes corridors in a region and can provide information down to the individual intersection level, while most regional travel demand models use the metropolitan region as the study area. There are two types of discrete modeling: traffic simulation and site traffic analysis. These two types of modeling are discussed in more detail in the following two sections.

Traffic Simulation Models

Microscopic traffic simulation models are very data intensive programs and require a large amount of information to provide the best results. At the same time, these traffic simulation models are an invaluable resource when presenting results to community groups and civic leaders using computer animation graphics. In addition, traffic simulation models allow transportation planners and traffic engineers to better reflect the quality of traffic conditions on a congested corridor. The required input data includes roadway geometry, traffic volumes, signal timing data, and other operational characteristics (such as transit vehicles and pedestrian movements). Some of the required data inputs are:

- *Roadway geometry*—includes the number of lanes, lane designations, turn bay lengths, distances between intersections, and roadway speeds.

- *Traffic volumes*—include peak-hour turning movement volumes, heavy truck percentages, and peak-hour factors.

- *Signal timing*—includes the existing coordinated signal timing plan, peak-hour cycle lengths, phase splits, and left-turn and right-turn phasing (exclusive, permissive, or exclusive/permissive).

- *Transit characteristics*—include the typical length of the vehicle, operational speeds, peak-hour headways, station locations, and expected dwell times.

- *Pedestrian movements*—include the number of pedestrians per hour by crosswalk, average walk time, and length of pedestrian crosswalk.

There are several traffic simulation models now being used, and all have various distinctive applications. Some of these models include CORFLO,[10] ITRAF,[11] and modules within TEAPAC.[12] Other traffic operation simulation models exist that provide support in the analysis of traffic to both the transportation planner and traffic engineer. The optimization of traffic signals can be modeled through the use of many software packages. One such package is Synchro,[13] which provides a complete implementation of the 1994 HCM, Chapter 9. In addition to calculating capacity, Synchro can also optimize cycle lengths and splits that eliminates the need for multiple timing plans. The software package also provides coordination between other software packages, such as TRAF-NETSIM,[14] PASSER 2,[15] and TRANSYT 7F.[16]

Site Traffic Analysis

The transportation professional often needs a software tool that will efficiently provide the following support when conducting site traffic analyses.

- To conduct traffic impact studies.

- To conduct small size, citywide traffic forecasts using historical and existing traffic volume and socio-economic data.

- To rapidly forecast the traffic impacts of new developments.

- To calculate level of service at critical signalized and unsignalized intersections and on arterials.

- To interactively test different mitigation measures.

- To determine traffic impact fees for individual development projects.

In most cases the data in the software program can be stored in a GIS format in which the user must first draw a network (or code a network in a batch file) before data can be input. If a GIS data base is not available, then the data can be pulled from existing maps and non-GIS data bases. All of the software programs perform four functions critical in the engineering and planning evaluation of all highway and land use development projects: traffic forecasting, intersection and arterial level of service analysis, mitigation, and impact fee calculation.

The analyst draws a road network on screen that consists of development zones, critical intersections, and gateways where new traffic enters and leaves the study area. Land uses, trip generation rates, and trip distribution percentages are input for each development zone. The most likely paths that the traffic will take from each development zone to each gateway are also coded. The A.M. and P.M. peak-hour traffic is assigned to the street system, and the level of service is calculated.

Traffic Forecasting

The following procedures are used when completing a site impact analysis.

- Determine the study area, and select the network to be coded.

- Draw the network using a batch process or an on-screen editor, and create zones.

[10] Developed by the Oak Ridge National Laboratory, University of Tennessee Transportation Center, Oak Ridge Institute of Science and Education and Viggen Corporation, Version 1.03, April 1997.

[11] Developed by the Oak Ridge National Laboratory, University of Tennessee Transportation Center, Oak Ridge Institute of Science and Education and Viggen Corporation, Version 2, April 1997.

[12] Developed by Strong Concepts, April 1995.

[13] Developed by Trafficware, Version 3, 1996-1997.

[14] Developed by the Oak Ridge National Laboratory, University of Tennessee Transportation Center, Oak Ridge Institute of Science and Education and Viggen Corporation, Version 2, April 1997.

[15] Developed by the Transportation Research Center, University of Florida at Gainsville, Florida, March 1998.

[16] Developed by the Transportation Research Center, University of Florida at Gainsville, Florida, March 1998.

- Enter the intersection data, including the number of turn and through-lanes and the length of turn lanes.

- Select the arterial analysis routes or the primary roadways that will be used for site generated traffic.

- Enter the trip generation rate data (most software programs contain trip generation data; however, user trip generation data can be entered). Alternatively, vehicle trip generation rates may be used from ITE.[17]

- Enter the paths between all zones and all gateways.

- Enter the directional distribution data from existing traffic counts; census data; or if a regional model exists in the area, use distribution data from the model.

- Assign the traffic on the roadway network.

- Analyze the level of service for individual intersections and arterials, and develop appropriate mitigation measures.

The site traffic analysis software packages provide an invaluable tool for the transportation professional when a regional model is not available. There are many site traffic software packages available. Some of the programs that can be used for site traffic analysis include: SITE[18] as part of the battery of TEAPAC programs, TRANMAP,[19] and TRAFFIX.[20] All of the site impact analysis software allow roadway levels of service to be calculated simultaneously for both baseline and future (no-build and build) scenarios at signalized and unsignalized intersections, on both urban and suburban arterials.

Level of Service Analysis

The level of service for signalized intersections is calculated using one of five different methods: 1994 HCM[21] Planning and Operations, 1985 HCM[22] Planning and Operations, TRB Circular 212[23] Planning and Operations, and two Intersection Capacity Utilization methods. Arterial level of service is also calculated according to either the 1994 or 1985 HCM methods.

Mitigation

After assigning the traffic to the transportation network using the site traffic impact analysis software, the level of service is calculated for all major roadways and intersections. After the initial traffic forecast and level of service are calculated, various test street improvements and signal timing changes for mitigating the impacts at an intersection can be completed.

Impact Fees

Impact fee calculations can be performed and the establishment of development requirements, such as additional traffic signals or traffic lanes, can be developed since the traffic impact software can trace the traffic generated by a new development through each critical intersection on the street network.

---

[17] *Trip Generation Manual,* 6th Edition (Washington, D.C.: Institute of Transportation Engineers, 1997).

[18] Developed by Strong Concepts, June 1993.

[19] Developed by the BA Consulting Group, Ltd. September 1997.

[20] Developed by Dowling Associates, Version 7.0, September 1997.

[21] *Highway Capacity Manual,* Third Edition, Special Report 209 (Washington, D.C.: Transportation Research Board, 1994).

[22] *Highway Capacity Manual,* Special Report 209 (Washington, D.C.: Transportation Research Board, 1985).

[23] *Circular 212* (Washington, D.C.: Transportation Research Board, January 1980).

Post Processors

Once the regional travel demand model or the microscopic traffic simulation model is developed, a number of postprocessing tools can be used for further analysis. The areas where postprocessing tools can be useful include the following:

- Presentation of results in a GIS-format.

- Calculation of roadway v/c ratios.

- Completion of regional air quality conformity analyses.

- Calculation of economic analyses on potential roadway and transit projects.

- Evaluation of transportation systems.

Efforts to combine regional travel demand models and GIS data bases continue to be a major research and development program for many software vendors, as well as for academic entities. Most meshing of transportation or traffic models and GIS have occurred on a project-by-project basis with no direct link of the models and GIS. In most cases, the model output must be taken and adjusted to fit the parameters of the GIS data base. The reverse is true when GIS data is brought into a model.

Roadway v/c ratios can be calculated based on the modeled roadway volumes and the assumed capacities of the roadways. These are typically assigned a corresponding level of service in accordance with the HCM. A comparison of the existing and future year roadway deficiencies serve as the basis for transportation plans. Many times the regional or microscopic model can be used to directly calculate the v/c ratio on the roadways in the study area.

Air quality analyses can be completed using regional model output data. Once the traffic assignment is completed for various time frames (e.g., for base year and transportation plan horizon year) the following data are extracted from the regional travel demand model.

- Vehicle miles of travel by facility type.

- Vehicle hours of travel by facility type.

- Average operating speed by facility type.

Once the regional travel demand model output data are extracted and entered into the Volatile Organic Compounds Emission model, the air quality conformity analysis can be completed. The Clean Air Act Amendments (CAAA) of 1990 established the mandate for better coordination between metropolitan area air quality and long-range transportation planning. Under the legislation, all transportation plans and transportation investments must conform to the State Implementation Plan (SIP). The intent of the SIP is to develop an integrated, multimodal transportation system that results in reduced pollution emissions to meet National Ambient Air Quality Standards. A transportation plan must be established that results in improved air quality from the levels observed in 1990, not just stabilized levels. Refer to Chapter 8 for a detailed discussion of the CAAA.

The postprocessing tools used by transportation professionals today are continuing to evolve. It their desire that both the regional travel demand models and the microscopic traffic simulation models will one day provide a seamless link between all other models. This includes GIS, link and intersection v/c ratio calculation, air quality analysis, economic analysis, and system performance measurement.

Limitations of Models

As stated previously in this chapter, a regional transportation planning model consists of a complex series of steps with many built-in assumptions. When using a highway or transit model, the transportation professional should not be overly optimistic about matching the simulated traffic volume or ridership numbers to existing traffic counts or boardings and alightings. A reasonable expectation is for the model to be accurate enough so that it will not affect the number of lanes required to meet the traffic volume. Furthermore, a transit model should accurately predict the number of riders on a transit system to a certain level. Additionally, there are limitations to the discrete models that have been described in previous sections.

Many times traffic data and traffic operations data have not been collected with the required accuracy necessary to develop a reliable and believable microscopic traffic simulation model. Currently, there are no uniform standards for accuracy that can be applied to discrete models. A thorough review of all input data should be conducted before using the data within the model. Likewise, all output data from any model should be reviewed for reasonableness before officially releasing the results.

Each planning software package often has unique approaches and assumptions. They are based on similar theories of travel behavior. However, they are often very different in how the transportation professional accesses and uses the software. The user must avoid mistakes by fully understanding all the features of the software. If the model is not performing as expected and if the answer cannot be found within any reference manual, a person that is experienced in the field of modeling is often the best place to find the solution to a perplexing problem.

References

Beimborn, Edward, Rob Kennedy and William Schaefer. *Inside the Blackbox: Making Transportation Models Work for Livable Communities*. Citizens for a Better Environment, August 1996.

Federal Highway Administration. *Calibration and Adjustment of System Planning Models*. Washington, D.C.: FHWA, December 1990.

Institute of Transportation Engineers Technical Council Committee 6F-47. *Selection and Use of Regional Transportation Microcomputer Planning Packages*. Washington, D.C.: ITE, February 1995.

National Transit Institute and Parsons Brinckerhoff Quade & Douglas, Inc. *Training Program for Major Investment Studies, Course Manual*. Washington, D.C.: Federal Transit Administration and Federal Highway Administration. June 1997.

Oppenheim, Norbert and Robert Oppenheim. *Urban Travel Demand Modeling*. West Sussex, England: John Wiley & Sons, October 1994.

Ortuzar, Juan de Dios and Luis G. Willumsen. *Modelling Transport*. West Sussex, England: John Wiley & Sons, December 1994.

Papacostas, C.S. and P.D. Prevedouros. *Transportation Engineering and Planning*. New Jersey: Prentice Hall, 1993.

Parsons Brinckerhoff Quade & Douglas, Inc. *State of Oregon Travel Demand Model Development And Application Guidelines*. June 1995.

Parsons Brinckerhoff Quade & Douglas, Inc. *State of Oregon Travel Demand Model Development Procedures Manual*. December 1996.

Shunk, Gordon A. Edited by John D. Edwards, Jr. *ITE Transportation Planning Handbook,* Chapter 4. New Jersey: Prentice Hall, 1992.

Weiner, Edward and Frederick Ducca. "Upgrading Travel Demand Forecasting Capabilities, U.S. DOT Travel Model Improvement Program," *TR News*. Washington, D.C.: Transportation Research Board, September–October 1996.

CHAPTER 7
Planning Approach to Capacity[1]

Edited by
John D. Zegeer
Principal
Kittelson & Associates, Inc.

The planning approach to capacity represents a broad assessment of the Level of Service (LOS) and capacity of a roadway, transit facility, bicycle facility, or pedestrian facility. Capacity and LOS analysis in transportation planning address such questions as the following:

- What is the maximum number of people or vehicles that can be accommodated within a specified time period?

- What will be the future LOS on an existing or planned facility?

- What lane configurations or signalization characteristics are needed for various traffic flow levels on an arterial road?

Planning applications are frequently intended to produce estimates at the earliest stages of planning when the amount, detail, and accuracy of information are limited. Planning procedures are often based on forecasts of average annual daily traffic and on assumed traffic, roadway, and control conditions. During project planning and development stages, generalized planning applications should be refined as more information becomes available. The analytical process during these later stages may reach the design or operational analysis level.

Capacity and Level of Service Concepts

The capacity of a transportation facility reflects its ability to accommodate a moving stream of people or vehicles; it is a measure of the supply side of transportation facilities. LOS is a measure of the quality of flow. Capacity analysis addresses questions such as the following:

- What is the quality of service provided by an existing facility during peak periods, and how much traffic increase can be tolerated?

- What types of roadway or transit facilities are needed to accommodate a given level of person or vehicle flow?

- What lane configurations are needed for various levels of average daily traffic on freeways or arterial roads?

- What highway or street designs (and hence capacities) are needed to serve a planned development?

- How many buses or rail cars are needed to serve peak direction flow at the maximum load point, and can these transit vehicles be passed through the busiest station or other point of constriction?

---

[1] This chapter reflects current planning concepts for capacity as of the summer of 1998. The materials that form the basis for this chapter are taken from the documents cited as "References" at the end of this chapter. Revisions to many of the concepts are underway. Refer to the latest update to the *Highway Capacity Manual* for current information.

- How wide must the sidewalk be on a street with high pedestrian activity, and would the holding space at street corners of a signalized intersection be sufficient?

Facilities are classified into two categories of flow: uninterrupted and interrupted.

- *Uninterrupted flow* facilities have no fixed elements, such as traffic signals, that are external to the traffic stream and may interrupt the traffic flow. Traffic flow conditions result from the interactions among vehicles in the traffic stream and between vehicles and the geometric and environmental characteristics of the roadway.

- *Interrupted flow* facilities have fixed elements that may interrupt the traffic flow. Such elements include traffic signals, STOP signs, and other types of controls. These devices cause traffic to stop periodically (or slow down significantly), irrespective of how much traffic exists.

Uninterrupted and interrupted flows are terms that describe the type of facility, not the quality of traffic flow at any given time. Thus a freeway experiencing extreme congestion is still an uninterrupted flow facility because the causes of congestion are internal to the traffic stream. Transit, pedestrian, and bicycle flows are generally considered to be interrupted. Uninterrupted flow may exist under certain circumstances, such as in a long busway without stops or a long pedestrian corridor. However, in most situations, capacity is limited by stops elsewhere along the facility.

Definition of Capacity

The capacity of a facility is defined as the maximum hourly rate at which persons or vehicles can reasonably be expected to traverse a point or uniform section of a lane or roadway during a given time period under prevailing roadway, traffic, and control conditions. *Vehicle capacity* represents the maximum number of *vehicles* that can reasonably be expected to pass a given point during a specified period under prevailing roadway, traffic, and control conditions. This definition assumes no influence of downstream traffic operation, such as backing up of traffic over the analysis point. *Person capacity* represents the maximum number of *people* that can reasonably be expected to pass a given point during a specified period under prevailing conditions.

Definition of Levels of Service

The concept of LOS uses qualitative measures that characterize operational conditions within a traffic stream and the perception of these conditions by motorists and passengers. The descriptions of individual LOSs characterize these conditions in terms of such factors as speed and travel time, freedom to maneuver, traffic interruptions, comfort, and convenience. Six LOSs are defined for each type of facility for which analysis procedures are available. They are given letter designations, from "A" to "F," with LOS A representing very favorable operating conditions (although not necessarily perfect) and LOS F representing very poor operating conditions. Each LOS represents a range of operating conditions. The volume of traffic that can be served under the stop-and-go conditions of LOS F is generally accepted as being lower than possible at LOS E; consequently, service flow rate at LOS E is the value that corresponds to the maximum flow rate, or capacity, on the facility. For most design or planning purposes, however, service flow rates at LOS D or LOS E are usually desirable because they ensure a more acceptable quality of service to facility users. LOSs for uninterrupted and interrupted flow facilities vary widely in terms of both the user's perception of service quality and the operational variables used to describe them.

For each type of facility, LOSs are defined on the basis of one or more operational parameters that best describe the operating quality for the facility type. Although the concept of LOS attempts to address a wide range of operating conditions, limitations on data collection and availability make it impractical to treat the full range of operational parameters for every type of facility. The parameters selected to define LOSs for each facility type are called measures of effectiveness (or service measures) and represent available measures that best describe the quality of operation on the subject facility type or segment. Table 7–1 presents the primary measures of effectiveness used to define LOSs for each facility type or segment.

Transportation System Elements

The elements of a transportation system can be grouped into the following five categories:

- *Point:* a very short portion of a facility (e.g., an intersection, toll plaza, or bus stop) that uses a different analysis procedure than the facility as a whole.

- *Segment:* a linear, uniform portion of a facility (e.g., basic freeway segment, freeway weaving area, freeway ramp, multilane highway, two-lane highway or arterial).

- *Facility:* a modal element (e.g., roadway, pathway, or transit route) that has relatively similar physical or operating characteristics (e.g., number of lanes, pathway width, service frequency) over its length. Demand volumes can vary over the length of a facility. An example of a freeway facility is a group of freeway segments with different numbers of lanes and weaving areas.

- *Corridor (or Subsystem):* two or more facilities that are generally parallel to each other, belonging to one or more modes, that are analyzed as a single unit.

- *System:* all of the facilities of one or more modes within a specified area (e.g., a district, city, or metropolitan area) or of a specified functional type (e.g., freeway facilities, arterial facilities).

Table 7–1 Primary Measures of Effectiveness for LOS Definition

Type of Facility or Segment	Measure of Effectiveness
Freeways	
Basic freeway segments	Density (pc/km/ln)
Freeway weave segments	Density (pc/km/ln)
Freeway ramp junction segments	Density (pc/km/ln)
Freeway facilities	Average travel speed (kph)
Multilane highways	Density (pc/km/ln)
Two-lane highways	Time delay (percent)
Signalized intersections	Control delay (sec/veh)
Unsignalized intersections	Control delay (sec/veh)
Urban streets or arterials	Average travel speed (kph)
Pedestrian facilities	Average travel speed (m/s), space (m^2/p), or flow rate (p/min/m)
Bicycle facilities	Frequency of events (events/hr), control delay (sec/bicycle), or average travel speed (kph)
Transit systems	Average travel speed (kph), availability of service, quality of service

Selection of Analysis Period

An agency's design and analysis policies and available resources determine the selection of the analysis period. The American Association of State Highway and Transportation Officials (AASHTO) recommends the hour with the 30th highest volume in the design year for rural roads. AASHTO notes that the highest afternoon peak hour flow for a week is close to the 30th highest hour volume for urban streets. Exceptions may be made for roads with high seasonal traffic fluctuation. Note that using the 30th highest hour demand may result in a design that may not be economical to achieve. The state of Florida uses the 100th highest hourly volume of the year as being representative of a typical peak hour during the peak season in urban areas for many planning applications. Many agencies use a community of facility-wide peak to daily volume ratios (K factors) to determine the analysis period. Many agencies do not have annual traffic count information and rely instead on highest average weekday hour volume for analysis purposes.

Duration of Analysis Period

The duration of the analysis period is typically 1 hour but can be as short as 15 minutes, or extend for the entire multihour peak period. The duration of the analysis period should be at least twice as long as the estimated travel time to traverse the length of the facility being analyzed, so as to ensure that the computed operating conditions are applicable to the entire length of the facility for the entire analysis period. The analyst may find it desirable to evaluate the facility's operations over several sequential analysis periods.

Conversion of AADT to Analysis Period Demand

The Annual Average Daily Traffic volume (AADT) is converted to peak direction analysis period vehicle demand as follows:

$$V = AADT \times K \times D$$

Where

V = estimated peak direction analysis vehicle demand (veh/h)

$AADT$ = annual average daily two-way vehicle demand (veh/day)

K = ratio of analysis period vehicle demand to the AADT

D = ratio of the peak direction vehicle demand to the total two-way analysis period vehicle demand.

Table 7–2   Example of Florida K Factors

Area Type	K100
Rural undeveloped highways	0.100
Rural developed roadways	0.095
Transitioning/urban arterials	0.094
Urbanized arterials	0.093

Note: The area types in this table are defined as follows:
- Urbanized areas are the urbanized areas designated by the U.S. Bureau of Census.
- An urban area is a place with a population of at least 5,000 not already included in an urbanized area.
- Transitioning areas are the areas outside of, or urbanized areas expected to be included in, an urbanized area within twenty years.
- Rural areas are whatever is not urban, transitioning, or urbanized.

Total two-way analysis period demand is used for the analysis of two-lane highways, so the directional factor D is set to 1.00 in those situations. If annual average daily traffic is not known, it can be estimated from average weekday daily traffic (AWDT) using the following conversion factor derived from the Highway Performance Monitoring System.

$$AADT = AWDT/1.07$$

The K factor should be determined from local data for similar facilities with similar demand characteristics. In the absence of local data, the following factors developed by Florida for predicting the 100th highest hour may be appropriate (Table 7–2).

The directional factor D should be obtained from local data sources for similar facilities with similar demand characteristics. Typical directional factors range from 55 percent to 65 percent. The higher directional factors tend to occur on facilities leading to an urban area or a major recreational area. Florida has determined a default value for urban locations of 0.568 for the directional factor.

Urban Street Concepts

This section provides guidance on capacity and LOS concepts for urban streets (or arterials), signalized intersections, and unsignalized intersections.

Urban Streets or Arterials

Urban streets include arterial, collector, and local streets in an urban or suburban area. They primarily serve through-traffic and secondarily provide access to abutting properties. They are defined generally as facilities with:

- Lengths of at least 2 km in downtown areas and at least 3 km in other areas.

- A signalized intersection spacing as short as 60 m in downtown areas and 120 m elsewhere.

- A maximum signalized intersection spacing of 3.2 km (longer spacings should be analyzed with uninterrupted flow methods).

Table 7–3   Arterial Levels of Service by Arterial Classification

	I	II	III	IV
Range of free-flow speeds	90 to 70 km/h	75 to 55 km/h	55 to 50 km/h	55 to 40 km/h
Typical free-flow speed	80 km/h	65 km/h	55 km/h	45 km/h
LOS	Average Travel Speed (km/h)			
A	>72	>59	>50	>41
B	>56–72	>46–59	>39–50	>32–41
C	>40–46	>33–46	>28–39	>23–32
D	>32–40	>26–33	>22–28	>18–23
E	>26–32	>21–26	>17–22	>14–18
F	≤ 26	≤21	≤17	≤ 14

Arterial LOS is defined in terms of the average of travel speed of all through-vehicles on the arterial. It is strongly influenced by the number of signals per kilometer and the intersection control delay. On a given facility, factors such as inappropriate signal timing, poor signal progression, and increasing traffic flow can substantially degrade the arterial LOS.

Four arterial classes are defined on the basis of an arterial's function and design. Free-flow speed is the average speed of motorists over those portions of arterial segments that are not close to signalized intersections, and it is observed during very low traffic volume conditions when drivers are not constrained by other vehicles or by traffic signals. The average free-flow speed should approximate the average desired speed for the motorists on a given facility. Free-flow speeds may be measured by test cars or by spot speed observations away from the signalized intersections and other delay-creating features. There is a range of average travel speeds within each class (Table 7–3).

In all cases, the arterial should be classified first by functional category and then by design category. The functional category is either the principal arterial or the minor arterial. Table 7–4 should be used to determine the functional and design categories. Once the functional and design categories have been determined, the arterial classification may be established by referring to Table 7–5.

Table 7–4   Establishing Functional and Design Categories

	Functional Category			
Criterion	Principal Arterial		Minor Arterial	
Mobility function	Very important		Important	
Access function	Very minor		Substantial	
Points connected	Freeways, important activity centers, major traffic generators		Principal arterials	
Predominant trips served	Relatively long trips between major points, and through-trips entering, leaving, and going through the city		Trips of moderate length within relatively small geographical areas	

	Design Category			
Criterion	High Speed	Suburban	Intermediate	Urban
Driveways access density	Very low density	Low density	Moderate density	High density
Arterial type	Multilane divided; undivided or two-lane with shoulders	Multilane divided; undivided or two-lane with shoulders	Multilane divided or undivided; one-way, two-lane	Undivided one-way, two-way, two or more lanes
Parking	No	No	Some	Much
Separate left-turn lanes	Yes	Yes	Usually	Some
Signals per kilometer	1–2	1–3	2–6	4–8
Speed limits	75–90 km/h	65–75 km/h	60–65 km/h	50–55 km/h
Pedestrian activity	Very little	Little	Some	Usually
Roadside development	Low density	Low to medium density	Medium/moderate density	High density

A major difference between the planning analysis of signalized intersections and that of arterials is the treatment of turning vehicles. Whereas the purpose of a signalized intersection is to move vehicles (including turning vehicles) past a point, the purpose of an arterial is to move through-vehicles over a reasonable length of roadway. Because the emphasis of an arterial is on through-movement, the major simplifying assumption in the planning application for an arterial is that left turns are accommodated (e.g., by providing left-turn bays at major intersections and controlling the left-turn movement with a separate phase that is properly timed).

It should be noted that intersection and arterial LOS do not always correlate. For example, an arterial with many signalized intersections may operate at a considerably worse overall LOS than the individual intersections. This is a reflection on the negative effect of many closely spaced signals on an arterial flow and possibly poor signal progression. On the other hand, an arterial corridor may show an acceptable LOS when one or more intersections within it are operating at a very poor LOS.

The speed-flow curves shown in Figures 7–1, 7–2, and 7–3 illustrate the sensitivity of the estimated arterial mean speed to midblock free-flow speed, demand/capacity ratio, signal density, and arterial class. The curves are plotted using the volume/capacity ratio for the through-movement in the peak direction at the critical intersection on the arterial.

The urban street planning procedures are particularly appropriate for facility-level evaluations of arterials. They have become widely used for developing congestion management systems, for long-range planning purposes where detailed inputs may not be available or known, and for providing inputs to highway economic and environmental studies. They may also be applied to estimate transit vehicle running times and speeds along arterial streets, when combined with transit vehicle dwell time. Table 7–6 can be used to estimate the number of through-lanes required on an arterial to achieve a desired LOS. This table has been developed for four classes of arterials assuming a median and left-turn pockets for each arterial class.

Collectors and local streets serve the purpose of moving traffic over short distances. Their primary objective is to provide accessibility, not speed. Thus, the LOS criteria for arterials that are based upon minimum speed may not apply to local and collector streets. The selection of LOS criteria for local and collector streets is a local agency decision. If "livability" or pedestrian friendliness are key objectives, then the agency might base LOS criteria upon

Table 7–5   Arterial Classes Based on Functional and Design Categories

Design Category	Functional Category	
	Principal Arterial	Minor Arterial
High speed	I	N/A
Suburban	II	II or III
Intermediate	II or III	III or IV
Urban	III or IV	IV

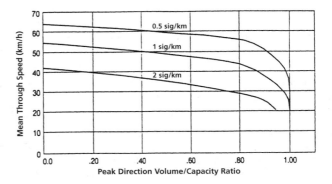

Figure 7–1   Speed-Flow Curves for Class II Urban Streets

Notes: Assumptions: 72 km/h mid-block free-flow speed, 10 km length, 120 second cycle, 0.45 g/C, arrival type 3, 0.925 PHF, left-turn pockets, 12% turns.

Source: "Production of the Year 2000 HCM," *Status Report*, Catalina Engineering, Inc., NCHRP 3-55 (6), May 30, 1998, Exhibit 15–10. Unpublished Interim TRB Committee on Highway Capacity and Quality of Service material.

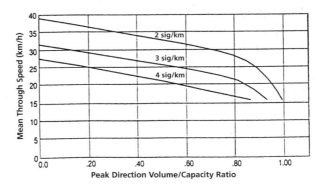

Figure 7–2   Speed-Flow Curves for Class III Urban Streets

Notes: Assumptions: 56 km/h mid-block free-flow speed, 10 km length, 120 second cycle, 0.45 g/C, arrival type 3, 0.925 PHF, left-turn pockets, 12% turns.

Source: "Production of the Year 2000 HCM," *Status Report*, Catalina Engineering, Inc., NCHRP 3-55 (6), May 30, 1998, Exhibit 15–11. Unpublished Interim TRB Committee on Highway Capacity and Quality of Service material.

maximum volumes and/or maximum speeds (rather than minimum speeds). The signalized and unsignalized intersection procedures for estimating delay can be used without adaptation for collector and local streets.

Signalized Intersections

The analysis of capacity and LOS at signalized intersections must consider a wide variety of prevailing conditions, including the amount and distribution of traffic movements, traffic composition, geometric characteristics, and the details of intersection signalization. A traffic signal essentially allocates time among conflicting traffic movements that seek to use the same physical space. The way in which time is allocated has a significant effect on the operation and the capacity of the intersection and its approaches. Capacity is evaluated in terms of the ratio of demand flow rate (volume) to capacity. This ratio (described as a v/c ratio) is one consideration in determining LOS. The measure of effectiveness for LOS is average control delay per vehicle (in seconds per vehicle).

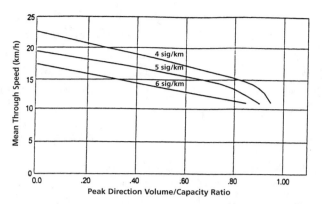

Figure 7–3   Speed-Flow Curves for Class IV Urban Streets

Note: Assumptions: 40 km/h mid-block free-flow speed, 10 km length, 120 second cycle, 0.45 g/C, pre-timed signals, arrival type 4, 0.925 PHF, left-turn pockets, 12% turns.

Source: "Production of the Year 2000 HCM," *Status Report,* Catalina Engineering, Inc., NCHRP 3-55 (6), May 30, 1998, Exhibit 15–12. Unpublished Interim TRB Committee on Highway Capacity and Quality of Service material.

Study of an intersection is done by designating "lane groups," which become the unit of analysis. A lane group consists of one or more traffic lanes on an intersection approach, or the approach as a whole. Each lane group is analyzed separately. For a given lane group at a signalized intersection, three signal indications are seen: green, yellow, and red. The red indication usually includes a short period during which all indications are red, referred to as an "all-red" interval, which, with the yellow indication, forms the change and clearance interval between two green phases. Definition of the variables and basic terms for describing traffic flow at signalized intersections are provided in Table 7–7.

Table 7–6   Service Volumes by Arterial Class

Class	Number of Lanes	One Direction Through Service Volume (veh/h)				
		LOS A	LOS B	LOS C	LOS D	LOS E
Class I	1	N/A	660	810	880	900
	2	N/A	1,470	1,760	1,890	1,890
	3	N/A	2,280	2,660	2,840	2,840
	4	N/A	2,840	3,280	3,480	3,480
Class II	1	N/A	N/A	460	760	840
	2	N/A	N/A	1,020	1,640	1,800
	3	N/A	N/A	1,550	2,510	2,710
	4	N/A	N/A	1,890	3,060	3,320
Class III	1	N/A	N/A	N/A	620	800
	2	N/A	N/A	N/A	1,390	1,740
	3	N/A	N/A	N/A	2,130	2,640
	4	N/A	N/A	N/A	2,600	3,230
Class IV	1	N/A	N/A	N/A	690	780
	2	N/A	N/A	N/A	1,540	1,700
	3	N/A	N/A	N/A	2,340	2,570
	4	N/A	N/A	N/A	2,860	3,140

Notes: Class I assumes: 5 intersections at 1.08 km spacing, cycle length = 120 s, free-flow speed = 75 km/h, g/C = 0.45, and arrival type of 3. Class II assumes: 5 intersections at 0.54 km spacing, cycle length = 120 s, free-flow speed = 65 km/h, g/C = 0.45, and arrival type 4. Class III assumes: 5 intersections at 0.32 km spacing, cycle length = 120 s, free-flow speed = 55 km/h, g/C = 0.45, and arrival type 4. Class IV assumes: 5 intersections at 0.22 km spacing, cycle length = 120 s, free-flow speed = 50 km/h, g/C = 0.45, and arrival type 4.

N/A = LOS cannot be achieved.

Table 7–7 Symbols, Definitions, and Units for Fundamental Variables of Traffic Flow at Signalized Intersections

Name	Symbol	Definition
Cycle		Any complete sequence of signal indications
Cycle length	C	The total time for the signal to complete one cycle
Interval		A period of time during which all signal indications remain constant
Phase		The part of a cycle allocated to any combination of traffic movements receiving the right-of-way simultaneously during one or more intervals
Change and clearance interval	Y_i	The "yellow" change time plus "all red" clearance time intervals that occur between phases for the lane group to provide for clearance of the intersection before conflicting movements are released
Green time	G_i	The time within a given phase, for a lane group, during which the green indication is shown
Lost time	L	The time during which the intersection is effectively not used by any movement, which occurs during the change and clearance intervals, and at the beginning of each phase
Start-up lost time	l_1	The time during which the lane group vehicles are not flowing effectively, as the first few vehicles in a standing queue experience start-up delays
Clearance lost time	l_2	The portion of the change interval at the end of a phase during which the lane group vehicles have effectively stopped flowing in anticipation of the red indication
Effective green time	g_i	That time that is effectively available for movement of vehicles of a given lane group
Extension of effective green time	e	The amount of the change and clearance interval, at the end of the phase for a lane group, that is usable for movement of its vehicles
Effective red time	r_i	The time during which the vehicles of a given lane group are effectively not permitted to flow into the intersection
Saturation flow rate	s_i	The maximum rate of flow for a given lane group, that can occur under prevailing traffic and roadway conditions, with 100 percent green time (expressed as passenger cars per hour of green time per lane)
Control delay	d_i	Delay experienced by vehicles in a lane group while decelerating to join a queue, while in the queue, and while accelerating to regain desired speed

Modern traffic signals allocate time in a variety of ways, from the simplest two-phase, pretimed mode to the most complex multiphase actuated mode. There are three types of traffic signal controllers:

- *Pretimed*—in which a general sequence of phases is displayed in repetitive order. Each phase has a fixed green time, change, and clearance interval that are repeated in each cycle to produce a constant cycle length.

- *Fully-actuated*—in which the timing on all of the approaches to an intersection is influenced by vehicle detectors. Each phase is subject to a minimum and maximum green time. Some phases may be skipped if no demand is detected. The cycle length for fully-actuated control will vary from cycle to cycle.

- *Semi-actuated*—in which some approaches (typically on the minor street) have detectors, and some do not. Minor street approach phase lengths vary according to demand.

Definition of Key Terms

Saturation flow is a basic parameter used to drive capacity. It is determined based upon the minimum headway that the lane group can sustain across the stop line, as the vehicles depart the intersection. Saturation flow rate is determined for each of the lane groups from field measurements, or a default value may be used. This "base" value is then adjusted for a variety of factors that reflect geometric, traffic, and environmental conditions specific to the site under study.

Capacity at intersections is defined for each lane group. The lane group capacity is the maximum rate of flow for the subject lane group that may pass through the intersection under prevailing traffic, roadway, and signalization conditions. The rate of flow is generally measured or projected for a 15-minute period, and capacity is stated in vehicles per hour (veh/h). The analysis of capacity in this section focuses on the computation of saturation flow rates, capacities, v/c ratios, and LOS for lane groups at the intersection.

LOS is determined by estimating the average control delay for motor vehicles entering signal-controlled intersections. Control delay is that portion of the delay attributed to traffic signal operation (i.e., it does not consider delay due to roadway geometry or traffic incidents). The average control delay per vehicle entering the intersection is computed based upon the vehicular demand, intersection geometry, and signal control characteristics. The hourly vehicle demand is adjusted using the peak hour factor (PHF) to obtain the peak 15-minute flow rate expressed in terms of vehicles per hour. The intersection geometry (lanes, lane widths, and grades) plus other data on the percentage of heavy vehicles, parking maneuvers per hour, buses stopping per hour, area type, pedestrian flows, and signal phasing types are used to compute the adjusted saturation flow rate for each approach to the intersection. The capacity of each approach is then computed based upon the saturation flow rate, the green time per cycle, cycle length, and lost time per cycle.

Definition of Levels of Service

LOSs are defined to represent reasonable ranges in control delay:

- *LOS A*—describes operations with very low control delay, up to 10 s/veh. This LOS occurs when progression is extremely favorable and most vehicles arrive during the green phase. Most vehicles do not stop at all. Short cycle lengths may tend to contribute to low delay values.

- *LOS B*—describes operations with control delay greater than 10 and up to 20 s/veh. This level generally occurs with good progression, short cycle lengths, or both. More vehicles stop than with LOS A, causing higher levels of delay.

- *LOS C*—describes operations with control delay greater than 20 and up to 35 s/veh. These higher delays may result from only fair progression, longer cycle lengths, or both. Individual cycle failures may begin to appear at this level. The number of vehicles stopping is significant at this level, though many still pass through the intersection without stopping.

- *LOS D*—describes operations with control delay greater than 35 and up to 55 s/veh. At level D, the influence of congestion becomes more noticeable. Longer delays may result from some combination of unfavorable progression, long cycle lengths, or high v/c ratios. Many vehicles stop and the proportion of vehicles not stopping declines. Individual cycle failures are noticeable.

- *LOS E*—describes operations with control delay greater than 55 and up to 80 s/veh. This level is considered by many agencies to be the limit of acceptable delay. These high delay values generally indicate poor progression, long cycle lengths, and high v/c ratios. Individual cycle failures are frequent occurrences.

- *LOS F*—describes operations with control delay in excess of 80 s/veh. This level, considered to be unacceptable to most drivers, often occurs with oversaturation, that is, v/c ratios with many individual cycle failures. Poor progression and long cycle lengths may also be major contributing causes to such delay levels.

  It is possible to have delays in the range of LOS F (unacceptable) while the v/c ratio is below 1.0, perhaps as low as 0.75 to 0.85. Very high delays may occur at such v/c ratios when some combination of the following conditions exists: the cycle length is long, the lane group in question is disadvantaged by the signal timing (has a long red time), and the signal progression for the subject movements is poor. The reverse is also possible: a saturated lane group (i.e., v/c ratio greater than 1.0) may have low delays if the cycle length is short, or the signal progression is favorable for the subject lane group, or both. Thus, the designation LOS F does not automatically imply that the intersection, approach, or lane group is over capacity; nor does a LOS better than E automatically imply that there is unused capacity available.

Identification of Critical Movements

The critical movements at a traffic signal are determined by first computing the v/s ratio for each through and left turn movement at the intersection. (The v/s ratio is the ratio between demand volume and saturation flow rate.) Then the left turn and opposing through-v/s ratios are summed to determine the pair of movements for each street that has the highest sum. The pair of critical movements for each street is the pair of left and opposing through-movements with the highest total v/s ratio. The sum of the critical movement v/s ratios for each street is the value used to compute the cycle length for the intersection. Figure 7–4 shows an example of the identification of critical movements. The critical pair of left and through-movements in the east/west street are the eastbound through and the westbound left. The critical north/south pair is the southbound left and the northbound through. Together, the critical movements sum to 1.00 (0.50 N/S + 0.50 E/W) for this example. This simplified procedure is not designed to address the subtleties of left turns from a shared lane, permitted lefts opposed by heavy through volumes, permitted plus protected phasing, or other more complex signal phasing strategies or street geometries. In many cases, these subtleties must be removed from consideration in a planning-level analysis.

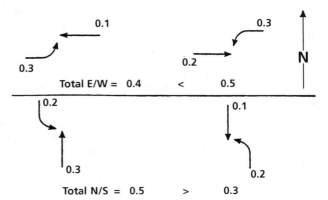

Figure 7–4 Calculation of Critical Movements Using V/S Ratios

Source: "Production of the Year 2000 HCM," *Status Report,* Catalina Engineering, Inc., NCHRP 3-55 (6), December 12, 1997, Exhibit 8–12. Unpublished Interim TRB Committee on Highway Capacity and Quality of Service material.

Table 7–8 shows the maximum service volumes that can be accommodated at a signalized intersection for a given LOS. It illustrates the relative sensitivity of LOS to traffic demand, the number of through-lanes, and the presence or absence of left-turn lanes.

Table 7–8 Signalized Intersection Maximum Service Volumes (Single Approach)

Left-Turn Lane Present?	Number of Through-Lanes	Maximum Service Volume (veh/h)				
		LOS A	LOS B	LOS C	LOS D	LOS E
No	1	N/A	390	480	520	540
No	2	N/A	680	770	810	850
No	3	N/A	990	1,310	1,410	1,490
Yes	1	N/A	N/A	570	680	740
Yes	2	N/A	N/A	1,040	1,220	1,320
Yes	3	N/A	N/A	1,410	1,650	1,770

Notes: N/A = not achievable given assumed signal timing.
Assumptions used to generate the values in Table 7–8 are:
1. Entries are total hourly volume for subject approach, including turns.
2. All approaches to intersection have the same demand as the subject approach.
3. Left turns equal 10 percent of approach demand. Right turns equal 10 percent of approach demand.
4. Phasing is permitted lefts in absence of exclusive left-turn lane; protected lefts when left-turn lane is present.
5. All approaches are two-way streets.
6. Cycle length = 100 s, lost time = 6 s without protected lefts or 12 s with protected lefts. Actuated, isolated signal, arrival type 3, in urban non-CBD area. Green/cycle length times computed to equalize degree of saturation.
7. Saturation flow computed assuming: 1,900 base saturation, 3.6 m lane widths, 2 percent heavy vehicles, 0 percent grade, 20 parking movements per hour, no local buses, no pedestrians.
8. Peak hour factor = 0.90. Lane utilization factors = 1.05 for two lanes, 1.10 for three lanes.

Unsignalized Intersections

This section describes capacity and LOS concepts for three types of unsignalized intersections: two-way stop-controlled (TWSC) intersections, all-way stop-controlled (AWSC) intersections, and roundabouts.

TWSC Intersections

A TWSC intersection occurs when the major street approaches are uncontrolled and the minor street approaches are controlled by STOP signs. These can be either intersections with four legs or T-intersections (with a single stop-controlled minor street approach as the stem of the T). Some of the right-turn movements on the minor and major street approaches may have YIELD signs, but the primary control for the minor street approaches must be STOP signs.

TWSC intersections assign the right-of-way among conflicting traffic streams according to the following hierarchy:

- *Rank 1*—All conflicting movements yield the right-of-way to any through- or right-turning vehicle on the major street approaches. These major street through- and right-turning movements are the highest priority movements at a TWSC intersection.

- *Rank 2*—Vehicles turning left from the major street onto the minor street yield only to conflicting major street through- and right-turning vehicles. All other conflicting movements at a TWSC intersection yield to these major street left-turning movements. Vehicles turning right from the minor street onto the major street yield only to conflicting major street through-movements.

- *Rank 3*—Minor street through-vehicles yield to all conflicting major street through-, right-, and left-turning movements.

- *Rank 4*—Minor street left-turning vehicles yield to all conflicting major street through-, right-, and left-turning vehicles; and also to all conflicting minor street through- and right-turning vehicles.

Even though the hierarchy described above suggests that the highest priority movements experience no delay as they travel through a TWSC intersection, experience shows that their right-of-way is sometimes preempted by other conflicting movements. Such preemptions most often occur during periods of congestion when vehicles in the conflicting movements are experiencing long delays and queues.

There are four measures that are used to describe the performance of TWSC intersections—these are control delay, delay to major street through-vehicles, queue length, and v/c ratio. The measure of effectiveness that is used to provide an estimate of LOS is control delay. This measure can be estimated for any movement on the minor (i.e., the stop-controlled) street. By summing delay estimates for individual movements, a delay estimate for each minor street approach and for the entire intersection can be calculated.

The capacity of the STOP-sign controlled approaches is based on three factors: (1) the distribution of gaps in the major street traffic stream, (2) driver judgment in selecting gaps through which to execute the desired maneuvers, and (3) the follow-up time required by each driver in a queue. The gap acceptance method computes the potential capacity of each minor traffic stream. The potential capacity is dependent on the conflicting volumes for the movement, the critical gap, and the follow-up time. Values of critical gap and follow-up time for passenger cars are given in Table 7–9.

The potential capacity for each vehicle movement at two-lane and four-lane street intersections is given in Figures 7–5 and 7–6, respectively.

LOS for a TWSC intersection is determined by calculating average control delay for each minor movement. LOS is not defined for the intersection as a whole. LOS criteria are given in Table 7–10.

Table 7–11 shows how the minor street maximum service volumes vary by LOS for a T-intersection. These calculations are for a T-intersection, with a single-lane minor street approach, a single combined right-turn and through-lane on each major street approach, and a separate left-turn lane for the major street left-turn movement.

Table 7–12 shows how the maximum minor street service volumes vary for four-leg intersections. The addition of more through-lanes or major street-turn pockets does not significantly improve LOS.

LOS F exists when there are insufficient gaps of suitable size to allow a side street demand to safely cross through a main street traffic stream. This LOS is generally evident from extremely long control delays experienced by minor street traffic and by queuing on the minor street approaches. In most cases at TWSC intersections, the critical movement is the minor street left-turn movement. As a result, the minor street left-turn movement may control the overall LOS for the intersection.

AWSC Intersections

AWSC intersections occur when all approaches are controlled by STOP signs. These can be intersections with either three or four legs. Since each driver must stop at AWSC intersections, the judgment as to whether to proceed into the intersection is a function of the traffic conditions on the other approaches. If there is no traffic present on the other approaches, a driver can proceed immediately after the stop is made. If there is traffic on one or more of the other approaches, a driver proceeds only after determining that there are no vehicles currently in the intersection and that it is their turn to proceed.

Table 7–9 Critical Gaps and Follow-Up Times for TWSC Intersections

Vehicle Movement	Critical Gap (sec)		Follow-up Time (sec)
	Four-Lane Street	Six-Lane Street	
Left turn from major street	4.1	4.1	2.2
Right turn from minor street	6.2	6.9	3.3
Through-traffic on minor street	6.5	6.5	4.0
Left turn from minor street	7.1	7.5	3.5

Table 7–10 LOS Criteria for TWSC Intersections

LOS	Average Control Delay (sec/veh)
A	0–5
B	> 5–10
C	>10–20
D	>20–30
E	>30–45
F	>45

Table 7–11 Minor Street Service Volumes for TWSC T–Intersections

Major Street Two-Way Volume (veh/h)	Minor Street Maximum Service Volume by LOS				
	LOS A	LOS B	LOS C	LOS D	LOS E
200	105	410	580	650	710
400	—	270	430	490	550
600	—	150	300	360	410
800	—	40	200	260	300
1,000	—	—	120	170	210

Notes: Assumptions used to generate the values in Table 7–11 are: major street LTs and RTs are each 10 percent of the approach volume; PHF = 0.85; heavy vehicles = 2 percent; grade = 0 percent; pedestrian flow = 0 percent; no flared minor approach; and no channelization.

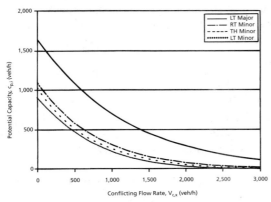

Figure 7–5 Potential Capacity for Two-Lane Streets

Source: "Production of the Year 2000 HCM," *Status Report*, Catalina Engineering, Inc., NCHRP 3-55 (6), May 30, 1998, Exhibit 17–5. Unpublished Interim TRB Committee on Highway Capacity and Quality of Service material.

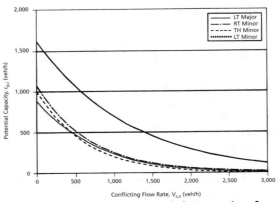

Figure 7–6 Potential Capacity for Four-Lane Streets

Source: "Production of the Year 2000 HCM," *Status Report*, Catalina Engineering, Inc., NCHRP 3-55 (6), May 30, 1998, Exhibit 17–6. Unpublished Interim TRB Committee on Highway Capacity and Quality of Service material.

Table 7–12 Major Street Service Volumes for TWSC Four-Leg Intersections

Major Street Two-Way Volume	Minor Street Maximum Service Volumes				
	LOS A	LOS B	LOS C	LOS D	LOS E
major street = one lane, minor street = one lane and no turn pockets					
500	N/A	200	400	400	400
1,000	N/A	N/A	100	200	200
1,500	N/A	N/A	N/A	N/A	N/A
major street = one lane, minor street = one lane plus turn pockets					
500	N/A	100	200	400	400
1,000	N/A	N/A	N/A	100	100
1,500	N/A	N/A	N/A	N/A	N/A
major street = two lanes plus turn pockets, minor street = one lane and no turn pockets					
500	N/A	200	400	400	400
1,000	N/A	N/A	100	200	200
1,500	N/A	N/A	N/A	N/A	N/A
major street = two lanes plus turn pockets, minor street = one lane plus turn pockets					
500	N/A	N/A	200	400	400
1,000	N/A	N/A	N/A	N/A	100
1,500	N/A	N/A	N/A	N/A	N/A

Notes: Assumptions used to generate the values in this table are: both approach legs of minor street have same volume; minor street LTs and RTs are equal to 33 percent of total minor street approach volume; major street LTs and RTs are each 10 percent of the approach volume; PHF = 0.85; a default PCE of 1.10 was used; no flared minor street approach; and no channelization.

N/A = not achievable under given conditions

Field observations show that AWSC intersections operate in either two-phase or four-phase patterns, based primarily on the complexity of the intersection geometry. Flows are determined by a consensus of right-of-way that alternates between the north-south and east-west streams (for a single-lane approach) or proceeds in turn to each intersection approach (for a multilane approach intersection). If traffic is present on the subject approach only, vehicles depart as rapidly as individual drivers can safely accelerate into and clear the intersection. If traffic is present on the other approaches, as well as on the subject approach, the saturation headway on the subject approach will increase somewhat, depending on the degree of conflict that results between the subject approach vehicles and the vehicles on the other approaches.

The capacity of a lane at an AWSC intersection is also dependent on the saturation headway of that lane. Since there is no traffic signal controlling the stream movement, or allocating the right-of-way to each conflicting traffic stream, the rate of departure is controlled instead by the interactions between the traffic streams themselves. There is a degree of conflict that can be observed that increases with the number of approaches that are loaded simultaneously. To a lesser extent, the geometry of the intersection itself controls this rate of departure. The capacity is computed as follows. The volume on the subject approach is increased incrementally until the degree of utilization on any one approach exceeds one. This flow rate is the maximum possible flow or throughput on the subject approach.

LOS for a AWSC intersection is based on the determination of average control delay. Control delay is defined as the total elapsed time from when a vehicle stops at the end of the queue until the vehicle departs from the stop line. This total elapsed time includes the time required for the vehicle to travel from the last-in-queue position to the first-in-queue position. Average control delay for any movement is a function of the capacity of the approach, and the degree of saturation. The LOS criteria for AWSC intersections are given in Table 7–13.

Table 7–14 can be used to estimate the number of through-lanes required to achieve a desired LOS for an AWSC intersection. The entries in the table are the maximum hourly approach volumes for any one of the four approaches to the intersection. As can be seen, adding through-lanes or turn pockets slightly improves the LOS at AWSC intersections.

Table 7–13 LOS Criteria for AWSC Intersections

LOS	Average Control Delay (sec/veh)
A	0–5
B	> 5–10
C	>10–20
D	>20–30
E	>30–45
F	>45

Table 7–14 Maximum Approach Service Volumes for AWSC Intersections

Through-Lanes	Left- and Right-Turn Pockets	LOS A	LOS B	LOS C	LOS D	LOS E
1	No	100	200	300	300	400
1	Yes	200	300	400	500	600
2	No	200	300	400	400	500

Notes: Assumptions used to generate the values in Table 7–14 are: equal demand on all four approaches; identical lanes on all four approaches; PHF = 0.85; 10 percent left turns; and 10 percent right turns.

Table 7–15 shows the intersection delay and the LOS for various combinations of total hourly volumes entering an AWSC intersection with a single lane on each approach. The demand split shows the percentage of total intersection demand on each street (pair of opposing approaches). Thus, a 50:50 split indicates that both intersecting streets have the same demand level. A 70:30 split means that the major street has more than twice the demand as the minor street. As can be seen, the demand split between streets does not significantly affect the total intersection delay for total entering volumes of 1,250 vph or less.

Modern Roundabouts

This section applies to single-lane roundabouts. There is not sufficient experience with multiple-lane roundabouts in the United States to support an analysis procedure at this time. The three main features of a roundabout are the central island, the circulating roadway, and the splitter island (Figure 7–7). The common characteristics that distinguish a modern roundabout from a traffic circle are as follows:

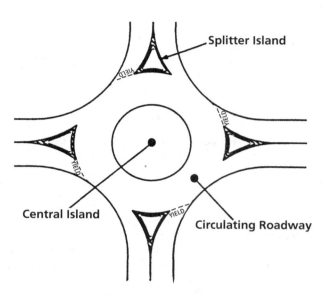

Figure 7–7 Modern Roundabouts

Source: "Production of the Year 2000 HCM," *Status Report*, Catalina Engineering, Inc., NCHRP 3-55 (6), June 23, 1997, Exhibit 17–35. Unpublished Interim TRB Committee on Highway Capacity and Quality of Service material.

1. Vehicles entering a roundabout on all approaches are required to yield to vehicles within the circulating roadway.

2. The circulating vehicles are not subjected to any other right-of-way conflicts and weaving is kept to a minimum. This provides the means by which the priority is distributed and alternated among vehicles.

Table 7–15 Intersection Delay (secs/veh) and LOS for Single-Lane AWSC Intersections

Demand Split	Total Volume Entering the Intersection (vph)									
	500	600	700	800	900	1,000	1,100	1,200	1,250	1,300
50:50	8.9 A	9.5 A	10.4 B	11.6 B	13.3 B	15.7 C	20.4 C	31.2 D	45.4 E	99.8 F
55:45	8.9 A	9.6 A	10.4 B	11.6 B	13.2 B	15.9 C	20.5 C	31.5 D	45.6 E	87.1 F
60:40	8.9 A	9.5 A	10.4 B	11.6 B	13.3 B	15.9 C	20.7 C	32.3 D	47.7 E	78.5 F
65:35	8.9 A	9.6 A	10.5 B	11.7 B	13.4 B	16.3 C	21.1 C	33.1 D	47.7 E	74.5 F
70:30	8.9 A	9.6 A	10.6 B	11.8 B	13.6 B	16.4 C	21.9 C	33.6 D	47.0 E	72.8 F

Note: Assumptions used to generate the values in Table 7–15 are: opposing approaches have equal demand; LTs and RTs are equal and are each 10 percent of the approach volume; PHF = 0.90; heavy vehicles = 2 percent; and T = 0.25.

3. The speed at which a vehicle is able to negotiate the circulating roadway is controlled by the location of the central island with respect to the alignment of the right entry curb and the circulating roadway cross section. It is important that the speeds of vehicles on the roundabout are low.

4. No parking is allowed on the circulating roadway.

5. No pedestrian activity takes place on the central island. Pedestrians are not intended to cross the circulating roadway.

6. All vehicles circulate counterclockwise, passing to the right of the central island.

7. Roundabouts are designed to properly accommodate specified design vehicles.

Table 7–16   Range of Critical Gaps and Follow-Up Times for Modern Roundabouts

	Critical Gap (sec)	Follow-Up Time (sec)
Upper-bound solution	4.1	2.6
Lower-bound solution	4.6	3.1

Table 7–17   V/C Ratios and Total Approach Volumes at Modern Roundabouts

Total Volume on All Approaches (veh/h)	Individual Approach v/c Ratio
1,600	0.60
1,770	0.70
1,940	0.80
2,090	0.90
2,240	1.00

Notes: Assumptions used to generate the values in Table 7–17 are: left turns and right turns are each 10 percent of the approach volumes; and PHF = 0.85.

8. Roundabouts have raised splitter islands on all approaches. Splitter islands are an essential safety feature, required to separate traffic moving in opposite directions and to provide refuge for pedestrians.

9. When pedestrian crossings are provided on the approach roads, they are placed approximately one car length back from the entry point.

Since roundabouts involve drivers making a right turn onto the roundabout, the gap acceptance characteristics of drivers are expected to be similar to drivers making right turns on the minor street approaches at TWSC intersections.

The approach capacity of a modern roundabout is dependent on the circulating traffic, critical gap, and follow-up time. Limited studies of U.S. roundabouts as well as comparisons with existing roundabout operations in countries indicate that a range of values for critical gap and follow-up time may be considered. The recommended range of values are given in Table 7–16.

Table 7–17 shows the v/c ratios for approaches on a roundabout with varying total volumes. These calculations are for four-leg intersections, with single-lane approaches and a single-lane circulating roadway. A roundabout with a single-lane circulating roadway can accommodate a higher volume on all approaches than an AWSC intersection.

Multilane Highway and Freeway Concepts

This section provides guidance on the capacity and LOS concepts for multilane highways and freeways. The following discussion provides brief definitions for some of the more frequently used terms in this section.

- *Multilane highway*—a facility with a free-flow speed of at least 70 km/h, with signalized or STOP-sign intersection interruptions located at least 3 km apart.

- *Freeway*—a divided highway with full access control and with two or more lanes in each direction.

- *Free-flow speed*—the mean speed measured for traffic when demand is low enough so that changes in demand do not affect the speed of traffic.

- *Mean speed*—the total travel time for all vehicles traveling the entire length of the facility divided by the number of vehicles traveling the entire length of the facility.

Multilane Highway Segments

Multilane highways in suburban and rural settings have different operational characteristics than do freeways, urban arterials, and two-lane highways. Multilane highways are not completely access controlled. At-grade intersections and, occasionally, traffic signals are found along these highways. Friction created by opposing vehicles on undivided multilane highways and the impact of access to roadside development contribute to a different operational setting than that found on freeways.

Multilane highways differ substantially from two-lane highways, principally because of the ability of a driver on a multilane highway to pass slower-moving vehicles without using lanes designated for oncoming traffic. Multilane highways also tend to be located adjacent to urban areas or to connect urban areas and often have better design features, including horizontal and vertical curvature.

The capacity of a multilane highway is the maximum sustained hourly rate of flow at which vehicles can be reasonably expected to traverse a uniform segment of roadway under prevailing roadway and traffic conditions. The time period used for analysis is 15 minutes. Free-flow speed is the speed of traffic as density approaches zero. Practically, it is the speed at which drivers feel comfortable traveling under the physical, environmental, and traffic control conditions existing on an uncongested section of multilane highway. Free-flow speeds will be lower on sections of highway with restricted vertical or horizontal alignments. Free-flow speeds tend to be lower when posted speed limits are lower. The importance of free-flow speed is that it is the starting point for the analysis of capacity and LOS. LOS is based on density. Density may be calculated by dividing the traffic flow per lane by speed.

Figure 7–8 shows the impact of v/c ratios on mean through-speed for multilane highways. Note that speed on higher-speed facilities is insensitive to demand until demand is at least 70 percent of capacity. The mean speed on lower-speed facilities is not sensitive to demand until the demand reaches at least 90 percent of capacity.

The capacity of a multilane highway segment is sensitive to the presence of a median (either a two-way, left-turn lane or a barrier) and the density of access points. The impacts of the presence of a median and access point density on capacity are illustrated in Figure 7–9. Control of side street and driveway access can increase multilane highway segment capacity by as much as 8 percent (when comparing capacity values for 24 access points per kilometer with capacity values for zero access points per kilometer).

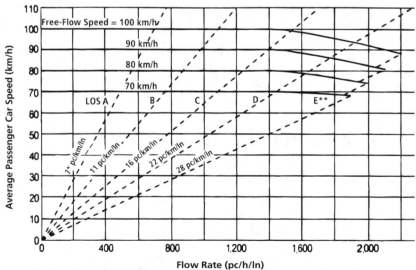

Figure 7–8   Speed-Flow Curves for Multilane Highway Segments

Notes: *   Maximum density for respective levels of service
    **   Maximum densities for LOS E occur at volume-to-capacity ratio of 1.0. They are 25, 26, 27, and 28 pc/km/lm at free-flow speeds of 100, 90, 80, 70 km/h, respectively.

Source: "Production of the Year 2000 HCM," *Status Report*, Catalina Engineering, Inc., NCHRP 3-55 (6), May 30, 1998, Exhibit 21–3. Unpublished Interim TRB Committee on Highway Capacity and Quality of Service material.

Definition of LOS

The measure of effectiveness that is used to provide an estimate of LOS is density. The three measures of speed, density, and flow or volume are interrelated. When values for two of these measures are known, a value for the remaining measure can be computed.

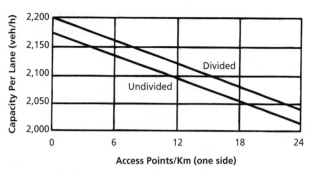

Figure 7–9 Effect of Access Control on Multilane Highway Capacity

Notes: Assumptions: 100 km/h speed, 3.6 m lane widths, 3.6 m lateral clearance (total).

Source: "Production of the Year 2000 HCM," *Status Report,* Catalina Engineering, Inc., NCHRP 3-55 (6), May 30, 1998, Exhibit 21–13. Unpublished Interim TRB Committee on Highway Capacity and Quality of Service material.

- *LOS A*—describes completely free-flow conditions. The operation of vehicles is virtually unaffected by the presence of other vehicles, and operations are constrained only by the geometric features of the highway and by driver preferences. Vehicles are spaced at an average of 143 m at a maximum density of 7 passenger cars per kilometer per lane (pc/km/ln). Maneuverability within the traffic stream is good. Minor disruptions to flow are easily absorbed at this level without a change in travel speed.

- *LOS B*—is also indicative of free-flow, although the presence of other vehicles begins to be noticeable. Average travel speeds are the same as in LOS A, but drivers have slightly less freedom to maneuver. Vehicles are spaced at an average of approximately 80 m at a maximum density of 12 pc/km/ln. Minor disruptions are still easily absorbed at this level, although localized deterioration in LOS will be more obvious.

- *LOS C*—represents a range in which the influence of traffic density on operations becomes marked. The ability to maneuver within the traffic stream is now clearly affected by the presence of other vehicles. Travel speeds begin to show some reduction for multilane highways with free-flow speeds over 80 km/h. The average spacing of vehicles is reduced to approximately 59 m at a maximum density of 17 pc/km/ln. Minor disruptions may be expected to cause serious local deterioration in service, and queues may form behind any significant traffic disruption.

- *LOS D*—represents a range in which ability to maneuver is severely restricted because of traffic congestion. Travel speed begins to be reduced by increasing volumes. The average spacing of vehicles is 48 m at a maximum density of 21 pc/km/ln. Only minor disruptions can be absorbed without the formation of extensive queues and the deterioration of service.

- *LOS E*—represents operations at or near capacity and is quite unstable. The densities at LOS E vary depending upon the free-flow speed. At LOS E, vehicles are operating with the minimum spacing at which uniform flow can be maintained. Disruptions cannot be damped or readily dissipated, and most disruptions will cause queues to form and service to deteriorate to LOS F. For the majority of multilane highways with free-flow speeds between 70 and 100 km/h, passenger-car mean speeds at capacity range from 68 to 88 km/h but are highly variable and unpredictable within that range.

- *LOS F*—represents forced or breakdown flow. It occurs either at a point where vehicles arrive at a rate greater than the rate at which they are discharged or at a point on a planned facility where forecast demand exceeds computed capacity. Although operations at such points (and on sections immediately downstream) will appear to be at capacity, queues will form behind these breakdowns. Operations within queues are highly unstable, with vehicles experiencing brief periods of movement followed by stoppages. Travel speeds within queues are generally less than 48 km/h. Note that the term "LOS F" may be used to characterize both the point of the breakdown and the operating condition within the queue.

Table 7–18 Service Volumes for Multilane Highways in veh/h/ln

Terrain	LOS	Free-Flow Speed = 100 km/h Percent Truck					Free-Flow Speed = 80 km/h Percent Truck				
		0	5	10	15	20	0	5	10	15	20
Level	A	630	610	600	590	570	500	490	480	470	460
	B	990	970	940	920	900	790	770	750	740	720
	C	1,420	1,380	1,350	1,320	1,290	1,150	1,120	1,100	1,070	1,050
	D	1,810	1,770	1,720	1,680	1,650	1,530	1,500	1,460	1,430	1,390
	E	1,980	1,930	1,880	1,840	1,800	1,800	1,750	1,710	1,670	1,630
Rolling	A	630	570	520	480	450	500	460	420	390	360
	B	990	900	820	760	710	790	720	660	610	560
	C	1,420	1,290	1,180	1,090	1,010	1150	1,050	960	880	820
	D	1,810	1,650	1,510	1,390	1,290	1,530	1,390	1,280	1,180	1,100
	E	1,980	1,800	1,650	1,520	1,410	1,800	1,630	1,500	1,380	1,290
Mountainous	A	630	500	420	360	310	500	400	330	290	250
	B	990	790	660	560	490	790	630	530	450	400
	C	1,420	1,130	940	810	710	1,150	920	770	660	580
	D	1,810	1,450	1,210	1,040	910	1,530	1,230	1,020	880	770
	E	1,980	1,580	1,320	1,130	990	1,800	1,440	1,200	1,030	900

Note: Assumptions used to generate the values in Table 7–18 are: for 100 km/h free-flow speed, highway has 0/km access points; for 80 km/h free-flow speed, highway has 15/km access points; lane width = 3.6 m, shoulder width > 1.8 m; divided highway; PHF = 0.90; all heavy vehicles are trucks; and regular commuters.

Service Volumes

Table 7–18 can be used to estimate the number of lanes required to provide a desired LOS for default conditions. The impact of different free-flow speeds, percent trucks, and terrain can also be determined with this table.

Basic Freeway Segments

Freeways provide for "uninterrupted" flow. There are no signalized or stop-controlled at-grade intersections, and direct access to and from adjacent property is not permitted. Access to and from the freeway is limited to ramp locations. Opposing directions of flow are continuously separated by either a raised barrier, an at-grade median, or a raised traffic island. Operating conditions on a freeway primarily result from interactions among vehicles and drivers in the traffic stream, and between vehicles and their drivers and the geometric characteristics of the freeway. Operations can also be affected by environmental conditions, such as weather or lighting; by pavement conditions; and by the occurrence of traffic incidents.

Although average travel speed is a major concern of drivers, freedom to maneuver within the traffic stream and proximity to other vehicles are equally noticeable concerns. These qualities are related to the density of the traffic stream. Unlike speed, density increases as flow increases up to capacity, resulting in a measure of effectiveness that is sensitive to a broad range of flows. LOS criteria are shown in Table 7–19.

For any given LOS, the maximum allowable density is somewhat lower than for the corresponding LOS on multilane highways. This reflects the higher quality of service that drivers expect when using freeways as compared to multilane highways. This does not imply that under similar conditions an at-grade multilane highway will perform better than a freeway with the same number of lanes. For any given density, a freeway will carry higher flow rates at higher speeds than will a comparable multilane highway.

Table 7–19 LOS Criteria for Basic Freeway Segments

LOS	Density Range (pc/km/ln)
A	0.0–9.0
B	>9.0–17.0
C	> 17.0–22.0
D	> 22.0–26.0
E	> 26.0–28.0
F	> 28.0

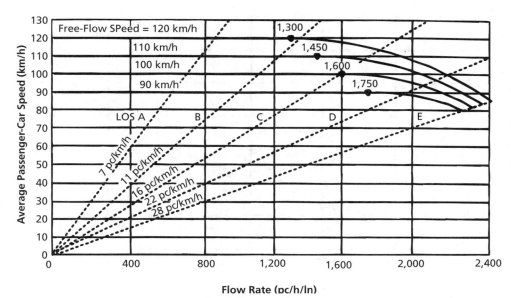

Figure 7–10　Speed-Flow Relationships for Basic Freeway Segments

Note: Capacity varies by free-flow speed. Capacity is 2,400, 2,350, 2,300, and 2,250 pc/h/ln at free-flow speeds of 120, 110, 100, and 90 km/h, respectively.

Source: "Production of the Year 2000 HCM," *Status Report*, Catalina Engineering, Inc., NCHRP 3-55 (6), May 30, 1998, Exhibit 23–3. Unpublished Interim TRB Committee on Highway Capacity and Quality of Service material.

The capacity of a basic freeway segment is determined from the computed free-flow speed of the segment. The computed free-flow speed varies according to the lane width, lateral clearance, and number of lanes. The demand for the segment is adjusted according to the peak hour factor, the percentage of heavy vehicles, specific grade, and driver population type. The capacity is not sensitive to the posted speed limit, the extent of police enforcement, or the presence of intelligent transportation system features related to vehicle or driver guidance.

Speed-Flow and Density-Flow Relationships

Speed-flow and density-flow relationships for a typical basic freeway segment in which the free-flow speed is known are shown in Figures 7–10 and 7–11. Recent freeway studies indicate that speed on freeways is insensitive to flow in the low to moderate range. This is reflected in Figure 7–10, which shows speed to be constant for flows up to 1,300 pc/h/ln for a 120 km/h free-flow speed. For lower free-flow speeds, the region over which speed is insensitive to flow extends to even higher flow rates. Free-flow speed is measured in the field as the average speed of passenger cars when flow rates are less than 1,300 pc/h/ln. Field determination of free-flow speed is accomplished by performing travel time or spot speed studies during periods of low flows and low densities.

A number of factors affect free-flow speed. These factors include number of lanes, lane width, lateral clearance, and interchange density or spacing. Under base traffic and geometric conditions, freeways will operate with capacities as high as 2,400 pc/h/ln. This capacity is typically achieved on free-flow speeds of 120 km/h or greater. As the free-flow speed decreases, there is a slight decrease in capacity. For example, capacity of a basic freeway segment with a free-flow speed of 90 km/h is expected to be approximately 2,250 ph/h/ln. The average speed of passenger cars at flow rates that represent capacity are expected to range from 85.7 km/h (free-flow speeds of 120 km/h or greater) to 80.4 km/h for a segment with a 90 km/h free-flow speed. Note that the higher the free-flow speed, the greater the drop in speed as flow rates move toward capacity. Thus, for a 120 km/h free-flow speed, there is a 34.3 km/h drop from low volume conditions to capacity conditions. The drop is only 9.6 km/h for a freeway with a 90 km/h free-flow speed.

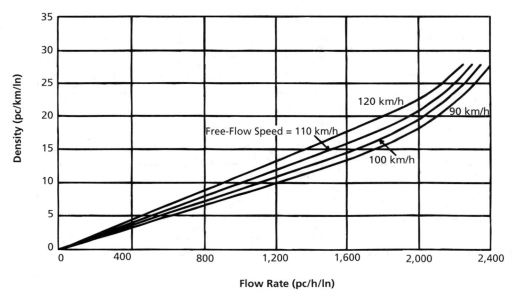

Figure 7–11 Density-Flow Relationships for Basic Freeway Segments

Source: "Production of the Year 2000 HCM," *Status Report*, Catalina Engineering, Inc., NCHRP 3-55 (6), May 30, 1998, Exhibit 11–3. Unpublished Interim TRB Committee on Highway Capacity and Quality of Service material.

LOS Definitions

The LOSs are defined to represent reasonable ranges in the three critical flow·variables: speed, density, and flow rate.

- *LOS A*—describes free-flow operations. Free-flow speeds prevail. Vehicles are almost completely unimpeded in their ability to maneuver within the traffic stream. Even at the maximum density for LOS A, the average spacing between vehicles is about 167 m, or 27 car lengths, which affords the motorist a high level of physical and psychological comfort. The effects of incidents or point breakdowns are easily absorbed at this level.

- *LOS B*—represents reasonably free flow, and free-flow speeds are maintained. The lowest average spacing between vehicles is about 100 m, or 16 car lengths. The ability to maneuver within the traffic stream is only slightly restricted, and the general level of physical and psychological comfort provided to drivers is still high. The effects of minor incidents and point breakdowns are still easily absorbed.

- *LOS C*—provides for flow with speeds at or near the free-flow speed of the freeway. Freedom to maneuver within the traffic stream is noticeably restricted and lane changes require more care and vigilance on the part of the driver. Minimum average spacings are in the range of 67 m, or 11 car lengths. Minor incidents may still be absorbed, but the local deterioration in service will be substantial. Queues may be expected to form behind any significant blockage.

- *LOS D*—the level in which speeds can begin to decline slightly with increasing flows and density begins to increase somewhat more quickly. Freedom to maneuver within the traffic stream is more noticeably limited, and the driver experiences reduced physical and psychological comfort levels. Even minor incidents can be expected to create queuing, as the traffic stream has little space to absorb disruptions. At the limit, vehicles are spaced at about 50 m, or eight car lengths.

- *LOS E*—at its highest density value, it describes operation at capacity. Operations in this level are volatile, as there are virtually no usable gaps in the traffic stream. Vehicles are spaced at approximately six car lengths, leaving little room to maneuver within the traffic stream at speeds that are still over 80 km/h. Any disruption to the traffic stream, such as vehicles entering from a ramp or a vehicle changing lanes, can

Table 7–20 Maximum Service Volumes for Basic Freeway Segments

	Interchange Density	Number of Lanes	Free-Flow Speed	Maximum Service Volumes (veh/h)				
				A	B	C	D	E
Urban	0.63	2	100	1,230	1,930	2,810	3,630	4,040
		3	102	1,882	2,960	4,300	5,480	6,090
		4	104	2,510	3,940	4,730	7,310	8,110
		5	107	3,290	5,170	7,470	9,290	10,250
	1.25	2	91	1,120	1,760	2,560	3,460	3,960
		3	93	1,710	2,700	3,920	5,260	5,970
		4	96	2,360	3,710	5,390	7,130	8,010
		5	98	3,020	4,730	6,880	8,990	10,060
Rural	0.31	2	120	1,390	2,190	3,050	3,640	3,980
		3	120	2,090	3,290	4,570	5,470	5,970
		4	120	2,790	4,380	6,090	7,290	7,960
		5	120	3,480	5,470	7,610	9,110	995
	0.63	2	117	1,360	2,140	3,000	3,620	3,960
		3	117	2,040	3,200	4,500	5,420	5,930
		4	117	2,720	4,270	6,010	7,230	7,910
		5	117	3,400	5,340	7,510	9,040	9,890

Notes: Assumptions used to generate the values in Table 7–20 are:

Urban—110 km/h base free-flow speed, 3.6 m wide lanes, 1.8 m wide shoulders, level terrain, 5 percent heavy vehicles, no driver population adjustment, and 0.90 PHF.

Rural—120 km/h base free-flow speed, 3.6 m wide lanes, 1.8 wide shoulders, level terrain, 5 percent heavy vehicles, no driver population adjustment, and 0.85 PHF.

establish a disruption wave that propagates throughout the upstream traffic flow. At capacity, the traffic stream has no ability to dissipate even the most minor disruptions, and any incident can be expected to produce a serious breakdown with extensive queuing. Maneuverability within the traffic stream is extremely limited, and the level of physical and psychological comfort afforded the driver is poor.

- *LOS F*—describes breakdowns in vehicular flow. Such conditions generally exist within queues forming behind breakdown points. Breakdowns occur for a number of reasons:

  - Traffic incidents can cause a temporary reduction in the capacity of a short segment such that the number of vehicles arriving at the point is greater than the number of vehicles than can move through it.

  - Points of recurring congestion, such as merge or weaving areas and lane drops, experience very high demand in which the number of vehicles arriving is greater than the number of vehicles discharged.

  - In forecasting situations, the projected peak hour (or other) flow rate can exceed the estimated capacity of the location.

Table 7–20 can be used to estimate the number of through-lanes required to obtain a desired LOS for basic freeway segments. The table can be used to test the effects of different interchange densities and is sensitive to the different operating characteristics of urban and rural freeways.

Pedestrian and Bicycle Concepts

This section describes capacity and LOS concepts for pedestrian and bicycle facilities. Chapter 16 contains more information on bicycle and pedestrian facilities. Pedestrian facility evaluation is a very complex matter that is affected by several factors. Research has indicated that gender differences affect walking speeds between male and female pedestrians. Another factor, aging, reduces the length of stride for a pedestrian and results in a commensurate reduction in walking speed. One can also divide pedestrians into groups by trip purpose. Commuting pedestrians exhibit higher walking speeds than shoppers. In addition, the presence of handicapped individuals could affect the performance of a pedestrian facility. Bicycle facility evaluation is affected by age, gender, and type of bicycles. Some pedestrian and bicycle facilities are shared paths that provide service for both pedestrians and bicycles. The interaction between bicycles and pedestrians on shared paths affects the performance of the facility.

Pedestrian Facilities

Pedestrian facility designers use body depth and shoulder breadth for minimum space standards. A simplified body ellipse of 50 cm × 60 cm, with total area of 0.30 m², is used as the basic space needed for a single pedestrian. In evaluating a pedestrian facility, an area of 0.75 m² for walking is used as the buffer zone needed for each pedestrian.

Pedestrian walking speed is highly dependent on the proportion of elderly pedestrians (65 years and older) in the walking population. If 0 to 20 percent of pedestrians are elderly, the average walking speed is 1.2 m/s. If elderly people constitute more than 20 percent of the total pedestrians, the average walking speed decreases to 1.0 m/s. In addition, on an upgrade of 10 percent or above, a walking speed reduction of 0.1 m/s is recommended. Pedestrian start-up time of 3 seconds is a reasonable midrange value for evaluation of crosswalks at traffic signals. A capacity of 75 p/min/m or 4,500 p/h/m is recommended and is used in this methodology. At capacity, a walking speed of 0.75 m/s is recommended.

Figure 7–12 illustrates the basic relationship between speed, flow, and density for pedestrian flow.

Sidewalks and Walkways

Sidewalks and walkways require computation of a clear effective walkway width. The lateral space actually available for pedestrian travel is the actual walkway width exclusive of both fixed and movable obstructions like street furniture. Sidewalk and walkway LOSs are defined by space (m²/p), flow rate (p/min/m), average speed (m/s), or volume to capacity ratio. Table 7–21 lists the sidewalk and walkway LOS criteria. These LOSs are illustrated in Figure 7–13.

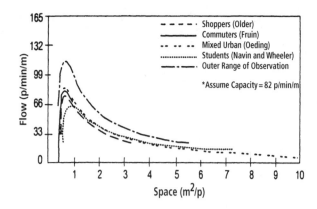

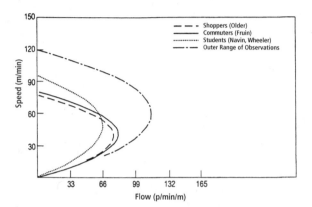

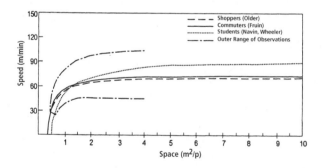

Figure 7–12   Relationships Between Pedestrian Speed, Flow, and Density (Space)

Source: "Production of the Year 2000 HCM," *Status Report,* Catalina Engineering, Inc., NCHRP 3-55 (6), May 30, 1998, Exhibits 9–2, 9–3, and 9–4. Unpublished Interim TRB Committee on Highway Capacity and Quality of Service material.

Flow in platoons increases with an increase in flow rate of a pedestrian facility. A rule of thumb that can be used to develop pedestrian LOS criteria for platoon flow is that pedestrian flow in platoons is approximately one service level lower than the average flow. LOS criteria for platoon flow on walkways and in transportation terminals is provided in Table 7–22. Table 7–23 provides stairway LOS criteria, including space (m²/p), flow rate (p/min/m), average horizontal speed (m/s), and volume to capacity ratio.

LEVEL OF SERVICE A

Pedestrian Space: > 5.6 m²/p   *Flow Rate:* ≤ 16 p/min/m

At a walkway LOS A, pedestrians basically move in desired paths without altering their movements in response to other pedestrians. Walking speeds are freely selected, and conflicts between pedestrians are unlikely.

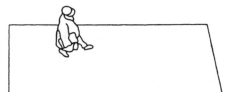

LEVEL OF SERVICE B

Pedestrian Space: > 3.7–5.6 m²/p   *Flow Rate:* > 16–23 p/min/m

At LOS B, sufficient area is provided to allow pedestrians to freely select walking speeds, to bypass other pedestrians, and to avoid crossing conflicts with others. At this level, pedestrians begin to be aware of other pedestrians, and to respond to their presence in the selection of walking path.

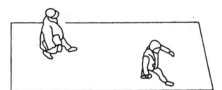

LEVEL OF SERVICE C

Pedestrian Space: > 2.2–3.7 m²/p   *Flow Rate:* > 23-33 p/min/m

At LOS C, sufficient space is available to select normal walking speeds, and to bypass other pedestrians in primarily unidirectional streams. Where reverse-direction or crossing movements exist, minor conflicts will occur, and speeds and flow rate will be somewhat lower.

LEVEL OF SERVICE D

Pedestrian Space: > 1.4–2.2 m²/p   *Flow Rate:* > 33–49 p/min/m

At LOS D, freedom to select individual walking speed and to bypass other pedestrians is restricted. Where crossing or reverse-flow movements exist, the probability of conflict is high, and its avoidance requires frequent changes in speed and position. The LOS provides reasonably fluid flow, but considerable friction and interaction between pedestrians is likely to occur.

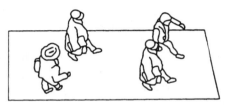

LEVEL OF SERVICE E

Pedestrian Space: > 0.75–1.4 m²/p   *Flow Rate:* > 49–75 p/min/m

At LOS E, virtually all pedestrians would have their normal walking speed restricted, requiring frequent adjustment of gait. At the lower range of this LOS, forward movement is possible only by "shuffling." Insufficient space is provided for passing of slower pedestrians. Cross- or reverse-flow movements are possible only with extreme difficulties. Design volumes approach the limit of walkway capacity, with resulting stoppages and interruptions to flow.

LEVEL OF SERVICE F

Pedestrian Space: ≤ 0.75 m²/p   *Flow Rate:* varies p/min/m

At LOS F, all walking speeds are severely restricted, and forward progress is made only by "shuffling." There is frequent, unavoidable contact with other pedestrians. Cross- and reverse-flow movements are virtually impossible. Flow is sporadic and unstable. Space is more characteristic of queued pedestrians than of moving pedestrian streams.

Figure 7–13   Pedestrian Walkway Levels of Service

Source: "Production of the Year 2000 HCM," *Status Report*, Catalina Engineering, Inc., NCHRP 3-55 (6), May 30, 1998, Exhibit 9–8. Unpublished Interim TRB Committee on Highway Capacity and Quality of Service material.

Bicycle Facilities

Bicycle facilities are divided into two major categories: uninterrupted and interrupted facilities. The uninterrupted facilities include exclusive off-street bicycle paths, shared off-street paths, and designated lanes (or paved shoulders). The interrupted facilities include signalized and unsignalized on-street designated bicycle facilities with or without exclusive right-turn lanes for motor vehicles traffic. Uninterrupted bicycle facilities use "frequency of events" as the service measure of effectiveness for all three types of facilities. Events are defined as bicycle maneuvers required by a bicyclist on a path including passing (same direction encounters) and meetings (opposite direction encounters). Interrupted bicycle facilities use control delay as the measure of effectiveness.

Exclusive Off-Street Bicycle Paths

Table 7–24 gives LOS criteria for exclusive off-street bicycle paths, and the relationships between "hindrance" and "events." "Hindrance" is the fraction of users over 1.0 km of a path experiencing hindrance because of passing and meeting maneuvers. "Events" is the number of times a bicycle is involved in passing and meeting maneuvers, which is strongly related to hindrance.

Table 7–21 Sidewalk and Walkway LOS Criteria

LOS	Space (m²/p)	Flow Rate (p/min/m)	Average Speed (m/s)	v/c Ratio
A	>5.6	≤16	>1.30	≤0.21
B	>3.7–5.6	>16–23	>1.27–1.30	>0.21–0.31
C	>2.2–3.7	>23–33	>1.22–1.27	>0.31–0.44
D	>1.4–2.2	>33–49	>1.14–1.22	>0.44–0.65
E	>0.75–1.4	>49–75	>0.75–1.14	>0.65–1.0
F	≤0.75	varies	≤0.75	varies

Table 7–22 Platoon-Adjusted Walkway LOS Criteria

| | Walkway | | Transportation Terminals | |
LOS	Space (m²/p)	Flow Rate[a] (p/min/m)	Space (m²/p)	Flow Rate (p/min/m)
A	>49	≤1.6	>2.3	≤0.37
B	>8–49	>1.6–10	>1.3–2.3	>37–5
C	>4–8	>10–20	>1.0–1.3	>57–68
D	>2–4	>20–36	>0.8–1.0	>68–75
E	>1–2	>36–59	>0.75–0.8	~75
F	≤1	≤59	≤0.75	>75

[a] Flow rates represent average flow rates over a 5–6 minute period.

Note that by these criteria, the LOS afforded to bicyclists in each direction is different unless the directional split is 50:50. Note also that three-lane bicycle paths will result in significantly higher service-flow rates for any given LOS. This is because many "events" on a three-lane bicycle path can occur without infringing on the lane of travel, in effect, without "hindering" the bicyclist.

Designated Lanes

Extended facilities (i.e., bicycle lanes on an urban street) use average bicycle travel speed, including stops, as the service measure of effectiveness. The average travel speed is simply based on the travel distance between two points and the average amount of time required to traverse that distance including stops at intersections. Table 7–25 provides the LOS criteria for extended bicycle facilities.

Table 7–23 Pedestrian Stairway LOS Criteria

LOS	Space (m²/p)	Flow Rate (p/min/m)	Average Horizontal Speed m/min	m/s	v/c Ratio
A	>1.9	≤16	≥32	≥0.53	0.33
B	>1.6–1.9	>16–20	≥32	≥0.53	>0.33–0.41
C	>1.1–1.6	>20–26	>29–32	>0.48–0.53	>0.41–0.53
D	>0.7–1.1	>26–36	>25–29	>0.42–0.48	>0.53–0.73
E	>0.5–0.7	>36–49	>24–25	>0.40–0.42	>0.73–1.00
F	≤0.5	varies	<24	<0.40	varies

Table 7–24 Levels of Service for Exclusive Bicycle Paths

LOS	Hindrance (%)	Frequency of Events Two-Way Two-Lane Paths (Events/h)*	Frequency of Events Two-Way, Three-Lane Paths (Events/h)*
A	≤10	≤40	≤90
B	>10–20	>40–60	>90–140
C	>20–40	>60–100	>140–210
D	>40–70	>100–150	>210–300
E	>70–100	>150–195	>300–375
F	>100	>195	>375

* A two-lane path is 2.4 m wide, and a three lane path is 3.0 m wide.

Signalized Intersections

Bicycle LOS at signalized intersections is defined by the average control delay experienced by bicyclists. Delay is especially important to bicyclists, as they are completely exposed to the elements. Excessive delays to bicyclists on designated bicycle facilities may cause them to disregard traffic control devices or use alternate routes not intended for bicycle use. Table 7–26 provides LOS criteria for a bicycle lane at a signalized intersection.

Table 7–25 LOS Criteria for Bicycle Lanes on Urban Streets

LOS	Average Travel Speed[a] (km/h)
A	>22
B	>15–22
C	>11–15
D	>8–11
E	≥7–8
F	<7

[a] Average travel speed includes stops. Average running speed assumed to be 25 km/h.

Transit Concepts

This section describes capacity and LOS concepts for transit modes that operate on public streets—bus, streetcar, and light rail—and therefore interact with other users of streets and highways. Consult Chapter 13 for more information on transit planning.

Transit plays two major roles in North America. The first is an efficiency role—the efficient use of road space or segregated rail rights-of-way. This role is dominant in the peak periods for work and school journeys and includes those who specifically use transit as an environmentally preferred way to travel. The other major transit role, a social role, provides basic mobility for those segments of the population that are young; too old; or otherwise unable to drive due to physical, mental, or financial disadvantages. Thirty-five percent of the population in the United States and Canada do not posses a driver's license and must depend on others to drive them; on transit; or on other modes, such as walking, bicycling, and taxis.

Table 7–26 LOS Criteria for Bicycles at Signalized Intersections

LOS	Control Delay per Bicycle (s)
A	<5
B	≥5–10
C	>10–20
D	>20–30
E	>30–45
F	>45

Transit comes in many varieties. *Bus* services can be provided by a number of vehicle types ranging from minibuses to articulated and double-deck buses. Standard 12-meter buses with over 35 seats are by far the dominant form of bus operated by U.S. transit systems and comprise over 80 percent of the national bus fleet. Articulated buses of 18 meters in length have been embraced by a smaller number of agencies, but their use is growing as agencies seek to improve capacity and comfort with relatively low increases in operating costs. *Double-deck buses* have been employed for trial applications but have not found widespread transit use in either Canada or the United States.

During the first half of the 20th Century, *streetcars* were a common sight in most larger North American cities. Their use nearly disappeared as automobile use became more common after World War II and as suburban growth occurred that was inefficient to serve by rail. The modern equivalent of these streetcars are the *light rail* systems that have opened since 1978. The two modes are very similar; however, light rail provides higher speeds and somewhat higher capacity than streetcars. Also, light rail tracks are separated from general traffic in North America (even when operating on the same street as other traffic), while streetcars sometimes share a lane with other traffic.

Heavy rail, also known as rail rapid transit, is by far the predominant urban rail travel mode in North America, in terms of system size and utilization. It is characterized by fully grade-separated rights-of-way, high-level platforms, and high-speed electric multiple-unit cars. *Commuter rail* is generally a long-distance transit mode using trackage that is part of the general railroad system but which may be used exclusively for passengers. As the name implies, service is heavily oriented towards the peak commuting hours, particularly on the smaller systems. *Automated guideway transit (AGT)* is the newest of the rail transit modes and has played a relatively minor role in North American transit. AGT is found most often at airports, but is also used in the downtown areas of Miami and Detroit. Cars are generally small, and the service is frequent. Depending on the application, *monorails* can be either heavy rail or AGT. Vehicles either straddle or are suspended from a single rail. Most applications in North America are for recreational uses, such as amusement parks.

Definitions of Capacity

Transit capacity is more complex and less precise than highway capacity. It deals with the movement of both people and vehicles, depends on the size of the transit vehicles and their frequency of operation, and reflects the interaction between passenger traffic concentrations and vehicle flow. Transit capacity depends on the operating policy of the transit agency, which normally specifies service frequencies and allowable passenger loadings. Accordingly, the traditional concepts applied to highway capacity must be adapted and broadened. Vehicle capacity reflects the number of transit units (buses, trains, and the like) that can be served by a loading area, transit stop, guideway, or route during a specified period of time. Person capacity reflects the number of people that can be carried past a given location during a given time period under specified operating conditions without unreasonable delay, hazard, or restriction, and with reasonable certainty.

Transit vehicle capacity is commonly determined for the following sets of locations:

- loading areas (berths),

- transit stops and stations,

- bus lanes and transit routes.

Each item in this list is directly influenced by the item preceding it: the vehicle capacity of a bus stop or rail station is controlled by the vehicle capacities of the loading areas provided at the stop or station, while the vehicle capacity of a bus lane or transit route is controlled by the vehicle capacity of the critical stops along the lane or route.

The two factors with the greatest influence on loading area vehicle capacity are dwell time and the g/c ratio (the ratio of the available signal green time to the signal cycle length) provided to the street that transit operates on. Of these two factors, dwell time—the time required to serve passengers at the busiest door, plus the time required to open and close the doors—is the factor with the greater influence on loading area vehicle capacity.

Person capacity is typically calculated for three locations:

- transit stops and stations,

- transit routes at their maximum load points,

- bus lanes at their maximum load points.

Bus Concepts

A loading area, or bus berth, is a space for buses to stop and board and discharge passengers. Bus stops contain one or more loading areas. The most common form of loading area is a linear bus stop along a street curb. In this case, loading areas can be provided in the travel lane (on-line), where following buses may not pass the stopped bus, or out of the travel time (off-line), where following buses may pass stopped vehicles. Loading areas in bus terminals may be linear, or they may take various other forms. Angle berths are limited to one bus per berth, and they require buses to back out. Drive-through angle berths are also feasible, and may accommodate multiple vehicles. Shallow "sawtooth" berths are popular in urban transit centers and are designed to permit independent movements into and out of each berth. Figure 7–14 illustrates common bus loading area configurations.

A bus stop is an area where one or more buses load and unload passengers. It consists of one or more loading areas. Bus stop capacity is related to the capacity of the individual loading areas at the stop, loading area design (linear or nonlinear), and the number of loading areas provided. Off-line bus stops provide greater capacity than do on-line stops for a given number of loading areas; but in mixed-traffic situations, bus speeds may be reduced if heavy traffic volumes delay buses exiting a stop. On the other hand, skip-stop operations are possible with off-line stops, but not with on-line stops.

Linear Berths

Sawtooth Berths

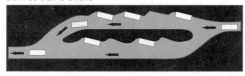

Angle Berths

Drive Through Berths

Figure 7–14   Bus Loading Area (Berth) Designs

Source: "Transit Capacity Concept," Final Draft Chapter for *HCM 2000*, Kittelson & Associates, Inc., September 1998, Exhibit 12–10.

The bus stop location influences capacity, particularly when passenger vehicles are allowed to make right turns from the curb lane (as is the case in most situations, except for certain kinds of exclusive bus lanes). Far-side stops have the least effect on capacity (when buses are able to use an adjacent lane to avoid right-turn queues), followed by midblock stops, and near-side stops.

Observed Bus and Passenger Flows

Observed bus volumes on urban freeways, city streets, and bus-only streets clearly show the reductive effects of bus stops on bus vehicle capacity. The highest bus volumes experienced in a transit corridor in North America—735 buses per hour through the Lincoln Tunnel and on the Port Authority Midtown Bus Terminal access ramp, in the New York metropolitan area—are achieved on exclusive rights-of-way where buses make no stops (and where an 800-berth bus terminal is provided to receive these and other buses) (Table 7–27). Where bus stops or layovers are involved, reported bus volumes are much lower.

When intermediate stops are made, bus volumes rarely exceed 120 buses per hour. However, volumes of 180 to 200 buses per hour are feasible where buses may use two or more lanes to allow bus passing, especially where stops are short. Several downtown streets carry bus volumes of 80 to 100 buses per hour, where there are two or three boarding positions per stop, and where passenger boarding is not concentrated at a single stop. (This frequency corresponds to about 5,000 to 7,500 passengers per hour, depending on passenger loads.)

Peak hour bus flows observed at 13 major bus terminals in the United States and Canada range from 2.5 buses per berth at the George Washington Bridge Terminal in New York to 19 buses per berth at the Eglinton Station in Toronto. The

Table 7–27 Observed Peak Direction Peak Hour Passenger Volumes on U.S. and Canadian Bus Transit Systems—1997 Data

City	State or Province	Agency	Route	Number of Peak Hour Peak Direction Buses	Peak Point Peak Direction Passengers	Bus Type
New York Area	NY/NJ	NJ Transit and Private Buses	Lincoln Tunnel	735	34,000*	Cruisers/Suburbans
New York Area	NJ	NJT/Private	Highway 9 routes	35	1,344	Cruisers
Pittsburgh	PA	PA Transit	East Busway	105	5,400	
Dallas	TX	DART	I-30 WB routes	50	2,730	Standards 12 m
Oakland	CA	AC Transit	82/82L	30	1,287	Articulated
Ottawa	Ontario	OC Transit	#95	20	1,500	Standard 12 m
Vancouver	BC	BC Transit	Boundary/UBC #9	24	1,500	Trolleybus
Washington	DC	WMATA	A-2, 3, 4, 6, 7, 8	31	1,122	Standard 12 m
Boston	MA	MBTA	#39	18	1,000	9 m
Denver	CO	RTD	15/15LTD	12	500	Standard 12 m

* No stops.

high berth productivity in Toronto reflects the special design of the terminal (with multiple positions in each berthing area); the wide doors on the buses using the terminal; and the free transfer between bus and subway, which allows use of all doors and separate boarding and alighting areas. The relatively low productivity at the New York terminals reflects the substantial number of intercity buses that use the terminals (which occupy berths for longer periods of time) and the single-entrance doors provided on many suburban buses. This experience suggests an average of 8–10 buses per berth per hour for commuter operations. Intercity berths typically can accommodate 1–2 buses per hour.

General Capacity Ranges

Table 7–28 identifies maximum bus vehicle capacity at loading areas, based on various values of dwell time and g/C ratio. Other values not provided in the table may be interpolated.

Table 7–29 provides estimated vehicle capacities of on-line linear bus stops. This exhibit shows the number of buses per hour for various numbers of loading areas, dwell times, and g/C ratios. As can be seen, increasing the number of loading areas at a linear bus stop has an ever-decreasing effect on capacity as the number of loading areas increase (i.e., doubling the number of loading areas at a linear bus stop does not double capacity). Nonlinear designs are 100 percent efficient—doubling the number of loading areas doubles the stop's capacity.

Table 7–28 Estimated Maximum Vehicle Capacity of Loading Areas (Buses Per Hour)

Dwell Time (s)	g/C = 0.5	g/C = 1.0
15	63	100
30	43	63
45	32	46
60	26	36
75	22	30
90	19	25
105	16	22
120	15	20

Note: Assumes 15-second clearance time, 25 percent queue probability, and 60 percent coefficient of variation.

Table 7–29 Estimated Maximum Capacity of On-Line Linear Bus Stops (Buses Per Hour)

Dwell Time (s)	Number of Loading Areas									
	1		2		3		4		5	
	g/C 0.50	g/C 1.00	g/C 0.50	g/C 1.00	g/C 0.50	g/C 1.00	g/C 0.50	g/C 1.00	g/C 0.50	g/C 1.00
30	43	63	79	117	105	154	117	173	128	189
60	26	36	48	67	64	89	71	100	78	109
90	19	25	35	47	46	62	51	70	56	76
120	15	20	27	36	36	48	40	54	44	59

Note: Assumes 15-second clearance time, 25 percent queue probability, and 60 percent coefficient of variation. To obtain the vehicle capacity of nonlinear on-line bus stops, multiply the one-loading-area values by the number of loading areas provided.

Table 7–30   Illustrative Busway Capacities

Stations: On-Line/Off-Line	Loading Condition							
	A		B		C		D	
	On	Off	On	Off	On	Off	On	Off
Passengers boarding at heaviest CBD station:								
Boarding passengers per bus	20	20	20	20	20	20	30	30
Boarding time per passenger(s)	2.0	2.0	1.2	1.2	0.7	0.7	0.5	0.5
Dwell time(s)	40.0	40.0	24.0	24.0	14.0	14.0	15.0	15.0
Vehicle Capacity:								
Loading area capacity (bus/h)	40	40	60	60	87	87	83	83
Effective loading areas	2.45	2.60	2.45	2.60	2.45	2.60	2.45	2.60
Station capacity (bus/h)	98	104	147	156	213	226	203	215
Passenger/hour—maximum load point:								
Peak—flow rate (15 min × 4)	4,210	4,470	6,320	6,700	9,150	9,710	12,180	12,900
Average—peak hour (with PHF)	2,820	2,990	4,230	4,490	6,130	6,510	8,160	8,640

Loading condition A: Single-door conventional bus, simultaneous loading and unloading
Loading condition B: Two-door conventional bus, both doors loading or double-stream doors simultaneously loading and unloading
Loading condition C: Four-door conventional bus, all double-stream doors loading.
Loading condition D: Six-door articulated bus, all doors loading.

Note: Assumes 15-second clearance time; 7.5 percent failure rate; 60 percent coefficient of variation; 3 linear loading areas; g/C = 1.0, PHF = 0.67; 50 percent of passengers board at heaviest CBD station; 43 seats per conventional bus; 60 seats per articulated bus; and no standees allowed.

Illustrative busway vehicle and person capacities for central areas are given in Table 7–30 for a variety of bus types and service conditions.

Light Rail and Streetcar Concepts

Light rail transit (LRT) started as a modification of street car operation to allow higher speeds by separating it from street traffic. LRT is characterized by its versatility of operation as it can operate separately from other traffic below-grade, at-grade, on an elevated structure, or together with road vehicles on the surface.

Observed Passenger Flows

The operating experience for typical LRT and streetcar lines in the United States and Canada are given in Table 7–31. This table gives typical peak-hour, peak-direction passenger volumes, service frequencies, and train lengths for principal U.S. and Canadian LRT lines.

General Capacity Ranges

The capacity of a rail line is determined by station capacity or way capacity, whichever is smaller. In most cases, station (or stop) capacity governs. Capacity depends on: (a) car size and station length, (b) allowable standees as determined by scheduling policy, and (c) the minimum spacing (headway) between trains. This minimum headway is a function not only of dwell times at major stations, but also train length, acceleration and deceleration rates, and train control systems.

LRT trains usually are limited to a maximum of three cars, where on-street operation is involved. Longer trains usually cannot operate on city streets without simultaneously occupying more than the space between adjacent cross streets when traversing short blocks, cannot clear at-grade intersections rapidly, and require long platform lengths at stations. Minimum headways for light-rail systems will depend on train length, platform and car design (high-floor versus low-

Table 7–31   Observed U.S. and Canadian LRT Passenger Volumes Peak Hour at the Peak Point for Selected Lines (1993–96 Data)

City	Location (may be trunk with several routes)	Trains/h	Cars/h	Avg. Headway(s)	Pass/Peak Hour Direction	Pass/m of Car Length
Calgary	South Line	11	33	320	4,950	6.8
Denver	Central	12	24	300	3,000	4.7
Edmonton	Northeast LRT	12	36	300	3,220	4.0
Los Angeles	Blue Line	9	18	400	2,420	5.4
Boston	Green Line Subway*	45	90	80	9,600	5.3
Newark	City Subway	30	30	120	1,760	4.6
Philadelphia	Norristown	8	8	450	480	3.3
Philadelphia	Subway-Surface*	60	60	60	4,130	5.0
San Francisco	Muni Metro*	23	138	156	13,100	4.8
Sacramento	Sacramento LRT	4	12	900	1,310	4.9
Toronto	Queen at Broadway*	51	51	70	4,300	6.1
Portland	Eastside MAX	9	16	400	1,980	5.1

* Trunks with multiple-berth stations.

Note: In a single hour, a route may have different lengths of trains, or trains with cars of different lengths or seating configurations. Data represent the average car. In calculating the passengers per meter of car length, the car length is reduced by 9 percent to allow for space lost to driver cabs, stairwells, and other equipment.

floor), fare collection methods (prepayment versus pay on train), wheelchair accessibility provisions, and headway controls (manual versus block signals). Under manual operations, 80–100 single-unit cars per track per hour could be accommodated. When trains run under block signal controls, as is common with rapid transit systems, 120-second headways are possible. Shorter headways can be realized with moving block signals. Most North American light rail systems are signaled for a minimum headway of 3–3$\frac{1}{2}$ minutes.

At 120-second headways, a light rail system operating on mainly reserved right-of-way with three-car trains would have a line capacity of up to 7,500 seated and 15,000 total passengers per hour (thirty 3-car trains at 170 persons/car). Under single-vehicle manual operation at lower speeds, closer headways are feasible. At 60-second headways, single LRT units have a capacity of 4,000 seated and 10,000 total passengers per hour (schedule load). However, in practice these capacities are not realized because of limited ridership demands. Typical ranges in person capacities are shown in Table 7–32.

Table 7–32   Typical Light Rail Transit Person Capacities 30 Trains per Track per Hour, 28–30 Meter Articulated Cars

Cars/Train	Passengers/Car				
	75*	100	125	150	175
1	2,250	3,000	3,750	4,500	5,250
2	4,500	6,000	7,500	9,000	10,500
3	6,750	9,000	11,250	13,500	15,750
4	9,000	12,000	15,000	18,000	21,000

*All passengers seated.

Current operating experience in the United States and Canada suggests maximum realizable capacities of 12,000 to 15,000 persons per track per hour. However, the European experience shows up to 20,000 persons per hour.

Quality of Service Concepts

Quality of service related to transit reflects the passenger's perception of transit performance. It measures both the availability of transit service and its comfort and convenience. Quality of service depends to a great extent on the operating decisions made by a transit system, especially decisions on where transit service should be provided, how often and how long transit service should be provided, and what kind of service should be provided.

LOS is often used literally to mean the amount of service both in frequency and hours of coverage—the latter sometimes referred to as the "span" of service. Quality of service can be used to refer to performance measures developed to evaluate transit service efficiency from the *passenger point of view*. The *operator point of view* encompasses the measures routinely collected for the FTA's National Transit Database (formerly Section 15) annual reporting process. Most of these measures relate to economy or productivity. The *vehicle point of view* includes measures of vehicular speed and delay routinely calculated for streets and highways using the procedures given in the *Highway Capacity Manual*. This point of view also includes measures of facility capacity in terms of the number of transit vehicles that can be accommodated. The passenger point of view, or quality of service, directly measures passenger's perception of the availability, comfort, and convenience of transit service.

Transit Trip Decision-Making Process

The first step in the process is to decide whether or not transit is a possibility for the trip. This step assesses the availability of transit service and is illustrated in Figure 7–15.

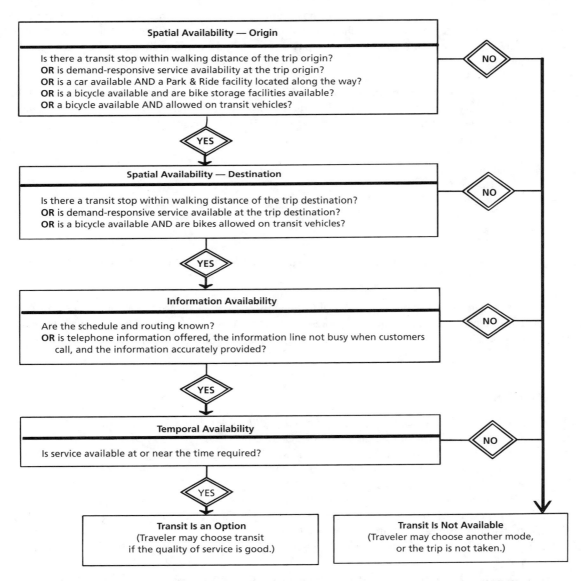

Figure 7–15   Transit Trip Decision-Making Process: Transit Availability

Table 7–33   Transit Quality of Service Framework

Category	Service and Performance Measures		
	Transit Stop	Route Segment	System
Availability	FREQUENCY Accessibility Passenger loads	HOURS OF SERVICE Accessibility	SERVICE COVERAGE Percent person–minutes of availability indexes
Quality	PASSENGER LOADS Amenities Reliability	RELIABILITY Travel speed Transit/auto travel time	TRANSIT/AUTO TRAVEL TIME Travel time Safety

This figure indicates, that there are a number of factors that enter into determining whether or not transit service is available. If any one of these factors is not met, transit is not a viable mode for the trip and the traveler will either use another mode or will not make the trip. If however, transit service is available at the trip origin and destination (or the traveler can use another mode to get to and from transit); if information is available on where, when, and how service is provided; and if transit service is provided at or near the time the trip needs to be made, then transit becomes an option. Assuming the latter is true, the decision-making process moves to step two, weighing the comfort and convenience of transit service against competing modes.

Quality of service is divided into two main categories: availability and quality. The availability measures address the spatial and temporal availability of transit service. The quality measures can be used to evaluate a user's perception of the comfort and convenience of his or her transit experience. Different elements of a transit system require different performance measures. They include:

- Transit stops.

- Route segments.

- System.

Combining the two performance measure categories with the three transit system elements produces the matrix shown in Table 7–33.

Some measures appear in more than one cell of the table, but only one service measure is assigned to each cell (the first measure shown in each cell). The service measure represents the performance measure that best describes the passenger's point-of-view of availability or convenience for a particular transit element.

References

Adolf D. May. *Performance Measures and LOS in the Year 2000 HCM—Final Report*. Washington, D.C.: National Cooperative Highway Research Program, 3-55 (4), October 31, 1997.

Catalina Engineering, Inc. "Production of the Year 2000 HCM." *Status Report*. Washington, D.C.: National Cooperative Highway Research Program, 3-55 (6), December 12, 1997.

Catalina Engineering, Inc. "Production of the Year 2000 HCM." *Status Report*. Washington, D.C.: National Cooperative Highway Research Program, 3-55 (6), May 30, 1998.

Transit Cooperative Research Program. "Transit Capacity Concept." Final Draft Chapter for *HCM 2000*. Washington, D.C.: Transportation Research Board, September 1998.

Transportation Research Board. *Highway Capacity Manual*, Third Edition, Special Report 209. Washington, D.C.: TRB, 1994 Update.

Transportation Research Board. *Highway Capacity Manual*, Third Edition. Washington, D.C.: TRB, 1998 Update.

CHAPTER 8
Environmental and Energy Considerations

Louis F. Cohn
Professor and Chairman
Roswell A. Harris
Professor of Civil and Environmental Engineering
Paul R. Lederer
Research Engineer
Department of Civil and Environmental Engineering
University of Louisville

Introduction

The size and scope of modern transportation systems are so immense that minor impacts from the use of a single automobile, the noise from a single airplane, or the removal of a single tree have been multiplied to an extent that our cities face ground-level ozone alerts, our neighborhoods face continual noise disruption, and our natural wildlife areas face permanent disruption of natural water flows and water quality. The plane, the train, and the automobile provide the mobility that our modern society and economy demand; but the proliferation of their use has turned minor environmental annoyances into potential or existing environmental and health hazards. The overdependence of the transportation system on petroleum, roughly 96 percent in the United States in 1995,[1] is a major source of many of the negative environmental impacts. "Using energy in today's ways leads to more environmental damage than any other peaceful human activity (except perhaps reproduction)."[2]

Modern transportation systems have evolved beyond the point where they can be designed only to expedite the mobility requirements of the population. The planner and designer must consider the impacts of the project on the people who live and work in the vicinity of it as well as those that will use it. These impacts range from pollutants that can directly affect human health and the environment, such as air pollutants and water pollutants, to more aesthetic effects that can influence the overall quality of life in the vicinity of the project.

Environmental analysis of transportation systems is a comprehensive and demanding task that has become an integral part of the planning process. Recent legislation and the resulting regulations now recognize that environmental concerns must be addressed during the planning and design stages. Transportation legislation, such as the Intermodal Surface Transportation Efficiency Act (ISTEA), now include provisions requiring environmental analyses in the planning stages. Environmental legislation such as the Clean Air Act Amendments of 1991 (CAAA) specifically address the impacts from transportation facilities. These laws have expanded the role of the environmental analyst beyond those specified in the National Environmental Policy Act (NEPA), in which an environmental analysis was required to merely assess the environmental impacts. The environmental analyst must now provide feedback to the transportation planner that will limit or prevent adverse environmental impacts.

The environmental impacts from transportation projects can cover a wide range of areas that require significant levels of analysis and research. The legal and analytical requirements continue to become more sophisticated and complex as both the methods for determining contaminant generation and pollutant dissemination are better understood. The impact areas

---

[1] *1997 National Transportation Statistics*, DOT-VNTSC-BTS-96-4 (Washington, D.C.: U.S. Department of Transportation, Bureau of Transportation Statistics, December 1996).

[2] "A Survey of Energy and the Environment," *The Economist* (August 31, 1991) through David L. Greene, *Transportation and Energy* (Lansdowne, Va.: Eno Transportation Foundation, Inc., 1996)

of noise analysis, air quality, and water resources are covered, reflecting the engineering-related issues of the environmental questions that generally concern civil engineers. In addition, energy considerations are discussed.

The results of environmental analyses, however, are highly dependent upon the project data provided by transportation planners and designers. Since much of this data emanates from traffic demand models that were not designed to provide inputs for environmental analyses, the environmental analyst must carefully and objectively examine this data and review the method of generating it. After establishing the relevance of the design data, he or she must then review existing environmental laws and regulations that may affect the project, make appropriate calculations of impact, compare impact values against acceptable criteria, and recommend mitigation where needed. This chapter will focus on information that assists the analyst in carrying out these functions when examining the impacts from highways, railways, and airports. This information includes a survey of relevant laws, an overview of the analytical demands, and direction for determining the appropriate prediction models and mitigation methods. While some consider the impacts from transit as a separate mode, air effects can be analyzed either as a highway vehicle for gasoline- or diesel-powered vehicles, or as stationary source for electric-powered vehicles where energy is generated from a central location. Water and noise impacts would be the same as for either highway or rail systems.

Purpose and Scope

This chapter is intended to outline and analyze the issues relating to environmental impacts that result from the implementation of proposed transportation projects. Within this scope, this chapter will help planners understand the basic engineering demands of the required environmental analysis. The modes of interest are limited to highways, railways, and airports, with the scope being confined to the impact areas listed above. This should not be construed to imply that other types of impacts, such as those on cultural and archeological resources, wildlife habitats, and historic places, are not important. Careful consideration of these impacts can, in fact, significantly reduce adverse visual impacts. They are not, however, subject to precise analytical methods and design criteria. The procedures for assessing and mitigating these impacts primarily fall within the scope of public participation where it is determined what items are of value that must be preserved.

The Concept of Impact Analysis

The method of determining the environmental impacts of transportation projects is the result of numerous important pieces of federal legislation including NEPA, CAAA, and ISTEA. These laws, and the regulations emerging from them, have established the requirement that environmental impacts be examined very early in the planning stages of transportation projects. NEPA requires the evaluation of environmental impacts and the examination of project alternatives, but these environmental analyses were only performed after the project had been included in the transportation plan. The passage of CAAA and ISTEA moved the environmental analysis up into the project selection process by requiring impact analyses of reasonable alternatives. In addition, these laws require the limitation of adverse impacts of transportation projects and public participation in the planning process.

The Public's Role in Impact Analysis

The public's role in environmental impact analyses has been continuously evolving since the 1960s when public outrage over environmental exploitations began to be publicized with the publication of books like Rachel Carson's *Silent Spring*. The Federal Aid Highway Act of 1962 initiated the transportation planning procedure and the involvement of the community in that process.[3] NEPA took it a step further by including requirements for public participation during federal aid project development. Public participation during the examination of environmental impacts for these projects is specifically required. Each state must have Federal Highway Administration (FHWA)-approved procedures to carry out a public involvement/public hearing program.[4] This program must include:

---

[3] *Freeways in the Urban Setting*, Hershey Conference, Sponsored by the American Association of State Highway Officials, American Municipal Association, and National Association of County Officials, Automotive Safety Foundation (Washington D.C.: June 1962).
[4] 23 CFR 771.111(h)(1).

- Coordination with the entire NEPA process.

- "Early and continuous opportunities during project development for the public to be involved in the identification of social, economic, and environmental impacts."

- "One or more public hearings or the opportunity for hearing(s) to be held by the State highway agency at a convenient time and place for any Federal-aid project which . . . has a significant social, economic, environmental, or other effect."

- "Reasonable notice to the public of either a public hearing or the opportunity for a public hearing."

- "An explanation at the public hearing of the . . . social, economic, environmental, and other impacts of the project."[5]

NEPA also laid the groundwork for the *Environmental Impact Statement* (EIS), which requires the evaluation of environmental impacts of federally funded projects and the presentation of the result of the EIS to the public. The EIS has proved to be a potent weapon in the hands of project opponents. Local communities have used this public access to the predicted environmental impacts to arouse public opposition to projects in their areas that they deem to have excess negative impacts. Frequent challenges to the completeness of the environmental impact statement have allowed them to effect significant construction delays. Community groups remain concerned about proposed projects, and they expect transportation agencies to examine potential impacts adequately and correctly. The passage of CAAA and the Intermodal Surface Transportation Efficiency Act of 1991 has enhanced public participation by allowing it greater input in the planning stages of a project.

Environmental Laws and Regulations

The laws and regulations that are most relevant to environmental analysis as practiced in the areas of noise analysis, air quality, and water resources are listed in Table 8–1; and the resulting regulations are shown in Table 8–2. Included in these lists are general environmental laws and regulations, such as NEPA and the Council of Environmental Quality guidelines, as well as those that affect specific environmental areas. These laws and resulting regulations have provided a framework for the development of a body of analytical methods, procedures, and computer programs that can currently be used by the environmental analyst.

Table 8–1 Federal Environmental Legislation Influencing Transportation

The Rivers and Harbors Act of 1899

Water Pollution Control Act of 1948

Water Pollution Control Act Amendments of 1956

Fish and Wildlife Coordination Act of 1958

Federal Aid Highway Act of 1962

Clean Air Act of 1963

Wilderness Act of 1964

Water Quality Act of 1965

Land and Water Conservation Act of 1965

Housing and Urban Development Act of 1965

Department of Transportation Act of 1966

Air Quality Act of 1967

Control and Abatement of Aircraft Noise and Sonic Boom Act of 1968

Wild and Scenic Rivers Act of 1968

National Flood Insurance Act of 1968

National Environmental Policy Act of 1969

Federal Aid Highway Act of 1970

Executive Order 11514, "Protection and Enhancement of Environmental Quality," 1970

Airport and Airway Development Act of 1970

Clean Air Act Amendments of 1970

Noise Control Act of 1972

Federal Water Pollution Control Act of 1972

Coastal Zone Management Act of 1972

The Endangered Species Act of 1973

Coastal Zone Management Act Amendments of 1976

Executive Order 11988, "Floodplain Management," 1977

Executive Order 11990, "Protection of Wetlands," 1977

Clean Air Act Amendments of 1977

Clean Water Act Amendments of 1977

Executive Order 11991, "Protection and Enhancement of Environmental Quality" (amended), 1977

Quiet Communities Act of 1978

Aviation Safety and Noise Abatement Act of 1979

Airport and Airway Improvement Act of 1982

Emergency Wetlands Resources Act of 1986

Water Quality Act of 1987

Airport Noise and Capacity Act of 1990

Clean Air Act Amendments of 1990

Intermodal Surface Transportation Efficiency Act of 1991

Energy Policy Act of 1992

Executive Order 12898, "Environmental Justice," 1997

Source: Louis F. Cohn (as amended).

---

[5] 23 CFR 771.111(h)(2)(i).

The impacts of many of the laws and regulations listed in Tables 8–1 and 8–2, and their historical context, are discussed in the publication *Urban Transportation Planning in the U.S.— A Historical Overview*[6] and *Summary of Environmental Legislation Affecting Transportation*.[7] The role of the federal government in environmental protection has been one of increasing prominence through the passage of more stringent environmental laws written for specific purposes and through the re-interpretation of existing laws for environmental applications. For example the Rivers and Harbors Act of 1899, originally intended to provide protection for marine vessels in navigable waterways, has more recently given the U.S. Army Corps of Engineers control to restrict construction, dumping, and dredging in the navigable waters of the United States for environmental purposes. The Fish and Wildlife Coordination Act of 1958, promulgated to protect endangered or threaten species, required consultation with the U.S. Fish and Wildlife Service when any body of water in the United States was to be modified in any way. This consultation was to be with "a view toward conservation of wildlife resources by preventing loss of and damage to such resources. . . ." This consultation requirement, along with the increased public concern for the environment has lead to the inclusion of environmental impacts in the planning process.

The Federal Aid Highway Act of 1962 created the 3C Planning Process, mandating that projects in urban areas must be developed through a continuing, cooperative, and comprehensive effort. "Comprehensive" was later defined by ten basic elements that included environmental amenities and aesthetics. The Control and Abatement of Aircraft Noise and Sonic Boom Act of 1968 mandated aircraft noise emission limits on aircraft that were type certified after December 31, 1969. This requirement has been the most significant of any legislative efforts in lowering airport noise levels.

Table 8–2 Federal Environmental Regulations and Directives Influencing Transportation

USGS Section 9 Bridge Permit, 1967

FAR PART 36, "Noise Standards: Aircraft Type and Airworthiness Certification," 1969

FHPM 7-7-1, "Process Guidelines," 1974[b]

USCOE/EPA Section 404, 1977[a]

DOT Order 5660.1A, "Preservation of the Nation's Wetlands," 1978

EPA/DOT, "Transportation-Air Quality Guidelines," 1978

CEQ Guidelines, "Regulations for Implementing the Procedural Provisions of NEPA," 1978[a]

DOT Order 5610.1C, "Procedures for Considering Environmental Impact," 1979[a]

DHUD, Noise Criteria and Standards, 1979[a]

FHPM 7-7-9, Air Quality Guidelines, 1979[a,b]

FHPM 7-7-3-2, "Location and Hydraulic Design of Encroachments on Floodplains," 1979[b]

DOT, F&W Compliance Procedures, 1979 (draft)[a]

EPA, "Noise Emission Standards for Interstate Rail Carriers," 1980

FHPM 7-7-2, "Environmental Impact and Related Statements," 1980[a,b]

23 CFR 771, "Environmental Impact and Related Statements," 1980[a]

FAA Order 1050.1D, "Policies and Procedures for Considering Environmental Impacts," 1983[a]

FAR Part 150, "Airport Noise Compatibility Planning," 1984

FHWA Technical Advisory T 6640.8A, "Guidance for Preparing and Processing Environmental and Section 4(f) documents," 1987

14 CFR 91, "Transition to an All Stage III Fleet Operating in the 48 Contiguous United States and the District of Columbia," 1991

14 CFR 161, "Notice and Approval of Airport Noise and Access Restrictions," 1991

23 CFR 772, "Procedures for Abatement of Highway Traffic Noise and Construction Noise," 1991 (formerly FHPM 7-7-3) as amended 1997

[a] Represents revision of earlier version.
[b] Since withdrawn in regulation reduction effort.

Source: Louis F. Cohn (as amended).

Environmental impact analysis became significantly more important to the planning process with the passage of NEPA. NEPA required the preparation of an EIS for "any major Federal action that may significantly affect the environment." This watershed law has had more impact on public works project development than any law in U.S. history. The completeness and accuracy of the EIS has proven to be vital to the successful completion of large-scale projects. Litigation challenging the thoroughness of an EIS has lead to significant delays in the completion of many projects. The Federal Aid Highway Act of 1970 implemented NEPA for the highway program; and it required the Secretary of Transportation to "promulgate guidelines designed to assure that possible adverse economic, social, and environmental effects . . ."[8] be fully considered. Quantitative guidelines were specified in the areas of air, noise, and water pollution.

---

[6] *Urban Transportation Planning in the U.S.—A Historical Overview*, DOT-T-93-02 (Washington, D.C.: U.S. Department of Transportation, November 1992).

[7] *Summary of Environmental Legislation Affecting Transportation* (Washington, D.C.: U.S. Department of Transportation, Federal Highway Administration, February 1996).

[8] 23 U.S.C. Sec. 109(h).

Table 8–3　Noise and Air Quality Models for Transportation

NCHRP 78 (Noise), 1969	MOBILE 2 (Air), 1980
NCHRP 117 (Noise), 1971	STAMINA 2.0/OPTIMA (Noise), 1982
CALINE (Air), 1972	INM 3.8 (Noise), 1982
TSC Model (Noise), 1972	TEXIN (Air), 1983
NCHRP 144 (Noise), 1973	EDMS (Air), 1985
Hiway (Air), 1975	INM 3.9 (Noise), 1988
NCHRP 173/174 (Noise), 1976	CALINE 4 (Air), 1989
CALINE 2 (Air), 1977	MOBILE4 (Air), 1989
FHWA Model (Noise), 1978	MOBILE4.1 (Air), 1991
EPA Volume 9 (Air), 1978	CAL3QHC (Air), 1991
MOBILE 1 (Air), 1978	MOBILE5 (Air), 1992
INM (Noise), 1978	MOBILE5a (Air), 1993
SNAP and STAMINA 1.0 (Noise), 1979	PART5 (Air), 1994
CALINE 3 (Air), 1979	BASINS (Water), 1996
INM 2.7 (Noise), 1979	INM 5.1 (Noise), 1997
IMM (Air), 1978	TNM (Noise), 1998
HIWAY 2 (Air), 1980	BASINS 2.0 (Water), 1998

Source: Louis F. Cohn (as amended).

Executive Order 11990, "Protection of Wetlands," 1977, draws its legislative authority from NEPA; and like all executive orders it has the force of law. The order requires federal agencies to "take action to minimize destruction, loss, or degradation of wetlands, and to preserve and enhance the natural and beneficial values of wetlands . . ."[9] and to develop an integrated, public-oriented process. Executive Order 11990 defines wetlands to include "swamps, marshes, bogs, and similar areas such as sloughs, potholes, wet meadows, river overflows, mud flats, and natural ponds."[10]

CAAA of 1970 ushered in a new era, as the federal government effectively took over control of the air pollution problem from state and local governments. These amendments required that all Air Quality Control Regions (AQCRs, the nation's urban areas), attain the National Ambient Air Quality Standards (NAAQS) for transportation-related pollutants by May 31, 1975. These pollutants include carbon monoxide (CO), hydrocarbons, nitrogen oxides (NO_x), and photochemical oxidants. A State Implementation Plan (SIP), which includes transportation control plans, was required for AQCRs not in compliance by 1970. The 1977 Amendments moved the date of compliance back to 1982 and additionally required an analysis of eighteen very specific "Reasonably Available Control Measures" for possible implementation. These measures included the requirement for the implementation of a motor vehicle inspection and maintenance program if compliance were not possible by 1982, in which case compliance could be delayed until 1987.

The Aviation Safety and Noise Abatement Act of 1979 shifted much of the activity involved in aviation noise control to local and regional airport authorities. The opportunity to create an optional Airport Noise and Land Use Compatibility Program was authorized in this law and codified in Part 150 of the Federal Aviation Regulations. A successfully completed "Part 150" study makes an airport eligible for significant extra federal funds for noise abatement purposes.

The Concept of Predictive Modeling

The purpose of impact analysis is to evaluate the likely results of implementing proposed transportation actions. Therefore, it is necessary for the environmental analyst to look into the future in a quantitative way to perform the necessary evaluations and compare the results with the guidelines and standards set forth in the environmental laws and regulations. This is accomplished through the use of algorithmic prediction models that are usually available in computer program form. Table 8–3 contains a list of the major computer models that have been developed for noise analysis and air quality within the last thirty or so years. In 1996, the EPA issued its first version of Better Assessment Science Integrating Point and Nonpoint

---

[9] Executive Order 11990, *Protection of Wetlands*, May 24, 1977, Sec. 1(a).

[10] Executive Order 11990, *Protection of Wetlands*, May 24, 1977, Sect. 7(c).

Sources (BASINS) to provide a model capable of analyzing an integrated watershed analysis including both point and nonpoint pollutant sources.

Noise Analysis

Basics of Sound

Sound, as we usually think of it, is the propagation of air pressure waves through the air, caused by a vibration or disturbance. The sound may be pleasurable or annoying; the latter is generally referred to as noise. Community noise is a mixture of varied, unrelated sounds, the sources of which are numerous. The primary concerns are transportation noise, industrial noise, and noises typical of community living such as the sounds of children playing, air conditioners, and fan noise. Each source has its own specific characteristics that contribute in combination with all of these community noise sources, which is also known as the loudness of the sound.[11] Some basic concepts are presented here to help understand the nature of sound.

Frequency, loudness, and duration are important considerations when dealing with sound impacts. The combination of these characteristics determine whether the sound is pleasant, informative, or annoying. Frequency, the number of oscillations per second of a periodic wave, refers to the tonal quality of noise. Frequency, the speed of sound, and wavelength are all interrelated, as illustrated by the following mathematical relationship:

$$f = c/\lambda \qquad (8{-}1)$$

where: f = frequency (Hz)

c = speed of sound (feet or meters per second)

λ = wavelength (feet or meters)

Table 8–4   One-Third Octave Band Characteristics

Lower Band Limit	Center	Upper Band Limit
14.1	16	17.8
17.8	20	22.4
22.4	25	28.2
28.2	31.5	33.5
35.5	40	44.7
44.7	50	56.2
56.2	63	70.8
70.8	80	98.1
89.1	100	112
112	125	141
141	160	178
178	200	224
224	250	282
282	315	355
355	400	447
447	500	562
562	630	708
708	800	891
891	1,000	1,122
1,122	1,250	1,413
1,413	1,600	1,778
1,778	2,000	2,239
2,239	2,500	2,818
2,818	3,150	3,548
3,548	4,000	4,467
4,467	5,000	5,623
5,623	6,300	7,079
7,079	8,000	8,013
8,913	10,000	11,220
11,220	12,500	14,130
14,130	16,000	17,780
17,780	20,000	22,390

The units of frequency, Hertz (Hz), are equivalent to cycles per second (i.e., 1,000 Hz means that the sound wave is oscillating one thousand times each second). For analytical purposes, frequencies are commonly grouped in octave bands or 1/3-octave bands. Table 8–4 displays the frequency ranges for 1/3-octave band groupings.

As for the human ear, low and high frequencies are "filtered-out" on the A-weighted scale. Figure 8–1 contains a plot of this weighting scheme and two other weighting schemes (B and C) used for other purposes. Figure 8–2 shows typical noise levels to provide the reader with a reference.

The Sound Pressure Level (SPL), or amplitude, is a measure of the strength or magnitude of the pressure wave of sound; and it is described by the man-made unit, a decibel (dB). SPL, in decibels, is calculated from the square of the ratio of the acoustic air pressure (p) to a reference pressure (p_o, generally 2×10^{-5} Newtons/meter^2) placed on a logarithmic scale, and then multiplied by 10. Mathematically:

---

[11] L.L. Beranek, Ed., *Noise and Vibration Control,* Revised Edition (Washington, D.C.: Institute of Noise Control Engineering, 1988).

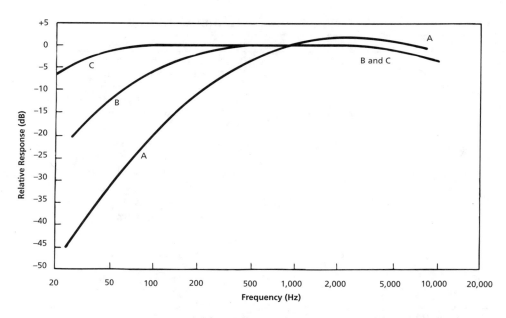

Figure 8–1 Sound Level Frequency Spectrum

$$SPL(dB) = 10 \log_{10}(p/p_o)^2 \qquad (8\text{–}2)$$

This relationship is important because it indicates that decibels do not add algebraically, but logarithmically. Mathematically:

$$SPL(dB) = 10 \log_{10}\left(\sum_{i=1}^{N} 10^{SPL_i/10}\right) \qquad (8\text{–}3)$$

where: SPL_i = any partial sound pressure level that adds to the total sound level

It is important to note that if the source number doubles, only a 3 dB increase in noise levels would be expected if all other parameters remain constant. This relationship is especially important when considering that the human ear also performs in a logarithmic manner. When the noise source is doubled, a 3 dB increase occurs; and a healthy ear can just perceive the change in intensity. A 10 dB change in noise levels is perceived as a doubling of noise to the same ear but would require ten times the number of sources.

The duration of the sound is also an important factor in assessing the impacts. If a sound lasts only for a fraction of a second (impulse noise), it may be briefly disturbing (e.g., a firecracker); but it usually would not interfere with ongoing activities. Noise that persists for long time periods (e.g., traffic noise), however, can have an impact on activities. The analyst usually takes this element into consideration using descriptors that will be discussed later. The remainder of this chapter will concentrate on the transportation-related noise associated with aircraft, trains, and automobiles. Other concepts will be presented as needed to provide the reader with an understanding of terms, methodologies, and regulations.

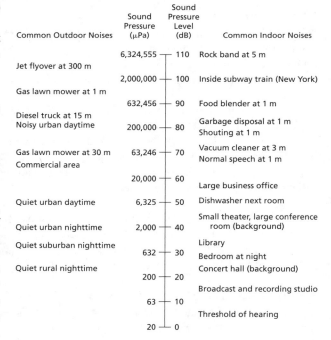

Figure 8–2 Common Indoor and Outdoor Noises

Table 8–5   Noise Abatement Criteria

Activity Category	$L_{eq}(h)^1$	$L_{10}(h)^1$	Description of Activity Category
A	57 (exterior)	60 (exterior)	Lands on which serenity and quiet are of extraordinary significance and serve an important public need and where the preservation of those qualities is required if the area is to continue to serve its intended purpose
B	67 (exterior)	70 (exterior)	Picnic areas, recreation areas, playgrounds, active sports areas, parks, residences, motels, hotels, schools, churches, libraries. and hospitals
C	72 (exterior)	75 (exterior)	Developed lands, properties, or activities not included in categories A and B table
D	—	—	Undeveloped lands
E	52 (interior)	55 (interior)	Residences, hotels, motels, public meeting rooms, schools, churches, libraries, hospitals, and auditoriums

^{1} Defined in the previous section.

Source: Title 23 United States Code, Chapter 772.

Highway Traffic Noise Analysis

Sounds emanating from highway traffic must be considered for two prime reasons: (1) the conscientious traffic/design engineer wants to build the best highway with the least negative impacts to the community as possible; and (2) many times needed funding depends on the successful completion of project environmental assessments, including the analysis of the impact of traffic noise on area residents.

Although there is no one national policy or methodology for all types of community noise analysis, the most used and relevant for traffic noise are the FHWA regulations. These regulations, included in Title 23 of the U.S. Code of Federal Regulations, Part 772,[12] prescribe Noise Abatement Criteria (NAC) as well as an analysis methodology. Table 8–5 shows the abatement criteria levels. It should be noted that the NAC levels are not standards, but they are levels at which FHWA has determined that noise is of sufficient magnitude that abatement must be considered. The regulation itself (23 CFR 772) is the noise standard mandated by federal law.

The methodology prescribed by 23 CFR 772 requires that priority consideration be given to outdoor areas where human activity usually occurs. If outdoor activity does not occur on a regular basis, the indoor criteria must be evaluated. The reader should note that the criteria levels are given as A-weighted decibels (i.e., weighted in a similar fashion that the human ear would perceive the noise).

The FHWA methodology specifies a detailed analysis procedure to evaluate traffic noise. First, existing "baseline" traffic noise levels are established. Modeling is permissible to determine the existing traffic noise levels if no other significant noise source is in the area of evaluation. Otherwise, measurements should be taken.

Once existing levels are established, future levels based on expected traffic growth are calculated and compared to both the existing noise level and the criteria. This comparison will determine if an impact will occur as a result of the proposed highway project. An impact will occur under either of two conditions. First, a future noise level that represents a "substantial increase" over existing noise levels (defined as 10 to 15 decibels by most state highway agencies), regardless of the beginning noise level, is considered an impact. Secondly, if the NAC are approached or exceeded (Table 8–5), abatement measures must be investigated. The NAC are expressed in two descriptors (L_{10} and L_{eq}) for both indoor and outdoor locations and various land use types.

[12] 23 CFR 772, 1997.

Other criteria for community noise levels have been established in states, local municipalities, and other countries. For example, the Department of Housing and Urban Development (HUD) have developed criteria specific to that agency's housing projects. The noise analyst should be aware that other criteria exist because any highway project generating noise that would affect another agency's project may also require an assessment of additional noise criteria. Accordingly, the traffic engineer should always review all applicable criteria before final design.

The FHWA Traffic Noise Methodology

The FHWA methodology is more than just a mathematical model. It is a method for evaluating existing and future traffic noise, determining the effects a project might have on abutting land use, and providing guidance on when noise abatement should be considered.[13]

As with all evaluation methods, a base case must be established for comparative purposes. In traffic noise evaluations the base case is usually defined as the existing noise environment. If a highway already exists in the planned corridor, it should be determined if the traffic is the major noise source. If the noise levels of the highway exceeds other continuing community noise levels by 10 dBA, then the highway should be considered the dominant noise source. If there is no existing highway, measurements should be made to establish the existing noise levels. Measurements should be carefully made and should be representative of the area. Many times, existing noise contours are desirable for use in the required environmental documentation; and this procedure requires multiple samples. During measurements, care should also be taken to use the proper equipment (at the proper settings), weather observations should be recorded, and careful calibrations are a must.[14]

If a highway already exists in the corridor of interest, and it is the major noise source, the FHWA permits modeling to be used to establish the existing noise environment. In this case, and for future predictions, the FHWA Traffic Noise Model in the form of a computer model is used.

Manual calculations have all but disappeared because of implementation of computer programs representing the FHWA model. The most used of these models is a program called the Transportation Noise Model (TNM). TNM predicts the traffic noise level at specified points (receivers), based on the user's representation of the study site. Complete details on the programs and their use are included in the user manual.[15]

One additional consideration is that the FHWA regulation 23 CFR 772 specifies the analysis period should be ". . . the worst hourly traffic noise impact on a regular basis for the design year. . . ." This is usually taken to mean that the loudest hour should be considered in noise evaluations. Of significance is that the loudest hour does not always occur during rush hour because vehicle noise emission is directly dependent upon speed. As the Level of Service decreases, noise levels may also decrease. Traffic conditions in which large trucks are at their daily peak and in which a Level of Service E exists will usually represent the loudest hour.

The descriptor used is also very important. The L_{10} (1 hour) descriptor is allowed for FHWA analysis, and specifies a percentile noise level that is exceeded for ten percent of the time. However, the L_{eq} (1 hour) descriptor has become the preferred traffic noise descriptor. The descriptor L_{eq} is based on the average acoustic intensity over time. Or more simply put, the equivalent noise energy of a steady, unvarying tone, over the same time period. This descriptor is represented mathematically by:

$$L_{eq} = 10 \ \log \frac{1}{t_2 - t_1} \int_{t_1}^{t_2} 10^{Li/10} \qquad (8\text{–}4)$$

---

[13] C.W. Menge et al., *FHWA Traffic Noise Model, Version 1.0, Technical Manual*, DOT-VNTSC-98-2 (Washington, D.C.: Federal Highway Administration, 1998).

[14] C.S.Y. Lee and G. Fleming, *Measurement of Highway-Related Noise*, FHWA-PD-96-046, DOT-VNTSC-FHWA-96-5 (Washington, D.C.: Federal Highway Administration, 1996).

[15] G. Anderson et al., *FHWA Traffic Noise Model, Version 1.0, User's Manual*, DOT-VNTSC-98-1 (Washington, D.C.: Federal Highway Administration, 1998).

where:
L_{eq} = the equivalent sound level over time period t [dB]

t = time period of consideration (usually one hour)

L_i = the A-weighted sound level over a short interval [dB]

In practice, the integral is evaluated as a summation of a finite number of time intervals.

Another descriptor commonly used in HUD community analysis is the L_{dn} or DNL (day-night level). The L_{dn} is simply the hourly L_{eq}s for twenty-four consecutive hours, logarithmically averaged, and a 10 dB penalty added from 10:00 P.M. until 7:00 A.M. (defined as "nighttime" hours). Mathematically:

$$Ldn = DNL = 10 \ \log \frac{1}{24} \left[\sum_{7 \ a.m.}^{10 \ p.m.} 10^{\frac{Leq \ (1 \ hour)}{10}} + \sum_{10 \ p.m.}^{7 \ a.m.} 10^{\frac{Leq \ (1 \ hour)}{10}} \right]$$ (8–5)

Traffic Noise Abatement

If an impact (as defined earlier) is identified, then abatement must be considered. Abatement can be accomplished at the source (e.g., quieter vehicles), along the sound path, or at the receiver. The noise analyst generally does not have control over the noise levels generated by individual vehicles. In contrast, a number of abatement options for the propagation path and receiver have been in wide use for a number of years. Abatement measures suggested by FHWA[16] include:

- traffic management measures (e.g., restriction or banning of truck traffic, a reduction in speed limits, exclusive lane designations),

- changes in the horizontal or vertical alignment of the highway,

- acquisition of property rights to allow construction of noise barriers,

- construction of noise barriers inside the right-of-way,

- acquisition of property for buffer zones, and

- noise insulation of public or nonprofit institutional structures.

The abatement measure selected must be feasible (practical) and reasonable (cost-effective). If the above listed measures are not determined to be both reasonable and feasible, then other innovative abatement measures may be recommended.

In practice, it is often not practical to implement traffic management measures, change the highway alignment, or insulate adjacent structures. As a result, noise barriers are the most frequently considered abatement measure. The use of diffractive barriers (walls or earth berms) have been used successfully to "block" the sound propagation path. Figure 8–3 depicts the typical use of a highway noise barrier. The "shadow zone" refers to the area of decreased noise levels caused by the barrier diffraction.

Detailed analysis is required to properly design these barriers. The TNM computer program was developed for this purpose and is used for most noise barrier designs in the United States. When the TNM is initially run, options are available to include a base height barrier and up to three iterations of a user input height increment. From this input, the acoustic contributions to a receiver noise level for the nonbarrier case, the base case, and up to six evenly spaced increments from the base case are calculated and stored in a separate output file. This file can be used by the TNM in an interactive session to evaluate each roadway segment contribution to each receiver, while varying the height of each noise barrier section over the limits of the input. Also shown by Figure 8–3 are transmittal and reflected wave paths. To allow for an

---

[16] *Procedures for Abatement of Highway Traffic Noise*, Title 23 Code of Federal Regulations, Part 772 (Washington, D.C.: Federal Highway Administration, 1997).

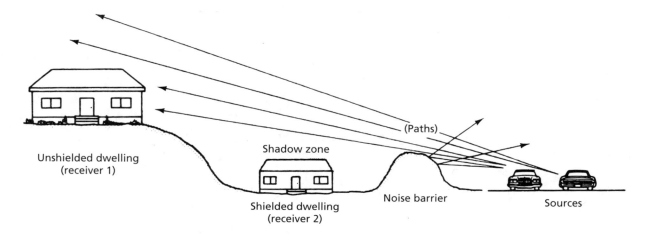

Figure 8–3   The Effect of a Noise Barrier on Approaching Sound

efficient barrier, the barrier must be acoustically opaque. That is, a material of sufficient mass, with no openings or cracks, must be used. Materials that have been used along highways include earth berms, concrete, masonry walls, steel, wood, glass, and plexiglass. Reflection from these walls (excluding earth berms) may cause increased noise levels or reduced barrier effectiveness on the other side of the roadway. If this reflective wave is determined to be a problem, absorptive treatment or tilting of the wall (at about 15 degrees) have both been used as a remedy.

During analysis of any transportation noise problem, other considerations are often present that are not included in the previously described models or methodology. For example, little consideration has been given to using vegetation as an alternative noise abatement measure. In fact, in certain situations, sufficient noise reduction is attained with properly planted and maintained vegetative screens.[17] Application of vegetative screens for noise abatement will often provide real noise abatement benefits to areas otherwise considered ineligible for noise abatement because of excessive cost of conventional abatement measures.

Airport Noise Analysis

The evaluation of aircraft noise is similar to that of traffic noise, except that the analysis is usually only performed when the aircraft is near the earth's surface, such as in the vicinity of an airport. With the rapid growth of air traffic, airport noise is becoming a major consideration for noise-sensitive areas located close to busy airports.

As with traffic noise evaluations, a base case must be established. Future predictions of alternate scenarios, including the do-nothing scenario, must be evaluated for some future year and compared to existing conditions. While measurements are made at some airports, modeling is often used to establish existing aircraft-generated noise levels. The Federal Aviation Administration's (FAA) preferred model for airport noise evaluations is the Integrated Noise Model (INM) version 5.1.[18]

The noise and operational characteristics of most commercial aircraft have been defined and are contained in the INM data base.[19] The operational mode of the aircraft is also extremely important when considering sound levels. Generally, as power increases, so does the sound level. This means that on takeoff, with near 100 percent throttle settings, and because of the close proximity to receivers, sound levels are the loudest and of the greatest concern.

---

[17] R.A. Harris and L.F. Cohn, "Use of Vegetation for Abatement of Highway Traffic Noise," *Journal of Urban Planning and Development*, Vol. 113, No. 2 (New York, N.Y.: American Society of Civil Engineers, 1987), pp. 127–138.

[18] N. Olmstead, *Integrated Noise Model, Version 5.1 User's Manual*, FAA-AEE-96-02 (Washington, D.C.: Federal Aviation Administration, 1996).

[19] Olmstead (1996).

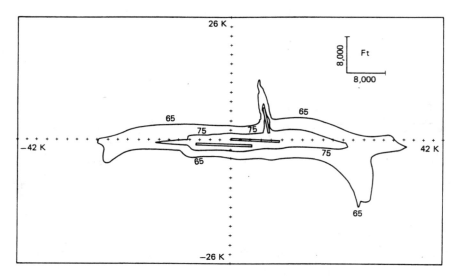

Figure 8–4 A Plot of Noise Contours Using the Integrated Noise Model

As with traffic noise, several descriptors are used in quantifying aircraft-generated noise. The L_{dn} is the most commonly used descriptor. Two other descriptors, the Composite Noise Rating (CNR) and the Noise Exposure Forecast (NEF), are seldom used in analysis today but are briefly discussed for completeness.

The CNR has been used for both military and commercial airports since the early 1960s. CNR is a 24-hour measure and is calculated from the Perceived Noise Level (PNL) near airports; it depends on daytime and nighttime aircraft operations where nighttime and ground runup operations are penalty weighted. The PNL (in dB) is a rating of the "noisiness" of sound and is calculated from sound pressure levels measured in 1/3-octave frequency bands.

The NEF is also a 24-hour descriptor with nighttime and runup operation penalties. It is based on the Effective Perceived Noise Level (EPNL) measure. EPNL is a single number loudness rating of the complex aircraft flyover sound. It is calculated allowing for the duration of flyovers and the presence of audible pure tones.

Another descriptor that is in common use in California is the Community Noise Equivalent Level (CNEL). This is a 24-hour descriptor that incorporates an energy average, with penalty weighting for nighttime hours much like L_{dn}. CNEL differs from L_{dn} in that the evening penalty weighting is a 3 dB step function to account for activity interference.

Other descriptors exist, and the analyst must be sure to use the proper descriptor to comply with project requirements. Airport noise models, such as INM, allow a selection of the output descriptor. Although local and state ordinances must be reviewed, the primary review agency in the United States is the FAA. The impact criterion established by FAA is the 65 L_{dn}.

It is usually not practical to select all individual receivers for study in an airport noise analysis. Instead, a typical output of INM is the plotting of a noise contour. A typical noise contour output is shown by Figure 8–4. This contour is plotted to a scale corresponding to a local land use map, and overlain on that map. Using this "noise exposure map," neighborhoods that are located inside a specific noise contour, such as the 65 dB contour, can be determined.

Airport Noise Abatement

FAA has identified thirty-seven noise control strategy categories (Table 8–6) applicable to airport noise abatement efforts. These abatement strategies focus on the propagation path (and distance) as well as control at the receiver. Control at the source has also been quite effective for aircraft. Federal Aviation Regulations (FAR), Part 36, mandated procedures to gradually introduce quieter aircraft into the U.S. fleet. These regulations are based on three stages, and Stage III is the quietest aircraft. Stage III aircraft (e.g., a Boeing 757) are now dominating the fleet, and Stage I and II aircraft have all but disappeared in commercial operations in the United States. These quieter aircraft have greatly reduced noise impacts in the vicinity of airports; however, increased development in the vicinity of airports has limited the overall benefits.

The FAA has made funds and assistance available for airport noise control under FAR, Part 150. By following a prescribed evaluation plan and the implementation of selected measures outlined in the 37 abatement categories, funds are available to assist individual airports in addressing noise problems.

Rail Noise Analysis

Rail noise analysis is very similar to that of highway traffic noise because each is a line source. That is, each must move along predetermined paths. However, rail noise evaluation is complicated by classification yard activities, wheel squeal, vibrations, and for the catenary noise of electric engine operations.

As with the other forms of transportation noise analysis, the existing case should be established first so that predictions of project impacts can be evaluated. Because of the lack of a good prediction model, measurement of the existing condition is highly recommended. Along tracks, these measurements should be typically made at 100 feet from the centerline. At classification yards the measurements should be made at the property line. These locations are suggested so that a comparison to the Federal Railroad Administration (FRA) Standards is possible. It should be noted that problems usually occur only for improperly operating locomotives because the standards are not restrictive. Typical levels are lower than the standards for train passbys and at classification yards.

Table 8–6 FAA Noise Control Strategy Categories

Category Number	Description
1	State noise law
2	Local noise law or ordinance
3	Airport master plan
4	ANCLUC plan
5	Part 150, Noise exposure map approved
6	Part 150, Noise compatibility plan approved
7	Development of an EIS
8	Noise monitoring equipment: Temporary or permanent
9	Restriction on ground runup
10	Limit on the number of operations by hour, day, month, year, or noise capacity
11	Preferential runway system
12	Runway restrictions imposed for specific aircraft type
13	Use restriction by aircraft type or class
14	Use restriction based on noise levels
15	Use restriction based on Part 36
16	Use restriction based on AC 36-3
17	Complete curfew
18	Arrivals and/or departures over a body of water
19	Displaced runway threshold
20	Rotational runway system
21	Maximum safe climb on takeoff
22	Takeoff thrust reduction
23	Reverse thrust limits
24	Flight training restriction
25	Weight or thrust limit
26	Informal flight operation restriction
27	Zoning
28	Purchase land for noise control
29	Use of capital improvements to direct development
30	Building codes and permits to control noise
31	Noise easements
32	Purchase assurance
33	Soundproofing programs
34	Noise use fees
35	Shift operations to a reliever airport
36	Local pattern restrictions
37	Navigational aid assisted departure

Source: Federal Aviation Administration, *Noise Abatement and Compatibility for Airports,* Advisory Circular AC-150/50204, 1983.

Although no formal FRA model exists for predicting noise levels along tracks, it has become common to use a 30 log speed relationship for conventional diesel operations.[20] That is:

$$L_{max} = 30 \log V + \text{constant} \tag{8–6}$$

where: V = speed in mph

This relationship does not hold for the newer high-speed rail evaluations and a 40 log V relationship is suggested.[21] Measurements at classification yards may be "scaled" according to the future level of operations for a particular project. This may be done using Equation 8–3. Other analysis ideas for urban rail transit are presented in a Federal Transit

---

[20] C.E. Hansen, *Environmental Noise Assessment of Railroad Electrification,* Inter-Noise '76 Proceedings (Washington, D.C.: Institute of Noise Control Engineering, 1971).

[21] R.L. Wayson and W. Bowlby, "Noise and Air Pollution of High Speed Rail Systems," *ASCE Journal of Transportation Engineering,* 115(1) (Washington, D.C.: American Society of Civil Engineers), pp. 20–36.

Administration handbook.[22] Vibration and infra-noise are also considerations when dealing with rail activities. Many times the vibration effects overshadow the noise considerations. The analyst must be careful not to overlook such problems during analysis.

Rail Noise Abatement

Four prime areas of abatement have been used for railroad noise. These are: (1) diffraction, using walls or berms; (2) reduction of rail squeal with special track; (3) dampening of track noise with special fasteners, ties, or wheels; and (4) increased separation distance to the receiver. The use of walls or berms is applied as with traffic noise with one significant exception. The guided system allows walls to be placed very close to the rails and makes the barrier much more effective for a smaller height of wall. Rail/wheel interaction causing squeal may be reduced with lubrication, special track, dampened wheels, or the use of barriers. Track noise, caused by vibration of the track, may be reduced with stiffer fasteners, rubber pads, or wheel dampeners. Increased separation relies on decreased noise levels at the receiver due to increased distance and, hence, increased geometric spreading. The exact abatement measure, or combination of measures, usually depends on the project. Accordingly, the analyst should be careful to pick the best method for the least cost.

Air Quality

The 1990 Clean Air Act Amendments and the Intermodal Surface Transportation Efficiency Act of 1991

The passage of CAAA and ISTEA effected significant changes in the requirements for both the planning and analysis of proposed transportation projects. The CAAA are important because they provide more stringent sanctions for a failure to attain NAAQS. In the past, sanctions could only be applied for the failure to submit a SIP. Under the CAAA, sanctions can be applied if a state fails to make all required submissions, the EPA disapproves of a SIP, or an area fails to attain the NAAQS. Nonattainment areas are now classified according to the type of pollutant exceeding the NAAQS and by the level of severity of the exceedance.

While areas with higher levels of pollution have longer periods of time to reach attainment, the penalties for failure to achieve attainment are more severe. In addition, areas must now show how they will meet the attainment deadline and display adequate real progress in the interim. Specific transportation sanctions, such as withholding of approval of federal aid highway projects, are now included for a failure to demonstrate reasonable progress towards attainment.

The CAAA addresses the transportation planning issue in Section 108(e) where it directs the EPA to "maintain a continuous air-transportation quality planning process, update the 1978 Transportation-Air Quality Planning Guidelines and publish guidance on the development and implementation of transportation and other measures necessary to demonstrate and maintain attainment of National Ambient Air Quality Standards." Such guidelines include:

- methods to identify and evaluate alternative planning and control activities;

- methods of reviewing plans on a regular basis as conditions change or new information is presented;

- identification of funds and other resources necessary to implement the plan, including interagency agreements on providing such funds; and

- methods to assure participation by the public in all phases of the planning process.

The overall effect of the CAAA is to require that transportation planning incorporate air quality improvement needs along with mobility and capacity needs. All resulting plans must adhere to this requirement; and transportation plans cannot

---

[22] C.E. Hansen, *Transit Noise and Vibration Assessment*, DOT-T-95-16 (Washington, D.C.: Federal Transit Administration, 1995).

create new NAAQS violations, increase the frequency or severity of existing NAAQS violations, or delay attainment of the NAAQS. A major impact has been to shift a greater responsibility for improving air quality to the transportation community. In addition, the CAAA places greater accountability on state and local governments to provide the planning that will bring an area into attainment.

Under the CAAA, the U.S. Department of Transportation (DOT) may exempt grants from sanctions for safety projects, if the primary purpose of the project is to solve a demonstrated safety problem. In addition, the U.S. DOT may also grant exemptions for the following project types:

- capital programs for public transit,

- construction or restriction of bus or high-occupancy vehicle roads or lanes,

- planning to reduce employee work–trip-related vehicle emissions,

- traffic flow improvements that achieve a net emission reduction,

- fringe parking facilities,

- programs to limit vehicle use in downtown or other congested areas, and

- programs for accident management that would reduce congestion.

In addition, the EPA may also elect to exempt transportation-related projects that could demonstrate an improvement in air quality. In summary, the sanctions are aimed at the development and implementation of projects that move people while discouraging capacity increases for single occupancy vehicles.

The 1970 CAAA requires implementing federal agencies to ensure that an action is in conformance with an approved SIP. The conformity provisions of the 1990 CAAA shift the emphasis from conforming to a SIP to conforming to a SIP's purpose of eliminating and reducing the severity and number of violations of the NAAQS.[23] This provision places a greater burden on the transportation program by shifting the conformity process from a plan comparison during the system planning process, to an analytical process during the development of plans, programs, and projects. As a result, it will significantly increase the contributions that transportation plans, programs, and projects must make toward air quality improvements in nonattainment areas.

ISTEA provides state and local officials with a funding system that allows greater flexibility to include alternative modes of transportation in the Transportation Implementation Plan (TIP). It also requires that the planning processes consider such factors as land use and the "overall social, economic, energy, and environmental effects of transportation decisions."[24] Going even further, Michael D. Meyer states in *Moving Urban America* that "the federal program historically emphasized transportation investments as an end in itself; ISTEA provides transportation funds to meet other societal goals, thus viewing transportation as a means of achieving some greater aim."[25] For those concerned with direct environmental impacts, ISTEA specifically links transportation funding to the goals set forth in the CAAA. In addition, the act strengthens the role of the Metropolitan Planning Organization (MPO) in developing the TIP. Finally, ISTEA established the Congestion Mitigation and Air Quality Program that provides funds for transportation projects and programs such as transportation control measures (TCMs) that are likely to contribute to the attainment of the NAAQS in ozone and CO nonattainment areas.

[23] J.M. Shrouds, *Transportation Provisions of the Clean Air Act Amendments of 1990* (Washington, D.C.: Federal Highway Administration, November 1990).

[24] 23 U.S.C. 135(c)(11).

[25] Michael D. Meyer, "Planning: The Challenge of Being the Glue," *Moving Urban America*, Transportation Research Board Special Report 237 (Washington, D.C.: National Academy Press, 1993).

Description of Air Pollutants

An air pollutant can be defined as any natural atmospheric component that reaches such a concentration that it adversely affects human health or public welfare. Accordingly, many atmospheric components that were once not considered pollutants are now a concern. A good example of this is carbon dioxide and its effect on the global warming problem. Because of this, the air quality analyst must define all relevant pollutants during the analysis.

The pollutants that are of concern when assessing the impacts of transportation projects are CO, NO_x, suspended particulate matter (PM_{10}), lead (Pb), and ozone (O_3). Volatile organic carbons (VOCs) are a concern because they are a direct precursor for ozone, a secondary pollutant (formed after being emitted). Ozone is indirectly controlled by limiting the two prime precursors from transportation, NO_x and VOCs. Sulfur oxides are also a regulated air pollutant, but they are not emitted in substantial amounts by transportation sources and generally are neglected during analysis. Pollutant amounts are reported in concentration units distributed in an air volume. Two common units are used: (1) micrograms per cubic meter and (2) parts per million. Micrograms per cubic meter is a mass per unit volume unit and changes with parameters such as temperature. Parts per million is a volume ratio of the pollutant to the air of concern and does not vary with temperature. The NAAQS are reported in both units and are listed in Table 8–7. Table 8–8 shows the relative transportation contribution of these pollutants.

Carbon Monoxide

Carbon monoxide (CO) is a colorless, odorless gas and is emitted primarily from the incomplete combustion of fossil fuels. Incomplete combustion is most likely to occur when the air–fuel ratio of vehicle engines is low. Significant emissions of CO can occur during vehicle starts, especially cold starts, rapid accelerations, operation under poor maintenance conditions, and at high altitudes where the "thin" air reduces the availability of oxygen. Nationwide, eighty percent of CO emissions are from transportation sources with over sixty percent of total emissions coming from highway sources.[26] CO is absorbed

Table 8–7 National Ambient Air Quality Standards

Pollutant	Standard Value		Standard Type
Carbon Monoxide (CO)			
8-hour Average	9 ppm	10 mg/m^3	Primary
1-hour Average	35 ppm	40 mg/m^3	Primary
Nitrogen Dioxide (NO_2)			
Annual Arithmetic Mean	0.053 ppm	100 μg/m^3	Primary & Secondary
Ozone (O_3)			
1-hour Average*	0.12 ppm	235 μg/m^3	Primary & Secondary
8-hour Average	0.08 ppm	157 μg/m^3	Primary & Secondary
Lead (Pb)			
Quarterly Average		1.5 μg/m^3	Primary & Secondary
Particulate < 10 micrometers (PM_{10})			
Annual Arithmetic Mean		50 μg/m^3	Primary & Secondary
24-hour Average		150 μg/m^3	Primary & Secondary
Particulate < 2.5 micrometers ($PM_{2.5}$)			
Annual Arithmetic Mean		15 μg/m^3	Primary & Secondary
24-hour Average		65 μg/m^3	Primary & Secondary
Sulfur Dioxide (SO_2)			
Annual Arithmetic Mean	0.03 ppm	80 μg/m^3	Primary
24-hour Average	0.14 ppm	365 μg/m^3	Primary
3-hour Average	0.50 ppm	1300 μg/m^3	Secondary

* The ozone 1-hour standard applies only to areas that were designated nonattainment when the ozone 8-hour standard was adopted in July 1997. This provision allows a smooth, legal, and practical transition to the 8-hour standard.

Source: U.S. Environmental Protection Agency (EPA), Office of Air Quality Planning and Standards, January 6, 1998.

---

[26] *National Air Pollutant Trends, 1900–1995* (Washington, D.C.: U.S. Environmental Protection Agency, October 1996).

Table 8–8 National U.S. Emissions Estimates, 1995 (Thousands of Metric Tons per Year)

Source Category	SO$_2$	NO$_x$	VOCs	CO	Particulate Matter PM$_{10}$	PM$_{2.5}$*
Transportation						
Highway	276	6,899	5,537	53,183	276	266
Aircraft	7	138	191	953	44	
Railroad	65	898	41	118	45	266
Other	192	1,682	1,812	13,101	268	
Subtotal	541	9,617	7,580	67,355	632	532
Stationary source fuel combustion						
Electric utilities	10,898	5,645	32	294	234	100
Industrial furnaces	2,763	2,846	122	610	217	161
Commercial	380	281	15	122	30	
Residential	164	360	474	2,566	339	459
Subtotal	1,420	69,133	643	3,592	820	720
Industrial processes						
Chemical & allied product mfg.	427	257	1,467	2,029	60	39
Metals processing	653	76	70	2,017	132	87
Petroleum & related industries	349	83	570	344	24	19
Other industrial processes	397	293	383	696	357	228
Subtotal	1,827	709	2,489	5,086	572	373
Waste disposal & recycling	34	77	2,187	1,602	230	179
Storage & transport	5	3	1,636	59	54	24
Miscellaneous						
Forest fires	0	0	124	1,180	—	
Slash/prescribed burning	0	0	162	3,901	—	
Other burning	7	207	117	775	660	6,651
Agriculture & forestry	—	—	—	—	7,610	
Fugitive dust	—	—	—	—	26,135	
Miscellaneous organic solvents	1	3	5,801	2	2	2
Subtotal	8	210	6,204	5,858	34,407	6,653
Wind erosion	—	—	—	—	1,962	706
Total	16,620	19,748	2,040	83,551	38,677	9,186

* PM$_{2.5}$ emission totals are for 1990.

Source: U.S. EPA, *National Air Pollutant Emissions Trends, 1900–1995*, October, 1996.

into the blood stream through the respiratory tract and reacts primarily with the hemoglobin in the red blood cells, decreasing the blood's oxygen-carrying capacity. Carbon monoxide can impair visual perception, learning functions, and manual dexterity especially in infants, the elderly, and persons with heart or respiratory diseases.

Suspended Particulate Matter

Suspended particulate matter may be any solid or liquid that is dispersed in the air. The particles created by combustion sources are small and may remain suspended in the atmosphere for relatively long time periods. The particulate matter of concern can be divided into two categories: particles under 2.5 micrometers in diameter—PM$_{2.5}$, and particles less than 10 micrometers in diameter—PM$_{10}$. PM$_{10}$ greater than 2.5 micrometers usually come from traffic-generated dust from unpaved roads or from agricultural fields. PM$_{2.5}$ are emitted from vehicle exhaust as well as industrial and residential combustion. They may also result from chemical reactions in the atmosphere involving combustion-generated sulfur dioxide, NO$_x$, and VOCs. The Environmental Protection Agency's (EPA) scientific review concludes that the fine particle, PM$_{2.5}$, can penetrate deeply into the lungs and can cause premature death and respiratory problems.[27] PM^{10} can aggravate asthma, increase respiratory problems in children and the elderly, and result in lower respiratory tract defense levels.

[27] *EPA's Updated Clean Air Standards* (Washington, D.C.: U.S. Environmental Protection Agency, July 16, 1997).

Volatile Organic Carbons

VOCs are usually the result of incomplete combustion of petroleum products (excluding methane) or from volatilization. At low concentrations, typical of transportation sources, VOCs are not particularly harmful; but they are a major element in the formation of atmospheric free radicals that may react with other compounds to form ozone. High ambient levels of VOCs, especially ethylene, may cause vegetation damage. Hydrocarbons may be emitted when fuels are not completely oxidized during combustion or from evaporative losses.

Nitrogen Oxides

Nitrogen oxides (NO_x) are primarily nitric oxide (NO) as emitted from transportation sources, but with an almost immediate transformation into nitrogen dioxide (NO_2). The amount of NO_x emitted from transportation sources depends on the temperature (ambient and engine), humidity, residence time in the engine, and combustion chamber design. NO has not been shown to constitute any adverse health effects at the concentrations typical near transportation systems; however, the resulting concentrations of NO_2 may have adverse effects on the respiratory system. Exposure to NO_2 at levels near the NAAQS has been shown to reduce breathing efficiency and increase lung irritation in the elderly and people with pre-existing pulmonary problems as well as to increase respiratory illness, lung congestion, and bronchitis in children. NO_2 is also a prime precursor for ozone. NO_2 is a light-brown gas that can cause decreased visibility. Damage to plant life and dye fading and discoloration of white fabrics may occur at high NO_2 concentrations.[28]

Ozone

Ozone is formed in the atmosphere by a complex set of photochemical reactions involving VOCs and NO_x in the presence of sunlight. Since ozone is not directly emitted by sources, it is defined as a secondary pollutant. Violations of the ozone NAAQS usually occur in the summer months when temperature and the amount of sunlight are highest. Even at low levels, ozone can cause respiratory problems and aggravated asthma in the elderly, children, and others with respiratory disease. Long-term exposure can cause loss of lung function, lowered immunity to disease, asthma attacks, and respiratory problems. The oxidants can also cause damage to vegetation and deterioration of materials. Ozone has a light gray appearance and can cause decreased visibility.

Lead

The use of unleaded gasoline and other fuels has all but eliminated emissions of lead from transportation systems. Accordingly, transportation-related analyses no longer consider this pollutant to be transportation related and will not be considered further.

Emissions

Direct emissions from highway vehicles, rail sources, and aircraft must be determined as the basis for several levels of analyses that are required to assess the impacts of transportation on air quality. On a regional scale, the emissions from these sources can be used to develop an emissions inventory for an area. In addition, the VOC and NO_x emissions, along with information on the emission locations, can be used in large-scale dispersion models like the Urban Airshed Model to evaluate ozone levels. On a smaller scale, CO emissions are used in models like CALINE4 and CAL3QHC to determine localized concentrations of CO along roadways and at intersections, respectively.

The initial step in determining the impacts of transportation-related activities is to calculate the direct emissions from the sources. For highways, the sources are the vehicles that travel the various segments of the transportation system under scrutiny. Railroads must be analyzed for the emissions from trains along the main transportation lines as well as from activities at the rail yards. Aircraft analyses must include consideration of ground-level activities that include additional power generation, airport traffic operations, and ground support equipment. Emission rates must be determined from all of these types of equipment with consideration given for the type of equipment used and the mode of operation. An extensive compilation of emission rates expressed as emission factors can be found in the EPA publication *Compilation*

---

[28] Joel L. Horowitz, *Air Quality Analysis for Urban Transportation Planning* (Cambridge, Mass.: The MIT Press, 1982).

of Air Pollutant Emission Factors, Volume II: Mobile Sources (commonly referred to as "AP-42"). This volume has two sections: I, Highway Vehicles and II, Non-road Mobile Sources. Section I provides extensive information about the highway vehicle emission factor model, currently MOBILE5a; and it includes numerous tables of both values used and produced by the model. Section II provides emission factor information for a wide range of non-road mobile sources (including agricultural equipment, construction equipment, lawn and garden equipment, aircraft and aircraft engines, locomotives, marine vessels, and miscellaneous types of equipment).

Highway Vehicles

Highway vehicle emissions result primarily from the incomplete combustion of the fuel and from fuel evaporation and are generally referred to as exhaust emissions and evaporative emissions, respectively. Since evaporative emissions do not involve any combustion process, they only contain hydrocarbon emissions. The factors that affect the evaporative emission rates are the same that usually affect evaporation such as temperature, altitude, and the vapor pressure of the fuel. Evaporative emissions are subdivided into the following six categories:

1. Hot soak emissions—evaporation of fuel in areas like the fuel injector or carburetor after a hot engine is turned off.

2. Diurnal emissions—diurnal temperature variations cause gas in the fuel tank to expand and escape at the gasoline tank vent; the vapors are routed to a charcoal canister where they are absorbed and purged to the running engine.

3. Running losses—fuel in the tank volatilizes in the tank and is routed to the charcoal canister where they are absorbed; emissions occur when the rate of formation exceed the capacity of the canister to purge them to the engine.

4. Resting losses—result from vapors penetrating parts of the evaporative control system, migrating out of the carbon canister, or evaporating liquid fuel during vehicle inactivity.

5. Refueling losses—vapors in the fuel tank that are displaced by the added liquid; also from spillage.

6. Crankcase emissions—result from defective positive crankcase ventilation systems.

Exhaust emissions are also divided into categories. Four categories are associated with engine mode operations:

1. Cold starts—emissions resulting from starting the engine when it has been allowed to cool for at least four hours for noncatalyst vehicles or at least one hour for catalyst vehicles; under these conditions a rich fuel mixture is required causing higher emission levels.

2. Hot starts—emissions resulting from starting the engine when it has only been off a short time; the emission levels are not as high as for a cold-start.

3. Hot stabilized—emissions from operation of the vehicle after the engine and emission control system have reached operating temperatures; these emissions are highly dependent on vehicle speed and power demand.

4. Idle emissions

Since the exhaust emissions result from the combustion process, the emission levels are dependent on any factors that affect the ability of the engine to consume the fuel efficiently. Determining the emissions for a large number of vehicles under actual driving conditions becomes a very complex procedure. Exhaust emission may vary with the type of vehicle, the manner in which the vehicle is driven, the type of facility on which the vehicle is driven, the Level of Service of the facility on which it is driven, the age and wear on the vehicle, and the speed and acceleration of the vehicle. Both the evaporative and exhaust emission categories and the types of pollutants emitted are listed in Table 8–9.

The current method for determining these highway vehicle emissions is through the use of the MOBILE5a computer program (except in California where the EMFAC7g program is used). Both programs determine an emission rate for a particular vehicular fleet mix in grams per mile. Since MOBILE5a is more widely used, important aspects of the specific methodology will be discussed. The core of the program is a set of Basic Emission Rates (BERs), or Baseline Exhaust Emission Rates, that are derived from actual vehicles. The BER is basically a linear or piecewise linear curve representing increases in the emission rate in grams per mile as the accumulated vehicle mileage increases. The BERs are defined by a zero-mile level, measured from new vehicles, and one or two deterioration rates that represent the expected increase in emissions from reduced efficiency of the emission control system along with increased emissions from the engine.

Since the emission rates were developed under standard test conditions, they have to be adjusted to more closely represent actual use, such as the ambient temperature, the fuel type, and the type of inspection and maintenance program implemented in the area. In addition, the vehicle fleet is represented by eight vehicle types:

1. light-duty gasoline vehicles,

2. light-duty gasoline trucks under 6,000 lbs. gross vehicle weight,

3. light-duty gasoline trucks with a gross vehicle weight between 6,000 lbs. and 8,500 lbs.,

4. heavy-duty gasoline vehicles,

5. light-duty diesel vehicles,

6. light-duty diesel trucks,

7. heavy-duty diesel vehicles, and

8. motorcycles.

Table 8–9 Emission Producing Vehicle Activities

Emission Producing Vehicle Activity	Type of Emissions Produced
Vehicle Miles Traveled	Running Exhaust Emissions (CO, VOC, NO_x, PM_{10}, SO_x) Running Evaporative Emissions (VOC)
Cold Engine Starts	Elevated Running Exhaust Emissions (CO, VOC, NO_x, PM_{10}, SO_x)
Warm or Hot Engine Starts	Elevated Running Exhaust Emissions (CO, VOC, NO_x, PM_{10}, SO_x)
Engine "Hot Soaks" (shut-downs)	Evaporative Emissions (VOC)
Engine Idling	Running Exhaust Emissions (CO, VOC, NO_x, PM_{10}, SO_x) Running Evaporative Emissions (VOC)
Exposure to diurnal and Multi-Day Diurnal Temperature Fluctuation	Evaporative Emissions (VOC)
Vehicle Refueling	Evaporative Emissions (VOC)
Modal Behavior (e.g., High Power Demand, Heavy Engine Loads, or Engine Motoring)	Elevated Running Exhaust Emissions (CO, VOC, NO_x, PM_{10}, SO_x)

Source: Guensler, R., Vehicle Emission Rates and Average Vehicle Operating Speeds, Institute of Transportation Studies, University of California, Davis, Ph.D. Dissertation, (Sacramento, CA: December, 1993), UCD-ITS-RR-93-24.

Local vehicle registration numbers can be used to determine the percentage of the vehicle fleet for each vehicle type. The vehicle age distribution can be defined from the local registration information as well and used in the program. In addition, the vehicle miles traveled (VMT) percentage for each vehicle type is included.

Other inputs are many and varied and become quite involved. These include all of the previously mentioned variables as well as inputs for control device tampering, gasoline volatility class, percentage of hot starts and cold starts, inspection maintenance parameters, percentage of catalyst and noncatalyst vehicles, air-conditioner use, extra loads on vehicles, and low versus high altitudes.

After the program is successfully and properly executed, an output file lists the exhaust, refueling, and evaporative emissions for each vehicle type. Also included is a composite emission factor that is a weighted average based on the VMT mix input. Emission factors in grams per mile are generated for HCs, CO, and NO_x. These emission factors are then multiplied by the VMT for the area under study to arrive at the total weight of pollutants emitted.

Rail Sources

In 1990, the CAAA required that the EPA establish emission standards for newly manufactured and newly remanufactured diesel-powered locomotives and locomotive engines that had previously been unregulated. Subsequently, the EPA issued new standards and emission factors for locomotives in December 1997. As can be seen in Tables 8–10 and 8–11, NO_x emissions are the primary area of concern. The emission standards were developed along the lines of the standards for heavy duty trucks with emissions levels expressed in terms of grams per brake-horsepower-hour. These standards become effective in the year 2000, and in order to allow manufacturers time to adapt to them, different standards were developed for the three different tiers shown in Table 8–12. Separate standards were also devised for differences in the primary usage of the locomotive for either line-haul duties or switch duties. The EPA developed test cycles for the line-haul and switch duties to test individual engines. The standards for the combined tier levels and duty cycles are shown in Table 8–13 and Table 8–14.

People mover systems and high-speed ground transportation systems (commonly called high-speed rail, but including magnetic levitation) can also be analyzed using AP-42 in an indirect way. Since most of these systems are electric in

Table 8–10   1995 National Emission Inventories: All Sources, Mobile Sources, and Locomotives (Millions of Metric Tons)

Emission	Total from All Sources	Mobile Sources	Locomotives
NO_x	19.7	9.62	0.90
PM_{10}	38.7	0.63	0.045
VOC	20.7	7.58	0.041
CO	83.6	67.36	0.118

Source: *National Air Pollutant Emissions Trends, 1900–1995*, Washington, D.C.: U.S. Environmental Protection Agency, October 1996.

Table 8–11   Locomotive Contributions to National Inventory in 1995 as a Percentage of All Sources and of Mobile Sources

Emission	Percentage of All Sources Contributed by Locomotives	Percentage of Mobile Sources Contributed by Locomotives
NO_x	4.57	9.36
PM_{10}	0.12	7.14
VOC	0.20	0.54
CO	0.14	0.18

Source: *National Air Pollutant Emissions Trends, 1900–1995*, Washington, D.C.: U.S. Environmental Protection Agency, October 1996.

Table 8–12   Tier Levels for Locomotive Engine Standards

Standard	Affected Locomotives
Uncontrolled	Manufactured before 1973, Electric Locomotives, and Historic Steam-Powered Locomotives
Tier 0	Manufactured from 1973 through 2001
Tier 1	Manufactured from 2002 through 2004
Tier 2	Manufactured after 2004

Source: *Final Emissions Standards for Locomotives*, EPA-420-F-97-048, Washington, D.C.: U.S. Environmental Protection Agency, December 1997.

Table 8–13   Exhaust Emissions Standards for Locomotives

| Tier and Duty-Cycle | Gaseous and Particulate Emmissions (g/bhp-hr) | | | |
	HC^1	CO	NO_x	PM
Tier 0 line-haul duty cycle	1.00	5.0	9.5	0.60
Tier 0 switch duty cycle	2.10	8.0	14.0	0.72
Tier 1 line-haul duty cycle	0.55	2.2	7.4	0.45
Tier 1 switch duty cycle	1.20	2.5	11.0	0.54
Tier 2 line-haul duty cycle	0.30	1.5	5.5	0.20
Tier 2 switch duty cycle	0.60	2.4	8.1	0.24

[1] HC standards are in the form of THC for diesel, bio-diesel, or any combination of fuels with diesel as the primary fuel; NMHC for natural gas, or any combination of fuels where natural gas is the primary fuel; and THCE for alcohol, or any combination of fuels where alcohol is the primary fuel.

Source: *Final Emissions Standards for Locomotives*, EPA-420-F-97-048, Washington, D.C.: U.S. Environmental Protection Agency, December 1977.

Table 8–14   Smoke Standards for Locomotives (Percent Opacity—Normalized)

	Steady-State	30-Second Peak	3-Second Peak
Tier 0	30	40	50
Tier 1	25	40	50
Tier 2	20	40	50

Source: *Final Emissions Standards for Locomotives*, EPA-420-F-97-048, Washington, D.C.: U.S. Environmental Protection Agency, December 1997.

nature, an energy consideration analysis must first be conducted. Then, the incremental requirements at the power plant, allowing for line loss and power plant efficiency, can be calculated. The additional emissions can then be equated to the electric rail system.

Aircraft and Support Facilities

Air travel in the United States grew at a rate of about five percent per year over a decade, from 1985 to 1995,[29] resulting in greater concerns about the environmental impacts associated with it. This increase in air travel, along with the commensurate growth in airport capacities and support services, has led to increased concern in recent years about the air quality impacts of these facilities. The primary pollutants that need to be considered from aircraft operations are CO, NO_x, VOCs, and particulate matter under ten microns in diameter. Sometimes small amounts of sulfur dioxide may be emitted as a result of sulfur in the jet fuel, but it usually does not need to be considered in an analysis.

Since the total operations of an airport include fixed ground-based activities and facilities as well as mobile sources such as the aircraft, the air quality impacts of airports must be considered from both the perspective of a stationary and a mobile source. If the airport is located in a nonattainment area, the stationary source must conform to the SIP by ensuring that any emissions resulting from an airport project must not exceed the emission forecast in the emission budget for that airport. There are general conformity threshold rates, as shown in Table 8–15, that presume conformity for projects that do not exceed these rates. Also, any airport access project in a nonattainment or maintenance area that is "reasonably significant" (i.e., a transportation project that serves regional transportation needs and would normally be included in the modeling of a metropolitan area's transportation network[30]) must also satisfy a transportation conformity analysis. In order to determine the emissions inventory, the air quality impacts must be considered for both the operation of the aircraft and for the equipment and facilities that comprise the support services. The sources of emissions may include:

- aircraft,
- ground support equipment,
- ground access vehicle, and
- stationary sources.

Table 8–15   General Conformity Threshold Rates

Nonattainment Status	VOCs (Ozone Nonattainment Areas)	NO_x (Ozone Nonattainment Areas)	Carbon Monoxide	Sulfur or Nitrogen Oxides (SO_2 or NO_x)	Particulate Matter
Extreme	10	10	NA	NA	NA
Severe	25	25	NA	NA	NA
Serious	50	50	100	NA	70
Marginal (inside an ozone transport region)	50	100	NA	NA	NA
Marginal (outside an ozone transport region)	100	100	NA	NA	NA
Moderate (inside an ozone transport region)	50	100	100	100	100
Moderate (outside an ozone transport region)	100	100	100	100	100
Maintenance (inside an ozone transport region)	50	100	100	100	100
Maintenance (outside an ozone transport region)	100	100	100	100	100

Source: *Air Quality Procedures for Civilian Airports and Air Force Bases*, FAA-AEE-97-03, Washington, D.C.: U.S. Department of Transportation, Federal Aviation Administration, April 1997.

[29] *National Transportation Statistics 1997*, DOT-VNTSC-BTS-96-4 (Washington, D.C.: Bureau of National Statistics, December 1996).

[30] FAA-AEE-97-03 (Washington, D.C.: Federal Aviation Administration, April 1997).

Aircraft Emissions

The process of determining aircraft emissions begins with determining the makeup of the aircraft fleet that typically utilizes the airport. The mix of the commercial fleet can be found in *Airport Activity Statistics of Certified Route Air Carriers*[31] that is published annually by the FAA. The emission factors for each aircraft, however, are dependent on the type of engine used by the aircraft, and determining the engine type may be difficult. If specific engine data are not available, the EPA-recommended procedure is to use the frequency of occurrence of each engine type on a particular aircraft as provided in *Air Pollution Mitigation Measures for Airports and Associated Activities*[32] and *Procedures for Emission Inventory Preparation, Volume IV: Mobile Sources*.[33] These publications also include information on alternative engine types if emission data are not available for the required aircraft.

The airport activity report also lists the number of takeoffs for each type of aircraft that is equivalent to the number of landing and takeoff cycles (LTO). The operations of aircraft within the atmospheric mixing zone, approximately 2,000 feet in height,[34] are defined as the LTO. There are six operating modes included in the typical LTO cycle:

1. Approach—from the moment the aircraft enters the mixing zone until it begins to land with the aircraft in a low-power mode.

2. Reverse thrust—approximately 15–30 seconds after touchdown when engines are engaged in high-power operation to slow the aircraft.

3. Taxi/idle-in—a low-power operation as the aircraft proceeds to the gate.

4. Taxi/idle-out—a low-power operation as the aircraft proceeds to the runway.

5. Takeoff—a high-power operation lasting from 30–45 seconds for commercial carriers.

6. Climbout—a high-power operation lasting from takeoff until the aircraft exits the mixing zone.

The emission inventory can then be calculated by determining the emission factor for each operational mode for each engine type and multiplying it by the time in each mode that each aircraft spends. The emission factors (listed in pounds of pollutant per 1,000 pounds of fuel) and fuel consumption (listed in pounds per minute) for commercial aircraft can be found in EPA's *Procedures for Emission Inventory Preparation*, Volume IV, Chapter 5, and in the International Civil Aviation Organization *Engine Exhaust Emissions Databank*.[35] Both the emission factors and fuel consumption are listed for each aircraft operating mode except for reverse thrust, which should use the same takeoff emission factors and fuel consumption rates. The emission factor for SO_x for all operation modes, based on the national average sulfur content of aviation fuels, is 0.54 lb/1000 lb.[36]

The emission inventory can be calculated in the same way for general aviation and air taxi aircraft if specific aircraft information is available, but the information is difficult to locate. The resulting inventory values may not differ significantly from the emissions calculated using a representative fleet mix.[37] While some information is available in *Procedures for Emission Inventory Preparation*, Volume IV, Chapter 5, the factors listed below, from the same reference, can be used. The airport activity for general aviation and air taxis can be found in *FAA Air Traffic Activity*.[38]

---

[31] *Airport Activity Statistics of Certified Route Air Carriers, Calendar Year 1994*, NTIS Report Number ADA 310183 (Washington, D.C.: Federal Aviation Administration, 1994).

[32] *Air Pollution Mitigation Measures for Airports and Associated Activity—Final Report*, ARB/R-94/534 or NTIS Number PB94-207610 (Sacramento, Calif.: California State Air Resources Board, May 1994).

[33] *Procedures for Emission Inventory Preparation, Volume IV: Mobile Sources (Revised)* (Ann Arbor, Mich.: U.S. Environmental Protection Agency, 1992).

[34] *Regulatory Support Document for Direct Final Rule for Control of Air Pollution from Aircraft and Aircraft Engines; Emission Standards and Test Procedures* (Washington D.C.: Environmental Protection Agency, April 29, 1997).

[35] D.H. Lister and R.J. Murrell, *ICAO Engine Exhaust Emissions Databank*, First Edition, Draft, prepared for the International Civil Aviation Organization (United Kingdom: Defense Research Agency, December 1993).

[36] Federal Aviation Administration (1997).

[37] *Air Pollution Mitigation Measures for Airports and Associated Activity—Final Report*.

[38] *FAA Air Traffic Activity Fiscal Year 1989*, NTIS Report Number ADA 226063 (Washington, D.C.: Federal Aviation Administration, 1989).

For general aviation aircraft:

- HC = 0.394 pounds per LTO
- CO = 12.014 pounds per LTO
- NO_x = 0.065 pounds per LTO
- SO_2 = 0.010 pounds per LTO

For air taxi aircraft:

- HC = 1.234 pounds per LTO
- CO = 28.130 pounds per LTO
- NO_x = 0.158 pounds per LTO
- SO_2 = 0.015 pounds per LTO

The actual computation of the emissions for the inventory can be attained through the use of the EPA and FAA preferred guideline model, *Emission and Dispersion Modeling System* (EDMS). EDMS contains information of the aircraft and engine emission factors, as well as assignments of ground support equipment and aerospace ground equipment.

Ground Support Equipment

Emissions from ground support equipment (GSE) are approximately 2 to 6 percent of total emissions at commercial airports.[39] Table 8–16 shows some of the more common types of GSEs. In addition, there is a wide range of equipment (e.g., generators, pickups, lawnmowers) for various airport support services, such as administration. The majority of GSEs are powered by either conventional diesel or gasoline motors, but some are powered by alternative fuel or electric motors. The main factors that affect the emissions of conventional and alternative fuel GSEs are brake-horsepower, load factor, usage, and emissions index. Site-specific data on the GSE types, brake-horsepower, load factor, and usage may be obtainable from aircraft and airport operators; and it should be used if it is available. In the absence of site-specific data, this information can be obtained from the FAA and EPA's *Technical Data to Support FAA's Advisory Circular on Reducing Emissions from Commercial Aviation*.[40] Emission factors can also be found in this circular as well as in *Regulatory Strategies for Off-Highway Equipment*[41] and *Feasibility of Controlling Emissions from Off-Road, Heavy-Duty Construction Equipment*.[42]

Ground Access Vehicles

Ground access vehicles include vehicles in parking lots and on airport and airport-access roadways. The emissions from these vehicles can be determined using the same process used for highway vehicles.

---

[39] *Air Pollution Mitigation Measures for Airports and Associated Activity—Final Report.*

[40] *Technical Data to Support FAA's Advisory Circular on Reducing Emissions from Commercial Aviation* (Washington, D.C.: U.S. Department of Transportation and U.S. Environmental Protection Agency, 1996).

[41] *Regulatory Strategies for Off-Highway Equipment,* prepared for California Air Resources Board (Arlington, Va.: Energy and Environmental Analysis, Inc., 1992).

[42] *Feasibility of Controlling Emission From Off-Road, Heavy-Duty Construction Equipment*, prepared for California Air Resources Board (Arlington, Va.: Energy and Environmental Analysis, Inc., 1988).

Table 8–16 Airport Ground Support Equipment

Air Start Units	Provide large volumes of compressed air to an aircraft's main engines for starting. Air start units are also called air compressors.
Air Conditioning Units	Provide conditioned air to ventilate and cool parked aircraft.
Aircraft Tugs	Tow aircraft in the terminal gate area or on the tarmac. They also tow aircraft to and from hangers for maintenance. These are broken into two categories: tugs for narrow body aircraft and tugs for wide body aircraft.
Baggage Tractors	Equipment used at airports to haul baggage between the aircraft and the terminal.
Belt Loaders	Mobile conveyor belts used at airports to move baggage between the ground and the aircraft hold.
Buses	Shuttle personnel between facility locations.
Cargo Moving Equipment	Various types of equipment employed to move baggage and other cargo around the facility and to and from aircraft. This category includes forklifts, lifts, and cargo loaders.
Cars	Move personnel around the facility.
De-icers	Vehicles used to transport, heat, and spray de-icing fluid.
Ground Heaters	Mobile units that provide heated air to heat the parked aircraft.
Ground Power Unit (GPU)	Mobile ground-based generator units that supply aircraft with electricity while they are parked at the facility. GPUs are also called generators.
Light Carts	Mobile carts that provide light.
Other	Small miscellaneous types of equipment commonly found at facilities such as compressors, scrubbers, sweepers, and specialized units.
Pickups	Move personnel and equipment around the facility.
Service Vehicles	Specially modified vehicles to service aircraft at facilities. This category includes fuel trucks, maintenance trucks, service trucks, lavatory trucks, and bobtail tractors.
Vans	Move personnel and equipment around the facility.

Source: *Air Quality Procedures for Civilian Airports and Air Force Bases,* FAA-AEE-97-03, Washington, D.C.: U.S. Department of Transportation, Federal Aviation Administration, April 1997.

Stationary Sources

Stationary sources can be divided into two main categories: combustion and noncombustion sources. Combustion sources primarily include boilers, incinerators, generators, and space heaters. Emission factors for these sources can be found in AP-42 and then multiplied by the fuel usage rate to obtain the total emission. Noncombustion sources include fuel storage tanks, coating or painting operations, deicing operations, solvent degreasers, and sand or salt piles. Emission factors for these operations can be found in FAA's *Air Quality Procedures for Civilian Airports and Air Force Bases.*

Dispersion Modeling

Dispersion modeling is required to determine the pollutant concentrations in the area of the emission source so that these levels can be compared to the NAAQSs. The pollutants that are of primary concern at transportation sources are CO, NO_x, PM_{10}, and possibly SO_2. The emissions inventory discussed previously are used in area-wide planning, but these values cannot be directly compared to the NAAQS. Dispersion modeling is required to determine ambient concentrations caused by transportation systems in a micro-scale analysis. Pollutant concentrations are dependent on several meteorological factors and the rate at which pollutants are emitted. Therefore, dispersion modeling requires a determination of the relevant meteorological factors and the selection of the proper dispersion technique that will most closely represent the dispersion characteristics at the site under study.

Meteorology

The primary meteorological parameters that determine atmospheric dispersion are wind speed, wind direction, turbulent mixing, and the mixing depth. Relative humidity and barometric pressure are key parameters for chemical reactions and engine emissions, but they are usually neglected during the actual dispersion modeling process.

Wind direction is important because it determines the direction of pollutant transport (i.e., the pollutant plume moves downwind of the source). Determination of proper wind direction to use during project analysis is a simple matter for straight highways or rail lines; however, this process becomes more complex near intersections or airports where determining the worst-case may require significant analysis. For example, vehicle queuing, vehicle delay, shifting wind directions and speeds, as well as combinations of these parameters must be considered for each leg of an intersection. Some dispersion computer models will make this determination for the user. Other programs require multiple runs to determine the worst-case scenario.

Wind speed is important for two reasons. First, downwind concentrations are inversely proportional to the wind speed. In general, pollutants are dispersed over greater areas at a faster rate under greater wind speeds resulting in lower concentrations. Conversely, higher concentrations will be present under lower wind speeds. For a worst-case analysis, a wind speed of 1 meter per second is often used. Second, wind speed directly affects convective mixing of the pollutants. This is a complex relationship between surface roughness, the wind speed, and the thermal stability of the atmosphere. Higher surface roughness and wind speed along with lower atmospheric stability will promote more mixing and, therefore, lower surface pollutant concentrations.

Mixing height is the vertical distance at which pollutant mixing is expected to occur. This information is hard to determine and a worst-case scenario of 500 to 1,000 meters is used in most analyses. Selection of this parameter should be based on local experience and can be crucial in air quality analysis.

A wide variety of dispersion computer models exists for the analysis of air quality from transportation sources. Many of these are based on the Gaussian dispersion model, which assumes that pollutant concentrations are distributed normally about the emission source. Adaptations to this basic model have led to the development of various analytical tools. The user should be acquainted with the limitation and assumptions of each before selecting one for analysis. In addition, local or state guidelines may be specific on which models are acceptable for an analysis; and the user must be careful to contact the controlling authorities before proceeding with the analysis.

Highways

EPA recommends the use of the dispersion model CALINE3, which analyzes highways as line sources of pollutant emissions. This model requires some familiarity to use accurately, and the reader is directed to the user manual *CALINE3—A Versatile Dispersion Model for Predicting Air Pollutant Levels Near Highways and Arterial Streets*[43] for details. Appropriate discussion, however, is pertinent here.

Modeling of emissions as a line source simply represents all of the individual vehicle emissions over a finite highway segment as a uniform emission rate spread over the length of the segment. CALINE3 also assumes that all of the emissions are uniformly mixed in a zone extending to 3 meters on each side of the highway. The additional width accounts for horizontal dispersion resulting from the vehicle wake effect. The emission concentrations then decrease with distance from the mixing zone. Inputs to CALINE3 include the traffic parameters as well as X,Y coordinates to delineate the relationship of the highway geometry and the receptors. Weather parameters must also be included along with other variables, such as surface roughness, settling velocity, and mixing width.

It should be noted that these dispersion models require emission factors as an input and usually work in conjunction with the emission factor models discussed previously. Accordingly, outputs are usually limited to only predicting concentrations for CO, NO_x and VOCs. In practice, CO is usually the only pollutant predicted for micro-scale analysis due to the high reactivity of both the NO_x and VOC components that react to form ozone. Since ozone is a secondary pollutant dependent upon photochemical reactions, micro-scale modeling is not required.

Since the highest pollutant concentrations generally exist near intersections, considerable activity has occurred in recent years to develop models that address this situation. The EPA-recommended program, CAL3QHC, an intersection modeling program, is actually a variant of CALINE3 that uses CALINE3 along with a signalized intersection analysis

---

[43] *CALINE3—A Versatile Dispersion Model for Predicting Air Pollutant Levels Near Highways and Arterial Streets*, Report No. FHWA/CA/TL-79/23 (Sacramento, Calif.: Office of Transportation Laboratory, November 1979).

technique and Deterministic Queuing Theory to model traffic delays at intersections. Inputs to these intersection models are more complex than the free-flowing traffic models. Length of queue lines, delay times, intersection geometry, approach speeds, and many other parameters may all be required input according to the situation and the model selected. The reader is referred to *User's Guide to CAL3QHC Version 2.0: A Modeling Methodology for Predicting Pollutant Concentrations Near Roadway Intersections*[44] for details. Accordingly, the user must be aware of how the model is actually predicting to insure an understanding of the output. This is especially true since some of the outputs are several pages long and provide data in various formats.

Parking lots are generally modeled as area sources or multiple line sources. CALINE4 and PAL are most often used in this type analysis. Additional input variables are required to define the parking lot, vehicle movement, and rates of usage. A more complex problem is that of underground or stacked parking garages.

Rail Sources

No formal dispersion models have been developed for analysis of conventional rail. The Gaussian model, however, can be easily adapted to allow for rail yard analysis, where worst-case conditions are certain to occur. Also, the Gaussian equation can be adapted for use along rail lines to determine the worst-case conditions. In the case of electric operations, the same analysis needed for emission factors for on-site power production should be employed; and then one of the available EPA Gaussian Equations computer algorithms may be used for the dispersion analysis.

Aircraft

The primary dispersion model in common use in the United States is EDMS, which has been previously discussed. The complexity of using this model arises from determining, with reasonable accuracy, the frequency and magnitude of the emission sources resulting from runway usage and the presence of other sources, such as service vehicles, accessing motor vehicles, fueling operations and storage, and local stationary sources on airport property. The determination of the spacial and temporal distribution of these sources can be quite complex. Added to these problems is the added input requirement of determining the fleet mix, fleet schedule, and engine types. Engine types can change with aircraft types, year of manufacture, retrofitting, and customer preference. The collection of this data can be as demanding as the analysis. Meteorology, on the other hand, is usually readily available from the airport and is thus specific for a particular problem.

Analysis

In the preceding sections, the terms "micro-scale" and "worst-case" have been used as they apply to the overall analysis and reporting needed to accomplish project planning, environmental consideration, and needed regulatory concurrence. The following section addresses this terminology more specifically as it applies to a given project. However, the analyst should contact the controlling authorities before project analysis is begun to insure that the worst-case assumptions are acceptable.

Definition of Analysis Nomenclature

During project analysis only a small area, usually directly abutting the emission source, is analyzed. This small-scale analysis is known as a micro-scale analysis. MPOs and other government agencies that must deal with air pollution on a regional basis perform general analyses over much larger regions, and these are known as meso-scale analyses.

Meso-scale analysis is usually a very general planning procedure and often stops at the emission inventory stage. An emission inventory is a summation of the total pollutant load of a specified area using emission factors that are based on rates of activities. Emissions from all sources are summed for a defined area, much like an accounting procedure.

---

[44] *User's Guide to CAL3QHC Version 2.0: A Modeling Methodology for Predicting Pollutant Concentrations Near Roadway Intersections*, EPA-45 4/R-92-006 (Research Triangle Park, N.C.: U.S. Environmental Protection Agency, 1992).

This procedure provides the local planning authority with data on the total amount of emissions being emitted, usually on an annual basis. The emission inventory predictions required to show "reasonable further progress" are determined in the same manner, except that the analyst is required to make assumptions about the number and type of emission sources that will be present. Emission inventories are not directly comparable to the NAAQS because the data are in the form of total amounts (e.g., tons per year) of each regulated pollutant and not in the form of ambient concentrations. However, emission inventories are quite useful for planning because the planner may:

- determine a baseline of emission in the area for future planning,

- use the inventories to compare future area alternatives,

- determine if projects will allow the area to be in compliance with the SIP, and

- determine the effectiveness of TCMs.

Recently, use of area grid models, such as the Urban Airshed Model, in meso-scale planning has become common; and it is required in some nonattainment areas. This concept allows not only the area-wide emissions to be analyzed, but also allows estimates of the areal concentrations to determine if violations of the NAAQS will occur. The problem to date has been that the required gross assumptions lead to very inaccurate predictions. Continuing developments in computer technology and geographic information systems should help alleviate this problem.

During micro-scale analysis, worst-case scenarios are often used for analysis. The idea behind using a worst-case condition is that if the NAAQS are not violated in this case, then there is no worry of the standard being violated in the typical or real-world case. The problem is in defining the worst-case scenario. Worst-case assumptions usually include:

- a wind speed of 1 meter per second directly toward the receptor (or, in the case of intersections or airports, that direction which predicts the greatest concentration),

- a stable stability class (sometimes neutral ([D]) in urban areas),

- highest vehicle or aircraft movement hour of the day, and

- a mixing height of 500 to 1,000 meters.

The analyst should be aware that during micro-scale analysis local area background concentrations must be included. Once the project contribution to the local concentrations is calculated, it must be numerically summed with the local background. The background concentration will never be zero in an urban area, and it may actually be quite high. The background concentration accounts for other area activities and, when summed with the project concentration, predicts the overall pollutant concentration. This concentration is the value that should be compared to the NAAQS to determine if a violation of the specific pollutant standard will occur.

Highways

Local and state requirements for analysis of air quality from highways can vary from region to region; however, when dealing with projects that involve federal funds, FHWA is the lead agency. Any project that requires federal funds or approval must satisfy the conformity rule defined in 40 CFR 93. The conformity rule defines specific requirements that regulated highway projects must meet to establish that the project will not contribute to increases in air quality violations.

Actual project analysis can be stated in simplified terms as: (1) determine the worst hour of traffic; (2) perform dispersion modeling using the worst-case meteorology and the nearest sensitive receptors; and (3) if the NAAQS are approached or exceeded, evaluate possible mitigation measures. Actual procedures may be quite involved. Figure 8–5 is a flowchart of how project analyses might evolve. As mentioned above, the project must be shown to be in conformity with the SIP. Conformity with the SIP is a legal requirement (23 CFR part 770 and 49 CFR part 623) to ensure that projects are only implemented if they will not interfere with areas in violation of the NAAQS. Sanctions (the withholding of federal funds) can be implemented if these guidelines are not followed. Figure 8–6 is a flowchart of the procedures that should be followed to ensure compliance.

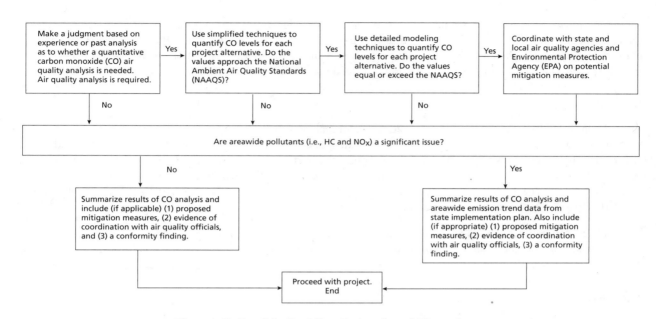

Figure 8–5   Air Quality Procedural Flowchart

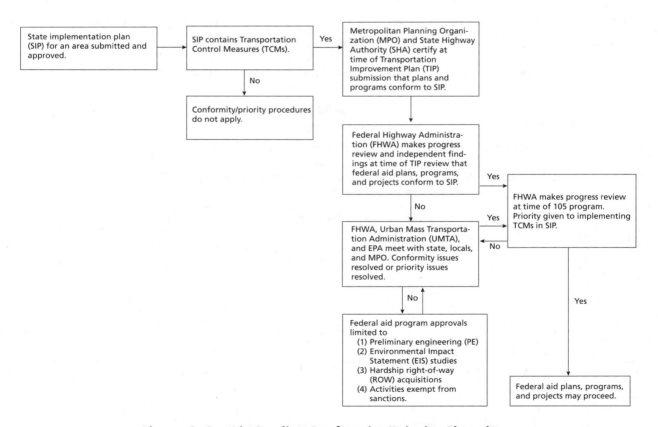

Figure 8–6   Air Quality Conformity/Priority Flowchart

Mitigation measures can be many and varied. Among the more significant are the reduction of congestion or delay; reduction of total vehicles (e.g., use of mass transit); changes in vehicle emissions (e.g., alternative fuels); and change in the distance between the traffic facility and the receptor, which allows more ventilation and reduced concentrations. In some places, such as tunnels or parking garages, forced ventilation may be required.

Rail Sources

The EPA has provided estimated average emission rates for locomotives in the three-tier levels as well as for uncontrolled locomotives as estimated in Table 8–17. These emission rates can be applied to the specific fleet mix and usage expected at the area under study to determine the contribution of rail activities to the emission inventory. Specifically, the expected fuel consumption of locomotives in each tier can be multiplied by the estimated emissions factor in grams per gallon. The EPA has developed fleet-average emission factors that consider the gradual introduction of controlled locomotives into the national fleet.

The analysis of rail operations is analogous to the highway environment. If a problem occurs, it will most likely be near a yard because of the actual numbers of locomotives. Violations, except under extreme conditions, are not likely. Mitigation options are limited.

Aircraft

In almost all cases, the FAA's guidelines are used during project analysis due to extensive use of federal funds at major airports. An airport survey[45] concluded that air quality analysis in U.S. airports primarily occurs only because of needed project environmental concurrence by regulating agencies. Several helpful documents are available from FAA for the analysis requirements, with the two most important being the *Airport Environmental Handbook*[46] and *Air Quality Procedures for Civilian Airports and Air Force Bases.*[47] AP-42 is also helpful.

The procedure for evaluating airport operations on ambient air quality can be summarized in four steps:

1. Determine if the airport exceeds 1,300,000 enplanements per year or 180,000 operations per year.[48]

2. If so, conduct an emission inventory; and check to see if the airport project conforms with the SIP requirements. Include both direct and indirect sources.

3. Conduct dispersion modeling at locations on and around the airport where vehicles slow down and idle, particularly roadway intersections. Dispersion modeling is typically done only for CO.

4. If the NAAQS are exceeded, evaluate mitigation measures.

Table 8–17   Estimated Emission Rates for Locomotives

	HC		CO		NO$_x$		PM	
	g/bhp-hr	g/gal	g/bhp-hr	g/gal	g/bhp-hr	g/gal	g/bhp-hr	g/gal
Uncontrolled line-haul*	0.48	10	1.28	26.6	13.0	270	0.32	6.7
Uncontrolled switch**	1.01	21	1.83	38.1	17.4	362	0.44	9.2
Tier 0 line-haul	0.48	10	1.28	26.6	8.6	178	0.32	6.7
Tier 0 switch	1.01	21	1.83	38.1	12.6	262	0.44	9.2
Tier 1 line-haul	0.47	9.8	1.28	26.6	6.7	139	0.32	6.7
Tier 1 switch	1.01	21	1.83	38.1	9.9	202	0.44	9.2
Tier 2 line-haul	0.26	5.4	1.28	26.6	5.0	103	0.17	3.6
Tier 2 switch	0.52	11	1.83	38.1	7.3	152	0.21	4.3

* Line-haul locomotives over the line-haul duty-cycle.
** Switch locomotives over the switch duty-cycle.

Source: *Emission Factors for Locomotives,* EPA-420-F-97-051 Washington, D.C.: U.S. Environmental Protection Agency, December 1997.

---

[45] R.L. Wayson and W. Bowlby, *Airport Air Quality Policy, Modeling, and Monitoring,* Project 90-180-6, Public Works (Canada: Nov. 1990).

[46] *Airport Environmental Handbook,* FAA Order 5050.4A (Washington, D.C.: Federal Aviation Administration, 1985).

[47] *Air Quality Procedures for Civilian Airports and Air Force Bases.*

[48] *Air Quality Procedures for Civilian Airports and Air Force Bases.*

As with highways, mitigation measures are numerous. The report *Air Pollution Mitigation Methods for Airports and Associated Activity*,[49] completed for the California Air Resource Board, presents several options for reducing emissions from aircraft use, changes in operational procedures, and changes in ground support equipment. Some of these options are the use of newer aircraft, reduced taxi/idle times (by airport layout, pushback before starting engines, high speed taxiways, and so forth), separation of the receptors and the airfield, and use of alternative fuels or electric motors for service vehicles. Other measures may also be used on a project-by-project basis.

Water Quality

Transportation systems can have significant effects on water quality through several mechanisms that can occur during construction, operation, and maintenance of the system. The problems that may arise are varied and are subject to a wide range of federal and state requirements that can slow or even stop a project. As is the case with many environmental laws, much of the legislation was developed with other objectives in mind; but they are now applied actively to transportation projects. It is important that the transportation planner be aware of the laws pertaining to water quality and be knowledgeable of some basic methods to limit the impacts of the transportation project on water quality. Table 8–18 lists the major legislation dealing with water quality that can affect the development of transportation projects.

Transportation projects can affect water quality through a wide range of direct and indirect causes that not only affect the quality, but also the quantity of water. Transportation projects, especially paved roads and highways, usually increase the volume of runoff in an area because of an increased amount of concrete surfaces, the removal of indigenous vegetation, and the increased compaction of the surrounding soil during construction. The increased runoff levels then carry elevated levels of pollutants into nearby bodies of water. Wetlands can be destroyed by the addition of fill material during construction or polluted from excess runoff. In addition, scenic rivers and lakes in protected wildlife areas may be considered by users as more valuable for wildlife habitats or recreational uses than the increased mobility resulting from the planned project. In some cases, the planner must show that no feasible alternative to the proposed

Table 8–18   Legislation and Regulations Concerning Water Quality

Legislation	Regulations Reference
Rivers and Harbors Appropriations Act of 1899	23 CFR 650 Subpart D and H; 33 CFR 114-115
The Clean Water Act 　Water Pollution Control Act of 1948 　The Federal Water Pollution Control Act of 1961 　The Clean Water Restoration Act of 1966 　Water Quality Improvement Act of 1970 　The Federal Water Pollution Control Act Amendments of 1972 　The Clean Water Act of 1977 　The Water Quality Act of 1987	DOT Order 5660.1A; 23 CFR 650; 　Subpart B, 771; 　33 CFR 209, 320–323, 325, 328, 329; 　40 CFR 121–125, 129–131, 133, 135–136, 230–23
The Coastal Zone Management Act of 1972, as amended in 1990	15 CFR 923, 926, 930
Endangered Species Act of 1973, as amended	7 CFR 355, 50 CFR 17, 23, 81, 222, 225–227, 402, 424, 450–453
Wild and Scenic Rivers Act	36 CFR 251, 297; 43 CFR 8350
Land and Water Conservation Fund Act	N/A
Executive Order 11988: Floodplain Management 　as amended by Executive Order 12148	DOT Order 5650.2; 23 CFR 650 Subpart A; 　23 CFR 771
Executive Order 11990: Protection of Wetlands	DOT Order 5660.1A; 23 CFR 777
Emergency Wetlands Resources Act of 1986	N/A
Intermodal Surface Transportation Efficiency Act of 1991, 　Wetlands Mitigation Banks, Sec. 1006–1007	23 CFR 771
Fish and Wildlife Coordination Act	N/A
Section 4(f) of the Department of Transportation Act	23 CFR 771.135

---

[49] *Air Pollution Mitigation Measures for Airports and Associated Activity—Final Report.*

project exists. The actual impacts of each project are dependent on the type of transportation project, the type of environment in which it is located, the construction methods that are employed, as well as the overall scale of the project.

EPA is emphasizing the analysis of water quality impacts within a watershed framework. It introduced software in 1996 for a more complete analysis of both water quality and flow changes resulting from project effects. This software, BASINS, is a geographic information system-based software that has the following attributes:

- facilitates examination of environmental information,

- provides an integrated watershed and modeling framework, and

- supports analysis of point and nonpoint source management alternatives.[50]

Runoff

Runoff is defined as a nonpoint source of pollutants because the effects on water quality are the result of the increased runoff over a large area, and the entry point into the environment is at an infinite number of locations that cannot be controlled individually. Changes in runoff resulting from a project can affect surface water quality, groundwater quality, flooding, and streambank/shoreline erosion. The increase in impermeable surface material results in higher peak flows during storm events.

The most common contaminants in highway runoff are heavy metals, inorganic salts, aromatic hydrocarbons, and suspended solids.[51] Solid materials, including heavy metals, result from the regular usage and passage of highway vehicles that drop oil, grease, rust, metals from brakepads and other parts that wear, and rubber particles. Highway maintenance operations can leave residues from salting and de-icing methods that result in residues of chlorine, calcium, and sodium.

Contaminated runoff can affect surface waters such as streams, rivers, ponds, and lakes that directly receive the pollutants. Some highways that connect developed areas follow valleys or terrain where topography tends to be less rugged and construction is less expensive. Consequently, highways are often in close proximity to streams, lakes, and wetlands offering little opportunity for the effects of runoff to be mitigated by natural infiltration and dispersion.

The introduction of contaminants into these waters can result in both contamination of the water itself and in contamination of the silt and mud at the bottom of these waters. Contaminated silt and mud can then re-introduce the contaminants into the water during construction activities that disturb the soil. Groundwater can be affected by contaminants that percolated through the soil and reach the water table. Because of the filtration effect of the soil, groundwater contamination from highway surface runoff is usually not a concern except possibly in areas with fractured rock or sinkholes in Karst that allow rapid drainage through the surface with little or no filtering. Considerable information about the amount of runoff and the concentrations of various pollutants in highway runoff can be found in the online report by the Center for Water Resources (CRWR), *A Review and Evaluation of Literature Pertaining to the Quantity and Control of Pollution From Highway Runoff and Construction.*[52]

Runoff can be controlled by a number of structural and nonstructural best management practices (BMPs) that can be found in FHWA's *Environmental Technology Brief*, "Is Highway Runoff a Problem?" Structural BMPs collect and capture the runoff until pollutants can settle or be filtered out. The use of structural BMPs can often require considerable open space, and they may therefore be limited to rural areas. Nonstructural BMPs are techniques that control the source of the pollutants. Some examples of each type are listed in Table 8–19. Further information concerning the performance

---

[50] U.S. Environmental Protection Agency, *About BASIN S 2*, Office of Water, http://www.epa.gov/OST/BASINS/basinsv1.htm.

[51] *Environmental Technology Brief*, "Is Highway Runoff a Serious Problem?," FHWA, Office of Engineering R&D, http://www.tfhrc.gov/hnr20/runoff/runoff.htm.

[52] Michael E. Barrett, Robert D. Zuber, E.R. Collins III, Joseph F. Malina Jr., Randall J. Charbeneau, and George H. Ward, *A Review and Evaluation of Literature Pertaining to the Quantity and Control of Pollution from Highway Runoff and Construction*, 2nd Edition, CRWR Online Report 95–5 (Austin, Texas: Center for Research in Water Resources, Bureau of Engineering Research, The University of Texas at Austin, April, 1995), http://www.ce.utexas.edu/centers/crwr/reports/online.html.

Table 8–19   Examples of Best Management Practices (BMPs) for Surface Runoff

Structural BMPs

Vegetated swales and infiltration ditches—placed along the roadside they allow the runoff time to settle and be filtered by the grass and soil.

Retention and detention basins—can control the volume of runoff and decrease the rate at which it enters the system. Allowing more time for runoff to evaporate, infiltrate, or be absorbed; and for heavier particles to settle out.

Wetland and shallow marsh systems—allow the vegetation to remove some of the contaminants.

Filtering systems—are fabricated systems that are used in conjunction with a sedimentation area to filter and remove contaminants.

Nonstructural BMPs
- Street sweeping
- Land use planning
- Vegetated buffer areas
- Fertilizer application controls

Sources: Michael E. Barrett, Robert D. Zuber, E.R. Collins III, Joseph F. Malina Jr., Randall J. Charbeneau, and George H. Ward, *A Review and Evaluation of Literature Pertaining to the Quantity and Control of Pollution from Highway Runoff and Construction,* 2nd Edition, CRWR Online Report 95–5, Austin, Texas: Center for Research in Water Resources, Bureau of Engineering Research, The University of Texas at Austin, April 1995, http://www.ce.utexas.edu/centers/crwr/reports/online.html; G.K. Young, S. Stein, P. Cole, T. Kammer, F. Graziano, and F. Bank, *Evaluation and Management of Highway Runoff Water Quality,* Washington, D.C.: U.S. Department of Transportation, Federal Highway Administration, 1996.

and design of each type of BMP can be found in *Evaluation and Management of Highway Runoff Water Quality* and in the CRWR online report.

In addition to the effects of runoff during use of the system, the effects of the construction process must also be considered. The construction process can change soil moisture conditions in several ways and, therefore, affect runoff volumes. If a roadway embankment restricts the flow of surface water, storm water will tend to pond upslope from the embankment, thereby increasing the average moisture content of the affected soil. Also, roadway drainage facilities can direct runoff to concentrate in an area that previously did not receive runoff from such an extensive area. If construction of a roadway embankment significantly compacts (i.e., reduces the porosity) the underlying strata, the ability of that strata to conduct groundwater flow may be reduced, thus causing an increase in water table elevation upslope from the embankment. Construction of sloped drainage ditches that intersect the water table can lower the local water table as well as create a possible ponding problem elsewhere downstream.

The construction process impacts on water resources should include important off-site activities and effects. Significant impacts may also be associated with the acquisition of fill from borrow pits or, conversely, with the disposal of excess or unsuitable materials removed from the construction site. There may also be impacts associated with induced development from the new or improved transportation facility. Fortunately, severe groundwater impacts from transportation systems are rare. The recharge lost to the groundwater system as runoff from paved surfaces may still percolate into the system at some later time. In regard to the potential reduction in aquifer transmissibility due to compaction of an embankment, those materials that tend to make good aquifers also tend to resist compaction.

In the construction of any transportation facility, it is important to avoid the interruption of natural drainage patterns. Failure to place a culvert where an embankment crossed even the most intermittent stream may cause ponding that will disrupt local vegetation and wildlife.

Erosion and Sedimentation

Erosion and sedimentation are perhaps most often associated with construction-related activities. The various techniques for erosion control include minimization of clearing, especially during rainy periods; quick reestablishment of vegetative cover; use of protective mulches; minimization of exposed slope length; avoidance of erodible soils; and management of on-site drainage through construction and use of channels, pipes, sedimentation ponds, filter fabrics, silt curtains, and so forth. These techniques are well known and are part of the standard contract specifications for virtually all major highway or airport construction projects.

Techniques for the prediction of the amount of erosion, turbidity, or sedimentation associated with transportation project construction are uncertain at best. As a result, the usual solution to construction-related turbidity impacts is to call for extensive erosion control and treatment measures (e.g., siltation ponds) in sensitive areas. In some instances, it may even be appropriate to ban construction activities during the spawning periods of important species.

Flood Control

Assessment of changes in surface hydrology expected to result from project construction can be performed by using one of several available models. Use of these models is usually a design-related task, and they are not generally used by the transportation planner. Flood impact studies for the 50- and 100-year storms are regularly performed for major projects using the Hydrologic Engineering Center (HEC) models of the U.S. Army Corps of Engineers. Studies for floods of shorter return periods (e.g., mean annual flood) can also be performed. If it can be shown that the additional (or reduced) flooding expected as the result of the project is insignificant in comparison to year-to-year variations in flood level, then it can be assumed the project will not have a significant effect on the surrounding environment.

The impacts of roadway construction on major floods are most often considered in connection with bridge design. Of particular concern is the potential for channel constriction by a too-short bridge structure that could cause flooding upstream from the constriction. These impacts can usually be quantified using the Corps HEC Models.

Transportation projects may also contribute to flooding by directly and indirectly causing a net increase in runoff due to a decrease in pervious area, especially if local storm water facilities have already reached capacity. As a basin becomes more urbanized, higher peak flows can be expected. The basin's time of concentration may also decrease, thus increasing maximum potential runoff intensity expected in a particular basin.

The most practical means of mitigating problems of increased runoff due to decreases in pervious areas is usually to design storm drainage in such a way as to retain the runoff on site. An example of such means would be through the construction of retention ponds, which may also serve to mitigate water quality problems associated with the first flush of pollutants from a paved area.

Wetlands

The conservation of wetlands in the United States has become a national priority with the aim to prevent further loss of wetlands in the country. Most of the adverse impacts on wetlands result from siltation, pollutants, excess nutrients, and changes to water flows including more frequent inundation and increased turbidity.[53] All of these impacts can result from the construction of transportation projects if proper precautions are not taken.

Usually steps should be taken to select corridors and alternative alignments that avoid wetlands to the extent practical. For impacts that are unavoidable, there are mitigation techniques available that attempt to recreate the basic ecological features of the wetland as it existed prior to construction. These mitigation techniques include restoration of the original water circulation conditions, introduction of preexisting plant species, and the creation of new wetland habitats.

Permits

The federal government has enacted several laws that have been applied to transportation systems to limit any adverse environmental effects. The ones listed below may be required and are discussed in more detail.

- Clean Water Act, Section 404—regulates the discharge of dredged and fill material into waters of the United States, including wetlands.

- Clean Water Act, Section 402—established the National Pollutant Discharge Elimination System to control discharge to surface waters from conveyance systems, including storm water runoff from transportation systems that is carried by municipal separate storm sewer collection systems.[54]

---

[53] U.S. Environmental Protection Agency, *Wetlands and Runoff*, Office of Water, http://www.epa.gov/OWOW/wetlands/facts/fact22.html.

[54] U.S. Environmental Protection Agency, Pollution Control Programs for Roads, Highways, and Bridges, Nonpoint Source Pollution Control Program, Office of Water (November, 1995), EPA-841-F-95-088c, http://www.epa.gov/OWOW/NPS/education/control.html.

- Clean Water Act, Section 401—requires a state certification when anyone applies for a federal license or permit to conduct any activity that may result in a discharge of a pollutant into waters of the United States.

- Rivers and Harbors Appropriations Act of 1899, Section 9—requires that a permit be obtained from the U.S. Coast Guard for the improvement or construction of a bridge or causeway in navigable waters.

- Rivers and Harbors Appropriations Act of 1899, Section 10—requires that a permit be obtained for construction or modification of structures or work on structures, such as piers, floats, intake pipes, outfall pipes, pilings, bulkheads, dredging dolphins, or fills, in navigable waters of the United States.

Section 404 Permits

Section 404 of the Clean Water Act requires that a permit be received for any project that involves the discharge of dredged or fill material into waters of the United States; and it gives the U.S. Army Corps of Engineers the authority to issue permits for any project that affects any body of water, including wetlands. In general the application for a permit must show that the project planners have:

- avoided any impacts to wetlands where practicable,

- minimized potential impacts to wetlands, and

- included plans to restore or create wetlands to compensate for any unavoidable impacts.[55]

In order to determine the applicability of any permit, the following definitions apply.

- Discharge of dredged material—includes, but is not limited to, the following:

    - The addition of dredged material to a specified discharge site located in waters of the United States.

    - The runoff or overflow from a contained land or water disposal area.

    - Any addition, including any redeposit, of dredged material, including excavated material, into waters of the United States that are incidental to any activity, including mechanized land clearing, ditching, channelization, or other excavation (33 CFR 323.2 [d] [1]).

- Fill material—Any material used for the primary purpose of replacing an aquatic area with dry land or of changing the bottom elevation of a body of water (33 CFR [e]).

- Wetlands—Areas that are inundated or saturated by surface or ground water at a frequency and duration sufficient to support, and that under normal circumstances do support, a prevalence of vegetation typically adapted for life in saturated soil conditions. Wetlands generally include swamps, marshes, bogs, and similar areas (40 CFR 230.3).

The Section 404 permit can be issued as either an individual or general permit by the Corps of Engineers. Individual permits are usually required for projects that will have potentially significant impacts. General permits are granted by the Corps of Engineers for projects that will only minimally affect water quality. These can be issued at a nationwide, regional, or state level; and they must satisfy specific conditions to be applicable. The general permit program, as described in 33 CFR Part 330, is the primary method of eliminating unnecessary paperwork for activities that are too minor to justify individual review. A general permit contains general and special conditions with which a proposed project must comply to qualify under its provisions. For example, a special condition could stipulate that not more than

---

[55] U.S. Environmental Protection Agency, *Section 404 of the Clean Water Act: An Overview,* Office of Water, http://www.epa.gov/OWOW/wetlands/wet10.html.

125,000 cubic yards of material may be discharged within the 100-year flood plain. The Corps of Engineers has published a list of nationwide permits with restrictions and limitations as guidance for project planners pursing the expedited permit procedure. Certain nationwide permits that result in a discharge will require a state 401 water quality certification, or waver thereof, prior to the issuance of the permit. More detailed descriptions of types of nationwide permits are listed in the *Federal Register: December 13, 1996* (volume 61, number 241, notices, pages 65873–65922); and a table summarizing this information can be found at the Website of the Ohio EPA Department of Water, http:/www.chagrin.epa.state.oh.us/programs/nwp.html.

The individual permit includes all projects that are not covered under general permits. Individual permits are required for situations that are usually of a larger magnitude than those falling under the other types, although the Corps may require an individual permit in any situation that it deems appropriate. Individual permits require a separate public interest review (often including a public hearing) and individual analysis by the Corps. This process is normally used only when impact-related aspects of a project indicate the possibility of character altering environmental consequences.

A decision on the permit application is made in most cases by the appropriate Corps District Engineer. In situations where another federal agency has objections about the application, the approval decision is referred to the Corps Division Engineer level, where attempts are made to resolve the objection through mediation. If this mediation is unsuccessful and objections still remain, the application may be referred to the Corps Chief of Engineers.

The 1977 amendments to Section 404 of the Clean Water Act also included a provision for the Corps to transfer permitting responsibilities to the states in a gesture to increase the states' roles in the regulatory process. This option is strictly voluntary, and it must be documented that it follows the same procedures as the Corps' 404 permit process. From the perspective of the Corps, the permit requirement is comprehensive under Section 404 in that activities related to Section 10 of the Rivers and Harbors Act, as well as Section 401 of the Clean Water Act, are also provided for under the Section 404 permit procedure. Thus, only one permit is required from the Corps.

An integral part of the 404 permitting process is the assessment of potential wetland impacts. This assessment will generally consider the following four factors: (1) wetland acreage affected, (2) relative productivity of the wetland and its importance to protected species, (3) relationship between the wetland and other regional ecosystems, and (4) potential enhancement of the wetland through project design. Adherence to this process ensures that the destruction, loss, or degradation of the wetland will be minimized. More detailed information on wetlands, Section 404 regulations, wetland delineation, mitigation procedures, and technical guidance documents are available at the EPA Website of the Office of Water: Wetlands, http://www.epa.gov/OWOW/wetlands/regs.html.

NPDES Permits

Section 402 of the Clean Water Act requires that sources of pollution that discharge at "point sources" (i.e., through pipes or other conveyances) have a discharge permit. Storm water runoff from highways, roads, and bridges that is carried by municipal separate storm sewer collection systems serving populations of over 100,000 must be permitted. Also, construction projects that disturb five acres or more must be permitted under this section.

Section 401 Certification

The Section 401 certification must be obtained from the state in which the discharge originates, and it must state that the discharge will comply with the applicable effluent limitations and water quality standards. It is required for any activity that may result in a discharge of a pollutant into waters of the United States. The certification obtained for the construction must also pertain to the subsequent operation of the facility. No permit will be issued until this certification has been granted or waivered. The required information is often submitted to the Corps of Engineers with the Section 404 information.

Section 9 Permits

The Rivers and Harbors Act of 1899, as amended by the Department of Transportation Act of 1966, requires that the U.S. Coast Guard approve the plans for the construction of a bridge over any navigable waters in the United States. Unlike the Section 404 process, "navigable waters" in this case are limited to those whose general character is "navigable, and which, either by themselves or by uniting with other waters, form a continuous waterway on which boats or vessels may navigate or travel between two or more states, or to or from foreign countries."

The courts have allowed this definition to stand because the purpose and scope of Section 9 are very narrow. Simply stated, the law is intended to protect navigation activities on the nation's waterways. The primary purpose of Section 9 is to provide a means of preventing the construction of bridges or other types of structures that may obstruct the safe passage of vessels.

Neither the Rivers and Harbors Act of 1899, the Department of Transportation Act of 1966, nor 33 CFR Part 114 contain specific guidance as to acceptability criteria for bridges and their effects on navigation. Nor do they contain any guidance as to how a permit application should be prepared or what it should contain. However, the appropriate details are available at the Coast Guard district level.

Upon receipt of an application, the Coast Guard initiates a review of navigational and environmental impacts, performs site inspections, and coordinates activities with other government agencies and special interest groups. Once the application has been reviewed and accepted as satisfactory, the public involvement process is initiated by issuing a public notice. Comments are received on the proposal for a 30-day period. The Coast Guard attempts to provide a forum that is conducive to the resolution of adverse comments, but it does not require resolution prior to making its decision. The Commandant of the Coast Guard makes the decision, after receiving a recommendation from the District Commander, who will recommend (a) issuance of the permit, (b) denial of the permit, or (c) that a public hearing be held to gather additional data.

It should be kept in mind that the Section 9 bridge permit process concerns primarily the effects on navigation. The information gathered in the environmental assessment phase is important, and it could preclude the construction of a bridge. The bridge itself, however, could be totally acceptable from the Section 9 perspective. Conversely, a bridge project determined to be nonmajor by FHWA, and therefore insignificant in impact, could be quite significant and major with respect to the Coast Guard.

Energy Considerations

Any discussion of transportation-related energy usage in the United States must begin with two irrefutable facts: transportation is almost exclusively powered by petroleum, and highway vehicles are the primary users of petroleum. The use of petroleum as an almost sole source of energy leaves the system open to disruption from abrupt changes in the world markets for petroleum. In addition, the continued use of the internal combustion engine in highway vehicles means that environmental problems still persist even with the significantly lower levels of emissions in today's vehicles.

Petroleum Dependence

The annual transportation consumption of petroleum in the United States has exceeded the annual domestic production of petroleum every year since 1976. As shown in Figure 8–7 and in Table 8–20 with information from the *Transportation Energy Data Book: Edition 17*,[56] this "transportation oil gap" has been continually increasing since 1982; and the petroleum use by transportation now exceeds domestic production by almost 73 percent. The supply from this oil gap is provided by imports that reached a high of 46.2 percent in 1996. In addition, transportation comprises 66 percent of domestic production (Table 8–21). Despite the recent emphasis on developing vehicles that are powered by alternate fuels, the transportation sector remains almost exclusively dependent on petroleum. Petroleum usage accounts for approximately 97 percent of energy usage; a figure that has been relatively constant since 1973 when it was almost

---

[56] Stacy C. Davis, *Transportation Energy Data Book: Edition 17* (Center for Transportation Analysis Energy Division, Oak Ridge National Laboratory, September 1997).

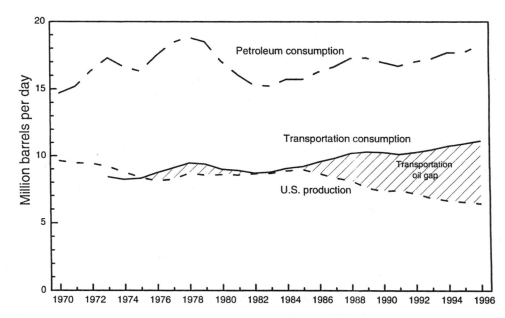

Figure 8–7   United States Petroleum Production and Consumption, 1973–1996

Source: Stacy C. Davis, *Transportation Energy Data Book, Edition 17,* Center for Transportation Analysis, Energy Division, Oak Ridge National Laboratory, September 1997, Table 2.2.

96 percent.[57] During the time period from 1970 to 1996, transportation energy consumption has increased over 50 percent from 16.07 quadrillion Btu to 24.44 quadrillion Btu as shown in Table 8–22. Even with the increases in energy efficiency, the average annual percentage increases from 1986 to 1996 are essentially unchanged from the previous period.

This almost total reliance on petroleum as an energy source is important because there are economic and political costs associated with this dependency. Economically, world oil prices are sensitive to disruptions in supply as was the case during the 1970s when OPEC restricted oil production, and in 1990–1991 when the loss of production in Iraq and Kuwait resulted in a short-term doubling of prices. The price shocks of the seventies resulted in gas lines that restricted mobility, significantly increased the cost of transportation in the United States, and brought about more government regulation that changed the shape of the vehicle fleet. David L. Greene estimates that the economic costs to the United States have been about $4 trillion as a result of monopoly pricing since 1972. He also states "since the fundamental facts of the world oil situation have not changed, there is good reason to anticipate additional costs of oil dependence in the future."[58]

Consumption Analysis

Transportation energy consumption is dominated by the highway sector as can be seen in Tables 8–23, 8–24, and 8–25. The highway sector accounts for over 75 percent of transportation energy usage with automobiles and light-duty trucks representing about 77 percent of the highway energy consumption. Air transportation is the next largest user with an 8.7 percent share of the total transportation energy use. Despite the efforts in many major cities to increase the use of buses and rail transportation, these sectors use only about 0.9 percent and 2.3 percent, respectively. Furthermore, there has not been a significant shift in the energy usage over the years among the modes of travel. The annual average energy usage of the highway sector has increased at the same percentage as the overall average annual rate of the entire transportation industry at 1.8 percent from 1985–1995. This picture of the transportation changes little if one looks at it in terms of vehicle-miles or passenger-miles, as can be seen in Table 8–26.

---

[57] Davis, *Transportation Energy Data Book*: *Edition 17.*

[58] David L. Greene, *Transportation and Energy* (Lansdowne, Va.: Eno Transportation Foundation Inc., 1996).

Table 8–20 United States Petroleum Production and Consumption, 1973–1996 (million barrels per day)

Year	Domestic Crude Oil Production	Net Imports Crude Oil	Net Imports Petroleum Products	Net Imports Total	Exports Crude Oil	Exports Petroleum Products	U.S. Petroleum Consumption[a]	World Petroleum Consumption	Net Imports as a Percentage of U.S. Petroleum Consumption	U.S. Petroleum Consumption as a Percentage of World Consumption	Transportation Petroleum Use as a Percentage of Domestic Production[b]
1973	9.21	3.24	2.78	6.03	0.00	0.23	17.31	56.39	34.8%	30.7%	91.5%
1974	8.77	3.47	2.45	5.89	0.00	0.22	16.65	55.91	35.4%	29.8%	93.7%
1975	8.37	4.10	1.75	5.85	0.00	0.20	16.32	55.48	35.8%	29.4%	99.4%
1976	8.13	5.28	1.81	7.09	0.00	0.22	17.46	58.74	40.6%	29.7%	107.6%
1977	8.25	6.57	2.00	8.57	0.05	0.19	18.43	61.63	46.5%	29.9%	110.2%
1978	8.71	6.20	1.80	8.00	0.16	0.20	18.85	63.30	42.4%	29.8%	108.7%
1979	8.55	6.28	1.70	7.99	0.24	0.24	18.51	65.17	43.2%	28.4%	109.6%
1980	8.60	4.98	1.39	6.37	0.29	0.26	17.06	63.07	37.3%	27.0%	104.4%
1981	8.57	4.17	1.23	5.40	0.23	0.37	16.06	60.87	33.6%	26.4%	103.7%
1982	8.65	3.25	1.05	4.30	0.24	0.58	15.30	59.50	28.1%	25.7%	100.6%
1983	8.69	3.17	1.15	4.31	0.16	0.58	15.23	58.74	28.3%	25.9%	101.1%
1984	8.88	3.25	1.47	4.72	0.18	0.54	15.73	59.84	30.0%	26.3%	102.3%
1985	8.97	3.00	1.29	4.29	0.20	0.58	15.73	60.10	27.3%	26.2%	102.6%
1986	8.68	4.02	1.41	5.44	0.15	0.63	16.28	61.76	33.4%	26.4%	110.3%
1987	8.35	4.52	1.39	5.91	0.15	0.61	16.67	63.00	35.5%	26.5%	118.1%
1988	8.14	4.95	1.63	6.59	0.16	0.66	17.28	64.82	38.1%	26.7%	125.4%
1989	7.61	5.70	1.50	7.20	0.14	0.72	17.33	65.92	41.5%	26.3%	135.7%
1990	7.36	4.79	1.38	6.17	0.11	0.75	16.99	65.99	42.1%	25.1%	140.0%
1991	7.42	5.67	0.96	6.63	0.12	0.89	16.71	66.58	39.7%	25.1%	136.6%
1992	7.17	5.99	0.94	6.94	0.09	0.86	17.03	66.74	40.8%	25.5%	143.7%
1993	6.85	6.69	0.93	7.62	0.10	0.90	17.24	67.04	44.2%	25.7%	153.1%
1994	6.66	6.96	1.09	8.05	0.10	0.84	17.72	68.31	45.4%	25.9%	161.9%
1995	6.56	7.13	0.75	7.88	0.10	0.86	17.73	69.38	44.4%	25.6%	167.1%
1996	6.47	7.37	1.05	8.42	0.11	0.87	18.23	c	46.2%	c	172.7%
Average Annual Percentage Change											
1973–96	-1.5%	3.6%	-4.1%	1.5%	—	6.0%	0.2%	0.9%[d]			
1986–96	-2.9%	6.2%	-2.9%	4.5%	-3.1%	3.3%	1.1%	1.3%[d]			

a Best estimate for U.S. petroleum consumption is the amount of petroleum products supplied to the U.S. in a given year. This is not the sum of crude oil production and net imports due to processing gain and stock changes.

b Transportation petroleum use can be found on Table 2.5.

c Data are not available.

d Average annual percentage change is for years 1973–1993 and 1985–1993.

Source: Stacy C. Davis, *Transportation Energy Data Book, Edition 17*, Center for Transportation Analysis Energy Division Oak Ridge National Laboratory, September 1997.

Table 8-21   Consumption of Petroleum by End-Use Sector, 1973–1996 (Quadrillion Btu)

Year	Transportation	Percentage	Residential and Commercial	Percentage	Industrial	Percentage	Electric Utilities	Percentage	Total	Total in Million Barrels per Day[a]
1973	17.83	51.2%	4.39	12.6%	9.10	26.1%	3.52	10.1%	34.84	16.46
1974	17.40	52.0%	4.00	12.0%	8.69	26.0%	3.37	10.1%	33.46	15.81
1975	17.61	53.8%	3.81	11.6%	8.15	24.9%	3.17	9.7%	32.74	15.47
1976	18.51	52.6%	4.18	11.9%	9.01	25.6%	3.48	9.9%	35.18	16.62
1977	19.24	51.8%	4.21	11.3%	9.77	26.3%	3.90	10.5%	37.12	17.53
1978	20.04	52.8%	4.07	10.7%	9.87	26.0%	3.99	10.5%	37.97	17.94
1979	19.83	53.4%	3.45	9.3%	10.57	28.5%	3.28	8.8%	37.13	17.54
1980	19.01	55.6%	3.04	8.9%	9.53	27.9%	2.63	7.7%	34.21	16.16
1981	18.81	58.9%	2.63	8.2%	8.29	26.0%	2.20	6.9%	31.93	15.08
1982	18.42	60.9%	2.45	8.1%	7.79	25.8%	1.57	5.2%	30.23	14.28
1983	18.59	61.9%	2.50	8.3%	7.42	24.7%	1.54	5.1%	30.05	14.19
1984	19.22	61.9%	2.54	8.2%	8.01	25.8%	1.29	4.2%	31.06	14.67
1985	19.50	63.1%	2.52	8.2%	7.81	25.3%	1.09	3.5%	30.92	14.61
1986	20.27	63.0%	2.56	8.0%	7.92	24.6%	1.45	4.5%	32.20	15.21
1987	20.87	63.5%	2.59	7.9%	8.15	24.8%	1.26	3.8%	32.87	15.53
1988	21.63	63.2%	2.60	7.6%	8.43	24.6%	1.56	4.6%	34.22	16.16
1989	21.87	63.9%	2.53	7.4%	8.13	23.8%	1.69	4.9%	34.22	16.16
1990	21.81	65.0%	2.17	6.5%	8.32	24.8%	1.25	3.7%	33.55	15.85
1991	21.46	65.3%	2.15	6.5%	8.06	24.5%	1.18	3.6%	32.85	15.52
1992	21.81	65.0%	2.13	6.4%	8.64	25.8%	0.95	2.8%	33.53	15.84
1993	22.20	65.6%	2.14	6.3%	8.45	25.0%	1.05	3.1%	33.84	15.98
1994	22.82	65.7%	2.09	6.0%	8.85	25.5%	0.97	2.8%	34.73	16.41
1995	23.20	66.9%	2.12	6.1%	8.69	25.1%	0.66	1.9%	34.67	16.38
1996	23.66	66.2%	2.22	6.2%	9.11	25.5%	0.73	2.0%	35.72	16.87
Average Annual Percent Change										
1973–1996	1.2%		−3.1%		0.0%		−6.6%		0.1%	0.1%
1986–1996	1.6%		−1.4%		1.4%		−6.6%		1.0%	1.0%

[a] Calculated from Total column. One million barrels per day of petroleum is approximately 2.117 quadrillion Btu per year.

Source: Stacy C. Davis, *Transportation Energy Data Book, Edition 17,* Center for Transportation Analysis, Energy Division, Oak Ridge National Laboratory, September 1997, Table 2.5.

In contrast to air quality concerns, changes in the modal makeup of the transportation fleet will not have a major impact on energy usage. Greene states in *Transportation and Energy*[59] that the energy efficiencies of different modes for the same function have little variability. This can be demonstrated by the data in Table 8–27, which is displayed graphically in Figure 8–8. With the exception of intercity buses, the primary modes of passenger travel have been converging since 1970. Only large changes in passenger choices, like one from airlines to intercity buses, would have any significant effects.

Highway usage is dominated by light-duty vehicles, particularly automobiles. Table 8–28 shows the distribution of VMT by mode, as well as the rates of increase. While there has been some shift from automobiles to light-duty trucks, such as minivans and sports utility vehicles, the differential rates of growth among the various modes are not great enough to effect any relevant changes in energy usage in the near future.

The actual calculation of any values for fuel consumption can be difficult because of the wide range of variables that must be considered. Some overall fleet information is available and can be used to estimate the energy impacts from a project. The fleet characteristics in a specific area will affect the anticipated energy usage. One source of information is the Corporate Average Fuel Economy (CAFE). CAFE values are the fleet averages that result from the government requirements for energy usage. The results of industry attempts to meet this regulation are shown in Table 8–29 for both domestic and imported vehicles. This information can be used in conjunction with an estimate of the characteristics of the local vehicle fleet to determine the overall mile per gallon for the local vehicle fleet.

---

[59] Greene, *Transportation and Energy.*

Table 8–22   Consumption of Total Energy by End-Use Sector, 1970–1996

Year	Transportation	Percentage Transportation of Total	Residential and Commercial	Industrial	Total
1970	16.07	24.2%	21.71	28.65	66.43
1971	16.70	24.6%	22.59	28.59	67.88
1972	17.70	24.8%	23.69	29.88	71.27
1973	18.61	25.1%	24.14	31.53	74.28
1974	18.12	25.0%	23.73	30.69	72.54
1975	18.24	25.9%	23.90	28.40	70.54
1976	19.10	25.7%	25.02	30.24	74.36
1977	19.82	26.0%	25.39	31.08	76.29
1978	20.61	26.4%	26.08	31.39	78.09
1979	20.47	25.9%	25.81	32.62	78.90
1980	19.70	25.9%	25.66	30.61	75.96
1981	19.51	26.4%	25.24	29.24	73.99
1982	19.07	26.9%	25.63	26.15	70.85
1983	19.13	27.1%	25.63	25.76	70.52
1984	19.80	26.7%	26.47	27.87	74.14
1985	20.07	27.1%	26.70	27.21	73.98
1986	20.81	28.0%	26.85	26.63	74.30
1987	21.45	27.9%	27.62	27.83	76.89
1988	22.31	27.8%	28.93	28.99	80.22
1989	22.56	27.7%	29.40	29.35	81.33
1990	22.54	27.7%	28.79	29.94	81.27
1991	22.12	27.3%	29.42	29.57	81.12
1992	22.46	27.3%	29.10	30.58	82.14
1993	22.88	27.3%	30.23	30.75	83.86
1994	23.57	27.5%	30.43	31.58	85.59
1995	23.96	27.5%	31.31	31.92	87.19
1996	24.44	27.2%	32.84	32.58	89.89
Average Annual Percentage Change					
1970–96	1.6%		1.6%	0.5%	1.2%
1986–96	1.6%		2.0%	2.0%	1.9%

^a Electrical energy losses have been distributed among the sectors.

Source: Stacy C. Davis, *Transportation Energy Data Book, Edition 17,* Center for Transportation Analysis, Energy Division, Oak Ridge National Laboratory, September 1997, Table 2.8.

In addition, studies have shown that vehicle fuel efficiency varies with the speed of the vehicle. Results of the three studies in Table 8–30 and Figure 8–9 show that energy usage reaches a peak and then declines at higher speeds. The two earlier studies, in 1973 and 1984, predict that the maximum energy efficiency will be reached around 35 to 40 mph; but a more recent study, performed by West et al.[60] in 1997, puts this maximum around 55 mph. Truck and bus usage and energy consumption are shown in Tables 8–31 and 8–32.

[60] B.H. West, R.N. McGill, J.W. Hodgson, S.S. Sluder, and D.E. Smith, *Development and Verification of Light-Duty Modal Emissions and Fuel Consumption Values for Traffic Models* (Washington, D.C.: Federal Highway Administration, April 1997).

Table 8–23   Domestic Consumption of Transportation Energy by Mode and Fuel Type, 1995 (Trillion Btu)

	Gasoline	Diesel Fuel	Liquefied Petroleum Gas	Jet Fuel	Residual Fuel Oil	Natural Gas	Electricity	Methanol
Highway	14,492.0	3,820.3	25.5			3.0	1.2	0.7
Automobiles	8,434.3[b]	113.7				1.9		0.0
Motorcycles	24.5							
Buses	44.0	168.8	0.2			1.0	1.2	0.7
Transit	5.4	79.0	0.2			1.0	1.2	0.7
Intercity[c]		25.4						
School[c]	38.6	64.4						0.0
Trucks	5,989.2	3,537.8	25.3			0.1		0.0
Light trucks[d]	5,405.2	205.7	12.2			0.1		0.0
Other trucks	584.0	3,332.1	13.1			0.0		0.0
Off-Highway	150.8	570.1[e]						
Construction	35.0	178.5[e]						
Agriculture	115.8	391.6[e]						
Nonhighway	318.0	778.1		2,084.0	962.7	722.1	310.0	
Air	33.2			2,084.0				
General aviation	33.2			73.4				
Domestic air carriers				1,710.7				
International air carriers[f]				299.9				
Water	284.8	274.3			962.7			
Freight		274.3			962.7			
Recreational	284.8							
Pipeline						722.1	248.4	
Rail		503.8					61.6	
Freight (Class I)		485.9						
Passenger		17.9					61.6	
Transit							43.6	
Commuter		8.7					14.7	
Intercity[c]		9.2					3.3	
Total	14,960.8	5,168.5	25.5	2,084.0	962.7	725.1	311.2	0.7

[a] Civilian consumption only. Totals may not include all possible uses of fuels for transportation (e.g., snowmobiles).
[b] Includes gasohol.
[c] Estimated using vehicle travel information.
[d] Two-axle, four-tire trucks.
[e] 1985 data.
[f] Represents an estimate of energy purchased in the U.S. for international air carrier consumption.

Source: Stacy C. Davis, *Transportation Energy Data Book, Edition 17*, Center for Transportation Analysis, Energy Division, Oak Ridge National Laboratory, September 1997, Table 2.9.

Table 8–24   Transportation Energy Use by Mode, 1994–1995[a]

	Trillion Btu		Thousand Barrels per Day Crude Oil Equivalent[b]		Percentage of Total	
	1994	1995	1994	1995	1994	1995
Highway	18,010.3	18,342.7	8,507.5	8,664.5	76.0%	75.7%
Automobiles	8,449.3	8,549.9	3,991.2	4,038.7	35.7%	35.3%
Motorcycles	25.6	24.5	12.1	11.6	0.1%	0.1%
Buses	202.1	215.9	95.5	102.0	0.9%	0.9%
Transit	86.7	87.5	41.0	41.3	0.4%	0.4%
Intercity	24.7	25.4[c]	11.7	12.0	0.1%	0.1%
School	90.7	103.0[c]	42.8	48.7	0.4%	0.4%
Trucks	9,333.3	9,552.4	4,408.7	4,512.2	39.4%	39.4%
Light trucks[d]	5,574.4[c]	5,623.2	2,625.1	2,656.2	23.5%	23.2%
Other trucks	3,775.9	3,929.2	1,783.6	1,856.0	15.9%	16.2%
Off-Highway	716.4	720.9	338.4	340.5	3.0%	3.0%
Construction	211.8	213.5	100.0	100.9	0.9%	0.9%
Agriculture	504.6	507.4	238.4	239.7	2.1%	2.1%
Nonhighway	4,971.3	5,174.9	2,348.3	2,444.4	21.0%	21.3%
Air	2,056.0	2,117.2	971.2	1,000.1	8.7%	8.7%
General aviation	95.3	106.6	45.0	50.4	0.4%	0.4%
Domestic air carriers	1,671.9	1,710.7	789.7	808.1	7.1%	7.1%
International air carriers	288.8	299.9	136.4	141.7	1.2%	1.2%
Water	1,413.8	1,521.8	667.8	718.8	6.0%	6.3%
Freight	1,171.1	1,237.0	553.2	584.3	4.9%	5.1%
Recreational	242.7	284.8	114.6	134.5	1.0%	1.2%
Pipeline	955.2	970.5	451.2	458.4	4.0%	4.0%
Rail	546.3	565.4	258.1	267.1	2.3%	2.3%
Freight	465.4	485.9	219.8	229.5	2.0%	2.0%
Passenger	80.9	79.5	38.2	37.6	0.3%	0.3%
Transit	43.9	43.6	20.7	20.6	0.2%	0.2%
Commuter	23.2	23.4	11.0	11.1	0.1%	0.1%
Intercity	13.8	12.5[c]	6.5	5.9	0.1%	0.1%
Total	23,698.0	24,238.5	11,194.1	11,449.5	100.0%	100.0%

[a] Civilian consumption only. Totals may not include all possible uses of fuels for transportation (e.g., snowmobiles).
[b] Thousand barrels per day crude oil equivalents based average on Btu content of a barrel of crude oil.
[c] Estimated using vehicle travel information.
[d] Two-axle, four-tire trucks.

Source: Stacy C. Davis, *Transportation Energy Data Book, Edition 17,* Center for Transportation Analysis, Energy Division, Oak Ridge National Laboratory, September 1997, Table 2.10.

Table 8–25   Transportation Energy Consumption by Mode, 1970–1995

Year	Automobiles	Motorcycles	Buses[a]	Light Trucks[b]	Other Trucks	Total Highway	Air	Water	Pipeline	Rail[c]	Total Nonhighway	Total Transportation[d]
1970	8,527	7	109	1,540	1,503	11,688	1,307	753	985	558	3,603	15,291
1971	8,971	9	108	1,687	1,568	12,343	1,304	698	1,007	560	3,569	15,912
1972	9,583	11	106	1,895	1,684	13,279	1,314	703	1,039	583	3,639	16,918
1973	9,891	13	109	2,105	1,844	13,962	1,377	827	996	619	3,819	17,781
1974	9,440	14	113	2,083	1,791	13,441	1,254	804	932	624	3,614	17,055
1975	9,611	14	119	2,239	1,789	13,772	1,274	851	835	563	3,523	17,295
1976	10,020	15	129	2,522	1,949	14,635	1,333	1,001	803	585	3,722	18,357
1977	10,108	16	132	2,739	2,156	15,151	1,411	1,103	781	595	3,890	19,041
1978	10,267	18	135	3,009	2,408	15,837	1,467	1,311	781	589	4,148	19,985
1979	9,719	22	137	3,095	2,510	15,483	1,568	1,539	856	613	4,576	20,059
1980	9,037	26	139	2,951	2,425	14,578	1,528	1,677	889	596	4,690	19,268
1981	8,927	27	143	2,964	2,461	14,522	1,455	1,562	899	565	4,481	19,003
1982	8,814	25	146	2,982	2,430	14,397	1,468	1,290	853	488	4,096	18,493
1983	8,762	22	145	3,196	2,598	14,723	1,505	1,187	738	482	3,912	18,635
1984	8,613	22	154	3,463	2,837	15,089	1,633	1,251	780	523	4,187	19,276
1985	8,673	23	161	3,630	2,924	15,411	1,678	1,311	758	487	4,234	19,645
1986	8,917	23	154	3,785	3,007	15,885	1,823	1,295	738	423	4,329	20,214
1987	8,836	24	157	4,036	3,132	16,185	1,894	1,326	775	485	4,480	20,665
1988	9,005	25	159	4,114	3,315	16,618	1,978	1,338	878	498	4,692	21,310
1989	9,106	26	163	4,139	3,386	16,820	1,981	1,376	895	501	4,753	21,573
1990	9,010	24	163	4,130	3,366	16,693	2,059	1,487	928	492	4,966	21,659
1991	8,845	23	174	4,080	3,302	16,424	1,926	1,567	864	463	4,820	21,244
1992	9,237	24	182	4,155	3,381	16,971	1,971	1,641	849	476	4,937	21,908
1993	9,204	25	192	4,563	3,542	17,527	1,996	1,473	889	513	4,871	22,399
1994	8,449	26	202	5,557	3,776	18,010	2,056	1,414	955	546	4,971	22,981
1995	8,550	25	216	5,623	3,929	18,343	2,117	1,522	971	565	5,174	23,517
Average Annual Percentage Change												
1970–1995	0.0%	5.2%	2.8%	5.3%	3.9%	1.8%	1.9%	2.9%	-0.1%	0.0%	1.5%	1.7%
1985–1995	-0.1%	0.8%	3.0%	4.5%	3.0%	1.8%	2.4%	1.5%	2.5%	1.5%	2.0%	1.8%

[a] Beginning in 1992, data became available on alternative fuel use by transit buses.
[b] Light trucks include only those trucks that have two-axles and four-tires. Starting in 1993, this category includes minivans and sports utility vehicles.
[c] This data have changed from previous editions due to a change in source for Class I freight railroad energy use. Previous estimates were based on sales.
[d] Total transportation figures do not include military and off-highway energy use and may not include all possible uses of fuel for transportation (e.g., snowmobiles).

Source: Stacy C. Davis, *Transportation Energy Data Book, Edition 17*, Center for Transportation Analysis, Energy Division, Oak Ridge National Laboratory, September 1997, Table 2.11.

Table 8–26   Passenger Travel and Energy Use in the United States, 1995

	Number of Vehicles (thousands)	Vehicle-Miles (millions)	Passenger-Miles (millions)	Load Factor (persons/vehicle)	Energy Intensities (Btu per vehicle-mile)	(Btu per passenger-mile)	Energy Use (trillion Btu)
Automobiles	136,066.0	1,541,458	2,466,333	1.6	5,547	3,467	8,549.9
Personal trucks	43,592.8	477,092	715,638	1.5	8,067	5,378	3,848.8
Motorcycles	3,767.0	9,797	13,716	1.4	2,501	1,786	24.5
Buses	647.6	8,428	142,818	16.9	24,063	1,420	202.8
Transit	67.1	2,178	18,818	8.6	40,175	4,650	87.5
Intercity	20.1	1,250	29,000	23.2	20,320[a]	876[a]	25.4[a]
School	560.4	5,000	95,000	19.0	18,120[a]	954[a]	103.0[a]
Air	[b]	7,927	415,188	52.4	229,254	4,377	1,817.3
Certificated route	[b]	4,629	403,888	87.3	369,562	4,236	1,710.7
General aviation	181.3	3,298[c]	11,300	3.4	32,323	9,434	106.6
Recreational boats	11,700.0	[b]	[b]	[b]	[b]	[b]	284.8
Rail	18.1	1,193	25,067	21.0	66,639	3,172	79.5
Intercity[d]	2.3[e]	283[f]	5,401[g]	19.1	44,170	2,315	12.5[a]
Transit[h]	11.2	572	11,419	20.0	76,224	3,818	43.6
Commuter	4.6	238	8,247	34.7	98,319	2,837	23.4

[a] Estimated using vehicle travel data.
[b] Data are not available.
[c] Nautical miles.
[d] Amtrak only.
[e] Sum of passenger train cars and locomotive units.
[f] Passenger train car-miles.
[g] Revenue passenger miles.
[h] Light and heavy rail.

Source: Stacy C. Davis, *Transportation Energy Data Book, Edition 17*, Center for Transportation Analysis, Energy Division, Oak Ridge National Laboratory, September 1997, Table 2.13.

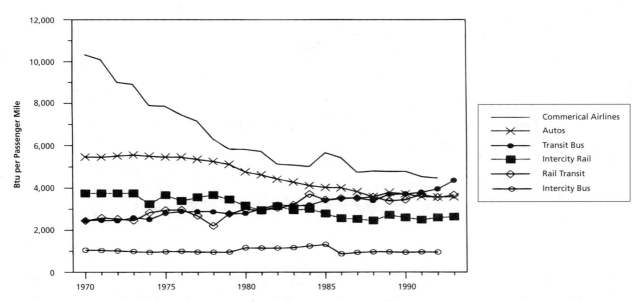

Figure 8–8   Efficiency Trends of Passenger Modes (Btu per passenger mode)

Sources: David L. Greene, *Transportation and Energy*, Landsdowne, Va.: Eno Transportation Foundation, 1996; Stacy C. Davis, *Transportation Energy Data Book, Edition 15*, Table 2–15.

Table 8–27 Energy Intensities of Passenger Modes, 1970–1995

Year	Automobiles (Btu per vehicle-mile)	Automobiles (Btu per passenger-mile)	Transit[a] (Btu per vehicle-mile)	Transit[a] (Btu per passenger-mile)	Intercity Buses (Btu per passenger-mile)	School Buses (Btu per vehicle-mile)	Certificated Air Carriers (Btu per passenger-mile)	General Aviation (Btu per passenger-mile)	Intercity Amtrak (Btu per passenger-mile)	Rail Transit (Btu per passenger-mile)
1970	9,302	5,472	31,796	2,472	1,051	17,857	10,351	10,374	[b]	2,453
1975	9,295	5,468	33,748	2,814	976	17,040	7,883	10,658	3,677	2,962
1976	9,293	5,467	34,598	2,896	996	17,051	7,481	10,769	3,397	2,971
1977	9,113	5,360	35,120	2,889	961	16,983	7,174	11,695	3,568	2,691
1978	8,955	5,268	36,603	2,883	953	17,018	6,333	11,305	3,683	2,210
1979	8,727	5,134	36,597	2,795	963	16,980	5,858	10,787	3,472	2,794
1980	8,130	4,782	36,553	2,813	1,069	16,379	5,837	11,497	3,176	3,008
1981	7,894	4,644	37,745	3,027	1,155	16,385	5,743	11,123	2,957	2,946
1982	7,558	4,446	38,766	3,237	1,149	16,296	5,147	13,015	3,156	3,069
1983	7,314	4,302	37,962	3,177	1,174	16,236	5,107	11,331	2,957	3,212
1984	7,031	4,136	37,507	3,204	1,247	14,912	5,031	11,912	3,027	3,732
1985	6,880	4,047	38,862	2,421	1,324	16,531	5,679	11,339	2,800	3,461
1986	6,853	4,031	39,869	3,512	869	15,622	5,447	11,935	2,574	3,531
1987	6,519	3,835	38,557	3,542	939	15,615	4,753	11,218	2,537	3,534
1988	6,299	3,705	39,121	3,415	965	15,585	4,814	11,966	2,462	3,585
1989	6,162	3,851	36,583	3,711	963	15,575	4,796	10,984	2,731	3,397
1990	5,954	3,721	36,647	3,735	944	16,368	4,811	10,146	2,609	3,453
1991	5,768	3,605	36,939	3,811	978	16,419	4,560	9,556	2,503	3,710
1992	5,770	3,606	40,472c	4,303c	978	16,386	4,482	8,582	2,610	3,575
1993	5,948	3,418	39,005	4,257	972	19,093	4,304	9,343	2,646	3,687
1994	5,628	3,517	40,102	4,604	876	20,591	4,455	9,825	2,351	3,828
1995	5,547	3,467	40,175	4,650	876	20,600	4,236	9,434	2,341	3,818
Average Annual Percentage Change										
1970–1995	-2.0%	-1.8%	0.9%	2.6%	-0.7%	0.6%	-3.5%	-0.4%	-2.1%[d]	1.8%
1985–1995	-2.1%	-1.5%	0.3%	6.7%	-4.0%	2.2%	-2.9%	-1.8%	-1.8%	1.0%

[a] Series not continuous between 1983 and 1984 because of a change in data source by the American Public Transit Association (APTA).
[b] Data are not available.
[c] Beginning in 1992 data became available on alternative fuel use by transit buses.
[d] Average annual percentage change is for years 1973–1995.

Source: Stacy C. Davis, *Transportation Energy Data Book, Edition 17*, Center for Transportation Analysis, Energy Division, Oak Ridge National Laboratory, September 1997, Table 2.15.

Table 8–28   Highway VMT by Mode, 1970–1995 (million miles)

Year	Automobiles	Motorcycles	Two-Axle, Four-Tire Trucks	Other Single-Unit Trucks	Combination Trucks	Buses[a]	Total
1970	916,700	2,979	123,286	27,081	35,134	4,544	1,109,724
1971	966,340	3,607	137,870	28,985	37,217	4,792	1,178,811
1972	1,021,365	4,331	156,622	31,414	40,706	5,348	1,259,786
1973	1,045,981	5,194	176,833	33,661	45,649	5,792	1,313,110
1974	1,007,251	5,445	182,757	33,441	45,966	5,684	1,280,544
1975	1,033,950	5,629	200,700	34,606	46,724	6,055	1,327,664
1976	1,078,215	6,003	225,834	36,390	49,680	6,258	1,402,380
1977	1,109,243	6,349	250,591	39,339	55,682	5,823	1,467,027
1978	1,146,508	7,158	279,414	42,747	62,992	5,885	1,544,704
1979	1,113,640	8,637	291,905	42,012	66,992	5,947	1,529,133
1980	1,111,596	10,214	290,935	39,813	68,678	6,059	1,527,295
1981	1,130,827	10,690	296,343	39,568	69,134	6,241	1,552,803
1982	1,166,256	9,910	306,141	40,212	66,668	5,823	1,595,010
1983	1,198,023	8,760	327,643	43,409	69,754	5,199	1,652,788
1984	1,224,919	8,784	357,999	46,560	77,367	4,640	1,720,269
1985	1,260,565	9,086	373,072	46,980	79,600	4,876	1,774,179
1986	1,301,214	9,397	389,047	48,308	81,833	5,073	1,834,872
1987	1,355,330	9,506	415,449	49,537	86,064	5,318	1,921,204
1988	1,429,579	10,024	439,496	51,239	90,158	5,466	2,025,962
1989	1,477,769	10,371	454,339	52,969	95,349	5,659	2,096,456
1990	1,513,184	9,557	466,092	53,443	96,367	5,719	2,144,362
1991	1,533,552	9,178	472,848	53,787	96,942	5,743	2,172,050
1992	1,600,839	9,557	478,193	53,691	99,112	5,759	2,247,151
1993	1,547,366	9,906	573,398[b]	56,781	103,123	6,126	2,296,700
1994	1,501,402	10,240	669,321[b]	61,284	108,932	6,409	2,357,588
1995	1,541,458	9,797	686,977[b]	62,706	115,454	6,383	2,422,773
Average Annual Percentage Change							
1970–1995	2.1%	4.9%	7.1%	3.4%	4.9%	1.4%	3.2%
1985–1995	2.0%	0.8%	6.3%	2.9%	3.8%	2.7%	3.2%

Source: Stacy C. Davis, *Transportation Energy Data Book, Edition 17,* Center for Transportation Analysis, Energy Division, Oak Ridge National Laboratory, September 1997, Table 3.1.

Table 8–29   CAFE Standards Versus Sales-Weighted Fuel Economy Estimates for Automobiles and Light Trucks, 1978–1997[a] (miles per gallon)

Model Year	Automobiles CAFE Standards	Automobiles CAFE Estimates[c] Domestic	Automobiles CAFE Estimates[c] Import	Automobiles CAFE Estimates[c] Combined	Light Trucks[b] CAFE Standards	Light Trucks[b] CAFE Estimates[c] Domestic	Light Trucks[b] CAFE Estimates[c] Import	Light Trucks[b] CAFE Estimates[c] Combined
1978	18.0	18.7	27.3	19.9	[d]	[e]	[e]	[e]
1979	19.0	19.3	26.1	20.3	[d]	17.7	20.8	18.2
1980	20.0	22.6	29.6	24.3	[d]	16.8	24.3	18.5
1981	22.0	24.2	31.5	25.9	[d]	18.3	27.4	20.1
1982	24.0	25.0	31.1	26.6	17.5	19.2	27.0	20.5
1983	26.0	24.4	32.4	26.4	19.0	19.6	27.1	20.7
1984	27.0	25.5	32.0	26.9	20.0	19.3	26.7	20.6
1985	27.5	26.3	31.5	27.6	19.5	19.6	26.5	20.7
1986	26.0	26.9	31.6	28.2	20.0	20.0	25.9	21.5
1987	26.0	27.0	31.2	28.5	20.5	20.5	25.2	21.7
1988	26.0	27.4	31.5	28.8	20.5	20.6	24.6	21.3
1989	26.5	27.2	30.8	28.4	20.5	20.4	23.5	20.9
1990	27.5	26.9	29.9	28.0	20.0	20.3	23.0	20.8
1991	27.5	27.3	30.0	28.4	20.2	20.9	23.0	21.3
1992	27.5	27.0	29.2	27.9	20.2	20.5	22.7	20.8
1993	27.5	27.8	29.6	28.4	20.4	20.7	22.8	21.0
1994	27.5	27.5	29.6	28.3	20.5	20.5	22.0	20.7
1995	27.5	27.7	30.3	28.6	20.6	20.3	21.5	20.5
1996	27.5	28.3	29.7	28.7	20.7	20.5	22.1	20.7
1997	27.5	27.9	30.1	28.6	20.7	20.2	22.2	20.4

[a] Only vehicles with at least 75 percent domestic content can be counted in the average domestic fuel economy for a manufacturer.

[b] Represents two- and four-wheel drive trucks combined. Gross vehicle weight of 0–6,000 pounds for model year 1978–1979 and 0–8,500 pounds for subsequent years.

[c] All CAFE calculations are sales-weighted.

[d] Standards were set for two-wheel drive and four-wheel drive light trucks separately, but no combined standard was set in this year.

[e] Data are not available.

Source: Stacy C. Davis, *Transportation Energy Data Book, Edition 17,* Center for Transportation Analysis, Energy Division, Oak Ridge National Laboratory, September 1997, Table 3.40.

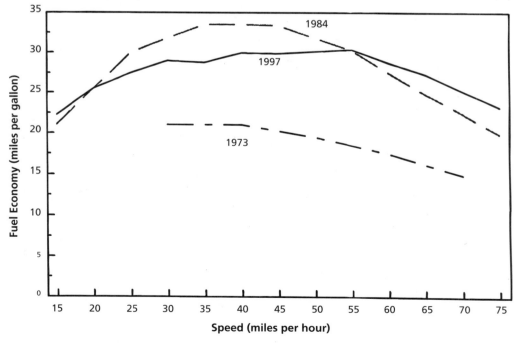

Figure 8–9   Fuel Economy by Speed, 1973, 1984, and 1997

Table 8–30 Fuel Economy by Speed, 1973, 1984, and 1997 (Miles per Gallon)

Speed (miles per hour)	1973 (13 vehicles)	1984 (15 vehicles)	1997 (8 vehicles)
15	d	21.1	22.3
20	d	25.5	25.5
25	d	30.0	27.5
30	21.1	31.8	29.0
35	21.1	33.6	28.8
40	21.1	33.6	30.0
45	20.3	33.5	29.9
50	19.5	31.9	30.2
55	18.5	30.3	30.4
60	17.5	27.6	28.8
65	16.2	24.9	27.4
70	14.9	22.5	25.3
75	d	20.0	23.3
Fuel Economy Loss			
55–65 mph	12.4%	17.8%	9.9%
65–70 mph	8.0%	9.6%	7.7%
55–70 mph	19.5%	25.7%	16.8%

[a] Model years 1970 and earlier automobiles.
[b] Model years 1981–1984 automobiles and light trucks.
[c] Model years 1988–1995 automobiles and light trucks.
[d] Data are not available.

Source: Stacy C. Davis, *Transportation Energy Data Book, Edition 17,* Center for Transportation Analysis, Energy Division, Oak Ridge National Laboratory, September 1997, Table 3.45.

Table 8–31 Truck Statistics by Gross Weight Class, 1992

Manufacturer's Gross Vehicle Weight Class	Number of Trucks	Percentage of Trucks	Average Annual Miles per Truck	Average Fuel Economy	Gallons of Fuel Used (millions)	Percentage of Fuel Use
6,000 lbs and less	37,068,163	62.61%	12,739	17.23	27,397	44.76%
6,001 – 10,000 lbs	17,519,216	29.59%	11,610	13.00	15,646	25.56%
10,001 – 14,000 lbs	349,301	5.90%	15,814	9.48	583	0.95%
14,001 – 16,000 lbs	127,219	0.21%	14,420	9.19	200	0.33%
16,001 – 19,500 lbs	209,158	0.35%	4,876	8.21	124	0.20%
19,501 – 26,000 lbs	1,859,529	3.14%	11,746	7.26	3,008	4.91%
26,001 – 33,000 lbs	197,985	0.33%	30,074	6.64	897	1.46%
33,001 lbs and up	1,870,183	3.16%	39,832	5.58	13,353	21.82%
Total	59,200,755	100.00%	13,281	12.85	61,206	100.00%

Source: Stacy C. Davis, *Transportation Energy Data Book, Edition 17,* Center for Transportation Analysis, Energy Division, Oak Ridge National Laboratory, September 1997, Table 3.25.

Table 8–32   Summary Statistics on Buses by Type, 1970–1995

Year	Transit Motor Bus[a]	Intercity Bus	School Bus
		Number in Operation	
1970	49,700	22,000	288,700
1975	50,811	20,500	368,300
1980	59,411	21,400	418,255
1985	64,258	20,200	480,400
1990	58,714	20,680	508,261
1992	63,080	19,904	525,838
1993	64,850	19,119	534,872
1994	68,123	19,146	547,718
1995	67,086	20,138	560,447
		Vehicle-Miles (millions)	
1970	1,409	1,209	2,100
1975	1,526	1,126	2,500
1980	1,677	1,162	2,900
1985	1,863	933	3,448
1990	2,123	991	3,800
1992	2,178	974	4,400
1993	2,210	1,065	4,300
1994	2,162	1,216	4,400
1995	2,178	1,250	5,000
		Passenger-Miles (millions)	
1970	18,210	25,300	[b]
1975	18,300	25,400	[b]
1980	21,790	27,400	[b]
1985	21,161	23,800	[b]
1990	20,981	23,000	74,200
1992	20,336	22,600	90,000
1993	20,247	24,700	94,200
1994	18,832	28,200	85,000
1995	18,818	29,000	95,000
		Energy Use (trillion Btu)	
1970	44.8	26.6	37.5
1975	51.5	24.8	42.6
1980	61.3	29.3	47.5
1985	72.4	31.5	57.0
1990	78.9	21.7	62.2
1992	87.5[c]	22.1	72.1
1993	86.2	24.0	82.1
1994	86.7	24.7	90.6
1995	87.5	25.4[d]	103.0[d]

[a] Data for transit buses after 1983 are not comparable with prior data. Data for prior years were provided voluntarily and statistically expanded; in 1984 reporting became mandatory.
[b] Data are not available.
[c] Beginning in 1992, data became available on alternative fuel use by transit buses.
[d] Estimated using vehicle-miles.

Source: Stacy C. Davis, *Transportation Energy Data Book, Edition 17,* Center for Transportation Analysis, Energy Division, Oak Ridge National Laboratory, September 1997, Table 3.32.

CHAPTER 9
Financial and Economic Considerations[1]

Gregory P. Benz, AICP
Senior Vice President
Parsons Brinckerhoff

Introduction

The other chapters in this handbook describe the importance of transportation systems to society and, in particular, the supporting role they play in our economy. Given this importance, planners and engineers often spend a great deal of time analyzing the advantages and disadvantages of particular transportation measures, identifying those actions that have best addressed the established needs and opportunities. Not only is there a need to determine on a comparative basis which action is the most beneficial investment, but given limited budgets, decisions must also be made on which projects from a list of recommended projects should receive priority over the others. This chapter describes the general issues and analytical approaches used in making these determinations. It starts with a review of capital and O&M (operating and maintenance) costs as they are major inputs, along with mobility benefits (discussed in other chapters), in the evaluation of alternatives to select projects for implementation and priority setting. The following section on funding sources and financial planning discusses options for covering these costs. Then, sections on evaluation methods, priorities settings, and implementation programming provide the context and methods in which this information is used for decision making. The chapter concludes by discussing uncertainties in using planning-level information in making decisions and priority setting.

The 1991 landmark Intermodal Surface Transportation Efficiency Act (ISTEA) and its reauthorizing legislation in 1998, the Transportation Equity Act for the 21st Century (TEA-21) have emphasized using planning information in decision making, especially in the use and allocation of limited financial resources. In particular, the Metropolitan Planning Regulation that emerged from ISTEA strongly linked collaborative multimodal planning within the context of financial constraints and the development of long-range metropolitan transportation plans. As part of the metropolitan planning process, where a more focused examination of a corridor or subarea of the region is needed to address mobility and related needs and problems, a major investment study (MIS) is often employed. The purpose of an MIS is to identify a transportation improvement project from a set of alternatives considered for inclusion in the long-range metropolitan plan. While TEA-21 may result in changes to the term "MIS" and some other features of MISs, it retains the basic principles. Many of the methods and levels of detail for generating planning level cost, financial information, and evaluation that are discussed in this chapter are appropriate for MISs.

For those interested, many of the concepts presented in this chapter are discussed in greater detail in other publications. See the list at the end of this chapter for further reading. Many of these referenced planning and engineering economy texts have detailed discussions on capital investment analysis.

Cost Estimating

This section discusses the estimation of capital costs, O&M costs, and life-cycle costing in transportation planning studies. The generation of reliable capital and O&M cost estimates represents an important element in the transportation investment decision process. The information generated as part of the transportation planning process is essential to determining the cost-effectiveness and the financial feasibility of the proposed alternatives. More specific discussions and examples of highway and transit costs are included in Chapters 12 and 13 of this handbook.

---

[1] Portions of this chapter were originally presented in Chapter 14, "Financial and Economic Considerations" prepared by Michael Meyers, in the First Edition of ITE's *Transportation Planning Handbook*. Added material has been drawn from the National Transit Institute's *Major Investment Study Reference Manual*, by Gregory P. Benz and James M. Ryan. Some parts of this chapter include excerpts from FTA's *Procedures and Technical Methods for Transit Project Planning*, by James M. Ryan, Donald Emerson, et al.

Capital Cost

Good methods and reliable capital cost information are particularly important when comparing cost-effectiveness and financial consequences among alternatives in a transportation planning study. These comparisons require cost information that is compatible among alternatives and representative of actual construction and procurement costs for each proposed alternative under study. The goal is to minimize the differences between the planning phase estimates and actual construction cost.

Framework for Capital Costing

In a transportation planning study, a set of transportation improvement alternatives is identified for analysis and evaluation. Some level of conceptual engineering is needed to physically define the alternatives as the basis for the capital cost estimates. As part of this physical definition, it is necessary to have a good concept of the transportation mode and technology, general alignment, and general design standards of each alternative. A service and operational definition is also needed in many cases where the vehicle and equipment needs are to be included in the capital cost estimate. (A service and operational definition will be needed for the O&M costing discussed later.)

For most alternatives identified in a transportation planning study, it will be possible to identify a number of segments of the alignments and other components that are typical, such as a four-lane at-grade arterial roadway with a median and a similar section without the median, or a two-track elevated light rail transit guideway structure. Of course, there will be many special or nontypical situations, such as a complex interchange structure or a traffic operations control center.

A useful method for conceptual engineering analysis and the development of capital cost estimates in a transportation planning study is to develop typical section costs that are then applied on a cost-per-unit basis, where applicable. A similar unit-cost approach could also be used for other typical items, such as bridge structures (which could vary by type of structure and span length), park-and-ride lots (with varying number of parking spaces), and transit stations (at-grade, elevated, subway). With the use of the conceptual engineering drawings, the respective lengths and quantities of each can be determined for each alternative. These typical segment or item capital costs usually do not include costs related to rights-of-way, special utility relocation, systemwide elements, and other add-on cost items. Figures 9–1

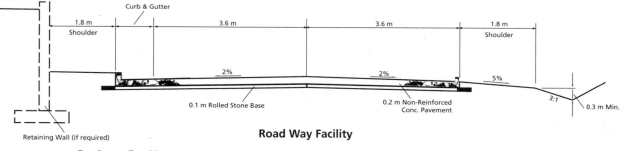

Road Way Facility

Southwest Corridor
Roadway Section Type 1

Item	Unit Cost	Quantity	Cost per Linear Meter
Clearing and Grubbing	$815/ha	15 m width	$7.60
Grading	$5.40 m²	15 m width	$82.00
Pavement	•	•	•
Shoulders	•	•	•
Fencing	$20.00 m	1 m	$20.00
Lighting	•	•	•
•	•	•	•
•	•	•	•
•	•	•	•
Section Cost per Linear Foot			\<Column Sum\>

Note: Cross-section and unit costs are for purposes of example only.

Figure 9–1   Typical Section and Composite Unit Costs for Roadway Section

Source: *Procedures and Technical Methods for Transit Project Planning,* Washington, D.C.: Federal Transit Administration, 1986.

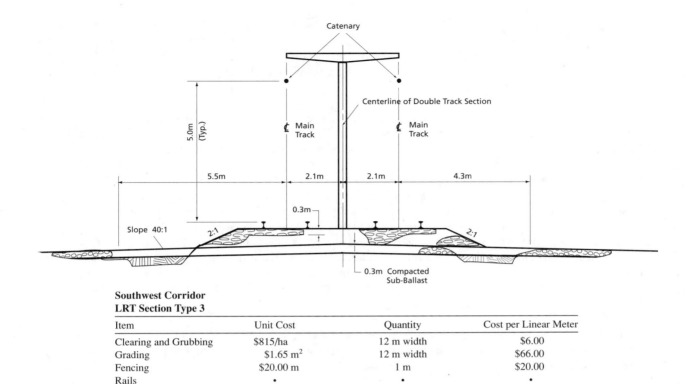

Southwest Corridor
LRT Section Type 3

Item	Unit Cost	Quantity	Cost per Linear Meter
Clearing and Grubbing	$815/ha	12 m width	$6.00
Grading	$1.65 m^2	12 m width	$66.00
Fencing	$20.00 m	1 m	$20.00
Rails	•	•	•
Ties	•	•	•
Ballast	•	•	•
•	•	•	•
•	•	•	•
•	•	•	•
Section Cost per Linear Foot			<Column Sum>

Note: Cross-section and unit costs are for purposes of example only.

Figure 9–2 Typical Section and Composite Unit Costs for Transit Section

Source: *Procedures and Technical Methods for Transit Project Planning,* Washington, D.C.: Federal Transit Administration, 1986.

and 9–2 illustrate the typical cross-section and composite unit cost for a roadway section and a light rail transit section.

Segments or areas, including certain areas of mitigation, cannot be handled by the typical section or item approach and will require special analyses to obtain a reliable estimate of capital costs. These segments or areas are usually costed in more detail by using the drawings (possibly at a larger scale), detailed quantities, and unit costs for each quantity item. These special segments or area capital costs usually do not include cost related to the rights-of-way, special utility relocation, systemwide elements, and other add-on-items.

Estimates of right-of-way cost should include allowances for appraisals, negotiations, and residential and business relocation in the capital cost estimate. Costs related to utility disruption and relocation and the effects of "master agreements" (agreements with the local government, utilities, or railroads on handling interfaces, disruption, and relocation) should be identified and costed.

The cost of systemwide elements is usually estimated on a unit-cost basis. For transit alternatives this could include vehicles, power distribution systems, train control systems, fare collection devices, maintenance facilities, and communications. For highway alternatives this could include central control equipment, loop detectors, data communications, closed-circuit television cameras, changeable message signs, an operations control center, and the like.

Add-on items consist of contingency allowances and other costs related to engineering, construction management, project mobilization, traffic management, agency administrative cost, insurance and other matters. These costs are usually estimated as a percentage of the direct construction costs. Typical percentages of add-on allowances are 20 percent for engineering and construction management, 10 percent for project mobilization and traffic management, and 10 percent for agency administration and insurance.

Contingency allowances for construction, right-of-way, utilities, purchase of vehicles, and other items will vary from 15 to 40 percent, based on the uncertainty attached to the complexity of the item, with 25 percent a typical average. Each element of the estimate can have a contingency factor based on the degree of risk or uncertainty at this stage of the planning process.

In order to prepare realistic comparative capital cost estimates for each alternative, data from current similar local and remote projects should be used as a basis for the unit costs. The local transportation agency with experience in the planning, design, and construction of transportation projects is usually the best source of data for developing unit costs (the state department of transportation, county or municipal highway and public works department, or a transit agency). If data from other geographical areas need to be used because of the lack of actual local construction experience or a very small local data base, those costs will need to be adjusted to reflect the following: scale of the alternative, local conditions, market changes, construction seasons, availability and local cost of materials, and labor and equipment, as well as escalation factors (using documented construction cost indices) to convert from past years and other locations to the local area and base year of estimate.

Usually, capital unit costs and the capital cost estimates are initially prepared in current dollars (i.e., the present year) for evaluation purposes. For financial planning, however, the estimates are escalated to reflect actual construction schedules. The transformation of these costs is discussed below.

Transformation of Capital Costs

The major uses of the capital cost estimates will be as input to the evaluation of the alternatives and the financial planning analysis. To support these efforts, annual capital cost projections may be needed for each alternative. Realistic implementation schedules for the design and construction of alternatives may need to be prepared in conjunction with the planned operational date and the financial planning activities. The schedules (cash flows) and cost components (e.g., design, construction, vehicles) are broken out to allow financial planning efforts to apply different revenue sources to different cost components as appropriate. The cost component breakdowns should be done in consultation with the financial planners before the capital costs are finalized.

The evaluation and financial planning analyses may require that the capital cost estimates be presented in different forms to allow for the analysis of the cost and benefits of each alternative. Two methods are typically used: (1) direct annualization of the capital costs based on the expected usable life of the cost component and (2) the concept of the net present value (also called present worth) over a predefined period.

Based on the capital cost and annual capital cost projections developed for each alternative, the values for both methods can be determined depending on the assumptions for discount rates and the economic life of each capital cost component.

For evaluation of any project advanced for federal funding, the U.S. Office of Management and Budget currently requires that federal agencies use a discount rate of 7 percent. Since this rate is used with cost expressed in constant dollars, it represents a rate of return net of inflation. Table 9–1 summarizes annualization factors (assuming a 7 percent discount rate) for various lives.

Table 9–2 illustrates the application of the annualization factors to components of a capital cost estimate. Each item (or category of construction) of the capital cost estimate is deemed to have a useful life ranging from twelve years for a bus vehicle to structures with a 30-year life. Right-of-way is assumed to have a 100-year life. "Soft" costs such as engineering and construction management and contingencies are allocated to the "hard" cost because they are developed in conceptual level capital cost estimating as a function (percentage) of capital cost. At a 7 percent discount rate, the $346,532,000 total capital cost (in present dollars) shown in Table 9–2, has an equivalent annualized capital cost of $28,768,100.

O&M Cost Estimating

In many transportation planning studies, a reliable estimate of the costs of operating and maintaining each alternative is important in the accurate assessment of its cost-effectiveness and financial implications. In some situations, estimates of O&M costs are unlikely to help distinguish among the alternatives and consequently may not be part of the technical work supporting the study.

Therefore, an important initial question regarding O&M costs is whether or not an effort to develop cost estimates is appropriate in a particular study. O&M cost estimates are likely to be useful for:

- major changes in the transit system and introduction of new transit modes;

- major highway alternatives in a study considering both highway and transit options; and

- highway alternatives that include significant traffic-management components (including intelligent transportation system [ITS] strategies such as incident management, control centers, special police enforcement, and reversible high-occupancy vehicle [HOV] lanes).

Table 9–1   Annualization Factors

Discount Rate: 0.07

Asset Life (years)	Annualization Factor
1	1.070
2	0.553
3	0.381
4	0.295
5	0.244
6	0.210
7	0.186
8	0.167
9	0.153
10	0.142
11	0.133
12	0.126
13	0.120
14	0.114
15	0.110
16	0.106
17	0.102
18	0.099
19	0.097
20	0.094
25	0.086
30	0.081
40	0.075
50	0.072
75	0.070
100	0.070

O&M cost estimates for major changes in the transit system are usually very important both for the assessment of relative costs and benefits and for financial planning. Analogous estimates are usually needed for major highway alternatives in a multimodal transportation planning study, since an even-handed comparison of highway and transit options should be done with an accounting of all costs for both modes. Where traffic management features are likely to involve additional staffing and equipment, an estimate of O&M costs is a necessary element of the costs involved.

For studies that do not include major transit alternatives or major highway options with significant operational features, O&M cost estimates for the highway options may be much less important *at the corridor or subarea levels*. Differences in O&M costs among highway options are often modest. Further, because individual highway projects represent relatively modest additions to the highway system (from either the statewide or regionwide perspective), the financial implications for any individual alternative are usually very modest.

Table 9–2   Example of Annualized Capital Cost Development

Item	Assumed Useful Life	Annualization Factor	Total Cost	Annualized Cost
ROW	100	0.07	31,959,000	$2,237,100
ROW Preparation	100	0.07	included in ROW above	
Structures	30	0.081	181,954,000	14,738,300
Trackwork	30	0.081	21,079,000	1,707,400
Signals/Electrical	30	0.081	15,837,000	1286,800
Pavement	25	0.094	55,837,000	5,226,700
Rail Vehicle	25	0.086	36,261,000	3,170,000
Buses	12	0.126	3,189,000	401,800
Contingencies	NA*			
Engin/Const. Mgmt.	NA*			
Total			$346,532,000	$28,768,100

*These costs are allocated to the elements above.

The discussions below outline two approaches—cost-allocation and resource build-up—that are available for O&M costing in transportation planning studies where these cost estimates are needed.

General Approach

Figure 9–3 provides an outline of the work related to O&M costing within the overall context of the development and refinement of the alternatives. Initial work on the development of O&M cost estimates involves a preliminary analysis that identifies a service and operating plan for each alternative that is a major component of the detailed definition of alternatives. Subsequent work focuses on two different activities that are largely independent of each other.

One activity involves the analysis of travel forecasts and refinement of service policies that lead to a final operating plan that optimizes the performance of each alternative. This work involves detailed coding and analysis of the highway and transit networks, preparation of travel forecasts, and adjustments to operating plans (HOV requirements, time-of-day restrictions, transit services, and so forth). It concludes with the development of supply characteristics that are the necessary inputs to the models of O&M costs. Supply characteristics typically include, for highway facilities, the number of lane kilometers of new facility, the number of new structures, enforcement or maintenance policies, snow removal policies, and so forth. For transit

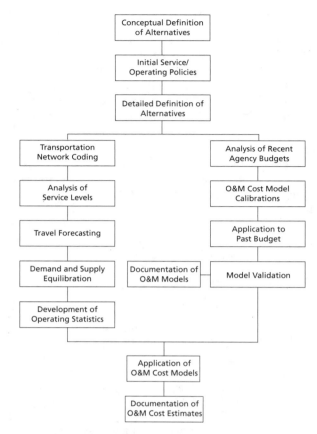

Figure 9–3   Estimating O&M Costs

facilities and services, supply characteristics typically include vehicle-kilometers; vehicle-hours (or a term more related to the operator and driver time called platform hours); and peak vehicles, often stratified by vehicle type (standard-size bus, articulate bus, minibus, van, and rail.)

The other activity involves the development of the O&M cost models themselves. This effort requires a detailed operating agency budget statement and an accurate estimate of service characteristics from a recent fiscal year. To the extent possible, the chosen fiscal year should be both stable—in that no significant changes in service levels, labor productivity, or wage rates occurred—and representative, in that service characteristics are similar to the current operation. Where the alternatives include modes or operating practices that are new to the local area, the model will also require data from other urban areas where these modes and practices are in place.

The O&M cost models are calibrated simply by identifying those costs that are variable with service levels and then attributing each variable cost item to the service characteristic to which it is most closely tied. The resulting unit costs can then be applied to variations in service characteristics to estimate the O&M cost of the alternatives.

Ideally, the O&M cost models should be validated by applying them to a past fiscal year in which service levels were somewhat different and examining how well the estimated costs match the actual expenditures for that year. Obvious candidates for the fiscal year selected for the validation work are those prior to major expansion or contraction of service. Difficulties may arise in obtaining cost records in the same accounting format and staffing records in sufficient detail to examine changes in labor productivity. The effort should be made, however, because the validation of the cost models against an operation that is somewhat different from that in the calibration year adds substantial credibility to its estimates for the alternatives.

Application of the O&M cost models is straightforward. The service characteristics for each alternative are used in the models to estimate staffing levels, labor costs, and material costs.

Aggregate Cost-Allocation Models

The most common O&M cost models employ a "cost-allocation" approach in which: (1) each line item of O&M costs from a recent budget year is allocated to one of several service variables and (2) the costs assigned to each variable are then summed and divided by the annual total for that service variable. The resulting model therefore consists of a set of aggregate unit costs taking, as general examples, the following forms:

- *Highway example—*
  Total O&M Cost = $\quad C_m \times$ (Lane Kilometers)
  $+ C_p \times$ (Pavement Area)
  $+ C_s \times$ (Major Structures)

- *Transit example—*
  Total O&M Cost = $\quad C_m \times$ (Vehicle Kilometers)
  $+ C_h \times$ (Vehicle Hours)
  $+ C_v \times$ (Peak Vehicles)
  $+ C_p \times$ (Passengers)

It is important to recognize that there are limitations to this approach, most of which stem from the highly aggregate nature of the resulting model. First, it is difficult to adjust the model for service conditions that are quite different from those that prevail in the system on which the model was calibrated. For example, embedded in the aggregate unit cost per vehicle-kilometer are average levels of police enforcement and the average fuel economy of current buses operating in mixed traffic. Where a transportation planning study considers a barrier-separated HOVway that carries significant bus volumes, adjustments to the per-lane-kilometer and per-vehicle-kilometer costs are necessary to reflect the higher level of police enforcement on the facility and the better fuel economy of buses separated from stop-and-go traffic. However, in aggregate cost-allocation models, the appropriate adjustments are obscured by the aggregation of maintenance, fuel, and other related costs into a single factor.

Second, the aggregate nature of the model makes checks on labor productivity levels difficult. These checks are important when the year on which the cost model is calibrated includes anomalies. One example is the extra staffing of operators and mechanics in training, preparatory to a significant expansion of transit services. Unit costs would be abnormally high in a model calibrated on this year since these staff positions contribute to costs while not yet providing additional service levels. A second example is the calibration of cost models from budget years in which wage rates have been frozen. In this case, it would be desirable to test alternative future wage rates given the uncertainty of the long-range change in wages. Again, however, the aggregate approach to O&M cost models obscures labor and material productivity and unit costs to an extent that problems may arise in the accurate calibration and applications of the models.

Resource Build-Up Models

In transportation planning studies where accurate forecasts of O&M costs are important, consideration should be given to development of cost models that use a resource build-up approach. Resource build-up models compute costs by estimating the labor and materials needed to provide a given level of service and maintenance and then applying projected unit costs of labor and material. In its most detailed form, a resource build-up model represents costs in a series of equations:

$$\text{O\&M Cost} = \text{(unit of service)}$$
$$\times \text{(productivity ratio: resources per unit of service)}$$
$$\times \text{(resource unit cost)}$$

Units of service typically include the same characteristics as found in cost-allocation models. They are derived from both the physical description and the final operating plan for each alternative. The resource-required-per-unit-of-service is a productivity measure expressed, for example, in such terms as "pavement-maintenance crews per thousand lane-kilometers," "police officers per lane-kilometer of HOVway," "mechanics per vehicle-kilometer," and "liters of diesel fuel per vehicle-kilometer." These productivity ratios are derived from local budget documents and, in the case of new modes, from data obtained from similar facilities and services in other areas. Unit costs are expressed in such terms as "average annual wages per maintenance worker" and "average price per liter of diesel fuel." They are also derived from recent budget documents, supplemented where necessary with data from other areas.

When cost data from other agencies are used for new modes or operating policies, it is important that the appropriate mix of new and older systems are represented in estimating the unit and productivity costs. The objective is to develop a process that accurately predicts long-term O&M costs for the system of concern. For example, rail maintenance costs should not be derived from systems recently opened because these costs are likely lower than the long-term costs. Similarly, cost data from older systems, which incur higher than normal costs due to deferred maintenance practices, should not be used exclusively. Because judgment is required in deciding these issues, it is important that the justification for using one system over another, or for using a mix of systems, is properly documented in the methodology report describing how the O&M costs are to be developed.

Short-Term Forecasts

Productivity ratios are central to the resource build-up approach and describe the manner in which labor and material requirements vary with service levels. In the short term these relationships can take one of three forms—continuously variable, step-wise variable, and fixed. Continuously variable items are those for which the added cost of an additional service unit—a lane-mile—remains the same over the entire range of service levels. Such items as pavement maintenance, vehicle maintenance, and so forth, are well represented as continuously variable cost items.

Items that vary in steps have costs that vary in steps. A common example is the cost tied to the operation of maintenance facilities themselves (as distinct from materials storage and vehicle maintenance done at the facility). These costs include utilities, janitorial staff, security, and other items that increase only when a larger or added facility is needed. Thus, it would be incorrect to assign these costs to a continuous variable—lane-miles—since every additional lane-mile would incorrectly add to the cost of these items. The correct approach is to vary the facility costs with larger increments (or steps) of lane-miles, where the step size is the number of additional lane-miles that would require the opening of an additional maintenance facility.

Finally, fixed items are those whose marginal cost is zero over the expected range of system variables. Staffing in administrative positions—the district manager's office, personnel, legal, and so forth—is likely to fall within this category.

Long-Term Forecasts

While the differentiation of costs into continuous, step-wise, and fixed categories is appropriate for short-range projections involving annual cash flows, it is likely that all agency costs vary continuously over the 15- to 20-year planning period of major transportation investments. Consequently, typical practice in economic analysis treats all operating costs as variable in the long term. Long-term service expansion is an increase in real terms (net of inflation) in the salaries of department heads and other positions that do not otherwise increase in number. For example, a general manager's salary is likely to increase in real terms as the size of the agency increases. Similarly, if the agency became significantly smaller, the general manager's salary would likely decrease. It is difficult to predict the size of the increase or decrease, but relating the cost of these positions to a continuous service variable is a straightforward way of recognizing this effect.

An Example

Table 9–3 illustrates one approach to modeling the costs of bus maintenance and servicing for a representative transit operation. For each cost item, the third column identifies the service variable to which the cost has been assigned. The "model" itself consists of the productivity ratios and unit costs in the next two columns. Outputs from the model are the labor requirements (if any) for each category and their estimated cost.

This table shows several options for portraying costs. In this example, all labor unit costs include both wages and fringe benefits. Thus the model would not be transparent in illustrating the effect of changes in the fringe ratio (relation of fringe benefits cost to wages)—a limitation likely to be quite acceptable in a planning analysis. An alternative specification would be to use separate line items for the wages and fringes in each labor category. The added flexibility of this specification must be traded-off, however, against the relatively large number of line items that would be added to the model. A useful compromise may be to use the more detailed specification for vehicle operators only, reflecting the magnitude of this expense and the variability of operator fringes.

Also in this example, all staff positions within a fixed line item are counted and costed together. Thus, in the office of the director of operations, the model does not identify individual positions or salaries and would not be able to illustrate the effects of different staff mixes. Again, this limitation would have no effect on the usefulness of the model in a planning analysis; and a more detailed specification of the fixed offices could be used in situations where the staffing mix was an issue.

Table 9–3   Sample Sections of a Detailed O&M Cost Model

Acct	Resource Category	Variable Service	Resource Productivity	Unit Cost	Staff	Cost ($000)
010	office of director of operations	peak vehicle	*1 staff* per 200 peak veh	*$47,000/* staffer		
	schedulers	peak vehicle	*1 staff* per 65 peak veh	*$28,700/* staffer		
	shift supervisors	garage	*3 supervisors* per garage	*$38,400/* supervisor		
	street supervisors	vehicle-hour	*1 supervisor* per 0.14MM veh-hr	*$34,100/* supervisor		
	support staff	garage	*5 staff* per garage	*$22,000/* staffer		
032	fuel	vehicle-kilometer	*0.31 liter* per veh-km	*$0.94/* gal		
	lubrication	vehicle-kilometer		*$0.012/* veh-km		
033	tires and tubes	vehicle-kilometer		*$0.021/* veh-km		
042	office of director of maintenance	peak vehicle	*1 staff* per 250 peak veh	*$38,000/* staffer		
	maintenance supervisor	garage	*3 supervisors* per garage	*$36,200/* supervisor		
	support	garage	*2 staff* per garage	*$22,000/* staffer		
050	service mechanics	peak vehicle	*1 serv. empl.* per 11 peak veh	*$24,600/* service empl		
	cleaning	peak vehicle	NA	*$0.213/* veh km		
060	bus mechanic	vehicle kilometer	*1 mechanic* per MM veh-km	*$29,600/* mechanic		
	parts	vehicle-kilometer		*$0.213/* veh-km		

This table also illustrates several forms of productivity ratios. These arise from an effort to keep the ratios in meaningful units. For labor items in which there are several staff positions associated with each service unit, the numerator of the productivity ratio is greater than 1. For example, operations supervisors are represented as three positions per garage, rather than one position per 0.333 garages. The converse occurs when there are several units of service associated with one position. Service mechanics, for example, are specified at 1 position per 11 buses rather than 0.09 positions for each bus. In both examples, the two specifications are equivalent and the model would yield the same result. However, the preferred specifications yield ratios that are much more easily interpreted.

Finally, Table 9–3 also presents the difficulty in computing productivity ratios for many material line items. While some items—diesel fuel, for example—have natural productivity ratios, many do not. Maintenance parts and cleaning supplies in this case cannot be quantified in any single unit. Their productivity ratio, then, is expressed directly in terms of costs-per-service-unit ($/vehicle-kilometers and $/peak vehicle, respectively).

Estimating Input Variables for Service and Maintenance

Many of the input variables for O&M cost models are physical attributes of the alternatives—lane-kilometers, track-kilometers, number of major structures, number of stations, and so forth. These variables are readily prepared from the descriptions of the alternatives. Other variables are operating characteristics for each alternative—hours of operation of HOV lanes; ITS operations; and a range of transit service variables, including vehicle-hours, vehicle kilometers, and peak vehicles. For transit alternatives, estimates of these service variables usually rely on the mathematically coded network representations used in demand forecasting.

A large number of simplifying assumptions are made in developing these coded networks, assumptions that overlook many of the nuances of transit scheduling. Coded networks used for patronage forecasting cannot begin to describe all of the route variations, headway changes, deadheading, and other details found in a real transit schedule. An understanding of the importance of these details helps to minimize their potential for introducing errors into the estimates of service variables. Often, it is necessary to perform additional calculations with the service characteristics estimated by the coded networks. Separate, spreadsheet-based analyses are useful for capturing the variety of transit service variations that are not coded explicitly into the networks. Calibration of the relationships in the spreadsheets can be done with the base-year transit system and its coded network representation. It is important that the service characteristics are derived from the final operating plan for each alternative—after completion of all level-of-service analyses, supply and demand balancing, and service refinements.

Life-Cycle Costing

Life-cycle costing analysis combines the initial (construction) cost of a project with its ongoing O&M costs, plus future capital facilities replacement and rehabilitation costs. Life-cycle costing provides a way of examining the trade-off between capital investment and O&M cost over some period of time. For instance, a high initial investment, in automated systems for example, would allow lower ongoing O&M costs. On the other hand a low initial investment might entail a higher level of O&M expenditures and perhaps sooner obsolescence, replacement, or rehabilitation. Those costs that occur at some point in the future will expend future dollars. A dollar spent at some point in the future is worth less than a dollar spent sooner. Thus, in life-cycle costing, each of the future O&M costs are discounted back to current dollars to provide a common basis for comparing other investment options or strategies. (Discounting is discussed later in the section titled "Economic evaluation tools.")

Life-cycle costing can be used in many ways. Within the context of evaluation and financial planning for a transportation planning study, the key is to clearly establish a performance standard that the transportation services and facilities are intended to meet over the lifetime of the analysis. The performance standard usually establishes the acceptable reliability, capacity (throughput) or equipment availability, operating speed, and safety level. Such standards affect the capital costs (the size, amount of redundancy, level of design, quality of material and equipment) and O&M costs (number and expertise of staffing, level of upkeep). The higher the standard, the higher the capital cost and/or O&M cost to maintain the standard over the analysis period of the service and/or facility.

The method to prepare a life-cycle cost analysis typically involves preparing a schedule of costs—implementation (design and construction) and the ongoing O&M cost from the start-up of operations through continuing service. At the end of the useful life of the facility or equipment, there may be future capital costs to rebuild, rehabilitate, or replace it. Operating costs usually increase as usage of the facility increases. Maintenance costs usually increase as the facilities and equipment get older or more heavily used. Each of these future costs is then discounted from its year of expenditure back to a present year cost using a discount rate (interest rate or cost of money.)

An example of useful life are transit vehicles: transit buses are considered to have a useful life of about twelve years while a rail transit vehicle has a twenty-five-year life. Usually a rail vehicle will require some midlife rehabilitation and technology upgrade. The degree of rehabilitation or the timing of when it needs to occur depends on the previous level of upkeep and maintenance performed on a regular basis.

The U.S. Federal Transit Administration (FTA) uses a cost-effectiveness measure for considering candidate projects for discretionary federal capital funding. The FTA approach uses a relatively straightforward method using an "annualization factor" to convert the total capital cost into an *equivalent annual capital cost* (see the earlier section titled "Transformation of capital costs") that can then be combined with the annual O&M cost to create an equivalent total project cost. The $346,532,000 total capital cost (in present dollars) converted to an equivalent annualized capital cost of $28,768,100 shown in Table 9–2 could be combined with an annual O&M cost of $15,483,000 for a total equivalent annualized cost of $44,251,100. This measure is later described in the discussion on cost-effectiveness in the section titled "Multiple measure evaluation framework."

Funding Sources and Allocation

One of the fundamental characteristics of constructing or implementing any transportation action is the requirement for funding. Despite substantial investment in transportation—highways, transit, railroads, airport, and port facilities—from the federal, state, regional, and local levels of government as well from the private sector, the need for new transportation facilities and for improving existing facilities often exceeds the funds available. Even with the substantial levels of funding in recently passed federal transportation authorization bills (see Chapter 20, "Regulatory and Legal Issues"), the funding needs are greater than the available funding and requires that steps be taken to allocate existing resources in the most cost-effective manner possible. Evaluation, programming, and priority setting are discussed later in this section; but first, funding sources and mechanism are reviewed.

Funding Mechanisms

The governmental and private sectors invest large sums of money in transportation. In TEA-21 over the next six years, the U.S. federal governments will invest $218 billion in surface transportation. This level of authorization represent a 40 percent increase over the previous funding levels provided in ISTEA, which in itself was a substantial increase over earlier funding levels. Of this, $174.6 billion is for highways, $41 billion for mass transit programs, and $2 billion for safety programs. As in the past, a large portion of the revenue for this funding is the federal gasoline tax of 18.3 cents per gallon.

In the public sector, the availability of funding for specific transportation projects depends to a large extent on the source of that funding. Funds for transportation projects come from many different sources and levels of government. In some cases, the funds are raised through property or sales taxes and become available through a community's general budgeting process. In other cases, funds become available through taxes on the users of the system (e.g., taxes on gasoline consumption). More recently, private sector groups like developers and business associations have been making substantial contributions to support transportation projects.

Some of the major mechanisms for funding transportation projects and operations include the following:[2]

---

[2] *Understanding the Highway Finance Evolution/Revolution* (Washington, D.C.: American Association of State Highway and Transportation Officials, 1987).

1. *User fees*—taxes on gasoline have traditionally been the single largest source of highway revenues since governments began large-scale construction of highways. Such taxes are applied mainly by the federal and state governments, and the proceeds are often placed in trust funds that serve as the source of funds for project support. For transit, user fees are the fares charged to riders.

2. *Registration and ad valorem taxes*—vehicle registration fees are the earliest form of user fees. In most cases, these fees are applied at a "flat" rate; however, in some states these fees are applied to vehicles on the basis of weight or some combination of weight, age, horsepower, and value. Ad valorem taxes are applied as a percentage of the vehicle sales price and thus represent a form of user taxation that keeps pace with inflation.

3. *Weight-distance taxes*—these taxes are applied on the basis of vehicle weight and distance moved by the vehicle. This tax is applied most often to heavy trucks. This is a relatively new form of taxation, but one which is being considered by many states and by the federal government.

4. *Tolls*—one of the earliest sources of revenue for highway and bridge construction, tolls have more recently served only a limited role in the nation's highway system mainly because of a federal prohibition on the use of tolls on highways and bridges constructed with federal funds. In recent years, however, officials have once again begun to look at the use of tolls as a means of providing highways and bridges.

5. *Nonuser tax sources*—over 23 percent of the funds used to support the highway system comes from general funds (i.e., monies allocated from the general treasury by legislative or executive bodies). This source of funds is used mainly at the local level where user taxes are not feasible. The most important sources of funds for the general treasury include property taxes, income taxes, sales taxes, and severance taxes.

6. *Debt financing*—to obtain the often large sums of funds that are needed to support a transportation investment program, governments sometimes issue bonds that provide the purchaser of the bonds a guaranteed rate of return. The return to the investor is guaranteed based on the revenue income of the governmental body (called general obligation bonds) or the revenue income from a particular project (e.g., tolls or a program; dedicated sales; or tax for transportation purposes, called revenue bonds).

7. *Private sector contributions*—in recent years, private sector groups such as developers, business associations, and major employers have been making substantial contributions in support of transportation projects. These contributions have taken several forms, including donations, cost-sharing, negotiated investments, benefit assessment fees, and impact fees.

The mechanisms for funding transportation projects vary from one jurisdiction to another, but in most cases the funding source will be one or more of the seven listed above. A recent assessment of the many types of funding mechanisms available to public officials is shown in Figure 9–4. As illustrated in this figure, there are many advantages associated with some funding mechanisms over others, and similarly there are also disadvantages. Perhaps the most important criteria for an effective funding technique are that it (1) provides stable levels of funding to accomplish program objectives, (2) is sensitive to inflation, and (3) is politically acceptable to elected officials and the general public.

Funding Programs

An important characteristic of transportation funding is that many of the federal and state funds for transportation are allocated on the basis of funding categories. Thus, for example, federal funds are available for specific types of projects (e.g., bridges) or for specific highway classifications (e.g., the primary versus secondary highway system). Other categories often found at the state level include funds for specific purposes (e.g., economic development), by mode (e.g., transit versus highway), and by organizational function (e.g., construction versus maintenance).

It is important to understand that the determination of how much money goes into which category for what purpose is fundamentally a political decision. Many of the categorical funds are allocated on the basis of formulae that try to incorporate some estimate of need into the allocation. However, even these allocation formulae are determined through the political process. Thus, one will often find funds allocated to specific projects or geographic regions that reflect more the requirements of the political decision-making process than it does any engineering rationale for transportation needs.

Figure 9–4 Evaluation of Alternative Financing Techniques

Alternative Finance Techniques	Description	Benefits[1]	Shortcomings[1]
User Fees			
Vehicle registration fees	A variety of fees and taxes imposed by most states on vehicle owners as part of the vehicle registration process. Can include a graduated tax on vehicle weight or distance traveled. Usually considered a charge for access to system and not based on use of system. Provides stable source of revenue.	1, 12	5, 10, 11
Fuel taxes	Levied by all states on fuel sales. Some local governments are authorized to impose motor fuel taxes and share in state fuel tax revenues. Are easily administered and produce substantial revenues.	2, 3, 18	9, 15
Parking taxes, fees, fines	Imposed by local governments on vehicle drivers or facility operators. Can yield significant revenue in large urban areas but may have adverse impact on local businesses.	4, 21	1, 2, 5, 18
Tolls	Fees charged to users of a facility. Generally based on size, weight, number of axles, and distance traveled. Can produce high amounts of revenue and are particularly useful where revenue lags behind increased traffic demand.	3, 11, 12, 14, 17, 18	5
Transit fares	Involves patronage fares, passes, and surcharges for peak-hour use. A combination of several alternatives may be necessary to maximize return.	7, 18	5
Utility fees	Transportation tax added to water and sewer fees based on consumption. Could include street utility fees.	2	2
Nonuser Fees			
Property taxes	Levied on both real and personal property. May be imposed by states, local governments, or transportation authorities, although some states have rate limitations. Revenues are inflation sensitive.	5, 1	23
Income or payroll taxes	Includes employer payroll taxes and employee income taxes. Can produce substantial revenue due to large base; however, few local governments are authorized to use income taxes for transportation.	3	2, 15
Sales taxes	Imposed on general merchandise, specific services, and luxury items by most states and many local governments. Some portions may be diverted or dedicated for transportation. Easily administered and responsive to inflation.	1, 2, 5	22
Severance taxes	Levied on removal of minerals and natural products from land or water. Can be imposed on resource-extracting industries.	30	12
Special Benefit Fees			
Tax increment financing	Earmarked revenues from taxes on personal and real property based on increases above a fixed base attributable to transportation improvement. Must be authorized by the state and can be used only by jurisdictions with ad valorem taxing authority. Can be used to secure bonds.	6, 7	4, 15, 16
Special assessments	Charges to the owner of a property that benefits from an improved transportation facility. Can be based on frontage, area, value or a combination of factors. Can be used to support bond issues, although special legislation is usually required.	16	7, 14
Traffic impact fees	Imposed on private developers to mitigate impacts of the development on local service. Can be in the form of tax on area, sponsorship of a transportation program, or improvements to adjoining facilities. Can be used as a condition for obtaining site plan approval or building permit.	6, 7, 8, 9	2, 4, 6, 13, 15
Service charges	Charges on properties for direct access to a transportation facility. May be assessed as a lump sum contribution to a capital item or an annual fee to cover operating costs.	26	15
Private Financing			
Developer financing	Payment of capital transportation improvement costs by private developers in return for dedicated land, construction of specific facilities, traffic control measures, changes in existing zoning and building regulations, or subsidized facilities. May be voluntary or required by law. May result in reduction of public expenditures but can be inequitable to developers.	13, 15	2
Negotiated investments	Contributions by private developers to the cost of public transportation improvements in return for changes in existing zoning and building regulations. Revenue potential opportunities may be limited by growth, construction rate, mobility requirements, and location desirability.	15	2, 13

[1] See list of benefits and shortcomings on pages 14 and 15.

Source: J. Mason, et al. "Traffic Management," report prepared for the State Transportation Advisory Committee, Pennsylvania Transportation Institute, April 1989.

Figure 9–4   Evaluation of Alternative Financing Techniques *(continued)*

Alternative Finance Techniques	Description	Benefits[1]	Shortcomings[1]
Private ownerships	Includes sharing ownership costs between transportation agencies and private entrepreneurs, employer subsidies for transportation, or development of a private consortium with authority to finance, construct, and charge fees to provide transportation. Eligible for specific depreciation and investment tax credit.	20	
Private donation	Land or capital contributions by businesses and private citizens for improvements that have strong private interest. Donors benefit from tax deductions and access.	19, 20	17
Debt Financing			
Bonds	Appropriate for high front-end capital expense where a tax or fee can be pledged for debt service. Good source for obtaining the large amounts of revenue quickly' although local government's authority is usually regulated by the state.	10, 25	8, 26
Zero coupon bonds	Issued by public agencies at a price below face value and at a deferred unspecified interest rate. Discounting maturity value provides competitive, tax-exempt yield.	25	26, 27
Interest arbitrage	Investment of borrowed funds at a higher interest rate than is being paid. Can generate significant amounts of revenue, although public agencies face severe penalties for use other than to reinvest debt service reserve funds or to temporarily reinvest unspent bond proceeds.	3	25
Vendor financing	Loan provided by manufacturer for value of equipment. Often used to gain competitive bidding advantage. Does not generally require specific revenue pledge although local agencies need authority to issue.	29	28
Private leasing	Ownership of equipment or building by a private firm that then secures a bond and leases equipment or building to agency. Lease agreement is structured so that bond proceeds pay for most of the purchase price. Private firm benefits from accelerated depreciation allowances.	24, 27, 28	27
Private Property Utilization			
Leasing or selling rights	Involves the sale or lease of undeveloped land. subsurface rights, or air rights surrounding a public facility. Can generate site-specific revenue and can provide a steady, long-term cash flow.	22, 24	15, 27
Leasing/selling existing facilities	Can be potential revenue source, although it may require capital outlays and sophisticated real estate and development skills. Amount of revenue is affected by availability and condition of facilities, characteristics of local real estate market. May require approval if facilities are funded by federal or state sources.	23, 24	20, 21, 27
Special Revenues			
Advertising fees	Includes charging fees or taxes on billboard advertising and renting space on public facilities such as parking meters, bus shelters, vehicles, and terminals. Local government may require authority to monitor advertisements.	1, 2	19
Lottery	Allowed by several states although very few allocate revenue to transportation. Can result in substantial revenue although state legislation is required and operation involves close control and management.	3	3, 15, 24

Benefits
1. Stable source of revenue for public agency.
2. Easy for a public agency to administer.
3. Provides substantial revenues for a public agency.
4. Can yield significant revenues in large urban areas.
5. Revenues are inflation sensitive.
6. Taxes are based on benefits received by an owner, attributable to transportation improvements.
7. Can be used to secure bonds.
8. Mitigates impacts of specific developments on local service.
9. Can be used by a public agency as a condition for obtaining a site plan or building permit.
10. Good source for obtaining large amounts of revenue quickly.
11. Can be structured to encourage the use of high-occupancy vehicles.
12. Can be graduated according to the size or weight of the vehicle.
13. Developer is directly responsible for assisting in providing roadway improvements for at least part of the traffic from the development.
14. Improvements can be built quickly by a private developer.
15. Developer may have some voice concerning the improvements that are selected.

---

[1] See list of benefits and shortcomings on pages 14 and 15.

Source: J. Mason, et al. "Traffic Management," report prepared for the State Transportation Advisory Committee, Pennsylvania Transportation Institute, April 1989.

Figure 9–4 Evaluation of Alternative Financing Techniques *(continued)*

Alternative
Finance Techniques | Description | Benefits[1] | Shortcomings[1]

16. Costs are shifted to a group of property owners in return for special benefit that accrues to their property as a result of nearby, publicly constructed physical improvements. Cost may be shifted only to the extent of benefits received.
17. Enables a government to raise more funding for road construction than would be possible through ordinary public financing.
18. Those who use the roads or services pay for their upkeep.
19. Provides a means to complete infrastructure improvements more quickly.
20. Eligible for specific depreciation, investment tax credit, or tax deductions.
21. Can alter travel behavior.
22. Can benefit both employers and employees by providing prime location real estate to developers, office and retail space to employers and transportation facilities to workers.
23. Governmental agency realizes a cost savings since it does not have to buy land or condemn land for transportation purposes.
24. Offers the lessor a number of options for earning tax-exempt interest, plus claiming depreciation and tax investment credits.
25. IRS considers the income to be tax-exempt for bonds issued by public entities.
26. Developer is responsible for the cost of obtaining access to the system.
27. Effective way for government to acquire assets for the least amount of up-front capital investment.
28. May reduce maintenance and administrative problems.
29. Provides flexibility in negotiating since one bidder might offer a lower price, but no financing, and another could provide delivery at a reasonable price and extremely attractive financing.
30. Taxes are generally used to maintain roads used in extracting and hauling the taxed products.

Shortcomings
1. May have adverse impacts on local businesses.
2. Potential for economic inequality.
3. Involves close control and management.
4 Difficult to administer.
5. Collection of revenue can be labor intensive or costly.
6. Monies paid by the developer might not be used for roadway improvements near the development.
7. Statutes may limit using this device: for example, road construction may be authorized, but widening or repair and repaving may not.
8. Creates a long-term liability for the agency.
9. When not associated with inflation, the revenue can fail to keep pace with repair costs.
10. Fees do not generate revenues that are proportional to highway use unless the weight of the vehicle and the mileage driven are taken into consideration.
11. Certain "flat taxes, taxes not related to the amount of road use incurred by a motor carrier, have been found unconstitutional—for example, Pennsylvania's truck axle tax and decal fee.
12. Revenue is unpredictable.
13. Legal issues can arise in regard to the extent which a governmental body can attach conditions to zoning approvals.
14. State enabling legislation is required for the creation of Special Benefit Assessment Districts. Property owners frequently challenge the establishment of these in court.
15. Requires enabling legislation.
16. Difficult to separate transportation improvement induced benefits from other economic forces at work. Other tax jurisdictions. such as school districts or hospital districts that will be deprived of additional income, resist the creation of tax increment districts.
17. Transit agency must possess the legal power to accept donations.
18. Can discourage downtown shopping and job seeking and thus, in an overall sense, be counterproductive.
19. Kiosk advertising can hinder security by shielding areas from the view of security cameras and guards. Vandalism is a major problem.
20. Requires close interaction, persuasive powers, and political sensitivity with all parties involved.
21. Governmental agencies need special authority.
22. Sales tax tends to be regressive and the services taxes revenue do not generally benefit those who pay the taxes.
23. Property tax is one of the most unpopular taxes. It has been the focus of voter resistance in the recent past. Since it is a general tax, property tax payers do not necessarily receive equal public services for equal contribution.
24. Potential for strong opposition from religious groups and from those who feel it will attract organized crime or hurt the poor.
25. Must follow *strict,* narrowly defined IRS rules. The change in tax law will likely complicate use of this finance technique.
26. Bond issue often involves voter referendums or special authorization.
27. Tax laws were revised several times in the previous years.
28. Requires legislation: several debates have been held in Congress on the technique.

---

[1] See list of benefits and shortcomings on pages 14 and 15.

Source: J. Mason, et al. "Traffic Management," report prepared for the State Transportation Advisory Committee, Pennsylvania Transportation Institute, April 1989.

Public Sources

Federal funds typically come from either formula or discretionary programs. *Formula* programs allocate funds to state departments of transportation, or to a transit agency, to be used for specified types of programs or projects. Most U.S. DOT highway funds that come to state DOTs are allocated on a formula basis, and thus the state can reasonably plan on a certain amount of money each year. A *discretionary* program allocates a pool of money to specific projects, although projects must compete for an allocation of those funds. The U.S. DOT's FTA Section 5309 program, the primary source of capital funds for "New Start" transit projects, is a discretionary program. Competition for these funds is very strong nationally, with the dollar amount of the requests outstripping the amount available severalfold.

Most federal programs require some minimum match from local (non-federal) sources. For example, federal funds from FTA's discretionary Section 5309 program must be matched by a minimum of 20 percent non-federal funds. This means for $4 of federal funds, there must be a $1 match of non-federal funds. On the highway side there are similar local match requirements for the formula funding programs.

From time to time, "demonstration" funds from federal sources have been available to implement projects. Such a program is often framed to promote the development or practical application of a new or advanced technology. These funds can be in the form of outright grants or may be loans to be repaid over time.

State and local governments may have similar types of formula and discretionary funding programs. The state of Maryland funds transportation projects and operations through the Maryland Transportation Trust Fund, programmed each year through the Maryland Department of Transportation's Consolidated Transportation Program (CTP). The CTP is approved annually by the Maryland Governor and General Assembly.

Public development corporations or other agencies and authorities with the power to issue bonds, often with some level of tax-exempt interest payment to investors, can be used to raise capital funds for the project. However, there has to be a revenue source to pay the interest and principal on the bonds. This revenue could come from user fees, like tolls or fares; general tax revenue; or dedicated sales tax, real estate tax (property or hotel room tax), or amusement taxes.

Transportation projects are usually funded through a combination of federal, state, and local sources. Nonpublic (private) sources can also be included in helping to leverage public monies. Federal funds for support of O&M are being phased out as a matter of federal policy so that state and local sources are used to fill the gap between the costs and revenue generated from fares and other sources.

Private Sources

In private industry, investment in a capital project is made with the expectation that revenue generated from the operation of the project will exceed the costs of repaying any loans, including interest and the day-to-day O&M cost so as to provide a "profit." Private investments often employ tax strategies involving deductions and credits for interest and depreciation that are not used in typical publicly financed projects and do not have a comparable tax liability.

Private funding sources for public transportation investment could come from conventional investment loans, equipment manufacturers and vendors, and construction companies involved in the implementation of the project. These financial and implementation packages are usually selected in a competitive procurement process. What these lenders or investors do is provide up-front capital for construction, often structuring the loans to take advantage of interest and depreciation tax deductions and various investment credits, although there remains the need for a revenue stream to pay a return to the investors over time.

Public–Private Ventures

As discussed above, groups of investors, construction ventures, equipment vendors, and other associated interests will form teams to take on the entire implementation of a project in conjunction with public financial support to repay the investors over the long term. This approach, which has many forms and names (such as "DBOM" for "design-build-operate-maintain"), offers potentially faster implementation, up-front capital, and lower initial costs. While fares and advertising can provide some of the revenue needed to support private funding, traditional public sources are usually needed to provide the revenue stream to meet the entire need over time. In conjunction with public sector enabling capabilities, mechanisms to generate the revenue stream to support the debt and O&M costs can include:

- general tax revenue;

- sales tax;

- real estate tax, including a tax to capture the increased property values brought about by proximity to the transit line's stations;

- tax or fee from a special assessment or benefit district; and/or

- selling of air rights or related development rights associated with the transit project.

One possible mechanism is to allow an office or hotel developer with access to public transit to reduce the amount of on-site parking required. In lieu of building the full allotment of parking in areas where land could be expensive or scarce, the developer could contribute some portion of the cost of that parking toward the transit project or pay an annual fee, providing a revenue stream.

With private funds, many of the federal and other governmental approval requirements do not apply. This can reduce the amount of time needed to implement the project. If public funding is involved, or if public actions and approvals are required, however, many of the requirements still apply.

Financial Analysis

In considering the cost, benefits, and effects of transportation improvement alternatives, the financial wherewithal— the actual availability of funds and the legal and political ability to spend them—needs to be considered. In a transportation planning study financial analysis, the principal objective is to reveal to all participants and decision makers the financial consequences and implications of transportation investment alternatives. Where existing and planned funding sources are not sufficient to accomplish the alternatives, the financial analysis element can offer an opportunity to explore new funding options.

Analysis Framework

In the metropolitan areas, a transportation planning study financial analysis is conducted within the context of the region's financially constrained long-range plan. The financial analysis provides the necessary information to select a preferred alternative that fits within the fiscally constrained transportation plan and Transportation Improvement Program (TIP). Also, the financial analysis can provide the project-level financial information for FTA New Starts in the case of major transit improvements. (See the section later in this chapter on "Setting priorities and developing and implementing programs" and Chapter 12, "Urban Transportation," for further details on TIPs.)

A region's financially constrained long-range plan can be expected to include information that demonstrates a balance of *cost (need) cash flow* and *funding cash flow.*

- The plan's *cost cash flow* includes the funding needs for the list of projects in the adopted plan, as well as funding reserved for any placeholders identified for specific corridors or subareas. The schedule of funding needs for each project and placeholder—both construction and O&M—are shown. These needs are combined with the annual O&M, rehabilitation, and replacement needs of the existing transportation system. Combined, the costs for the existing and new systems constitutes the plan's cost cash flow needs.

- The plan's *funding cash flow* includes the stream of funding from established funding sources. The plan may also identify funding streams from new or additional sources that are expected to be available over the schedule of the plan.

A financially constrained long-range plan has the plan's cost cash flow needs in balance with the plan's funding cash flow.

The scope and extent of a transportation planning study financial analysis depend on the particular corridor or subarea and on what the plan includes for that corridor or subarea—either no funding or a "placeholder" amount. A general framework for the analysis of potential funding sources and any "shortfall" includes:

- Develop cost estimates for the alternatives—both construction and O&M needs.

- Develop the cash flow of the annual funding needs—based on the implementation schedule and operations.

- Identify existing sources of funding to meet those needs.

- Evaluate options, where shortfall exists, possibly including—

    Reallocation of funding priorities established in the long-range plan.

    Identification of the new regional sources.

    Identification of new corridor and subarea sources, such as local initiatives, taxing districts, toll/fare strategies, private sector, and joint development.

    Evaluation of new financing options, such as bonding, short-term notes, and leasing, for revenue generation potential, timing, stability, and equity.

At the end of the transportation planning study, a funding strategy is identified along with a preferred transportation strategy. Specific issues and considerations in developing and conducting a financial analysis are reviewed below.

Issues, Procedures, and Assumptions

The discussion that follows is not intended as a work plan. Instead, it provides a list of procedural and technical issues, questions, and typical concerns. In addition, it provides some general guidance with respect to certain major assumptions.

Which Alternatives are Analyzed?

Unlike other effects addressed in a transportation planning study, it is not always necessary to perform a financial evaluation of every alternative. Sometimes, it is only necessary to evaluate the most costly alternative, under the assumption that if funds are available for the most costly option, then funds will be available for less costly alternatives. However, there may be exceptions to this approach. For example, where there are major modal differences among the alternatives—such as highway versus light rail transit—it may be appropriate to examine at least one highway and one rail alternative. This is because certain funding sources may be available to one mode, but not another.

If the higher cost alternatives push the limit of feasibility, it may be desirable to do a financial analysis of a lower cost alternative that could be more feasible from a funding perspective. Such an analysis would identify the point at which the cost of an alternative exceeds a realistic projection of revenues.

Another example might be where one alternative has high capital costs, versus an alternative with high O&M costs. In some instances, a transportation systems management (TSM) alternative could also be evaluated, if for no other reason than to provide a basis of comparison with the built alternatives.

Begin with the Incremental Funding Needs of the Alternatives

An initial step of the financial analysis is to set forth the funding requirements for the alternatives. For the alternatives evaluated, capital and operating funding requirements are typically displayed on an annual flow-of-funds basis, over at least 20 years. For purposes of the TIP, capital, operating costs, and subsidies are expressed in nominal (inflated) or year-of-expenditure dollars. However, it is usually easier to perform the entire analysis in constant dollars and to convert to nominal dollars at the very end. An exception is if there are reasons to think that some of the costs—labor, for example—will rise either faster or slower than general inflation.

The initial flow of capital and operating funding will often reflect a *technically* driven construction schedule, such as might be generated by a critical path methodology (i.e., how quickly construction contracts can be let, how long it may take to perform each of the major construction activities, and other issues). This is a good place to start, especially if it reflects official objectives. The initial engineering-driven schedule can then be modified, if necessary, based on financial constraints that may require phasing or staging of implementation to match the availability of funds.

Conduct the Analysis within a Regionwide Context

It is typically necessary to place the financial analysis within a regionwide context. Are new funds going to be needed just for investments in the study corridor, or is there a larger "basket" of unfunded transportation needs that will be competing for any source of new funding? In the case of the former, major new regionwide sources of funding may not be needed or appropriate. Instead, corridor-specific sources, such as extended project phasing or changes in overall program prioritization, may be the appropriate approach. Where there is a substantially larger basket of unfunded high-priority needs, new broad-based state or local sources are perhaps more appropriate. This evaluation may be done separately from any particular study corridor analysis, in order to encompass the full regional context. However, it may not be possible to add the project recommended by the study to the plan and TIP until the regional analysis is completed and a funding plan or strategy is adopted. In the metropolitan areas, a transportation planning study financial analysis is conducted within the context of the region's financially constrained long-range plan.

Consider Fare and Pricing Options

One of the methods of closing an operating funding gap, which is sometimes overlooked, is to change the fare or toll structure. Small increases in systemwide transit fares may yield more than enough to offset any subsidy increase associated with a corridor alternative. It may be possible to impose tolls or fees for single-occupant vehicle (SOV) use of HOV lanes, where the HOV facility is expected to have some excess capacity available. (That is, excess HOV capacity can be "auctioned" to SOVs with the highest value of time.) Pricing assumptions used in the financial analyses would be carried through to the demand and related analyses so there is internal consistency.

Consider Private Sector Participation and Innovative Financing

The analysis could consider the potential for private sector participation and other innovative financing. While there are many possibilities here, assumptions ought to be realistic as to potential contributions of these sources, especially if legislative or regulatory changes are needed.

Link Financial Analysis to the Public Involvement Program

Where substantial regionwide funding shortfalls are evident, new regionwide sources may be needed. The real challenge is to build support for the funding plan and, in particular, for new sources of funding. Where new sources of funding are being considered, it is important to involve officials, stakeholders, and the public in that process. What new sources are likely to be politically acceptable? Analyzing "new" sources that have no support—or that are not likely to gather support in the future—could end up being an academic exercise and probably not worth the effort. Testing the waters for potential new sources, and even using formal survey techniques to rate the sources in terms of political acceptability, can be incorporated into the analysis.

Do Sensitivity Analysis

The analysis should include alternative scenarios. Variables that should be varied for sensitivity testing can include the capital costs, patronage and fare revenues, interest rates (where debt financing is an option), inflation assumptions, and economic variables that can affect the state and local transportation tax base. As always, the particular variables that are most critical will vary with the specifics of the transportation planning study. (See the section "Dealing with uncertainties" later in this chapter.)

Evaluation Methods and Their Purposes

The evaluation of alternatives is a continuing element of the work in transportation planning. In many ways, it is the central, organizing activity throughout the entire study program. Ideally, the very early work in a transportation planning study should develop a plan for the evaluation of alternatives. Some of the last work in the study invariably involves the comparison of the cost, benefits, and other effects of the alternatives. Most of the technical work in between focuses on developing the information to complete this evaluation. The evaluation has at least five specific roles in the conduct of a transportation planning study:

- Development of the evaluation plan entails organizing the goals and objectives that are implicit or explicit in the public involvement program. Early work to develop a plan for the evaluation generally attempts to identify a clearly stated set of goals and objectives for transportation improvements in the corridor. These goals and objectives are often distilled from a wide variety of perspectives and interests that are represented among the participants in the study. Consequently, the evaluation plan can help to synthesize the early inputs received in the public participation program and ensure that all questions will be addressed in the analysis.

- The evaluation plan identifies the information that is to be produced in the technical analysis. Given a clear statement of goals and objectives, a key step in the development of an evaluation plan is the identification of performance measures that will be used to examine the success with which the alternatives meet each objective. These performance measures effectively provide an inventory of the information to be developed and, therefore, the technical work to be done during the study.

  The evaluation criteria provide the basis for continual assessment and refinement of the alternatives as the work progresses and more information becomes available. It is useful to recognize that the evaluation phase of transportation planning—and of any assessment of complex options—is not restricted to the final phase of the analysis. Rather, it is a continuous and comprehensive process within which the technical work proceeds. The process is continuous in that there is a series of decisions that must be made throughout the analysis—alignment variations, design standards, operating policies, and the like—that together shape the nature and performance of each alternative. It is comprehensive in that the final evaluation of alternatives considers a broad range of criteria—transportation, environment, costs, finances, and other factors—that require a broad perspective. Clearly then, the ongoing decision making should be carried out with regard to its ultimate effect on the evaluation of each alternative and should be reviewed by the study participants in that light.

  The evaluation of the alternatives organizes the presentation of technical conclusions. The nature of corridor planning—a detailed assessment of complex alternatives in several technical aspects—can lead to an overabundance of information that loses its usefulness in decision making. The evaluation of alternatives plays a critical role in sifting and organizing this information to help highlight the key differences among the alternatives.

- The evaluation plan ensures that the transportation planning study develops whatever additional information may be needed by federal agencies or congressional committees as discussed in the section on FTA New Starts Criteria. While the structure and content of the evaluation is determined largely by the information needs for local decision making, the evaluation plan should also provide for the development of any additional information that might be required by federal agencies or congressional committees. Typically, the information requested by the federal government is the same as—or can be easily derived from—the information needed for local decision making. Consequently, a coordinated effort to develop all of the information can help to avoid follow-up work to answer additional questions.

There is no standard content for the evaluation of alternatives in a transportation planning study. The general goal is to produce the information needed by participants in the study so that they can get on with decision making at the end of the technical work. This audience includes local officials, local and state agencies, affected residents and businesses in the corridor, the general public, and (where certain types of federal funds may be sought for a major investment) both the executive and legislative branches of the federal government.

Role of Goals, Objectives, Needs, and Problems Definitions

While many transportation professionals are accustomed to a strict focus on transportation problems and their solutions, transportation planning studies are increasingly identifying broader sets of factors to be considered in making decisions about major investments. Several of these factors introduce considerations that extend well beyond immediate transportation concerns. Further, initial public involvement activities in a study may identify a broader set of perspectives that participants in the study bring to the table and that are included in the goals and objectives for transportation improvements in the corridor. A key issue in a transportation planning study, therefore, is the integration of the central emphasis on transportation problem solving with the broader context of goals and objectives for a corridor and subarea.

Several goals are commonly found in a planning study statement of goals and objectives for transportation improvements in a corridor. These include:

1. Improvements in mobility (or accessibility);

2. Support for economic development; and

3. Preservation of the environment.

The first goal easily accommodates the central focus on transportation problems and their solutions. The second is often included to recognize the interactions between transportation and land development. The third goal easily accommodates the requirements under the federal National Environmental Policy Act or local requirements to consider the environmental consequences of the alternatives in decision making.

Typically, a number of objectives are identified within each of the goals to call out the specific considerations that are important in the corridor of interest. The transportation goal, for example, may include a number of objectives that identify specific travel markets within the corridor. One objective may address commuter travel, a second suburb-to-suburb travel, and so forth. This approach is a useful way to organize the objectives that the alternatives will attempt to address and the evaluation measures that will be developed to quantify the degree of success of each alternative.

The principle here is to recognize concerns that will play a role in decision making of various participants in a transportation planning study and to provide sufficient information to support informed decision making. A careful approach to the structuring of the goals and objectives early in the study will provide a solid foundation for the development of alternatives that respond directly to the transportation problems and other goals in the corridor, the selection of evaluation measures that effectively present the technical results, a technical approach that focuses on the important issues, and a public involvement program that effectively communicates the information needed for decision making.

There are many methods that have been used by engineers and planners to answer these questions. Some have been used more than others, and each has its advantages and limitations. Before discussing these methods, however, some attention must be given to how benefits and costs are defined.

Definitions of Benefits and Costs

In its broadest sense, a benefit is a desirable effect of an investment, where "desirable" is defined as a positive effect on a society, a community, or an agency. Costs are usually defined as the dollar expenditures for both construction and O&M of a particular alternative. An analyst must be aware of several basic characteristics of benefit and cost measurement.

- *Real vs. pecuniary*—real benefits are those realized by the final consumers of a project, while pecuniary benefits are those gained at the expense of other individuals or groups. A good example of a pecuniary benefit is the increased value of land resulting from improvements to the transportation system. Although the owners of the land will benefit monetarily from these improvements, consumers of this land will ultimately pay higher rents or acquisition costs. From society's point of view then, there will be no net gain for the economy.

- *Direct vs. indirect*—direct benefits and costs are those specifically related to the investment, while indirect benefits and costs occur as "by-products." For example, improvements to a road or transit facility could have a direct benefit *to the users* of reduced travel times and a direct cost *to the implementing agency* of "x" dollars for construction. Indirect benefits might be the time savings *to other road users* caused by commuters diverting to the new facility (and thus reducing congestion on other routes). Indirect costs might be the cost *to other agencies* (e.g., police) that need to change operations because of the new project.

- *Tangible vs. intangible*—in economic terms, tangible benefits and costs are those that can be assigned a monetary value. Intangible benefits and costs are thus those where monetary values cannot be assigned (e.g., aesthetic design of a transit station). Although not defined monetarily, these intangible effects are often extremely important to decision makers and thus should be included in the evaluation in some form.

- *User vs. nonuser*—the "user" vs. "nonuser" distinction is an important concept in the transportation evaluation process. For example, many investments have been justified based on the monetary value of savings in user travel time. More recently, however, the benefits and costs affecting nonusers (e.g., the general community or specific neighborhood groups) have become very important in evaluation.

- *Total vs. incremental*—an estimate of total benefits and costs includes every effect that can be associated with a particular project. Incremental benefits and costs are those additional benefits and costs that are associated with a proposed change to an existing system. A transit example of an incremental cost assessment would be the estimation of the added costs associated with adding an express bus route to the services provided by the agency. These incremental costs would accrue to the transit operator, the agency responsible for freeway operations (assuming the express bus used the freeway), the freeway users, and the users of transit.

- *Initial vs. life-cycle costs*—the initial costs of a project are the capital costs associated with its construction. However, a better representation of project costs should include the costs of operation, maintenance, and rehabilitation. This type of costing procedure is called life-cycle costing. It allows the analyst, for example, to determine how much cost savings will occur with higher initial capital costs, if these higher costs result in lower overall maintenance expenditures.

The above characteristics of benefits and costs apply in general terms to all evaluation studies. But as noted above, a commonly used measure of transportation benefit is that which directly affects the user of the facility. There are many texts that examine in detail the economic theory underlying project evaluation (most often focussing on the concept of consumer surplus). It is beyond the scope of this chapter to review these concepts. However, it is important to know *that the quantifiable evaluation of user benefits is primarily a process of determining the reduction in negative effects that will occur if an improvement is made.* From the perspective of the user, reductions in the number of accidents, travel costs, and travel time comprise the most direct benefits of transportation projects. In most cases, the most significant of these is the reduction in user travel times. It has been estimated, for example, that between 72 and 81 percent of the calculated benefits of the U.S. interstate highway system have been attributed to travel time savings.[3]

Once the reduction in travel time, accidents, or travel cost is determined, it is multiplied by a unit value to determine a total savings for this measure. Of course, the validity of this approach depends to a great extent on the appropriateness of these unit values. It has been the determination of these values that has created considerable controversy among professionals. Of particular interest are the *value of time* and the *value of human life*.

- *Benefits from travel time savings*—the underlying basis for assigning a monetary value to travel time is that time not spent in travel can be used for other activities having economic value. Studies have shown that the value of time is sensitive to trip purpose, a traveler's income level, and the amount of time savings per trip.[4] In the case of work trips, the value of time is most often estimated as some portion of the average travelers' wage. For other trip purposes (e.g., shopping and recreational), the value of time is less obvious. Although a value of time that varies by traveler's income and amount of time savings theoretically is the most correct, for computational purposes it is usually assumed that the value of time is a constant, with one value for work trips and another for nonwork trips.

[3] G. Fallon et al., "Benefits of Interstate Highways," *Committee Print 91-41* (Washington, D.C.: U.S. Government Printing Office, 1970).

[4] T. Thomas and G. Thompson, "The Value of Time for Commuting Motorists as a Function of Their Income Level and Amount of Time Saved," *Highway Research Record 314* (Washington, D.C.: Highway Research Board, 1970).

Table 9–4 Comparison of Freeway and Truck Management Strategies
(Millions of Dollars Annually)

| | Economic Effects[1] | | | | | | | |
| | Freeway | | Direct | | Indirect | | | |
Strategy	Feasible	Congestion Relief	Motor Carriers	Other Vehicles[2]	Shippers/ Receivers[3]	CA Business Sales[4]	Air Quality[5]	Implementation Cost[6]
Traffic Management[7]	Yes	++	$8	$121	+	$8	+	$20–40
Incident Management[7]	Yes	+	$4	$44	+		+	$3–5
Night Shipping and Receiving[8]	Maybe	+	$3	+	–$2,200	–$913	+	$2–3
Peak-Period Ban *Core Freeways[8,9]	Unlikely	+	–$43	$7	–	–$28	–	$2–3

Notes: ++Significant positive effect.
   +Modest positive effect.
   –Modest negative effect.

[1] Dollars.

[2] Time and vehicle operating cost savings (+) or cost increases (–).

[3] Logistics cost savings (+) or cost increases (–).

[4] Changes in volume of business sales (output) in 1988 relative to baseline forecast. Traffic and incident strategies were combined because their individual direct (motor carrier) effects were too small to be modeled reliably.

[5] Not quantified.

[6] Ten-year annualized implementation costs.

[7] Los Angeles, San Francisco, and San Diego.

[8] Los Angeles and San Francisco only.

[9] Assumes eighty percent of peak-period truck kilometers of travel are diverted to arterials; twenty percent diverted to off-peak periods (midday or night).

Source: Cambridge Systematics, Inc., *Urban Freeway Gridlock: Summary Report,* report prepared for the California Department of Transportation, 1988.

- *Benefits from reduction in accidents*—just as the value of time differs by trip and traveler characteristics, the benefits of accident reduction also vary by certain characteristics, the most important being by type of accident and by the area where the accident occurred. In the case of fatal accidents, the analyst is faced with the difficult task of estimating the value of a human life. In addition, some choices have to be made on including *net future* earnings vs. *total future* earnings of victims, nonmonetary items such as loss to family or community service, and values associated with pain and suffering.

- *Benefit from reduced cost of vehicle operation*—included in this category of benefit is the reduction in the user costs of fuel, oil, maintenance and repairs, and depreciation. Typical unit values for operating costs vary by type of vehicle, roadway design and traffic characteristics, driver and trip characteristics, and the costs in an urban area for each component of the operating costs. Unit values and how they are used can be found in many handbooks.[5]

A study on the effect of trucks on freeway congestion in Los Angeles illustrates many of the above concepts associated with the definition of benefits and costs.[6] Table 9–4 shows a comparison of the effect of the different strategies considered in this study. The direct economic cost or benefit was defined as the time or vehicle cost savings or increase associated with each strategy. The analysis assumed a $20 value of time for motor carriers and a weighted average for all other vehicles

---

[5] See, for example, *Characteristics of Urban Transportation Systems* (Washington, D.C.: U.S. DOT, FHWA, 1988); *A Policy on Design of Urban Highways and Arterial Streets* (Washington, D.C.: American Association of State Highway and Transportation Officials, 1973); E. Morlok, *Introduction to Transportation Engineering and Planning* (New York, N.Y.: McGraw-Hill, 1978); and *State Highway Cost-Allocation Guide* (Washington, D.C.: U.S. DOT, FHWA, October 1984).

[6] *Urban Freeway Gridlock: Summary Report,* report prepared for the California Department of Transportation (Cambridge, Mass.: Cambridge Systematics, Inc., 1988).

of $10 per hour. Vehicle operating costs were defined as the wear and tear on tires and fuel. The indirect effects were defined as the changes in regional employment, personal income, and business sales as the direct costs and benefits that accrue to the motor carriers work their way through the regional economy. The implementation costs were mainly associated with the equipment and personnel needed to put each strategy in place. The air quality, freeway congestion relief, and feasibility assessments were simply judgments on the likely positive or negative effect of each strategy.

All of the benefit and cost measures discussed so far have one common characteristic—they can be expressed in dollars. Of course, many project decisions depend on more than just an economic analysis of costs and benefits. Importantly, other measures of project effect, most often not expressed in dollar terms, must be included in project evaluation. As noted by Meyer and Miller:[7]

> . . . the most important consequences of changes to the transportation system are not necessarily those measured strictly in monetary terms . . . . Nonmonetary effectiveness and equity implications can be much more important than an efficient expenditure of funds.

Nonetheless, the estimate of the monetary value of the benefits and costs associated with project alternatives and their consequent relevant worth is a significant component of evaluation efforts. The use of monetary value for benefits and costs leads to another important concept in evaluation—discounting and capital recovery.

Economic Evaluation Tools

Discounting and Capital Recovery

The costs and benefits associated with transportation projects can vary over time. For example, the often substantial capital costs occur at the beginning of a project's life cycle with the subsequent costs (O&M) occurring over the remainder of the project life in varying levels. Likewise, the benefits of a project are often the greatest at some point in the future when the facility is operating at near capacity. Because of this variation in the value of benefits and costs, the evaluation process must provide a benchmark that can be used to compare alternatives. This benchmark is developed by discounting the sums of money that exist at different points in time to a reference time period. This is done by using Equation 1.

Equation 1:
$$F = P \times (1 + r)^n$$

where:

F = future amount of money

P = present amount of money

r = discount rate

n = periods of repayment or project life

Thus, for example, if one invests $10,000 today with an interest rate of 10 percent for a one-year period, the investment at the end of that one year will be worth $10,000 \times (1 + 0.1)^1 = $11,000. The $10,000 today is equivalent to $11,000 in one year's time, or the $10,000 is the present or discounted value of the future $11,000. By rearranging Equation 1, the present value of future cost or revenues is

Equation 2:
$$P = \frac{F}{(1+r)^n}$$

In Equation 2, the factor $1/(1 + r)^n$ is called the *present worth factor* and is found in tabular form for different discount rates in many project evaluation texts (Table 9–5). In addition, most handheld calculators or computer programs

---

[7] M. Meyer and E. Miller, *Urban Transportation Planning: A Decision-Oriented Approach* (New York, N.Y.: McGraw-Hill, 1984).

contain present worth factors, thus there is often no need to look for a reference text.

Another important concept in project evaluation is knowing the present value of a constant stream of equal payments over several periods. The relationship between an initial investment and the annual payment over "n" years needed to repay the value of this initial investment is given by:

Equation 3: $A = P \left[\dfrac{r(1+r)^n}{(1+r)^n - 1} \right]$

where A is the uniform payments required over "n" periods. The term $[r(1 + r)^n / [(1 + r)^n - 1]$ is referred to as the *capital recovery factor* and represents the proportion of an initial investment that has to be recouped as benefits in each of "n" periods in order to return the same value as was invested. For example, the annual payment required to return the value of a present amount of $10,000 over ten years assuming an interest rate of 10 percent would be:

Table 9–5   Present Worth and Capital Recovery Factors

	Present Worth Factors				
Year	5%	8%	10%	12%	15%
1	.9524	.9259	.9091	.8929	.8696
2	.9070	.8573	.8264	.7972	.7561
3	.8368	.7938	.7513	.7118	.6575
4	.8227	.7350	.6830	.6355	.5718
5	.7835	.6806	.6209	.5674	.4972
10	.6139	.4632	.3855	.3220	.2472
15	.4870	.3152	.2394	.1827	.1229
20	.3769	.2145	.1486	.1037	.0611
50	.0872	.213	.0085	.0035	.0009
	Capital Recovery Factors				
Year	5%	8%	10%	12%	15%
1	1.0500	1.0800	1.1000	1.1200	1.1500
2	.5378	.5607	.5762	.5917	.6151
3	.3672	.3880	.4021	.4163	.4380
4	.2820	.3019	.3155	.3292	.3503
5	.2310	.2505	.2638	.2774	.2983
10	.1295	.1490	.1627	.1770	.1993
15	.0963	.1168	.1315	.1468	.1710
20	.0802	.1019	.1175	.1339	.1598
50	.0548	.0817	.1009	.1204	.1501

$$A = (\$10,000) \left[\frac{(0.1)(1.10)^{10}}{(1.10)^{10} - 1} \right] = \$1,627$$

Capital recovery factors are shown in Table 9–5.

For evaluation purposes, the benefits and costs associated with alternatives are assumed to occur at a single point in time, either expressed as present values or equivalent annual values. The present value method assumes all benefits and costs over the project life occur at the present time, while the equivalent annual cost method determines the series of payments over the project life that would have the same present values as the time stream of costs and benefits expected to occur if the project were implemented.[8] It is important to note that the estimation of the time stream of benefits and costs for a project can be quite complex. For example, many projects can experience costs (e.g., maintenance) that increase arithmetically or geometrically over time. In such cases, special equations can be used (found in engineering economy texts) that discount these costs to the present time.

For both of these methods, and for any approach that discounts benefits and costs, one of the key issues is what discount rate to use. The major options available to selecting discount rates, expressed as net of inflation, include:

1. The percentage rate of return that the investment would otherwise provide in the private sector.

2. The government borrowing rate for capital.

3. The "social discount rate" that recognizes the additional societal value of investment in public services and infrastructure.

4. A discount rate explicitly chosen to reflect the risk associated with an alternative.

---

[8] D. Shupe, *What Every Engineer Should Know About Economic Decision Analysis* (New York, N.Y.: Marcel Dekker, 1980).

In most cases, the government borrowing rate for capital is the rate used. However, planners and engineers must recognize that the selection of a discount rate is in essence a decision of weighting present versus future effects. The discount rate can significantly influence the desirability of one project over another, and thus extreme care should be used in selecting this rate. At a minimum, a sensitivity analysis should be undertaken to determine how project desirability varies with different discount rates.

Classical Benefit/Cost Comparisons

Each of the evaluation methods discussed below uses all or most of the discounting and capital recovery concepts discussed above. For purposes of illustrating the following methods, assume that a project has a time stream of benefits and costs as shown in Figure 9–5. The costs are defined as the initial capital costs of construction and the continuing costs of O&M. The benefits represent the benefits to users in terms of reduced travel time and travel costs. Using Equation 2, the discounted costs and benefits can be defined as:

$$\text{Present value benefits} = \sum_{t=0}^{n} \left(\text{pwf}_{r,t} \right) \left(\text{benefits}_{y,t} \right)$$

$$\text{Present value costs} = \sum_{t=0}^{n} \left(\text{pwf}_{r,t} \right) \left(\text{costs}_{y,t} \right)$$

where: $\text{pwf}_{r,t}$ = present worth factor with discount rate r and time t

       $\text{benefits}_{y,t}$ = benefits of project y in time period t

       $\text{costs}_{y,t}$ = costs of project y in time period t

       n = economic life of project y

For purposes of comparison, the same economic life should be used for all projects under consideration. In those situations, where this is not the case, project strategies can be used to provide the same project life period. For example, if one is comparing a 1-in. pavement resurfacing project with an economic life of three years to a 2-in. resurfacing project with an economic life of six years, the analysis could include the discounted costs of two 1-in. resurfacing projects over a six-year period compared to similar costs for one 2-in. resurfacing project. Alternatively, and in practice used most often, both projects could be analyzed based on the equivalent annual benefits and costs, thus reducing the time period for comparison to one year.

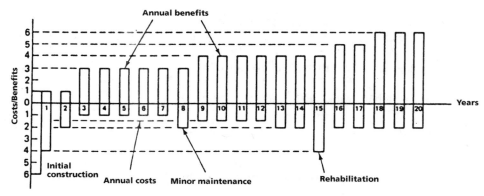

Figure 9–5   **Time Streams of Benefits and Costs for a Hypothetical Project**

Source: Institute of Transportation Engineers, *Transportation Planning Handbook*, First Edition, Englewood Cliffs, N.J.: Prentice Hall, 1992.

Net Present Worth or Discounting

The net present worth or discounting method uses the chosen discount rate to convert the project costs and benefits to its equivalent present value and then compares these values. The present value of the benefits and costs is equal to the summation of the value of these effects multiplied by the present worth factor appropriate to the period over which the costs and benefits occur. The net present worth then equals the difference between the present value benefits and costs. The net present value of the project shown in Figure 9–5 is represented mathematically by:

Equation 4:
$$NPV = \sum_{t=0}^{n}\left(pwf_{r,t}\right)\left(benefits_{y,t}\right) - \sum_{t=0}^{n}\left(pwf_{r,t}\right)\left(costs_{y,t}\right)$$

where: NPV = net present value with discount rate r

A net present value greater than 0 indicates that a project will present net benefits to society.

Benefit/Cost Analysis

The evaluation method most often used by engineers is benefit/cost (B/C) analysis. Put simply, the B/C method compares the discounted benefits and costs for each project and then compares each alternative to another. The best alternative is the one that has a B/C ratio greater than 1.0 and whose B/C ratios with all other lower cost alternatives are also greater than 1.0. Thus, for each alternative the B/C ratio would be:

Equation 5:
$$B/C = \sum_{t=0}^{n}\left(pwf_{r,t}\right)\left(benefits_{y,t}\right) / \sum_{t=0}^{n}\left(pwf_{r,t}\right)\left(costs_{y,t}\right)$$

Alternatively, if the capital recovery approach is to be taken, the discounted benefits and costs are summed and multiplied by the appropriate capital recovery factor to get annual cost and benefit values. A B/C ratio is then developed based on these values.

If a particular alternative has a B/C ratio less than 1.0, it should be rejected as a viable candidate. Each successive pair of projects is then compared with each other such that the B/C ratio between projects "i" and "j" is defined as:

Equation 6:
$$B/C_{i,j} = \frac{B_i - B_j}{C_i^1 - C_j^1}$$

This B/C ratio must be greater than 1.0 if project "i" is preferred over project "j." To avoid inconsistencies, the higher cost alternative should always be compared to the lower cost alternative. That is, alternative "i" in Equation 6 is the higher-cost alternative. As noted previously, the best alternative, from an economic evaluation perspective, is the one having a B/C ratio over 1.0 and whose B/C ratios with all lower cost alternatives are also greater than 1.0. Figure 9–6 presents an example application of B/C analysis.

Note in this example that the alternative with the highest B/C ratio when compared to the "do nothing" alternative (alternative 0) did not result in the "best" alternative. This is an important observation in that one of the most common mistakes in evaluation practice is to end the analysis after comparing the alternatives with the "do nothing" alternative. The relative worth of each alternative as compared with every other alternative must be examined in order to determine the one having the most benefit.

B/C analysis is a valuable tool for determining the relative worth of alternatives. However, such an analysis approach also involves risks, in particular the risk of the analyst misinterpreting the analysis results. Starling provides some useful caveats in the use of B/C analysis:[9]

---

[9] G. Starling, *The Politics and Economics of Public Policy* (Homewood, Ill.: Dorsey, 1979).

	Present Value of Costs ($ millions)		
Alternative	User Cost	Operating and Maintenance	Capital
0 do nothing	250	150	5
1	150	140	10
2	200	135	15
3	100	105	20
4	110	135	22

(a)

	Benefit/Cost Comparison with "Do Nothing"		
Alternative	Change in User O & M Costs	Change in Capital Costs	Benefit/Cost Ratio
0			
1	80	5	16.0
2	35	10	3.5
3	165	15	11.0
4	125	17	7.4

(b)

	User + O&M Costs	Cap. Costs	Benefit/Cost in Comparing Alternatives		
Alternative			Alt. 2	Alt. 3	Alt. 4
1	290	10	$-\$45/5 = -9.0$ (no benefit)	$\$85/10 = 8.5$	$\$45/12 = 3.8$
2	335	15		$\$135/5 = 27.0$	$\$90/7 = 12.9$
3	205	20			$-\$40/2 = -20.0$ (no benefit)
4	245	22			

(c)

Note: Alternative 2 is not justified because it shows no benefit over alternative 1. Alternative 3 is possibly justified because it dominates alternatives 1 and 2. Alternative 4 also dominates alternatives 1 and 2 and has a negative benefit/cost ratio with alternative 3. Therefore, alternative 3 is the best alternative based on economic efficiency. Note that the alternative with the highest benefit/cost ratio when compared with the do-nothing alternative did not result in the best alternative.

Figure 9–6   Example Application of B/C Analysis

Source: Institute of Transportation Engineers, *Transportation Planning Handbook*, First Edition, New Jersey: Prentice Hall, 1992.

Some analysts want to believe that the benefit/cost ratio is the rule that solves all problems, but that can (also) depend on budgetary constraints. Other analysts want to believe benefit/cost analysis is highly accurate, but we have seen that discount rates can make a decision difference . . . . Still other analysts want to ignore the very important relationship between equity and efficiency. On equity grounds, a technical school project having 1.5:1 benefit/cost ratio might be preferable to a technical school project having a benefit/cost ratio of 5:1 if the former resulted in additional income to a disadvantaged segment of the population . . . .

It was some of these concerns about the use of B/C analysis that led to the development of other methods of economic evaluation.

Cost-Effectiveness

The primary result of a cost-effectiveness analysis is the identification of the alternative that gives the greatest return in value for each dollar spent. Of course, the important question is "what value?" In transportation, the cost-effectiveness approach is concerned with how each alternative contributes to the goals and objectives of a community, organization, or study.[10] The basis of this assessment is the identification of the criteria (i.e., measures of effectiveness) that will be

[10] E. Thomas and J. Schofer, *Strategies for the Evaluation of Alternative Transportation Plans, National Cooperative Highway Research Program Report 96* (Washington, D.C.: Highway Research Board, 1970).

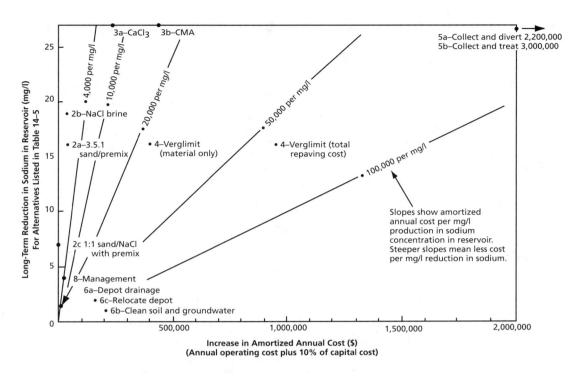

Figure 9–7   Cost-Effectiveness Analysis of Highway Snow Removal Strategies and Water Quality

Source: Institute of Transportation Engineers, *Transportation Planning Handbook*, First Edition, Englewood Cliffs, N.J.: Prentice Hall, 1992.

used to measure the effect. The "effectiveness" of an alternative is usually represented as a scaled quantity relating to a specific objective (e.g., number of car pools formed and reduction in pollutant concentrations). Cost-effectiveness ratios can thus be calculated to show the degree of goal attainment per dollar of net expenditure.[11]

An example of a cost-effectiveness analysis is shown in Figure 9–7 and Table 9–6. The purpose of this study was to determine the best strategy for maintaining water quality in a reservoir adjacent to a major state highway. In particular, the study emphasized the alternative approaches that would meet the water quality objective but would also allow the state highway agency to keep the road surface in usable condition during the winter months. As can be seen in Figure 9–7 the most cost-effective strategy lies to the left of the $10,000 per mg/l cost line in that alternatives to the right of this line are less attractive than alternatives 3a and 3b. The exact alternative or group of alternatives to be selected will depend on the availability of capital funds and the degree to which long-term reduction of sodium is important to the highway agency.

The most important characteristics of the cost-effectiveness approach are that it (1) indicates which alternatives clearly dominate the others, (2) illustrates the possible trade-offs between level of effectiveness and costs, and (3) directly links the evaluation process with the goals and objectives that are important in the decision-making process.

Societal Quantification of Costs and Benefits

Benefits and costs associated with transportation and related improvement alternatives can be categorized into three groups:

1. *Transportation users*—those that accrue directly to people or entities who use transportation services or facilities.

---

[11] B. Hudson, M. Wachs, and J. Schofer, "Local Impact Evaluation in the Design of Large-Scale Urban Systems," *Journal of the American Institute of Planners,* vol. 40, no. 4. (July 1974).

Table 9–6 Summary of Alternatives, Hobbs Brook Reservoir Sodium Chloride Study

Alternative	Long-Term Change in Sodium (mg/l)	Long-Term Reservoir Sodium (mg/l)	Capital Cost ($)	Annual Cost Increase[1] ($)	Cost per mg/l Sodium Reduction[2] ($ in 1985)	Level of Service for MDPW Roads Relative to Current Salting
1. No action. continue straight salt	0	43	0	0	—	No change
2a. 3.5:1 sand/premix (4 NaCl:1 CaCl$_2$)	−16	27	0	27,000	1,700	Reduced due to slipperiness
2b. NaCl Brine	−19	24	200,000	6,000	1,400	No change
2c. Prewet NaCl or sand and NaCl	−7	36	20,000	4,000	900	No change
3a. Calcium chloride (CaCl$_2$)	−27	16	150,000	200,000	8,000	Reduced due to slipperiness
3b. Calcium magnesium acetate	−27	16	150,000	409,000	15,700	Reduced due to slipperiness
4. Pavement additive (Verglimit)	−16	27	4,750,000	−52,000	26,400	Reduced due to slipperiness
5a. Collect highway runoff and divert to Charles River	−27	16	19,850,000	200,000	80,900	No change
5b. Collect highway runoff and treat by reverse osmosis	−27	16	19,100,000	1,100,000	111,500	No change
6a. Modify depot drainage	−2	41	150,000	0	7,500	No change
6b. Clean depot soil and groundwater	−1	42	354,000	100,000	135,400	No change
6c. Relocate depot	−2	41	600,000	0	30,000	No change
7a. Waltham to CaCl$_2$	−3	40	50,000	25,000	10,000	No change
7b. Lexington and Lincoln to CaCl$_2$	−2	41	50,000	20,000	12,500	No change
7c. Commercial to CaCl$_2$	−2	41	0	20,000	10,000	No change
8. Improve management practices	−4	39	0	20,000	5,000	No change

[1] Current 1985 annual cost estimated to be S250,000/year.

[2] Increased annual cost plus 10% of capital cost divided by long-term reduction in sodium concentration.

Source: Institute of Transportation Engineers, *Transportation Planning Handbook*, First Edition, Englewood Cliffs, N.J.: Prentice Hall, 1992.

2. *Transportation providers*—those that accrue directly to public agencies or private concerns that provide, operate, and maintain the transportation service or facilities.

3. *Secondary and indirect*—those that accrue indirectly to the users or providers or to society at large as a result of the transportation services or facilities.

These categories will be discussed further below. Careful accounting of costs and benefits should begin with clear definitions of both terms. Clearly stated definitions are important because casual discussions of the "costs" of major transportation alternatives often include a wide range of effects of the strategies.

Costs

Costs include the changes in capital and O&M expenses associated with transportation improvement. These costs usually increase as the result of a major investment, though O&M costs might decrease for certain kinds of capital projects. Two other kinds of "costs" are sometimes included as well:

1. Users of the transportation system incur costs, and these costs may change as a result of major transportation improvements. Highway users pay for fuel and the maintenance of vehicles. (Transit users pay fares, but these "transfer payments" are usually not counted as costs, since they are simply reimbursements to transit operators for costs they incur in providing services.) Both highway users and transit riders expend travel time that could be included in a generalized definition of costs. For careful accounting of costs and benefits, however, it is probably most useful to define costs to include only expenses incurred by transportation providers, and exclude from the definition costs incurred by users of the transportation system. This approach keeps all costs borne by users, both out-of-pocket expenses and time expenditures, consistently on the benefits side of the calculations—an outcome preferable to one that defines highway out-of-pocket expenses as costs and highway travel time savings as benefits.

2. Costs have sometimes been defined more broadly to include any negative effects of the improvement—an increase in air pollutant emissions, for example. The difficulty with this approach is that it is difficult to apply

consistently. Some alternatives may reduce emissions, while others may increase them. Obviously, it is undesirable to count the effects on air quality as a "cost" in some alternatives and a "benefit" in others. A better approach, therefore, is to define costs to include only the change in direct expenses associated with building, operating, and maintaining the improvements. All effects are then classified as benefits, whether they happen to be positive or negative.

Calculations on the cost side are reasonably simple in that all measures are expressed in a common unit—the dollar—and basic techniques of engineering economics are available to account for the schedule on which the costs are incurred over the project lifetime. The classical methods for comparing all costs and benefits typically compute the present value of all costs and all benefits, discounted to represent the time value of money. Simpler methods might be used with cost-effectiveness indicators. The FTA uses a measure of cost-effectiveness, for example, that converts total capital costs of a project into an annualized equivalent cost that can be used directly with other annual measures—O&M costs and new trips. This approach effectively ignores the distribution of costs over time and, while it would not be sufficient for the strict accounting of costs and benefits in the classical methods, is consistent with the less rigidly structured nature of cost-effectiveness measures.

The U.S. Office of Management and Budget has set the discount rate to be used in these calculations at 7 percent (as of FY98) for projects that are advanced for federal funding assistance, although this may be updated from time to time.

Benefits

Calculations on the benefits side are made quite challenging by the wide range of effects associated with major transportation projects: congestion relief, economic development, changes in land use patterns, improved travel times, changes in energy consumption, reduced pollutant emissions, and so forth.

For *direct benefits to users* of the transportation system, several measures have been used routinely, such as reductions in aggregate travel time for highway users and transit riders, and the number of new transit riders. These measures have generally been employed in studies that have considered only one mode—highway improvements or transit alternatives—and will continue to be useful in studies where conditions suggest that a multimodal set of alternatives is not appropriate.

In many other studies where multimodal options are reasonable, however, broader measures of direct user benefits are necessary. Composite measures of user benefits are available from the travel forecasting procedures used to predict traffic volumes, HOV volumes, and transit ridership. The component of these procedures commonly used to estimate the share of trips using each available mode (the "mode choice model") develops a measure of overall "impedance" for travel between all subareas of the region. This composite impedance measure reflects all attributes of all modes—the travel times, auto-operating costs, parking costs, transit fares, walking times to and from transit, and so forth. The value of this measure changes in response to changes in any attribute of any mode. Consequently, changes in this composite impedance measure well represent the overall benefits (or disadvantages where transportation accessibility became worse) associated with each alternative.

For *other benefits*, beyond those accruing to users of the transportation system, the necessary calculations may be captured by the overall measure of cost-effectiveness that is employed. For the classical methods that attempt to provide an indication of the absolute merits of each alternative, it is necessary to value each benefit (and disadvantage) in dollar terms. Unfortunately, no compiled source of standard unit values is currently available for this purpose, but work is underway in the federal government to identify standard values.

Multiple Measure Evaluation Framework

Outlined below is a framework for the evaluation of alternatives that attempts to structure the information in a way that can be understood by the many nontechnical participants in a transportation planning study. This framework provides a structure upon which the evaluation is built. The goals, objectives, evaluation criteria, and discussions that make up the evaluation are necessarily determined by local officials and staff to focus on the local decisions that must be made.

Several possible approaches might be considered for the evaluation of transportation improvements, ranging from (1) a free-form discussion of the options to (2) a very structured analysis complete with weighting and scoring of project attributes to (3) the calculation of numerical measures intended to compare all costs with all benefits. However, experience with transportation planning studies suggests that significant problems exist with all three of these approaches. With a generally unstructured approach, there is significant risk that the evaluation will degenerate into a rambling, unfocused discussion that more often repeats rather than interprets the data. With complex "weighting and rating" methods, the approach tends to mask rather than illuminate the issues and often only tenuously relates to the realities of decision making. Finally, with strict cost-versus-benefits approaches, the task of quantifying all costs and benefits in terms of equivalent dollar values introduces much uncertainty and opportunity for disagreement on the appropriate valuation of the variety of benefits and disadvantages.

Table 9–7 Typical Goals and Objectives Summarized by Perspective

Goals for the Corridor
1. Improve transportation service levels.
2. Stimulate economic development.
3. Preserve and protect the environment.

Cost-Effectiveness
4. Obtain a reasonable return for the cost incurred.
5. Identify a sound funding package (capital and O&M).
6. Distribute costs and benefits fairly.

Consequently, a more useful approach might be to use multiple measures of the performance of each alternative. The multiple-measures approach provides some structure to organize the evaluation but avoids complexities in the structure that might obscure the information on effects and trade-offs needed to make decisions.

This approach relies on two simple principles:

1. The measures should provide all information needed to describe the performance of the alternatives with respect to local goals and objectives.

2. The presentation of goals, objectives, and measures should be organized in a way that permits a coherent discussion.

The first principle simply recognizes the importance of the goals and objectives identified by participants in the transportation planning study. The evaluation should be able to describe how well each alternative performs with respect to these goals and objectives. Table 9–7 is a list of typical goals and objectives identified for the evaluation of alternatives in transportation planning studies. These six goals are commonly identified by participants in transportation planning studies and generally cover the range of interests in transportation improvements: transportation service levels, economic development, environmental protection, cost-effectiveness, financial feasibility, and equity. The specific objectives within each of the goals refer to specific conditions in the corridor and, therefore, differ widely across studies. The second principle further recognizes that there are different kinds of goals and that there are often conflicts among the various goals. The evaluation should be sufficiently well structured to identify commonalities, differences, and trade-offs that exist among the alternatives with respect to the various goals and objectives. Often, the goals themselves can be used to organize the evaluation. For example, it might be useful to structure the evaluation plan and all subsequent documentation around each of the six goals in Table 9–7. Alternatively, and particularly where the list of goals becomes longer, it might be better to organize the evaluation around a smaller number of "perspectives" that can be used to group related goals together. Experience with corridor planning suggests that four perspectives may be useful:

1. *Effectiveness*—compares alternatives in terms of how well they address the established problems identified at the outset (mobility, environmental protection, urban development, energy conservation, and so forth).

2. *Cost-effectiveness*—compares alternatives in terms of whether the benefits are commensurate with the costs, both capital and operating.

3. *Financial feasibility*—compares alternatives in terms of the availability of funds for construction and operation.

4. *Equity*—compares alternatives in terms of the distribution of costs and benefits across different population groups.

Among the six goals identified in Table 9–7, the first three would be included in a discussion of effectiveness, while the fourth, fifth, and sixth correspond (in order) to cost-effectiveness, financial feasibility, and equity. That is why the table identifies the first set of goals as corridor goals while the second set is geared to the evaluation of transportation improvements. Subject to the goals and objectives of local participants, *these perspectives are independent and equal in their importance.* Significant trade-offs may exist among the alternatives in that some may perform well with respect to one goal, while others may perform well on other goals. For example, one alternative may have low capital and operating costs, produce modest benefits, and therefore achieve a high level of cost-effectiveness. A second alternative might have significantly higher costs, much higher benefits, and therefore achieve a modest level of cost-effectiveness. The trade-off that will have to be addressed by participants in the transportation planning study is whether the first alternative is preferred because it is the most efficient use of resources or the second because it provides the largest improvements in the corridor.

Effectiveness

Goals and objectives related to effectiveness both establish the reasons why major transportation improvements are being considered and identify ancillary concerns that constrain the options. Transportation concerns—like congestion and mobility—are the primary basis for consideration of a major action in a corridor. Some other concerns—typically urban development—are often identified as motivating factors as well. A third set of concerns often constrains the improvements—typically those related to such environmental effects as noise, intrusion on parklands and historic sites, air pollutant emissions, and so forth.

There are several considerations in the selection of evaluation measures related to the effectiveness of alternative investments:

- *The measures should be developed early in the analysis with appropriate input from local decision makers.* This is an obvious step to ensure the relevance and usefulness of the information. The evaluation methodology should be a high-priority item in the early stages of the analysis. Development of a written explanation of the evaluation process is often the catalyst for local officials to come to grips with the specific measures that are of importance for local decision making.

- *The measures should be comprehensive in that they address all of the stated objectives, but they should be structured to avoid simple restatements of the same benefits.* Many potential effectiveness measures are highly interrelated. In some cases, there is good reason to include measures of the same effect that portray the effect from different perspectives. For example, the increased development potential of an area may be due primarily to the improvement in transportation accessibility to that site. While including both measures of accessibility and measures of development potential likely double-counts some benefits, both may be of sufficient interest to warrant their use in the effectiveness analysis. In other cases, two candidate measures may be purely redundant. As an extreme example, it is unnecessary to include both "total transit trips" and "transit trips diverted from autos" since the second measure is a direct mathematical derivation from the first.

- *To the extent possible, the measures should quantify the effects rather than express subjective judgments on the nature of the effect.* Many of the important objectives of an improvement can be difficult to quantify and the consequent temptation is to use subjective evaluation measures: significant or not significant, desirable or not desirable, and so forth. However, it is often more useful to provide measurements rather than judgments to local officials and the public. The relocation of a single residence for a major project may not appear to be "significant"—except to the people who live there.

- *The measures should provide the proper perspective on the magnitude of the effects.* Many of the effects of transportation improvement occur in terms of numbers that are large in an absolute sense but are relatively small when placed in perspective. For example, pollutant reductions expressed in terms of thousands of pounds per day may appear to be a large benefit; but they should also be expressed in terms of their effect on regionwide air quality if the reduction constitutes less than 0.1 percent of total emissions in the region.

- *Finally, discussion of the measures should reflect the magnitude of differences in the measures compared to the likely error levels they may contain.* Varying degrees of uncertainty exist in all information used in planning. The presentation of effectiveness measures should be accompanied by a well-written discussion that both highlights the major differences between alternatives and indicates where the differences are small given the levels of uncertainty. Minor differences in traffic volumes and transit patronage, for example, are usually within the error of the estimates.

Within these general guidelines, the identification of specific measures of effectiveness depends only on the identified goals and objectives, together with the judgment of analysts and officials on the most useful ways of portraying the effectiveness of each alternative.

Cost-Effectiveness

The term *cost-effectiveness* is intended here to refer generally to the extent to which transportation improvements produce benefits that are commensurate with—or "justify"—their costs. Three primary issues arise in any attempt to fashion measures of cost-effectiveness:

- The specific method used to calculate numerical measures of relative costs and benefits.

- The quantification of costs and benefits.

- The approach to recognizing trade-offs among alternatives.

As with the overall structure of the evaluation, there is no specific approach that is the "best" way to examine cost-effectiveness. A variety of approaches can be used, subject to several considerations that determine their technical soundness and usefulness to decision makers. The central consideration with any approach, however, is the same: the purpose of an assessment of cost-effectiveness is to communicate to all participants in the study a reasonable understanding of the trade-offs between the costs and benefits of each alternative. The specific measures used in the analysis are simply tools to help identify these trade-offs. *The specific measures are not themselves the focus of the analysis, nor do they represent its conclusion.* Rather, they are tools that provide the basis for careful thought and well-written discussion that are necessary to fully develop a clear understanding of the trade-offs among the alternatives.

Measures of Relative Costs and Benefit

A major question in this evaluation is development of measures that examine the trade-offs between costs and benefits. It is important to recall that this discussion is within the context of a multiple-measures approach. The task is therefore to develop appropriate measures of costs versus benefits that can be used in conjunction with the various other measures dealing with effectiveness, financial feasibility, and equity.

A number of the "classical" approaches discussed earlier are available for comparing costs and benefits such as the B/C ratio, net present value, and the internal rate of return. These measures are based on a strict accounting of all costs and benefits. Because these approaches are designed to determine whether the benefits of an improvement exceed the costs in absolute terms, they must attempt to carefully count all benefits and convert each into its monetary equivalent. This task is both a strength and a difficulty with these classical methods. It is a strength in the sense that it provides a way of counting all benefits—transportation, economic development, pollutant reductions, and so forth—so long as reasonable ways can be found to value the benefits in terms of dollars. An explicit accounting might serve to highlight all the benefits—both direct and indirect—accruing from an improvement, including those that might otherwise receive little attention. Further, the valuation of each benefit provides a way to represent the implications of differences between corridors and subareas. For example, the elimination of a ton of pollutant emissions might be more valuable in a nonattainment area than in an attainment area.

The dollar valuation of all benefits is a weakness of the classical methods in that it requires insights that may not be attainable. It requires knowledge of the appropriate values to assign to a human life saved, a ton of emissions removed in a nonattainment area, a significant visual intrusion, and so forth. Consequently, it is very difficult to implement these classical approaches in the comparison of costs and benefits. A possible solution to these difficulties may lie in current efforts of the federal government to develop appropriate dollar-valuations of various benefits. When these efforts are completed, the estimated values may support a commonly accepted approach to the three classical methods for comparing costs and benefits.

Cost-Effectiveness Measures

An alternative that does not require the valuation of benefits employs a cost-effectiveness measure. This approach uses a measure of benefits that captures, both directly and indirectly, as large a share of the expected benefits as possible. A ratio between this measure of benefits and a measure of costs provides an indicator of the relative performance of alternative improvements:

$$\text{Cost effectiveness indicator} = \frac{\text{Cost measures}}{\text{Benefit measures}}$$

where the benefit measure is not valued in terms of dollars. The challenge here is to find a measure of benefits that is sufficiently representative of the potentially broad range of effects of transportation improvement. It is important to recognize that using multiple cost-effectiveness measures can introduce situations where each would compare all costs with a subset of benefits. For example, separate indicators might be computed in terms of (1) dollars-per-kiloton-of-emissions-reduced, and (2) dollars-per-barrels-of-oil-saved. However, both measures load all of the costs of the improvements onto a single, narrowly focused benefit. The resulting indicators would overstate the costs of producing each benefit, since they would not address the summation of all benefits. Consequently, cost-effectiveness indicators are likely to be useful only when they directly represent a large segment of the benefits and are reasonable proxies for large portions of the indirect benefits. For example, the FTA uses "new transit trips" to represent overall benefits in the cost-effectiveness measure developed for all major transit projects proposed for discretionary FTA funds. In addition, FTA also uses total hours saved for existing and new transit users and for existing auto and truck trips. Similarly, "savings in highway travel time" might be a useful measure of overall benefits for a set of alternatives that include only highway improvements. A measure that incorporates overall travel benefits of multiple transportation modes is outlined in the next section.

In the interim, it may be useful to use direct user benefits as a proxy for indirect benefits, at least in studies where the appropriate set of alternatives includes only a single mode. Obvious questions arise as to the extent to which a single measure, no matter how broadly defined, can capture the wide variety of benefits resulting from major transportation improvement. In response, it is important to recognize that the direct benefits of transportation improvement are savings in travel impedances (time and costs) and that the indirect benefits are consequences of these mobility improvements. For example, where significantly improved transit service reduces travel impedances for substantial numbers of both existing and new transit riders, there will be associated benefits—less highway congestion, lower energy consumption and pollutant emissions, and so forth—whose magnitude depends directly on the magnitude of the ridership gain and associated user benefits. Even an indirect effect such as economic development is related to changes in user benefits. The likelihood that a project will have significant effects on development patterns is largely determined by its ability to provide significant increases in accessibility.

In other settings, a simple cost-effectiveness measure may be insufficient. For highway alternatives, it is not always the case that mobility improvements are associated with positive indirect benefits—pollutant emissions, for example, may increase rather than decrease. Further, in multimodal evaluations many of the indirect consequences may differ significantly between highway and transit alternatives.

Recognition of All Alternatives

Virtually all methods of evaluating trade-offs in costs and benefits focus on the *differences* between alternatives. Consequently, it is necessary for each alternative to identify a basis for comparison. At least four reasonable choices are available for use as the baseline in evaluating each alternative:

1. *The no-build alternative*—this approach puts all of the alternatives, including the TSM option, on an even footing and presents all of the alternatives as full-fledged options for implementation.

2. *The TSM alternative*—this approach better isolates the costs and benefits associated with major improvements, since it would separate the benefits that can be achieved with low-cost approaches.

3. *The next-lower-cost alternative*—this approach focuses on the marginal return on *each additional* increment of investment.

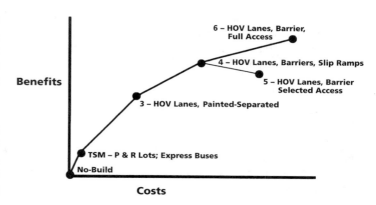

Benefits

6 – HOV Lanes, Barrier, Full Access

4 – HOV Lanes, Barriers, Slip Ramps

5 – HOV Lanes, Barrier Selected Access

3 – HOV Lanes, Painted-Separated

TSM – P & R Lots; Express Buses

No-Build

Costs

Figure 9–8 Cost-Effectiveness Comparison of Alternatives

4. *A composite of all lower-cost alternatives*—this approach recognizes that trade-offs exist among all of the lower-cost alternatives.

Regardless of the baseline, a useful tool is a graphical method illustrated in Figure 9–8. Much can be discovered about the relationships among the alternatives by examining the alternatives in order of increasing cost. This approach begins with the *no-build* alternative and examines the productivity of increasing levels of investment. In this example, the TSM alternative generates significant benefits relative to its costs—hence the relatively steep slope of the line between the *no-build* and *TSM* alternatives. With higher levels of investment, alternatives 3, 5, and 7 produce the largest added benefits compared to the added costs. Alternative 4 produces added benefits compared to alternative 3, but not at as high a rate as alternative 5. Alternative 6 actually produces fewer benefits than alternative 5, even though it costs more. Perhaps the most useful information for decision-makers is a well-thought-out discussion of these differences, including explanations of *why* the differences arise. For example, alternative 3 might be a reversible HOV lane built from the central business district to the region's beltway, while the remaining alternatives might be more ambitious HOV facilities that add more HOV lanes and extend beyond the beltway. A thorough discussion of the incremental costs and benefits would highlight the lower return in benefits compared to costs of these more ambitious alternatives—and may help decision makers select the appropriate scope of the necessary improvement.

Clearly, calculation of cost-versus-benefit against any single baseline alternative masks many of these trade-offs. Calculations against either the *no-build* or *TSM* option ignores all of the other alternatives. Calculations against the next-lower-cost alternative would better focus on the added benefits produced by each increment in costs (though this must be done carefully for alternative 6, since it has negative benefits compared to alternative 5.) This approach seems highly desirable, since it would directly support a careful discussion of the merits of each increment of investment. The potential difficulty of this approach is that it does not produce a single number that represents the overall cost-effectiveness of each alternative. For some types of cost-effectiveness measures, it is possible to compute the weighted averages of their values over several alternatives. For example, if benefits are expressed in terms of travel time savings, an average cost-per-hour-of-time-savings could be computed for alternative 5 as a weighted average of that measure computed for (1) *TSM* versus *no-build*, (2) alternative 3 versus TSM, and (3) alternative 5 versus alternative 3. The appropriate weights in this calculation are the incremental costs of each alternative. Similar weighted averages can be computed for B/C ratios, internal rates of return, and various cost-effectiveness measures (cost-per-new-transit-rider, for example). A weighted average is not possible, however, for the net-present-value approach.

The larger problem, however, may be the setting where a single measure of cost-effectiveness becomes the focus in lieu of a thorough understanding of the trade-offs in costs and benefits. The solution, then, is to avoid single measures of trade-offs between costs and benefits in the evaluation of a complex set of major investment alternatives and to focus instead on careful explanations of the incremental differences.

Financial Feasibility

The financial analysis establishes (1) the funding requirements for both the capital and operating costs of each alternative, (2) the projected yields from existing sources of funds used to support transit, (3) the potential yield from other possible funding sources in cases where existing resources are not sufficient, and (4) measures of the feasibility of the alternative financing packages assembled for each alternative.

The remaining task in the evaluation of the alternatives is to use the measures of financial feasibility to examine the likelihood that sufficient existing and, where necessary, additional funding sources would be available to cover the capital and operating costs of each alternative. The selected measures should include relatively few key indicators of financial effects. Three kinds of indicators can be used in this analysis. First, for existing sources that are dedicated entirely to a particular transportation mode, the surplus or deficit of projected funds compared to projected needs is likely the best indicator of financial capability. For new sources, discussion of the steps necessary to develop the source is a primary concern. This discussion would identify the necessary major actions—such as referenda, local legislation, and state legislation—and, to the extent possible, the likelihood of success given past experience with similar efforts. Finally, for new sources or existing sources that are not dedicated entirely to a particular mode, ratios can be constructed to illustrate the size of the modal requirement in comparison with various measures of financial capability. For example, where a particular mode is currently funded as a budget line item of local government, a useful measure is the current and projected percentage of the total budget necessary for the mode. This measure reflects the need for modal assistance, the total resources available to the local government, and the needs of other local governmental functions. A second example would be measures of the financial feasibility of value capture mechanisms that indicate the fractional change in profitability of development within a special taxing district.

In sum, the evaluation of financial feasibility presents measures of the effect of projected funding needs on existing and potential sources of funds. While the measures themselves are rarely conclusive indicators of financial feasibility, they help to define for local and federal decision makers the financial context in which the selection of an alternative is made.

Equity

Equity issues are those concerned with the distribution of the costs and benefits of an alternative across the various subgroups in the region. Equity considerations generally fall within three classes. First is the extent to which the transportation investments improve transportation service to various population segments—for example, the extent to which transit improvements benefit those who are transit-dependent. Second is the distribution of the costs of the project across the population through whatever funding mechanism is used to cover the state and local contributions to construction and operation. Third is the incidence of significant environmental effects.

Each of these classes of effects should be pursued to the extent that they are identified as areas of concern through the public participation process. Where appropriate, analytical techniques are available to quantify several measures of the distribution of costs and benefits. For the distribution of service improvements, the demographic data and transportation network information developed in the travel forecasting work provide a wealth of data on service changes for individual market segments. The tax-burden implications of any funding mechanism can be explored to the extent necessary with standard financial analysis techniques. Finally, the environmental analysis provides an inventory of likely effects on neighborhoods, residences, and businesses that can be used to quantify the extent to which specific population groups would be adversely affected by any of the alternatives.

Trade-Off Analysis

The purpose of the trade-off analysis is to pull together the key differences among the alternatives across the previously defined perspectives. It is designed to take the broadest view possible, highlighting for decision makers the advantages and disadvantages of each option and pointing out the key trade-offs of costs and benefits that must be made in choosing a course of action.

As in much of the evaluation, the content and approach to the analysis is dependent upon local goals and objectives and the alternatives considered. Perhaps the most important component of a successful trade-off analysis is its assignment to an analyst who is able to take a broad perspective on the purpose of the transportation improvements and the merits of the alternatives and who has strong writing skills. Together with reviews by study committees, the analyst's insight and reasoning are indispensable to a result that aids local officials in the choice of an alternative.

Several examples can be used to illustrate the kinds of trade-offs that might be found in a set of alternatives. One frequently found trade-off is that between effectiveness and cost-effectiveness. One alternative may yield a modest level of transportation improvement at a highly cost-effective return on the investment, while a second may yield greater improvements at such a high cost that its overall cost-effectiveness is lower. In this case, the trade-off analysis should point out that the second alternative provides a higher level of benefits, but that the marginal benefits are purchased at a relatively costly rate of return.

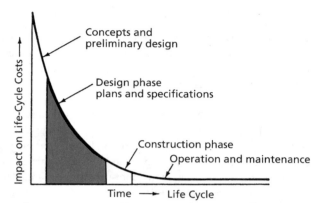

Figure 9–9   Value Engineering Savings on Project Cost

Source: Institute of Transportation Engineers, *Transportation Planning Handbook*, First Edition, Englewood Cliffs, N.J.: Prentice Hall, 1992.

Another frequent example is the trade-off between effectiveness and financial feasibility. Often, the alternative providing the greatest improvements in transportation service is also the most costly and would require a significant increase in the annual investment in transportation made by the local area. The trade-off analysis would highlight the additional commitment by the local governments—and possibly the equity implications of the means used to finance this commitment—necessary to implement this alternative.

The major task of the trade-off analysis then is to reduce (to the extent possible) the vast amount of information developed during the analysis to those essential differences between the alternatives. Its purpose is to frame the decision on a preferred alternative in terms of the advantages of choosing one option compared to the foregone advantage of options not chosen.

Value Engineering

Value engineering is a systematic cost control technique that is performed by a group of independent professionals experienced in the design and construction of the type of facilities that are under consideration.[12] As such, value engineering is not really an economic evaluation method designed to assess relative worth among several alternatives. Its intent is to reduce the capital costs without compromising quality, to decrease operating expenses, and to improve project reliability. An example of the effect of value engineering is found in the program established by the Environmental Protection Agency (EPA) that provided oversight to $9.3 billion worth of construction from 1977 to 1984. A total savings of $538 million were identified from the value engineering effort, with the average savings per project close to 5.6 percent.

The scope of the value engineering effort depends on the complexity of the project under consideration. As shown in Figure 9–9, the earlier in the project development process that savings can be identified, the greater the effect on the project's life-cycle costs.

A similar result to that of the value engineering team approach is obtained through Value Engineering Change Proposals. Often referred to as "contractor incentive clauses," these clauses in a contract provide an incentive (sharing in some portion of the costs saved) to the contractor to identify cost saving measures that will still produce the same project and project quality, only at a reduced cost. Such clauses are being used in many transportation projects around the country.

---

[12] S. Ostheim, et al., *Value Engineering Process Overview*, Report UMTA-DC-06-0483-88-1, prepared for the Urban Mass Transportation Administration (Washington, D.C.: UMTA, January 1988).

Summary

The evaluation methods discussed above are the major means engineers and planners have of determining the relative value of individual alternatives and the desirability of one alternative over another. Value engineering allows an agency to identify cost savings in projects while not sacrificing quality. The primary purpose of evaluation is to provide information to those making the investment decisions. This means that the evaluation process should provide information on the effects, likely trade-offs, and areas of uncertainty in the analysis. The ultimate decision, however, is often a political one, and thus subject to the political characteristics of the decision at hand. As noted in a Transportation Research Board synthesis of practice:[13]

> . . . technical and institutional factors are constantly interacting, and many final decisions are intuitive. It is rare that a decision regarding a major project is based on technical data only, although technical data can have a strong influence on a go- or no-go decision. Also, technical factors are often the major determinants of priority of hundreds of smaller projects. However, a nontechnical factor—for example, the inappropriateness of a project for the time or conditions—can terminate the technical analysis of that project . . . .

The information produced in the evaluation process should thus be considered as one—albeit an important—input into the decision-making process.

Setting Priorities and Developing and Implementing Programs

Programming has been defined as "the matching of available projects with available funds to accomplish the goals of a given period."[14] This definition pinpoints two major purposes of the programming process. First, the programming process must take into account the *resource availability* of funds among modes, functional systems, political jurisdictions, and specific project types. Second, the programming process must be concerned with *the staging of projects over time* in such a way that the interdependence of the projects is clearly recognized.

The process by which a program is developed and implemented needs to have a "vision" for the overall program, including developing a consensus on what the program is trying to achieve, establishing the means of setting parameters in which the program is to work, and conveying a sense of direction. The programming process should be open by actively seeking opinions from a variety of interests. It needs to have some quantitative basis for developing the process, but it must also recognize that by necessity there have to be some qualitative "factors" and that the ultimate decision-making authority may rest somewhere else and not necessarily solely use the "planning" information as the basis for choices.

The programming process typically includes:

- project initiation and definition;

- financial analysis of both revenues and costs;

- project readiness, phasing, and scheduling;

- prioritization;

- program approvals; and

- monitoring and modification.

One of the most important tasks in the programming process is the setting of priorities for project selection. There are several methods that can be used to establish such priorities. These are covered in the next section.

---

[13] *Priority Programming and Project Selection, National Cooperative Highway Research Program Synthesis of Highway Practice 48* (Washington, D.C.: Transportation Research Board, 1978).

[14] Ibid.

Setting Priorities

Given unlimited funding, establishing project priorities would not be an important consideration in project decision making. Every project would be constructed. However, in many cases, not only is the funding available for transportation purposes limited, but overall funding levels are declining over time. In addition, most transportation agencies have limited capacity to design facilities or to monitor the design process. The limited level of funding and the constrained organizational capacity to produce projects thus requires some sense of where limited resources should be allocated.

Ideally, the results of the economic evaluation process, using one or more of the methods discussed earlier, can be used to establish project priorities. The results of this evaluation process provides important information on the contribution of each project to society's net welfare. Thus, B/C assessments or cost-effectiveness analyses can be used to determine the relative importance of one set of projects over another. Thus, those projects that provide the greatest achievement of the desired objective for every dollar expended would receive the top priority in the project listing. However, there are often other objectives or measures, sometimes conflicting, that become important to decision makers when deciding which projects should be implemented (funded) before others. Program development may have to contend with:

- geographic balance vs. transportation needs,

- rural vs. urban needs,

- capital maintenance needs vs. capital expansion,

- technical needs vs. political realities, and/or

- highway vs. transit needs (and perhaps other transportation needs like port and airport).

Planners and engineers have used a variety of approaches to incorporate these measures into a prioritization scheme. One approach to ranking projects is based on the development of a *priority index*. Points are assigned (most often subjectively) to several measures that are characteristic of each project. The project that receives the most points receives the greater priority in implementation. An example of the results of such an approach is shown in Figure 9–10. This figure shows the ranking of noise barrier projects that are to be constructed along a state's interstate highway system.[15] Points were assigned to each project as shown in Table 9–8.

A cost-effectiveness rating, defined as the cost-per-reduction-of-noise-per-dwelling-unit, was calculated and used to distinguish between projects where there was little or no difference in the assignment of priority points. In such cases those projects having a lower cost received a higher priority.

Another example of the use of priority indices is found in the southeastern Michigan priority programming process. Eight criteria are used in this process with the maximum allowable points assigned to each as follows:

- Congestion and traffic operations improvements   Maximum: 30 points

- Safety   Maximum: 30 points

- Minimize cost   Maximum: 20 points

- Air quality   Maximum: 5 points

- Energy conservation   Maximum: 5 points

- Social, economic, and environment   Maximum: 5 points

- Maintenance and service   Maximum: 10 points

- Intermodal coordination   Maximum: 5 points

---

[15] *Evaluation and Ranking of Noise Barriers* (Boston, Mass.: Massachusetts Department of Public Works, 1988).

The total points assigned between the first two criteria cannot exceed 50 points, thus assuring that a project will not receive more than 100 points. The project scores are then used to rank the most desirable projects for inclusion in the transportation program.

Another approach to setting priorities is establishing priority categories or problem areas and assessing all projects to be programmed against these categories. For example, in some areas of the country, the effect of particular projects on improving air quality is an important consideration to regional and local decision makers. Thus, many regional planning agencies have established air quality effect as a priority category. Those projects that contribute to the greatest improvement in air quality receive greater priority.

Figure 9–10 Priority Setting for Noise Barrier Projects

Barrier Priority and Number of Priority Points		Barrier Number on Second Figure	Barrier Information					Supplementary Rating: Cost/Reduction/Unit ($/dB/unit) (lower is better)
			Location		Approximate Height and Length (feet)*		Estimated 1987 Total Cost (rounded)	
1	842	34	Milton/Quincy	I-93	12	3,400	$ 600,000	1,000
2	794	33	Milton	I-93	12	3,900	$ 700,000	1,300
3	756	32	Milton/Quincy	I-93	18	6,300	$1,600,000	1,500
4	745	27	Boston	I-93	14	2,700	$ 500,000	700
5	743	28	Boston	I-93	18	1,700	$ 500,000	2,400
6	576	16	Lynnfield	I-95	14	5,500	$1,100,000	1,700
7	545	26	Woburn	I-93	14	3,500	$ 700,000	1,000
8	407	38	Wellesley/Newton	I-95	24	3,100	$1,100,000	7,400
9	397	17	Lynnfield	I-95	18	2,800	$ 700,000	2,200
10	374	12	Wakefield	I-95	14	6,700	$1,300,000	2,800
11	351	1	Fall River	I-195	16	3,400	$ 800,000	1,100
12	349	37	Wellesley/Newton	I-95	14	3,700	$ 700,000	1,100
13	319	23	Medford	I-93	18	2,900	$ 900,000	1,000
14	311	25	Stoneham	I-93	24	4,200	$1,400,000	1,300
15	288	31	Boston	I-93	18	4,300	$1,300,000	2,000
16	286	21	Lowell	I-495	16	3,400	$ 700,000	1,700
17	277	22	Boston	I-93	24	1,900	$ 600,000	3,600
18	269	5	Wakefield	I-95	10	1,200	$ 200,000	1,500
19	261	14	Lynnfield	I-95	16	4,000	$ 900,000	5,100
20	259	30	Boston	I-93	20	3,200	$1,100,000	4,700
21	254	8	Wakefield	I-95	14	1,200	$ 200,000	2,300
22	254	29	Boston	I-93	14	4,100	$ 900,000	2,700
23	252	15	Lynnfield	I-95	26	2,000	$ 700,000	6,500
24	250	13	Lynnfield	I-95	24	4,000	$1,400,000	76,400
25	216	41	Newton	I-95	14	1,400	$ 300,000	1,700
26	210	52	Woburn/Reading	I-93	16	5,000	$1,100,000	2,300
27	208	6	Wakefield	I-95	20	1,700	$ 500,000	1,700
28	206	11	Lynnfield/Wakefield	I-95	20	1,300	$ 400,000	14,900
29	198	4	Reading	I-95	22	2,000	$ 600,000	3,900
30	196	51	Chelmsford	I-495	20	3,100	$1,000,000	9,200
31	189	7	Wakefield	I-95	26	1,800	$ 600,000	2,300
32	187	9	Wakefield	I-95	20	2,200	$ 600,000	4,000
33	187	10	Lynnfield/Wakefield	I-95	18	1,800	$ 500,000	5,300
34	185	48	Chelmsford	I-495	26	7,900	$2,900,000	5,300
35	183	24	Medford	I-93	12	2,200	$ 400,000	700
36	172	20	Lowell	I-495	16	3,600	$ 800,000	2,600
37	169	42	Wilmington	I-93	20	3,600	$1,000,000	4,700
38	165	43	Wilmington	I-93	18	4,600	$1,100,000	3,000
39	162	45	Wilmington	I-93	18	2,300	$ 600,000	3,600
40	161	50	Chelmsford	I-495	20	1,900	$ 600,000	5,500

*1 foot = 0.3048 meters.

Source: Institute of Transportation Engineers, *Transportation Planning Handbook,* First Edition, Englewood, N.J.: Prentice Hall, 1992.

A common approach to developing some sense of project priority in regional programming documents is to assign a "high," "medium," or "low" rating to projects in the list. This rating is a subjective assessment of how individual projects help achieve specific objectives. For example, projects can be rated by how they help promote economic development opportunities, contribute to the regional versus the local transportation system, how they provide more equitable distribution of government resources in a region, or as before how they help attain air quality objectives. One of the challenges in this approach is identifying what groups will assign the project ratings and what criteria will be applied in the rating process.

More sophisticated models have been developed that attempt to maximize the net benefits of an investment program over time. Many states use these models not only to establish project priorities but also to stage projects over time.

Table 9–8   Point Assignment for Noise Barrier Project Priority Setting

1.	Five points for each year that a sensitive land use has been exposed to noise effect.	
2.	For residences of all types,	
	Each residence now experiencing 68-72 dBA Leq	1 point
	Each residence now experiencing 73-77 dBA Leq	5 points
	Each residence now experiencing over 77 dBA Leq	25 points
3.	For places of worship,	
	Each place of worship now experiencing 68-72 dBA Leq	5 points
	Each place of worship now experiencing over 72 dBA Leq	25 points
4.	For schools, hospitals, nursing homes, libraries, or recreational areas of all types,	
	Each location now experiencing 68-72 dBA Leq	10 points
	Each location now experiencing over 72 dBA Leq	50 points

Programming Document

The federal government has required that all urban areas receiving federal transportation funds must have a TIP. The TIP is intended to serve several purposes:[16]

1. Identify transportation improvements recommended for advancement during the program period (usually three to five years).

2. Indicate an urban area's priorities with respect to transportation.

3. Group improvements of similar urgency and anticipated staging into appropriate staging periods.

4. Include realistic estimates of total costs and revenues for the program period.

5. Include a discussion of how projects recommended in the transportation plan were merged into the TIP.

There are six characteristics of an effective programming process and of the resulting document. First, the programming process must be closely linked to the planning steps that precede it. That is, projects that are programmed for implementation should already have been subjected to analysis and evaluation. Second, the program should have a multiyear framework that integrates projects over time. The different stages of project development—preliminary engineering, right-of-way acquisition, and construction—should also be identified by project in the program. Third, trade-offs and the necessity of establishing priorities among policy and agency objectives are critical components of the programming process. What must be avoided is the "shot gun" approach—the allocation of small amounts of resources to a large number of projects in order to satisfy everyone, but not enough resources to complete the implementation of any projects. Fourth, for the programming process to be credible, the estimate of the funds available must be realistic. This requires a good understanding of the many sources of funds that can be used to finance transportation projects. Fifth, the programming document can also be used as a way of monitoring the progress of projects through the project development process and as a means of identifying the obstacles that stand in the way of successful implementation. Finally, because the programming process is an important decision-making process, opportunities should be provided to interested parties to comment on the final decisions. (For more information on TIPs, see Chapter 12, "Urban Transportation Studies," and Chapter 20, "Regulatory and Legal Issues.")

---

[16] "Transportation Improvement Program," *Federal Register* (Washington, D.C.: U.S. DOT, September 17, 1975).

Program area		Short-range plan objective				Long-range plan objective				Priority	Current costs ($000)			
Project description	Lead agency	1	2	3	4	1	2	3	4		Fed.	State	Local	Total

Escalated costs	Program year					Environmental documents
	1992-1993	1993-1994	1994-1995	1995-1996	1996-1997	

Figure 9–11   Example Format for a TIP

Source: Institute of Transportation Engineers, *Transportation Planning Handbook,* First Edition, Englewood Cliffs, N.J.: Prentice Hall, 1992.

Although the format of a programming document will out of necessity reflect the requirements of local transportation agencies, Figure 9–11 provides an example of what such a document might look like. One should note that the projects listed in the program are associated with the objectives of the transportation plan, that a lead agency is identified for every project, that the costs are given in current and inflated dollars so that a true indication of the funding required to complete the project is presented, and that any required environmental documents are indicated. As can be seen in Figure 9–11, the programming document can be used not only as a mechanism to define a region's strategy of project implementation, but also as a management tool to monitor the progress of program completion.

Federal Metropolitan Planning Regulations

The Federal Metropolitan Planning Regulations provide the framework and principles for transportation planning and programming in metropolitan areas. Section 450.318 of the joint Federal Highway Administration (FHWA)/Federal Transit Administration (FTA) Final Rule on Statewide and Metropolitan Planning issued in the *Federal Register* on October 28, 1993 and effective November 29, 1993 derived from the ISTEA and the 1990 Clean Air Act (CAA) Amendments policies.[17]

As presented in the joint FHWA/FTA planning regulations governing the development of transportation plans and programs for urbanized areas (23 CFR Part 450 and 49 CFR 613), the metropolitan transportation planning process includes the development of a transportation plan addressing at least a 20-year planning horizon. The plan includes both long-range and short-range strategies and actions that lead to the development of an integrated intermodal transportation system that facilitates the efficient movement of people and goods. The transportation plan is to be reviewed and updated at least triennially in nonattainment and maintenance areas and at least every five years in attainment areas to confirm its validity and consistency with current and forecasted transportation and land use conditions and trends, and to extend the forecast period. The transportation plan must be approved by the region's Metropolitan Planning Organization (MPO).

[17] TEA-21, the 1998 legislation which reauthorized the ISTEA program, retained the principles of the metropolitan planning regulations although some of the specific items may be modified in further regulations.

The metropolitan planning process identifies corridors or subareas that merit consideration for major capital investments. An MIS[18] is then required to support these decisions. Where federally funded major transportation investments are being contemplated, the MIS should identify all reasonable alternative strategies for addressing the transportation demands and other problems. The MIS should produce information on the costs, benefits, and effects of these alternatives so that an informed choice can be made. The *result* of the MIS is selection of a proposed project or set of improvements—a major investment or perhaps something of less cost—to be incorporated into the metropolitan plan and into the TIP. States then adopt MPO TIPs and incorporate them into the state TIP.

If an area is in nonattainment, the metropolitan plan, the TIP, and the Statewide Transportation Improvement Program, including a newly incorporated project resulting from MISs, must pass the EPA air quality conformity test.

Financial Constraint

The MPO's plan, the TIP, and the state TIP must be financially constrained. The TIP must be financially constrained by year and include a financial plan that demonstrates which projects can be implemented using current revenue sources and which projects are to be implemented using proposed revenue sources (while the existing transportation system is being adequately operated and maintained). The results of MISs will not always be available in time for inclusion in the update of the MPO's plan; and a place holder, either a no-build or "most promising" alternative, may be assumed and included in the plan. Inclusion of this assumed project allows the financial constraint test to be applied to the plan and reserves certain funds for the corridor or subarea. The plan will have to be amended once the MIS is completed and must continue to meet the financial constraint test.

Air Quality Conformity

Conformity is the process to assess the compliance of any transportation plan, program, or project with air quality control plans and goals. The conformity process is defined by the CAA and related amendments and EPA regulations. U.S. EPA has developed "Criteria and Procedures for Determining Conformity" to state or federal implementation plans of transportation plans, programs, and projects funded or approved under Title 23 U.S.C. This rule also establishes the process by which FHWA, FTA, and the local Metropolitan Planning Organization (MPO) determine conformance of highway and transit projects. Conformity is defined as conformity to a State Implementation Plan's (SIP) purpose of eliminating or reducing the severity and number of violations of the National Ambient Air Quality Standards (NAAQS) and achieving expeditious attainment of such standards. In addition, federal activities may not cause or contribute to new violations of air quality standards, exacerbate existing violations, or interfere with timely attainment or required interim emissions reductions towards attainment.

Thus, "conformity" means conformity to the SIP for attaining and maintaining clean air. Conformity determinations must be made for: plans, programs, and projects that receive ISTEA funding; federal projects that require FHWA and FTA approval; and regionally significant projects sponsored by a recipient of federal highway and transit funds.

The SIP allocates emission reduction requirements among mobile and stationary sources and commits to achieve necessary mobile source reductions. The emissions budget acts as a ceiling on transportation plan and TIP emissions. (This emissions budget acts in the SIP in much the same way as the financial constraint acts in the metropolitan plan and TIP.) An increase in emissions caused by a proposed project could be allowed if the total plan and TIP emissions, including project emissions, are within the overall SIP emissions budget.

Discretionary Program Allocation: FTA New Start Criteria

A *discretionary* funding program allocates a pool of money among projects or programs. To allocate a discretionary pool of funds, a consistent framework for evaluating candidate investments is needed to help ensure that available resources are directed to the candidate projects and programs that offer the greatest return on the investment.

---

[18] TEA-21 retained the basic principles of a MIS, but some changes are expected in its relation to the preparation of any associated NEPA environmental document—Environmental Impact Statement or Environmental Assessment.

The FTA's Section 5309 New Starts program, the major source of federal capital funds for transit projects, is a discretionary program. Requests for funds under this program historically far outstrip the available funds, requiring FTA to recommend to Congress the allocation of each year's program pool of funds. Competition for these funds is very strong nationally, with the dollar amount of the requests outstripping the amount available severalfold. To assist FTA in making its recommendations, they created a framework to develop consistent and comparable information and measures on the candidate projects; this framework is called Section 5309 New Starts Criteria. These criteria, and the technical guidance to prepare them, are intended to ensure that the information submitted on each candidate project is developed in a manner that enables comparisons with projects from other metropolitan areas. These criteria, reflecting federal interest, are distinct from the local evaluation criteria used to select a preferred investment strategy, based on local goals, objectives, established needs, problems, and opportunities for the corridor or locality.

FTA applies a multiple measure method, in which New Start projects are analyzed against several evaluation criteria and results are displayed and reported. Starting in FY1999, the set of criteria was established reflecting a comprehensive set of quantitative and qualitative measures:

- mobility improvements,

- environmental benefits,

- operating efficiencies,

- cost-effectiveness,

- transit-supportive land use and future patterns,

- other factors (optional),

- local financial commitment.

These are illustrated in Figure 9–12. Specific guidance on the methodologies to develop and present this information was provided by FTA to provide consistency among the candidate projects.

Dealing with Uncertainties

Creditability of Information Used for Evaluation

Planning analysis and evaluation, almost by definition, is fraught with uncertainty because of the nature of the information that is available, developed, and used. Forecasting future conditions, demographics, travel patterns, costs, funding sources, revenues, and effect levels is based on many assumptions, extrapolation of past behavior, and less-than-perfect understanding of causal relationships. At the level of detail in which the information and data used in most planning analyses is developed, that there is "uncertainty" is the one certainty. While we can try to minimize the uncertainty, it is a planner's responsibility to recognize and understand the uncertainty that is inherent in the information. Decision makers need to be aware of the nature and degree of uncertainty in the information they are using to make their choices so they can be comfortable using the information.

As an illustration, Figure 9–8 showed an example of a cost-effectiveness diagram. In the diagram, the cost and benefit information were shown as points, implying a degree of precision. In reality, the inherent uncertainty in the planning-level cost and benefits information means the estimates are less specific points and more brackets or ranges of costs and benefits, as shown in Figure 9–13. When the bracket of one alternative is distinct (not overlapping) with another alternative as in alternative 3 or 4 in Figure 9–13, then the decision makers can have a degree of confidence using that information. When they overlap as in alternatives 5 and 6, they cannot be sure their choice would remain the same as more detailed and accurate information that would later be developed on a selected project.

Figure 9–12 FTA New Starts Criteria

Criteria	Performance Measure	Measurement
1. Mobility Improvements	Value of travel time savings	New Start compared to No-Build and TSM
	Low-income households served	Number within ½ mile of boarding points
2. Environmental Benefits	Change in pollutant emissions	New Start compared to No-Build and TSM
	Change in regional energy consumption, expressed in BTUs.	New Start compared to No-Build and TSM
	EPA air-quality designation for region	Current EPA designation
3. Operating Efficiencies	Operating cost per passenger-mile	New Start compared to No-Build and TSM
4. Cost Effectiveness	Incremental cost per incremental passenger in forecast year	New Start compared to No-Build and TSM
5. Transit-Oriented Land Use	Rating on transit-supportive existing land use and future patterns	Combined rating on a set of factors: • Existing land use • Containment of sprawl • Transit-supportive corridor policies • Supportive zoning regulations • Tools to implement land use policies • Performance of land use policies
6. Other Factors	Optional consideration of other factors	Local policies, programs, and factors relevant to the success of the project
7. Local Financial Commitment	Proposed local share of project costs	Percent of capital funds from non-Federal (non-Section 5309) sources
	Stability and reliability of capital financing	High, medium, low ranking
	Stability and reliability of operating funds	High, medium, low ranking

Source: *Technical Guidance on Section 5309 New Starts Criteria*, Washington, D.C.: Federal Transit Administration, 1997.

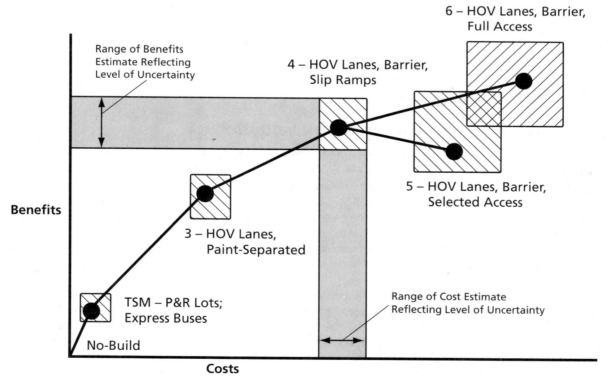

Figure 9–13 Recognizing Uncertainties in Cost-Effectiveness Evaluation

There are a number of approaches and techniques that can be developed within each planning study work program to control, manage, and understand the uncertainty. One method is to use independent peer reviews (expert panels) of assumptions, data sources, estimating methodologies, and results at various milestones in the study process. Many planning studies have employed peer review panels, such as for travel forecasting activities, and found them to very effective in establishing the adequacy and credibility of the methodologies, assumptions, and the results. Methodology and results reports can be useful documents to support reviews and quality control.

Contingency and Cost Ranges

Because of the continuing concern about the differences in capital cost estimates between the planning (decision) phase and actual construction, it is important to understand what the uncertainties are in these planning-level estimates and to develop ways of reducing those uncertainties while acknowledging any remaining issues. For planning-study construction cost estimates, these uncertainties can be related to changes in project scope, design standards, errors in unit cost assumptions, errors in quantities, inadequate allowances for environmental mitigation, underestimation of right-of-way and utility costs, unforeseen implementation problems, and the like.

Use of contingencies, discussed earlier in the section on capital cost estimating, is a common way that uncertainty is addressed. Based on local experience with similar projects and consultation on lessons learned from other areas, such as by the use of peer review or expert panels, planners and engineers can identify the areas of greatest uncertainty, given the level of conceptual engineering and other technical studies being performed. While contingency is commonly applied to cost estimating, it can be applied to any estimating or forecasting activity as well.

A way to recognize the presence of uncertainty is to develop a range of capital cost estimates—"low," "high," and "most-likely"—for each alternative. The lower cost estimate can be based on reasonable assumptions (defined and used consistently on all alternatives) and decisions that are uniformly favorable toward lower capital costs, while the higher cost estimate could be based on reasonable but uniformly unfavorable outcomes. As these estimates evolve over the course of the study, reviews by the local agencies, local officials, and the public can lead to a most-likely estimate that lies somewhere between the bounds. The most-likely estimate is usually the one used as the primary planning capital cost estimate in the other components of the planning study, such as evaluation. A major benefit of developing the lower- and upper-bound costs, even though the basic unit cost assumptions are agreed upon, is that there is still a level of uncertainty based on the level of engineering and technical analyses conducted in the study.

Risk and Sensitivity Analysis

While introducing contingency into planning estimates is prudent, it does not provide any indication of the variability or sensitivity of the estimates to changes in assumptions or input values. The reasonableness or degree of certainty of key assumptions or factors can be assessed in a risk analysis. Risk and sensitivity analyses are often performed on:

- Demand and revenue assumptions,
- cost and financial assumptions.,
- environmental and community effects, and
- political factors.

As an illustration of risk and sensitivity analyses in the financial area, some ideas in conducting risk and sensitivity analyses are presented in the following sections.

Be Conservative with Respect to Discretionary Funding Assumptions

Discretionary funding sources, such as FTA Section 5309, can have a high degree of uncertainty associated with them. In a financial analysis, it may be prudent to treat discretionary funding as a "gap-filler" after state, local, federal formula, and flexible funding sources are exhausted. Even then, a "reasonability" test of any assumptions about availability is prudent. For example, the analysis would want to be cautious in having discretionary funding exceed a reasonable percent of the nationwide total in any given year. The analysis might examine the region's past success in obtaining discretionary funds and the level of authorized but uncommitted funds that might be available. Sensitivity tests, exploring the implications of various discretionary funding levels, are also suggested.

Perform Reasonability Tests of Flexible Funding Sources

While the Surface Transportation Program (STP), Congestion Management and Air Quality Improvement Program (CMAQ), Donor State Bonus, Section 9, Minimum Allocation, and the like are formula-allocated, the actual programming of flexible funds for specific purposes and projects is largely at the discretion of state transportation officials and MPOs. Here again, consider the regionwide context. Use of any of these sources for the alternatives means less funding is available for something else. It is prudent to perform a reasonability test, so that unrealistic assumptions are not made with respect to the proportion of these funds that may be diverted from other important transportation purposes. It is good to work with a policy advisory committee of some sort to test the reasonableness of any assumptions about the future programming of these funds.

Considerations in Evaluation and Programming

Planners and engineers have adopted several approaches for dealing with uncertainties in the evaluation and programming process:[19]

1. Assume the useful life of a project is less than its economic life. By so doing, the initial capital outlay must be recouped over a reduced period of time, and the benefits of the project must therefore be greater to justify the project.

2. Add a "risk" premium to the discount rate used in the economic evaluation. Increasing discount rate reduces the expected value of net benefits and thus requires larger expected future benefits to justify the project.

3. Stage projects over time so that the completion of one stage can initiate a reexamination of the feasibility of further project stages.

4. Use scenarios to identify alternative future characteristics and the effect of these alternative futures on facility or system design.

5. Undertake sensitivity analysis of the important evaluation variables (e.g., the discount rate and value of time) to determine how the evaluation results vary with changes in key input parameters.

6. Use decision theory techniques (e.g., decision flow diagrams and game simulation) that employ probability distributions of events occurring to incorporate uncertainty into the analysis.

One of the most important approaches to uncertainty in design is the staging of projects. An investigation of project staging in the planning process entails a systematic examination of alternative strategies for system or project development over the long-term and a consideration of short-term actions that do not foreclose future options. In some sense, a staging strategy is adopting a concept of incremental development where a particular operations improvement or design would occur only in those corridors in which the need was justified in the short term. Each corridor or project location would receive the level of improvements appropriate to their needs, with the design and level of service upgraded as demand developed.

An example of project staging as it has been applied to transit investment is shown in Figure 9–14. This figure shows how several corridors in a metropolitan area have various levels of planning, policy, operational, or construction activities planned over the next 20 years. In addition, because it is difficult in some cases to determine the exact nature

---

[19] M. Meyer and E. Miller, *Urban Transportation Planning: A Decision-Oriented Approach* (New York, N.Y.: McGraw-Hill, 1984).

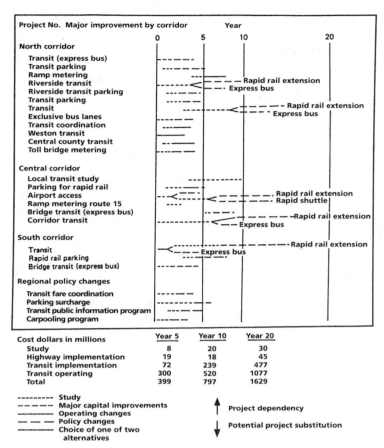

Figure 9–14   Project Staging Applied to Transit Investments

Source: Institute of Transportation Engineers, *Transportation Planning Handbook,* First Edition, Englewood Cliffs, N.J.: Prentice Hall, 1992.

of the demand and thus the type of facility design that is warranted, the staging strategy provides for the option of adopting two approaches when more detailed information is available. For example, the Bell Creek Jackson transit route in the North Corridor is scheduled to be studied from year four to year eight, with the most likely options being a rail rapid transit extension or the initiation of an express bus. By adopting such a staging strategy, planners and engineers provide a great deal of flexibility in determining the most appropriate investment and facility design strategy for a region. It allows for the identification of alternative project substitutions, operating and policy changes, and decision points where decisions between alternatives can be made.

Summary

This chapter has focused on the financial and economic analysis considerations that are important in evaluating transportation improvement alternatives and strategies and the selection and programming of projects for implementation. In an environment of constrained fiscal resources, it is important in transportation planning to establish the effectiveness, cost-effectiveness, financial feasibility, and equity measures of all those strategy options available to decision makers. Massive amounts of money are spent on transportation by all levels of government and by the private sector. These funds come from a variety of sources (most importantly user fees like gasoline taxes) and are dispensed on the basis of numerous formulas and decision criteria.

There are many different ways that projects can be evaluated for selection and programming. Given the many stakeholders and their varied sets of values and concerns, a multiple measure evaluation framework can provide varied decision-makers and other interested parties with the trade-offs among benefits, costs, effects, and financial considerations. Planning level information, though, inherently has uncertainties in the data and estimates that need to be recognized and managed in its analysis and presentation so that decision-makers can feel comfortable using this information.

No matter how sophisticated the methodology or the analysis, many of these decisions are political in nature and thus subject to factors often outside the control of the analyst.

Further Reading

American Association of State Highway and Transportation Officials. *Manual of User Benefit Analysis of Highway and Bus Transit Improvements.* Washington, D.C.: AASHTO, 1977.

B. Hudson, M. Wachs, and J. Schofer. "Local Impact Evaluation in the Design of Large-Scale Urban Systems," *Journal of the American Institute of Planners*, vol. 40, no. 4. Chicago, Ill.: July 1974.

M. Meyer and E. Miller. *Urban Transportation Planning: A Decision-Oriented Approach.* New York, N.Y.: McGraw-Hill, 1984.

M. Wohl and C. Hendrickson. *Principles of Transportation Systems Investment.* Englewood Cliffs, N.J.: Prentice Hall, 1984.

Transportation Research Board. *Methods for Capital Programming and Project Selection, National Cooperative Highway Research Program Synthesis* 243. Washington, D.C.: TRB, 1977.

CHAPTER 10
Statewide Multimodal Transportation Planning

Michael D. Meyer, P.E.

Professor and Chair

School of Civil and Environmental Engineering

Georgia Institute of Technology

Introduction

Beginning in the early 1900s with the planning for the first state-level highway systems, state transportation planning has played an important role in helping define today's national highway network. In many states, such planning in recent years has also included efforts to improve other components of a state's transportation system, including airports, transit facilities and services, intercity passenger and freight rail, ports, and inland water navigation. With the passage of the Intermodal Surface Transportation Efficiency Act (ISTEA) in 1991, which for the first time required that statewide transportation planning occur as part of the federally supported transportation program, this *multimodal* nature of statewide transportation planning has become even more important. This characteristic of statewide transportation planning was reaffirmed by Congress when it passed the Transportation Efficiency Act for the 21st Century (TEA-21) in 1998. The purpose of this chapter is to identify the key elements of a statewide multimodal transportation system, describe the basic steps included in statewide multimodal transportation planning, and the key issues related to the implementation of statewide transportation programs.

A State Transportation System Defined

State departments of transportation (DOTs) focus most of their resources on fairly well-defined elements of their state's transportation system. For example, state officials are usually most concerned with those facilities and services that have state-level significance (as defined by an assessment of the importance of their role in the movement of people and goods, or as defined by legislation). For highways, the functional classification of roads often indicates what level of governmental entity has responsibility for their construction and upkeep. So, for example, the interstate highway system and other high speed, multilane highways are the responsibility of the state, whereas collector and local roads are most often the responsibility of local governments. For airports, states are often concerned with those airports having a threshold level of passenger or freight operations. For transit, state planning roles vary significantly from one locale to another. In some situations, state transportation agencies are the operating authority, while in others the state provides funding support, but local transit operators or metropolitan planning organizations conduct the planning. For rail, water and nonmotorized transportation, states have different planning roles depending on legislative mandate and the agency's historical interest in that mode of transportation.

Although state transportation agencies only have jurisdictional responsibility over a subset of a state's transportation system, in reality, all system components are important to state transportation planners. In particular, the *connectivity* of the transportation system, an important state transportation goal, requires the effective operation of all such components. For example, intercity highway travel (the responsibility of the state) must be complemented with effective local access roads (the responsibility of local governments). Or the ability of ports and airports to handle large levels of passengers and goods is affected by the performance of the highway, transit or rail access linkages. Thus, one will often find statewide transportation planners not only concerned with the planning for state-operated transportation facilities, but also with a variety of transportation issues that occur at the regional or local levels.

The following three examples illustrate this concept of defining the transportation system components that are of state interest.

Vermont

The Vermont Agency of Transportation has adopted the following classification scheme for the state's transportation system. This approach is an adaptation of the highway functional classification concept only broadened to include transportation corridors.

- *Class 1: major multimodal corridors and transport centers* — these corridors represent the core of the state's transportation system in that they handle the most travel demand. Transportation investment in these corridors emphasizes the goal of "moving people and goods in the most efficient and environmentally responsible manner."[1] In Vermont, these corridors include the national highway system (NHS) routes, a network of intermodal centers and public transit (bus and rail) links, railways, and pedestrian and bicycle facilities.

- *Class 2: other major routes and facilities* — these routes are primarily highways that are on the designated state highway system (other than the NHS routes). In rural areas, these routes will be the means of accommodating bicycles and pedestrians (along the highway shoulders). In addition, these routes will provide opportunities for rail service (where such facilities already exist), as well as public transit and park-and-ride lots that can provide support services for travel feeding into the Class 1 corridors.

- *Class 3: minor routes and collectors* — these routes are mainly two-lane rural or urban routes that connect to higher classed facilities. Any accommodation of pedestrians, bicycles, and public transportation on these routes would have to be done after careful study.

- *Class 4: local* — these roads are primarily intended to provide access to land. They carry low traffic volumes and serve mainly as feeder routes of local significance.

- *Class 5: town, village and urban centers* — these centers are located in areas with the greatest population in the state and thus present unique transportation problems of access and circulation. The transportation facilities and services in these centers would have to accommodate multiple users and serve multiple functions.

Oregon

The three components of Oregon's transportation system include:[2]

- *Corridors* — which serve statewide functions and are defined as broad bands through which various modal links provide important connections for passenger or freight services.

- *Facilities* — which are of statewide function and are individual modal or multimodal terminals that, even by themselves, are of a sufficient level of importance to be of statewide functions.

- *Systems* — which are of statewide function and are collections of links, services, or terminals that taken as a whole are of statewide function, even though individual corridors, facilities or services that make up the systems are not of statewide function.

Transportation corridors, facilities, and systems serving statewide functions were delineated by considering the importance of each element in terms of: (1) connecting major cities or urban areas within or outside Oregon; (2)

[1] *Vermont's Long Range Transportation Plan* (Montpelier, Vt.: Vermont Agency of Transportation, August 1995).

[2] *Oregon Transportation Plan* (Salem, Ore.: Oregon Department of Transportation, September 1992).

volumes of passengers and freight; (3) contribution to important environmental, land use and development goals; and (4) accessibility provided to regions of Oregon and other states and nations.

Ohio

The Ohio Transportation Plan identified the transportation system of state interest to consist of three distinctive elements:[3]

- *Corridors* — major intercity linear elements of highway, rail, and waterway routes.

- *Hubs* — major intermodal facilities that comprised airports, waterports, foreign trade zones, and railroad intermodal facilities.

- *Clusters* — county-level aggregations of public transportation systems within the seven largest metropolitan areas.

Corridors were identified based on whether or not they served the goals relating to economic development; preservation of the state's competitive advantages; and service to international, interstate and intrastate travel. The criteria also struck a balance between preservation and enhancement of the state's major developed economic centers and the economic development desires of the more rural parts of the state. Criteria were established for identifying which transportation corridors were the most critical from a statewide perspective. Designated corridors included those that had the highest weights associated with the targeted criteria and that provided important interconnectivity between Ohio's economic activity sites and other parts of the country and world. The designated Ohio macro-level corridors are shown in Figure 10–1. Eighty-four percent of Ohio is located within ten miles of a macro-highway corridor.

Identifying intermodal facilities was an important step in the process of defining significant hubs. In total, the Ohio DOT identified 639 intermodal facilities that were considered of state significance. These included airports, waterports, Amtrak stations, intercity bus stations, rail intermodal yards, park-and-ride lots, and truck terminals. In each case, a set of threshold criteria was used to define "state significance." For example, a threshold of 15,000 or more annual flights was applied to identify significant airports; or only those truck terminals with fifty or more tractor units registered were included in the inventory of intermodal facilities.

In summary, a state's transportation system should be viewed as consisting of all modes of transportation and intermodal connections that provide mobility and accessibility. Those portions of this system that are of primary concern to the state DOT will vary from one state to another and will reflect historical, institutional, and regulatory influences. Many states have adopted a transportation corridor approach as one element of the system designation process. In addition, many of these corridors have included multimodal transportation designations, which is an important evolutionary step in meeting the planning principles of ISTEA. In some cases, these corridors are being identified not only because of the types of transportation facilities and services that are present, but also because of the activities occurring in the corridor that are of state interest (e.g., population centers, economic activity).

What Is Statewide Multimodal Transportation Planning?

Transportation planning, at all levels of government and in both the public and private sectors, occurs for a variety of reasons. At its most basic level, the purpose of transportation planning is to outline the strategic investments in facilities and services that are necessary to meet expected future deficiencies, and to identify the operational and technological changes in the existing network that will improve transportation service. The planning process is thus an opportunity to participate in and influence the allocation of investment dollars. It provides some sense of where society is heading and how transportation fits into this future. Planning can link the many individual decisions made by groups and organizations into a common vision of how each will help achieve a desired set of goals. Indeed, planning can help define these goals.

---

[3] *Access Ohio, Ohio Multi-Modal State Transportation Plan to the Year 2020* (Columbus, Ohio: Ohio Department of Transportation, October 1993).

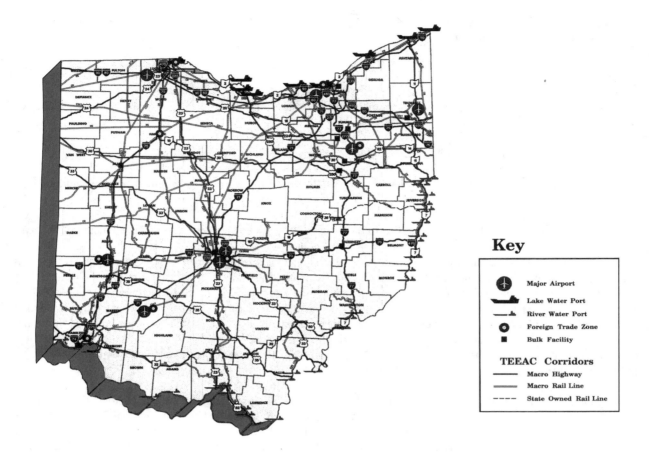

Figure 10–1   Access Ohio Transportation Corridors and Hubs

Source: *Access Ohio, Ohio Multi-Modal State Transportation Plan to the Year 2020,* Columbus, Ohio: Ohio Department of Transportation, October 1993.

Planning is also a process of answering very basic questions about the future and what society wants for this future. For example, the Florida Transportation Plan was designed to answer four basic questions:[4]

- *Where are we now?* This question concerns trends and conditions relating to population characteristics, demographics, and the transportation system.

- *Where do we want to go?* This question concerns major issues, public outreach results, obstacles, and opportunities.

- *What will guide us?* This question concerns the mission statement, goals, and long-range objectives.

- *How will we get there?* This question concerns revenue estimates, program and resource plan, and the next steps.

For the purposes of this chapter, statewide multimodal transportation planning will be defined as follows:

Statewide multimodal transportation planning is the process of identifying the most cost-effective and appropriate set of transportation strategies that will provide a desired level of performance for the state's transportation system in relation to a set of desired goals and outcomes, thus helping the state meet the needs of its citizens and of those dependent upon the state's products for their livelihood.

---

[4] *Implementing the 2020 Florida Transportation Plan* (Tallahassee, Fla.: Florida Department of Transportation, undated).

In the context of this definition, planning is primarily a process of determining desired goals, gathering data on the performance of the transportation system, analyzing this data, relating the analysis results to desired outcomes, and then producing the information that can be used by decision makers to choose the best course of action. This process includes very specific technical steps that must be undertaken to assure valid results. However, the process must also be structured to provide system users and stakeholders with opportunities to influence the results of the planning effort. This often implies the creation of mechanisms such as advisory boards or task forces that are formally charged with providing input; and entails extensive, proactive efforts at public involvement.

With limited resources, state DOTs are often faced with the prospect of not having sufficient funds to meet all the transportation needs of the state. The planning process examines each of the prospective improvement strategies from the perspective of whether or not the associated costs provide sufficient achievement of stated desirable outcomes to warrant serious consideration. In addition, the process assesses the appropriateness of different strategies for meeting estimated needs. An effective statewide transportation planning process must thus have some analytical capability in providing such assessment. In some cases, this capability could consist of fairly sophisticated statewide models, while in others this capability might simply be a structured approach at data analysis.

One of the key phrases in the above definition is "providing a desired level of performance." Traditionally, transportation system performance was defined primarily in relation to the level of congestion on individual facilities. Volume-to-capacity (v/c) measures provided useful information on how individual parts of the network were performing with regard to efficiency of operation. However, the concept of "system performance" has been broadened in recent years. Ultimately, this performance relates to economic development, environmental quality, and quality of life goals that motivate transportation investment in the first place. Levels of system performance in some states now include not only measures of operational efficiency, but also measures of how effective the transportation system is in meeting such goals.

Products of the Planning Process

A major product of statewide multimodal transportation planning is information to decision makers, stakeholders, transportation system customers, and the general public on the transportation and societal consequences of proposed actions (or inaction). This information can be provided in many ways—through formal documents and hearings and marketing materials, as well as through informal discussions with transportation system users and those affected by the current performance and condition of the network. There are many different types of plans that can be produced by the transportation planning process.

- *Policy plans*—these plans provide a policy framework to guide transportation planning and decision-making.

- *Action plans*—these plans recommend action steps that will be undertaken to implement policies and goals.

- *Corridor plans*—these plans identify investment strategies at a macro-corridor level where the corridors are identified as being of statewide significance.

- *Needs plans*—these plans develop an assessment of needs that are primarily associated with the condition of the transportation infrastructure.

- *Systems plans*—these plans provide a statewide systems perspective on the problems and opportunities associated with the transportation system. This approach focusses on the interrelationships among the different components of the system.

- *Project plans*—these plans identify and evaluate specific projects that have been determined to have statewide significance.

As part of every state's planning program, the state DOT is required by the U.S. DOT to produce two documents that establish both the strategic transportation direction for the state — the Statewide Transportation Plan (STP) — and the near-term program of projects to be implemented — the Statewide Transportation Improvement Program (STIP).

Statewide Transportation Plan

The STP provides a blueprint for the type, magnitude, and timeframe of improvements that will preserve and/or enhance the state's transportation system.[5] The plan should cover at least a twenty-year horizon and be statewide in scope so that system connectivity is achieved. The plan should also:

- Focus on those issues and system characteristics that are of *state concern* (e.g., the state's designated NHS).

- Consider *all modal components* of a state's transportation system that could affect the performance of the system identified as of state concern.

- Be *intermodal* in that consideration is given to elements of and connections between different modes of transportation.

- Describe the *availability of financial and other resources* needed to implement the plan.

- Be *coordinated and integrated* with metropolitan transportation plans.

Given the important role that metropolitan areas play in a state's economy and the concentration of transportation assets found in such areas, this latter characteristic of the plan becomes very important. Some principles for the coordination and integration of statewide and metropolitan transportation planning include:

- Develop a shared and consistent data collection and analysis strategy.

- Define transportation networks with identical facilities and facility data.

- Develop a common set of assumptions for socioeconomic and demographic forecasts.

- Establish common performance measures and evaluation criteria for system and project selection.

- Exchange information on the latest developments regarding the application of advanced technologies.

- Establish a periodic process of meeting with planning counterparts to exchange information.

- Use each plan as input into the development of other plans.

- Develop a formal process of public participation to allow maximum exposure to plan elements.

- Relate all plans to financial strategies and realistic estimates of funds available to implement the program.

One of the important components of transportation planning at the metropolitan level is establishing the planning linkage between transportation and land use. This means that one of the first steps in metropolitan transportation planning is determining the likely or desired land use patterns over the planning time frame and then relating these land use patterns to the type and number of trips using the transportation system. In some states, such as Oregon and Washington, state laws have required that there be a strong linkage between statewide transportation planning and local land use plans in recognition of the fact that providing new access to land via improvements to the transportation system will clearly influence development patterns. State DOTs not only have important influence at the level of regional transportation investment, but also can influence development patterns at the corridor and subarea level through their permitting process associated with changes to site access. For example, most state DOTs require a permit when a driveway to a state highway is constructed or altered and when a site development served by a driveway is changed in terms of size or use to cause significant negative impact on the adjacent road system. Many states have adopted policies relating to access management that regulate the spacing, location and design of driveways, medians and median

---

[5] Federal Highway Administration and Federal Transit Administration, *A Guide to Statewide Transportation Planning Under ISTEA* (Washington, D.C.: U.S. Department of Transportation, 1996).

openings, intersections, traffic signals, and freeway interchanges.[6] Thus, state DOT officials play an important role in the policy leverage that can be applied to guide urban development patterns and, therefore, in the metropolitan transportation planning process as well.

The Statewide Transportation Plan should also reflect the needs and desires of a wide variety of stakeholders and transportation system customers. Through a comprehensive public involvement effort, those most affected by the performance of the transportation system along with those who provide transportation services should be given numerous opportunities to contribute to the development of the plan.

Statewide Transportation Improvement Program

The STIP describes those projects that will be implemented over (at least) the following three years. Metropolitan planning organizations (MPOs) in the state's urban areas also produce a Transportation Improvement Program (TIP). These are included in the STIP. The STIP includes all capital and noncapital projects or phases of transportation project development that will use federal transportation dollars. In addition, the STIP must include all regionally significant transportation projects requiring federal approval or permits, even if no federal dollars are to be used in the construction. A regionally significant project is defined as a project on a facility that serves regional transportation needs and that would normally be included in the modeling of a metropolitan area's transportation network. Importantly, the STIP should be financially constrained to available revenues for each year found in the document. This means that information should be provided on which projects will be implemented using available revenues and which are to be implemented using proposed new revenues. In both cases, the existing transportation system must be shown to be adequately operated and maintained; that is, system performance and condition should not suffer because needed funds were transferred elsewhere.

The type of information provided for each project in the STIP includes: project description, estimated cost, federal funds for each year, category of federal funds and source of nonfederal funds for year one, likely sources of funding beyond year one, and responsible agency for project implementation. Given the importance of the STIP in setting transportation priorities over the short-term (and thus providing the most immediate means of beginning to achieve the strategic directions of the STP), the STIP becomes an important indicator of progress toward meeting air quality goals. For projects included in the TIPs for metropolitan areas in nonattainment of air quality goals, a conformity finding must have already occurred prior to a project being included in the STIP. A conformity finding means that through analysis of a project's effects, it is determined that the project will not worsen air quality in the metropolitan area (see Chapter 12, "Urban Transportation Studies," for more discussion on the relationship between the TIP, STIP, and air quality concerns).

Basic Components of Statewide Transportation Planning

Recent experience with statewide transportation planning shows that there are some basic planning steps that are common to most states. Figure 10–2 shows the most important steps that will be discussed in this section. In each of these steps, involving the public and stakeholder groups is an important characteristic of successful planning. Such public involvement should be proactive and provide complete information, timely public notice, full public access to key decisions, and opportunities for early and continuing involvement. These procedures should not be targeted solely to the general public, but should also provide opportunities for participation to affected agencies, private providers of transportation, and those individuals and groups having a stake in the outcome of the planning process. In particular, the public involvement processes should:

- Provide reasonable public access to technical and policy information.

- Show how public opinion was considered and responded to by state officials.

- Seek out and consider the needs of those traditionally underserved by existing transportation systems (e.g., low-income and minority households).

---

[6] See, for example, *Model Land Development & Subdivision Regulations That Support Access Management* (Tallahassee, Fla.: Florida Department of Transportation, January 1994).

- Be coordinated with public involvement activities undertaken at the metropolitan level.

- Periodically evaluate the effectiveness of the approaches being used to provide public opinion opportunities.[7]

Step One: Establish Vision, Goals, and Objectives

Planning is undertaken to accomplish societal goals and objectives or, more broadly, to identify transportation's role in achieving a vision of what a state or community wants to be. This vision and the identification of more specific goals and objectives will reflect the historical, economic, and political characteristics of a particular state. Thus, this first step in the transportation planning process is the one most often heavily engaged with public involvement and stakeholder issue identification efforts. A credible and effective planning process depends on an initial understanding of desired directions for the transportation system and on the acceptable roles for transportation investment in meeting broader societal goals.

Planning goals can reflect numerous concerns, although most state transportation goals focus on such things as economic development, environmental quality, and safety. State transportation planners use a variety of methods to identify the most appropriate set of planning goals and objectives. Active outreach to the users of the transportation system and to the general public is a critical ingredient of successful planning. Telephone surveys, focus groups, market research, public meetings, and a variety of other techniques can be used to assess the degree of public satisfaction with a state's transportation system, to identify perceived problems with this system, and to gauge public sentiment on what actions should be taken. The goals that result from this public process should reflect the different concerns that are expressed by system users and by the public. Especially important is a strong consideration for the efficient movement of goods. In order to best reflect the importance of freight transportation in a state's transportation plan, representatives of the freight movement industry (e.g., shippers, manufacturers, carriers, port authorities) should be actively involved throughout the process. In addition to public outreach efforts, a working partnership between the state DOT and the state's MPOs will provide an important linkage to those concerns of greatest importance to the state's urban areas. Many state DOTs have used MPO-identified transportation issues and corresponding goals and objectives as an important point of departure for their own planning efforts.

The following two examples illustrate the types of goals that are often found in statewide transportation planning.

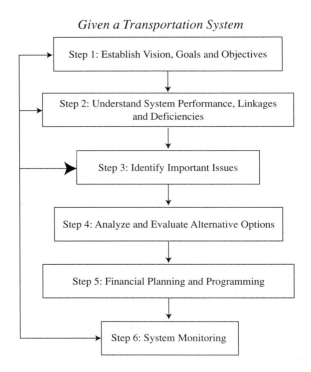

Given a Transportation System

Step 1: Establish Vision, Goals and Objectives

Step 2: Understand System Performance, Linkages and Deficiencies

Step 3: Identify Important Issues

Step 4: Analyze and Evaluate Alternative Options

Step 5: Financial Planning and Programming

Step 6: System Monitoring

Figure 10–2 Steps in Statewide Transportation Planning

Texas

The Texas DOT used an extensive public involvement process to identify the key goals and issues that were of concern to the state's citizens. The following seven goals were adopted by the Texas Transportation Commission as representing

---

[7] Some good references on different techniques for providing public involvement opportunities include: K. Stein-Hudson, et al., *Customer-Based Quality in Transportation, National Cooperative Highway Research Program Report 376* (Washington, D.C.: Transportation Research Board, 1995); Federal Highway Administration, *Innovations in Public Involvement for Transportation Planning* (Washington, D.C.: U.S. Department of Transportation, January 1994); and see Chapter 12, "Urban Transportation Studies," in this handook.

the desired direction for the state's transportation system. These goals became the fundamental purpose of transportation planning at all levels of the process.[8]

- *Mobility and accessibility* — to develop a multimodal transportation system that meets the mobility and accessibility needs of all Texans.

- *Effectiveness and efficiency* — to maximize the use of existing transportation facilities and services and ensure that investment decisions are based on efficient solutions.

- *Choice and connectivity* — to maximize the modal options available to individual and business transportation system users to ensure that all modes are efficiently connected to provide for easy transfers and timeliness.

- *Safety* — to ensure that all modes of transportation and transfers between modes are safe for transportation users and providers.

- *Environmental and social sensitivity* — to provide a transportation system that is environmentally energy efficient and sensitive to community needs and issues.

- *Economic growth and international trade* — to build a transportation system that maximizes opportunity for economic growth, international trade, and tourism.

- *New technology* — to take advantage of emerging and new technologies that increase the efficiency, safety, and attractiveness of the transportation system.

Oregon

The state of Oregon is one of the few states in the United States having a strong linkage between growth management and state investment policies. Accordingly, the Oregon Transportation Plan is the implementation tool for assuring that transportation investment achieves the vision articulated by the state's Land Conservation and Development Commission, the body empowered to establish planning goals and benchmarks. There are four goals for the state's transportation system:[9]

- *Goal 1* — enhance Oregon's comparative economic advantage and quality of life by the provision of a transportation system with the following characteristics: balance, efficiency, accessibility, environmental responsibility, connectivity among places, connectivity among modes and carriers, safety and financial stability.

- *Goal 2* — develop a multimodal transportation system that provides access to the entire state, supports acknowledged comprehensive land use plans, is sensitive to regional differences, and supports livability in urban and rural areas.

- *Goal 3* — promote the expansion and diversity of Oregon's economy through the efficient and effective movement of goods, services, and passengers in a safe, energy efficient and environmentally sound manner.

- *Goal 4* — implement the Transportation Plan by creating a stable but flexible financing system, by using good management practices, by supporting transportation research and technology, and by working cooperatively with federal, regional and local governments, Indian tribal governments, the private sector, and citizens.

There are 116 specific action strategies associated with these four goals, ranging from "preserve corridors" to "establish a demonstration program to encourage alternatives to the use of the automobile."

[8] *The Texas Transportation Plan* (Austin, Texas: Texas Department of Transportation, 1994).

[9] *Oregon Transportation Plan* (Salem, Ore.: Oregon Department of Transportation, September 1992).

Step Two: Understand System Performance, Linkages and Deficiencies

Understanding the performance and condition of the transportation system and the relationship between this system and other important phenomena (e.g., environmental quality, economic development, and community quality of life) often become the basic point of departure in identifying needs and opportunities. This step thus entails large amounts of data collection on transportation system deficiencies and where major improvements can be made to enhance system performance. Given a multimodal transportation system, statewide transportation planning should provide information profiles on all relevant modes and modal interconnections that indicate current status, likely trends, and key issues as they relate to the total system. Many states are commissioning or sponsoring the development of policy or sector analyses that focus on the contextual relationships with the transportation system. Broadening the planning perspective to include issues beyond those simply focussed on the transportation system will require opportunities for the involvement of stakeholders representing these sectors and issues.

An important characteristic of transportation planning in some cases is the strong linkage between transportation planning and a state's achievement of air quality targets. The process by which this linkage is most often established is called the "conformity determination." No transportation project to be implemented in a part of the state found to be in noncompliance with nationally defined air quality standards can be included in a STIP until that project is found to conform to a State Implementation Plan (SIP). The purpose of the SIP is to outline a strategy for eliminating or reducing the severity and number of violations of these standards. In urban nonattainment or maintenance (previously nonattainment but redesignated as attainment) areas, the MPO and the U.S. DOT have direct responsibility for ensuring such conformity. For projects outside MPO boundaries but still in nonattainment or maintenance areas, the project sponsor and the U.S. DOT make this determination. For state highways, this most likely means the state DOT. Regulations provide very specific criteria that must be met for transportation plans, programs, and projects. Even if the state DOT is not the project proponent, consultation procedures are to be in place that ensure coordination and cooperation.

System performance and areas of potential improvement can be defined and analyzed in many different ways. The following example from Montana shows how one can approach this step.

Montana

The Montana transportation plan devoted considerable attention to better understanding the performance and condition of the state's transportation system, its relationship to the state's economy, and potential deficiencies in meeting expected demands.[10] Figure 10–3 shows typical information that is used as part of the analysis of the transportation system. Included in this information for Montana are data relating to the performance and condition of the highway and bridge system, transit services, airports, freight and passenger rail, and pipelines. The existing and forecasted demands on these elements of Montana's transportation system provide a good indication of the current situation and likely future trends.

In addition to the data collected on the transportation system, substantial analysis was undertaken on the economic, environmental, and social considerations that would likely affect the management and development of Montana's multimodal transportation system. The following information was used in the planning process.

- *Economic and demographic considerations –*
    Expected statewide economic and population growth.
    Projections for Montana's traditional economic base (natural resources).
    Measures of the rise of an emerging service economy.
    Population trends affecting transportation system needs (urbanization and aging).
    Growth in tourism and recreational travel.

- *Environmental considerations –*
    Land ownership (state, tribal, federal and local ownership of substantial land in the state).
    Air, water, water quality, and energy effects.

---

[10] *Tran Plan 21 Transportation System Analysis* (Helena, Mont.: Montana Department of Transportation, 1995).

Wetlands, flood plains, wild, and scenic rivers.
Endangered species.
Historic and archeological sites.
Hazardous waste sites.
Visual quality and aesthetics.

- *Social considerations –*
  Values and priorities of citizens for the future of transportation in Montana.
  Tribal governance issues.

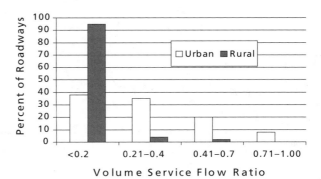

Figure 10–3   Montana DOT's Analysis of the Transportation System

Source: *Tran Plan 21, Transportation System Analysis,* Helena, Mont.: Montana Department of Transportation, 1995.

Step Three: Identify Important Issues

By its very nature, statewide transportation planning should focus on those issues, challenges, and opportunities that are most relevant to an individual state. For example, a state that is a major tourist destination might provide some emphasis on this issue in the planning process; whereas another state that is primarily a natural resource exporter might focus attention on the movement of bulk commodities throughout the nation. No matter what issues are emphasized, it is likely that the statewide transportation plan will consider a range of transportation options to meet the transportation needs of the state.

Traditionally, the primary purpose of transportation planning has been to improve the performance and condition of the transportation system. Increasingly, however, transportation planning is also being tied to other societal goals (e.g., improve air quality or enhance economic development opportunities) such that transportation system performance and condition is now just one of the many issues that transportation planning often analyzes. One of the first activities in planning is thus to define the issues that will be addressed during the planning process. The following examples illustrate how this step can be accomplished.

California

The California Transportation Plan was based on an iterative process that included the participation of numerous agencies and groups throughout the state. A synthesis was prepared of the issues, concepts, and strategies that had been identified in the plans of all of the 43 regional transportation planning agencies in California. In addition to this synthesis, each planning agency was asked to identify the five most significant issues in their region, which resulted in 68 separate issues being identified.

Given the size and diversity of California, the issues and concerns common to geographic areas were grouped together resulting in eight well-defined geographic clusters of common issues. The North Coast region, for example, a relatively low populated area dependent on traditional industries such as logging and fishing, identified the following top issues:

- insufficient transportation funding;
- transit services;
- development, safety, and maintenance of the highway system;
- dealing with growth.

The Sierra Nevada and Cascades region, a large tourist area, identified the following key issues:

- maintenance, improvement, and expansion of the highway system;
- funding inadequacies;

Ridership of Transportation Services for the Elderly and Disabled, 1990 to 1993

System	Annual Ridership		Percent Change
	1990	1993	1990 to 1993
Area VII Agency on Aging	2,067	11,715	440.6
Big Horn County Council on Aging	11,289	4,795	-57.5
Blackfeet Nursing Home	8,348	6,621	-20.7
Community Memorial Hospital	Not in Operation	8	Not Applicable
Community Medical Center	Not in Operation	1,596	Not Applicable
Dawson County Urban Transportation District	Not in Operation	5,234	Not Applicable
Fallon County Council on Aging	12,114	2,309	-80.9
Golden Years, Incorporated	4,707	2,602	-44.7
Great Falls Senior Center Transportation	8,675	10,743	23.8
Hollowtop Senior Center	Not in Operation	7,430	Not Applicable
Hospitality House	Not in Operation	4,214	Not Applicable
Human Resources Council, District 12	0	0	0
Judith Basin Senior Citizen Center	Not in Operation	249	Not Applicable
Kootenai Senior Citizens Insurance	95	2,219	2,235.8
Lake County Council on Aging	Not in Operation	978	Not Applicable
Liberty County Council on Aging	3,741	2,558	-31.6
Agency on Aging Area II (Musselsbell County)	5,377	3,756	-30.2
Native American Senior Center	955	1,589	66.4

Accidents, Injuries, and Accidents in Montana, 1992

	1992 Accidents		1992 Injuries		1992 Pedestrian	
	Fatal	Non-Fatal	Fatal	Non-Fatal	Fatal	Non-Fatal
Rural	152	3,932	171	6,057	8	49
Urban	20	1,983	21	2,958	6	70
Total	172	5,915	192	9,015	14	119

Pavement Conditions on Primary and Interstate Roadways
Average Serviceability of Statewide System (Pavement Serviceability Index)

Roadway Classification	1983–1984	1985–1986	1988	1990	1992
Primary System	2.6	2.8	3.0	3.4	3.3
Interstate System	3.6	3.8	3.7	3.7	3.6
Secondary System			Information Not Available		

Selected Transit System Performance Measures, 1990 and 1993

System	Operating Costs Per Passenger		Operating Costs Per Mile		Riders Per Mile	
	1990	1993	1990	1993	1990	1993
Urban Transit						
Great Fall Transit District	$2.26	$2.92	$2.55	$2.73	1.1	0.9
MET Transit (Billings)	1.80	2.48	2.42	2.66	1.3	1.1
Mountain Line Transit (Missoula)	2.44	3.29	1.83	2.61	0.8	0.8
Urban Transit – Average	2.08	2.83	2.24	2.66	1.1	0.9
Rural Transit						
Area IX (Eagle Transit)	3.44	3.91	1.46	1.90	0.4	0.5
Big Dry Transit	3.58	5.63	1.38	1.54	0.4	0.3
Blackfeet Transit	4.80	3.60	1.27	2.16	0.3	0.6
Butte-Silver Bow	1.75	2.43	2.14	2.67	1.2	1.1
City of Helena Dial-A-Ride	4.08	5.47	2.64	3.07	0.6	0.6
Fergus County Council on Aging	Not Funded	2.03	Not Funded	1.84	0.7	0.9
Fort Peck Transportation System	9.33	7.17	2.13	1.81	0.2	0.3
Powder River Transportation	6.26	1.06	1.52	1.32	0.2	1.2
Valley County Council on Aging	2.57	2.89	1.21	1.49	0.5	0.5
(Rural Transit) Average	2.75	3.24	1.80	2.21	0.7	0.7
Elderly/Disabled Service Average	3.03	3.16	1.21	1.00	0.4	0.3

Figure 10–3 Montana DOT's Analysis of the Transportation System (continued)

Source: *Tran Plan 21, Transportation System Analysis,* Helena, Mont.: Montana Department of Transportation, 1995.

- reduction of growth and visitor effects;

- difficulties of providing transit options;

- need for support of aviation;

- increasing bicycle use.

Not surprisingly, the issues identified in each region are tied closely to the local economy, the status of the transportation system, and the values of the people who live in the region. A statewide transportation planning process must be sensitive to this range of issues.

Vermont

The Vermont Agency of Transportation conducted two public opinion surveys as part of its public involvement process for transportation planning. In addition, the agency conducted three focus groups that investigated important transportation issues in depth. The opinion survey reached 1,200 citizens and was designed to be statistically representative of five different geographic areas of Vermont. Some of the results of the survey are shown in Figure 10–4. These results were incorporated into the goals setting and issues identification phases of the planning process.

Georgia

The Georgia Transportation Board and the Georgia DOT formed the Transportation 2000 Commission to achieve a consensus on future state transportation directions. The Commission consisted of representatives from the development community, financial institutions, contractors, modal agencies, local and state governments, environmental and public interest groups, and the general public. The Commission sponsored 15 regional meetings with over 1,000 citizens attending. Participants were asked to answer specific transportation-related questions. From these meetings, and from other outreach efforts, the Transportation 2000 Commission developed a comprehensive vision to guide the state's transportation program.[11] The specific goals that surfaced from this process were classified into five major areas — economic development, environment and energy efficiency, finance, human resources, and public involvement and relations. Unlike the previous example from Vermont, the survey of participants was not a statistically valid representation of the state's population; however, the results were indicative of those who are active in transportation planning and thus of the state's opinion-makers. Example results from this data collection effort are shown in Figure 10–5.

Step Four: Analyze and Evaluate Alternative Options

The key analytical foundation for transportation planning is an analysis and evaluation methodology. This process usually entails a large amount of data collection to calibrate models and for forecasting future consequences of alternative investment or operational options. Not all analysis, however, must be based on modeling efforts. For example, very few states currently have statewide models that include both metropolitan and rural areas. The more usual analysis approach is to develop an analysis methodology for specific study areas (e.g., corridors) or for specific issues (e.g., access to the state's largest seaport).

Because state DOTs plan for many projects that will be constructed in metropolitan areas, state officials will often be major participants in a major investment study (MIS). A major investment is defined as "a high-type highway or transit improvement of substantial costs that is expected to have a significant effect on capacity, traffic, level of service or mode share at the transportation corridor or sub-area scale" and where federal funds are potentially involved. Examples of such investments include new or partially controlled access principal arterials, construction or extension of a high-occupancy vehicle (HOV) facility, addition of lanes to an existing freeway, or building a light rail line. The purpose of the MIS is to better understand the transportation needs in a metropolitan corridor, analyze alternative strategies for addressing these needs,

---

[11] *Vision Statement for George's Future Transportation Program* (Atlanta, Ga.: Georgia Transportation 2000 Commission, May 1994.)

and present the resulting information in an understandable way to decision-makers (see Chapter 12, "Urban Transportation Studies," for more detail on MIS studies).

A planning partnership between the state DOT and the state's MPOs will be an important framework for undertaking an MIS. The MIS should be viewed as a collaborative process involving the many groups and agencies having interests and concerns in the transportation corridor. In particular, the MPO will play a lead role in the MIS decision process; and although specific responsibilities will be worked out on a case-by-case basis, it is clear that the state DOT and MPO must work closely together in making the MIS a success. Some examples of the analysis and evaluation step are as follows:

Wisconsin

The Wisconsin long-range transportation plan provided "a broad planning umbrella — with a unified vision and set of goals throughout — from which individual modal plans for highways, airports, railroads, bikeways, and transit were to be shaped."[12] The major elements of this plan included the development and implementation of the following:

- multimodal intercity freight plan,
- multimodal intercity passenger plan,
- strategic issue analysis,
- metropolitan planning assistance,
- financial planning,
- system level environmental evaluations,
- public participation.

The following four "visions" guided the analysis process in terms of assessing alternative strategies for improving the state's transportation system.

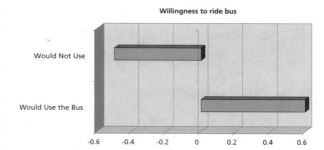

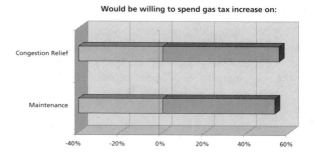

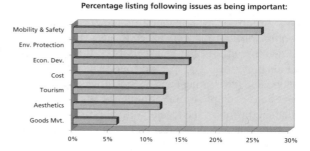

Figure 10–4   Public Opinion Survey Results in Vermont's Transportation Planning Process

Source: *Vermont's Long Range Transportation Plan,* Montpelier, Vt.: Vermont Agency of Transportation, August 1995.

- *Vision 1: a market-based approach —* Wisconsin's transportation system would be guided by a market-driven approach. A strict "burden of proof" (in terms of cost-effectiveness) would determine which investments would be made.

- *Vision 2: maintain current policies —* Wisconsin's 21st century transportation system would be developed and planned largely according to existing state policies, programs, and strategies.

- *Vision 3: more transportation choices —* Wisconsin's 21st century transportation system would offer a greatly expanded range of transportation choices wherever economically and environmentally feasible.

- *Vision 4: environmental and social focus —* Wisconsin's 21st century transportation system would offer the widest possible array of choices and opportunities, with environmental and social values as the primary focus.

---

[12] *Translinks 21, A Multimodal Transportation Plan for Wisconsin's 21st Century* (Madison, Wis.: Wisconsin Department of Transportation, February 1995).

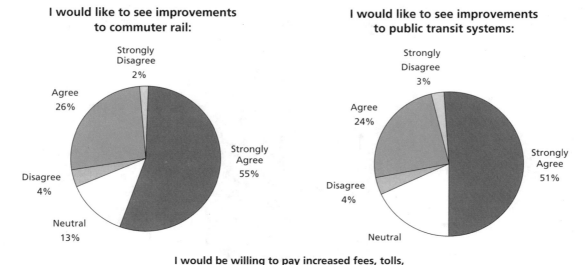

I would like to see improvements to commuter rail:

Strongly Disagree 2%
Agree 26%
Strongly Agree 55%
Disagree 4%
Neutral 13%

I would like to see improvements to public transit systems:

Strongly Disagree 3%
Agree 24%
Strongly Agree 51%
Disagree 4%
Neutral

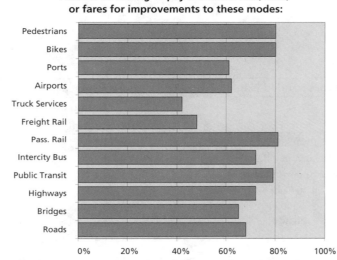

I would be willing to pay increased fees, tolls, or fares for improvements to these modes:

Pedestrians
Bikes
Ports
Airports
Truck Services
Freight Rail
Pass. Rail
Intercity Bus
Public Transit
Highways
Bridges
Roads

0%   20%   40%   60%   80%   100%

Figure 10–5   Data Collected as Part of Statewide Transportation Planning in Georgia

Source: *Vision Statement for Georgia's Future Transportation Program,* Atlanta, Ga.: Georgia Transportation 2000 Commission, May 1994.

Based on these visions, four plan alternatives were defined and analyzed. The analysis framework used by the Wisconsin DOT (WisDOT) in developing the state's multimodal transportation plan is an excellent example of how analysis tools can be used to identify issues and assess potential solution strategies. Importantly, the WisDOT analysis approach explicitly considered the interaction between modes of transportation when evaluating alternative plan scenarios. Integrated data sets were developed that included data on passenger rail, freight rail, intercity bus, auto, truck, air passenger, air cargo, and waterborne freight. For intercity passenger analyses, current ridership data was augmented with data from an extensive statewide travel preference survey. Survey respondents (only those traveling between counties) were asked their mode preference given varying levels of travel time, cost, and service frequency.

The analysis of freight movements was based on trend forecasts tied to state and county employment forecasts adjusted for industry productivity differences. These trends were then reviewed by a freight industry expert panel that adjusted the trends based on expected developments in freight moving technology and emerging economic expectations. For example, this panel adjusted the trends to reflect an increasing reliance on truck and rail intermodal partnerships.

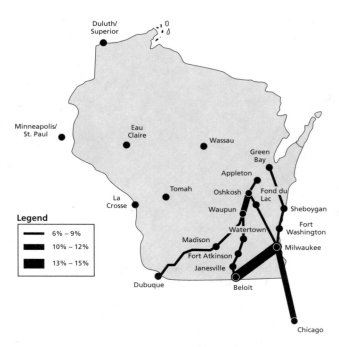

Results of Recommended Plan on Trend Truck Volume Forecast 2020			
		Reduction in Trend	
Route		Intercity Auto	Total Traffic
I-43	Beloit to Milwaukee	14.1%	1.5%
I-43	Milwaukee to Green Bay	8.3%	0.9%
Hwy 41	Milwaukee to Fond Du Lac	7.4%	0.5%
Hwy 41	Fond Du Lac to Oshkosh	8.8%	0.2%
Hwy 26	Janesville to Waupun	6.9%	0.7%
Hwy 26	Waupun to Oshkosh	11.0%	1.1%
I-94	Illinois Line to Milwaukee	11.4%	1.0%

Figure 10–6   Freight Forecasts for the Wisconsin Statewide Transportation Planning Process

Source: *Translinks 21, A Multimodal Transportation Plan for Wisconsin's 21ˢᵗ Century,* Madison, Wis.: Wisconsin Department of Transportation, February 1995.

The recommended transportation plan focussed on the completion of the state's proposed Year 2020 highway network, passenger rail improvements, feeder bus service to high-speed rail, and intercity bus service to all communities over 5,000 population. Figure 10–6 shows the results of the intercity passenger and freight analysis. The addition of high-speed rail shows a significant diversion from air travel to rail and a reduction of 2.7 million auto trips due to passenger rail and intercity bus service improvements. Not only does this analysis examine statewide totals with regard to forecasted results, but expected results were also estimated for selected critical corridors.

The freight analysis followed a similar approach in estimating results. Figure 10–7 shows the difference between the trend mode share and the forecasted mode share given plan implementation. This figure shows the relatively modest shift from trucking to rail with plan implementation (explained in part by the relatively short distances involved with typical truck movements). On a corridor basis, the results of plan improvements are more pronounced.

The results of this analysis were exposed to numerous groups in Wisconsin through a comprehensive public involvement program. In addition, representatives of the freight industry were participants in the process of defining expected trends in commodity flows. Public involvement was thus an important ingredient in the Wisconsin statewide transportation planning process.

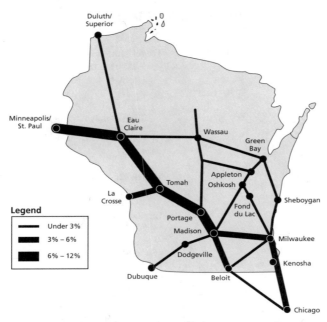

Impact of Recommended Plan on Trend Intercity Auto Forecast 2020			
		Reduction in Trend	
	Route	**Intercity Auto**	**Total Traffic**
I-90/94	Madison to Portage	6.6%	4.2%
Hwy 18/151	Madison to Dodgeville	0.5%	0.3%
I-94	Madison to Milwaukee	5.5%	4.4%
I-90/94	Portage to Tomah	12.4%	6.5%
I-94	Kenosha to Milwaukee	2.9%	1.9%
I-90	Beloit to Madison	5.1%	3.9%
Hwy 29	Wausau to Green Bay	0.3%	0.1%
Hwy 41	Fond Du Lac to Milwaukee	1.3%	0.6%
Hwy 51	Portage to Wausau	2.5%	1.4%

**Figure 10–7   Intercity Forecasts for the
Wisconsin Statewide Transportation Planning Process**

Source: *Translinks 21, A Multimodal Transportation Plan for Wisconsin's 21st Century,* Madison, Wis.: Wisconsin Department of Transportation, February 1995.

Maryland

The Maryland DOT's statewide planning study examined 24 transportation corridors that were facing serious traffic congestion problems.[13] Each corridor was studied with the same study approach to maintain complete and uniform analysis of transportation improvements both within and among corridors. The demand modeling approach used for this study was a traditional transportation modeling approach. Population and employment growth over the study time horizon had to be estimated so that future travel demands could be forecasted. Projections for the year 2010 showed that population and employment growth would continue to focus around Baltimore and Washington, D.C. These population and employment growth patterns were used to distribute the resulting trips on the transportation network. Based on statewide figures for mode choice, these travel demands could be predicted by mode of travel and then assigned to individual routes through the transportation network. The following steps were undertaken for each of the corridor studies.

---

[13] *Maryland Statewide Commuter Assistance Study,* Executive Summary (Baltimore, Md.: Maryland Department of Transportation, 1990).

Table 10–1   Quantitative Data for Maryland Commuter Study

Screenline Volume/Capacity Ratio
Screenline 1(Capital Beltway)
    Northbound
    Southbound
Screenline 2 (HD 223)
    Northbound
    Southbound
Screenline 3 (Charles/Prince Georges)
    Northbound
    Southbound
Screenline 4 (HD 225)
    Northbound
    Southbound

Annualized Cost/Trip Served
Transit Trips Only

Annualized Cost/Trip Mile Served

% of Highway Lane Miles Operating at:
    LOS A
    LOS B
    LOS C
    LOS D
    LOS E
    LOS F

Person Miles Traveled (AM Peak Hour)
    Low-Occupancy Vehicle (LOV)
    High-Occupancy Vehicle (HOV)
    Transit

% of Commuter Miles Earned by:
    LOV Operating at LOS D or better
    HOV
    Transit

Travel Times for Selected Locations
Waldorf to D.C.
    LOV
    HOV
    Transit
T.B. (Brandywine) to D.C.
    LOV
    HOV
    Transit

Vehicle Hours Traveled (A.M. Peak Hr)
Change from null alternative

Capital Cost ($ millions)
    Highway
    Transit
    Bus
    Commuter Rail
    Light Rail
    Heavy Rail

Annual Operating Cost ($ millions)
    Highway
    Transit
    Bus
    Commuter Rail
    Light Rail
    Heavy Rail

Ability to Meet 50% Cost/Revenue Ratio

Cost Effectiveness Index

Enhancement of Access to Area of Economic Development

Compatibility With Local Plans

Fatal Flow Evaluation

Right-of-Way Opportunities

Other Issues Including Safety

Source: Maryland Department of Transportation, *Maryland Statewide Commuter Assistance Study,* Executive Transit Summary, Baltimore, MD 1990

- *Identification of alternatives* — based upon the information compiled in the corridor profile and derived from the travel demand forecasting process, a range of transportation improvement alternatives were developed for each corridor. These alternatives were developed based upon an examination of existing and future congestion levels, development patterns, commuting trends, and right-of-way opportunities and constraints in the corridor.

- *Evaluation of alternatives* — each alternative was then evaluated based upon measurements of its effect on the problem, its practicality, and cost. The alternative's impact were measured in terms of its effect on future congestion levels as well as its projected usage. The practicality measures included compatibility with local plans, physical and environmental feasibility, and right-of-way opportunities. Measures of cost include total and annualized capital and operating costs.

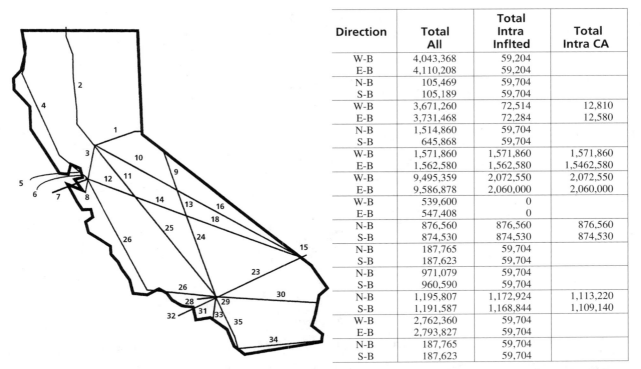

Direction	Total All	Total Intra Inflted	Total Intra CA
W-B	4,043,368	59,204	
E-B	4,110,208	59,204	
N-B	105,469	59,704	
S-B	105,189	59,704	
W-B	3,671,260	72,514	12,810
E-B	3,731,468	72,284	12,580
N-B	1,514,860	59,704	
S-B	645,868	59,704	
W-B	1,571,860	1,571,860	1,571,860
E-B	1,562,580	1,562,580	1,5462,580
W-B	9,495,359	2,072,550	2,072,550
E-B	9,586,878	2,060,000	2,060,000
W-B	539,600	0	
E-B	547,408	0	
N-B	876,560	876,560	876,560
S-B	874,530	874,530	874,530
N-B	187,765	59,704	
S-B	187,623	59,704	
N-B	971,079	59,704	
S-B	960,590	59,704	
N-B	1,195,807	1,172,924	1,113,220
S-B	1,191,587	1,168,844	1,109,140
W-B	2,762,360	59,704	
E-B	2,793,827	59,704	
N-B	187,765	59,704	
S-B	187,623	59,704	

Figure 10–8   Example Information from California's Intermodal Transportation Modeling

Source: *ITMS Users' Guide*, Sacramento, Calif.: California Department of Transportation, April 1996.

The first two categories of evaluation measures were developed from the corridor profile and travel demand forecasting materials outlined above. The cost measures used information from those two elements of the study, but initially required the development of a detailed capital and operating cost model based on national and state construction and operation experiences.

Table 10–1 shows the quantitative measures that were used to evaluate different alternatives (and thus the type of data that had to be produced from the analysis).

California's ITMS Methodology

The California Department of Transportation has developed a quick-response statewide sketch planning tool to assist planners in evaluating different strategies for improving California's transportation system.[14] The Intermodal Transportation Management System (ITMS) was designed to examine the effect of such strategies on both person travel and freight transportation. Importantly, the ITMS forecasts transportation demand for ten-, twenty-, and thirty-year time horizons. For passenger travel, the state was divided into passenger corridors and key origin-destination data were used to determine the overall patterns of demand in these corridors. For example, data used for air passenger transportation included data from an origin-destination 1992 survey and airport terminal forecasts from the Federal Aviation Administration. An example of the air corridors and of the types of forecasts that could come from this approach is found in Figure 10–8. A similar approach was followed for freight transportation with data coming from government data records; a proprietary data base that covered rail, truck, air, and water freight origin and destinations; and a forecast of the U.S. economy. In both the passenger and freight planning efforts, the ITMS allows planners to determine how many passengers and commodities will shift from one mode to another given different transportation strategies.

---

[14] *ITMS User's Guide* (Sacramento,Calif.: California Department of Transportation, April 1996).

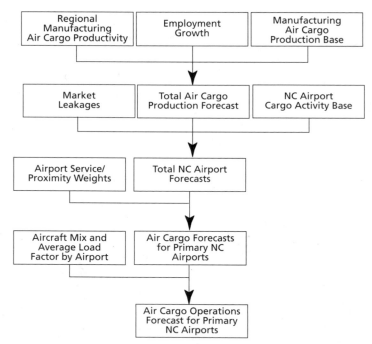

Figure 10–9 Forecasting Methodology for North Carolina's Air Cargo System Plan

Source: *North Carolina Air Cargo System Plan,* Raleigh, N.C.: North Carolina Department of Transportation, February 1992.

North Carolina's Air Cargo System Plan

The previous examples illustrate the analysis and evaluation of statewide multimodal transportation systems. The California and Wisconsin examples, in particular, show how freight considerations can be integrated into a planning framework with passenger planning. In many cases, however, state transportation planners examine individual modal systems as a targeted planning effort. So, for example, one can often find state rail plans, airport system plans, and port and waterborne transportation plans. A study commissioned in 1991 by the North Carolina DOT that focussed on the air cargo system in the state provides a useful example of how such planning can occur.[15]

The Air Cargo System Plan was based on a thorough analysis of air cargo flows, facilities and services, and a forecast of air freight traffic and related aircraft operations through the year 2010. The forecasting and allocation model used in this study is shown in Figure 10–9. The primary variable that was the foundation of the analysis was "air cargo pounds" produced by manufacturing industries for each county in the state. For any given year in the forecast time frame, a heuristic procedure was employed to allocate cargo traffic to and from each of the state's three primary airports. This model was calibrated and validated on 1990 data (with validation occurring on a subset of this data) with favorable results. The types of data needed for this study included:

- Detailed outbound air cargo flow data for (a) North Carolina counties, (b) selected regional market area counties, and (c) the total United States.

- Historical trends in air cargo productivity for the top two North Carolina market areas.

- Industry-specific employment forecasts for counties and market areas in North Carolina and the surrounding states.

- Import and export air cargo statistics for the Wilmington Customs District and the total United States.

---

[15] *North Carolina Air Cargo System Plan* (Raleigh, N.C.: North Carolina Department of Transportation, February 1992).

- Commodity and port of export statistics for North Carolina-originating air exports.

- State of origin export statistics for North Carolina airports.

- U.S. domestic and international air cargo activity statistics by carrier for North Carolina airports.

- Published U.S. domestic and international air cargo forecasts from secondary sources.

- Average driving distances between the major North Carolina airports and the origin and destination areas (counties, population centers).

In addition to this data, a survey was sent to a large number of companies representing manufacturers and shippers, agribusiness, freight forwarders, couriers, surface carriers, and warehousing and distribution operations. Ninety-five percent of the firms surveyed used air freight services. The survey also indicated the types of improvements that were desired in such services.

Of special concern in this study was enhancing the intermodal character of transportation services that was defined as "the integration of activities in a distribution chain, which facilitates the business transactions which move goods from origin to destination, both domestically and internationally."[16] The need for integrating carrier- and commodity-specific transportation systems was based on several factors:

- There are various types of "intermodal bridges" that have emerged, including: (a) a transfer of cargo involving ocean and land carriage to an interior point, (b) a transfer of cargo involving ocean and land carriage that originate or terminate at a coastal area, and (c) a transfer between two ocean movements joined by a transcontinental land transport system that requires handling of cargoes at two additional ports.

- Intermodal bridges are also rapidly developing with sea and air and also land and air links, in the latter case combining the lower costs of truck transportation and the speed of air transportation to produce low cost and efficient reliable door-to-door service. This includes both small package and document business as well as the larger air freight shipments.

- Double-stack rail services designed to reduce the cost of ocean carrier landbridge services have been expanded to domestic cargoes based on marginal cost efficiencies.

- Automated cargo-handling systems and automated terminals utilizing conventional vessels, conventional railcars, and aircraft have resulted in tremendous advances in productivity due to the application of advanced computerized and mechanized materials handling concepts.

- Trailer-truck on rail car systems exploit the larger cubic capacity and weight payloads of motor carriers to meet the needs of specific shippers and commodities.

The plan recommended that special efforts be undertaken to develop all air cargo aviation facilities where appropriate. In addition, the plan recommended a further effort to develop a global air cargo industrial complex that would position the state to capitalize on this growing freight sector.

Oregon Freight Rail Plan

One of the important elements of a state's transportation system, but one not under the direct control of the state DOT, is the rail system. However, given the critical role that rail transportation has in supporting a state's economy, state transportation planners often develop policies and investment programs designed to enhance the performance of rail transportation. These efforts are heavily dependent upon the participation of railroad companies and their customers in the planning process. This is one form of the public-private partnership that is the foundation for planning success.

[16] *North Carolina Air Cargo System Plan* (Raleigh, N.C.: North Carolina Department of Transportation, February 1992).

In 1994, the Oregon DOT updated the Oregon Freight Rail Plan, which was first developed in 1978.[17] The Oregon rail system is comprised of 2,600 route miles operated by 21 different railroads. An indication of the dynamic nature of rail planning was that over the eight years since the last update, the following characteristics of the rail system had changed:

- The rail mileage was 300 miles shorter due to line abandonment.

- More railroads were operating in the state.

- Rail traffic increased by 28 percent with traffic originating in Oregon decreasing, while terminating traffic increased twofold.

- Wood and farm products declined in relative importance to the transport of other commodities, such as chemicals.

In order to comment on the state's planning process, the Oregon DOT had established a Rail Freight Advisory Committee consisting of suppliers and users of rail service along with government agencies involved in rail freight issues (e.g., the Port of Portland). This Advisory Committee made recommendations relating to rail investment programs and to overall state policy relating to the rail system. For example, the plan included the following policies regarding rail freight:

- *Policy 1: increase opportunities for the state by having a viable and competitive rail system.*

  1. Stabilize and improve Oregon's access to the national rail system by maintaining a competitive environment for rail customers, assuring a level playing field for each mode, and assisting in removing capacity restraints.

  2. Promote intermodal centers where freight may be interchanged between rail and other modes by identifying suitable locations with adequate potential volumes and, if necessary, funding rail improvements and providing adequate highway access.

  3. Identify opportunities for improved rail service to Oregon's deep water ports that will promote foreign trade by funding support facilities to reduce congestion and increase efficiency.

- *Policy 2: strengthen the retention of local rail service where feasible.*

  1. Where necessary, seek alternative ownership or operation of rail facilities in order to preserve service.

  2. Encourage increased use of rail service by promoting rail service opportunities, providing a wide range of intermodal facilities, and assisting localities and rail users to understand railroad economics, revenue needs of individual lines, and land use requirements.

  3. Utilize federal or state funds for rail service continuation assistance as appropriate. Preference should be given to those lines that upon analysis have a positive benefit over cost ratio and will not require public assistance for ongoing operations.

- *Policy 3: protect abandoned rail rights-of-way for alternative or future use.*

  1. Ensure that political jurisdictions and private groups are familiar with how to preserve and convert abandoned rail rights-of-way for public use and interim trail use, as allowed under federal law.

  2. Use federal, state, and local funds to preserve rail rights-of-way for future transportation purposes.

- *Policy 4: integrate rail freight considerations in the state's land use planning process.*

  1. Recognize the social, economic, and environmental importance of rail freight service.

  2. Encourage land use zoning and ordinances that enhance and protect existing rail freight service.

  3. Work with communities to minimize conflicts between railroad operations and other urban activities.

[17] *1994 Oregon Freight Rail Plan* (Salem, Ore.: Oregon Department of Transportation, July 1994).

4. Assist in removing constraints to improve railroad operating efficiency within urbanized areas. Work with communities to consolidate or close existing grade crossings and prevent the establishment of unjustified new grade crossings.

5. Encourage local jurisdictions to identify alternative uses for low density branch line rights-of-way.

The analysis and evaluation step in this planning process was very different from that found in other types of statewide transportation planning. As noted in the plan, it is difficult to predict rail freight movements in that so many market forces influence the use of rail. International trade heavily influences movement through Oregon's ports. Domestic mergers and consolidations could dramatically change how freight is transported. And technological advances (e.g., container transportation and truck-on-railcar) could significantly alter the type of service offered. The basis for the analysis in the Oregon Rail Freight Plan was a commodity-by-commodity assessment of likely growth or decline in rail traffic. These trends were used to determine the overall originating and terminating rail tonnage, and the consequent loads on rail lines. The analysis indicated a 27 percent increase in tonnage from 1992 to 2000. Transportation planners were then able to identify rail line capacity restricted clearance and port access issues that needed to be addressed.

Corridor 18

Historically, transportation system connectivity meant making sure that the same designated highway in two states met at the same state border location. Increasingly, in today's international marketplace, system connectivity means getting passengers and commodities from one location in the United States to another location, most often involving travel among many states. In addition, with international trade agreements, increased cross continent freight movement can be expected. One of the planning responses to this potential travel demand has been the use of multistate corridor studies. Such studies have also been used to examine the application of intelligent transportation system (ITS) technologies to freight movement (e.g., the application of electronic bar code technology to monitor vehicle weight and safety permitting from one state to the next).

Corridor 18 is an example of multistate corridor planning with terminus locations in Indianapolis and Houston.[18] This corridor, which serves local, regional, national, and international demands for transportation, is difficult to model at a high level of detail. Therefore, a model was developed based on all national highway system routes in the study area as the modeled network. Interstate highways connecting to areas outside of the study boundary were considered external nodes. Two geographic levels of traffic analysis zones were used. Inside the study area, the traffic analysis zone was based on counties or parishes. Outside the study area, the zones were defined by the Bureau of Economic Analysis (BEA) zones. External zones were used to represent international movements to and from Canada and Mexico.

A model was developed based on separate trip matrices for auto and truck traffic on the highway network. For auto trips, an inter-urban travel model was used to estimate trips up to 725 km (450 miles). Longer trips used the results of the 1990 National Personal Travel Survey and then adjusted to match ground counts at calibration points in the network. Truck movements were estimated based on truck tonnages reported moving to and from the BEA zones. International truck trips were estimated using cross-border truck volumes.

For projections, auto trips were assumed to increase based on expected population growth and the increase in vehicle miles traveled per person. Truck trips were projected to increase proportional to the increase in gross national product. Cross-border truck movements were more difficult to project because of the uncertainty associated with economic conditions in Mexico and an increasing reliance on truck and rail intermodal services. An external study on the expected high-growth export market to Mexico was used as a benchmark for the percent increase in cross-border truck traffic to and from Mexico. The Canadian market, being more established than that with Mexico, was assumed to expand at a more modest rate.

New highways and improvements to existing highways were incorporated into the network model and future trip matrices were used to assess the likely effects of these improvements.

---

[18] *Corridor 18 Feasibility Study,* Final Report (Columbia, S.C.: Wilbur Smith & Associates, October 1995).

The Corridor 18 study illustrates the important characteristics of transportation planning at larger scales of analysis: (1) it is highly aggregate in terms of zonal definitions and network description, (2) travel growth is tied closely to economic surrogate variables, (3) trip matrices are assumed to reflect increases in population percentages and indicators of economic activity, and (4) high levels of uncertainty are often associated with projections in areas where external factors can have a significant effect on the resulting estimate (e.g., the state of the Mexican economy). See Chapter 11 for more detail on intercity travel.

Step Five: Financial Planning and Programming

One of the key steps in taking a project from initial concept to implementation is identifying the magnitude and source of funding for its implementation. Financial planning and the programming of a project in the transportation improvement program is the process by which this occurs. Because the STP is closely linked to the transportation plans of a state's metropolitan areas, the STIP is also closely integrated to the transportation improvement programs of these same areas. Figure 10–10 shows an example from Florida of how the state's transportation plans and programs rely on inputs from other planning activities in the state.

Both the STP and the statewide TIP must be financially constrained. For the statewide TIP this means that the source of revenues to fund proposed projects, while at the same time operating and maintaining the transportation system at an adequate level, should be indicated. Financial constraint is an important characteristic of transportation plans and programs. Such constraint provides a credibility check on what is being produced. Financial planning should consider not only traditional sources of funds, but also the potential of innovative and nontraditional sources of finance. Relating the desired system performance levels to costs directly conveys what is needed to satisfy customers' expectations of system performance and condition.

The state DOT must have a process for estimating expected revenues from all sources of funds and for projecting these revenues over the time frame of the program. In those instances where projects are to be funded from proposed new funding sources, the statewide TIP should identify the strategies that will be used to ensure their availability.

One of the most important trends in transportation finance over the past 10 years has been the increasing use of innovative or nontraditional sources of funding. Innovation in funding has occurred in three areas:

- *New revenue sources* — principally tolls, value capture, and cost-sharing with those who benefit from an improvement.

- *New roles* — for the public and private sectors that support the tapping of new resources, financial and entrepreneurial; especially increasing roles for the private sector beyond design and construction to include sharing in development, finance, and ownership.

- *New financing structures and techniques* — that leverage existing revenue sources and encourage private investment — both equity and debt.

An example of the packaging of different revenue sources for highway projects is found in a study for a major bypass around the Atlanta metropolitan area. As part of this study, the following potential revenue sources were identified: project debt, toll revenue, investor equity, state and federal loans, donated rights-of-way, development fees, air rights leasing, concession rights leasing, fiber optic cable rights leasing, fiber optic cable shared capacity leasing, and tax increment financing. At the state level, one of the more promising approaches is the use of an infrastructure bank that would allow the state to provide loans, enhance credit, and pay bond or debt incurred by agencies using resources to construct projects.

The statewide transportation planning process has an important role to play in defining which strategies are most appropriate. This often means that unique partnerships will have to be established to provide the institutional mechanisms that will allow public and private sector cooperation. To be successful, these partnerships will rely on mutual understanding of what is to be accomplished and an agreement on the respective roles that each partner will play in the cooperative adventure.

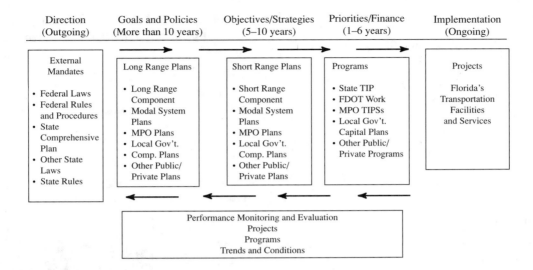

| Direction (Outgoing) | Goals and Policies (More than 10 years) | Objectives/Strategies (5–10 years) | Priorities/Finance (1–6 years) | Implementation (Ongoing) |

External Mandates

- Federal Laws
- Federal Rules and Procedures
- State Comprehensive Plan
- Other State Laws
- State Rules

Long Range Plans

- Long Range Component
- Modal System Plans
- MPO Plans
- Local Gov't.
- Comp. Plans
- Other Public/ Private Plans

Short Range Plans

- Short Range Component
- Modal System Plans
- MPO Plans
- Local Gov't.
- Comp. Plans
- Other Public/ Private Plans

Programs

- State TIP
- FDOT Work
- MPO TIPSs
- Local Gov't. Capital Plans
- Other Public/ Private Programs

Projects

Florida's Transportation Facilities and Services

Performance Monitoring and Evaluation
Projects
Programs
Trends and Conditions

Figure 10–10   Florida's Integrated Transportation Planning and Programming Process

Source: *Implementing the 2020 Florida Transportation Plan,* Tallahassee, Fla.: Florida Department of Transportation, undated.

Another important element of statewide transportation planning and programming is the selection of projects. Project selection procedures for state DOT investment programs can vary widely. A study of the many different techniques that can be used to establish priorities in state DOTs found the following distribution.[19] (Table 10–2.)

The following state examples illustrate how project selection and financial planning occurs in selected instances.

Wisconsin

The transportation planning process for Wisconsin included an examination of four plan alternatives.[20] Two of the plan alternatives assumed no revenues other than those expected from current funding programs. Two alternatives involved increased funding. (Table 10–2.) The final recommended plan required increased funding in the range between alternatives 3 and 4, about $8.9 billion in addition to the $30.1 billion from current sources, plus adjustments for inflation. The financing plan associated with the plan anticipated that revenue increases would be achieved gradually, in a series of steps over the 25-year planning period. (Figure 10–11.)

As an illustration of explaining how such an increase in financing would affect the average citizen, the plan stated for an assumed increase in the motor fuel tax:

> If this were done, the average one-car household in Wisconsin would see its motor vehicle fuel tax payments increased by $20 annually (or about four cents per gallon) every five years. In 2020, with the Translinks 21 plan in place, that one-car household's annual motor vehicle fuel tax payment would have increased by a total of $100 over current levels, plus inflation.

The plan presented a short "shopping list" of funding options, including:

- fuel tax,
- vehicle registration fees,

[19] Lance Neumann, *Methods for Capital Programming and Project Selection, Synthesis of Highway Practice 243* (Washington, D.C.: Transportation Research Board, 1997).

[20] *Translinks 21, A Multimodal Transportation Plan for Wisconsin's 21st Century* (Madison, Wis.: Wisconsin Department of Transportation, February 1995).

- supplemental sales tax on new and used vehicles,

- truck weight-distance tax,

- motor vehicle title tax,

- toll roads,

- bonding,

- state general funding,

- regional transportation authorities.

Washington State

The Washington State Transportation Commission adopted 10 service objectives and 51 action strategies in describing the desired services to be provided by the state's highway system plan.[21] According to the "needs" that surfaced from the planning process, it was estimated that the expected revenues over the 20-year life of the plan would be exceeded by $9 billion in needs. Therefore, the commission prioritized the recommended projects and established a six-year plan that fed into a two-year budget. (Figure 10–12.) The trade-offs made by the commission were to fully fund maintenance, operations, and preservation activities; all core high-occupancy vehicle lane projects and safety projects were to be fully funded; and only 40% of the mobility projects received funding.

Step Six: System Monitoring — the Feedback Loop

Transportation planning includes continually monitoring the performance of the transportation system to determine the progress being made in improving system performance and to identify additional areas of improvement. This system monitoring can take many forms. Every state DOT has a comprehensive traffic data collection system that collects data on traffic volumes, vehicle classification, and vehicle weights. This data can be collected through long-established counting programs (e.g., continuous and coverage count traffic data collection) or special data collection efforts (e.g., special vehicle classification studies). It is likely that some future data collection will occur through the use of ITS technologies.

Table 10–2   Different Techniques Used to Establish Priorities in State DOTs

Technique	Number of States Out of 39 That Use Them
Benefit and cost ratios:	33
Cost and effectiveness ratios:	20
Sufficiency and deficiency ratios:	22
Management systems:	38

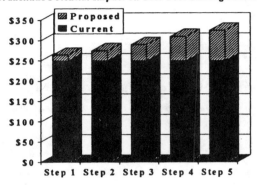

Translinks Potential Impact on User Fees Through 2020 (millions)

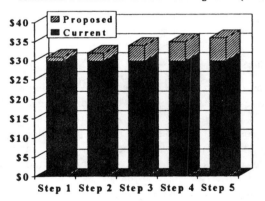

Translinks Potential Investments Through 2020 (Billions)

Figure 10–11   Plan Investment Scenarios in Wisconsin

Source: *Translinks 21, A Multimodal Transportation Plan for Wisconsin's 21st Century*, Madison, Wis.: Wisconsin Department of Transportation, February 1995.

Many states have begun to use management systems as a means of monitoring system performance and of feeding this information into the decision-making process. Typical management systems are targeted on key policy or program issues, for example, pavement and bridge condition, safety or accident monitoring, and more recently congestion and intermodal connectivity. Key to the operation of a management system is the identification of performance or condition measures that reflect important considerations for establishing priority investments.

[21] *Washington's Transportation Plan,* 1997- 2016 (Olympia, Wash.: Washington State Department of Transportation, April 1996).

Table 10–3 Wisconsin Plan Alternatives and Associated Costs

Table 10–3   Wisconsin Plan Alternatives and Associated Costs

Plan Components		Plan Alternative	Base Case (Alt. 1)	Alternative 2	Alternative 3	Alternative 4
INTERCITY PASSENGER TRANSPORTATION						
Highways	Corridors 2020 Expansion	Same as Base Case	$4,000: Corridors 2020 backbone complete by 2005	-$2,320: Delay corridors 2020: Reduce highway construction	Same as Base Case	Same as Base Case
	Other Improvements	$250: Interchange access $175: Country roads		Same as Base Case	$250: Interchange access	$250: Interchange access $150: Country roads
	Highway Rehabilitation	+$2,060: Increased rehab	$9,800: All state highways	Same as Base Case	+$1,600: Increased rehabilitation	+$2,800 Increase rehabilitation
	Local Road Improvements	+$2,000	$9,500: Local road maintenance improvements	Same as Base Case	+$1,060: Expand local road program	+$2,000: Expand local road program
Intercity Bus		+$160: Phase in service to 45 cities	$6: Decline in service possible	+$110: Restore service and add new service	+$75: Some service restored	+$160: Phase in service in 45 cities
Rail	High speed rail	+$475: High speed rail-Chicago-Milwaukee-Madison	No high speed rail	$250: Chicago/Milwaukee	+$120: Chicago/Milwaukee, Smaller state share	+$420: Milwaukee /Chicago/Twin Cities
	Conventional Rail	+$115: New service-Madison, Green Bay, Expand service: Chicago, Milwaukee, and Twin Cities	$20: Milwaukee-Chicago operating assistance	+$220: New service; Appleton, Green Bay, Madison, Tomah, La Crosse, Expand to Twin Cities	+$180: New service: Madison, Green Bay, Expand service to Twin Cities, Feeder bus service	+$440: New service-Madison, Green Bay, north central WI, Expand service to Twin Cities, Feeder bus service
Intermodal Stations		$25: New station facilities				
Air Passenger		+$90: Aggressively promote air travel	$870: State Airport System Plan	Same as Base Case	+$250: Expand airport improvements	+$140: Airport improvements including second runway at Milwaukee
INTERCITY FREIGHT TRANSPORTATION						
Highways		$60: All season highways				$130: All season highway
Rail Freight		Same as Base Case	$400: Increase freight rail program, grade crossing safety improvements	$140: Continue rail assistance grant/loan program	+$190: Increased funding for intermodal projects	+$250: Alt. 3 plus freight car acquisition
Air Freight		$25: Navigational improvements	Same as air passenger (above)	Same as Base Case	+$25: Improved freight facilities	+$50: Create Essential Air Services Program and facility improvements
Harbors		+$50: Expand Harbor Assistance Program	$50: Harbor Assistance Program	Same as Base Case	+$45: Physical improvements	+$60: Physical improvements
Intermodal Facilities		+$60: Improve highway access to facilities	Limited support	Same as Base Case	+$30: Improve highway access	+$50: Improve highway access
URBAN TRANSPORTATION						
Highways	Milwaukee Co. freeways	+$1,290: Modernization and rehabilitation	$750: Minimal rehabilitation	Same as Base Case	+$750: Increased rehabilitation	+1,210: Modernization rehabilitation
	Other	$250: Urban amenities				$250: Urban amenities
Transit	Urban Transit	+$925: Stabilize transit finance, marketing, expand service	$1,900: Maintain existing service	+$1,350: Improved transit in urban areas including LRT in Madison and Milwaukee	+$700 Increased operating assistance and improved service	+$1,520: Major transit improvements including LRT in Madison and Milwaukee
	Elderly and Disabled	+$220: Increase aids program	$170: Specialized transportation programs	+$190: Increased aids program	+$130: Increased aids program	+$260: Increased aids program
Bike/Ped		+$100: New state program	$100	+$140: New state program	+$80:New state program	+$120: New state program
TDM		+$70: Research and assistance	+$28: Technical support and research	+$80: Research and assistance	Same as Alt. 2	Same as Alt. 2

Source: *Translinks 21, A Multimodal Transportation Plan for Wisconsin's 21st Century,* Madison, Wis.: Wisconsin Department of Transportation, February 1995.

The following examples show the characteristics of management systems as they relate to planning and decision-making.

Maryland Congestion Management System

Maryland's Congestion Management System (CMS) uses performance measures to evaluate corridors and facilities, with the severity or type of congestion triggering progressively more detailed analysis. CMS performance measures were selected based upon the extent to which they were:

- Consistent with the Maryland Transportation Plan.

- Good indicators of congestion and capable of reflecting degrees of severity.

- Useful in comparing modes.

- Sensitive to changes in supply and demand caused by implementing congestion management strategies.

- Derived from or applicable to existing data bases.

- Easy to collect and periodically measure.

- Derived from travel demand modeling to gauge future congestion and be able to measure the effectiveness of alternative strategies.

The selected performance measures were categorized into three major groups: travel time and speed measures, system usage and capacity measures, and other measures. (Table 10–3.)

Oregon Intermodal Management System

The Oregon DOT has developed a statewide management system that focuses on the intermodal connections in the state transportation system. The purpose of this management system is to monitor the performance of the transportation system and to identify problems by relating system performance to a predetermined set of performance measures. The target of this management system was the intermodal facilities and services that provided the connections between modes in the state. Five categories of performance measures were used to assess the level of facility interconnectiveness—capacity, accessibility, connectivity, time delay, and safety. The specific values of the measures for each facility were compared to threshold criteria that then provided indications of where additional studies might be necessary to improve system performance. An example of these thresholds as applied for passenger rail stations is shown in Figure 10–13.

Conclusions

The purpose of the U.S. transportation system is to provide for the efficient and economic movement of people and goods. State DOTs have a very important role in providing the desired levels of mobility and accessibility afforded by this system. Statewide multimodal transportation planning is the process by which the performance of a state's transportation system is assessed and strategies are identified for improvement. Statewide transportation planning is to be closely linked to a state's economic strategy as well as to environmental, social, and land use policies that guide development in the state. The state DOT's planning process should be coordinated with other planning efforts undertaken by public and private sector groups that could have some effect on how the state's transportation system is used. The MPOs have a critically important role to play in defining the transportation needs of the state's major metropolitan areas, most often the areas with the most congested road system and in need of the greatest mobility and accessibility enhancements.

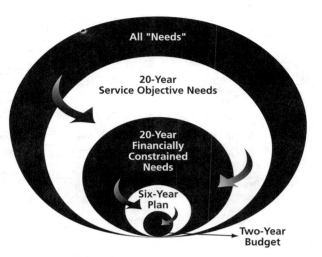

State Highway System Plan Trade-Off Decisions
(1995 Billion Dollars)

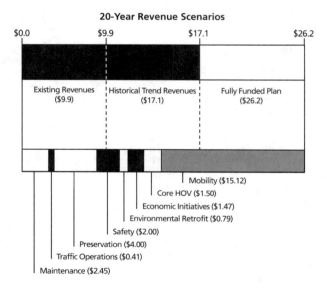

Figure 10–12   Washington State Financially Constrained Planning

Source: *Washington's Transportation Plan,* 1997-2016, Olympia, Wash.: Washington State Department of Transportation, April 1996.

Table 10–4 Maryland's Performance Measures for Congestion Management

Performance Measure	Collected Data	Corridor Level Analysis	Facility-Level Analysis	Measures of Strategy Practicality or Effectiveness
Travel Time-Related Measures				
Travel Time by Mode	X	X	X	X
Delay		X	X	X
System Capacity and Usage Measures				
Traffic Volume	X			
Volume to Capacity		X	X	X
Level of Service		X	X	X
Vehicle Occupancy	X		X	X
Vehicle Miles Traveled		X	X	X
Person Miles Traveled		X	X	X
Transit Ridership/Capacity	X		X	X
PMT by Transit Load Factor	X	X		X
Modal Shares	X	X		X
Other Important Measures				
Air Quality Rating			X	X
Annualized Cost/Trip				X
Consistency with Local Plans				X
Fatal Flaw Evaluation				X
No. & Avg. Duration of Incidents	X	X		X
No. of Congested Major Intersections		X	X	X

Source: *Maryland Statewide Commuter Assistance Study, Executive Summary*, Baltimore, Md.: Maryland Department of Transportation, 1990.

The statewide transportation plan should provide a strategic perspective on state transportation system investment over at least a 20-year time horizon. A statewide transportation plan should consider a wide range of investment, operational, and technology options that can meet the multimodal transportation needs of transportation system users. Statewide transportation planning should consider all modes of transportation in a coordinated fashion, and develop an overall strategy that best meets the needs of transportation markets. In addition, comprehensiveness means looking not only at alternatives that require physical changes to the transportation system, but looking also at enhancements to the operations or use of the system as well as increased efficiencies and safety that could occur through application of advanced technologies.

Finally, the users and stakeholders of the transportation system should be given ample opportunity to participate in the planning process. This participation is not only afforded to the general public, but also to agencies and groups not usually included in the planning process — private freight providers, operators of transportation facilities and services, and environmental constituencies. This is perhaps the most important characteristic of the transportation planning process. It is to be an open process, with provisions made to allow maximum input into the desired visions and directions for transportation system investment.

Mode Connection	Performance Measures	Threshold	Type of Measure
Whole facility	Square footage of terminal space per peak hour passenger	<1.5 sq. feet per passenger	Condition
	% of statewide annual facility injury accident rate	>150%	Condition
	% of statewide annual facility fatality accident rate	>150%	Safety
	% of statewide average annual facility property damage accident rate	>150%	Safety
	% of statewide average annual facility theft rate	>150%	Safety
Passenger Car	Curbside availability?	No	Condition
	Linear feet of passenger car space for Curbside availability per peak hour passengers	<0.3'/passenger <100' minimum	Condition
	Average daily peak % v/c total for parking	>0.9	Performance
	Average minutes to park	>10 minutes	Performance
Public transit	Curbside availability?	No	Condition
	Linear feet of transit space for curbside availability per peak hour passengers	<0.03'/passenger <50 minimum	Condition
	% of trains met by transit within an hour before and after arrival	<100%	Performance
	Integrated ticketing?	No	Condition
	Integrated baggage handling?	No	Condition

Figure 10–13 An Example of Performance Measures for Intermodal Transportation: State of Oregon

Source: *Oregon Transportation Plan*, Salem, Ore.: Oregon Department of Transportation, September 1992.

References

Federal Highway Administration and Federal Transit Administration. *A Guide to Statewide Transportation Planning Under ISTEA*. Washington, D.C.: U.S. Department of Transportation, 1996.

National Academy of Public Administration, et al. *State Departments of Transportation: Strategies for Change, National Cooperative Highway Research Program Report 371*. Washington, D.C.: Transportation Research Board, 1995.

Transportation Research Board. *Transportation Planning, Programming, and Finance; Proceedings of a National Conference, Transportation Research Circular 406*. Washington, D.C.: TRB, 1993.

Transportation Research Board. *Statewide Transportation Planning, Proceedings of a National Conference, Transportation Research Circular 471*. Washington D.C.: TRB, 1997.

CHAPTER 11
Intercity Passenger Travel

Alan E. Pisarski
Consultant

Introduction

Scope of Consideration

This chapter presents material describing the characteristics of intercity passenger travel activity. Because the term "intercity" is so amorphous, several elements of travel activity are treated here to cover its broad meaning. Included in the discussion are: basic intercity travel, as defined below; international travel to, from, and between the United States and other countries with emphasis on our North American neighbors Mexico and Canada; and some consideration of local rural travel, which, while not truly intercity in character, is often indistinguishable from intercity travel as a result of the shared use of intercity surface facilities.

Exclusions from Consideration

Given the definitions above, it is clear that local metropolitan passenger travel is the most significant travel activity to be excluded by the definition employed. There are boundary issues to be resolved—one issue is between local and intercity transportation as their distinctions blur over time and another issue is between freight and passenger movements as more and more passenger travel occurs in trucks and vans. Also, the reader is advised to carefully look at the definitions provided with each data source that will explain which groups are included and excluded. Travel survey data will differ from tourism border-crossing data or from carrier count data in definition as well as in data collection methods.

Definitions

The term "intercity transportation" is understood in a general way by most English-speaking people, whether they are transportation professionals or not. They understand that it relates to the term "interstate," which is sometimes called "interurban" and may include international travel; and that it mostly means "not-urban" or "not-local" travel activity. The term "rural" itself is often linked to intercity as the space between metropolitan areas, and it is defined in various ways. Here it is accepted as meaning nonmetropolitan. This usage is closest to the general popular understanding but varies from some U.S. Bureau of the Census definitions.

Highway travel has perhaps been the greatest cause of confusion in the definition of intercity travel for passengers or freight. In nonhighway modal areas, the mode fundamentally defines the nature of the travel. Air passenger service, Amtrak service in the United States, and most shipborne travel are treated as intercity in their character. But the highway-related modes cause overlap and confusion, particularly between local rural and intercity travel on scheduled buses or in autos or trucks. Increasingly there is a blending of Amtrak functions as well, where many so-called long-distance Amtrak routes serve substantial numbers of daily commuters.

The components of a more rigorous definition of intercity travel generally involve the use of distance and time criteria. Distance definitions have been used by the Bureau of the Census and private surveyors to make the distinction from local travel. Usually a distance of 75 or 100 miles is used as the threshold of intercity travel. Given the small size of their countries, many European surveys typically use much shorter distances as their cut-off criteria, such as 75 or even 50 kilometers (approximately 50–33 miles). The 1995 American Travel Survey (ATS) used a distance threshold of

100 miles. But there are clearly some "local" trips that exceed those distances and some "intercity" trips less than that distance.

One "time" criterion employed identifies travel activity that is nonrepetitive as being of interest, seeking to avoid the daily travel activity typical of most households. The travel industry, which has a serious interest in properly defining its market, often uses a time criterion based on overnight stays, accepting all trips with an overnight stay as intercity but not excluding some without an overnight stay. Typically an additional distance criterion of 75 to 100 miles is used to capture nonovernight intercity travel, sometimes called excursion or same-day travel.

Internationally accepted definitions, based on government interests in international tourism and the balance of payments to travel and transportation accounts, have historically used geographic or jurisdictional boundaries as criteria for defining intercity travel more than distance or time criteria. Conventionally, trips across national borders are treated as part of intercity travel, although the actual trips might involve only very short-distance travel such as work trips or shopping trips between the United States and Canada. The way that these trips factor into national accounts, specifically by balance-of-payments calculations, leads to their inclusion.

The World Tourism Organization Definitions

In 1991 the World Tourism Organization (WTO), a United Nations (UN) chartered agency, sponsored a world conference in Ottawa, Canada attended by over 100 nations, which adopted a set of definitions and statistical standards regarding long-distance travel. Those definitions and statistical standards have now been published in six or seven languages in a UN and WTO publication.[1] This document draws from a long history of attempts to define tourism travel, exhaustively starting with the League of Nations in 1937. Its definition of tourism is germane because it officially links to many other related international standards that affect intercity travel, such as the International Monetary Fund, which along with other partners defines common definitions and internationally adopted standards for balance-of-payments calculations; and other UN agencies such as the High Commission for refugees, which differentiates travelers from immigrants, refugees, and nomads.

The WTO definition of a tourist shown below provides valuable guidance in the understanding of intercity travel.

> Tourism comprises the activities of persons traveling to and staying in places outside their usual environment for not more than one consecutive year for leisure, business and other purposes.[2]

This definition, which will be surprising to some, encompasses *all* trip purposes—not just leisure travel. After excluding some travel as defined by international convention, (i.e., diplomats, migrants, refugees, and nomads), it counts all travel *outside the usual environment* as tourism travel (excluding those who will be paid at the destination, like guest workers). Thus, the travel industry's definition of the term "tourist" does not follow the popular understanding of the word as a person on vacation seeing the sights. The key is the concept of *usual environment* and the distinction between travel within it and travel beyond it. Those accustomed to urban travel studies will immediately accept the concept of usual environment as the basis for local metropolitan travel; just as they will accept the concept of *outside the usual environment* as the basis for intercity travel without a hard, fast, exhaustive definition of what *usual environment* entails. These definitional elements are important to recognize, especially when viewing any national or international sources of tourism and travel statistics. *It is this definition that will be employed here as the basis for intercity travel.*

Other Definitions

As noted earlier, international passenger flows are often defined more by balance-of-payment accounting concepts, and statutory customs requirements than by transport or tourism characteristics. The main distinctions made in international statistical structures are a function of the permanence of the stay, either establishing residence or receiving pay at the destination site. This is an important accounting distinction in that expenditures by "foreign" tourists in a country or a

---

[1] *Recommendations on Tourism Statistics* (New York, N.Y.: United Nations Statistical Commission and the World Tourism Organization, 1994).
[2] Ibid.

state represent an "export" by that state or country, whereas spending by a visitor earning income at the destination constitutes domestic consumption. All of this international terminology is symmetric in domestic travel as well. The definitions can be applied with equal validity to travelers visiting Florida from Washington or visiting France from Washington.

An increasingly significant distinction in European concerns is that between international and intercontinental transport. "International" indicates movements within the Common Market area, whereas intercontinental travel implies noncommon market or non-European flows. A similar distinction is used in the U.S. international market to differentiate Canadian and Mexican travel from "overseas" travel.

Dimensioning Existing Intercity Passenger Travel

Data Sources

It is obligatory to review the current state of statistical programs in this sector of transportation at the outset, to examine the trends in the nature of the ability to describing current national intercity passenger activity, and to identify the sources of the data employed here.

The U.S. statistical data base for transportation, and particularly for intercity travel, has been weak, at least since the late seventies. This status is a result of deregulation of many of the transport modes and of the decline in funds available for data collection in national transportation agencies. Many of these sources had been moribund and in need of serious review and modification.

A very positive shift in our knowledge base and the availability of travel data has come about as a result of the U.S. Department of Transportation's (DOT) new Bureau of Transportation Statistics (BTS). This agency was created by the Intermodal Surface Transportation Efficiency Act (ISTEA) to respond to many of the data needs that developed over the last 20 years. Its major intercity passenger travel product is the 1995 ATS. (The reporting year for the last public national survey of long-distance travel in the United States was 1977.)

Canada's system of national statistics has been the more effective in developing a comprehensive ongoing national transportation data base, although it is also undergoing substantial change. Downsizing has been severe with the Canadian National Tourism Agency being privatized, and both Statistics Canada (the equivalent to our Bureau of the Census) and Transport Canada (the equivalent to our DOT) have been sharply affected by staff and budget cuts. However, the travel survey programs have been sustained. The work of Statistics Canada in their domestic and international travel surveys has been supported by Transport Canada and the new Canadian Tourism Commission, a joint public-private agency.

Mexico's National Agency for Statistics and Geographic Systems (INEGI) has not yet produced a full national travel survey.

Many of the data programs of Europe and Asia are premised on customs and other border control operations of the national government. This arrangement may work where long-distance trips are almost by definition transborder trips, but it would be ineffective in very large countries like Canada and the United States. Border authorities obtain such data as traveler nationality, age, sex, residence, destination, trip purpose, mode of travel, and length of stay. The loss of statistical control as a result of the decline in border barriers in Europe in 1992 is of great concern among European analysts, both for transportation and tourism as well as for balance of payments applications. At this time the European community's statistical agency, Eurostat, is pursuing research on the use of traditional travel surveys or technological substitutes to replace border control statistics.

Passenger Travel Data Sources

A review of major passenger sources and their current status appears below. A list of Web sites and general guides to travel data appears in this chapter's appendix.

The availability of the 1995 ATS has filled a 20-year void in terms of access to useful detailed information on long-distance travel in America. The survey sponsored by BTS and conducted by the Bureau of the Census collected long-distance travel information over the full-year period of 1995, interviewing 80,000 households each quarter to obtain data on their long-distance trips from the previous three months. Long distance was defined as trips over 100 miles in length; the Oak Ridge National Laboratory (ORNL) calculated actual route distances for highway travel and developed the ability to display through-trips by area. The extensive scale of the survey was designed to provide state-to-state, long-distance travel flows and metro-level origins and destinations in order to permit delineation of major travel corridors. A key product is the collection of modal data for airport, rail, bus terminal access, and egress trips. It is intended that the survey will be conducted every five years into the future, although with possible redesigning. The survey is made available in print and electronic media, one of the most useful of which is a state profile series.

National Travel Survey

The original National Travel Survey (NTS) produced by the Bureau of the Census came to a close in 1977 due to a lack of funds; and it is now superseded by the ATS, discussed above. The best industry substitute is the NTS produced annually by the U.S. Travel Data Center of the Travel Industry Association since 1979. It is conducted monthly and produces about 1,500 observations per month. Other industry-monitoring-type surveys obtain aspects of intercity travel data primarily for travel industry advertisers and market analysts, but none approach the sample size and transportation coverage of the new BTS survey. However, most have the advantage of currency in that they obtain annual and even quarterly or monthly data produced on a rapid turnaround rate. The combination of the ATS, conducted every five years as a benchmark, and the NTS, as an annual monitoring tool, could be a formidable resource if managed effectively.

Statistics Canada surveys Canadian domestic and international travelers. Both the U.S. and Canadian Price Index surveys include intercity travel expenditures by households as part of their analyses of personal consumption patterns and costs.

Air Travel

The Federal Aviation Administration and the Office of Information Management at the U.S. DOT, now part of the BTS, produce a family of statistics on airport operations, air carrier and charter activity, and passenger origin and destination (O-D) patterns. Through a 10-percent sample of all air carrier tickets, a very detailed O-D airport-to-airport flow is produced. This data set was found to be outmoded in a 1998 audit report of the DOT Inspector General, and an improved approach has been recommended. The main data set is the T100 data set derived from the original form 41 system of the former Civil Aeronautics Board. This data set contains traffic information from large U.S. and foreign carriers. A parallel data set is produced by the Aviation Statistics Centre of Statistics Canada for Canadian aviation. As is typical with such operations-based data, they contain no associated demographic information.

Rail Travel

All of the old Interstate Commerce Commission (ICC) reporting, including that of Amtrak data, has been shifted to the BTS. Amtrak retains most sources of rail data reporting, providing limited data in annual reports. The data are not broadly disseminated because of proprietary marketing concerns. The demise of Via Rail in Canada leaves open the question of rail passenger activity statistics in Canada.

Intercity Bus Travel

Almost all significant reporting of intercity bus travel was abolished at the ICC before its demise. Industry attempts to revitalize a reporting program have been unsuccessful, nor have Bureau of the Census efforts to establish a bus industry survey succeeded to date. The only reporting available consists of summary statistics on Class I carrier revenues and passengers, retained by BTS from the former ICC program. In Canada, intercity bus property activities are included in the reporting of urban transit by Statistics Canada. Data include passenger volumes and miles traveled and industry financial statistics.

Intercity Auto Travel

The main source of personal travel in America remains the National Personal Travel Study (NPTS) conducted over the years at the Bureau of the Census under the joint sponsorship of a number of U.S. DOT agencies, led by the Federal Highway Administration. The survey was shifted to private contractors by DOT for the 1990 survey and again for 1995. Only a limited portion of the survey addresses intercity travel, but the survey is invaluable because it links intercity travel characteristics to extensive demographic and local travel characteristics. Its limited sample size does not permit the identification of origin-destination patterns.

A series of conferences and papers were sponsored by the Transportation Research Board's Task Force on National Statistics examining the ramifications of melding the DOT survey of local travel, the NPTS, and the ATS data sets to establish a smooth trip-length continuum of travel survey data for the nation.

International Travel

A number of official sources provide counts of international arrivals and departures in the United States and Canada. These are monitored as part of the tourism, balance-of-payments, and immigration programs of both countries. The On-board Travel Survey of the former U.S. Travel and Tourism Administration, now the Travel Industries office of the International Trade Administration of the Department of Commerce, provides expenditure and other travel information on air visitors to the United States, including Canadians. This survey is based on questionnaires administered on departing flights from the United States. Statistics Canada provides an annual survey of visits to the United States and other foreign destinations by Canadians. Previous joint surveys by Canada and the United States in major traveling countries to assess market potential for visits to the North American continent have ended with the effective dissolution of the programs.

Dimensioning the Existing Passenger System

The national transportation system can be construed as a multimodal set of systems providing passenger and freight services to serve local, intercity, and international needs. There are certainly components of the system that are primarily focused on intercity passenger activity, such as Amtrak; but the system is largely one that serves all needs—or what might be called markets—simultaneously. Therefore, this chapter does not provide a detailed description of the U.S. transportation system and its services. The subject is treated briefly and the reader is directed to those sources—mostly annual reports that maintain an inventory of the system, the rights-of-way, the fleets of vehicles, the condition of the components, and the services provided.

A growing interest in intermodal connectivity has raised the greatest concern in the public sector about system connectivity on the passenger side, where most often the linkages must be provided by the public sector. Generally, where the private sector provides intermodal interfaces, they work relatively well. As an example, perhaps the model for a "seamless" interface is provided by the air-rental car connection.

The annex to this chapter provides a brief summary of the main passenger-related elements of the national transportation system.

Characteristics of Intercity Travel

Overall Scale of Intercity Travel

As a rough guide to the reader, the 1995 NPTS places U.S. national travel at about one billion trips *per day*—or about four one-way trips per capita per day. Conveniently the ATS was conducted in the same year and places long-distance travel at one billion trips *per year,* based on a round-trip definition of a trip. An estimated average round-trip length of roughly 800 miles for trips over 100 miles in length yields a coarse estimate of more than 800 billion person-miles per year. Preliminary ATS analysis places this at about 25 percent of all national passenger travel. More detailed values for long-distance travel based on trips of over 100 miles (one-way trip length) are shown in Table 11–1.

Table 11–1 Intercity Travel Summary (annual values)

Measure	Value	
All Person-Trips	1,042,615	(Thousands)
Foreign	41,296	(Thousands)
Domestic	1,001,319	(Thousands)
All Person-Miles	827,000,00	(Thousands)
Per Capita Trips	4	
Per Capita Miles	3,147	
Mean Trip Length	827	miles
Median Trip Length	425	miles

Source: *American Travel Survey,* Washington, D.C.: U.S. DOT, Bureau of Transportation Statistics, 1995.

Another perspective on long-distance travel trends is shown in Figure 11–1. This figure shows intercity passenger-miles per capita and intercity passenger-miles per unit GDP (Gross Domestic Product) on an index basis with constant dollar GDP trends shown for reference. The figure shows that there has been appreciable growth, roughly 40 percent from 1980 to 1996, in intercity passenger-miles per capita; and lower but still significant growth of 13 percent in intercity passenger-miles per unit of GDP based on reporting by the Eno Transportation Foundation.[3]

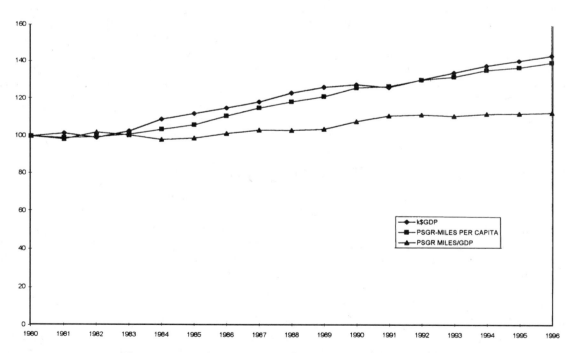

Figure 11–1   Passenger Mile–GDP Index Trends

Source: Eno Transportation Foundation, Washington, D.C.: ETF, 1997.

[3] *Transportation in America, Annual* (Washington, D.C.: Eno Transportation Foundation, Inc.).

Modal Trends of Common Carriers

The ETF provides mode usage data in intercity travel by summarizing intercity passenger carrier statistics. The ETF provides annual measures of carrier passengers carried, passenger-miles traveled, and revenues based on carrier reporting. A 20-year overview from 1976 to 1996 indicates that overall long-distance passenger travel including private vehicles has increased by 80 percent, from 1.3 trillion passenger-miles to 2.4 trillion, with two-thirds of the growth coming after 1986. Essentially all of the growth has occurred in the private auto and air modes with roughly three-fourths of the growth in autos and the remainder in air. This has resulted in an increased share for air over time—from under 12 percent in 1976 to over 18 percent by 1996. Despite strong growth, the auto mode has continued its long-term decline in share, which peaked at 90 percent in 1960, was down to 86 percent by 1976, and declined further to just above 80 percent by 1996. Private air, bus, and rail travel make up the remainder of passenger-miles of travel. Figure 11–2 traces the passenger-miles provided by the carrier modes over the long term starting in 1950.

A large part of the growth in passenger-miles has resulted from increases in average trip length, rising from about 700 miles in 1976 for air carriers to about 840 miles in 1996. Amtrak and bus travel saw similar increases—from 230 to 270 miles for Amtrak and from 120 to 140 miles for buses.

Overall Personal Travel Spending

A review of personal transportation spending indicates that American households spend about $6,000 per year for all personal travel-related activities, based on the Consumer Expenditure Survey (CEX), the data source for the computation of the consumer price index, conducted annually by the Bureau of the Census for the Bureau of Labor Statistics (BLS). The vast majority, roughly 93 percent, of all household personal transportation spending is related to the acquisition, operation, and upkeep of motor vehicles. About 5 percent of transportation spending goes to purchased intercity travel. The remainder goes to local transit, about 1 percent, and miscellaneous purchases and rentals, also amounting to about 1 percent. Figure 11–3 provides more detail on the distribution of consumer expenditures for transportation in 1995, the latest year for which data are available. Table 11–2 provides totals for 1995 and detail-by-income quintiles, a division

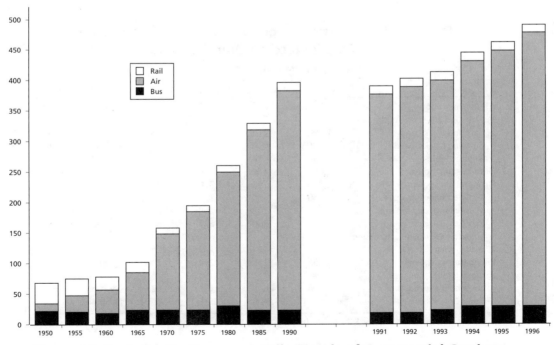

Figure 11–2   Intercity Passenger Mile Trends of Commercial Carriers

Source: Eno Transportation Foundation, Washington, D.C.: ETF, 1997.

of the population into five equally sized groups based on income. These data vary significantly from year to year and have shown variations in share of transportation in total consumer spending in a range from 17 to 19 percent.

Expenditures for purchased intercity travel in Table 11–2 are included under public transportation and need clarification. First, they include local as well as long-distance expenditures for purchased transportation. Second, they include only the household personal consumption expenditures of residents and therefore represent only a portion of all expenditures for intercity person travel in the United States. Roughly speaking, about 80 percent of the public transportation spending in the survey is intercity in nature with the remainder local transit, taxi, and school buses. There are some other elements that could be included in this count but are instead counted elsewhere in the survey such as auto, motorcycle, and recreation vehicle rentals out of town. These add only a few percent to the overall estimated spending.[4] The detailed elements of the survey under public transportation are shown in Table 11–3, with their estimated shares of public transportation spending.

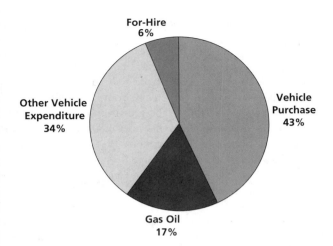

Figure 11–3   Consumer Expenditures for Transportation, 1995

Source: *Consumer Expenditure Survey,* Washington, D.C.: Bureau of Labor Statistics, 1995.

The values for public transportation spending in the CEX would need to be expanded in the following three ways to approach a complete estimate of total intercity travel spending: (1) business travel would need to be added, such as that travel paid for by an employer, amounting to about 25 percent of all intercity miles of travel; (2) intercity travel within the United States by nonresident visitors would also need to be added; and, most importantly, (3) a significant portion of the auto expenditures that dominate total travel spending would need to be allocated to intercity travel. These elements will be treated below.

Table 11–2   Consumer Expenditures for Transportation by Type by Income Quintile, 1995
(annual average household spending $)

	All	Lowest	Second	Third	Fourth	Highest
All transportation	6,014	2,021	4,025	5,745	7,639	11,155
Vehicle purchases (net outlay)	2,638	654	1,775	2,702	3,401	4,841
Cars and trucks, new	1,198	216	862	838	1,426	2,619
Cars and trucks, used	1,406	430	900	1,846	1,903	2,169
Other vehicles	34	8	13	17	72	54
Gasoline and motor oil	1,006	470	716	985	1,275	1,621
Other vehicle expenses	2,015	752	1,320	1,823	2,603	3,813
Vehicle finance charges	260	60	127	271	393	482
Maintenance and repairs	653	302	469	621	851	1,130
Vehicle insurance	712	266	527	673	895	1,267
Vehicle rent, leasing, licensing, other charges	389	124	197	257	464	934
Public transportation	355	145	214	234	360	879
Average annual total household expenditures	$32,264	$14,607	$22,126	$29,125	$39,395	$62,639
% Trans	18.64%	13.84%	18.19%	19.73%	19.39%	17.81%

Source: *Consumer Expenditure Survey,* Washington, D.C.: Bureau of Labor Statistics, 1995.

---

[4] It should be noted that the values in the survey are averages per spending unit. Thus a high-level expenditure engaged in by a very small share of households (e.g., cruise travel or the use of a personal aircraft) will yield a small annual average spending estimate per household.

Price Trends

Figure 11–4 presents the trends in travel prices per passenger-mile in the intercity carrier modes over the last ten years. This figure shows the dramatic convergence of all public carrier modes in that period around an average fare cost of 10 cents per mile. This extraordinary situation explains the extreme popularity of air travel and the relative decline of bus travel. Air travel, although highly variable in price from market to market, is often able to compete on price with buses or Amtrak; and it has become the mass transit mode of intercity travel. The Amtrak rates exclude public subsidies that make up a major part of their revenue per passenger. Auto costs per passenger-mile of travel are dependent on the number of travelers in the vehicle sharing the vehicle operating cost. For auto to be competitive with the travel party costs at 10 cents per mile per person would require about two persons per vehicle. Given that about 80 percent of intercity travel consists of two or more persons, the auto is highly price-competitive for most trips.

Table 11–3 Public Transportation Elements of the Consumer Expenditure Survey

Public Transportation Category of CEX	Share of Spending
Intercity	
Air	60%
Intercity Bus	2%
Mass Transit Out of Town	1%
Taxi Fares Out of Town	5%
Intercity Train	5%
Ship	6%
Local	
Mass Transit	17%
Taxi Fares	2%
School Bus	2%
Total	100%

Source: Unpublished tables, *Consumer Expenditure Survey,* 1992.

Intercity Travel Trends

The ATS is the first government-sponsored survey of long-distance travel since the quinquennial Economic Census dropped the NTS after 1977. The two surveys, bracketing almost a 20-year period, provide a valuable look at travel change over that period. Table 11–4 provides a comparison to the 1977 survey and shows growth rates over the period.

Some parts of the terminology in this table need further explanation. The first row identifies "household trips." This term refers to group trips made by the household (e.g., if a single individual in the household made a trip, that would count as one household trip and one person-trip, but a trip made by both parents and two children would count as just one household trip but four person-trips). Thus household trips, unlike local travel surveys, are not the sum of person-trips.

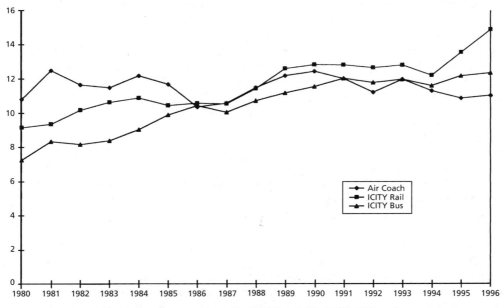

Figure 11–4 Revenue per PSGR Mile Trends

Source: National Transportation Statistics, Washington, D.C.: Bureau of Transportation Statistics.

The decline in average household size for the period would have affected these trends.

The second row makes a distinction that is a more significant one than in local travel surveys. It differentiates households *without any trips in the year* that meet the criteria of the survey. This is analogous to a nontrip-making household *on a survey day* in a local travel survey. Given the long-distance character of the survey trips, it is not surprising that some households will not make such a trip in a year's time. The data in the table indicate that in 1977 only 72 percent of households made trips over 100 miles in length. That has grown to 80 percent by 1995, but it is still very significant that in 1995 20 percent of households did not make a trip farther than 100 miles in the entire year. This makes a further important distinction between the nature of local and long-distance surveys. It is useful in a local survey to get travel data over a considerable time period in order to capture seasonal change and establish a solid average daily trip rate; but it is rarely seen as crucial to trace the same household, in that daily rates are seen as relatively stable. There is no such stability in long-distance travel, except perhaps arbitrarily at the annual level. However, given the intermittent nature of the causes of long-distance travel, we cannot infer that one month's trip observations can be multiplied by 12 to get annual household travel rates.

Table 11–4 National Long-Distance Travel Trends (trips over 100 miles)

Measure (annual)	1977	1995	% Change
Household* Trips	4.1	5.5	34.1%
% Households Making Trips	72	80	11.1%
Trips/Trip Making Households	5.7	6.9	21.1%
Trips/Capita	2.4	4.0	66.7%
Trips/Traveler	4.0	4.8	20.0%
Miles/Traveler	2,836	3,943	39.0%
Miles/Capita	1,737	3,147	81.2%
Miles/Trip	709	827	16.6%

* See text for definitions.

Sources: *National Travel Survey,* Washington, D.C.: U.S. Bureau of the Census, 1977; *American Travel Survey,* Washington, D.C.: U.S. Department of Transportation, Bureau of Transportation Statistics, 1995.

Table 11–5 Travel Growth Elements*

	Persons (millions)	Annual Trips/Person	TRIP Length/ Trip (miles)	Person Miles (millions)
1977	220	2.4	709	374,352
1995	263	4.0	827	870,004
% Change	19%	60%	16%	116%

* See text for discussion of terms.

Source: *American Travel Survey,* Washington, D.C.: U.S. DOT, Bureau of Transportation Statistics, 1995.

Deconstructing the Trend

The data provided give enough information to deconstruct the elements that have driven the growth trend. If person-miles is accepted as total persons multiplied by trips per person multiplied by average trip length per person-trip, then the growth rates for these elements in the period are as shown in Table 11–5.

Overall, these figures suggest that the dominant factor in the substantial change in travel has been the growth in the annual trip-making rate, with population growth and trip-length growth playing lesser, although still significant, parts. As Table 11–4 indicates, the per-person trip-rate trend itself can be seen as the product of the trip-making rate of trip makers and the proportion of trip makers in the population.

Intercity Travel by Purpose

Perhaps the most important distinction to be made in intercity travel is between business and personal travel. An important part of this distinction is in the fact that personal travel is generally self-funded and initiated, whereas business travel is determined and paid for by others. As a result, the cost factors and time pressures are very different and manifest themselves in ways that make for sharp distinctions in travel behavior.

This being said, the whole area of description of long-distance travel suffers from a lack of sound, discrete trip purposes. In these purposes leisure activities may be confused with specialized terms such as "holiday" or "vacation;" and the distinctions between business and leisure may be blurred by convention, seminar, and conference attendance; and such modern phenomena as incentive awards and the tendency to meld business and leisure travel. There are also new terms in such specialized areas as cultural tourism, heritage tourism, and eco-tourism that have only weakly defined meanings and boundaries. This development is cause for great caution when examining travel by purpose.

Overall travel shares by a number of measures by broad purpose categories are shown in Table 11–6 from both the ATS of the BTS and the NTS of the Travel Industry Association of America. The ATS distributions are differentiated by person-trips, person-miles, and household trips to demonstrate the variation that these perspectives induce. The term used in the ATS component of the table that may need further explanation is *Personal Business,* which can include trips for medical care, banking, or to attend a wedding or funeral in a distant location. The NTS of the Travel Industry Association of America uses a slightly differing classification of purposes.

The distributions for each column category for the ATS data indicate that one must investigate each to gain a full understanding of trends. Each category indicates something about trip lengths and about party size in the different trip purposes. It is clear that business trips with greater share of person-miles than person-trips tend to have longer average trip lengths and that the other purposes tend to have larger travel-party sizes.

Intercity Travel by Mode

The amounts and shares of travel by mode for person-trips, person-miles, and household trips are shown in Table 11–7. This table represents some aggregation of modes, given that many modes account for only a very small share of travel. As can be seen from the table, the personal-use vehicle dominates person-trips, and with air travel it accounts for almost 98 percent of trips. When perspective shifts to person-miles, the two modes retain their dominance, but air gains a far greater share of total travel given its greater average trip length. Among the other modes, elements of interest are that charter and tour buses account for as much as they do, and that scheduled bus and intercity rail (Amtrak) account for as little as they do, together accounting for less than 1 percent of travel.

The private air mode, differentiated from commercial services and not shown in the table, actually accounts for a significant share of travel in all categories. The BTS's *National Transportation Statistics* identifies general aviation as having more than 170,000 aircraft in 1994, flying almost 24 million aircraft hours and over 11 billion passenger-miles in 1995 in corporate, business, and personal aircraft.[5] (Not all of these miles would qualify as intercity travel. The ATS shows roughly 7 billion passenger-miles.) This is in contrast to the almost 400 billion passenger-miles flown

Table 11–6   Intercity Travel by Purpose—ATS

Purpose	Person-Trips	Person-Miles	Household Trips
Visit friends and relatives	33.03%	32.02%	29.78%
Leisure travel	29.90%	29.29%	26.98%
Business	22.45%	25.66%	29.33%
Personal business	14.62%	13.02%	13.91%
All	100.00%	100.00%	100.00%

Source: *American Travel Survey,* Washington, D.C.: U.S. DOT, Bureau of Transportation Statistics, 1995.

Intercity Travel by Purpose—NTS

Purpose	Person-Trips
Pleasure travel	70%
Visit friends and relatives	(36)
Outdoor recreation and sightseeing	(10)
Entertainment	(24)
Business	23%
Business	(20)
Convention	(3)
Other, personal	7%

Source: *National Travel Survey,* Washington, D.C.: Travel Industry Association of America, 1997.

Table 11–7   Intercity Travel by Mode, 1995

	Person-Trips (millions)	Person-Miles (billions)	Household Trips (millions)
Personal-use vehicles	813.9	451.6	505.5
Commercial air	161.2	355.3	129.2
Intercity bus	3.2	2.7	2.8
Charter bus	14.2	9.4	11.9
Train	5	4.4	4.2
Ship and boat	0.6	1.8	0.4
Total	1,001.3	826.8	656

	Person-Trips (percentages)	Person-Miles (percentages)	Household Trips (percentages)
Personal-use vehicles	81.54%	54.73%	77.29%
Commercial air	16.15%	43.06%	19.76%
Intercity bus	0.32%	0.33%	0.43%
Charter bus	1.42%	1.14%	1.82%
Train	0.50%	0.53%	0.64%
Ship and boat	0.06%	0.22%	0.06%
Total	100.00%	100.00%	100.00%

Source: *American Travel Survey,* Washington, D.C.: U.S. DOT, Bureau of Transportation Statistics, 1995.

---

[5] *National Transportation Statistics, Annual* (Washington, D.C.: U.S. DOT, Bureau of Transportation Statistics).

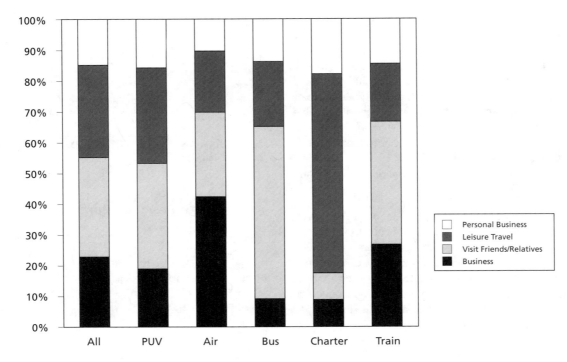

Figure 11–5   Trip Purpose by Mode of Travel

Source: *American Travel Survey,* Washington, D.C.: U.S. DOT, Bureau of Transportation Statistics, 1995.

domestically in that year by commercial carriers on about 5,500 aircraft. The Eno Transportation Foundation cites 10.6 billion and 435 billion passenger-miles, respectively, for 1996.

Trip Purpose and Modal Use

As Figure 11–5 shows, there is considerable variation in the significance of the various purpose categories within each mode. While business travel accounts for about 22.5 percent of all travel, it is over 43 percent of air travel and almost 27 percent of rail travel, but less than 19 percent of private vehicle travel. Visiting friends and relatives is the most important purpose for intercity bus travel, accounting for 56 percent of scheduled bus trips. Train travel also has a larger-than-average dependence on visiting friends and relatives but less-than-average involvement in leisure travel. Leisure travel is most important for charter buses, accounting for almost 65 percent of bus travel, often as part of package tours.

Trip Length Variations in Modal Use

The effects of trip length have been noted as a factor in a number of the elements previously discussed. Trip length has a strong influence in both modal choice and its relationship to trip purpose. Figure 11–6 shows the distribution of mode usage by trip length, with the bus and rail modes grouped together. Again, the limited role of these modes is seen. The trend pattern is clear: as trip length increases, the role of air travel increases; but it is also notable that for round trips of up to 2,000 miles, the private vehicle still accounts for a greater share of trips than air travel. Private vehicles claim a 97 percent share of trips below 300 miles, dropping to about 93 percent for trips in the 300–500 mile range as air begins to make inroads and rail and bus have some role. In the 500–1,000 mile range, private vehicle drops to about 77 percent as air jumps to an almost 20 percent share, and all other modes have their greatest effect at 3.5 percent of trips. At 2,000 miles or greater, air finally reaches dominance at 75 percent, while private vehicles still carry 23 percent of trips and the surface carrier modes decline to a 1.5 percent share.

The overall characteristics of the modes by distance are significantly different. Table 11–8 depicts the roles played by each trip length range in the travel activities of each mode, along with the mean and median trip lengths for each mode. For some modes the great majority of activity occurs at trip lengths below 1,000 round-trip miles. Almost 90 percent of private vehicle trips and 80 percent of surface rail and bus trips are below that level. Air travel has almost the reverse pattern, with 73 percent of its trips having round-trip lengths *above* 1,000 miles. Cruise ship and ocean liner travel have the most specialized pattern, with heavy levels of use at the lowest and the highest ranges, about 30 percent each at less than 300 miles and over 2,000 miles. As noted in the table the surface carrier modes have mean and median trip lengths most like those of the total, with private-vehicle and air trips being skewed on the low and high sides, respectively. The shipborne travel mode, reflecting the bimodal character of its trip-length distribution, shows the greatest ratio of mean to median, more than double, suggesting that some very long trips distort the distribution.

This is all based on person-trips by mileage category rather than person-miles of travel. Note that if person-miles are tabulated by these mileage categories rather than trips, the picture shifts substantially. Figure 11–7 depicts the pattern shift. The outstanding feature of this graphic is that trips of over 2,000 round-trip miles, while accounting for less than 10 percent of trips, account for almost 42 percent of all travel miles. The average trip length of trips over 2,000 miles slightly exceeds 3,500 miles; note that this excludes international travel. Trips of over 1,000 round-trip miles account for 60 percent of travel miles.

Business Travel

The significant variation in the patterns of mode use by purpose is clearer when stratified by trip length. The case of

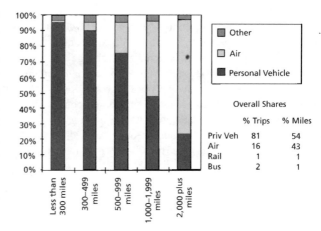

Figure 11–6   Means of Transport by Round-Trip Distance

Source: *American Travel Survey,* Washington, D.C.: U.S. DOT, Bureau of Transportation Statistics, 1995.

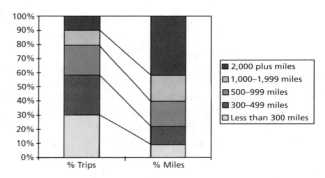

Figure 11–7   Person-Trips versus Person-Miles Relationships

Source: *American Travel Survey*, Washington, D.C.: U.S. DOT, Bureau of Transportation Statistics, 1995.

Table 11–8   Trip-Length Distribution of Trips by Mode

Round Trip Length	Personal Vehicle	Commercial Air	Intercity Bus	Charter Bus	Train	Ship and Boat	Person-Trips
Less than 300 miles	36.37%	1.21%	22.04%	26.38%	22.54%	30.94%	30.60%
300–499 miles	31.53%	5.41%	28.58%	30.62%	34.49%	6.84%	27.37%
500–999 miles	21.43%	20.73%	31.35%	25.87%	22.92%	13.03%	21.37%
1,000–1,999 miles	7.46%	28.17%	8.45%	12.91%	8.33%	19.38%	10.82%
2,000 plus miles	3.21%	44.48%	9.59%	4.22%	11.71%	29.80%	9.84%
	100.00%	100.00%	100.00%	100.00%	100.00%	100.00%	100.00%
Mean trip length	553	2,222	839	653	869	2,005	827
Median trip length	369	1,794	481	442	448	951	425

Source: *American Travel Survey,* Washington, D.C.: U.S. DOT, Bureau of Transportation Statistics, 1995.

business travel is the most important. While commercial air reaches a 20 percent overall share of all travel, this varies sharply by distance as shown previously in Table 11–8. But stratification by business purposes indicates that business travel accounts for 43 percent of air travel, a percentage that varies substantially by trip length. American business travel is fundamentally based on auto and air travel. The auto and air combination accounts for 97 percent of all travel overall and only varies narrowly between 96.3 percent and 98 percent in any trip-length range. But the variation in share between auto and air shifts substantially. Air only accounts for 1.4 percent below 300 round-trip miles; but it jumps to over 9 percent in the 300–499 mile range, and to over 36 percent in the 500–999 range. Above 1,000 round-trip miles it accounts for the majority of travel, at 68 percent for trips in the 1,000–1,999 range and 85 percent above 2,000 round-trip miles. It is worth noting that private auto use still accounts for two-thirds of all business travel use, and 80 percent of all round trips less than 1,000 miles. Even in the range of 500–999 round trip miles, private auto use accounts for more than 60 percent of the business travel.

Highway Travel Flows by State

It is difficult to portray the rich level of flows data that can be generated by the ATS. Its large sample size permits measures of substantial geographic detail, such as highway corridor flows for the country and for states. No previous national surveys have been able to provide such geographic detail. Table 11–9 summarizes long-distance highway passenger-miles of travel occurring within a state's boundaries, differentiating those that lie wholly within the state from the travel miles within the state for those trips leaving or destined to the state, including personal vehicles and buses. In a separate column the table shows long-distance travel passing through the state as modeled from the ATS origin-destination patterns by the Oak Ridge National Laboratories. This provides extraordinary insight into the effect of intercity travel on major roads within a state. To accomplish this the ORNL created a simulated national highway computer network that permits allocation of individual vehicle trip origins and destinations to specific highway route segments.[6] This then permits calculation of more detailed miles of travel and allocation by highway segment. For example, a highway trip from Pittsburgh to Minneapolis would be assigned to the most likely (shortest, in time or distance) travel route and the amount of travel in each state traversed could be allocated to that state. The final column in the table provides a summary of per capita intercity travel by all modes for each state, contrasted to the national average of 3,100 miles per capita. Inspection of the rankings of states show the strong influence that size of state and incomes have on long-distance travel. Almost all of the states with per capita long-distance travel above 4,000 miles are in the west, and Alaska tops all of course with over a 7,000 mile per capita annual average.

Demographic Characteristics of Intercity Travel

The tendencies to travel over long distances show significant demographic variation. Not surprisingly, income and profession affect business travel strongly, and income and age affect leisure travel just as strongly. The following sections briefly presents some of the demographic variation in long-distance travel.

Male-Female Patterns

In the 1977–1995 period, women's business travel rates increased at twice the rate (170 percent) of their travel rate growth for all trips (85 percent) and far faster than men's growth rates in business travel (95 percent). But men still make about 4.3 trips per year, contrasted to women's rate of 3.4. The ratio of women's travel to men's has remained roughly stable at 63 percent of men's since the 1977 survey. The major cause of that difference in trip making is still largely due to business travel, where men's rate is 1.23 trips per year contrasted to women's 0.5 trips per year, despite the rapid growth in women's travel. The remaining difference is explained by a greater annual trip-making rate (0.33) for outdoor recreation for men and almost double that for women (0.18).

---

[6] This system is called the Oak Ridge National Highway Network and represents roughly 437,000 miles of U.S. highways; about 50,000 miles of Canadian highways; and 17,000 of Mexican highways in the system. At the time of the geocoding of the ATS, the system was slightly smaller.

Table 11–9   State Passenger Travel Flows

State	Within	From	To	Thru	Total	Miles per Capita
Alabama	2,087	2,008	1,925	3,872	9,892	2,413
Alaska	514	87	483	0	1,084	7,207
Arizona	3,063	1,753	1,621	2,379	8,816	4,117
Arkansas	1,276	1,057	1,213	2,459	6,005	2,762
California	20,932	10,141	5,125	858	37,056	3,517
Colorado	2,234	1,718	2,395	1,707	8,054	4,919
Connecticut	28	997	794	2,461	4,280	3,151
Delaware	16	108	588	1,430	2,142	2,324
District of Columbia	0	9	36	16	61	4,108
Florida	8,381	3,905	7,204	32	19,522	3,104
Georgia	2,850	3,555	3,013	6,781	16,199	2,773
Hawaii	18	0	0	0	18	4,752
Idaho	938	491	669	1,356	3,454	4,241
Illinois	3,714	3,959	2,602	5,278	15,553	3,064
Indiana	2,226	2,212	2,007	5,307	11,752	2,610
Iowa	1,652	1,324	1,231	3,191	7,398	3,235
Kansas	1,451	1,190	1,081	2,249	5,971	3,607
Kentucky	1,512	1,486	1,527	4,268	8,793	2,491
Louisiana	1,818	1,272	1,497	1,357	5,944	2,498
Maine	602	536	1,114	241	2,493	2,838
Maryland	736	1,553	1,008	3,883	7,180	2,931
Massachusetts	626	1,404	1,582	1,598	5,210	2,745
Michigan	7,562	2,803	2,085	246	12,696	3,258
Minnesota	4,718	1,740	1,597	859	8,914	4,005
Mississippi	1,263	1,093	1,122	2,618	6,096	2,427
Missouri	3,768	2,309	2,959	3,785	12,821	3,284
Montana	1,550	550	947	1,252	4,299	5,060
Nebraska	1,124	768	663	3,205	5,760	3,954
Nevada	448	434	1,951	1,848	4,681	4,093
New Hampshire	196	244	738	608	1,786	3,137
New Jersey	782	1,572	2,234	3,504	8,092	2,776
New Mexico	1,729	803	1,175	2,799	6,506	4,376
New York	5,026	3,260	2,647	2,663	13,596	2,346
North Carolina	4,061	2,493	2,900	4,794	14,248	2,708
North Dakota	751	318	413	680	2,162	4,066
Ohio	4,389	3,565	3,196	4,809	15,959	2,619
Oklahoma	2,096	1,669	1,442	3,054	8,261	3,469
Oregon	2,308	1,172	1,292	1,300	6,072	4,250
Pennsylvania	3,457	3,812	3,558	5,837	16,664	2,419
Rhode Island	0	78	100	289	467	2,362
South Carolina	1,768	1,479	2,810	4,646	10,703	2,469
South Dakota	963	366	785	640	2,754	4,162
Tennessee	1,995	1,752	2,656	4,582	10,985	2,765
Texas	20,833	6,593	4,420	2,357	34,203	3,440
Utah	1,551	1,112	1,084	2,894	6,641	4,749
Vermont	74	320	611	252	1,257	3,235
Virginia	2,685	3,123	2,878	6,888	15,574	3,749
Washington	4,106	2,082	1,358	591	8,137	4,498
West Virginia	425	460	981	2,466	4,332	1,914
Wisconsin	4,275	2,006	2,373	1,891	10,545	3,222
Wyoming	595	479	825	2,386	4,285	5,521

Some of these differences carry over into modal use. Women who made only 45 percent of all long-distance trips made over 62 percent of rail and 53 percent of bus trips.

Travel Party Size

Most intercity travel is conducted by individuals traveling alone (39 percent) or two adults traveling together (30 percent). Thus only about 30 percent of all intercity travel involves children, either traveling with one or more adults or traveling alone. Not surprisingly the carrier modes, air, rail, and intercity bus, have much higher percentages of single travelers, all above 60 percent, given their tendency to support work-related purposes, to serve younger and older riders, and the fact that as party size increases the cost advantage of a private vehicle grows substantially.

The 1995 ATS indicates that average travel party sizes vary from a low of 1.3 for intercity buses, to 1.5 on trains and tour buses, 1.6 on airplanes, and jumping to 2.3 for private vehicles.

Income Patterns

Income is of course an important factor in levels of travel activity and the nature of that travel. However, it should be noted that while inflation-adjusted disposable personal incomes increased by only 40 percent from 1977 to 1995, travel grew by more than 116 percent. Overall travel increases rapidly with income: quadrupling from 1.5 trips per year for those under $25,000 to 6.0 per year for those over $50,000. Private vehicle travel jumps rapidly from 1.3 trips per year for those with incomes under $25,000 to 4.1 trips per year for those between $25,000–$50,000 and increasing slightly to 4.6 trips for those over $50,000. In air travel there is a rapid progression with income from 0.2 below $25,000 tripling to 0.6 for the group between $25,000–$50,000 and more than doubling to 1.5 trips per year for those over $50,000. These rates are summarized in Table 11–10. The surface carrier modes are used more frequently by lower-income groups. Those who are below $25,000 in income compose 16 percent of all trip makers but compose 54 percent of those on buses and 23 percent of train riders.

Racial and Ethnic Variations

Again, as with the low-income groups cited above, minorities are differentially represented in the surface for-hire modes. Minorities compose 15 percent of trip makers but account for 52 percent of intercity bus riders and 32 percent of train riders. Trip-making rates grew faster for minorities between 1977 and 1995 than for the white population. Black travel grew from 1.1 to 2.0 trips per year, an 81 percent growth; Hispanics increased from 1.4 to 2.4, a growth rate of 71 percent; while the White non-Hispanic rate increased 67 percent from 2.7 to 4.5 trips per year. But the average minority travel rate in 1995 *was still below that of Whites in 1977.*

All racial and ethnic groups have about the same level of private-vehicle use, between 80 and 85 percent of trips. But Blacks and Hispanics used air travel less than average, more in the range of 11 to 12 percent rather than the 15 to 16 percent for all users.

Age Variations

Age-specific trip rates are shown in Table 11–11 for both 1977 and 1995. The interesting difference is that the peak-per-person travel rate in 1977 was the 35 to 44 age group, whereas in 1995 the peak occurred at 45 to 54 years of age. All of the major growth has occurred in the age groups over 45. This is due to many factors. Some of them include increasing vigor of older Americans, greater wealth, greater freedom to pursue leisure travel, and greater ease of travel. These data are all the more compelling given that the population bubble known as the "baby boom" is just now moving into this age

Table 11–10   Average Annual Long-Distance Trip Making Rates by Mode and Income*

Selected Modes	Under $25,000	$25,000–$50,000	Over $50,000
Private vehicle travel	1.3	4.1	4.6
Air travel	0.2	0.6	1.5
All travel	1.5	4.6	6.0

* Numbers may not add up due to rounding.

Source: *American Travel Survey,* Washington, D.C.: U.S. DOT, Bureau of Transportation Statistics, 1995.

period. In the decade 1995–2005 the number of persons in their fifties will increase by 50 percent.

International Travel Trends

U.S. and World Trends

The United States, as one of the wealthiest nations in the world and also one with a large population and a large, attractive spatial area, is a major player in world travel as both a generator and host of world travel. It has ranked first or second over the years among the world's top spenders on foreign travel and first in revenues received from foreign visitors. This travel is a major factor in U.S. balance of payments, generating a substantial positive balance in favor of the United States, the most important source of exports of services, and the third largest export overall.

Table 11–11   Annual Person Trip Rates by Age Group

Age Group	1977	1995	% Change
under 18	1.8	2.3	28%
18–24	2.3	3.7	61%
25–34	3.3	4.2	27%
35–44	3.7	4.7	27%
45–54	3.4	5.7	68%
55–64	2.8	5.1	82%
65+	1.5	2.8	87%

Source: *American Travel Survey,* Washington, D.C.: U.S. DOT, Bureau of Transportation Statistics, 1995.

U.S. International Travel

There were about 52 million outbound trips crossing the nation's borders by U.S. residents in 1996, based on data from the Travel Industries office of the International Trade Administration and the Immigration and Naturalization Service. Outbound travel has risen slowly but steadily over the years from just more than 40 million in 1988, roughly a 29-percent increase. As Figure 11–8 shows, that travel activity has three major components: Mexico, Canada, and total "overseas" travel (i.e., those trips leaving North America). That growth has been very uneven, consisting of an almost static trend of travel to Canada oscillating in the range of 12–13 million per year over the entire period, exhibiting basically zero growth; Mexican growth has been volatile, with brief ups and downs but with overall growth of about 46 percent from 13.5 million in 1988, reaching almost 20 million in 1996; and overseas travel, although showing a slight dip in the 1991 recession, exhibiting a very healthy 37-percent growth for the period.

Among the factors that affect these trends are overall economic trends in the sending economy, changing tastes about attractive destinations, relative exchange rates with countries visited, and political or social problems in potential travel destinations. The total U.S. earnings from visitors, including travel to the United States on U.S. carriers and spending in the United States, is above $90 billion; and, after subtraction of U.S. residents' spending abroad of about $70 billion, yields a positive contribution to balance of payments of more than $25 billion in 1996, $27.2 billion in 1997 and, after a brief dip in 1998 due to the Asian crises, forecasted to rise again to just below $30 billion in 1999. This has been growing since the late eighties, when for the first time the United States shifted from negative to positive in the tourism balance of payments.

Foreign Visitors to the United States

The United States is the world's most important international travel destination. Although France received more visitors than the United States in 1997 (67 million visitors versus 48 million), U.S. visitor revenues, at $75 billion, were almost triple France's; and, according to the World Tourism Organization, they amounted to about 17 percent of all international tourism receipts, excluding transportation costs between countries. Visitors to the United States grew dramatically in the last decade, increasing almost 80 percent from 1986 to 1996. The dominant sources of travel to the United States, not unexpectedly, are Mexico and Canada. Both grew about 40 percent in visits during the period. But other sources grew far faster; with Europe and South America increasing by more than 160 percent; Latin American travel doubling; and the greatest growth in visitors coming from the Far East, more than tripling in travel volumes, from 2.25 million to over 7.5 million in the ten-year period. Figure 11–9 depicts these growth trends over the decade.

The use of the intercity transportation system by foreign visitors is a significant component of intercity planning. Based on the in-flight survey of the Travel Industries office of the International Trade Administration, about 12 percent of the

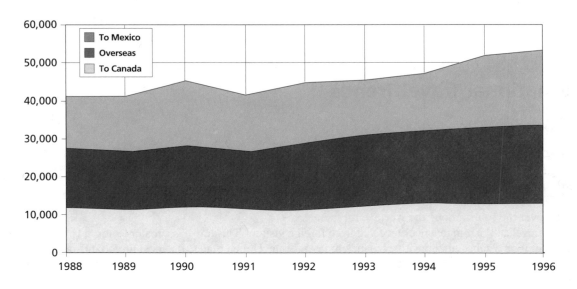

Figure 11–8   U.S. Resident Outbound Trends, 1988–1996

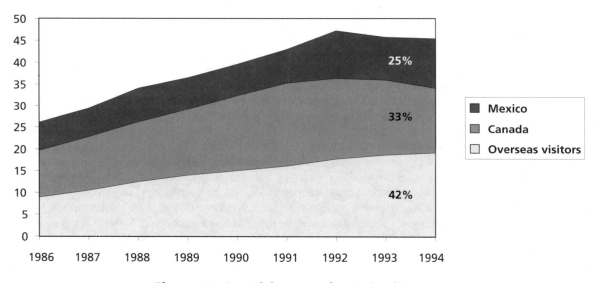

Figure 11–9   Visitors to the United States

Source: Travel Industries Office, Washington, D.C.: U.S. International Trade Administration.

expenditures of foreign visitors while in the United States go to travel payments. At some time during their stay visitors use a variety of modes—approximately 31 percent of foreign visitors use domestic air travel; 38 percent use taxicabs; 5 percent use intercity rail; 12 percent use intercity bus; and 36 percent use rental cars. In addition, 36 percent travel in the vehicles of residents. As expected, the tendency to use the different modes varies substantially by country of origin and trip purpose. The United States is of increasing interest as a destination for driving. Relatively inexpensive fuel and car rental costs, and relatively excellent and uncongested roads by world standards, make auto touring on scenic highways a major potential U.S. tourism attraction. Many states enjoy the benefits of foreign traveler spending. The top ten states in overseas visitors, which excludes Canada and Mexico, are shown in rank order in Table 11–12. California receives more than 6 million visitors while Pennsylvania receives on the order of 700,000. Not surprisingly, the top cities parallel the top states.

Canadian and Mexican Visitation

As noted, visits from Canada and Mexico comprise about one-half of all foreign visits to the United States and showed reasonable growth when comparing the end points of the period; but that observation misses the fact that both countries saw peaks in their travel in the 1991–1992 periods, reaching above 28 million visitors before declining to above 23 million in 1996. The trends in both countries are the product of reverses in economic trends and particularly losses in exchange value with the dollar in the period. Much of the loss in visitors from Canada and Mexico after 1991–1992 were day-trippers driving into the United States for shopping and recreation. Since the 1995 liberalization of Canadian-U.S. air travel restrictions, air travel to the United States boomed, rising 18 percent in 1996 and rising again in 1997 to reach more than a 25-percent share of all Canadian arrivals. Mexican arrivals showed similar trends with a decline in short-stay border crossing traffic of 25 percent in 1997, largely due to exchange rate changes, but a rise of 19 percent in air travel for longer stays.

Table 11–13 shows the mode shares indicated in the ATS for travel by U.S. residents traveling to Canada and Mexico. Not shown in the table is that more than half of travel to Mexico was generated from Texas and California, whereas Canadian travel was more dispersed in its origins, given the many states bordering that country. Data from Statistics Canada on Canadian mode choice outbound to the United States indicates that almost all day-trippers are auto-oriented, as expected; but of the 14.7 million overnight visitors to the United States, about 9.7 million (66 percent) were by auto, 3.8 million (26 percent) by air, and 650,000 (4 percent) by bus, not terribly dissimilar to the U.S. mode flow northwards. An important factor in Canadian international statistics is that 52 percent of all visitors to Canada who are not U.S. residents arrive via the United States. Data are more sparse regarding Mexican travel to the United States. Indications are that most overnight stays from Mexico are for longer distances and tend to be air-related (71 percent) with the remainder in surface modes.

Table 11–12 Top States and Areas and Top Cities Visited in 1997 by Overseas Visitors

Top States and Areas Visited	Visitors (millions)	Top 10 Cities Visited
California	6.4	New York City
Florida	6.1	Los Angeles
New York	5.3	Miami
Hawaii	3.1	San Francisco
Nevada	2.2	Orlando
Guam	1.4	Honolulu
Massachusetts	1.2	Las Vegas
Ilinois	1.1	Washington, D.C.
Texas	1.0	Chicago
		Boston

Source: Travel Industries Office, Washington, D.C.: U.S. International Trade Administration.

Table 11–13 U.S. Travel Mode Shares to Neighboring Countries

	Canada	Mexico
Private vehicle	60.4%	51.8%
Commercial air	32.4%	40.6%
Bus	5.6%	3.0%
Train	0.5%	—
Ship and ferry	0.9%	4.1%

Source: *American Travel Survey,* Washington, D.C.: U.S. DOT, Bureau of Transportation Statistics, 1995.

Table 11–14 Trip Purpose Share Comparisons

Trip Purpose	U.S.–U.S.	U.S.–Canada	U.S.–Mexico
Business	29.3%	19.1%	15.1%
Visit friends/rels	29.8%	17.6%	31.5%
Leisure activities	27.0%	54.3%	40.5%
Personal business	13.9%	9.0%	13.0%

Source: *American Travel Survey,* Washington, D.C.: U.S. DOT, Bureau of Transportation Statistics, 1995.

Mode choice to Canada and Mexico varies widely depending on trip purpose and the state from which travelers emanate. Overall, trip purposes do not vary widely from domestic U.S. long-distance travel; the greatest factor is the smaller level of business travel and greater emphasis on leisure activities. Table 11–14 summarizes the overall patterns.

Local Rural Travel versus Intercity Travel in the United States

Local rural travel needs consideration in intercity travel because it shares the highway system with true intercity trips, and it is often a part of rail and bus intercity travel as well. The rural share of national population over 50 years is shown in Figure 11–10. In this figure, the metropolitan portion has been subdivided between its suburban and central city elements.

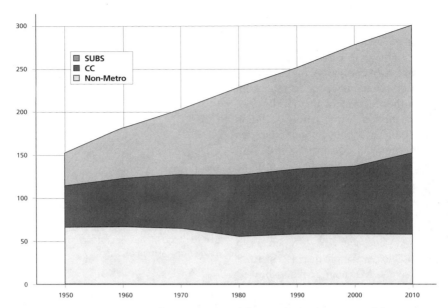

Figure 11–10   Long-Term Population Trend by Major Geographic Area, 1950–2010

Source: 1998 Stat. abstract, Washington, D.C.: U.S. Bureau of the Census.

Population Trends

In 1950, the national population consisted of a "rural" or nonmetropolitan population that was 44 percent of the national total of 151 million and a metropolitan population containing the remaining 56 percent.[7] By 1990, the metropolitan population had reached 77 percent of the national population and was receiving 86 percent of national growth. The nonmetropolitan population had declined from approximately 66 million to 56 million people, and it represented only about 23 percent of the population. In 1996, metropolitan population had reached 80 percent of total population, and rural population at 20 percent equaled roughly 54 million.

One part of the "decline" in rural population is in fact not decline at all. For example, in 1995–1996 metropolitan areas actually lost population (about 0.25 million) to rural areas given an imbalance of out-migrants to in-migrants. It is the absorption of formerly rural populations into the metropolitan complex as suburban development expands into rural areas that has often caused a shift of population from the rural category to the metropolitan category. Thus a prosperous and growing rural population is almost a statistical impossibility, because if it prospers and grows it will outgrow its rural definition and become urban. Often rural population growth is led by those counties just adjacent to the edge of the metropolitan areas of the country and represent the leading edge of metropolitan growth. These areas are statistically rural but are increasingly metropolitan in their orientation and are likely candidates for metropolitan status after the 2000 census.

An important aspect of this trend and the overall outward growth of metropolitan areas is the growing interaction between formerly intercity, rural, and metropolitan travel. As metro areas grow outward and suburban work trips reach farther out into rural areas, these trips increasingly interact with intercity trips—both passenger and freight traffic on highways, and in some important cases rail. Thus, growing metropolitan congestion is becoming an increasingly important factor for intercity travel in terms of the effects on the scheduling of intercity trips and overall travel times. Neither long-distance trucks or intercity buses can be scheduled around the peak period in a metro area once the peak has spread beyond acceptable limits. The reintroduction of intercity traffic, passenger, and freight into the peak stream adds to already-serious congestion.

---

[7] The census uses a definition of rural that defines all areas outside out of urban centers as rural. This both overstates and understates rural population (e.g., towns of 5,000 can be called urban, but at the same time outer portions of major metropolitan areas might be called rural) and leads to a definition of rural of about 25 percent of the population. The definition used here for rural is all areas outside metropolitan areas.

As noted, rural populations have declined to about 20 percent of national population over recent years. One part of this trend has been the decline in farm populations. In the eighties, farm populations declined by 2.5 percent a year compared to 2.9 percent in the seventies. Farm populations consisted of about 5 million persons in 1990, constituting about 2 percent of the national population, contrasted to 30 percent in 1920. Clearly then, only about 10 percent of our rural population is oriented to farming. It is estimated that about one-third of rural counties are farm oriented for the dominant share of their economic activities. With increasing frequency rural counties are business- and manufacturing-oriented. About one-third of rural counties are focused on manufacturing, rather than farming. Thus questions of rural transportation access and service needs are questions that affect the manufacturing sector of the economy as well as the agricultural, mining, forestry, and fisheries sectors. In a recent study, the State of Wisconsin conducted an analysis of the rural portions of the state and the linkages to the state's major four-lane highway system; and found that even in the smallest towns there were establishments with a major part of their output oriented to exports that had great dependence on highways for shipping around the nation and the world.

Table 11–15   Urban Rural Transportation Comparisons, 1995

	Urban	Rural
Number of units* (thousands)	88,629	14,495
Income before taxes	$38,001	$29,975
Age of reference person	47.6	50.1
Persons per unit	2.5	2.6
Persons 65 and over	0.3	0.4
Earners	1.3	1.3
Vehicles	1.8	2.5
Percent homeowner	61	80
At least one vehicle owned	85	92
Average annual expenditures	$33,101	$27,160
Transportation	18.16%	22.20%
Vehicle purchases (net)	7.81%	10.89%
Gasoline and motor oil	2.95%	4.36%
Other vehicle expenses	6.23%	6.39%
Vehicle finance charges	0.75%	1.26%
Maintenance and repairs	2.01%	2.08%
Vehicle insurance	2.18%	2.38%
Vehicle rent, leasing, licensing, other charges	1.28%	0.67%
Public transportation	1.17%	0.56%

* Units are roughly equivalent to households.

Source: *Consumer Expenditure Survey,* Bureau of Labor Statistics, 1995.

Comparison of consumer spending between urban and rural populations is revealing. Total rural income and spending per household is considerably less than the average for urban, based on comparisons in the CEX of the BLS. Table 11–15 shows some of the more significant differences. The key finding is that while rural incomes and spending are sharply lower than urban (84 percent of national spending), their actual transportation outlays slightly exceed those of urban dwellers. Their expenditures are also far greater in shares of total spending, with more than 22 percent of rural household spending going to transportation, contrasted to about 18 percent for urban dwellers. (It is notable that both are down in share from past trends.)

The typical rural household has slightly older members than its urban counterpart, with higher levels of home ownership, the same number of workers in the household, but with lower education levels. In transportation the households own far more vehicles (2.5 versus 1.8 per household), and as a result they spend more on fuel and insurance. Their vehicles are more likely to be used trucks. They compensate for these greater levels of spending by spending less on leased vehicles and on purchased transportation, both metropolitan and intercity carriers. In large part they seem to compensate for higher levels of transportation spending with lower shares of income going to home ownership. If transportation is seen as a substitute for housing costs, as it often is in suburban and rural situations, it is clear that the strategy has an advantage, with housing costs an 8-percent share less than urban shares, more than compensating for a 4-percent share difference in transportation. With the exception of higher medical costs, all other costs in terms of share of spending tend to be about the same as urban shares.

Trends Affecting Future Intercity Travel

All travel will be affected by a number of important trends that will develop in the nineties and into the new century. In many cases intercity travel will be the form of travel most affected by these trends. Changing demographic and employment patterns will affect the scale and character of intercity travel. Other factors including the growth trends in tourism will also play a role.

Demographic Trends

The population growth rate continues to decline since the baby boom period of the forties and fifties. Census middle series projections for the population show that, roughly speaking, we will add about 25 million per decade out to 2030 and beyond.[8] Current annual growth rates are less than 1 percent per year and declining, with upwards of 40 percent of growth attributable to foreign immigration.

Although the declining rate of overall population growth must be considered to be a stabilizing factor, not significantly affecting travel demand, changes in the distribution of the population will be important to intercity travel, increasing and changing the character of demand. Population will change in stages pivoting around the year 2010.

In the first stage national patterns will be characterized by the maturing of the workforce as the baby boomers move into their most productive work years. In the period from 1986 to the year 2000, persons in the 40-year-old age group will grow by 60 percent; and those in the 50-year-old age group fall to just below 40 percent. In the decade after 1995, 50-year-olds will increase by 50 percent and will be a major factor in intercity travel given their high propensity to travel. This period will be characterized by a mature population with few dependents and with considerable financial independence. This suggest high effects on travel with vacations, weekend travel, and domestic and international tourism playing major roles.

Employment Change

Although the growth rate of the work force will decline as a result of the baby boom age shift, changes in the character of work may have more sweeping effects. The shift to occupations and industries typically associated with business travel is a key element. Technical managerial functions are the groups that will grow vigorously to the year 2000. These are the occupations with the highest long-distance business travel tendencies. Occupations with low propensities for business travel such as those in agriculture, mining, and manufacturing will tend to decline.

While transportation occupations themselves are not considered to be a major growth field, primarily due to consolidations in rail employment, operators of long-distance truck and aviation pilots and air personnel will be significant growth areas.

Drivers Licenses and Vehicles

By the year 2000 it is expected that we will have an effective saturation of vehicles and drivers licenses in the United States. The young first-time drivers will be a very small group in absolute terms and as a share of total population. Possession of licenses among all groups over eighteen should be nearly universal. The last of the age groups without almost universal drivers licenses are those over seventy with rates slightly above 60 percent, while those just below that age have rates above 80 percent. However, saturation at this time is mostly an attribute of the white non-Hispanic population. Licensing rates tend to be in the 80-percent range for minority males and in the 70-percent range for minority females. This will be the major growth area in licensing for the future.

Effective vehicle saturation can be expected also as vehicles available already exceed drivers. While auto ownership will continue to grow, as vehicles become increasingly specialized, miles traveled per vehicle should decline as driving is distributed among a larger available fleet. Again there are major pockets of auto-less households largely in our central cities in low-income households. Whether these will make the transition to auto ownership over time is problematic.

Pleasure Driving and Tourism

Prospective growth in intercity travel as a function of population age, discretionary income, and time is a driving factor for prospects of increased tourism. Other factors also need consideration. Among these is the trend in recent years toward shorter weekend-oriented vacation trips, rather than the traditional long family vacation. This is explained by

---

[8] The Bureau of the Census provides population projections in a high, low, and middle series.

a number of factors. Two-worker households are argued to have more difficulty organizing long trips and are more likely to have quick trips on the spur of the moment. Because 70 percent of American workers live in households with two or more workers, this is an important factor. Also, the rise in ownership of weekend homes has been accompanied by an increase in fixed recreational patterns. At the same time the rise in ownership of recreation vehicles and the growing interest in identifying and marking scenic roads of recreational interest (scenic byways movement) suggest that long-distance travel is still very popular, along with increasing average trip lengths in air and rail travel.

The WTO shows very extensive growth for international travel for this region of the world. They indicate that even with the current financial conflicts in East Asia, world growth in tourism will be on the order of 4.3 percent per year through 2020; and in the Americas growth will be lower but still substantial, in the range of 3.8 percent, with expected growth of over 18 percent for the period 1995 to 2000. Intercity travel and tourism can be expected to be a major part of American travel well into the future.

Annex: Major Intercity Transportation Statistics Sites

Bureau of Transportation Statistics—http://www.bts.gov

Tourism Industries Office—http://tinet.ita.doc.gov

Oak Ridge National Laboratories—http://www-cta.ornl.gov

National Personal Travel Survey—http://www-cta.ornl.gov/npts

Federal Highway Administration—http://www.fhwa.dot.gov

Travel Industry Association—http://www.tia.org

Bureau of the Census—http://www.census.gov

Bureau of Labor Statistics, Consumer Survey—http://www.bls.gov/csxhome.htm

World Tourism Organization—http://www.world-tourism.org

Appendix: Major Elements of the Transportation System, 1996

Mode	Major Defining Elements	Components
Highways[1]	Public roads and streets; automobiles, vans, trucks, motorcycles, taxis, and buses (except local transit buses) operated by transportation companies, other businesses, governments, and households; garages, truck terminals, and other facilities; or motor vehicles	**Public roads[2]** 46,036 miles of interstate highways 112,467 miles of other national highways **System roads** 3,760,947 miles of other roads **Vehicles and use** 130 million cars, driven 1.5 trillion miles 69 million light trucks, driven 0.8 trillion miles 7.0 million commercial trucks with six tires or more, driven 0.2 trillion miles 697,000 buses, driven 6.5 billion miles
Air	Airways and airports; airplanes, helicopters, and other flying craft for carrying passengers and cargo	**Public-use airports** 5,389 airports **Airports serving large certificated carriers[3]** 29 large hubs (72 airports), 417 million enplaned passengers 31 medium hubs (55 airports), 89 million enplaned passengers 60 small hubs (73 airports), 37 million enplaned passengers 622 nonhubs (650 airports), 15 million enplaned passengers **Aircraft** 5,961 certificated air carrier aircraft, 4.8 billion miles flown[4] **Passenger and freight companies** 96 carriers, 538 million domestic revenue passenger enplanements, 12.9 billion domestic ton-miles of freight[4] **General aviation** 187,300 active aircraft, 3.5 billion miles flown
Rail[5]	Freight railroads and Amtrak	**Miles of track operated** 126,682 miles of major (Class I)[6] railroads 19,660 miles of regional railroads 27,554 miles of local railroads 24,500 miles of Amtrak **Equipment** 1.2 million freight cars 19,269 freight locomotives **Freight railroad firms** Class I: 9 systems, 182,000 employees, 1.4 trillion ton-miles of freight carried Regional: 32 companies, 10,491 employees Local: 511 companies, 13,030 employees **Passenger (Amtrak)** 23,000 employees, 1,730 passenger cars,[7] 299 locomotives,[7] 19.7 million passengers carried[7, 8]
Transit[9]	Commuter trains, heavy-rail (rapid-rail) and light-rail (streetcar) transit-systems local transit buses, vans and other demand response vehicles, and ferry boats	**Vehicles** 43,577 buses, 17.0 billion passenger-miles 8,725 heavy rail and light rail, 11.4 billion passenger-miles 4,413 commuter rail, 8.2 billion passenger-miles 68 ferries, 243 million passenge-miles 12,825 demand response, 397 million passenger-miles
Water	Navigable rivers, canals, the Great Lakes, the St. Lawrence Seaway, the intracoastal waterway, and ocean shipping channels; ports; commercial ships and barges, fishing vessels, and recreational boating	**U.S.-flag domestic fleet[10]** Great Lakes: 730 vessels, 58 billion ton-miles Inland: 33,323 vessels, 297 billion ton-miles Ocean: 7,051 vessels, 408 billion ton-miles Recreational boats: 11.9 million[11] **Ports[12]** Great Lakes: 362 terminals, 507 berths Inland: 1,811 terminals Ocean: 1,578 terminals, 2,672 berths
Pipeline	Crude oil, petroleum product, and natural gas lines	**Oil** Crude lines: 114,000 miles of pipe (1995), 338 billion ton-miles transported (1996 Product lines: 86,500 miles of pipe (1995), 281 billion ton-miles transported (1996) 160 companies,[13] 14,500 employees **Gas** Transmission: 259,400 miles of pipe Distribution: 952,100 miles of pipe 20.0 trillion cubic feet, 138 companies, 171,600 employees

[1] *Highway Statistics,* Washington, D.C.: U.S. Department of Transportation, Federal Highway Administration, 1996.

[2] Does not include Puerto Rico.

[3] Large certificated carriers operate aircraft with a seating capacity of more than sixty seats. *Airport Activity Statistics of Certificated Air Carriers, 12 Months Ending December 31, 1996,* Washington, D.C.: U.S. Department of Transportation, Bureau Sixty of Transportation Statistics, Office of Airline Information, 1997.

[4] Preliminary data.

[5] Except where noted, figures are from *Railroad Facts: 1997,* Washington, DC: Association of American Railroads, 1997.

[6] Includes 891 miles of road operated by Class I railroads in Canada.

[7] Fiscal year 1996. *Twenty-Fifth Annual Report, 1996,* Washington, DC: Amtrak, 1997.

[8] Excludes commuter service.

[9] Data for 1995. *National Transit Summaries and Trends for the 1995 National Transit Database Section 15 Report Year,* Washington, D.C.: U.S. Department of Transportation, Federal Transit Administration, 1997.

[10] Excludes fishing and excursion vessels, general ferries and dredges, derricks, and so forth used in construction work. Vessel data from *Transportation Lines of the United States,* New Orleans, LA: U.S. Army Corps of Engineers, 1998. Ton-miles data from *Waterborne Commerce of the United States 1996,* New Orleans, LA: U.S. Army Corps of Engineers, 1997.

[11] *Boating Statistics,* Washington, D.C.: U.S. Department of Transportation, U.S. Coast Guard, 1996.

[12] Data for 1995, from *A Report to Congress on the Status of the Public Ports of the United States, 1994–1995,* Washington, D.C.: U.S. Department of Transportation, Maritime Administration, October 1996.

[13] Regulated by the Federal Energy Regulatory Commission.

Source: Unless otherwise noted, *National Transportation Statistics 1997,* Washington, D.C.: U.S. DOT, Bureau of Transportation Statistics, December 1996.

CHAPTER 12
Urban Transportation Studies

Steven Gayle
Executive Director
Binghamton Metropolitan Transportation Study

Introduction

The purpose of this chapter is to provide those involved in urban transportation planning an overview of the process of developing a transportation plan and some related products, and an explanation of how the plan is implemented. Many references discuss the transportation planning process in isolation. Yet, as the discipline of urban transportation planning has matured, its practitioners have come to understand that those who implement their plans, whether they are local elected officials or state transportation agencies, and those who benefit from those plans, including the general public in all of its facets, care primarily about the products of the planning process.

The job of the urban transportation planner has many aspects. In broad terms, the planner acts as a focus of public desires, helping to elicit and interpret how the neighborhood, the community, and the metropolitan area want to approach the future. The planner is an investment manager, helping public decision makers understand how best to invest the public resources at their disposal to achieve the community's goals. The planner is a lookout, serving to alert those decision makers about the unforeseen consequences of their actions. At the core of the planners' work is the understanding that each community in which they work is different. This chapter will explore each of those roles in the context of the development and implementation of a regional transportation plan.

The urban transportation planner must complete a variety of tasks in the daily work of developing plans and programs. These tasks include such diverse elements as establishing a vision of the future, defining goals and objectives, collecting and organizing data, forecasting travel demand, developing financial plans, completing air quality conformity determinations, testing plans, and conducting a public participation process. This chapter will address each of these tasks, providing both general guidance and references to more in depth material.

Urban transportation planning is serious work. Investments in transportation infrastructure last a long time and change the face of the region. These choices may also either enable or constrain future alternatives. Deciding whether or not to construct a new expressway or a light rail line will shape the elemental form and structure of your community. A decision to construct a network of bicycle paths or develop a new paratransit service will affect the public's view of the quality of life in your community. A decision to improve a port or rail terminal will affect the commerce of your community. Reaching the best decisions for your community requires both analytical capability and political acumen.

Background

Urban transportation planning is a discipline that has evolved over a number of decades. Much of that evolution has been driven by federal transportation law, as Congress recognized the need to accompany massive capital investment by a rational process to select the location and type of facilities to be built. Much of the content of urban transportation studies, as well as the process by which they are developed and adopted are mandated by law and regulation.

- The Federal Aid Highway Act of 1962 established what would become known as the "3-C" planning process. Federal transportation spending in urbanized areas with population greater than 50,000 would have to be based on transportation plans that were continuing, comprehensive, and a cooperative venture of state and local government. This was quite a dramatic statement of the importance of the planning that should accompany transportation investment and location decisions. Plans were to consider social, economic, environmental, and land use factors. They were to be updated to continually reflect growth in the urban region and changing travel patterns. Perhaps most unique was the requirement that both state and local governments cooperate in these plans. This recognized the technical expertise of the state highway department in studying corridors and designing facilities, but also the necessity of input from local officials in relating projects to community development plans and goals.

- The Federal Aid Highway Act of 1973 required the creation of Metropolitan Planning Organizations (MPOs) to carry out the 3-C process. MPOs would become the focus of both the technical process and the political forum that came to characterize urban transportation planning.

- The Clean Air Act Amendments of 1990 required that metropolitan areas not in attainment of National Ambient Air Quality Standards (NAAQS) use transportation control measures to help control their pollution levels. Transportation plans were compelled to demonstrate conformity with the approved State Implementation Plan (SIP).

Table 12–1   ISTEA Planning Factors

1. Preservation of existing transportation facilities and using existing transportation facilities more efficiently.
2. The consistency of transportation planning with energy conservation programs, goals, and objectives.
3. The need to relieve congestion and prevent congestion from occurring where it does not yet occur.
4. The likely effect of transportation policy decisions on land use and development plans.
5. The programming of expenditure on transportation enhancement activities.
6. The effects of all transportation projects to be undertaken within the metropolitan area, without regard to whether such projects are publicly funded.
7. International border crossings and access to ports, airports, intermodal transportation facilities, major freight distribution routes, national parks, recreation areas, monuments, historic sites, and military installations.
8. The need for connectivity of roads within and outside the metropolitan area.
9. The needs identified through use of the management systems.
10. Preservation of rights-of-way for construction of future transportation projects and corridors.
11. Methods to enhance the efficient movement of freight.
12. The use of life-cycle costs in design and engineering.
13. The overall social, economic, energy, and environmental effects of transportation decisions.
14. Methods to expand and enhance transit services.
15. Capital investments in increased security in transit systems.

Source: Intermodal Surface Transportation Efficiency Act, Public Law 102–240, §134(f).

- The Intermodal Surface Transportation Efficiency Act of 1991 (ISTEA) was viewed by many as watershed in urban transportation planning, an act of Congress that both empowered MPOs and gave them new responsibilities. While MPOs were still required in all metropolitan areas with more than 50,000 people, those above a population threshold of 200,000 were designated "transportation management areas" (TMAs) and given additional authority and responsibility. The current approach to urban transportation plans is very much governed by ISTEA.

ISTEA imposed a list of fifteen specific factors that MPOs were required to address in their plan. (Table 12–1.) While each MPO was given the leeway to determine the appropriate means and level of incorporating each factor, there would nonetheless be a commonality among all metropolitan plans. Of equal significance, long-range plans were required to be constrained by estimates of reasonably available financial resources. Previous long-range plans were often no more than wish lists, since it was frequently more politically palatable to include candidate projects than to make hard choices. Fiscal constraint imposed those hard choices, and in doing so it forced the plans to be more realistic.

It is, however, clear that the fiscally constrained plan can be surrounded by a vision plan, one that outlines a more optimistic view of investment resources and engages policy makers in discussions of new initiatives and concepts. Such vision plans are important in that they have the potential of catalyzing a search for innovative ways to finance a desired but otherwise unreachable project.

ISTEA also imposed a new perspective on investing in the transportation system. With the interstate highway system essentially complete and a view that large new construction projects would be few, the outlook shifted from "build and rehabilitate" to "manage and operate." The belief was that, while new capacity was still sometimes necessary, there was much to be gained from a strategy of efficient management. MPOs and states were required to create and implement management systems for pavements, bridges, safety, congestion, public transportation facilities, and intermodal facilities. These systems would rationalize data that in many cases were already being collected and help the MPO identify and address current system deficiencies in a systematic fashion. Coupled with funding flexibility, the output of the management systems would help decision makers weigh trade-offs when faced, for example, with choosing between a bridge rehabilitation and a bus purchase project. Thus, the management systems would influence the implementation of the transportation plan.

ISTEA created some entirely new funding categories in the Federal Highway Administration (FHWA) program. While the national highway system (NHS) and Surface Transportation Program (STP) were not very different from the Federal-Aid Primary, Secondary, and Urban System programs they replaced, the STP-Enhancement and Congestion Mitigation and Air Quality (CMAQ) programs were entirely new. The Enhancement program required states to dedicate a minimum of ten percent of their STP allocation to projects that would enhance the transportation system: bicycle and pedestrian facilities, landscaping, historic preservation, and similar activities. CMAQ funding was allocated only to those metropolitan areas designated in nonattainment of NAAQS, to be spent on projects that contribute to achieving or maintaining attainment per the approved SIP. The new act otherwise allowed unprecedented flexibility in allocating funding to projects. Where planners had previously been constrained to match investment needs to strictly defined categorical funding opportunities, ISTEA's provisions allowed FHWA program funds to be spent on transit and Federal Transit Administration (FTA) funds to be used for roadway projects, as long as certain conditions were met.

Finally, ISTEA opened up the decision-making process and brought new stakeholders to the table. While public participation was not a new concept, ISTEA's requirements went beyond previous regulations. MPOs were required to involve "citizens, affected public agencies, representatives of transportation agency employees, private providers of transportation, and other interested parties" in the development of the transportation plan. It is left to the individual MPO to develop effective public involvement mechanisms. The STP-Enhancement program in particular brought to the MPO table many groups that had never previously been interested in urban transportation planning and programming. And while these people may have come to the MPO forum interested only in natural resources, or a bicycle trail, or an historic railroad station, in many cases they left with a broader understanding of and ongoing interest in urban transportation planning. At the same time, MPO staff and decision makers gained an understanding of the true breadth of the metropolitan transportation system.

- The National Highway System Designation Act of 1995 made continued development and implementation of ISTEA's management systems optional, in addition to designating those roadways that would comprise the NHS. The only exception was that TMAs were still required to maintain congestion management systems. This act also added a sixteenth planning factor to the MPO planning menu—consideration of tourism and recreational travel.

- The Transportation Equity Act for the 21st Century (TEA-21) reauthorized the federal surface transportation programs for a six-year period beginning with federal fiscal year 1998. TEA-21 in general retains the planning provisions created by ISTEA. Following are notable changes for the urban planning process:

  - *Planning factors.* The sixteen planning factors described above are changed to seven issue areas of consideration, which MPOs must provide for in the development of their transportation plans. These areas are enumerated in Table 12–2. The language of TEA-21 explicitly states that while MPOs "*shall* provide for consideration," failure to do so is not reviewable by any court.

  - *Transportation Improvement Program (TIP).* While the requirement that the TIP be fiscally constrained to estimates of available resources is retained, as are air quality conformity requirements in nonattainment areas, the MPO may include additional projects for "illustrative purposes." These are projects for which funding is not immediately available but that are identified as the MPOs' next priority if additional resources are found. These resources may result from bid savings, deferral of already programmed projects, or creation of new revenue sources. There is no requirement that such projects be selected for implementation; but if they are selected, the approval of the U.S. DOT is required. Bicycle and pedestrian projects are singled out with a requirement for special consideration in the TIP development process.

- *Public participation.* The broad requirement for public involvement in the development of transportation plans and programs is reaffirmed. Freight shippers, providers of freight transportation services, and representatives of users of public transit are added to the list of stakeholders who must be consulted.

- *Metropolitan areas under 200,000 population.* MPOs in smaller metropolitan areas that are also air quality attainment areas retain the opportunity to develop abbreviated plans and TIPs. The U.S. DOT must review and approve these documents and make a determination that they are appropriate in light of the complexity of transportation problems in the area.

Table 12–2 Transportation Equity Act for the 21st Century, Planning Considerations

(A) Support the economic vitality of the metropolitan area, especially by enabling global competitiveness, productivity, and efficiency.

(B) Increase the safety and security of the transportation system for motorized and nonmotorized users.

(C) Increase the accessibility and mobility options available to people and for freight.

(D) Protect and enhance the environment, promote energy conservation, and improve quality of life.

(E) Enhance the integration and connectivity of the transportation system across and between modes and for people and freight.

(F) Promote efficient system management and operation.

(G) Emphasize the preservation of the existing transportation system.

Source: Transportation Equity Act of the 21st Century, Public Law 105–178, §1203(f).

- *Project development streamlining.* There has been broad concern about the time required to move projects from plan to construction, and the cost of producing the necessary studies and documents in the planning and preliminary engineering phases. Much of the attention has focussed on the overlap of environmental requirements imposed by National Environmental Policy Act (NEPA) and those created by U.S. DOT. One of these, the major investment study (MIS), discussed later in the chapter, is eliminated as a stand-alone requirement by TEA-21. However, the essential elements of the MIS process are retained.

What may be most important is that the drafters of TEA-21 recognized that the metropolitan planning process that grew out of the historical sequence of transportation legislation as finally defined by ISTEA has proven effective in guiding public investment in metropolitan transportation systems.

TEA-21 also retains the principle of flexible funding established in ISTEA, reaffirming the responsibility of state and local decision makers to select the best transportation investments for an area without being strictly bound by categorical funding. Perhaps the biggest change with respect to funding is the creation of a "firewall" around most of the TEA-21 program. Previous to this legislation, congressional appropriators could limit the amount spent annually on transportation programs regardless of either authorized spending levels or the availability of money in the Highway Trust Fund (HTF). Because the HTF is included in the Federal Unified Budget, there had been an incentive to retain a balance of unspent funds. Language in TEA-21 leaves the HTF in the Federal Unified Budget, but it prevents savings from being used as budgetary offsets and essentially requires that the previous year's HTF receipts be appropriated. This provides planners with increased certainty about available funds over the life of TEA-21.

Understanding the Urban Transportation Plan

The long-range regional transportation plan is the essential product that must be produced in all metropolitan areas. As previously noted, ISTEA imposed and TEA-21 continues numerous requirements for the development and contents of the plan, but there is no "cookie cutter" approach to this effort. If done properly, this plan will elicit the region's goals and objectives as they relate not only to the transportation system, but also to broader issues of urban form, economic development, and quality of life. It will form the foundation for many subsequent products, from MISs to capital programs. In approaching the task of creating a long-range plan, the planner must be aware of certain issues.

- *Uncertainty in predicting the future.* Policy makers often assume that planners have the training and skill to accurately predict the future upon which their plans are based. In fact, much of what drives the demand for transportation facilities and services is external to the transportation planning process. Will there be unanticipated changes in technology? How rapidly will the implementation of intelligent transportation system (ITS) technology proceed? What will the cost and availability of fuel be in twenty years? Will the efficiency of travel be affected by technological advances in vehicle propulsion systems? Can the condition of the local, regional, and national economy be forecasted with confidence? Are predictions of growth in population and employment reasonable? How will changing societal values affect travel demand? Looking back a number of decades, could planners have been reasonably expected to predict the entry of large numbers of women into the workforce, or the influence of a newly heightened view of environmental quality or urban ecosystems? The list of issues could go on, but the point should be well taken: the planner must be honest about the effect of unpredictable events on plan scenarios and devise methods to address that uncertainty in developing the plan.

- *Limitations of analytical processes.* Computerized travel demand models, which are described at length in Chapter 6, form the technical foundation of the long-range plan. Because it is numerical, the model output is often viewed by both staff and decision makers as being more accurate than is the case. Even with advances in model development, the ability to forecast travel is limited. Travel behavior is complex, affected by the full range of exogenous variables discussed above, and cannot be entirely described by the mathematical relationships in a model. Yet planners routinely accept the notion that a model calibrated to replicate current travel behavior will accurately predict future behavior. Unfortunately, models sometimes do only a fair job of producing acceptable base year volumes. Factors that are used to calibrate the base year volumes to ground counts, such as travel time or link speed, are sometimes artificially imposed on the network, then carried forward to future year forecasts. Trips made by shared modes like transit and ridesharing are typically not fully mathematically developed and therefore have their effect minimized. Bicycle and pedestrian trips are nonexistent in many models and therefore are not measured as part of the transportation system. Taken together, these deficiencies of the model may result in overprediction of vehicle trips, leading to a perceived need for more highway facilities. This is not to say that models cannot provide valuable information for transportation decisions, but rather that both planners and decision makers must use caution in viewing the outputs, be they traffic volume or transit ridership, as unrealistically precise. The question is not whether the forecasted annual average daily traffic on an arterial street is 20,000 or 22,000, but rather the need for investigating capacity solutions along a corridor or for an additional river crossing. The same may be said of other post-processor analytic tools that are used to forecast plan implementation outcomes, including air emissions models and accessibility measures.

- *Influence of the political process.* In establishing the 3-C urban planning process, the federal government created the MPO as an explicitly political forum, in which state representatives and local elected officials have to reach an agreement on regional plans. The planner must recognize the political agendas of the policy level participants. A preconceived bias toward a given project or solution may skew the process. For example, a powerful mayor who has decided that a light rail project is a desirable development for the city, and who is skilled in using the media, may choose to ignore a technical solution that points in a different direction, dismissing the forecasts as meaningless. Thus, communications and political skills are as important to planners as are technical skills.

The point of this discussion is to help the planner understand that creating a long-range urban transportation plan cannot be approached as a technical project with a deterministic outcome, but rather as a dynamic process that guides decision making. As a result of growing understanding of the planning process and how it leads to investment decisions, new ways of approaching planning have developed. These include, in addition to the traditional planning process, performance-based planning and strategic planning. The planner should consider these methodologies in developing the best approach to creating the long-range plan for the metropolitan area. Attributes of the traditional long-range plan include:

- *Recognition of the role of the metropolitan transportation system.* A plan that addresses only the quality of the transportation system has missed its mark. The system must be viewed in terms of the important roles it plays in the community, from the neighborhood scale to the region and beyond. Through providing for the mobility of persons and goods, the transportation system supports the regional economy, both internally and in its ability to participate in and, perhaps, compete in the national and global market. It is a determinant of the quality of life of its residents, through the accessibility it provides to opportunities throughout the region and through the effects it has on the natural environment. The plan must acknowledge these roles and relate the proposed investments to the achievement of desired mobility and quality of life.

• *A horizon of twenty years.* Despite the uncertainty associated with forecasting travel demand and behavior, an uncertainty that increases as the forecast period lengthens, the generally accepted twenty-year horizon is now required by federal regulation. While the plan may include shorter-range elements, the longer horizon allows the community to identify long-terms needs and recognizes that major capital investments, like new rail systems or expressways, take a long time to progress from plan to construction.

• *An update cycle of three to five years.* The most appropriate way to address the uncertainty surrounding the conditions and assumptions upon which long-term travel forecasts are based is through relatively frequent updates. Demographic, economic, structural, and societal trends must be periodically reevaluated. Are changes in land use tracking with the input that was used for the travel forecasts, or must an adjustment be made? Have new population forecasts been developed? Is it time to perform a new survey of household travel behavior? Are there societal trends that will affect travel behavior that were not apparent when the previous plan was done? For example, a plan that missed the trend of women entering the workforce in large numbers would have quickly outgrown its usefulness and credibility.

• *A multimodal and intermodal approach.* Long-range plans cannot be limited to the traditional highway and transit elements. For a plan to encompass the metropolitan transportation system, it must deal with forecasts of travel not only by automobile and transit, but also by pedestrian and bicycle movements. It must consider freight movement by truck, rail, air, and where applicable, water. Finally, there must be an examination of the ease with which people and freight may transfer from one mode to another, and whether new terminal facilities would enhance these intermodal transfers, leading to what has been referred to as "seamless transportation."

• *A linkage to land use plans.* There is a dynamic relationship between transportation and land use, as each influences the other. Thus, the transportation plan ought to be linked to a regional land use plan. All else being equal, increased accessibility increases land value and in turn the potential intensity of development. Such accessibility can result from a new freeway interchange or a new rail transit station. Plans for transportation investment should be responsive to the spatial development patterns the community desires.

• *Fiscal constraint.* This ISTEA requirement forces the planning effort to be realistic. It must address the region's ability to finance its transportation needs and to confront the necessary tradeoffs that must be made with limited resources. Estimating reasonably available resources is a challenge in itself. Making assumptions about formula-based revenues from federal and state sources is easier than assigning plausible numbers to either project-based discretionary funds, local revenue sources, or the money that may be raised from private-sector contributions and through innovative means. Reaching consensus on the financial plan is a key decision early in the process.

• *Vision.* While ISTEA does not require vision, the planner should avoid a plan that is simply a statement of what is required to maintain the existing transportation system. Such a plan is unlikely to engage the community or its leaders or encourage them to openly discuss what transportation investment can accomplish. While fiscal constraint may limit initiatives, the requirement for fiscal constraint does not proscribe creating a companion vision plan. A plan with a twenty-year horizon should explore the opportunities available to the community and the region, what changes are desired, and what part transportation investment can play in achieving that vision. Such a plan may act as a catalyst for innovative ideas directed toward raising additional revenue for a desired action.

• *Broad involvement of the public and stakeholders.* Planners have long known that plans created in a vacuum, regardless of their technical proficiency, are not likely to succeed. ISTEA reinforces this notion with its mandate for public involvement. The goals and objectives that drive the long-range plan must properly arise from the community itself. The vision of the community's structure, how it functions, and what quality of life it offers is not for the planner to construct. It is rather the planner's job to make the connection between improving the transportation system and achieving those goals. Nor is public involvement a one-time effort. There must be continued feedback as the plan is developed. Not only does this ensure that the plan reflects the community's image, but it also gains credibility for the effort and enhances support for the plan's implementation.

Performance-Based Planning

The development of performance-based planning is primarily attributable to the notion that government should be more like business, that efforts to meet the needs of the investors (tax payers) and customers (transportation system users) must be measured and ought to show a positive result. This approach differs from the traditional planning process by focusing on outcomes rather than outputs. It also includes an iterative loop that feeds the measurements of performance back into the planning process. (Figure 12–1.) Performance-based planning is still very much in its infancy, with continuing research into appropriate performance measures, data collection, and analysis techniques. This research begins with the understanding that we tend to plan what we can measure; thus, we need to get better at measuring what we truly need to plan. Transportation plan outputs may include:

- Improvements to the infrastructure in terms of lane miles of pavement reconstructed or resurfaced and average pavement sufficiency; number of deficient bridges replaced or rehabilitated and reductions in number of deficient bridges; and number of buses replaced and average fleet age.

- Improvements to person and vehicle flow, in terms of total miles of vehicle and person travel, average trip time and distance, and vehicle and person hours of delay.

- Transit utilization in terms of passenger trips, revenue miles and hours of service, or farebox recovery ratio.

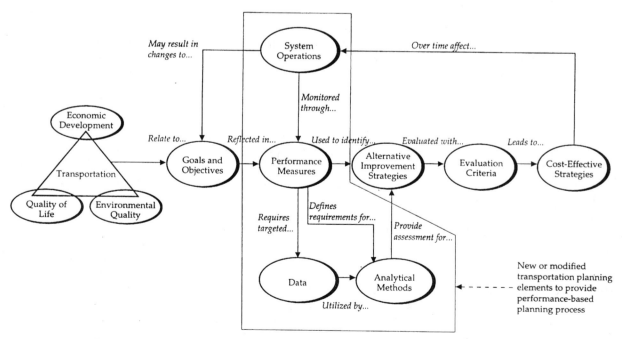

Figure 12–1   Elements of a Performance-Based Planning Process

Source: "Multimodal Transportation: Development of a Performance-Based Planning Process," *National Cooperative Highway Research Program Project 8–32(2)A*, Washington, D.C.: National Academy Press, 1997.

While these are important measures of the efficiency of the metropolitan transportation system, their use may result in both the planner and the implementing agencies narrowing their focus, and missing the broader issues of mobility and quality of life. The performance-based plan's measurement of *outcomes* addresses this narrow perspective. For example, while mobility can be measured in terms of congestion, travel time and cost, it can also be viewed in terms of the extent to which desired trip ends are linked by multiple mode choices for all population groups. What is the degree of accessibility of the region's employers to the region's workforce? Is commodity flow being supported through modal and intermodal investments that maintain a high degree of competitiveness for regional shippers and receivers? Do planned transportation investments contribute to the community's objectives in managing or encouraging growth, and to the creation of a chosen urban form? Does the transportation plan contribute to environmental sustainability in the region, or accelerate the degradation of the urban ecosystem? These kinds of measures, though more difficult to develop and analyze, include much of what we should expect our customers to look for in an urban transportation plan.

The performance-based plan does not exclude analysis of outputs as factors to be fed back into the planning process and used to evaluate investment, but rather it adds the measurement of outcomes. In both cases it is necessary to establish a performance baseline from which to measure change as plan elements are implemented. Establishment of baseline measures does not prevent the evolution of better performance measures for outcomes. These are likely to be refined as we learn more about the causal relationship between improvements or changes to the transportation system and the outcomes we are seeking in mobility, economic activity, environmental quality, and so forth.

An appropriate location for delineation of outputs, which will influence outcomes, is a final chapter of the plan document, which may outline implementation strategies. Achievement of desired outcomes can then be monitored in an annual effectiveness review. The Wilmington (Delaware) Area Planning Council performs such a review. This review documents the implementation of both transportation and land use actions; and then it quantifies resulting outcomes in terms of such parameters as mode share, vehicle travel, and air quality.

Strategic Planning

The strategic planning approach is designed to address the inherent uncertainty of the forecasting methodology and the tendency in the traditional planning process to treat numerical predictions as more accurate than they are. Defining a strategic vision is an element common to each of the approaches to the long-range plan. The community, its elected officials, and various stakeholders must reach an agreement on the desired future state of the region. As noted earlier, the vision is not limited to the metropolitan transportation system; but it must incorporate land use, the regional economy, and quality of life issues.

Strategic planning differs from the traditional plan by explicitly identifying uncertainties. This may be expressed as using a range of assumptions rather than a specific set of parameters as the basis for forecasts. For example, the planner may use a range of population and employment growth figures. The plan may then define with relative certainty the deficiencies of the existing transportation system and the needs for the first five-year increment. The mid- and long-range elements, with horizons of ten and twenty years respectively, would be portrayed with less certainty, using a number of scenarios for each. The strategic plan's recommendations should not unnecessarily foreclose future options to satisfy long-range needs. Early corridor preservation is an example of maintaining flexibility while studies are performed to determine the best modal solution in the corridor. Incremental development, to the extent that it is possible, should be considered for major capital investments like fixed guideway rail systems or new expressways. This again keeps future options open, recognizing that these investments have a long life and profound effect on the community's form and quality of life.

Peer Review

While it may be difficult to achieve, having the urban transportation planning process and plan reviewed by peers in the profession has merit. The planning staff can become too close to the process to realize its own biases. Inviting planners from other communities for occasional reviews can reveal such biases and result in a better plan.

Public Participation

Devising and conducting an effective public participation process is of pivotal importance to developing a credible urban transportation plan. As noted in Table 12–3, the FHWA and FTA joint regulations implementing the urban planning process are very explicit in describing the required public participation process. Transportation planners have understood since long before the passage of ISTEA that the development of a credible plan cannot proceed in a vacuum; public participation is a long-standing attribute of the planning process. The key word is "effective." For example, it is inadequate to simply post an MPO meeting announcement in the newspaper and hold a pro forma public hearing on the draft plan. It is equally infeasible to survey every household in the metropolitan area to determine the residents' transportation needs and ideas. Yet we must elicit from both stakeholders and the general public their opinion on goals and objectives, their perspective on the transportation needs of various groups across a spectrum from neighborhood to region, and their views on competing alternative investment strategies. The planner must recognize and enumerate the stakeholders throughout the region and devise a process that will

Table 12–3 Federal Regulations Concerning Public Involvement in the Planning Process (CFR 450.316)

"The metropolitan planning process shall:

(1) Include a proactive public involvement process that provides complete information, timely public notice, full public access to key decisions, and supports early and continuing involvement of the public in developing plans . . . ;

    (ii) Provide timely information about transportation issues and processes to citizens, affected public agencies, representatives of transportation agency employees, private providers of transportation, other interested parties and segments of the community affected by transportation plans.

    (iii) Provide reasonable public access to technical and policy information used in the development of plans . . .

    (iv) Require adequate public notice of public involvement activities and time for public review and comment at key decision points . . .

    (v) Demonstrate explicit consideration and response to public input received . . .

    (vi) Seek out and consider the needs of those traditionally underserved by existing transportation systems, including but not limited to low income and minority households."

actively engage them. Even more of a challenge is achieving meaningful involvement of the "traditionally underserved." While some may believe that a robust public participation process adds too much time to developing the long-range transportation plan, such participation permits early identification of conflicts, permitting time to be focussed on their resolution. The result can be a plan that is more credible and less likely to be subject to litigation and other delays later in the process.

Much research has been done in the area of public participation, and numerous techniques have been developed. Many of these are applicable to the development of the urban transportation plan. The most effective process will use a variety of approaches; any single strategy will not be adequate. While stakeholder groups like freight shippers or private transit providers will have a working knowledge of at least their part of the transportation system and the related infrastructure, special efforts must be made to reach and educate the general public. Presenting purely technical information to a public gathering will serve only to confuse and alienate rather than enlighten the audience. Innovative use of video, computer graphics, and games have all proven valuable in explaining technical issues to a lay audience. Other useful techniques include:

- Task forces and advisory committees.

- Targeted surveys.

- Taking the plan to the community.

- Use of print and electronic media.

- Use of the Internet.

Whichever techniques are chosen, it is important to remember that they all require staff and monetary resources. The planning agency must consider how much it can budget for this task within the overall context of producing the transportation plan.

Task Forces and Advisory or Steering Committees

Because of the number of topics that are investigated in depth in the course of preparing an urban transportation plan, this is one of the most productive ways to involve both stakeholders and the general public. Task forces are selected to focus on each of the main topics in the plan, from land use to transit to freight to transportation infrastructure and so on. Task force members can be selected in various ways, from appointment by the MPO Board to open self-selection. It is often best to use a combination of those approaches. Stakeholders are appointed to the appropriate task force to make sure they are represented and to offer valuable expertise. Citizens can be recruited through newsletters and the media and asked to choose a task force on which they would like to serve. (Table 12–4.)

A significant limitation of the task force approach is that the process is usually quite lengthy and involves a number of meetings. Concern is expressed that only "professional meeting goers" will stay with the process, resulting in certain perspectives dominating the outcome. One response is to utilize other approaches to gain the opinions of those who cannot commit to a long series of meetings, and then ensure that those opinions are transmitted to the task forces and given legitimate weight in their deliberations. While the composition of task force membership is important, a key to success is establishing how these bodies will operate. A strong chair with good meeting facilitation skills is important to keeping the work of the group on track. MPOs that choose to rely heavily on the task force approach to citizen participation should consider investing in facilitation training for their chairs. Operating rules are typically established and consented to at the initial meeting of the group. These must include the imposition of a timeframe on the work of the task force, with due dates for certain products. Chairpersons must know what is expected of them and what resources are available to them. Beyond the provision of support for meeting logistics, this can involve bringing in outside expertise to advise the group on a specific topic in their area of interest. Finally, members must be made to feel that their contributions are meaningful. If it becomes clear to members that the ideas they are generating are never seriously considered by the planners or decision makers, they will quickly lose interest. This does not mean that everything a task force generates must be accepted out of hand, but that rejection of products must be accompanied by a thoughtful explanation. Another advantage of this technique is that stakeholders and community leaders become involved in and accountable for the plan. The sense of ownership they develop may well influence the plan's acceptance by the public.

The planning agency must consider the costs, primarily in terms of staff time and monetary resources, of establishing a large task force or advisory committee effort. How many committees will you create, how often will they meet, and what is the result in staff time required simply to attend the meetings? Will your agency find it difficult to provide the level of support expected? Consider the public relations consequences if your staff cannot keep up with simple housekeeping tasks like generating announcements, minutes, and reports.

The Capital District Transportation Committee of Albany, New York used the task force approach as the core of its *New Visions*[1] transportation plan. Task forces were established for these nine subject areas:

- Demographics, land use, and growth futures.

- Infrastructure renewal.

Table 12–4 Stakeholders in the Urban Planning Process

- Local elected officials
- Transit operators
- Transit employees and unions
- Private transportation providers
- Major employers
- Freight shippers
- Freight carriers
- Port operators
- Airport operators
- Human service agencies
- Economic development officials
- Environmental organizations
- Motorist advocates
- Bicycle and pedestrian advocates
- Senior citizens advocates
- Advocates for the disabled
- Emergency service providers

---

[1] *New Visions for Capital District Transportation, Regional Transportation Plan* (Albany, N.Y.: Capital District Transportation Committee, March 20, 1997).

- Transit futures.

- Special transportation needs.

- Expressway management.

- Arterial corridor management.

- Goods movement.

- Bicycle and pedestrian issues.

- Urban issues.

The planning staff recognized that there would be areas of overlap between these subjects and advised the task forces accordingly. When appropriate, joint meetings were held to review draft reports. Task forces were given a mission to accomplish, which included:

- Identifying issues relevant to both near-term and long-term regional vision, policy, and investment strategy. Modify the definition of these issues in response to public opinion.

- Proposing planning and investment principles to provide implementation guidance towards creating a future regional vision.

- Objectively analyzing the issues and options, using a set of core performance measures as the yardstick.

- Outlining feasible and potentially desirable actions and identifying strategies where an apparent consensus exists. Where the Capital District Transportation Committee faces a major policy choice, making no recommendations but instead providing performance-based information to guide a public dialogue that will lead to policy direction.

- Recommending action regarding the ultimate status of the task force beyond *New Visions*. Continue to provide a discussion and advisory forum, revise participation or focus, or dissolve.

In carrying out this mission, each task force was expected to address safety, land use, social justice and equity, resource efficiency, and environmental effects. This exercise involved over 125 individuals in the private and public sectors; and it generated a series of white papers and contributions to technical reports, forming the core direction of the plan.

Taking the Plan to the Community

A successful public participation plan must include appropriate outreach activities. Planners are often disappointed that attendance at public forums is low, despite efforts to advertise such events. While many of the representatives of stakeholder groups are willing to attend such meetings, it is especially difficult to attract representatives of the traditionally underserved community as well as the general public. Having to travel to a meeting can be a barrier, as can the time involved, particularly when the value of the participation is unknown. Many MPOs have demonstrated the value of special outreach techniques to engage target community groups, including minority and immigrant neighborhoods, low-income households, and senior citizens. The Metropolitan Washington Council of Governments undertook a special project to develop and evaluate such techniques.[2] The project had the following objectives:

- To ensure that the transportation system proposed in the plan would broadly serve the community.

---

[2] P. Lebeaux, *A System That Serves Everyone Attracting Nontraditional Participants into the Regional Transportation Planning Process* (Washington, D.C.: Metropolitan Washington Council of Governments, December, 1996).

- To improve the likelihood that the plan would receive broad political support, thereby increasing the likelihood of implementation.

- To look for new sources of ideas about meeting the transportation needs of the citizenry.

They began by targeting selected neighborhoods for enhanced outreach, realizing that in a large metropolitan area it is impossible to directly involve the entire region. These included a suburban neighborhood with a growing Latino population; a pair of inner-city, low-income, predominately African-American neighborhoods; a community with a large concentration of new immigrants; and a far suburban, low-density area where senior citizens were having mobility problems. Planners working in a smaller metropolitan area may still find it useful to target specific groups or neighborhoods. Even though the entire community is more accessible, staff and monetary resources are proportionately smaller. Project outreach techniques included:

- Community brainstorming meetings.

- A travelling van exhibit.

- A brochure distributed in the community.

- A postcard questionnaire.

- A random telephone survey.

Project findings that are relevant to other planners in developing community outreach efforts include:

- It was much easier to involve participants in one-time or occasional community events, such as brainstorming sessions or focus groups, than for ongoing participation in a task force.

- Considerations in the success of brainstorming sessions include: using a captive audience already attending an event (by holding the event immediately after a church service, for example), providing child care and food, being sensitive to language issues (sessions in the Latino neighborhood were conducted in Spanish with interpreters), and involving community groups in planning and cosponsoring the sessions.

- The travelling van exhibit was effective in attracting the interest of participants, but it was expensive to operate and inflexible as far as scheduling. It was felt that a portable display was a better alternative.

- Focus groups, using trained community facilitators, were used as a follow up to brainstorming sessions. They provided useful details and drew out reasons for opinions expressed at the previous sessions.

- Postcard questionnaires distributed at community meetings and van appearances generated similar comments to the random telephone survey.

This project demonstrates that "taking the plan to the community" in a thoughtful way can generate a great deal of success in eliciting opinions from the "traditionally underserved." The enhanced outreach process generated a significant proportion of the new ideas offered through the overall public participation process for the vision planning exercise. Planners should be aware that transportation needs identified by these groups often tend to be short term in nature. There was not so much interest in a long-term vision for the regional transportation system as in immediate improvements that would affect respondents' ability to travel to work or to meet other needs. The planner should remain open to all ideas that are put forward, even if they do not directly relate to the long-range plan. To the extent that suggested short-term improvements are valuable and can be implemented, the planning agency's credibility in the underserved neighborhood will be enhanced. This can in turn benefit future rounds of involvement in long-range planning. Planners involved in community outreach efforts must keep an accurate record of the comments made and the disposition of those comments. This record should be appended to the plan document.

The planning agency should be as creative as resources will allow in reaching out to the community. Taking a discussion of the plan to a high school civics class or a university class in environmental planning may generate unexpected interest and opinion. The outreach arena is also one where agencies have effectively used a game approach to elicit comments without overwhelming the participants with technical information. One such game allows participants at a public meeting to select among alternative transportation investments in the context of fiscal constraint. After the planner reviews alternative plan actions, each of which is illustrated on a separate display, participants are given an amount of play money ("MPO $") equal to the total resources available. They can then spend it on the various plan alternatives, each of which has a specified cost. This helps bring home the point of tradeoffs, that investing in a new light rail system, for example, may mean foregoing the desired level of highway and bridge infrastructure sufficiency. This hands-on exercise is more effective than the planner offering a verbal explanation of why the plan cannot be an endless wish list.

Use of the Print and Electronic Media

The media can be an important tool for achieving effective public involvement. The planner must distinguish between the use of free news coverage and special uses of the media that may require payment. Positive news coverage by the print and electronic media can best be achieved by understanding their business and developing a good working relationship. Learn when newspaper, radio, and television news deadlines are. When you have meetings for which you want news coverage, make sure you schedule them to permit deadlines to be met. Provide complete and adequate notice in a press release preceding the meeting. Information must be conveyed to the media in an appropriate format. Giving a reporter a fifty-page report will not be as effective as providing a bullet list of talking points. When interviewed, the planner must keep comments brief, not overly technical, and politically neutral. Keep in mind how your use of the media relates to your overall public participation plan. Providing timely information to the public early in the process of developing goals and objectives requires a different approach than when seeking their opinions on a short list of final alternatives.

The media can be used in a positive way beyond news coverage to inform the public and to elicit their responses. Some MPOs have used a televised town meeting format. This can combine a studio audience with an opportunity for viewers to call in with questions and comments. Careful preparation is necessary to ensure the information you want to convey is well presented. Do not waste the visual nature of a televised presentation on "talking heads." If this is being used to initiate your plan, consider paying for production of a video that explores the community's transportation system, highlighting both positive and negative aspects. Such a video can also be used effectively in community meetings, as people learn well from a visual medium. If you are using this format later in the plan development process to present alternative investments, consider the use of computer graphics to display what a facility, corridor, or community model may look like. In a smaller community where the planning budget does not allow for video production, consider at least using visual renderings of the plan alternatives. Another caveat related to this format is managing the call-in portion of the show to ensure that a single caller or those advocating a single point of view do not dominate the discussion. Make sure you are prepared to answer the questions that are likely to be asked, and do not allow yourself to be drawn into a confrontational interaction.

While not as engaging as television, the newspaper can be used in a similar manner. It is valuable because of its wide circulation. Discuss with the publisher and editor the opportunity for a special report at appropriate times during the planning process. Once again it is important to be clear about what you want to present, to avoid lengthy technical descriptions or explanations, and to use an attractive format. Consider using the services of a graphic arts consultant. Photographs can be used to document current conditions, while renderings can depict plan alternatives. Some MPOs have used a clip out/mail back form in the special section to elicit public response. Be aware of limited circulation newspapers in your community. Neighborhood, ethnic, or foreign language publications can be a valuable tool to reach underserved communities. Consult with the editors of those publications on how your information may be modified to work effectively for the target audience.

Use of the Internet

A growing number of MPOs have found an Internet presence to be a useful tool in fostering two-way communication with the public. An MPO Web site can present a large amount of material in a variety of ways, depending on how much the planning agency can invest in its creation and maintenance. As it relates to the transportation plan, the material can include anything from outlines of goals and objectives, graphic portrayals of plan alternatives, maps, and finance charts, to a full draft text that can be downloaded. Items that are open for discussion can be highlighted. The site can be linked to sites of local governments, related planning agencies, and neighborhood or community groups to increase the potential audience.

Before the planning agency establishes a Web site, it is important to research the costs not only of creating the site, but also of maintaining it. Sites that are infrequently updated lose their appeal and their audience. Finally, the planner should realize that this approach, while an excellent supplement to the public involvement process, will only reach a relatively small number of people in the community.

Goals and Objectives

The starting point for the urban transportation plan is the development of goals and objectives. This is a critical and difficult task. It has been said that a skilled planner can write a plan that can take a community in any direction, a plan that will support growth management or unbridled expansion, a plan that directs investment toward major enhancements in transit service or one that relies entirely on freeway expansion. It is the goals and objectives that define the plan, that make the plan uniquely that of its community. Allentown and Albuquerque may share the same technical approach to travel demand modeling, but have entirely different philosophies on how transportation investments should be made in their metropolitan regions. It is not the role of the planner to devise the goals and objectives, but to facilitate a process that elicits them from the public and their leaders, to translate them into the language of planning, and to use them to guide the technical process.

In the ideal setting, transportation plans are developed in concert with regional comprehensive plans. In that case broad planning goals are generated first, and it becomes clear how investment in the metropolitan transportation system can support achievement of those goals. However, it is often the case that transportation plans are left to proceed on their own. This was particularly true in response to the requirements of ISTEA, which established absolute deadlines for such plans. Many communities were not prepared to undertake a regional comprehensive plan in time to provide a foundation for the transportation plan. In some cases there were comprehensive plans that were relatively recent, but in others they were outdated or nonexistent. The transportation planner must be prepared to address the development of regional goals and objectives in the absence of a comprehensive plan.

Using the public participation process discussed above, it is valuable to approach goal development in terms of broad subject areas. These may include:

- Personal mobility.

- Freight mobility.

- Safety and security.

- System integrity and preservation.

- Economic growth or viability.

- Land use and urban structure.

- Environmental protection or enhancement.

- Social equity.

Such an approach puts the planning effort on a more sound footing than setting facility-oriented goals like "build twenty miles of freeways" or "purchase fifty new buses," which are outputs rather than outcomes.

Personal Mobility

What affects mobility in your region? This goal area should include statements related to traffic congestion, transit capacity and service parameters, accessibility for people with disabilities and those without cars, travel by nonmotorized modes, and system connectivity. The latter may include such diverse subjects as convenient intermodal connections, or the lack of a bridge connecting communities separated by a river. Goal statements should recognize the role ITS technology may play in enhancing system performance.

Freight Mobility

While the majority of freight moves by truck, metropolitan areas may also have railroad freight terminals, airports with cargo operations, coastal or inland ports, and pipelines. While truck movement is affected by congestion, there are also issues of system connectivity, bridge clearances and weight restrictions, hazardous materials considerations, and travel limitations imposed by local ordinance in terms of truck routes or restricted delivery times. Delivery in congested business districts with limited curb space and lack of off-street facilities can create significant congestion. ITS technology also operates in the commercial vehicle arena and should be considered. Intermodal connections are key to the operations of rail terminals and ports. Goals may also address the need for expansion of port or rail facilities, dredging of a harbor, extension of an airport runway, or the capacity of an international border crossing.

Safety and Security

Safety goals typically relate to the reduction of the number and severity of motor vehicle crashes and accidents involving pedestrians and bicyclists. This may in turn incorporate discussions of freeway incident management or of improving emergency service response through-traffic signal preemption. Highway-rail grade crossing safety remains an area of concern, and it should be considered in the context of goals that may result in increased freight or passenger train movements or the construction of a light rail system. Safety of transit system users must also be addressed, including in-vehicle issues, bus stop safety, and station security.

System Integrity and Preservation

This group of goal statements describes the investment necessary to maintain the physical infrastructure of the transportation system in a state of good repair. This encompasses preventive maintenance, rehabilitation, and replacement of pavements; bridges; transit vehicles, guideway, and fixed facilities; pedestrian and bicycle facilities; and traffic control systems and related advanced technologies. In certain areas of the country there are special infrastructure needs that fall in this category, like seismic retrofit in earthquake-prone regions. These goals should also recognize the need to dedicate sufficient resources to the continued operation of the transportation system, particularly to the extent that traffic control centers and related systems are in place.

Economic Growth or Viability

There are many ways to get at the dynamic relationship between the regional economy and its transportation system. Commerce requires transportation of raw materials, finished products, employees, and customers. Availability of system capacity and connectivity contribute to business location decisions. Understanding logistics requirements of existing or sought after industries may shape the modal focus of these transportation goals. Growth may also create demands for new capacity. This set of goals will reflect the state of the region's economy. Regions whose economies are stagnant may consider investing in transportation improvements in the hopes of attracting new businesses. Regions that are growing rapidly may have to judge how much they have to invest to keep up with demand.

Land Use and Urban Structure

Some of these issues are similar to economic goals, but they have more far-reaching consequences. Again, the relationship is dynamic and long-standing. The extent to which a community spreads out or remains compact by

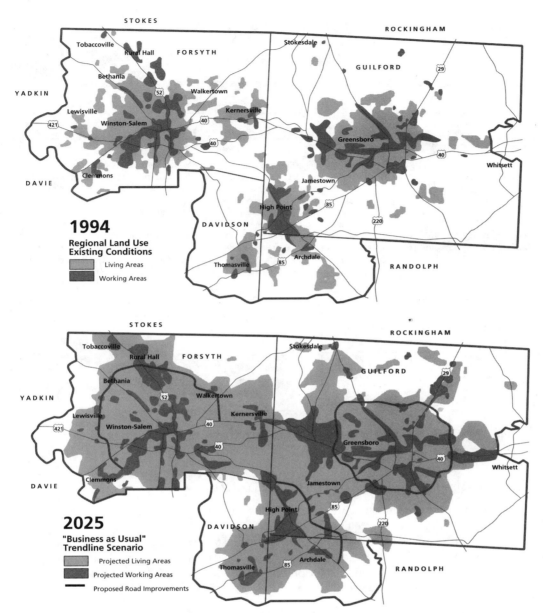

Figure 12–2   Effective Graphic Presentation of a Land Use Forecast

accommodating growth within existing boundaries, is automobile reliant or transit friendly, provides for access to employment for those without cars, and balances employment and housing within its community are all outcomes of land use decisions that affect the transportation system. Goal statements that reflect an understanding of those effects are key. In many communities, land use decisions are made without consideration of transportation and other infrastructure costs. There has been an expectation that land development, even in terms of widely spread low-density uses, has benefits to the community that outweigh the costs of providing infrastructure. This perspective is generally no longer the case. In terms of transportation, understanding has increased about the correlation between low-density development, not only the capital cost of building roads, but also longer trip length, increases in vehicle-miles-traveled, lack of alternative modes, and greater congestion. The Piedmont Triad Regional Transportation Study used a graphic representation to depict current land use and the forecasted result of "business as usual" land development at the plan horizon. (Figure 12–2.) This was supplemented with a discussion of the transportation implications of that development pattern. (Figure 12–3.)

The Piedmont Triad Regional Transportation Study

Implications of the Trend Line
(Business-as-Usual) Land Use Scenario

Key Elements :

- Increasing congestion and gridlock
- Increasing auto-dependence & cost
- Continued low-density development
- Isolated clusters of segregated uses
- Continued loss of open space
- More time in cars & longer commutes
- Inefficient public service provision
- Loss of existing community identity
- Increasing air pollution
- Encroachment into watersheds

Key Implications :

- Ineffective transit due to continued low-density development patterns
- Loss of identity & sense of community
- Continued loss of mixed-use areas and deterioration of downtown areas.
- Continued suburban sprawl and loss of open space & countryside
- Short-term attractiveness by allowing development of large lot.subdivisions
- High traffic volumes on Interstates
- Lower average operating speeds
- More expansive infrastructure needed

Year	Population	Vehicle Miles Traveled	Vehicle Hours Traveled
1994	704,000	16.5 million VMTs	377,500 VHTs
2025	866,000	29.7 million VMTs	782,000 VHTs
% Increase 1994 - 2025	+23%	+80%	+107%

Figure 12–3   Informing the Public: Implications of Land Development

Environmental Protection or Enhancement

These goals will consider the connection between construction, operation, and use of the metropolitan transportation system and the natural environment. The requirements of the NEPA and the Clean Air Act as amended have been in place long enough that both planners and elected officials generally understand the relationships. Statements should relate to air quality; energy consumption; and effects on land, water, noise, and cultural resources. The fundamental point is the realization that transportation investment cannot only avoid environmental degradation, but also contribute to environmental enhancement and improvements to the community's quality of life.

Social Equity

How do transportation investments affect different segments of your metropolitan community? Do suburban residents receive a greater benefit than people who reside in the urban core? Are the needs of low-income residents addressed? How about those of senior citizens, school-age children, or persons with disabilities? Are there geographic concentrations of minority citizens? If so, how do they fare in the provision of appropriate transportation services? These goals will recognize the diversity of the community and its transportation needs. Even a small metropolitan area has various and sometimes conflicting needs. A new expressway may well prove to be the best way to serve suburban activity centers, while elderly residents of the urban core need paratransit service. A freight rail terminal may require improved access to the interstate highway, but the connection may negatively affect an adjacent minority neighborhood. Planning goals will highlight and help to resolve these conflicts.

The next issue is the construction of goal statements. Should they be broadly or narrowly focused? Goals should be clear statements of policy, while the accompanying objectives must have measurable outcomes. There is, however, a danger in making statements that are too simple. While everyone can agree with goals like "repair our bridges" or "improve highway safety," they offer little guidance to the planner. Remember that the goals are the foundation for investment priorities. Therefore, an acceptable goal statement might be: "It is the highest priority to maintain the existing highway and bridge infrastructure in a state of good repair." A related objective could be: "Reduce the number of deficient bridges on principal arterials by eight percent during the first five years of the plan." A sample array of goal and objective statements, not intended to be complete, is found in Table 12–5.

Financial Plan

Because of the financial constraint requirement imposed by ISTEA, a financial plan must be developed and adopted early in the planning process. This provides the target for investment. The plan must be based on estimates of reasonably available funding from all levels of government. The state DOT and the MPO are required by federal mandate to work together to develop these estimates. These estimates are important because they turn the plan from merely a "wish list" of projects to a realistic representation of the facilities and services that the region can support. The plan's estimates must include the following programs:

- Federal funds allocated to the states, including:

  – Interstate maintenance.

  – NHS.

  – Unattributed STP, including transportation enhancement and safety set-asides.

  – Bridge program.

  – FTA formula funds.

  – FHWA and FTA discretionary program funds. These estimates must be treated differently than formula allocations in developing estimates.

- Federal funds allocated directly to MPOs, including:

  – Attributed STP.

  – CMAQ.

  – Congressional demonstration project or similar earmarked funds. These must be placed in the context of the true estimated cost of the subject project.

Table 12–5 Sample Long-Range Plan Goals and Objectives

PERSONAL MOBILITY

GOAL: Maintain travel time between representative locations for peak hour travel at 1998 level.
OBJECTIVES:
- Institute operational improvements on both limited access and signalized arterials to increase capacity.
- Within five years, add 200 intersections to the Centralized Signal Control System.
- Within three years, develop a plan for the use of Intelligent Transportation System technology to enhance freeway capacity.
- Develop and implement a Freeway Incident Management Plan to address non-recurrent peak-hour congestion.
- Manage demand to limit growth in number of single occupant vehicles on the system during peak periods.
- Expand existing Ride/Share program to twenty new locations.

GOAL: Increase public transit's share of person travel.
OBJECTIVES:
- Identify and develop park-and-ride locations with express bus service along Freeway Corridors A and C.
- Implement peak period reverse commute bus service from "Inner City Neighborhood" to "Suburban Commercial Center."
- Maintain an equitable transit fare structure.

GOAL: Increase pedestrian and bicycle share of person travel.
OBJECTIVES:
- Complete construction of Bicycle Paths A and D.
- Develop model "pedestrian friendly" zoning and subdivision codes for suburban communities.

SYSTEM INTEGRITY

GOAL: Maintain the metropolitan surface transportation system in a state of good repair.
OBJECTIVES:
- Reduce the number of deficient bridges by 7% within ten years.
- Maintain pavement sufficiency on principal arterials at no more than 10% poor.
- Improve the pavement sufficiency on arterial streets to no more than 15% poor within five years.

GOAL: Maintain the metropolitan transit system in a state of good repair.
OBJECTIVES:
- Do not exceed current Federal guidelines in scheduling bus replacement projects.
- Construct a new bus maintenance/storage facility to replace Garage B.

SAFETY

GOAL: Reduce motor vehicle crash rates on principal arterials.
OBJECTIVES:
- Identify and address all current high accident locations within three years.

GOAL: Reduce personal injury pedestrian and bicycle accidents by 10%.

OBJECTIVES:
- Identify and address all current high-accident locations within three years.
- Provide funding support to Health Department public education campaign directed toward high-risk pedestrian groups, including children and senior citizens.

- State revenues for transportation purposes, including:

  - State match for federal funds.

  - Highway programs, which may provide separate funding for state highway system and local road projects.

  - Transit programs, which may provide separately for capital and system operating costs.

- Regional transit authority revenues from other than federal and state sources, including local government payments and fares.

- Toll authority revenues.

- Unique local programs like a dedicated sales tax for transportation purposes.

- Private sources of funds. These may include traffic impact fees and leveraged private investment.

It is not necessary to account for local tax revenues that are used for routine local street maintenance programs.

It may be difficult to reach an agreement on reasonable estimates, given the difficulty of forecasting revenues from that broad variety of fund sources over a twenty-year period. There is no single acceptable methodology. Some agencies choose to estimate conservatively, using a minimal growth rate from a known point in time like the current year or the last year of authorizing legislation. There may be political pressure to increase estimates, allowing the incorporation of more projects and actions in the final transportation plan. Given that financial constraint is the key to developing a realistic plan rather than a wish list, such pressure must be minimized as much as possible. There is likely to be some negotiation in reaching a financial plan that the MPO is able to adopt. Once adopted, there must be a clear explanation given in regard to the eligible uses of each fund source, in that the final plan is constrained not to the total funds available, but to each fund source. This is especially important for single purpose fund sources, like a state transit operating assistance program.

Metropolitan Transportation System

With the advent of ISTEA and its focus on intermodal and multimodal transportation, the notion of a metropolitan transportation system was developed. Instead of looking at a series of individual systems, including the freeway system, the surface arterial system, the local road system, the transit system, and so forth, planners began to adopt the perspective of a unified metropolitan transportation system. This system encompasses all the modes in the region, is free of jurisdictional limits, and recognizes the integration of the modes. Thus, the planner must deal with the fact that an urban bus transit system runs on local streets and arterials, and therefore transit operations cannot be analyzed independently of arterial congestion. Similarly, a plan that addresses arterial access management must also provide for appropriate pedestrian facilities and operations. The resulting conflicts are often difficult to resolve, as a single facility is expected to provide for contradictory roles. But by addressing the transportation system as a single entity of interrelated elements, the planner becomes more aware of potential conflicts in the planning stage, rather than finding unexpected consequences when a given project is being designed or built.

The planner must understand the characteristics of each system or facility type and the potential interrelations with other systems. This may be addressed in terms of system users and their needs.

Personal mobility:

- *Pedestrian* — continuous system of sidewalks and related facilities, connecting primary generators; crosswalks; adequate green time at signalized intersections; grade-separated facilities as necessary; accommodation per the Americans with Disabilities Act.

- *Bicyclist* — in most states, a bicycle is considered a vehicular user of the roadway, except where prohibited, typically on limited access facilities. Provision may be made for both on-street travel and separate bicycle paths. The on-street system should consider connectivity, signs and pavement markings, and specialized detectors for actuated signals. Bicycle parking and storage at various locations should be included.

- *Transit user* — paratransit, fixed route bus, and fixed guideway systems. All except the latter utilize the street system; light rail may also be on and interface with the street system. Route structure and total travel time are key determinants in usage.

- *Motorist* — consider a functional classification hierarchy of the street and highway system, trip purposes, and internal and external trips. Parking is an often overlooked element. Intermodal connections, as at park-and-ride lots, must also be considered.

Freight mobility:

- *Trucks* — require generalized access, may be restricted from local streets, consume more capacity than cars, and consider different operating characteristics in terms of safety.

- *Rail* — interface with street system at grade crossings, and truck access to terminals is important.

- *Air* — truck access to freight terminals is important.

- *Water* — truck and rail access to port facilities is important.

Travel Characteristics

Having developed a sense of the metropolitan transportation system, the planner must next examine the travel characteristics of system users and the factors that influence their travel decisions. Travel characteristics involve the often complex relationship of the user to the system. There is, for example, the interaction between the spatial array of land use, roadway classification, and trip patterns. In addressing mode choice trends, the planner may need to examine the importance of telecommuting in the region, as well as the influence of parking cost and availability. Modal characteristics of freight movement must be analyzed. The reader is referred to Chapter 4 for a thorough discussion of urban travel characteristics.

Inventories

The initial step of the technical process of the urban transportation plan is the development of inventories of the plan components. These inventories establish the baseline of the urban plan, both in terms of performance and infrastructure. Investment performance will be measured against this baseline, as will the timing of the next plan update. Inventories can be considered in the following categories: demographics, land use, transportation network, and travel behavior. The planning agency must determine what data sources are available for this step. Much of the data is likely to be already on hand, unless the agency is newly constituted (as is the case when new MPOs are designated after the decennial census). Data sources may also include other public agencies in the metropolitan area, state agencies, national default data, or data purchased from commercial sources.

Demographics

Demographic information describes the population of the urban area and therefore drives much of the demand side of the plan. The first level of demographic source information is the U.S. Census, which provides not only raw population, but also a great deal of descriptive information cross referenced by location. Typically, this information is translated from census geography to traffic analysis zones (TAZ), a task accomplished through the provision of an equivalency list to the Census Bureau. The information that is critical to plan development includes:

- Population.

- Employment.

- Age distribution.

- Racial and ethnic group distribution.

- Disability.

- Number of households.

- Household size and composition.

- Household income.

- Household auto ownership.

- Workers by household.

The availability of this information from the Census Bureau on CD-ROM greatly simplifies the process of analysis of demographic data, particularly in combination with the use of a geographic information system (GIS). The GIS permits graphic display of all of this information and is invaluable in managing network-based spatial data. Visual representation can serve to educate both planners and decision makers about the demographic structure of the community. For example, GIS can make it easy to identify concentrations of the traditionally underserved, by mapping household income and auto ownership, racial and ethnic groups, and populations greater than 75 years-of-age. Maps can be developed for population density or distribution of household size. An example is shown in Figure 12–4.

The other important set of demographic information is employment. The planner will need to know the distribution of employment sites in the urban area by number and type of employees. The number of employment type categories will depend on the input requirements of the travel demand model, but they may include at a minimum, manufacturing, commercial, and retail. This information may be obtained from the state department of labor or regional economic development agency.

Land Use

Complementing the spatial distribution of the population is the spatial distribution of activity, interpreted as land use data. The data will be inventoried by TAZ in order to match the spatial input to the travel demand model. The inventory must show current land use by type: residential by dwelling unit type (single or multiple family), retail, commercial, industrial, institutional, and special uses. The level of detail must be balanced with the resources required to create the inventory and keep it up to date. For example, within institutional uses, a church, a university, a nursing home, and a prison all have markedly different trip generation characteristics. The land use inventory must also include current zoning codes and maps. This information will facilitate the forecasting of the potential build-out of various subareas or corridors.

Transportation Network

An inventory of the physical infrastructure and operating characteristics of the elements of the metropolitan transportation system is vital. A decision must be made early on regarding the level of detail that is necessary for the effort. There is no need, for example, to include every local street in the street system inventory, as they will not be directly affected by the regional transportation plan. The network map, or spatial inventory, will again relate to the required input of the travel demand model. It will include all principal arterial freeways, expressways, and highways; some or all arterial streets; and possibly some collector streets. The network's physical inventory will include a physical description, including number of lanes; level of access and tolls; presence of HOV lanes, bus lanes, or other special uses; type of traffic control; and presence of bicycle and pedestrian facilities. There will also be an operational description including average daily and peak-period traffic volume, free flow and operating speed, percent commercial traffic, and presence of bus routes.

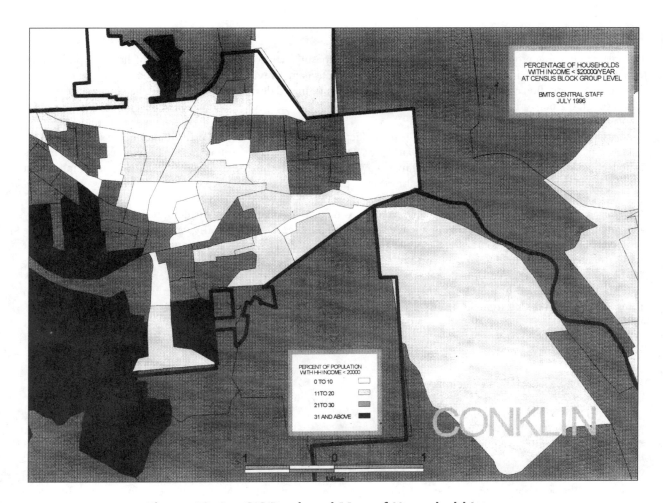

Figure 12–4   GIS Produced Map of Household Income

The transit system's spatial inventory will include a complete map of fixed guideway systems, if any, and stations; bus routes and terminals; and park-and-ride lots. Paratransit service is noted as a separate element. Physical inventory includes number and age of vehicles in the transit fleet, garage and maintenance facilities and vehicles, stations and shelters, and related items. The operational inventory will include hours of operation of each service, revenue miles, headways, capacity, fare structure, and ridership.

The freight system's spatial inventory will include location of railroads, ports, airports, and truck routes and restrictions. There will be a list of freight terminals by type: truck, rail, air, water, and intermodal. It may also include the location of major shippers and receivers. The operational inventory will focus on ton-miles by mode and commodity class.

Facilities dedicated to bicycles and pedestrians will also be inventoried. To the extent that bicycle lanes are on-street facilities, they will be denoted as an element in the highway and street network physical inventory. Any off-street bicycle paths or trails should be inventoried separately. It is not generally necessary to inventory sidewalks; but it will be important to know about the presence of sidewalks in critical corridors and special pedestrian facilities like pedestrian bridges, skywalks, or trails.

Travel Behavior

The last critical inventory element is travel behavior, as the planner combines knowledge of how people use the transportation system with the spatial and operational characteristics previously described. Behavior can be viewed in terms of the production and attraction of travel demand, the origin and destination of trips, and the choice of mode and path through the network.

Land use and demographic data determine trip production and attraction rates. For example, home-based trips are produced in zones where there are residential land uses. The rate of trips per household is then determined by such factors as household size, income, and auto ownership. Likewise, trips may be attracted to zones where there are employment land uses and may be modified by number of jobs by type.

A key issue in developing a travel behavior inventory is the use of local data versus default data. The use of locally generated data is ideal, but the planning agency has to weigh the cost of statistically valid travel surveys against the perceived benefits. Survey types may include home interview, employee worksite interview, on-board transit, or activity center focused. In choosing a course of action, relevant questions include how many years have elapsed since the previous survey was performed and whether that information still produces valid forecasts. Journey-to-work information is included in the U.S. Census. Default information may be obtained from the Nationwide Personal Transportation Survey and from the Transportation Research Board. If a survey is planned, consider the following issues and elements:

- Sample size.

- Sample selection methodology.

- Design of questionnaire or other data collection forms.

- Data handling requirements.

While travel survey techniques have become standardized over time, the planning agency must consider retaining a consultant if the necessary expertise does not exist on staff. In many instances, a local college or university may be able to provide assistance in both designing and administering the survey. Proper design of the questionnaire is critical. It must ensure that all required data items are collected, that the person being interviewed understands the questions (especially true for self-administered surveys), and that analysts can easily and accurately code the data. A final consideration is the opportunity for cost sharing. There may be another agency that can benefit from surveying the same target audience by adding some questions. It is important, however, to keep the survey instrument from becoming too long or unwieldy.

Travel behavior as it relates to freight movement is also important but harder to obtain. Publicly or commercially available commodity flow data may be at too gross a level of detail to be useful in network planning. Consideration should be given to a survey of major businesses in the region to collect data on logistics patterns, modes, and volume. The planner must understand that private businesses may be reticent to provide proprietary information about their business activity. One key to success is the initiation of a formal freight stakeholders group through which the private sector learns how it can realize direct benefits from involvement in the planning process. It is also helpful to use a direct interview technique rather than a mail back survey, where assurances regarding confidentiality can be made to the interviewee. Finally, ask only what you need to know: numbers and types of inbound and outbound vehicles by time of day and preferred route.

Forecasting Travel

Having established the goals and objectives for your plan, and having gathered a baseline of data, the major technical process of the urban transportation plan is forecasting travel by mode and across the network. See Chapter 6 for a thorough discussion of travel demand modeling and forecasting. Issues to be considered in addition to the construction, calibration, and use of the model are:

- Base assumptions. It is important to be explicit about forecasting assumptions and to reach consensus at the technical advisory committee about those assumptions. These assumptions may include:

  - Population growth in terms of both a regional control total and a distribution of the total growth among subunits for each time period in the forecast. Municipal growth forecasts can then be translated into numbers of households and distributed to the TAZ level.

  - Economic growth in terms of new employment by employer type, using the range of employer types incorporated in your model. Employment growth must also be distributed from a control total to the TAZ.

  - Overall urban development patterns as reflected in land use forecasts that have the concurrence of local and regional governments. Note especially significant changes that may be contemplated. Examples include institution of an urban growth boundary or explicit support of neotraditional development in specific areas.

- Factors affecting travel behavior:

  - The external cost of travel, including fuel price and use, tolls and other pricing schemes, parking, and transit pricing.

  - The effect of ITS technology on capacity of highways and transit system operations.

  - Changes in air quality attainment status leading to controls imposed on the transportation sector by the SIP.

- Factors external to the metropolitan area. Societal trends of the recent past like women entering the workforce in large numbers have had a marked effect on travel behavior. The aging of the population in the coming decades may have an equally significant effect. While these trends may be difficult to identify, they should be noted to the extent that agreement is reached. Another factor is major development outside the area that will affect traffic volumes. For example, the construction of a new major tourist attraction fifty miles away may significantly increase the volume of external through-traffic on a metropolitan area freeway.

- Recognition of the limits of the model in accurately predicting transit, bicycle, and pedestrian trips on a traffic analysis zone level. This in turn may limit the model's efficacy in the area of multimodal transportation alternatives and linkage to land use plans.

The initial task is the calibration of the base year model and the development of future year null forecasts. These are forecasts of future demand with no changes to the system beyond projects currently programmed but not yet constructed. A decision must also be reached regarding the time increments to be forecasted. For a smaller, low-growth metropolitan area, a single twenty-year forecast may be adequate. More typically, a ten-year forecast will also be developed. This horizon not only offers a forecast with a greater level of confidence but also a period for which major investment decisions may be required in the near term.

Plan Development and Testing

All of the pieces should now be in place to develop sets of alternative actions that will be included in the draft final plan. The goals and objectives have been established that the plan is intended to meet and by which its performance will be measured. A financial plan has been agreed to, establishing the amount of money available for investment. Current demographic and transportation system data has been collected and analyzed. Forecasts of future system demand have been developed. The public and the MPO decision makers should have been involved throughout each of these activities, providing for a sequential buy-in.

The development and testing of alternatives may follow a stepwise pattern, depending in part on the size and complexity of the metropolitan area. An initial step may be a broad allocation of resources to general areas of need identified in goal and objective statements. Following an earlier example, in which a high priority was assigned to maintaining the highway and bridge infrastructure in a state of good repair, with objectives of reducing the number of deficient bridges and miles of poor pavements, a specified number of dollars or percentage of programs could be assigned to this use. For example, "40 percent of NHS and STP funds and 50 percent of State highway funds will be utilized in the first ten years of the plan for the rehabilitation and/or replacement of deficient bridges and pavements. This may be modified if pavement and/or bridge sufficiency objectives are reached earlier." The same step would be taken in relation to each set of goals and objectives. Thus, allocations would be made for safety improvements, congestion management, freight mobility, environmental protection, and so forth.

This is an important point for involvement and review by MPO decision makers. There should be agreement that the broad funding allocation mirrors the adopted plan goals. The cost of trade-offs will begin to become more clear. The planner must remain flexible as adjustments to the allocations are considered. For example, an elected official may discover that assigning the highest priority to infrastructure maintenance results in not being able to fund a new river crossing in his community within a ten-year timeframe. Plan objectives may be modified to achieve a better fit to available resources. It may be useful for the planner to provide a variety of options to the public and decision makers. The process of reducing these options to a final draft plan can allow for reaffirmation of goals and objectives.

The next step is to begin identifying actions. In many cases, that will involve selecting specific projects for inclusion in the plan. In some instances, however, the plan may simply identify deficient corridors or subareas, and include an agreement to develop a solution based on the outcome of an MIS (discussed in a subsequent section). The plan may state "Corridor A is identified as a major capacity deficiency. There is a commitment to conduct a planning study to identify the best solution for personal and freight mobility in the corridor within 3 years, and to initiate construction of the selected solution within the first 10 year phase of the Plan." There will be parts of the plan that commit to investment but do not identify specific projects, such as pavement rehabilitation or transit operations. Finally, actions may be identified that are desired, but they are outside the scope of the implementing agencies. An example may be the construction of an intermodal rail-truck freight terminal, which will be constructed by the railroad if they determine the market will support it.

The performance of the transportation system must then be evaluated with the inclusion of the selected actions. This is an iterative process, as improvements are sequentially added to the network, and their composite effect is modeled and analyzed. The planner is referred to the discussion of the metropolitan transportation system and the need to identify the effect of improvements to one subsystem on other components. In air quality nonattainment areas, this analysis must be accompanied by a conformity analysis, determining the effect on emissions of the proposed "build" plan. An equity analysis may also be conducted to determine whether there are disproportionate effects on low-income or minority neighborhoods or other selected communities of interest.

This may also be the point at which the planner discusses a *vision plan* with decision makers. It will become clear what actions can be accommodated in the fiscally constrained plan and what is likely be left out. As discussed earlier, the vision plan may include actions for which there is a significant degree of support, but for which funding cannot be identified. The vision plan must be clearly identified and explained as such. It is valuable to formally include these initiatives. Doing so tells the public that actions they may have supported have not been ignored, provides an orderly basis for moving projects into the plan as new funding is identified or as updates occur, and may create a catalyst for developing an innovative financing mechanism not previously identified.

Decision Making and Plan Adoption

As the draft plan begins to take shape, it should be reviewed both with technical advisory committees and through the public participation process. The planner must be able to present the draft plan in a way that makes clear the relationship between the proposed system improvements and the investment goals. Forecasts of system performance must be provided on a variety of scales. These will include measures of congestion as applied to both personal and freight mobility, infrastructure sufficiency, air quality and other environmental factors, and measures of effect on the regional economy

Table 12–6 Performance Objective for Plan Evaluation

SELECTED CORE MEASURES		2015 Performance Goals and Qualifications	Change, 1996 to 2015		
			Comparable Progress Scenario, Steady State Funding	Full Implementation Scenario	
TRANSPORTATION SERVICE					
Access	Percent of PM Peak Hour Trips Transit Accessible	Increase from 1996 levels.	✗	✓✓	*
	Percent of PM Peak Hour Trips with Non-Drive Advantage	Increase from 1996 levels.	✓	✓✓✓✓	*
	Percent of PM Peak Hour Trips Accessible by Bicycle and Walking	Increase from 1996 levels, and improve quality of facilities.	✓✓	✓✓	*
Accessibility	Travel Time between Representative Locations by best mode on typical PM peak hour, including exposure to incident delay	As with congestion measures, maintain close to 1996 times and increase predictability.	✗		*
Congestion	Daily Recurring Excess Person Hours of Delay	Maintain close to 1996 levels.	✗✗✗✗		*
	Excess Person Hours of Peak Hour Delay Per PMT	Maintain close to 1996 levels.	✗✗✗✗		*
	Daily Excess Vehicle Hours of Delay by Truck	Maintain close to 1996 per VMT.	✗✗✗✗		*
Flexibility	Reserve Capacity on the Urban Expressway and Arterial System (PM Peak Hour Vehicle Miles of Capacity)	Accept some decline in exchange for greater reliability & route, mode choice.	✗✗	✗	*
RESOURCE REQUIREMENTS					
Safety	Estimated Annual Societal Cost of Transportation Accidents, Millions of 1996 $	Reduce from 1996 per capita levels.	✗	✓	*
Energy	Daily Fuel Consumption (thousands of gallons)	Reduce from 1996 levels.	✗	✓	*
Economic Cost	Annual Vehicle Ownership and Operating Costs for Autos and Trucks, Millions of 1996 $	Reduce total monetary costs, public and private, direct and indirect, from 1996 per capita levels.	✗	✓	*
	Other Monetary Costs of Transport: Highway and Transit Facilities and Service, Parking Facilities, Environmental Damage, Millions of 1996 $		✗✗	✓	*
EXTERNAL EFFECTS					
Air Quality	Daily Hydrocarbon (HC) Emissions (kg)	Reduce well below 1996 levels.	✓✓✓✓	✓✓✓✓	*
	Daily Nitrogen Oxide (NO_x) Emissions (kg)	Reduce well below 1996 levels.	✓✓✓	✓✓✓	*
Land Use	Residential Use Traffic Conflict: Miles at LOC "E" or "F"	Reduce from 1996 levels.	✓	✓✓✓	*
	Arterial Land Access Conflict: Miles at LOC "E" or "F"	Reduce from 1996 levels.	✓	✓✓✓	*
	Dislocation of Existing Residences and Businesses	Enhance rather than dislocate existing properties.			*
	Community Quality of Life: Factors that reflect community quality of life in the central cities, inner & outer suburbs, small cities & villages, & rural areas	Contribute significantly and explicitly.		✓	
Environment	Number of Major Environmental Issues to be Resolved with Existing Commitments	Use transportation investment to enhance the environment.			*
Economic	How Does the Transportation System Support the Economic Health of the Region?	Contribute significantly and explicitly.		✓	

✓✓✓✓	Positive impact > 50%, 2015 relative to 1990
✓✓✓	Positive impact between 20% and 50%
✓✓	Positive impact between 10% and 20%
✓	Positive impact < 10% or not quantified
	Negligible impact expected
✗	Negative impact < 10% or not quantified
✗✗	Negative impact between 10% and 20%
✗✗✗	Negative impact between 20% and 50%
✗✗✗✗	Negative impact > 50%, 2015 relative to trend
*	Indicates impact has been quantified

Notes:
1. Quantification of many impacts is dependent upon the recommended actions related to the Northway. A Major Investment Study is required to determine the extent to which a major highway or transit investment is warranted in this critical corridor.
2. The Comparable Progress Scenario, with Steady State Funding, and the Full Implementation Scenario are described in the Budget section of this document.

Source: *New Visions for Capital District Transportation*, Regional Transportation Plan, Albany, N.Y.

and urban growth and development. A sample display of performance objectives is shown in Table 12–6. Remember that the concern of both the public and its elected leaders is not the plan itself, but the resulting performance of the transportation system and its effect on their communities. The planner must demonstrate that the proposed investments will lead toward the desired performance, allowing for expected uncertainty.

Once the final draft plan has been reviewed by the technical advisory committees and public participation structure, it will be brought to the MPO Policy Board for final approval. While this is an overtly political process, to the extent that the Board

Table 12–6   Performance Objective for Plan Evaluation *(continued)*

		Current Condition	2015 Performance Objective	Change 1996 to 2015
INFRASTRUCTURE				
HIGHWAY	Max % of Interstate roads in poor condition	5%	0%	✓✓✓✓
	Max. % of other NHS roads in poor condition	12%	< 5%	✓✓✓✓
	Max. % of other principal arterials in poor condition	15%	< 10%	✓✓✓
	Max. % of other federal-aid roads in poor condition	17%	< 12%	✓✓✓
	Max. % of local (non federal-aid) roads in poor condition	9%	< 15%	See note 1
	Max % of all roads in poor or fair condition	22%	< 20%	✓
	% of busiest 400 intersections that accommodate the mobility-impaired	0-5%	80-100%	✓✓✓✓
	% of highway signs meeting visibility standards	0-5%	80-100%	✓✓✓✓
	% reduction of high speed Amtrak grade crossings		100%	✓✓✓✓
	% reduction of freight main line grade crossings		> 25%	✓✓✓
	% reduction of vertical, horizontal and load restrictions on NHS and high-truck state routes		80-100%	✓✓✓✓
	Lane-miles of state road reconstructed for multi-modal accommodation		550	✓✓✓✓
	Lane-miles of non-state road reconstruction for multi-modal accommodation		550	✓✓✓✓
	Center-line miles with full bicycle accommodation		> 353	✓✓✓✓
	Centerline miles of system with Intelligent Transportation System features (smart signals, message signs, incident management, etc...)		260	✓✓✓✓
BRIDGE	Max. % of state bridges rated deficient	38%	<20%	✓✓✓✓
	Max. % of local bridge rated deficient	42%	<20%	✓✓✓✓
	Max. % of all bridges rate seriously deficient		0%	✓✓✓✓
	% reduction of vertical restrictions on bridges over freight main lines		80-100%	✓✓✓✓
TRANSIT	% of equipment that is over age	0%	0%	✓✓✓✓
	% of fleet that is wheelchair accessible	12%	100%	✓✓✓✓
	Number of shelters at human service facilities	12	All	✓✓✓✓
SERVICE				
TRANSIT	% of service that is wheelchair accessible	7	100%	✓✓✓✓
HUMAN SERVICE	Number of agencies coordinating service	7	all	✓✓✓✓

✓✓✓✓	Positive impact greater than 50%, 2015 relative to 1996.
✓✓✓	Positive impact between 20% and 50%.
✓✓	Positive impact between 10% and 20%.
✓	Positive Impact less than 10% or not quantified.
	Negligible impact expected.

Notes:
1. While 15% poor is defined as acceptable, forecasts indicated that current conditions could generally be maintained.

Source: *New Visions for Capital District Transportation,* Regional Transportation Plan, Albany, N.Y.

has been involved in the development of the plan and has provided approval for various actions during the process, final approval may be easily managed.

The typical plan development process, incorporating each of the elements discussed in this chapter, is depicted in Figure 12–5.

A decision will be made on the physical publication of the plan. Most MPOs publish their plans in more than one form. There is typically a short version relying heavily on maps and graphics that is easily comprehensible by the public. There may also be an executive summary, a full printed plan, and various technical appendices. The planner must then turn to implementation activities, as described in subsequent sections. These actions and strategies should be included as a closing chapter in the plan document. This helps make both the public and decision makers aware of the fact that the plan is intended to guide actions, that it is not in itself a final product.

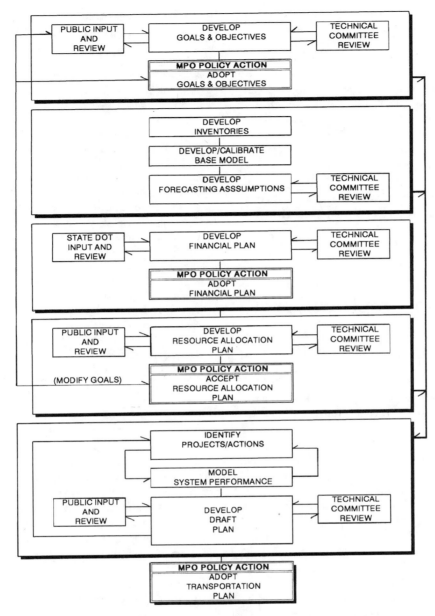

Figure 12–5   The Urban Planning Process

Major Investment Study

As noted earlier, the plan may state a commitment to improving travel in a given corridor or subarea; but it may recognize that more work is needed before choosing the best solution. ISTEA and its subsequent regulations (23 CFR 450.318) established a process that filled the gap between the plan and the NEPA-driven project development process—the MIS. The MIS, while conducted under the auspices of the MPO, was designed to refine the plan and lead to a decision on the design concept and scope of the investment. A cooperative process is mandated to fairly evaluate a variety of modal solutions for a given problem.

TEA-21 includes language specifically requiring the elimination of the MIS as a stand-alone process, but also requiring the promulgation of new regulations to include its essential elements. Chapter 20 reviews this legal issue in greater detail. Regardless of the ultimate outcome of these new regulations, the planner should recognize that it is important to have an open process that broadly examines corridor solutions without preconceived biases.

The MIS is reserved for situations where it is clear that a large investment will be required and offers a rigorous method to evaluate the trade-offs, for example, between additional expressway lanes, HOV lanes, or fixed guideway rail transit. Just as the public and stakeholder groups were involved in the development of the plan, this same requirement exists on a more focused basis for the MIS. In addition, environmental resource and permitting agencies are brought to the table. The benefit of involving these parties early in the scoping process is that controversies that tend to arise later and delay project development schedules may be avoided.

Implementation: The Transportation Improvement Program

In metropolitan areas, the primary way that the transportation plan is implemented is through the sequential addition of appropriate projects to the MPO's Transportation Improvement Program (TIP). Required by federal law, the TIP must meet a number of criteria established in law and regulation. (Table 12–7.)

Table 12–7   Federal Requirements for the Transportation Improvement Program
23CFR Part 450.324

- Cover a minimum time period of three years and be updated at least every two years.
- Allow for reasonable opportunity for public comment on the proposed TIP.
- Be financially constrained by year and include a financial plan. The state and transit operator must provide the MPO with estimates of available federal and state funds.
- Include all federal-aid projects inside the metropolitan area boundary funded under Title 23 (FHWA) and the Federal Transit Act.
- Projects must be consistent with the transportation plan.
- Include all projects of regional significance regardless of fund source where federal approvals are required and all other projects of regional significance for informational purposes.
- Represent a priority listing of projects—at a minimum assigning priority in order of program year.
- In air quality nonattainment areas, demonstrate conformity to the approved SIP.
- Identify the criteria and projects for prioritizing implementation of transportation plan elements.
- Provide detailed information on project description, phasing, and funding.

This capital program is subject to the same MPO cooperative decision-making process as that described for the transportation plan. This establishes the opportunity for MPO participants to understand the continuity of the process. They will move from adopting the goals and objectives that drive the plan, to adopting a financial plan that constrains it, to the plan itself, and then to the selection and programming of projects that implement the adopted plan. While the plan is not the only source of TIP candidate projects, it must guide the establishment of investment priorities. Other sources of candidate projects include the output of pavement, bridge, safety, and other management systems, which systematically identify current system deficiencies; and solicitations from private transit operators, local jurisdictions, and the public, which may identify needs that have been otherwise missed.

The relationship between the plan and the TIP development process is anchored in the methodology that is used to identify project priorities. For example, the plan may not identify specific pavement rehabilitation projects. But if it states a goal of maintaining the highway infrastructure in a state of good repair, and an objective of reducing the lane miles of poor pavement by seven percent over the first ten years of the plan period, then the TIP will reflect that priority through the inclusion of appropriate pavement projects.

Some MPOs use a goal-oriented project screening and rating system. A set of screening criteria and a point system are developed that reflect the goal structure of the transportation plan. A sample point system is shown in Table 12–8. Points are awarded in concert with the importance of the objective to be accomplished. Candidate projects are solicited and passed through a preliminary screening process that eliminates those that do not meet defined threshold conditions. Projects that pass the screening are then scored and ranked. This provides an ordered list from which the draft TIP will be developed. It must be understood by both the planner and the decision makers that the rank-ordered list is not automatically converted into the program. The scoring system provides guidance, but it does not make choices. Projects that clearly meet plan objectives should rise to the top, and those that do not should drop to the bottom. But developing the draft program will take a great deal more work.

While TEA-21 continues a good deal of flexibility in the use of federal-aid fund sources, TIP projects must still be matched to available funds. Fiscal constraint requires that projects must fit into the financial plan. A high-cost project, particularly in a smaller metropolitan area with a modest allocation of funds, may distort priorities for a given year. Air quality conformity findings may also alter the final choice of projects, as may concerns about social or political equity. There are also practical considerations related to producing the program. Implementing agencies, whether the state DOT or local jurisdictions, must be consulted with regard to project scheduling to avoid imposing unrealistic design and letting dates.

A typical structure uses a subcommittee of the MPO Planning or Technical Committee to work with staff to develop the draft TIP. The process may seem akin to completing a jigsaw puzzle, as the rank-ordered project list is balanced against the various constraints noted above. The draft TIP must show a clear relation to the transportation plan, and it must also demonstrate how project implementation is prioritized.

Once the draft TIP is accepted, the public must be given the opportunity to review it and comment. Even if the plan was recently updated and a robust public involvement process was used, the planner may discover a different public response to the draft TIP. People may not understand planning concepts as well as the proposed construction of a project in their neighborhood. For example, support in the planning process for enhancing freight mobility through the construction of an intermodal freight terminal may turn into opposition in the neighborhood that is adjacent to the selected site. The planner must be prepared to address the comments on the draft TIP while avoiding getting involved in controversy over individual projects. It may help to keep the community involved throughout the process and to educate people about the planning continuum from the plan, through MIS (where it is utilized), to TIP development, to project development activities including NEPA requirements. However, the planner must also be honest that inclusion of a project in the TIP represents a commitment by the MPO and the implementing agency; and that while specific concerns will be addressed in the project development process, there may be a reluctance to withdraw the project entirely once it is included.

A final draft TIP that reflects any changes made in response to comments from stakeholders and the public is then presented to the MPO Policy Committee. Upon adoption, it will be incorporated into the Statewide Transportation Improvement Program (STIP) required by TEA-21. An extract from a TIP is shown in Table 12–9.

Table 12–8 1998–2002 Transportation Improvement Program Project Scoring System

INFRASTRUCTURE MAINTENANCE	POINTS
[Maximum score 35 points]	
Bridge Rehabilitation	
> Priority deficient [per State DOT standard] within TIP timeframe	35
> Not priority deficient	15
Bridge Replacement	
> Priority deficient [per State DOT standard] within TIP timeframe	35
> Not priority deficient	15
Pavement Rehabilitation	
> Sufficiency rating Poor (5 or less) and AADT>10000	25
> Sufficiency rating Poor (5 or less) and AADT<10000	15
> Sufficiency rating Fair (6) and AADT>10000	15
> Sufficiency rating Fair (6) and AADT<10000	5
Transit Vehicle Replacement	
> Transit coach, age > 12 years	30
> Paratransit vehicle included in ADA Plan, age > 5 years	30
> Paratransit vehicle not included in ADA Plan	5
SYSTEM SAFETY	
[Maximum score 25 points]	
Highway/Street Projects	
> Project correcting statistically verified High Accident Location	25
> Railroad grade crossing elimination	20
> Geometric improvement with accident reduction potential	10
Median barrier where there is a history of crossover accidents	
Safety widening	
Center bidirectional turn lane	
Intersection turn lanes	
Alignment or sight distance improvements	
Signing/pavement marking improvements	
Installation of warranted signal	
Guiderail improvement	
Transit Projects	
> Bus stop turnouts in high traffic volume locations	20
Terminal or bus stop improvements	10
Loading area safety improvements	10
> Maintenance facility safety improvements required by OSHA or local co	20
Maintenance facility safety improvements not mandated	10
Pedestrian and Bicycle Projects	
> Construct pedestrian or bicycle facilities that are recognized as high priority actions in the BMTS Pedestrian and Bicycle Plan	20
> Construct pedestrian or bicycle facilities that are recognized as medium priority actions in the BMTS Pedestrian and Bicycle Plan	10
> Construct pedestrian or bicycle facilities that are recognized as low priority actions in the BMTS Pedestrian and Bicycle Plan	5
SYSTEM EFFICIENCY (TSM/TDM)	
[Maximum score 15 points]	
Highway Projects on NHS/principal arterials	
> Reduce current (or forecasted in TIP timeframe) LOS E/F vhd	15
Ramp metering	
Interchange improvements	
Construct/improve park and ride facility	
Implement incident management plan	
Highway Projects on surface arterials	
> Reduce current (or forecasted in TIP timeframe) LOS E/F vhd	10
Signal progression/optimization	
Turn lanes/channelization	
Access control/parking prohibition	
Transit Projects	10
Reduce peak period headway on congested routes	
Reduce transit travel time	
Add express bus service on arterials	
Improve intermodal transfer facilities	
SYSTEM EXPANSION	
[Maximum score 15 points]	
Highway Projects	5-15
> Reduce LOS E/F vehicle hours of delay per standards	
Construct arterial lane	
Corridor preservation activity	
Construct new bridge	
Transit Projects	5-15
> Expand fixed route bus service	
Construct surface arterial bus lane	
Expand bus fleet to serve enlarged service area	
> Expand paratransit service	
Expand paratransit fleet to increase service hours or area	
INTERMODAL FACILITIES AND GOODS MOVEMENT	
[Maximum score 10 points]	
Highway/Bridge projects on designated truck network	10
> Bridge rehabilitation/replacement which eliminates substandard clearance	
> Bridge rehabilitation/replacement which eliminates load posting	
Highway/Bridge projects anywhere on network	5
> Bridge rehabilitation/replacement over railroad to achieve clearance for double-stack trains	
> Highway rehabilitation which improves truck access to terminals	
> New highway facilities which significantly improve truck access to designated network	
OTHER FACTORS	
[Maximum score 10 points]	
> ISTEA enhancement activity	10
> Accessibility included in adopted ADA plan	10
> Air quality improvement/emissions reduction	5
> Private financing (minimum 25% contribution)	5

Source: *Binghamton Metropolitan Transportation Study 1998–2002.*

| | | | Project cost in $ millions
P=Scoping, PE, Design
R=Right of Way Acquisition | | | C=Construction   T=Total Cost
I=Construction Inspection | | | |
| | | STP
Fund
Source | Obligated
Element
FFY 1997 | Annual
Element
FFY 1998 | FFY 1999 | FFY 2000 | FFY 2001 | FFY 2002 | 1998-2002
Program
Total |
Project Code	Project Description/Type								
STP-9	Bicycle Plan Implementation	Small							0.224 T
	• Bicycle route signing	Urban							0.000 P
	• Bicycle route map								0.000 R
	PIN 9752.27			0.200 C					0.200 C
				0.024 I					0.024 I
STP-10	US 11 (Front St) R&P	Small							4.367 T
	• I-81 Exit 5 to Broome Comm College	Urban							0.000 P
	• Full R&P		0.084 R						0.000 R
	Town of Dickinson			3.899 C					3.899 C
	PIN 9043.23			0.468 I					0.468 I
STP-11	Clinton Street Reconstruction	Small							4.400 T
	• Front St to Glenwood Avenue	Urban							0.000 P
	City of Binghamton			3.929 C					3.929 C
				0.471 I					0.471 I
STP-12	Conrail over Old Vestal Road	Small							1.133 T
	• Remove RR overpass,								
	Improve road alignment	Urban	0.288 P						0.000 P
	Old Vestal Road, NY 201 to Campus Plaza		0.100 R						0.000 R
	• Intersection Improvements, Turn Lanes			1.012 C					1.012 C
	PIN 9751.68			0.121 I					0.121 I
STP-13	NY 12A over Thomas Creek	Flex							4.951 T
	• Replace bridge			0.118 P					0.118 P
	• Widen to 3 lane section			0.169 R					0.169 R
	Town of Chenango					4.016 C			4.016 C
	PIN 9002.09					0.482 I			0.482 I
						0.166 F			0.166 F
STP-14	Main Street over Apalachin Creek	Small							1.393 T
	Bridge Rehabilitation	Urban	0.050 P	0.133 P					0.133 P
	Town of Owego		0.010 R	0.010 R					0.010 R
	PIN 6752.45					1.117 C			1.117 C
						0.133 I			0.133 I
STP-15	NY 7, Sandy Beach to CR 313	Flex							2.533 T
	Town of Conklin								0.000 P
	• R&P			0.014 R					0.014 R
	• Widen to 3 lane section					2.249 C			2.249 C
	PIN 9306.63					0.270 I			0.270 I
STP-16	Harry L Drive R&P	Flex							4.478 T
	Stella Ireland Rd to Toys R Us								0.000 P
	Village of Johnson City			0.078 R					0.078 R
	PIN 9751.87					3.924 C			3.924 C
						0.476 I			0.476 I

Source: *Binghamton Metropolitan Transportation Study 1998–2002.*

The TIP is a not a static document that can then be ignored until the next update cycle. The planning agency must invest resources in monitoring the implementation of TIP projects in terms of both schedule and cost. This requires close communication with the implementing agencies. Schedule changes and cost overruns or savings make program management an important task. Effective program management will lead to the most efficient use of resources. The TIP may be amended by the MPO between update cycles, and these amendments are then carried into the STIP.

The Continuing Process

The urban transportation planning process is one of continuous analysis and reconsideration. As noted earlier, the need for updating the transportation plan results from the inability to forecast the future with certainty. The MPO or planning agency must have in place processes that monitor all of the basic determinants of the plan.

- Is population accurately following forecasts in terms of both numbers and distribution?

- Is the same true of economic activity and employment?

- Are land use decisions following the framework on which the plan's assumptions are based?

- Have there been changes in resource availability that are significantly different from the adopted financial plan?

It is equally necessary to monitor system performance in terms of all modes. The planner is interested in both the degree to which background growth of each mode is following forecasts and the extent that system operation is responding to the implementation of plan elements as predicted.

- Is traffic volume on key facilities within a reasonable range of predictions? How about vehicle- or person-hours of delay and other congestion measures?

- Is transit ridership on various routes and modes within a reasonable range of predicted utilization?

- Have crash rates responded to safety initiatives?

- Have travel demand management programs had the expected effect on travel behavior?

- Have travel pricing programs had the expected effect on travel behavior?

- Has the installation of ITS technology had the expected effect on traffic operations?

- Has the construction of new pedestrian or bicycle facilities resulted in the forecasted shift of person travel to those modes?

Finally, the political climate changes over time. Support for specific actions in the plan, particularly major investments, may change as a result. The planner must recognize that implementation of such an action may become impossible, even if it is still technically justified.

The Annual Effectiveness Review utilized by the Wilmington Area Planning Council, discussed earlier, is a good example of such a monitoring mechanism. The MPO's Unified Planning Work Program, through inclusion of technical studies and monitoring activities, provides for the continuing work that will analyze transportation needs and possibly discover new ones once the plan is adopted.

The planning agency may begin with a predetermined schedule of plan update activities, on a five-year cycle for example. However, by continuously monitoring the information and issues noted above, a decision may be made that an update should be initiated sooner or that it can be delayed because conditions are relatively static.

References

Binkley, Lisa and Sarah Jo Peterson. "TransLinks 21: Description and Alternative Land Use and Transportation Policies." Madison, Wis.: Wisconsin Department of Transportation, 1993.

Boyd, David and Amy Gronlund. "The Ithaca Model: A Practical Experience in Community Based Planning," *Transportation Research Record, No. 1499.* Washington, D.C.: National Academy Press, 1995.

Capital District Transportation Committee. "Transportation Improvement Program Project Selection Process," *Metropolitan Planning Technical Report, No. 4.* Washington, D.C.: Federal Highway Administration, 1994.

Capital District Transportation Committee. "New Visions for Capital District Transportation: Regional Transportation Plan." Albany, N.Y.: CDTC, 1997.

Center for Urban Transportation Research. "A New Strategic Urban Transportation Planning Process." Tampa, Fla.: University of South Florida, 1995.

Codd, Ned and C. Michael Walton. "Performance Measures and Framework for Decision Making Under the National Transportation System," *Transportation Research Record, No. 1518.* Washington, D.C.: National Academy Press, 1996.

"Consideration of the 15 Factors in the Metropolitan Planning Process," *National Cooperative Highway Research Program Synthesis 217.* Washington, D.C.: National Academy Press, 1995.

Decorla-Souza, Patrick. "The Impact of Alternative Development Patterns on Highway System Performance," *Metropolitan Planning Technical Report, No. 1.* Washington, D.C.: Federal Highway Administration, 1993.

Decorla-Souza, Patrick and others. "Evaluating the Options in Urban Areas with Financial Constraints," *Transportation Research Record, No. 1518.* Washington, D.C.: National Academy Press, 1996.

Federal Highway Administration. "A Guide to Metropolitan Transportation Planning Under ISTEA," Report No. FHWA-PD-95-031. Washington, D.C.: FHWA, 1995.

Federal Highway Administration and Federal Transit Administration. "Innovations in Public Involvement for Transportation Planning." Washington, D.C.: FHWA and FTA, 1994.

Federal Transit Administration. *Working Together on Transportation Planning: An Approach to Collaborative Decision Making,* Report No. FTA-DC-26-6013-95-1. Washington, D.C.: FTA, 1995.

Giuliano, Genevieve. "Relationships Between Urban Form and Transportation: Implications for Long Range Planning," *Metropolitan Planning Technical Report, No. 1.* Washington, D.C.: Federal Highway Administration, 1993.

Howe, Linda K., and Richard Brail. "Intermodal Surface Transportation Efficiency Act and Interactive Transportation Planning and Decision Support: A New Conceptual Model," *Transportation Research Record, No. 1466.* Washington, D.C.: National Academy Press, 1994.

Lebeaux, Pamela. "A System That Serves Everyone: Attracting Non-Traditional Participants into the Regional Transportation Planning Process." Washington, D.C.: National Capital Region Transportation Planning Board, 1996.

Mackett, Roger. "Land Use Transportation Models for Policy Analysis," *Transportation Research Record, No. 1466.* Washington, D.C.: National Academy Press, 1994.

Metropolitan Transportation Commission. "Maximizing Regional Transportation Investments in the ISTEA Era: A Guide for Programming ISTEA's Flexible Funds," *Metropolitan Planning Technical Report, No. 4.* Washington, D.C.: Federal Highway Administration, 1994.

"Multimodal Transportation: Development of a Performance-Based Planning Process," *National Cooperative Highway Research Program,* Project 8-32(2)A. Washington, D.C.: National Academy Press, 1997.

National Academy Press. "Response of Small Urban Area MPOs to ISTEA," *National Cooperative Highway Research Program Synthesis 252.* Washington, D.C.: National Academy Press, 1998.

Nelson, Dick and Don Shakow. "Least Cost Planning for Metropolitan Transportation Decision Making," *Transportation Research Record, No. 1499.* Washington, D.C.: National Academy Press, 1995.

U.S. Advisory Commission on Intergovernmental Relations. "Planning Progress: Addressing ISTEA Requirements in Metropolitan Planning Areas." Washington, D.C.: U.S. Advisory Commission on Intergovernmental Relations, 1997.

Wilmington Area Planning Council. "Annual Effectiveness Review of the 2020 Metropolitan Transportation Plan." Wilmington, Del.: WILMAPCO, 1997.

CHAPTER 13
Urban Transit

Thomas F. Larwin,[1] P.E.
General Manager
San Diego Metropolitan Transit Development Board

Introduction

Public transportation systems are the common carriers of passengers in urban areas. As such, public transportation is not a distinct technology, but an operational and institutional concept related to the movement of groups of people. It relies upon highway and railroad engineering extensively, and it applies the operations and management methods employed by common carriers for other transport modes.

This chapter provides information on the physical and operational characteristics of urban transit systems. It defines the important terms; overviews transit's role in the urban setting; surveys physical characteristics such as rights-of-way, vehicles, stops, and performance; and presents service planning guidelines, fare pricing concepts, and operational procedures. It then describes transit planning methods and the economic and management aspects that define transit's role in providing urban mobility. References for further reading are set forth at the end of the chapter, and footnote sources offer the reader opportunities for extended study.

The reader should be particularly familiar with the Transit Cooperative Research Program (TCRP), which issued its first report in 1993; the TCRP is managed by the Transportation Research Board (TRB) and funded by the Federal Transit Administration (FTA). A wealth of new research and data emerging from the TCRP relates to current and evolving transit procedures, practices, trends, and improvements. Many of these TCRP reports are used as references and are cited at the end of this chapter. Primary statistical references are also cited and include the American Public Transit Association's annual *Fact Book,* Canadian Urban Transit Association's annual *Transit Fact Book,* FTA's annual *Transit Profiles,* International Union of Public Transport's annual *Urban Public Transport Statistics,* and U.S. Department of Transportation (DOT), Bureau of Transportation Statistics' *Annual Reports.*

The reader is referred to other chapters for further details on transportation planning studies (Chapter 5), travel demand and modal choice models (Chapter 6), transit capacity (Chapter 7), major investment studies (Chapter 9), intercity passenger systems (Chapter 11), and off-street terminals (Chapter 18).

Transit in Cities

Urban transit is an essential public service. It is necessary for the modern metropolitan area to function, and it serves several primary purposes:

- It increases transportation capacity in heavily traveled corridors.

- It reduces reliance on car trips.

- It supports and fosters densely developed areas, especially city centers.

- It provides mobility for the elderly, handicapped, and others who are unable to drive.

---

[1] Thomas F. Larwin acknowledges the significant contributions made by Herbert S. Levinson as author of Chapter 5, "Urban Mass Transit Systems," in the 1992 *Transportation Planning Handbook* and the use of material from that edition in this update.

Strategic Role

The role and importance of public transit varys among cities throughout the world. Relevant factors affecting its use include: (1) per capita incomes and car ownership, (2) patterns and intensities of land uses, (3) employment and population concentrations and compactness, (4) topography, (5) adequacy of the street and highway system, (6) parking availability and pricing, and (7) the quantity and quality of transit service provided.

Local policies have a strong, direct effect on transit's importance in the community. Transit can influence urban form, and the design of the urban environment can encourage transit use and reduce dependence on the automobile. Public policies can support more compact urban form, a greater land use mix, and transit-friendly design.

Canada and Europe provide numerous examples of cities that have placed an emphasis on transit investments and supportive land use and development patterns. In the United States, cities such as Portland, Sacramento, and San Diego are pursuing "transit-oriented developments" (TODs). These provide walkable neighborhoods and easy to access urban transit.

In Hong Kong, with unusually high densities, major physical barriers, limited road and living space, and low car ownership, public transit carries more than 85 percent of all person trips. In Beijing and Shanghai, public transport accounts for about 30 percent of all person trips; this figure increases to more than 75 percent when walking and bicycle trips are excluded. By contrast, in most U.S. urban areas, transit accounts for about 2 percent of the total person trips. Table 13–1 provides comparisons to other European countries, showing that the United States has the lowest transit use (as a percentage) of total trips.

Even so, the usage figures in Table 13–1 mask the importance of public transit in serving certain travel markets. This table also shows the proportion of commuter trips in the United States using transit, and it is 5 percent on a national basis and 12 percent for central cities. For example, transit vehicles carry two-thirds or more of all peak-hour, peak-direction travelers entering (or leaving) the downtown areas of large cities such as New York, Chicago, Toronto, and Montreal; and they account for more than one- third of all travelers entering the central business districts of many U.S. cities. In addition, transit serves many school and personal business trips in large central cities.

Benefits

Transit provides important benefits to its riders, the adjacent land development, and the community, such as the following.

- *Social benefits.* Transit acts as a "safety net" for individuals who cannot afford an automobile, who are handicapped, or who are too young or old to drive.

- *Congestion relief benefits.* Transit reduces the numbers of vehicles on streets and highways, especially in high travel demand corridors, and into high activity centers.

- *Environmental benefits.* Transit makes contributions to reductions in air pollutants.

- *Economic benefits.* Transit is a significantly less expensive alternative than using an automobile at a total cost of $0.36 to $0.46 per km (American Automobile Association, 1995).

- *Energy benefits.* Transit reduces oil consumption.

Table 13–1   Public Transit's Role in Urban Trip Making

Country	Percentage of Total Person Trips
Italy	21
Switzerland	20
England	20
Denmark	14
Austria	13
France	12
Germany	11
Sweden	11
Netherlands	8
Norway	7
United States	2[1]
As a percentage of commuter trips:	
Nationwide	5[2]
Metropolitan areas	6[2]
Central cities	12[2]
Suburbs	3[2]

[1] 1995 Nationwide Personal Transportation Survey.
[2] Mode used to commute to work, 1990.

Sources: John Pucher and Christian Lefevre, *The Urban Transport Crisis in Europe and North America,* Houndmills, Basingstroke, Hampshire, and London: MacMillan Press, 1996. Alan Pisarski, *Commuting in America,* Lansdowne, Va.: Eno Transportation Foundation, Inc., 1996. *Our Nation's Travel, 1995 NPTS Early Results Report,* Washington, D.C.: Federal Highway Administration, 1997.

Defining Transit

Detailed definitions of urban public transportation are contained in a glossary published by the U.S. DOT's Bureau of Transportation Statistics in 1996.[2] Many of these definitions can be defined according to general function, technology, right-of-way, and type of service.

Functions

Urban public transportation consists of the movement of people in vehicles that are available to the general public at usually prescribed rates of fare. In this regard, it is to be distinguished from private passenger transportation, in which people travel on foot or in vehicles not available to the general public, as well as from freight transportation. Public transportation has two subcategories—transit and paratransit.

Transit (or mass transportation) is public transportation for the carriage of passengers and their incidental baggage, operating on established routes and fixed schedules, and serving prescribed stops at prescribed rates of fare. Transit includes such modes as local bus, semirapid bus, electric trolley bus, streetcar, light rail transit, rail rapid transit, and regional (commuter) rail.

Paratransit encompasses diverse forms of public transportation that fill the niche between private transportation and transit. It includes such modal families as internal circulators (e.g., elevators, people movers in controlled environments), subscription transportation (e.g., vanpools, school buses), for-hire transportation (e.g., taxis, rental cars), and public paratransit (e.g., jitneys, dial-a-ride).

Right-of-Way and Technologies

The various forms of transportation are generally categorized into a number of discrete modes. There are three defining characteristics of mode of transportation: right-of-way, technology, and type of service.[3] As a convenience, the general technology of the vehicle is often the only characteristic used in distinguishing between modes, but the situation is really more complex. For example, the bus—commonly spoken of as a distinct mode of transit—is actually a generic term that in reality has many variations and applications. Buses can operate on diverse types of right-of-way (such as city streets in mixed traffic, reserved lanes, or exclusive busways), vary in their technology (being powered by diesel engines, alternative fuels, and electricity), and provide different kinds of service (such as locals, expresses, short-range shuttles, or charters). Thus, what is apparently one mode is really several related modes centered around one general technological family. This complexity should be kept in mind in any reference to a particular "mode."

Right-of-way-related definitions are as follows:

- *Right-of-way* refers to the land used by transit systems. It may be shared (street transit), semiexclusive, or semirapid transit (e.g., light rail transit, buses, and high-occupancy vehicles on reserved lanes), and exclusive or rapid transit.

- *Guideway* or infrastructure refers to the right-of-way plus the special improvements required for operations (e.g., tracks, power distribution, control system). For purposes of this chapter, this term also refers to any technology that is "guided" by a rail(s), beam, or side curbs.

Technologies relate to the *vehicles* or the rolling stock operating on streets and highways or guideways that furnish the actual passenger transportation. Transit revenue service includes individually scheduled units, which may be a single vehicle or a *train* of vehicles. The following vehicles are commonly used:

---

[2] *Transportation Expressions* (Washington, D.C.: U.S. Department of Transportation, Bureau of Transportation Statistics, 1996); *Transportation Acronym Guide* (Washington, D.C.: U.S. Department of Transportation, Bureau of Transportation Statistics, 1996).

[3] Vukan R. Vuchic, *Urban Public Transportation, Systems and Technology* (Englewood Cliffs, N.J.: Prentice-Hall, 1981).

1. Road-based vehicles

    a. *Articulated bus:* a transit bus (diesel or electric) with a permanently attached semitrailer, with full interior passenger circulation.

    b. *Dual-mode bus:* a transit bus that can be propelled by electricity or by an engine.

    c. *Transit bus:* a vehicle usually propelled by an engine that is generally designed for frequent-stop service with front and center doors and without luggage storage compartments or rest room facilities. A transit bus generally less than 7.6-m long is called a *minibus*. An *over-the-road* bus is characterized by an elevated seating area located over a baggage compartment and is usually used in longer distance, express service operations.

    d. *Trolley bus:* a transit bus propelled by electricity obtained from overhead wires.

    e. *Van:* a passenger vehicle on an automobile or light truck chassis, propelled by an engine, with a capacity of 8 to 15 persons.

2. Rail and fixed guideway vehicles

    a. *Automated guideway transit (AGT):* small- and medium-sized vehicles that operate fully automatically on guideways with exclusive rights-of-way generally on a loop or as a shuttle within central business districts, airports, or other high activity centers and in some line-haul applications.

    b. *Monorail:* can be considered a subset of AGT and is differentiated by being suspended from or supported by a guideway formed by a single beam or rail.

    c. *Commuter railroad car:* a standard railroad passenger car with high-density seating. It may be selfpropelled (by electricity or diesel engines) or designed for haulage by a locomotive.

    d. *Rail transit car (rapid transit car, heavy-rail transit car):* an electrically propelled vehicle usually operated in trains on exclusive right-of-way. For purposes of this chapter, these cars are referred to as "rapid rail transit."

    e. *Streetcar and light rail vehicle (LRV):* an electrically propelled rail vehicle operated singly or in trains on shared, semi-exclusive, or exclusive right-of-way. *Vintage trolleys* used in historic applications also fit in this category.

    f. *Guided Bus:* a standard bus that has horizontal guidewheels in front of the front wheels to control the steering; side concrete curbs guide the vehicle.

3. Other vehicles

    a. *Ferryboat:* a passenger-carrying marine vessel that provides short-distance service over a fixed route and on a published schedule between two or more ports.

    b. *Funicular (or inclined plane):* a passenger mode that consists of a pair of rail vehicles permanently attached to two ends of the same cable, acting as a counterbalance to each other. Applications are usually found in situations with steep gradients (e.g., Pittsburgh, Los Angeles, Zurich, Paris, Hong Kong, Napoli).

    c. *Aerial tramway:* a passenger cabin that is suspended and towed by an overhead cable. Applications are typically where topography is mountainous or across a river (e.g., Roosevelt Island in New York City).

Services

Public transportation can provide different kinds of services and varying service levels. Key definitions pertaining to service follow.

- *Local transit service* operates on streets or other right-of-way with frequent stops and at relatively low speeds; it serves adjacent land uses within acceptable walking distances. Shuttle services within business districts or connecting high activity centers functionally fall within this category.

- *Express service* does not attempt to serve all land areas through which it passes, but it offers faster speeds to a selected number of stops spaced more widely apart. It includes limited-stop and nonstop services.

- *Basic service* comprises routes that operate all day (although the length of the "day" may vary from about 14 to 24 hrs.) and at least five days per week.

- *Headway* is the time interval between transit revenue vehicles passing a stop or station.

- *Peak service* comprises routes that operate during peak demand periods only. The *base period* is between the morning and afternoon peak periods.

- *Special service* comprises irregular routes operated for special events or for seasonal traffic generators.

Markets

Urban transit can be oriented to serve specific markets. These include central business district-oriented (CBD) work trips; service to, from, and within low-income or high-density neighborhoods; service to schools, medical facilities, and shopping areas; connections with high activity centers; and commuters in high travel demand corridors. Typically, the focus of urban transit in U.S. cities has been increasingly for home-to-work trips as the urban area size increases, as shown in Figure 13–1.

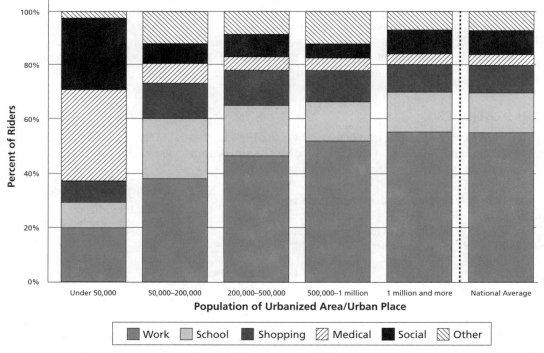

Figure 13–1   Purpose of Transit Trips by Population Group

Source: *Americans in Transit, A Profile of Public Transit Passengers,* Washington, D.C.: American Public Transit Association, December 1992, p. 6.

Groups of users, or markets, that have been found to be more likely to use transit as their principal mode to work are as follows:[4]

- Workers with low incomes.

- Workers with college educations.

- Hispanics.

- Workers, ages 17–29.

- Asians.

- Workers with mobility or work limitations.

- Workers with no household cars.

- African-Americans.

- Workers with graduate school educations.

- Women.

- Immigrants (under ten years in the United States).

Transit Use and Performance Trends

Public transport within U.S. and Canadian cities is used extensively for trips to and from the city center and in larger central cities for school, shopping, and work trips to other destinations. Figure 13–2 indicates trends in the use of public transport by persons entering central cities as compared to suburbs and areas outside of metropolitan zones. Between 1990 and 1995, the share of person trips using transit reversed a decline in central cities that was found between 1983 and 1990. The work trip to the city center is where transit is most effective in U.S. and Canadian cities. Similarly, transit provides effective service to high activity centers, such as outlying business and employment districts, airports, and stadia. Relatively good transit service (often on exclusive rights-of-way), high parking costs, and central city highway congestion often collectively give public transit the edge over the car.

General Statistics

Trends in transit service in the United States between 1985 and 1996 are shown in Table 13–2. The 11-year history shows that service (vehicles and vehicle-km) have increased while ridership has declined 8 percent. On the other hand, passenger km increased 4 percent over this 11-year period.

Pertinent statistics for U.S. and Canadian transit systems are summarized in Table 13–3. U.S. public transport is provided by a fleet of 121,994 transit vehicles that operated some 5,907 million vehicle-km and carried 7,975 million passengers in 1996. The Canadian transit fleet of 13,147 vehicles operated 755 million vehicle-km and carried 1,348 million passengers in that same year.

Table 13–2   Change in U.S. Transit Service
(all modes)

	1985	1990	1996	% Change 1985–1996
Active Vehicles in Rush-Hour Service	94,368	92,961	119,556	27
Vehicle-Kilometers Operated (millions)	4,493	5,186	5,907	31
Passenger Kilometers (millions)	63,725	66,240	66,509	4
Annual Riders (millions)	8,636	8,799	7,975	–8

1.0 kilometer = 0.62 miles.

Source: *Transit Fact Book, Annual,* Washington, D.C.: American Public Transit Association.

---

[4] The Drachman Institute with G. J. Fielding, *Transit Markets of the Future—The Challenge of Change, Transit Cooperative Research Program Report 28* (Washington, D.C.: Transportation Research Board, 1998).

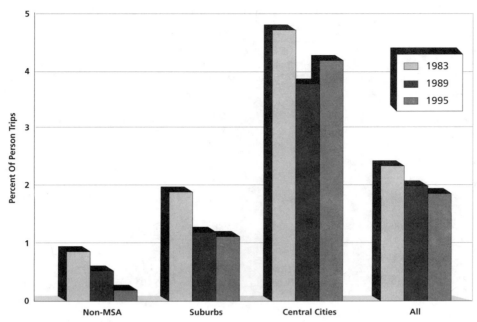

Figure 13–2   Transit Shares of All Travel by Place of Residence—1983, 1990, 1995

Sources: Alan E. Pisarski, *Travel Behavior Issues in the 90s,* Washington, D.C.: Federal Highway Administration, July 1992. Nationwide Transportation Survey, 1995.

Table 13–3   Profile of U.S. and Canadian Transit Operations by Mode, 1996

Item	Light Rail	Heavy Rail	Commuter Rail	Trolley Bus	Motor Bus	Demand Responsive	Ferry Boat	Other[1]	Total	Canada Total
Number of Systems (Agencies)	22	14	17	5	2,248	5,228	26	15	5,918[2]	86
Vehicles Owned or Leased	1,312	10,388	4,864	1,001	70,850	33,284	109	186	121,994	13,147
Vehicle-Kilometers Operated (millions)	60	876	390	22	3,492	995	4	68	5,907	755
Passenger Fares ($ millions)	144	2,322	1,145	55	3,446	210	54	30	7,406	1,576[3,4]
Operating Expenses ($ millions)	447	3,402	2,296	135	10,660	1,292	183	60	18,475	2,752
Unlinked Passenger Trips (millions)	261	2,157	352	117	4,887	93	49	32	7,948	1,348
Estimated Passenger-Kilometers (millions)	1,538	18,597	13,502	297	30,421	1,338	412	36	66,141	NA
Estimated Trip Length (Kilometers)	6.0	8.5	38.2	2.6	6.1	14.0	8.5	1.6	8.3	NA

Notes: 1.0 kilometer = 0.62 miles.
NA – Not Available.
Preliminary Data
[1] Includes cable car, inclined plane, automated guideway transit, aerial tramway, and monorail.
[2] Total is not sum of all modes since many systems (agencies) operate more than one mode.
[3] Canadian dollars.
[4] Non-governmental operating funding.

Source: *Transit Fact Book, Annual,* Washington, D.C.: American Public Transit Association.

Tables 13–4 and 13–5 give basic trends in U.S. transit service provided and consumed, respectively, since 1960. Table 13–4 shows a rise in operating costs from $1.10 per vehicle-km in 1960 to $2.63 per vehicle-km in 1996 (in constant 1990 dollars). However, since 1980, the unit operating cost has declined (in constant 1990 dollars) from $2.93 to $2.63. During this same period, as shown in Table 13–5, the operating revenues per vehicle km in constant 1990 dollars fluctuated, but decreased from $1.19 to $1.05, and the farebox recovery ratio remained relatively stable around 0.40.

Table 13–4 Profile of U.S. Transit Service Produced, 1960–1996

	1960	1965	1970	1975	1980	1985	1990	1996[2]
Active Pasenger Vehicles								
Rail[1]	11,866	10,664	10,548	10,617	10,654	10,043	11,332	11,341
Motor Bus	53,426	51,053	50,750	51,514	60,234	64,258	58,714	67,874
Other	[3]	[3]	[3]	[3]	[3]	16,033	18,500	35,676
Commuter Rail	[3]	[3]	[3]	[3]	[3]	4,035	4,415	4,665
Total	65,292	61,717	61,298	62,131	70,888	94,369	92,961	119,556
Vehicle-Kilometer (millions)								
Rail[4]	750	703	709	719	647	752	903	937
Motor Bus	2,699	2,529	2,321	2,480	2,720	3,023	3,428	3,492
Other	[3]	[3]	[3]	[3]	[3]	447	544	1,087
Commuter Rail	[3]	[3]	[3]	[3]	[3]	295	343	390
Total	3,449	3,232	3,031	3,200	3,367	4,517	5,218	5,906
Employees[5]								
Numbers	156,400	145,000	138,040	159,800	187,000	262,037	262,176	297,447
Operating Cost, per vehicle-kilometer,								
all modes	$0.40	$0.45	$0.66	$1.17	$1.85	$2.74	$3.02	$3.16
1990 dollars[6]	$1.10	$1.19	$1.46	$2.01	$2.93	$3.33	$3.02	$2.63

1.0 kilometer = 0.62 miles.

[1] 1985 and 1996 data contain paratransit services, including employees.

[2] 1996 data are preliminary

[3] "Other" data and commuter rail not available before 1985; including demand response, cable car, ferry, trolley bus, inclined plane, and automated guideway. Data for 1975, 1980, 1985, and 1996 include commuter rail.

[4] Includes rapid rail and light rail.

[5] Full-time employee equivalents through 1990; overall in 1996.

[6] Consumer Price Index base year 1990 = 1.00.

Sources: *Transit Fact Book,* 1998 Edition, Washington, D.C.: American Public Transit Association, February 1998; Gordon J. Fielding, *Managing Public Transportation Strategically,* San Francisco, Calif.: Jossey Bass, Inc., 1987.

Table 13–5 Profile of U.S. Transit Service Consumed, 1980–1996[1]

	1980	1985	1990	1996
Total (unlinked) Passenger Trips (millions)[2]	8,567	8,636	8,799	7,975
Passenger Revenue (millions)	$2,556.8	$4,574.7	$5,890.0	$7,416.8
Average Fare/Passenger Trip (cents)	30	53	73	93
Passenger Trips per Vehicle-Kilometer	2.53	1.91	1.69	1.35
Passenger Revenue per Vehicle-Kilomete				
all modes 1990 dollars[3]	$0.75	$1.01	$1.13	$1.26
	$1.19	$1.23	$1.13	$1.05
Ratio: Passenger Revenue to Operating Cost	0.41	0.37	0.37	0.40

1.0 kilometer = 0.62 miles.

[1] 1996 data are preliminary.

[2] Includes cable car, inclined plane, automated guideway, ferryboat, and commuter rail for 1985, 1990, and 1996. Data for 1985, 1990, and 1996 includes demand response.

[3] Consumer Price Index Base year 1990 = 1.00.

Source: *Transit Fact Book,* 1998 Edition, Washington, D.C.: American Public Transit Association, February 1998.

Modal Trends

Throughout the world, the last few decades have seen an upgrading of bus systems and an expansion of rail transit systems. In Europe, Asia, and South America, rail transit development has been triggered by urban growth, often at high densities, coupled with centralized development patterns, and employment growth in the city center. In the United States and Canada, transit investment reflects expansion of downtown office space, suburban and urban traffic congestion, the desire to provide a viable alternative to the car and freeway, and the realization by governments at many levels that the automobile cannot exclusively provide commuter transportation.

Table 13–6 Bus Transit (Large Systems): Ridership and System Profiles, 1995

Area	System	Maximum Revenue Vehicles in Service	Annual Revenue Vehicle-Kilometers (000)	Annual Unlinked Rides (000)	Unlinked Rides per Veh-km
Atlanta	MARTA	565	40,871	73,253	1.79
Baltimore	MTA	762	32,742	86,974	2.65
Boston	MBTA	871	42,440	106,279	2.50
Chicago	CTA	1,657	113,745	306,076	2.68
Cleveland	RTA	591	32,960	46,577	1.41
Dallas	DART	741	43,082	50,996	1.18
Denver	RTD	683	46,214	62,765	1.36
Detroit	D-DOT	384	26,243	57,027	2.17
Houston	METRO	985	60,307	79,569	1.31
Los Angeles	LACMTA	1,843	124,814	344,346	2.75
Miami	MDTA	508	37,294	62,258	1.67
Milwaukee	MCTS	431	28,275	56,019	1.98
Minneapolis	MCTO	849	36,892	61,110	1.66
New Jersey Transit	NJT	2,767	196,524	189,821	1.05
New York City	NYCDOT	893	34,384	76,984	2.23
New York City	NYCTA	3,094	142,285	658,519	4.62
Oakland	AC TRANSIT	585	37,093	61,943	1.67
Orange County, CA	OCTA	508	37,294	62,258	1.67
Philadelphia	SEPTA	1,110	54,953	163,123	2.96
Pittsburgh	PAT	726	38,610	64,357	1.66
Portland	TRI-MET	522	33,649	56,217	1.67
San Francisco	MUNI	373	19,548	90,579	4.63
San Diego	MTS	594	34,202	58,900	1.72
San Jose	SCVTA	393	28,029	39,387	1.40
Seattle	METRO	847	46,806	57,467	1.23
St. Louis	BI-STATE	561	30,965	39,913	1.28
Washington	WMATA	1,283	57,644	146,590	2.54

1.0 kilometer = 0.62 miles.

Sources: *Transit Profiles: The Thirty Largest Agencies,* Washington, D.C.: Federal Transit Administration, December 1996; *Short Range Transit Plan,* San Diego, Calif.: San Diego Metropolitan Transit Development Board, September 1998.

Bus Transit

Bus transit is the dominant form of public transport in most North American cities. Within the United States, buses carry about 65 percent of the annual passenger trips. Table 13–6 gives salient facts for bus transit systems in larger U.S. cities.

Light Rail Transit

There are approximately 350 light rail transit (LRT) and streetcar systems found throughout the world. Characteristics of light rail (and streetcar) systems operating in the United States and Canada are summarized in Table 13–7 (Group I systems have generally higher average speeds than the Group II systems). In addition to the systems shown, new LRT starts have been opened in Denver (1994) and Dallas (1996).

Vintage trolley systems have also had a resurgence in urban applications, especially in CBDs, and are found in over twenty U.S. communities, including Dallas, Detroit, Portland, San Francisco, San Jose, and Seattle.

Rapid Rail Transit

Rapid rail transit (sometimes referred to as "metro" or "heavy rail") km have more than doubled throughout the world since 1960. Over two-fifths of the new construction occurred in newly urbanizing parts of the world, but an equal share was found in urban areas with high automobile use in Europe and Canada. *Janes World Railways* identified more than 90 rail transit systems in 39 countries in 1995, and another 18 new start systems under construction or in design.[5]

[5] Janes, *Urban Transport Systems* (Frome and London, Great Britain: Butler and Tanner Limited, 1997–1998).

Table 13–7 Light Rail Transit System Profiles and Productivity Indicators

City/System	Parameters			Statistics		
	One-Way Line km	No. of Cars	Rides/Weekday	Cars/km	Rides/km	Rides/Car
LRT–Group I						
Baltimore, Central Corridor[d]	35.4	35	20,000	1.0	565	571
Calgary, C-Train[a]	29.3	85	114,500	2.9	3,908	1,347
Cleveland, Shaker Rapid[b]	21.1	48	9,900	2.3	469	206
Denver, MAC[d]	8.5	11	15,000	1.3	1,765	1,364
Edmonton, LRT[a]	12.3	37	36,000	3.0	2,927	973
Los Angeles, Long Beach[a]	35.4	54	42,000	1.5	1,186	778
Neward, City Subway[b]	6.9	24	16,800	3.5	2,435	700
Philadelphia, Media–Sharon Hill[b]	19.2	29	8,200	1.5	427	283
Portland, MAX[a]	24.3	26	24,500	1.1	1,008	942
Sacramento, RT Metro[a]	29.5	36	24,300	1.2	824	675
St. Louis, MetroLink[d]	29.0	31	40,000	1.1	1,379	1,290
San Diego Trolley[a]	55.4	71	45,000	1.3	812	634
San Jose, Guadalupe[a]	32.2	50	20,000	1.6	621	400
Subtotals/Averages	338.5	537	416,200	1.6	1,230	775
LRT–Group II						
Boston, Green Line[b]	40.1	220	213,000	5.5	5,312	968
Boston, Mattapan–Ashmont[b]	4.3	12	7,000	2.8	1,628	583
Buffalo, MetroRail[a]	10.3	27	28,000	2.6	2,718	1,037
Fort Worth, Tandy	1.6	8	5,900	5.0	3,688	738
New Orleans, St. Charles/Riverfront[b]	14.0	41	26,000	3.1	1,857	634
Philadelphia, Subway-Surface[b]	35.9	112	77,500	3.1	2,159	692
Pittsburgh, South Hills[b]	31.2	71	29,000	2.3	929	408
San Francisco, Muni Metro[c]	39.1	128	134,300	3.3	3,435	1,049
Toronto, Streetcars	75.5	267	307,100	3.5	4,068	1,150
Subtotals/Averages	252.0	886	827,800	3.5	3,285	934
Totals/Averages	590.5	1,423	1,244,000	2.4	2,107	874

1.0 kilometer = 0.62 miles.
[a] New start opened since 1977.
[b] Major reconstruction/rehabilitation since 1977.
[c] Upgraded from streetcar to LRT standards since 1977.
[d] New start opened since 1992.

Source: John W. Schumann and Suzanne R. Tidrick, "Status of North American Light Rail Transit Systems: 1995 Update," *Seventh National Conference on Light Rail Transit,* vol. 1, Washington, D.C.: Transportation Research Board, 1995.

Figure 13–3 shows the 1975 patterns of transit use in the Soviet Union, Europe, Latin America, Asia, and North America.[6] Even though the statistics are now somewhat dated, the graphic comparisons remain basically the same today:

1. In newly urbanizing parts of the world, systems tend to be short, with very heavy loads per km of line.

2. In the Soviet Union with crowded urban conditions and low auto ownership, loads averaged 90 million passenger km of travel per km of line per year (pkm/km).

3. In Latin American, with heavily used short systems, there were nearly 70 million pkm/km annually, due in part to additional midday trips. Systems in Asia (Japan and Korea) average 60 pkm/km of line per year. The 39-km-long Hong Kong system had more than 110 pkm/km of line in 1986.

---

[6] Boris S. Puskarev, Jeffrey M. Zupan, and Robert S. Cumella, *Urban Rail in America: an Exploration of Criteria for Fixed-Guideway Transit* (Bloomington, Ind.: Indiana University Press, 1982).

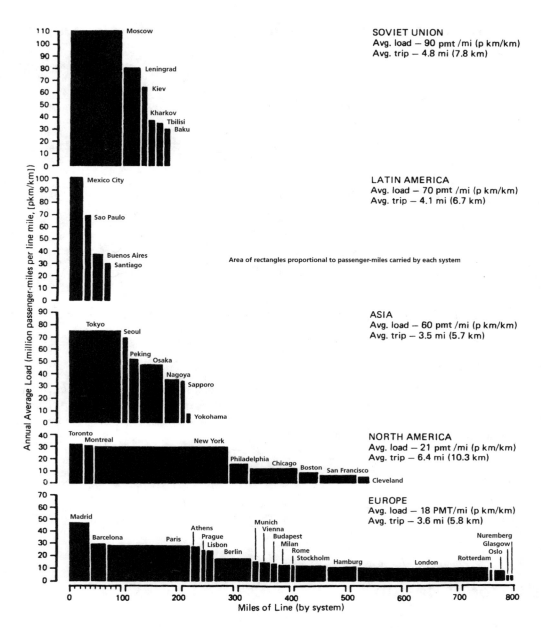

Figure 13–3 World Rapid Transit Use by Urban Area, 1975

Source: Pushkarev, Boris S. with J.M. Zupan and Robert S. Cumella, *Urban Rail in America: An Exploration of Criteria for Fixed Guideway Transit,* Bloomington, Ind.: Indiana Univeristy Press, 1982; Institute of Transportation Engineers, *Transportation Planning Handbook,* Englewood Cliffs, N.J.: Prentice-Hall, 1992.

4. In countries with older urbanization and stronger economies, the system extent corresponds more closely to the geographic extent of the urbanized areas. Thus, trips are longer and loads are lighter in the United States, Canada, and Western Europe.

Table 13–8 gives rail rapid transit ridership and system profiles for principal rapid transit systems operating in the United States and Canada. Analysis of ridership for these systems indicates that approximately 20 to 30 percent of inbound riders cross the CBD cordon within the A.M. peak hour (8–9 A.M.). Approximately 75 percent of all riders begin or end their trips within the CBD.

Table 13–8 Rapid Rail Transit Ridership and System Profiles, 1995

Study Area	System	Directional Kilometers	Number of Stations	Maximum Revenue Vehicles in service	Annual Revenue Veh km (000)	Annual Unlinked Rides (000)	Unlinked Rides per Veh km Traveled
Atlanta	MARTA	130.0	33	158	35,210	70,354	2.00
Baltimore	MTA	47.3	14	54	6,411	10,556	1.64
Boston	MBTA	122.0	53	310	47,976	113,440	3.38
Chicago	CTA	334.3	145	803	7,287	135,462	1.85
Cleveland	RTA	61.5	18	35	3,198	6,949	2.16
Lindenwold/Philadelphia	PATCO	50.7	13	102	6,748	10,881	1.61
Los Angeles	LACMTA	9.7	5	16	1,118	5,888	5.25
Miami	MDTA	67.9	21	80	9,381	14,204	1.51
New Jersey/New York	PATH	46.0	13	282	20,628	64,734	3.13
New York City	Staten Island	46.0	22	36	3,966	5,069	1.71
New York City	NYCTA	793.2	468	4816	486,604	1,234,599	2.53
Philadelphia	SEPTA	122.5	76	287	23,616	86,611	3.66
San Francisco	BART	228.5	34	406	70,568	76,332	1.08
Washington	WMATA	286.8	74	588	66,907	198,380	2.96

1.0 kilometer = 0.62 miles.

Source: *Transit Profiles: The Thirty Largest Agencies,* Washington, D.C.: Federal Transit Administration, December 1996.

Automated Systems

AGT systems are generally smaller vehicle systems that operate in controlled or concentrated environments (e.g., airports, large institutions, leisure and entertainment parks, CBDs). A roster of daily ridership figures for North American automated systems in a variety of operating environments is shown in Table 13–9, and more details for those operated by transit agencies are included in Table 13–10.

Commuter Rail

Table 13–11 gives annual ridership statistics for commuter rail systems operating in U.S. cities. Commuter rail lines in the United States carried 353 million passengers in 1996. The New York/New Jersey and Chicago regions accounted for about 79 percent of the ridership.

Transit Modal Design

Right-of-Way Characteristics

This section gives geometric right-of-way characteristics and guidelines for selected transit technologies. Table 13–12 shows the types of right-of-way where specific transit vehicles operate. Table 13–13 gives illustrative geometric standards and right-of-way requirements for busways and rail transit. Although these values reflect current practice, individual circumstances for different applications may vary. Preparation of specific, detailed geometric criteria is desirable for each new transit service and facility application; these standards should reflect specific local conditions.

Streets and Highways

Most bus service operates in mixed traffic over streets and highways. Bus priority lanes are used on downtown streets in many large cities (e.g., New York, Paris, Singapore), and bus (or HOV) lanes are provided along radial freeways in many cities (e.g., Houston, Los Angeles, San Diego, Seattle, Washington). Busways (sometimes called transitways) are found in Adelaide (Australia), Houston, Ottawa, Pittsburgh, Port of Spain, and Runcorn (England). A bus tunnel, including five bus stations, opened in downtown Seattle in 1990.

Buses on all types of public streets and highways generally operate effectively within the ranges of geometric values set forth in Chapter 11 of the *Traffic Engineering Handbook*. LRT on-street operation requires similar treatments as with exclusive bus lanes, plus additional design for safety purposes and placement of poles for the catenary wire.

Special design considerations for buses include:

1. The swept paths and horizontal clearance requirements of transit vehicles, especially where making right turns.

2. The acceleration characteristics of transit vehicles in relation to geometrics of acceleration lanes and merging areas.

3. The load limits of bridges.

4. The pavement strength (i.e., depth and type) at bus stops and on local streets.

Generally, the majority of buses operating in urban applications today are 2.6-m wide. Minimum lane width of 3.0 m is desirable. However, practical compromises involving reduced speeds sometimes must be made in situations where buses must use narrower lanes. The speed, capacity, and reliability of buses (and on-street LRT) can be enhanced by a variety of *priority* techniques, such as:

1. Exclusive or preferential transit lanes on sections of streets and freeways.

2. Exclusive transit turns at intersections.

3. Metered freeway entry with bus preference.

4. Passive traffic signal priority measures, such as cycle-length adjustments, split phases, and timing plans selectively favoring buses (or LRT).

5. Active traffic signal priority measures, such as unconditional or conditional signal preemption by buses (or LRT).

6. Exclusive transit streets, malls, and ramps.

7. Exclusive busways.

Frequently, the application of the first three techniques is limited to peak periods or directions where transit patronage is relatively high. Other HOVs are sometimes permitted to share use of preferential transit lanes, ramps, and bypasses on freeways.

Table 13–9 Daily Ridership for North American Automated Guideway Transit Systems

Category	Location	Ridership
Airport	Atlanta, GA	109,000
Airport	Chicago-O'Hare, IL	12,000
Airport	Cincinnati, OH	30,000
Airport	Dallas–Fort Worth, TX	50,000
Airport	Denver, CO	50,000
Airport	Houston, TX	8,500
Airport	Las Vegas, NV	15,000
Airport	Miami, FL	15,000
Airport	Orlando, FL	49,000
Airport	Pittsburgh, PA	50,000
Airport	Seattle–Tacoma, WA	43,000
Airport	Tampa, FL	71,000
Airport	Tampa-parking, FL	8,000
Institutional	Duke University Hospital, NC	2,000
Institutional	Harbour Island, Tampa, FL	2,000
Institutional	Pearlridge Mall, HI	4,000
Institutional	Senate Subway, DC	10,000
Leisure	Bronx Zoo, NY	2,000
Leisure	Busch Garden, VA	6,000
Leisure	CalExpo, CA	4,000
Leisure	Carowinds, NC	7,000
Leisure	Circus-C., Las Vegas, NV	11,000
Leisure	Circus-C., Reno, NV	6,000
Leisure	Circus-Water Park, Las Vegas, NV	2,000
Leisure	Disneyland, CA	15,000
Leisure	Disney World, FL	20,000
Leisure	Hershey Park, PA	8,000
Leisure	Kings Dominion, VA	5,000
Leisure	Kings Island, OH	7,000
Leisure	Luxor-Excalibur, Las Vegas, NV	10,000
Leisure	Magic Mountain, CA	8,000
Leisure	Memphis/Mudd Island, TN	2,000
Leisure	Miami Zoo, FL	1,200
Leisure	Minnesota Zoo, MN	1,000
Leisure	Mirage, Treasure Island, Las Vegas, NV	8,000
Leisure	Toronto Zoo, ON	2,000
Transit	Detroit Mover, MI	9,000
Transit	Jacksonville, FL	1,100
Transit	Miami Metromover, FL	12,000
Transit	Morgantown, University of West Virginia	16,000
All	Total	691,800

Source: *Transit Pulse, 1995 Transit Profiles*, Washington, D.C.: Federal Transit Administration, December 1996.

Table 13–10 Automated Guideway (Transit Agencies) Operating Profiles, 1995

Area	System	Directional Route-Kilometers	Vehicles in Maximum Service	Passenger Trips/Vehicle-Kilometer
Jacksonville	JTA	1.9	2	2.31
Miami	MDTA	13.7	20	3.79
Tampa	Hartline	1.5	2	5.98
Detroit	DTC	4.7	6	3.45

1.0 kilometer = 0.62 miles.

Source: *Transit Pulse*, Boston, Mass.: newsletter published bimonthly. *Transit Profiles*, Washington, D.C.: Federal Transit Administration, December 1996.

Table 13–11 Commuter Rail Ridership for U.S. Systems, 1995

City	System	Unlinked Trips Annual (000s)	Passenger Trips per Revenue Vehicle Kilometer	Passenger-Miles per Revenue Vehicle Kilometer	Number of Stations[1]
Boston	MBTA	25,495	1.02	19.08	102
Chicago	METRA	67,138	1.21	26.20	223
Chicago	NICTD	2,604	0.78	21.76	18
New Haven	ConnDOT	292	0.43	08.83	7
Los Angeles	SCRRA	4,402	0.68	23.81	41
Miami	Tri-Rail	2,735	0.69	21.93	15
New Jersey	NJTransit	47,551	0.71	17.48	163
New York	LIRR	97,736	1.09	24.77	134
New York	Metro North	62,409	0.94	30.29	107
Philadelphia	SEPTA	23,301	1.13	16.03	181
San Diego	NCTD	178	0.58	15.80	8
San Francisco	CalTrain	5,539	0.92	20.84	34
Washington DC/Baltimore	MTA	4,800	0.64	19.27	40
Washington DC/Virginia	VRE	1,840	1.10	37.39	17

1.0 kilometer = 0.62 miles.

[1]1997 APTA Data.

N/A—Data not available.

Source: *Transit Profiles: The Thirty Largest Agencies,* Washington, D.C.: Federal Transit Administration, December 1996.

Busways

The technology of line, station, and terminal facilities for exclusive busways continues to undergo development. Where busways are used by carpool drivers, their design must allow for the presence of mixed traffic streams. Where bus volumes are relatively heavy (i.e., 40 or more buses in the peak hour and direction, and buses stop en route), it is better to limit busway use to buses.

Busway stations normally require a loading-unloading lane separate from the through-lane in each travel direction. Different platform berth layouts have different geometric and right-of-way requirements. The number of loading berths to be provided depends on design patronage volumes, minimum bus headways, peak bus accumulations, plans of operation, loading and fare collection characteristics, types and locations of stations, berth design, number of routes, and other factors. Busway stations usually require acceleration and deceleration lanes and tapers for satisfactory transition between line and station operations. (Chapter 18 contains information on the planning of terminals for bus operations.)

Busway stations in CBDs generally require more elaborate facilities and space than stations located elsewhere. If CBD penetration involves subway structures, then ventilation, delivery, and station design problems may be severe and costly. Because of this, CBD delivery is often provided by means of streets with curbside stops or through elevated terminals. Seattle's bus tunnel provides electric propulsion power to dual-mode buses and is designed to accommodate future LRT vehicles.

Figure 13–4 shows busway designs used in Ottawa, Canada. Shown in Figure 13–5 are several photos of priority busway operations in Curitiba, Brazil. These photos demonstrate the integrated concept used in Curitiba to fit the priority busway into the city and with special stations that facilitate boarding. The transit facilities there were part of a coordinated busway-land development plan.

Table 13–12 Vehicle Application Matrix

Vehicle	Right-of-Way Options				
	Shared Street Right-of-Way	Protected Street Right-of-Way	Semi-Private Right-of-Way/or HOV Lane	Exclusive Right-of-Way	Shared Railroad Right-of-Way
Motor Bus	X	X	X	X	
Trolley Coach	X	X	X	X	
Light Rail/ Streetcar	X	X	X	X	X
Heavy Rail				X	X
Commuter Rail				X	X
Automated or Advanced Rapid Transit			X		

Table 13–13 Typical Basic Geometric and Right-of-Way Characteristics for Selected Transit Facility Types

Characteristic	Unit	Exclusive Busway	Light Rail Transit In-Street Center Reservation	Light Rail Transit Exclusive Right-of-Way	Rapid Transit
Access control	—	Full	Partial	Full	Full
Number of lanes or tracks	—	2	2	2	2
1. Width					
a. Transit Vehicle	m	2.6	2.9	2.9	3.1
b. Lane envelope clearance[1]	m	3.7	3.4	3.8	4.1
c. Track gauge	m	—	1.4	1.4	1.4
d. Emergency walkway	m	2	None	0.8	0.8
e. Minimum shoulders (each)[2]	m	0.8	None	None	None
f. Border barriers or fencing (each)	m	0.6	None	0.3	0.3
g. Overall minimum right-of-way[3]					
(1) Aerial	m	10	—	7.3	7.9
(2) At-grade	m	10	6.7	9.2	9.8
(3) Subway	m	12	—	11.6	25
2. Stations[4]					
a. Side platform width	m	3	3	3.7	3.7
b. Center platform width	m	—	—	7.3	7.3
c. Platform length	m	37	122	122	152–183
3. Minimums					
a. Vertical clearance	m	4.3	4.3	4.3	4.3
b. Design speed	km/h	37	25	37	37–50[6]
c. Horizontal curve radius (for new construction)	m	122	61	152	122–183[6]
4. Maximum grade	%	4	6–7[5]	6[5]	4.0

1.0 meters = 3.28 feet; 1.0 km/h = 0.62 mph.

[1] Overall vehicle clearance requirements on tangent line.
[2] Emergency walkway for busways is incorporated in busway shoulders.
[3] Minimums based on normal structural requirements for tangent-line sections without stations and without station acceleration and deceleration lanes and tapers for busways. Special drainage provisions, side slopes, or retaining walls on cuts and fills and any subway lateral ventilation requirements are excluded.
[4] Typical line stations. In CBD's busway station requirements and rail platform widths may be greater. Off-board lifts/ramps for wheelchair boardings require special design consideration.
[5] Depends upon specific LRV, and is for short lengths.
[6] Higher end of ranges for regional rapid transit.

Source: Vanous databooks, inventories, reports, and criteria.

Guided Bus

Guided bus applications exist in Essen, Germany (opened in 1980); Adelaide, Australia (opened in 1986); and Ipswich, England (opened in 1995). The guideways require curbing on each side of a single-lane roadway, with the pavement width (i.e., curb-to-curb) sized to fit the distance between horizontal guidewheels that guide the bus. The bus size can vary, as long as the horizontal guidewheels are uniformly spread. The principal advantages of this application are: (1) increased travel comfort, (2) speed, (3) flexibility of the bus to also use normal streets and highways, and (4) decreased right-of-way width.

Light Rail Transit

LRT uses predominately reserved, but not necessarily grade-separated, rights-of-way. Alternative right-of-way

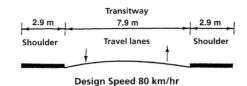

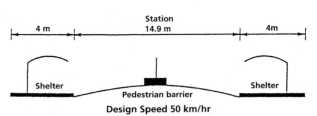

Figure 13–4 Typical Busway Cross Sections

Source: Ottawa and Carleton Regional Transit Commission.

Figure 13–5   Bus Boarding Station in Curitiba, Brazil

Source: Photo: Martha Welborne

types for LRT application are shown in Figure 13–6. Electrically propelled rail vehicles operate singly or in trains. Thus, a major feature or LRT is its flexibility and versatility. LRT operating in exclusive right-of-way becomes similar to rapid rail (heavy rail) transit design, except that power distribution systems and station platform lengths and heights may differ—normally allowing higher capacity for rapid rail.

The versatility of LRT operations in North America is shown in Table 13–14. Subway LRT operation in the city center is found in Boston, Cleveland, Edmonton, Los Angeles, Newark, Philadelphia, Pittsburgh, and San Francisco. In contrast, Baltimore, Buffalo, Calgary, Dallas, Denver, Portland, Sacramento, St. Louis, San Diego, and San Jose operate on private rights-of-way in outlying areas and on-street downtown, usually in reserved lanes or in transit only streets. Descriptive characteristics of U.S. LRT systems are provided in Table 13–15.

Most LRT systems have street-level station platforms. However, in a few cases (e.g., San Francisco) LRT serves both high- (no steps between platform and vehicle) and low- (where steps are required to board) level platforms. The Calgary, Edmonton, Los Angeles, and St. Louis systems use high-level platforms throughout.

Shared on-street track alignment is primarily determined by the geometry of the streets available for the route. Turning radii can be quite short, but track spacing at sharp curves must be increased so that the front and rear overhangs of one vehicle do not collide with the center portion of a vehicle on the adjacent track. This may preclude simultaneous 90-degree turns at intersections of two narrow streets and dictate single-track, alternate movement, or other design solutions.

Semiexclusive route sections can be placed in the median strip of wide arterials with crossings at grade. In this case, tracks are usually laid on open railroad-type rock ballast between intersections, both for low-cost profile and to prevent private vehicles from encroaching on the tracks. Curve geometrics usually are designed for somewhat higher speeds (larger radii), but clearances of vehicles at curves can still be a problem.

Methods of priority treatment for buses can apply to on-street LRT operations. This applies particularly to traffic signal priority measures and exclusive use of streets or lanes in downtown areas. Low-cost LRT applications normally rely upon shared use of existing transportation rights-of-way (e.g., reuse of an existing freeway, railroad, or street corridor). A summary of different approaches to use of railroad rights-of-way is provided in Table 13–16. Figure 13–7 provides illustrative examples of pedestrian treatments in a combined railroad and LRT operating environment.

LRT speeds and track capacities are generally lower than rapid rail transit in the same alignment. More direct service with branch or parallel lines often can be provided; stops may be located more convenient to development and spaced

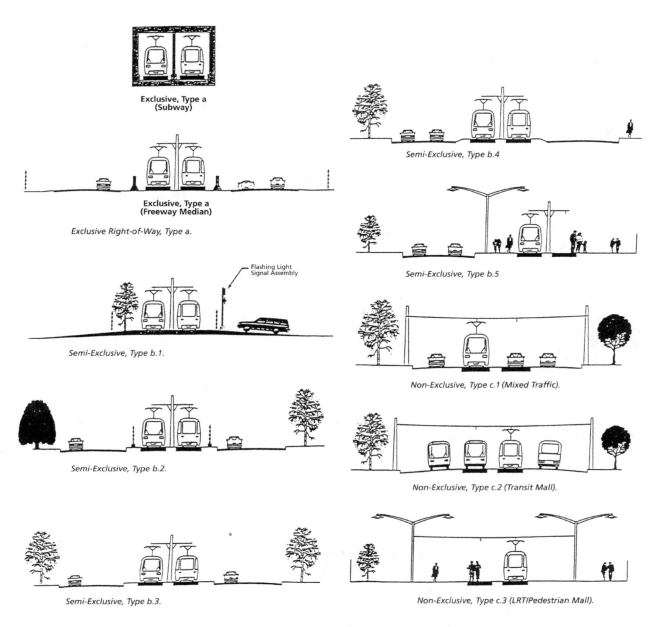

Figure 13–6   Alternative Right-of-Way Types for LRT

Source: Hans W. Korve, et al. *Integration of Light Rail Transit into City Streets, Transit Cooperative Research Program Report 17.* Washington, D.C.: Transportation Research Board, 1996.

more closely to reduce walking distances. Thus, overall door-to-door travel times for urban trips up to perhaps 10 km may be in the same range as those provided on fully grade-separated urban rapid transit facilities. Attractive linear park treatments, such as along St. Charles and Carrollton Avenues in New Orleans and Beacon Street in Boston-Brookline, can provide additional amenities along and in the streetcar right-of-way located in street medians.

Rapid Rail Transit

Rapid rail transit is the main peak-hour travel mode for CBD travelers in most large cities. Its high capacity and ability to operate below ground make it possible to support a large CBD employment; conversely, ridership correlates closely

Table 13–14 U.S. LRT Systems Right-of-Way Characteristics

City/System	km of Line						
	Subway/ Tunnel	Exclusive ROW[a]	Private ROW[b]	Street or Highway Median[c]	Reserved St. Lanes or Mall[d]	Mixed Traffic[e]	Total
LRT–Group I							
Baltimore, Central Corridor	—	—	32.2	—	3.2	—	35.4
Calgary, C-Train	1.9	1.3	13.2	10.5	2.4	—	29.3
Cleveland, Shaker Rapid	—	11.3	—	9.8	—	—	21.1
Denver, MAC	—	—	5.6	—	2.9	—	8.5
Edmonton, LRT[f]	4.7	—	7.6	—	—	—	12.3
Los Angeles, Long Beach	0.8	—	29.8	3.2	1.6	—	35.4
Neward, City Subway	2.1	4.8	—	—	—	—	6.9
Philadelphia, Media–Sharon Hill	—	—	16.3	—	0.3	2.6	19.2
Portland, MAX	—	8.7	3.7	8.4	3.4	0.1	24.3
Sacramento, RT Metro	—	9.5	12.4	1.0	1.8	4.8	29.5
St. Louis, MetroLink	1.3	16.0	11.7	—	—	—	29.0
San Diego Trolley	—	—	51.8	1.6	2.0	—	55.4
San Jose, Guadalupe	—	15.8	1.8	13.5	1.1	—	32.2
Subtotal	10.8	67.4	186.1	48.0	18.7	7.5	338.5
LRT–Group II							
Boston, Green Line	7.2	17.1	—	11.4	—	4.4	40.1
Boston, Mattapan–Ashmont	—	4.3	—	—	—	—	4.3
Buffalo, MetroRail	8.4	—	—	—	1.9	—	10.3
Fort Worth, Tandy	0.6	—	1.0	—	—	—	1.6
New Orleans, St. Charles/Riverfront	—	—	3.5	9.0	0.2	1.3	14.0
Philadelphia, Subway-Surface	4.0	—	—	1.9	—	30.0	35.9
Pittsburgh, South Hills	3.4	—	22.2	—	—	5.6	31.2
San Francisco, Muni Metro	10.2	—	1.2	6.3	—	21.4	39.1
Toronto, Streetcars	1.0	—	2.6	4.0	—	67.9	75.5
Subtotals	34.8	21.4	30.5	32.6	2.1	130.6	252.0
Totals: km	45.6	88.8	216.6	80.6	20.8	138.1	590.5
% Total	8	15	37	14	3	23	100

1.0 kilometer = 0.62 miles.

[a] Aerial or surface with no grade crossings.
[b] Surface, LRT private ROW with grade crossings.
[c] Surface, reserved medians of highways and streets with grade crossings.
[d] Surface, reserved lanes (other than medians) and LRT/pedestrian malls.
[e] Street lanes shared by LRT and other traffic; "streetcar" operations.
[f] Saskatchewan river bridge included under Subway.

Source: John W. Schumann and Suzanne R. Tidrick, "Status of North American Light Rail Transit Systems: 1995 Update," *Seventh National Conference on Light Rail Transit*, vol. 1, Washington, D.C.: Transportation Research Board, 1995.

with office employment in the city center. Speed, service reliability, and the ability to alleviate street congestion and affect land development are among its desirable attributes. Because it is costly and time consuming to develop, it becomes practical only where there is extensive street congestion, high employment and residential densities, and overloaded or slow surface transit operations. Typical standards, such as those shown in Table 13–13, are used to determine horizontal alignment. Vertical alignment design should balance land, construction, and environmental costs.

Construction costs are least at grade, but this requires permanent occupancy of a strip of land and building of grade separations for all crossings. It is generally feasible only in outlying areas where land is relatively inexpensive, or in freeway medians where the cost of land and grade separations can be shared with the highway. Elevated construction costs can be twice as much as for facilities at grade; but the land below can be used for a street, for parking or industrial uses, or even for linear parks. The BART (San Francisco Bay Area Rapid Transit) system in Albany and El Cerrito, California, is an example of the latter.

Table 13–15 U.S. LRT Systems Descriptive Characteristics

City/System	Portion of ROW Reserved (%)	Average Stop Spacing (km)	Double Track (%)	Through Service Routes (No.)	Number of Cars: 4-axle[a] (No.)	Number of Cars: 6-axle[b] (No.)	System Average Speed (km/hr)
LRT–Group I							
Baltimore, Central Corridor	100	0.7	61	1	0	35	35
Calgary, C-Train	100	0.9	100	3	0	85	29
Cleveland, Shaker Rapid	100	0.8	100	2	0	48	30
Denver, MAC	100	0.8	94	1	0	11	23
Edmonton, LRT	100	1.3	100	1	0	37	30
Los Angeles, Long Beach	100	1.6	100	1	0	54	34
Neward, City Subway	100	0.6	100	1	24	0	28
Philadelphia, Media–Sharon Hill	87	0.4	71	2	29	0	26
Portland, MAX	99	0.9	89	1	4[c]	26	30
Sacramento, RT Metro	84	1.0	68	1	0	36	34
St. Louis, MetroLink	100	1.5	97	1	0	31	43
San Diego Trolley	100	1.6	99	2	0	71	30
San Jose, Guadalupe	100	1.1	95	2	6[c]	50	32
Subtotal/Averages	98	1.0	90	19	63	484	—
LRT–Group II							
Boston, Green Line	89	0.5	100	4	0	220	22
Boston, Mattapan–Ashmont	100	0.5	100	1	12	0	20
Buffalo, MetroRail	100	0.7	100	1	27	0	20
Fort Worth, Tandy	100	0.3	100	1	8	0	17
New Orleans, St. Charles/Riverfront	90	0.2	100	2	41	0	15
Philadelphia, Subway-Surface	17	0.2	100	5	112	0	18
Pittsburgh, South Hills	82	0.5	88	4	16	55	26
San Francisco, Muni Metro	45	0.2	100	5	0	128	18
Toronto, Streetcars	10	0.1	100	10	215	52	15
Subtotal/Averages	48	0.2	97	33	431	455	—
Totals	77	0.4	93	52	494	939	—

[a] Nonarticulated, rigid body.
[b] Articulated.
[c] Vintage trolley cars for downtown loop, not included in totals.

Source: John W. Schumann and Suzanne R. Tidrick, "Status of North American Light Rail Transit Systems: 1995 Update," *Seventh National Conference on Light Rail Transit,* vol. 1, Washington, D.C.: Transportation Research Board, 1995.

In densely built-up and environmentally sensitive areas, including CBDs, the adverse effects of noise and reduced daylight usually preclude elevated construction. A doubling or even tripling of costs (relative to aboveground construction) occurs where underground alignments are considered. However, land costs are minimized by the use of street rights-of-way, easements under private property instead of outright purchase, and development of air rights over those parcels that must be acquired. Environmental deterioration is minimized, although it must be recognized that underground travel is not as attractive to passengers as moving in natural light. This is sometimes alleviated by developing underground retail establishments along concourses and passageways to reduce "tunnel effects."

Toronto developed many sections of its Bloor and Yonge subways by acquiring a strip of land near and parallel to each street, constructing the subways, and then selling the land for joint development. This method of construction minimized disruption of street traffic and transit during the period that the subways were built.

Junctions between rapid transit routes and branching of lines or services should be minimized. Where lines cross, tracks should generally be grade separated and must be grade separated where headways are less than three minutes. Careful junction design is essential to avoid creating capacity bottlenecks.

Table 13–16 Summary of Approaches to LRT Use of Railroad Right-of-Way

Approach	Issues
1. Parallel Operation	• To help protect itself from liability, railroad operator may require horizontal separation of up to 40 feet and possible installation of a crash barrier. • Railroad may require LRT agency to assume total liability and/or to carry very high insurance coverage. • Railroad may require that proposed LRT at-grade crossings (especially pedestrian crossings near station platforms) to be reconfigured to grade separated crossings. • Adjacent land owners accustomed to rail traffic. • At-grade rail crossings grouped together. • At-grade rail service to freight customers located on the side of the LRT corridor is problematic. • Railroad-oriented development potential of land adjacent to the LRT system may be compromised.
2. Relocate Railroad	• Existing utilities, because many have been located along the railroad ROW as linear features, might easily be avoided. • Following construction of LRT, redevelopment along the corridor can proceed unimpeded by freight service influences/impacts. • Negotiations with the railroad can be slow. • The costs associated with relocation of the railroad service tracks may not be justifiable.
3. LRT/Railroad Shared Use	• May be the only approach if ROW is limited and abandonment not possible. • Efficient use of track facilities. • Operating considerations different dependent upon whether the railroad operations include freight or passenger services. • Car design pertaining to buff impact loads must conform to Federal Railroad Administration (FRA) requirements if traffic intermingles without separation on different tracks or by time of day. • Extent of FRA regulation of transit operator is dependent upon segregation of LRT and railroad operations and whether trackage is connected to the "general system of railroads" regulated by the FRA. • Track design and conflicts with system components such as catenary and passenger facilities such as station platforms, including horizontal and vertical clearance requirements, on sections utilized by railroad operations must conform to FRA freight regulations. • FRA regulation may extend to elements of the transit system which affect railroad operations, including signals, track, and dispatch.
4. Railroad Abandonment	• Affected railroad will be responsive once formal proceedings are submitted to the Interstate Commerce Commission. • If successful, the LRT can be constructed as under Approach 2, *Relocate Railroad*. • Approval process can be slow. • On-line freight customers, existing and potential, may petition to maintain rail service.

Sources: Adapted from Richard D. Pilgrim, Lonnie D. Blaydes, and William D. Burgel, "Issues Associated with Light Rail Transit Use of Freight Railroad Right-of-Way," *Seventh National Conference on Light Rail Transit,* vol. 1, Washington, D.C.: Transportation Research Board, 1995; Baltimore Mass Transit Administration, Baltimore, Md.; San Diego Metropolitan Transit Development Board, San Diego, Calif.; BRW, Inc., 1994.

For both LRT and rapid rail transit planning, an operational analysis should determine the need for crossovers and storage tracks. The former are needed primarily for track maintenance purposes, while the latter provide opportunity for turning trains back short of the end of the line or for storing disabled vehicles. As a rail transit system expands, more operational flexibility is required in order to provide reliable service and respond to disruptions.

There is a growing similarity between heavy and light rail transit. Several light-rail systems have underground routes, high platforms, and completely (or virtually completely) separated rights-of-way. Manila's LRT system plus San Diego's 1997 extension to Mission Valley are examples.

Automated Systems

Automated systems provide urban transit service in several cities, and they also operate in controlled environments such as airports and entertainment activities (e.g., Disney World) and institutional settings (e.g., Duke University Hospital, West Virginia University in Morgantown). Downtown people movers operate in Detroit, Jacksonville, and Miami. People movers operate in numerous airports including Atlanta, Chicago O'Hare, Dallas-Fort Worth, Houston, Newark, Orlando, Pittsburgh, Seattle-Tacoma, and Tampa. Intermediate capacity systems operate in Lille, France (the "VAL" system); Docklands, London; Toronto and Vancouver; and several communities in Japan.

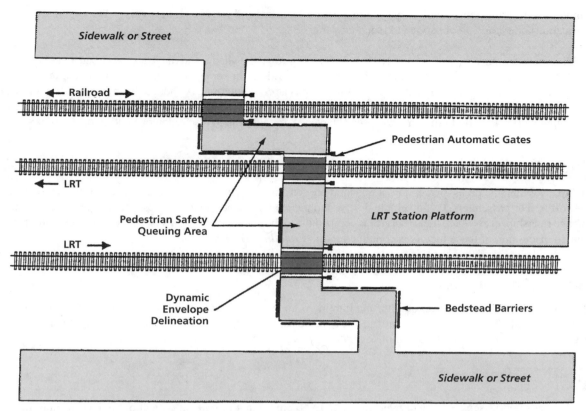

Figure 13–7 Illustrative Pedestrian Treatment in Combined Railroad and LRT Corridor

Source: Hans Korve, et al., "Pedestrian Control Systems for Light Rail Transit Operations in Metropolitan Environments," *Seventh National Conference on Light Rail Transit,* vol. 2, Washington, D.C.: Transportation Research Board, 1997.

The right-of-way for automated systems requires grade separation. However, the vehicle size is generally smaller than an LRV or rapid rail car and results in less right-of-way width. Right-of-way complications exist where switching occurs, depending upon the guideway technology involved. There are several urban examples of automated transit being designed and built to be an integral part of CBD office and retail buildings in Detroit, Miami, and Jacksonville. Toronto and Vancouver both have applications that are more traditional fixed route transit. Standards have been published to identify the minimum requirements for design, construction, operation, and maintenance of automated people mover systems.[7]

Commuter Rail

Commuter rail operations take advantage of existing railroads. Commuter rail lines are sometimes commingled with main-line rail and passenger services, may be diesel or electrically propelled, and generally serve suburban areas. Systems are found in large U.S. and Canadian metropolitan areas; and in major cities such as Berlin, Brussels, Frankfurt, Hamburg, London, Munich, and Paris in Europe; Rio de Janeiro in South America; Melbourne and Sydney in Australia; and Tokyo in Asia. Systems in several cities—including Brussels, Copenhagen, Frankfurt, London (Thames Link), Melbourne, Paris (RER), and Philadelphia—provide service through the city center.

Many of the commuter lines operate in railroads originally located to serve intercity travel; and in generating urban land uses along their corridors, they found themselves serving increasing numbers of local trips. Up to about 1920, some railroads added routes in the suburbs where they found sufficient demand. However, since that time many routes have been abandoned because of the high costs of railroad operation, reduced ridership, and the reluctance by management to allow long-distance passengers and freight customers to subsidize urban transportation. Most of the older U.S.

---

[7] *Automated People Mover Standards, part I* (Washington, D.C.: American Society of Civil Engineers, 1997).

commuter rail improvements involve upgrading existing facilities and fleet (e.g., new cars, better signals, additional electrification) or expansion of service to reach new markets.

New U.S. commuter rail systems have started up in Dallas, Los Angeles, Miami, and San Diego as urban areas have looked for ways to enhance lightly used existing freight railroad corridors. In some cases, for example, the San Diego–Los Angeles corridor, freight and Amtrak also use the same tracks as commuter rail. An added feature with such multiple use is enhanced multimodal transportation terminals. In San Diego and Los Angeles, both terminals also link with the local rail transit networks. For additional reference, see Chapter 18 for a thorough discussion of multimodal terminals.

Vehicle Design Factors

Ridership levels and the public perception of transport are sensitive to vehicle design and to the comfort and convenience that are offered to passengers. Good vehicle design and passenger accommodation is essential since poor design may discourage ridership, even where transit service is competitive to the automobile in terms of cost, expediency, and reliability. A detailed discussion of these factors is contained in the *Canadian Transit Handbook*.[8]

Passenger Environment

Control over noise, temperature, air quality, and lighting is an integral part of vehicle design. Sixty-five dBA (decibels, A-weighted) is the upper range of the comfort zone for noise. Interior temperature should fall within a close range of 20 degrees C, and there should be a complete air change every 1 to 2 min.

Seats

Widths of seats per passenger typically vary from 40 to 60 cm, with 43 to 50 cm typical of vehicles used in local and high-density service, and wider seats in buses and rail vehicles designed for longer suburban runs. The spacing distance between backs on transverse seats typically varies from 66 to 86 cm, with the lower half of this range most common for vehicles used in high-density service. Accordingly, the area per seated passenger typically varies from 0.3 to 0.5 sq m, with from 0.3 to 0.4 sq m appropriate for local service vehicles.

Passenger seats are arranged transversely or longitudinally in relation to the vehicle body length. Transverse seating is preferred for passenger comfort; but vehicle narrowness, planned high proportions of standees, wheel housings, or other spatial considerations often impose longitudinal seating in portions or the entirety of vehicles. Pairs of transverse seats are occasionally notched (longitudinally offset from each other by several inches) to save space or to improve comfort in reaching the seats farthest from the aisle. The dimensions of such seats fall within the ranges given above.

Standing Area, Aisles, and Doors

The number of riders who must stand for all or part of their journey is a major consideration in transit system design. The area per standing passenger under crush peak-period conditions can be as little as 0.15 sq m. The minimum area per standing passengers under easy standing conditions for "schedule design" purposes varies from about 0.23 to 0.36 sq m per person. Crush loads of under 0.28 sq m per person should be tolerated only for very limited durations or for special events. The minimum aisle widths on transit vehicles, usually between transversely positioned seats, typically range from 53 to 79 cm.

On most transit vehicles, doorway widths per passenger lane for boarding and alighting vary from 56 to 76 cm, with the lower half of this range typical on vehicles used in local transit. In the United States, single-channel doors predominate on buses. In some other countries, double-channel doors are used; in these cases the clear width per

---

[8] *Canadian Transit Handbook*, 3rd Edition (Toronto: Canadian Urban Transit Association, 1993).

channel or lane is slightly less than for single-lane doors. Rail transit vehicles have doors 1.2- to 1.5-m wide every 4.6 to 7.6 m of vehicle length.

Endedness

A trade-off is possible in rail vehicles between passenger space and operational flexibility. LRVs and streetcars can be designed with a single end for driving and doors only on one side, thereby, providing more space for seats and standees; however, route terminals must permit turning such vehicles through loops or turning "wyes." Rapid transit vehicles also can be simplified by having driving equipment at only one end and operating permanently in "married pairs;" this again results in a slight increase in the available passenger space. Double-ended vehicles allow for simple turnbacks at terminal stations, and they can offer dual side loading where stations are designed to permit (e.g., stations with a center platform also, as in San Diego).

Wheelchair Access

With passage of the Americans with Disabilities Act (ADA), all transit vehicles in the United States require wheelchair accessibility. This is provided in various ways:

- For most rapid transit systems and some LRT systems, the vehicles and platforms are both high-level, and the design requires off-platform lifts, elevators, or ramps to reach the platform.

- For buses and most LRT systems, the vehicles are high-level and the platforms are low-level, and special devices are needed to lift the wheelchair patron from the sidewalk or platform to the floor of the vehicle; in San Diego, onboard lifts are used; in Sacramento, mini high-level platforms with ramps are used; and in San Jose, lifts are used.

- Modern bus and LRT operations are increasingly moving toward low-floor vehicles that obviate the need for a lift or special platform.

Vehicle Dimensions, Capacities, and Features by Mode

Typical ranges for key dimensional and capacity characteristics of transit vehicles currently in significant use are indicated in Table 13–17. Lengths and widths shown are external body dimensions. Heights are from pavement or top of rail to roof. The lower end of the ranges of number of seats shown and the upper end of the ranges for standees generally apply to vehicles used on high-volume routes in large cities. The largest number of seats and lowest number of standees occur on longer suburban routes or where, for policy reasons, high levels of comfort are to be offered. Table 13–17 also shows the maximum length of trains in common use and the resulting total passenger capacity per train.

Motor Bus

Figure 13–8 shows dimensions of standard and articulated bus vehicles. Motor buses have a number of common features. These include rubber-tired suspension and guidance systems under the control of a human operator and an internal combustion engine or electronic propulsion.

Due to air quality concerns, increasing numbers of North American transit operators are moving toward use of alternative fuel buses (e.g., compressed natural gas, liquified natural gas). Other emerging technologies include zero-emission fuel cell buses that convert hydrogen into electricity without combustion and without pollutants (demonstration initiated in Chicago in 1997). Also, ethanol-powered buses have been tested in Peoria, Illinois; while West Covina, California has plans to deploy hybrid buses that use natural gas engines to generate electricity for an electric motor. Similarly, in 1997 there were 169 electric battery-operated buses operated.[9] Low-floor buses have become popular due to accessibility concerns. (Figure 13–9.)

---

[9] Heidi Tolliver-Nigro, "Riding into the 21st Century, Electric and Hybrid Innovations," *Mass Transit* (Fort Atkinson, Wis.: Cygrus Publishing, Johnson Hill Press Division, January/February 1998, pp. 22–23).

Table 13–17   Characteristics of Typical Transit Vehicles

Type of Vehicle	Length (m)	Width (m)	Seats	Standees[2]	Total	Remarks
			Typical Capacity[1]			
Minibus—short haul	5.48–8.84	1.98–2.44	15–29	0–15	15–44	
Transit bus (high floor)	9.14	2.44–2.59	35	19–25	54–60	
	10.67	2.44–2.60	39	25–33	64–72	
	12.19	2.44–2.61	43	32–47	75–90	New Flyer Industries—C40 HF, 1995
Transit bus (low floor)	9.14	2.44–2.59	30	19–25	49–55	
	10.67	2.44–2.60	34	25–33	59–67	
	12.19	2.44–2.61	38	32–47	70–85	New Flyer Industries—C40 LF, 1995
Articulated transit bus	16.76	2.61	64–66	34–42	98–108	Chicago–a.m. General-MAN
	18.29	2.61	65	32–47	97–112	New Flyer Industries—D60, 1993
Street car	14.23	2.74	59	40–80	99–139	P.C.C.[3]
Light rail car train (high floor)	97.52–98.76	2.65	256	344–544	600–800	San Diego-6-axle car, 4-car train Siemens)
Light rail car train (low floor)	56.08	2.7	144	166–246	310–390	Portland-6-axle car, 2-car train SD100 (Siemens)
Rail rapid transit train	184.40	3.05	500	1,300–1,700	1,800–2,200	10-car train, IND New York
	182.89	3.05	576	1,224–1,664	1,800–2,240	8-car train, R-46 cars, New York
	136.73	3.14	504	876–1,356	1,380–1,860	8-car train, Toronto
	117.04	2.84	312	600–1,100	912–1,412	CTA, 1994-8—car trains
	117.04	2.84	376	610–1,200	986–1,576	CTA, 1970-8—car trains
Commuter rail train (single-level)	250.91	3.20	1,100	200–1,100	1,300–2,200	Regular car, 10-car train Budd trains, Chicago METRA
Commuter rail train (bi-level)	250.91	3.20	400–1,440	200–1,400	1,600–2,840	Bombardier Bilevel Commuter Coach (NCTD Coaster, Toronto's GO Transit 10-car train

[1] In any transit vehicle the total passenger capacity can be increased by removing seats and by making more standing room available, and vice-versa.

[2] Higher figures denote crush capacity; lower figures, schedule-design capacity.

[3] Presidents' Conference Committee Cars.

Sources: Adapted from the Institute of Transportation Engineers, *Transportation Planning Handbook,* Englewood Cliffs, N.J.: Prentice-Hall, 1992.

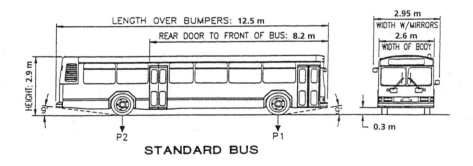

STANDARD BUS

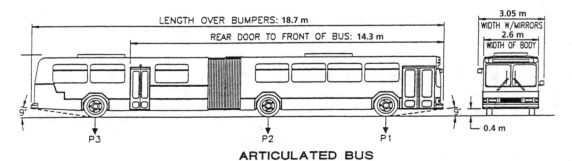

ARTICULATED BUS

Figure 13–8   Various Bus Vehicle Profiles (Standard, Articulated, Trolley Coach)

Source: *Designing for Transit, A Manual for Integrating Public Transportation and Land Development in the San Diego Metropolitan Area,* San Diego, Calif.: San Diego Metropolitan Transit Development Board, July 1993.

Trolley Bus

Electric trolley buses, or trolley coaches, are powered by rotary DC electric motors, typically one per vehicle; and they obtain power from overhead lines at 550-600 volts DC. As Figure 13–10 shows, because the vehicle is isolated from ground, a double overhead power distribution system is used, with two spring-tensioned trolley poles mounted on the vehicle roof, one for collection and one for power return, to complete the circuit.

The "dual-mode" bus has both electric and diesel motors. This feature helps to eliminate one of the trolley coach's major operational disadvantages compared to the motor bus—the inability to bypass downed overhead wires or disruptions such as road construction and traffic accidents. Dual-mode buses operate in Vancouver, Lyon (France) and in Seattle's bus subway.

Paratransit

These services use a variety of vehicle types, including sedans, vans, and small-sized buses. The smaller vehicles are generally suited to the low number of passengers carried with this type of service. An example is shown in Figure 13–11.

Light Rail Transit

Common features of LRVs include: (1) steel-wheel, steel-rail suspension guidance; (2) electric propulsion; (3) overhead power supply (most applications); (4) train operation; and (5) ability to operate in either shared or right-of-way. Light rail transit is a very versatile form of transit and can combine the benefits of rail transit (greater capacity, high speed) with some benefits of motor buses (use of readily available at-grade rights-of-way, minimal environmental effect). However, improperly used, it can have the disadvantages of both modes—costs of fixed guideways and track and slow-speed operations in mixed traffic.

Figure 13–9 Examples of Low-Floor Buses

Source: EG&G Dynatrend and Crain & Associates, Inc., *Transit Operations for Individuals with Disabilities, Transit Cooperative Research Program Report 9,* Washington, D.C.: Transportation Research Board, 1995.

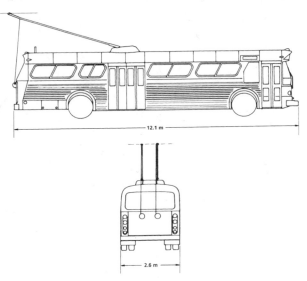

Figure 13–10   Trolleybus Coach Profile and End View

Source: Institute of Transportation Engineers, *Transportation Planning Handbook,* Englewood Cliffs, N.J.: Prentice-Hall, 1992, p. 138.

Due to accessibility concerns, *low-floor LRVs* are becoming increasingly prevalent. While up to 25 percent more expensive than regular LRVs, their operational advantages in boarding have proven attractive. Three types exist: (1) partly low floor with level access through at least one door, (2) mainly low floor with level access through all doors, and (3) fully low floor (i.e., 100 percent). An example of an LRV with a low floor over 65 percent of its length is shown in Figure 13–12. In 1998, Portland, Oregon became the first North American LRT operator to move toward low-floor LRVs. Wheelchair accessibility features of other North American LRT operations include ramps (e.g., Baltimore, Sacramento), platform lifts (e.g., San Jose), and onboard lifts (e.g., San Diego).

Vintage Trolleys

Vintage trolleys are historic (or historic appearing) trams or streetcars. They are normally nonarticulated, two-axle, and used in museum or downtown applications. The design focus is more on historical relevance than on performance.

Rapid Rail Transit

Common features of rapid rail transit vehicles include: high capacity; track-based guidance and suspension systems; wayside power collection (third rail or overhead catenary); and extensive supporting infrastructure. Most rapid rail transit cars operate on steel rails for both guidance and suspension. Several systems—Montreal, Mexico City, and some lines in Paris—use a rubber-tired suspension system with separate rubber guide wheels and steel wheels and

Figure 13–11   Low-Floor Small Bus

Source: EG&G Dynatrend and Crain & Associates, Inc., *Transit Operations for Individuals with Disabilities, Transit Cooperative Research Program Report 9,* Washington, D.C.: Transportation Research Board, 1995.

rails for switching. The Sapporo system contains rubber wheels only. The diversity of North American rapid rail equipment is shown in the dimensions provided in Table 13–18, and a Toronto vehicle is shown in Figure 13–13.

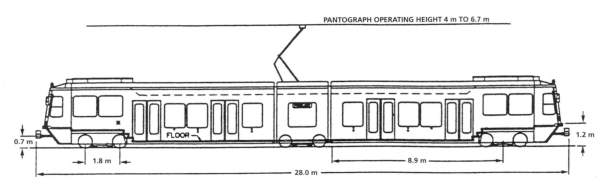

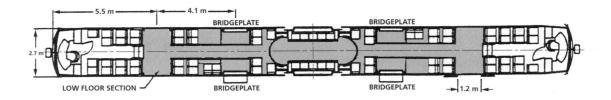

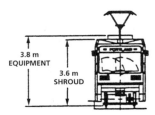

Figure 13–12   Low-Floor Light Rail Vehicle

Source: Dennis L. Porter, "Introduction of Low-Floor Light Rail Vehicles to North America: History and Status of the Portland Type 2 Vehicle," *Seventh National Conference on Light Rail Transit,* vol. 1, Washington, D.C.: Transportation Research Board, 1995.

All doors on most rapid rail transit trains can be controlled from a single point. Train operation with one person is common both in North America and abroad. Although some of the new systems are fully automated (e.g., BART), a train operator usually controls opening and closing of the doors.

Automated Systems

The various AGT and advanced rapid rail transit systems, while differing in their technological and operational features, share several common elements: automated control systems; exclusive right-of-way; frequent service; and relatively small, lightweight guideways and vehicles.

Table 13–19 gives vehicle characteristics for three basic types of automated guideway systems. Group I, intermediate capacity systems, is the most widely applied. The Group II systems include minirail and monorail technologies. The Group III systems are likely to be more extensively applied in the future.

Table 13–18 Rapid Rail Equipment Summary

Area	Length (m)	Width (m)	Seats
Atlanta	22.5	3.2	64–68
Baltimore	22.5	3.1	76
Boston	14.6–20.9	2.8–3.1	42–64
Chicago	14.4	2.8	39–51
Cleveland	14.6–22.5	3.1	54–84
Los Angeles	22.5	3.2	59
Miami	22.5	3.1	72
New York City	15.3–22.4	2.6–3.0	28–76
New York/New Jersey PATH	15.4	2.8	31–32
Philadelphia/New Jersey PATCO	20.3	3.1	72–80
Philadelphia/SEPTA	16.5–20.3	2.7–3.0	50–65
San Francisco BART	21.0–22.5	3.2	64–72
Washington	22.4	3.1	68–80

Source: *Transit Vehicle Data Book,* Washington, D.C.: American Public Transit Association, 1997.

The Vancouver and Toronto AGT vehicles are functionally similar to heavy-rail vehicles, except that the cars are shorter (17- vs. 12.7-m long). They provide high-level loading with doors on both sides. Features include linear induction motor propulsion, radial or steerable trucks, and fully automated train control.

Commuter Rail

Commuter rail vehicle technology must be compatible with conventional passenger rolling stock. Electrically operated lines provide multiple train controls. Diesel locomotive propelled trains are often operated in a push-pull configuration. Bilevel coaches are used on commuter lines in Europe and in Chicago, Los Angeles, Miami, San Diego, San Francisco, and Toronto; the Dallas commuter rail operation uses single-level coaches, as do most Eastern U.S. cities. Because of the relatively long trip lengths and high average speeds compared to other urban transit services, commuter rail vehicles are generally designed for higher comfort levels than other rail vehicles. Seated vs. standee ratios are higher, seats are

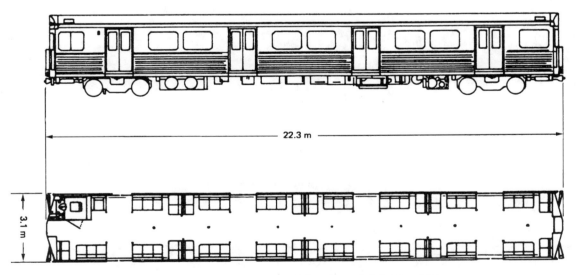

Figure 13–13 Rapid Rail Vehicle Profile

Source: Institute of Transportation Engineers, *Transportation Planning Handbook,* Englewood Cliffs, N.J.: Prentice-Hall, 1992, p. 138.

wider, and cars may be equipped with washrooms. A 2-2 or 3-2 transverse seating arrangement is common. Typical bilevel and single level commuter rail cars are shown on Figure 13–14.

A new generation of selfpropelled rail transit vehicles are being evaluated by several urban areas. They are sometimes referred to as "diesel multiple units" (DMU) or "light weight diesel" cars. Functionally, DMUs are a hybrid of LRT and commuter rail, with the major distinctive feature being DMU's ability to propel itself without the need for an external power source. However, certain design elements restrict application of DMUs (e.g., long tunnels, sharp curves, steep gradients) as opposed to LRTs. Dimensional contrasts of typical diesel locomotives, LRVs, and DMUs are shown in Figure 13–15.

Commuter rail vehicle data for North American operations finds the vast majority of cars are 25.91 m in length, and width is generally at 3.2 m. However, there is a wide variance in seating capacity (the bilevels seats 148–162 persons, while the others seat 93–127 persons).

Table 13–19 Characteristics of Selected Automated Guideway Transit Systems

Item		Group I		Group II		Group III	
Definition		• Intermediate transit capacity • Technologically mature • Relatively extensive applications		• Smaller transit capacity • Limited applications		Likely systems in the near future	
						Magnetic levitated	Personal rapid transit
Representative System		Kobe Portliner	Miami Metro-mover	Dortmund H-Bahn	Sydney Mini-monorail	M-Bahn	Morgantown PRT
	Purpose	Feeder to rapid transit; intra-island loop	Feeder to Metro rail; DBD loop	Feeder to S-Bahn, shuttle in campus	Feeder to MRT, CBD loop	Feeder to S-Bahn, experimental line	Intra-area service
	Route length (km)	64	3.0	1.1	3.5	1.6	6.4
	Station spacing (m)	945	365	1,036	457	792	3,048
System Outline	Route configuration	double-track loop/shuttle	double-track loop	Single-track shuttle	Single-track loop	Double-track shuttle	Double-track shuttle
	Guidance	Lateral guidance	Central guidance	Running beam	Running beam	Lateral guidance	Central guidance
	Car support	Rubber (stuffed)	Rubber tire (air)	Rubber (solid)	Rubber	Magnetic (levitated)	Rubber
	Power	3 ph. alt. 600V	3 ph. alt. 380V	3 ph. alt. 500V	3 ph. alt. 500V	DC 960V	3 ph. alt. 575V
	Automation	Full	Full	Full	Full	Full	Full
Vehicle	Size: L×W×H (m)	8.4×2.4×3.2	11.9×2.9×3.6	8.2×2.1×5.0	3.2×2.1×2.3 (7 units/train)	11.8×2.3×2.3	4.7×2.0×5.4
	Weight (metric tons)	10.5	14.5	7.3	22/train	7.5	3.9
	Capacity/car	75	100	42	170 train	71	21
	Max. Speed (kph)	60	95	50	32	N/A	48
	Acc. kph/sec	3.5	3.2	3.5	2.6	4.7–5.6	2.3
	Dec. kph/sec	3.5	2.4	7.2	2.6	3.5	4.3
	Propulsion	90 kw × 8/train	75 kw × 2/car	23 kw × 4/car	37 kw × 6/train	Linear motor	454 kw/car
Structure	Guideway	Concrete, partially steel	PC concrete and steel box	Steel	Steel	Steel	PC concrete
	Max. Gradient (%)	5.0	10.0	4.5	Up 4.4, down 6.0	12.0	10.0
	Min. Curvature (m)	30	24	30	20	30	9
Current Status		In operation since 1985	Operated only 1986	Commercial within university; extension planned	Commercial operation started July 1, 1988 Sentosa Monorail[1]	In operation since started July 1, 1974	1988
		Osaka New Town Yukarigaoka VONA Saitasa Ina Line	Atlanta airport Tampa airport Seattle airport Changi airport				

1.0 kilometer = 0.62 miles.
N/A = Not Available.
1 = Singapore

Source: *Singapore Urban Transport Improvement Study,* Executive Summary, Japan: Japan International Cooperation Agency, November 1988.

Ferryboats

A few cities in North America provide ferry service; these include Boston, New York, San Francisco, Seattle, and Vancouver. A modern vehicle, Vancouver's "sea bus," was specially designed for high-capacity waterborne transit. This vehicle, shown in Figure 13–16, has a capacity of 400 seated passengers. Six double rows of doors per side allow flow-through passenger loading and unloading, and minimize terminal times. A double-ended catamaran configuration provides maximum capacity for a given length and good resistance to the hull while loading and unloading. Two ferries operating from specially designed terminals provide a capacity of 2,400 passengers per hour each way.

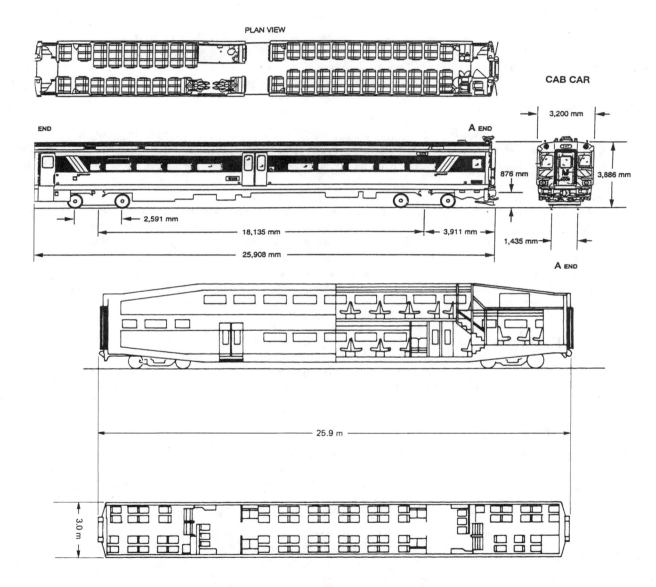

Figure 13–14   Bilevel and Single-Level Commuter Rail Vehicle Profile and Layout

Sources: New Jersey Transit Corporation, Newark, N.J.; Adapted from the Institute of Transportation Engineers, *Transportation Planning Handbook,* Englewood Cliffs, N.J.: Prentice-Hall, 1992.

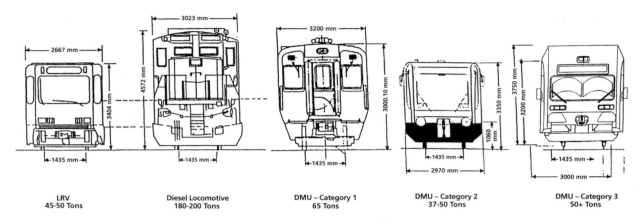

Figure 13–15   Dimensional Contrasts of Various Rail Vehicles

Source: Edwards and Kelsey, *Transit Cooperative Research Program, Project A-17*, in progress.

Vehicle Performance

Transit travel times and capacities depend upon vehicle performance, dwell times, stop spacing, route geometry (curves, grades), legal or design speed limits, and traffic delays. Transit operations in mixed traffic are particularly susceptible to delay, while efficiently operated services on exclusive rights-of-way normally experience only delays connected with passenger stops.

The maximum rates of acceleration, deceleration, and jerk (rate of change in acceleration or deceleration) in normal transit service must be related to the tolerance of a standee who is not able to hold on to a hand grip. This condition frequently occurs when passengers have both hands full (e.g., with bundles), when such passengers cannot reach a hand grip, or when a hand grip is not available. Acceleration and deceleration rates of from 4.8 to 5.6 $km/h/s^2$ are usually considered appropriate upper limits under such conditions. The jerk rate is even more critical to passenger comfort; a preferred maximum jerk rate is 3.2 $km/h/s^2$, and an allowable maximum jerk rate is about 50 percent above this value.

System Design

A basic understanding of the foundation for producing transit rides requires knowledge of the interdependence of land uses and the transit system, the effect of access relationships, and the connectivity of the transit system.

Land Use and Transit Systems

Transit investments can promote compact, mixed-use, and transit-supportive development. Such development, in turn, can induce transit ridership. This symbiotic relationship is ongoing, with transit and urban form continually reinforcing, reshaping, and helping to reconstitute each other. Figure 13–17 shows the interrelationships among various land use design aspects and transit patronage.

While a great deal of a metropolitan area's urban form is already in place, thousands of individual investment decisions continue to be made every year, each of which contributes to the evolution of urban America. Under a different set of rules and policies governing urban development, a differently built environment would emerge that existing and future transit investments could effectively support the mutual optimization of urban livability.

Meaningful coordination of transit-urban form relationships must take place within a larger systems context. Initiatives to coordinate transit investments and urban development should be framed more globally in terms of such complementary initiatives as travel demand management planning, road pricing, regional growth management, and community redevelopment.

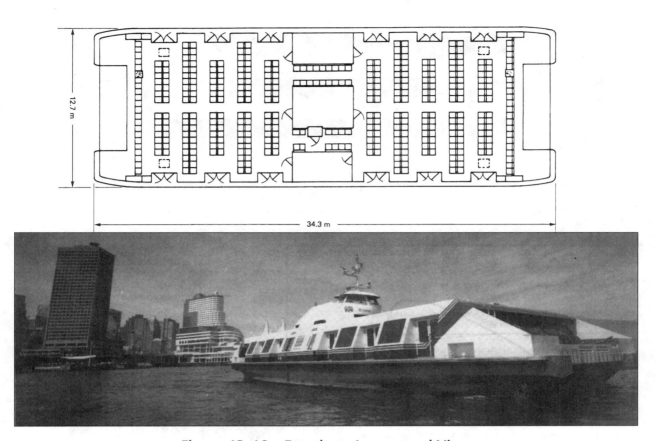

Figure 13–16   Ferryboat Layout and View

Source: Institute of Transportation Engineers, *Transportation Planning Handbook,* Englewood Cliffs, N.J.: Prentice-Hall, 1992.

Transit and urban form always have and always will best complement each other when tied to a larger policy agenda aimed at improving the quality of urban environments. Strengthening future transit and urban form interactions will hinge on recognizing these systemic relationships, and putting in place the package of public programs and private initiatives necessary to accomplish these goals.

Figure 13–18 shows the importance of transit-oriented land use design. Traditional residential neighborhoods and transit-oriented developments in the San Francisco Bay Area favor walking and transit use. A comparison of an auto-dependent neighborhood design with transit-oriented development is shown in Figure 13–19. This figure shows that street system design can foster transit system connectivity and access as depicted by the lower half schematic.

High density is a factor that is often associated with high transit ridership. This does not mean that only high-rise apartments and office buildings should be constructed near transit stops. However, for transit to be cost-effective, certain thresholds of development should be encouraged.

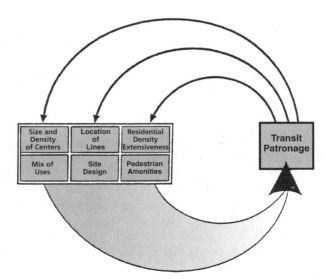

Figure 13–17   Transit Development: Relationships

Source: Parsons, Brinckerhoff, Quade & Douglas, Inc., *Transit and Urban Form, Transit Cooperative Research Program Report 16,* vols. 1 and 2, Washington, D.C.: Transportation Research Board, 1996.

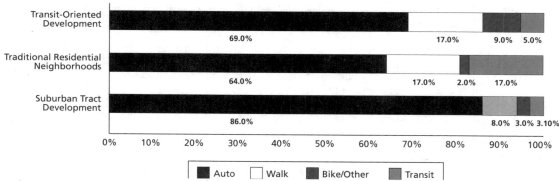

Transit-Oriented Development: 69.0% Auto, 17.0% Walk, 9.0% Bike/Other, 5.0% Transit

Traditional Residential Neighborhoods: 64.0% Auto, 17.0% Walk, 2.0% Bike/Other, 17.0% Transit

Suburban Tract Development: 86.0% Auto, 8.0% Walk, 3.0% Bike/Other, 3.10% Transit

Legend: Auto, Walk, Bike/Other, Transit

Figure 13–18   Daily Trip Generation by All Modes in the San Francisco Bay Area

Source: Robert Cervero and Samuel Seskin, *An Evaluation of the Relationships Between Transit and Urban Form, Transit Cooperative Research Program Research Results Digest No. 7,* Washington, D.C.: Transportation Research Board, June 1995.

Table 13–20 summarizes proposed relationships between land densities and different types of transit services. While these thresholds may be superseded by other site-related circumstances, such as topography or good feeder bus service, they provide useful guidelines. A gradient of densities should exist within the walking radius of a transit stop, with the highest intensity of use located nearest the transit facility.

In some instances, density is indicated in the table by the type of urban environment within which it is located. Three such environments have been distinguished: (1) "urban centers" (such as a CBD) are characterized by a concentration of high-intensity buildings with mixed uses in close proximity, (2) "urban areas" (i.e., in the "ring" surrounding the CBD) consist of moderately dense clusters of single- and multi-family houses and related commercial districts, and (3) "suburban areas" are low- to moderate-density areas in which single-family homes predominate. The relationship between distance from a transit station and the propensity to use transit is displayed in Figure 13–20.

Access Relationships

Transit-focused development can be described as development, generally within half a mile of rail transit stations, that provides sufficient densities and mixes of activities and convenient pedestrian linkages to support significant transit ridership. Focusing development in proximity to transit stations can create interesting and

Figure 13–19   Comparison of Auto-Dependent Areas with Transit-Oriented Development

Source: Adapted from Frank Spielberg, The Traditional Neighborhood Development: How will Traffic Engineers Respond?, *ITE Journal,* Washington, D.C.: Institute of Transportation Engineers, September 1989.

functional urban centers, diminish environmentally damaging urban sprawl, and play a major role in realizing regional development strategies.

Many older cities sustaining rapid growth from the late 1800s onward developed in conjunction with the invention and spread of rail transit. Development patterns of the older parts of cities like Boston, Chicago, New York, and Philadelphia are closely integrated with transit service. However, development around transit stations since World War II has been markedly successful in certain areas and not so in others.

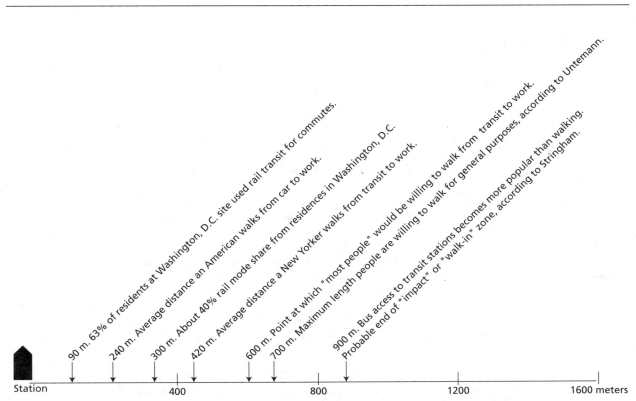

Figure 13–20   Empirical Evidence on Ridership by Distance

Notes: 1.0 kilometers = 0.62 miles; 1.0 meters = 3.28 feet

Source: Robert Cervero and Samuel Seskin, *An Evaluation of the Relationships Between Transit and Urban Form, Transit Cooperative Research Program Research Results Digest No. 7,* Washington, D.C.: Transportation Research Board, June 1995.

Table 13–20   Relationship Between Residential Land Densities and Different Types of Transit Services

Service Levels	Density Thresholds
Bus: minimum service, 0–8 km between routes, 20 buses/day	4 dwelling unit/residential acre
Bus: intermediate service, 0.8 km between routes, 40 buses/day	7 dwelling unit/residential acre
Bus: frequent service, 0.8 km between routes, 120 buses/day	15 dwelling unit/residential acre
Light rail: 5-minute peak headways	9 dwelling unit/residential acre; 65–250 square km corridor
Rapid rail: 5-minute peak headways	12 dwelling unit/residential acre; 250–350 sq km corridor
Commuter rail: 20 trains/day	1–2 dwelling unit/residential acre existing track

The Institute of Transportation Engineers (1989) recommends the following minimums:

1 bus/hour	4–6 dwelling unit/residential acre	465,000 to 745,000 square meters of commercial/office
1 bus/30 minutes	7–8 dwelling unit/residential acre	745,000 to 1.9 million square meters of commercial/office
Light rail/feeder buses	9 dwelling unit/residential acre	3.2 to 4.5 million square meters of commercial/office

1.0 kilometers = 0.62 miles.
0.93 square meters = 1.0 square foot.

Source: J. Holtzclaw, *Using Residential Patterns and Transit to Decrease Auto Dependence and Costs,* San Francisco, Calif.: Natural Resources Defense Council, 1994.

Transit-focused development generally leads to enhanced ridership:

- When stations are located in prime regional and community nodes of activity (retail, business, education, service) attractive to typical market forces.

- When these nodes are designed to promote pedestrian movements between uses and between the uses and the transit steps.

- When the regional and local real estate market is active.

- When public policies and regulations permit or encourage intensive development around station areas.

- When transit extends into areas *before* they are developed.

When development focuses on areas in which stations are located, governmental action can help promote station-area development. In areas attracting development interest, local governments have adopted public programs and regulations that permit an intensively built mix of activities around stations, promote transit-friendly design, and control provision of parking to generate transit usage. Cleveland's Tower City Center, a joint developer, transit, and government project, created a 33,480 sq m regional mixed-use center (transit, retail, office, hotel) around restored city landmarks, including its 1920s rail terminal. In San Diego, the LRT system has two CBD nodes where multistory development has been placed over two stations; both were public-private ventures. In station areas where developer interest is lacking, public actions can underwrite redevelopment costs and improve accessibility to and the appearance of the station.

Transit extensions into suburban communities can provide opportunities for station-area development as part of community business district revitalization efforts. Small-scale infill residential projects can build densities and ridership along light-rail lines, as demonstrated in Portland, Oregon. In some areas, it may be possible to retrofit built-up or partly developed neighborhoods to support transit service.

There are many ways that the design of new development can encourage greater use of public transportation. Most involve little cost or effort if they are followed early enough in the planning of a project. It is usually cheaper and easier to design something in advance than it is to try to fit it in later. The task in transforming existing development is often more challenging, but the transportation rewards are just as great.

Success in encouraging transit use through land use design requires a change in how the issue of transportation planning is approached. Instead of relying upon a single-minded effort to accommodate automobiles, both public planners and private developers must consider reopening the urban area to travel of all sorts. Plans should reflect the needs of pedestrians, transit riders, and bicyclists. Although much "lip service" has been paid to other modes of travel, the design of newer communities has discouraged their use.

Key principles for developing more transit-oriented communities are as follows:

1. Create a pedestrian-friendly environment.

2. Make pedestrian facilities a priority.

3. Design building sites to serve many users.

4. Encourage a mixture of land uses.

5. Encourage appropriate densities.

6. Interconnect the street system.

7. Narrow the neighborhood street.

8. Be cautious of major streets.

9. Integrate transit into the community.

10. Consider transit linkage in advance.[10]

---

[10] *Designing for Transit, A Manual for Integrating Public Transportation and Land Development in the San Diego Metropolitan Area* (San Diego, Calif.: San Diego Metropolitan Transit Development Board, July 1993).

System and Network Design

These are three typical transit network concepts, as depicted in Figure 13–21:

1. *Grid,* with most service focused on a CBD, along with non-CBD cross-town routes, but traveling on a street system developed on a grid basis. Some travel to the CBD requires a transfer.

2. *Radial,* with all service focused on the CBD, regardless of the underlying street system.

3. *Modified radial,* with most service still focused on the CBD, but some routes serving a cross-town function. Another variation of this concept is "hub and spoke," where the hubs serve as points of timed connections.

Good transit system design requires good *connectivity* between routes. With the multiplicity of destinations that exist, networks cannot be practically designed to provide nontransfer trips for all travelers. *Transfers* are often necessary to complete trips; however, travelers perceive them as negative experiences. Travelers dislike the time and cost required for transferring, but they also dislike the need for added trip planning, the possibility of a missed connection, the uncertainty of arrival time at their destination, exposure to weather and crowding, the need to find the next vehicle, difficulty of baggage handling, and waiting in unfamiliar or hostile surroundings. A well-designed transit station or bus stop, with coordinated transfer times, can decrease the unpleasantness of the transfer by directly addressing the above reasons why travelers avoid transfers.

The difficulty of making a trip is referred to as the trip's *disutility.* It is known that the disutility of any trip can be influenced by the conditions of travel. Waiting and walking accrue greater amounts of disutility than riding the same amount of time. Poor weather, crowding, and congestion can increase disutility, too. The requirement to spend money increases disutility.[11] *Timed transfer* points can offset this disutility associated with transferring by having the route connections timed to meet. Timed transfers are similar to coordination if air travel at "hubs" where routes are scheduled to arrive within a prescribed time window to facilitate interchange among the routes with minimum waiting time.

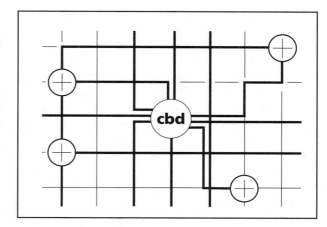

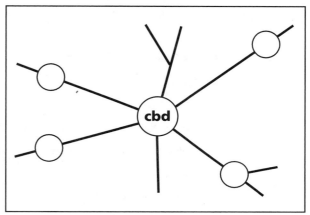

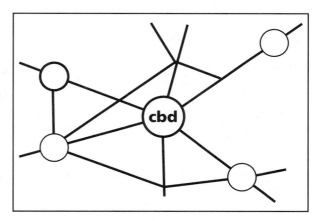

Figure 13–21   Alternative Transit System Networks

Source: *The Canadian Transit Handbook,* Third Edition, Canada: Canadian Urban Transit Association, 1993.

---

[11] Alan J. Horowitz, et al., *Evaluation of Intermodal Passenger Transfer Facilities* (Washington, D.C.: Federal Highway Administration, 1994).

Many factors will influence the overall transit route structure. The configuration is defined in terms of time (periods and schedules of service), space (routes, stops, and fixed-facility geography), technology, service type, and other characteristics. Spatially and geographically, transit networks may vary widely in complexity and in interrelationships with other transportation networks. Major considerations include:

1. The area to be served, its geography, topography, land use, and development density.

2. Location of major traffic generators.

3. Demand patterns in time and space.

4. Policies and master plans regarding land use and transportation.

5. Service area coverage standards.

6. Accessibility standards and resulting stop and station locations.

7. Service headway standards.

8. Vehicle types, sizes, and capacities.

9. Streets and other rights-of-way available for transit use.

10. Land available for yards and maintenance facilities.

11. Role of other urban transit systems.

12. Transfer opportunities to other routes.

13. Interfaces with intercity transportation systems.

Table 13–21 Typical Maximum Distance Traveled to Reach Urban Transit Stops and Stations

Access Mode	Most Patrons (km)	Some Patrons (km)
Walk	0.6–1.0	1.0–1.6
Bicycle	1.6–3.2	3.2–4.8
Feeder transit; motorcycle	3.2–6.4	6.4–13
Auto Kiss-ride; taxi	4.8–6.4	6.4–10
Park-ride	6.4–10	10–16

1.0 kilometer = 0.62 miles.

Sources: Henry D. Quinby, "Coordinated Highway-Transit Interchange Stations," *Origin and Destination: Methods and Evaluation*, Highway Res. Rec. 14, Washington, D.C.: Highway Research Board, National Research Council, 1966, pp. 99–121; Various other reference data were used in this table.

Service Area Coverage

Service area coverage indicates how well a transit system reaches its market. It is defined by the distribution of stops or stations in space, and by the distance that people are willing to walk to these points. To reach a stop or station, patrons will usually travel up to the maximum distances shown in Table 13–21; Figure 13–20 also shows the relationship between the propensity to use transit and access mode. Acceptable walking distances from origin to boarding stop and from alighting stop to destination are usually taken to be 0.5 to 0.6 km; such figures, of course, do not apply to the elderly and handicapped.

The acceptable walking distance is also affected by the quality of the transit service (patrons may walk farther for better service than for very poor service), grades, quality of the traveled access ways, perceptions of security enroute and at the stop, available alternatives, weather conditions, and other factors. The combined access time to and from transit stops at both ends of a trip may exceed the time spent on the transit vehicle itself, especially if the latter is relatively fast and involves no transfers.

Transit Planning

The planning for transit services is more complicated than for highways or streets in that consideration must be given to key elements such as: route alignment, stop locations, stop design, fare levels and fare payment systems, service levels, and vehicle configuration and capacity. The various approaches and considerations involved in planning for new, enhanced, or expanded transit services is covered in this section.

Major Investment Studies

Transit planning efforts in the United States must comply with the requirements set forth in the Intermodal Surface Transportation Efficiency Act of 1991 (ISTEA), as updated in 1998 by the Transportation Equity Act for the 21st Century, whenever federal funds are sought. In particular, the federal criteria for major transit investments for "new starts" require detailed analyses of transportation alternatives for corridors where fixed guideway facilities are proposed. These alternatives must include both "build" and "no-build" alternatives, as well as a transportation system management option that involves better management and operation of the existing facility such as through provision of high-occupancy vehicle lanes.

The analysis should assess each alternative's capital and operating costs, ridership attraction, capital and operating efficiency and productivity, effects on modal choice, and levels of automobile use. An accompanying environmental statement analyzes environmental effects and energy consumption, effects on land use and development patterns, extent of neighborhood disruption and displacement, job creation effect, and other factors considered important by the local community. In the end, the analysis should also compare the relative cost and effectiveness of each alternative, in terms of ability to serve the public and to meet public policy objectives.

This increasingly formalized and rigorous planning process is intended to ensure cost-effective decisions at each stage of project development. Federal financial support is available for conducting the studies required; detailed review of these studies and formal consent by the FTA is required for a local agency to progress to each subsequent stage.

Whether in the United States or elsewhere, the procedures for selecting the optimum transit investment entail the design of a variety of alternative transit improvement projects. These alternatives must then be evaluated on the basis of their forecasted costs and performance in meeting state and local transportation objectives. The preferred project is then selected by local decision-makers in a process that weighs each alternative's projected benefits against its projected costs: the chosen alternative is normally referred to as the "locally preferred alternative." Specifics with regard to the alternatives analysis, federal major investment studies process, and related cost-effectiveness evaluation are covered in more detail in Chapter 9.

Service Planning Approaches

Transit planning takes many forms. It includes *strategic planning,* which takes a broad global look at how an agency might function in its surrounding environment; *long-range planning,* which generally relates to major facility development (and in the U.S. FTA's major investment studies) in a 5- to 10-year time frame; *short-range planning,* which traditionally produces a 5-year transit development plan; and *service or operations* planning, which looks at service changes on a continuing basis. All types of planning are closely linked to system finance and administration.

The transit planning effort should reflect specific local circumstances and needs. It should assess existing problems and how they are likely to change, identify improvement options, and suggest directions. It should provide essential information to decision-makers relative to ridership, cost, performance, and environmental and economic aspects. It should produce transit plans that are compatible with an area's needs, goals, and resources.

Short- and long-range transit planning studies traditionally include: (1) setting goals and objectives; (2) conducting system inventories; (3) surveying travel patterns, especially those of transit patrons; (4) identifying existing needs and problems; (5) forecasting future ridership; (6) identifying and assessing improvement alternatives; (7) developing improvement programs; and (8) preparing financial analyses. It may lead to environmental impact assessments of proposed system developments.

The system planning process involves planners, transportation engineers, transit users, citizens, and public officials. Collectively, these groups should identify the most promising candidate plans for decision-makers to examine and from which to select the most appropriate improvements.

Strategic management and planning have been applied increasingly to the transit industry in recent years. They involve identifying the organization's basic mission; pinpointing internal and external factors that influence this mission;

adopting a set of master strategies, policy goals, and objectives; developing and implementing functional strategies; and reviewing and evaluating performance.

The strategic approach to management and planning calls for a look at the external environment in which transit operates—how this environment affects the transit system and how these effects will change. It also looks at the internal agency environment—including management capabilities, resource availability, and management practices. It assesses organizational strengths and weaknesses and identifies future strategies. It includes situation assessment, fiscal planning, management appraisal, and performance evaluation. (Figure 13–22.)

Within the strategic planning process, there are various levels of analysis. (Table 13–22.)

- *Trip-level* analyses that can lead to operational adjustments of service; these operational needs tend to be of an urgent nature because they affect the quality of the service offered.

- *Route-level* analyses that can lead to service enhancements, reductions, and restructuring.

- *Regional and subregional* analyses that can lead to metropolitan-wide service improvements, new transit services, and capital programs for the development of regional facilities.

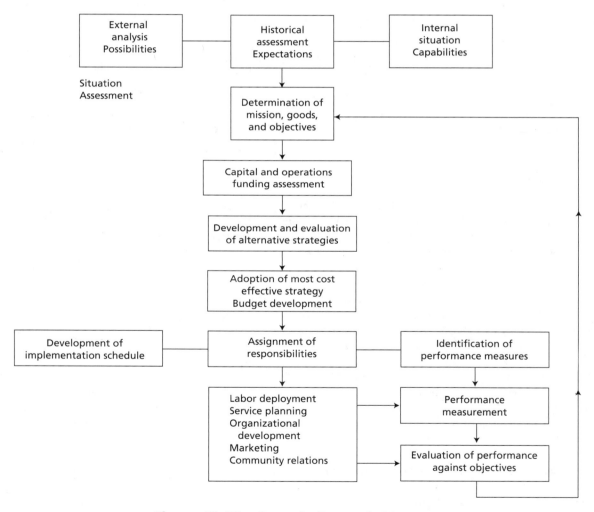

Figure 13–22   Steps in Strategic Management

Source: Institute of Transportation Engineers, *Transportation Planning Handbook,* Englewood Cliffs, N.J.: Prentice-Hall, 1992, p. 171.

Table 13–22 Summary of Evaluation Procedures and Measures for Transit Service Modification

Evaluation Procedures	Frequency	Evaluation Measures	Possible Outcomes and Actions
Trip Level			
Passenger complaints	As received	• Identification of problems to be checked	• Operations adjustments
Driver and supervisor reports	As received	• Identification of problems to be checked	
Operators' time checks	As needed	• Percent of trips missed/on-time	
Operators' load checks	As needed	• Peak load counts • Peak occupancy	
Route Level			
Public comments	As received	• Identification of potential improvements	• Service enhancements, reductions, restructuring • Market research and advertising
Operators suggestions	As received	• Identification of potential improvements	
Farebox/vendomat counts	Daily	• Number of passengers by type of fare	
Route Evaluation Report	Annually	By route: • Passenger boardings/revenue kilometer • Passenger kilometers/seat kilometer • Subsidy/boarding passenger	
On/off counts	Annually	• Bus stop/rail station counts • Loading profiles • Peak load counts • Average trip lengths • Vehicle seat kilometers of service • Percent of trips on-time	
Regional or Subregional Level			
Quarterly reports	Quarterly	By operator: • Total passengers • Farebox recovery ratio • Subsidy/boarding passenger • Passenger boardings/revenue kilometer	• Market research • Planning studies • Service enhancements, reductions, restructuring • New service proposals • Capital facility proposals
Area planning studies	As needed	• Service proposals and analyses (subregional)	
Short-range transit plan	Annually	• Service proposals and analyses (regionwide)	
Regional transportation plan	Two years	• Service and facility proposals and analyses (regional)	
Onboard survey	Five years	• Trip patterns • Trip purpose and frequency • Demographics and attitudes • Mode/distance to/from stops • Fare type	

Source: San Diego Metropolitan Transit Development Board, San Diego, Calif.

Service Planning Considerations

Bus transit service planning should reflect the specific needs and operating requirements of each urban area. Suggested bus service planning guidelines based on U.S. and Canadian practice are summarized in Table 13–23. These guidelines provide a point of departure in developing service plans or making specific changes in routes, stops, or service frequencies.

For rail transit service planning, rail transit lines typically extend 19 to 32 km of travel from the city center (and longer for commuter rail) with a 30- to 40-minute running time. In developing and configuring new lines, it is important to maximize ridership. Lines should generally radiate from the city center, penetrating major employment areas, high activity centers (e.g., universities, medical centers), and residential markets. For service *through* the city center (rates that terminate by going through it or around it) it is desirable to (1) capitalize on costly underground construction by enabling the same tunnel to serve two or more corridors, (2) avoid having to turn trains back, (3) provide its own collector-

Table 13–23 Suggested Bus Service Planning Guidelines

1. Route Directness—Simplicity
   a. Routes should be direct and avoid circuity. Routes should be not more than 20 percent longer in distance than comparative trips by car.
   b. Route deviation should not exceed 8 minutes per round trip, based on at least 10 customers per round trip.
   c. Generally, there should be not more than two branches per trunk-line route.

2. Route Length
   a. Routes should be as short as possible to serve their markets; excessively long routes should be avoided. Long routes require more liberal travel times because of the difficulty in maintaining reliable schedules.
   b. Route length generally shall not exceed 40 kilometers round-trip or two hours.
   c. Two routes with a common terminal may become a through route if they have more than 20 percent transfers and similar service requirements, subject to (b). This usually results in substantial cost savings and reduces bus movements in the central business district.

3. Route Duplication
   a. There should be one route per arterial except on approaches to the CBD or a major transit terminal. A maximum of two routes per street (or two branches per route) is desirable.
   b. Express service should utilize freeways or expressways to the maximum extent possible.
   c. Express and local services should be provided on separate roadways, except where frequent local service is provided.

4. Service Period
   a. Regular service: 6:00 a.m. to 11:00 p.m./midnight, Monday–Friday.
   b. Owl service: selected routes, large cities—24 hours
   c. sSuburban feeder service: weekdays 6:00–9:00 a.m.; 4:00–7:00 p.m. (Some services 6:00 a.m. to 7:00 p.m.)

   d. Provide Saturday and Sunday service over principal routes except in smaller communities, where Sunday service is optional.

5. Loading Standards
   a. Peak 30 minutes: 150 percent
   b. Peak hour: 125–150 percent
   c. Transition period: 100–125 percent
   d. Midday/evening: 75–100 percent
   e. Express: 100–125 percent
   f. Suburban: 100 percent

6. Service Reliability
   a. Peak: 80 percent of buses 0 to 3 minutes late.
   b. Off-peak: 90–95 percent of buses 0 to 3 minutes late.

7. Passenger Shelters
   a. Provide at all large-volume downtown stops.
   b. Provide at major inbound stops in residential neighborhoods.
   c. At stops that serve 200 to 300 or more boarding and transferring passengers daily.

8. Bus Route and Destination Signs
   a. Provide front-, rear-, and side-mounted signs.
   b. Front sign should give at least route number and general destination; side sign should give route number and name (front sign may give all three types of information); rear sign should give number.

9. Passenger Information Service
   a. Provide telephone information service for period that system operates.
   b. Ninety-five percent of all calls should be answered in five minutes.

10. Route Maps and Schedules
    a. Provide dated route maps annually.
    b. Provide printed schedules on a quarterly basis or when service is changed.
    c. Schedules should provide route map (for line).

Note: Policy headways may result in considerably lower load factors.

Source: Adapted from *Bus Route and Schedule Planning Guidelines, NCHRP Synthesis 69,* Transportation Research Board, National Research Council, Washington, D.C., 1980.

distribution function, and (4) provide through-transit service for riders. Park-and-ride facilities and feeder bus services should be provided at outlying stations where population densities are too low to attract walk-on riders.

The number of different services that operate along a single track should be kept to a minimum. A "single route" per track simplifies scheduling, equalizes train loads, and is easiest to understand. In some cases, however, it is necessary to operate several lines on the same route. A good rule is not to operate more than two services (or branches) per trunk line route. "Trunks" with many branches should be avoided.

Several transportation planning concerns apply specifically to LRT systems. These include identifying when and where to grade separate; type of protection for at-grade intersections; signal preemption opportunities; methods of signal control; treatment, design, and operation of on-street reservations; affects to street traffic; and methods of signal control. Ideally, the amount of street running should be minimized in order to enhance reliability. However, this is where cost trade-offs may force lower cost choices at the expense of potential service interruptions. Single-track operations should also be minimized since they limit service frequency and operating flexibility, but they may be an acceptable cost trade-off. San Diego initiated its LRT operations with about 50 percent of its 26.5-km new start in 1981 as a single-track operation. By 1983, it was largely double-tracked. Certain parts of its expanded system, and that of Sacramento's, remains single-tracked.

An Institute of Transportation Engineers informational report[12] suggests that where cross-street volumes are lower than 15,000 to 20,000 average daily traffic volume on multilane streets, at-grade light rail operations are usually feasible for even long trains (three to four cars) and short headways (three to six min.). These guidelines—which generally result in peak-hour volumes per lane of 300 to 400 vehicles—also apply to LRT alignments in street medians. For higher volumes, grade separation may be desirable. Obviously, engineering analysis that considers train and highway speeds, proximity of other signalized intersections, and queuing space must be considered in deciding when and where to grade separate.

The hours of operation and the size of trains are normally set by policy. Some systems operate 24 hrs. (e.g., New York City), while in most U.S. cities and in London, Toronto, Hong Kong, and Singapore the service day is 18 to 20 hrs.

Cities with heavy ridership (e.g., New York, Toronto, Hong Kong), operate constant length train consists throughout the day. Systems in cities with fluctuating ridership levels (e.g., Atlanta, Boston, Chicago, Cleveland, PATCO, San Diego) vary train lengths to maintain frequent service throughout the day.

Route Planning

Geographic Characterization

Geographically, several kinds of transit routes can be identified:

1. *Radial routes* that normally radiate from the CBD. These are typically the "backbones" of a transit network and usually carry the largest numbers of passengers per unit length of route because of connection with the CBD. They may have one terminal in the CBD, or they may serve two different radial corridors by running through the CBD. Rail transit routes are almost always radial.

2. *Circumferential routes* provide service between different outlying areas without requiring travel through the CBD. By intercepting radial routes, they also serve as feeder and distributors for the latter. In very large metropolitan areas, complete circles are sometimes formed; in Europe, where these circles often connect a group of railroad terminals, such circular routes are sometimes operated by rail transit.

3. *Crosstown routes* are similar to circumferential routes, except that they are usually short routes on fairly straight alignment, tangential to the CBD and perpendicular to the radial routes. Increasingly common are suburb-to-suburb routes that connect major suburban communities and activity centers that characterize our large metropolitan areas.

4. *Feeder routes* connect outlying areas to radial or crosstown routes where through-routing to the CBD is infeasible.

5. *Shuttle routes* provide service between two major generators, such as between the CBD and an outlying parking facility or railroad terminal.

Service and Functional Characterization

Service on the various transit routes may include one or more of the following types:

1. *Local service* serves all stops along a route. It is the basic and preponderant form of service in an urban transit network. In off-peak or evening periods, sometimes these local services can provide "route deviation"

---

[12] *LRT Grade Separation Guidelines* (Washington, D.C.: Institute of Transportation Engineers, June 1990).

service where the bus is permitted to leave the basic route (up to two or three blocks) to serve an exiting passenger.

2. *Express service* becomes feasible when radial routes extend more than about 5.0 to 6.5 km from the CBD, and when passenger volumes are large enough (especially with longer than average trip lengths) to sustain such service. Often such routes operate limited-stop or express in the inner area and as a local service beyond the terminal of a parallel local line. Thus, there are sometimes two or more "rings" of local service— the inner ring being served directly by local routes and the outer ring(s) by routes that operate limited or express service in the inner ring. These patterns are highly developed in cities, such as Chicago and Cleveland, and the San Francisco Peninsula suburban area. Often, limited-stop and express service is warranted only during peak periods; although special service, such as to airports, will be scheduled all day.

"Limited-stop" bus service operates along city streets with stops mainly at major transfer points beyond the CBD. Express service involves even faster operation, typically on freeways or other major highways parallel to the local route that it supplements. Often, express services are oriented to outlying park-and-ride lots. These services are characterized by little or no turnover of passenger loads. (Houston and Seattle have an extensive system of park-and-ride, peak-hour express bus routes operating largely on transitways or HOV lanes.)

3. *Rapid rail transit services* provide longer spacing between stops than urban bus services and, typically, longer than LRT station spacing. Rapid rail (and commuter rail) trains may operate as *locals*, as an alternate stop service, or as a form of *zone express*. Multitrack rapid transit and commuter rail lines operate zone express services to increase speeds. Some rail transit lines employ skip-stop operations on two-track lines to accelerate service, especially when stations are closely spaced. Half of the trains along the route in such an operation do not stop at one group of stations; the other half bypasses the other stations. All trains make important stops in CBDs and at major transfer and terminal points. Skip-stop service (as in Philadelphia and New York) tend to equalize loads on successive trains. Such services may be inconvenient for passengers who wish to travel between stations in different skip-stop groups, for they must transfer at a station where all trains stop; but these disadvantages may be more than balanced by the travel-time savings obtained.

4. *Secondary distribution routes* include internal service within major activity centers (e.g., CBDs, airports). They may also provide connections between such centers and transportation terminals or major parking facilities.

5. *Other types* of transit routes may be provided for special events, "owl" periods, outlying employment locations at shift-change times, and similar special situations which suggest the tailoring of service to the demand.

6. *Suburb-to-suburb* services provide an emerging challenge to operators due to the typically low-density conditions that face such service areas. Productivity is typically low compared to other routes in the urban area, but it is enhanced when combined with a transit center concept.

Ridership Estimating

Estimating transit ridership is both art and science. The choice of method depends upon the nature and extent of the planning project or the fare and service change. *Analogy* methods are useful in assessing the ridership for small-scale changes in service coverage or frequency. *Market-based* estimates, such as *trip rates,* can assess the ridership of transit service extensions into new areas. *Elasticities* provide a reliable means of quantifying ridership response to changes in fares or frequency. *Mode split* models are used in estimating future transit ridership resulting from major new transit system development, population growth, and employment change. Travel surveys provide the basis for developing models and forecasts (see Chapters 5 and 6).

Analogy Methods

When minor service extensions or route cut backs are proposed, a transit property may want to review patronage impacts for similar changes and apply them to the service under consideration. Often the average number of riders per km in similar rates can be used to estimate the performance of an extension.

Market Analyses

Ridership potentials for service extensions into new areas can be estimated by studying the market served. Where new offices, schools, or industrial plants are developed, surveys can assess likely ridership. The number of residents served, their income and car ownership characteristics, and similar data should be obtained. Trip rates then can be used to determine the ridership propensity of each market segment. These rates can be stratified by car ownership, household size, distance from the bus stops, and peak versus off-peak travel.

Table 13–24 gives an example of transit trip rates per dwelling unit stratified by car ownership and persons per household. Figure 13–23 shows how transit route ridership can be estimated based upon market and rider characteristics.

Mode Split Models

Mode split models use more elaborate methods for determining the projected use of transit vis-a-vis auto. Such modes are a staple of the long-range planning process and are discussed in Chapter 6.

Service Levels

Service frequency and its reciprocal, transit vehicle or train *headways,* is affected by:

1. Patronage (demand) volumes in different time periods.

2. Transit unit (vehicle or train) capacity.

3. Minimum possible headway at busiest stop or station.

4. Maximum or "policy" headway.

5. Headways of and timed transfers with connecting routes.

Table 13–24   Montreal Home-Based Weekday Transit Trips per Dwelling Unit by Car Ownership and Persons per Household, 1978

	Cars per Household		
Persons/D.U.	0	1	2+
On-lsland Sectors			
1	1.04	.28	.17
2	1.86	.95	.29
3	2.75	1.51	.88
4	3.80	2.12	1.77
5	5.00	3.49	3.28
Off-lsland Sectors			
1	.35	.06	.00
2	.80	.31	.10
3	1.27	.45	.26
4	1.56	.60	.39
5	2.63	.90	.85

D.U. = dwelling unit.

Source: N. Monkman and J.H. Shortreed, "Transport Impacts of Changing Household Structure," *Proceedings of the International Symposium on new Directions in Urban Modeling,* Waterloo, Ont.: University of Waterloo, 1983.

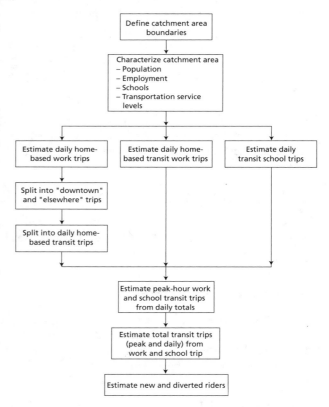

Figure 13–23   Transit Route Ridership Estimation Procedure

Source: Institute of Transportation Engineers, *Transportation Planning Handbook,* Englewood Cliffs, N.J.: Prentice-Hall, 1992, p. 164.

Table 13–25 Typical Maximum Headway Policy

| | Maximum Headways | | | | | | | | |
| | Arterial Routes | | | Feeder Routes | | | Express Routes | | |
Time of Day	M–F[1]	Sat[1]	S&H[1]	M–F[1]	Sat[1]	S&H[1]	M–F[1]	Sat[1]	S&H[1]
6:00 a.m. to 9:00 a.m.	15	30	30	30	60	60[2]	15	—	—
9:00 a.m. to 4:00 p.m.	30	30	30	60	60	60[2]	—	—	—
4:00 p.m. to 7:00 p.m.	15	30	30	30	60	60[2]	15	—	—
7:00 p.m. to 12:00 a.m.	30	30	30	60[2]	60[2]	60[2]	—	—	—
12:00 a.m. to 6:00 a.m.	60[2]	60[2]	60[2]	—	—	—	—	—	—

[1] M–F = Monday through Friday; Sat = Saturday; S&H = Sundays and holidays.
[2] Maximum headway if service is justified at all.

Source: Institute of Transportation Engineers, *Transportation Planning Handbook,* Englewood Cliffs, N.J.: Prentice-Hall, 1992, p. 151.

The first three factors are discussed in preceding sections. The maximum or policy headway is established by the governing board or regulatory agency as representing the minimum level of service that is considered adequate, or can be afforded, for various types of routes. A typical policy is shown in Table 13–25. Shorter headways are provided whenever justified by demand.

When transit patrons know that the service they wish to use is scheduled at headways of about 10 min. or less, they usually arrive at the stop or station at random. Average waiting times of one-half the service headways may be assumed under these circumstances. Since the public is not concerned about precise timetables in such situations, headways are selected to correspond as precisely as possible to demand at the maximum load point. The resulting headway may be an integer or even fractional number of minutes.

When service headways lengthen to intervals greater than 10 min., patrons will tend to consult timetables and arrive at the transit stop shortly before the vehicle or train is scheduled to arrive. A reasonable approximation of the passenger waiting time is the square root of the headway. Thus, if service operates every 30 min., passengers will arrive about five to six min. before the train or bus arrives.

Transit schedules that use headways that are divisible into 60 min. (i.e., "clock headways") are more easily remembered by patrons and therefore minimize the need for timetables. Hence, headways of 12, 15, 20, 30, or 60 min. are normally used; and other values are avoided. They are desirable when headways exceed 10 min.

Travel Time Considerations

Passenger service times while transit vehicles are stationary can account for a significant portion of the total trip time. Principal impediments to rapid boarding and alighting are restricted door widths, steps, bunching of passengers in doorway areas, and methods of fare collection.

Passenger Service Times

Table 13–26 summarizes typical loading and unloading times per passenger per lane or channel of door space for transit vehicles. The minimum times and maximum flow rates are obtained with high platforms (no steps to negotiate) and prepaid or postpaid fares. Pronounced crowding inside or immediately outside the vehicle may markedly increase the boarding-alighting times cited in this table.

Vehicle Dwell Times

The standing time of a transit vehicle making a passenger service stop includes time for: (1) opening and closing of doors (usually from 1 to 4 seconds per stop); (2) alighting and boarding of passengers; and (3) sometimes additional delays such as waiting to start, maneuvering into moving traffic (for buses only), or waiting ahead of the stop because of preceding vehicles or trains not having cleared the area.

Although passengers, especially in peak periods, try to optimize their spatial distribution for boarding, alighting, or traveling on transit vehicles, imbalances in these functions frequently occur, resulting in varying demands for space at different doors. This imbalance must be taken into account when computing dwell time, either by identifying the passenger flow at the busiest door(s) or by adding 10 or 15 percent to the times obtained for the average value per door, lane, or channel.

Dwell times at a rail transit stop may exceed 60 sec. at the busiest CBD or terminal station during peak hour. Values of 40 sec. at major stops and 20 sec. at other stops are more common during busy times.

Travel Time and Delay

Table 13–27 shows bus travel times spent enroute for cities in the United States. Delay rates in minutes per mile for U.S. cities are also shown in this table.

Passenger dwell times at stops should be minimized to optimize transit speeds. Techniques are: use of passes or fare cards or selfservice fare collection, wide multichannel doors, low-floor vehicles, and sufficient number of stops to distribute passenger loads. It is desirable to separate local and express bus stops where the respective services may have widely varying dwell times. Bus lane speeds can also be enhanced by providing alternate skip-stops to better distribute

Table 13–26 Average Boarding and Alighting Intervals[1] for Transit Vehicles

Operation	Physical Conditions	Operational Conditions	Seconds/ Passenger/ Lane[2]
Boarding	High-level platform (rapid transit)	Fares paid at fare gates	1.0
		Fares paid off vehicle (at fare gates or by passes)	2.0
	Low-level or no platform (buses and streetcars)	Single-coin or token fare paid on vehicle	3.0[2]
		Multiple-coin fare paid on vehicle	4.0[2]
		Zone fares prepaid; tickets registered on vehicle	4.0–6.0
		Zone fares paid on vehicle	6.0–8.0[3]
Alighting	High-level platform	No ticket checking at vehicle doors	1.0
	Low-level or no platform	No ticket checking at vehicle doors	1.7
		Ticket checking or issue of transfers at vehicle doors	2.5–4.0

[1] Intervals in this table do not apply to disabled individuals boarding or alighting by wheelchair; times for wheelchair access will vary but normally will be between one and two minutes.
[2] A lane represents one file of persons, 55–60 cm wide. Assumes that all lanes are used equally; however, allowance is usually made for the fact that whereas some lanes are used to capacity, others operate below that flow rate.
[3] Where "exact fares" are required and drivers do not make change, times may be somewhat less.

Source: Herbert S. Levinson, et al., *Bus Use of Highways: Planning and Design Guidelines, NCHRP Report 155,* Washington, D.C.: Transportation Research Board, National Research Council, 1975.

Table 13–27 Travel Time and Delay for Typical Bus Routes

Bus Location/Year	Routes or (Streets)	Avg. Time Min./Km	Percentage of Journey Time Spent			Remarks
			Traffic Delays	Passenger Stops	Moving	
Alameda-Contra Costa County, CA, Transit (Oakland) 1979	4	3.08	19.4	26.7	53.9	Suburban
Minneapolis, MN, 1977 (CBD)	1	1.97	18.6	23.6	57.9	Intercity
Phliadelphia, PA, 1977 (CBD)	(3)	7.03	25.8	24.0	50.2	Central Business District
Santa Clara, CA, 1969	(2)	7.07	26.5	25.8	47.7	Central Business District
St. Louis, MO, 1957–1958	3	2.72	16.2	9.1	74.7	Suburban
New Haven, CT, 1979–1980	20	3.39	12.1	17.9	70.0	City lines
	2	3.81	19.0	18.4	62.6	Urban–Suburban

1.0 kilometer = 0.62 miles.

Source: Herbert S. Levinson, "Analyzing Transit Travel Time Performance," *Urban Buses—Planning and Operation,* Transportation Research Record. 915, Transportation Research Board, National Research Council, 1983.

crowding, and by increasing stop spacing. The location of bus stops can affect speeds; curb bus lane speeds can be improved by restricting right turns at major boarding points, or by going to far-side stops.

It is clear that the fare collection procedures influence the proportion of total time spent at stops. As might be expected, the lowest proportion of travel time attributable to traffic delays occurs when buses operate outside the central area of the city.

Variations from the average travel time are important since passengers are concerned about arriving at destinations on time. They may evaluate a transit service more in terms of the 95th or 99th percentile travel time than by the mean value. Schedule makers must allow for late running in calculating layover time at terminals and, therefore, also must consider travel-time deviations. Such deviations are largest in mixed-traffic situations and least for operations in exclusive rights-of-way.

The following formulas are used to calculate bus travel times and speeds along a bus route:

$$TT = T_f + N_s (T_s + T_{AD}) + T_D, \text{ in min. per km}$$

$$V = \frac{60}{TT} \text{ in km per hr.}$$

where:

T_f = free flowing travel time, min. per km

T_s = time spent at stops, min. per km

T_{AD} = time lost accelerating and decelerating, min. per km

N_s = number of stops per km

T_D = traffic delays, min. per km

TT = total travel time, min. per km

V = speed, km per hr.

Table 13–28 summarizes maximum vehicle performance speeds, platform speeds, and stop spacings for the various types of public transport service.

Table 13–28 Typical Vehicle Velocities and Stop Spacings

Transit Vehicle and Service Type	Maximum Performance Speeds (km/h)	Platform Speeds (km/h)	Linear Stop Spacing		
			CBDs (m)	non-CBD	
				Traditional Practice in North America (m)	Some Modern Systems with Longer Stop Spacings (m)
Urban bus					
Local	80–105	13–22	120–240	150–250	300–450
Limited stop	80–105	19–29	120–240	350–900	600–1500
Express	80–105	26–51	[1]	1200–9000	1500–4500
Streetcar, local	64–95	13–34	120–240	150–250	300–450
Light rail transit	80–105	24–55	300–600	—	600–1500
Heavy rail transit	80–105	24–55	300–750	500–1100	1100–2400
Regional rapid transit	115–135	55–89	600–900	—	1800–9000
Commuter railroad	115–160	40–105	[1]	1200–4500	2400–9000

1.0 kilometers = 0.62 miles.
1.0 meters = 3.28 feet.
[1] Usually stops at only one or two terminals in or adjacent to CBD.

Total Trip Time

Two types of travel time are of concern in analyzing transit system performance. Transit travel time is the time consumed in traveling within the transit system. Total trip time, measured from origin to destination of a trip, may include the following components:

1. Access from trip origin to boarding transit stop.

2. Walking within larger transit stations.

3. Waiting for the next transit service.

4. Travel on the transit system.

5. Transferring if a route change is involved.

6. Access from final alighting stop to destination.

At change-mode points, such as rail transit stations where passengers may transfer between rail service and feeder buses or automobiles, the time involved (items 2 and 5) may become substantial. Transfer time (item 5) also includes a new waiting time (item 3), unless schedules are so closely coordinated that the connecting service departs as soon as passengers have boarded from the arriving service (i.e., "timed transfers").

Access Time

Access time depends on access mode. Walking speeds are assumed to be in the range of 3.25 to 4.75 km per hr., bicycling about 20 to 28 km per hr. Speeds for auto and bus access must be measured from field conditions, and allowance must be made for walking between these access modes and the stop or station entrance. Waiting time is a function of service headways.

Transit Stop and Station Planning

The spacing, location, design, and operation of transit stops have major effects on transit vehicle and system performance (as previously discussed). In the intensive urban areas, stop location and spacing effect door-to-door travel times and, hence, transit ridership. However, in suburban areas, North American operating practices allow operators to bypass stops at which no one wants to board or alight.

Spacing

Transit stops should be spaced as far apart as practical. Close spacing is desirable where people must walk to buses and trains; wider spacing should be provided where people drive to stops or stations. Land use, population density, and terrain influence bus and rail stop spacing in practice.

The spacing of transit stops should reflect the intensity of development and passenger modes of arrival at stops. Wider spacing allows higher transit speeds, but it is not practical where bus or rail lines rely on walk-on riders—especially in high density areas.

The goal should be to minimize the tradeoff between the passenger time on the system and the time required to reach it. (Figure 13–24.) Precise mathematical formulations are difficult in view of the many assumptions about access distances, walking speeds, and vehicle performance.

Figure 13–25 shows the effects of station spacing on rail transit speed as a function of top car speeds. For example, negligible operating speed gains are obtained with close station spacing (0.5 km) regardless of whether the vehicle's top speed goes beyond 48 km per hr.

Location and Design

Transit stops may be located on-street (bus or streetcar stop) or off-street (bus terminal, rail transit station, or commuter rail terminal). Guidelines for on-street stops follow. Chapter 18 contains guidelines for grade-separated stations and ones in exclusive right-of-way, and for off-street stops and stations, including the locations and design of bus stops along freeways.

Key planning and design considerations for on-street transit stops are provided below:

1. *Bus stops.* Bus stops are usually located adjacent to the curb for direct, safe passenger access to and from sidewalks. Where sidewalk width permits, shelters and benches are desirable at busy stops, especially where service headways exceed a few minutes. Shelter walls offer space for the transmission of more detailed information, such as maps, schedules, notices from transit management to the public, and advertising.

   Stops may be located on the near side or the far side of an intersection or at midblock locations. The choice is based upon an assessment of relative traffic, transit, environmental, and physical factors.

   - *Traffic factors* include: bus and car turning movements at intersections, type and status of cross street, type of traffic control (signal or stop sign), presence or absence of curb parking, and truck and car loading requirements. Intersection capacity may also be affected by the location of a bus stop; the *Highway Capacity Manual*[13] and Chapter 7 should be used as a reference.

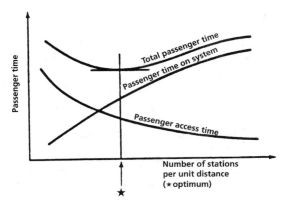

Figure 13–24   Relationship Between Passenger Travel Time and Station Spacing

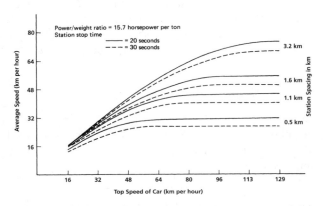

Figure 13–25   Top Speed, Station Spacing, and Average Speed—Rail Transit

Source: *Transportation Planning Handbook,* Institute of Transportation Engineers, Englewood CLiffs, N.J.: Prentice-Hall, 1992, p. 144.

   - *Transit-related factors* include: locations of stops for intersecting bus routes and proximity to rail transit station entrances.

   - *Environmental factors* include: type of adjacent land uses, proximity to large traffic generators, and passenger origins and destinations.

   - *Physical factors* include: adequacy of sidewalk, and locations of driveways, utility poles, trees, and hydrants.

   - *Near-side stops* are preferable where bus flows are heavy and where parking is permitted during busy traffic periods. They are desirable at intersections with one-way streets moving from right to left and at locations where buses make a right turn. They enable buses to rejoin the traffic flow where parking is allowed, since the buses can use the intersection for maneuvering.

   - *Far-side stops* are preferable where traffic flows are heavy and where curb parking is prohibited during busy traffic periods. They are desirable where there are heavy turning movements off the street, at intersections with one-way streets moving from left to right, and where buses make left turns.

---

[13] *Highway Capacity Manual,* Special Report 209 (Washington, D.C.: Transportation Research Board, 1985 and updated).

- *Midblock stops* are rarely used and are never at major transfer points. They may be justified in long blocks at the center of where major traffic demand is generated or where space is insufficient at adjacent intersections.

- *Special bus stops* are sometimes provided in freeway rights-of-way, either along the main travel lanes within interchange areas or along parallel frontage roads. Design and location should minimize time losses to buses, minimize delays to general traffic, and maximize benefits to transit riders.

Figure 13–26 gives the minimum lengths for bus turnouts at street curbs; dimensional aspects of bus stops without turnouts are provided in Table 13–29.

2. *On-street LRT station stops.* Some of the considerations for bus stops may apply to on-street LRT stops. However, tracks are usually located adjacent to the street centerline, and boarding and alighting areas must be accommodated within the roadway. However, numerous examples of side-running or curb-running LRT exist (e.g., Los Angeles, Sacramento, San Diego). In either case, locational considerations are somewhat different than for bus stops. Chapter 18 contains additional detail related to LRT station types.

Capacity

Transit agencies are concerned with (1) the number of vehicles needed to serve passengers on a given line at the maximum load point and (2) the ability to accommodate these vehicles at major passenger boarding points or junctions. Capacity standards and computational approaches vary among properties. Methods of calculating transit capacity and assessing levels of service are more fully explained in Chapter 7.

In its simplest form, and for most practical U.S. applications, transit capacity is a function of three items: (1) the seating and standing size of vehicles, (2) whether the vehicles can be entrained, and (3) the headway of the service. However, it is influenced by the concentrations of passengers at major boarding points, track and terminal configurations, and the presence of other traffic in the transit right-of-way. It also reflects the operating policies of the transit agency that normally specifies service frequencies and passenger loading standards.

Estimating Capital Costs

Capital costs are subject to many factors that differ from one system to another. Although basic bus costs are fairly similar, they vary substantially with engine type, optional equipment ordered, and from year to year with inflation. Civil engineering construction for guideways, stations, terminals, and maintenance facilities are also functions of the topography and soil conditions of the site, of the prices of construction materials, and of the level of construction wages. Total rapid rail transit and LRT project costs largely depend upon the amounts of surface, elevated, and subway construction; and right-of-way acquisition costs. A rail transit capital cost index study, summarized in Table 13–30, found that about 22–23 percent of project costs (based upon recent projects) are so-called "soft costs" (e.g., feasibility studies, engineering, construction management, project management, start-up). As shown on Table 13–30 due to the total grade-separated nature of rapid rail, the stations represent a significant project cost (23.57 percent) as compared to LRT (5.81 percent).

Table 13–29 Minimum Desirable Lengths for Bus Stops

Curb-Side Bus Stop Type	No Parking Zone Dimensions
Near-side Stop	30.5 meters
Far-side Stop	27.5 meters
Mid-block Stop	45 meters

* plus 1.5 meters from edge of crosswalk or end of radius, whichever is further from the intersection.

1.0 meters = 3.28 feet.

Sources: Texas Transportation Institute, Texas A&M University, *Guidelines for the Location and Design of Bus Stops, Transit Cooperative Research Program, Report 19,* Washington, D.C.: Transportation Research Board, 1996.

Table 13–30 Rail Transit Capital Cost Components

Project Cost Categories	Category Weights	
	LRT	Rapid Rail
Guideway	25.65%	25.58%
Yards and Shops	5.56%	2.58%
Systems (Signals, Electrification, Communications, Revenue Collection)	11.37%	9.24%
Stations	5.81%	23.57%
Vehicles	13.86%	8.41%
Special Conditions (Utility, Relocation, Demolition, Landscaping)	6.36%	3.21%
Right-of-Way	8.99%	4.73%
Soft Costs	22.40%	22.68%

Source: Booz, Allen & Hamilton, Inc., *The Transit Capital Cost Index Study,* Washington, D.C.: Federal Transit Administration, July 1995.

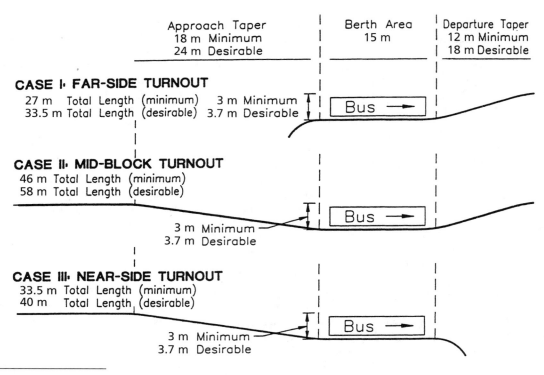

Approach Area Note: Dimensions of taper assume that buses will decelerate mostly in the approaching travel lane.

Berth Area Notes: Add 6 m to length of berth area if articulated buses will use turnout; add 21 m more for each additional articulated bus expected to use the turnout at the same time; Add 15 m for each additional standard bus expected to use the turnout at the same time.

Departure Area Note: Dimensions of taper assume that buses will accelerate mostly in the departing travel lane.

General Note: Bus turnouts are widened sections of roadway designed for buses to pull out of the traffic stream. While advantageous to general traffic, turnouts make it difficult for buses to re-enter the flow of traffic. They should therefore be used only under special circumstances.

Figure 13–26   Bus Turnout Designs

Source: *Designing for Transit,* San Diego, Calif.: Metropolitan Transit Development Board, 1993.

A summary of actual unit costs (1996–97 dollars) are as follows:

1. *Total project costs.* Rail transit costs per route mile will vary widely as indicated above. Table 13–31 reflects cost experience since 1989 on rapid rail and LRT projects.

2. *Vehicle costs.* Capital costs of various transit vehicles are estimated as follows (1998 dollars):

• Commuter rail (unpowered)	$1.1–$2.0 million
• LRV articulated	$1.9–$3.0 million
• Rail rapid transit car (23 m)	$1.1–$2.3 million
• Rail rapid transit car (15 m)	$0.7–$1.4 million
• Articulated bus (with air conditioning)	$375,000–$400,000
• Standard bus (with air conditioning)	$220,000–$280,000
• Standard bus (compressed natural gas)	$260,000–$360,000
• Medium bus	$150,000–$290,000
• Mini- and small bus or van	$ 50,000–$225,000
• Trolley bus	$500,000-$600,000

Table 13–31   Costs of Recent U.S. Rail Projects

Project	Initial Project Cost	Route Length (Km)	No. of Stations	Year in Service
Commuter Rail				
Tri-Rail, Miami	$78 million	107	15	1989
Virginia Twy. Exp., Washington DC	$131 million	131	16	1992
Metrolink, Los Angeles	$1,300 million	666	46	1992
Coaster, San Diego	$189 million	67	8	1995
West Coast Express, Vancouver	$100 million	7	8	1995
Trinity Twy. Exp., Dallas	$74 million	16	3	1996
Light Rail Transit				
Blue Line, LA–Long Beach	$912 million	35	22	1990
Central Line, Baltimore	$360 million	36	24	1992
MetroLink, St. Louis	$351 million	29	18	1993
Metro. Area Connection, Denver	$117 million	8	11	1994
Green Line, Los Angeles	$718 million	32	14	1995
Orange Line (Santee), San Diego	$109 million	5	3	1995
Blue Line (Old Town), San Diego	$113 million	5	3	1996
Red & Blue Lines, Dallas	$854 million	32	21	1996
Waterfront Extension, Cleveland	$70 million	3.5	5	1996
Central Line Extensions, Baltimore	$106 million	12	8	1997
Blue Line (Mission Valley West), San Diego	$220 million	10	7	1997
Westside MAX, Portland	$964 million	29	20	1998
Mather Field Ext., Sacramento	$34 million	3	1	1998
Rapid Rail Transit				
Orange Line (Midway), Chigaco	$493 million	15	8	1993
Red Line (Segment 1), Los Angeles	$1,450 million	7	5	1993
Metro Extension, Baltimore	$326 million	2.4	2	1994
Pittsburg/Antioch Extension, BART	$506 million	12	2	1996
Colma Station Extension, BART	$170 million	3	1	1996
Red Line (Segment 2), Los Angeles	$1,660 million	11	8	1996
Dublin/Pleasanton Extension, BART	$517 million	22	2	1997
Red Line (Glenmont),Washington DC	$291 million	2.6	1	1997
Blue Line (Franconia-Springfield), Washington DC	$166 million	5	1	1997

1.0 kilometer = 0.62 miles.

Sources: Individual transit agencies.

Estimating Operating Costs

Transit operating costs in 1996 averaged $3.16 per vehicle km (for all modes). Labor constituted 80.0 percent; material and supplies, 10.0 percent; utilities, 4.0 percent; services, 5.2 percent; and other costs, 0.8 percent.[14] Because transit systems are highly labor-intensive, total operating expenses depend very much on labor costs and labor efficiency.

There are differences in the *distribution* of labor costs for the various transit modes. As shown in Table 13–32, the operation function represents the greatest costs for all systems. However, nonvehicle maintenance (i.e., way and structures) adds significantly to rail system costs.

Unit operating and maintenance costs are normally derived through a cost allocation process. Each cost category is assigned (or allocated) to a unit of output or system size expense item such as vehicle hrs., vehicle km, peak vehicles, and for rail transit track km. (Table 13–33.) The costs in each category are then summed and related to the total number of units. The total operating cost then takes a form such as the following:

$$\text{Cost} = A \times H + B \times M + C \times V$$

---

[14] *Transit Profiles for the 1995 National Transit Database Report Year* (Washington, D.C.: Federal Transit Administration, December 1996).

Table 13–32 Breakdown of Operating Expense by Mode, 1996

Operating Function	Bus	Heavy Rail	Light Rail	Commuter Rail	Ferryboat
Operations	52%	41%	40%	35%	68%
Maintenance	19%	16%	22%	20%	12%
Nonvehicle Maintenance	4%	27%	20%	16%	4%
General Administration	18%	16%	18%	15%	12%
Purchased Transportation	7%	0%	0%	14%	4%

Source: *Transit Fact Book,* Washington, D.C.: American Public Transit Association, 1996.

where:

H = vehicle hrs.

M = vehicle km

V = peak vehicles

A, B, and C are the coefficients derived from the cost allocation analyses.

This model is then applied to estimate the cost effects of specific service charges. More refined analyses divide the costs into variable, direct overhead, and indirect overhead. The variable and indirect overhead costs are then used to assess the incremental effects of service changes.

Transit Operations

Transit operations activities include providing and supervising service, setting schedules and fares, maintaining fleet and plant, assuring system safety, and dealing with operating personnel. An efficient transit operation calls for effectiveness in all these areas.

Fleet Requirements

The number of individual transit units needed for a given route varies directly with the length of route and inversely with the average speed (including layover time). It can be estimated from the following formula:

$$N = \frac{nL_R}{V} \times \frac{60}{h}$$

where:

N = transit units needed

h = headway in min.

V = average vehicular speed over entire route in km per hr.

L_R = round-trip length of route km

n = number of cars per unit

Table 13–33 Example of Fully Allocated Approach for Expense Assignment

Function and Expense Object Class[1]	Vehicle Hours	Vehicle Kilometers	Peak Vehicles
501 Labor			
010 Vehicle operations	X		
041 Vehicle maintenance		X	
042 Nonvehicle maintenance			X
160 General administration			X
502 Fringe Benefits			
010 Vehicle operations	X		
041 Vehicle maintenance		X	
042 Nonvehicle maintenance			X
160 General administration			X
503 Services			X
504 Materials and supplies			
010 Vehicle operations		X	
041 Vehicle maintenance		X	
042 Nonvehicle maintenance		X	
160 General administration			X
505 Utilities			X
506 Casualty and liability costs	X		
507 Taxes			
010 Vehicle operations	X		
041 Vehicle maintenance		X	
042 Nonvehicle maintenance			X
160 General administration			X
508 Purchased transportation	X		
509 Miscellaneous expenses			X
510 Expense transfers			X
511–516 Total reconciling items			X

[1] Section 15 Reporting System, Level R.

To this must be added the number of units waiting in the terminal plus any spares for vehicles that might be laid up (e.g., 10 percent).

For example, on a 30-km-round-trip bus route with five-min. service and a 25-km-per-hr. operating speed, the required fleet size (N) is estimated as follows:

$$N = \frac{1 \times 30 \times 60}{25 \times 5} = 14.4 \text{ or } 15 \text{ buses}$$

One or two "spare" buses should be added to this number (i.e., around 10 percent).

Scheduling Service

The scheduling function provides the detailed framework for the conduct of daily operations. Transit scheduling involves separate but closely related preparation of schedules of the service itself (timetables), the equipment needed to furnish that service, and the daily and weekly tours of duty of the personnel to operate the equipment involved. Required inputs include patronage estimates, network information (such as bus travel times including traffic conditions, schedules of connecting services), vehicle capacity and availability data, policy on headways and load factors, and provisions of the labor agreement concerning working conditions.

Public timetables can be developed from the schedule considering the following additional factors:

1. Transition between peak and off-peak periods.

2. Possible sharp fluctuation in demand within a period (e.g., during shift changes at factories).

3. Connections with intersecting routes where numbers of transfers can be estimated to be substantial. (This is especially important when headways are long.)

4. Schedule coordination of coinciding portions of routes to equalize headways.

5. Opportunities for turning some trips back short of the terminals.

6. Traffic flow differences that affect travel time.

The assignment of operators to transit vehicles is far more complex than determining service frequencies. Once largely or completely a manual process, "cutting" driver runs from a schedule is now largely computerized.

The schedule department of a transit system also conducts field checks of passenger volumes past maximum and other load points; of transit vehicle running times at various times of the day; special surveys; and operator work signups. It may also house a relatively large reproduction activity because of the volume of scheduling and signup materials, public timetables and maps, forms, bulletins, and other materials requiring printing.

Supervision

The conduct and supervision of transit operations is the function of the transportation department of a transit agency. Major activities include dispatching, supervision, central control, communications, and security and safety.

Dispatching involves getting trains and buses into service properly and on time, receiving them when vehicle runs are completed for the day, and maintaining a variety of records required in this activity. Dispatchers manage the "extra board," which furnishes replacements for operators who are absent for any variety of reasons. They may keep constant running records of the status and availability of every vehicle for assignment to individual runs. Often, they supervise the makeup of materials that are given to each operator before initiating a vehicle run (pouches of transfers, schedule paddles, instructions, etc.).

Field supervisors or inspectors are responsible for service reliability, elimination of bunches and gaps in service, service restoration following accidents or other emergencies, handling disabled transit vehicles, reassigning vehicles and operators when necessary, and similar field operational activities. Inspectors may cover an assigned district in a radio car or they may be stationed at critical transit intersections or in a central walkable zone. They work closely with the central control facility.

Good schedule adherence—particularly avoidance of running ahead of schedule—helps to minimize patron waiting time at stops. Achieving such reliability requires careful supervision of line operations for and frequent monitoring of the scheduling process.

The *central control* office is the nerve center of a transit system. It is in two-way communication by radio with all or most transit vehicles or trains, and it is usually on separate radio channels with every field inspector, maintenance vehicle (including road-call trucks for disabled vehicles), top- and middle-management vehicle in the field, security police, revenue collection vehicles, and so on. Central control provides support, general direction, coordination and, where necessary, appropriate strategies regarding any kind of emergency on the transit system. Records should routinely be kept of all service delays, interruptions, emergencies, and of all communications both ways on the radio system.

Communications can be enhanced through automatic vehicle location and control systems that provide real-time monitoring of transit performance. These systems operate in Toronto and San Antonio, as well as numerous other cities in North America, Western Europe, and Canada.

Automatic passenger counting equipment is used by several U.S. and Canadian properties to provide a data base on schedule adherence and passenger loads. This information is valuable to the planning and scheduling departments. The counters record the number of passengers entering and leaving the buses, as well as the bus arrival times.

Emerging Technologies

Recent transit vehicle technology improvements have focused on low-floor interiors (bus and rail) and alternative fuels for buses. New efforts continue refinements to low-floor technology, weight reduction, life-cycle costs of components, modular bus chassis, and the passenger interface (i.e., Intelligent Transportation Systems [ITS] advances). For more complete information on ITS, refer to Chapter 16 of the *Traffic Engineering Handbook.*

Advances in automatic vehicle location (AVL) will enable transit operations in various ways: (1) public safety forces can be given precise vehicle location in case of emergency, (2) street supervisors can be advised of mechanical failures, (3) arrival information can be transmitted to stops or stations, and (4) more accurate data can be collected for planning and operational purposes. Global positioning systems provided the basic technology for AVL. An example of an AVL configuration in Houston is shown in Figure 13–27. In Denver, Colorado, AVL is being used for emergency purposes, microphone monitoring, immediate communications to the dispatcher, and to generate an icon on the dispatcher's graphic map showing the alarming vehicle's location. A 1997 survey indicated that 69 U.S. transit agencies were considering installing an AVL system, in the process of implementing one, or already had an operational system.

ITS applications in transit are widespread and exist in all aspects of an operation. Specific operating applications of ITS in transit include:

1. Transit route deviation and dynamic stop requests.

2. Real-time bus location information.

3. Timed transfer management. (Figure 13–28.)

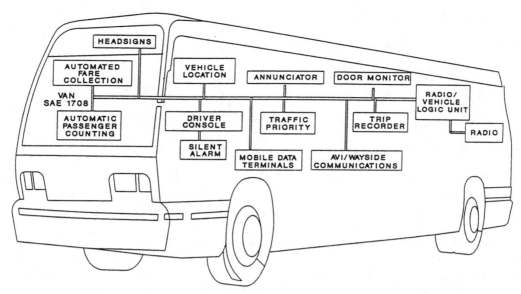

Figure 13–27   AVL Schematic Configuration on Bus

Source: Paula E. Okunieff, *AVL Systems for Bus Transit, Transit Cooperative Research Program, Synthesis of Transit Practice 24,* Washington, D.C.: Transportation Research Board, 1997.

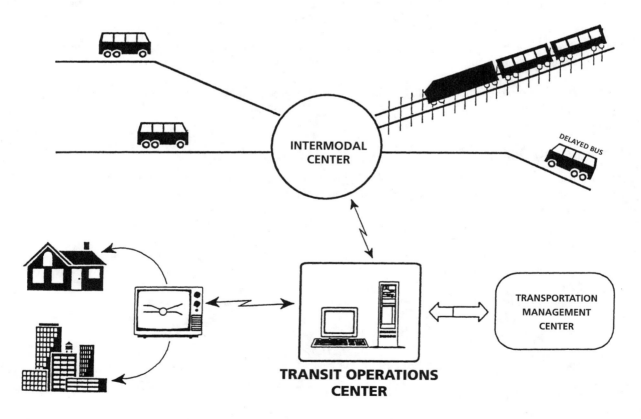

Figure 13–28   Intermodal Center Timed Transfer Management with ITS

Source: Bellomo-McGee, Inc., *Responsive Multimodal Transportation Management Strategies and IVHS,* Washington, D.C.: Federal Highway Administration, February 1995.

4. Transit parking space reservation.

5. Smart Card fare collection.

6. Transit priority on signalized networks.

7. Transit vehicle information displays.

8. Transit schedule reliability.

9. Improved transit management information.

10. Automatic accident data recording.[15]

Security

Crimes may be classified into two major groups: those against persons and those against property. Either type may occur on transit vehicles, in transit stations and stops, and their vicinity. In the first category, the most common crimes involve theft, ranging from picking pockets to assault and robbery. The second category includes vandalism—damage to and destruction of transit property or of vehicles parked on station property.

Record Keeping

Beginning in January 1998, all U.S. transit operators were required to report to FTA on security as part of Section 15 reporting. The events are divided into two parts, for both in-vehicle and in-station incidents:

- *Part 1 (violent and property crime reports):* homicide, forcible rape, robbery, aggravated assault, burglary, larceny and theft, and motor vehicle theft.

- *Part 2 (arrests):* other assaults, vandalism, sex offenses, drug abuse violations, drunkenness, disorderly conduct, trespassing, fare evasion, and curfew and loitering laws.

Planning and Design

Reducing fear of crime is an important part of inviting people to use public transport. Typically, it is the public's perception that a stop, station, or system is unsafe that is worse than the actual case. Factors that can affect this perception include:

- sensationalist news reporting,

- poor nighttime lighting at stops,

- a lack of good public information,

- inadequate signing,

- no uniformed staff on premises or on the vehicle,

- a general sense of isolation due to the environment,

- no direct communication to the control center.

---

[15] *Responsive Multimodal Transportation Management Strategies and IVHS* (Washington, D.C.: Bellomo-McGee, Inc., prepared for Federal Highway Administration, February 1995).

Several of these factors can be treated with design, while others require labor. Importantly, new stops or stations should be designed in a way to enhance the feeling of security. Oftentimes, the local police department will aid in such a design review.

On-vehicle design features to minimize crime and deter vandalism include: perimeter seating in the rear or buses, plastic window guards, security cameras, and intercoms on rail transit vehicles.

Security Operations

The effort to prevent crimes requires police patrol work. In small systems, municipalities may be requested to furnish this service and to respond to specific incidents when called by vehicle operators or the central controller. Rapid transit systems, because of the large areas of special property (e.g., stations, parking areas) involved, must usually furnish their own protection and therefore establish their own police force. This protection can be provided in several different ways: contract with local police department, agency staff with or without peace officer status, contract with private security, or some combination of these forms. They also avail themselves of closed-circuit television equipment to survey and control station areas.

Two-way radios on buses can serve as a crime deterrent. Operating shorter rail transit trains during evening and overnight (reducing the cars per operating personnel) and roving security police are used by some transit agencies.

Many transit vehicles are equipped with some form of a "silent alarm," actuated covertly by operators when crime problems threaten or occur on or about their vehicles. Increasingly, bus and rail vehicles are outfitted with cameras that record during operation.

Safety

Three types of accidents can occur in transit systems:

1. *Vehicle collision accidents:* Transit vehicles in mixed traffic may collide with other vehicles, pedestrians, or fixed objects; moreover, vehicles overturning or leaving the roadway are usually included in this category. Rail transit vehicles may collide with other cars or trains, with service vehicles, or with pedestrians.

2. *On-board passenger accidents:* passengers may suffer injury when entering or leaving vehicles or while on board. A common cause of accidents is the closing of doors while passengers are moving through them or tripping on vehicle stairs.

3. *Nonvehicle station accidents:* passengers or employees may be injured in bus or rail stations, especially on stairs and escalators.

Some of the accidents result from acts of nature (e.g., snow storms, floods) that are difficult to avoid through design or training. However, the first two of these accident types can be reduced to some extent by safety training of vehicle operators; special emphasis in this training is placed on proper procedures for decelerating, opening and closing doors, and accelerating, since many accidents are caused during these parts of the operating cycle. In addition, the training should include methods for operators to deal with stress. Nonvehicle station accident problems must be addressed through design changes, such as better lighting and marking of obstacles; signing; and, in critical situations, redesign and reconstruction of the hazardous areas, including possible fire proofing.

Garaging

There is a need to store (park) vehicles when not in use. The location of bus or rail vehicle yards is usually combined with the site of maintenance facilities. Rooms for dispatchers and vehicle operators reporting for work are provided. Some systems also acquire or lease bus parking space near the CBD (perhaps under an elevated freeway or transit structure) where buses not needed in the middle of the day can be stored between the two commute peaks; such parking areas usually do not include any facilities for vehicle fueling or maintenance. Space facility needs can be determined through the help of guidelines based upon a given number of buses as shown in Table 13–34.

Maintenance

The success of transit systems depends on the quality with which rolling stock and fixed facilities are maintained and vehicle breakdowns are kept to a minimum. The public becomes quickly aware of scheduled trips not made. A common reason for the failure of a system to fill all scheduled trips is the unavailability of sufficient pieces of rolling stock in acceptable running condition. Rail systems must also maintain tracks, guideway structures, and stations in a safe and sanitary state. As a general rule, there should be a zero-tolerance policy towards graffiti since it breeds additional graffiti and disrespect of the system.

Table 13–34 Bus Maintenance Facility Planning Guidelines

Space	Ratios	Standard
General Repair Bays	1 Bay/20 Buses	6 m × 17 m
PM/Inspection Bays	1 Bay/50 Buses	6 m × 17 m
Major Repair Bays	1 Bay/60 Buses	6 m × 17 m
Brake Repair Bays	1 Bay/100 Buses	6 m × 17 m
Brake Shop	0.33 m²/Bus	37 m² Minimum
Tire Repair Bays	1 Bay/200 Buses	6 m × 17 m
Tire Shop/Storage	0.37 m²/Bus	37 m² Minimum
Common Work Area	0.56 m²/Bus	37 m² Minimum
Equipment Storage	0.47 m²/Bus	19 m² Minimum
Body Repair Bays	1 Bay/75 Buses	6 m × 17 m
Body Shop	0.37 m²/Bus	27 m² Minimum
Parts Storeroom	1.9 m²/Bus	93 m² Minimum

Source: Matt Geyer, "How to Estimate Bus Maintenance Needs," *Metro*, Torrance, Calif.: A Bobit Publication, January/February 1998, p. 64.

Maintenance of Rolling Stock

The most successful transit systems practice "preventive maintenance" in addition to taking care of problems as they arise. Each vehicle is scheduled for different levels of maintenance at various intervals of service.

Administration of vehicle maintenance programs of any appreciable size is usually computerized. By input from dispatchers, or from a computerized scheduling program, vehicles due periodic maintenance can be identified. Fuel and oil consumption can be recorded and analyzed to identify possible deterioration of engine performance. Spare parts inventories and purchasing requirements are also processed by computer.

Maintenance of Plant and Fixed Facilities

All plant and fixed facilities (including the maintenance shops themselves) must be kept clean and in working order. In rail systems, a major effort is also expended in maintaining the stations, track, and guideway. Such activity is subdivided into the following major parts:

1. Track inspection and replacement.

2. Inspection and maintenance of power distribution (third rail or overhead).

3. Mechanical maintenance, including ventilation and air-conditioning equipment, escalators, elevators, and the like.

4. Trash collection, cleaning, and repairing damage in stations and right-of-way.

5. Inspecting and maintaining fire hoses, water lines, and related safety equipment.

To perform these activities efficiently, a right-of-way maintenance yard is provided, combined with a rolling-stock maintenance yard. Special-purpose vehicles, including a variety equipped to use the rails (termed "hi-rail" vehicles), are also needed.

Labor

Transit systems are highly labor-intensive. In the United States, 80 percent of all transit operating costs was represented by payroll, taxes, and fringe benefits in 1995.[16]

Most nonmanagement employees in the transit industry of the United States and many other countries are unionized. In addition to wage levels, labor contracts generally specify maximum number of hours of unpaid breaks, maximum length of "spread" (the time between first reporting to work and last leaving it), length of rest periods, overtime and night differentials, the minimum proportion of straight shifts to be scheduled, and other factors affecting platform costs.

Although employees and their union representatives would prefer a system in which all worked straight shifts of eight hrs., passenger demand calls for peak employee needs between 0600 and 0900, and again between 1600 and 1900. Meeting these demands require scheduling many split shifts with large spreads and large unpaid breaks. Negotiating the compromise is often difficult and is bound to result in less-than-optimum labor costs.

Part-time employment can alleviate some of these problems; it had almost disappeared from U.S. labor contracts until 1978, when the Seattle Metro Transit System was able to include a provision for some part-time bus operators in its settlement with the union. Most other systems have since obtained similar concessions.

Another unique contract provision is one used by San Diego Transit Corporation for "community-based drivers." These drivers have lower wage rates than the regular operators. Certain new, suburban routes are classified for these drivers. As a result, the cost performance of these typically lower used routes is benefited.

Fare Payment

The governing board of a transit agency sets the basic fare policy and approves each element of the fare structure. The level and structure of fares determine the passenger volumes attracted and the revenues generated. Critical to enhancing ridership is the ability to have a "seamless" structure where transfers can be made among all routes in the metropolitan system with little or no fare upgrade. Also, passes should be interchangeable. Fare collection procedures may also affect revenues produced and influence transit operating speeds, capacity of stops and stations, and operating costs.

Fare Policies

The level of fares is commonly a secondary factor affecting trip making and modal choice, since the market is somewhat inelastic. Most transit systems in the world are subsidized: thus, maximizing profits is not a factor in establishing fare levels.

Increasingly, public transit agencies are adopting fare structures that relate more to marketing than to revenue goals. Fare policies vary widely from one agency to another, but they are generally organized into four areas:

1. *Customer-related.* The focus of this policy area is to respond to the following: increasing ridership, maximizing social equity, increasing the convenience for users, offering significant discounts, and making fare payment easy.

2. *Financial.* Here the emphasis is placed on increasing revenue and would include fare structure components that would minimize evasion, reduce the cost of fare collection (e.g., printing, labor), and increase prepayment of fares.

3. *Management-related.* This area focuses on: ease of control by bus drivers and other transit personnel, expediting patron flow, and improving the reliability of fare payment data.

4. *Political.* The political focus relates to: producing a specific sum or a given proportion of operating cost and the perceived acceptance by political constituents to accepting changes and increases to various fare levels of the fare structure.

---

[16] *Transit Profiles for the 1995 National Transit Database Report Year* (Washington, D.C.: Federal Transit Administration, December 1996).

The policy of setting a fare structure is where marketing, budgeting, and planning all come together to determine future ridership and revenue for the transit system. Fare structures can be:

- distance-based,

- time-based,

- service-based,

- market-based,

- a simple flat fare.

The nonflat fare-based structures are more equitable for travelers but are more complicated for the customer to understand. Table 13–35 gives the advantages and disadvantages of the alternative strategies. Generally speaking, commuter rail systems employ distance-based structure; while bus and rail transit systems employ many variations, with flat fares being the most common.

Collection Types

Fare collection systems may be divided into manual and automatic methods, on-board vehicles, or off-board vehicles. There is a great variety of collection systems in each of these categories. Table 13–36 provides a matrix of basic fare systems. The different types of equipment for fare collection include:

- Ticket vending machines, common with proof of purchase systems.

- Turnstiles, common with barrier systems (with increasing use of stored value magnetic fare cards).

- Fareboxes, common with payment on entry systems.

- Validators, common with proof of payment systems.

- Ticket office machines, commonly used in conductor validated systems with designated ticket agents.

Table 13–35   Advantages and Disadvantages of Alternative Fare Structure Strategies

| | Fare Strategy Options | | | | |
	Flat Fare	Market Based	Distance Based	Time-Based	Service Based
Advantages	• Easiest to Understand • Simplest and least expensive to implement and administer • Lowest level of fare abuse	• Generally considered equitable; offers ability to pay less • Can make fare increase politically acceptable • Can minimize ridership loss with fare increase • Maximizes prepayment • Most convenient option	• Should produce greatest revenue • Considered equitable; longer trip has higher cost	• Should increase ridership • Allows management of fleet usage through shift to off-peak • Considered equitable; commuters pay more	• Relatively easy to understand • Considered equitable; higher quality or higher priced service has higher cost • High revenue potential; low fare abuse
Disadvantages	• Places inequitable burden on those making short trips • Increase will cause greatest loss of riders	• Generally produces least revenue • Potentially high level of fare abuse • Requires extensive marketing to maximize ridership • Highest media production and distribution cost	• Difficult to use • Difficult to implement and administer; may require special equipment • Potentially high level of fare abuse • May be unpopular with users with long trips	• Potential for conflicts with drivers • Potential for fraud (agents on rail) • May require equipment modifications (or new equipment)	• May be unpopular among users of higher cost service • Complicates transfers (e.g., may require payment of "upgrade" fare in transferring)

Source: Daniel Fleishman, et al., *Fare Policies, Structures, and Technologies*, TCRP Report 10, Washington, D.C.: Transportation Research Board, 1996.

Table 13–36 Basic Fare Systems

System Name	Most Common Single-Ride Fare Media	Modes Served in North America	Equipment Required	Other Possible Equipment
Proof of Purchase	Paper Ticket	Light Rail Commuter Rail Rapid Transit	Ticket Vendor	Ticket Office Machine Validator Central Computer
Payment on Entry (farebox)	Bills and Coins Tokens Paper Tickets	Bus Light Rail	Farebox	Central Computer Transfer Issuer Validator
Conductor Validated	Paper Tickets	Commuter Rail	Ticket Office Machine	Ticket Vendor Central Computer Handheld Devices
Barrier	Magnetic Ticket	Rapid Transit Light Rail	Ticket Vendor Gates	Addfare Machine Central Computer

Source: R. Scott Rodda, "Evolving Fare Technologies," *Transportation Research Circular No. 421*, Washington, D.C.: Transportation Research Board, April 1994.

Fares may be paid in cash, tickets, or tokens; by showing a prepaid pass or season ticket; by canceling a ticket on board the vehicle; by magnetically encoded tickets; or by Smart Card technology. Most North American surface transit systems now require the payment of exact fares; vehicle operators do not carry or make change. The exact-fare system has practically eliminated assaults on drivers; however, it represents some inconvenience to passengers. Bulk sale of tickets or tokens off vehicles partly alleviates this inconvenience.

There is a worldwide trend toward more prepayment and automatic payment of fares and away from on-board and manual fare payment. In many European countries (e.g., Germany) and on almost all North American LRT lines, a self-service, barrier-free fare collection system is employed. Sometimes referred to as "proof of payment," this system relieves operators or conductors of all fare collection responsibilities, and fare gates are not needed in rail stations. Passengers either use prepaid tickets or passes, or they purchase tickets from machines at stops or stations. Fare payment is checked at random by roving inspectors. Underpayment or nonpayment, when discovered, subjects the offender to a substantial fare surcharge (and embarrassment) on the spot or, if there is failure to pay, to an even greater penalty in subsequent proceedings. The practicality of such a system varies with different social environments. The older rail transit systems in the United States and Canada utilize flat fares—usually paid to turnstiles or agents. Newer systems (e.g., BART, Washington METRO) have distance-based fares, with special card-reading equipment. Some lightly traveled lines have on-train fare collection in off-hours.

Use of prepayment and off-vehicle fare collection reduces dwell time at stops, with resulting higher travel speeds for passengers and better utilization of vehicles by the transit agency. In addition, use of prepayment schemes brings cash to the transit agency at an earlier date than conventional fare payments.

Measuring Performance

The traditional measure of performance, the "bottom line" of the annual financial statement, must be augmented by other indicators to justify investments and service levels, to determine priorities, and to evaluate performance. *Efficiency* measures evaluate the quality of system management and operation; indicators relate the quantity of service to the resources required to accomplish this effort (e.g., operating cost per vehicle hour, vehicle hours per employee). *Effectiveness* indicators quantify the success of systems to serve the public and to fulfill the policy objectives (other than internal efficiency) established for them (e.g., passengers per vehicle hour). Finally, *cost-effectiveness* provides an overall measure of performance (e.g., operating cost per passenger).

Measures to improve efficiency include the following:

1. Improved selection and training of managers.

2. More freedom for transit management to manage, within broad policy guidelines; greater use of modern management techniques.

3. Better training programs, including sensitivity and motivational training for nonmanagement personnel; better motivational strategies for employees.

4. Better labor utilization through increased use of high-capacity vehicles.

5. Greater standardization of vehicle design for more efficient operation and maintenance; further improvements in design.

6. Joint bulk procurement of vehicles, spare parts, and other items, especially for smaller systems.

7. Prompt adjustment of services—additions, cutbacks, changes—in response to changing demands.

8. Increased efficiency in scheduling of operators and vehicles.

9. More productive and cost-effective labor contract provisions.

10. Compulsory arbitration when necessary and effective to avoid strikes; use of thoroughly qualified arbitrators jointly approved by management and labor.

11. Selective use of part-time labor.

12. Improved field supervision of operations and traffic control devices to reduce delays, gaps in service, and bunching; improved vehicle monitoring and control.

13. Simplified fare collection methods to accelerate passenger flow at bus stops and in stations.

Measures to improve effectiveness include the following:

1. Most of the efficiency measures listed above, in as much as they will result in better and, perhaps, lower-priced service.

2. Improved and new services to generate new demand (as distinguished from the response to demand changes), including the use of paratransit and experimental service strategies where appropriate.

3. Improved marketing strategies.

4. Improved transit information systems and communication between transit management and passengers.

Performance Audits

Performance audits of transit operators have become increasingly typical as agencies providing subsidy resources have wanted evidence of cost-effective use of their contributions. For example, California has required triennial audits of each operator since 1978. In the first phase of the audit, five indicators are composed with data from three years ago for the following:

1. operating cost per passenger,

2. operating cost per vehicle hr.,

3. passengers per vehicle hr.,

4. passengers per vehicle km,

5. vehicle hr. per employee.

Paratransit Service

General Purpose Services

Paratransit covers a wide range of collective passenger movement types. These include:

- School buses.

- Social and health agency and related special bus and van services.

- Community and neighborhood services by small buses and vans.

- Jitneys.

- Demand-responsive services by buses or vans.

- Shared taxis and regular taxi services.

- Van pools.

- Organized rideshare (hitchhiking) services.

Many of these services are organized or operated by private companies, social agencies, or welfare organizations. Many transit operators have been exploring opportunities for paratransit services that can utilize the equipment that is available to them.

A bus operating on a fixed route or schedule may, for example, be programmed to deviate from that route up to a certain distance to pick up and deliver passengers, and still operate within the general framework of the route and schedule involved. This is sometimes called "route deviation" service.

Still more freedom from route and schedule constraints is introduced by "dial-a-ride" or demand-responsive service. Routes are determined dynamically by current demand, and schedules may only provide for vehicles meeting each other or fixed route service at some interval, such as once an hour; in some cases, there is no schedule at all. Service may focus on one or on a few traffic generators ("many-to-few" service) or may be unconstrained within the area served ("many-to-many" service). Dial-a-ride service approaches the characteristics of on-call taxi service, except that several passengers and their individual origins and destinations are served on the same trip in a sedan or van. Adopted criteria for the maximum duration between phone calls for immediate service and vehicle arrival for pickup ("response time") usually help determine the size of the service area for individual dial-a-ride vehicles.

Manual or computer dispatching, or both, are required to translate passengers' calls for service into efficient temporal and spatial distribution of that service; costs per passenger served are thereby increased. If fares are kept within or near the framework of customary transit fares, or if regular transit wages are paid, flexible route (particularly dial-a-ride) services are likely to be considerably more expensive than fixed route transit service per passenger carried.

Paratransit should complement conventional transit service where the latter exists, each undertaking the functions best performed by it. Paratransit may have advantages when providing service in places or at times when conventional transit cannot provide them, meeting needs of special groups of travelers and helping to make more efficient use of existing or potential transportation resources. In some instances, privately run paratransit service has been operated in direct competition with conventional transit. In high-density corridors, this may not be detrimental; but in medium- and low-density markets, such competition has usually proved to be unsustainable.

Shared taxis are sometimes provided at airports, train stations, and other points of major passenger concentration. These and regular taxi services are provided by private owners under the jurisdiction of a regulatory body, such as a public service commission, city department, county authority (e.g., Orange County Transportation Authority in California), or transit agency (e.g., Metropolitan Transit Development Board in San Diego). Taxis provide a high degree of passenger flexibility and convenience, but at a far higher cost per passenger than traditional transit service.

Van pools and bus pools are normally employer-sponsored and work best where employment at a single location is high.

Americans with Disabilities Act (ADA) Requirements

Essential elements of a transit system that is accessible to the disabled include accessible vehicle and facility design, equipment maintenance, employee training, and information communications. Parallel complementary curb-to-curb service is also required by ADA within 1.2 km of any fixed route service that exists.[17]

Accessible Vehicle and Facility Design

For transit providers in the United States, ADA regulations specify minimum accessibility design standards for vehicles and facilities. Vehicles and facilities should meet or exceed these minimum standards. In Canada, the Ontario Ministry of Transportation has developed recommendations for improved access to transportation systems as part of its Easier Access Program.

Equipment Maintenance

To attract persons with disabilities to transit, and to fixed route systems in particular, service must be safe and reliable. All access features, including lifts and ramps, wheelchair securement systems, kneeling features, and information and communications systems must be maintained in working order. Each feature should be checked regularly as part of any daily inspection, and malfunctions should be reported and repaired promptly. For all transit providers in the United States, the ADA regulations include provisions specific to lift and equipment maintenance.[18]

Employee Training

Adding lifts, ramps, and other features to vehicles and facilities is only the first step in providing transportation services that are truly accessible. A well-trained work force is also essential to ensure that equipment is used correctly and that all customers, including those with disabilities, receive appropriate assistance and are served courteously. ADA also requires announcement of major stops for the convenience of blind passengers, which is a new challenge in the training of bus drivers.

All transportation providers in the United States are required by ADA regulations to train employees "to proficiency." Training should address use of all access equipment, providing appropriate assistance to individuals with disabilities, knowledge of system policies and practices, and basic customer service and sensitivity skills.

Accessible Information and Communications

To be able to understand and use the transit system, customers (including those with vision, speech, and hearing impairments) need to have access to service information. This includes written materials, schedules, and any other communications that may be provided, such as those in terminals at transit stops and in vehicles.

Section 37.167(f) of the U.S. DOT's ADA regulations includes specific requirements for ensuring access to information and communications. Information must be provided in formats usable by the person with a disability and must be provided in formats appropriate to their use. Systems and technologies must be employed to ensure that individuals with hearing and speech impairments have equal access to any communications provided both prior to the trip and during the trip.

---

[17] EG&G Dynatrend and Crain & Associates, Inc., *Transit Operations for Individuals with Disabilities, Transit Cooperative Research Program Report 9* (Washington, D.C.: Transportation Research Board, 1995).

[18] Section 37.161 of the U.S. DOT's regulations contains general provisions that apply to all providers of transportation services. Section 37.163 details additional requirements for public entities.

Organization and Financing

The design and delivery of public transport service is influenced by the way that the transit agencies are organized, the legal definitions of the agencies' responsibilities, and the relationships among agencies that play a role in providing service. They are also influenced by the attitudes of the communities and governments involved and the financial resources committed by each.

Organizational Models

Transit management actions and styles have changed dramatically since the early 1960s as transit passed from private to public ownership in North America. However, there are numerous efforts in the United States to reintroduce private sector involvement through the competitive bidding of some transit services. In other parts of the world (e.g., United Kingdom, Japan) whole transit systems have been "privatized." Also, the recent "design, build, operate, and maintain" rail transit contracts in New Jersey and Puerto Rico demonstrate a continuing interest in a private sector approach to management, even if the funding is largely from public sources.

Basic single operator public ownership options include: (1) a city or county department (e.g., San Francisco, Milwaukee County), (2) a municipal corporation (e.g., Montreal, Quebec), (3) a regional or subregional transit authority (e.g., Houston METRO, Toronto Transit Canadian, San Francisco BART), and (4) a state agency (e.g., Rhode Island Public Transit Authority, New Jersey Transit, Connecticut Transit). Each form of ownership has its own strengths and weaknesses in terms of accountability to the community, freedom to act, and financial resources. Choice will depend upon geography, precedent, and community attitudes.

Many transit systems currently operate under some sort of regional authority that enables the service to cross municipal boundaries and provides a broader constituency and revenue base. Still, many authorities are faced with the very problems they sought to avoid. An effective authority needs a board that sets policy, is not polarized, and lets the general manager oversee the operation.

Hybrid ownership and operations options that have emerged in response to the changing transit environment include:

1. *Superagencies that separate policy and planning from operations or balance city and suburban interests.* Examples include the Metropolitan Transportation Authority, New York; Regional Transportation Authority, Chicago; and the Regional Transit Board in Minneapolis and St. Paul. The Metropolitan Transit Development Board is the overall coordinating agency for the San Diego area. It establishes policy, designs and constructs the light-rail lines, and assumes responsibility for short-range planning and financing. It owns the assets of the San Diego Transit Corporation (the major bus operator) and San Diego Trolley, Inc. (the light rail operator), as well as buses and facilities for contract services.

2. *Coordination of municipal providers.* Examples include the Metropolitan Transportation Commission in the San Francisco Bay Area, the Metropolitan Transportation Authority in greater New York, and the "transit federations" throughout Germany.

3. *Broadened role of transit agency as a "mobility manager."* Several transit agencies have expanded their role to focus on bus and mobility objectives. The array of mobility functions possible is shown in Table 13–37. Essentially, the organizational approach is to respond to and influence the demands of the urban travel market by offering a range of options to the single-occupant automobile.

The principal activities of a transit system are best understood within the context of an internal organization structure.

Figure 13–29 gives a generalized arrangement for a typical property, including basic departments for transportation, maintenance, finance, administration, and planning. Many different variations are possible.

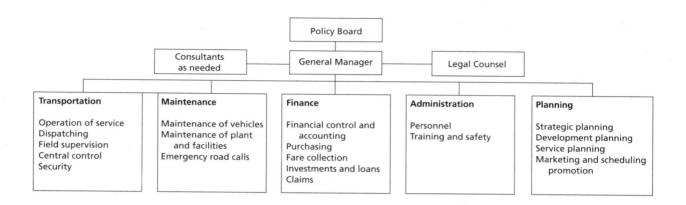

Figure 13–29 Typical Transit Agency Organization

Source: H. Levinson, *Transportation Planning Handbook,* Washington, D.C.: Institute of Transportation Engineers, 1992, p. 171.

Table 13–37 Mobility Management Functions

	Mobility Management Strategies	Supportive Actions
Operational		
Nontraditional methods of service delivery, which are generally not fixed routes and may include collaboration with other partners	Ridesharing Subsidies to vanpoolers Subscription buses Subscription buses with paid, nonagency drivers Coordination with private shuttles Operation of shuttles funded by private sector Facilitation of casual carpooling Dial-a-ride for late night and low density trips Demand-responsive feeders Checkpoint dial-a-ride Service routes/community buses Service integration with jitneys Assistance for volunteer and community-based transportation services	Guaranteed ride home Schedule coordination with intermodal facilities (train depots, airports, ports) Supporting bicycle commuting Reverse commute programs
Technological		
Increased travel options or convenience through use of technical advancements	Telecommuting centers Real-time rideshare matching Multi-provider trip reservation and integrated billing	Integration of transit into traffic management centers Integrated fare media
Informational/Programmatic		
Expanded mode choices resulting from more complete information and broader-based-marketing	Collaborative arrangements with ridesharing agencies for trip planning Transit telephone center with information on all modes, providers	Trip-planning kiosks at activity centers Joint programs with the private sector Supporting Transportation Management Associations (TMAs)
Land Use		
Techniques to foster transit ridership through linkages with land development	Transit villages in joint ventures Influencing transit-friendly development	Intermodal facility siting

Source: Gail Murray, David Koffman, and Leiff Chambers, *Strategies to Assist Local Transportation Agencies in Becoming Mobility Managers, TCRP Synthesis of Transit Practice 21,* Washington, D.C.: Transportation Research Board, 1997.

In large systems, main departments may be broken into smaller units with several deputy general managers, each responsible for two or more departments, reporting to the general manager. In small systems, there may be only an operations department, with other functions conducted by appropriate offices within municipal government; some functions, such as maintenance, fare collection and banking, and accident claims, may be contracted out to private industry.

Competitive Award of Services

Competition works in the private sector to keep prices and costs as low as practical for customers. Similarly, many transit properties use competition to obtain the lowest costs for quality services, which might include: provision of fixed route services, vehicle cleaning, professional services (e.g., auditing, legal, planning, security), and printing. In Phoenix, all bus operations are awarded on a competitive award basis and three operators provide service.

Competitive award normally means use of the private sector to perform the contracted services. However, in some cases, the public sector can perform the service and is considered an eligible bidder (e.g., London Transport has contracted with London Bus; and in California, Chula Vista Transit has contracted with San Diego Transit Corporation). The key to an effective competitive award process is to maintain some minimum standard of quality. Therefore, a two-step process is preferred where qualifications of potential contractors are first used to screen down to a list of experienced firms and entities. Then, a second step is where costs are used to select a low bidder.

Financing

Urban transit system finance in North America has generally followed an historic path consisting of three stages:

1. In their early years, systems were profitable and attracted private capital for construction and operation. Oftentimes, too, the city's electric utility company was involved as an owner or partner due to the preponderance of electric street railway systems beginning in the late 1800s.

2. With the advent of competition from private automobiles, profits disappeared more or less rapidly. At this point, generally after World War II, most systems became publicly owned and entered a stage in which it was felt both justifiable and practical to expect passengers to pay only for the cost of operation and perhaps make some contributions toward capital costs; however, government assumed the financing of most of the capital burden.

3. Since the 1970s, operating expenses have risen due to service expansion and inflation. During the same period, public policies were generally adopted against raising fares appreciably, if at all, because of increased concern about air pollution, energy conservation, and various social goals. As a result, for this phase, most systems in the United States and in many other countries entered a third financial phase, making no attempt to have users pay the full amount of operating expenses. Government—national, state, local, or a combination of these—assumes the responsibility of making up the deficits through subsidy grants.

The U.S. transit industry as a whole was in the second stage until the middle of the 1960s, but it has since become dependent on government subsidies for operations. In 1996, operating subsidies (federal, state, and local) totaled $11.1 billion,[19] or about 56 percent of the total operating costs.

The trends in average fares charged in relation to operating costs and inflation are shown in Figure 13–30. Since 1984 fares have generally outpaced inflation and unit operating costs. The widening gap largely results from the need of policy boards to raise fares to make up for the loss of subsidy funding, and recessionary impacts in the early 1990s.

Resources and Subsidies

Low transit fares enhance the attractiveness of using transit but increase the need for outside subsidy. Accordingly, subsidies in one form or another have been found in transit system accounts in the past. For example, commuter railroad operation generally has been supported by profits made from freight service. Municipally owned utilities, such as gas and electricity supply, have assisted transit budgets, perhaps by cash transfers or by setting artificially low prices for electricity consumed by trains and streetcars. However, most public transit today requires that substantial cash subsidies be made by national, state, or local governments.

Grants or subsidies for capital investments are common throughout the world. They are usually made by a higher level of government (e.g., national, state, provincial) and are accompanied by conditions as to the type of project to be

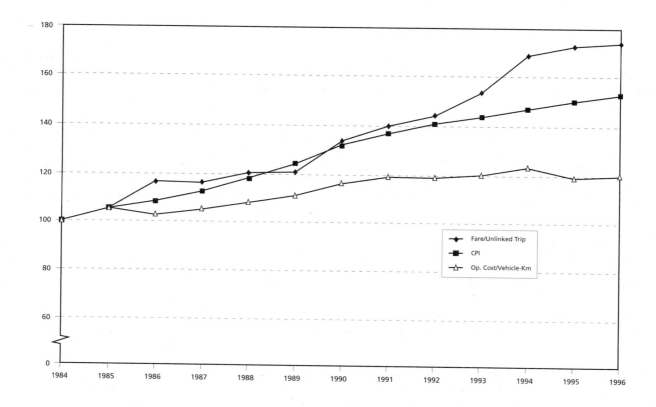

Figure 13–30   Change in Transit Fare Compared with Operating Costs and Inflation

Source: *Transit Fact Book,* Washington, D.C.: American Public Transit Association, February 1998.

financed and the size of the local contribution. In the United States, federal capital grants were initiated in 1965 and have increased in size considerably since then; Table 13–38 shows federal transit funding experience since 1984, including the flexible provisions contained in the ISTEA of 1991.

The sources of subsidies for operating expenses, the methods of raising them, and the conditions attached to granting them vary greatly within any country and among different countries. Each method is the result of the goals, needs, and political climate of the area involved.

Subsidies may be generated within the system or within the next larger organization of which the system is a part. This occasionally still involves transfer of utility profits; toll bridge revenues; or profits from other operations, such as freight transportation. Alternatively, the transit agency may have the power to levy taxes directly; for example, real estate, sales, income, fuel, and motor vehicle registration taxes are levied in various parts of the United States.

Subsidies may also be derived from local, state, provincial, or national governments. In some cases, general funds are used; while in other cases, the proceeds of special taxes are used. To assure that these subsidies are truly needed and effectively spent, the granting agency usually attaches certain conditions to the grants. Also, some programs provide funds specifically for subsidizing the money "lost" by the charging of concessionary fares to the elderly, the handicapped, students, or other groups.

State operating assistance programs vary widely. Each program reflects specific traditions, political arrangements, and economic circumstances. Farebox recovery ratios are used as targets or requirements in several states. They are mandates in California, Illinois, Maryland, and Pennsylvania; and they serve as guides in Connecticut and Ontario. Local cost recovery requirements or targets range from under 20 percent in California; 33 percent in Connecticut; and 50 percent

Table 13–38   Federal Funding Commitments to Transit

Federal Capital Grant Approvals by Program (millions)

Federal Fiscal Year	Discretionary[a]	Formula[b]	Other[c]	Total
1984	$1,096.0	$1,339.2	$440.8	$2,876.0
1985	727.7	1,491.6	291.0	2,510.3
1986	1,132.3	1,324.8	680.2	3,137.3
1987	694.5	1,376.5	403.7	2,474.7
1988	875.4	1,380.6	264.8	2,520.8
1989	1,199.7	967.7	422.1	2,589.5
1990	1,169.4	962.6	248.0	2,380.0
1991	1,108.4	1,035.0	253.0	2,396.4
1992	1,027.3	1,207.7	377.9	2,612.9
1993	1,792.8	1,426.5	245.8	3,465.1
1994	1,606.0	1,647.4	323.9	3,577.3
1995	2,666.2	2,462.4	352.6	5,481.2
1996	1,742.5	2,067.6	315.0	4,125.1
1997	1,771.6	2,074.7	202.4	4,048.7
1996 % of Total	42.3%	50.1%	7.6%	100.0%

Flexible Highway Funds Obligated to Transit (millions)

Fiscal Year	Congestion Mitigation & Air Quality Improvement Program	Surface Transportation Program	Interstate Substitute & Earmarked Federal Highway Administration Funds	Total
1992	$176.9	$ 25.1	$101.7	$303.7
1993	298.4	146.9	23.9	469.2
1994	317.0	183.2	109.5	609.7
1995	484.1	200.3	117.4	801.8
1996	344.6	324.2	111.3	780.1
1997	257.9	207.9	48.3	514.1
1997 % of Total	50.2%	40.4%	9.4%	100.0%

[a] 49 USC 5309 and 5310 through 1991; 49 USC 5309 only beginning in 1992.
[b] Federal Transit Act Sections 5 and 9A and 49 USC 5311 and 5336 through 1991; 49 USC 5311 and 5336 beginning in 1992.
[c] Federal Aid Highway Act of 1973, as amended; Federal Aid Urban Systems and Interstate Transfer; and National Capital Transportation Act of 1969, as amended.

Source: U.S. Department of Transportation, Federal Transit Administration.

or more in Illinois, Maryland, and Ontario. These targets or requirements are designed to improve operating efficiency and limit reliance on state subsidy.

As transit agencies look for financial help for new projects and services, unique resources may be found.

- *Public–private partnerships.* Special assessment financing districts for major urban transportation improvements are emerging as a means of generating contributions to transit development costs. For example, the Embarcadero station on BART in San Francisco was financed by this method.

- *Sale-leaseback transactions.* Numerous transit agencies have reaped a one-time benefit from sale-leaseback transactions, in which the assets of transit vehicles are "sold" and then leased back, resulting in a one-time net gain for the agency.

- *Joint development projects.* These types of projects can also generate an ongoing revenue stream to a transit system where a private development on transit property enjoys beneficial use of the real property paying a lease or rental income stream. Additional benefit for transit is the production and attraction of revenue trips to the system.

Community Planning with Transit in Mind

There is a broad range of societal, economic, and institutional factors that will affect the use of transportation systems and facilities. The rapid and continuing change in the computer and telecommunications industries may affect the way in which people work, travel, and interact with one another.

The post World War II trends of urban sprawl, rising car ownership, and development of the interstate highway system significantly contributed to the increase of personal automobile use. Correspondingly, transit use has declined. These trends, as a view of the future, show that transit planners will be faced with new challenges, most of which will make it increasingly difficult to attract customers to transit. City land use planners will have to team with the transit planners in order to flexibly and effectively respond to these trends.

A primary challenge for transit planners and policy makers in the 21st century will be to look at transit in a different way than in the past. As a high capacity transportation mode, it is prudent to look for more effective ways to shape urban areas by integrating public transit into the community planning process:

- Through use of the pedestrian- and transit-oriented land use design in new suburban development and in redevelopment of older neighborhoods.

- By designing transit to serve special event generators where large numbers of people are oriented (e.g., stadia, ballparks, convention facilities).

- By intensifying land uses around existing transit nodes in CBDs and in outlying business districts.

- By connecting with intercity bus, rail, and air terminals.

Suggested References for Further Reading

Transit Cooperative Research Program Reports

Howard P. Benn. *Bus Route Evaluation Standards, Transit Cooperative Research Program, Synthesis of Transit Practice 10.* Washington, D.C.: Transportation Research Board, 1995.

Booz, Allen & Hamilton, Inc. *Applicability of Low-Floor Light Rail Vehicles in North America, Transit Cooperative Research Program Report 2.* Washington, D.C.: Transportation Research Board, 1995.

Cambridge Systematics, Inc. *Transit Ridership Initiative, Transit Cooperative Research Program, Research Results Digest No. 4.* Washington, D.C.: Transportation Research Board, February 1995.

Cambridge Systematics, Inc. and Apogee Research, Inc. *Measuring and Valuing Transit Benefits and Disbenefits, Summary, Transit Cooperative Research Program Report 20.* Washington, D.C.: Transportation Research Board, 1996.

Cambridge Systematics, Inc., et al. *Economic Impact Analysis of Transit Investments: Guidebook for Practitioners, Transit Cooperative Research Program Report 35.* Washington, D.C.: Transportation Research Board, 1998.

Robert Cervero and Samuel Seskin. *An Evaluation of the Relationships Between Transit and Urban Form, Transit Cooperative Research Program Research Results Digest No. 7.* Washington, D.C.: Transportation Research Board, June 1995.

Judy Davis. *Consequences of the Development of the Interstate Highway System for Transit, Transit Cooperative Research Program Research Results Digest No. 21.* Washington, D.C.: Transportation Research Board, August 1997.

John J. Dobies. *Customer Information at Bus Stops, Transit Cooperative Research Program, Synthesis of Transit Practice 17.* Washington, D.C.: Transportation Research Board, 1996.

John T. Doolittle, Jr. and Ellen Kret Porter. *Integration of Bicycles and Transit, Transit Cooperative Research Program, Synthesis of Transit Practice 4.* Washington, D.C.: Transportation Research Board, 1994.

The Drachman Institute with G. J. Fielding. *Transit Markets of the Future—The Challenge of Change, Transit Cooperative Research Program, Report 28.* Washington, D.C.: Transportation Research Board, 1998.

EG&G Dynatrend and Crain & Associates, Inc. *Transit Operations for Individuals with Disabilities, Transit Cooperative Research Program Report 9.* Washington, D.C.: Transportation Research Board, 1995.

Rebecca Elmore-Yalch. *A Handbook Using Market Segmentation to Increase Transit Ridership, Transit Cooperative Research Program Report 36.* Washington, D.C.: Transportation Research Board, 1998.

Daniel Fleishman, et al. *Fare Policies, Structures, and Technologies, Transit Cooperative Research Program Report 10.* Washington, D.C.: Transportation Research Board, 1996.

Ronald J. Hartman, Elaine M. Kurtz, and Allen B. Wynn. *The Role of Performance-Based Measures in Allocating Funding for Transit Operations, Transit Cooperative Research Program, Synthesis of Transit Practice 6.* Washington, D.C.: Transportation Research Board, 1994.

Katherine S. Hooper. *Innovative Suburb-to-Suburb Transit Practices, Transit Cooperative Research Program, Synthesis of Transit Practice 14.* Washington, D.C.: Transportation Research Board, 1995.

Rolland D. King. *Bus Occupant Safety, Transit Cooperative Research Program, Synthesis of Transit Practice 18.* Washington, D.C.: Transportation Research Board, 1996.

Hans, W. Korve, et al. *Integration of Light Rail Transit into City Streets, Transit Cooperative Research Program Report 17.* Washington, D.C.: Transportation Research Board, 1996.

KRW, Inc. *Guidelines for Transit Facilities Signing and Graphics, Transit Cooperative Research Program Report 12.* Washington, D.C.: Transportation Research Board, 1996.

Multisystems, Inc., et al. *Multipurpose Fare Media: Developments and Issues, Transit Cooperative Research Program, Research Results Digest No. 16.* Washington, D.C.: Transportation Research Board, June 1997.

Gail Murray, David Koffman, and Cliff Chambers. *Strategies to Assist Local Transportation Agencies in Becoming Mobility Managers, Transit Cooperative Research Program Report 21.* Washington, D.C.: Transportation Research Board, 1997.

Jerome A. Needle and Renee M. Cobb. *Improving Transit Security, Transit Cooperative Research Program, Synthesis of Transit Practice 21.* Washington, D.C.: Transportation Research Board, 1997.

Paula E. Okunieff. *AVL Systems for Bus Transit, Transit Cooperative Research Program, Synthesis of Transit Practice 24.* Washington, D.C.: Transportation Research Board, 1997.

Tom Parkinson with Ian Fisher. *Rail Transit Capacity, Transit Cooperative Research Program Report 13.* Washington, D.C.: Transportation Research Board, 1996.

Parsons, Brinckerhoff, Quade & Douglas, Inc. *Guidelines for Development of Public Transportation Facilities and Equipment Management Systems, Transit Cooperative Research Program Report 5.* Washington, D.C.: Transportation Research Board, 1995.

Parsons, Brinckerhoff, Quade & Douglas, Inc. *Transit and Urban Form, Transit Cooperative Research Program Report 16,* vols. 1 and 2. Washington, D.C.: Transportation Research Board, 1996.

Douglas R. Porter. *Transit-Focused Development, Transit Cooperative Research Program, Synthesis of Transit Practice 20.* Washington, D.C.: Transportation Research Board, 1997.

Price Waterhouse, Multisystems, Inc., and Mundle & Associates, Inc. *Funding Strategies for Public Transit, Transit Cooperative Research Program Report 31,* vols. 1 and 2. Washington, D.C.: Transportation Research Board, 1998.

Project for Public Spaces, Inc. *The Role of Transit in Creating Livable Metropolitan Communities, Transit Cooperative Research Project Report 22.* Washington, D.C.: Transportation Research Board, 1997.

Charles River and Associates, Inc., *Building Transit Ridership, An Exploration of Transit's Market Share and the Public Policies that Influence It, Transit Cooperative Research Program Report 27.* Washington, D.C.: Transportation Research Board, 1997.

Kevin St. Jacques and Herbert S. Levinson. *Operational Analysis of Bus Lanes on Arterials, Transit Cooperative Research Program Report 26.* Washington, D.C.: Transportation Research Board, 1997

John J. Schiavone. *Monitoring Bus Maintenance Performance, Transit Cooperative Research Program, Synthesis of Transit Practice 22.* Washington, D.C.: Transportation Research Board, 1997.

Richard Stern. *Passenger Transfer System Review, Transit Cooperative Research Program, Synthesis of Transit Practice 19.* Washington, D.C.: Transportation Research Board, 1995.

Texas Transportation Institute, Texas A&M Research Foundation, and Texas A&M University. *Guidelines for the Location and Design of Bus Stops, Transit Cooperative Research Program Report 19.* Washington, D.C.: Transportation Research Board, 1996.

Statistical References

American Public Transit Association. *Transit Fact Book, Annual*. Washington, D.C.

Canadian Urban Transit Association. *Transit Fact Book, Annual*.

Federal Transit Administration. *Transit Profiles for the National Transit Database Report Year*, Washington, D.C.: FTA, Annual.

International Union (Association) of Public Transport. *Urban Public Transport, Statistics 1997*, vol. 1 and 2. 1997.

Edited by Geoffrey Freeman Allen, Janes Transport Data—Janes Information Group Limited. *Janes World Railways*. Coulsdon, Surrey, United Kingdom.

Bureau of Transportation Statistics. *National Transportation Statistics*. Washington, D.C.: U.S. DOT, BTS, Annual.

Bureau of Transportation Statistics. *Transportation Statistics Annual Report*. Washington, D.C., U.S. DOT, BTS, Annual.

Reports

Bellomo-McGee, Inc., prepared for Federal Highway Administration. *Responsive Multimodal Transportation Management Strategies and IVHS*. Washington, D.C.: FHWA, February 1995.

Canadian Urban Transit Association. *The Canadian Transit Handbook*, Third Edition. 1993.

Institute of Transportation Engineers. *Transit ITS Compendium*. Washington, D.C.: ITE, April 1997.

Hans Korve, et al. "Pedestrian Control Systems for Light Rail Transit Operations in Metropolitan Environments," *Seventh National Conference on Light Rail Transit*, vol. 2. Washington, D.C.: Transportation Research Board, 1997.

David S. Phraner. "Vintage Trolleys: A National Overview," *Transportation Research Record No. 1361*. Washington, D.C.: Transportation Research Board, 1992.

San Diego Metropolitan Transit Development Board. *Designing for Transit, A Manual for Integrating Public Transportation and Land Development in the San Diego Metropolitan Area*. San Diego, Calif.: July 1993.

John W. Schumann and Suzanne R. Tidrick. "Status of North American Light Rail Transit Systems: 1995 Update," *Seventh National Conference on Light Rail Transit*, vol. 1. Washington, D.C.: Transportation Research Board, 1995.

Transportation Research Board. *Workshop on Transit Fare Policy and Management, Transportation Research Circular Number 421*. Washington, D.C.: TRB, April 1, 1994.

CHAPTER 14
Parking

Mary Smith, P.E.
Senior Vice President
Walker Parking Consultants, Inc.

Planning for parking has been a concern of communities, property owners, and all those who provide goods and services to their communities since the days of the horse and buggy. Parking is a major determinant in density of land use; a typical suburban office building may have at least as much land or floor area in parking as it has leasable office space. A regional shopping center will typically have 1.5 sq m of parking for every sq m of leasable retail space, while restaurants and entertainment facilities can have 4 to 7 sq m of parking for every sq m of occupied space.

This chapter reviews the principles of planning for parking facilities. Included are discussions of the role of parking in transportation and urban systems, characteristics of parking, parking needs, zoning requirements, cost and financing issues, parking policies, and management strategies. Two related topics are not addressed herein: parking studies and parking design. Instead these two topics are covered in the *Transportation Engineering Handbook,* prepared by the Institute of Transportation Engineers (ITE).

Introduction

Types of Parking

The ancestor of modern parking is the barn, shed, or stable of the horse and buggy days. Not far behind, however, was the development of the first *on-street parking* space—the hitching post—and the first *off-street parking facility*—the livery stable. Off-street parking facilities today range from driveways, carports, and multicar garages at residences to *parking structures* in excess of 10,000 spaces. The largest multifacility systems generally serve transit or university parking needs. For example, BART, in San Francisco, manages 42,230 spaces while the Ohio State University parking system has more than 26,000 parking spaces. The largest individual parking facilities in the United States are likely to be found at airports and theme parks. The largest single parking complex, with 21,000 spaces in two connected structures, is at Universal Studios in Orlando, Florida.

Parking may be provided in *public parking facilities* that serve any and all who wish to use them or in *private parking facilities* that are reserved for specific users. *Commercial* facilities are those operated for a profit, often by a *professional parking operator.* Commercial facilities are usually public; however, some commercial facilities may be entirely reserved (usually leased on a monthly basis) to a specific group of users and therefore are "private."

The vast majority of parking in the United States is provided in *surface lots* and is "free"— to the user, that is. The cost of building and operating "free parking" is either borne by the landowner or passed through to the tenants in the lease rate. As land cost and density increase, multistory parking structures are more likely to be viable from a development perspective. As will be discussed later in this chapter, owning and operating a space in a parking structure costs *at least* double that of a surface lot, excluding land. There is, therefore, substantially more incentive for the owner or manager of the property to decide to charge the user for parking in a structure. An owner may also decide to charge for parking as part of a strategy to control who parks where or as part of an employee trip reduction program.

In most cases, the parking fee is still subsidized below the actual cost of owning and operating the space, due to market forces—when most of the other parking in the community and parking at competitors is free, it is difficult to charge the user the full cost. There are two general exceptions: (1) core areas of our largest cities where monthly parking charges exceed $150 per month and (2) airport parking. It is a little known fact that parking is often among the biggest generators of net revenue to support airport operations.

The vast majority of parking facilities are operated as *self-park*. *Valet* parking has become more common in recent years as a customer service tool at places with parking shortages or long walking distances. In the 1950s, *mechanical* parking structures employed elevators and other devices to move the vehicle away to parking stalls not accessible by pedestrians. This facility type fell out of favor due to reliability problems and the high cost of maintenance as the facilities aged. Electronics and other technological advances have made these structures feasible again in the 1990s, especially where there is not an adequate site for a traditional self-park structure.

Figure 14–1   Parking Facility at the University of Virginia

Building codes distinguish *parking garages* (underground structures that must have sprinklers and mechanical ventilation) from *open parking structures* (above grade multistory parking facilities that are naturally ventilated.) *Mixed-use* parking structures may include other land uses at grade, which helps to create a more pedestrian-friendly building at street level. Other uses may also be built over parking structures, although usually with a substantial premium cost for developing the parking levels. An excellent example is the University of Virginia, where a new campus bookstore was built on top of a parking structure set against the side of a hill. The bookstore is at the same level as the adjacent plaza of the student union. (Figure 14–1.) Another example is the placement of the athletic facilities, such as tennis courts, on the roof. There are also regional variations in the terms used for parking facilities; for example, parking structures may be called parking *decks* or *ramps* in certain areas, while the British term is *car park*.

Definitions

Central Business District

A *central business district* (CBD) is the traditional heart of the business, commercial, financial and administrative activity of a community. A *fringe* area may extend the CBD another two or three blocks in each direction. The fringe area often includes industrial and other lower density uses and may have substantial on-street and surface parking serving the core area at lower rates.

Activity Center

An *activity center* is a relatively large concentration of development that is a major focus of activity within an urban area. While CBDs are historically the dominant form of activity center, the suburban activity center is the most prevalent form of commercial development in North America today. Suburban activity centers typically have multiple land uses and may consist of multiple mixed-use developments. Institutions such as major government centers, colleges, universities, and medical centers also create activity centers.

Intermodal

Intermodal is an adjective describing the change of mode from one form of transportation to another; an *intermodal parking facility* typically allows change of mode from private vehicle to public transit of one type or another. However, parking facilities at airports, train stations, and other terminals are also intermodal.

Parking Capacity and Supply

Parking capacity is the number of vehicles that can be parked in a given facility; *parking supply* is the total number of spaces available to serve a destination.

Effective Supply

Effective supply is the level of occupancy for optimum operating efficiency. A parking facility will be perceived as full at somewhat less than its actual capacity, generally in the range of 85 to 95 percent full, depending on various factors. For example, a parking supply broken into many small lots with many of the spaces reserved for specific users operates far less efficiently than a large single facility with all spaces available to any user. The cushion of extra spaces reduces the need to search an entire system for the last few available spaces. It further provides for operating fluctuations, vehicle maneuvers, and vacancies created by reserving spaces for specific users such as disabled parking, losses due to misparked vehicles, snow cover, and so on. Therefore, users may perceive that there is a serious or even severe parking problem even though there are almost always spaces available somewhere in that system. The effective supply cushion in a system also provides for unusual peaks in activity (i.e., above the design day need); on such days, the parking system may not operate efficiently but can absorb periodic higher accumulations.

Parking Demand

Parking demand is a term that has not always been well defined in the industry—is it the peak accumulation of vehicles or the number of spaces that should be provided? *Webster's*[1] defines demand as "the quantity of goods wanted at a given price." The qualifier of price is especially significant in parking planning because the price of parking has a major effect on demand. Therefore, we shall hereinafter define parking demand as the number of spaces that should be provided to serve a use or group of uses under a specific set of circumstances, including pricing. *Parking generation* is the accumulation of vehicles. Parking demand then is equal to the *peak generation rate* on a design day plus a five to ten percent effective supply cushion. The parking generation rates periodically published by ITE[2] are the number of occupied spaces per unit of independent variable (e.g., per employee, per sq m) found in data bases collected by ITE members. While they typically reflect the peak accumulation on the survey date, that date may or may not be the appropriate design day (see section below). Therefore ITE's data on parking generation rates are not necessarily parking demand ratios, and care must be taken in application thereof.

Parking Adequacy

Parking adequacy is determined by comparing the demand to the supply. Where appropriate, an equally acceptable approach is to compare the peak generation rate on the design day to the effective supply.

Design Day

Design Day is the level of parking generation that recurs frequently enough to justify providing parking spaces at that level. One does not want to build for an average day and have an insufficient supply for fifty percent of the days of year. Conversely, it is not appropriate to design for the peak accumulations that could conceivably never occur. Further, that unusual peak may only last for an hour or so. Neighbors of an office building, hospital, or university will not complain if parking spills out into the neighborhood on rare occasions, but they will not accept it every day. The design day is typically selected from among the top ten to twenty activity days per year.

Utilization and Occupancy

Utilization is the usage of a space or facility over a given period of time. *Occupancy* may be measured and recorded at hourly intervals or only at the expected peak period.

---

[1] *Webster's II New Riverside Dictionary,* Office Edition (New York, N.Y.: Berkley Books, 1984, p. 188).
[2] *Parking Generation,* Second Edition (Washington, D.C.: Institute of Transportation Engineers, 1984, p. viii.)

Duration

Duration is the length of time a vehicle is parked. *Average stay or average duration* is the average length of time all vehicles are parked in a facility over a specific period. *Short-term parking* is generally defined as parking for 2.99 hours or less; *long-term* parking is generally defined as parking for 3.0 hours or more. *All-day* parking refers to vehicles parked for the hours of a typical working day. *Visitor parking* is usually short term; however, it may be long term at an ambulatory surgery center, airport, or a hotel. Similarly *employee parking* is usually, but not always, long-term parking.

Turnover

Turnover is the number of different vehicles parked in a specific area or facility over a given period of time divided by the number of spaces. Turnover may be calculated over the course of an entire day or separately for daytime and evening parking. If parking spaces in a facility are underutilized, the turnover rate will be very low. A common misconception is that turnover can be calculated by dividing the time period by the average stay (e.g., 8 hours divided by 2 hours average equals four turns per day.) This is really the maximum or *potential turnover* possible in a given time period and can only be achieved when the spaces are 100 percent occupied throughout the time period. Employee parking typically turns over 1.1 to 1.2 times per day due to in and out activity, while customer parking may turn over three to seven times per day. Multiday parking, as occurs at airports and hotels, will turn over less than one time per day, while airport short-term parking may turn over 10 or more times per day if effective segregation of long- and short-term parkers is achieved.

The Automobile and Parking: Facts of Life

It is acknowledged in transportation and urban planning that our resources are not limitless and that greater efficiency in the use of transportation resources must be achieved. How to achieve this goal is, of course, the controversial issue. Parking availability and price are key determinants in mode choice, which in turn, is a most fundamental element in transportation planning. Reliance on the personal automobile—and the need to park it at both ends of each trip—has increased in the last decade even as transportation demand management (TDM) and reduction of single-occupant vehicle (SOV) trips have been a focus of transportation and urban planners.

The largest single factor in these trends is suburbanization. The population in the central city where transit is more widely available and price incentives to use alternative modes exist has declined. Virtually all metropolitan growth between 1980 and 1990 occurred in the suburbs.[3] Likewise, suburban areas constituted 42 percent of the jobs in 1990, up from 37 percent in 1980. Other factors contributing to the increased reliance on the personal automobile are maturation of baby boomers, more women in the workforce, more trip chaining, higher levels of automobile ownership, the democratization of mobility,[4] the shift from an industrial to a service-based economy, and corporate downsizing and re-engineering. All have combined with suburbanization to increase the modal split of SOV trips.

And all contribute to the ever-increasing need for parking. While there are signs that the demographic trends have leveled out,[5] "signs of a turnaround in suburbanization or travel behavior changes are scarcely evident anywhere but in the fantasies of planners."[6]

As a result, parking planning today is more controversial than ever. The traditional and still widely held view is that adequate and convenient parking must be provided for commerce—and a community—to survive, let alone thrive. A survey conducted by the Downtown Research and Development Center ranked parking as the second most crucial issue that downtowns face.[7] The American Planning Service[8] says it "receives hundreds of requests each year about off-street

---

[3] A. E. Pisarski, *Commuting in America II* (Washington, D.C.: Eno Foundation for Transportation, Inc., 1996, p. 18).
[4] Ibid., pp. XI–XVI.
[5] Ibid, p. XI.
[6] S. Polzin, "We Aspire to Build Rail Transit—Do We Aspire to Live Where Rail Transit Will Work?," *Urban Transportation Monitor* (Burke, Va.: Lawley Publications, December 5, 1997, p. 4).
[7] M. Barr, *Downtown Parking Made Easy* (New York, N.Y.: Downtown Research and Development Center, 1997, p. 1).
[8] D.C. Shoup, "The High Cost of Free Parking," *Parking Today* (Los Angeles, Calif.: Bricepac, Inc., April 1997, p. 20).

parking requirements for different land uses—in fact, we receive more requests year after year on this topic than any other." Research conducted by the Downtown Partnership of Baltimore in 1996 found that downtown "will continue to lose companies and fail to capture new growth until parking problems are resolved."[9] In 1996 alone, six companies (with a total of 600 employees) cited parking as the primary reason for their decision not to locate downtown.

Conversely, Shoup, among others, has argued that the incorporation of minimum parking requirements in American zoning ordinances and the false mantra of "free parking" are primary causes of suburban sprawl, difficulty achieving TDM objectives, and all of the negative effects resulting from transportation via SOV. Putting aside "the chicken or the egg" arguments, it is certainly true that providing abundant free parking and surrounding new buildings with seas of asphalt make solo trips the preferred, if not only, option available to many people. Transit service is not economically viable at lower land use densities, and the true cost of parking is not borne by the person making the mode choice.

Moreover, studies back up the informal opinion of many planners that zoning ordinances require too much parking. One such study[10] concluded:

> By "conservatively" over-requiring parking, many zoning codes increase the cost of development, encourage solo driving, lower density, and worsen environmental quality. When too much parking is required, parking management and pricing strategies become difficult to implement. How can a developer or employer charge for anything so oversupplied? Developers do not usually object to providing more parking than is needed because they are responding to inflated perceptions of demand by themselves, tenants, lenders, and others.

A 1986 survey of members of the National Association of Industrial and Office Parks found that most developers want more parking than zoning ordinances require.[11] Out of 57 responses on office building parking, 39 percent agreed with their local zoning ordinance ratio, 42 percent felt the requirement was too low and provided more than was required, and only 19 percent thought the ratio was too high. This perceived need for as much or more parking as zoning requires is most likely the result of low land costs at suburban locations, which make it feasible to provide generous surface parking as an amenity or competitive advantage. Developers in CBDs often are not required to provide any parking but find it necessary to develop and subsidize at least some very expensive parking to market the building, albeit far less than required in the suburbs.

However, when land cost or availability trigger the need to use structured parking, developers are far more likely to question the required number of spaces, develop shared parking or TDM solutions, or pass along the cost of parking to the users via fees. The market ultimately decides how much new office space is developed downtown without free parking as opposed to in the suburbs with free surface parking.

The fundamental reason why jobs move to the suburbs is not free parking but because the "American dream" is to live in the country. The vast majority of Americans seek to live in the area of lowest density that they can afford. The jobs follow the labor supply. Low density means low land cost, and low land cost usually means free parking. Thus free parking, zoning requirements, land value, and density are so subtly intertwined in the market lease rate of new space in a particular locale that one cannot point to any one factor, such as free parking, as the dominant one causing all of the deleterious effects of SOV trips.

It is unlikely that a fundamental shift in the equation will occur without government intervention; efforts thus far to change commuting habits have seen only limited success. Meanwhile, there is significant grassroots opposition to efforts to force such change. In 1990, the federal government mandated that states require employee SOV commute reduction plans by large employers in areas of nonattainment as part of the Clean Air Act. However, those requirements were changed to voluntary in 1995; many states, including the most ecologically conscious, rescinded their requirements shortly thereafter.

---

[9] *Gateway to Growth: Improving Parking in Downtown Baltimore* (Baltimore, Md.: Downtown Partnership of Baltimore, September 1997, p. ii).
[10] R. Wilson, *Suburban Parking Economics and Policy: Case Studies of Office Worksites in Southern California* (Washington, D.C.: Federal Transit Administration, 1992, p. 46).
[11] J. Casazza, *Parking for Industrial and Office Parks* (Arlington, Va.: National Association of Industrial and Office Parks/Educational Foundation, 1986, p. 116).

An initiative by three federal agencies to lower the "cap" on tax-free, employer-provided parking from $165 per month to $135 per month or less has not found the support of Congress and has languished without definitive action. That program would have had miniscule effect on commuting patterns—less than 0.5 percent reduction in mode split to SOV was projected.[12] Almost all locations where the market rate for employee parking exceeds $135 per month are in urban downtowns; lowering the cap on employer-paid parking, thus, will only affect locations where parking is already market-priced and significant transit use and trip reduction already occurs. This, in turn may encourage more tenants to move to the suburbs where parking is free, subverting the whole plan. A Baltimore study[13] found that tenants are moving to the suburbs because of parking hassles even as it has constructed a new subway system; significantly increasing parking cost may be the last straw. In the words of one 24-year tenant: "We have decided that due to the high cost of parking to consider relocation to the county."

Unless and until government has the will to tax *all* employer-provided parking—which will require imputing a value of "free parking" in the suburbs—there can be no means of ensuring that the typical commuter considers the price of parking in modal choice. In sum, one can conclude that, as long as America has a free market economy and a political system that bends to its constituencies' wants and desires, the vast majority of parking will be free parking in suburban locations, where transit is not economically viable and carpooling is not an acceptable choice for most commuters. In turn, parking will continue to be a major issue to transportation planners. However, transportation planners can and should work to minimize the three primary reasons that parking is all too often inefficiently provided:[14]

1. Underpricing of parking.

2. Oversupply of parking.

3. Lack of shared parking.

Transportation Characteristics

As noted by Pisarski,[15] commuter trips are more important in transportation planning than would be indicated by their proportion of total trips. This is because of the effect commuting has on the economy and development within a community, congestion at peak hours, and in turn air pollution problems. From a parking perspective, significantly more parking spaces are required per commuting trip than per shopping or other personal trip, since commuter space turnover is so much lower. That is, a commuter space only serves one to two trips per day whereas a customer space may serve three to ten trips per day. Also, commuter parking is generally far more price-sensitive than customer parking and more easily influenced by local transit alternatives.

According to the 1995 Nationwide Personal Transportation Survey (NPTS),[16] Americans average 1,572 personal trips per year, including commuting, or 4.3 trips per person per day. Nine hundred sixty-five or 61.3 percent were as a personal vehicle driver, thus representing a trip requiring parking spaces at one or both ends. Only 21.3 percent of trips are commuting or work-related. Even more startling, NPTS found that only 37 percent of person trips between 6 A.M. and 9 A.M. were journey-to-work trips. A primary factor in this low number is trip chaining; the NPTS counts each segment of a multistop trip as a separate trip with a distinct purpose. Additional relevant statistics from the 1990 census indicate that there were 115 million working adults and 165 million registered drivers. A conservative appraisal, based on this data, estimates that nonresidential parking spaces are used at least 300 million times each day in the United States.

From 1960 to 1995 the percentage of workers commuting to work in private automobiles increased from 70 to 91 percent. Another 3.1 percent used transit systems, but a number of those users drove to and parked in commuter parking facilities. The percentage driving alone was up much more sharply, from 64.37 percent in 1980 to 73.19 percent in 1990

[12] Association for Commuter Transportation, *Commuter Choice Initiative* (Washington, D.C.: Federal Transit Administration, Federal Highway Administration, and U.S. Environmental Protection Agency, June 1996, p. 13).

[13] *Gateway to Growth* (Baltimore, Md.: Downtown Partnership of Baltimore, September 1997, p. ii).

[14] John G. Shaw, *Planning for Parking,* (Des Moines, Iowa: University of Iowa Public Policy Center, 1997, p. 6).

[15] Pisarski, *Commuting in America II* (Washington, D.C.: Eno Foundation for Transportation, Inc., p. 3).

[16] *"Our Nations Travel: 1995 NPTS Early Results Report"* (Washington, D.C.: Federal Highway Administration, undated).

and 75 percent in 1995. All other alternative modes to the SOV commute declined except working at home, which increased from 2.26 percent in 1980 to 2.96 percent in 1990.[17]

Parking Needs

There exists a wide variation in parking demand among otherwise similar land uses. The variations reflect differences in density of development, availability of public transportation, local policies, price of parking, and local economic vitality levels. In areas with a mix of land uses, such as the CBD, parking demand is often reduced because of the interrelationship of the activities present. Parking demand also varies over time as employment densities, transportation management issues, and car ownership levels change. Density of employees per unit floor area in offices, for example, has dropped from about 6.5 employees per 100 sq m (6 employees per 1,000 sq ft) to 3.8 employees per 100 sq m (3.5 employees per 1,000 sq ft) over the past forty years, but the recent trend is back toward higher employee density.[18] At hospitals and medical centers, the longtime standard for determining the number of parking spaces was the number of beds. But treatments on an outpatient basis have increased dramatically since 1980, resulting in increased demand for parking with no increase—and often a decrease—in beds.

Setting Parking Demand Formulas

It is generally accepted that a formula should be used relating parking spaces required to some quantitative measure of the land use. A variety of issues that affect the specific formulas used for determining parking requirements are discussed in the following paragraphs.

Units

Parking demand and generation rates are generally stated as a ratio of x spaces per y units, with the unit being an appropriate measure for that particular land use. The unit in the vast majority of cases is building area (sq m or sq ft). Other units employed include dwelling units, hotel rooms, seats, or persons. It is highly desirable that the unit be something calculable at the time of planning. In general, demand ratios based on numbers of employees, which are often highly variable over time, should be avoided. However, certain land uses—specifically hospitals, schools, and other institutions—are so variable that allotments per employee, student, and patient are the only reasonable determinants. In some cases, particularly those of assembly space such as auditoriums, there will be a capacity in persons that is licensed or posted by governmental units to serve as the basis for parking requirements.

In the past, parking ratios tended to be stated as one space for each y sq ft. However, most in the industry now prefer to use a ratio stated as x spaces per 1,000 sq ft. It is simply easier for the average person to multiply than to divide. Therefore the more recent studies of parking requirements, such as *Parking Generation*[19] and *Shared Parking*[20], have generally employed the spaces-per-1,000-sq-ft convention. As America converts to metric ratios, the best conversion appears to be parking spaces per 100 sq m. Hereinafter, that basis will be employed. Another aspect of ratios based on sq m is how area is calculated. Because there is wide variation among both national standards and zoning ordinances on this issue, the modifiers "gross," "net," "leasable," and "rentable" are frequently added to clarify the term "floor area." The Urban Land Institute (ULI) provides the following terminology with respect to floor area:[21]

- *Gross Floor Area (GFA):* Total, gross floor area, including the exterior building walls, of all floors of a building or structure.

- *Gross Leasable Area (GLA):* The gross floor area that is available for leasing to a tenant.

[17] Ibid, p. 49.
[18] R. Weant and Herbert Levinson, *Parking* (Westport, Conn.: Eno Foundation for Transportation, 1990, p. 119).
[19] *Parking Generation* (Washington, D.C.: Institute of Transportation Engineers, 1987).
[20] *Shared Parking* (Washington, D.C.: The Urban Land Institute, 1983).
[21] M. Smith, "Zoning Requirements," *The Dimensions of Parking* (Washington, D.C.: The Urban Land Institute, 1993, p. 51).

- *Net Floor Area (NFA):* The total floor area, excluding exterior building walls.

- *Net Rentable Area:* The net floor area that is available to a tenant. Also called net leasable area.

Thus, GFA is calculated "out-to-out," and NFA is calculated "in-to-in" of exterior walls. For purposes of calculating parking requirements, the vehicular parking and loading areas and the floor area occupied by mechanical, electrical, communications, and security equipment are deducted from either GFA or NFA, as these spaces do not contribute to parking demand. While older ordinances tended to use NFA, most industry standards today (e.g., ULI; ITE; National Parking Association, known as NPA) use GFA or GLA.

The use of leasable or rentable adjustments has become important with the trend to large, multiple-tenant building developments. Generally, GLA is GFA minus the floor area of elevator shafts and stair towers, public restrooms, permanently designed corridors, public lobbies, and common mall areas. Merely enclosing the space connecting the tenant spaces does not add significantly to parking demand. For example, if GLA is the same, the common mall areas of enclosed shopping centers do not generate significantly more demand than either a shopping center with open-air courtyards or a strip center with all stores opening to the parking lot. Likewise, connecting the lobbies of a pair of office towers with an atrium does not generate additional parking demand; thus, the atrium should be excluded from parking demand calculations. In smaller buildings, the difference between GLA and GFA is negligible.

Design Day and Design Hour

The traffic engineer does not design the street system to handle the peak volume that will ever occur; instead, the activity that represents the 85th or 90th percentile of peak-traffic volume is used for design. *Shared parking*[22] employs the 90th percentile ratio of the peak hour occupancies observed. *Parking generation*[23] presents regression curves for the average of the peak accumulations observed; however, in a subsequent article, the ITE committee[24] suggested the 85th percentile as an appropriate design standard. Weant and Levinson[25] and Smith[26] generally employ the 85th percentile, as does the Parking Consultants Council (PCC).[27] Figure 14–2 documents the cumulative distribution of parking generation rates in the ITE data base for office buildings as a demonstration of the 85th percentile.[28]

Effective Supply

When determining the adequacy of a parking system, a parking consultant will usually assign "effective supply factors" to each of the different facilities to determine the overall effective supply, then compare these factors with a "design day parking generation rate." It is not practical to require such analysis for each and every development project. Therefore, requirements in zoning ordinances should include an effective supply factor of five to ten percent over the anticipated peak accumulation of parked vehicles on the design day, within the stated requirement. NPA's *Recommended Zoning Ordinance Provisions* reflects such a factor. However, ITE's *Parking Generation* reports accumulations of vehicles and, thus, should be factored upwards to serve as zoning or planning standards. For smaller or single-tenant buildings, a ten percent factor is appropriate; while in larger, multitenant developments, a five percent factor can be used.

Size

The size of a development project influences more than the effective supply factor. The peak accumulation of vehicles at a large multitenant building is much more likely to fit a standard than is the peak accumulation of parking in a small building within the same land use category. It is simply a case of probability; among fifty small office buildings, a number

---

[22] *Shared Parking* (Washington, D.C.: Urban Land Institute, p. 13).
[23] *Parking Generation* (Washington, D.C.: Institute of Transportation Engineers, 1987, p. vii).
[24] "Using the ITE *Parking Generation* Report," *ITE Journal* (Washington, D.C.: Institute of Transportation Engineers, July 1990, p. 25).
[25] R. Weant and Herbert Levinson, *Parking* (Westport, Conn.: Eno Foundation for Transportation, 1990, p. 94).
[26] M.S. Smith. "Zoning Requirements," *The Dimensions of Parking* (Washington, D.C.: The Urban Land Institute, 1993, p. 51).
[27] Parking Consultants Council, *Recommended Zoning Ordinance Provisions for Parking and Off-Street Loading Spaces* (Washington, D.C.: National Parking Association, 1992, p. 5).
[28] "Using the ITE *Parking Generation* Report," *ITE Journal* (Washington, D.C.: Institute of Transportation Engineers, July 1990, p. 27).

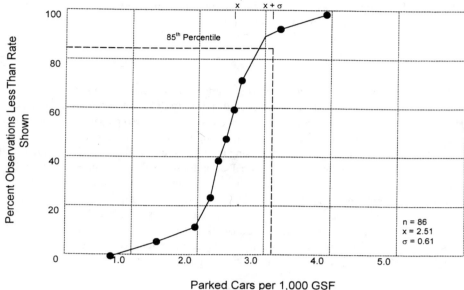

Figure 14–2   Design Day Definition

Source: Special tabulations of data from *Parking Generation,* Washington, D.C.: Institute of Transportation Engineers, 1987.

will have a demand high enough to justify a 3.9 spaces per 100 sq m (3.6 spaces per 1,000 sq ft) zoning requirement. If the tenants of those fifty buildings move into a large building, the accumulation of vehicles will average out; and a 3.2 spaces per 100 sq m (3.0 spaces per 1,000 sq ft) supply will be sufficient. It is entirely appropriate, therefore, for a community to have a higher ratio for smaller concentrations of a specific land use than that required for larger buildings. Single-tenant buildings, especially larger ones, may need special study. When there are multiple departments with different functions, the parking needs will be similar to a large multitenant building; however, a single-tenant building that houses one large function may have higher needs. It should be noted that size has the reverse effect on shopping centers. This is because the size of the center usually reflects its focus—neighborhood, community, or regional—and, thus, reflects differences in shopping and parking patterns. (Table 14–1.)

Accessory Uses

Accessory uses are areas within a specific land use that are not the principal activity generator but are necessary to the successful tenancy of that land use. Examples are storage, stock, office, and kitchen spaces. Some will argue that this floor area should be calculated at different rates. Most national standards have been based on studies wherein these areas

Table 14–1   Characteristics of Shopping Centers

Center Type	Leading Tenant (basis for classification)	Typical GLA	General Range in GLA	Usual Minimum Site Area	Minimum Support Required
Neighborhood Center	Supermarket or drugstore	5,000 sq m (53,820 sq ft)	3,000–10,000 sq m (32,292–107,639 sq ft)	1 hectare (2.5 acres)	2,500–40,000 people
Community Center	Variety, discount, or jr. department store	15,000 sq m (161,569 sq ft)	10,000–30,000 sq m (107,639–322,917 sq ft)	4 hectares (9.9 acres)	40,000–150,000 people
Regional Center	One full line department store of at least 10,000 sq m (107,639 sq ft) of GLA[1]	40,000 sq m (430,556 sq ft)	30,000–1000,000 sq m (107,639–1,076,391 sq ft) or more[1]	12–20 hectares (30–50 acres)	150,000 or more people

[1] Centers with more than 69,677 sq m (750,000 sf) GLA usually include three or more department stores and hence are super regionals.

Source: Adapted from *Parking Requirements for Shopping Centers,* Washington, D.C.: The Urban Land Institute, 1982, p. 27.

have been considered as part of the floor area used to calculate parking ratios; therefore, it is usually appropriate to include accessory areas in the floor area calculations for the primary use.

Complementary Uses

A complementary use is a space that is used or leased by a different land use designed to serve or enhance the primary one. Although the complementary use normally would have substantially different parking characteristics from those of the primary land use, the interrelationship with the primary use results in lowered parking demand, primarily through captive market effects. For example, a deli or sandwich shop that might otherwise require more parking spaces per unit floor area can be allowed in an office building without increasing the ratio of the primary activity generator. ULI's *Parking Requirements for Shopping Centers* studied this issue specifically and found that small concentrations of complementary uses do not change the parking requirements from those of the primary land uses. It should be noted that the full GLA (i.e., the sum of the primary and complementary uses) should be multiplied by the ratio for the primary use. There should be a limit on the percentage of leasable space occupied by complementary uses. Using the above example, a single strip center should not be allowed to lease a substantial portion of its space to restaurants without meeting the parking requirements for restaurants. The NPA recommends that a maximum of ten percent of the GLA be occupied by complementary uses without viewing the tenancies with separate ratios.[29]

Common Uses

Table 14–2 summarizes data from ITE's *Parking Generation*,[30] which represents peak observed accumulations and not necessarily "demand" or "required spaces" for zoning. Special considerations for determining parking demand for some of the more common uses is discussed in the following sections.

Retail

For shopping centers, the most definitive and widely accepted reference on parking demand is *Parking Requirements for Shopping Centers,* which was published by ULI in 1982. This report recommended a parking demand ratio varying from 4.3 spaces per 100 sq m (4.0 spaces per 1,000 sq f) GLA for smaller centers to 5.4 spaces per 100 sq m (5.0 spaces per 1,000 sq ft) for larger centers. Tables 14–3, 14–4, and 14–5 present important data from that study relating to parking at retail uses.

However, since the publication of that document there have been substantial changes in retailing that have affected parking demand, including changes in operating hours on peak days and increased evening parking demand on weekdays. Of even greater impact is the incorporation of increasingly larger dining and entertainment components, a trend that is epitomized by Mall of America and urban retail/entertainment (URE) centers such as City Walk at Universal Studios in Los Angeles. *Parking Requirements for Shopping Centers* looked at the effects of limited amounts of entertainment uses (food court, cinema, and restaurant uses) on shopping centers under the paradigm of 1970s development. Depending on the relative proportions of traditional retail uses and entertainment uses, there may be dramatic deviations in parking needs from those found in the ULI recommendations. In some cases, the peak parking accumulation will not even occur during the Christmas shopping season.

Therefore, analysis of parking needs in today's URE centers is often most accurately determined by evaluating the parking needs of the individual and specific combination of uses at different times of day and seasons of the year to determine the peak accumulation of vehicles. This is basically a "shared parking analysis" as commonly used for downtown and mixed-use projects.

---

[29] *Recommended Zoning Ordinance Provisions* (Washington, D.C.: National Parking Association, 1992).
[30] *Parking Generation* (Washington, D.C.: Institute of Transportation Engineers, 1987).

Table 14–2 ITE Parking Generation Rates

Use	Unit	Period	Peak Accumulation[a] (85% tile)	Spaces per Unit (Recommended Ratio[b])
Commercial Airport	Enplaning passengers	Weekday	0.64	0.70
	Enplaning passengers	Saturday	1.48	1.62
	Enplaning passengers	Sunday	2.05	2.26
Light Industry	100 sq m (1,000 sq ft) GLA	Weekday	2.61(2.43)	2.87(2.67)
	Employee		1.00[c]	1.10
Industrial Park	100 sq m (1,000 sq ft) GLA	Weekday	2.27(2.11)	2.50(2.32)
	Employee	Weekday	0.80	0.88
Manufacturing	100 sq m (1,000 sq ft) GLA	Weekday	2.45(2.28)	2.70(2.51)
	Employee	Weekday	1.00[c]	1.10
Low-Rise Apartment	Dwelling unit	Weekday	1.38	1.52
		Saturday	1.53	1.68
High-Rise Apartment (central area)	Dwelling unit	Weekday	0.59	0.65
Residential Condominium	Dwelling unit	Weekday	1.41	1.55
		Saturday	1.23	1.35
Convention Hotel	Room	Weekday	1.10	1.21
Motel with Restaurant/Lounge	Rooms	Weekday	1.49	1.64
Movie Theater	Seats	Weekday	0.30	0.33
		Saturday	0.37	0.41
Sports Club/Health Spa	100 sq m (1,000 sq ft) GLA	Weekday	6.86(6.37)	7.55(7.01)
Church/Synagogue	Attendees	Sunday	0.62	0.68
Hospital	Beds	Weekday	2.48	2.73
Medical-Dental Clinic/Office	100 sq m (1,000 sq ft) GLA l	Weekday	5.92(5.50)	6.51(6.05)
General Offices Building	100 sq m (1,000 sq ft) GLA	Weekday	3.23(3.00[d])	3.55(3.30)
	Employees	Weekday	0.93	1.02
Office Park	100 sq m (1,000 sq ft) GLA	Weekday	3.53(3.28)	3.55(3.30)
Hardware/Paint/Home Improvement Store	100 sq m (1,000 sq ft) GLA	Weekday	3.48(3.23)	3.82(3.55)
	100 sq m (1,000 sq ft) GLA	Saturday	4.51(4.19)	4.96(4.61)
Shopping Center	100 sq m (1,000 sq ft) GLA	Weekday	4.77(4.43)	5.24(4.87)
	100 sq m (1,000 sq ft) GLA	Saturday	5.49(5.10)	6.04(5.61)
Quality Restaurant	100 sq m (1,000 sq ft) GLA	Weekday	18.73(17.40)	20.60(19.14)
	100 sq m (1,000 sq ft) GLA	Saturday	21.65(20.11)	23.81(22.12)
	Seats	Weekday	0.54	0.59
		Saturday	0.61	0.67
Family Restaurant	100 sq m (1,000 sq sq ft) GLA	Weekday	12.00(11.15)	13.20(12.26)
	Seats	Weekday	0.42	0.46
Fast Food Restaurant (without drive-in window)	100 sq m (1,000 sq ft) GLA	Weekday	14.27(15.36)	15.70(16.90)
	Seats	Weekday	0.77	0.85
Bank—with drive-in & walk-in facilities	100 sq m (1,000 sq sq ft) GLA	Weekday	5.88(5.47)	6.48(6.02)
Fast Food Restaurant (with drive-in window)	100 sq m (1,000 sq ft) GLA	Weekday	14.38(13.36)	15.83(14.70)
	Seats	Weekday	0.70	0.77

[a] Average rate plus one standard deviation. Transportation Engineers, *Parking Generation*, 2nd Edition.
[b] Ten percent effective supply factor. May not be needed in all cases (i.e., residential).
[c] Adjusted to 1.00 space/employee.
[d] Adjusted to 3.00 spaces/1,000 sq ft of building area.

Source: Weant & Levinson, *Parking*.

Table 14-3 Shopping Center Parking

GLA	Spaces/100 sq m GLA (/1000 sq ft)
2,500–40,000 sq m (26,910–430,556 sq ft)	0.0 (4.0)
40,000–50,000 sq m (430,556–538,196 sq ft)	0.0 (4.5)
50,000–120,000 sq m (538,196–1,291,669 sq ft)	0.0 (5.0)
Over 120,000 sq m (1,291,669 sq ft)	Special study
Offices	Up to 10 percent of gross area require no added spaces.
Cinema	For under 10,000 sq m (107,639 sq ft) center/ complex, add three spaces per 100 seats of up to 10 percent of cinema area.
	For 10,000–20,000 sq m (107,639–215,278 sq ft) center, add three spaces per 100 seats above 250.
	For over 20,000 sq m (215,278 sq ft) center, add three spaces per 100 seats above 750.
Food Services	For 2,500 – 10,000 sq m (26,910 to 107,639 sq ft) center, add 10.8 spaces per 100 sq m (10/1,000 sq ft) of food service tenant area. For 10,000 – 20,000 sq m (107,639–215,278 sq feet) center, add 6.5 spaces per 100 sq m (6/1,000 sq ft) of food service area.
	For 20,000 – 60,000 sq m (215,278–645,835 sq ft) no added spaces needed.
	For 60,000 sq m (645,835 sq ft) and over, reduce basic supply of 5.4 spaces to 4.3 spaces/100 sq m (5.0 spaces to 4.0 spaces per 1,000 sq ft) food service area.

Source: Adapted from *Parking Requirements for Shopping Centers*, Washington, D.C.: The Urban Land Institute, 1982.

Eating and Drinking Establishments

Restaurants are significant components of commercial developments in the 1990s and are indeed a major component of the URE center. A major driver of this phenomenon is the changing American family. In 1967 only 29.2 percent of the total food dollar was spent away from home; by 1990 that figure had climbed to 42.5 percent.[31]

While there are numerous variations in types of restaurants, the following classifications combine categories developed by the ITE for *Parking Generation* and U.S. Census Bureau reporting categories. These groupings have reasonably similar parking demands. Given that parking planning may begin long before a particular restaurant tenant lays out seating areas, spaces/unit area is the most appropriate unit for parking demand ratios.

"Fine Dining Establishments" are premier, "white tablecloth" or gourmet restaurants serving food and beverage at relatively high cost. Some of these restaurants only serve dinner, and many do not have a significant bar area. These restaurants are typically designed with lower density and require reservations at busy times. For this type of restaurant, an appropriate design standard would be 21.5 spaces per 100 sq m (20 spaces per 1,000 sq ft).

"Eating and drinking establishments" bridge the gap between fine dining and family restaurants, with more moderately priced meals and kid's menus but extensive beverage service. Many of these restaurants are heavily themed, following on the Hard Rock Café model, with entertainment as part of the dining experience. Because they typically do not take reservations, there may be long

Table 14-4 Monthly Shopping Center Sales Variations, Percent of Peak Month by Type of Center

Month	Neighborhood up to 10,000 sq m (107,639 sq ft)	Community 10,000–30,000 sq m (107,639–322,917 sq ft)	Regional 30,000–75,000 sq m (322,917–807,293 sq ft)	Super Regional over 75,000 sq m (807,293 sq ft)
January	51%	41%	37%	36%
February	49	41	36	36
March	56	46	44	44
April	57	49	43	43
May	58	52	45	44
June	53	50	44	44
July	53	49	45	42
August	58	56	50	49
September	56	52	47	48
October	56	54	49	47
November	69	65	62	56
December	100	100	100	100

Source: Adapted from *Parking Requirements for Shopping Centers*, Washington, D.C.: The Urban Land Institute, 1982, p. 47.

[31] *ICSC Research Quarterly*, Volume 2, Number 3 (International Council of Shopping Centers, Fall 1995).

waiting lines and heavy activity in the bar at busy times. This can result in peak parking needs reaching 26.9 spaces per 100 sq m (25 spaces per 1,000 sq ft) GLA.

"Family restaurants" are at the lowest end of the sit-down scale, usually serving breakfast as well as lunch and dinner, and typically without any alcoholic beverage service. With little or no waiting and no bar area, 16.1 spaces per 100 sq m (15 spaces per 1,000 sq ft) GLA is an appropriate design standard.

"Fast-food" restaurants generally have counter ordering, with a self-serve seating area; restaurants of this type usually have drive-through service. Due to the variations in designs, seats are part of the recommended ratio for demand. The recommended peak parking ratio is 10.8 spaces per 100 sq m (10 spaces per 1,000 sq ft) of kitchen, counter and waiting area plus 0.5 spaces per seat provided.

Table 14–5 Monthly Shopping Center Traffic Trends

Month	Percent of Annual Traffic
January	7.8%
February	7.4
March	7.8
April	7.9
May	7.9
June	7.9
July	8.2
August	8.5
September	7.7
October	8.7
November	8.9
December	11.4
	100.0%

Source: Adapted from *Parking Requirements for Shopping Centers,* Washington, D.C.: The Urban Land Institute, 1982, p. 46.

Entertainment Uses and Special Event Facilities

Multiscreen cinema complexes providing thousands of seats are a significant development trend with parking needs that have outpaced the available planning literature. The increasing size of cinemas and the changing design practices—epitomized by stadium seating, branded fast-food, and the like—makes a ratio based on seats the most appropriate. Where seats are not available, a good rule of thumb for conversion of GLA to seats is 18.6 sq m (20 sq ft) per seat. Another ratio unit sometimes used is screens, but seats per screen varies widely, and multiscreen cinemas often have larger and smaller auditoriums in the same complex.

A cinema is a classic example of a land use where size has a tremendous effect on parking needs. While a single or small multiscreen cinema can fill virtually every seat through the evening by running the latest blockbusters on each screen, this becomes increasing unlikely as 15 , 20, or 30 screens are provided. Moreover, with the rotating schedules of the cineplex, those arriving early to wait in line for the next show on screens 1, 2, and 3 can take parking spaces vacated by those exiting from an earlier showing on screens 10, 11, and 12. Thus, while a peak parking demand of one space for every two seats is appropriate for a single screen theatre and one space per three seats, as given in *Parking Generation* and *Shared Parking,* is appropriate for a theatre with up to five screens, the ratio can be reduced as the number further increases.

Live performance theatres are typically single auditoriums requiring a ratio of one space per two seats. Where multitheatre complexes exist, adjustment of this ratio for likely simultaneous use—or lack thereof—may be appropriate with documentation. (Table 14–6.)

A one space per two seat ratio is also appropriate for other places of assembly in smaller facilities (e.g., churches, synagogues).

Table 14–6   Auditorium Parking

	Maximum Seating Capacity	Parking Spaces				Transport Modes	Seats per Space	Spaces per Seat
		Adjacent	Vicinity	On-Street	Total			
Cleveland Arena	11,000	4,000	1,000	500	5,500	Auto, bus	2.0	0.5
Civic Auditorium—San Francisco	8,000	854	414	—	1,268	Auto	6.3	0.2
Coliseum—Richmond, KY	9,500	1,500	500	200	2,200	Auto	4.3	0.2
Cow Palace—San Francisco	15,000	7,000	150	850	8,000	Auto, bus	1.8	0.6
Maple Leaf Gardens—Toronto	19,500	350	3,500	—	3,850	Auto, bus, rail	5.1	0.2
Municipal Auditorium—Dallas	11,000	1,100	7,610	740	9,450	Auto, bus	1.2	0.8
O'Keefe Centre—Toronto	3,155	2,000	150	—	2,150	Auto, bus	1.5	0.7
Place des Arts—Montreal	3,000	389	725	250	1,364	Auto, bus	2.2	0.5
Veterans Memorial—Columbus, OH	3,964	1,200	300	1200	2,700	Auto, bus	1.5	0.7

Source: Adapted from *Traffic Considerations for Social Events,* Washington, D.C.: Institute of Transportation Engineers, 1976.

Convention centers have widely varying parking demand by type of event. These facilities are constructed to draw regional if not national tourists for conventions. The parking demand for a regional event where many people drive in for the day will be considerably higher than for a large national event where most delegates fly in and take shuttles from hotels. Certain types of conferences may also have significantly higher demands, such as religious groups and franchise or distribution network meetings. However, the peak parking demand for a convention center almost always occurs with the "public show" booked into the facility in periods of low convention activity. These "filler events" such as boat and home shows draw local residents, most of whom drive and park. There are also differences between convention centers, which have a combination of exhibit and meeting space, and exposition halls that are predominately exhibit halls.

There will be relatively low turnover for a national convention (1.5 to two turns per day) with peak arrivals in the morning and peak departures in the afternoon, while the boat show will have higher turnover (three to five turns per day) and in and out activity all day long.

Conversely, by their very nature, convention centers have tended to be located in larger activity centers with convenient hotels. The center's dedicated parking may be designed for the needs of a moderate, midweek national convention, with the higher needs of public shows on the weekend accommodated by other parking resources in the vicinity. When a "mega-show" is scheduled, a parking and transportation management plan is developed by the center's management and the show organizer to provide an alternative mode of travel to the center. Therefore, no one recommended ratio is provided; the number of spaces is best determined by a site-specific parking study.

The parking demand at arenas and stadiums is generally calculated by defining the design event (i.e., not the Super Bowl but a sellout regular season game). An appropriate adjustment for local transit service and charter bus service is taken, and then the mode split to personal vehicle is divided by expected auto occupancy. Vehicle occupancy at these facilities can vary substantially by type of event as seen in Tables 14–8. Therefore required parking varies as well (Table 14–9), but one space per three seats is a good starting point.

Commercial sporting facilities for amateur sports such as tennis, basketball, and indoor soccer are becoming common. Given that games in many of these facilities are tightly scheduled, with overlap of those waiting for the next game or match, two parking spaces per team member are required for a single-field venue. As multiple fields are developed, staggered scheduling of games may lower the ratio.

Casinos are another "new" problem for local officials. While land-based casinos have relatively low turnover (twenty percent or less of the spaces turn over in the peak hour), and a ratio of parking spaces to licensed occupancy can be determined, riverboats may—or may not—have a significant overlap of gamblers arriving for the next cruise before the debarkation of those on the previous cruise. The degree of overlap is significantly influenced by the embarkation and debarkation procedures and the time in port. For example, if gambling is allowed only while in motion, the casino will be organized around a short turnaround time, and there can be a peak accumulation of vehicles exceeding one space per attendee on a single cruise. Conversely, when gambling is allowed to continue in port while patrons debark, the debarkation will spread out, lowering the peak traffic volumes in short periods as well as the peak parking accumulation. Additional factors are the percentage of users expected to arrive by charter bus and any additional amenities nearby.

Hotels

Determining parking demand for hotels is complicated by the variety of hotel products in the marketplace, from the low budget, no frills motel to the largest convention hotels. In 1986, Barton-Aschman Associates[32] determined that demand for hotel parking was directly related to demand of the "component uses" of the particular hotel. They suggested that parking demand could be determined by a "shared parking" analysis of the hotel (and its particular components). The basic components of hotels are the number of guestrooms, restaurant(s) and lounge(s), employees, and convention or meeting rooms. Ratios for these components as presented in ULI's *Shared Parking* are presented in Table 14–10.

---

[32] Gerald Salzman, "Hotel Parking: How Much Is Enough?" *Urban Land* (Washington, D.C.: Urban Land Institute, January 1988, pp. 14–17).

Table 14–7   National Draw Convention Transportation Characteristics

Daily attendee presence at peak hour	80%	McCormick Place East Parking Study, Walker Parking Consultants, 1990
	70%	Anaheim Convention Center Parking Study, Walker Parking Consultants, 1993
	46%	Currigan Hall, Denver, Walker Parking Consultants, 1990
	70%	Cobo Hall, Walker Parking Consultants, 1993
	50%	Portland Convention Center, Carl H. Buttke, Inc., 1985
Driving ratio	24%	McCormick Place East Parking Study, Walker Parking Consultants, 1990
	25%	Anaheim Convention Center Parking Study, Walker Parking Consultants, 1993
(PM peak) >	44%	Orange County Convention Center, Transportation Consulting Group, January 1998
Daily >	74%	Orange County Convention Center, Transportation Consulting Group, January 1998
	15–25%	Cobo Hall, Walker Parking Consultants, 1993 (anecdotal)
	72%	Cobo Hall, Walker Parking Consultants, 1989 (SAE Convention)
(AM peak, inbound) >	40%	Riviera Hotel and Casino Convention Center, G.C. Wallace, Inc., 1990
(PM peak, outbound) >	15%	Riviera Hotel and Casino Convention Center, G.C. Wallace, Inc., 1990
	15–20%+	Las Vegas Convention Center, G.C. Wallace, Inc., 1994
	20%	McCormick Place, Barton-Aschman Associates, Inc., 1992
	25%	Pennsylvania Convention Center, Orth-Rodgers Associates, Inc., 1990
	10%	Portland Convention Center, Carl H. Buttke, Inc., 1985
(includes taxis) >	15%	Washington State Convention and Trade Center, City of Seattle, 1995
	16%	New York Exposition and Convention Center, Final Environmental Impact Statement
Persons/car	2.5	McCormick Place Parking Study, Walker Parking Consultants, 1990
	1.5	Anaheim Convention Center Parking Study, Walker Parking Consultants, 1993
	1.9	Orange County Convention Center, Transportation Consulting Group, January 1998
96 Outlier? >	2.3	(People/hotel room—business travel) Orlando CBV Research Dept.—1.8/'95 & 1.9/'94
	1.5	Currigan Hall, Denver, Walker Parking Consultants, 1990
(AM peak, inbound) >	2.2	Riviera Hotel and Casino Convention Center, G.C. Wallace, Inc., 1990
	2.5	Riviera Hotel and Casino Convention Center, G.C. Wallace, Inc., 1990
(AM inbound) >	2.5	Las Vegas Convention Center, G.C. Wallace, Inc., 1994
(PM outbound) >	2.5	Las Vegas Convention Center, G.C. Wallace, Inc., 1994
	2.5	McCormick Place East Parking Study, Walker Parking Consultants, 1990
	1.4	Pennsylvania Convention Center, Orth-Rodgers Associates, Inc., 1990
	2.0	Portland Convention Center, Carl H. Buttke, Inc., 1985
	1.5	Washington State Convention and Trade Center, City of Seattle, 1995
	1.8	New York Exposition and Convention Center, Final Environmental Impact Statement
Daily exhibitor presence at peak hour	80%	McCormick Place East Parking Study, Walker Parking Consultants, 1990
	69%	Currigan Hall, Denver, Walker Parking Consultants, 1990
Ratio of attendees to exhibitors	4:1	McCormick Place East Parking Study, Walker Parking Consultants, 1990
	22:1	Currigan Hall, Denver, Walker Parking Consultants, 1990 (4,400—attendee trade show)
	12:1	Currigan Hall, Denver, Walker Parking Consultants, 1990 (21,000—attendee consumer show)
	4:1	Cobo Hall, Walker Parking Consultants, 1993 (ratio of '88 attendees to '88 "delegates")
	7:1	Portland Convention Center, Carl H. Buttke, Inc., 1985
Employees as a % of daily attendance	5.0%	McCormick Place East Parking Study, Walker Parking Consultants, 1990
	2.3%	Denver Convention Center, Walker Parking Consultants, 1990
	1.5%	Portland Convention Center, Carl H. Buttke, Inc., 1985

Notes:

+ Percent is likely higher because substantial numbers of delegates parked north of the site and walked to the site. These delegates were counted as pedestrians even though they drove a vehicle.

Source: Walker Parking Consultants, Inc., 1999.

Similarly an "analytical approach" to determining parking demands for hotels, as discussed by Geok Kuah,[33] follows the logic for mixed-use development. This approach goes a step further, separating demand for employees and guests, and may be somewhat more accurate as a result. The following is a list of components and factors that may be considered when determining demand for hotels, all of which must be determined for weekday versus weekend to determine the overall peak.

---

[33] Geok K. Kuah, "Estimating Demand For Mixed Use Developments," *The Parking Professional* (Fredericksburg, Va.: International Parking Institute, September 1991, pp. 16–22).

Table 14–8   Mode of Arrival to Various Special Events

Location	Type of Event	Percent of Persons Arriving by Private Vehicle
Oakland, CA[a]	Pro-football	88
	Pro-baseball	97
Shea Stadium, NY[a]	Pro-football	65
	Pro-baseball	65
San Diego, CA[a]	Pro-football	85
	Pro-baseball	97
Yankee Stadium, NY[a]	Pro-football	10
	Pro-baseball	40
Anaheim Stadium, CA[a]	Pro-baseball	100
	Football	100
Atlanta Stadium, GA[a]	Pro-football	66
	Pro-baseball	87
Dodger Stadium, CA[a]	Pro-baseball	85
Los Angeles Coliseum, CA[a]	College football	95
	Pro-football	90
Nets Stadium, NJ[a]	Pro-basketball	90
	Concert	70
Kansas City, MO[a]	Pro-football	60
Edmonton, Canada[a]	Pro-football	50
	Soccer	80
Mile High Stadium, CO[a]	Pro-football	82
	Baseball	100
Orange Bowl, FL[a]	Pro-football	73
	College football	78
	High school football	75
Cotton Bowl, TX[a]	Pro-football	82
	College football	87
Ohio State University, OH[a]	College football	84
Weber State, UT[a]	College football	75
Ware Memoriala[a]	College football	73
Memorial Stadium, PA[a]	College football	68
Meadowlands, NJ[a]	Horse racing	80
American Museum of Natural History, NY[b]	Museum	73
Hagley Museum, DE[b]	Museum	49
Milford, CT[b]	Jai Alai	88
Husky Stadium, Seattle, WA[c] (1984)	College football	76
(1987)	College football	65

[a] *Traffic Engineering Magazine,* June 1975. Technical Council Committee Report 6A5.

[b] Wilbur Smith and Associates' Studies.

[c] Michael E. Williams, *Husky Stadium Expansion Plan and Transportation Management Program* (Seattle, WA: University of Washington, Transportation Office, August 1988).

- Number of guestrooms:

    Occupancy percentage.

    Percentage of guests who drive and park.

- Employees:

    Number of employees per occupied room (hotel only).

    Number of employees for restaurant and lounge per shift.

    Percentage that drive.

Table 14–9   Parking Provisions of Selected Stadiums

	Seating Capacity	Parking Spaces On Site	Parking Spaces Vicinity	Total Spaces Per Seat	Auto Occupancy Football	Auto Occupancy Baseball	Distance From CBD	Served Rail Transit
Anaheim, CA	43,300	12,000	0	0.28		3.4		
Atlanta, GA	58,800	4,400	5,500	0.17	2.7	3.0	1 mile	
Cincinnati, OH	56,200	4,800	20,000	0.44	3.25		Adjacent	
Dallas, TX	72,000	4,000	10,600	0.20	3.6–3.8		2 miles	
Denver, CO	51,000	2,700	9,300	0.24	3.0	1.9	2 miles	
Edmonton, Alta	33,100	7,000	8,000	0.45			1.5 miles	LRT
Houston, TX	53,000	30,000	0	0.57			6 miles	
Kansas City, MO	78,200	16,000	0	0.20			10 miles	
Los Angeles, CA								
Coliseum	93,000	11,000	26,500	0.40	2.6		3.5 miles	
Dodger Stadium	56,000	16,000	0	0.29		2.6	1.5 miles	
Meadowlands, NJ	76,000	20,800		0.27				
Miami, FL	80,000	3,000	2,100	0.06	2.5	2.1	1.5 miles	
New Orleans, LA	78,000	5,000	0	0.06			Adjacent	
New York, NY								
Shea Stadium	60,000	7,400	1,000	0.14				NYCTA
Yankee Stadium	65,000	2,000	300	0.04				NYCTA
Oakland, CA	54,000	8,000	18,000	0.48	3.5	3.2		BART
Orchard Park, NY	80,000	15,000		0.19				
Philadelphia, PA	65,300	11,000	5,000	0.25	2.8	2.8	3 miles	SEPTA
Pittsburgh, PA	50,300	4,400	24,000	0.56		3.47	Adjacent	
St. Louis, MO	50,100	7,500	10,000	0.35			Adjacent	
San Diego, CA	54,000	14,700	500	0.28	2.5–3.1	2.8–3.0	6 miles	
Seattle, WA	65,000	2,300	5,500	0.12		2.8	1 mile	
Washington, DC								
(R.F. Kennedy)	50,000	10,000		0.20				
Seattle-Husky Stadium	58,500	11,325	9,170	0.35				

Sources: Adapted from *Traffic Considerations for Special Events*, Washington, D.C.: Institute of Transportation Engineers, 1976; Whitlock, E. M., *Parking for Institutions and Special Events*, Westport, Conn.: Eno Foundation for Transportation, 1982.

Adjustment for optional mode choice.

Adjustment for absenteeism.

- Restaurant and lounge patronage:

  Number per guest (part of shared parking).

  Peak hour percentage.

  Nonguest diners percentage.

  Nonguest drivers percentage.

- Convention and meetings:

  Number of attendees or area of meeting space.

  Nonguest percentage.

  Nonguest driver percentage.

Table 14–10   Hotel Parking Ratios

Guest room	1.25 spaces per room
Restaurant/lounge	10.75 spaces per 100 sq m (10/1,000 sf) GLA
Conference rooms	0.5 spaces per seat
Convention area	32.3 spaces per 100 sq m (30/1000 sf) GLA

Source: Urban Land Institute, 1982.

Office Parking

There are significant variations in density of employees as well as presence by type of office space. One variable is lease rate; a multitenant general office building, originally class A but now older and dated compared to the newer market entries, will be likely to have a higher density of employees than the newer class A, a "luxury" building occupied by law and financial firms. Of course, this merely points out that densities tend to increase over time as the building ages without substantial reinvestment. A building with a corporate headquarters as its single tenant will often have lower densities than a multitenant building of the same size; however, a building solely occupied by back-of-house operations such as data processing and telemarketing may have significantly higher densities.

A study of ten office buildings in southern California in 1992[34] found employment densities ranging from 2.2 to 8.8 employees per 100 sq m (2.0 to 8.2 employees per 1,000 sq ft). The peak parking accumulation at buildings in the 2.9 to 3.2 employees per 100 sq m (2.7 to 3.2 employees per 1,000 sq ft) density range all had peak parking accumulations of 2.2 to 2.4 spaces per 100 sq m. There was considerable variation in the other results. A building with 1.9 employees per 100 sq m (2.0 employees per 1,000 sq ft) had a peak demand of 1.7 spaces per 100 sq m (1.8 spaces per 1,000 sq ft), while another with 5.4 employees per 100 sq m (5 employees per 1,000 sq ft) had a demand of 1.5 spaces per 100 sq m (1.4 spaces per 1,000 sq ft). The use with higher total employment had significantly lower employee presence and parking needs, apparently due to multiple shifts.

Presence factors are also directly influenced by size of office. As previously noted, it is far more likely that most of the employees in a small office building will be present at the same time than at a large, multitenant building. The added presence of visitors further complicates the issues. Medical office buildings may have a presence of more than 1 visitor per employee. The typical office building will have only five to seven visitors per 100 employees present at the typical peak hour for parking needs (late morning) while back-of-house operations may have negligible visitor parking. Offices of consumer service providers—insurance and employment agencies, real estate offices, and the retail bank branch— will have similar employment density but visitor demand between that of general offices and medical offices. In the California study, visitor parking demand typically ranged from 1.0 percent to 9.9 percent with one site out of range at 33.4 percent. Interestingly the latter site still had only 1.9 spaces per 1,000 sq m (1.8 spaces per 1,000 sq ft) occupied at the peak time of accumulation.

Medical office parking may also vary by site. Space located on hospital campuses is more likely to be leased to physicians who have to spend significant time at the hospital, such as surgeons, who in turn have more restricted office hours than a neighborhood medical office occupied by family physicians.

For all of these reasons, it is recommended that any all encompassing "office" ratio be subdivided into discrete categories. ITE broke its data for *Parking Generation* into three office categories: (1) medical and dental offices, (2) general office building, and (3) government office buildings and office parks. The NPA considered it appropriate to separate consumer service offices and further varies the requirement for most of the uses by size. A new category added herein is for data processing and telemarketing office tenants.

Historic studies by ULI in 1983 and ITE in 1987 determined that average parking accumulations for general office buildings were 2.7 and three spaces per 100 sq m (2.5 and 2.79 spaces per 1,000 sq ft) GLA, respectively. ULI recommended the 90th percentile ratio from their study of 51 freestanding buildings at 3.2 spaces per 100 sq m (3.0 spaces per 1,000 sq ft).

No ratio is provided herein for government offices. Rather, a shared parking analysis by type of office is appropriate. Areas where the public goes to receive services should be treated as consumer offices, areas generally used only by employees would be general offices, and meeting and assembly spaces would be evaluated based on design attendance and time of day factors.

---

[34] Richard E. Willson, *Suburban Parking Economics and Policy* (Washington, D.C.: Federal Transit Administration, September 1992, FTA-CA-11-0036-92-1, pp. 21–22).

Industrial Uses

A 1988 study by ITE[35] looked at the differing needs of land uses within employment centers that include office, warehouse, and industrial buildings as well as hybrid buildings designed to serve either. It found the employment densities seen in Table 14–11 and average parking accumulations found in Table 14–12.

Educational Institutions

Table 14–13 summarizes data on various parking parameters at selected institutions. The traditional unit of measure for parking at educational institutions is the enrollment of students. *Parking for Institutions and Special Events*[36] noted a variety of factors influencing demand, including types of students (e.g., residential, commuter, evening), administrative policies (e.g., vehicle registration and parking fees), and other socioeconomic factors. It recommended that parking demand for universities be individually determined for faculty and staff, resident students, and commuter students based on data collected at the institution.

In a 1993 review of data from multiple parking studies, Dorsett[37] used regression analysis to determine how strong a relationship exists between total student, staff population, and parking demand and found that the statistician's regression line would have predicted the actual number

Table 14–11 Variation of Employment with Building Area and Type of Use

Type of Use	Number of Studies	Average Number of Employees Per 100 sq m (per 1,000 sq ft) of Gross Floor Area
Warehouse	16	0.9/100 sq m (0.8/1,000 sq ft)
Heavy manufacturing	47	1.4 (1.3)
Light manufacturing	25	2.4 (2.2)
Industrial park	30	2.3 (2.1)
Research and development	6	3.4 (3.2)
General manufacturing	82	4.0 (3.7)
Total	206	—

Source: Adapted from *Employment Center Parking Facilities,* Washington, D.C.: Institute of Transportation Engineers, 1988.

Table 14–12 Industrial Parking Demands

Type of Industry	Per Employee	Per 100 sq m (per 1,000 sq ft) GFA
	Average Number of Spaces Used	
Warehouse	1.0	0.5 (0.5)
Light manufacturing	0.8	1.6 (1.5)
Industrial	0.7	1.6 (1.5)
General manufacturing	0.7	1.7 (1.6)

Source: Adapted from *Parking Generation,* 2nd Edition, Washington, D.C.: Institute of Transportation Engineers, 1987.

Table 14–13 Summary of Parking Survey Data by Student Enrollment

Parameter	Less Than 5,000	5,000–9,999	10,000–19,999	Greater Than 20,000
	Range of Student Enrollments			
Average number of registered vehicles	2,922	5,298	10,899	22,381
Average number of parking spaces	1,779	3,856	6,602	13,187
Ratio of vehicles per space	1.64	1.37	1.65	1.69
Average parking fees				
Reserved spaces	No data	$136	$175	$211
Student spaces	$68	$86	$118	$67
Visitor spaces	Free	$2/day	$.50/hr	$.50/hr
Number of colleges with garages	1	None	10	12
Average number of garage spaces	No data	None	956	1253
Parking fines	$5–50	$5–50	$3–50	$4–50
Towing charges	$25–65	$35–40	$20–40	$15–55
Number of colleges in survey	15	10	26	16

Sources: A Survey of 100 Colleges and Universities' Parking, Williamsburg, Va.: William and Mary College Office of Auxilliary Services, 1987; Clark, J. E. and L. K. Freeman, *The Experience of Changing from a No-Fee to a User-Fee Campus Parking System,* Washington, D.C.: Transportation Research Board, National Research Council, January 1990.

---

[35] "Employment Center Parking Facilities," *ITE Journal* (Washington, D.C.: Institute of Transportation Engineers, June 1988, pp. 29–35).

[36] Edward M. Whitlock, *Parking for Institutions and Special Events* (Westport, Conn.: Eno Foundation for Transportation, Inc. 1982, pp. 23–32).

[37] John Dorsett, "Predicting Parking Demand for Universities," *The Parking Professional* (Fredericksburg, Va.: International Parking Institute, October 1993, pp. 28–33).

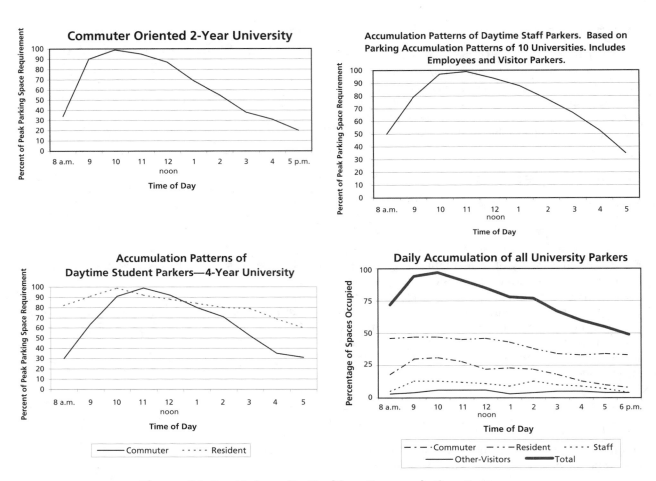

Figure 14–3   University Parking Accumulation Patterns

Source: Whitlock, Edward M., *Parking for Institutions and Special Events,* Westport, Conn.: Eno Foundation for Transportation, 1982, p. 26.

of occupied parking spaces only 13 out of 22 times with a twenty percent margin of error. The remaining nine cases fell outside the twenty percent margin of error. This is an extremely high variation that virtually any planner would consider unacceptable. Dorsett noted city and campus transit system strength, student and staff ratios, parking policies, class schedules, and availability of other sources (primarily on-street parking in nearby neighborhoods) as influences on demand. Therefore, while data from these studies is presented in Figure 14–3, it is provided in broad ranges rather than a single ratio for predicting demand on a specific campus. Parking characteristics at universities are also presented in Tables 14–14, 14–15, and 14–16.

Medical Institutions

Whitlock[38] concluded that a single ratio relating demand to the traditional variable, number of beds, was unreliable. He recommended a more definitive analysis based on four variables: typical daily staff population, typical daily visitor population, percent of staff driving, and percent of visitors driving. Travel modes from that work are formed in Table 14–17. Since that study, there has been a "revolution" in the delivery of health care in the United States.

Dorsett[39] recommends studying each of four user groups (i.e., employees, physicians, visitors and patients) and identifying when and in what quantities each user group is on campus and the percentage of each that drive and park.

---

[38] Edward M. Whitlock, *Parking for Institutions and Special Events* (Westport, Conn.: Eno Foundation for Transportation, Inc. 1982, pp. 12–16).

[39] John Dorsett, "Predicting Parking Demand for Hospitals," *The Parking Professional* (Fredericksburg, Va.: International Parking Institute, October 1995, pp. 28–34).

Table 14–14 Ranges in Peak-Parking Demand at Colleges and Universities

	Units	Average (rounded)	Eno Range (rounded)	85% Design Values	Urban Land Institute
Commuter Students	per student	0.30	.15 – .45	0.37	0.25 – 0.50
Resident Students	per student	0.25	.15 – .40	0.36	0.05 – 0.40
Faculty/Staff	per faculty/staff }	0.70	.50 – 1.00	0.92	0.30 – 0.90
Visitors	per faculty/staff }		N/A	N/A	0.02 – 0.05

Sources: Adapted from research from the Eno Foundation for Transportation and the Urban Land Institute.

Table 14–15 Percentage of Parking Spaces Required for Long- and Short-Term Parking by User Group

	Length of Stay Per Total Vehicles Parked (Percent of Daily Parkers)		Length of Stay Per Peak Parking Demand (Parking Space Allocation)	
User Group	Short-Term 0–3 Hours (Percent)	Long-Term 3.1+ Hours (Percent)	Short-Term 0–3 Hours (Percent)	Long-Term 3.1+ Hours (Percent)
Faculty/Staff	46.7%	53.3%	16.2%	83.8%
Resident Students	40.2%	59.8%	13.4%	86.6%
Commuter Students	50.7%	49.3%	20.8%	79.2%
Public/Visitor	80.0%	20.0%	47.4%	52.6%
General Parking	54.8%	45.2%	20.4%	79.6%

Source: Richard T. Klatt and Mary S. Smith, "Priority Parking for Universities," *The Parking Professional*, June 1992.

Table 14–16 Summary of Duration and Turnover for Universities

User Group	No. of Loc.	Total Capacity	0–1	1–2	2–3	3–4	4–5	5–6	6–7	7+	Total Different Vehicles Observed	Avg. Stay Hours	Turn Over	All-Day[1] Parkers No.	%	Footnotes
Faculty/ Staff	5	2,429	1,061	612	539	690	399	186	202	1,050	4,739	3.83	1.95	1,252	26%	
Percent			22%	13%	11%	15%	8%	4%	4%	22%	Range:	3.65–4.31	1.59–2.24			
Resident Students	1	106	32	34	26	17	22	12	14	72	229	4.54	2.16	86	38%	2
Percent			14%	15%	11%	7%	10%	5%	6%	31%	Range:	N/A	N/A			
Commuter Students	3	1,424	529	488	389	379	235	188	154	413	2,775	3.53	1.95	567	20%	
Percent			19%	18%	14%	14%	8%	7%	6%	15%	Range:	2.92–4.62	1.66–2.21			
Public/ Visitor	10	4,507	5,936	3,448	1,811	979	652	389	326	457	13,998	1.96	3.11	783	6%	3,5
Percent			42%	25%	13%	7%	5%	3%	2%	3%	Range:	1.43–3.19	2.31–4.32			
General Parking	4	1,287	704	482	291	310	172	117	123	495	2,694	3.36	2.09	618	23%	4
Percent			26%	18%	11%	12%	6%	4%	5%	18%	Range:	2.80–3.93	1.69–2.94			

Notes: [1] Six hours or more.

[2] Small sample, only one location.

[3] Generally, F/S and students can park if they pay the hourly fee.

[4] Includes F/S, students and visitors.

[5] Three locations had parking time limits.

Source: Richard T. Klatt and Mary S. Smith, "Priority Parking for Universities," *The Parking Professional*, June 1992.

(Figure 14–4.) Because many hospitals have multiple lots, with each reserved for specific users, it is particularly important to look at the demand in similar groupings. The peak hour demand for each user group differs; therefore, the outpatient lot may need to be designed for parking demand at 10 A.M. and the employee lot for demand at the 3 P.M. shift change. The formula presented in NPA's *Recommended Zoning Requirements* provides an order of magnitude guide, but there is no substitute for a study calibrated to actual activity on the campus.

Residential

The influences on residential parking demand are many, but the primary ones are socioeconomic and availability of alternate transportation modes; both will affect auto ownership levels by tenants. The "democratization of auto ownership" as cited by Pisarski[40] would indicate that there has been an increase in parking needs at residential land uses over the last 35 years. In 1960, 21 percent of households in the United States had no vehicle; in 1990 only 11 percent were without vehicles. Moreover, a disproportionate share of households without vehicles is comprised of elderly women living alone. Another group that is more likely to be vehicle-less is recent immigrants. Geographically, most households (59 percent) without vehicles are renters in central cities, with the New York metropolitan area accounting for one-fifth of all zero vehicle households. One interesting reversal of trends is that the percentage of households with three vehicles has stabilized—actually it dropped one percent in 1990 as compared to 1980—after periods of extraordinary growth (jumping from 1.3 million households to over 14 million in 1980.) These households tend to be in rural farming areas, although midwestern states are above average as well. Only California seems to have high shares of urban households with three or more vehicles.

Recommended ratios for parking demand at multifamily housing units are based on the number of bedrooms. Adjustments should be made based on the socioeconomics of the tenants and the availability of transit in the vicinity of the site.

Table 14–17   Travel Modes of Hospital Visitors and Employees

	Employee Staff	Visitor
	Percent by Car	
14 General Hospitals	58–91	48–81
14 Medical Centers	45–91	42–83
3 Specialty Hospitals	49–75	25–52
3 Extended Day Care Facilities	65–81	50–67
	Percent Auto Drivers	
6 Hospitals	78–84	87–95

Sources: E. M. Whitlock, *Parking for Institutions and Special Events,* Westport, Conn.: Eno Foundation for Transportation, 1982; Hunnicut, J. M., "Parking, Loading and Terminal Facilities," *Transportation Engineering Handbook,* Washington, D.C.: Institute of Transportation Engineers, 1982.

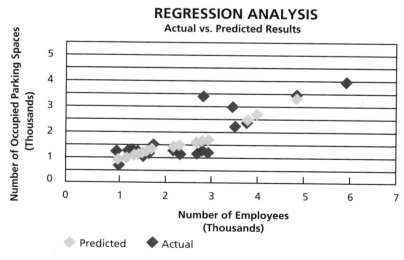

Figure 14–4   Hospital Parking per Employee

Note: Excludes medical office building employees and spaces.

Source: Walker Parking Consultants.

[40] Alan E. Pisarski, *Commuting in America II* (Washington, D.C.: Eno Foundation for Transportation, Inc., 1996, p. 18).

Intermodal Parking

Intermodal parking facilities are increasingly common. In an effort to facilitate use of both new and existing rail transit, the federal government has encouraged development of parking at rail stations in order to increase the convenience and attractiveness of this mode choice. Parking-to-bus and parking-to-shuttle intermodal facilities are also being developed.

The parking demand of a commuter station is generally stated as a ratio of spaces per embarking passenger on the average day of the peak month of ridership. There is no single ratio that can be applied. (Table 14–18.) Mode of travel varies substantially. (Table 14–19.) The demand at two successive stops on the same line can be dramatically different, due to the nature of the communities and market areas each serves, as well as the parking availability and policies in place. A market study that specifically addresses the competitive position of the station being studied with alternative station

Table 14–18   Parking Provisions of Selected Rail Transit Stations

Region	Location	Boarding Passengers per Weekday	Off-Street Parking Spaces	Parking Spaces/ Passenger Boarding
Atlanta	Avondale	9,700	1,180	0.12
	Eastlake	2,800	610	0.22
	Hightower	10,300	1,400	0.14
	Chamblee	8,000	1,520	0.19
	Brookhaven	4,200	1,700	0.40
	Lenox	10,900	800	0.07
	Lindbergh	11,100	1,470	0.13
	Lakewood	4,300	1,900	0.44
	College Park	7,700	2,120	0.28
Boston	Wollaston	2,700	500	0.19
	North Quincy	2,400	800	0.33
	Quincy Center	7,500	930	0.12
	Commuter Rail—North[a]	11,000	3,360	0.31
	Commuter Rail—South[a]	3,800	2,640	0.69
Chicago	Ashland	4,750	264	0.06
	Cicero-Berwyn	2,700	360	0.13
	Cumberland	5,500	828	0.15
	Dempster	3,200	594	0.19
	Des Plaines	4,750	596	0.13
	Howard	9,600	300	0.03
	Kimball	4,100	180	0.04
	Linden	3,500	456	0.13
	River Road	3,900	747	0.19
Cleveland	West Side (5 stations)	20,000	6,400	0.32
	East Side (3 stations)	10,000	900	0.09
Philadelphia	Bucks County[a]	4,000	1,800	0.45
	Chester County[a]	3,900	1,100	0.28
	Delaware County[a]	15,500	2,200	0.14
	Montgomery County[a]	19,500	4,300	0.22
	Lindenwold (New Jersey)	20,000	9,000	0.45
San Francisco	Concord line (6 stations)	20,360	6,555	0.32
	Richmond line (5 stations)	9,130	3,381	0.37
	Alameda line (8 stations)	27,100	7,562	0.28
	Oakland line (3 stations)	7,300	1,087	0.15
	Daly City	8,860	1,877	0.21
Toronto	Islington	23,500	1,300	0.06
	Warden	24,600	1,500	0.06

[a] Commuter railroad stations.

Sources: Herbert S. Levinson, "Planning Transit Facility Parking for the Boston Metropolitan Area," *Transportation Research Record 601*; San Francisco data from BART, 1980; Transportation Research Board, 1976; Chicago data from Chicago Transit Authority, 1985; Atlanta data from Metropolitan Atlanta Rapid Transit Authority, June 1990.

Table 14–19 Overview of Travel Characteristics of Park-and-Ride Users

Characteristics	Range	Number of Lots[a]	Average[a]
Previous mode of travel			
Drove alone	11% to 65%	305	49.2%
Carpool/vanpool	5 to 28	303	23.2%
Transit (bus or other)	5 to 49	304	10.4%
Did not make trip	0 to 29	303	14.9%
Arrival mode to facility			
Drove alone	38 to 91	146	72.6%
Shared ride	3 to 36	146	11.0%
Dropped off	0 to 31	117	11.1%
Walked	0 to 21	132	4.4%
Bus	0 to 10	132	1.3%
Trip purpose			
Work or business	83 to 100	107	97.2%
School	0 to 11	80	2.3%
Other	0 to 17	80	0.5%
Travel frequency (rd.-trips/wk.)			
Three or less	2 to 15	101	6.6%
Four	3 to 16	86	7.6%
Five or more	71 to 93	86	86.8%
Home-to-lot distances (miles)			
Three or less	6 to 74	163	46.4%
Four to six	18 to 42	162	22.8%
Six or more	8 to 69	162	29.2%
Lot-to-destination distances (miles)			
Less than 10	0 to 100	190	6.9%
10 to 30	0 to 100	190	63.2%
30 or more	0 to 51	177	30.4%

[a] The "average" values shown are weighted by the number of park-and-ride lots surveyed. Partial or missing data from certain studies may cause the percentage not to total 100.

Source: Charles E. Bowler, Errol C. Noel, Richard Peterson, Dennis Christiansen, *Park-and-Ride Facilities— Guidelines for Planning, Design and Operation,* Washington, D.C.: Federal Highway Administration, U.S. Department of Transportation, 1986.

choices is often necessary to project parking demand. See Chapter 10 of this handbook for more information on terminal facilities.

Railroad stations serving long-distance routes have somewhat different parking demands than commuter rail stations according to the differences in length of stay and in pick-up and drop-off characteristics. (Table 14–20.) Many stations serve both, and a blend of both needs must be met.

Airport parking facilities are also intermodal facilities, as they facilitate the connection between air travel and personal vehicle travel. Airport parking demand is highly complex, being both a captive market and a lucrative one that has attracted competition by off-airport commercial providers. Because the revenue stream from parking is often critical to the financial health of the airport as a whole, there is a high degree of market analysis required to project demand. Generally, airport public parking demand is evaluated in three areas:

1. *Hourly* or short-term parking serves "kiss and fly" as well as "meeters and greeters" who stay three hours or less. This group may comprise seventy to eighty percent of the total number of parkers, but the turnover is very high (ten or more turns per day.) The number of spaces required is thus a relatively small proportion (twenty to thirty percent) of the total spaces required. It is generally considered best to segregate parking for these users in the most convenient location, making it easier for the short-term parker to find the available space. This reduces congestion on the arrivals and departures roadways. In order to keep these spaces turning over,

Table 14–20 Parking Demand at Railroad Stations

Station	Daily Parking Space Demand[a]			
	Amtrak	Commuter	Combined Amtrak and Commuter	Spaces Per Boarding Passenger
Wilmington, DE	0.33	0.31	0.32	.32
New Haven, CT	0.27	0.32	0.30	.30
Providence, RI	0.20	0.42	0.24	.24
Stamford, CT	0.34	0.42	0.41	.42
New Carrollton, MD	0.52	—[b]	0.52	.53

[a] Number of daily parking spaces demanded per daily boarding passenger by type.
[b] Amtrak station only.

Sources: L.K. Carpenter, *Planning Rail Station Parking: Approach and Application*, New Haven, Conn.: Wilbur Smith & Associates; *Parking Feasibility Study—New Carrollton Station*, Washington, D.C.: James Madison Hunnicutt & Associates, October 1978; *Stamford Railroad Station Parking Feasibility Study*, Washington, D.C.: Hunnicutt-Davis Associates, November 1978.

they are generally priced with a modest hourly rate that accumulates to a hefty sum for travelers, such as $1 per hour to a maximum of $20 or more per day.

2. *Daily* parkers typically are willing to pay a relatively high rate for convenient terminal parking. The demand by this group is price-sensitive. Pricing daily parking at the terminal at a rate considerably below that for short-term parking, such as $10 per day, will generally keep most of the daily parkers out of hourly parking. A good starting point for calculating daily demand is to look at parkers who stay 3–24 hours, who typically comprise up to twenty percent of the volume of parkers. Ultimately pricing and relative convenience of access to the parking—both pedestrian and vehicular—will be the determinant of daily parking demand.

3. *Remote* parking is generally provided for multiday stays. Although they may comprise only ten percent of parkers, those with stays over 24 hours typically require sixty to seventy percent of the spaces. The quantity of remote parking at an airport can be greatly affected by commercial, off-airport parking.

Table 14–21 Parking Spaces per Originating Enplanement

Size of Airport (annual orig. enp.)	Spaces Per Originating Enplanement		
	Lowest	Median	Highest
175 k to 900 k	0.12	0.70	1.33
900 k to 3.5 m	0.14	0.56	1.18
3.5 m up	0.11	0.43	0.82

Source: Adapted from Larry Donoghue, "U.S. Airports Parking Statistics Analysis," *The Parking Professional*, February 1997, p. 20.

Employee parking is generally provided off-site with shuttle service. Overall ratios of public parking per originating enplanement at various airports are presented in Table 14–21.

Summary of Recommended Parking Ratios

Table 14–22 presents recommended[41] ratios for parking supply on a design day for various uses. The ratios are adjusted to provide an effective supply factor over the design accumulation of vehicles. These ratios are intended to be maximum ratios and should always be adjusted for expected mode splits as well as any anticipated differences in presence, vehicle occupancy, and other such factors.

Shared Parking

Shared parking methodology allows for the adjustment of demand projections for time of day, day of week, season, and interaction in mixed-use developments to identify when the peak accumulation of vehicles will occur. Although the analysis approach was developed in the 1980s, the concept is not really new—a fundamental principle of downtown planning going back to the earliest days of the automobile has always been to share parking resources rather than have each use

[41] Parking Consultants Council, *Recommended Zoning Ordinance Provisions* (Washington, D.C.: National Parking Association, pp. 16–20).

Table 14–22   Summary of Table Uses and Space Requirements

Use	Parking Spaces Required
Residential	
Single Family Dwelling Unit	2 / Dwelling Unit
Multi-Family Dwelling Unit	
Studio	1.25 / Dwelling Unit
1 bedroom	1.5 / Dwelling Unit
2 or more bedrooms	2 / Dwelling Unit
Accessory Dwelling Unit	1 / Dwelling Unit
Sleeping Rooms	1 / Unit or Room plus 2 for owners/managers
Commercial Lodgings	1.25 / Sleeping Room or unit plus 10.8 /100 sq m GLA (10/1,000 sq ft) rest/lounge/meeting room plus 32.3 space/100 sq m GLA (30/1,000 sq ft) convention
Elderly Housing	0.5 / Dwelling Unit
Group, Convalescent and Nursing Homes	0.33 / Resident
Day Care Center	1 space per employee plus 1.2 space per person licensed capacity enrollment, plus drop-off spaces equal to one for each eight enrollees permitted
Hospital /Medical Center	0.4 / Employee plus 1 space / 3 beds plus 1 space / 5 average daily outpatient treatments plus 1 space for each 4 members of medical staff. (Medical centers and teaching hospitals add 1 space for each student, full-time faculty/staff)
Retail Service	
General Retail	3.6 /100 sq m (3.3 / 1,000 sq ft) of GFA
Convenience Retail	4.3 / 100 sq m (4/1,000 sq ft) of GFA
Service Retail	2.6/100 sq m (2.4 / 1,000 sq ft) of GFA
Hard Goods Retail	2.7/ 100 sq m (2.5 / 1,000 sq ft) GFA interior sales space plus 1.6/100 sq m (1.5 / 1,000 sq ft) of interior storage and exterior display / storage areas
Shopping Center	4.3/100 sq m (4 / 1,000 sq ft) of GFA for centers with up to 37,000 sq m (398,296 sq ft); 4.8/100 sq m (4.5 / 1,000 sq ft) of GLA for centers 37,000 to 55,750 sq m (398,296–600,088 sq ft); 5.4 /100 sq m (5.0 / 1,000 sq ft) of GLA for centers with over 55,750 sq m (600,088 sq ft)+B41
Personal Care Services	2 / Treatment station but not less than 4.3/100 sq m (4 / 1,000 sq ft of GFA)
Coin Operated Laundries	1 space / 2 washer and dryer machines
Other Retail / Service Uses	As determined by the Zoning Administrator
Temporary Retail	3.6/100 sq m (3.3 / 1,000 sq ft) of GFA
Motor Vehicle Sales and Service	2.7/100 sq m (2.5 / 1,000 sq ft) of GFA interior sales space plus 1.6/100 sq m (1.5 / 1,000 sq ft) of external display (does not include stock areas closed to the public) plus 3 / service bay
Motor Vehicle Laundries	1 space per each 2 peak shift employees plus queue space for vehicle count equal to one and one-half times the maximum hourly capacity of the facility
Food and Beverage	
Fine Dining	21.5/100 sq m (20 / 1,000 sq ft) GLA plus any spaces required for any banquet and meeting rooms
Eating and Drinking	26.9/100 sq m (25 / 1,000 sq ft) GLA plus any spaces required for any banquet and meeting rooms
Family Restaurant	132.9100 sq m (12 / 1,000 sq ft) GLA plus any spaces required for any banquet and meeting rooms
Fast food	10.8/100 sq m (10 / 1,000 sq ft) GLA for kitchen, serving counter and waiting area plus 0.5 / seat provided
Office and Business Services	
General Business Offices	3.9/100 sq m (3.6 / 1,000 sq ft) of GFA for GFA up to 3,000 sq m (32,292 sq ft); 3.2/100 sq m (3/1,000 sq ft) GLA for GFA over 3,000 sq m (32,292 sq ft)
Consumer Service Offices	4.3/100 sq m (4 / 1,000 sq ft) of GFA for GFA up to 3,000 sq m (32,292 sq ft); 3.6/100 sq m (3.3 / 1,000 sq ft) GLA for GFA over 3,000 sq m (32,292 sq ft)
Data Processing / Telemarketing / Operations Offices	7.5/100 sq m (7 / 1,000 sq ft) of GFA for GFA up to 3,000 sq m (32,292 sq ft); 6.5/100 sq m (6/1,000 sq ft) GLA for GFA over 3,000 sq m (32,292 sq ft)

Source: Adapted from *Recommended Zoning Ordinance Provisions for Off-Street Loading Space,* Washington, D.C.: National Parking Association.

Table 14–22 Summary of Table Uses and Space Requirements (continued)

Use	Parking Spaces Required
Medical Offices (not part of hospital campus)	For buildings with 500 sq m (5,382 sq ft) or less GFA, 6.5 spaces/100 sq m (6/1,000 sq ft) of GFA; for buildings greater than 5,000 sq m (5,382 sq ft) GFA, 5.9/100 sq m (5.5 / 1,000 sq ft) GLA
Medical Offices (on hospital campus)	For buildings with 500 sq m/ (5,382 sq ft) or less GFA, 5.9/per 100 sq m (5.5/1,000 sq ft) of GFA; for buildings greater than 500 sq m (5,382 sq ft) GFA, 5.4/100 sq m (5 / 1,000 sq ft) GLA
Industrial	
	2.2/100 sq m (2 / 1,000 sq ft) GFA plus any required spaces for office, sales, or similar use or as special conditions as the use may require
Storage / Wholesale Utility	
	0.5/100 sq m (0.5 / 1,000 sq ft) GFA plus any required spaces for offices, sales, etc.
Mini Warehouse	3 spaces at the office; access to individual storage units must provide for loading of vehicles without impeding traffic flow through the facility
Governmental	
	As determined by the Zoning Administrator
Educational	
Elementary and Secondary Schools	1 / classroom and other rooms used by students and/or faculty plus 0.25 per student over the driving age
College and University	To be established by the Zoning Administrator based on a study of parking needs prepared specifically for the subject institution
Cultural / Recreational / Entertainment	
Public Assembly	.25 / person in permitted capacity
Cinemas	Single screen: 1 space / 2 seats Up to 5 screens: 1 space / 3 seats Over 5 screens: 1 space / 3.5 seats
Theatres (live performance)	1 space / 2 seats
Arenas and Stadiums	1 space / 3 seats
Recreation facilities	2 spaces per player or 1 space / 3 persons in permitted capacity

Source: Adapted from *Recommended Zoning Ordinance Provisions for Off-Street Loading Space*, Washington, D.C.: National Parking Association.

or building have its own parking. Shared parking is a vitally important way to reduce density and waste of resources devoted to parking.

The shared parking demand methodology developed by ULI is designed to determine the peak accumulation of vehicles for a specific mix of uses proposed for a development. Factors that affect the peak parking demand for mixed-use projects include: the time of year, the day of the week, and the hour of the day. The fact that parking demand for each component may peak at different days of the week or hours of the day generally means that fewer parking spaces are needed for the project than would be required if each component were a freestanding development. An obvious example is that restaurant parking needs peak in the evening when office parking needs have declined.

Figure 14–5 presents the typical variation of parking needs by time of day for some of the more common uses occurring in shared parking situations. These variations are different according to whether it is a weekday or weekend. Figure 14–6 presents typical variations by month of year.

It should be noted that while the factors presented are based predominately on the ULI *Shared Parking* report, some of the adjustment factors have been modified based on more recent experience and trends. The parking demand at retail uses in the evening hours has been increased to reflect changes in shopping patterns that have occurred since the publication of both *Parking Requirements for Shopping Centers* and *Shared Parking*. The factors for hotel guestrooms

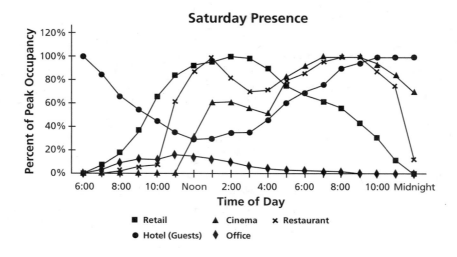

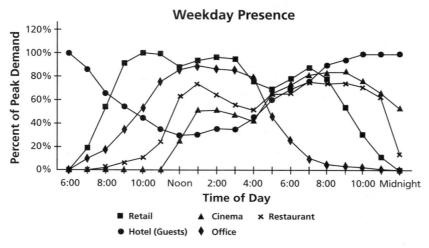

Figure 14–5   Variation of Parking Demand by Time of Day

Source: Adapted from *Shared Parking,* Washington, D.C.: Urban Land Institute, 1983.

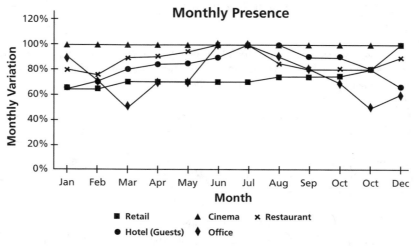

Figure 14–6   Variation of Parking Demand by Month of Year

Source: Adapted from *Shared Parking,* Washington, D.C.: Urban Land Institute, 1983.

have been adjusted to reflect a subsequent and more detailed study of hotel parking by Barton-Aschman Associates.[42] The factors for cinemas have also been adjusted, based on studies of parking needs at today's multiscreen megaplexes: the time of day and seasonal adjustment factors in *Shared Parking* are too low in places and can result in an underestimation of the parking needs of today's cinemas.

Captive Market

The term "captive market" was originally borrowed from market researchers to describe people who are already present in the immediate vicinity of a development and are likely patrons of a new use. In shared parking analysis it is used to reflect the adjustment of parking needs due to the interaction among uses. Captive market effects not only accrue from the on-site development but also from nearby uses such as office buildings. In parking analysis, planners use the complementary factor (i.e., the noncaptive ratio), which is the percentage of users who are *not* already counted as being parked. Generally, the planner considers vehicles as being generated by the land use that was the primary trip purpose.

Mode Split

A factor is applied to adjust the design ratio, which assumes virtually 100 percent private auto arrival. Availability of local transit and price of parking would be the primary considerations. The mode-split adjustment should also account for differences in auto occupancy. In some cases, it is appropriate to separate the ratio into customer and employee components and adjust the mode split separately for each.

Development Synergy and Multipurpose Trips

Certain developments achieve much greater interaction between uses than others. When such synergy exists, a successful project may have lower parking demands than if the uses were built separately and achieved more typical patronage levels when standing alone. For example, a restaurant may have greater noontime patronage than it would otherwise have, because it is located within walking distance of a large employment center. It may have more customers per day while having a low noontime parking demand. Similarly, employees of retail tenants form a major component of the patronage of a food court at a shopping center.

Today's URE center is predicated not only on the possibility of multiple destinations being visited on single trips, but also on multiple destinations being visited simultaneously. A family visiting a URE on a Saturday afternoon may split up with the children going to the cinema, one parent going shopping and the other catching a game in the sports bar. The length of stay is longer and the planner must consider the effects of *sequential* visits (which add to parking needs without generating vehicle trips) as well as *simultaneous* ones (which generate no additional parked vehicles or trips) in the parking analysis.

The shared parking methodology, including the effects of captive market was recently reviewed and validated by a subcommittee of ITE.[43] The methodology is presented in a flow chart in Figure 14–7.

As noted previously, CBDs are among the best examples of successful shared parking. In addition to public transportation, the ability to carpool and choose alternative modes is maximized in the CBD. As a result overall parking demand ratios range from 1.5 to 3.5 spaces per 100 sq m, with 2 to 2.5 spaces per 100 sq m being most common.

Zoning Requirements

Zoning is the means by which cities ensure that a new development meets the community's standards. It has been termed "a preventive approach for achieving planned and orderly development."[44]

---

[42] Gerald Salzman, "Hotel Parking: How Much is Enough" (Washington, D.C.: Urban Land Institute, pp.14–17).

[43] *Shared Parking Planning Guidelines* (Washington, D.C.: Institute of Transportation Engineers, August 1995, pp. 1–3).

[44] Weant and Levinson, *Parking* (Westport, Conn.: Eno Foundation for Transportation, 1990, p. 35).

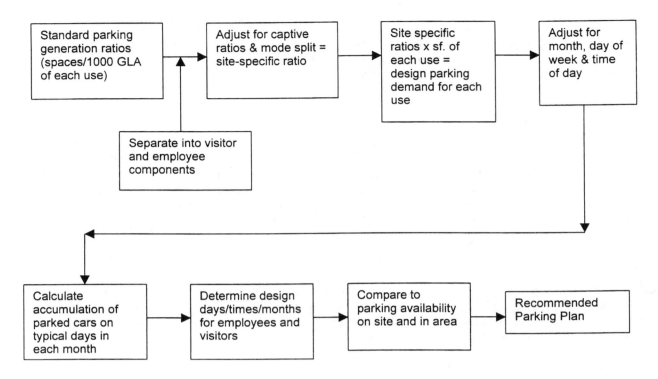

Figure 14–7   Shared Parking Analysis Methodology

Source: Adapted from *Shared Parking,* Washington, D.C.: Urban Land Institute, 1983.

With respect to parking, zoning standards typically establish formulas for determining how many parking spaces must be provided for specific types of land uses. The intent of most local governments is to require property owners to provide sufficient off-street parking spaces without spillover parking—overflow onto public streets or adjacent private property. Zoning policies that require an excessive amount of parking space waste resources. While a necessary component of development, land area and resources devoted to parking reduce the amount of development each particular site can support. Even when local zoning policies will not permit more development on a site, relative costs (both capital and operating) are affected by local zoning requirements. Excessive paved parking areas are undesirable to the community from both the aesthetic and environmental perspectives.

Shoup[45] has shown that minimum requirements and free parking lower density, increase development costs, and reduce land values. Based on studies of density before and after parking requirements were added to the zoning ordinance of Oakland, California, requiring parking increased the cost per dwelling unit by 18 percent, decreased density by 30 percent, and land values fell by 33 percent. A more recent study by Willson[46] estimates that increasing the parking requirement for an office building from 3.7 to 4.1 spaces per 100 sq m (2.5 to 3.8 per 1,000 sq ft) would reduce density by 18 percent and land values by 32 percent. And as previously discussed, market pricing of parking would significantly affect mode choice, but it is very difficult to charge the real cost of providing parking when it is oversupplied.

Therefore it behooves the local government to carefully adopt parking requirements, weighing the problems of spillover parking against the potential negative effects of over-requiring parking. In a 1964 report on off-street parking requirements, the American Society of Planning Officials (now known as the American Planning Association) warned against trying to employ a single standard for parking space requirements.[47]

[45] Donald Shoup, "The True Cost of Free Parking" *Parking Today* (August 1997, p. 33).

[46] Willson, "Suburban Parking Requirements: A Tacit Policy for Automobile Use and Sprawl," *APA Journal* (Chicago, Ill.: American Planning Association, Winter 1995).

[47] Weant and Levinson, *Parking* (Westport, Conn.: Eno Foundation for Transportation, 1990, p. 37).

No one set of standards, with the exception of off-street parking for industrial use, is recommended. The underlying assumptions used in drafting local regulations are often unknown and may not be applicable to other localities. The best approach, of course, is to develop off-street parking requirements based on local parking and traffic studies and the characteristics of the various zoning ordinance use districts.

Adopting another community's ordinance wholesale is inadvisable. In *Flexible Parking Requirements,* the American Planning Association recommended taking the following steps in revising a local zoning ordinance.[48]

1. Determine generic development characteristics (land uses present, employment densities, mode of travel, cost of parking, and so on).

2. Review parking experience (e.g., studies, literature, and zoning ordinances) elsewhere.

3. Survey parking generation rates and problems at existing uses that may be applicable.

4. Establish parking policy regarding level of service to be provided.

5. Determine zoning requirements.

6. Monitor parking standards.

A sensible approach to step 5 is to start with the ratios included in Table 14–22, which assume essentially a modal split of 100 percent personal automobile use, adjust for patterns of local automobile use as determined in step 1, and then develop a preliminary model. The model should then be tested via occupancy studies at existing land uses in the community.

Flexibility in Requirements

There will still remain variations in demand within a community, so that a single, set formula may not adequately cover all situations for each land use. Some of the variables are size of building, access and distance to public transit, ridesharing patterns, shared parking, and zoning districts. If fees for parking are changed in a CBD or activity center, the required parking can and should be substantially different than in another activity center with free parking. The traditional means of accommodating such variations include:

*   Varied requirements in different zoning districts.

*   Planned unit development permits.

*   Special and conditional use permits.

The American Planning Association, in *Flexible Parking Requirements,* urges that more flexibility be built into zoning ordinances. It discusses zoning ordinances that have provided mechanisms for adjusting parking requirements. The initial impetus for these approaches is to achieve specific land use and traffic management objectives, rather than flexibility to meet local parking demand variations. However, these built-in or preapproved adjustments also provide a means of eliminating the adversarial nature of zoning variance procedures. Some of the provisions by which cities are building flexibility into parking requirements include the following:

*   Shared parking.

*   Fees-in-lieu.

*   Off-site parking.

---

[48] T.P. Smith, *Flexible Parking Requirements,* Planning Advisory Service Report No. 377 (Chicago, Ill.: American Planning Association, 1983, pp. 23–24).

- Credits for ridesharing programs.

- Credits for public transportation accessibility.

- Accepting a credible parking study that evaluates the site-specific circumstances and demand.

Flexible Parking Requirements presents a discussion of some of the means by which these adjustments are being accommodated in various communities.

Recommended Zoning Ordinance Provisions has language to protect the city's interests while allowing flexibility to address the most common circumstances that influence parking demand. In addition to providing language addressing the ownership and land use change issues, the PCC recommends that certain adjustments to parking requirements be handled by setting a specific credit that can routinely be taken, but also allowing consideration of an analysis of parking demand by a qualified parking or traffic consultant. Further, the use of this adjustment will require the developer to pledge to provide additional parking up to the unadjusted standard if the city finds later that the projected demand is being exceeded.

The latter requirement is called the "land bank" provision because the developer is required to submit a plan detailing how the additional spaces could later be provided in either surface lots or structures in conformance with all other requirements in the ordinance. The developer who does not wish to accept the land bank condition must go through the normal variance procedure, usually to a zoning board of appeals or the city council, to receive a permanent, irrevocable reduction in the requirements.

In some cases, land banking provides all parties with a necessary level of comfort for a lower parking ratio. The developer can provide more green space on the site initially and then apply for permanent variance after a period of successful operation at the lower ratio has occurred.

Following are some of the circumstances in which flexibility in requirements may be appropriate.

- *Shared parking:* ULI's *Shared Parking* report provides a methodology for calculating shared parking effects without resorting to an inflexible formula.

- *Captive market:* The captive market is a component of shared parking effects; however, it does not require that parking be shared to achieve a reduction in demand. It often occurs among land uses that are not self-contained within a development. The captive market effect is one of the most significant determinants of parking demand in CBDs. Therefore, a zoning ordinance should allow parking requirements to be adjusted for captive market effects independent of shared parking effects.

- *Fees-in-lieu:* It may be in the best interests of a city to develop public parking in a densely developed activity center, rather than have each property owner provide sufficient parking for each building. With the high cost of constructing parking, and with the competing demands on city resources, a number of cities have asked the developers who will directly benefit to pay the city some or all of the cost of developing parking in municipal facilities.

  A significant problem has occurred in situations where there was slow, small, or random development; money dribbled into the fund and was not sufficient to cost-effectively develop parking in reasonable proximity to each development. The developer who has contributed $50,000 to the fund in lieu of ten parking spaces does not want it to sit in a fund for five years waiting for more money to come in, nor to go into a structure six blocks away. Success of this method is much more likely when rapid development is expected in a definable area, and when an off-street parking facility is or will be available on a definable schedule and within acceptable proximity.

- *Off-site parking:* Many cities have added clauses allowing off-site parking to be substituted for on-site parking under certain conditions.

- *Ridesharing:* The term "ridesharing" generally refers to various forms of carpooling, van pooling, and subscription bus service associated with employees' trips to and from work. Properly formulated ridesharing programs can reduce both traffic and parking demand. Zoning credits for ridesharing programs are a particularly effective means of achieving transportation management goals. Ridesharing credits are also a means of allowing the adjustment of parking requirements for any land use that runs a dedicated shuttle. The most common application is hotels that cater to those wanting convenient access to an airport. However, other uses may also run shuttles and may merit reduced parking requirements.

- *Transit:* Even smaller communities may have areas that are well-served by public transit, while other areas are not. A reasonable reduction in the parking requirements when a land use is within a certain distance of a regularly scheduled transit service may then be considered.

The Cost of Parking

Before discussing the art and science of managing parking resources, it is beneficial to place the cost of parking in proper context. The cost of parking has become an issue as the efficiency of transportation has become a priority. Many of those concerned with encouraging alternative modes argue that the user should be charged the actual cost to own and operate a parking space in order to make a fair comparison between mode choices. In other cases, institutions and communities have faced substantial "sticker shock" when looking at the cost of building structured parking to serve their users. Therefore, an understanding of the cost of parking is important to the efficient use of parking resources, which may in turn reduce or even eliminate the need for new spaces.

The cost of parking facilities has two distinct components: the capital cost (or cost to own, which includes construction and financing) and the operational cost. Discussion of construction and operational costs herein is provided primarily for comparison of options and understanding the order of magnitude of parking costs. The numbers should be considered no more than a "snapshot in time."

Capital Cost

The *construction cost* is the total amount paid to the contractor(s) for building a parking facility. The *project cost* adds so-called soft costs, beginning with the design fee and reimbursable expenses, the cost of surveys, geotechnical testing, and other factors; and materials testing during construction. Additional services not covered by the standard design contract, such as full-time on-site representation and feasibility studies, are also added. The cost of land acquisition, demolition, and site preparation are also considered part of project costs. Finally, financing costs are added.

Construction costs for parking structures vary substantially by locality, primarily due to labor costs and construction practices. The northeast has higher union costs than the southeast; the midwest has higher costs for durability issues than the southwest. California and Florida lead the country in the delivery of parking projects by the design/build delivery system; this has allowed designers to put the lessons of construction efficiency into practice on traditional design/bid projects, resulting in generally lower costs.

Market factors also can cause significant variations even within one construction season. Because 60 percent or more of a parking structure's cost will be in the structural system and associated items like expansion joints and sealers, the capabilities and workload of local cast-in-place and precast concrete contractors will have a substantial effect on the cost of the facility. Timing is everything; if a structure is bid after most of the contractors have booked work for the season, the bids will escalate.

The construction cost is usually stated in cost per sq m (sq ft), and cost per space for comparison with industry norms and other projects. Cost per sq m gives an idea of the basic elements and amenities incorporated into the design—for want of a better term, the quality of the finished building. The cost per space reflects both the *efficiency* (sq m or sq ft of parking area per space) of the parking design and the cost per sq m. In two different projects, the same level of

Table 14–23   Construction Cost per Parking Space

		Sq M/Space	25.0	27.5	30.0	32.5	35.0	37.5	40.0
		Sq Ft/Space	270.6	297.7	324.7	351.8	378.8	405.9	433.0
Cost/Sq M	Cost/Sq Ft								
Surface Lots									
$ 50	$ 4.62		$ 1,250	$ 1,375	$ 1,500	$ 1,625	$ 1,750	$ 1,875	$ 2,000
$ 75	$ 6.93		$ 1,875	$ 2,063	$ 2,250	$ 2,438	$ 2,625	$ 2,813	$ 3,000
$ 100	$ 9.24		$ 2,500	$ 2,750	$ 3,000	$ 3,250	$ 3,500	$ 3,750	$ 4,000
Above Grade Structures									
$ 200	$18.48		$ 5,000	$ 5,500	$ 6,000	$ 6,500	$ 7,000	$ 7,500	$ 8,000
$ 225	$20.79		$ 5,625	$ 6,188	$ 6,750	$ 7,313	$ 7,875	$ 8,438	$ 9,000
$ 250	$23.10		$ 6,250	$ 6,875	$ 7,500	$ 8,125	$ 8,750	$ 9,375	$10,000
$ 275	$25.41		$ 6,875	$ 7,563	$ 8,250	$ 8,938	$ 9,625	$10,313	$11,000
$ 300	$27.72		$ 7,500	$ 8,250	$ 9,000	$ 9,750	$10,500	$11,250	$12,000
$ 325	$30.03		$ 8,125	$ 8,938	$ 9,750	$10,563	$11,375	$12,188	$13,000
$ 350	$32.34		$ 8,750	$ 9,625	$10,500	$11,375	$12,250	$13,125	$14,000
Below Grade Structures									
$ 300	$27.72		$ 7,500	$ 8,250	$ 9,000	$ 9,750	$10,500	$11,250	$12,000
$ 400	$36.95		$10,000	$11,000	$12,000	$13,000	$14,000	$15,000	$16,000
$ 500	$46.19		$12,500	$13,750	$15,000	$16,250	$17,500	$18,750	$20,000
$ 600	$55.43		$15,000	$16,500	$18,000	$19,500	$21,000	$22,500	$24,000
$ 700	$64.67		$17,500	$19,250	$21,000	$22,750	$24,500	$26,250	$28,000
$ 800	$73.91		$20,000	$22,000	$24,000	$26,000	$28,000	$30,000	$32,000
$ 900	$83.15		$22,500	$24,750	$27,000	$29,250	$31,500	$33,750	$36,000
$1,000	$92.39		$25,000	$27,500	$30,000	$32,500	$35,000	$37,500	$40,000

architectural, durability, and engineering systems can be provided resulting in a similar cost of say $300 per sq m ($28 per sq ft). However, if one achieves an efficiency of 27.7 sq m per space (300 sq ft per space) and the other 32.3 sq m per space (350 sq ft per space), the more efficient design will cost $8,160 per space or 16 percent less than the $9,690 per space cost of the less efficient design. Table 14–23 compares efficiency and cost per unit area to cost per space.

Surface lot parking is obviously the least expensive to construct; in 1998 dollars, the range is $50 to $100 per sq m (approximately $5 to $10 per sq ft) depending on requirements for drainage, lighting, and landscaping. Above-grade, open-air structures typically cost $200 to $350 per sq m with the low end typically only occurring in simple, two-level structures or in very large, repetitive structures (over 5000 spaces.) Underground parking costs vary widely; the number of floors below grade and the soil conditions affect the cost dramatically. It is not uncommon for underground garages to cost $500 to over $1000 per sq m.

The efficiency of parking designs varies widely. Note that any mixed-use area should not be included in the efficiency calculation to avoid distorting comparisons. A typical surface lot or structure with circulation through the parking areas can achieve efficiencies of 25 to 33 sq m per space (270 to 350 sq ft per space). Efficiencies below 28 sq m per space were almost never seen prior to the downsizing of the automobile in the 1970s and the subsequent development of compact-only stalls. Given that the latter are now in disfavor in many locales, efficiencies of 28 to 30 sq m per space (300 to 325 sq ft per space) are the goal of most designs at the turn of the millenium. Efficiencies of over 30 usually reflect a site constraint requiring short rows or single-loaded aisles and should be avoided if at all possible. Short-span garages (with columns between parking spaces rather than between bays) will have efficiencies over 30 sq m per space, but they may be dictated by mixed use above the parking use. Facilities with special requirements for express ramps and loss of parking areas to toll plazas or other parking-related functions will also have efficiencies of 30 to 35 sq m per space.

During the planning stage, the project budget will include an *estimated construction cost* that represents an estimate of what a contractor would bid for the project based on the contract drawings plus *design contingencies* (for issues not yet addressed in the design) and the *field contingency* for unforeseen site conditions and design changes during construction. The design contingency is generally carried as 15 percent of the estimated cost at completion of the schematic phase, 10 percent at the end of design development, and 5 percent at the end of preparation of construction documents to allow for market conditions at the time of bid.

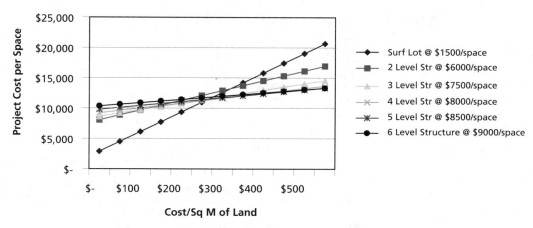

Figure 14–8 Land Cost impact on Project Cost

Traditionally, once the project was bid and awarded, correction of minor errors and omissions in the design drawings was paid out of the field contingency. A federal study[49] of design-caused changes concluded that the owner should anticipate and carry at least a two percent contingency for deficiencies in designs produced in accordance with customary architectural/engineering practices. The report notes that almost every design is unique and that it would be "prohibitively expensive and time consuming" to require the design team to produce "perfect" plans and specifications. This is not to say that the owner should not seek a designer with a superior track record in the quality area, which today is usually measured by monitoring design-caused change orders.

Exclusive of land and financing costs, the project cost will typically be 10 to 15 percent over the construction cost at the completion of the project. Land costs can dramatically affect the capital cost of parking. As seen in Figure 14–8, assumptions have been made for the cost per space for facilities ranging from surface lots to six-level structures. A 15 percent factor for project costs (on both construction and land cost) is included. There is a convergence of all options at a land cost of $325 per sq m ($30 per sq ft) wherein virtually all the options have the same overall project cost per space of about $12,000. Below this land cost, surface parking is the most cost-effective, and there is some cost benefit in going out on a couple levels rather than up to four or more levels. Above land costs of $325 per sq m, higher structures are more feasible, and the cost of multistory structures converge so there is not much difference according to number of levels.

Another issue that is important in evaluating alternative sites and options for parking expansion is the *cost per added space*. When there is existing parking on the site of a proposed structure, those spaces must first be torn up and rebuilt at new construction costs before any new spaces are added. Table 14–24 gives a comparison of five alternative parking options to gain 500 spaces at a hospital that is located on the fringe of a business district. Option A is building on a site already owned but without parking, which is obviously the most cost-effective at $2,875 per added space. Option B is to assemble a site by acquiring a full block of older tract housing and develop a 500 space surface lot. Land acquisition and demolition costs $100 per sq m and results in a cost per added space of $6,555 for B1. If the land costs $200 per sq m as in B2, the cost per added space jumps to $10,235, more than building a structure. Option C is to develop a structure on part of the raw ground used for surface parking in option A; the cost per space and the cost per added space are identical at $9,775. Option D is to build a structure on the site of an existing 100-space parking lot. A 600-space, seven-level structure would be required to add 500 spaces, at a project cost per added space of $11,730 per added space, about $2,000 more per added space than option C. For interest's sake, a final option E has been included—acquiring a similar sized parcel and building a six-level structure for 500 spaces. It is assumed that this is on the side of the hospital towards the business district and has a land cost of $325 per sq m. This option has a project cost per added space of just over $12,000 per space.

---

[49] Committee on Construction Change Orders, Building Research Board, National Research Council, *Design Deficiencies for Construction Contract Modifications* (Washington, D.C.: National Academy Press, 1986, p. 1).

Table 14–24 Comparison of Parking Alternatives

		Site A	Site B1	Site B2	Site C	Site D	Site E
Footprint (metric)		80 m by 200 m	80 m by 200 m	80 m by 200 m	36.5 m by 76 m	36.5 m by 76 m	36.5 m by 76 m
Footprint (English)		263′ by 658′	263′ by 658′	263′ by 658′	120′ by 250′	120′ by 250′	120′ by 250′
Existing Parking Spaces		none	none	none	none	100	none
Land Acquisition		no	yes	yes	no	no	yes
Size of Structure		500	500	500	500	600	500
Number of Floors		surface	surface	surface	6 levels	7 levels	6 levels
Land Cost /sq m		—	$ 100	$ 200	—	—	$ 325
Construction Cost /Space		$ 2,500	$ 2,500	$ 2,500	$ 8,500	$ 8,500	$ 8,500
Construction Costs		$1,250,000	$1,250,000	$1,250,000	$4,250,000	$5,100,000	$4,250,000
Land Acquisition		—	$1,600,000	$3,200,000	—	—	$ 970,900
Other Project Costs	15%	$ 187,500	$ 427,500	$ 667,500	$ 637,500	$ 765,000	$ 783,135
Total Project Cost		**$1,437,500**	**$3,277,500**	**$5,117,500**	**$4,887,500**	**$5,865,000**	**$6,004,035**
Project Cost Per Space		**$ 2,875**	**$ 6,555**	**$ 10,235**	**$ 9,775**	**$ 9,775**	**$ 12,008**
Project Cost Per Added Space		**$ 2,875**	**$ 6,555**	**$ 10,235**	**$ 9,775**	**$ 11,730**	**$ 12,008**
Financed Amount	7%	$1,581,250	$3,605,250	$5,629,250	$5,376,250	$6,451,500	$6,604,439
Annual Cost of Project		$ 225,134	$ 425,015	$ 624,895	$ 507,480	$ 608,976	$ 623,412
Annual Capital Cost per Space		**$ 450**	**$ 850**	**$ 1,250**	**$ 1,015**	**$ 1,015**	**$ 1,247**
Annual Operating Cost per Space		**$ 350**	**$ 350**	**$ 350**	**$ 500**	**$ 500**	**$ 700**
Total Annual Cost per Space		**$ 800**	**$ 1,200**	**$ 1,600**	**$ 1,515**	**$ 1,515**	**$ 1,947**
Monthly Revenue Per Space to Break Even		**$ 67**	**$ 100**	**$ 133**	**$ 126**	**$ 126**	**$ 162**

As noted, building surface parking on raw land already owned is the most cost-effective, but it is also the least realistic—few owners with parking problems would have this much raw, undeveloped land available! It might be somewhat easier to find a location on an existing campus for the structure in option C, which is similarly the most cost-effective among the structure alternatives. Building a surface lot on low cost ground is also very cost-effective. In addition, it has the advantage of "banking the land" for future expansion of the hospital. Even with expensive land, option E at $12,008 per added space is only a little more expensive than option D's $11,730 per space, because the latter requires building twenty percent more spaces to replace those lost on the surface lot. If for example, the commercial area around site E was a retail, dining, and entertainment area, the facility could capture parkers on evenings and weekends, more than offsetting the incremental capital cost.

Financing costs include the cost of obtaining the financing; where reasonably conventional financing is to be obtained, the cost of financing would typically be added into the amount borrowed and is another 10 to 15 percent of the project cost. For early project planning, a factor of 25 percent to 35 percent for design, financing, and miscellaneous project costs over an estimate based on the typical construction cost per space is a reasonable assumption. Financing methods are further discussed later in this chapter. However, for the purposes of determining the cost to own and operate parking, a total project cost, including a 25 percent factor for all soft costs, will be financed at a cost of funds of 7 percent over twenty years for the structures and land acquisition but over ten years for the lots. Parking facilities are rarely financed for longer terms because they typically begin to require significant restoration and refurbishing at that age. The cost of financing each project has been added to Table 14–24. Note that both the annualized capital cost per space as well as the cost per added space is given so that one can begin to understand the revenue that must be generated from each space to pay for it.

Operating Costs

Several factors contribute to the variability in operating expenses among different parking facilities. First, one must consider the size of the facility. There are some economies of scale that allow larger facilities to have lower costs per space. The ownership of a facility can influence operating costs; a lot or structure that is part of a parking system, whether municipal, institutional, or private, will cost less to operate versus a facility that is independent. Location is also an important consideration: above ground or below, warm weather climate or the snow belt, high or low crime, high wage scale or low. Hours of operation, ratio of contract parking patrons to daily parking patrons, and automated payment versus cashiers or even whether fees for parking are charged at all, all influence operating expenses.

To determine operating expenses for parking facilities, one must first define what is included. The following categories are included in operating expenses:

- labor costs (wages and benefits),

- management fees and costs,

- security costs,

- utilities,

- insurance,

- supplies,

- routine maintenance,

- structural maintenance,

- snow removal,

- elevator and parking equipment maintenance, and

- other expenses.

Table 14–25 Operating Expenses for Parking Structures

	Median Annual Cost Per Space
Cashiering Salaries & Benefits	$119.57
Management Costs	$ 76.67
Security Costs	$ 67.49
Utilities	$ 58.42
Insurance	$ 15.78
Supplies	$ 7.58
Routine Maintenance	$ 18.70
Structural Maintenance	$ 50.00
Snow Removal	$ 3.90
Elevator/Parking Equipment Maintenance	$ 10.61
Other Expenses	$ 64.40
	$493.12

Source: Walker Parking Consultants, *1996 Operating Expense Survey*.

Taxes, whether sales, property, parking, or some other type, are not included here due to the wide range of taxes among facilities. A municipally owned structure, for instance, would likely pay no property tax; while a privately owned structure could have a substantial property tax bill. Pittsburgh, Pennsylvania, has a fairly (or unfairly, from the owner or operator's point of view) substantial 20.6 percent parking tax, while other locales may have little or no such tax. Debt service is also not included in these figures, as it is not considered an operating expense.

The data in Table 14–25 was gathered from a survey sent to operators of parking structures throughout the United States.[50] The numbers reflect responses from 17 states with data on 59 parking structures. They differ in size from 208 spaces to 3,000 with a median size of 632 spaces. The oldest facility on which information was provided was opened in 1945, while the median age of the structures is 17 years.

According to this recent survey, the overall operating expenses for a typical parking structure were close to $500 per space annually as of 1996. More than half of the operating costs ($263.63) are associated with revenue collection and security. The "Basic Operating Expense" for a nonattended facility with no security cost was $230 per space per year in 1996 dollars. Larger structures located in warm climates may have lower costs than this, but smaller structures located in the snow belt can expect to spend a greater amount per space, especially if an adequate amount is spent on structural maintenance.

The size and age of a structure make a difference; but clearly, hours of operation and type of use have the greatest effect on the bottom line. A facility with the primary purpose of providing parking for frequent events requires more cashiers than a general parking facility. If the cashiers are paid a higher wage and benefits are provided, the increased hours of operation can increase expenses in a hurry. Security costs can be huge factor, ranging from $0 to $250 per space. Utility costs, again because of location and type of structure, also have a significant effect on the total picture. They ranged from less than $4 to over $200 per space in this survey.

Many of the respondents reported little or no cost in one or more areas, presumably because accounting practices do not "charge" the parking system for those expenses. Therefore, an operating cost for each of the scenarios has been

---

[50] Laughlin et al, "Operating Costs for Parking Structures Vary Significantly," *Parking* (Washington, D.C.: National Parking Association, May/June 1997, pp. 18–20).

Table 14–26   Monthly Revenue Required per Space

Project Cost/Space	Annual Operating Cost per Space												
	$ 50	$100	$150	$200	$250	$300	$400	$500	$600	$700	$800	$900	$1000
$ 1,000	$ 14	$ 18	$ 22	$ 26	$ 31	$ 35	$ 43	$ 51	$ 60	$ 68	$ 76	$ 85	$ 93
$ 2,000	$ 24	$ 28	$ 32	$ 36	$ 40	$ 45	$ 53	$ 61	$ 70	$ 78	$ 86	$ 95	$103
$ 3,000	$ 34	$ 38	$ 42	$ 46	$ 50	$ 54	$ 63	$ 71	$ 79	$ 88	$ 96	$104	$113
$ 4,000	$ 43	$ 48	$ 52	$ 56	$ 60	$ 64	$ 73	$ 81	$ 89	$ 98	$106	$114	$123
$ 5,000	$ 53	$ 57	$ 62	$ 66	$ 70	$ 74	$ 82	$ 91	$ 99	$107	$116	$124	$132
$ 6,000	$ 63	$ 67	$ 71	$ 76	$ 80	$ 84	$ 92	$101	$109	$117	$126	$134	$142
$ 7,000	$ 73	$ 77	$ 81	$ 85	$ 90	$ 94	$102	$110	$119	$127	$135	$144	$152
$ 8,000	$ 83	$ 87	$ 91	$ 95	$ 99	$104	$112	$120	$129	$137	$145	$154	$162
$ 9,000	$ 93	$ 97	$101	$105	$109	$113	$122	$130	$138	$147	$155	$163	$172
$10,000	$102	$107	$111	$115	$119	$123	$132	$140	$148	$157	$165	$173	$182
$12,500	$127	$131	$135	$140	$144	$148	$156	$165	$173	$181	$190	$198	$206
$15,000	$152	$156	$160	$164	$168	$172	$181	$189	$197	$206	$214	$222	$231
$17,500	$176	$180	$185	$189	$193	$197	$205	$214	$222	$230	$239	$247	$255
$20,000	$201	$205	$209	$213	$217	$222	$230	$238	$247	$255	$263	$272	$280
$22,500	$225	$230	$234	$238	$242	$246	$255	$263	$271	$280	$288	$296	$305
$25,000	$250	$254	$258	$262	$267	$271	$279	$287	$296	$304	$312	$321	$329
$27,500	$275	$279	$283	$287	$291	$295	$304	$312	$320	$329	$337	$345	$354
$30,000	$299	$303	$307	$312	$316	$320	$328	$337	$345	$353	$362	$370	$378

Note: Interest Rate = 7%.

Source: Walker Parking Consultants, 1999.

estimated for Table 14–24. Note that capturing the evening and weekend revenue from the commercial district increases the operating cost of option E.

Summary

Combining the construction, financing, and operating costs for the options in Section 14–6 gives a picture of the overall annual cost per parking space. The monthly revenue to break even gives a pretty good idea of what would have to be charged to employees if the spaces are largely used by employees. Table 14–26 cross-tabulates project cost per space versus annual operating cost per space to show the monthly revenue required per space to break even.

Parking Management

"Parking management tactics" is a term adopted by the Federal Highway Administration[51] to describe the variety of parking policies and actions that can be employed by cities to alleviate parking and other related transportation problems. Most of these tactics are equally applicable to major activity centers, both institutional and commercial. The five main categories or tactics pertain to:

1. pricing;

2. on-street supply;

3. enforcement and adjudication;

4. off-street supply:

   • within the activity center,

   • fringe and corridor parking;

5. marketing.

---

[51] John F. DiRenzo, Bart Cima, and Edward Barber, *Parking Management Tactics* (Washington, D.C.: Federal Highway Administration, 1981).

There is no one tactic that can simultaneously achieve all hypothetically desired goals (minimize auto usage and traffic congestion, maximize transit patronage, provide adequate parking, and foster economic growth). This is partly due to some fundamental conflicts among various goals. For example, tactics that increase the parking supply are likely to reduce the incentive to use mass transit. Some of these strategies may be quickly discarded for failure to meet the goals and objectives of a community or institution. Others require more detailed consideration.

Pricing Tactics

Pricing is a major force in determining parking conditions, especially in the dynamic circumstances found in activity centers where fees are charged for parking. Generally speaking, there may be one or more purposes in pricing of parking: generating revenue, controlling who parks where, and encouraging alternative modes of transportation.

Short-Term Pricing

Visitor parking should generally be available close to destinations; the fee structure of a particular facility or system is often set to make sure that visitors' needs are met first. Short-term parkers are not as price-sensitive as long-term parkers. In many cases there is a compelling reason to come to the activity center that is little influenced by the price of parking. Certainly if a competitive destination has equally acceptable products and services, short-term parking cost may be an influence on choice of destination.

Table 14–27   Types of Parking Management Actions

On-Street Parking Supply	Off-Street Parking Supply in Activity Centers	Fringe and Corridor Parking	Pricing	Enforcement and Adjudication	Marketing
Add or remove spaces	Expand or restrict off-street supply in CBD and activity centers	Fringe parking	Change parking rates	Enforcement	Advertising
Change mix of short- and long-term parking		Park-and-ride parking	Increase rates	Non-police enforcement personnel	Brochures Maps Media
Parking restrictions	Zoning requirements Minimum requirements Maximum requirements Joint use	Carpool/vanpool parking	Parking price increase Parking rate structure revision	Ticketing Towing Booting	Convenience programs (i.e., monthly contracts)
Peak-period restrictions			Parking tax		
Off-peak restrictions	Constrain normal growth in supply		Parking surcharge	Adjudication Administrative Judicial	
Alternate side parking by time of day and/or day of week	Maximum ceiling (i.e., freeze) on CBD spaces		Decrease rates		
Permissible parking durations	Reduced minimum parking requirements through HOV and transit incentives		Free parking in CBD		
Prohibitions on parking before specified hours	Restrict principal-use parking facilities		Differential pricing programs		
Residential parking permit programs	Construct new lots and garages		Short-term vs. long-term rates Carpool/vanpool discounts		
Carpool/vanpool preferential parking	Change mix of short- and long-term parking		Vehicle size discounts Geographically differentiated rates		
Carpool/vanpool m Carpool/vanpool stickers	Restrict parking before or during selected hours of the day		Monthly contract rates		
Loading zone regulations Bus Taxi Delivery Diplomat	Preferential Parking Carpool/vanpool parking Handicapped parking Small vehicle spaces		Merchant shopper discounts Stamp programs Token programs		
			Employer parking subsidies Reduce subsidies Transit/HOV subsidies		

Source: DiRenzo, John F., Bart Cima, and Edward Barber, *Parking Management Tactics,* Washington, D.C.: Federal Highway Administration, 1981.

However, even retail can be a strong destination. When Circle Centre, a public–private joint venture, retail and entertainment center in downtown Indianapolis was about to open, there was much speculation in the press regarding whether or not it could succeed with the relatively modest parking fee of $1 for the first three hours. The fee structure then jumps to $2 per hour; discouraging parking longer than three hours was considered necessary to keep the more than 50,000 downtown employees out of the parking intended for visitors to the center and downtown. Richard Feinberg, director of Purdue University's Retail Institute, was quoted as saying "Where else in Indianapolis do you have to pay to shop?"[52] However, in the end, the parking fee was a not an issue to shoppers; and the project is among the top five percent of retail centers nationally, in terms of annual sales per sq ft.

Long-Term Pricing

Pricing of parking can and does play a major role in mode choice and parking location by employees and other long-term parkers. In large activity centers like the CBD, these parkers usually have a variety of choices. If price is a concern, an employee can find very reasonably priced, if not free, parking on the perimeter of the activity center and walk three or more blocks to his or her place of employment. Shuttle and park-and-ride programs may make low-cost perimeter parking more accessible in large CBDs. A People Mover, such as in Detroit, also provides easy and convenient access to parking throughout the CBD. On the other hand, if proximity to the workplace is a concern to an individual, higher-priced parking can be found near the workplace.

True market-pricing generally only exists in older CBDs of major cities where commercial parking comprises the majority of the supply. Many of the properties in these areas were developed before the private automobile became the predominant mode of transportation and, therefore, do not provide adequate parking for tenant and customer needs by today's standards. Private enterprise stepped in to fill that void. Off-street commercial parking pricing is usually not much influenced by on-street meter rates set by the municipality; generally, if a commercial facility exists, it is because the on-street parking alone cannot serve the needs of the area.

However, in many communities, the municipality has intervened in the market and provided public parking. Reasons for such intervention are discussed in section 14.7.4, Off-Street Supply Tactics. Pricing of parking in municipally-owned facilities is, of course, set by public policy but often is restrained well below what the market would otherwise bear. Sometimes this is by specific intent; the community wishes to maintain a viable CBD and therefore subsidizes the real cost of parking out of concern that those prices might otherwise discourage business and commerce from locating in the CBD.

In other cases, parking pricing may have originally been set for a specific reason long since forgotten and then rarely raised. The cost of parking in real dollars then consistently declines over time, making it all the more difficult (politically) to raise. Only when the parking system is required to finance capital expenditures for construction of new structures or restoration and repair of older ones does the community stop and consider the cost and market value of providing parking. Meanwhile, because pricing of privately-owned and operated facilities is influenced and restrained by municipal parking rates, commercial parking cannot be viable, and thus the burden of providing parking falls increasingly on the shoulders of the municipality.

Similarly, most institutions do not charge the full cost of providing parking to users and eventually all parties may face sticker shock in attempting to finance a much needed structure. The ideal, of course, is to charge market rates for parking, raising them *every year* to keep pace with inflation and market factors, and to develop reserves to finance new projects and capital maintenance and repair.

Pricing and TDM Plans

Of equal interest in this age of increasing reliance on personal vehicles is the need to encourage alternate modes of travel by commuters. Where TDM is contemplated, parking pricing is often critical to success. Studies of TDM have

---

[52] Mary S. Smith, "Circle Centre," *Parking* (Washington, D.C.: National Parking Association, September 1996, p. 28).

consistently shown that free parking is the single largest deterrent to success of a TDM program.[53] The following options for parking pricing should be considered for incorporation in TDM plans:

- *Fees for parking:* The available information indicates that a fairly high increase in cost is required to achieve a significant reduction in SOV commuting.[54] Demand elasticity for parking appears to be very situation-dependent, reflecting the cost of alternative modes, commuting distances, and market pricing at competitive facilities.

- *Discounts for ridesharing:* Discounts, if not elimination of parking charges, should be considered for carpools and vanpools. This strategy is often most effective when combined with other nonpricing strategies, such as preferential locations and aggressive rideshare matching programs. The planner must also be concerned with cost-effectiveness of such programs. When the California Department of Transportation added a discount and preferential parking program for carpool parking, 90 percent of the spaces were used by existing pools, and two-thirds of the new pool participants switched from transit. Trips to the site actually increased and transit use declined by over 200 persons per day.[55]

- *Transit subsidies:* In addition to raising the cost of parking, lowering the cost of transit by either subsidizing or paying the full cost of transit can be a critical component to a successful TDM plan. Again, the "first in line" for such subsidies will generally be those who already use transit, and it will be critical to combine this tactic with increasing the cost of SOV parking to achieve any real benefit.

- *Transportation allowances:* Rather than target a single mode of transportation, the transportation allowance is a cash payment to each employee to be used to pay for parking, transit, or to be pocketed with a mode choice of walking or bicycling. It is important with this type of system that SOV parking be a substantially more expensive option.

- *Cash-out programs:* Similar to the transportation allowance, the cash-out program is a monthly payment equal to the monetary value of the previously free parking space. Employees can then spend it on parking at that rate, use it for other modes of transportation, or simply pocket it.

- *Parking taxes or surcharges:* In a community where commercial parking exists but fees are still not adequate to encourage alternative modes, parking taxes or surcharges can be used to force the market rates to a more acceptable level. However, it must be applied to a broad area. When Madison, Wisconsin applied a peak period surcharge to four of its municipal garages, some commuters switched to transit, but many more simply switched parking location.[56] The EPA proposed parking taxes in the 1970s as a means of improving air quality but dropped the proposal due to opposition from Congress. Those in the parking industry argued that the wholesale imposition of parking taxes across the country would most affect downtowns, where parking is already market-priced and significant utilization of transit already exists. As with the income tax-free cap on employer-provided parking, until Congress has the will to impute the value of free parking and apply the tax program to all employers, this type of program may simply encourage more employers to move to the suburbs where parking is "free."

On-Street Supply Tactics

On-street parking is often a critical parking resource to activity centers despite the limited capacity it can provide. Older CBDs and institutional activity centers often have streets intentionally designed to provide on-street parking in addition to moving traffic lanes. However, on-street parking rarely if ever is solely adequate for even the smallest downtown. Generally, the goals for management of on-street parking relate to controlling who parks where and preventing spillover

---

[53] John G. Shaw, *Planning for Parking* (Des Moines, Iowa: University of Iowa Public Policy Center, 1997, p. 24).

[54] Ibid, p. 24.

[55] Ibid, p. 25.

[56] Ibid, p. 26.

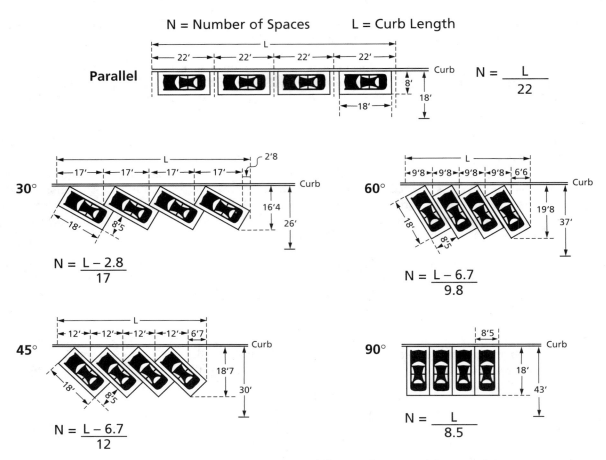

Figure 14–9   Street Space Used for Various Parking Positions

Source: Burrage, Robert H. and Edward G. Mogren, *Parking,* Westport, Conn.: Eno Foundation for Transportation, 1957.

parking into adjacent neighborhoods. Parking management strategies involving the on-street supply include: adding or removing spaces, changing the permitted time limit, restricting parking to certain times or users, and employing on-street spaces for preferential carpool parking.

Adding and Removing Spaces

In smaller towns and cities, adding on-street parking via angled parking stalls where parallel parking stalls previously existed may be one of the most cost-effective means for adding parking. A relatively minor reduction in sidewalk or parkway may allow angled parking to be developed. Angled parking also has a traffic calming effect and is promoted by neotraditionalists for that reason. Given that this approach would only be applied on streets where desired vehicle speeds are low, relatively narrow traffic lanes are appropriate as well. Generally a shallower parking angle is preferred to coordinate with the narrow traffic lanes and make it only accessible to users in the adjacent lane of traffic. Perpendicular parking, although more efficient, is usually avoided because of the increased traffic conflicts.

Conversely, on-street parking does affect traffic movement on streets critical for through-traffic movement, and conflicts over use of curb space for bus stops and deliveries can be a significant issue. In larger cities, prohibiting parking in peak hours has often been used to provide a compromise between peak hour traffic needs and convenient parking for storefront businesses. Following the "Great Chicago Flood" of 1992, when a construction accident flooded the underground tunnel system and, in turn, the basements of buildings in the downtown area, on-street parking was temporarily removed from many streets. Commercial operators were happy to capture the additional short-term parkers in off-street facilities, even at reduced rates negotiated as part of the agreement to remove the on-street parking supply.

The parking system adjusted to the loss of spaces with market pricing pushing employees in successive pricing tiers each a little farther away. It was perceived to be such a success in improving traffic flow that the prohibitions on on-street parking were extended.[57]

It is also very important for city parking officials to periodically review on-street restrictions for real need rather than habit. The dedicated loading zone required for retail tenancy along the block may no longer be necessary when the use changes to office; the street traffic in an area may no longer require peak period prohibitions. Prior to opening Circle Center, the city of Indianapolis conducted a block-by block review of on-street parking controls and removed fifty percent of the rush hour restrictions on on-street parking. Enforcement of meters was privatized. These improvements reduced complaints about parking from 172 to 22 per month and reduced towing from 1,000 to 160 vehicles per month.[58]

Metered and Time Limit Parking

The most common parking management tactic for on-street spaces is the parking meter. The primary purpose of on-street meter is to keep the spaces available for short-term users, by facilitating enforcement of the time limit. Originally, at least, revenue generation was solely intended to cover the cost of enforcement. Over time, many cities developed a significant revenue source in parking meter revenue.

More recently, as CBDs struggled to compete with suburban shopping centers, the parking meter has become a contentious issue in many cities. "Give us free parking instead of meters and we'll be able to compete," the merchants argue. Quite frankly, the short-term parker is not price sensitive, but rather convenience sensitive. If there is any negative effect of parking in downtowns vis-a-vis the suburban shopping center, it is lack of *convenient* parking, not lack of *free* parking. On-street parking is usually not convenient enough to serve thriving store-front retail much less a restaurant in that space. Removing meters does not solve that problem and only exacerbates the problem of financing off-street parking at reasonable rates to a public used to free on-street parking.

Moreover, removing meters makes enforcement significantly more difficult, both operationally and politically. Tire chalking is more time consuming and easily removed; time limits are often evaded by moving the car every couple of hours. Technological means have been invented to track length of stay in zones and specific stalls by license plate and automate the issuance of tickets. However, the parking meter has the added advantage of pricing a resource in short supply. This not only supports but helps to finance the eventual development of market-priced public parking off-street. Another disadvantage to removing meters is that, without the revenue stream paying for enforcement, the temptation is strong and ever-constant to reduce enforcement, which will quickly lead to more violation of the time limits.

It is again advisable for the municipality to periodically review its meter and time limit system for currency and efficiency. Given the political process, it is all too easy for the city to grant requests for special time limits: the five-minute meter in front of the copy shop, a 15-minute limit at the meat market. Aside from the fact that these limits are almost never enforced, the proliferation of multiple meter limits and fees only adds confusion and complication to the on-street parking system. Wherever possible, meter limits should be simplified to say one-hour and two-hour limits for short-term parking and 10-hour limits for peripheral meters that can be used by employees.

Preferential Parking

Some cities, notably Portland Oregon, have successfully adopted programs that reserve on-street parking (typically in peripheral areas that would otherwise be 10 hour meters) for carpools.

Residential Parking Permits

One of the almost inevitable results of parking shortages in activity centers is spillover parking into adjacent neighborhoods. Where those neighborhoods are residential, the residential parking permit (RPP) program is among the

---

[57] "Chicago Continues with Downtown Parking Ban," *The Urban Transportation Monitor* (July 24, 1992, p. 1).

[58] "At Your Service: Beauty, Convenience and Safety Distinguish a New Downtown," *Indianapolis Monthly* (Indianapolis, Ind.: Emmis Publishing Group, July 1996).

Table 14–28   Characteristics of Selected Residential Parking Permit Programs

City	Responsible Agencies	Activity Generating Impacts	Criteria	Hours	Geographic Area	Permit Fee	Non-resident Parking Privileges	Penalty for Parking Violations
Alexandria, VA	Traffic	CBD	Park occupancy 75% Nonresident 25%	M–F 8 a.m.–5 p.m.	2 Districts	$2/year	3 Hours Visitor permits	$15.00
Arlington, VA	Traffic Engineering	Employment Center	Peak occupancy 75% Nonresident 25%	M–F 8 a.m.–5 p.m.	7 Districts Total of 100 blocks	None	Visitor permits	N.A.
Baltimore, MD	Transit and Traffic	Hospital	Peak occupancy 80% Nonresident 25%	M–F 24 hours	Neighborhood 20 Blockfaces	$10/year	Visitor permits	$7.00
Boston, MA	Traffic and Parking	CBD	Administrative discretion	24 hours	Citywide Neighborhood (1 program)	None	2 Hour (citywide) 2 spaces/block (neighborhood)	$5.00 (citywide) $10.00 (neighborhood)
Cambridge, MA	Traffic and Parking	University Transit stations Retail areas	Administrative discretion	M–F 24 hours	Citywide	$1/year	Visitor permits	$15.00
Eugene, OR	Traffic	University	Administrative discretion	M–F 9 a.m.–3 p.m.	33 blocks	$5/year	2-hour parking	N.A.
Milwaukee, WI	Public Works	University Hospital Industrial area Retail area	Min. 150 spaces Nonresident 20% Transit nearby	Except Sunday 8 a.m.–5 p.m.	11 districts	$6/year	2-hour parking	$20–40 for falsification of application
Montgmery County, MD	Traffic Engineering	Hospital High school	Average occupancy 8 a.m.–5 p.m. > 50% Nonresident 50%	M–F 9 a.m.–5 p.m.	2 districts	$5/year	Visitor permits	$10
San Francisco, CA	Traffic Engineering	Transit stations CBD University	Peak occupancy 80% Nonresident 50%	M–F 8 a.m.–9 p.m.	3 separate districts	$5/year	2-hour parking	$10
Vancouver, B.C.	City Engineering	Local generators	Petition from 213 residents	24 hours	150–200 RPDs Each RPS is generally 2–3 spaces	None	None	$25
Washington, DC	D.C. DOT	CBD Transit stations Other generators	Peak occupancy 70% Nonresident 10%	M–F 7 a.m.–6:30 p.m.	Multiple areas covering 12–15% of all residential streets	$5/year	2 hours Visitor permit	$5

Source: DiRenzo, John F., Bart Cima, and Edward Barber, *Parking Management Tactics*, Washington, D.C.: Federal Highway Administration, 1981.

most viable strategies for controlling the problem. Where the spillover is almost entirely employee, the on-street spaces may be restricted to one- or two-hour parking or a residential permit holder. The restrictions may only apply during certain hours of likely problems, such as 8 A.M. to 6 P.M. Area residents pay a modest fee for a residential permit that allows the vehicle to be parked on the street. The time limit allows short visits by service vehicles and guests of the residents; longer stays require the parker to obtain a RPP visitor pass card from the resident and return to place it in the vehicle. In other cases, the time limit does not work well. For example, where the spillover is largely composed of university students parking for a single class, or tourists to a destination lacking adequate parking, all users may be required to display a permit. The environment of the residential neighborhood is not only enhanced by the reduction of nonresident parking, but also by the reduction of vehicular traffic seeking a parking space. State or local enabling legislation may be required to implement an RPP.

Enforcement

Cheating parking meters is a folk-crime: shaving the payment for the expected stay or not paying the meter is perfectly fine to the vast majority of Americans, if you get away without a ticket! Turnover studies routinely find substantial overtime parking at meters even with extensive enforcement. Illegal parking not only allows parkers to avoid paying their fair share and subverts the entire parking management system, but it may also negatively affect traffic flow on critical streets.

Parking management agencies have increased enforcement over the past decade, so that those who try to abuse the system find that they are likely to get a ticket virtually every time they try to avoid paying the fee. They vigorously pursue collecting fines from offenders; it is only fair to those that abide by the rules. Experience in many cities has shown that strict enforcement more than pays for itself.

An extensive study of the statistical relationship between parking revenues, fee schedules, fines, and enforcement practices was published by Adiv and Wan.[59] This study indicates that the level of enforcement and the rate schedule are more important determinants of parking behavior than the fine schedule. That is, the fee is more likely to be paid up front with high enforcement than with high fines. Therefore, while increasing the fine will obviously increase total revenue compared to what might have been collected with the lower fines, strict enforcement and higher fees are more beneficial to a system as a whole. Also the study concluded that despite the fact that about one in three users either parked for free or exceeded the time limit, the meters were effective in their major goal: keeping the spaces available for short-term parking. It is impossible to achieve perfect compliance with meters or time limits; however, with optimum enforcement, the offenders are reduced to those with short stays who are more likely to arrive and depart between enforcement tours.

One concern regarding strict enforcement often occurs when ticketing is performed by police officers. Writing parking tickets is not the highest or best use of a highly trained police officer's time and talents. Therefore, ticketing should be done by trained parking enforcement officers. A related issue with enforcement is adjudication of tickets once issued. Adjudication is the process of judgement for disputed tickets and the penalty and pursuit process.[60] Often, parking tickets are administered via the courts, which consider them to be a waste of valuable, indeed scarce, resources. Some judges routinely throw out tickets on almost any excuse; other agencies make little effort to collect outstanding tickets. As a result, the prompt voluntary payment of tickets is generally very low, between 10 and 33 percent.[61] Scofflaws may accumulate hundreds of dollars in unpaid parking tickets.

The most successful strategy for resolving problems in collection is to establish either an in-house bureau dedicated to ticket collection or retain a professional ticket collection firm to aggressively pursue ticket collection. A key component of the programs also is a towing or booting program. As tickets are issued, the enforcement personnel check the license plate against a "hot list" of scofflaws; when a vehicle is identified as frequent violator or associated with significant unpaid tickets, the vehicle is towed and impounded or immobilized via a "boot" applied to one wheel until outstanding tickets have been paid. In some states, such as California, vehicles cannot be reregistered if there are unpaid parking tickets.

---

[59] Aaron Adiv and Wenzhi Wang, "On-Street Parking Meter Behavior," *Transportation Quarterly* (Washington, D.C.: Eno Transportation Foundation, July 1987, p. 305).

[60] Weant and Levinson, *Parking* (Westport, Conn.: Eno Foundation for Transportation, 1990, p. 268).

[61] Ibid, p. 268.

On the adjudication side, many communities have effectively decriminalized parking tickets by establishing a procedure for resolution at an administrative rather than court level. A trained, paralegal officer or panel hears evidence in disputed ticket cases and has authority to determine fault and assess fines as appropriate. Generally, the procedure allows the parking ticket or the computerized ticket writer's log to be *prima facie* evidence and the ticket writer need not be present at the hearing.[62] Enabling legislation for administrative adjudication is usually required. Some cities have made the process extremely citizen-friendly, allowing walk-in hearings, write-in explanations, periodic amnesty programs, and credit card payment of outstanding tickets and fines.

Off-Street Supply Tactics

Although the city can cause expansion or restriction of supply as deemed appropriate to local needs, the first decision, of course, must be which of the two approaches best meets the goals and objectives of the community. Area-wide parking caps are generally employed when the street system is grossly inadequate. For example, in the city of Boston there is a limited number of parking spaces permitted in central areas. Developers who wish to build parking must buy a license(s) held by existing parking facilities that must then close. Restrictions on parking supply also imply the responsibility of local government to provide alternative modes of transportation. In most cases, where restrictions are used, both commuter rail and bus services are available.

Those controlling parking in institutional activity centers can also use restrictions on supply to foster development of alternative modes. In the early 1990s, the University of Illinois—Champaign-Urbana made a decision to stop building more parking, at least on an interim basis, and used the pressure of parking shortages to help fuel development of an award-winning public transportation initiative. Rather than setting up its own shuttle system, the University worked with the local transit agency to expand routes to provide not only area-wide transit but also shuttle service between outlying commuter and student lots and campus buildings. All students are assessed a transportation fee as part of annual fees and receive a pass for free use of the entire transit system; faculty and staff can purchase a subsidized pass for the system. The University has recently resumed construction of additional parking but primarily to replace spaces lost to building construction.

Local officials can also restrict supply by setting *maximum* rather than minimum parking requirements in the zoning process. Minimum requirements normally give the right to the developer to provide more spaces. Seattle and Belleview, Washington as well as Portland, Oregon have adopted maximum limits for parking provided in new commercial developments.[63]

As discussed earlier in this chapter, more efficient use of parking resources has been mandated both by public opinion and federal initiatives such as the Intermodal Surface Transportation Efficiency Act. Where local officials choose to set minimum parking requirements, it is important that they be carefully constructed to not require excessive parking and to foster shared parking and TDM goals.

Marketing

While marketing in itself will not increase parking supply or reduce demand, it will be very valuable to publicize any and all steps taken to improve parking in an activity center. The negative effect of increased parking fees on employee recruitment should be minimized as much as possible by explaining the need for the increase and the overall benefits of changes in parking policies to the individual, the business, and the activity center.

Summary of Parking Management Tactics

As discussed herein, there are tactics available to meet almost any parking management goal for an activity center or a community. Obviously, the first step is to articulate the goals. One community that has both articulated its goals well

[62] Ibid, p. 269.

[63] Ibid., p. 44.

and made substantial progress towards meeting those goals is Portland, as seen in Table 14–29.

When Parking Development Is Required

Conceptual Parking Supply Models

An infinite number of solutions can be envisioned that might alleviate projected parking shortages in CBDs and activity centers. Six conceptual models of parking development were defined and analyzed for a downtown parking study for the city of Denver in 1992.[64] These models provide a useful means of evaluating alternatives for parking expansion. Note that different strategies may be required for long- and short-term parking. (Table 14–30.)

1. *Laissez faire:* The baseline model allows the market to determine how much parking is provided. The private sector and financing requirements for new development dictate how much and what type of parking is provided to satisfy new and existing parking demand. Parking is neither required nor constrained by zoning, but it is allowed as a use by right. The laissez faire model currently flourishes in many cities, such as Denver.

Table 14–29 Guiding Principals for a Parking System: The Portland Example

Portland Parking Policies are intended to manage parking and stimulate economic development in Portland's Central City area. Parking policies are intended to:

- "Pinch" the parking supply to encourage the use of alternative modes of travel, i.e., transit, bicycling, walking and carpooling.

- Allow new surface parking to meet the particular needs of individual districts while acknowledging that:
  — All newly-developed surface parking will be landscaped;
  — Buildings should be oriented to pedestrians and transit;
  — New, free-standing commercial commuter surface lots are prohibited; and
  — New, large surface lots must be part of phased developments to ensure that future phases will replace them with higher-density development.

- Establish a system of parking ratios for office uses throughout the Central City.

- Support parking structures, in the Downtown, as the preferred form of parking, and allow new surface lots (greater than 20 spaces) only as part of a phased development or for large-scale residential development.

- Manage on-street parking to support land use activities within each district and mitigate spillover impacts on adjacent neighborhoods.

- In districts with maximum ratios and paid parking, new parking will be allocated through the ratios and managed to maximize utilization.

- New parking for visitors, customers and clients will be approved based on a parking demand analysis.

Source: *Gateway to Growth: Improving Parking in Downtown Baltimore,* Baltimore, Md.: Downtown Partnership of Baltimore, September 1997.

Table 14–30 Matching Long- and Short-Term Parking Strategies

		Short-Term Parking					
		Laissez Faire	Area Shared	Destination Shared	Central	Intercept CBD	Intercept Regional
Long-Term Parking	Laissez Faire	●	◓	●	◓	◓	◓
	Area Shared	○	○	●	◓	◓	◓
	Destination Shared	○	◓	●	◓	◓	◓
	Central	◓	◓	◓	◓	◓	◓
	Intercept CBD	○	○	●	◓	◓	◓
	Intercept Regional	○	○	●	◓	◓	◓

Key:
- ● Scenario worthy of further analysis.
- ◓ Scenario has disadvantages that outweigh advantages.
- ○ Scenario does not support goals.

Source: *Downtown Denver Parking Strategy,* Indianapolis, Ind.: Walker Parking Consultants, June 1992, pp. V–1 to V–12.

---

[64] *Downtown Denver Parking Strategy* (Indianapolis, Ind.: Walker Parking Consultants, June 1992, pp. V–1 to V–12).

The laissez faire solution is essentially market-driven and as such parking locations are completely flexible and unplanned, the product of economic development, demolition of buildings, and specific parking needs as required by financial institutions and developers for new private-sector projects.

2. *Area–shared:* An area-shared facility would be intended to provide parking for essentially all uses within a reasonable walking distance. This model is often that employed by cities who provide parking for the business district, but it is also that employed where commercial operations provide parking for a particular area. Public-private joint ventures are also an option.

An excellent example of an area-shared project is the Post Office Square facility in Boston. Developed by a public-private consortium known as Friends of Post Office Square, an inadequate and antiquated 750 space above-ground parking structure was torn down and replaced by a 1,400 space underground garage. At street level, a full-block park themed as a public square was developed.[65]

3. *Destination–shared:* Similar to the area-shared model, the destination-shared model targets a specific project or several uses in proximity of each other. This model suggests private-sector development rather than public involvement. However, some destination-shared parking facilities might be a joint public-private venture.

The destination-shared model is intended to minimize many of the problems of laissez faire parking occurring indiscriminately throughout the CBD. The destination-shared model is based upon the conventional developmental context, wherein each individual project is constructed with its own individual parking facilities. The difference between this model and the laissez faire model, however, is that the destination-shared concept specifically identifies where parking structures will be permitted and these structures are built in such a manner as to permit sharing between a number of destinations.

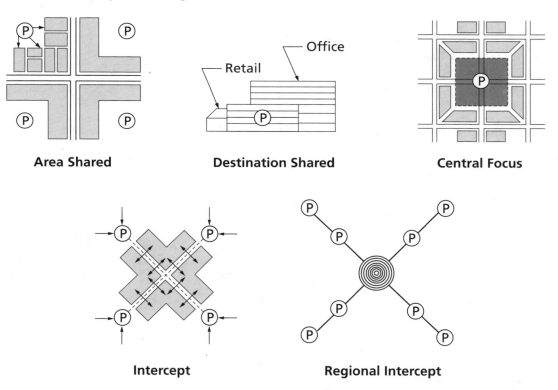

Figure 14–10   Parking Development Options

Source: *Downtown Denver Parking Strategy,* Indianapolis, Ind.: Walker Parking Consultants, June 1992, pp. V–1 to V–12.

---

[65] "Friends of Post Office Square," *Parking* (Washington, D.C.: National Parking Association, May 1995, p. 39).

Destination-shared parking facilities could be built by either the public or the private sector or a public–private partnership. Public–private partnership could occur where a specific project receives a subsidy to build parking, or where the city builds a parking structure and leases the air rights for a mixed-use development built by a private developer. An excellent example is the World of Wonders garage at Circle Centre, in downtown Indianapolis. The World of Wonders garage not only serves Circle Centre, but also the nearby RCA Dome and Convention Center.

4. *Central focus:* This model satisfies parking demand in one large parking reservoir in the centroid of the activity center. The central focus concept creates a large, centralized parking facility in the center of the zone with a major pedestrian distribution system that emanates from this facility to the many diverse destinations within the core.

   A good example of this facility type is the Grant Park Parking Facility in Chicago, Illinois, which runs several blocks on the lakefront in the Loop, providing substantial parking for many uses within the area that do not have their own parking facilities. The central focus parking concept could be a depressed, below-grade structure with either air rights development or park and green space over the top of a parking facility.

   A key to the success of this type of facility is good vehicular access to the very center of activity. Otherwise, by bringing all of the vehicles within the core, the centralized parking facility could encourage additional congestion, air pollution, and other negative effects. As such, it requires a fairly unique combination of circumstances.

5. *Intercept:* This model intercepts parkers at the perimeter of the activity center. In larger cities where the intercept would occur over 1,000 ft from the core, the intercept model is dependent on a shuttle system to move the parker conveniently, quickly, and economically to destinations within the core.

   The intercept model is based upon the philosophy that auto congestion within the core creates negative effects, air pollution, and unnecessary congestion; and that the environment within the activity center should be kept pedestrian in scale and free of auto traffic. If this parking is inexpensive, convenient, and directly connected to the activity center via shuttle service or a pleasant pedestrian walking experience, the concept would be successful.

   However, given the laissez faire parking development policy in many activity centers today, there is simply too much parking available within the core to make an immediate change to the intercept concept viable. In order to encourage the use of intercept parking, parking rates within the core must be considerably higher in price than the parking spaces available within intercept lots. Likewise, the availability of surface parking lots and parking structures within the core must be reduced, so as to force long-term employee parking to the perimeter intercept lots. Simply providing intercept parking is not enough; the program must be accompanied by disincentives to park within the core.

   Shorter term shopping trips or residential parking in close proximity to residential units simply do not work with intercept parking; therefore, the intercept parking concept generally is combined with short-term parking within the core and destination-shared parking near residential units. This is the model employed in larger cities such as Chicago where monthly parker rates in the central core are as high as $250 per month, but all day parking in the fringe is available for as low as $100 per month (1998 dollars.)

6. *Regional-intercept:* Much like the intercept model, the regional-intercept model intercepts parkers further from the core of the activity center. The benefits are similar to the intercept model, in addition to further improving air quality. The key to this model being a viable solution is a regional transportation system that would offer convenient access to the activity center. This approach would offer close-in destination-shared parking for short-term and residential parking needs; while long-term employee parking would be intercepted at regional facilities built along HOV and transit corridors and at the intersections of major accessways that are used for commuting.

The construction of regional-intercept parking facilities relies upon a regional transportation system that offers direct, convenient, and fast access from the parking sites directly into the core in very close proximity to the ultimate destination. It is not likely that this connection can be provided solely by bus; and most of those cities that currently employ this strategy successfully have rail transit, including New York City, Washington, D.C., and San Francisco.

Urban Design Issues

Parking as a building type can either have a negative effect on the area or a positive contribution in terms of urban design improvements to a given area. Urban design issues related to parking facilities have to do with the overall design of the building, its scale and massing, and the way in which the parking facility is blended into the fabric of existing buildings. Of particular importance is the treatment of the street level and whether the parking facility creates an intrusion into the overall streetscape scale and character of a given area. Another major issue is whether the parking structure is a singular use, auto-oriented facility, or whether it becomes a mixed-use project or a part of a new redevelopment effort, included as only one part of a number of new elements in a given project.

A parking facility can also become a catalyst for major public improvements such as the creation of a new public open space or park, or the infill of large voids in the urban fabric, by the construction of a new parking facility that fills the gap. Parking can also become a major form-giver, such as parking structures often do in major sports facilities, airport projects, or other destination uses. Within an urban activity center, parking can form a transition buffer between two different land uses, or it can define a major public space. On the other hand, parking can also have a negative effect, creating a wall of inhospitable, nonpedestrian space that takes away light from the street and creates imposing facades upon an otherwise pedestrian environment. This is generally the type of environment that has been created along streets where the parking structures have been built as a backside of major developments on the more prominent street. In essence, the secondary street becomes the back door of the city, relegated to parking activities.

From an urban design perspective, the imposition of surface parking upon the street has several problems. First of all, the surface parking lot removes a large "chunk of fabric" from the streetscape continuity of urban building form. These lots are generally not well-landscaped and have a negative effect on the overall quality of the environment. In addition, congestion and a proliferation of curb cuts also negatively affect the pedestrian walkway system.

In order to mitigate the above problems, several specific urban design limitations should be placed on the construction of parking structures or surface parking lots. These include:

- Requirements for extensive landscaping along the buffer of lots; however, landscaping needs must also be cognizant of security and life safety concerns.

- Limitation of curb cuts across pedestrian walkways.

- Requirements that existing buildings may not be torn down for the use of surface parking, unless it is simply an interim use leading to the construction of a new building.

- New parking structures within the activity center should include mixed-use development at street level and design treatment to the building itself to minimize its effect upon the overall fabric and character. Height, massing, and the use of materials would be controlled through design standards.

- The development of above-grade parking structures should be prohibited from major pedestrian streets and directed instead to secondary streets dedicated more to auto access.

- Incentives would need to be created to encourage below-grade parking structures, combined with mixed-use projects, or public open space.

- In terms of access, parking facilities should be located to coincide with major access streets and those service roadways intended to carry major traffic into the core.

Table 14–31 Alternative Parking Development Scenarios

Goals	Laissez-Faire (ST) Laissez-Faire (LT)	Destination-Shared (ST) Laissez-Faire (LT)	Destination-Shared (ST) Area-Shared (LT)	Destination-Shared (ST) Destination-Shared (LT)	Destination-Shared (ST) CBD-Intercept (LT)	Destination-Shared (ST) Regional-Intercept (LT)
1. To facilitate access to downtown while meeting air quality goals, including strategies to promote transit and ridesharing.	■	■	○	■	○	√
2. To coordinate parking facility development with transportation systems (vehicular and pedestrian) to and within downtown.	■	■	√	■	√	√
3. To coordinate parking facility development with the development or redevelopment of other downtown property and desired density patterns.	■	■	√	○	√	√
4. To develop parking facilities which serve shared parking needs.	■	○	√	√	○	○
5. To integrate appropriately designed parking (structure and surface) as a suitable land use (permanent or temporary).	■	■	√	○	○	√
6. To create mechanisms to assure that the appropriate amount of storage is provided for various classifications fo vehicles (short-term parkers, long-term parkers, HOV, buses, etc.) which enter downtown.	■	■	√	√	√	√
7. To provide a financially self-supporting parking system.	■	○	○	√	○	○
8. To minimize impact on residential areas from parking generated by commercial land uses.	■	■	■	■	○	√

Key: √ Supports goal; ■ Opposes goal; ○ Neither supports nor opposes goal.

Source: Chance Management Advisors, May 1991.

- Parking facilities should be located where they would offer the greatest opportunity to identify a given land use and provide clear definition of form, linkages, and connections.

- Parking facilities should be located where they have a positive urban design effect on a given area, such as the infill of gaps in the streetscape.

Comparison of Alternative Scenarios

Table 14–31 demonstrates how the scenarios were evaluated for the degree to which each alternative supports the parking strategy goals of Denver. A marking of (√) indicates that the alternative supports goals for both short-term and long-term parking. The reverse, a marking of (■), indicates that the alternative is in opposition to the goal. A marking of (○) indicates that the alternative is neutral concerning the goal involved.

Parking Management Organizations

When a municipality or institution has substantial parking resources, people are required to manage the resources. In many cases, the duties are fragmented among numerous departments or agencies. In the municipal case (with institutional

Table 14–32   Characteristics of Effective Parking Management Systems

Characteristic	Standard	Sample of Jurisdictions
Experienced Staff	Executive-level parking professional with minimum 15 years' related experience	Boston, Cincinnati, Minneapolis, Montgomery County, Prince George's County, Philadelphia
Representative leadership/oversight and coordination among relevant partners	Public–private board of directors or partnership	Denver, Kalamazoo, MI, Minneapolis, Philadelphia, Portland, OR, Pittsburgh, Wilmington, Prince George's County
Effective Organizational Structure	Non-profit organization	Denver, Kalamazoo, Portland
	Independent Parking Authority	Philadelphia, Pittsburgh, Wilmington, Prince George's County
Clear goals, objectives and guiding	Emphasis on economic development and planning	Minneapolis, Pittsburgh, Portland, San Antonio, Prince George's County, Denver, Montgomery County
Planning, evaluation, and proactive development	Five-year plan with annual review of benchmarks	Cleveland, Milwaukee, Minneapolis, Pittsburgh, Portland, San Antonio, Seattle, Wilmington, Montgomery County, Prince George's County
Development Ratios and Requirements	Standard industry development ratios	Boston, Chicago, Cincinnati, Cleveland, Denver, Milwaukee, Minneapolis, Montgomery County, Pittsburgh, Philadelphia, Portland, Seattle

Source: *Gateway to Growth: Improving Parking in Downtown Baltimore*, Baltimore, Md.: Downtown Partnership of Baltimore, September 1997.

equivalent in parentheses), Public Works (Building and Grounds) may control most of the "physical" aspects—building and maintaining on- and off-street facilities; The Police Deptartment (Security) provides enforcement and security; and Finance (Business Office) is responsible for revenue collection. Typically, parking is far down the list of concerns and priorities of each department. The process is often politicized and lacks clarity of goals and attention to implementation.

A more successful model is a professional organization hereinafter called Parking Management that is responsible for all or nearly all functions associated with parking management. Where it is necessary and appropriate to have separation of function, (for example, planning and zoning will continue to administer parking requirements), Parking Management must have a designated liaison to coordinate and personally contribute to policy decisions.

There are a variety of types of successful parking organizations that will be discussed and compared herein. Table 14–32 summarizes the characteristics of effective parking management organizations.[66] The following goals are also typically held in common by all of these options.

- Revenue should be tied to expenses and operations as closely as possible. For example, parking meter revenue should be evaluated in terms of potential or expected revenue, as well as compared to the expense of obtaining the revenue. This principle holds true for all parking management functions—even those that have less revenue than expenses. The only way to enhance cost and benefit ratios is to know how to control both revenue and expenses—and their analysis.

- Budget preparation, analysis, allocation, and adjustment should be under the control of Parking Management.

- The locations of parking management functions within the city governmental structure should be equivalent to the importance of parking management issues as they are perceived in the city.

- Parking Management may have personnel demands based upon air quality requirements and possibly other monitoring requirements. The structure and budget of Parking Management should be flexible enough to meet these demands whenever they are promulgated by regulatory or governmental agencies other then the city.

[66] *Gateway to Growth: Improving Parking in Downtown Baltimore* (Baltimore, Md.: Downtown Partnership of Baltimore, September 1997, p. ii).

- Where Parking Management and other agencies will try to encourage change and alter behavior in some ways that people are going to want to resist, it should be "protected" from political pressure as much as possible. Getting people to alter their driving and parking patterns is not easy. Agreeing to the plan and making it happen are two different things. If actions to accomplish goals can be overturned for political reasons, it will be impossible to implement parking and transportation plans.

Table 14–33 further discusses strengths and weaknesses of the various models.

Parking Authority

There is no inherent magic to a parking authority, but it does offer more independence than a city department or division. An authority is a "cousin" to city government. As part of the extended family, it can have the same personnel policies (if desired), particularly if most or all of the personnel have been in city departments previously.

Table 14–33   Strengths and Weaknesses of Organizational Structures

	Strengths	Weaknesses
Independent Parking Authority	Parking functions are placed in an entity with one purpose—to deliver parking.	Responsible for debt.
	Can maintain some independence while also working closely with the city.	New legislation is often required (state and local).
	Requires a Board of Directors to set policy, maintain fiscal responsibility and guide staff.	Board of Directors can sometimes be unwieldy or cumbersome depending upon requirements.
	Easy to create new positions, set salary scales different from government, and initiate rewards based on merit.	Civil service may make transferring employees difficult and cumbersome.
	Can make decisions and implement programs quickly.	
	Has power to issue bonds to finance projects. Can also benefit from city guarantee.	
Non-profit Organization	Parking functions are placed in an entity with one purpose—to deliver parking.	The ability to issue bonds, while possible, may be more difficult and complex.
	Can maintain some independence while also working closely with the city.	New legislation could be required to delegate functions.
	Flexibility regarding the size and characteristics of the board of directors.	Civil service may make transferring employees difficult and cumbersome.
	Easy to create new positions, set salary scales different from government, and initiate rewards based on merit.	
	Can make decisions and implement programs quickly.	
City Department	Easy to transfer employees from other city departments.	Parking gets buried in bureaucracy and does not receive the needed attention.
	New positions can be created under civil service regulations, which are less subject to political pressure.	Parking policy more likely to remain the purview of staff and elected officials unless citizen advisory committee formed.
	Easy to earmark revenues for general fund activities.	Civil service and budgeting process can be cumbersome and time consuming.
		Financing for parking facilities must compete with other municipal projects if general obligation bonds are requested.

Source: Chance, Barbara, "Organizational Alternatives for Public Parking Management," *Parking Professional,* Fredericksburg, Md.: 1986.

A Parking Authority is only as good as the planning and people that go into it. Some authorities across the county are very professional and have excellent reputations. Others are political patronage havens with reputations for squandering money and living on the edge of scandal. This organizational structure allows for a lot of flexibility and ability to respond to issues quickly. However, that is only an advantage if it is used well and in the pursuit of important goals.

Nonprofit Organization

One of the more recent models is a nonprofit organization (NPO) that is charged with dealing with the specific needs and concerns of an activity center such as a downtown. Parking is often one of the priorities of these organizations. Aside from the legalities of the enabling legislation, the main difference between an NPO and a Parking Authority is that the NPO may have a broader perspective on issues than a Parking Authority focused solely on parking. Both may be concerned with supporting and encouraging the economic vitality of an activity center, but the NPO may have a more balanced approach because it manages more elements than parking.

Separate Department

Many cities have separated transportation or parking functions from public works or similar functions and created a department devoted solely to those issues, including splitting off the functions in Public Works or another department to create a new department.

The primary advantage of such a restructuring would be to emphasize the importance of transportation and parking issues for the city and its citizens. Generally, there will be less conflict of interest and more focus on those issues. Above all, there will be fewer layers between the parking manager and the "CEO" (Mayor) and "COO" (City Manager) of the municipality.

The creation of a new department would require an appropriate process, based upon municipal law. Such actions might be perceived by the public as creating more municipal bureaucracy and needless additional or overlapping jobs. Clear goals and objectives for the results of a new department would have to be part of the public information process. There may be sufficient changes and planning necessary to justify a separate department, but the manner in which it would be created would be crucial for its acceptance.

Parking Management as an Enterprise Fund

Government accounting differs from business accounting, since government is not concerned with profits, and instead is concerned with assuring that revenues are sufficient to meet expenses. The National Council on Governmental Accounting has defined the various kinds of fund accounting used in governmental units. An enterprise fund is described as "a fund where ongoing activities operated like a business are recorded." Activities that are funded by user charges are most often defined as enterprise funds. Proceeds from revenue bond issues, and their disposition, are often accounted for in such a fund.

Parking Management could operate as an enterprise fund while operating under any of the previously discussed organizational structures. The defining characteristic of an enterprise fund organization is that it must generate sufficient revenue to cover its immediate expenses and to prepare for the future as necessary. In the case of parking, an enterprise fund would need to cover operating costs, debt service, debt service reserve funds (or any other required funds connected with bind issues), and sinking or reserve funds for future significant construction or maintenance.

Unlike the general fund, which primarily uses taxes to cover costs from many activities that do not raise revenue, a parking enterprise fund would require that parking activities be self-sufficient and that they be managed like a "business"—to generate income in excess of expenses. This would not mean that the primary purpose of Parking Management would be to generate profit; it would mean that parking functions would always need to consider the relationship of resources to desired activities and expenses. There could be no "deficit funding" or " bailouts" from other governmental funds.

Parking is one of the few governmental activities that can be operated as an enterprise fund, which is often the most desirable fund accounting method for parking activities. The positive aspects of an enterprise fund structure are as follows:

- Parking Management is different from many other functions in government—it has the responsibility to produce revenue as well as spend it. More pointedly, it must control the ratios of revenues to costs—including the addition and deletion of positions and people. As an example, each parking enforcement officer produces revenue at a multiple of the position salary. If enforcement officer positions are cut, it "saves" personnel costs but "loses" revenue. Very often, the relationships between certain types of positions and the production of revenue are not understood by budget bureaus whose normal method to cut operating costs is to reduce personnel. Further, a continuing danger to parking management organizations is the temptation for "raids" on what looks like excess revenue over expenses. It is sometimes difficult to keep funds within a budget for long-term maintenance, replacement of equipment, construction seed money, unanticipated studies or consulting, and other reserves.

- It will be extremely important for Parking Management to monitor its revenues, expenses, maintenance funds, and development funds as a parking strategy is carried forward. Parking Management will be expected to fund management and operations changes, some or all of new construction, additional incentives for ride sharing, and other activities. It must keep a very close watch on cost and benefits of existing programs and anticipated new or improved ones. It needs a budget structure that it controls, which in turn affects responsibility and accountability.

Sometimes there is reluctance in governmental units to establish enterprise funds. If the functions to be accounted for in this manner have been generating revenue that has flowed directly to the general fund, this revenue stream process is altered.

However, the general fund also loses the expenses associated with the activities, and this would be viewed as positive. In some cases, the executive order or legislation creating an enterprise fund specifies the degree of excess revenue that may remain in the enterprise fund and the disposition of any additional revenue. Other aspects of the fund that are usually specified include the goals and objectives of the fund, any limitations on activities, and some general operating procedures. The issue to be considered is whether or not it is desirable to have parking functions operated in such a way that they pay for themselves and generate excess revenue to be used in the future to provide additional services or to maintain the desired level of service.

Financing Parking Facilities

According to Heeseler,[67] "the parking industry has been characterized as a real estate business with very high tenant turnover." Parking facilities are difficult to finance because they are specialized and uniquely subject to changes in the parking demand of the generators they serve, which in turn make them relatively high risks in the eyes of the financial markets. Lenders and investors will be very concerned with both the strength and longevity of the intended market for the facility as well as the possible alternative users or uses of the parking facility itself. In most cases, however, the general credit of the owner will be equally if not more important than the projected revenue and expenses of the parking facility itself. When a parking facility is constructed as part of a private development, it is generally a relatively minor part of the project financing package. Lenders may be more interested in the number of spaces provided being adequate to market the retail or office space, for example, than in the line item projections for parking revenues and expenses in the project pro forma.

When a parking facility is being financed with public bonds, few if any facilities can show adequate coverage of the debt service to be secured solely by the parking revenues of the facility itself. These difficulties often necessitate

---

[67] E. Carlton Heeseler, *Financing Parking Facilities* (N.Y.: Van Nostrand Reinhold, 1991, p. 1).

alternate approaches such as general obligation (G.O.) bonds or system revenue bonds. The lenders will typically be far more interested in either the credit rating of the municipality (in the case of G.O. bonds) or the finances of the parking system as a whole (with revenue bonds) than in the projections of revenues and expenses for the parking facility itself.

Conversely, in those situations where a parking facility can be profitable, the financial markets of the 1990s have seen investment opportunity. Parking-centered real estate investment trusts have been established and several commercial parking operators have done (or are reputed to be preparing for) initial public offerings on the various stock exchanges. The key to these investments has been careful assessment of the strength of the parking management team and the assets: both owned properties and long-term leases and contracts for managing properties.

Public Financing

As previously noted, municipal parking structures would not be self-supporting at most of the rates charged in activity centers; and they would likely have to be subsidized by other sources. The most common are:

- General fund/obligation of the city, county, or state.

- Revenues from other parking facilities and meter revenues.

- In lieu and impact fees.

- Taxes, including:

  - Ad valorem (property taxes; most general fund pledges are ad valorem).

  - Special assessment district (where property owners are taxed to supply any deficits).

  - Tax increment district (the additional sales and property taxes generated by private redevelopment in the district are dedicated to paying for associated municipal expenditures).

  - Sales taxes in a defined or general area.

  - Hotel and lodging taxes in a defined or general area.

Other revenue sources such as grade level retail space income, development fees, or income from air rights can help to finance parking facilities.

Types of Public Financing

When public financing is contemplated, a key decision is what type of bonds would be issued. Table 14–34 summarizes the four main types of public parking financing, and some of the key issues related to each. The cost of financing with a G.O. bond—backed by the full faith and credit of the entity—either as the sole pledge or as a back-up to specified revenues will usually be significantly lower than with "pure" revenue bonds—backed solely by a specified stream of parking revenue.

In the former case the lenders will be principally interested in the credit rating of the issuing municipality or entity. With revenue bonds, lenders typically require that there be coverage, or a margin of safety by which either gross or net revenue exceed the annual payment of debt service. Projected pledged net revenues after operating expenses generally must be 1.5 to 2 times the annual debt service to gain capital market access through revenue bond financing. Additionally, the lender may impose what can be significant covenants on parking revenue bonds, including:

Table 14–34   Municipal Bonds for Parking

	General Obligation Bonds	Revenue Bonds	General Obligation Revenue Bonds	Certificates of Participation
Definition	Pledge the full faith and credit and unlimited taxing power to pay debt service.	Pledge the revenues of a specified source to pay debt service. Additional assurances are covenanted within the bond documents.	Pledge specified revenues and the issuer's full faith and credit and unlimited taxing powers.	A government agency enters into an agreement with another party (lessor) to lease an asset. Lease payments are sufficient to pay the purchase price and associated interest cost of acquiring the assset.
Source of Payment	Property taxes	Specified revenues	Specified revenues and property taxes	Tax revenues subject to annual appropriations (budget process)
Purposes	Projects that benefit whole community	Projects that benefit specific users	Whole community and/or specific areas	
State Law/Charter	Debt limit?	Debt limit?	Debt limit?	Not subject to debt limit
	Voter approval required?	Voter approval required?	Voter approval required?	No voter approval required
Risk/Cost	Highest security— lowest cost	Higher than general obligations because of limited revenue stream. The degree of risk depends on the individual financing package. Investors require coverage usually in the range of 125% to 200%	Same as general obligations	Higher than general obligation depending on essentiality of project/use
Credit Rating Impact	Full impact	Credit rating is dependent on the degree of security the financing package has. The credit rating for a revenue bond is independent of an issuer's general obligation rating.	Usually a full impact on the credit rating. May be mitigated depending on the revenue stream.	Full impact, usually half grade to full grade lower than general obligation.

Source: Schaefer, Michael, *Municipal Bond Basics for Parking Providers,* Springsted Public Finance Advisors.

- *Debt service reserve fund:* The entity is required to maintain a fund with an amount sufficient to pay one year's debt service. (Federal tax laws sets a three-fold limit.)

- *Operating reserve fund:* The entity is required to maintain a fund of two to three months' operating expenses.

- *Capital maintenance fund:* The entity is required to maintain a fund for periodic major maintenance and restoration so the parking facility can continue to generate sufficient revenue to repay the bonds.

- *Parking rate covenant:* Knowing that, historically, parking demand can be volatile and municipalities may have failed to raise rates sufficient enough to keep pace with inflation of costs, lenders may impose a requirement that rates will be adjusted as required to pay operating expenses and maintain all required reserve funds.

A key concept of "net revenue bonds" is that operating expenses are paid first to protect the revenue generating capacity of the facility. A "gross revenue bond" presumes a third party will guarantee the revenue generating capacity.

The disadvantages to G.O. Bonds are (1) they often require voter approval, and (2) most jurisdictions have many competing demands on their G.O. pledge from nonrevenue generating facilities (e.g., local government services, schools, parks). Special assessment and tax-increment bonds may be attractive to the municipality and the general public because there is no burden placed on the typical homeowner; however, opposition from the affected tax payers or tax receiving agencies (such as school districts) can make implementation of these districts problematic.

Cooperation between public agencies with bond authority may also be used to structure financing. Lease revenue and economic development bonds may be issued whereby one tax-exempt agency constructs the facility and leases it to the other, subject to statutory powers. The lease payments become a contingent liability on the leasing agency's balance sheet, contingent on the terms of the lease.

Certificates of participation (COP) are a lease arrangement that still qualifies for tax-exempt bonds if the appropriate tests are met. The private entity is the developer, lessor and nominal owner of the facility, while the public agency leases the facility for a specified term. The public agency may operate the facility or may retain a parking management firm to operate it. The title to the completed parking facility is in the name of the public agency and held by a trustee over the term of the lease. The purchasers or investors in the COPs provide the funds for the construction and are repaid from the lease payments. Generally, COPs are backed by a pledge of the public entity to pay the lease from general funds if parking revenues are insufficient to repay the bonds. While not a general obligation, the credit rating of the municipality would be seriously affected by a failure to appropriate funds to pay the lease. These bonds can achieve an investment grade rating with a great deal of flexibility and without the restrictions of general obligation bonds.[68] They are thus an attractive form of public financing for parking facilities for communities.

Tax-Exempt Bond Requirements

Another critical decision that must be made early is whether or not tax-exempt or taxable bonds can be used. The Tax Reform Act (TRA) of 1986 significantly tightened the rules under which tax-exempt financing can be used. While a bond counsel should review all proposed projects for conformance, the following list outlines the general requirements that must be met to use tax-exempt bonds:[69]

- Not less than ninety percent of the spaces must be available to the general public on a daily, monthly, or yearly basis, excepting only governmental and not-for-profit institutional uses. If monthly spaces are offered on a first-come, first-served basis and many or even most of them are leased by employees of a single corporation, that is still generally considered public use. The complications come with agreements to lease parking spaces *directly* by a single corporation itself.

- Not less than 95 percent of the bond proceeds must be spent on the public parking facility. This test can be complicated where a public-private joint development occurs, and it is difficult to trace the uses of the funds. For example, a public parking facility is to be constructed with street-level retail leased to tenants and apartments built in the air-rights. The parking spaces are shared and serve area parkers in the daytime and the residents at night. How much of the land acquisition, foundation, and site utilities—much less the construction cost of the parking facility—can or should be allocated to the parking facility and how much to the private development components?

- No more than ten percent of the annual debt service may be paid for or guaranteed by a corporate or nonpublic entity. Thus, when revenue from retail or air-rights development is expected to help repay the bonds, it may comprise no more than ten percent of the total revenue stream to retain tax-exempt financing. Also, even if all spaces are to be used by the public on a daily fee basis, the bonds cannot be guaranteed by a corporation in excess of this threshold to reduce the municipal or investor risk, without losing the tax-exempt status.

- Agreements for the management and operation of the facility may not exceed a five-year term, must provide for payment to the operator by either a periodic fixed fee or fixed percentage of the gross revenue, and must give the public entity the option to cancel at the end of any two-year period. Because concession-style and long-term agreements cannot be used with tax-exempt financing, the interest in and viability of leaseback arrangements with commercial parking operators has been sharply reduced.

---

[68] Ibid, p. 93.

[69] Ibid, p. 30.

Obviously, the structure of the deal in a public–private partnership is critical to obtaining tax exempt financing, which can carry an annual interest rate of as much as two percent less than taxable financing. It should be noted that combinations of taxable and tax exempt bonds can still be issued for public–private developments where the strict tests for tax exempt bonds cannot be met (for example, a taxable series of bonds funds from a garage leased or reserved for a private entity, while the tax-exempt series goes towards the public portion of the garage). Also, tax increment districts with single or limited development projects may run afoul of the test relating to sources of funds for repayment of the bonds, jeopardizing tax-exempt financing.

Sizing a Bond Issue

The typical bond issue includes a number of different elements. As discussed previously, construction cost, land acquisition, related design fees, and miscellaneous expenses are considered part of the *project cost*. The project cost will typically be 10 to 15 percent greater than the land and construction cost. There are also *costs of issuance* for counsel, printing, rating agency and trustee fees, and closing costs that are typically one-half to one percent of the amount financed. Other expenses related to the issuance include the underwriter's spread and bond insurance, which can help hold down the interest rate.

It is typical for bond issues to be sold prior to the start of construction. Much of the preparatory and design costs may have already been incurred; therefore it is important to carefully track such expenses for incorporation in the bond amount. Because the bond payment may occur during construction or before sufficient patronage is built to develop funds to pay the first annual payment, it is common to structure the bond payments to defer prinicipal payments for a year or two and to include in the bond an amount sufficient to make interest payments in that period. This is known as "capitalized interest." When bonds are not sold early in the process, "bond anticipation notes" may be issued that provide the necessary funds for cash flow, until the bonds are sold. Interest on this interim financing would then be included in the permanent financing.

Conversely, since the bond funds are paid to the municipality, they may be invested until required to pay contractors. A 1984 study[70] found that owners should estimate the potential interest earned during the construction draw down using percentage curves given in the study rather than a straight line monthly draw down. Also, there would be interest earned during the first year on the debt service reserve and the capitalized interest. These deductions from the bond amount help to moderate the overall total of funds to be borrowed. Note that one of the arbitrage provisions of the TRA of 1986 is that the short-term investment of such funds cannot return an interest of more than the interest rate paid to the bond holders.

As seen in Table 14–35, the differences in financing requirements can make a significant difference in the amount of funds that must be borrowed as well as the interest rate. In order to put the cost of financing a parking structure in proper perspective, the amount of financing and the necessary monthly income required per space necessary for the facility to be financed without subsidy from other sources is calculated for a 1,000 space structure under three scenarios: G.O. bond, parking revenue bond, and COP, all of which are tax exempt. Clearly the lowest cost option is the G.O. bond, but the COP is only marginally more expensive. Primarily because of the coverage requirements, the structure built with parking revenue bonds would have to yield more than twice the revenue of the tax-exempt G.O. bond to be financed as a stand-alone facility.

Not-for Profit Entities

Traditionally, institutions tended to view parking simply as a cost of operating the institution, but they increasingly finance new parking facilities by spreading the burden to all parkers in the system. Where the new parking structure represents a fairly small proportion of the total system spaces, the incremental cost to all users can be quite small. For example, if the 1,000 space structure in Table 14–34 is built with tax-exempt bonds by a university with 20,000 annual permit

[70] E. Carlton Heeseler and William Arons, *Parking Facility Construction Payment Schedule Study* (Washington, D.C.: National Parking Association, 1984).

Table 14–35 Project and Financing Costs for Typical 1,000 Space Structure

(1998 dollars)	Tax-Exempt G.O. Bond		Tax-Exempt Revenue Bond		Tax-Exempt COP		Private Mortgage Financing		(Private Mortgage row label)
Construction Costs	$8,500 /space	$8,500,000	$8,500 /space	$8,500,000	$8,500 /space	$8,500,000	$8,500 /space	$8,500,000	Construction Costs
Land Cost		$1,000,000		$1,000,000		$1,000,000		$1,000,000	Land Cost
Special Equipment or Furnishings		$300,000		$300,000		$300,000		$300,000	Special Equipment or Furnishings
Architectural and Engineering Fees	5% Const cost	$425,000	5% Const cost	$425,000	5% Const cost	$425,000	5% Const Cost	$425,000	Architectural and Engineering Fees
Project Representative during Construction	$20,000 /month	$180,000	$20,000 /month	$180,000	$20,000 /month	$180,000	$20,000 /month	$180,000	Project Representative during Construction
Permits and Fees		$—		$—		$—	1.50% Const Cost	$127,500	Permits and Fees
Surveys and Testing		$100,000		$100,000		$100,000		$100,000	Surveys and Testing
Design Contingency	2.5% Const cost	$212,500	2.5% Const cost	$212,500	2.5% Const cost	$212,500	2.5% Const Cost	$212,500	Design Contingency
Field Contingency	5% Const cost	$425,000	5% Const cost	$425,000	5% Const cost	$425,000	5% Const Cost	$425,000	Field Contingency
Total Project Cost		**$11,142,500**		**$11,142,500**		**$11,142,500**		**$11,270,000**	**Total Project Cost**
Project Cost/Space		$11,143		$11,143		$11,143		$11,270	
Financing and Other Costs	20 year g.o. bond		20 year rev bond		20 year cop		20 yr mortgage		**Financing and Other Costs**
Equity	7% 0% Proj Cost	$—	8.5% 0% Proj Cost	$—	7.5% 5% Proj Cost	$557,125	9% 10% Proj Cost	$(1,127,000)	Equity
Developer Fee	0% Proj Cost	$—	0% Proj Cost	$—	0% Proj Cost	$—	5% Proj Cost	$563,500	Developer Fee
Feasibility Study		$25,000		$25,000		$25,000		$25,000	Feasibility Study
Administrative Cost	$10,000 /month	$180,000	$10,000 /month	$180,000	$10,000 /month	$180,000	$10,000 /month	$180,000	Administrative Costs
Costs of Finance Issuance	1% of amt finan	$121,150	1% of amt finan	$138,750	1% of amt finan	$127,600	1% Proj Cost	$112,700	Legal Fees
Capitalized Interest	1 yr interest	$848,050	1 yr interest	$1,179,375	1 yr interest	$957,000	5% Const Cost	$425,000	Interim Const Financing Cost
Underwriter's Spread	1.50% bond amt	$181,725	1.50% bond amt	$208,125	1.50% bond amt	$191,400	2% Mort Amt	$233,700	Mortgage Fees
Bond Insurance	0.50% prin & int	$114,357	1.00% prin & int	$293,237	1.00% prin & int	$250,331			
Debt Service Reserve	1 yr payment	$—	1 yr payment	$1,466,185	1 yr payment	$—			
Construction Fund Earnings	5.6% Const Cost	$(623,980)	5.6% Const Cost	$(623,980)	5.6% Const Cost	$(623,980)			
Debt Service Reserve Earnings	5% Reserve	$—	5% Reserve	$(73,309)	5% Reserve	$—			
Capitalized Interest Earnings	5% Cap Int	$(42,403)	5% Cap Int	$(58,969)	5% Cap Int	$(47,850)			
Subtotal Financing and Other Costs		**$803,900**		**$2,734,414**		**$1,616,626**		**$412,900**	**Subtotal Financing and Other Costs**
Total Financing Required		**$11,946,400**		**$13,876,914**		**$12,759,126**		**$11,682,900**	**Total Financing Required**
Financing and Other Costs, % of project		7%		24.5%		15%		4%	Financing and Other Costs, % of project
Total Amount Financed		**$12,115,000**		**$13,875,000**		**$12,760,000**		**$11,685,000**	**Total Amount Financed**
Annual Debt Service		**$1,143,570**		**$1,466,185**		**$1,251,656**		**$1,280,051**	**Annual Debt Service**
Annual Income on Reserve Funds		$—		$(73,309)		$—		$1,051,650	Interest on Annual Debt
Annual Operating Expense	$500 /sp/yr	$500,000	$500 /sp/yr	$500,000	$500 /sp/yr	$500,000		$269,841	Annual Depreciation (straight line for 31.5 yrs)
								$1,168,290	Property Taxes
Total Annual Expenses and Debt Service		$1,643,570		$1,892,876		$1,751,656	$500 /sp/yr	$500,000	Operating Expenses
								$2,989,781	Total Annual Capital and Operating Expenses
Monthly Income Required Per Space	1.0 coverage	$136.96	2.0 coverage	$315.48	1.0 coverage	$145.97	15% IRR	$169,050	Required Annual Return to Investors
								$3,158,831	Annual Income req'd to satisfy investors
								$249.15	Monthly Income to satisfy investors

Source: Walker Parking Consultants, 1999.

holders, the $1.4 million annual cost could be recouped by increasing fees for all users by $70 per year or less than $10 per month for the normal school year. However, if the same structure is built by a hospital with 3,000 employees and rates for visitors are not raised, each of the employees would have to pay another $460 per year or about $39 per month more for the parking improvement. That might not seem like much to those paying $100 per month or more to park in a CBD, but it can cause significant labor unrest at an institution where parking fees were previously $10 per month. (Everything is relative!) One of the biggest challenges for not-for-profits seeking financing of parking improvements is that due to the typically low rates and small size of the system they usually present significant risks to investors.

Private Financing

Because of the differences in financing and taxation of private developments, there are significant differences between the way publicly and privately financed projects are structured, not the least of which is that the pro forma statement of income and expenses is stated in a completely different manner. Most public entities are not concerned with the income tax implications of owning real estate, but private investors are. The investment decision for a privately financed (nontax-exempt) facility considers the depreciation of the asset and the income and property taxes paid. Moreover, the private investor is concerned with making an adequate return on the investment, while a public entity usually just wants to break even.

Prior to the TRA of 1986, it was quite possible for a private investor to build and finance a parking facility and lease it to a public entity or not-for-profit institution for less than the public entity would pay in debt service for tax-exempt financing. The TRA significantly closed this gap so that the "leaseback" option will usually cost the entity a little more than public bond financing. However there may remain other advantages to doing private financing under a leaseback arrangement, primarily in procurement efficiencies (i.e., they are not subject to the nuances of procurement regulators). Also, they preserve the entity's credit rating or debt capacity to finance other projects, since the financing would be "off the balance sheet" of the municipality or not-for-profit institution.

CHAPTER 15
Activity Centers

Robert T. Dunphy
Resident Fellow, Transportation
Urban Land Institute

Centers of economic activity require significant levels of transportation access in order to serve a large market—in some cases an entire region. Their size makes them significant traffic generators, highly visible compared to individual strip shopping centers, industrial plants, and highway-oriented developments that collectively cause much more traffic. The traditional activity center is represented by the skyline of a downtown central business district (CBD) or by specialized facilities, such as transportation terminals, medical centers, and academic complexes. Recently, much of the urban growth has been in suburban clusters of regional shopping centers, office parks, and industrial users.

The location of activity centers follows the real estate maxim of "location, location, location." The effect, however, is "traffic, traffic, and traffic"—either vehicular, transit, or both—which necessitates the planning, design, and implementation of major transportation infrastructure improvements. The economic success of many suburban centers has created traffic problems that could lead to their undoing or at least limit their potential. The perception of gridlock and parking problems may encourage businesses to leave for more distant locales and for governments to limit further development. While inadequate attention to the transportation needs of activity centers can make them seem like a transportation problem, many communities have determined that clustering of development into activity centers is part of the solution for coping with growth.

This chapter discusses activity centers in general—both the traditional form in downtowns and the "suburban activity centers" (SACs) or "edge cities." This latter type is clearly the most prevalent emerging urban form of commercial activity in North America. These centers have located along major highway corridors, often at the intersection of two freeways; and they must cope with both the transportation demands of their own businesses and residents, as well as regional traffic on the periphery.

Development and Types of Activity Centers

The term "activity center" refers to a relatively large concentration of development, usually containing a mix of land uses, especially office and retail. When cities were dominated by their downtown (and smaller cities still are), the CBDs contained the major businesses and retailers in the region. Following the expansion of the suburban population after World War II, retailing followed in the 1950s, and businesses were not far behind. Downtowns are probably still the largest activity centers in most regions, although the overwhelming majority of future development is likely to be in the suburbs, which are the major focus of this chapter. Activity centers may also be institutional complexes, such as major government centers, colleges and universities, and medical centers. As an example of their prominence as traffic generators, the San Diego Association of Governments estimated that the top ten activity centers accounted for 6 percent of regional miles traveled. Moreover, this definition, topped by the major airport, four military facilities, two universities, and four shopping centers, did not take into account the extensive office development around these regional shopping centers, or the downtown.[1]

One of the most recent developments in activity centers is urban entertainment centers, which offer a combination of entertainment, dining, and retail—the "trinity of synergy"—within a pedestrian-oriented environment. The early urban

---

[1] San Diego Region Activity Centers, map (San Diego, Calif.: San Diego Association of Governments, April 1997).

entertainment centers have been in urban districts, often parts of revitalized downtowns such as One Colorado in Pasadena and Santa Monica's Third Street Promenade, both in California; and Times Square in New York City. Urban entertainment complexes, in contrast, are cohesive, managed properties with tenants, often located on "greenfield" sites as part of activity centers. Examples of these include three in California—Ontario Mills in Ontario, Universal City Walk in Hollywood, and the Entertainment Center at Irvine Spectrum in Irvine.[2] In addition to entirely new complexes, urban and retail uses are being added to existing shopping centers and large mixed-use developments. One of the challenges of such developments to transportation planners is that they are so new, their effects on traffic and parking are still being understood.

The largest activity centers typically cover no more than 6 square miles. They typically have:

- more jobs than resident labor force;

- major amounts of retail;

- some master planning;

- mixed office and retail, and often hotel, residential, or other commercial uses;

- higher development densities than surrounding areas;

- recognition as a focal point for activity within the community.

Most often activity centers are in one or more of the following forms:

- CBD;

- office park of several hundred or more acres;

- retail center of 100 or more acres;

- mixed-use center of several hundred to thousands of acres;

- large office corridor stretching a mile or more;

- major activity center or "outlying downtown";

- university, medical center, or other institutional complexes;

- major recreational facility with ancillary uses.

Activity Centers, Corridors, and Subareas

Major traffic generators can include centers as well as corridors or subareas. Such subtle distinctions may be useful to planners but probably have little relevance to citizens, elected officials, or transportation professionals. If the area has an identity and generates large amounts of traffic, it will probably need to be addressed as a unique transportation need. *Centers*, as defined by Cervero, tend to be well-defined, focused concentrations of development, with relatively high density and a mix of land uses, such as Perimeter Center situated 12 miles north of downtown Atlanta.[3] By 1998, the Central Perimeter submarket was the largest in Atlanta, with 19 million sq ft of office space.[4] *Corridors*, on the other hand, include sprawling developments such as the Route 1 corridor outside Princeton, New Jersey, which runs for 8 miles and contained 10 million sq ft of office development in the 1980s.[5] The Princeton Area office market was estimated to

---

[2] Michael D. Beyard, et al., *Developing Urban Entertainment Centers* (Washington, D.C.: Urban Land Institute, 1998, pp. 23, 24, 27).

[3] Robert Cervero, *America's Suburban Centers: The Land Use-Transportation Link* (Boston, Mass.: Cambridge University Press, 1989, p. 16).

[4] *ULI Market Profiles 1998: North America* (Washington, D.C.: Urban Land Institute, 1998, p. 7).

[5] Robert Cervero, *America's Suburban Centers: The Land Use-Transportation Link* (Boston, Mass.: Cambridge University Press, 1989, pp. 96, 99).

have growth to 25 million sq ft of space by 1996.[6] *Subareas* may follow transportation or topographic corridors and boundaries and typically may be an entire community. Subareas are an important part of the urban transportation planning process, typically involving a much greater area than that of activity centers.

There are a number of types of activity centers. These include downtowns, education institutions, medical centers, airports, industrial parks, theme parks, stadiums, and other major facilities. Each is very specialized in nature. Most vary significantly from facility to facility and warrant highly individualized study. While it is beyond the scope of this handbook to treat each of these in depth, the first three listed above are covered in overview form in the following sections of this chapter. Generally, the methodology outlined in the latter part of this chapter is applicable to most activity centers. As stated earlier, the major orientation of this chapter is for the SAC, where the most change is expected. However, since many of the older centers are evolving into more urbanized developments, it is important for planners to recognize some of the best transportation practices in downtowns and adapt as appropriate.

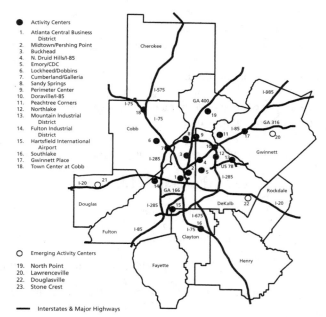

Figure 15–1   Atlanta's SACs

Source: Atlanta Regional Commission, 1998.

Central Business Districts: The Original Activity Centers

Downtowns have historically been the largest and oldest activity centers within urban areas. Many date from preautomobile history when travel distance limitations virtually required nearly all businesses to be located in one central area. Most *urban area* downtowns (as distinguished from suburban business districts or downtowns) have evolved under different development and transportation policies than those of the suburbs. Most have also been located at what became the hub of the area transportation system. Atlanta, for example, was originally named Terminus because it served as the center of a 19th century railroad network. Atlanta's downtown is now the crossing of three interstate routes and one other radial freeway, compared to its suburban centers that are typically located along one major route or at the crossing of a radial and a circumferential route, as shown Figure 15–1.

Real Estate Market Trends

Traditionally the dominant business and industry center of a region, downtowns are struggling to recast their roles and functions in the economy and society of metropolitan areas. Demographic trends have eroded their prime market, and suburban centers have increased competition for traditional users. Technology has allowed businesses to move large numbers of workers to "back office" locations, linked through telecommunications. Downtown is being redefined in many communities as one of many "cities of the mind," which include urban universities, museums, and hospital complexes.[7] Canadian cities, which, unlike their American counterparts, have not lost their appeal as places to live, work, and visit, face similar economic challenges. McKellar reported that "the split in office market absorption between downtown and the suburbs over the last decade is remarkably similar in Canada and the United States." This suggests similar economic trends related to office markets, with the result that "suburbs are hot, downtown is not."[8]

---

[6] *Princeton Area Real Estate Market* (Princeton, N.J.: GMH Realty, 1996, p. 1).

[7] *ULI on the Future* (Washington, D.C.: Urban Land Institute, 1993, pp. 52–55).

[8] James McKellar, "Downtowns Emerging in New Forms," *Ivy Business Quarterly* (London, Ontario: Ivey School of Business, University of Western Ontario, summer 1996).

To real estate professionals, the bottom line for downtowns is the performance of the property market. ERE/Yarmouth ranked CBD office markets based on over 100 respondents' ratings of property values, rents, and future conditions; and they found that "with a few exceptions, suburban markets continue to outperform downtown markets." The *exceptions* (i.e., the downtown markets that are attracting new development, more investors, supporting higher rents, and providing competitive yields on investments), were identified as 24-hour cities. Their common characteristics included a critical mass of residential, office, and retail uses within walking distance, good public transportation use, and low crime rates. The city centers in the major U.S. metro areas meeting these criteria were: Boston; New York; Washington, D.C.; Miami; Chicago; Minneapolis; Seattle; and San Francisco. Other cities in range of the 24-hour city status that were not included in the surveys but met the requirements were: Baltimore, Cincinnati, Philadelphia, Portland, Spokane, San Jose, and San Diego.[9]

Employment Trends

A healthy real estate market does not necessarily lead to increased travel, however, unless real estate values increase enough to justify the construction of additional space. Downtown office employment in both the United States and Canada has been recently driven by growth in just two sectors of the economy: finance, insurance, and real estate (FIRE); and business services. While business service growth will be healthy, FIRE employment has been flat.[10] These overall trends are, of course, subject to the economy of individual markets. At the end of the 1990s, for example, Boston was considered one of the strongest downtown office markets in the eastern United States. Strong leasing activity was absorbing much of the available vacant space, and new buildings were under development. Improving market conditions in Seattle caused several developers to dust off long-standing plans, and thirteen buildings were proposed for an additional 3.3 million sq ft of space. One of the worst performing downtown office markets had been Dallas. Even there, however, rents started to rise and absorption turned positive in 1996, leading to a hope that "the Dallas CBD may be positioned for a comeback."[11] The leading markets in 1998 are shown in Table 15–1.

Population Trends

Most CBDs have experienced a loss of population during the last several decades as residents moved out to suburban locations. This trend erodes the market for retail and other services, causing them to leave and making the downtown even less attractive to residents. Preserving the central area as the heart of the community is becoming better understood as the responsibility of elected leaders and the private sector. This "core" focus is an important part of many regional transportation strategies as well, since getting people downtown offers the widest options to driving; and keeping them there allows many trips to be made without moving the car. To counter powerful economic trends, a public strategy is essential, backed up by private investment. Retail, sports, and entertainment are often part of downtown revitalization plans. To succeed, however, it is essential to maintain the population base. For example, successful redevelopment in Fort Worth covered a 14-block area of buildings built or renovated to capture much of its frontier history and included cinemas, restaurants, nightclubs,

Figure 15–2 New urban entertainment projects, such as this one by Forest City Development, have contributed to the revitalization of Times Square.

Source: *Developing Urban Entertainment Centers,* Urban Land Institute, 1998.

---

[9] *ULI on the Future: Smart Growth* (Washington, D.C.: Urban Land Institute, 1998, p. 54).

[10] James McKellar, "Downtowns Emerging in New Forms" (London: Ivey Business Quarterly, summer 1996).

[11] *ULI 1997 Real Estate Forecast: Mid Year Outlook by Sector, Area, and Enterprise* (Washington, D.C.: Urban Land Institute, 1997).

museums, apartments, and office buildings. However, a strong market is provided by the fact that 750,000 people reside within 15 minutes of downtown; and it has been growing larger and richer.[12]

The challenge of maintaining a population base is shown by St. Louis, where regional population has been stagnant until recently. Despite some significant achievements in revitalizing downtown neighborhoods during the 1980s, St. Louis has seen an erosion of the inner city population, with growth occurring on the periphery of the region (Figure 15–3). The population the area is losing is not only the primary support for downtown retailers, but also the prime transit market.

Characteristics of Downtowns

Downtowns typically exhibit the following characteristics:

- highest concentration of employment within the area;

- high concentration of work trips;

- high development density;

- synergy among downtown development;

- focus of highway and transit systems;

- highest transportation accessibility within the urban area;

- highest transit utilization within the area;

- extensive network of sidewalks and other pedestrianways;

Table 15–1   Downtown Office Markets with Lowest Vacancy Rates, 1998 (Ranked in Order from the Lowest)

San Jose
San Francisco
Boston
Charlotte '
Salt Lake City

Source: CB Commercial Office Vacancy Rate, cited in Dean Schwanke, *ULI 1998 Real Estate Forecast*, Washington, D.C.: Urban Land Institute, p. 30.

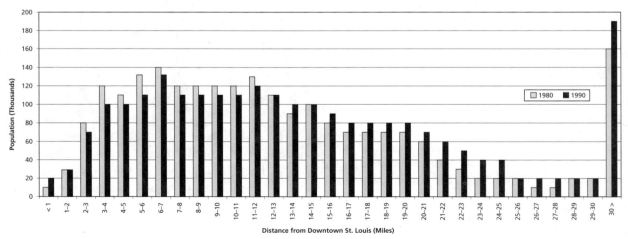

Figure 15–3   Population Trends in St. Louis

Source: Robert T. Dunphy, et al., *Moving Beyond Gridlock: Traffic and Development*, Washington, D.C.: Urban Land Institute, page 101.

---

[12] Thomas Black, *Fort Worth: Maintaining Downtown Vitality* (Washington, D.C.: Urban Land Institute, February 1998, p. 79).

Table 15–2 Peak-Hour Person Trips by Mode to Selected Central Business Districts

	Year	Peak One-Way Persons	Peak Auto	Peak Transit	Peak Percent Auto	Peak Percent Transit
New York	1971	805,300	64,424	740,876	8%	92%
1 hour peak period	1974	738,500	73,850	664,650	10%	90%
	1982	749,100	89,892	659,208	12%	88%
	1994	636,317	n/a	n/a	n/a	n/a
	1996	629,628	80,774	547,776	13%	87%
Washington	1983	169,000	114,920	54,080	68%	32%
3 hour peak period,	1990	403,300	280,000	123,300	69%	32%
except for 1 hour peak	1993	473,000	297,000	176,000	63%	37%
period reported in 1983	1996	429,600	288,000	141,600	59%	41%
Boston	1972	114,736	52,791	61,945	46%	54%
1 hour peak 8-9:00 am	1982	122,035	61,689	60,346	51%	49%
Toronto	1985	228,100	37,700	190,400	17%	83%
3 hour peak period	1991	295,100	54,000	241,000	18%	82%
	1995	302,100	50,500	251,600	17%	83%
Houston	1976	670,741	574,825	95,916	86%	14%
11.5 hour survey period	1979	659,932	572,821	87,111	87%	13%
for 1982 & 1986	1982	649,107	550,443	98,757	85%	15%
	1986	701,465	514,174	187,018	73%	27%

Source: Cordon counts conducted by respective MPO's/cities, compiled by ULI.

- shared or other public parking;

- high percentage of land dedicated to transportation right-of-way—often up to 25 percent allocated to streets, sidewalks, and alleys;

- less off-street service and loading facilities than suburban areas;

- more widely spread peak period travel demand than outlying business districts.

The net result of changes in the CBD differs for each city. In general, travel patterns have changed and trip purposes are somewhat different; but overall travel levels remain the same or have increased. The problem faced by transportation planners is to provide services to meet the new characteristics of the CBD.

Travel Characteristics at CBDs

CBD trips may be made by a wide range of modes including auto, taxi, truck, transit, bike, or walk. In the largest urban areas, transit is often the dominant mode for workers to the CBD. Canadian cities of comparable size show higher use of transit to the downtown areas than do U.S. cities. Table 15–2 summarizes data for several North American cities. Four of these are among the leading rail transit cities. The longest available trend data is from New York City, where the number of persons entering midtown Manhattan declined from 805,000 in 1971 to 630,000 in 1996. While the overwhelming means of access to the New York CBD is transit, the number of transit trips declined by 26% over the quarter century, and the number of persons entering by auto increased by 25%. The percent of peak hour trips entering the New York CBD by transit declined from 92% in 1971 to 88% in 1982, and has remained relatively stable since then. Toronto, on the other hand has seen continued growth in the number of persons entering the downtown, despite the lingering effects of the 1990s recession, with both auto and transit trips increasing by about one third. While not generally considered a mjaor transit city, Houston's aggressive transit investments in the 1980s resulted in a sharp jump of persons entering downtown Houston by bus — a gain of 88,000 daytime riders between 1982 and 1986.

During the last two decades, as the CBD's role as part of the region has changed, land uses have changed signficantly, along with travel patterns. Between 1980 and 1990, the number of regional commute trips made within or to the central city increased by 7.5 percent. (Although it was not possible to separate out the CBD in the 1990 Census, it was surely the dominant work destination.) Intrasuburban trips over the same time period increased by 27.5 percent, to almost the level of city-destined commutes. In 1990, about three-quarters of metro transit commuting was destined to the city, most likely to the CBD.[13]

Travel patterns in Atlanta showed similar trends. In 1960, three counties (suburban Fulton, DeKalb, and Clayton) sent more than 30 percent of workers to jobs in Atlanta. By 1990, only DeKalb had such high rates of out-commuting, while suburban DeKalb, Cobb, and Clayton counties emerged as work destinations.[14]

A comparison of downtown destinations with suburban centers in Charlotte found that work trips dominated CBD travel, accounting for 51 percent of all trips but only 18 percent in Southpark, a suburban shopping and office center.[15]

Among U.S. metropolitan areas in 1990, the suburb-to-suburb flow is the dominant market. However, the central city ranked close as a work destination in 1990, accounting for 38 percent of work locations, compared to 41.5 percent for

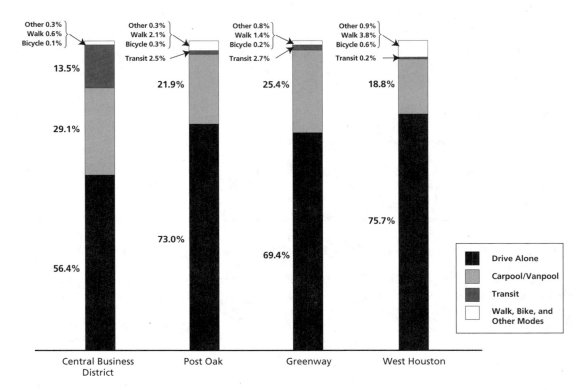

Figure 15–4   Commuting Modes for Downtown Houston and Major Activity Centers

Source: Calthorpe Associates, *Design for Efficient Suburban Activity Centers: Phase I Report*, Washington, D.C.: Federal Transit Administration, March 1997, p. 9.

[13] Charles River Associates, Inc., *TCRP Report 27: Building Transit Ridership* (Washington, D.C.: National Academy Press, 1997, p. 19).

[14] Tadashi Fujii and Truman A. Hartshorn, "The Changing Metropolitan Structure of Atlanta, Georgia: Locations of Functions and Regional Structure in a Multinucleated Urban Area," *Urban Geography* (Silver Spring, Md.: Urban Geography, V.H. Winston & Son, 1995, p. 698).

[15] Wayne A. Walcott and Sallie M. Ives, "The Transportation Service Needs of Non Central Business Districts Activity Centers," *Compendium of Technical Papers* (Washington, D.C.: Institute of Transportation Engineers, 1988, p. 42).

suburban jobs. Trips entirely within the central city were still the dominant travel flow market among metro areas of over one million in population, as well as those under one-half million.[16]

The Commuter and Downtown Travel

CBD workers have many more travel options than those working elsewhere. Driving and parking is often difficult and more expensive than other locations, while transit service is the most convenient in the region. Consequently, commuters are least likely to drive alone and more likely to car pool or ride transit. In Houston for example, a city where the car is considered to be king, one out of seven commuters to downtown rode public transit, compared to less than 3 percent at the largest suburban centers, as shown in Figure 15–4.

A comparison of workers in downtown Washington, D.C., with those in a suburban CBD, a close-in suburban office campus, and a more distant office research park illustrates such sharp differences. As shown in Table 15–3, the majority of workers

Table 15–3   Midday Trip Making in Washington, D.C., Area Activity Centers

	CBD	Suburban CBD	Campus	Park
Midday Trips per Employee	1.4	1.3	1.2	0.9
Midday Vehicle Trips per Employee	0.1	0.3	1.1	0.8
Midday VMT per Employee	0.9	3.5	6.4	12.7
Midday Trips per Employee vs. CBD	1.0	0.9	0.9	0.6
Veh. Trips per Employee vs. CBD	1.0	3.3	11.1	7.8
VMT per Employee vs. CBD	1.0	4.0	7.5	14.9

Source: Douglas and Evans, "Urban Design, Urban Form, and Employee Travel Behavior," TRB Transportation Planning Applications Conference, Washington, D.C.: U.S. Department of Transportation, 1997.

to the CBD (57 percent), rode transit—a mix of heavy rail, bus, and commuter rail. Transit use for the suburban CBD was 14 percent, but only 2 percent for the other two lower density areas. Over 90 percent of workers at the two lower density suburban locations drive to work alone, while only 30 percent of those working in downtown Washington did. Walking trips were virtually nonexistent in the two campus settings, but 3–4 percent in the suburban and urban CBDs respectively.

The mode of travel for commuting workers reflects the downtown density, demographics in the labor shed for downtown commuters, the cost of downtown parking, and the level of transit service. Table 15–4 depicts mode of travel data for selected cities. These data represent weekday commuting trips to downtown, in contrast to Table 15–2 which reports only peak hour trips, but includes non-work trips and through trips as well. The cities which both sets of data are available show similar patterns, with New York and Toronto having the highest transit share of commute trips to the CBD, followed by Chicago, Montreal, San Francisco, Boston, Washington and Vancouver, B.C. For other cities reporting 1990 CBD commuting data, transit use was reported by fewer than one third of workers, with most of the rest driving to work. Among the cities for which comparative data was available, only Houston

Table 15-4   CBD Work Trips by Transit

	1980	1990
Atlanta	n/a	16%
Boston	58%	43%
Calgary	44%	n/a
Chicago	74%	61%
Dallas-Ft. Worth	19%	n/a
Denver	n/a	17%
Edmonton	50%	30%
Houston	15%	17%
Los Angeles	24%	15%
Montreal	67%	58%
New York	60%	80%
Ottawa	54%	31%
St. Louis	27%	11%
San Diego	14%	n/a
San Francisco	52%	50%
Toronto	75%	64%
Vancouver	46%	35%
Washington, DC	43%	36%
Phoenix	n/a	5%
Portland*	32%	*

* Note: 1990 JTW mode split to the CBD is inconsistent with other data, and may have been subject to Census Bureau geo-coding errors.

Sources: 1980 CBD Work Trips taken from Susan Hanson, ED. *The Geography of Urban Transportation* (New York: Guilford Press), p. 232 and Robert Cervero, "Urban Transit in Canada: Integration and Innovation at Its Best," Transportation Quarterly, July 1986, p. 294. 1990 CBD Work Trips taken from Jorney-to-Work Census Transportation statistics gathered from individual metropolitan planning organizations.

[16] Alan E. Pisarski, *Commuting in America II: The Second National Report on Commuting Patterns and Trends. Lansdowne, Virginia* (Lansdowne, Va.: Eno Transportation Foundation, Inc., 1996, pp. 75–76).

showed an increase in the transit share among downtown commuters — a consequence of a major transit expansion and freeway bus service.

Perhaps of even greater significance than the commute was the opportunity for midday trips once downtown. Workers in the Washington CBD actually made more than 40 percent more trips than their suburban counterparts in the suburban office research park, but the bulk of them (80 percent) were walk trips. One half of the CBD trips were to eat lunch, while most people working in the suburban office settings reported eating at their desks. The combined midday trip comparisons show how dominant the private auto is, not just for getting to work but for other work and nonwork needs. Employees in the suburban office research park made eight times as many vehicle trips per worker and drive 15 times more miles than downtown workers, just during the day.[17] Similar results were found in Houston, where a survey of workers in the CBD and selected suburban centers found that downtown workers made 12 percent more trips—primarily nonwork pedestrian trips within the downtown.[18]

A survey of the effect of a new retail center that opened in 1995 in downtown Indianapolis found that Circle Centre captured a significant share of the lunch crowd—21 percent of office workers reported eating lunch there at least once the previous week. More significantly, Circle Centre had a dramatic effect on midday shopping by office workers, which increased from 20 percent before the center's opening to 33 percent afterwards. In addition, 12 percent reported shopping at other times during the day, up sharply from 8 percent before.[19]

Like SACs, travel characteristics for downtowns vary substantially. Size, density, parking, transit availability and fares, accessibility by available travel modes, and local policy affect mode choice, vehicle occupancies, and parking characteristics as does the very nature of downtown activities. Small downtowns may generate their peak period travel demand over concentrated periods as short as 15 or 20 minutes. Larger more diverse downtowns generate their peaks over as long as 2 hours or more. With this range in characteristics, transportation planning efforts should be based on careful studies and accurate data for the specific downtown being considered.

Planning Concepts and Principles

Urban area downtowns require a different approach due to their generally different nature. Nevertheless, many of these access principles will be the same as for SACs. Concepts and principles that may differ are:

- Major access and circulation routes should be concentrated on or near the periphery of the area.

- The core area should be devoted to high intensity uses, with major reliance on transit and pedestrian circulation in large downtowns.

- Transit service, where available, should be provided to at least major concentrations of employment and patron- or visitor-oriented businesses; transit utilization should be encouraged, especially where roadway level of service, air quality, or other conditions would significantly benefit.

- Transit priorities and amenities should be provided where transit usage is being encouraged.

- Continuity of pedestrian circulation in plan and elevation should be provided.

- Parking should be separated for long-term (employee), short-term (visitor or patron), and errand or service purposes. The most convenient parking, on- or off-street, should be reserved for short-term and errand parking.

- Curb-loading zones should be provided in accordance with actual loading activity and be located to minimize conflicts with pedestrian and vehicle circulation.

---

[17] Douglas and Evans, "Urban Design, Urban Form, and Urban Travel Behavior," *Proceedings of the 6th TRB Conference on the Application of Transportation Planning Methods* (Washington, D.C.: TRB, 1997, pp. 298–306).

[18] Rice Center, Houston's *Major Activity Centers and Worker Travel Behavior* (Houston, Texas: Houston Galveston Area Council, 1987, pp. V–72).

[19] Tom Dwyer, "Downtown Shopping: The Impact of Circle Centre," *ICSC Research Quarterly* (New York, N.Y.: International Council of Shopping Centers, Winter 1996, p. 8).

Table 15–5   Transportation Planning Principles for Typical Downtowns

Traffic Circulation Principles
- A hierarchy of downtown streets should be established (for example, major arterials, minor arterials, collector and distributor streets, and local streets) that defines the relative importance of moving through traffic and providing access to property. This hierarchy should be implemented through the use of street design techniques, traffic control measures, and parking regulations.
- The CBD street system should have sufficient* traffic capacity to minimize congestion and handle peak-hour traffic loads during the planning period.
- Non-CBD traffic should be directed away from the core area utilizing alternative or bypass routes.
- The CBD street system should provide adequate* access and circulation for CBD traffic.
- The central area street system should provide direct access for emergency and service vehicles.
- The CBD circulation system should connect with both existing and proposed major thoroughfares beyond the CBD (i.e., radial freeways and principal arterial streets).
- The CBD street system should provide more than one opportunity to reach a destination.
- The CBD circulation pattern should be easily comprehended by the average driver and provide relatively direct routings without circuitous travel.
- The circulation plan should be designed for incremental implementation with individual elements available for use as they are completed.
- Streets should be designed to provide continuous routings and continuity of capacity.
- The CBD circulation plan should allow drivers to circulate around the blocks or areas that generate high traffic volumes.
- Major downtown streets should be free from conflicts with major at-grade railroad crossings.
- Complex intersections and multiphase signals should be avoided.
- Streets and land development should be designed to complement each other. Arterial streets should border rather than sever CBD land use activity areas. Land parcels should not be so large as to make circulation difficult; the street pattern should not cut land areas into parcels too small to permit sound development.

Parking Principles
- CBD parking should be accessible from the primary CBD approach routes and located in direct contact with major vehicle entry points.
- CBD parking facilities should be distributed in relation to the directional distribution of vehicular approach to the area.
- The parking system should provide space for explicit use of long-term, short-term, visitor, and errand parking.
- CBD parking system should have sufficient capacity* to accommodate present and future peak parking demands.
- CBD parking, where possible, should facilitate dual or shared usage of facilities.
- Shuttle buses should connect peripheral commuter parking facilities with ultimate CBD destinations.
- Parking should not be permitted on major thoroughfares of medium and large downtowns, where priority is given to through-movements* rather than local access.
- Facilities must be provided to accommodate the needs of regular delivery vehicles, quick-stop service (such as mail and newspaper trucks), and special purpose vehicles such as construction and maintenance trucks.

Pedestrian Circulation Principles
- Continuity of pedestrian circulation between downtown destinations should be a priority.
- A suitable environment for pedestrians should be established. This should include, in addition to other amenities, protection from weather, especially in high pedestrian volume areas.
- Pedestrian access from major CBD parking facilities and transit stops or stations to CBD land uses should be located to avoid traffic* conflicts and enhance safety.
- Major pedestrianways should be properly defined and identified by landscaping and lighting.
- To maintain safe and convenient pedestrian crossings, streets should have no more than four moving lanes, unless medians with suitable pedestrian refuges are provided.

Transit Principles
- Surface transit should be given priority to use street facilities.
- Direct transit access should be provided to primary CBD destination areas for the convenience of passengers.
- Land uses should be located to capitalize on transit facilities as well as to maximize the market for transit.
- To the extent possible, the principle of through-routing should be applied to all CBD transit facilities to avoid looping and artificial doubling of transit vehicle loads.

* The degree of preference to transit and pedestrians compared to motor vehicles varies greatly for different downtowns. The clearest indication of the extent to which vehicles will be served is in the level of service (LOS), which is generally lower in downtown than anywhere else in the region. Cities may prefer to be even more restrictive, limiting parking and vehicle access. An example is the 1972 downtown plan for Portland, Oregon, which called for reducing reliance on the automobile and increasing transit travel—including a lid on downtown parking. The principles indicated here require judgments on the relative priority given to motor vehicles compared to pedestrians, transit, and "quality of life" values. Such conflicts should be established as part of the downtown plan.

Source: Adapted from the Institute of Transportation Engineers, *Transportation Planning Handbook*, Englewood Cliffs, N.J.: Prentice-Hall, 1992.

- Parking should be utilized on a shared basis rather than restricted to individual businesses to achieve maximum effectiveness of available facilities; lots or garages serving the public should be encouraged.

- Employee parking should be located away from the immediate downtown core area to the extent practical to reduce traffic circulation there.

- In larger downtowns, free intra-CBD transit service, local bus circulator service, and closer spacing of rail transit stops can enhance circulation.

- Total parking demand rates will be lower than for suburban locations; in large areas, the ratio may be as low as one-half of suburban levels. In a few of the largest downtowns, it is a small fraction of corresponding demand rates due to mode splits and vehicle occupancies.

- Access to downtown developments should link directly to parking or transit facilities where possible to facilitate access.

- Pedestrian facilities should be provided with adequate capacity and minimum conflicts with other modes. Grade-separated pedestrian system segments may be appropriate in some larger downtowns.

Colleges, Universities, and Medical Centers

Colleges, universities, and medical centers represent a specialized form of activity center. They are located in downtowns and SACs as well as on separate campuses in cities, suburbs, and rural locations. As with downtowns, the high degree of variability makes each academic and medical institution and individual case for planning. One significant difference is that such institutions are more likely to operate under centralized management, providing greater leverage for transportation options and a higher degree of central planning. The specific characteristics of the institution, its policies, and the surrounding environment need to be known in order to provide a basis for planning. In that respect, it is similar to a traffic access study for a major development, with the potential that the ownership has a greater degree of control over the end users than a major landowner or developer. Surveys of existing characteristics are usually necessary before transportation planning can be initiated for existing institutions; for new medical and academic campuses, characteristics may be inferred from comparable projects and adjusted to reflect policies anticipated for the new campus.

College Operations, Policies, and Transportation Markets

Colleges and universities can generally be classified as resident, commuter, or combination campuses. This classification refers to the predominant makeup of the students studying there. Schools with high percentages of commuting students require much more external access capability and, in most cases, substantially more campus parking. Some "resident" campuses may have a large percentage of their students living in on-campus dormitories—generally within walking distance of classes. Others may rely on off-campus housing. Universities with extensive off-campus housing or remote parking facilities often operate a campus transit system to serve them.

The campus population is made up of three basic components: students, faculty, and staff—each with their own unique travel patterns and transportation needs. Transportation planning is facilitated by the fact that there is usually good information on the class and staff locations and schedules. These can be supplemented by counts of persons or vehicles entering and exiting the campus throughout the day and provide more accurate indications of campus activity.

There are two primary types of travel to be considered: access to and from campus and internal travel within campus. In an ideal setting, much of the internal travel is on foot, placing a premium on good pedestrian access between major internal destinations, as well as to parking and external transit terminals. Campus travel is also subject to seasonal peaks during exams or registration, as well as special events such as graduation and sporting events.

Planning transportation for college and university campuses involves not only technical analyses, but also evaluation of existing and potential campus policies. Especially important are university policies toward transportation on- and off-

Table 15–6 Typical College, University, and Medical Campus Transportation Planning Principles

Pedestrian Circulation

1. Continuous pedestrianways (at-grade, below-grade, or above-grade) should link all major activity nodes, including major transit stops and parking facilities.
2. Parking facilities, vehicular circulation routes, bicycle routes, and buildings should be arranged to minimize conflicts between pedestrian and vehicular movements.
3. In academic settings, to adequately accommodate walking between consecutive classes during typical scheduled 10-minute breaks, all classroom buildings should be located within a diameter of approximately 1,500 feet. (This suggests that classroom buildings should be clustered in the core of the campus with supporting buildings [e.g., gymnasiums, practice buildings, laboratories] located toward the periphery).
4. Provisions for handicapped persons should be made where appropriate when designing or modifying pedestrianways.
5. Major pedestrianways should be defined by landscaping and lighting and integrated with the open space system. This will provide a unifying element, linking areas that are not visually linked.
6. Provisions for handicapped persons should be made where possible when designing or modifying pedestrianways.

Transit

1. Campus transit routes should facilitate people-movement to and within the campus and between major parking facilities and trip destinations.
2. Bus stops should be located as near activity nodes as possible.
3. Bus stops should be located to avoid conflicts between passengers and parking maneuvers, driveway access, service vehicle access, or major traffic movements.
4. Commuter bus stops should be as centrally located (in relation to activity intensity) as possible.
5. Major bus stops should be provided with shelter from weather.
6. Partnerships with local transit operators should be pursued.

Bicycles

1. Bicycle transportation to and from medical and academic campuses should be encouraged.
2. Separation of bicycle and pedestrian paths should be provided within the campus when both are provided; bicycles should not be permitted to be ridden on high-volume pedestrian walkways within the campus.
3. Bicycle storage facilities should be located along major campus access routes as close to major buildings or building complexes as possible, for convenience and security.
4. Fees for bicycle storage should be avoided, in order to avoid any impediments to bicycle use.
5. Bicycles should not be permitted to be chained to doors (restrict access), trees (bark is stripped off and trees eventually die), or any fixed structure in a pedestrianway (block passage). Strict enforcement is necessary.

Parking

1. Parking facilities should meet campus needs on-site and discourage the use of adjacent neighborhoods for campus parking unless such parking is acceptable to the community.
2. Parking should be located, designed, and controlled according to two basic categories—long-term and short-term (there may be further subdivisions within each).
3. Parking facilities should be planned to be accessible from the primary approach routes and within acceptable walking distance of building entrances.
4. Street access to major parking facilities should be located and designed to minimize conflicts with pedestrians and not disrupt other on-street traffic movement. Adequate queuing capacity should be designed into each ingress and egress point.
5. Parking facilities should be easily identified by infrequent users of the facilities.
6. Parking facilities should offer security for users and protection of property.
7. Parking regulations and enforcement should ensure that the parking system operates according to the goals of the institution.
8. Shared parking should be encouraged, especially where there are nearby uses whose demands peak at different times of the day, week, or year.

Emergency Access (Medical Centers)

1. The emergency access facility must be easily accessible from all major approach routes. The route(s) leading to emergency entrance(s) must be clearly marked and free of sharp turns or visibility obstructions.
2. The emergency access facility and/or its principal access points should be as far as possible from major intersections and other points of traffic conflict.
3. The emergency access drive should be physically separated from parking facilities, pickup/drop-off areas, truck dock facilities, and any other internal circulation roads used by the public. The emergency access drive should not conflict with significant pedestrian movements.
4. The emergency access drive should provide for "through-movement" for exiting vehicles rather than requiring turning or backing-up maneuvers. An adequate number of bays should be provided to accommodate the peak demand.

Goods and Services

1. Buildings requiring direct deliveries from outside the campus should have convenient access to streets and off-street loading areas.
2. Service functions should be provided from areas away from pedestrianways.
3. Service "spines" or cores should be planned to minimize the number of service areas on-campus.
4. Adequate parking space should be provided adjacent to every loading dock or service door so the anticipated number of service vehicles can be accommodated. Enforcement should prevent unauthorized parking.
5. Building storage areas and mechanical and electrical systems should all be serviceable from the outside service area. Building architectural design should incorporate this principle.
6. Vertical and horizontal alignments and widths of service roads should be designed to accommodate the appropriate vehicles adequately. Obstructions (existing and future) such as low-hanging trees above ground architectural features and other lateral and vertical clearance constraints should be avoided.
7. Deliveries and service to buildings with service access along or crossing major pedestrianways should be prohibited during the hours of maximum pedestrian volumes.

Source: Adapted from the Institute of Transportation Engineers, *Transportation Planning Handbook*, Englewood Cliffs, N.J. Prentice-Hall, 1992.

campus, including student auto ownership, parking availability and financing, transit availability and financing, and parking priorities. Local government policies affecting campus transportation conditions include campus use of municipal parking, resident parking, limited or full-street closures, and transit operating hours. Coordination of campus, municipal, and neighborhood interests is especially critical in serving the overall community transportation needs, as well as preserving "town" and "gown" harmony—and many such conflicts have to do with traffic and parking.

There is such a wide variation in travel modes and parking requirements that it is imperative to recognize the unique nature of each institution's current needs as well as their future operational strategies that may relate to transportation. There may, however, be potential for transferring good ideas from similar settings. For example, the University of Washington's U-PASS provides extensive mobility for students through the regional transit system, helping both the campus and the city. Similar approaches have succeeded at the University of Illinois at Champaign, the University of South Florida, and elsewhere. In Boise, such a program is supported by Boise State, as well as St. Luke's Regional Medical Center, and Saint Alphonsus Regional Medical Center, and ten other major traffic generators.

Transportation planning for a college or university campus is much more transit- and pedestrian-oriented and less auto-dependent than for a downtown. Generally, personal vehicular traffic is either limited or prohibited in campus core areas; only service and emergency vehicles are provided access to every facility. Parking is usually very limited in the core and most spaces are located peripherally. Campus core movements are primarily on foot. Table 15–6 provides a list of planning principles for internal transportation.

Medical Center Operations, Policies, and Transportation Markets

Medical centers have many similarities to colleges and universities in terms of the unique clientele as well as the centralized management. Some have evolved into massive proportions, such as the Texas Medical Center in Houston. Consisting of 42 institutions that collectively employ over 50,000 workers, in addition to over 9,000 volunteers, and served 4.5 million patient visits in 1998, this facility is the size of a small downtown. Its 675 acres contain over 20 million sq ft of space in 100 buildings, as well as 37,000 parking spaces.[20]

Some of the key factors affecting the health care industry are restructuring, increased cooperation, and managed care.[21] Restructuring is likely to lead to a greater emphasis on bottom-line financial performance, possibly including the development of underutilized facilities. Increased cooperation among existing colocated facilities will place a premium on better transportation access. Managed care will continue to reduce the length of stay and increase the share of outpatient services, leading to further requirements for a responsive transportation system.

Medical center transportation must serve a wide variety of clients, including physicians, nursing staff, inpatients, outpatients, and service personnel. Certain facilities may also have significant levels of ambulance and emergency vehicle traffic, as well as students. As discussed in Chapter 14, it is important to recognize the unique needs for parking of different groups—for example designing the employee lot to accommodate afternoon shift time, and the outpatient lot for a morning peak. Those facilities specializing in elective treatment sometimes exhibit fluctuations by season and by strength of the economy. Surveys of such facilities should recognize such fluctuations.

Emergency access is critical to medical centers; usually it takes top-access priority. Usually minimization of conflicts with other vehicles and pedestrians is a requirement; emergency rooms are generally located away from outpatient, visitor, and employee entrances.

The automobile is the dominant mode of travel by certain segments of the medical center clientele—especially physicians and patients. However, transit access is important for many users of urban facilities and even in some suburban institutions for patients and staff without cars. Once there, pedestrian access should be favored for internal travel. The priority placed on pedestrian access has resulted in enclosed or grade-separated walkways in some institutions.

---

[20] Current data available from the Texas Medical Center Web site at http://www.tmc.edu/tmc-visitor.html.

[21] *San Antonio Medical Foundation Advisory Services Report* (Washington, D.C.: Urban Land Institute, 1997, pp. 9–10).

Figure 15–5   Texas Medical Center and Downtown Houston

Source: Landiscor©, 1998.

As indicated above, the changing nature of the health care industry makes it imperative that medical centers adapt to a more competitive environment. One aspect of this is the relationship to the physical and economic aspects of the surrounding community. From the institution's perspectives, three key objectives are that (1) they need to respond to growth demands at existing locations or new branches elsewhere, (2) they need compatible surrounding land uses, and (3) they should be a positive force for community development.[22]

Parking is a frequent subject of conflict. The cost of providing parking on overcrowded sites has resulted in a tendency to rely on off-site curb parking. This may congest or preempt parking for adjacent residential or commercial neighborhoods affecting viability or attractions. If a potential for this may occur, measures should be provided to prevent the undesirable effects. Typical transportation planning principles for medical centers are similar to those of universities as shown in Table 15–6.

Suburban Activity Centers

Following World War II, the federal highway program, water and sewer grants, and mortgage assistance combined with a pent-up demand for housing and a baby boom to make suburban tract housing the defining land use of the period. This was followed, according to sociologist and real estate consultant Nina Gruen, by four other periods. The first saw the development of shopping centers as retail followed the population to the suburbs. This was followed by the information age, when offices and industrial research and development operations moved to the suburbs, often in new activity centers competing with the traditional downtown. The horizontal "flex tech space" was then followed by high-rise, mixed-use developments.[23] These centers have been variously termed "suburban subcenters," "megacenters," "SACs," or simply "suburban business districts." During the 1980s, SACs attracted the attention of geographers, transportation analysts, and planners. The phenomenon was probably most publicly articulated by *Washington Post* writer Joel Garreau. Garreau's 1989 book, *Edge Cities: Life on the New Frontier*, attracted a wider, even popular audience to a development pattern that was not new but was now recognized as a development pattern to be addressed by public policy.[24] Such "suburban" activity centers were typically located at high accessibility locations, usually major highway interchanges

[22] "Update: Consulting Services to Hospitals and Medical Centers," *Development Strategies Review* (St. Louis, Mo.: Development Strategies Inc.: winter 1988, p. 9).

[23] Nina Gruen, "Real Estate Grows Against the Backdrop of a Changing Culture," *Real Estate Forum* (New York, N.Y.: Real Estate Forum, September 1996, p. 93).

[24] Joel Garreau, *Edge City: Life on the Frontier* (New York, N.Y.: Doubleday, 1991).

to serve a large geographic market. As major nodes of activity, they became major traffic generators, adding significantly to the loads on the facilities that serve as their lifelines to their market. This section addresses suburban multiple use activity centers that typically consist of retail, office, lodging, restaurant, and entertainment uses.

Origins and Development of Suburban Activity Centers

The first stage of suburbanization in the United States began prior to World War II with the "streetcar suburbs" and shops, housing, and businesses that were within an easy walk of the streetcar. Suburbs such as Pasadena, California; Shaker Heights, Ohio; and Bethesda, Maryland developed in this fashion. Beginning in the 1950s and concurrent with the development of the interstate highway system and freeway systems in many larger cities, activity centers have developed at or near intersections of freeways or regional thoroughfares to take advantage of the high level of regional access inherent in such locations. Most of these activity centers started to develop when they were on the periphery of urban development and large tracts of land (called "greenfield sites") could be assembled.

The timing of the beginning of development has a lot to do with the character of activity centers and the appropriate transportation facilities. The real estate firm of Robert Charles Lesser & Co., which uses the term "metro cores" to include the region serving downtowns, edge cities, and industrial activity centers, identifies four generations of such developments, beginning with the traditional downtowns that controlled such jobs until the 1960s. Beginning in the 1960s, this analysis observes that a new generation of office and industrial space began to locate 2 to 6 miles from downtown, offering the first alternative uptown or midtown rival to downtown. Examples include Mid-Wilshire in Los Angeles, Midtown Atlanta, and Country Club Plaza in Kansas City. The third generation began in the 1970s, when "the explosive growth of office oriented metro cores was the big real estate story of the 1970s and 1980s. . . . Every U.S. metropolitan area

The Evolution of a Highway Corridor . . .
Where Does Your Community Fit In?

The evolution of a highway is an example of why we need to look beyond the short-term plan for a community. As an area develops, transportation and community plans are often motivated by congestion after the fact. The bucolic two-lane county crossroad in a rural village.(phase I) typically has a few small shops that serve a small regional area.

As the area grows, the two-lane historic post road becomes too congested and traffic is rerouted to a new four-lane highway on the outskirts of town (phase II). As most of the traffic is directed to the new highway, it provides an opportunity for new shopping centers, fast-food restaurants, car dealerships and other highway-related uses.

Regional traffic increases cause conflicts with the local traffic which now must fight for left and right turns into the commercial properties. An increase in accidents will necessitate a dedicated center lane for left turns. The traffic will eventually become too intense, and a concrete barrier will be installed to prohibit left turns.

Intersections are then improved with jughandles. As congestion on the four-lane highway continues to increase (phase III), a limited access superhighway is constructed to accommodate regional traffic, presenting an opportunity for a large regional mall, sports complex and hotels.

The evolution of a corridor takes many years, and illustrates the need for each community to anticipate its long-term growth. County and regional master plans will play an important role in your long-term planning, because these plans typically encompass a ten- to twenty-five-year growth projection.

The choices are in your hands, and you have the opportunity to employ aggressive and creative approaches to shaping the direction of your community.

Figure 15–6   Evolution of a Greenfields SAC

Source: *Managing Transportation in Your Community: A Municipal Handbook,* Trenton, N.J.: New Jersey Department of Transportation, January, 1989, p. 5.

sprouted one, even Tyler, Texas." Some of these were urban or urbanizing, such as Buckhead in Atlanta and Century City in Los Angeles, while suburban office centers included City Post Oak in Houston; Bellevue, outside Seattle; and Perimeter Center outside Atlanta. During this period, some industrially oriented suburban centers also developed along freeways, most prominently Silicon Valley South of San Francisco but also including Peachtree Corners northeast of Atlanta. In the 1980s, a fourth generation of office-oriented metro cores emerged, 4 to 12 miles farther out, some with a semirural character such as Plano, outside Dallas. In the early 1990s, when little office development took place, the vast majority of corporate relocations and expansion took place in these areas. J.C. Penney moved to Plano and Sears moved 45 miles from downtown Chicago to Hoffman Estates.[25]

As indicated in Figure 15–6, activity centers have developed generally through market pressures to take advantage of prior transportation investments, like prime freeway locations. A typical example is probably the South Coast metropolitan area in central Orange County, California, which is intersected by three freeways. The land was controlled by two families, who farmed it until there became a market for development. The principal owners enticed high visibility tenants, required signature architecture and landscaping, and created a privately financed cultural center. Despite the extraordinary commercial success of this area as the premier entertainment and shopping area for Orange County, "planning for the area has consisted of a number of general plan amendments, zoning changes, EIRs, and development agreements with (the) two property owners."[26] One of the consequences has been that public improvements for roads and traffic have often been retrofitted, rather than planned in advance. Rather than a typical downtown street grid, which offers many options to drivers and good pedestrian connections, many suburban centers are built on a superblock model, which offers neither. Often built aside major highways themselves and unable to keep up with regional growth, traffic congestion at these suburban centers often becomes an issue to the surrounding community and an impediment to their full development.

Suburban Activity Center Characteristics

Broadly defined, SACs can cover a wide array of different types, including mixed office and retail centers, industrial centers, large office parks and even corridors. The most prominent of these typically:

- Contain significant levels of office development, hotels, and other commercial uses.

- Contain major amounts of retail.

- Have more jobs than resident labor force.

- Are perceived as a "destination" by businesses and visitors.

A 1987 survey of 57 suburban employment centers (a somewhat more inclusive term than activity centers) by Cervero classified them into six categories. The category most closely approximating the mixed-use centers discussed in much of the real estate literature are called "subcities," described as "secondary office and retail centers within their respective markets. Even though they rival the downtown in terms of many medium-sized cities in size and density." Such subcities included Post Oak in Houston, now known as Uptown Houston; Bellevue, outside Seattle; South Coast Metro in Orange County, California; Warner Center outside Los Angeles; and Perimeter Center north of Atlanta. The nine subcities, including older downtowns of Stamford, Connecticut, and Towson, Maryland, all contained a premium-quality regional shopping mall, at least one conference hotel, and over 5 million sq ft of office and commercial space. The higher densities also meant decked parking charging commercial rates. Finally, a quality indicator was a "feel" for being a downtown setting and a reputation for being the "other" central place outside downtown.[27]

A survey for a 1989 National Cooperative Highway Research Program (NCHRP) project identified over seventy SACs in the United States, each containing at least 5 million sq ft of office and retail space. Nearly all have developed in the thirty largest metropolitan areas of the United States. Canada has similar activity centers in its largest cities.[28] The Edge

[25] Christopher B. Leinberger, "The Changing Location of Development and Investment Opportunities," *Urban Land* (Washington, D.C.: Urban Land Institute, May 1995).

[26] Calthorpe.

[27] Robert Cervero, *America's Suburban Centers* (Boston, Mass.: Unwin Hyman, 1989, pp. 85–86).

[28] K.G. Hooper, *Travel Characteristics at Large-Scale Suburban Activity Centers, NCHRP Report 323* (Washington, D.C.: Transportation Research Board, National Academy of Sciences, October 1989).

Table 15–7 Transition of Urban Cores

	Urban	Suburban Office-Dominated	Suburban Industrial-Dominated	Semi-Rural
1st (Before 1960s)	Original downtown office and industrial cores			
2nd (1960s)	Clayton (St. Louis) Country Club Plaza (Kansas City) Mid-Wilshire (Los Angeles) Towson (Baltimore) White Plains (New York)	Bala Cynwyd (Philadelphia)	City of Commerce (Los Angeles) City of Industry (Los Angels) South San Francisco (San Francisco)	
3rd (1970s)	Century City (Los Angeles) Las Colinas (Dallas)	Bellevue (Seattle) Camelback (Phoenix) Denver Tech (Denver) Hunt Valley (Baltimore) King of Prussia (Philadelphia) Newport Beach/Costa Mesa/Irvine (Los Angeles) Perimeter Center (Atlanta) Post Oak (Houston) Tyson's Corner (Washington, D.C.) Walnut Creek/Concord (San Francisco)	Kent Valley (Seattle) Ontario (Los Angeles)[1] Peachtree Corners (Atlanta) Silicon Valley (San Francisco) Ventura Tech Corridor (Los Angeles)	Maryland Farms (Nashville) Princeton (New York) Redmond (Seattle)
4th (1980s)		Mesa (Phoenix) Ontario (Los Angeles) Owings Mills (Baltimore) Reston (Washington, D.C.) Warner Center (Los Angeles)	Sugarland (Houston) Sunset Corridor (Portland, Oregon) 290 Corridor (Houston) Valencia (Los Angeles)[2]	Fair Oaks (Washington, D.C.) Georgia 400 North (Atlanta)

[1] In the 1980s, Ontario became an office-dominated core.
[2] In the 1990s, Valencia will become an office-dominated core.

Source: Christopher B. Leinberger, "Urban Cores: Development, Trends and Opportunities in the 1990s," *Urban Land Magazine,* Washington, D.C.: Urban Land Institute, December 1990, p. 6.

City Group has identified 173 "edge cities," each containing at least 24,000 employees in 34 metropolitan areas of the United States. "Urban cores" at different stages of development as defined by Robert Charles Lesser & Co. are shown in Table 15–7.

Table 15–8 shows some of the development characteristics of two of the largest SACs—Uptown Houston and Dallas' Parkway Center. Each has about two-thirds the office space of the CBD in its own area. Not all activity centers are as large in size as compared to the CBD. Nevertheless, most are at least subregional centers.

Figures 15–7 and 15–8 show aerial views of Uptown Houston and Parkway Center. Each typifies locational characteristics of most activity centers and interfaces with the regional transportation system.

Table 15–8 SACs—Houston vs. Dallas

	Uptown Houston	Dallas Galleria
Office (square ft)	23 million	13.9 million
Retail (square ft)	4.0 million	5.7 million
Hotel Rooms	5,600	2,718
Residential units	9,000	14,581
Industrial/warehouse (square feet)	0	9.3 million
Employees	80,000	90,000
Residents	17,000	30,000

Sources: Current data from Uptown Houston Association, 1990 data for Dallas Galleria; Nina J. Gruen, et al., *Housing in Suburban Centers: Development Opportunities and Constraints,* Washington, D.C.: Urban Land Institute, 1995.

Uptown Houston is located at the intersection of two freeways (including the inner circumferential freeway 5 miles from the CBD) and is penetrated by the most heavily traveled arterial in the city. It is directly served by five full interchanges and one partial interchange. Arterial street spacing averages nearly one mile—typical of the spacing planned for the suburban residential area originally anticipated to develop there. Like most SACs, Uptown Houston is sparingly served by transit; all routes pass through on the way elsewhere (typically, the CBD).

Figure 15–7   Uptown Houston

Source: Uptown Houston Association.

The Galleria Area, one of three major urban centers in the Dallas region, is located at the intersection of the Dallas North Tollway and the LBJ Freeway about 10 miles from downtown. It serves as the "downtown" of North Dallas, an upscale residential address served by prestigious offices and high-end shops. While the Parkway Center area was upzoned intentionally to try to concentrate the North Dallas office development in one area, the roadway network density was only modestly intensified at the time zoning decisions were made—only rights-of-way for some streets were widened. There is a transit center in the Galleria, but the center is not near any of the ultimate work trip ends. Bus routes are not currently designed to serve Parkway Center as a destination; the area bus system has a strong CBD focus and uses the transit center primarily for transfers. An extension of the Dallas Light Rail system will be located several miles to the east.

Most newer SACs have developed in what have been some of the most "auto-accessible" locations in suburbia. They are typically along an expressway—often at or near the intersection of two expressways. This has provided the regional or subregional accessibility needed for a successful activity center. The activity centers have developed because the

Figure 15–8   Aerial View of Dallas Galleria

Source: Dallas Galleria.

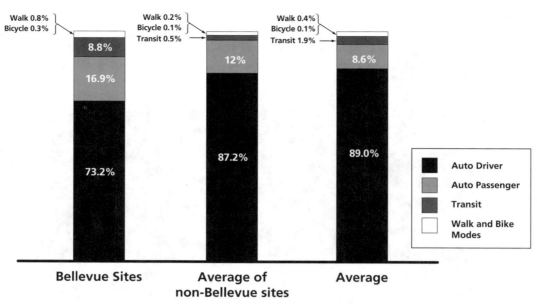

Figure 15–9   Mode of Access Comparisons

Source: Calthorpe Associates, *Design for Efficient Suburban Activity Centers: Phase I Report*, Washington, D.C.: Federal Transit Administration, March 1997.

population, especially office workers and middle- and upper-income shoppers, have located in suburbs as urban areas have grown. The suburban population expansion, high roadway accessibility, and attractive development opportunities have all led to the development of SACs in larger urban areas. Transit has rarely played as much of a factor as it did in the earlier "streetcar suburbs." There are some exceptions, as well as many cases where transit is being retrofitted into suburban centers without it or where existing transit-served centers are being redeveloped with more of an urban focus.

Travel Characteristics at Suburban Centers

Travel demand at activity centers is driven by three major factors: through-trips, density, and auto dependency. Since most emerging centers are designed around the automobile, auto and truck traffic are the dominant components of weekday traffic. In the past, the formula has been pretty simple: calculate the parking and traffic demands based on the assumption that everyone will drive, and size the roads accordingly. This simple formula is changing, however, just as the centers are becoming more complex. It appears that for the near term much of the development in suburban centers will consist of infill and redevelopment, calling for much greater attention to creating a sense of place, with the appropriate parking, traffic, and even transit access. Carrying out this emphasis on place, there is likely to be more attention to creating "walkable" destinations, even for those who drive to the center. In this way, suburban centers will become much more like traditional downtowns, where it is possible to leave the car at work or at the first stop and conduct business; complete errands; and enjoy meals, drinks, or entertainment in a "one-stop shopping" environment. Urbanizing centers in this fashion will require much greater emphasis on planning among developers, retailers, corporate users, and governments; and better integration of transportation facilities into the development programs.

The Changing Suburban Center Commute

The highway-oriented suburban centers that began around a mall and filled in with office and industrial parks left few options to get to or around them than individual cars. There is now greater attention to integrating transit as the center develops or at least retrofitting it in appropriate places. Figure 15–9 compares the mode of access to five typical auto-oriented suburban centers surveyed in 1988 with one, Bellevue, that had aggressively created options. As indicated, transit was negligible (0.5 percent) at the five suburban sites; but it accounted for 8.8 percent of commuters to Bellevue, while 87 percent of the non-Bellevue commuters drive alone vs. 73 percent in Bellevue.

A 1998 study examined thirty SACs and selected six as "exemplary sites" of efficiency. As shown in Figure 15–10, driving alone is much less common. (Not surprising, since this was one of the criteria for selection.) Driving alone ranged from a high of 76 percent in downtown Bellevue to around 60 percent in Kendall Square, Cambridge, an older urban center outside Boston, and in downtown Santa Monica. In addition, residents of most of these suburban centers were even less likely to drive alone, in some cases by a wide margin. In the 2 older trolley suburbs, Cambridge and Bethesda, driving alone by residents was about 25 percentage points lower than by employees based in the activity centers.

Once there, workers in such "efficient" suburban centers have many choices for lunch and errands, and they have less of a need to get in their cars. As indicated above in the comparison between workers in downtown Washington and three suburban centers in Maryland, those in more urbanized Bethesda had many more choices. About two-thirds of their midday trips were made as pedestrians, compared to less than one out of four who drove. The midday patterns for the others were just the opposite—about one in ten walked, and over 80 percent drove for midday trips. It is often heard that the worst traffic congestion at suburban centers is during the day rather than in the rush hour. Perhaps this helps explain why: because commute trips are spread over a period of perhaps two hours at each end of the day, while lunch hour travel generally clusters both within a much shorter time period. Of course, traffic count data can be used to compare peaking at individual centers.

Besides lunch hour, the other best opportunity for running errands is on the way home. About half of workers in all four Washington area centers made an intermediate stop on the way home, an unexpected finding to the authors who assumed that the high level of midday travel in the more urban centers would substitute for evening errands.

In the survey of the six mostly auto-oriented centers sponsored by the NCHRP study, 37 percent of workers reported making a stop on the way home, most of them outside the center.[29] Median commute distances for office workers in both studies typically averaged 11 to 12 miles.

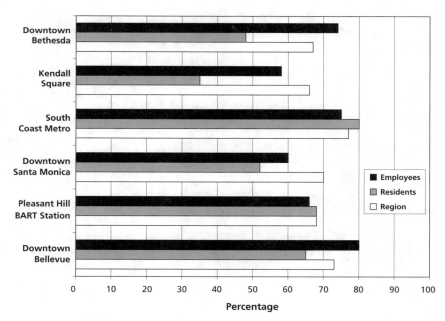

Figure 15–10 Solo Driving—Calthorpe Case Studies

Source: Calthorpe Associates, *Design for Efficient Suburban Activity Centers: Phase I Report,* Washington, D.C.: Federal Transit Administration, March 1997.

---

[29] K.G. Hooper, *Travel Characteristics at Large-Scale Suburban Activity Centers, NCHRP Report 323* (Washington, D.C.: Transportation Research Board, National Academy of Sciences, October 1989, p. 35).

Retail Center Trips

Retail centers are often the core of suburban centers, just as the major department stores were typically located at the prime downtown locations. Massive parking facilities and extensive major road networks are required to adequately serve them. This becomes a special concern when an expansion is considered. With limited room for expansion, many malls require the addition of parking decks, adding significantly to the expansion costs. The expansion of Tyson's Corner Center, the heart of a suburban center in Washington's Virginia suburbs, required 6,000 new spaces in parking decks. At a construction cost of $48 million, this accounted for over one-fourth of the total development cost.[30] Figure 15–11 depicts a typical regional retail center roadway network.

Workers represent a significant share of traffic and parking at suburban centers. The NCHRP survey of suburban centers found that during the evening peak hour, trips to and from work by suburban center employees averaged about 12 percent at regional centers. It was even higher at the specialty centers surveyed—20 percent.[31] Workers account for an even higher share of peak parking demand, so it is in the interest of the retailers to encourage other modes during peak seasons or at least peripheral parking. A 1994 survey of employees at the South Coast Metro activity center, where transit use among office workers was virtually nonexistent, found that 4 percent of retail workers rode transit, and 20 percent used carpools or vanpools, compared to 15 percent of office workers.[32] See Chapter 14 for a discussion of parking requirements for retail centers.

Trips to the mall offer a good example of "efficient" travel behavior. Shoppers tend to double-up, combine trips, and travel during off-peak hours; and shopping trips are fairly short. Nationally, one-third of all shopping trips in 1995 consisted

Figure 15–11   Regional Shopping Center and Road System

Source: Kravco Company, King of Prussia, Pa.

---

[30] Dean Schwanke, *Remaking the Shopping Center* (Washington, D.C.: Urban Land Institute, 1994, p. 120).

[31] K.G. Hooper, *Travel Characteristics at Large-Scale Suburban Activity Centers* (p. 86).

[32] Calthorpe Associates, *Design for Efficient Suburban Activity Centers: Phase I Report* (Washington, D.C.: Federal Transit Administration, March 1997, p. 128).

of two or more occupants.[33] Once at the mall, shoppers visit 2.5 stores per trip and spent about $60, an average including those who simply window-shopped.[34]

Nearby workers provide an important built-in market for retailers in suburban centers. A 1988 survey found that suburban office workers located within 2 miles of a major regional mall spent about $2,000 annually per worker on retail purchases made during the workday. Even office workers in areas with limited retail facilities spent $1,800 annually. The largest component of this was lunch purchases. It was estimated that about half of workers went to lunch outside their building on an average day, and 85 percent got there by private auto. Thirty-five percent of the suburban workers reported shopping during the day, of which 60 percent of the trips were during the lunch hour. This was a heavily auto-dependent market, with 93 percent driving their own car home. These workers reported a wide variety of other stops on the way home—54 percent stopped for groceries the previous week; 33 percent shopped for other things; and 28 percent went to a health club, movie, or other activity. While not all of the shopping was nearby, 14 percent of office workers in ample retail areas reported stopping for dinner or drinks close to the office, and 7 percent went shopping in the area. As shown in Table 15–9, among office workers in the six suburban centers in the NCHRP survey, half reported making midday trips, and 20–33 percent of these were within the activity center.

Midday trips to and from regional retail centers in the (admittedly auto-oriented) SACs of the 1989 NCHRP were almost entirely by auto and pedestrian. Only three of the six centers surveyed in the study showed even 1 percent of trips by transit. Walk percentages in the range of 2 to 5 percent were representative for typical suburban regional retail malls. One center within a high-density mixed-use development and a hotel had a 17-percent walk trip share and another center with extensive bus service had 5-percent transit trips. Small retail centers had virtually no transit trips and 4 to 9 percent walk trips.[35] This, however, reflects a significant information gap, since there are very few published studies of nonauto travel in more pedestrian-oriented centers. To offset the negative impression of transit riders held by many retailers and shopping center managers, the Metropolitan Transit Development Board in San Diego surveyed bus riders at seven malls in 1994. They found that 51 percent were shoppers at the mall who spent an average of $56. A survey of riders at trolley stations near two malls in December 1997 found an even higher percentage of shoppers—79 percent with a spending average of $79.

The proportion of retail center trips that are internal to the activity center ranges greatly, apparently by activity center size. Table 15–10 shows that retail centers in the three large activity centers studied by NCHRP draw about twice as much from

Table 15–9 Office Employee Trips Within SACs

| | Percentage of Employee Trips | |
Trip	Total	Within Activity Center
Intermediate stops on trip to work	22%	8–13%[1]
Midday trips	50	20–33[2]
Intermediate stops on trips from work	37	10–15[1]

[1] Low limit is for activity center with significant retail activity immediately outside activity center boundaries; high limit has no such retail nearby.

[2] Low limit has less than 60 percent of employees in technical, profesional, manager, administrative positions; high limit is for activity centers with over 60 percent.

Source: K.G. Hooper, *Travel Characteristics at Large-Scale Suburban Activity Centers, NCHRP Report 323,* Washington, D.C.: Transportation Research Board, National Academy of Sciences, October 1989, p. 35.

Table 15–10 Internal Activity Center Trips to Major Retail Centers

	Trips from Within Activity Center	
	Midday	Evening
Large activity center (between 13 and 17 million SF office)	47%	31%
Small activity center (between 3 and 5 million SF office)	23	14

Source: K.G. Hooper, *Travel Characteristics at Large-Scale Suburban Activity Centers, NCHRP Report 323,* Washington, D.C.: Transportation Research Board, National Academy of Sciences, October 1989, p. 37.

---

[33] Office of Highway Information Management, *Our Nation's Travel: 1995 NPTS Early Results Report* (Washington, D.C.: Federal Highway Administration, 1997, p. 25).

[34] "The 1996 Mall Customer Shopping Patterns Report," *ICSC Research Quarterly* (New York, N.Y.: International Council of Shopping Centers, winter 1996, p. 3).

[35] K.G. Hooper, *Travel Characteristics at Large-Scale Suburban Activity Centers, NCHRP Report 323* (Washington, D.C.: Transportation Research Board, National Academy of Sciences, October 1989, p. 37).

Table 15–11 Regional Retail Center Trip End Distribution

Land Use	Midday Peak Small SAC	Midday Peak Large SAC	P.M. Peak Small SAC	P.M. Peak Large SAC
Office	14%	35%	9%	16%
Home	55	39	58	57
Shop/bank/restaurant	18	13	16	13
Other	13	13	17	14

Source: K.G. Hooper, *Travel Characteristics at Large-Scale Suburban Activity Centers, NCHRP Report 323*, Washington, D.C.: Transportation Research Board, National Academy of Sciences, October 1989, p. 38.

Table 15–12 Hotel Internal Activity Center Trips

	Trips to and from Points Within Activity Center A.M. Peak Hour	Trips to and from Points Within Activity Center P.M. Peak Hour
Large activity center	37%	36%
Small activity center	19	27

Source: K.G. Hooper, *Travel Characteristics at Large-Scale Suburban Activity Centers, NCHRP Report 323*, Washington, D.C.: Transportation Research Board, National Academy of Sciences, October 1989, Table 41.

within the activity centers as they do in the three small-sized activity centers. The sources of these trips appeared to vary, perhaps due to the extent and mix of other land uses within the varying-sized activity centers. It should be pointed out that these and other data presented herein are for a typical period, not a seasonal peak period used for design purposes.

Regional retail center trip origins and destinations determined from the same surveys also show differences between large and small activity centers. Table 15–11 shows the variations. Consistent with the Table 15–10 data, larger activity centers appear to provide greater percentages of the retail market than do small activity centers. During the midday peak, 35 percent of the trips to the large activity centers came from offices, compared to only 14 percent at the smaller centers.

Midday auto occupancy for retail centers ranged from 1.15 to 1.44; vehicle occupancies for regional shopping centers ranged between 1.23 and 1.20. The P.M. peak-hour occupancies were similar to slightly higher, ranging from 1.26 to 1.45 for regional malls and 1.18 to 1.51 for smaller centers.

Pass-by trips are those that are drawn from traffic passing a site on the way from an origin to a primary destination; no route deviation is necessary to make a stop along the way. Midday pass-by trips ranged between 15 and 25 percent for regional centers. Evening peak-hour pass-by trips ranged between 10 and 30 percent of total trips.[36] For smaller retail centers, the pass-by trips averaged 26 percent for midday and 36 percent for P.M. peak hour. See Chapter 5 for a discussion of models and trip generation.

Hotels in large activity centers drew about one-third of all peak-hour trips from these activity centers, as reported in Table 15–12 for the six activity centers surveyed by the NCHRP. This is even more "self-contained" than office workers in those same SACs. Hotels in smaller activity centers have less but still significant synergy with these activity centers; about 20 percent of the A.M. hour internal trips are to and from the activity center and about 27 percent are in the P.M. peak.[37]

Residential

A survey of nineteen multifamily residential complexes located in the six suburban centers surveyed by the NCHRP found 30 percent of residents reported actually working in the nearby centers. Hooper, the survey director, pointed out, however, that the effect of this high level of nearby commuting on suburban center travel was minimal because the number of residences is too small and is completely dwarfed by the extensive number of jobs, so that local residents would account

---

[36] K.G. Hooper, *Travel Characteristics at Large-Scale Suburban Activity Centers, NCHRP Report 323* (Washington, D.C.: Transportation Research Board, National Academy of Sciences, October 1989, p. 39).

[37] K.G. Hooper, *Travel Characteristics at Large-Scale Suburban Activity Centers, NCHRP Report 323* (Washington, D.C.: Transportation Research Board, National Academy of Sciences, October 1989, Table 41).

for only a relatively small share of the number of in-commuters.[38] However, developing a better balance of housing near suburban centers can help reduce regional travel and contribute to environmental goals, as well as create a better market to enhance the market success of the center. Housing development within and nearby the center often faces both political and financial challenges, however. Commercial development is often preferred over residential by local residents and government because it generates higher tax revenues to the local government and because office parks are perceived to offer less intrusion in the adjacent residential areas. Many suburban centers are located in upscale communities who prefer to accept only housing that maintains the exclusive character of the community, limiting the number of potential buyers.[39] Finally, as office and retail development matures, land prices often escalate beyond the levels at which residential development is feasible.

Parking Characteristics

Parking in downtowns is often provided at a fee in lots or garages that serve many destinations. There are strong financial incentives to ensure that parking is adequate to serve downtown needs, but not excessive. Parking problems are often addressed by a parking study, which often involves analysis of supply vs. demand, site alternatives, and financial feasibility. In the suburbs, however, "free" parking is expected by shoppers and workers. Each development is assumed to meet their parking needs on-site, and the amount of parking is established by codes rather than by studies. As a result, suburban areas are often criticized for providing excessive amounts of parking, which virtually precludes any options to driving. In low-density areas with surface parking provided by the developer or building owner, the financial effect may be minimal. Property managers responsible for maintaining suburban campus grounds often claim that it is "cheaper to pave it than to mow it." Once it becomes necessary to build parking structures, however, "free" parking becomes an expensive item that must be added on the occupancy costs. A study of parking at higher density sites in Orange County, California, for example, estimated a break-even cost for one parking structure in Costa Mesa at $235 per commuter, while the owner billed tenants $60 a month.[40]

The two major constituencies for parking at suburban sites are users and nearby residents, and both would prefer more to less parking. Building managers never want to hear complaints from users that they had a hard time finding a space, and developers need to make a similar case to potential clients. Local residents also want to ensure that on-site parking is adequate so that there will be no spillover into their neighborhoods. In the case of expanding suburban centers, however, it is often necessary to build up, not out, meaning finding a place for additional parking. This can often involve buying expensive land to expand parking supply, or building parking structures on existing lots, an even more expensive option. In such cases, it is important for the financial viability of the project, and often for its approval, to avoid unnecessary parking.

One example of grappling with such difficult choices is parking for shopping centers, a stereotype of suburban development. Retailers wish to ensure that there is never a time when a customer cannot find a parking place, even at the height of the holiday season. As a result, the design standard established in a 1965 study was the tenth highest hour. A 1982 study, however, reflecting both shifting demand patterns as well as a greater tolerance for encouraging shopping at less busy hours, selected a twentieth highest hour for design. It was estimated that with this level of parking, over half the spaces would be empty during 40 percent of the hours of operation, and that during nineteen hours each year some patrons would be inconvenienced. These new ratios ranged from 4.0 to 5.0 spaces per thousand sq ft (93 sq m) of gross leasable area, depending on the size of the center.[41,42]

One of the opportunities for reducing parking requirements at suburban centers might be to charge for parking. This would certainly reduce the demand, although there might be some concerns that an undesirable side effect might also be to reduce business. Another option is the sharing of parking by different uses, especially developments whose parking requirements peak at different times. Such a methodology was developed by the Urban Land Institute to serve mixed-use developments

---

[38] K.G. Hooper, *Travel Characteristics at Large-Scale Suburban Activity Centers, NCHRP Report 323* (Washington, D.C.: Transportation Research Board, National Academy of Sciences, October 1989, p. 3).

[39] Nina Gruen, et al., *Housing in Suburban Employment Centers: Development Opportunities and Constraints* (Washington D.C.: Urban Land Institute, 1995, p. 5).

[40] Robert T. Dunphy, *No More Free Parking* (Washington, D.C.: Urban Land Institute, September 1993, Vol. 52–9, p. 9).

[41] *Parking Requirements for Shopping Centers: Summary Recommendations and Research Report* (Washington D.C.: Urban Land Institute, 1982, p. 12).

[42] Note: metric not used because it is not yet standard in real estate. See discussion in Chapter 14.

with a common parking facility.[43] A 1995 Institute of Transportation Engineers (ITE) survey of local governments found that 41 percent of those surveyed (admittedly not statistically representative) offered reduced requirements for shared parking. In four regions—the Northwest, the West, the Midwest, and the Mid-Atlantic—more than half of local governments reduced the parking requirements for shared parking. Of those allowing shared parking, half required a parking study, with about one-third of those requiring the book *Shared Parking* as a guide. This broader interpretation of shared parking among land use with complementary demand patterns offers advantages to local governments and the public as well as developers. It has the potential for reducing the cost and land area for parking and allowing more attractive designs. In addition, greater mixing of uses can limit the number of access points and improve traffic flow.[44] Cities can take more active roles to encourage shared parking by developing municipal facilities and parking assessment districts—a role traditionally limited to downtowns. An even more aggressive city could identify shared parking potential, adopt area plans that encourage it, and even serve as a liaison among property owners and developers.

Changing development regulations from requiring all parking to be provided on-site to encouraging convenient facilities shared among several users could have a significant effect not only on reducing overall parking supply, but also in creating more of a pedestrian environment.

Transportation Planning for Activity Centers

Transportation planning for activity centers is best done as part of a top-down regional visioning exercise that considers the role of the activity center in the region, outlines a framework for serving its traffic needs, and brings a coherent public policy and private interest to bear. However, such planning is more often done in isolation, as a bottom-up series of negotiations among developers, local government, and local citizens. Developer Wayne Snyder, chairman of the Kravco Company in King of Prussia, Pennsylvania, points out that "the cities at the nexus of major transportation routes attract powerful office and retail development, which overwhelms the municipality and its residents. Traffic is the big issue in citizen opposition."[45] Well-organized plans can help avoid such confrontation and facilitate orderly development while addressing the concerns of the community in advance, before it becomes a pitched battle over individual developments.

Transportation improvements in activity centers usually involve a blend of fixing preexisting problems and providing expanded transportation capacity to serve growth. Many of these "built-in" problems date to the development of the center. For instance, many CBDs grew up before the freeway era and usually have a well-developed surface street system that has evolved over many years. In contrast, most SACs began in rural or suburban areas at the junction of two expressways or an expressway and a major arterial. As a result, usually there is limited arterial street capacity in suburban centers, and a tendency of overdependence on the freeways to provide accessibility. This results in "fractured" arterial street planning, high congestion at the ramp terminals with the expressway, and concentration of traffic at a few points on the road network rather than the dispersion of traffic over an integrated road network. Moreover, some suburban business districts have evolved according to a "superblock" development pattern, which favors cars but serves as an obstacle to pedestrian movements and a sense of place. These problems and other issues must be addressed for most SACs in the transportation planning process for the area. Typical issues are listed in Table 15–13.

Perhaps the most serious and most challenging issue that affects the future transportation scenario for all activity centers is the ability to accommodate the private automobile. It often seems that development wants to happen, in terms of proposed projects, where traffic congestion is already bad. In good times, it may be possible to create special assessments or partnerships among property owners to help finance road and transit projects. In a slow economy, development is often seen as a way to help energize the economy, and the associated transportation effects are often given much lower priority by local and state governments. It is within this maelstrom of conflicting demands that transportation professionals must attempt to adhere to a long-range vision of providing adequate transportation systems for through-movements and local access, often without much guidance on a longer term development program.

---

[43] *Shared Parking* (Washington, D.C.: Urban Land Institute, 1983).

[44] ITE Committee 6F-52, *Shared Parking Planning Guidelines: An Informational Report* (Washington D.C.: Institute of Transportation Engineers, 1995).

[45] Wayne Snyder, interview with author (May 17, 1998).

Table 15–13 Typical Activity Center Transportation-Related Issues

- Projected activity center size and character
    Degree of concentration or sprawl (mixed use vs. multi-use)
    Densities and square footage by use (actual vs. zoned, announced, or planned)
    Rate of development
- Travel projections
    Trip generation
    Internal trip making
    Ride sharing
    Vehicle occupancies
    Travel demand management potential (and commitment)
- Regional access to the activity center
    Expressway (overall capacity and number and capacity of interchanges)
    Arterial (capacity, continuity)
    Transit (quantity and directness of service linkages served)
    Other modes
- Through traffic
    Conflicts with access and internal circulation
    Priority given to through versus local movements
    Bypasses for through traffic
- Internal circulation
    Roadway system
    Pedestrian system needs, potential, and priority
    Transit functions, productivity, and cost factors
    Transit priority treatment
    Conflicts with through and regional access traffic
- General roadway system characteristic
    Capacity to accommodate further density increases
    Spacing of expressway interchanges, arterials, collectors, and local streets

- Continuity
    Special treatments (e.g., grade separations, one-way streets)
    Potential for operational improvements
- Property access
    Access on major arterials
    Priority trade-offs between access and mobility
    Protection of roadway and intersection capacity
    Signal spacing
- Parking
    Ratios and synergy between adjacent developments
    Convenience
    Fees and impacts on both marketability and demand
    Conflicts with transit incentives
    Surface vs. structured supply
    Use of fringe parking
- Service
    Special service needs
    Separation of heavy truck traffic
- Transportation improvements
    Expressway interchanges (more, redesigned)
    Arterial street improvements
    Pedestrian system enhancement or expansion
    Additional streets or improved continuity
    Transit circulators
    Travel demand management
    Parking ratio reductions
    Provision of amenities to encourage transit use and walking for internal trips
    Improvement priorities
    Cost
    Source of financing for improvements

Source: Institute of Transportation Engineers, *Transportation Planning Handbook*, Englewood Cliffs, N.J.: Prentice-Hall, 1992.

A related challenge for the transportation professional is the extent to which transportation concerns, especially providing adequate parking and street capacity, are subordinated to broader community concerns, such as livability and community. One example is the popularity of traffic calming to slow traffic in areas, possibly with the use of impediments to speeding. In the planning area, this movement is often called the New Urbanism approach. It advocates the call for a return to "traditional" centers with on-street parking and a mix of traffic and pedestrians, a stark contrast to the typical mall or office park surrounded by a sea of parking. In addition to "lower" street standards, these approaches often call for limiting parking and new roads. One of the prime examples is Portland, Oregon, which adopted a lid on downtown parking in 1972, along with dropping all new freeways planned for downtown. Transportation planners who adhere to a "business as usual" approach are often considered to be obstructionist. This makes it essential to follow the general principles suggested here of being in touch with the community and fashioning a transportation approach that is both professional and consistent.

Transportation Planning Principles

Key issues need to be specified for each activity center and a set of objectives should be established to respond to these issues and needs. In Houston, for example, property owners supported by local businesses in the largest suburban center, Uptown Houston (also described as the nation's largest suburban activity center), identified three key strategies in the late 1980s to improve transportation:[46]

---

[46] Brian S. Bochner and John R. Breeding, "Solving Congestion in the Nation's Largest Activity Center," *ITE 1990 Compendium of Technical Papers* (Washington, D.C.: Institute of Transportation Engineers, 1990).

Table 15–14   Typical Transportation Planning Principles for Activity Centers

General

- Planning for activity center transportation systems should encourage coordination and most effective use of all appropriate modes and forms of transportation.
- The transportation and land use plans should be mutually supportive.
- Activity center transportation and land use should be arranged so that highest trip generating land uses are located nearest high accessibility transportation facilities, particularly transit routes and stations.
- The transportation facilities should be aesthetically attractive and, to the extent possible, blend in with or highlight the surroundings and topographic features through which they pass.
- The transportation system should be comprehensible and easy to use for both frequent users and unfamiliar visitors.
- Adequate system capacity and continuity should be ensured by defining and protecting sufficient future transportation right-of-way early; consistent with local policies on accommodating traffic and potential build-out of development.*
- All elements of the transportation plan should be consistent with political and financial realities.
- The plan must be stageable with individual elements to be usable as they are completed.

Roadway System and Traffic Circulation

- The activity center street system should provide adequate access and circulation for activity center traffic.*
- The activity center circulation system should connect with both existing and proposed major thoroughfares beyond the activity center (e.g., radial freeways and principal arterial streets).
- The activity center street system should be flexible by providing more than one opportunity to reach a destination.
- Through traffic should be directed away from the core area utilizing alternative or bypass routes.
- The activity center circulation pattern should be easily comprehended by the average driver and provide relatively direct routing without circuitous travel.
- The circulation plan should be designed for incremental implementation with individual elements available for use as they are completed.
- Streets should be designed to provide continuous routing and continuity of capacity.
- The activity center circulation plan should allow drivers to circulate around the blocks or areas which generate high traffic volumes.
- Emergency vehicles *must* be able to reach any portion of the activity center in a reasonably direct manner.
- Given streets should perform specific functions (for example, major arterials, minor arterials collector/distributor streets, local streets) to the extent that a hierarchy can be identified. This hierarchy should be implemented through the use of street design techniques, traffic control measures, and parking regulations. Streets should have an appearance consistent with their function. Major streets should have wider pavements, rights-of-way, and building setback than minor streets to give the appearance of a more important street function. Minor streets should encourage slower speeds and pedestrian movement.
- One-way streets should balance convenience to through-trips with inconvenience to local destinations.
- Complex intersections and multiphase signals should be avoided.
- Streets and land development should be designed to complement each other. Arterial streets should border rather than sever activity center land use activity areas. Land parcels should not be so large as to make circulation difficult: the street pattern should not cut land areas into parcels too small to permit sound development.
- Adequate spacing of arterial streets should be provided to meet both capacity and circulation needs.*
- Efficient use of existing facilities should be considered in addition to physical improvement or construction of new facilities.
- All major roadways should be improved or constructed to appropriate geometric and safety standards; however, needed improvements should not be discarded only because all design standards cannot fully be met due to right-of-way or other constraints.
- The activity center *freeway* system should recognize basic principles of continuity.
- Care must be exercised to ensure that there is sufficient capacity at interchanges. Collector-distributor facilities may be required to distribute the traffic from the freeway onto several arterial streets. Special ramp configurations, including direct connector ramps may be needed.
- Direct connections to the activity center by mass transit and high-occupancy vehicles should be considered during the planning stage of freeways to ensure good access by other modes.

Parking

- Activity center parking should be accessible from the primary activity center approach routes and located at major vehicle entry points.
- Activity center parking facilities should be distributed in relation to the directional distribution of vehicular approach to the area or development.
- Parking should provide explicit space for long-term, short-term, visitor, and errand parking.
- The activity center should have sufficient parking capacity to accommodate peak parking demands, consistent with adopted parking policies and the effectiveness of programs to reduce peak vehicle use.
- Activity center parking should facilitate dual or shared usage of facilities by the development and operation of facilities.
- Parking should not be permitted on major thoroughfares.
- Adequate off-street facilities must be provided to accommodate the needs of regular delivery vehicles, quick-stop service (such as mail and newspaper trucks), and special-purpose vehicles such as construction and maintenance trucks.

Transit

- Service should be directly oriented to major destinations in the activity center.
- The most direct possible to routing should be used.
- Routes should be designed to be comprehensible to those who are not familiar with the transit system.
- Transfers for activity center trips should be minimized.
- Conflicts of buses with traffic and pedestrians (heavy right turns, garage access, curb parking and loading, crosswalk conflicts, etc.) should be minimized.

* The degree of preference to transit and pedestrians compared to motor vehicles varies greatly for different downtowns. The clearest indication of the extent to which vehicles will be served is in the level of service (LOS), which is generally lower in downtown than anywhere else in the region. Cities may prefer to be even more restrictive, limiting parking and vehicle access. An example is the 1972 downtown plan for Portland, Oregon, which called for reducing reliance on the automobile and increasing transit travel—including a lid on downtown parking. The principles indicated here require judgments on the relative priority given to motor vehicles compared to pedestrians, transit, and "quality of life" values. Such conflicts should be established as part of the downtown plan.

Source: Institute of Transportation Engineers, *Transportation Planning Handbook*, Englewood Cliffs, N.J.: Prentice-Hall, 1992.

1. Create a special improvement district.

2. Adopt a plan of area transportation improvements.

3. Make transportation improvements in this area a higher priority for public agencies.

An improvement district was subsequently established, allowing property owners to pay for improvements and finance bonds. Between 1992 and 1998, Uptown Houston has leveraged $37 million in public infrastructure.[47] While this is probably an unusual example of concerted action by the private sector and public sector support, it certainly offers a good model of developing needed consensus on an action agenda and carrying it out.

Table 15–14 lists a number of generally applicable activity center transportation planning principles. These ideas can serve as a checklist, which should be adapted to fit each activity center. Most will be applicable regardless of size, land use mix, and urban area location.

Transportation planning objectives and principles should be combined and coordinated with the four system elements: streets, parking, traffic, and pedestrians. Each of these individual principles represent desirable results; but they will occasionally conflict with other transportation planning principles, development principles, or local policies. These conflicts need to be resolved as early in the planning process as possible. As indicated above, it is also critical to understand how transportation fits in with community goals.

These combined planning principles will serve to direct subsequent planning efforts.

Transportation Planning Methodology

Activity center transportation planning is often performed as part of any or all of the following efforts:

- A regional transportation plan.

- A subregional or subarea plan.

- An activity center plan.

- A corridor plan.

- Plans for anticipated development in an approval "pipeline."

- Comprehensive land use or zoning plan revisions.

Transportation planning for activity centers has its place and role relative to each. In each case, the same principles listed above should be considered. The level of detailed analysis may vary based on the specific purpose of the planning effort.

Planning Scope

The objectives of subarea and activity center transportation planning may include any or all of the following:

- Evaluate the effects of potential land use changes.

- Estimate the potential "build out" based on the current or proposed transportation system.

---

[47] *Uptown Houston Annual Report* (Houston, Texas: Uptown Houston, 1998).

- Evaluate the density (spacing) and structure of activity center transportation facilities.

- Determine the size of the transportation network facilities.

- Modify (usually intensify) an existing transportation plan or evaluate proposals on full sites.

- Evaluate roadway or transit system options and improvements.

- Evaluate the potential for transit.

- Develop a revised zoning strategy or plan.

- Analyze the potential of transportation management policies (e.g., pricing, parking ratio limits).

- Assess the cumulative effects of proposed developments of several sites within the activity center.

- Assess the effects of a major development within an activity center.

Each type of analysis will have its own specific objectives reflecting local policies and needs. In general, they should be consistent with the applicable planning principles listed previously. Reviewing the traffic effects of individual developments is best done if it reflects a refinement of previously established development plans and previously agreed upon transportation services.

Building for the Pedestrian

Many suburban centers and even some downtowns are criticized as being dominated by the automobile, with little consideration of the pedestrian. As with most issues concerning activity centers, it is best to address pedestrian needs up front rather than to try to fix problems later on. This issue goes beyond transportation, as businesses, developers, and designers, seek to create "walkable" centers that can differentiate their developments as unique, attractive destination environments, rather than simple suburban office locations or malls. Since all trips begin on foot, whether they are from a parking lot, a transit stop, or a nearby home or commercial building, it is important that pedestrian considerations be a continuing component of planning for activity centers. Moreover, it is a critical precondition for transit. It has been pointed out that "a healthy walking environment can succeed without transit, but a transit system cannot exist without the pedestrian."[48]

An illustration of an activity center developed under single ownership is the NASA Johnson Space Center outside Houston, described as a " typical SAC with multiple employment sites and parking facilities. As the central (mall) portion of the project developed under a master planning process, there was inadequate consideration of the relationship between parking facilities and building distances. As a result, surveys showed large walking distances with a mean of 800 ft. Planned expansion of the employment levels resulted in a more careful analysis of parking needs, including a parking simulation model for 51 work sites and 97 parking areas.[49]

Walking can be a significant share of trips within downtowns, but it is generally a very small share of trips in suburbia, including suburban centers. Among the six mostly auto-oriented suburban centers surveyed in the late 1980s, none reported that more than 1 percent of workers walked. Walking was significant for selected travel markets, however. It was estimated that 17 percent of midday trips to the Dallas Galleria walked there, probably because of the large amount of nearby offices and a hotel connected by enclosed walkways. Residents of downtown Bellevue and South Coast Metro making trips within those centers were estimated to walk 17 percent of the time, substantially higher than the 7 percent average for all

---

[48] Calthorpe Associates, *Design for Efficient Suburban Activity Centers: Phase I Report* (Washington, D.C.: Federal Transit Administration, March 1997, p. 14).

[49] Machemehl and Miller, *Evaluation of the Spatial Distribution of Activity Center Parking Facilities, Transportation Research Record 1404* (Washington, D.C.: Transportation Research Board, 1993, p. 46).

centers studied.[50] Another study of six suburban centers with more of a pedestrian orientation showed that while walking to work is relatively rare for workers, it is much more common among those living around the center. In Santa Monica, a walkable beach town near Los Angeles, 16 percent of residents walked to work in 1990, compared to a paltry 1 percent of workers at major employers. Another 2 percent of residents bicycled. A 1987 survey of workers in downtown Bethesda, Maryland, a thriving suburban center on Washington, D.C.'s Metrorail system, estimated that a mere 2 percent walked to work, compared to a substantial 15 percent of residents reported in the 1990 Census.[51]

While acceptable walking distances in shopping malls are considered to be 1,000 ft, walking distances in attractive suburban pedestrian environments (continuous walkways of adequate width for two-way travel with amenities and interesting features along the way) can be generally assumed to be 500 ft between buildings and not more than 2,000 ft overall. Most CBDs have contiguous buildings; continuous attractive pedestrian facilities should be provided in each block. Surface parking lots common in suburban centers tend to increase separation of buildings. This reduces pedestrian travel usage due to increased walking distances.

Development of a system of effective pedestrian circulation requires a fine grained, interconnected pattern of streets. The superblock pattern that is often the basis for newer suburban developments requires long, circuitous walking routes, even to reach buildings that are nominally adjacent. A block

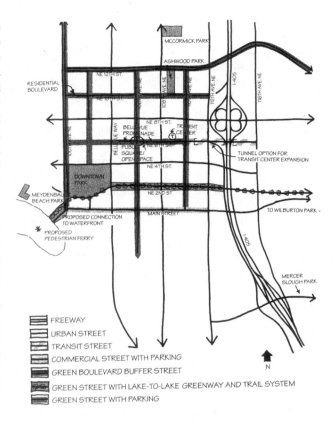

Figure 15–12   Bellevue—Pedestrian Scheme

Source: *Downtown Bellevue, Washington: An Evaluation of Development Potential and Recommendations for Strategies to Shape a Vibrant Central Business District*, Washington, D.C.: Urban Land Institute, 1997, p. 42.

pattern scaled to pedestrians, with buildings oriented to the street, can go a long way to creating attractive walking opportunities. Significant pedestrian linkages should be supported with pedestrian facilities that directly connect trip generators, provide shelter or other appropriate amenities, are interesting to walk along, and have a minimum of conflicts with vehicles. In the core of the South Coast Metro center, buildings are connected by a network of pedestrian paths separated from auto traffic. The pedestrian network ties into the mall's entrance through a long bridge and an adjacent street, built as a traffic mitigation measure by the developer to eliminate pedestrian crossings at a congestion. Many workers are able to use it to reach the mall at lunchtime.[52]

Figure 15–12 shows an example of a proposed street hierarchy for downtown Bellevue, Washington, which includes urban streets and "green" streets. The green streets would be pedestrian friendly with landscaping, lower speed limits, and on-street parking, as opposed to urban streets whose major focus is access and moving traffic.[53]

---

[50] K.G. Hooper, *Travel Characteristics at Large-Scale Suburban Activity Centers, NCHRP Report 323* (Washington, D.C.: Transportation Research Board, National Academy of Sciences, October 1989, pp. 39, 85).

[51] Calthorpe Associates, *Design for Efficient Suburban Activity Centers: Phase I Report* (Washington, D.C.: Federal Transit Administration, March 1997, pp. 115, 151).

[52] Calthorpe Associates, *Design for Efficient Suburban Activity Centers: Phase I Report* (Washington, D.C.: Federal Transit Administration, March 1997, p. 126–127).

[53] *Downtown Bellevue, Washington: An Evaluation of Development Potential and Recommendations for Strategies to Shape a Vibrant Central Business District* (Washington, D.C.: Urban Land Institute, 1997, p. 42).

Transit

A well-designed pedestrian system will also provide a significant edge to potential transit service, since both pedestrians and buses are often plagued by the lack of good connectivity common to many activity centers. Consideration of the role of transit in the development plans for an activity center can greatly facilitate the success of transit, just as failing to deal with it in advance can create impossible barriers to effective transit.

There are four major transit markets for an activity center: through-trips, destination trips by workers and visitors, originating trips by nearby residents, and internal trips. Figure 15–13 shows an estimate of trips destined and internal to the Nassau Hub at Hempstead, Long Island for office, retail, and school land uses.

Downtowns have traditionally been served by a radial route structure; this has, at least in part, resulted in downtowns attracting the largest transit mode split of any activity center. Other activity centers with the best transit service will be those on heavy bus or rail routes, preferably not too far from downtown. It is important for activity center stops to be located as close to major destinations as possible to serve local travelers, but not so roundabout as to unnecessarily inconvenience through-travelers. That is one of the major advantages of concurrent decisions about locating activity centers and major transit hubs—that they are recognized as major points of access to the transit system, in part because of having significant attractions nearby.

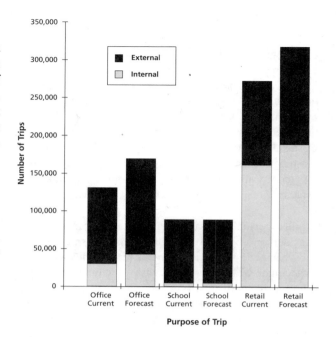

Figure 15–13 Nassau Hub Trip Destinations by Land Use

Source: *Nassau Hub Study*, Long Island, N.Y.: Long Island Regional Planning Board, January 1998, p. 62.

The key to attracting destination trips to transit is to provide direct service to and from the activity center from throughout the area in which employees and visitors live or park. Typically, this is within 10 miles or so for employees. For example, overall transit commuting to the South Coast Metro in Orange County, California, is negligible—only 1 percent. However, there is a greater concentration of low-income workers who live 2 to 5 miles away; and 1991 transit use from this distance was over 5 percent.[54] With direct, frequent service and supporting policies, transit may be able to attract significantly increased ridership. In Bethesda, Maryland, for example, high frequency bus and rail service combined with paid parking helped transit to capture a 16-percent share of all workers in 1987; and 27 percent of Bethesda residents used public transit for commuting in 1990.[55] This combination of high-density housing in the corridor, a short walk at both ends of the trip, and competitive service with the auto on a cost and time basis is the best way to encourage transit use to and from activity centers by workers, shoppers, visitors, and residents. Standard or customized travel models can use these factors to estimate potential transit use for a range of potential variables. Of course suburban centers like Bethesda are fairly rare, possibly illustrating how difficult it is to implement such aggressive protransit policies in the suburbs, where low density is common and free parking is the norm.

In Chicago, an opportunity for expanding transit service to a growing suburban center occurred with the opening of a new commuter rail station in the Lake-Cook Road corridor. Because the corridor extended for over 5 miles between Deerfield and Northbrook, most jobs were beyond a reasonable walking distance. A range of transit options was considered, and two transit ridership models were developed to test three service options: fixed route, van, and demand responsive. It was found that despite the high employment level of 30,000, only 25 percent lived within a convenient

---

[54] Nina Gruen, et al., *Housing in Suburban Employment Centers: Development Opportunities and Constraints* (Washington D.C.: Urban Land Institute, 1995, pp. 74, 78).

[55] Calthorpe Associates, *Design for Efficient Suburban Activity Centers: Phase I Report* (Washington, D.C.: Federal Transit Administration, March 1997, p. 151).

access to the trains. The recommended option consisted of seven van routes serving clusters along corridor, at approximately 20- to 30-minute headways. A demonstration project was established, with local employers providing the local match to a federal grant.[56]

As indicated earlier, most downtowns are compact. So once a commuter or visitor gets there, most midday trips can be made on foot. That is not the case in sprawling suburban centers, leaving a choice of driving or (where available) taking a bus. Providing such a midday service may share some of the same routes as commuting service, but a separate system may also be necessary for effective collection and distribution of access trips and to provide reasonably comprehensive coverage for internal trip making. Such an internal transit system also needs to provide convenient service, especially serving "time-starved" workers who need to be back at their desk in an hour. An example of such a customized service was instituted in the Oak Brook activity center outside Chicago; and it was subsequently cancelled, in part because it could not compete with workers' own cars.

Buses may be used to carry moderate volumes of internal trips at relatively low speeds. A much higher cost option for internal trips in an activity center is a dedicated fixed-guideway people mover, which could offer much higher speeds to selected destinations during the day, and connect transit riders to major bus or rail terminals, and even link drivers to peripheral parking lots. People movers developed under a federal demonstration program in Detroit and Miami were seen as the leading edge of a new technology that would be widely adopted in downtowns, airports, and suburban centers. However, while they have been incorporated into airports, none has yet to penetrate the suburban market. In fact, the first commercially adopted system in a mixed-use suburban center, Las Colinas, was discontinued. A new prototype of such systems, such as that serving the Getty Museum outside Los Angeles, may eventually lead to more common application in other downtowns and suburban centers. This, however, requires organizing development around such a transit system, which could involve a significant reordering of current patterns. For example, planners for the Nassau Hub center in Long Island acknowledged "the center is so vast, it can easily accommodate the ambitious growth model postulated for the 21st Century Suburban Center," and that growth trends did not contribute to the Hub as a place that is pleasing to visit or has any kind of positive identity. As an alternative, a transit-friendly center was proposed, as shown in Figure 15–14 where new development is concentrated around places that are already the focus of activity, reinforcing the potential of those places to become transit stops.[57]

Managing Demand

The confluence of a strong economy, declining public finances, and the emergence of suburban growth centers in the 1980s led to a growing involvement of suburban businesses in transportation in general and especially in creating programs to get their employees to work. During this period, a number of business organizations began actually operating commuter transportation services; and by 1990, there were an estimated dozen organizations dedicated to transportation services at activity centers, all but one in the suburbs. In addition, there were another twenty-two startups, all in the suburbs, as well as a longer list of organizations waiting in the wings. The list has expanded since then, and there has been some consolidation as groups ceased because of finances or lack of support. Typical programs include subsidizing transit services or fares, organizing and supporting vanpools, matching potential applicants for carpools or vanpools, offering free rides home in case of emergencies, preferential parking, and getting businesses more engaged in transportation issues. In many cases, development approvals were conditioned on developers' setting up such programs and getting new businesses involved.[58]

Vanpools have been most successful in attracting commuters when supported and encouraged by employers. Large employers (over 500) in Houston, where in the early 1980s over 2,000 vanpools were in operation, were able to attract over 30 percent of employees for trips to and from work when active employer-sponsored programs reached maturity.[59] Employees of smaller organizations were attracted in much fewer numbers—about 5 percent in organizations with 250 to 500 employees and insignificant numbers of smaller employers. While third-party vanpool sponsorship produced a

[56] Cindy Fish, Fred Dock, and William Baltutis, *Lake—Coor Corridor Suburb to Suburb Demonstration Project, Transportation Research Record 1496* (Washington, D.C.: Transportation Research Board, pp. 162–163).

[57] *Nassau Hub Study* (Long Island, N.Y.: Long Island Regional Planning Board, January 1998, p. 62).

[58] Robert T. Dunphy and Ben Lin, *Transportation Management through Partnerships* (Washington, D.C.: Urban Land Institute, 1990, pp. 43–50).

[59] Brian S. Bochner and Jose A. Soegaard, "Increasing Vehicle Occupancy—Vanpools as a Major Travel Mode," *ITE Compendium of Technical Papers, 51st Annual Meeting* (Washington, D.C.: Institute of Transportation Engineers, 1981, p. 2).

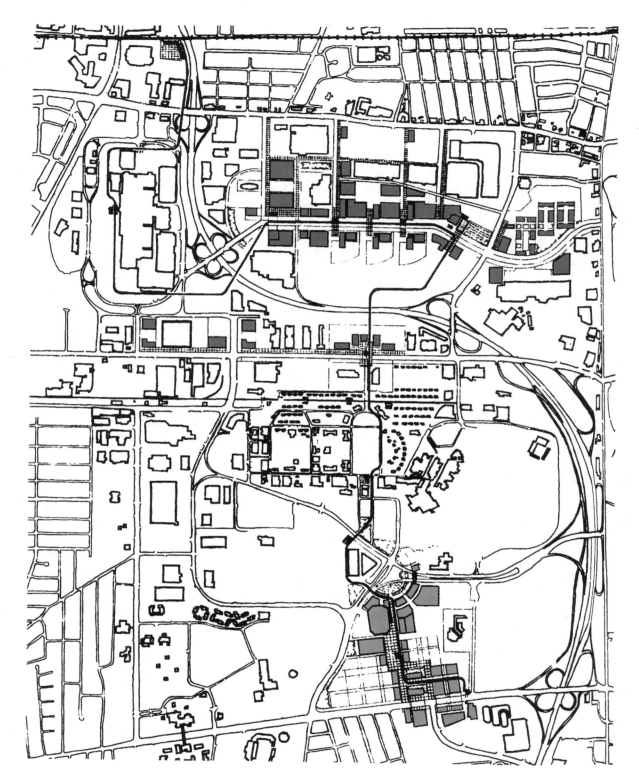

Figure 15–14   Development Supporting Transit-Friendly Scenario—Nassau Hub

■ Existing Buildings
▨ New Transit-Friendly Development in Nassau Hub

Source: *Nassau Hub Study,* Long Island, N.Y.: Long Island Regional Planning Board, January 1998, p. 62.

significant number of vanpools, the *percentage* of total work trips represented never reached significant levels. The economic slump in Houston took some of the congestion incentive and a lot of the market from such programs. However, there have been calls for current travel surveys that can help clarify the market demand for vanpools, carpools, and transit.

The Orange County Transit District in Orange County, California, supported ridesharing programs by assisting in market demand studies for their suburban centers, which approach the size and density of traditional CBDs. In the South Coast Metro Area, for example, the South Coast Metro Alliance was formed in 1985 to market the area, but also in response to an Orange County Transit District study concluding there was potential for TMA to be effective in alleviating traffic demand. This TDM market study led to a joint private-public field office to implement a TMA strategy.[60] Soon after this program was established, the South Coast Air Quality District implemented a regulation requiring all large employers to implement ridesharing programs, a big boost to the TMA program. In 1996, the program was terminated, the same year that the air district lifted the regulation on sites with 100–249 workers, although some firms continued their interest through Southern California Rideshare. In addition to assisting in organizing carpools, the other significant incentive for carpooling is a dedicated high-occupancy vehicle (HOV) lane, which offers a time advantage. Orange County has developed a transitway development program of freeway-based commuter lanes and transitways, focusing on major SACs; and they developed a travel forecasting methodology sensitive to changes in corridor level and site specific characteristics, such as the ability of transitways to provide higher levels of service to activity centers. This tool was used to help determine locations for direct HOV access ramps, including one serving the South Coast Metro Area, which is now in the planning stage.[61]

Streets and Highways

All trips that cannot be accommodated by walking or transit will be made by automobile or other personal vehicle (hereafter simply preferred to as auto). In most U.S. and Canadian cities, trips as an auto driver or passenger may amount to as much as 90 percent or more of all trips to, from, and within a medical or suburban activity center unless significant transit and pedestrian provisions are made. These auto trips must be accommodated on the streets, adjacent highways, and parking facilities of the activity center.

The high density of activities and trip generation at activity centers commonly necessitate much closer spacing than that of the typical suburban roadway system, which may range from 4 to 8 miles for expressways and 1 mile for arterials. A significant difference in establishing political and business support for highways serving activity centers is that on radial arterials, most of the traffic is probably destined downtown. On suburban freeways serving activity centers, most of the traffic is probably not destined there, so improving such freeways requires gaining support of a broader constituency. Bellevue, Washington, for example, grew from a suburban to a regional center with direct access to I-405. As Bellevue has matured, the freeway is reaching capacity, a condition that is expected to limit growth unless it is addressed. Widening the freeway, however, becomes a regional transportation issue, which requires Bellevue to gain broader support.[62]

Arterial spacing almost always needs to be less than one-half mile and often one-quarter mile in SACs, but no more than three to four blocks apart in CBDs. As indicated earlier, such spacing decisions are best made as part of an overall development plan, which makes it possible to ensure route continuity and adequate rights-of-way. As new districts within an activity center are developed, it is then possible to stage the expansion of roads to serve the development. In some cases, developers will be expected to contribute rights-of-way or fund road improvements through impact fees or other conditions of approval. Such a combination of private, local, and state improvements makes an organized staging plan even more important. Intersection capacity needs should be based on estimated peak-hour intersection approach volumes, and they should consider both A.M. and P.M. peaks as well as any other peaks that may occur due to specific land use. Because some intersections will need extra turn lanes, attempts should be made to identify the needs of such locations. Heavy turn locations are best identified from the current turning volume patterns, appropriately expanded to account for planned development. Basic and intersection lane requirements for arterials and other major streets should

---

[60] Valdez and Wang, *Comparison of TDM Market Research Study Results and TMA Development in 3 SACs, Transportation Research Record 1212* (Washington, D.C.: Transportation Research Board, pp. 1–10).

[61] Christine Huard-Spenser, *Transportation Planning Methods for Improving Mobility in Developing Activity Centers in OC, CA, Transportation Research Record 1283* (Washington, D.C.: Transportation Research Board, 1990, p. 37).

[62] *Downtown Bellevue, Washington: An Evaluation of Development Potential and Recommendations for Strategies to Shape a Vibrant Central Business District* (Washington, D.C.: Urban Land Institute, 1997, p. 43).

be sufficient to accommodate projected traffic at the desired level of service in the horizon year. Sufficient right-of-way should be reserved for *ultimate* needs, including special provisions for property access. This means that likely access provisions should be generally included in the analysis process, as should provisions for pedestrian and transit facilities. Urban design and other amenities should also be included in the right-of-way. If needed and appropriate, building setbacks may also need to be specified to help meet the expected needs. An example of arterial improvements based on planned development patterns is shown in Figure 15–15 for Perimeter Center (or Buckhead), a major suburban center north of Atlanta.

Parking

Parking code requirements in downtowns assume significant use of other, often commercial facilities; shared parking that allows multiple trips without moving the car; and often significant use of transit. These same principles should apply in suburban centers, although parking code requirements are often based on satisfying all needs on-site, creating the box

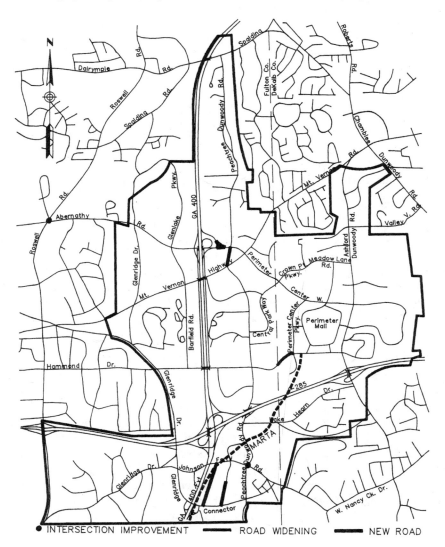

Figure 15–15   Planned Highway Improvements—Perimeter Center

Source: The Long Island Regional Planning Board.

Table 15–15 Selected Activity Center Analyses and Methods

Analysis	Methods
Trip generation (total or by purpose), including impacts of various demand-related policies	ITE *Trip Generation,* NCHRP Report 323, special local studies, regional travel model trip generation techniques imported adjustment factor from other surveys, validated model imported from another area and validated locally, other locally acceptable methodology. May be daily or peak hour, weekday, weekend, or seasonal peak.
Travel patterns	Activity center origin destination surveys (employees, visitors, and/or residents), regional origin-destination data applied to activity center, regional travel model (regional or study area validation), manually determined distribution based on locally acceptable surrogate data, other locally acceptable method.
Land use and demographic projections, including zoning strategy analyses	Activity center-based real estate market study, regional market study considering activity center, zonal allocation made based on region or subregion control totals, local agency estimate, other locally acceptable method. Primary projections may be land use or demographic; may need to be convened for trip generation purposes. [Zoning strategy analysis may be percentage of maximum zoning intensity as basis for estimate; if so, percentage of maximum density actually realized should be based on experience and timing should be based on projected absorption rates.]
Transit ridership	Regionally calibrated mode-split model, mode based on activity center attitude surveys backed by experience in similar areas elsewhere, model imported from another similar area validated locally if possible, default model from computer software package validated locally, other locally acceptable model.
Facility traffic or transit volume estimates	Assignment using region, subregion, or activity center model on mainframe or microcomputer with locally acceptable software (should be validated if other than calibrated regional model) refined with volume smoothing technique (e.g., NCHRP report 255),[1] manual adjustment of agency traffic assignments (for minor network variations only); manual assignment for limited number of zones using surrogate data or distribution from prior regional, subregional, or activity center assignment; other locally acceptable method. May be daily, peak-hour based on relevant peak-hour percentages and directional splits, or direct peak-hour assignments.
System capacity analysis	For roadways, daily link equivalent of peak-hour directional volumes factored using appropriate signal splits, directional splits, and peak-hour percentages, daily capacities accepted for regional planning; peak-hour directional or nondirectional capacities using appropriate signal splits and general approach conditions—all generalized for application where turning volumes cannot be accurately estimated. Where short-term intersection analyses are to be made and turning volumes can be projected with reasonable accuracy, use current Highway Capacity Manual (HCM)-based analyses techniques or other locally acceptable method or a system-based method using signal progression to set signal splits (e.g., PASSER).[2] For transit, use combination of (policy) headway, peak-load local points, and station stop boarding and *HCM* analysis technique or other acceptable method. For pedestrian system, use current *HCM* pedestrian procedure.
Traffic signal system	Requires reasonably accurate estimates of hourly directional volumes including turn movements. Use software such as TRANSYT for signal network analyses and PASSER for route analyses.
Parking	Start with ITE *Parking Generation,*[3] ULI *Parking Requirements for Shopping Centers,*[4] or other acceptable source and adjust for internal trips and shared parking using data presented earlier in this chapter or other locally acceptable research.

[1] N. J. Pederson and D. R. Samdahl, *Highway Traffic Data for Urbanized Area Project Planning and Design,* NCHRP Report 225 (Washington, D.C.: Transportation Research Board, December 1982).

[2] *Highway Capacity Manual,* Special Report 209 (Washington, D.C.: Transportation Research Board, 1985).

[3] *Parking Generation* (Washington, D.C.: Institute of Transportation Engineers, 1985).

[4] Walker Parking Consultants, *Parking Requirements for Shopping Centers* (Washington, D.C.: Urban Land Institute, scheduled 1999 publication).

Source: Institute of Transportation Engineers, *Transportation Planning Handbook,* Englewood Cliffs, N.J.: Prentice-Hall, 1992.

in a sea of parking model. The results of such thinking can ensure adequate parking while creating other problems. In Bellevue, Washington, where it is possible to walk between some offices and retail, propriety lots linked to individual buildings force shoppers to move their cars as they shop or attend meetings. This generates midday traffic jams and a perception that parking is a hassle.[63]

Mixed-use developments planned with ULI's "Shared Parking" technique or similar methods create development districts with the possibility of shared parking. An ITE survey of 143 communities across the United States and Canada found that 41 percent allowed reductions in parking requirements if shared parking was implemented. In three regions—the Mid-Atlantic, the Midwest, the Northwest, and California—over half of the local governments indicated that shared parking was allowable. A case study of Downtown Oakland using ULI shared parking rates, adjusted to reflect observed demand, found offices in mixed-use projects had 10 percent lower parking demand than in stand-alone projects, restaurant demand was 85–90 percent lower, and location near a BART station reduced office parking demand by 40 percent.[64] Similar adjustments can be made to conventional methods of estimating parking (e.g., ITE's *Parking Generation*) to account for above-normal transit, ride sharing, pedestrian mode shares, and applicable shared parking.

The issue of charging for parking, common in CBDs, is favored by those who advocate less reliance on the automobile; and there are some suburban business groups that are willing to consider it. The challenge is to make it work for businesses; their workers; and clients, who are likely to have other free parking options.

Other Activity Center Planning Issues

Transportation is only one of the considerations in activity center planning. Real estate market demand, land use mix, local site characteristics, the surrounding area, design opportunities and constraints, environmental aspects, and economics all enter the total analysis. Transportation is one of the most important factors, but far from the only one. As a result, transportation should be planned jointly with other plan components.

Appropriate effects of interactive planning may include but are certainly not limited to those listed in Table 15–15. These vary by activity center.

Perhaps the most difficult single factor to deal with is the uncertainty of the real estate market. Over the long term, good planning can create a vision for an activity center as well as a "build out" scenario that estimates the ultimate development levels. Transportation improvements are staged to provide facilities over a fairly long time (short-term capital programs can be 6 years). The real estate market and financing can deliver developments much more quickly. If they are in the "wrong" place from the transportation planner's perspective, this creates two problems: unexpected traffic congestion around the new development and an unnecessary transportation investment elsewhere—at least in the short term.

Local and regional planning agencies can help to overcome this dilemma by requiring planned transportation facilities to be in place before granting development approvals. Some agencies approve zoning with the contingency that the landowner commit certain improvements. Others require right-of-way dedications, financial contributions, or other participation to support the overall plan. Such approaches can help bring order to a seemingly chaotic process. On the other hand, there is often a community desire for certain developments, especially during economic downturns.

As difficult as it often is to focus public and private interest and efforts on activity center planning, even successful collaborations require follow up, an even more difficult challenge. Such continuing programs are critical to ensure timely implementation of transportation projects are regular updates on changes in development plans. Uptown Houston, for example, has a full-time traffic engineer dedicated to carrying out plans of both the public and private owners. Such a continuing planning effort needs to involve at one time or another the property owners, developers, and businesses, as well as appropriate public agencies, area residents, and sometimes the general public.

---

[63] *Downtown Bellevue, Washington: An Evaluation of Development Potential and Recommendations for Strategies to Shape a Vibrant Central Business District* (Washington, D.C.: Urban Land Institute, 1997, p. 34).

[64] ITE Committee 6F-52, *Shared Parking Guidelines: an Informational Report* (Washington, D.C.: Institute of Transportation Engineers, 1995, Appendix).

Implementation of Transportation Plans

Transportation plans for activity centers invariably involve a cooperative effort among private- and public-sector entities. The cooperation starts during planning, but extends into funding, construction, operation, and other areas. For this reason, priorities, strategies, and responsibilities for implementation should be agreed to by all parties during the planning process. It is seldom possible for the parties to make binding financial commitments very far into the future due to all the uncertainties that surround both public- and private-sector funding. Nevertheless, each entity should agree to the responsibilities for right-of-way, funding, construction, operation, and maintenance of each plan component. In many cases joint responsibility may be appropriate. Priorities should be set using criteria consistent with overall participant and activity center objectives with the understanding that (1) the activity center systems must function with each increment of improvement and (2) there must be ability to adjust implementation in response to changing conditions.

Institutional Instruments

All institutional instruments should be established prior to actual need. Some require complex legal and political efforts; others may exist in or near the needed form. These instruments may include:

- Zoning overlay district (area with special zoning provisions) or special district with special provisions to facilitate or ensure plan implementation.

- Special assessment or improvement district.

- Model joint access agreements.

- Development agreements between developers and local governments to guide long-term, multiphase projects.

- Revised subdivision platting or access policy components or powers.

- Special public authority for district.

- Transportation or thoroughfare plan amendments.

- Urban design guidelines.

- Special transportation system standards or design criteria.

- Additional development review or approval stages.

- Creations of district association.

The Goal Is a Process, Not Just a Plan

One of the great advantages of CBDs is that there is only one in a city (and a region). Downtown development and transportation issues as a result often receive prominent attention by the mayor and council, the media, downtown businesses, and the public. In contrast, there are often many suburban centers. They usually fall in different cities or in the unincorporated area of the county, and their dominant businesses are frequently branches of a firm headquartered downtown or elsewhere. With development densities second only to the downtown, such centers are in the dilemma of needing city services but getting country management. The kind of police and fire, trash collection, and property maintenance services required can be taxing on a suburban government. Beginning in the 1970s, downtowns in Toronto, New Orleans, and elsewhere were faced with similar problems because of deteriorating municipal finances; and they recognized that the businesses would need to pay to ensure adequate services to maintain a healthy business district. The result was the creation of a business improvement district (BID), which allowed property owners to tax themselves to provide the kind of services that could no longer be provided by the city. Originally, such programs emphasized trash collection and security, the most visible services to the public. Recently, some have recognized the need for broader involvement in longer term planning and economic development. Such an institution, with official sanction, may present an excellent means of bringing businesses, developers, and city officials together to address critical needs for downtowns. To date, however, these BIDs are largely a city phenomenon, although there are some suburban examples, such as the Cumberland Galleria outside Atlanta.

For growing suburban centers, the pressing need has been traffic, not trash; and the creation of Transportation Management Associations (TMAs) served a similar purpose in the suburbs to that of the BIDs downtown. While most of the focus has been on operating or promoting commuter assistance programs, some of the early TMAs, including ones in Princeton, the Baltimore/Washington International Airport, and El Segundo, California took an active role in addressing longer term transportation needs. The proliferation of such TMAs creates a built-in institution in many suburban growth centers that not only can help in identifying needs but also in advocacy for implementing plans. Where there is not a formal institution such as a BID or a TMA, it may be useful to create at least an informal group that can help carry a vision and pressure the appropriate parties to implement their plans when the initial enthusiasm has waned.

CHAPTER 16
Bicycle and Pedestrian Facilities

Jennifer L. Toole, AICP and Bettina Zimny, AICP
The RBA Group
Morristown, NJ

Introduction

Bicycling and walking are basic, fundamental forms of transportation that are sometimes overlooked in this age of high-tech motorized travel. Yet these human-powered transportation modes are important to the success of the transportation system as a whole. All travelers are pedestrians at some point during their trip—even if it is between their parking space and their office building. According to the 1990 Nationwide Personal Transportation Survey, one in ten households do not own a vehicle and therefore must rely on alternative forms of transportation.[1] Add to this the number of people who are either too old or too young to drive, and one realizes that for quite a sizable number of U.S. citizens, the ability to walk or bicycle to a destination is critical to their freedom of mobility. Transportation planners and engineers therefore have the same level of responsibility to provide for the safety of bicyclists and pedestrians as they do for motorists.

There are growing efforts throughout the United States to improve conditions for bicycling and walking. Congress recognized this need in 1991 when it passed the Intermodal Surface Transportation Efficiency Act (ISTEA)—a spending package that increased the responsibilities of local and state governments to plan and implement bicycle and pedestrian facilities. The funding infusion provided by ISTEA and continued by Transportation Efficiency Act for the 21st Century (TEA-21) in turn fueled even stronger efforts to build trails and to renovate streets and roadways for bicycling and walking.

Goals for Bicycling and Walking

In a comprehensive, national study on bicycling and walking, the U.S. Department of Transportation (DOT) found that "increased levels of bicycling and walking transportation would result in significant benefits in terms of health and physical fitness, the environment, and transportation-related effects." The U.S. DOT set the following goals as a result of this study:

- To double the percentage of total trips made by bicycling and walking in the United States—from 7.9 to 15.8 percent of all travel trips.

- To simultaneously reduce by ten percent the number of bicyclists and pedestrians killed or injured in traffic crashes.[2]

Current levels of bicycling and walking in the United States are low (7.9 percent of total trips) when compared to the number of people who say they would bicycle or walk if there were safe facilities available. In a 1995 poll conducted by Rodale Press, 31 percent of all Americans whose primary means of transportation is driving alone in their car would prefer to commute and run errands using some other means of transportation. Among bicyclists who do not currently commute, forty percent (representing over 25 million people) say they would start commuting if they had access to safe bicycle facilities. In the noncyclist category, over one-third (22.7 million people) say they would start riding to work if they had access to safe bike lanes on roads and highways. This represents a tremendous opportunity to reduce single occupant vehicle trips.

---

[1] The actual figure is probably higher than this, since low-income households have a higher nonresponse bias to surveys.

[2] U.S. Department of Transportation, Federal Highway Administration, *The National Bicycling and Walking Study—Final Report* (Washington, D.C.: U.S. DOT, Federal Highway Administration, 1994), pp. VI.

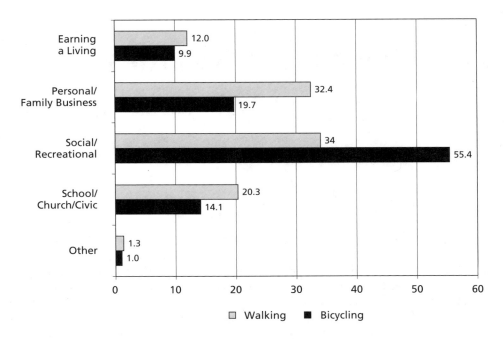

Figure 16–1 Walking and Bicycling Trips by Purpose

Source: *National Bicycling and Walking Study*, Washington, D.C.: U.S. Department of Transportation, Federal Highway Administration, 1994.

People choose to bicycle and walk every day, either out of convenience, necessity, or for other reasons. There are nine million daily bicycle trips and 56 million daily walk trips in the United States each day. Thirty-two percent of the walk trips are for personal and family business, and 55 percent of the daily bike trips are for social or recreational purposes.[3] (Figure 16–1.) The combined number of people who bicycle and walk every day is greater than the amount of people who use transit.

Bicyclists and Pedestrians at Risk

Bicycle and pedestrian safety is a growing concern for many communities. In 1996, 82,000 pedestrians were injured and over 5,400 were killed in the United States. On average, a pedestrian is injured in a traffic crash every six minutes in this country. Children and seniors are at great risk—one-third of pedestrian injuries and fatalities in 1996 were children under the age of 16.

Bicycle safety is also a problem, although far fewer are killed each year than pedestrians. In 1996, 761 bicyclists were killed and 59,000 were injured in traffic crashes. As with pedestrian crashes, children between the ages of 5 and 15 are at the highest risk—nearly one-third of the bicyclists killed in traffic crashes in 1996 were in this age range.[4] Since most crashes involve a motor vehicle, safety improvements for bicyclists and pedestrians are important for everyone on the road.

Global Perspective

The U.S. is not alone in its efforts to encourage more bicycling and walking for transportation. In 1997, the British Parliament approved the Road Traffic Reduction Act. The act requires local traffic authorities to undertake reviews of current and future traffic levels on local roads in their area, and to produce a report containing targets for reducing levels

---

[3] *National Personal Transportation Survey* (Washington, D.C.: U.S. DOT, Federal Highway Administration, 1995).

[4] National Highway Traffic Safety Administration, *NHTSA Traffic Safety Facts* (Washington, D.C.: NHTSA, 1996).

or rates of growth. In 1998, the British Government enacted measures to include bike lanes on all new roads and to require trains to transport bicycles. Their long-term goals are to have twenty percent of all trips conducted by bicycle.[5]

Bicycling and walking play key roles in the transportation systems of other developed nations, including Japan, the Netherlands, and many European countries. In Japan an estimated 15 percent of workers rely on bicycles for their commute to work, and in Dutch cities between twenty and fifty percent of all trips are typically made by bicycle.[6]

Many countries are finding that traffic calming plays an important role in increasing the levels of bicycling and walking. Slower traffic is a critical factor in pedestrian and bicyclists' comfort level—therefore traffic calming can often do as much to encourage bicycling and walking along a corridor as upgraded sidewalks or designated bicycle facilities. The choice to bicycle or walk has much to do with the quality of the environment between the origin and destination. The principles of traffic calming (as described in Chapter 17) should be implemented in conjunction with improvements to the streetscape and removal of barriers to bicycling and walking.

In a growing number of communities, bicycling and walking are considered as solid indicators of a community's livability. In cities and towns where people can regularly be seen out bicycling and walking, there is a palpable sense that these are safe and friendly places to live and visit.

Bicycle and Pedestrian Planning Theory

Planning opportunities for enhancing the bicycle and pedestrian experience can include many avenues: urban design, facility design, public involvement, traffic calming, traffic engineering, landscaping, funding, bicycle and pedestrian behavior studies, and more. (Figure 16–2.) Although they share some similar issues, one common misconception is that both bicycling and walking issues should be addressed under one heading. In reality they are separate and distinct modes of transportation that should be studied individually. For example, pedestrian access to transit will logically require more sidewalk connections and improvements to roadway crossings in the immediate vicinity of the station and bus stop, while bicycle improvements might include bike lanes in a wider radius and bike parking facilities at the station itself.

Bicycling and walking are not functionally different from other transportation modes: the same basic assumptions that allow planners to predict the outcome of transport decisions for other modes can be applied to bicycling and walking. After fifty years of evolution, very few stones have been left unturned in motor vehicle traffic modeling.[7] In contrast, bicycle and pedestrian transportation planning theory is in its formative years. Even the most basic planning theories for bicycling and walking are still evolving.

Providing Balance Among Transportation Modes

The underlying principle of bicycle and pedestrian planning is to provide a system that allows a choice in modes and a reasonable balance in accommodations, without favoring one mode to the expense of all others. In order to achieve this balance, bicycling and walking must become more attractive alternatives, which requires considerable retrofit in most communities.

In many cases, creating a reasonable balance means more than simply installing sidewalks or designated bicycle facilities. For the pedestrian, it means increased attention to factors that have—in the past—been beyond the domain of responsibility for engineers. It means making streetscape improvements—an area in which engineers are not typically trained, but must now become more proficient in with the assistance of planners, landscape architects, and urban designers.

---

[5] "Britain Passes Historic Legislation to Reduce Traffic," *Pro-Bike News,* vol. 18, no. 2 (Washington, D.C.: Bicycle Federation of America, February 1998).

[6] U.S. Department of Transportation, Federal Highway Administration, *The National Bicycling and Walking Study—Final Report* (Washington, D.C.: U.S. DOT, Federal Highway Administration, 1994), pp. 130–132.

[7] Bruce Epperson, "Bicycle Transportation: A Qualitative Approach" (unpublished work, 1996).

It is important to remember that, despite the lack of facilities, pedestrians and bicyclists will continue to use streets that have no accommodations, and they are within their rights to do so. In some cases, they have no other choice in order to get to their destination. In other cases, they may have an alternative route, but that route is circuitous and indirect. Pedestrians and bicyclists almost always take the most direct route, because to do otherwise they must expend more of their own time and energy.

Design imperative

- *Transportation planners should not fail to provide a facility because of a concern that it would encourage walking and bicycling in a dangerous location. Pedestrian and bicycle travel will occur regardless, and the burden of responsibility is to accommodate that travel in the best way possible.*

Transportation planners should not fail to implement bicycle and pedestrian improvements because of liability concerns. National standards clearly state that, when designing bike lanes and paved shoulders for bicycle use, any additional space for bicycles is better than none. ADA also provides a clear imperative to provide facilities for the disabled within the public right-of-way, facilities that will benefit all pedestrians.

Bicycle and Pedestrian Travel Demand Simulation and LOS Analysis

While bicycle and pedestrian planning research has not yet developed to the same level as motor vehicle planning, some sketch planning techniques do exist. When planning bicycle and pedestrian facilities, it is important to remember that current volumes usually do not reflect demand for two reasons:

1) There is an overall lack of accommodations throughout most communities, resulting in fewer numbers of bicyclists and pedestrians.

2) Dispersed land uses create trip distances that are perceived as being too far to make on foot or by bicycle.

Travel demand modeling and Level of Service (LOS) analysis for bicycling and walking are emerging areas of study that are being used by more and more by transportation planning agencies to forecast areas needing improvements and to determine what types of improvements are needed. There are two statistically calibrated mathematical equations currently in use that determine the relative comfort of a bicyclist given the conditions of a particular street segment: the Bicycle Compatibility Index[8] and the Bicycle Level of Service (BLOS) model.[9] These equations are very similar. They measure variables in the street cross section that affect bicycling, such as amount of motor vehicle traffic, traffic speed, the amount of separation between the bicyclist and moving traffic, the percentage of heavy vehicles, presence of on-street parking, and the condition of the pavement surface.

Pedestrian suitability models are in a more formative stage. Early research focused primarily on quantifying walkway space, flow characteristics, and pedestrian capacity analysis.[10] *The Highway Capacity Manual* provides procedures for operational analysis of walkways, crosswalks, and intersections that illustrate the LOS for such spaces. More recent pedestrian analysis has examined factors that affect a pedestrian's level of comfort in a given road corridor. These models, such as Portland's Land Use, Transportation, Air Quality Connection (LUTRAQ) and others, examine quality-related comfort, convenience, and safety factors of the pedestrian environment. Further details on travel demand modeling and LOS analyses for the bicycle and pedestrian modes are provided later in this chapter.

---

[8] Alex Sorton, "Bicycle Stress Level as a Tool to Evaluate Urban and Suburban Bicycle Compatibility," *Transportation Research Record 1438* (Washington, D.C.: Transportation Research Board, 1994).

[9] Bruce W. Landis, "Real-Time Human Perceptions: Toward a Bicycle Level of Service," *Transportation Research Record 1578* (Washington, D.C.: Transportation Research Board, 1997).

[10] John J. Fruin and G. Benz, "Pedestrian Time-Space Concept for Analyzing Corners and Crosswalks," *Transportation Research Record 959* (Washington, D.C.: Transportation Research Board, 1984).

Regional Transportation Patterns

Land Use

Facility Design/Engineering

Community Support/Encouragement

Education

Enforcement

Figure 16–2   Bicycle and Pedestrian Planning Issues

Source: The RBA Group, Morristown, N.J.

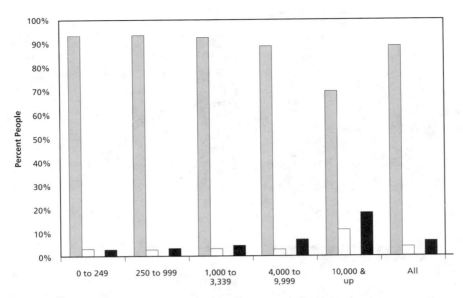

Figure 16–3   Mode of Transportation by Population Density

Source: *NHTSA Traffic Safety Facts*, Washington, D.C.: National Highway Traffic Safety Administration, 1996.

Land Use

Bicycle and pedestrian trips are typically characterized by short trip distances: approximately one quarter-mile to one mile for pedestrian trips and one quarter-mile to three miles for bicycle trips. Land use patterns therefore have a critical effect on bicycle and pedestrian circulation. Current development trends such as suburban sprawl and decentralization result in inconvenient linkages between residential areas and shopping and employment centers, and they create disincentives for bicycling and walking. The 1995 *National Personal Transportation Survey*[11] shows that levels of bicycling and walking increase as population density increases. (Figure 16–3.)

Opportunities to provide accessible, safe, convenient, and inviting environments for walking and bicycling should include adoption of effective land use planning and design standards. Research has shown that land use strategies involving mixed-use development with high densities, suitable job and housing balance, effective parking management, and transit-oriented design can reduce auto trips by as much as 18 percent.[12]

Education and Enforcement

Training and education of bicyclists, pedestrians, and motorists, and enforcement of existing laws and regulations are essential. Different types of users need different kinds of facilities, training, and programs in order to bicycle, walk, and drive safely and efficiently, with confidence. Needs vary for each user type. For example, children, older adults, recreational bicyclists and walkers, and commuters each have different skill levels, experience, and perceptions of risks. An understanding of these varying types of users and their needs is necessary in order to provide resources, programs, and facilities to accommodate everyone.[13]

Education, safety and security needs are frequently identified by communities. Bicycle and pedestrian accidents and injuries, hazardous traffic conditions, lack of enforcement of traffic laws, poor maintenance of walkways and bicycle routes, insufficient lighting and security along facilities, and lack of bicycle and pedestrian training programs are problems that contribute to confidence and security-related needs.

---

[11] National Highway Traffic Safety Administration, *NHTSA Traffic Safety Facts* (Washington, D.C.: NHTSA, 1996), p. 12.

[12] Federal Transit Authority, *Planning, Developing and Implementing Community-Sensitive Transit* (Washington, D.C.: FTA, 1996).

[13] John Williams, *Balancing Engineering, Education, Law Enforcement and Encouragement—National Bicycling and Walking Case Study No. 11* (Washington, D.C.: U.S. Department of Transportation, Federal Highway Administration, 1994.)

Bicycle and Pedestrian Transportation Planning Studies

The rising awareness of bicycle and pedestrian issues in transportation planning has brought with it a new era of planning for these modes. In most states and many local and regional areas, transportation agencies are becoming more responsive to improving conditions for bicyclists and walkers. Many of these projects have started with planning studies, whether they were small scale (such as a study to improve bicycle and pedestrian access to a neighborhood bus stop) or large scale (such as a statewide master plan for bicycling and walking).

While there are some common elements (such as public participation) that nearly all bicycle and pedestrian planning projects should include, they otherwise can vary greatly depending upon the particular needs of the community. The following are a variety of different planning studies that may be initiated by transportation planners to better meet the needs of people on foot and bicycle, with descriptions of important issues and topics to cover in these studies.

The Statewide Bicycle and Pedestrian Master Plan

Many parts of the United States have programs to promote bicycling and walking. Generally, the focus has been on bicycling, with the recent addition of pedestrian programs. The more successful programs are characterized by comprehensiveness, stable funding, development of facilities, and other components. These have evolved in response to a variety of circumstances. In Florida, accident statistics have been the spur to action. In Minnesota, the economics of encouraging bicycle use have appealed to advocates, politicians, and agency staff alike.[14] More recent plans and programs, such as New Jersey, Pennsylvania, and Oregon are based on target usage goals, performance measures and implementation programs.

The following elements should be part of a statewide planning process:

- *Vision*—an overall statement of the state's desires for nonmotorized travel.

- *Goals and objectives*—detailed steps for how the agency plans to fulfill the vision.

- *Performance measures*—— the "report card" by which progress towards the objectives, goals, and vision can be measured.

- *Current conditions*—data relating to levels of use, safety problems, the suitability of the existing on- and off-road physical network of facilities, and policies and practices for nonmotorized travel.

- *Strategies and actions*—potential and proposed bicycle- and pedestrian-related changes to the physical environment and institutional practices.

- *Implementation*—identification of physical and programmatic activities that can be funded to help reach the vision, goals, and objectives. These may include both pilot projects and implementation tools, such as facility design guidelines, mapping, and technical training and assistance.

- *Evaluation*—assessment of progress in moving towards the vision and goals, using the performance measures as guides.[15]

Local Bicycle Network Plans

The first step in improving local conditions is to determine where improvements should go and what they should consist of. In most communities, there's no shortage of locations that need sidewalks and bikeways, therefore decisions must be made as to which locations should receive first priority for funding, and which improvements can be incorporated

---

[14] U.S. Department of Transportation, Federal Highway Administration, *The National Bicycling and Walking Study—Final Report* (Washington, D.C.: U.S. DOT, Federal Highway Administration, 1994).

[15] U.S. Department of Transportation, Federal Highway Administration, *Bicycle and Pedestrian Planning Under ISTEA*, FHWA Publication No. FHWA-HI-94-028 (Washington, D.C.: U.S. DOT, FHWA, 1994.)

in other ongoing highway or development projects. Some communities develop independent bicycle and pedestrians master plans, while others address these issues in conjunction with their overall transportation planning effort.

A route improvement plan is a critical first step in developing a network of local and regional facilities. A bicycle network plan typically identifies streets that need improvements and establishes a prioritized schedule for installing the new facilities.

Local bicycle network plans primarily focus on improvements within the street cross section ("on-road" improvements), however they may sometimes include a trail and greenway ("off-road") element (see the following description of a trail plan). In addition to providing a more efficient network for bicycle transportation, planning and installing on-road bicycle facilities can help to alleviate conflicts between bicyclists and pedestrians in areas where sidewalk bicycling is common.

There are several key issues in determining which streets should receive the highest priority for new bicycle facilities.

1) *Bicycle travel demand:* an estimate of latent demand for bicycling should be made in order to determine locations where bicycle facilities are most needed to serve travel needs. As mentioned earlier in this chapter, demand cannot be accurately measured by counting the numbers of bicyclists using streets that are currently unimproved, since they are often in poor condition and discourage bicycle travel. A more detailed description of bicycle travel demand analysis is provided later in this chapter.

2) *Existing conditions and bicycle suitability analysis*: an important step in determining locations that are in need of bicycle facilities is to evaluate current conditions on candidate roadways. This should include both an overall assessment of compatibility as well as locations with special problems for bicyclists, such as narrow bridges, freeway interchanges, or other obstacles. With this information, decisions can be made regarding locations that may need only minimal improvements to serve bicyclists, versus streets that would require more extensive improvements. A more detailed description of bicycle suitability analysis is provided later in this chapter.

3) *Public opinion and political support:* public opinion is important during the development of a bicycle network plan, not only for the sake of knowing the public's preferences for new facilities, but also in order to develop a base of popular support for alternative transportation. Local community groups, bicycle advocates, and other interested citizens should be given the opportunity to set goals and objectives for planning efforts, and to provide meaningful ideas on locations needing improvements throughout the community.

4) *Route continuity and directness:* a successful bicycle network includes continuous routes that provide direct access to destinations throughout the community. Although during the early stages of implementation gaps in the system are inevitable, eventually the bicycle network should enable a bicyclist to travel between destinations and residential areas with a high level of comfort, and with few delays. Detours that route cyclists a considerable distance away are not desirable, since bicyclists will usually continue to take the most direct route or not ride at all. (Figure 16–4.)

Connections between the on-road network and local trails are critical, since trail entrances often attract bicyclists from nearby residential areas. The bicycle network plan should link trails to nearby employment centers and transit stations as well.

5) *Cost effectiveness:* one of the most important factors in developing an on-road bicycle facility network is cost effectiveness. In addition to developing special bicycle improvement projects that may involve roadway widening, opportunities can be sought to implement facilities during regularly scheduled roadway improvements, such as the following.

- Capacity improvements: when adding lanes and improving intersections to ease motor vehicle congestion, additional width can be provided for bike lanes or wide curb lanes.

Why bicyclists and pedestrians prefer to stay on the thoroughfare:

- The thoroughfare provides the most direct route for bicyclists and pedestrians;
- There may be destinations along the thoroughfare that are inaccessible from side streets;
- Less-traveled streets will often have many stop signs, whereas traffic on the through street has the right-of-way or signals that favor through traffic; and
- Potential conflict points are increased with rerouting, especially for cyclists and pedestrians who must cross the thoroughfare (some cyclists have the added difficulty of additional left turns).

Consequences of rerouting without providing adequate facilities:

- Many cyclists and pedestrians stay on the thoroughfare, causing possible safety problems and reduced capacity (bicyclists riding slowly in a narrow travel lane can cause traffic delays);
- Pedestrians and bicyclists may be routed through uncontrolled crossings of thoroughfares;
- Circuitous route signing that is ignored breeds disrespect for other signing;
- Some motorists will not respect bicyclists or pedestrians who are perceived to be where they don't belong; and
- The importance of bicyclists and pedestrians in the transportation network in diminished.

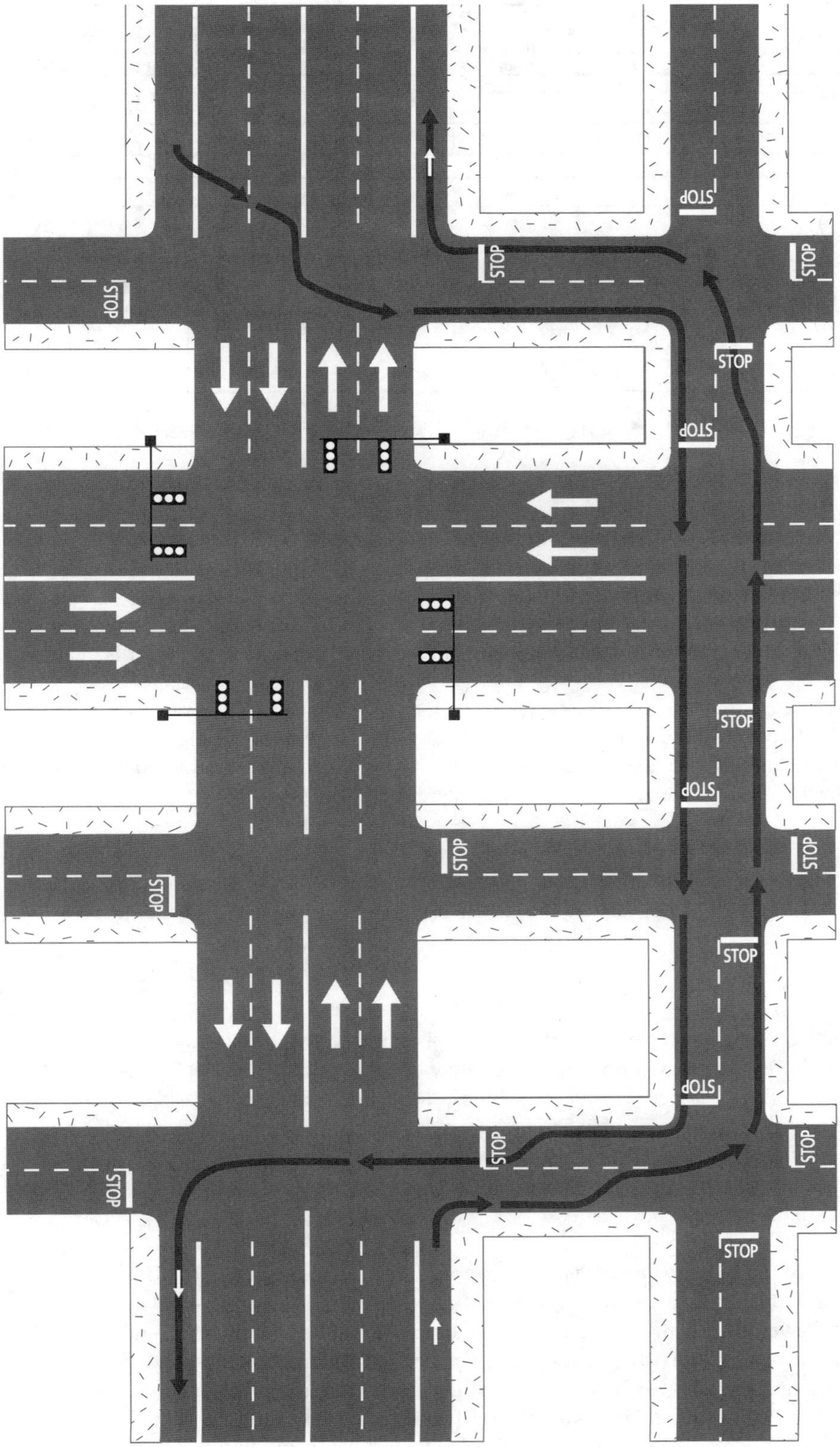

Figure 16–4   Routing of Bicyclists on Thoroughfares

Source: *Oregon Bicycle and Pedestrian Plan*, Salem, Ore.: Oregon Department of Transportation, 1995.

Route Name	From (N or W)	To (S or E)	Len. (Ls) (Mi)	Lanes (L) Th #	Con	Traffic Data Vol. (ADT) (vpd)	Pct. (HV) (%)	Post. Spd. (SPp) mph	Width of Pavement (Wt) (ft)	(Wl) (ft)	(Wps) (ft)	Occu. OSP % (OSPA) (%)	Pvmt. Cond. (PRs) (1..5)	Lane? (Y/N)	BLOS Score	Grade (A..F)
Existing Conditions															####	####
Transit Road	Sheridan Road	Main Street	1.00	4	U	15,000	3	40	12.0			0	4.0		4.27	D
Alternatives Evaluation																
Alternative A :															####	####
Example: 14 foot curb lane			1.00	6	D	17,140	3	45	14.0			0	5.0		3.80	D
Alternative B :															####	####
Example: 12 foot outside lane and 3 foot paved shoulder			1.00	6	D	17,140	3	45	15.0	3.0		0	5.0		3.16	C
Alternative C :															####	####
Example: 12 foot outside lane and 6 foot bike lane			1.00	6	D	17,140	3	45	18.0	6.0		0	5.0		1.90	B

Figure 16–5   BLOS Alternatives Comparison

Source: New York State Department of Transportation, Albany, N.Y.: 1997.

- Street resurfacing: when resurfacing and restriping streets, roadway space can be reallocated to provide on-road bicycle facilities without physically widening the road. Capacity analysis should be done to insure that changes to lane configuration do not create unacceptable delays for motorists. If a bicycle suitability analysis has been done for the roadway, it is also possible to calculate the resulting benefits to bicycle LOS. (Figure 16–5.) More information on street restriping is provided later in this chapter.

- Shoulder paving: a few extra feet of paved roadway shoulder can greatly benefit bicycle travel—as little as three feet of smoothly paved shoulder to the right of the edge line can enable the bicyclist to move out of the travel lane, given that this area does not include rumble strips, which make the shoulder impassable for bicyclists. Paved shoulders of four to six feet in width are preferred.

Upon developing a target network of proposed bicycle facilities, a list of short-term projects can be developed for early implementation. Decisions about which projects should receive the highest priority are usually based on a combination of the factors listed above. These projects will move forward into the funding and design development phases.

Local Pedestrian Plans

It is important for local governments to assess the current condition of the pedestrian transportation system and develop a master plan for future pedestrian improvements. Current conditions may be measured by a variety of factors. These include security and safety factors that relate to properly designed facilities, such as sidewalks and crossings; convenience and access factors that are associated with connectivity between land uses, access to destinations and intermodal links; and qualitative factors such as aesthetics, streetscape treatments, and pedestrian-scale amenities that are associated with pedestrian comfort levels. Elements of the local pedestrian plan that provide both a qualitative and quantitative assessment of these factors include the following.

- *Sidewalk and crosswalk inventory and improvements*: an inventory should be conducted to identify locations of existing sidewalks and crossings, as well as those that are in need of repair. A plan for pedestrian improvements should be developed, with a phased implementation schedule. Municipally funded sidewalk construction should focus on gaps in the existing sidewalk system, particularly in areas that show a high demand. Sidewalks and safe crossings should also be installed within a one-mile radius of schools, in business districts, and in areas where connections between existing facilities are not likely to occur through new development. Techniques such as "walkability audits" and tools that assess a community's walkability, such as the checklist in Figure 16–6 are readily available and easily adapted to any community. [16]

[16] Dan Burden and Michael Wallwork, *Handbook for Walkable Communities and Pedestrian Facilities Design* (High Springs, Fla.: Campaign to Make America Walkable, 1997).

- *Pedestrian LOS and travel demand:* transportation modeling and quantitative travel demand tools for pedestrian planning have only recently begun to be researched, developed, and utilized. Though research exists for pedestrian capacity analysis *(Highway Capacity Manual)*[17] and travel demand (Zupan and Pushkarev)[18], findings are primarily related to very defined urban environs (e.g., sidewalks, crosswalks, street corners) or geographic areas. A detailed discussion of these pedestrian planning studies may be found in Chapter 5.

More recent efforts in pedestrian trip generation research include Portland's LUTRAQ travel demand model [19] and a "Sketch Plan Method for Estimating Pedestrian Traffic."[20] Also emerging is a Roadside Pedestrian Conditions model[21] that begins to quantify the "perceived safety" of pedestrians through utilization of a number of factors relating to safety, comfort, and convenience.

Components of many of these tools include:

- relationships between land use patterns and household travel behavior,
- ease of street crossings,
- sidewalk continuity,
- local street characteristics and configurations,
- topography,
- trip purpose,
- trip distance,
- weather,
- time of day and illumination. [22]

Pedestrian Task Force Committee

Walkability Checklist

The goal of the pedestrian audit is to assess the quality of the walkable environment in our chosen study areas. Facilities, safety, security, aesthetics, pleasure, motorist behavior, and access to transit all contribute to walkability. Furthermore, a good pedestrian environment should be useable and safe for all including the young, the elderly and those with disabilities.

Getting Started:
Go to your designated starting area. Look over the checklist and the map so that you are familiar with the questions and your route. As you walk, check the problems you encounter for each section of the route. The sections are marked on the map. Note locations of things you would like to see changed right on the map.

How to use the Audit:
◊ Note section numbers (from map) on the audit form.
◊ For each section, use a check mark to indicate the specific problems encountered.
◊ Note comments and mark problem locations on map.
◊ Assign an overall rating for each of the six basic questions by circling one option.

	Section	Section	Section	Section	Section
1. Is there a place to walk?					
• No sidewalks					
• Sidewalks are discontinuous					
• Sidewalks are blocked					
• Sidewalks are in bad shape					
• **Overall Rating:** **1** awful; **2** many problems; **3** some problems, not too bad; **4** good; **5** very good					
2. Is it possible to cross the street safely?					
• No crosswalks where needed					
• No ped signal on traffic light					
• Light not timed adequately					
• Road/intersection too wide					
• **Overall Rating:** **1** awful; **2** many problems; **3** some problems, not too bad; **4** good; **5** very good					
3. ADA access, needs of elderly and children are accommodated?					
• Curb cuts/ramps not available					
• Ramps lead to traffic lane rather than crosswalk					
• Width or condition of sidewalk inadequate					
• Sidewalk/street boundary is not discernable to blind					
• Signal actuators are not accessible					
• Timing of lights is inadequate for slower walkers					
• **Overall Rating:** **1** awful; **2** many problems; **3** some problems, not too bad; **4** good; **5** very good					
4. Is it pleasant and convenient to walk?					
• Needs more grass, flowers, trees					
• Dirty, litter and trash					
• Not well lit					
• Too much traffic					
• Pedestrian access lacking to key destinations					
• Walkways do not access buildings					
• **Overall Rating:** **1** awful; **2** many problems; **3** some problems, not too bad; **4** good; **5** very good					
5. Do drivers behave well?					
• Do not yield to crossing pedestrians					
• Block crosswalk with turning movements					
• Drive too fast for conditions					
• Back up without looking					
• **Overall Rating:** **1** awful; **2** many problems; **3** some problems, not too bad; **4** good; **5** very good					
6. Is transit access convenient?					
• Bus stop not served by sidewalk					
• Bus stop not close to destination					
• Difficult to get to bus stop					
• Bus shelter difficult to use					
• **Overall Rating:** **1** awful; **2** many problems; **3** some problems, not too bad; **4** good; **5** very good					

Figure 16–6 Walkability Checklist

Source: Suzan A. Pinsof, Evanston, Ill.

[17] Transportation Research Board, *Highway Capacity Manual,* National Research Council (Washington, D.C.: TRB, 1988).

[18] Zupan and Pushkarev, *Urban Space for Pedestrians* (Cambridge, Mass.: MIT Press, 1975).

[19] Friends of Oregon, *Making the Land Use Transportation Air Quality Connection—Modeling Practices* (Portland, Ore.: 1000 Friends of Oregon, 1993).

[20] Ercolano, Olson and Spring, "Sketch Plan Method for Estimating Pedestrian Traffic," 1997 Pedestrian Conference (Washington, D.C.: unpublished paper).

[21] Landis, Ottenberg and Vattikuti, "The Roadside Pedestrian Environment: Toward a Comprehensive Level of Service" (Washington, D.C.: Transportation Research Board, 1999).

[22] U.S. Department of Transportation, Federal Highway Administration, *A Compendium of Available Bicycle and Pedestrian Trip Generation Data in the U.S.* (Washington, D.C.: U.S. DOT, FHWA, 1994).

These methodologies may be used to:

- evaluate pedestrian facilities' LOS,

- determine pedestrian trip generation rates for various types of pedestrian activity centers.

A local pedestrian planning process is also an excellent way to bring pedestrian issues into the public forum. The process should include opportunities for local citizens to voice their concerns. It is particularly important to solicit the involvement of the less affluent portions of town: the urban poor are often pedestrians out of necessity. They can provide valuable insights regarding barriers to pedestrian travel. A pedestrian master planning project also provides the opportunity to discuss and implement policy changes.

State and Local Policy Plans

Some states and local governments find that in addition to making physical improvements to their transportation infrastructure, a variety of their policies affecting bicycle and pedestrian transportation have become outdated or do not support alternative transportation. Policy changes can include a number of elements, such as the following.

- *Goals that emphasize alternative transportation*: revisions to transportation goals and objectives that include encouraging alternative transportation. It is helpful to establish measurable goals for increasing bicycle and pedestrian travel and reducing crashes.

- *Changes to standard operating procedures:* policies for standardizing bicycle and pedestrian improvements through the regular activities of local, regional, and state governments. For example, some communities have made it standard transportation policy to include bicycle and pedestrian concerns during all transportation improvement studies, and to provide bicycle facilities and sidewalks whenever streets are constructed or maintained.

- *Revisions to zoning ordinance and street design standards*: revisions to zoning ordinances, subdivision regulations, and local street design standards to encourage or require development of bicycle and pedestrian facilities during development projects. Examples include bicycle parking ordinances, trail development ordinances, and residential street layout requirements that ensure continuity between adjacent developments so that bicyclists and walkers are provided with through-routes. (Figure 16–7). At the state level, roadway design standards can be revised to address bicycle and pedestrian needs as well as those for motor vehicles.

- *Changes to the motor vehicle code:* it is important to eliminate laws that are problematic for bicyclists and pedestrians, such as mandatory sidepath laws (requiring bicyclists to use sidepaths if they exist), or laws that require bicyclists to ride in bike lanes if they exist (this is a problem because bicyclists must merge into travel lanes when making left turns, or when there is debris in the bike lane). Motor vehicle laws should be designed to give pedestrians the right-of-way when crossing the street, and they should limit right-turn on red where appropriate.

Trail and Greenway Plans

Trails and greenways are becoming increasingly important as transportation corridors that traverse all types of land uses. In some communities, trail planning efforts begin with a single project, with additional trail projects coming to the surface after the first trail is successfully completed. Other communities develop a trails and greenway master plan that identifies a variety of potential off-road corridors that could be used for trail connections, such as river and stream floodplains, abandoned railroad corridors, utility rights-of-way, and public or private open space lands.

Greenway and trail projects typically proceed through a feasibility study process (or pre-engineering phase) during which a number of issues are addressed:

- physical suitability of the proposed trail route,

- requirements for land acquisition,

- ideas from local citizens and adjacent land owners,

- trail design features,

- marketing plan and funding strategy,

- maintenance and management plan,

- action plan and phased development strategy.

Final products of the planning process should include a thorough inventory and analysis, a graphic map showing the proposed location of the trail in relationship to adjacent properties, streets, built structures, and other features, and an action plan that defines how the project will move forward.

Transit Access Studies

Improving bicycle and pedestrian access to transit can broaden the service area for transit and provide people with a greater variety of travel options. The economic, transportation, and environmental benefits of pedestrian and bicycle-friendly transit have been well documented in both the United States and other countries.[23] Transit access improvements are relatively low-cost strategies that both promote public transit and lengthen distances for a typical bicycle or walking trip.

Elements of transit access studies include:

- bike-on-transit programs (Figure 16–8),

- bicycle and pedestrian access route improvements,

- bicycle storage facility plans,

- pedestrian-friendly site and station facility plans.

Arterial Corridor Plans

Corridor-wide bicycle and pedestrian plans are designed to improve the mobility of pedestrians and bicyclists, reduce traffic congestion, improve air quality, and enhance quality of life. For the purposes of this chapter, corridors are defined as urban or suburban, heavily trafficked arterials that act as a barrier to nonmotorized travel.

An open grid system (like the one in the bottom diagram) offers direct routes for bicyclists and pedestrians with minimal out-of-direction travel. Street patterns that include cul-de-sacs and dead-end streets (see top diagram) require a long circuitous route to cover a short distance, increasing travel distances for what could otherwise be a fairly short bicycle or walking trip.

One solution is to include off-road paths that link cul-de-sacs and dead-end streets, providing short cuts for bicyclists and pedestrians.

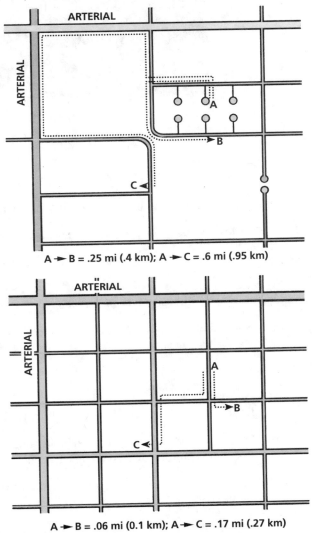

A → B = .25 mi (.4 km); A → C = .6 mi (.95 km)

A → B = .06 mi (0.1 km); A → C = .17 mi (.27 km)

Figure 16–7   Travel Distance Savings with an Open Street Grid

Source: *Oregon Bicycle and Pedestrian Plan*, Salem, Ore: Oregon Department of Transportation, 1995.

---

[23] Replogle and Parcells, *The National Bicycling and Walking Study—Case Study No. 9: Linking Bicycle/Pedestrian Facilities with Transit* (Washington, D.C.: U.S. Department of Transportation, Federal Highway Administration, 1992).

Figure 16–8   Bike-on-Transit

Source: Greenways Incorporated, Cary, N.C.

Primarily three types of pedestrian and bicycle travel patterns or movements occur in these corridors:

1) Movements along the corridor associated with sidewalks, shoulders, and bikeways.

2) Movements across the corridor associated with intersections, crosswalks, underpasses, and overpasses.

3) Movements to destinations within the corridor associated with on- and off-road linkages and between adjacent land uses. (Figure 16–9.)

Problems associated with each type of movement are design-related and operational. They include:

- Sprawling land uses that discourage walking and bicycling by increasing distances between origins and destinations.

- Wide, high-speed, at-grade crossings or intersections with high-speed merge areas, free right turns, double left turn bays, and other obstacles.

- Lack of sidewalks or bikeways and missing links or gaps in the network of bicycle and pedestrian facilities.

- Lack of aesthetic treatments such as lighting, landscaping, and other streetscape amenities that create an attractive, comfortable, and secure environ.

- Numerous driveway openings and curb-cuts that create conflicts between pedestrians, bicyclists, and motor vehicles.

- Inadequate signal timing that does not accommodate slower pedestrians.

- Marginal or inadequate facility provisions, such as narrow sidewalks with little or no separation from the travel lane.

Pedestrian and bicycle-friendly planning and design solutions include:

- Installation of striped crosswalks, medians and pedestrian signals, and adjustment of signal timing.

- Traffic calming treatments such as curb extensions that shorten crossing distances and increase the visibility of pedestrians.

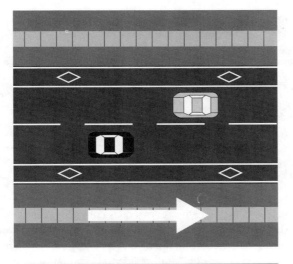

Axial Trips

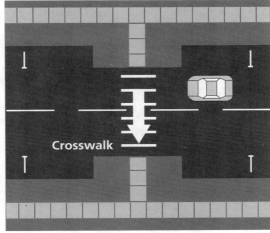

Cross-Corridor Trips

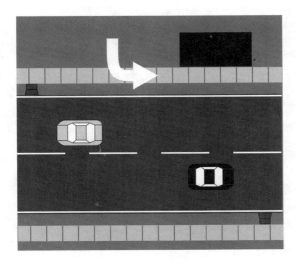

Radial Trips

Figure 16–9   Bicycle and Pedestrian Corridor Travel Patterns

Source: The RBA Group, Morristown, N.J.: 1998.

- Upgrading or enhancement of marginal facilities or substandard utility treatments to provide for bicycle-friendly drainage grates and remove poles and signs from the travelway.

- Provision of sidewalks, wide shoulders, or off-route trails parallel to corridors.

- Improved lighting and signage at over- and under-passes.

Further research and studies documenting these issues can be found in *TRB Report 294A-Planning and Implementing Pedestrian Facilities in Suburban and Developing Suburban and Rural Areas.*

Bicycle Travel Demand Analysis

There are two methods of determining demand for bicycle facilities: the intuitive approach versus the use of a demand forecasting model. The intuitive approach is less time consuming, however it does not yield precise results. For this method, destinations throughout the study area that would attract bicyclists are shown on a base map. Routes are selected that serve higher concentrations of destination points or that serve destinations that typically yield high numbers of bicyclists, such as universities. Emphasis should be placed on routes that link residential communities with destinations in a three-mile radius, since these represent a 10–15 minute bike ride for an average bicyclist.

Destinations should include colleges and universities, shopping centers, major employment centers (e.g., hospitals, business parks, major industries and corporations), schools (public and private), parks and recreation facilities, and trails or greenway connections. Public opinion is important to the success of this method. It is particularly important to gain opinions from a wide variety of local citizens (representing different geographic areas) who represent basic adult and youth riders as well as recreational bicycle enthusiasts.

The other method of estimating latent bicycle travel demand is to adjust conventional motor vehicle travel demand theory so that it applies to bicycle travel. Using a gravity model to measure latent bicycle travel demand can yield results that are more precise than the intuitive approach and compliment the type of analysis that is typically done for motor vehicle and transit travel simulation. This can be particularly important in cases where bicycle improvements are competing for similar funding mechanisms as other modes, since most transportation improvement programs make funding decisions based upon quantifiable results.

When evaluating a system of candidate routes, a model currently exists that effectively measures latent bicycle travel demand. The Latent Demand Score (LDS) has been used for a number of metropolitan bicycle network plans, including Birmingham, Alabama; Philadelphia, Pennsylvania; and Tampa, Florida. (Figure 16–10.) It is a probabilistic gravity model that estimates the relative amount of bicycle travel that would occur if conditions were ideal for bicycling. Similar to motor vehicle travel demand models, the LDS measures latent demand for four trip types:

- home-based work trips,

- home-based shopping trips,

- home-based recreational and social trips,

- home-based school trips.

Not only can a gravity model be used to justify expenditures, it can also help to prioritize future improvements. In addition, the LDS model can be used on trails that are proposed as part of the bicycle transportation network.[24]

Bicycle Route Suitability Analysis

Much progress has been made in developing statistically accurate models that measure bicycle route suitability. These equations measure the relative comfort of bicyclists given the conditions of a particular street segment. The scoring method is derived from a formula that uses variables in the street cross section that affect bicycling, including:

---

[24] Bruce W. Landis, "Bicycle System Performance Measures: The Interaction Hazard and Latent Demand Score Models," *ITE Journal,* vol. 66, no. 2 (Washington, D.C.: Institute of Transportation Engineers, Feb. 1996), pp. 18–26.

$$LDS = \sum_{n=1}^{4} TTS_n \times \frac{\sum_{n=1}^{4}(GA_n \times \overline{TG_n})}{(GA_n \times \overline{TG_n})} \times \left[\overline{TG_n}\sum_{d=1}^{l} P_{nd} \times ga_n\right]$$

n	=	bicycle trip purpose (e.g., work, personal/business, recreation, school)
TTS	=	trip purpose share of all bicycle trips
GA	=	number of generators or attractors per trip purpose
TG	=	average trip generation of attractor or generator
P	=	effect of travel distance on trip interchange, expressed as a probability
ga	=	number of generators or attractors within specified travel distance range
d	=	travel distance <u>range</u> from generator or attractor

Figure 16–10   Latent Demand Score

Source: "Bicycle System Performance Measures: The Interaction Hazard and Latent Demand Score Models," *ITE Journal*, Washington, D.C.: Institute of Transportation Engineers, February 1996.

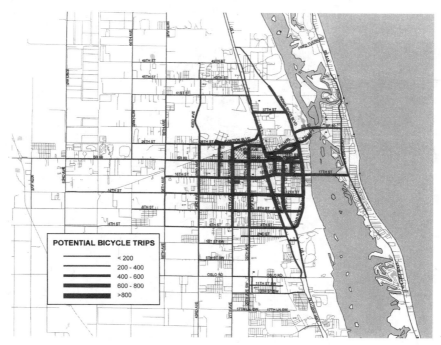

Figure 16–11   Potential Bicycle Trips

Source: *Bicycle and Pedestrian Transportation Plan,* Vero Beach, Fla.: Indian River County Metropolitan Planning Organization, 1997.

- amount of motor vehicle traffic,
- traffic speed,
- width of the right-hand travel lane,
- percentage of heavy vehicles,
- presence of on-street parking,
- condition of the pavement surface.

The formula for the BLOS model[25] is as follows:

$$BLOS = a_1 \ln(\text{Vol}_{15}/L_n) + a_2 SP_t(1 + 10.38HV)^2 + a_3(1/PR_5)^2 + a_4(W_e)^2 + C$$

Where:

BLOS	=	Bicycle Level of Service
Vol_{15}	=	volume of directional traffic in 15-minute time period

$$\text{Vol}_{15} = (ADT \times D \times K_d)/(4 \times PHF)$$

Where:

ADT	=	average daily traffic on the segment or link
D	=	directional factor
K_d	=	peak to daily factor
PHF	=	peak hour factor

L_n	=	total number of directional *through* lanes
SP_t	=	effective speed limit

$$SP_t = 1.1199 \ln(SP_p - 20) + 0.8103$$

Where:

SP_p	=	posted speed limit (a surrogate for average running speed)

HV	=	percentage of heavy vehicles (as defined in the 1994 Highway Capacity Manual)
PR5	=	FHWA's five-point pavement surface condition rating
W_e	=	average effective width of outside through lane:

Where:

$$W_e = W_v - (10 \text{ ft} \times \% \text{ OSPA}) - (W_g \times G_n/66L_s) \quad \text{for cases where } W_l = 0$$

$$W_e = W_v + W_l(1 - 20 \times \% \text{ OSPA}) - (W_g \times G_n/66L_s) \quad \text{for cases where } W_l > 0 \text{ and } W_{ps} = 0$$

$$W_e = W_v + W_l - 2(10 \times \% \text{ OSPA}) - (W_g \times G_n/66L_s) \quad \text{for cases where } W_l > 0 \text{ and } W_{ps} > 0 \text{ and a bike lane exists}$$

Where:

W_t	=	total width of outside lane (and shoulder) pavement
OSPA	=	percentage of segment with occupied on-street parking
W_l	=	width of paving between the outside lane stripe and the edge of pavement
W_{ps}	=	width of pavement striped for on-street parking
W_v	=	effective width as a function of traffic volume
W_g	=	average width of stormwater grates

---

[25] Bruce W. Landis, "Real-Time Human Perceptions: Toward a Bicycle Level of Service," *Transportation Research Record 1578* (Washington D.C.: Transportation Research Board, 1997).

$$G_n \;=\; \text{Number of stormwater grates}$$

$$L_s \;=\; \text{Length of segment in miles}$$

Where:

$W_v \;=\; W_t$		if ADT > 4,000 veh/day
$W_v \;=\; W_t\,(1\text{-}0.00025 \times \text{ADT})$		if ADT $\leq$ 4,000 veh/day, and if the street or road is undivided and unstriped

a_1: 0.507 a_2: 0.199 a_3: 7.066 a_4: –0.005   C: –0.005

$(a_1 - a_4)$ are coefficients established by a multivariate regression analysis

The equation defined above has a correlation coefficient of $R^2 = 0.77$.

The numerical result of the BLOS model is stratified into service categories "A, B, C, D, E, and F" according to the ranges shown in Figure 16–12. This stratification was established according to a linear scale that represents the aggregate response of bicyclists to roadway and traffic stimuli (for more information about the research methods used for this model or the Bicycle Compatibility Index, see the reading list at the end of this chapter).

Bicycle Facility Design

There are several sources of national design guidelines and standards that apply to bicycle facilities. The American Association of State Highway and Transportation Officials' (AASHTO's) *Guide for the Development of Bicycle Facilities* is a comprehensive, basic guideline to bicycle facility planning and design. The *Manual on Uniform Traffic Control Devices* (MUTCD) addresses bicycle facility signage and striping, both for on-road and off-road bicycle facilities. The *Americans with Disabilities Act Accessibility Guidelines* (ADAAG) should be consulted if the particular bicycle facility is also expected to accommodate pedestrians, such is the case with most trails.

When designing bicycle facilities, it is important to:

1. Know the operating characteristics of the bicyclist.

2. Follow design guidelines and standards that have been established in the United States for all bikeway types.

3. Make certain that transition areas (where facilities begin and end) are clear for both bicyclists and motorists.

4. Address not only the need for additional operating space, but also any existing spot hazards as well as ongoing maintenance of the facility.

Bicycles are legally classified as vehicles in most states and are therefore subject to the same rules and responsibilities as all other vehicles. One of the first steps in determining appropriate design for bicycle facilities is to determine the characteristics of the users. In a 1994 document, *Selecting Roadway Design Treatments to Accommodate Bicyclists,* the FHWA stated that "any roadway treatments intended to accommodate bicycle use must address the needs of both experienced and less experienced riders."[26] To implement this policy, the agency proposed the development of three different design cyclists—Groups A, B, and C.

Figure 16–12 Stratified Categories for the BLOS Model

LEVEL-OF-SERVICE	BLOS Score
A	≤ 1.5
B	> 1.5 and ≤ 2.5
C	> 2.5 and ≤ 3.5
D	> 3.5 and ≤ 4.5
E	> 4.5 and ≤ 5.5
F	> 5.5

[26] W.C. Wilkinson and others, *Selecting Roadway Design Treatments to Accommodate Bicycles* (Washington, D.C.: U.S. Department of Transportation, Federal Highway Administration, 1994), p. 1.

BLOS A

BLOS B

BLOS C

BLOS D

BLOS E

BLOS F

Figure 16–13   Bicycle Levels of Service A–F

Source: The RBA Group, Morristown, N.J.

- *Group A—advanced adult bicyclists*: Group A bicyclists are experienced riders who generally use their bicycle as they would a motor vehicle. Research has shown that Group A bicyclists are not necessarily more comfortable in traffic since they have a heightened awareness of potential danger. Despite this, Group A bicyclists are generally more willing to ride on roadways that have no bicycle accommodations. They ride for convenience and speed and want direct access to destinations with a minimum of detour or delay. They prefer to have sufficient operating space within the street cross section to eliminate the need for either themselves or a passing motor vehicle to shift position. The Bicycle Federation of America estimates that five percent of all bicyclists fall into the Group A category.[27]

- *Group B—basic adult riders*: Basic or less confident adult riders may still be using their bicycles for transportation purposes but have a relatively high aversion to interaction with traffic. These bicyclists have both a wide variation in skill and strength, and great differences in their self-assessment of skills. For these reasons, this category contains the broadest cross section of user profiles and operating characteristics.[28]

Basic riders are more comfortable riding on neighborhood streets and multi-use paths and prefer designated facilities such as bike lanes on busier streets. If possible, they avoid roads with fast and busy traffic unless they have additional space in which to operate. Despite their aversion to traffic, basic adult riders can still be expected to use major arterials. Many bicycle-dependent users are forced to travel on high-speed, high-volume streets in order to reach jobs or basic needs. Further compounding this problem is the fact that many of these bicycle dependents live in central city areas and are employed in service industries with nontraditional work hours, requiring them to make one or both commutes in the dark. Many bicycle-dependent users have little enthusiasm or skills for bicycling, and in many cases they are not aware that they are required to follow traffic laws.[29]

- *Group C—children riders*: For most children, bicycle use is initially monitored by their parents. While they may not travel as far as their adult counterparts, they still require access to key destinations in their community, such as schools, convenience stores, and recreational facilities. Child riders enter and exit the roadway frequently, often in crosswalks and from driveways. After age ten, the operating characteristics of Group C cyclists increasingly resemble those of Group B cyclists, especially for boys. By age twelve, children have acquired most of their adult-level physical skills, but continue to show a lower level of judgmental abilities in such tasks as gap acceptance and risk acceptance.[30] Residential streets with low vehicle speeds, linked with multi-use paths and busier streets with well-defined separation between bicycles and motor vehicles, can accommodate children without encouraging them to ride in the travel lane of a major arterial roadway.

The FHWA proposed a set of design treatments for roadways based on a two-tier system, with one set recommended as a minimum for all streets and highways where bicyclists are permitted to operate (based on the needs of Group A cyclists), and a second set of treatments for routes expected to serve Group B/C cyclists. These tables can be used as a guide for choosing design treatments (for more information, refer to FHWA Publication No. FHWA-RD-92-073, Selecting Roadway Design Treatments to Accommodate Bicycles).[31]

Choosing the Appropriate Bicycle Facility Type

When funding for new bicycle facilities is imminent and projects are ready to proceed to the design phase, the next step in the process is to select the appropriate type of bicycle facility. This has been the topic of some controversy over the years, as transportation planners in the United States have begun to learn more about bicycle travel behavior and preferences.

[27] Ibid, p. 5.

[28] Bruce Epperson, "Bicycle Transportation: A Qualitative Approach" (unpublished work, 1996).

[29] Ibid.

[30] Ibid.

[31] W.C. Wilkinson and others, *Selecting Roadway Design Treatments to Accommodate Bicycles* (Washington, D.C.: U.S. Department of Transportation, Federal Highway Administration, 1994), pp. 16–21.

There are basically four types of on-road bicycle facilities: bike lanes, wide curb lanes, bike routes (shared roadways), and paved shoulders for bicycle use (definitions of each type follow). It is not appropriate to choose one facility type and apply it to the entire bicycle network—for example, it is not recommended that communities only install wide outside lanes and no bicycle lanes, or vice versa. Several factors should be taken into consideration in choosing the target facility type.

- *What type of bicyclist is most likely to use this facility?*
  The Federal Highway Administration provides guidance in choosing the appropriate facility type based on the skills of the likely users, traffic volumes, traffic speeds and other factors in *Selecting Roadway Design Treatments to Accommodate Bicyclists.*[32] As a general guide, most communities choose to design their bicycle network to meet the needs of basic adult riders and youth bicyclists.

- *What type of improvement would work best to increase the comfort level of bicyclists on this particular segment?*
  If a bicycle suitability analysis has been performed, it is possible to show different design scenarios and their effect on the bicycle LOS for the given roadway segment. (Figure 16–5.)

- *What type of facility can be installed given current cost and right-of-way constraints for this roadway?*
  Cost constraints are an inevitable and important factor in the decision-making process

Effects of Bike Lane Striping on Comfort Level and Behavior

As recent polls have shown, most Americans are reluctant to ride bicycles in absence of designated bike lanes and separated pathways.[33] In fact, more and more communities have begun installing bike lanes not only for the additional operating space they provide for bicyclists, but also as a method to *encourage* more bicycle travel. In the past, Americans' preference for striped bike lanes was largely anecdotal with no solid evidence of bike lanes' effect on travel behavior or comfort level.

Several studies in recent years have shown results that quantify the benefits of providing bike lanes. A 1997 study on bicyclists' comfort level (as part of the BLOS model) indicates that a stripe between the travel lane and the area where a bicyclist typically rides increases the bicyclist's comfort level by more than thirty percent.[34] A 1996 study by the University of North Carolina Highway Safety Research Center for Florida DOT compared motorist and bicyclist interactions on wide curb lanes, bike lanes, and paved shoulder facilities. The study found several advantages to bike lanes and paved shoulders:

1) Motorists are less likely to encroach into the adjacent lane when passing a bicyclist on facilities with paved shoulders or bicycle lanes.

2) Motorists have less variation in their lane placement when passing a bicyclist on a paved shoulder or bicycle lane facility.

3) Bicyclists are more likely to ride further from the edge of the roadway in a bicycle lane or on a paved shoulder than they are in a wide curb lane. This increased distance only marginally reduces the separation distance between the bicyclists and motorists, but it significantly increases the distance to the right of the bicyclist that can be used, if needed, to maneuver around an object or debris in the lane.

4) In general, the presence of the stripe separating bicyclists from motor vehicles results in fewer erratic maneuvers on the part of motorists and enhances the comfort level for all roadway users.[35]

---

[32] W.C. Wilkinson and others, *Selecting Roadway Design Treatments to Accommodate Bicycles* (Washington, D.C.: U.S. Department of Transportation, Federal Highway Administration, 1994).

[33] Rodale Press, "Pathways for People" (Washington, D.C.: Rodale Press, 1995).

[34] Bruce W. Landis, "Real-Time Human Perceptions: Toward a Bicycle Level of Service," *Transportation Research Record 1578* (Washington, D.C.: Transportation Research Board, 1997).

[35] David L. Harkey and others, *Evaluation of Shared-Use Facilities for Bicycles and Motor Vehicles* (Chapel Hill, N.C.: University of North Carolina, 1996), pp. 22–23.

These results confirmed an earlier (1985) study by the Maryland State Highway Administration, which concluded that a bike lane stripe has a significant and positive effect on motor vehicle and bicycle tracking. Based on the observations made in that study, both vehicles appear to guide off the lane stripe rather than the other vehicle; and each appeared to have more confidence in the passing maneuver since the space in which each vehicle traveled was well-defined.[36]

Bikeway Types

There are a variety of types of facilities or roadway treatments that can be used to accommodate bicycles, as described in the following sections. This chapter gives an overview of design practices for these bikeways—for a more technical information on facility design the reader should reference the latest version of AASHTO's *Guide for the Development of Bicycle Facilities* and U.S. DOT's MUTCD.

The designer should note that lighting is an important consideration in the development of a bicycle transportation network. Utilitarian bicyclists often have no other choice than to ride at night during certain times of the year. Unlit roadways can be very dangerous for bicyclists, who despite standard bicycle headlamps and tail-lights are still nearly invisible to motorists until they are very close.

Shared Roadways

On shared roadways, bicyclists and motorists share the same travel lanes. A motorist will usually have to cross over into the adjacent travel lane to pass a bicyclist. All streets where bicyclists are permitted to ride are technically classified as shared roadways. However, there are several treatments that can enhance shared roadways for cyclists: bike routes, wide outside lanes, and bicycle boulevards.[37]

Bike Routes (Signed Shared Roadways)

Bike routes are shared roadways that meet a set of minimum design and operational criteria for bicycle compatibility, and which have been designated with bicycle route signs as connector routes within the bicycle facility network. Criteria are defined as:

- The street should provide a reasonably good LOS to bicyclists, as measured through a suitability rating system.

- Obstacles and barriers to bicycle travel should be addressed, including hazardous drainage grates, potholes, uneven manhole covers, angled rail-road crossings, and narrow bridges. Where certain obstacles cannot be improved but do not pose an undue risk to bicyclists, advance warning signs (as recommended by the MUTCD) should be used to alert bicyclists of their presence.

- The proposed bike route should be part of an interconnected system of bicycle facilities. Bicycle routes should not abruptly end at barriers.

- Future street maintenance and construction activities should consider and plan for safe transport by bicycles along this route.

Bicycle route signage should always include directional information such as an arrow and the name of the destination served and, if appropriate, the distance to the destination. Some communities have developed unique bike route signs, which is acceptable given that the design does not include an elaborate map that cyclists are unable to read without stopping.

---

[36] Steven R. McHenry and Michael J. Wallace, *Evaluation of Wide Curb Lanes as Shared Lane Bicycle Facilities* (Baltimore, Md.: Maryland State Highway Administration, 1985), p. 55.

[37] Oregon Department of Transportation, *Oregon Bicycle and Pedestrian Plan* (Salem, Ore.: Oregon DOT, 1995).

Figure 16–14   Shared Roadway Cross Section

Source: *Oregon Bicycle and Pedestrian Plan*, Salem, Ore.: Oregon Department of Transportation, 1995.

Figure 16–15   Bike Route Sign

Source: *Manual on Uniform Traffic Control Devices*, Washington, D.C.: U.S. Department of Transportation, 1988.

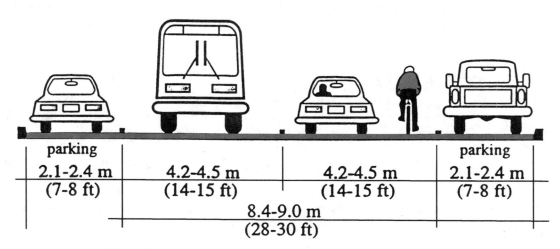

parking 2.1-2.4 m (7-8 ft)	4.2-4.5 m (14-15 ft)	4.2-4.5 m (14-15 ft)	parking 2.1-2.4 m (7-8 ft)

8.4-9.0 m
(28-30 ft)

Two-lane roadway with wide lanes and parking

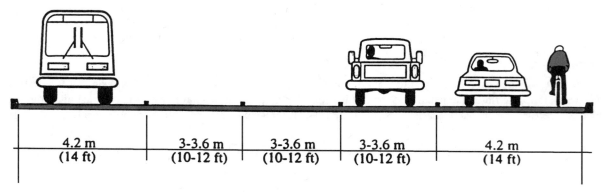

4.2 m (14 ft)	3-3.6 m (10-12 ft)	3-3.6 m (10-12 ft)	3-3.6 m (10-12 ft)	4.2 m (14 ft)

Figure 16–16   Wide Curb Lane Cross Section

Source: *Oregon Bicycle and Pedestrian Plan*, Salem, Ore.: Oregon Department of Transportation, 1995.

Wide Outside Lane

Outside lanes that are 4.3 m (14 ft) wide may be provided to allow an average size motor vehicle to pass a bicyclist without crossing over into the adjacent lane. Wide outside lanes are generally considered an appropriate facility for Group A advanced riders on busy urban arterials.

The wide curb lane is always the furthest right-hand *through* lane. There is no special "wide curb lane" sign; however, on high-volume urban arterials, the designer may choose to install "Share the Road" warning signs (standard bicycle warning plate with a subplate stating "Share the Road"). Where wide curb lane streets meet the minimum requirements for bike routes, they may be designated with signage as a bike route.

For retrofit projects where wide outside lanes are to be installed, the roadway may either be physically widened or re-striped to reduce the lane width of inner lanes and increase the width of outer lanes.

Bike Lanes

A bike lane is a portion of the roadway designated for preferential use by bicyclists, typically with a width of 1.2–1.5 m (4–5 ft). Bicycle lanes serve the needs of all types of cyclists in urban and suburban areas, providing them with their own travel lane on the street surface. They are designated with signage, edge striping, and bicycle icons to call attention to their preferential use by bicyclists. On two-way streets, bike lanes are always installed on both sides. Two-way bike lanes on one side of two-way streets create hazardous conditions for bicyclists and are not recommended.[38] In cases where a 1.5 m (5 ft) cannot be achieved for a bike lane, an unmarked lane of lesser width can be installed as an interim measure.

Regular maintenance is of the utmost importance to the success of a bicycle lane. A bicycle lane that has collected broken glass and debris is rendered useless and is unsuitable for bicyclists. A regular schedule of maintenance should be established for bike lanes. Some communities have developed "spot improvement" programs that enable local bicyclists to keep maintenance agencies informed of potholes and other maintenance problems by filling out a request card.

The needs of cyclists can be accommodated by retrofitting bike lanes onto existing urban streets. In many cases this can be accomplished without physically widening the roadway, but instead by restriping the existing cross section to add bike lanes. Significant opportunities are available in many parts of the country to do this, particularly in urban center city areas where traffic volumes are getting lower. In areas with higher traffic volumes, a cost-benefit analysis can be done to determine the relative benefits to the bicyclist versus the reduction in LOS for the motorist.

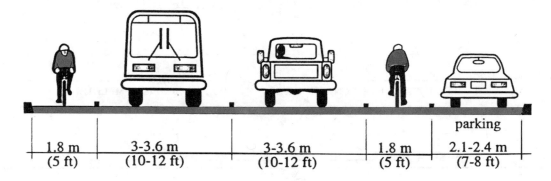

| 1.8 m (5 ft) | 3-3.6 m (10-12 ft) | 3-3.6 m (10-12 ft) | 1.8 m (5 ft) | parking 2.1-2.4 m (7-8 ft) |

Figure 16–17   Bike Lane Cross Section

Source: *Oregon Bicycle and Pedestrian Plan*, Salem, Ore.: Oregon Department of Transportation, 1995.

---

[38] American Association of State Highway and Transportation Officials, *Guide for the Development of Bicycle Facilities* (Washington, D.C.: AASHTO, 1991).

In Figure 16–19 (before restriping the road), the current motor vehicle LOS is C, and the bicycle LOS is D. In Figure 16–20 (after restriping the road), the motor vehicle LOS is D, and the BLOS rises to a B.[39]

When bike lanes are placed adjacent to parallel parked cars, bicyclists run the risk of getting "doored" by motorists who are getting out of their cars. Some communities have developed a bicycle lane design that uses a portion of their bike lane space as a "deterrent strip" next to parallel parked cars. This space is typically 0.6 m–0.7 m (2–2.5 ft) in width, and is distinguished by a different pavement surface (such as brick pavers) or marking.

Bike lane striping and signage are addressed in the MUTCD. For more detailed solutions on lane configurations, solutions for retrofitting urban streets to include bike lanes, and intersection layouts, the *Oregon Bicycle and Pedestrian Plan* (1995) is a comprehensive source of information.

PORTLAND BICYCLE PROGRAM
FACILITY IMPROVEMENT REQUEST FORM

The bicycle facility improvement program is intended to enhance bicycle safety and encourage bicycling through **low-cost**, small scale improvements suggested by concerned bicyclists (e.g., pavement maintenance and sweeping, hazard removal, bike rack installation, and grating repair).

Location: _____
　　　　　STREET

　　　　　_____
　　　　　CROSS STREET, ADDRESS, OR LANDMARK

Suggestion: _____

　　　　　_____

　　　　　_____

Requested by: _____
　　　　　NAME

　　　　　_____
　　　　　STREET　　　　　CITY　　　　　ZIP

　　　　　_____
　　　　　DAY PHONE　　　　　DATE

DO NOT WRITE BELOW THIS LINE—FOR OFFICE USE ONLY

Referred to: _____

Investigation: _____
　　　　　PDOT STAFF: LIST CONDITION BEFORE AND AFTER JOB IS COMPLETED

　　　　　_____

　　　　　_____

　　　　　Signed _____ Date _____

Figure 16–18　Spot Improvement Request Form

Source: Oregon Bicycle and Pedestrian Plan, Salem, Ore.: Oregon Department of Transportation, 1995.

---

[39] Baltimore Metropolitan Council, *Baltimore Regional Bicycle Suitability Analysis Report* (Baltimore, Md.: Baltimore Metropolitan Council, 1998).

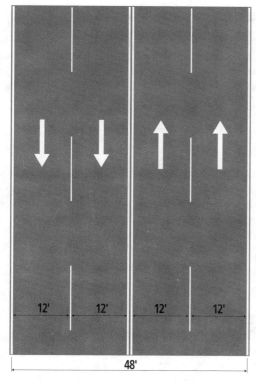

4 Lane Undivided — Before

ADT = 13,500

Motor Vehicle LOS = C

V/C Ratio = 0.40

Bicycle LOS = D

Figure 16–19   Four-Lane Undivided (Before)

Source: *Baltimore Regional Bicycle Suitability Analysis Report,* Baltimore, Md.: 1998.

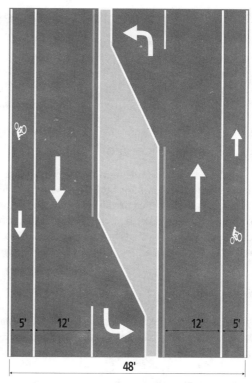

4 Lane Undivided — After

ADT = 13,500

Motor Vehicle LOS = D

V/C Ratio = 0.83

New Bicycle LOS = B

Figure 16–20   Four-Lane Undivided (After)

Source: *Baltimore Regional Bicycle Suitability Analysis Report,* Baltimore, Md.: 1998.

Paved Shoulders

Paved shoulders can also serve bicyclists' needs on streets with no curb and gutter, and particularly in rural areas. While any additional space is beneficial, a 1.2 m–1.8 m (4 ft–6 ft) shoulder is preferred. Paved shoulders should be included on both sides of the roadway. In addition to the benefits to bicyclists, paved shoulders can also serve the needs of motorists by extending pavement life and providing a break-down area. As with bike lanes, paved shoulders should be constructed to withstand heavy loadings (since trucks and service vehicles will occasionally use them) and should be free of surface irregularities. Regular maintenance is essential if paved shoulders are to be useful to bicyclists.

Paved shoulders that include rumble strips can be essentially useless to bicyclists. On shoulders where the rumble strip extends across the whole width of the shoulder, bicyclists typically ride in the travel lane rather than face the jarring effect of the strip. In most cases, rumble strips are not recommended on bicycle facilities unless they can be designed to provide bicyclists with an adequate amount of space in which to operate.

Spot Improvements for Obstacles to Bicycling

Sudden changes in pavement conditions can have a very detrimental effect on bicyclists, particularly when they occur with no forewarning. Unless quick evasive actions are taken, such obstacles and irregularities can cause bicyclists to crash. It can also be a problem when bicyclists suddenly swerve to avoid a hazardous condition, since this is an unpredictable movement and can result in a crash with a motor vehicle. The following are some examples of bicycle hazards (consult AASHTO's *Guide for the Development of Bicycle Facilities* for further detailed solutions).

Street Maintenance Work

Many urban streets are laid upon a maze of storm sewers and utilities. Maintenance on this vast infrastructure is frequent, causing problems for bicyclists who must maneuver across milled pavement, over sudden pavement changes and steel plate covers (which are slippery when wet), and through narrowed-down lanes. In general, bicycles are far more susceptible to sudden pavement changes in construction areas than motorists, since they have no suspension. Warning signs can help to give bicyclists advanced notice of upcoming pavement changes. When at all possible, a clear path should be maintained through construction areas for bicycle travel.[40]

At-Grade Railroad Crossings

Rough and uneven railroad crossings and those that are set at an acute angle to the roadway and are obstacles to bicyclists. Streets with inlaid rails (trolley streets) can also be difficult to negotiate on bike, if the rail is in the normal operating area for bicyclists or if pavement adjacent to the rail has deteriorated and left open cracks. Rail crossings should be made as smooth as possible. In some cases, filler material can be used to reduce the gap next to the rail. For diagonal crossings, the bicyclist should be given the alternative to cross the rail at a ninety-degree angle, by flaring the shoulder.

Bridge Crossings

Adequate space for bicycles and pedestrians should be a standard element for all new bridges where bicycles are permitted to operate, including both major and minor bridges. These guidelines should apply regardless of whether bicycle lanes or sidewalks connect to the bridge at the time it is built. Minimum accommodations for bicycles should include bike lanes and sidewalks on each side. It is also important to provide bike lanes where roadways pass beneath bridges, so that these areas do not present a barrier as well.

Surface conditions on bridges can also cause problems for cyclists. Steel decks are slippery when wet, and expansion joints can create a gap that is too wide.

Manholes and Utility Covers

Manholes that are lower or higher than the surrounding pavement create an obstacle to cyclists. This sometimes occurs during roadway resurfacing when a manhole is not raised to the new surface level. Local roadway engineers should develop specific design solutions to address the need for a level pavement surface, including raising manholes to meet the same grade as newly laid pavement.

Bicycle-Safe Drainage Grates

Some types of drainage grates can trap a bicycle wheel and cause a crash, particularly those with bars that are parallel to the direction of travel and with wide openings between the bars. Bicycle-safe drainage grate designs have been developed by many transportation agencies, and should be used wherever bicyclists are expected to ride. It is also important that drainage grates be placed on an even grade with the surrounding pavement.[41]

---

[40] Oregon Department of Transportation, *Oregon Bicycle and Pedestrian Plan* (Ore.: Oregon DOT, 1995).
[41] Ibid.

Multi-Use Trails

Multi-use trails are physically separated from motor vehicle traffic (except at crossings with streets) by an open space or barrier. They are usually built either within an independent right-of-way (such as a utility or railroad right-of-way), or along easements across private lands. Trails accommodate a variety of users for both recreation and transportation purposes. User groups can include pedestrians, joggers, skaters, bicyclists, horseback riders, and people in wheelchairs. Multi-use paths can provide a linkage through corridors not well served by the street system, and they are particularly helpful to bicyclists if they provide a direct, traffic-free route linking origin and destination points.

National guidelines for the design of multi-use trails are provided by AASHTO's *Guide for the Development of Bicycle Facilities* (1999). Nearly one-third of the guide is devoted to trail design, and the requirements are quite detailed.

The minimum width for two-directional trails is 3 m (10 ft), however 3.7 m–4.3 m (12–14 ft) widths are preferred where heavy or mixed traffic is expected. Due to the popularity of off-road trails, centerline stripes should be considered for paths that generate substantial amounts of pedestrian traffic. Trail etiquette signage should clearly state that bicycles should give an audible warning before passing other trail users, since they often travel considerably faster than other users.

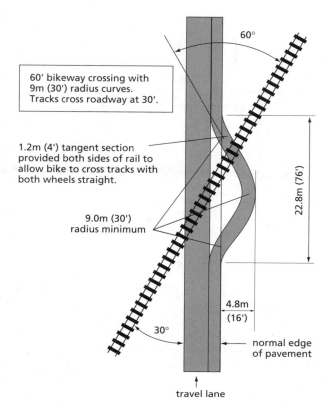

Figure 16–21   Bike Lane at Railroad Crossing

Source: *Oregon Bicycle and Pedestrian Plan*, Salem, Ore.: Oregon Department of Transportation, 1995.

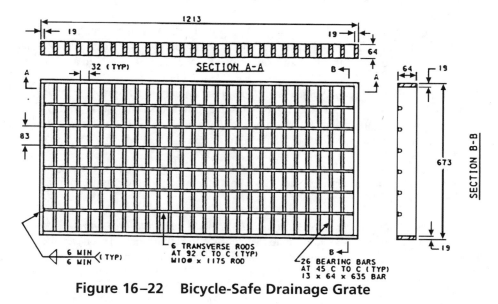

Figure 16–22   Bicycle-Safe Drainage Grate

Source: *Pennsylvania Bicycle Facility Design Guidelines,* Harrisburg, Pa.: Pennsylvania Department of Transportation, 1996.

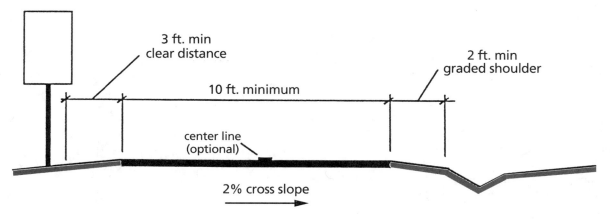

Typical bicycle path cross section

Figure 16–23   Multi-Use Trail Cross Section

Source: The RBA Group, Morristown, N.J.

In the past, bicycle sidepaths (bikeways immediately adjacent to roadways) were developed with the concept of separating cyclists from roadways in order to reduce opportunities for conflict. It is now widely accepted that bicycle paths immediately adjacent to roads or on sidewalks actually cause greater conflicts. For this reason, they are not recommended.[42]

Trail and roadway intersections can become areas of conflict if not carefully designed. For at-grade intersections, there are usually several objectives.

1. *Site the crossing area at a logical and visible location.* When at all possible, trails should be designed to meet roadways at existing intersections. If alternate locations for a bicycle path are available, the one with the most favorable intersection conditions should be selected. Midblock crossings should not be sited in close proximity to major intersections with other highways.

2. *Warn motorists and trail users of the upcoming crossing.* Warning signage and pavement markings that alert motorists and trail users of the upcoming trail crossing should be used in accordance with the MUTCD. Consistency in the use of this type of signage can help to alert bicyclists in advance of intersections.

3. *Maintain visibility between trail users and motorists.* Vegetation, highway signage, and other objects in the right-of-way should be removed or relocated so that trail users can observe traffic conditions, and motorists can see approaching trail users. Every effort should be made to locate midblock crossings on straight sections of roadway, rather than near curves where sight distance is limited.

4. *Intersections and approaches should be on relatively flat grades.* Bicyclists should not be required to stop at the bottom of a hill. Crossings should be made at a ninety-degree angle, in order to lessen the amount of exposure time for trail users.

5. *Wide intersections should be re-designed to provide adequate crossing time for trail users.* For wider crossings, a gap analysis should be done to determine the appropriate design treatment at intersections. If trail crossings are expected to be frequent (such as on the weekends), it may be necessary to provide a traffic signal that responds to bicycles or can be pedestrian-activated. Generally, if the intersection is more than 22.5 m (75 ft)

---

[42] American Association of State Highway and Transportation Officials, *Guide for the Development of Bicycle Facilities* (Washington, D.C.: AASHTO, 1991).

from curb to curb, it is preferable to provide a center median refuge area for trail users, per ADA (Americans with Disabilities Act) or ANSI (American National Standards Institute) standards.

6. *Intersections should be evaluated to determine if it would be more appropriate to give trail users the right-of-way and require motor vehicles to stop or yield.* Particularly in rural areas, trails sometimes cross roadways with extremely low volumes of traffic. In some cases, it is more appropriate to require motor vehicle traffic to stop or yield.

For high-speed, multilane arterials and freeways, the only viable solution may be a grade-separated crossing. Overpasses can be extremely expensive and marginally successful if users are expected to climb long entrance ramps. Underpasses should be of adequate width and should be well-lit with vandal-resistant fixtures. Approach ramps for grade-separated crossings must meet ADA or ANSI standards.

Bicycle Storage and Parking

Bicycle parking is an important investment to improve and encourage bicycle travel in urban areas. There is a severe shortage of bicycle parking in most parts of the country. Appropriate locations for bicycle parking facilities should be considered on a case-by-case basis, with an analysis of the specific design constraints at each location. The following general location criteria are recommended:

- Parking facilities should be located within 15 m (50 ft) of building entrances (where bicyclists would naturally transition into pedestrian mode).

- Parking facilities should be installed in a public area within easy viewing distance from a main pedestrian walkway, usually on a wide sidewalk with five or more feet of clear sidewalk space remaining. In general, sidewalks that are narrower than 3.7 m (12 ft) in width cannot accommodate bike racks.

- For bike parking facilities placed near walls or buildings, a minimum of 0.6 m (2 ft) clear space is needed between the bicycle rack and a parallel wall, and 0.8 m (2.5 ft) from a perpendicular wall.

- Bike racks should be placed on hard surfaces rather than in grassy medians or unpaved areas.

- Racks should be placed to avoid conflicts with pedestrians. They are usually installed near the curb and at a reasonable distance from building entrances. They should not be placed in a manner that interferes with pedestrian traffic exiting crosswalks.

- Bicycle rack placement within the right-of-way should not block access or obstruct movement. In general, bike racks should not be placed in front of doors (including cellar doors in urban downtowns) or in close proximity to fire hydrants, bus stop shelters, telephones, mailboxes, benches, newsstands, or subway exits. On streets with metered parking, racks placed between meter poles should be as close to mid-way as possible.[43]

Bicycle Parking Types

It is important to choose a bicycle rack design that is simple to operate. Bicycle racks should be designed to allow use of a variety of lock types. It may be difficult initially to determine the number of bicycle parking spaces needed: bicycle racks should be situated on-site so that more racks can be added if bicycle usage increases. There are three general types of bicycle parking facilities. The following provides information on each style.[44]

---

[43] Philadelphia Department of Streets, *Philadelphia Bicycle Facility Design Guidelines* (Philadelphia, Pa.: Philadelphia Department of Streets, 1998).
[44] "Bicycle Parking," *Pro-Bike News* (April 1996).

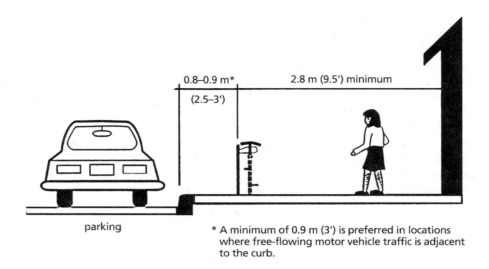

Figure 16–24   Bicycle Rack in the Right-of-Way

Source: *Philadelphia Bicycle Facility Design Guidelines*, Philadelphia, Pa.: Philadelphia Department of Streets, 1988.

- *Class I bicycle parking:* This category includes bike lockers or locked and guarded storage areas that provide high-security protection.

  - *Advantages*—High-security storage and ideal for long-term storage.

  - *Disadvantages*—Expensive.

- *Class II bicycle parking:* This category includes racks that secure both wheels and bicycle frame, which usually have moving parts and provide medium security with a user-supplied lock.

  - *Advantages*—Medium security and great when coupled with covered protection from the elements.

  - *Disadvantages*—Moving parts, complex design, and may not work with the common U-lock.

- *Class III bicycle parking:* The most common type of Class III rack are inverted "U"s.

  - *Advantages*—Simple design, affordable, can be manufactured by a local welder, and supports frame as well as wheel.

  - *Disadvantages*—Offers low-security for long-term parking.

Pedestrian Facility Design

There are a number of information sources for design guidelines that apply to pedestrian facilities. *Design and Safety of Pedestrian Facilities,* published by the Institute of Transportation Engineers, contains recommended practices for pedestrian improvements. The MUTCD and ADAAG also address a range of pedestrian facility design standards. However, many of these national resources have been written to deal primarily with motor vehicle design and contain limited pedestrian-related material, such as AASHTO's *A Policy on the Geometric Design of Streets and Highways* (also known as the *Green Book*). At the local level, it is often more common to find examples of comprehensive design practices that recognize pedestrian needs.

Pedestrian Characteristics

There are basic definitions of concepts and characteristics of pedestrian movement, their relationship to various land use contexts, and common pedestrian crash types to be considered when planning for pedestrian movement. These characteristics can be found in the AASHTO's *Green Book* and *Highway Capacity Manual* and include information on:

- Average pedestrian dimensions (the average pedestrian occupies a space of 450 mm × 600 mm or 18″ × 24″).
- Walking speeds.
- Capacities for pedestrian-related facilities.

Where pedestrian movement is very dense, such as on pedestrian bridges or tunnels, at intermodal connections, outside stadiums, or in the middle of downtown, then pedestrian capacity analysis may be needed. Research has developed a LOS concept for pedestrians that relates flow rate to spacing and walking speed.

An average walking speed of 1.2 m per sec. (4 ft per sec.) has been used for many years. There is a growing tendency to use 1.1 meters per second (3.5 ft per sec.) as a general value and 0.9 or 1.0 meters per second (3.0 or 3.25 ft per sec.) for specific applications such as facilities used by the elderly or handicapped.

Design consideration must also take into account characteristics of pedestrians with physical, visual, or mental disabilities. For example, average pedestrian dimensions increase for individuals using canes, walkers, wheelchairs, shopping carts, or baby carriages.[45] Pedestrians with ambulatory difficulties are sensitive to walking surfaces. Persons with hearing or visual impairments or learning disabilities may be less able to process typical sensory information, such as colors or signing.[46]

Pedestrian trip generation rates have been defined for different land uses. Where roads abut such uses, either existing or proposed, these numbers provide an indication of potential trip making activity. Chapter 7 of this handbook provides a summary of capacity; and the *Highway Capacity Manual* provides procedures for the operational analysis of walkways, crosswalks and street corners.

Specific crash classification types have been developed for pedestrian collisions.[47] Crashes often occur because of deficient roadway designs or traffic control measures, or they may result from improper behavior on the part of motorists and pedestrians. Examples of some of the more common types of pedestrian crashes and their likelihood of occurrence are shown in Figure 16–25.

Guidelines on the design of a range of specific pedestrian facilities, including sidewalks, shoulders, medians, crosswalks, curb ramps, and so forth are provided in this chapter.

Pedestrian Facilities

An individual's decision to walk is as much a factor of security, safety, and convenience as it is the *perceived quality* of the experience. Pedestrian facilities should be designed with the following factors in mind:

- *Sufficient width*: sidewalks should accommodate anticipated volumes based on adjacent land uses, and they should at a minimum allow for two adults to walk abreast. Greater detail on sidewalk dimensions is provided later in this chapter.

- *Protection from traffic:* high-volume or high-speed (>56 km/h or 35 mph) motor vehicle traffic creates dangerous and uncomfortable conditions for pedestrians. Physical (and perceptual) separation can be achieved through a

---

[45] Institute of Transportation Engineers, *Design and Safety of Pedestrian Facilities* (Washington, D.C.: ITE, 1998).

[46] Ibid, pp. 20–27.

[47] U.S. Department of Transportation, Federal Highway Administration, *Pedestrian Crash Types: A 1990's Information Guide*, FHWA Report No. FHWA-RD-96-163 (Washington, D.C.: U.S. DOT, FHWA, 1997).

combination of methods: a grassy planting strip with street trees, a raised planter, bicycle lanes, on-street parallel parking, and others. Intersection design should facilitate both vehicular and pedestrian movement with geometric dimensions that reduce pedestrian crossing distances and provision of median refuge islands.

- *Street trees:* street trees are an essential element in a high quality pedestrian environment. Not only do they provide shade, they also give a sense of enclosure to the sidewalk environment, which enhances the pedestrian's sense of walking in a protected environment.

- *Pedestrian-scale design:* large highway-scale signage reinforces the general notion that pedestrians are out of place. Signage should be designed to be seen by the pedestrian. Street lighting should likewise be scaled to the level of the pedestrian, instead of providing light poles that are more appropriate on high-speed freeways. Components such as street furniture, vistas, and landmarks should be incorporated into designs to help make walking routes interesting.

- *Continuity:* pedestrian facilities are often discontinuous, particularly when private developers are not encouraged to link on-site pedestrian facilities to adjacent developments and nearby sidewalks or street corners. New developments should be designed to encourage pedestrian access from nearby streets. Existing gaps in the system should be placed on a prioritized list for new sidewalk construction.

Midblock Dash
Frequency: 442 cases; 8.7% of all crashes
Severity: 37% resulted in serious or fatal injuries.

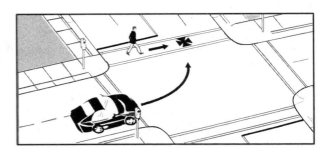

Vehicle Turn/Merge
Frequency: 497 cases; 9.8% of all crashes
Severity: 18% resulted in serious or fatal injuries.

Figure 16–25   Common Types of Pedestrian Crashes

Source: *Pedestrian Crash Types: A 1990's Informational Guide,* Washington, D.C.: U.S. Department of Transportation, Federal Highway Administration, 1997.

- *Clearances:* vertical clearance above sidewalks for landscaping, trees, signs, and similar obstructions should be at least 2.4 m (8 ft). In commercial areas and Central Business Districts (CBDs), the vertical clearance for awnings should be 2.7 m (9 ft). The vertical clearance for building overhangs that cover the majority of the sidewalk should be 3.6 m (12 ft).

- *Conformance with National Standards*: all pedestrian facilities should be consistent with *Americans with Disabilities Act* requirements. Specific guidance is provided by Architectural and Transportation Barriers Compliance Board's *Americans with Disabilities Act Accessibility Guidelines.*

Sidewalk Design Overview

Sidewalks not only encourage walking, but they also improve the safety of pedestrians. The safety benefits of sidewalks are well-documented: one study found that streets without sidewalks had 2.6 times more pedestrian and automobile collisions than expected on the basis of exposure, while streets with sidewalks on only one side had 1.2 times more pedestrian crashes.[48] In the United States 5,412 pedestrians were killed and 82,000 were injured in 1996. Most pedestrian fatalities in 1996 occurred in urban areas (71 percent).[49]

---

[48] Richard L. Knoblauch, et. al., "Investigation of Exposure Based Pedestrian Areas: Crosswalks, Sidewalks, Local Streets and Major Arterials," FHWA Report No. FHWA-RD-88-038 (Washington, D.C.: U.S. DOT, FHWA, 1988).

[49] National Highway Traffic Safety Administration, *NHTSA Traffic Safety Facts* (Washington, D.C.: NHTSA, 1996).

All roadways should have some type of walking facility out of the traveled way. A separate walkway is often preferable, but a roadway shoulder will also provide a safer pedestrian accommodation than walking in the travel lane.

Direct pedestrian connections should be provided between residences and activity areas. It is usually not difficult to ascertain where connections between residential areas and activity centers will be required during the early stages of development.

Development density can be used as a surrogate for pedestrian usage in determining the need for sidewalks. Local residential streets, especially cul-de-sacs, can accommodate extensive pedestrian activity on the street because there is little vehicular activity. Collector streets are normally used by pedestrians to access bus stops and commercial developments on the arterial to which they feed.

Sidewalks should be provided on all streets within a 0.4 kilometers (one quarter-mile) of a transit station. Sidewalks should also be provided along developed frontages of arterial streets in zones of commercial activity. Collector and arterial streets in the vicinity of schools should be provided with sidewalks to increase school trip safety.[50]

Sidewalk Obstacles

Street furniture and utility poles create obstacles to pedestrian travel when located directly on the sidewalk. At the very minimum there should be 0.9 m (3 ft) of sidewalk width to allow wheelchairs to pass. Where possible, utilities should be relocated so as not to block the sidewalk. Benches should not be sited directly on the sidewalk, but set back at least 0.9 m (3 ft).

The design of new intersections or re-design of existing intersections presents an opportunity to improve pedestrian circulation. Street furniture located near intersections can block sight lines. In general, the designer should consider the effect on sight distance for all features located in the vicinity of roadway intersections.

Sidewalk Pavement Design

Sidewalks and roadside pathways should be constructed of a solid, debris-free surface. Regardless of the type of surface chosen, it must be designed to withstand adequate load requirements. Standard depth of pavement should consider site-specific soil conditions and is therefore left to local discretion. Brick and concrete pavers are popular materials for more decorative sidewalks. (Figure 16–26.) The use of stylized surfaces is encouraged, however, they must be installed properly or they will deteriorate over time.

Pedestrian Facility Maintenance

Maintenance is an important aspect of creating adequate and comfortable facilities for pedestrians. A crumbling sidewalk is not only an eyesore but also a hazard to the pedestrian and a barrier to the disabled. Regular maintenance protects public investment and reduces liability risk.

A periodic inspection schedule for pedestrian facilities should be adopted by local jurisdictions. Crosswalks will need re-striping. A general maintenance budget should be allocated by each local government for use on a yearly basis, perhaps combined with a maintenance budget for bicycle facilities.

Sidewalk Width and Setback Guidelines

The following are recommended guidelines for sidewalk width and setback for a typical community. It is important to note that there are some areas that warrant wider sidewalks than the minimum. For example, sidewalks in and around local universities and colleges must accommodate a much higher volume of pedestrians, and therefore they warrant

---

[50] Transportation Research Board, *Planning and Implementing Pedestrian Facilities in Suburban and Rural Areas,* TRB Report No. 294A (Washington, D.C.: TRB, 1987).

Figure 16–26   Decorative Sidewalk Treatments

Source: The RBA Group, Morristown, N.J., Greenways Incorporated, Cary, N.C.

additional width. The recommendations below are based on ITE and ADA guidelines and common practices used by other pedestrian-friendly communities in the United States.

- *Sidewalks in CBDs.* Sidewalk widths in CBDs are, for the most part, already determined by building setback and street width. Should a reconstruction project warrant further study of sidewalk width in a CBD, service standards have been set by AASHTO's *Green Book.*

- *Arterial and collector streets in commercial and residential areas.* Sidewalks on arterial and collector streets in commercial and residential areas should be a minimum of 1.5 m (5 ft) wide. A minimum of a 0.6 m (2 ft) wide planting strip should be provided. If no planting strip is possible, the minimum width of the sidewalk should be 2.1 m (7 ft).

- *Sidewalks on local streets in residential areas.* On local streets in residential areas, sidewalk width may be based on the number of units per acre. For multifamily developments and single-family homes with densities that exceed 4 units per acre, the sidewalk should be a minimum of 1.5 m (5 ft) wide with a minimum setback of 0.6 m (2 ft). For densities up to 4 dwelling units per acre, the sidewalk should be a minimum of 1.2 m (4 ft) wide with a 0.6 m (2ft) setback.

- *Sidewalks on streets with no curb and gutter.* The setback requirements in this section are based on roadway cross sections that include curb and gutter. Sidewalks located adjacent to "ribbon pavement" (pavement with no curb and gutter) are not recommended. However, if no other solution is possible, sidewalks adjacent to ribbon pavement should have a much greater setback requirement, depending on roadway conditions. Engineers should consult AASHTO's *Policy on Geometric Design of Highways and Streets* for more specific guidelines.

- *Sidewalks in rural areas.* In most rural areas, the low volume of pedestrians does not warrant sidewalk construction. In most cases, 1.2 m (4 ft) wide paved shoulders can provide an adequate area for pedestrians to walk on rural roadways, while also serving the needs of bicyclists. Exceptions should be made in areas where isolated developments such as schools, ballparks, or housing communities create more pedestrian use. For example, motorists might regularly park along a rural road to access a nearby ballpark. A sidewalk may be warranted in this circumstance so that pedestrians can walk separately from traffic. Sidewalks in rural areas should be provided at a width based on the anticipated or real volume of pedestrians, with 1.5 m (5 ft) being the minimum width.

Continuity in Construction Zones

Work zone areas can disrupt pedestrian and bicycle circulation, and they often create total barriers for pedestrians. Just as traffic is re-routed during roadway construction, pedestrians and bicyclists should be provided a safe alternative through the work zone. If a safe alternative is not provided, they will often try to make their way across the site unprotected.

Pedestrians and bicyclists should be re-routed well in advance of the construction barriers, since most are unlikely to retrace their steps to get around the work zone. The MUTCD provides appropriate signage for these situations, and it provides limited guidance for pedestrian detours in Section 6C-9. If a path is to be provided within the work zone, it should be constructed of a smooth and even surface, with no gaps. Pedestrians should be protected from construction vehicle traffic, roadway traffic, and falling debris.

Construction sites are particularly difficult to traverse for disabled pedestrians. An alternate accessible route should always be provided when the main accessible route is interrupted by construction activities.

Intersection Design and Pedestrian Crossings

Intersection design is extremely important for the safety of pedestrians. No single feature creates a safe intersection for pedestrians—the design elements described in the next sections should be combined as site conditions warrant.

Crosswalks

Marked crosswalks should be provided at intersections that carry significant pedestrian volumes, or where newly installed sidewalks are likely to generate more pedestrian traffic.

Crosswalks can serve to channel pedestrian traffic through an intersection, as well as heighten the awareness of motorists of possible pedestrian crossing movements. It is important to note that, although crosswalks are an important element in intersection design, a crosswalk alone does not insure the safety of a pedestrian. Too often, crosswalks are the sole provision for pedestrians at intersections when other safety measures are also needed.

Paragraph 3B-18 of the MUTCD provides guidance on crosswalk design. High visibility designs are recommended. (Figure 16–27.) Crosswalk lines should be 0.3–0.6 m (1–2 ft) in width and spaced be 0.3–0.6 m (1–2 ft) apart. A nonskid, long-life striping material is the preferable marking material for bicycle and pedestrian facilities.

The optimum width of crosswalks is 3 m (10 ft) wide, with a minimum width (as set by the MUTCD) of 1.8 m (6 ft) wide. Wider crosswalks should be installed at locations with higher pedestrian volumes. At signalized intersections with stop bars, a minimum separation of 1.2 m (4 ft) is necessary between the stop bar and edge of the crosswalk. At midblock locations stop or yield bars should be placed to allow motorists adequate stopping time, particularly on multilane sections. Criteria for installing crosswalks is shown in Figure 16–28.

Curb Ramps

A deciding factor in the location and design of crosswalks is the placement of curb ramps at street corners. Curb ramps should always be placed so to lead the pedestrian directly into a striped crosswalk area. Corners should either include two curb ramps or one broad ramp that serves both crosswalks. Curb ramps should always be provided with a matching ramp on the opposite side of the road, as well as ramps at pedestrian refuge islands.

ADA provides federal guidance for curb ramp installation, and use of either guideline is acceptable. Current ADA standards state that the slope of curb ramps cannot exceed 1:12, with a maximum rise of 0.76 m (30 in). If the curb ramp is located in an area where pedestrians might typically walk, it must have flared sides that do not exceed a slope of 1:10. It is also extremely important that the bottom of the curb ramp be even with the street surface. A raised lip at the street edge can cause a wheelchair to tip over, even if it is only 6 mm (0.25 in) high.

Traffic Signals

Pedestrian safety at intersections depends in part on minimizing the length of time that the pedestrian is exposed in the street. One way of minimizing conflict and exposure at intersections is to improve the phasing of traffic signals. Traffic signal improvements for pedestrians may include the following provisions:

- Improvements to timing options and turn phasing.

- Elimination of right-turn-on-red movements.

- Elimination of free-right turning movements (with yield signs).

- Addition of pedestrian signals (walk and don't walk).

- Push-button signals that can be tripped by pedestrians.

- Reduced corner radii to shorten the distance the pedestrian must cross, therefore also shortening the signal interval.

- Construction of curb extensions to reduce "in-street" walking distance.

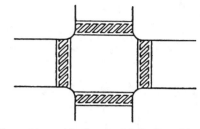

Crosswalk marking with diagonal lines for added visibility

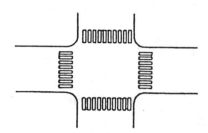

Crosswalk marking with longitudinal lines for added visibility

Figure 16–27 High Visibility Crosswalk Patterns

Source: *Manual on Uniform Traffic Control Devices*, Washington, D.C.: U.S. Department of Transportation, 1988.

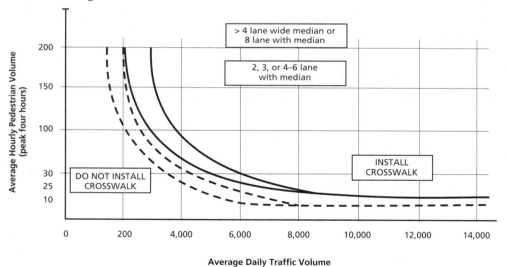

Criteria for Installing Crosswalks

- – – Location with predominantly young, elderly or handicapped Pedestrians.
- —— Other locations

Basic Criteria

1. Speed limit of 5 mph.
2. Adequate stopping sight distance.
3. For mid block preferred block lengths > .
4. Crosswalk adequately illuminated.
5. Minimal conflicting attention demands.

Figure 16–28 Criteria for Installing Crosswalks

Source: *Manual on Uniform Traffic Control Devices*, Washington, D.C.: U.S. Department of Transportation, 1988.

Extensive guidelines for traffic signalization to accommodate pedestrian crossings are provided in the MUTCD. Traffic engineering analysis is necessary on a case-by-case basis in order to determine the best signal option. Signalized intersection design and audible signals should be given special consideration in areas with higher numbers of senior citizens, school-age children, and disabled persons.

On-Street Parking

The presence of parked cars near intersections have been cited as a contributing factor in many pedestrian crashes in urban areas. Parked cars block visual access to oncoming traffic, so that both pedestrians and motor vehicles cannot see each other. Consideration should be given to removing parking in the immediate vicinity of crosswalks.

Corner Curb Radius

One aspect of intersection design that is often overlooked is the turning radii of corners. A wide turning radius can increase crossing distance, as well as increase the speed of turning traffic. However, a turning radius that is too small can cause long vehicles (such as flatbed trucks or buses) to jump the curb edge and eventually cause the curb to crumble, hit pedestrians waiting to cross, or hit and demolish street furniture (especially signal and lighting poles). The optimum design is a compromise between the two.

Curb Extensions

Curb extensions or "bulb-outs" are extensions of the sidewalk and curb into the street on both sides of a pedestrian crosswalk. Curb extensions have several advantages for the pedestrian. The primary benefit is a shorter crossing distance at an intersection. (Figure 16–29.) Shortening this distance decreases the amount of time the pedestrian is exposed to traffic. By narrowing the traffic lane and creating a smaller corner radius, curb extensions also reduce traffic speeds at the intersection. Curb extensions increase visibility for the pedestrian in areas with on-street parking by offering an unimpeded view of oncoming traffic (and allowing on-coming traffic to also see approaching pedestrians). Lastly, curb extensions can provide additional space for landscaping to improve the visual quality of the street.

Medians and Refuge Areas

In general, pedestrians are better accommodated when roadway width at intersections is narrower, thereby making medians unnecessary. Pedestrian refuge areas can be essential for large, multilane, urban and suburban intersections. These islands serve several purposes. They allow a resting area for slower pedestrians who cannot make it across the intersection within the time allotted. In wider urban intersections, refuge areas allow pedestrians to cross one direction of traffic at a time, and they provide a place to wait for the next pedestrian cycle. In this case, they also reduce the overall delay to motor vehicles that would otherwise have to stop for an interval in order to allow a pedestrian to cross the entire length of the intersection.

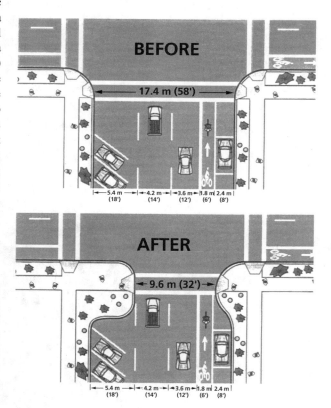

Figure 16–29   Curb Extension Reduced Crossing Distance

Source: *Oregon Bicycle and Pedestrian Plan,* Salem, Ore.: Oregon Department of Transportation, 1995.

Medians and refuge areas can be particularly important for urban intersections with center turn lanes and left turn signals. Traffic signals that serve these intersections often do not allow adequate time for the pedestrian to traverse the length of the intersection. The center median therefore provides a refuge for pedestrians who must wait through several cycles to complete a crossing.

A pedestrian refuge should be provided at intersections with crossing distances that cannot be made within the time allotted by the signal phasing (assuming a standard rate of travel at 1 m/3.5 ft per sec). Refuge areas should also be installed at intersections with crossing distances that exceed 22.8 m (75 ft), or with a high volume of elderly or disabled pedestrians.

The preferred width for medians is 1.8 m (6 ft), with 1.2 m (4 ft) being the minimum width. The length of the island should be based in part on the geometric design of the approaching traffic lanes, but it should not be less than 6 m (20 ft). The design of the island should meet ADA standards, with curb cuts provided. (Figure 16–30.)

Midblock Crossings

In situations where a midblock crossing formalizes a pedestrian activity that is already occurring on a frequent basis, midblock crossing provisions can be used to improve the visibility of the pedestrian. Midblock crossings are most appropriate in locations where a high pedestrian traffic generator is located directly across the street from a significant source of pedestrians. Examples would include a commercial area with fast food restaurants across the street from a university, or a shopping center across from a high school. However, due to the increased safety risk of a pedestrian crossing in midstream traffic, midblock crossings should be generally discouraged unless one or more of the following conditions apply:

- The location is already a source of a substantial number of midblock crossings, or it is anticipated to generate midblock crossings (for a new development).

- The land use is such that a pedestrian is highly unlikely to cross the street at an adjacent intersection, and when midblock crossings would be frequent.

- The safety and capacity of adjacent intersections creates a situation where it is dangerous to cross the street, except at a designated midblock location.

- Spacing between adjacent signals exceeds 600 feet.

- Other lesser measures to encourage pedestrians to cross at adjacent intersections have been unsuccessful.

Figure 16–30   Median Refuge Island

Source: The RBA Group, Morristown, N.J.

On-street parking can reduce sight distances at midblock crossings. In areas with on-street parking, midblock crossings should include highly visible crosswalk markings and a flared-out curb extension. (Figure 16–31.)

Another measure to improve motorist awareness of the midblock crossing is to erect overhead pedestrian crossing signs on span wires or mast arms above the street. In cases of extremely high pedestrian volume during certain times of the day, a signalized intersection with pedestrian push-buttons should be considered.

Grade-Separated Crossings

Convenience is essential in designing overpasses and underpasses. Studies have shown that pedestrians can rarely be convinced to use a poorly located crossing—and will almost never use an overpass if it takes fifty percent longer to cross than an at-grade crossing. Grade-separated crossings should be provided within the normal path of pedestrians wherever possible. Even for the most ideal overpass location, it may still be necessary to block pedestrian access to the at-grade crossing with fencing.

A 1988 study concluded that state and local governments usually consider grade-separated crossings in the following situations:

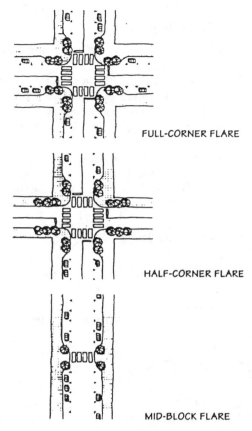

FULL-CORNER FLARE

HALF-CORNER FLARE

MID-BLOCK FLARE

Figure 16–31   Midblock Flare

Source: *Planning and Implementing Pedestrian Facilities in Suburban and Developing Rural Areas,* TRB Report 294A, Washington, D.C.: Transportation Research Board, 1987.

- Where there is moderate to high pedestrian demand to cross a freeway or expressway.

- Where there is a large number of young children (i.e., particularly near schools) who must regularly cross a high-speed or high-volume roadway.

- On streets having high vehicle volumes, high pedestrian crossing volumes, and where there is an extreme hazard for pedestrians (e.g., on wide streets with high-speed traffic and poor sight distance).

- Where one or more of the conditions stated above exists in conjunction with a well-defined pedestrian origin and destination (e.g., a residential neighborhood across a busy street from a school, a parking structure affiliated with a university, or apartment complex near a shopping mall).[51]

It is important to provide adequate lighting of the crossing to prevent crime and vandalism. Underpasses often need lighting 24 hours a day. Topography should be a major consideration in determining whether an underpass or overpass is more appropriate. These facilities are regulated by ADA standards, therefore extensive ramping is usually necessary to meet the grade requirements.

Expressway Ramps

Pedestrian safety is often jeopardized in areas where expressway ramps intersect with arterial, collector, and local streets. For new roadways and roadway widening projects, a pedestrian circulation plan should be developed for interchange exit and entrance ramp locations, particularly for areas with the following characteristics:

[51] C.V. Zegeer and S.F. Zegeer, "Pedestrians and Traffic Control Measures" (Washington, D.C.: Transportation Research Board, 1988).

- Areas with substantial pedestrian volume or nearby pedestrian attractors.

- Where existing sidewalks are located in the vicinity of expressway exits and entrances.

- Where new sidewalks are planned for the vicinity of expressway exits and entrances.

Several measures can increase the awareness of motorists and improve conditions for pedestrians at interchanges. Ramp width should be minimized to reduce the crossing distance for pedestrians. Warning signs should be posted on exit ramps to warn motorists of upcoming pedestrian crossings. Motorists should be encouraged to quickly reduce their vehicle speed after exiting the highway, both through signage and traffic calming methods.

It should be noted that it is difficult to correct all of the problems associated with expressway entrance and exit ramps on local streets. In some cases, these areas will always be unfriendly for pedestrians due to the limiting factors of high speed exiting traffic and poor sight distance. Extra care should be taken to improve these areas for pedestrians wherever possible.

Traffic Calming

Traffic calming is a relatively new and very different approach to managing the roadway environment. Traffic calming seeks to reduce the negative effects of motor vehicles. It employs a variety of physical measures or techniques to reduce vehicle speeds, alter driver behavior, and improve conditions for nonmotorized street users.[52] By their nature, therefore, "traffic calmed" roadways are more conducive to bicycling and walking. For a more detailed discussion of traffic calming practices, see Chapter 17 of this handbook.

Pedestrian Linkages

When a grid or other dense street network is not available, pedestrian linkages should be provided to maintain walking continuity. Cul-de-sacs, loop roads, and similar treatments that disrupt pedestrian continuity should incorporate pedestrian linkages such as "cut-throughs" to adjoining developments. (Figures 16–32 and 16–33.) These shortcuts enable pedestrians to travel by the most direct route between destinations. In most cases, routes will have fewer vehicular conflicts since the pedestrian does not have to use an arterial to get from one local street to another.

Similarly, large lot commercial developments, such as office buildings or shopping centers, should provide numerous linkages with surrounding residential areas to permit nearby residents to walk to the site. Linkages should also be provided between adjoining commercial, residential, and office uses; for example, walkways connecting an office building parking area with an adjacent restaurant. It is not necessary to demonstrate that there is a latent demand for walking. The linkage is required to service even the single trip if it is generated.

Policy for linkages can be defined in the land use element of municipal master plans, in the circulation element of municipal master plans, and on the official map.

Summary and Conclusions

The mandates of ISTEA, TEA-21, and other transportation-related and legislative measures, such as the Clean Air Act Amendments of 1990, provide planners with both flexibility and funding to implement a comprehensive planning approach that will result in a transportation infrastructure that is capable of accommodating the transportation and recreation needs of both bicyclists and pedestrians.

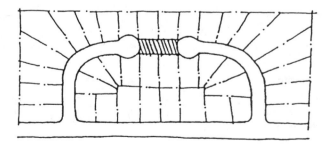

Figure 16–32   Pedestrian Linkages

Source: *Accommodating the Pedestrian*, New York, N.Y.: Van Nostrand Reinhold Co., 1984.

---

[52] Ian Lockwood, "ITE Traffic Calming Definition", *ITE Journal*, vol. 67, no. 7 (Washington, D.C. Institute of Transportation Engineers, July 1997) p. 22.

As described in this chapter, state-of-the-practice tools and guidelines relating to facilities design and the planning and maintenance of bicycle and pedestrian facilities have been developed and tested in a number of states, regions, and communities. Though these tools and guidelines exist, transportation policy changes at the state and local levels are also required to fully integrate bicycle and pedestrian concepts into the transportation planning process and move bicycle and pedestrian design beyond just marginal improvements.

It is important that bicycling and walking become a routine part of the transportation system rather than being treated as modes separate from other transportation systems. In the long term it would be preferable for bicycle and pedestrian facilities to be incorporated directly, based on their own merits, in all transportation plans, projects, and programs. Similarly, separate, dedicated funding for bicycle and pedestrian facilities, which may currently be needed to assure that improvements will be constructed, should over time cease to be needed as the merit of funding these improvements becomes generally accepted. It is necessary to address both bicycle and pedestrian transportation issues in a more systematic manner.

Suggested References for Further Reading

In addition to the following suggested references, also see the publications that are cited in the footnotes.

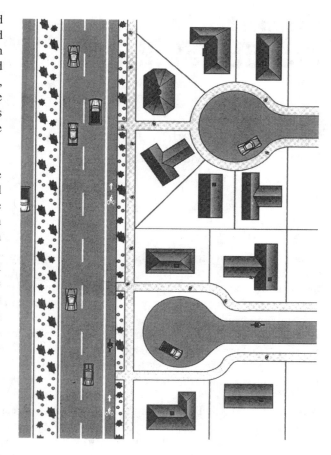

Figure 16–33   Cul-de-sac Connections

Source: *Oregon Bicycle and Pedestrian Plan*, Salem, Ore.: Oregon Department of Transportation, 1995.

American Association of State and Highway Transportation Officials. *Guide for the Development of Bicycle Facilities.* Washington, D.C.: AASHTO, 1999.

Institute of Transportation Engineers. *Design and Safety of Pedestrian Facilities: A Recommended Practice of the Institute of Transportation Engineers.* Washington, D.C.: ITE, 1998.

Institute of Transportation Engineers. *Review of Planning Guidelines and Design Standards for Bicycle Facilities.* Washington, D.C.: ITE, 1997.

John J. Fruin and G. Benz. "Pedestrian Time-Space Concept for Analyzing Corners and Crosswalks," *Transportation Research Record 959.* Washington, D.C.: Transportation Research Board, 1984.

Oregon Department of Transportation. *Oregon Bicycle and Pedestrian Plan.* Salem, Ore.: Oregon DOT, 1995.

Pedestrian Design Guidelines Notebook. Portland, OR, Office of Transportation Engineering and Development, Pedestrian Program, 1997.

Pedestrian Facilities Guidebook: Incorporating Pedestrians Into Washington's Transportation System. Washington State Department of Transportation, Puget Sound Regional Council, Association of Washington Cities, and County Road Administration Board, September 1997.

Rails-to-Trails Conservancy. *Trails for the 21st Century.* Washington, D.C.: Rails-to-Trails Conservancy, 1995.

U.S. Department of Transportation, Federal Highway Administration. *National Bicycling and Walking Study—A Final Report.* Washington, D.C.: U.S. DOT, FHWA, and associated case studies, 1994.

Transportation Research Board. *Bicycle Condition Index.* Washington, D.C.: TRB, 1998.

Transportation Research Board. *Planning and Implementing Pedestrian Facilities in Suburban and Developing Suburban and Rural Areas.* TRB Report No. 294A. Washington, D.C.: TRB, 1987.

CHAPTER 17
Traffic Calming

Crysttal Atkins
Project Manager, Traffic Calming Program
Bureau of Traffic Management
City of Portland, Oregon

Introduction

Over the last century transportation engineers have developed and built roadway designs that increased traffic speeds and volumes. These designs typically involve widening and straightening roads, thereby creating a roadway environment that feels safe and comfortable for higher speed driving. For example, until recently typical residential street width standards called for sufficient right-of-way to allow two vehicles to easily pass each other on the street, even when cars are parked on both sides of the street. This has clearly increased both capacity and speeds on the wider residential streets. At the same time that street designs made higher speed driving more comfortable, improved automobile designs have made cars that are more powerful and maneuverable. Plus, good planning principals have not always been used when additions to the transportation system were made or when new residential area streets were designed as well. All of these factors contribute and compound the problem of excessive traffic speeds and volumes on residential streets.

As traffic volumes and speeds increased on residential streets, so did resident complaints to public officials. Beginning in the late 1940s, U.S. cities such as Montclair, New Jersey; Grand Rapids, Michigan; and Richmond, California began traffic calming programs (although the term had not yet been invented) to address citizen concerns. In the late 1960s, the Dutch began to experiment with a higher level of traffic calming. Their *woonerf*, or "living yards," design turned roadways into shared spaces where cars were the invited guests rather than the predominant users of the space. The *woonerf* design proved quite successful, and the concept quickly spread throughout Europe. In the early 1980s, a few U.S. cities began traffic calming programs to address citizen concerns. At the end of the 20th century, traffic calming is part of a national change in the way the transportation system is viewed, as evidenced by the passage of the Intermodal Surface Transportation Efficiency Act of 1991 and the Transportation Equity Act for the 21st Century.

While the number of traffic calming programs in the United States has grown substantially over the last twenty years, a consensus of what is meant by traffic calming has yet to be reached by transportation professionals. A subcommittee of the Institute of Transportation Engineers (ITE) offered the following definition, which was published in the July 1997 issue of the *ITE Journal:*

> Traffic calming is the combination of mainly physical measures that reduce the negative effects of motor vehicle use, alter driver behavior and improve conditions for non-motorized street users.[1]

The subcommittee also provided their intended interpretation of the definition in the article, differentiating traffic calming from traffic control devices, streetscaping, and "route modification." There was no clear acceptance of this definition. Some transportation professionals felt that excluding devices such as diverters, street closures, and turn restrictions from the traffic calming toolbox was inappropriate. Others were concerned that the definition did not address the other two "Es"—enforcement and education.

---

[1] Lockwood, I.M., "ITE Traffic Calming Definition," *ITE Journal,* Vol. 67 (Washington, D.C.: Institute of Transportation Engineers, July 1997), pp. 22–24.

Reid Ewing offered another definition that deserves consideration in his presentation at the 1997 ITE Annual Conference in Toronto, Canada. Ewing's definition is:

> Traffic calming involves changes in street alignment, installation of barriers, and other physical measures to reduce traffic speeds and/or cut-through volumes, in the interest of street safety, livability, and other public purposes.[2]

Despite the fact that a consensus has yet to be reached, both of these definitions contain much commonality as they attempt to articulate the basic tenets of traffic calming. Each describe the engineering and physical change aspects of traffic calming measures, and each at least implies that traffic calming measures are self-enforcing. Two of the definitions express goals of altering motorist behavior and improving livability and conditions for the nonmotorist users of a street. As traffic calming techniques are used to meet different public goals, such as crime prevention, urban main streets, or urban redevelopment, we may find that even these two definitions are too narrowly defined.

Table 17–1   ITE District 6 Traffic Calming Survey Results

Type of Measure Reported	Number of Jurisdictions Reporting Use
Speed humps/tables	79
Diverters/closures	67
Traffic circles	46
Curb extensions/chokers	35
Engineering measures (any kind)	110
Total Response	153

Source: R.S. McCourt, "Neighborhood Traffic Management Survey," Washington, D.C., Institute of Transportation Engineers.

The Case for Traffic Calming

More and more transportation professionals throughout the country are using traffic calming measures to address traffic problems. When the ITE District 6 undertook a survey in 1996, asking jurisdictions if they had an active traffic calming program and what types of measures they used, 153 cities and counties nationwide responded. Of the respondents, 110 reported the use of one or more engineering measures. The remaining respondents used educational and enforcement activities that would fall within the broader definition of traffic calming. Table 17–1 summarizes the results of the survey, which would have been radically different if taken ten years ago.

Why are we seeing a movement toward traffic calming? There is often significant citizen demand for transportation professionals to "do something" about the speed and number of cars on the street, and traffic calming measures are the "something" that professionals can use to solve these problems. But in addition to the positive citizen reaction to traffic calming, there are good social and sound engineering reasons to apply traffic calming measures. For example, numerous studies have found that traffic calming measures increase safety for all users of the roadway. The positive social results are more difficult to quantify; but a few studies suggest that traffic calming measures can increase property values, decrease crime and noise levels, discourage urban sprawl, and promote a sense of community. These claims are examined in greater detail in the following sections.

Improving Livability

Traffic calming is most often touted as a way to increase or enhance livability in neighborhoods. "Livability" is one of those terms that is nearly impossible to define, as the definition will vary greatly depending on the individual and their values. However, some success in quantifying livability as it relates to traffic has been achieved through the 1972 research of Appleyard. Appleyard[3] looked at the environmental quality of San Francisco, California city streets. The findings of this study, which have been validated in a number of additional studies, are that residents are more satisfied with the street environment when traffic volumes and speeds are low to moderate. Residents are more likely to walk, bike, and play along such streets; and there is a greater sense of community. Appleyard concluded in his book *Livable Streets:*

> The environmental capacity of most residential streets might therefore be reached in the 500 to 800 vehicles per day range. The speed of drivers must also be considered. Speed limits for the top 15 percent should be in the 15 to 20 m.p.h. range for children to be secure.[4]

---

[2] Ewing, Reid, "Overview: Legal Aspects of Traffic Calming," *Compendium of Reference Papers*, 1998 ITE Annual Conference (Washington, D.C.: Institute of Transportation Engineers, 1998).

[3] Appleyard, Donald, *Livable Streets* (Berkeley, Calif.: University of California Press, 1981).

[4] Appleyard, *Livable Streets.*

A recent report on the benefits, costs, and equity effects of traffic calming found that communities that reduce automobile dependency tend to have roadway design features associated with traffic calming such as traffic speed and volume constraints, pedestrian friendly street environments, and higher density commercial and residential patterns. The report states:

> . . . Traffic calming can help reduce low density urban expansion (urban sprawl) by improving urban environmental quality, thus reducing the incentive for residents to move to suburban areas, although it's impact on the complex social forces contributing to sprawl are limited.[5]

Further, the study found that "Traffic calming tends to provide the greatest benefits to pedestrians, bicyclists and local residents, while imposing the greatest costs on automobile users, particularly those who drive more and faster than average."

Many European studies suggest that walking, cycling, and street life increases when traffic speeds and volumes are lowered after the streets are traffic calmed. For example, the Danish Road Directorate[6] conducted an experiment in speed reduction on highways passing through three towns. In Skærbæk, they studied the everyday outdoor activities along the main road before and after the installation of traffic calming. Activities were divided into two main categories: compulsory (such as shopping or delivery of mail) and optional (such as socializing or playing). They found a 16 percent increase in the number of persons using the main street for both compulsory and optional activities after the street was calmed. (Table 17–2.) In the town of Vinderup, it was found that pedestrian and cyclist activity increased as well. (Table 17–3.)

Table 17–2   Compulsory and Optional Activities and Persons, Before and After Conversion (Skærbæk, Denmark)

	Total		Compulsory		Optional	
	Before	After	Before	After	Before	After
Activities	1,432	1,668	727	926	413	503
Persons	2,167	2,499	1,058	1,257	744	858

Source: *Consequence Evaluation of Environmentally Adapted Through Road in Skærbæk,* Report No. 63, Shultz Grafisk A/S, Road Data Laboratory, January 1988. Records were collected from diaries of observers during 7.5 daytime hours.

Table 17–3   Number of Highway Crossings, Before and After Conversion (Vinderup, Denmark)

Pedestrians	Cyclists
Before – After	Before – After
1,062 – 1,935	840 – 1,168

Source: Counts were taken over 7.5 daytime hours. L. Herrstedt, "Traffic Calming Design—A Speed Management Method," *Accident Analysis and Prevention,* Vol. 24, No. 1, 1992, Road Data Laboratory, pp. 3–16.

Impact on Residential Property Values

Although not directly related to livability (some citizens might argue otherwise), several studies have found that residential property values increase with reduced vehicle traffic. One study from Grand Rapid, Michigan found that homes in the Dickinson neighborhood, which was traffic calmed with diagonal diverters, had an average value 18 percent higher than comparable homes in the Burton Heights neighborhood, a neighborhood with a nearly identical street network and land-use mix that was not traffic calmed; and this increment appeared to increase over time.[7] A second study looked at the effect of traffic volumes on housing prices and found that: ". . . city properties are discounted by 1.05 percent for each additional one thousand cars in the average daily traffic count . . . . that traffic has a higher proportional effect on higher valued properties . . . . A one percent increase in daily traffic causes a three basis point decline in house values."[8]

Crime Reduction

Several cities have reported the use of traffic calming measures to decrease crime within a neighborhood. To date, the results are mixed. The most successful intervention was reported by Dayton, Ohio in their Five Oaks Neighborhood Stabilization Plan. The plan closed and beautified streets, transforming an open grid system into a series of

---

[5] Litman, Tod, Traffic Calming Benefits, *Costs and Equity Issues* (Canada: Victoria Transport Policy Institute, 1997).

[6] *Consequence Evaluation of Environmentally Adapted Through Road in Skærbæk,* Report 63, Schultz Grafisk A/S (Road Data Laboratory, January 1988).

[7] Bagvy, Gordon, "Effects of Traffic Flow on Residential Property Values," *Journal of the American Planning Association* (January 1980).

[8] Hughes, William and C.F. Sirmans, "Traffic Externality and Single-Family Housing Prices," *Journal of Regional Science,* Vol. 32, No. 4 (1992).

mini-neighborhoods with a single entry off an arterial. The through-streets were treated with speed humps. Violent crime declined by 50 percent and nonviolent crime by 24 percent. Ft. Lauderdale unfortunately did not see the same results when streets were closed in 1988 in the Riverside Park neighborhood.[9] They found no drop in serious crimes, with a reduction in only prowler calls and traffic incidents.

Reducing Noise

Several cities have conducted noise studies to determine the effect of traffic calming measures on neighborhood noise levels. Charlotte, North Carolina found that noise levels did not change after speed humps were installed in two neighborhoods, and it showed a slight decrease in the third neighborhood. San Jose found that average noise levels fell from 77 to 75 dB(A) after speed humps were installed.[10] Beverly Hills, California reported no significant difference in noise levels between streets with speed humps and control streets.[11]

Speed Reduction

Most traffic calming projects are aimed at reducing traffic speeds. Speeding is not only a factor in the frequency and severity of traffic accidents, it is also the greatest cause of discomfort and concern for residents and nonmotorized users of the street. Many times residents will accept high traffic volumes as long as traffic speeds are reduced. Traffic engineers generally use the 85th percentile speed to represent traffic speeds on a particular street. Ideally, the 85th percentile speed on a street is equal to the posted speed limit, with only 15 percent of the vehicles traveling above the posted limit. Residents and pedestrians seem to feel uncomfortable when traffic speeds are near 30 mph or above. Whether by coincidence or by design, many traffic calming programs use a 30 mph 85th percentile speed as the minimum to qualify for a traffic calming project.

Figure 17–1   Example of a 14 ft Speed Bump

Source: Portland Traffic Calming Program, Bureau of Traffic Calming, City of Portland, Oregon.

Figure 17–2   Example of a 22 ft Speed Bump

Source: Portland Traffic Calming Program, Bureau of Traffic Calming, City of Portland, Oregon.

The speed reduction effect of a particular device will vary depending on the type and design of the device, the number and spacing of the devices within a project design, and the particular roadway characteristics of where the devices were installed. Nonetheless, as particular device designs are being used by a number of jurisdictions and more jurisdictions are reporting the results of their traffic calming projects, it is becoming easier to estimate what speed reduction results will be achieved by using a particular device. This is particularly true with regards to speed humps and tables. For example, Portland, Oregon reports an overall average speed reduction of 8 mph on streets treated with either speed humps or speed tables. Before and after studies done by Charlotte, North Carolina show that speed humps reduced speeds by approximately 5 to 6 mph. Charlotte is also testing chicanes on five neighborhood streets. They report an initial average speed reduction of 2 mph, although the results range from a 10 mph reduction to a 3 mph increase. Figures 17–1, 17–2, and 17–3 illustrate examples of devices being tested or used to slow traffic.

---

[9] R. Szymanski, *Can Changing Neighborhood Traffic Circulation Patterns Reduce Crime and Improve Personal Safety? A Quantitative Analysis of One Neighborhood's Efforts,* Master's Thesis, Florida International University (Ft. Lauderdale, Fla.: 1994).

[10] Ewing, Reid, "Interim Report on Chesbro Avenue Pavement Undulations," State of the Art Report.

[11] Ewing, Reid, "Speed Humps: Implementation and Impact of Residential Traffic Control"

Improving Safety

The sound engineering reasons to apply traffic calming measures focus on increased safety and improvement of the street environment for other modal users. The need to reduce traffic speeds for the benefit of the nonmotorized street user can be seen in recent accident statistics. A recent study found that "The chance of a pedestrian being killed by an automobile accident increases from 5% at 20 mph to 45% at 30 mph and 85% at 40 mph . . ."[12] Another study[13] found that between 1986 and 1995, approximately 6,000 pedestrians died every year in the United States after being hit by an automobile. In 1997, 30 percent of all the 5- to 9-year-old children who died in car crashes were pedestrians. Since 1986, 17 percent of all pedestrian fatalities, an average of approximately 1,033 per year, involve children under the age

Figure 17–3 Temporary One-Lane Chicane

Source: Photo Reid Ewing.

of 18. The average cost to society of a pedestrian–motor vehicle crash is $312,000, or a total of more than $32 billion per year. Nearly one-third of the bicyclists killed in motor vehicle crashes in 1997 were between 5 and 15 years old.

Traffic calming has also produced reductions in the number and rate of traffic accidents, a benefit for the motorized street user. Seattle, Washington has documented considerable success in reducing accidents through the use of traffic circles. As early as 1982, Seattle reported in the *ITE Journal* that "The total number of reported collisions was reduced from 33 to 3 as a result of the installation of the traffic circles, yielding a 91% decrease."[14] Similarly, the 1992 *Peer Review Report* on Portland's Traffic Circle Program found that the reported accident rate had decreased by 28 to 84 percent at intersections where circles had been installed.[15] The 1997 Surface Transportation Policy Project article, *Mean Streets—Pedestrian Safety and Reform of the Nation's Transportation Law,* reports that Seattle's traffic calming program reduced pedestrian accidents by more than 75 percent.[16]

Much of the evidence, indicating that traffic calming measures reduce the frequency and severity of accidents, comes from the reports on traffic calming studies conducted by other countries. For example, a study reviewing 600 Danish traffic calming projects found a 43 percent reduction in traffic crash casualties compared with untreated areas.[17] Similarly, the Insurance Corporation of British Columbia recently published a report in which it summarized 43 international case studies. Among the 43 cases, collision frequencies declined by 8 to 100 percent. (Figure 17–4.)

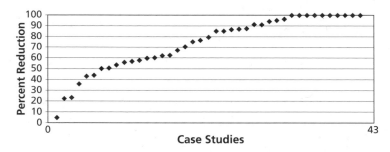

Figure 17–4 Reduction in Collision Frequency for All Researched Case Studies

---

[12] *Walking Tall: A Citizen's Guide to Walkable Communities* (Pedestrian Federation of America, 1995).

[13] *Mean Streets—Pedestrian Safety and Reform of the Nation's Transportation Law*, Surface Transportation Policy Project (Washington, D.C.: Environmental Working Group, April 1997).

[14] Dare, James and Noel Schoneman, "Seattle's Neighborhood Traffic Control Program," *ITE Journal* (Washington, D.C.: Institute of Transportation Engineers, February 1982).

[15] *Evaluation of the Neighborhood Traffic Management Program—Peer Review Analysis of the Traffic Circle Program* (Portland, Ore.: City Council of Portland, 1992).

[16] *Mean Streets—Pedestrian Safety and Reform of the Nation's Transportation Law.*

[17] *The Safety Benefits of Traffic Calming* (Road Safety Group, 1996).

Traffic Calming Programs

Conversations between traffic calming practitioners at transportation conferences tell of cities that installed their first traffic calming project and were subsequently inundated by citizen requests for a traffic calming project on their street. Many of these cities had to scramble quickly to develop guidelines, and ultimately traffic calming program procedures, to handle these requests. This is not necessarily the least stressful way to go about developing a new program!

Program Development

Developing a new traffic calming program requires much thought and reflection on what problems the program is designed to solve and what mechanisms will be used to solve them. Successful programs are structured enough to allow citizens, staff, and elected officials to be comfortable in moving forward with projects; but they are flexible enough to adjust to the challenges of each individual project.

The process of program development is essentially quite straightforward. The goal is to produce an integrated set of policies, objectives, and procedures that will provide the program's vision, a set of overall guidelines, and the policy basis for making future decisions. These provide consistency and the political and technical framework for decision-making. You need to know where you are going and what you hope to accomplish if you want your program to be successful. Table 17–4 outlines the types of program policy issues that need to be considered during program development.

Table 17–4   Traffic Calming Program Development
Typical Program Policy Issues

Policy	Issues to be Considered
Types/classification of eligible streets	• Which classification(s) of streets are eligible (i.e., local, collector, arterial)? • Is the predominant land use (i.e., residential, commercial, mixed-use) a factor in eligiblity?
Program response	• Will the program be *reactive* (responding to citizen requests for action) or *proactive* (with staff identifying problems and initiating action)? • Will project boundaries be narrowly focused (for example, by street segment), or will project boundaries by broadly focused (such as an area-wide project)?
Acceptable corrective measures (enforcement, education, and engineering)	• Will a combination of corrective measures be used, or will the program focus on only one type? • Does a street need to meet minimum speed and/or volume criteria to be eligible for corrective measures? • Does a street need to complete one type of corrective measure (for example, an education effort) to qualify for additional measures?
Traffic diversion allowed or prohibited	• If diversion is allowed, under what circumstances (for example, local streets only with more than 75% cut-through traffic)? • Will there be a minimum volume required to trigger diversion measures? • If project causes unintentional diversion, what remedies are provided? • How much volume increase on an adjacent street would be considered unacceptable? • Would remedies be automatic?
Parking removal	• Is on-street parking removal an issue for residents? • How will conflicts be resolved?
Accommodation for transit and other transportation modes	• Will the existence of other modes (i.e., transit service, bike lane, pedestrian path, truck route) on a street change its eligiblity? • Will some device choices be restricted to accommodate transit and/or other transp. modes? • How will traffic calming projects complement or enhance the use of transit or other transportation modes?
Accommodation for emergency response services	• How will the need for prompt emergency response be balanced with the need to slow traffic and/or reduce traffic volumes? • Will some device choices be restricted to accommodate emergency services?
Resource issues	• How will the program be funded? • Is the funding source(s) stable? • Will residents be required to participate in the project cost and/or maintenance?

Table 17–4   Traffic Calming Program Development
Typical Program Policy Issues (continued)

Policy	Issues to be Considered
Administration	• Are there applicable codes and related policies that need to be integrated into the program procedures? • Do any codes or policies need to be changed prior to adoption of the program? • Is there sufficient resource allocation for the program? • How will adherence to the minimum program procedures (e.g., project selection, notification area) be ensured? • How will the program be evaluated and on what timeframe?
Public involvement	• Who is involved? • When are they involved? • What decisions can they make? • How will the final decision be made (e.g., by a vote of a committee, a majority approval by ballot or petition, by City Council)?

Sample Traffic Calming Program Policies (Portland, Oregon)

The traffic calming program is guided by a set of council-adopted program policies. The program policies are as follows.

- Through-traffic should be encouraged to use higher classification arterials, as designated in the arterial streets classifications and policies (contained in the *Transportation Element of the City of Portland Comprehensive Plan*).

- A combination of education, enforcement, and engineering methods should be employed. Traffic calming devices should be planned and designed in keeping with sound engineering and planning practices. The city traffic engineer shall direct the installation of traffic control devices (signs, signals, and markings) as needed to accomplish the project, in compliance with the municipal code.

- Emergency vehicle access should be accommodated in keeping with the existing fire bureau response standards. If current emergency vehicle access does not meet the existing response standard, traffic calming efforts should not further degrade the response time.

- Transit service access, safety, and scheduling should not be significantly affected.

- Reasonable automobile access should be maintained. Pedestrian, bicycle, and transit access should be encouraged and enhanced wherever possible and within budget limitations. Projects should be coordinated with the bicycle and pedestrian programs where possible.

- Parking removal should be considered on a project-by-project basis. Parking needs of residents should be balanced with the equally important functions of traffic, emergency vehicle access, transit, bicycle, and pedestrian movement.

- Application of the traffic calming program shall be limited to those neighborhood collector streets that are primarily residential and to local service streets. Where appropriate, projects on neighborhood collector streets should be coordinated with projects on local service streets.

- Traffic calming projects on neighborhood collector streets shall not divert traffic off the project street through the use of traffic diversion devices. As a result of a project on a neighborhood collector, the amount of traffic increase acceptable on a parallel local service street shall not exceed 150 vehicles per day.

- Traffic may be rerouted from one local service street to another as a result of a traffic calming project. The acceptable traffic increase should be defined on a project-by-project basis. An "impact threshold curve" established by the Portland Office of Transportation shall serve as a guideline to determine the amount of rerouted traffic that is acceptable on local service streets.

- To implement the traffic calming program, certain procedures should be followed by the Office of Transportation in processing traffic calming requests in accordance with applicable codes and related policies and within the limits of available resources. At a minimum the procedures shall provide for submittal of project proposals, project evaluation and selection, citizen participation, communication of any test results and specific findings to project area residents and affected organizations before installation of permanent traffic calming devices, and appropriate city council review.

The traffic calming program has the following six objectives:

1. Improve neighborhood livability by mitigating the impact of vehicular traffic on residential neighborhoods.
2. Promote safe and pleasant conditions for residents, motorists, bicyclists, pedestrians, and transit riders on residential streets.
3. Promote and support the use of transportation alternatives to the single-occupant vehicle.
4. Encourage citizen participation in all phases of traffic calming program activities.
5. Make efficient use of city resources by prioritizing traffic calming projects.
6. Support the policies contained in the *Transportation Element of the City of Portland Comprehensive Plan* to "provide for the safe and efficient movement of people and goods while preserving, enhancing, or reclaiming the neighborhoods' livability" and to "guide the use of the city street system to control air pollution, traffic, and livability problems."

Obviously, it is best to start program development with a good definition of the problem and a review of existing, referent policies at the local and state level. From there, a series of questions need to be thought about and answered. Figure 17–5 shows an example of some existing traffic calming program policies.

Program Objectives

Objectives define what the program is trying to accomplish, and they are directly related to the program policies. Table 17–5 provides a list of some typical traffic calming program objectives and offers others for consideration. If program policies and objectives tell us where we want to go, program procedures tell us how we are going to get there. It is the nuts and bolts of the program, the "rules" that you and the citizens will follow when doing a traffic calming project. There are as many different program procedures as there are traffic calming programs. However, Table 17–6 summarizes the basic areas that need to be addressed in any set of program procedures.

Program Policies

- Use 3 E's
- Direct through traffic to arterials
- Accommodate emergency vehicle access
- Minimize impact on transit
- Enhance alternative transportation modes
- Balance parking needs and parking removal
- Limit re-routing and diversion impacts on adjacent streets
- Establish standard project procedures

Figure 17–5   Recommended Program Policies

Source: Portland Traffic Calming Program, Bureau of Traffic Calming, City of Portland, Oregon.

Public Involvement

Developing an effective public involvement process is critical to the success of any traffic calming program. Involving the public in project decision-making is time consuming and often frustrating, so jurisdictions are sometimes tempted to minimize the amount of public involvement required to complete a traffic calming project. This is a big mistake! Traffic calming projects are not like other types of construction projects that take place within the road right-of-way. Even the best-engineered traffic calming project—designs that would have had significant positive effects—have failed miserably because residents felt something was being done to them rather than for them.

Table 17–5   Traffic Calming Program Development Program Objectives

Typical Program Objectives	
Objective	Comments
Maintain/enhance neighborhood livability.	This objective may include more specific language, such as increase and enhance visual greenspaces, increase perception and reality of safety, or increase a resident's sense of community.
Enhance safety for residents, pedestrians, bicyclists, motorists, and school children.	
Environmental enhancement objectives, such as improve neighborhood aesthetics, increase greenspaces, decrease air pollution, or decrease noise.	It may be difficult to quantify a decrease in air pollution as a result of a traffic calming project.
Promote alternative transportation modes.	The language may specify the alternative modes.
Encourage public involvement.	
Other Program Objectives to Consider	
Objective	Comments
Increase property values.	This may be difficult to quantify in the short term.
Decrease crime.	
Enhance traffic safety for school children.	

Table 17–6 Traffic Calming Program Development Typical Program Procedures

Procedure	Issues to be Considered/Corollary Issues
How to handle project requests	**If program is reactive, who can submit a request?** **Are there pre-submittal requirements?** If yes, who needs to complete them? **How will problems be identified in disenfranchised neighborhoods?** **How will previously treated streets be handled if a new request is received?** Is there a time limit for reconsideration? **How will incident related or other special requests by handled?**
Evaluation and ranking of projects	**Will objective criteria be used?** Do these criteria reasonably represent the nature and extent of the problem? **Is the information easy to obtain and/or quantify?** Can it be easily understood? **Is the calculation used to rank projects easy to understand and perform?** Does it adequately rank the severity of the problem? **Is there a minimum score for eligibility for a project?** Are there different minimums for different types of project solutions? **Will the potential project list(s) rank projects city-wide or within specific boundaries (e.g., political boundaries, neighborhood association boundaries, geographic boundaries)?**
Project selection procedure	**How are projects selected (e.g., by a prioritized list, elected officials, neighborhood associations)?** **Is the procedure equitable?** **Is the procedure fair?** **Can projects be selected in conjunction with other projects?**
Public notification and involvement	**How will initial resident support for the project be determined?** How much support is needed for the project to proceed? **What citizen/resident notification method(s) will be used?** How far away from the project street will residents be notified about the project? **How will citizen/resident communications and involvement be handled throughout the project?** **Who can be directly involved in the project?** How will they be involved? How can other interested citizens/parties participate? Will businesses, the transit provider(s), the emergency response and other service providers be included? **How will the project design be determined?** Can residents influence the design? Can other citizens or interested parties influence the design? **How will support for the final project design be determined?** Will a ballot or petition be needed? Is there a minimum response rate? Is a simple majority approval sufficient, or is there a higher standard? Will City Council or other elected officials need to approve the project? **How will the project be evaluated following construction?** If new problems are inadvertently caused by the project, how will these be solved? **How will project results be communicated?** Who will receive the information?
Construction	**Will construction be completed by outside contractors or on-staff crews?** **Is there a significant delay between final project approval and final construction?** If yes, how will this information be communicated to residents and citizens? **Will temporary devices be installed to test a project design?** **Will temporary devices be installed as an interim measure pending final construction?** If yes, who will install the temporary devices? **Will the residents be responsible for the maintenance of the landscaping in the devices?** If yes, how will they be notified of their responsibility? Will they be required to sign a document agreeing to maintain the landscaping? How will conflicts be resolved? What happens if they fail to maintain the landscaping?
Ongoing program evaluation	**How will project results be reviewed and on what timeframe?** **How is political support assessed and retained?** **How are resident and citizen satisfaction assessed and retained?** **Will the program policies, objectives, procedures, and processes be reviewed periodically?** Who will be involved in the review? **How and who will keep the inventory of devices?** **Who will perform the routine review of the devices to assure compliance to standards?** How often will this review happen?

Most residents view the street space in front of their house as part of their property even though they intellectually understand that the street is public. A project that changes the street in front of their house causes many people to become quite emotional. Residents from adjacent streets may, understandably, be concerned that the traffic will be shifted to their street as a result of the project. Consequently, they may openly and actively oppose the project in an attempt to protect their self-interests. (This scenario is especially likely if the program policies and procedures do not address the diversion issue.) No matter where they may live in the neighborhood, nearly everyone feels strongly that they should have a say in what happens. It is important, therefore, to plan the public involvement process that balances the residents' need to have influence over the project design with the jurisdiction's need for a project that is safe, that does not negatively affect the overall transportation system, that can be constructed and maintained for a reasonable cost, and that generates the support of the majority of the residents in the neighborhood.

Liability Issues

It is important to work with legal counsel during program development. The legal issues associated with implementing a traffic calming program revolve around the issues of statutory authority, constitutionality, and tort liability. Obviously, a jurisdiction must first have adequate authority to implement traffic calming measures before proceeding. The degree of control a local jurisdiction has over its streets and highways varies by state. Some states have retained most of the control, while others have not. The local jurisdiction must also respect the constitutional rights of affected landowners and users of the roadways. Finally, like any other installation in the roadway, the jurisdiction has the responsibility to minimize the risk to roadway users. The risk of tort liability suits is generally the issue that concerns local jurisdictions the most.

Some transportation engineers and city attorneys are so concerned about the increased liability risk that they actively oppose the development of a traffic calming program. This is due in part to the lack of adopted standards like the Federal Highway Administration's *Manual on Uniform Traffic Control Devices* (MUTCD) or the American Association of State Highway and Transportation Officials' *A Policy on Geometric Design of Highways and Streets* (also known as "the green book") for traffic calming measures. So how much additional risk is a jurisdiction taking on by developing a traffic calming program? Reid Ewing and Charles Kooshian answered that question in their August 1997 *ITE Journal* article, "U.S. Experience with Traffic Calming," with ". . . 'You have little or no exposure, provided your traffic calming measures are well-designed, well-signed, well-lighted, and well-documented."[18]

In the absence of national standards, the best way for a jurisdiction to protect itself from legal challenges is to develop a rational, well–thought-out program planning and implementation process. Figure 17–6 is a flow chart showing Bellevue, Washington's thorough program procedures; and Figure 17–7 is Bellevue's "Traffic Calming Control Matrix." Adopted program policies, including minimum program procedures, limit a jurisdiction's exposure to tort liability suits by showing that the jurisdiction's actions were not arbitrary, capricious, or unreasonable. In addition to following adopted program policies and procedures, each project file should document the activities of the jurisdiction during the project. Table 17–7 shows the types of information that a project file should contain.

As with any other installation within the public right-of-way, traffic calming device installations should be periodically inspected and reviewed for maintenance and safety issues. Programs that are at risk of a legal challenge are those that: do not have a process for selecting project streets, but rely instead on neighborhood petitions or financial contribution to determine which project gets built; use casual, unquantifiable observations of traffic conditions to determine the nature and extent of traffic problems; have nonconsistent or ad hoc contacts with neighborhood residents and other stakeholders; allow project designs that do not provide adequate visibility delineation and warning so they are readily apparent to the motorist and provide adequate time for motorist response; do not measure or evaluate the effects of the project; and those that keep poor project records and documentation.

---

[18] Ewing, Reid and C. Kooshian, "U.S. Experience with Traffic Calming," *ITE Journal* (Washington, D.C.: Institute of Transportation Engineers, August 1997).

Project Development

Different programs use different processes for project development. Some programs use a "hands off" approach by requiring the residents or neighborhood groups to develop the proposed project design for staff review and approval, thereby limiting the amount of staff time devoted to the project. This approach gives the residents much ownership in the project, which is good; but it can also lead to difficulties if the staff rejects the proposed project design. Some programs are much more "hands-on" with staff interacting directly with the residents or neighborhood groups throughout project development and implementation. Obviously, this approach requires a substantial commitment of staff time. Some programs take the traditional "tell us the problem and we'll do whatever we think is best" approach, which requires less staff time than the hands-on approach. However, residents or neighborhood groups are often dissatisfied with the more traditional approach and may oppose the project even if the design is good. The project development process outlined below and summarized in Table 17–8 falls into the "hands-on" category. It is being presented because this approach may be less familiar to most transportation professionals than either of the other approaches. This project development process employs a volunteer traffic committee, made up of residents and other interested parties in neighborhood, to work with staff to identify the traffic problems, develop possible solutions, and select the preferred project design for approval.

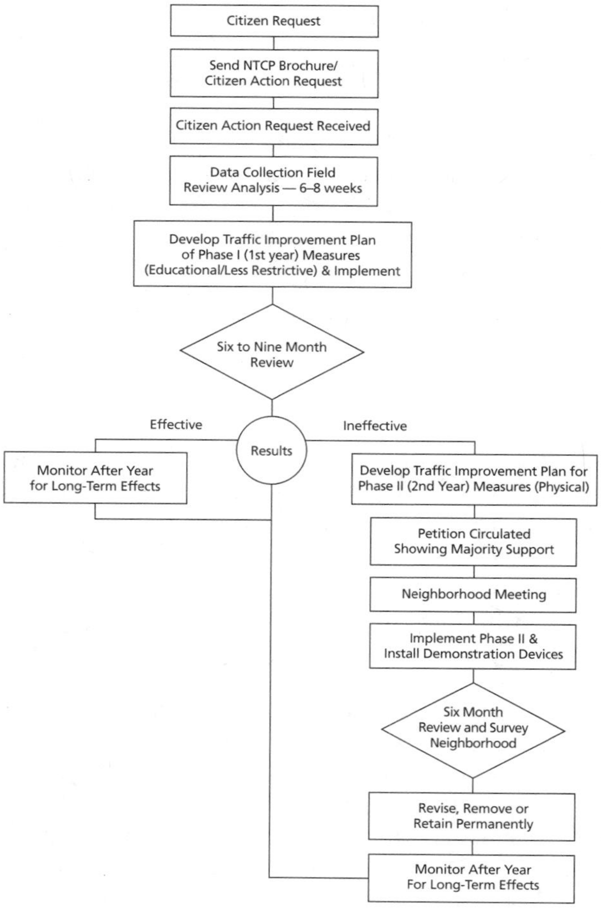

Defining the Project

There is much information that the traffic calming staff needs to gather and analyze prior to the first public meeting kicking off the traffic calming project. Depending on what information is used by the program to rank and select the project, the staff may need to have traffic speed and volume counts taken on the project street to identify or verify the traffic problems. Volume counts should also be taken on the adjacent parallel local streets and any other local streets that the staff suspects might be used as alternative routes when the project is constructed. These counts will be used to determine if the project has inadvertently caused a new problem on an adjacent street. Accident information for these streets should be collected

Figure 17–6   Program Procedures in Bellevue, Washington

Source: Bellevue, Washington Traffic Calming Program.

Table 17–7   Example of Information Contained in Project File

Information Type	Examples
Traffic studies	Speed and volume counts, screen-line volume counts, vehicle classification studies, pedestrian crossing gap analysis, accident analysis, or other traffic studies.
Project selection	Project score, ranking, and so forth showing how and why the project was selected over other pending projects.
Project alternatives	Development and consideration of project alternatives, results of any test installations that may have been tried, and how the final project design was selected.
Public input and review	Documentation of public process used, project traffic committee meeting minutes, open house summaries, project fact sheets, petition or ballot results, and so forth.
Evaluation of project effects and impacts	Speed and volume counts, screen-line volume counts, vehicle classification studies, pedestrian crossing gap analysis, accident analysis, other traffic studies, mitigation efforts taken to reduce unintended impacts, and so forth.

Land Use	Classification — Collector: Small Commercial Residential	Local Streets: Neighborhood Collector Residential	Local Streets: Local Access Residential	Curbs & Gutters	% Grade	Curvature of Street	School Bus Route/Metro	Adjacent Arterials	Previous Traffic Eng. Improve. Unsuccessful	Impacts to Police/Fire	Delay Accident	Homes Front Street	Acceptable Impacts	Control Device Use May Be Considered
Traffic Engineering & Specialized Improvements	Yes	Yes	Yes	—	—	—	—	—	—	—	—	—	—	High Speeds
Police Enforcement Neighborhood Speed Watch Program	Yes	Yes	Yes	—	—	—	—	—	—	—	—	—	—	High Speeds
Speed Humps	No	Vol. ≤ 3,000 vpd 85% ≥ 35	Vol ≥ 300 85% ≥ 35	Yes	Not > 10%	300–3,000	Yes	Yes	Yes	Yes	—	Yes	Yes	High Speeds & Cut-through volumes
Traffic Circles	No	Vol. ≤ 3,000 vpd 85% ≥ 35	Vol ≥ 300 85% ≥ 35	Yes	Not > 10%	—	Yes	Yes	Yes	Yes	—	Yes	Yes	Speeds or Accident History
Stop Signs	MUTCD	MUTCD	MUTCD	—	—	—	—	—	—	—	—	—	—	Accident History
Diverter	No	No	Vol ≥ 300	Yes	—	—	Yes	Yes	Yes	Yes	Yes	Yes	Yes	High cut-through volumes
One-Way/Chokers	No	Vol ≥ 2,500	Vol > 300	Yes	—	—	Yes	Yes	Yes	Yes	Yes	—	Yes	High cut-through volumes
Street Closure	No	Yes, If Vol ≥ 6,000 Non-local ≥ 20%	Yes, If Vol ≥ 3,000 Non-local ≥ 20%	—	—	—	Yes	Yes	Yes	Yes	Yes	Yes	Yes	High cut-through volumes

Notes: [1] All volumes in units of typical daily traffic volumes.

[2] Source for street type designation—City of Bellevue Street Classification.

[3] Control devices may be considered when either the speed criteria, volume criteria or both criteria are exceeded.

Figure 17–7   Traffic Calming Control Matrix

Source: Bellevue, Washington Traffic Calming Program.

and analyzed as well. Basic information about the project street should be gathered, such as street width; parking characteristics; adjacent land uses and the location of businesses; existence of transit, bicycle or pedestrian routes on the street; where the elementary school and the school crosswalks are located; the location and type of existing traffic controls; and the frequency and type of emergency services access. Consider also the street's role in the overall transportation network. How does the street relate to neighboring streets and properties; where and how does the street connect to higher classified arterials and collectors? How do these arterials and collectors currently function; does this affect the project street; and can improvements be made, if necessary?

Stakeholder information should also be gathered and will form the basis of the project mailing list. How is the project area defined? (Program guidelines may specify that only residents on the project street are within the project area, or the project area may extend beyond the project street boundary.) Who resides within the project area and do they own the property? (Program guidelines may require that nonresident owners be notified of the project.) What businesses on the project street might be affected by the project? Is the project notification area different from the project area? (Generally the project notification area is much broader than the project area.) Who lives within the project notification area? If the street is a transit route, who will represent the transit authority? Will the emergency service providers send representatives? Are there other service providers (the postal service, waste and recycling services, and so forth) that might want to participate? Will the school send a representative? Is there a neighborhood or business association in the area that will want to be involved?

Table 17–8 An Example of a "Hands-On" Traffic Calming Project Process (Portland, Oregon)

Step	Process
1) **Petition to proceed** (local service and neighborhood collector street projects)	A petition is circulated to all households and businesses on the project street to determine the level of support for the proposed project. Each household and business is entitled to one response. The project can go forward only if a majority of households and businesses sign the petition.
2) **Plan development** (local service and neighborhood collector street projects)	Traffic calming project staff work with interested residents to develop a traffic calming plan. Everyone in the project area is invited to participate in this process. A series of public meetings are held to exchange information and ideas, develop and refine plan alternatives, and identify the preferred traffic calming plan.
3) **Petition to test** (local service street projects only)	A test of the traffic calming plan is usually not required. However, a temporary test is conducted if the plan includes traffic diversion devices to ensure that an unacceptable amount of traffic is not shifting onto other local service streets. Each household and business is entitled to one response. The majority of the households and businesses must sign the petition in order for the test to proceed. If the required signatures are not obtained, the plan is modified or the project is discontinued. If the petition is successful, the test is installed for at least three months.
4) **Project ballot** (local service street projects)	An open house is held to present the proposed permanent traffic calming plan. For nondiversion projects, each household, business, and nonresident property owner on the project street, on cross streets up to the next parallel street, and on any other street that must use the project street as its primary access (for example, a dead-end street off the project street) receives a ballot asking if they support the project. For diversion projects, households, businesses, and nonresident property owners on any other streets that were affected during the test also receive a project ballot. A majority of those ballots returned must be in favor of the project for it to proceed to city council action.
(Neighborhood collector street projects)	An open house is held to present the proposed permanent traffic calming plan. Each household, business, and non-resident property owner on the project street receives a ballot asking if they support the project. A majority of those ballots returned must be in favor of the project for it to proceed to city council action.
5) **City council action** (local service and neighborhood collector street projects)	Traffic calming project staff prepare a report and recommendation for city council action. The public is notified of the opportunity to attend the city council hearing and comment on the proposal.
6) **Design and construction and implementation** (service and neighborhood collector street projects)	If the project is approved by the city council, the city designs and constructs the traffic local calming devices. Education and enforcement tools are also implemented.

Project Initiation

When the preliminary information has been collected and analyzed, the first project meeting can be scheduled. Generally it is best to schedule the project meeting at a location easily accessible to the project residents and at a time that is convenient to working adults. Be sure to look for meeting locations that are ADA-accessible, and be prepared to accommodate people who have special needs. Often schools, community centers, or churches will make space available for project meetings for a nominal fee. Welcome children into the process whenever feasible, as they can bring valuable information and insights (particularly regarding pedestrian crossing issues).

The focus of the first meeting should be information-sharing. Staff should explain the purpose of the project, how the project was selected (and if applicable, the extent of resident support as demonstrated by whatever method required by program procedures), the nature of the problem as they understand it, and the types of corrective measures available. Residents should identify specific problem locations and the nature of the problem as they understand it. Figure 17–8 illustrates the two-way communications taking place at an initial project meeting. Near the end of the meeting, staff should outline the roles and responsibilities of traffic committee members and ask for volunteers.

Use of Project Traffic Committee

The project traffic committee is the primary involvement method for residents and other interested parties during project development and implementation. This method offers several advantages, including the cultivation of a close working relationship between staff and the volunteer traffic committee. Initially a number of people may sign-up to serve on the traffic committee, and the interests of these volunteers may vary. Many will live on the project street and have a direct interest in the project. Some may live on adjacent local streets and may be concerned that the project will negatively affect them. Occasionally someone who opposes all traffic calming may sign-up for a traffic committee. As funny as it may sound, a project committee with one or two project opponents on it has the advantage over a committee comprised of only like-minded individuals. Others in the neighborhood will be just as skeptical as those on the committee who oppose the project. It is far more effective to listen and consider the opponents' concerns during alternative development than to discover a design flaw at the project's open house.

Figure 17–8 "Two-Way" Communication Between the Project Traffic Committee and the City's Staff

Source: Portland Traffic Calming Program, Bureau of Traffic Calming, City of Portland, Oregon.

Project Committee Organization

The first traffic committee meeting often has two goals. The first goal is committee organization. The group should discuss and decide on committee ground rules, membership (particularly how members may be added or removed), how formally or informally the meetings will be conducted, and how often the group would like to meet. The second goal is to decide on project goals and objectives. These goals and objectives give the committee some criteria to judge alternative designs by and will also be used to measure the success of the project. Frequently project goals are written fairly broadly, for example: reduce traffic speeds. Some groups prefer to write very specific goals, for example: reduce the 85th percentile speed to 25 mph. When groups write specific goals it is important for the group to acknowledge that the project may not fully attain the goal (a post-construction 85th percentile speed of 26 mph, for example) and still be considered a success. Figure 17–9 displays the project goals developed by a traffic committee.

As with all committee meetings, staff should carefully document the nature of the committee's discussions and any decisions that are made at the meeting. These meeting minutes are an important part of the final project file; as they document what alternatives were considered, how and why an alternative was chosen for the final design, and that the program procedures were followed. They may also be used as an ongoing communications tool to keep residents on the project street in touch with the committee's work, and by the committee and staff to bring new-comers to the project up-to-speed in short order.

Problem Definition

The next series of traffic committee meetings allow staff and the committee to educate each other regarding the problems and to engage in meaningful dialogue regarding possible solutions. Often additional data will be needed to understand the observed problems. For example, if the problem that is identified is cut-through traffic, a license plate study can be conducted to find out where vehicles observed on the project street are registered. Other types of traffic studies that may be needed are: intersection and turning movement counts, screen line volume counts, vehicle classification counts, pedestrian counts and gap studies, travel time studies, and origin and destination studies. Some of these counts and studies need to be completed by staff, some can be done jointly by traffic committee members and staff, and a few can be conducted by traffic committee members on their own (with direction from staff). As the problem is refined through the gathering and analyzing of additional information, a concurrent investigation process of the traffic calming devices available to the project and their uses will naturally take place by the group. This allows the traffic committee (and staff) to bounce various design ideas off each other. Each traffic calming device has benefits and downsides. As the group explores the various ideas, the pros and cons of using a particular device in a particular location can be discussed.

Formulating Solutions

Once staff and the traffic committee thoroughly understand the problem, the group can begin to formulate solutions. Actually, the basic design alternatives are often clear to both the traffic committee and staff by the time this stage is reached. (Sometimes there is only one design alternative.) The staff will usually present the traffic committee with drawings of the design alternatives under consideration. If an aerial photograph of the project street is available and the project design is straightforward, the staff and committee can "design" the alternative together at the meeting using the aerial and acetate device symbols. If driveway cuts, intersections, and even some utility manholes can be seen on the aerial, placement of the device symbols can be quite exact. Obviously the traffic committee feels much ownership of the design using this method.

No matter what method is used to present the design alternatives, the traffic committee and staff need to examine each alternative carefully and discuss the possible positive and negative aspects of each design before a decision is reached. An alternative design considered by a traffic committee is shown in Figure 17–10. Every traffic calming design has trade-offs. The best design alternative provides the residents with what they believe to be the most benefits for the least trade-offs. Part of the challenge of traffic calming is to design a solution that satisfies the unique needs of the neighborhood. Many of these needs are related to values held in common by the residents (their sense of community), and this is why the residents on two similar streets with similar problems on paper may decide on very different solutions!

Goals and Objectives
NE 7TH AVE

Neighborhood Traffic Management Project
As Adopted by the Traffic Committee, March 16, 1989

I. Improve vehicular & pedestrian safety along NE 7th Avenue

  A. Reduce vehicle velocities that contribute to collisions with fixed objects and pedestrians.

  B. Reduce Identifiable hazards created by current intersection designs.

  C. Improve visibility for drivers and pedestrians at 7th and Brazee and other intersections on 7th Avenue.

  D. Preserve pedestrian crossings at all locations where NTMP devices are located.

  E. Realign "angled" pedestrian crossings at offset intersections, if possible.

  F. Create a safe environment for bicyclists through a reduction in traffic speeds and appropriate design of NTMP devices.

II. Reduce vehicular velocities on the NE 7th Avenue, particularly where reduced speed will contribute to public safety.

  A. Reduce velocities such that 70 percent of vehicles traveling on NE 7th Avenue remain within the posted speed.

  B. Reduce the perception of NE 7th Avenue as wide-open through street that serves as a faster alternative to NE Martin Luther King Jr. Blvd.

III. Enhance the neighborhood environment along NE 7th Avenue through improved safety, lower vehicle speeds and the design of traffic management devices.

  A. Create a sense of neighborhood entrance and identity at NE Hancock, Knott and Fremont Streets.

  B. Reduce vehicular volume and speed to increase a feeling of safety along the street, on sidewalks and in front yards.

  C. Preserve and develop NE 7th Avenue as a safe and pleasant bicycle route.

IV. Stabilize or reduce traffic volumes on NE 7th Avenue

  A. Stabilize or reduce traffic volumes as much as possible through non-diversionary methods.

Figure 17–9   Example of Project Goals and Objectives

Source: Portland Traffic Calming Program, Bureau of Traffic Calming, City of Portland, Oregon.

Communicating the Proposed Solution

Once a design alternative is chosen, it is important to communicate the proposal project design to the neighborhood at large. It is best to utilize several different communication methods to ensure that as many residents are reached as possible. The traditional mailing of information to residents and placement of articles in local newspapers should be included, as these methods are broadly inclusive and easily documented in the project file. However, aside from the telephone calls that staff will receive from residents about the project, these methods do not allow much two-way conversation to take place between residents, the traffic committee, and staff. One easy way to facilitate two-way communication is to hold a project open house. An open house is an informal public meeting where people can review the project proposal, ask questions, and make comments on the proposal. Generally the open house does not have a formal presentation period. Instead the staff and traffic committee are available to answer questions and talk about the project for several hours, so neighbors can attend the open house when it is convenient for them and still get all the information.

The open house format has several advantages over other types of public meetings. Many people are uncomfortable asking questions in a formal public meeting setting. The open house gives them a friendly and informal setting where they can talk one-on-one with staff or traffic committee members about the project. Since there is no formal presentation period, there is no opportunity for those who like to grandstand to gain control of the meeting. The open house setting also lets the traffic committee present the project design to their neighbors. The committee has the opportunity to discuss why they made the decisions that they did, and why they support the project design.

Testing the Proposed Solution

Depending on the project design and the program requirements, a test of the proposed design may be required or desirable. Whenever the design proposes traffic diversion devices, the design should be tested to see whether or not the diverted traffic moves to an adjacent local street, an undesirable effect. If the traffic has not moved to an adjacent local street, it has probably moved to the higher classified arterial streets. Omitting the testing of a "diversion design" is disastrous! Generally the test needs to stay in place for 60 to 90 days before any conclusions can be drawn about the design's effects. Drivers may try several alternative routes, including an adjacent local street, before choosing a new route. Figure 17–11 shows a diversion device in test form, while Figure 17–12 shows the device when permanently constructed. Although test devices are rarely attractive, even under the best of conditions it is important to try to keep test devices from being out-and-out ugly.

It also makes sense to test any new devices that you are developing or have little experience with before adding

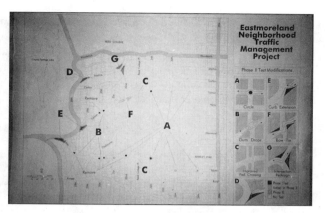

Figure 17–10   Example of Project Design Alternatives

Source: Portland Traffic Calming Program, Bureau of Traffic Calming, City of Portland, Oregon.

Figure 17–11   A Test of a Proposed Diverter

Source: Portland Traffic Calming Program, Bureau of Traffic Calming, City of Portland, Oregon.

Figure 17–12   The Permanent Diverter— After Construction

Source: Portland Traffic Calming Program, Bureau of Traffic Calming, City of Portland, Oregon.

them to your list of approved devices. Most residents and neighborhoods are honored to be the first to try a particular device, if you approach them correctly. Testing allows a conservative approach to be taken when experimenting with a new device you are developing or have little experience with. The test can be conducted on a low-volume street with a moderate speeding problem to limit potential problems. If the device has the desired effect, it can be tested on a street with more severe problems. If the device does not produce the desired effects, it can be modified or dropped from further consideration. (Whenever possible, build temporary test devices that can be easily modified or removed with little cost.)

Approval and Implementation

The final step in project development is the approval process. Depending on the program requirements, a petition or ballot may need to be approved by a majority (or higher percentage) of the residents, nonresident owners, and businesses within the defined project petition and ballot area. A sample petition and ballot are shown in Figures 17–13 and 17–14. Often the results of the petition or ballot are used as advisory information for the political body that must give final approval to the project. Once the appropriate approvals have been gained, the project design can move into the final design and construction phase. An evaluation of the project results should be conducted within a reasonable period after final construction is complete.

Temporary Device Installation

Program staff may want to consider the use of temporary devices as part of their project development process. Temporary devices can be used to bridge the gap between approval of the traffic calming project design alternative and actual construction of the project. For example, curb extensions can be used to narrow the roadway at elementary school crosswalk locations, thus decreasing the crossing time needed by children. Construction of the permanent curb extensions is best accomplished during the summer when children are out of school. However, the project development phase is often completed during the school year. Temporary curb extensions can be installed quickly and easily while the final design

Gwinnett County Speed Hump Program

Subdivision Name: ______________________

(Signature as appears on Tax Bill) Page ____ of ____

	Yes	No	
1. ______________ Print Name (First, Last)	☐	☐	______________ Witness
______________ Signature			______________ Lot #:
2. ______________ Print Name (First, Last)	☐	☐	______________ Witness
______________ Signature			______________ Lot #:
3. ______________ Print Name (First, Last)	☐	☐	______________ Witness

Figure 17–13 Example of Speed Hump Petition Used in Gwinnett County, Georgia

Source: Gwinnett County Department of Transportation.

NE 32/33/Hassalo Street
Traffic Calming Project Ballot

Should the NE 32/33 Hassalo Street Traffic Calming Project, consisting of seven 14′ speed bumps on NE 32nd/33rd Ave., and six 22′ speed bumps, eight median islands, and three curb extensions on NE Peerless Place/Hassalo Street (shown on the enclosed maps) be forwarded to City Council for approval to be constructed?

Yes: ____ No: ____

Signed: ______________________ Date: ____________

Please print your name and address: ________________

____

Please print the property address if different from above:

____

____

Figure 17–14 Example of Ballot Used in Portland, Oregon

Source: Portland Traffic Calming Program, Bureau of Traffic Calming, City of Portland, Oregon.

is being completed. The temporary devices, while not necessarily attractive, provide the benefit to the children immediately. The residents, parents, and school administrators that participated in project development are also rewarded by quickly seeing the results of their planning efforts. Figures 17–15 and 17–16 show temporary devices in place at elementary school crosswalks.

Traffic Calming Devices and Their Uses

Although every traffic calming project is unique in its own way, most projects do not require a new device design to solve them. Those streets with unique problems and characteristics are clearly a design challenge, and they often require a one-of-a-kind device design. For the most projects, though, project design becomes a matter of choosing the right device(s) for the problem(s) at hand, in keeping with the preferences of the residents. All traffic calming measures have some effect on both traffic volume and speed. However, most devices have a dominant effect and are usually categorized by this effect. For example, traffic speeds are controlled by modifying the roadway characteristics, such as narrowing the vehicular travel lanes or installing traffic circles or speed humps or speed tables. Cul-de-sacs, turn restrictions, and diverters at intersections are examples of devices that are primarily volume control measures. Some devices frequently used in traffic calming projects, such as curb extensions or pedestrian refuges, have little effect on traffic speed or volume but significantly enhance pedestrian visibility and safety. Information on other traffic calming devices that are rarely (if ever) used in the United States, such as the Dutch *woonerf*, may be found in traffic calming literature from Europe, Britain, and Australia. The *Urban Transportation Monitor* published the information presented in Tables 17–9 and 17–10, describing the likely results that will be achieved with passive and active traffic calming strategies.

One of the challenging elements for professionals in the traffic calming field today is that there is little standardization of traffic calming devices, including the names used to describe the devices. One jurisdiction's curb extension is another jurisdiction's choker. The third jurisdiction may use the same name but have different design standards for the device. Therefore, it is important to ask many specific questions when discussing the experience and results of a particular device with another traffic calming professional. On the negative side, it can be difficult to generalize the results that can be expected from the use of a particular device because each jurisdiction's design can be different. On the positive side, there are some innovative traffic calming device designs being tested or used by programs throughout the country. Do not hesitate to call another jurisdiction regarding their traffic calming program and devices. Almost without exception, traffic calming professionals are willing to share their designs and experiences (positive and negative) with others in the field.

Keeping in mind that there may be design differences between similar devices and that some devices fall into more than one category depending on what purpose they are being used for, the following section will describe the traffic calming devices used most commonly in the United States. Three categories will be used to group the devices—slowing, volume control, and other—with a very brief overview of some devices used in other countries finishing the section.

Figure 17–15   Temporary Pedestrian Refuge at a School Crosswalk

Source: Portland Traffic Calming Program, Bureau of Traffic Calming, City of Portland, Oregon.

Figure 17–16   Temporary Curb Extension at a School Crosswalk

Source: Portland Traffic Calming Program, Bureau of Traffic Calming, City of Portland, Oregon.

Table 17–9 Likely Results with Passive Traffic Calming Strategies

Strategy	Percent Volume Reduction	Percent Speed Reduction	Percent Accident Reduction
Traffic safety program	0	0	0
Active police presence	8	28	4
Speed watch	4	7	2
Speed alert—"smart trailer"	9	7	3
STOP signs	14	19	4
Street striping	6	7	4
Turn prohibitions	35	18	5
One-way streets	47	50	5

Source: *Urban Transportation Monitor*, Rathbone Publications, May 24, 1996. Copyright: Lawley Publications, t. (703) 764-0512, f. (703) 764-0516.

Table 17–10 Likely Results with Active Traffic Calming Strategies

Strategy	Percent Volume Reduction	Percent Speed Reduction	Percent Accident Reduction
Speed hump	9	22	3
Speed table	2	19	4
Chicanes	26	34	6
Diverters	28	22	3
Forced turn-islands	95	50	7
Street closure	7	5	4

Source: *Urban Transportation Monitor*, Rathbone Publications, May 24, 1996. Copyright: Lawley Publications, t. (703) 764-0512, f. (703) 764-0516.

Speed Reduction Devices

At its simplest, there are three strategies used to slow traffic. You can narrow the roadway (reduced vehicle lane), change the roadway so the driver needs to deviate from the straight line of travel (horizontal changes), or change the texture of the roadway (vertical changes). The narrowing strategy by itself seems to have the least effect on traffic speeds. Consequently, this strategy is often used in combination with the other two, either as part of the same device or as part of a design employing several different devices. Figure 17–17 illustrates the use of a narrowing strategy in conjunction with other traffic calming devices. Most of the narrowing strategies will be discussed as part of the "other" category.

Figure 17–17 Roadway Narrowing Used in Combination with Other Traffic Calming Devices

Source: Portland Traffic Calming Program, Bureau of Traffic Calming, City of Portland, Oregon.

Before discussing the types of devices that can be used to achieve speed reductions, it is necessary to discuss one that should not be used as a traffic calming device. That device is the STOP sign. STOP signs are traffic control devices that are used to assign right-of-way. The MUTCD explicitly states: ". . . STOP signs should not be used for speed control." While a few traffic calming programs choose to install STOP signs at unwarranted locations on low-volume residential streets in an attempt to slow traffic, this is not considered a good practice by most transportation professionals. Studies have shown little to no midblock speed reduction and many more rolling than complete stops. Driver noncompliance at STOP signs can create a very dangerous situation when pedestrians and other motorists expect drivers to stop and proceed accordingly.

Traffic Circles

Some of the earliest traffic calming programs used a traffic-slowing device that is still quite common today—the traffic circle. Traffic circles are used at intersections and cause drivers to slow down as they move out of the straight line of travel within a reduced width vehicle travel lane and navigate around the circle. In addition to slowing traffic speeds, traffic circles have the added benefit of substantially reducing intersection vehicle collisions.

Traffic circles can be landscaped to visually "break up" the straight line of sight along the street and add aesthetic value to the neighborhood. Some traffic calming programs provide ongoing maintenance of the landscaping, while others require the neighbors to maintain the landscaping. Parking must be removed along the curb on both sides of the circle to allow large vehicles to maneuver around the circle, which can be an issue for the adjacent property owners. Often traffic circles are designed with mountable curbs to accommodate emergency response and other large vehicles. Although costs will naturally vary depending on the design, traffic circles are considered by most programs to be an expensive device.

Signing, striping, and stop control varies from area to area. Some jurisdictions require left turns to take place in front of the traffic circle, while some require that a left turn be done after navigating the circle. Some jurisdictions use YIELD signs on all approaches to a traffic circle and some STOP control the minor legs of the intersection. The standard KEEP RIGHT sign is often used, although a number of traffic calming programs have adopted the Portland, Oregon flight of arrows sign for their traffic circles. It is important to be sure that intersections with traffic circles be lighted adequately.

One drawback to traffic circles is that bicyclists are forced to merge with the vehicular traffic around the circle. When a survey of commuter bicyclists was taken in Boulder, Colorado, traffic circles emerged as a device that bicyclists opposed. (Table 17–11.) Some pedestrians are concerned that drivers' cannot see them because of the traffic circle, but no problems have been reported by programs using these devices. A few residents report increased noise associated with the deceleration and acceleration of traffic, particularly large vehicles such as busses. Since the deceleration and acceleration profile of a vehicle around a traffic circle is less dramatic than that of a vehicle stopping for a STOP sign (see Figure 17–18), the incremental noise is probably less pronounced as well.

Traffic circles are generally used in a series along a street segment. Traffic speeds will be reduced at the traffic circles, but they will increase between the circles if no other devices are included in the design to keep the traffic speeds reduced. Odd-shaped traffic circles have been used at T-intersections with limited success. The flattened side of the traffic circle had less effect on traffic speeds than the round side of the circle.

Chicanes

A few programs are experimenting with or have used chicanes to slow traffic. Curb extensions or planters are used on alternate sides of the street to form s-shaped curves along the roadway. These devices are sometimes called serpentines, deviations, or reversing curves. Currently, limited information is available regarding the results achieved by programs using these devices in the United States. Charlotte, North Carolina is testing chicanes on five neighborhood streets. They report an initial average speed reduction of about 2 mph, although the results range from approximately a 10 mph reduction to a 3 mph increase. Some information is available on the use of chicanes in Europe, Britain, and Australia. Chicanes need to be designed carefully to prevent motorists from either circumventing the device by simply driving down the middle of the street or by testing their driving skills by racing through the sharp curves. Further, they need to be carefully located so that they do not unduly interfere with driveways and vehicle parking. Figure 17–19 illustrates a chicane.

Table 17–11   Bicycle Commuters' Views on Traffic Calming Measures (Boulder, Colorado)

street closures	mildly in favor as long as efficient through-connections are maintained for bicyclists
speed humps	strongly in favor as long as cross sections are not sloped across bike lanes
raised crosswalks (speed tables)	strongly in favor as long as cross sections are not sloped across bike lanes and crosswalks are not textured
raised intersections	opposed to due to their high cost
traffic circles	opposed to due to their high cost, danger to merging cyclists, and confusion for motorists—somewhat tolerable at low traffic volumes
neckdowns	mildly in favor as long as cyclists are not forced to merge with cars
medians (center islands)	non consensus—opposed if cyclists are crowded together with fast-moving cars
stop signs	mildly in favor
speed radar trailer	mildly in favor
photo radar	strongly in favor

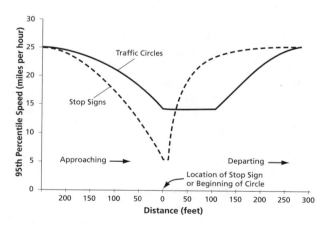

Figure 17–18   Comparitive Area of Influence—STOP Signs vs. Traffic Circles

Speed Humps and Speed Tables

Once considered to be too much of a liability problem to be used as a traffic calming device, speed bumps, humps, tables and, undulations are coming of age. Some people think of the jarring parking lot bumps when the name "speed bump" is used, but today's modern traffic calming speed bump or hump is generally 7.5 to 10 cm (3 to 4 in) in height and at least 3.66 m (12 ft) wide. Many programs use the name "speed hump" to try to differentiate between parking lot bumps and traffic calming devices. They have developed a sign that says "hump" to mark the devices. Some programs, like Portland, Oregon's, choose to use the standard "bump" sign and specify the bump size in the name, as in 14′ speed bump. No matter what they are called, these devices are being used across the United States with great success and with no greater liability issues than with any other traffic calming device.

ITE currently recommends only the 3.66 m (12 ft) Watts design speed hump. This design was developed and tested by Britain's Transport and Road Research Laboratory, and it is the most common hump design used in the United States today. It is 3.66 m (12 ft) wide (in direction of travel) and 7.5 to 10 cm (3 to 4 in) high, built in a parabolic curve shape, with a design speed of 24 to 32 km/h (15 to 20 mph). However, many jurisdictions have experimented with and are using other designs. For example, Portland uses a parabolic-shaped bump that is 4.27 m (14 ft) wide and 7.5 cm (3 in) high with a design speed of 32 to 40 km/h (20 to 25 mph). Toronto, Ontario, Canada introduced their new sinusoidal design speed hump at the 1997 ITE annual conference. As shown in Figure 17–20, this design is 4 m (13 ft) wide and 7.5 to 10 cm (3 to 4 in) high with a design speed of 30 km/h (19 mph).

One design that is quickly gaining wide popularity is Seminole County's (Florida) 22 ft speed table. (Figure 17–21.) This design is 6.71 m (22 ft) wide and 7.5 to 10 cm (3 to 4 inches) high, built with 1.83 m (6 ft) wide ramps at the ends and a 3.05 m (10 ft) flat "table" in the middle. The design speed is 40 to 48 km/h (25 to 30 mph).

Many other variations in width, height, and profile have been or are being tried by jurisdictions. Some are landscaping an area on each side of the hump to improve its appearance and enhance neighborhood aesthetics. Speed tables, in particular, are being modified with striping, textured, and colored pavement treatments and used as "raised crosswalks" by some programs. In general, the experience to date shows that the wider and lower the design, the smoother the "ride." Signing and striping for these devices varies widely from jurisdiction to jurisdiction.

Figure 17–19   Example of Chicane

Source: Photo Reid Ewing.

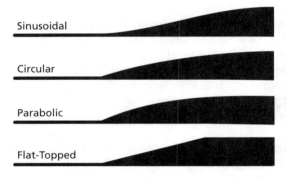

Figure 17–20   Speed Hump Profiles, Toronto, Ontario, Canada

Figure 17–21   School Bus Crossing a 22 ft Speed Table

Source: Photo Reid Ewing.

The second factor in overall speed reduction is how closely or far apart the devices are placed. As is probably obvious, the closer together, the greater the overall speed reduction; and the further apart, less overall speed reduction will take place. The graphs shown in Figures 17–22 and 17–23 delineate the speed reduction that Portland, Oregon has experienced using various spacings. There are certainly some limitations on where the devices can be located as well. Generally humps or tables should not be installed on roadways with more than two lanes of travel, on grades greater than 6 to 8 percent, on curves, at transit stops, intersections, or STOP signs. When possible, avoid utility manholes, driveway cuts, and drainage facilities as well when locating speed humps or tables.

Speed humps and tables are becoming the preferred traffic calming slowing device in many jurisdictions because they are inexpensive to install and very effective. Bicyclists generally favor speed humps over traffic circles. Residents like the fact that parking removal is not necessary for these devices (unless a landscaped area is included on each side of the hump) and that the fastest drivers on the street slow down (even though they may still be above the posted speed limit). Emergency service providers and transit authorities have had mixed reactions to the devices. Police agencies are generally neutral to supportive, while public works and other service providers are generally neutral.

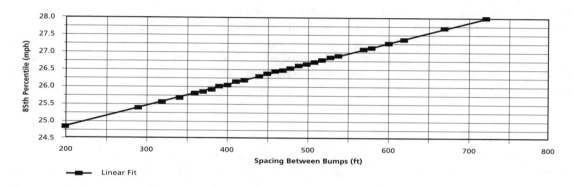

**Figure 17–22   Speed Hump Spacing vs. Speed—14 ft Hump
(Obervations on 29 Streets)**

Source: Portland Traffic Calming Program, Bureau of Traffic Calming, City of Portland, Oregon.

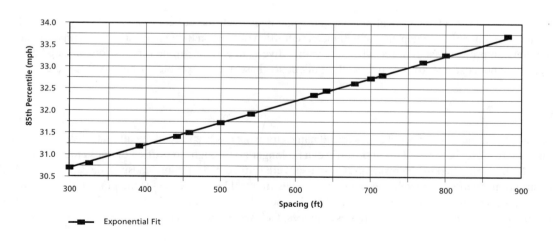

**Figure 17–23   Speed Hump Spacing vs. Speed—22 ft Hump
(Observations on 7 Streets)**

Source: Portland Traffic Calming Program, Bureau of Traffic Calming, City of Portland, Oregon.

Raised Intersections

A variation on the speed table (or maybe the raised crosswalk) is the raised intersection. This is an expensive device that literally raises the entire intersection (similar to the flat "table" portion of the speed table), with ramps on all approaches. Although expensive, the device effectively treats the two adjoining streets at once in that location. The intersection is often built using brick or other textured pavement treatments. Boulder, Colorado has recently built several raised intersections. A project in Toronto, Ontario, Canada installed a raised, textured intersection treatment at the T-intersection of two residential streets. All three legs of the intersection were narrowed with curb extensions to 8 m (26.25 in) in width. While the intersection is wide enough for two vehicles to pass comfortably, it visually appears to be much narrower.

Volume Control Devices

All traffic calming projects have the potential to affect traffic volumes, at least marginally. Even a project that uses the most benign traffic calming devices, such as curb extensions, may cause a few drivers to choose another route. Projects that reduce traffic speeds commonly reduce traffic volumes by a small percentage as well. The extent of the volume reduction will vary depending on the existence of convenient alternative routes, the increase in travel time caused by the speed reduction on the project street, and the personal preferences of individual drivers (some drivers detest going around traffic circles, for example). This small volume reduction on the project street is an added bonus, as long as the bulk of the traffic reduction is moving to higher classified arterials and not adjacent local streets. The only way to be sure that the adjacent local streets are not experiencing significant volume increases as an inadvertent result of a traffic calming project is to take before and after project construction volume counts.

Diversion Projects

Sometimes the primary goal of a traffic calming project is to reduce the volume on the street. Most jurisdictions are reluctant to intentionally divert traffic from one residential street to other streets, and some traffic calming programs do not allow traffic diversion projects at all. Other traffic calming programs allow diversion projects under certain circumstances, such as local streets with high traffic volumes that are being used as commuter cut-through routes. Diversion projects are always controversial, with some of the greatest controversy occurring within the project neighborhood. Although one might think that every resident on a local street with high volumes would welcome a diversion project; in fact, many residents are adamantly opposed. Diversion project designs affect everyone, residents and commuters alike. Many residents do not feel that the reduction of the traffic volume in front of their house is worth the additional personal inconvenience.

Residents who live on the adjacent local streets, and sometimes even the collector streets if they are residential in character, often strongly oppose any plan that will increase traffic volumes on their streets. It is very important, therefore, to test any diversion project design to see where the traffic diverts to and determine if new problems are being created by the design. It is not cost-effective, or politically prudent, to chase a traffic problem from street to street.

Cul-de-Sacs

Cul-de-sacs, dead-ends, and full street closures are all names for what has been called the ultimate diversion device. Cul-de-sacs completely close the street. Through-traffic can no longer go through, so traffic volumes are generally reduced to only that which is generated by the residents. Cul-de-sacs are formed by installing landscaped islands, gates, bollards, or other obstructions to motorized vehicles. Generally pedestrian and bicycle access is maintained through the device. Sometimes emergency service access is maintained by the use of locked gates, or "break-away" or removable bollards. Parking removal is not usually an issue with these devices. Cul-de-sacs are often expensive devices to install.

Diagonal Diverters

Diagonal diverters force traffic to turn rather than continue straight on a street. They are also sometimes called full diverters or diagonal road closures. These devices block the roadway by installing barriers diagonally across an intersection. Sometimes diagonal diverters are used on a number of different streets within a neighborhood to discourage cut-through traffic by making the route circuitous. This design has also been criticized for its "rat maze" qualities by some residents and professionals. Diagonal diverters are generally landscaped, with pedestrian and bicycle access allowed through the device. A minimal amount of parking may need to be removed to install the device. Diagonal diverters can be relatively inexpensive to install, depending on the location and the design of the device.

Figure 17–24   Example of Semi-Diverter

Source: Portland Traffic Calming Program, Bureau of Traffic Calming, City of Portland, Oregon.

Semi-Diverters

Semi-diverters, sometimes called half closures or partial closures, restrict one direction of travel, while allowing the other direction to continue. When the majority of the cut-through traffic occurs in the morning or the afternoon peak hours, these devices can be very effective by restricting that predominant movement. Portland, Oregon has also successfully used a series of semi-diverters around some elementary schools to control circulation and aid congestion around the school. Drivers can violate these devices easily when there is little opposing traffic and the one-way portion of the device is relatively short. As illustrated in Figure 17–24, semi-diverters are often landscaped and can be designed to allow the through-bicycle-movement and emergency vehicle access. There will likely be some parking removal required to install the device. These devices can be fairly expensive to install, depending on the design and size of the device.

Channelization Devices

There are many different types of channelization devices that can be used to divert traffic. Median islands can be built along the centerline to preclude left turn movements or cross street through-movements. They can be designed to allow the through-bicycle-movement. Median islands can also be used to eliminate sweeping turns at very large or off-set intersections. Pork chops are small median islands that force vehicles to turn in a particular direction (usually to the right). Some median island and pork chop channelization devices are large enough to be landscaped. Depending on the use and location of the device, some parking removal may be necessary. Generally these devices as inexpensive to install.

Other Traffic Calming Devices

Devices in this category do not generally cause significant traffic speed or volume reductions. These devices are used to provide a safer, more pleasant environment for residents, pedestrians, and bicyclists. They are frequently used in conjunction with speed reduction devices, but they can be used in situations where speed reduction is not possible or desirable—a pedestrian refuge on a higher classified arterial, for example. Some of these devices can be designed in such a way that they become a speed or volume reduction device. For example, when a textured gateway treatment is raised so that it becomes much like a speed hump, it will have a slowing effect on traffic. Finally, there are some design features that may be used to enhance a traffic calming project design that are not really traffic calming devices, such as planting of street trees along the project.

Curb Extensions, Chokers, and Lateral Shifts

Curb extensions are a commonly used traffic calming device that narrows the roadway width curb-to-curb. The curb is extended to the edge of the vehicle lane, generally at all four corners at an intersection or on both sides of the street at a midblock location. These devices are also called bulbouts, nubs, knuckles or intersection narrowings. The installation of curb extensions alone will have little effect on traffic speeds. They are used primarily at intersections or midblock pedestrian crosswalks to shorten the crossing distance for pedestrians. These devices let the driver and the pedestrian "see and be seen" by each other by bringing pedestrians out from behind the parked cars and up to the edge of the vehicle lane. At midblock locations, curb extensions can increase the crossing opportunities for pedestrians by reducing the length of gap needed for the pedestrian to cross. Curb extensions can be used in many different situations where increased pedestrian comfort and safety is desired—from downtown redevelopment projects to enhanced transit stop locations on neighborhood streets to improved traffic safety for school children at school crosswalks. An example of a curb extension is illustrated in Figure 17–25.

Figure 17–25   Example of a Curb Extension

Source: Photo Reid Ewing.

Curb extensions can be expensive to install, particularly if drainage facilities need to be relocated. Depending on the size of the curb extension, landscaping and street trees can be incorporated into the design. A small amount of parking removal is required to install the curb extensions, which can be of concern for the adjacent residents or businesses. Curb extensions can also cause conflicts for bicyclists and motorists if not carefully designed, particularly on high-volume streets.

A variation of the curb extension is the choker. A choker is a curb extension that extends far enough into the roadway to reduce the vehicle lane width. Chokers are also called midblock narrowings, midblock yield points, or pinch points, depending on how the choker is configured. If the choker is combined with a marked crosswalk, they are sometimes called safe crossings. Depending on how far the choker extends into the vehicle lane, these devices can become speed reduction devices. They can be designed to allow two vehicle lanes, with reduced lane widths, or they can reduce the street cross section to one lane of travel.

If the device narrows the street to one lane of travel, the lane can be parallel to the alignment or angled to the alignment. The former is called a parallel choker; the latter an angled choker, twisted choker, or angle point. One-lane chokers are very rare in the United States, although they are commonly used in other countries. Many jurisdictions are reluctant to test one-lane chokers because of the inherent conflict of two vehicles meeting and vying for the same lane space. In reality, vehicle queuing to negotiate a single lane width occurs naturally on narrow, low-volume residential streets when cars are parked on both sides of the street.

Another way in which curb extensions can be designed to affect traffic speeds are lateral shifts. Lateral shifts are curb extensions installed in such a way as to add curves to an otherwise straight street. The curb extensions forming the lateral shift cause the travel lanes to bend one way and then bend back the other way to return to the original direction of travel. They are occasionally referred to as jogs, staggerings, or axial shifts. Lateral shifts are one of the few measures that can be used on arterials or streets where high traffic volumes and high posted speeds preclude more abrupt measures.

Median Islands

Other types of roadway narrowing strategies include median islands, which are also called midblock medians, median slow points, median chokers, and center island narrowings. Median islands are exactly what the name implies, raised islands located along the centerline of the street that narrow the roadway. An example is shown in Figure 17–26. Median islands are generally less expensive to install than curb extensions, depending on their length and width, of course. This is because median islands rarely require the relocation of existing drainage facilities. These devices can be attractively landscaped, although the location of utility lines within the street may preclude the installation of street trees within the median island.

On-street parking may or may not be affected by the installation of median islands, depending on the roadway width and the width of the median island. Many residents and most fire departments prefer median islands broken into shorter segments along the street rather than long median islands that channelize traffic and separate opposing traffic flows. The residents prefer to turn into their driveways without a lot of inconvenience, and the fire department needs to be able to maneuver around traffic stopped in the travel lane. There is some evidence that long, unbroken median islands increase traffic speeds; while shorter median islands tend to slow traffic a little. Median islands can be installed at the entrance to the street to provide a gateway treatment. When placed just downstream of the intersection, the median island and gateway treatment causes drivers turning onto the street to turn at a 90° angle and thereby reduce their speed.

Figure 17–26   Roadway Narrowing Using a Median Island

Source: Photo Reid Ewing.

Pedestrian Refuges

Median islands can be designed to provide a pedestrian refuge in the center of the street. This feature can be particularly helpful on high-volume streets where gaps in traffic sufficient to cross both lanes of travel at once are rare. When used as a refuge, the median island provides a safe, comfortable space in the center of the street for the pedestrian to stand while waiting for traffic to clear. Pedestrian refuges have been successfully used at school crosswalk locations on streets with high volumes or with more than two travel lanes.

Textured Pavement Treatments and Gateways

Textured pavement treatments are used as gateway treatments, either alone or in combination with other devices such as a raised median island; or they can be used to call attention to midblock crosswalk locations. Textured treatments can be simply that, textured; or the treatment may be raised much like a speed hump. In theory textured treatments should reduce traffic speeds (old cobblestone streets usually do not have speeding problems); but when used as gateways and midblock crosswalks, the area of textured treatment is apparently so small that little or no speed reduction will result. However, textured treatments can provide a visual and auditory clue to drivers that they are entering a different driving environment, such as a residential neighborhood or commercial and shopping area with many pedestrians. Gateway treatments that include a median island along with the textured or raised treatment can add to the visual amenity and residential identity of the street.

Residents sometimes complain about increased noise caused by the vehicle tires crossing the textured pavement area. The traffic engineer for Beaverton, Oregon experimented with several stamped "brick" pavement texture treatments and found that tire noise increased when the long side of the "brick" ran perpendicular to the direction of travel. When raised and placed at a crosswalk location, textured treatments become raised crosswalks (although raised crosswalks do not have to be textured). The width and height of the rise will determine how much speed reduction will take place, just like a speed hump.

Street Trees, Bicycle Lanes, and Traffic Calming Signs

Street trees are a neighborhood amenity that increases livability by beautifying the streetscape and helping to reduce pollution levels. The existence of mature street trees does not seem to affect traffic speeds or volumes at all. The existence of street trees do make the environment more pleasant, especially for pedestrians, by creating shade and a barrier between traffic and the sidewalk.

Bicycle lanes help reduce conflicts between bicyclists and motorists by providing a dedicated space for bicyclists alongside the vehicle lanes. They are most often installed on through-streets with relatively high traffic volumes, particularly those direct routes that can be used by bicycle commuters. Depending on the width of the street, parking may need to be removed on one or both sides of the street to provide sufficient room for the bicycle lanes, which can make the installation of bicycle lanes somewhat controversial. When installed in conjunction with a traffic calming project, bicycle lanes can help reduce the roadway width both visually and physically. In some situations, the installation of bicycle lanes along with reduced vehicle lane widths will result in a modest speed reduction. The installation of a traffic calming project that reduces traffic speeds or volumes is obviously a benefit to the users of the bicycle lanes as well as the residents.

A number of traffic calming programs have developed special signage to remind drivers that they are in a residential or traffic calmed area. These signs are more educational than they are regulatory. They have a negligible effect on traffic speeds and volumes, but residents are often fond of them.

Nonengineered Traffic Calming Strategies

Most people, residents and professionals alike, think of the various engineering strategies when they refer to a traffic calming program or project. However, traffic calming literature often describes the "3E's"—engineering, enforcement, and education—as strategies that may be used to reduce traffic speeds. Many programs incorporate aspects of education and enforcement strategies within their procedures. Some programs even require that residents complete an educational effort before they can be eligible for an engineered traffic calming project. Even though educational and enforcement efforts are limited in their ability to bring about permanent speed reductions, they still have merit in their ability to raise resident and driver consciousness about speeding and its negative effects.

Neighborhood Traffic Safety Campaigns

Neighborhood traffic safety campaigns involve the distribution of personalized letters or general fliers to all households within a neighborhood, citing statistics on the prevalence of speeding in the neighborhood and appealing for compliance with speed limits and traffic laws. It is unlikely that this type of educational effort alone will bring about a reduction in speeding. However, it alerts neighbors that other residents are concerned about speeding and may help bring people together to work on the problem.

Neighborhood Speed Watch

This is an educational effort where residents borrow radar guns and record the speed, make, model, and license plate number of vehicles observed speeding through their neighborhood. The registered owners of the speeding vehicles are then sent a warning letter from the police department or other agency reminding them of the posted speed limit and the neighborhood's concern for safety and livability. The speed reduction effect of such an effort is fairly short-lived, if there is any effect at all. However, there is a benefit in raising the consciousness of drivers and the residents.

Speed Trailers

Speed trailers contain radar equipment to determine the speed of passing vehicles. Typically, the unit is set up to report each vehicle's speed on the external reader board. The appropriate speed limit sign is attached to the trailer near the reader board. The driver can readily see if their actual speed exceeds the speed limit. Speed trailers are often used as an educational tool. However, the unit can provide traffic speed and volume data if equipped to do so.

Other Strategies

Public safety ad campaigns or other advertising efforts are undertaken to raise awareness about various traffic-related issues. Different advertising mediums can be used to deliver the safety message. Figure 17–28 shows the use of "bus bench" advertising to deliver a public safety message. Often more than one medium is used during the same campaign. Sometimes a public safety ad campaign is coupled with increased enforcement of the particular issue raised by the campaign.

Emergency Response Issues

As traffic calming programs have become more common throughout the United States, the emergency response agencies have become more concerned and vocal. Many traffic calming projects have been stopped or postponed because agreement on the project could not be reached with emergency response agencies, particularly the fire department. The problem is particularly difficult because both services—traffic calming and emergency response—are needed and demanded by the public. The trick is to find the balance where both agencies can deliver the greatest benefits with the fewest trade-offs.

Figure 17–28   Example of One Medium Used During a Public Education Campaign

Source: Portland Traffic Calming Program, Bureau of Traffic Calming, City of Portland, Oregon.

Example of Emergency Response Concerns

In Portland, Oregon the traffic calming and the fire bureau staff had traditionally worked together on traffic calming projects. Perhaps this is because, unlike some jurisdictions, the fire bureau could not "veto" a traffic calming project. Through this working relationship, many project designs were modified based on the fire bureau's needs and preferences. In 1993, two events happened that severely taxed the working relationship between the agencies. First, Portland's traffic calming program expanded to begin treating residential collector streets. These through-streets carried fairly high volumes of traffic and were often used by the fire bureau to respond to emergencies. However, since these streets also had predominantly residential land uses along them and experienced high traffic speeds, the residents successfully demanded that the traffic calming program do something to solve their traffic problems and improve livability. Many residents made it very clear to fire bureau staff that they considered solving the traffic problems to be more important than maintaining the current level of emergency response. The fire bureau staff found this attitude very dismaying.

The second event was the approval to test, and subsequently use, two speed bumps designs as traffic calming devices. The fire bureau participated in the speed bump design tests and, while they did not like either design, they endorsed the use of the 22 ft speed bump on streets that they considered to be response streets. As speed bumps grew in popularity with residents and became the most frequently used traffic calming device, the fire bureau became very concerned that their overall response times would deteriorate because of the traffic calming projects. The traffic calming staff agreed that the fire bureau's concern may be valid, although data could not be produced to confirm or deny that fire vehicle response times were effected by traffic calming devices enough to deteriorate overall response times.

In 1995, the two agencies jointly conducted an extensive research project to document the average delay experienced by six typical fire vehicles when encountering traffic circles, 14 ft speed bumps, and 22 ft speed bumps. It was hoped that the results of the research shown in Tables 17–12, 17–13, and 17–14 could be used to plan future traffic calming projects. The thought process went something like this: The fire bureau has a goal of responding within 4 minutes. The current response time in this area is 2 minutes and 30 seconds. If six 22 ft speed bumps are installed on this street, response time will increase by 30 seconds. The project can be installed because the 4 minute response time goal is met. As one might expect, it is just not that simple! The data collected by the research project substantially increased the information available to both agencies about one aspect of the problem. For example, the agencies learned that the longer the vehicle's wheel-base, the greater the delay. However the information did not help with planning traffic calming projects, because there are many other factors that contribute to overall response time; and the two agencies could not agree on how to factor in the other variables.

In response to the high demand for traffic calming projects and the potential for delay in emergency response delivery, the Portland City Council took action to resolve this conflict. In April 1996, the Council directed the Portland Office of Transportation and the fire bureau to resolve this problem through a policy approach. Staff was directed to develop a new emergency response policy and street classification system for incorporation into the transportation element. Prior

Table 17–12 Typical Impacts of Traffic Circles on Emergency Vehicles

Vehicle	Lowest Speed (mph)	Desirable Speed (mph)	Travel Time Delay (seconds)	Impact Distance (feet)
Engine 18	14	25	2.8	261
	14	30	4.3	489
	14	35	6.1	671
	14	40	8.5	814
Rescue 41	16	25	1.3	170
	16	30	2.3	301
	16	35	3.1	467
	16	40	5.1	612
Squad 1	17	25	1.2	172
	17	30	2.3	326
	17	35	3.7	501
	17	40	5.3	776
Truck I	10	25	4.8	319
	10	30	6.4	524
	10	35	8.4	749
	10	40	10.7	1034
Truck 4	11	25	4.3	322
	11	30	6.2	549
	11	35	8.1	799
	11	40	10.3	1139
Truck 41	11	25	3.9	338
	11	30	5.2	555
	11	35	7.3	845
	11	40	9.2	1255

Lowest Speed:	This is the lowest speed a vehicle travels when navigating around a traffic circle.
Desirable Speed:	This is the speed a driver might wish to travel if there were no traffic circles.
Travel Time Delay:	This is the additional time required to travel to a destination due to a traffic circle's influence.
Impact Distance:	This is the length of street where a given vehicle cannot be driven at the desired speed because of the traffic circle's influence.

Source: Portland Traffic Calming Program, Bureau of Traffic Calming, City of Portland, Oregon.

to the adoption of the new emergency response route classification, there was no classification for emergency response routes in the transportation element of the comprehensive plan. The transportation element addressed the need for emergency vehicle access in describing how designated traffic streets should function. Having adopted policy language on emergency response, accompanied by an emergency response classification system, offered several benefits.

- It balanced the need for prompt emergency response with the need for slowing traffic on residential streets.

- It provided the city and its residents with clarity and certainty regarding streets' eligibility for traffic slowing devices.

- It ensured a basic network of emergency response streets, which can be used to help route response vehicles in an emergency and to help the city site future fire stations.

- It was incorporated into the transportation element, allowing emergency response needs to be considered with other modal needs when changes to a street are considered.

Table 17–13 Typical Impacts of 14-ft Speed Bumps on Emergency Vehicles

Vehicle	Lowest Speed (mph)	Desirable Speed (mph)	Travel Time Delay (seconds)	Impact Distance (feet)
Engine 18	13	25	2.3	236
	13	30	3.7	399
	13	35	5.2	581
	13	40	7.7	814
Rescue 41	17	25	1.0	147
	17	30	1.7	269
	17	35	2.9	483
	17	40	4.9	628
Squad 1	12	25	2.7	244
	12	30	4.1	436
	12	35	5.9	611
	12	40	8.3	852
Truck 1	11	25	3.4	269
	11	30	4.9	455
	11	35	6.6	646
	11	40	9.4	931
Truck 4	12	25	3.4	315
	12	30	4.9	485
	12	35	6.8	732
	12	40	9.1	1053
Truck 41	12	25	3.5	327
	12	30	4.7	472
	12	35	6.6	762
	12	40	8.6	1152

Lowest Speed:	This is the lowest speed a vehicle travels when crossing a 14-foot speed bump.
Desirable Speed:	This is the speed a driver might wish to travel if there were no speed bumps.
Travel Time Delay:	This is the additional time required to travel to a destination due to a 14-foot speed bump's influence.
Impact Distance:	This is the length of street where a given vehicle cannot be driven at the desired speed because of the speed bump's influence.

Source: Portland Traffic Calming Program, Bureau of Traffic Calming, City of Portland, Oregon.

Emergency Response Streets Classification Study

To assist in the study, a citizen advisory committee (CAC) was appointed consisting of seven members, representing the seven transportation districts of the city. Applicants were solicited through an established organization of neighborhood associations within the city. Aside from geographic representation, members were selected based on their interest in the study, their experience and active participation on committees, and their ability to see all sides of the issue.

The role of the CAC was to advise the study's technical advisory committee (TAC) in developing an emergency response policy and street classification system for incorporation into the transportation element. The TAC consisted of staff from transportation planning, the traffic calming program, and the fire bureau. The TAC sought CAC's advice in the following areas: policy language to address the need for prompt emergency response, criteria for selecting emergency response streets, and emergency response street classification descriptions. The CAC also played a leading role in developing the public review process for the study, helping the TAC to staff all of the public open houses, and responding to public feedback.

With the assistance of the CAC, a new emergency response policy was crafted for the transportation element. The policy recognizes the transportation system's role in facilitating prompt emergency response. It also defines how the emergency response classification system will be used. The policy is:

Table 17–14　Typical Impacts of 22-ft Speed Bumps on Emergency Vehicles

Vehicle	Lowest Speed (mph)	Desirable Speed (mph)	Travel Time Delay (seconds)	Impact Distance (feet)
Engine 18	21	25	0.8	136
	21	30	1.7	323
	21	35	3.0	505
	21	40	5.0	752
Rescue 41	34	25	0.0	0
	34	30	0.0	0
	34	35	0.3	118
	34	40	1.5	263
Squad 1	24	25	0.4	80
	24	30	1.0	214
	24	35	2.1	433
	24	40	3.4	708
Truck 1	22	25	0.6	137
	22	30	1.4	320
	22	35	3.0	600
	22	40	4.9	885
Truck 4	16	25	1.8	254
	16	30	3.4	449
	16	35	5.9	674
	16	40	7.7	1039
Truck 41	14	25	3.0	316
	14	30	4.8	622
	14	35	7.2	912
	14	40	9.2	1322

Lowest Speed:	This is the lowest speed a vehicle travels when crossing a 22-foot speed bump.
Desirable Speed:	This is the speed a driver might wish to travel if there were no speed bumps.
Travel Time Delay:	This is the additional time required to travel to a destination due to a 22-foot speed bump's influence.
Impact Distance:	This is the length of street where a given vehicle cannot be driven at the desired speed because of the speed bump's influence.

Source: Portland Traffic Calming Program, Bureau of Traffic Calming, City of Portland, Oregon.

Provide a network of emergency response streets that facilitates prompt emergency response. The emergency response classification system shall be used to determine whether traffic slowing devices can be employed, to guide the routing of emergency response vehicles, and to help site future fire stations.

In concert with the new policy language, two emergency response street classification descriptions were developed as the major emergency response streets were selected and mapped. These are used to describe how emergency response streets should function, to specify appropriate design treatments to facilitate prompt emergency response, and to indicate which streets are eligible for traffic-slowing devices and which are not. The two classification descriptions are shown in Table 17–15.

The classification map was developed by the staff and the CAC, which identifies major and minor emergency response streets. The designation of major and minor emergency response streets was a joint effort between the transportation and fire bureaus considering first, policy direction; and second, operational and programmatic needs. The classification designations offer clarity and certainty to both bureaus, as well as to the public about streets' eligibility for traffic-slowing devices.

Major emergency response streets were selected based on the following considerations: eligibility of streets for traffic slowing devices, spacing and connectivity, traffic classifications, location of fire stations, and topography. Under current policy, district collectors and higher arterials are ineligible for traffic-slowing devices; and they were therefore automatically

Table 17–15 Emergency Response Streets Classifications (Portland, Oregon)

Classification	Functional Purpose	Design Treatment and Operating Characteristics
Major emergency response streets	Major emergency response streets are intended to serve primarily the longer, most direct legs of emergency response trips.	Design treatments on major emergency response streets should enhance mobility for emergency response vehicles by employing preferential treatments such as Opticom. Major emergency response streets are not eligible for traffic-slowing devices.
Minor emergency response streets	Minor emergency response streets are intended to serve primarily the shorter legs of emergency response trips. All streets not classified as major emergency response streets are classified as minor emergency response streets.	Minor emergency response streets are designed and operated to provide access to individual properties. Minor emergency response streets are eligible for traffic-slowing devices.

designated as major emergency response streets. Neighborhood collectors that are not at least 75 percent residential are also ineligible for traffic-slowing devices. These collectors were designated as major emergency response routes where technical staff agreed that the higher arterial network did not provide adequate coverage. In cases where additional major emergency response routes were needed, neighborhood collectors were selected over local service streets, whenever possible.

The intent behind this selection process was to establish a major emergency response street network where emergency vehicles could make the longer legs of their trips on relatively higher-speed streets, reserving the shorter legs of their trips for more local streets where speeds would be lower. This resulted in an approximately half-mile spacing between major emergency response streets. Other considerations in developing the network were connecting all existing fire stations to major emergency response streets and avoiding streets whose topographic conditions would result in emergency vehicle response delays. All streets that were not selected as major emergency response streets were designated as minor emergency response streets.

Emergency Response Streets Classification Implementation

The CAC made several recommendations regarding the implementation of the new classification. They made the following recommendations.

- Streets rendered ineligible for traffic-slowing devices by their designation as major emergency response streets should be given higher priority for nonengineered solutions to problems of excessive speed (i.e., focus on education and targeted traffic enforcement in place of traffic-slowing devices).

- The five street segments that have been identified as major emergency response streets that currently have traffic-slowing devices will retain the slowing devices on these streets. However, these streets will not be eligible for additional traffic-slowing devices in the future.

- The traffic calming program, the fire bureau, and the police bureau will continue to cooperatively address problems of excessive speeds and volumes on residential streets. This will include, but is not limited to, the evaluation of all new devices intended to slow general traffic to determine their effect on emergency response providers and the development of cooperative educational programs.

What Was Learned Through This Process?

Finding a balance between the need to slow traffic on residential streets to increase neighborhood safety and livability, and the need to provide prompt emergency services is not easy; but it can be done. It takes a willingness on the part of all the service providers involved to understand and appreciate the various services provided and the constraints under which the provider works, an openness to change, and a commitment to finding a balanced solution. The success of this process goes well beyond the development of the emergency response classification. It has given the city council a successful model with which to resolve these types of conflicts between bureaus. However, perhaps the most important success of this process has been the forging of relationships between the bureaus that did not exist prior to this effort.

New Developments

Thus far, the discussion of traffic calming in this chapter has focused on retrofitting existing streets within an existing street system. Does traffic calming have a place in new developments? The answer appears to be "maybe," depending upon which choices are made regarding the street system within the development and how the development connects to the existing system.

There are several different street patterns that have been used over the years in subdivision layouts, with the two most common street patterns being the grid and the cul-de-sac or loop patterns. More recently, the use of several alternatives to the traditional "suburban sprawl" patterns—neotraditional development, pedestrian-oriented development, or transit-oriented development—have been promoted with some success. Transportation planners and engineers may want to also explore the shared street concept, such as the Dutch *woonerf*, as well before deciding on which type of street pattern to use.

If the transportation planner and engineer want to use the traditional grid and cul-de-sac or loop patterns, they need to take into account the positive and negative aspects of each, weigh the trade-offs between the two patterns, and decide how to best mitigate the negative aspects of the pattern that is chosen. For example, the grid pattern disperses traffic over a greater area within the neighborhood, thereby keeping traffic volumes low. The grid pattern also provides many connections; and if the blocks are kept short, this pattern can encourage pedestrian activity. On the other hand, the grid pattern can be readily abused if the higher classified arterials and collectors become congested. Many of the existing streets being traffic calmed today are part of a grid pattern.

The cul-de-sac or loop pattern has been widely criticized, but it offers some clear advantages to neighborhood residents. A recent study of street patterns indicates a significant resident preference for the cul-de-sac and loop development patterns. "The findings suggest that cul-de-sac streets, and especially the lots at the end, perform better than grid or loop patterns in terms of traffic safety, privacy, and safety for play. . . . People said they felt cul-de-sac streets were safer and quieter because there was no through traffic and it moved more slowly."[19] Traffic speeds and volumes will naturally be low on cul-de-sac streets; but the collector that serves the cul-de-sacs may experience significant speed and volume problems, particularly if the collector is wide and straight. In addition, the traditional cul-de-sac pattern has not provided adequate connections to encourage bicycle and pedestrian mode use.

Transportation planners and engineers can use the basic principals of traffic calming to design a street system that will overcome the downsides to either of these patterns. For example, the collector serving the cul-de-sacs can be designed with curves and traffic-slowing devices to keep traffic speeds low; and bicycle and pedestrian access can be provided between the ends of the cul-de-sacs to accommodate alternative mode uses.

Conclusion

As transportation professionals, our concepts about how the transportation system is supposed to function, and who routinely uses the system, are changing. More than ever before, we are thinking, planning, and building a multimodal system where automobiles share the system with the other users. We are also trying to deal with the problems that our culture's love and fascination with the automobile has brought us. Traffic calming is one strategy that we can use to help solve these problems, particularly when they exist in residential neighborhoods.

There is a substantial amount of information available to transportation professionals today that was not available even a decade ago, describing the various traffic calming programs and devices that are being used by cities across the

[19] Southworth, Michael and Eran Ben-Joseph, *Streets and the Shaping of Towns and Cities* (McGraw-Hill, New York, 1997).

United States. This body of experience shows us that traffic calming devices can increase safety and neighborhood livability and reduce the negative effects of excessive traffic speeds and volumes in residential neighborhoods. We can learn much from the examples of failed traffic calming experiments as well. Herein lies the exciting reality of traffic calming—there is much innovation, experimentation, and the re-evaluation of standard methods and practices left to be done! This is a dynamic area where new ideas are needed and welcomed by both the public and other transportation professionals. The work is challenging, to be sure; but the rewards are worth the effort!

Further Reading

Appleyard, Donald. *Livable Streets*. Berkeley, Calif.: University of California Press, 1981.

Bagvy, Gordon. "Effects of Traffic Flow on Residential Property Values," *Journal of the American Planning Association*. American Planning Association, January 1980.

Southworth, Michael and Eran Ben-Joseph. "Speed Humps: Implementation and Impact of Residential Traffic Control." *Streets and the Shaping of Towns and Cities*. McGraw-Hill, New York, 1997.

Dare, James and Noel Schoneman. "Seattle's Neighborhood Traffic Control Program," *ITE Journal*. Washington, D.C.: Institute of Transportation Engineers, February 1982.

Environmental Working Group. *Mean Streets—Pedestrian Safety and Reform of the Nation's Transportation Law*, Surface Transportation Policy Project. Washington, D.C.: Environmental Working Group, April 1997.

"Evaluation of the Neighborhood Traffic Management Program—Peer Review Analysis of the Traffic Circle Program." Portland, Oregon: City of Portland, 1992.

Ewing, Reid. "Interim Report on Chesbro Avenue Pavement Undulations," *State-of-the-Art Report*.

Ewing, Reid. "Overview: Legal Aspects of Traffic Calming," *Compendium of Reference Papers*. 1998 ITE Annual Conference. Washington, D.C.: Institute of Transportation Engineers, 1998.

Ewing, Reid and C. Kooshian. "U.S. Experience with Traffic Calming," *ITE Journal*. Washington, D.C.: Institute of Transportation Engineers, August 1997.

Hughes, William and C.F. Sirmans. "Traffic Externality and Single-Family Housing Prices," *Journal of Regional Science*. Volume 32, No. 4, 1992.

Litman, Tod. *Traffic Calming Benefits, Costs and Equity Issues*. Canada: Victoria Transport Policy Institute, 1997.

Lockwood, I.M. "ITE Traffic Calming Definition," *ITE Journal*. Washington, D.C.: Institute of Transportation Engineers, July 1997, pp. 22–24.

McCourt, R.S. ITE District 6. "Neighborhood Traffic Management Survey," *ITE Journal*. Washington, D.C.: Institute of Transportation Engineers, 1996. Available through DKS Associates, Portland, Oregon.

Pedestrian Federation of America. *Walking Tall: A Citizen's Guide to Walkable Communities*. Pedestrian Federation of America, 1995.

Road Data Laboratory. *Consequence Evaluation of Environmentally Adapted Through Road in Skærbæk*, Report No. 63. Schultz Grafisk A/S, January 1988.

Road Safety Group. *The Safety Benefits of Traffic Calming*. Road Safety Group, 1996.

Rathbone Publications. *Urban Transportation Monitor*. Rathbone Publications, May 24, 1996.

Szymanski, R. *Can Changing Neighborhood Traffic Circulation Patterns Reduce Crime and Improve Personal Safety? A Quantitative Analysis of One Neighborhood's Efforts*. Master's Thesis, Florida International University. Ft. Lauderdale, Fla., 1994.

CHAPTER 18
Transportation Terminals

Leon Goodman, P.E.
Principal Project Manager
Parsons Transportation Group
Jerome M. Lutin, P.E.
Senior Director, Planning, Research and Development
New Jersey Transit Corporation

Definition and Scope

Whether it's a simple corner bus stop, a complex multimodal downtown transportation center, a major international airport linking world capitals, or a busy marine cargo terminal, transportation interface areas are often the key to the success of transportation systems—local, intercity, or international. These places, where passengers (on foot or in vehicles) and freight enter and then leave or change modes within the system, may be called terminals, garages, lots, stops, transportation centers, stations, intersections, interchanges, complexes, depots, interfaces, activity centers, or other names not yet devised. Whatever they are called, they are the places where any capacity or efficiency problems will show up first; where safety is a particular concern because of the amount and complexity of the required maneuvers and movements; and where major capital and operating costs will be involved, particularly for the larger and more complex facilities. This chapter will deal with planning and design issues and techniques for terminals within the local (urban and suburban) systems and within the longer-distance (intercity and international) systems, for passenger and freight movement. Operational issues will be considered as they relate to assuring sound planning and design.

Urban and suburban systems include: the street and highway network (accommodating auto, bus, and truck movement); bus transportation systems; ridesharing; paratransit; rail systems (e.g., light rail, rail rapid, commuter rail, rail freight); passenger distribution systems (e.g., escalators, moving walks, people movers); waterborne systems; and new technology modes (e.g., dual-power, guided bus, magnetic levitation). Intercity and international systems include auto, bus, and truck travel via the nationwide street and highway network; intercity rail passenger and rail freight systems; intercity and international air transportation for passengers and cargo; and intercoastal and international marine cargo movement.

While local and longer-distance transportation systems are often institutionally distinct and can be considered and studied separately, there are considerable and frequent interactions and interrelationships between them. The highway system, for example, serves both movements. Sections of the rail network are used by long-distance and commuter rail services; and ground access modes at airports compete with "regular" urban transportation for the limited capacity of urban highways and transit systems. In addition to the management of this "sharing" of rights-of-way and service corridors, the local and longer-distance systems depend on well-planned and smoothly functioning interfaces to provide the total transportation service that users need and justifiably demand in the increasingly competitive business and transportation environment.

Throughout this necessarily brief overview of a complex and constantly changing area of transportation planning, attention will first be devoted to principles and techniques that are applicable to a number of modes and systems. After discussing these central concepts, the specifics applicable to particular modes and situations will be explored. While a balanced treatment of the "terminals" field has been the goal, there *are* differences in the level of information, at least in the level of published material, regarding local and longer-distance systems and regarding the various modes. Greater coverage is given, however, to those situations that are most likely to need significant planning and design efforts in the foreseeable transportation planning "world."

Terminal aspects for the street and highway mode and for transit modes (i.e., the "ground transportation" modes) are extensively covered in other chapters of this book. These include subjects such as parking, intersections and interchanges, transit planning, and toll plazas. Such matters will, therefore, be either omitted or treated briefly here. The material in this chapter is organized to cover:

- Planning studies for terminals.

- Modal ground and transportation terminals.

- Airports.

- Ports (marine terminals).

- Distribution systems.

Table 18–1 Terminal Elements for Different Combinations of Random and Batch Arrivals and Departures

	Random Arrivals	Batch Arrivals
Random departures	Parking garages	Exiting direction at transit stations, airports, ports, (container movements)
Batch departures	Entering direction at transit stations, airports, ports (container movements)	Transfer passenger at transit stations, airports, etc.

Planning Studies for Terminals

Terminal Concepts and Processes[A]

The concepts, processes, and analytical techniques reviewed here are generally applicable to all terminal areas, though they have greatest relevance to the more formal, more complex "terminals" of the various surface transportation modes.

Terminal functions include provisions for passengers and freight to (a) enter or leave a mode within the system, (b) interchange within a mode, or (c) interchange between or among modes. Examples of each would include: (1) a corner bus stop where a passenger walks from home and boards a local bus; (2) an express stop on a rail rapid transit line, where passengers can transfer between local and express trains; and (3) a major international airport where passengers can transfer from domestic and international flights to auto (e.g., parked, picked-up, rental), taxis, express and local bus, rail service, or helicopter. These examples further illustrate the range between "simple" interfaces or terminals and the complex facilities needed in large cities and at major activity centers.

For the more complex facilities, certain features become necessary either due to their financial and institutional framework, the number of alternative paths that might be selected, or the sheer amount of travel that needs to be accommodated. The cost of building and operating the terminal must be recovered by those governmental or private sector institutions responsible; so there needs to be design and operational consideration for collecting fares, tolls, rental fees, tariffs, and the like. It is also important to know the routing of passengers and freight through the terminal (or through a series of links and terminals). Choice of routes is done by the passenger, by the shipper, or by the carrier depending on the frequency and type of trip, the number of alternative routings available, the fare or rate structure, institutional traditions, the "image" of the terminal, and other factors. When alternatives are available, this route choice decision is a key determinant of the actual flow through a terminal and is, therefore, a key study item when estimating the market (i.e., the forecasted traffic) for a terminal.

Individual or "bunched" arrivals (or departures) to (or from) the terminal area have a significant effect on the planning, design, and operation of the facility. These are usually referred to as random or batch situations. Table 18–1 gives examples of interface elements for different combinations of random arrivals and departures and batch arrivals and departures.

For all terminals it is seldom practical for each unit being transported, whether passenger or freight, to get to the transportation loading or transfer point right at the time that the vehicle is ready to leave, so provisions have to be made for various types of waiting or holding facilities. Here again there is quite a range, from provision of adequate space on a rail rapid transit platform to accommodate passengers waiting for trains on a two-minute headway, to the elaborate waiting

---

[A] See reference list at the end of this chapter for source information for all sections labeled, A, B, C, etc.

rooms, restaurants, and hotels that are typically provided at major airports, where the interval between flights is measured in hours rather than minutes. The consumer services associated with large terminals (e.g., bus terminals, rail stations, airports) are more than a convenience for travelers. They provide, and are, a major source of the revenue needed to fund the building and operation of the terminal.

Freight terminals provide for direct transfer, from line-haul service to distribution service, and for longer-term storage. They may also function partially as warehouses and, as occurs at a large port or airport facility, there may be processing of the goods at an intermodal terminal. The shipment of freight, particularly in international trade, is increasingly done in containers that can be accommodated by a number of domestic and international carriers.

The functions of terminals and the common names of facilities performing these functions, in various transportation modes, are outlined in Table 18–2 and Table 18–3.

The *processes* by which passengers and freight move through terminal areas need to be well understood in order to analyze ways to accomplish the desired functions and to design (or evaluate) the physical and operational systems for

Table 18–2 Functions of Transportation Terminals

- Sorting of passengers and/or freight by trip length, destination, etc.
- Loading of passengers or freight onto transport vehicles (or belt, pipeline, etc.) and unloading
- Transferring from one vehicle to another
- Holding and/or storing of passengers or freight from time of arrival to time of departure
    - Possible processing of goods, packing for movement
    - Provision of comfort amenities for passengers (e.g., food service, other retail businesses)
- Documenting movement
    - Freight weighing, preparation of waybill, selection of route, billing
    - Passenger ticket sales, fare/revenue collection, checking reservations
- Handling vehicle (and other component) storage, maintenance, and assignment
- Concentrating passengers and freight into groups of economical size for movement (e.g., to fill a train or airliner) and dispersal at other end of trip
- Security processes, checking documents, checking for contraband

Source: Edward K. Morlok, *Introduction to Transportation Engineering and Planning*, McGraw-Hill, 1978.

Table 18–3 Common Names for Facilities Performing Terminal Functions of Transportation Modes

Major Mode	Facility	Modal Interface or Other Primary Function
Air	Airport } Air terminal }	Ground access modes and air connections
	Field	Airport with very limited facilities
	Hanger	Repair and servicing
	Heliport	Same as airport
	Seaplane base	Same as airport
Automobile (and other road vehicles)	Parking garage or lot	Vehicle storage, walking access
	Gas station	Vehicle repair and servicing
Bus	Toll plaza	Collection of fees
	Bus station } Bus terminal }	Intercity bus and access mode connections
	Bus stop	Walking access connections
Rail, passenger	Rail station } Transit station }	Local access modes and rail connections; sometimes includes other intercity modes (e.g., bus)
Rail, freight	Freight house	Local (truck) access
	Team tracks	Local (truck) access (open area as opposed to building)
	Private siding	Loading or unloading by shipper or receiver of freight
	Classification yard shops, rip track, etc.	Freight train connections Car repair and servicing
Water, freight	Port	Ground access modes (usually rail, truck, and/or pipeline) and sometimes vessel connections
	Dock, wharf, or pier	A single vessel loading-unloading facility
Water, passenger	Ferry terminal	Ground access (pedestrian, auto, bus, rail) to vessels

Source: Edward K. Morlok, *Introduction to Transportation Engineering and Planning*, McGraw-Hill, 1978.

a particular alternative. Terminals have, in fact, been viewed as processors of freight and passengers. This most often means processing of the vehicles or containers in which the freight or passengers are carried; but it can also mean, as in the case of pedestrian flow studies, directly analyzing the flow of passenger movement. The terminal performs this function utilizing a physical facility, labor, and specialized equipment. The times required for this processing (e.g., for passengers, for freight, for vehicle and equipment use) are of primary concern in the design and evaluation of terminals. These time factors, for the terminal operator and for the terminal user, are often the prime determinants of costs that, in turn, will determine the financial viability of a facility or system. Also, for the terminal user, the "in-terminal" and "access" times (and the reliability of those times) create a reality and a perception that greatly influences routing choices.

For all of the present and future modes and systems it is important to keep in mind the ultimate purposes of the process and to recognize that there may be several ways to achieve those purposes. The designer or evaluator should not get caught up in the present ways or the equipment that exists today. The use of the "mobile lounge" concept at airports, allowing a significant potential reduction in the extent and cost of terminal buildings, is an example of modifying procedures, equipment, and physical plant while still achieving the transportation "purpose." "Just-in-time" delivery and other business methods based on electronic information systems are continuing to change the planning of transportation terminals.

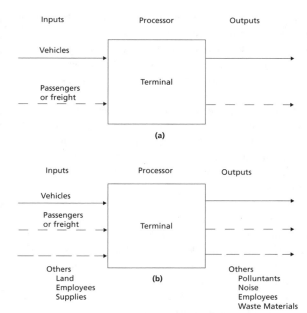

Figure 18–1 Simplified Process Flowchart of a Transport Terminal

Source: Edward K. Morlok, *Introduction to Transportation Engineering and Planning,* McGraw-Hill, 1978.

Analysis Techniques[A]

Process Analysis

An important tool for understanding terminals and other interface areas is the *process flowchart*. It shows the activities that a unit of traffic (e.g., passenger, box, vehicle, container) experiences as it proceeds through a facility. The chart shows the order of the activities and the potential alternative paths or sequences, and it may be used to develop process time requirements.

Process flowcharts can be very simple or quite complex depending on their purpose (i.e., how many individual steps are involved in the overall process). A simple flowchart will show the terminal as a single "black-box" processor with simple inputs and outputs of vehicles, passengers, and freight (as applicable). A more complete representation, useful for cost determination, might also include the "supporting" inputs and outputs (e.g., land, employees, and supplies [inputs]; environmental effects, employees, and waste materials [outputs]). Figure 18–1 shows simple process flow charts of both types (transportation flows only and all flows). For transportation planning purposes, this text will be concerned more with the transportation flows. There will be more focus on loading and unloading, ticketing, paper or computer processing of freight documentation, parking fee collection, and the like.

To depict more detail on a fuller type of process flowchart, a standard set of symbols has been developed and is shown in Figure 18–2. These symbols, representing different elements and processes in the interface, are combined with various types of lines and arrows to form the complete flowchart. The technique can be used in the analysis of many different transportation modes and in varying contexts.

Figure 18–3 shows a more detailed process flowchart, using the standard symbols and lines and arrows, for an intercity passenger terminal. It traces the flow from passenger arrivals to passenger departures; and it includes "subplots," such as passenger transfers to intracity distribution modes.

In addition to its use for analyzing a particular terminal configuration, the process flowchart is indispensable in evaluating alternative design schemes and operating plans. One might, for example, want to compare shipment of goods by rail either by "break-bulk" method or by use of containers.

Figure 18–4 shows process flowcharts for containerized movement and for the "break-bulk" method. Inspection of the flowcharts quickly reveals the reduction of the number and complexity of steps involved, if containerized movement is used. It does not, by itself, show which method has lower costs which would need to be looked at in a subsequent quantitative analysis of costs and levels of service.

Processing Times

Processing times are a major element in evaluating the level of service of a terminal. Theoretically one could estimate total processing time by summing up the times for each step shown on the flowchart. Each of those individual times, however, is subject to considerable variation due to system or user characteristics. Waiting for the vehicle needs to be accounted for, either because of the known service times (e.g., trains scheduled to arrive every five mins.) or the congestion delays that result from overloads. These "dependent-on-flow" waits can be a consequence of overloaded vehicles, resulting in a need to wait for the following vehicle; or they may be a consequence of vehicles that are behind schedule because of accidents, a system overload, or other factors.

When the waiting is in a specific line or location it is often referred to as queuing. Some processing time variation is due to individual choice as, for example, when different travelers arrive at different times for a specific scheduled vehicle departure time. This difference relates to varying personalities (some people like to arrive well in advance, while others will get there just in time) and to perceptions of the reliability of access modes. For a number of reasons, therefore, there are variations in processing times; and these are often expressed in distributions, either as a simple range of values or as formal, statistical distributions.

For individual processes with multiple activities it is also important to recognize which activities control the time

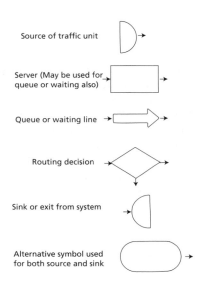

Figure 18–2   Standard Symbols Used in Process Flowcharts

Source: Edward K. Morlok, *Introduction to Transportation Engineering and Planning*, McGraw-Hill, 1978.

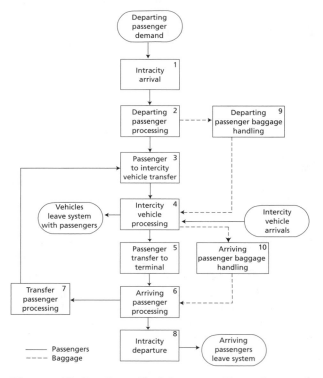

Figure 18–3   Detailed Process Flowchart of a General Passenger Terminal

Source: Edward K. Morlok, *Introduction to Transportation Engineering and Planning*, McGraw-Hill, 1978.

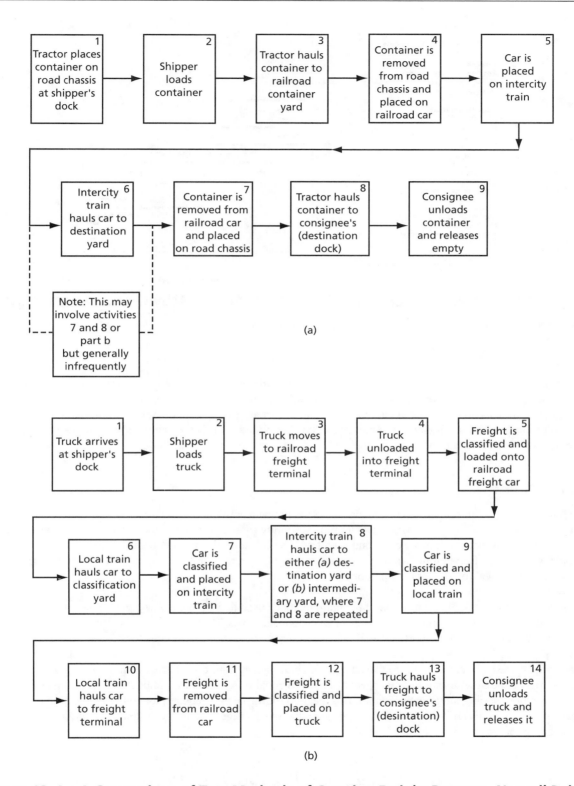

Figure 18–4 A Comparison of Two Methods of Carrying Freight Between Nonrail Points Using a Process Flowchart

Source: Edward K. Morlok, *Introduction to Transportation Engineering and Planning*, McGraw-Hill, 1978.

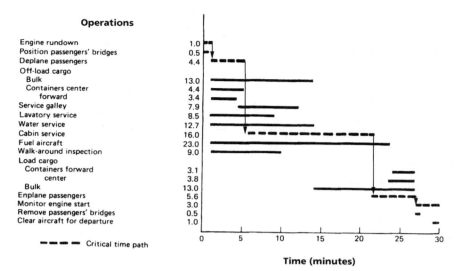

Operations

Engine rundown	1.0
Position passengers' bridges	0.5
Deplane passengers	4.4
Off-load cargo	
Bulk	13.0
Containers center	4.4
forward	3.4
Service galley	7.9
Lavatory service	8.5
Water service	12.7
Cabin service	16.0
Fuel aircraft	23.0
Walk-around inspection	9.0
Load cargo	
Containers forward	3.1
center	3.8
Bulk	13.0
Enplane passengers	5.6
Monitor engine start	3.0
Remove passengers' bridges	0.5
Clear aircraft for departure	1.0

– – – – Critical time path

Time (minutes)

Figure 18–5   Example of Critical Servicing Time: Aircraft Activities at a Terminal Gate

Source: Edward K. Morlok, *Introduction to Transportation Engineering and Planning*, McGraw-Hill, 1978.

required (i.e., which are on the critical path). Figure 18–5 provides an example for aircraft activities at a terminal gate. It shows that when two activities occur in parallel, the one needing the longer time is controlling. The activity time diagram must also take into account that certain activities can only start after others are completed. Following through in this fashion, the shortest time for the entire sequence can be determined. This is the *critical time*, and the sequence of the controlling activities is called the *critical time path*.

Waiting Times

In terminals, as in any transportation function, one seeks to eliminate or minimize unproductive time (e.g., delays, waiting, not moving). But, particularly in interfaces and terminals, waiting cannot be avoided and in fact, as described previously, may be an integral aspect of terminal design and operation. Thus, determining the amount of waiting time and the number of people, vehicles, or freight units waiting (or to be stored) is basic to terminal design, so that adequate capacity can be provided for the waiting or storage functions.

The cumulative flow-time diagram is one of the main methods used to estimate *waiting times* and the *number of units waiting*—both key factors in planning, designing, or evaluating terminals. The method can be outlined in a simple example based on a gate position at an airport terminal, where each plane needs thirty minutes for processing.

The use of this gate by aircraft can be portrayed on a diagram such as Figure 18–6 (a). The horizontal axis denotes time. For convenience the time unit in this figure was chosen to equal thirty minutes, although any scale can be used. The vertical axis represents aircraft using the facility. This diagram shows the time required for each traffic unit (in this example, aircraft) to be served. From it the average waiting time and the average time in the system (i.e., the time waiting plus the time being served) can be calculated:

$$\overline{w} = \frac{1}{N}\sum_{i=1}^{N}\left(E_i - A_i\right) = \frac{1}{N}\sum_{i=1}^{N}\left(D_i - A_i - S_i\right) \tag{18–1}$$

$$\overline{t} = \frac{1}{N}\sum_{i=1}^{N}\left(D_i - A_i\right) \tag{18–2}$$

where

$\overline{w}$ = mean waiting time

N = number of traffic units, $i = 1, 2, \ldots, N$

A_i = moment of arrival of unit i

D_i = moment of departure of unit i

E_i = moment unit i enters server

S_i = time required to serve unit i

$\overline{t}$ = mean time in the system

Formulas 18–1 and 18–2 hold even if the serving times are not constant; and they reveal the number in the waiting line at any point in time. The maximum might be used as a basis for designing the waiting area. The average number in the system during the period from arrival of 1, A_1, to departure of the last, D_N, is simply

$$\overline{n} = \frac{1}{D_N - A_1} \sum_{i=1}^{N} \left(D_i - A_i \right) \qquad (18\text{--}3)$$

where $\overline{n}$ is the mean number of traffic units in the system during the period $D_N - A_1$.

Figure 18–6(b) portrays the same situation except that instead of each traffic unit being represented as a discrete unit, the arrivals and departures are represented as a continuous flow. The cumulative arrival line passes through the points of arrival of traffic units in the discrete diagram; and the cumulative departure line passes through the times of departure. This representation is more commonly used where the number of traffic units is very large, which makes the approximation of a stepped line by a smooth line fairly good. The time of each traffic unit in the system is then approximated by the

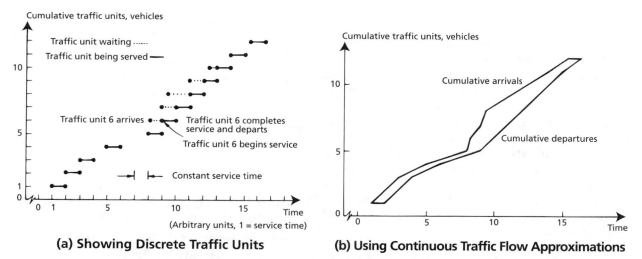

(a) Showing Discrete Traffic Units   **(b) Using Continuous Traffic Flow Approximations**

Figure 18–6(a) and (b)   Cumulative Flow-Time Diagrams

Source: Edward K. Morlok, *Introduction to Transportation Engineering and Planning*, McGraw-Hill, 1978.

horizontal distance between the two lines if the process is first in, first out; and the vertical distance is approximately the number in the system. In most applications of this form of the diagram, the lines are drawn as smooth curves rather than short straight-line segments. The average time and average number in the system can be approximated using the area bounded by the two cumulative curves divided by either the number of units or the time interval,

$$\bar{t} = \frac{Z}{N} \tag{18-4}$$

$$\bar{n} = \frac{Z}{D_N - A_1} \tag{18-5}$$

where Z is the area bounded by cumulative arrival and cumulative departure curves, the total traffic-unit-time-units spent in the system.

Capacity

The maximum possible flow of traffic units per unit of time through a terminal or other interface needs to be estimated (for planned facilities) or evaluated (for existing facilities). Capacity determinations need to be coupled with consideration of some idea of level of service, which is usually measured by waiting times or waiting delays. Thus level of service can be thought of as the maximum volume that can be accommodated with acceptable or tolerable patterns of delay. Before dealing with how "acceptable" or "tolerable" criteria might be developed, it is valuable to discuss the relation of traffic volume, service times, queues, waiting times, and the like.

Assume a single processor with a constant service time as in the previous aircraft example, and assume traffic units arrive at a constant time headway. As long as the headway is greater than the service time, all units can be served. However, if the headway is less than the service time, a queue will form, as in the case of vehicles 5 through 8 in Figure 18–6. If the volume continued indefinitely at this level, the queue would increase indefinitely in length, resulting in a total time approaching infinity. Of course, in actual systems the volume drops (headways increase) after a peak period, so the system can recover (Figure 18–6). If the average waiting and serving time were drawn relative to volume (the inverse of headway), the result would be as shown in curve 3 in Figure 18–7.

Delay and Service Times

In actual systems, time headways usually vary between arrivals of traffic units. Units sometimes bunch together, as do passengers departing from a vehicle. And there are simply random arrivals, resulting from many different people all deciding when to travel almost independently of one another. In the case of varying arrival headways, even if the volume yields an average headway greater than the (constant) service time, some delay is likely. This was shown in Figure 18–6, where delay occurred even though only 12 vehicles arrived in 15 time units, less than the 15 vehicles that theoretically could be accommodated in that period. As the volume increases the average headway drops, and the likelihood of delay increases. As a result, actual delay patterns appear as shown by curve 2 in Figure 18–7, delay increasing with volume and tending toward very large values near the maximum capacity.

Given a maximum tolerable average delay, curves such as 1 and 2 in Figure 18–7 can be used to specify a capacity, or maximum volume, which the processor can accommodate

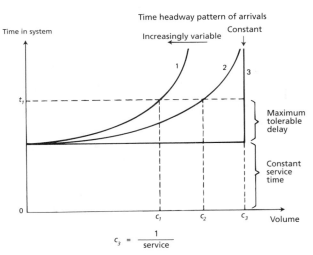

Figure 18–7   Typical Time-Volume Curves for Terminal Processor with Constant Service Times and Varying Arrival Time Headway Patterns

Source: Edward K. Morlok, *Introduction to Transportation Engineering and Planning*, McGraw-Hill, 1978.

in a "steady state" for a long time. The maximum volume will, of course, depend upon the choice of that maximum delay. In the processor shown in Figure 18–7, if the maximum time were selected as t_1 (with a corresponding maximum delay), the capacity with curve 1 would be c_1. The capacity will depend upon the peaking of traffic within the period of analysis, or more precisely upon the entire distribution of the headways. Given any maximum average delay, the greater the peaking, the lower the maximum capacity—as illustrated by c_1, the capacity with relatively high variability in headways; and c_2, the capacity with more moderate variability.

The service times at most terminal processors are not constant; constant service times were used in the discussion above to facilitate understanding of the operations. If the service time varies, the general form of the time in system versus volume curve remains the same as that illustrated by curves 1 and 2. It begins at zero volume at the mean service time and then increases as volume increases, usually slowly at first; and when the volume approaches the maximum throughput value (the inverse of the mean service time), the delays increase rapidly. Also, the more variable the arrival headways, the greater the delay. A similar relationship applies for the variability of the service times. Usually this is based on the average time in the system, but sometimes it is also based on the distribution of the time. This reflects the importance of the range and reliability of travel times as well as average travel time. However, in all cases it must be based upon judgment, perhaps aided by the use of economic criteria on the costs of the delays and the costs of adding additional servers.

Another useful relationship already implied by the foregoing discussion is that among the total time in the system, the delay, and the service time, for any individual traffic unit the total time is the sum of the delay and service times. As a result, mean times are also related by the sum

$$\bar{t} = \bar{w} + \bar{s} \qquad (18–6)$$

where

$$\bar{t} \quad = \quad \text{mean time in the processor system}$$

$$\bar{w} \quad = \quad \text{mean waiting time}$$

$$\bar{s} \quad = \quad \text{mean service time}$$

In using Formula 18–6, it is important to realize that in some situations the queue length may affect the length of service time, since servers tend to be more rapid when the line is long. For instance, in an airport check-in line or at a tollbooth, the agent may pause to exchange pleasantries if the line is short; but, if faced with a long line, the agent would instead concentrate on processing travelers as quickly as possible. Thus it is necessary that the mean service time used in the formula applies to the conditions being analyzed. This is merely a word of caution and is not meant to imply that service time will always depend upon the length of the queue. In many mechanized terminal processes, such as automated loading and unloading equipment in freight terminals, the serving times are not affected by the volume of traffic. So it is important to check whether or not the mean service times vary with the volume, the same as the delay does. Of course, for much capacity analysis, only the total time versus volume curve is important.

Simulation

The irregular occurrence of traffic, as earlier described, is the norm for the various types of passenger and freight transportation interfaces. This characteristic leads to the concept that the realistic, day-to-day capacity of a terminal is well below the theoretical maximum capacity because, otherwise, the potential traffic delays would be too large. One of the most useful analytical methods for modeling the performance of systems with irregular traffic flows is *simulation*. This technique has application in many fields, and the description used here conveys only the basic concepts as they apply to transportation.

The basic idea of simulation is to model a process, paying special attention to the various events that occur as the process continues. Thus in the context of transportation, the focus is typically on the arrival of vehicles or other traffic, placement in the appropriate serving facility, loading and unloading, departure of the vehicle, making the server available to another unit, and other such factors. An important distinction is made between two types of simulation:

one is deterministic, meaning that all events are characterized by certainty—as to when they will occur, how long each process will take, and so on. The other type is stochastic, meaning that there are possible variations in these characteristics of the system as it is represented in the simulation model. In particular, those characteristics that are modeled as variable (such as the time required to load and unload a vehicle) have probabilities associated with each of the possible values, the associated probability indicating the relative frequency or likelihood of each of the possible values.

Similarly, the results of the simulation are characterized by probabilities. For example, the result of a typical simulation might be that the probability of an aircraft having to wait more than 8 minutes after arrival at an airport until it is given clearance to land is 0.05.

Our attention will focus on stochastic simulation, which involves the use of probability concepts. In order to represent characteristics of the system that vary the *probability density function* is used. The most common probability density function used for traffic arrivals at transport terminals and other transport elements is the Poisson distribution. The variable is the number of traffic units that arrive in a given interval of time, given a particular mean arrival rate. The mathematical formula for the Poisson distribution is presented in Formula 18–7.

$$p(n) = \frac{(\lambda t)^{\mu} e^{-\mu}}{n!}, \text{ for } n = 0, 1, 2, \ldots \tag{18-7}$$

where

$p(n)$ = probability of n arrivals in a period of t

n = number of arrivals

λ = mean arrival rate (volume in our terminology)

t = time period

$n!$ = $n(n-1)(n-2) \ldots (2)(1)$ and $0! = 1$

e = base of natural logarithms

Any mathematical or other model of a system should be tested before it is used in engineering design or planning, for otherwise one can have little confidence that results of using the model will replicate real world phenomena.

With this very brief introduction to probability distributions, it is now possible to discuss simulation. This discussion will be presented in a very general form, one suitable for manual use, even though most simulations make use of computers. Extension to computer use is straightforward, with one of the computer languages that have been written especially for simulations.

As an example of simulation, suppose we are modeling the arrival of buses at a bus stop, and it has been determined that the buses arrive following the Poisson distribution at an average rate or volume of 83 buses per hour (0.02306 bus/second). In this case, the probability of a headway greater than or equal to t seconds will be, with $\lambda = 0.02306$ per second,

$$p(h \geq t) = e^{-0.02306t} \tag{18-8}$$

Transforming this, we have $\qquad \log_e [p(h \geq t)] = -.02306t \tag{18-9}$

and $\qquad t = 43.4 \ \log_e \frac{1}{p(h \geq t)}$

This equation can be used to find the headway t, which will be exceeded by a probability $p(h \geq t)$. Thus we can choose any value of $(p \geq t)$, substitute it into the equation, and obtain the desired time t.

To obtain a single headway to use in the course of simulating the arrivals of vehicles (buses) at a stop, we select a probability $p(h \geq t)$ and then use the equation to find the corresponding time period of no arrivals, t.

The process is continued until enough bus arrivals are generated for the purposes of the simulation. This number usually must be large enough so that the simulation results, which are often expressed in averages and perhaps distributions, have settled on reasonably stable values. Twenty bus arrivals and nineteen headways are shown in Table 18–4. As can be seen, the mean headway remains fairly stable in this example after about ten bus arrivals, the distribution mean being 43.4 seconds.

This example should provide enough information to show what simulation is capable of, and to demonstrate that at least small manual simulations can be performed. Computer "spreadsheet" programs are widely available to assist in such simulations.

Although simulation is probably the most widely used method for modeling stochastic traffic flows in transportation, such as those occurring at terminals, another important method is the use of *queuing theory*. Queuing theory deals with queues by deducing characteristics through mathematical analysis, attempting to find formulas that will directly provide information of the type we obtained from simulation. The queuing theory approach thus has the advantage of simplicity and ease of use over simulation; but as one might expect, it is only possible to derive such formulas for certain types of queues. And, of course, the entire problem must be described in mathematical formulas in order to use the equations of this theory.

Queuing theory formulas provide useful information for the design and analysis of waiting line systems, quite similar to the information obtained from the simulation example. For instance, the average number of traffic units in the queue and the average number in the system (queue and servers) is important in ascertaining the adequacy of waiting areas. The distribution of waiting times and the average are important in assessing the adequacy of the entire system in serving the traffic. The phenomenon of "relaxation time" also needs to be taken into account. From this distribution the probability of delays greater than any specified value can be obtained, and this permits the application of criteria such as those used for airport runways.

There are four characteristics of queues that must be specified in order to predict performance. One is the distribution of the headways of traffic arrivals, which may be uniform (i.e., with constant headway) or may follow the Poisson or random arrival pattern (i.e., negative exponential probability of headways), or some other pattern. A second characteristic

Table 18–4   Example Simulation of Arrival Times of Buses at a Stop

Bus Number	Random Number Drawn	Time Headway (seconds)	Arrival Time (seconds)	Cumulative Mean Headway (seconds)
1			0	
2	32	49	49	49.0
3	99	1	50	25.0
4	61	21	71	23.6
5	16	80	151	37.8
6	66	18	169	33.8
7	10	100	269	44.8
8	49	31	300	42.9
9	83	8	308	38.5
10	12	92	400	44.4
11	36	44	444	44.4
12	31	51	495	45.0
13	92	4	499	41.6
14	8	110	609	46.8
15	74	13	622	44.4
16	84	8	630	42.0
17	33	48	678	42.4
18	16	80	758	44.6
19	28	55	813	44.6
20	64	19	832	43.8

Note: Random numbers are integers drawn from the range 0 to 100, all with equal probability.

Source: Edward K. Morlok, *Introduction to Transportation Engineering and Planning*, McGraw-Hill, 1978.

is the distribution of service times (e.g., constant, Poisson). A third important characteristic is the number of serving channels or stations. The fourth characteristic is the so-called queue discipline, which specifies the order in which arriving traffic units will be served. In transport, this is usually the first to arrive, then the first to be served; but in other systems the order may be last to arrive, then first served, just as when mail is stacked in a pile and then sorted from the top down. In queuing theory terminology, the former discipline is usually referred to as "first in, first out" (FIFO); and the second as "last in, first out" (LIFO).

One important class of results is for the case of a single-server queue, with Poisson arrivals, negative exponential service times, and a FIFO discipline. Various measures of the performance of such a queue are presented in Table 18–5. Since the Poisson distribution has but one parameter, the mean, the only parameters in the model are the mean arrival rate λ and the mean service rate μ. These would both be expressed in traffic units per unit time, as vehicles per hour. The mean headway of arrivals is $1/\lambda$ and the mean service time is $1/\mu$. It should be noted that the mean time between departures from the servicing channel must be greater than $1/\mu$ since the server is not always in use. The mean departure headway must be equal to $1/\lambda$ since no more units can leave than arrive.

The various results given in Table 18–5 are essentially self-explanatory. These results are termed *steady-state results*, which means they are the results that would be observed after the system operated for such a long time that the averages or probabilities did not change as the system ran longer. In fact, they are actually derived from the situation of an infinite period of operation. It has been found useful to express many of the formulas in terms of ρ, ρ being equal to λ/μ, so as to simplify presentation. ρ is called *traffic intensity*. ρ must be less than 1.0; otherwise the waiting line would continually build up as time passed and a steady state would not exist. As can be seen from inspection, many of these performance measures would be quite useful in analyzing a facility.

Table 18–5 Single-Station Queuing Relationships with Poisson Arrivals and Exponential Service Times for Steady-State Conditions

Queuing Model		Description of Model
1	$p(n)=\left(\dfrac{\lambda}{\mu}\right)^{n}\left(1-\dfrac{\lambda}{\mu}\right)=(\rho)^{n}(1-\rho)$	$p(n)$ = probability of having exactly n vehicles in system
2	$\bar{n}=\dfrac{\lambda}{\mu-\lambda}=\dfrac{\rho}{1-\rho}$	$\bar{n}$ = average no. of vehicles in system
3	$\text{var}(n)=\dfrac{\lambda\mu}{(\mu-\lambda)^{2}}=\dfrac{\rho}{(1-\rho)^{2}}$	$\text{var}(n)$ = variance of n (no. of vehicles in system)
4	$\bar{q}=\dfrac{\lambda^{2}}{\mu(\mu-\lambda)}=\dfrac{\rho^{2}}{1-\rho}$	$\bar{q}$ = average length of queue
5	$f(d)=(\mu-\lambda)e^{(\lambda-\mu)d}$	$f(d)$ = probability of having spent time d in system
6	$\bar{d}=\dfrac{1}{\mu-\lambda}$	$\bar{d}$ = average time spent in system
7	$\bar{w}=\dfrac{\lambda}{\mu(\mu-\lambda)}=d-\dfrac{1}{\mu}$	$\bar{w}$ = average waiting time spent in queue
8	$p(d\leq t)=1-e^{-(1-p)\mu t}$	$p(d\leq t)$ = probability of having spent time t or less in system
9	$p(w\leq t)=1-\rho e^{-(1-p)\mu t}$	$p(w\leq t)$ = probability of having waited time t or less in queue

λ = average number of vehicle arrivals per unit of time

μ = average servicing rate, number of vehicles per unit of time

ρ = traffic intensity or utilization factor = λ/μ

Source: Edward K. Morlok, *Introduction to Transportation Engineering and Planning*, McGraw-Hill, 1978.

Another important set of results is for queues with Poisson arrivals, Poisson service times, and the FIFO queue discipline with many service channels. Here the FIFO discipline means that an arrival will enter the first available server, implying that there is one waiting line. Even though this is unlike many situations where there is a queue for each server, it often approximates such situations well.

The final type of queuing theory model covered here is the case of Poisson arrivals and constant service times. This is a more difficult system to model mathematically; and as a result, performance measures that can be estimated analytically are not as numerous as the other cases, but they are useful nevertheless.

Pedestrian Flow Analysis

The concepts, processes, and analytical techniques described up to this point have commonly been based on vehicles as the "traffic units." Vehicular capacity analyses can be carried out using the general techniques reviewed previously, together with the specific capacity analysis methods for particular modes, for example, the *Highway Capacity Manual*[1] for roadway systems. The movement of people on foot (i.e., pedestrian movement) is a critical element of passenger transportation interfaces and terminals.

There are two general conceptual approaches to pedestrian flow analysis: "linear" situations (e.g., walkways, stairways, corridors) and "area" situations (e.g., transit platforms, sidewalk corner areas, terminal areas). Pioneering studies by Dr. John Fruin and others in the early 1970s initially focused on the linear approach, and these studies led to material such as that contained in Chapter 13 of the *Highway Capacity Manual*. The time-space concept, particularly appropriate for area analyses, was described in a 1984 paper by Dr. Fruin and Gregory Benz[2] and further developed in a 1986 monograph by Benz.[3] Details of both the linear and area types of pedestrian analyses are presented elsewhere in this handbook.

Market Research (Demand Estimation)

Considering the varying numbers and sizes of potential transportation interfaces, and the many different transportation modes, it is not surprising that there are many techniques used to estimate the demand for interfaces or terminals. Projected terminal demand volume clearly relates to the expected usage of the overall system that the terminal is part of. System demand estimation involves surveys of existing usage, mathematical models (and the associated computer software), trend analysis, future market analysis, and considerable doses of engineering planning and policy judgment. The analyses will depend considerably also on whether the planner is dealing with modification or expansion of an existing system or with an entirely new terminal or system.

Typically, demand forecasts used in design of terminal facilities are estimated in three stages: (1) the overall travel magnitude and growth for the market of interest is estimated; (2) the market share that can be expected to be attracted to the facility under study is determined as a fraction of total demand; and (3) the peak period demand is estimated and expressed typically as a rate of flow for passengers, vehicles, and units of goods movement per unit of time.

Specifics of the demand projection methodologies are described in other chapters of this handbook and in the technical literature for the respective modes (e.g., Chapter 12, "Urban Transportation Studies," concerning overall area transportation needs; Chapter 7, "Planning Approach to Capacity," including links and nodes as intersections or interchanges; Chapter 13, "Urban Transit," covering links and nodes as stops or stations; Chapter 14, "Parking;" and other chapters). In each case there are some common types of demand data that need to be projected, for the short-term and for the long-term:

---

[1] *Highway Capacity Manual* (Washington, D.C.: Transportation Research Board, 1994).

[2] John J. Fruin and Gregory P. Benz, *Pedestrian Time-Space Concept for Analyzing Corners and Crosswalks* (Washington, D.C.: Transportation Research Board, Transportation Research Record 959, 1984).

[3] Gregory P. Benz, *Pedestrian Time-Space Concept* (Parsons Brinckerhoff Quade & Douglas, Inc., January 1986).

- Overall loading (e.g., passengers, tons, vehicles).

- "Type" of loadings (e.g., cars, trucks, buses; commuters, shoppers; frequent vs. occasional users).

- Time period volumes (e.g., annual, daily, peak period, peak hour).

- Reliability and predictability of flows.

Such estimates, where possible, need to be based on current usage data (from up-to-date surveys). The planner needs to not only assess the present patterns but also market the trends and future industry economic and technical developments, land use changes, and so on. Examples include the freight industry with its rapidly increasing intermodal linkages and highway interchange planning, where land use changes can make an adequate plan obsolete very quickly.

Finally, there should be a process in place for periodic updating of needs estimates. This process would not only update field traffic counts but would also look deeper to try to anticipate and respond to market forces. In today's fast-changing and highly competitive business environment, this requires looking beyond the immediate mode or industry to the overall market. Intercity bus and rail carriers, for example, need to be constantly assessing the short-distance air travel industry to see how their market is changing and will be changing.

Terminal Design[B]

Having discussed terminal planning concepts, planning studies for terminals, and demand estimation for terminals, it is appropriate now to review the principles of actually developing and evaluating functional layouts and physical designs for terminals. This section is meant only as a general review of how one should approach this task and what elements need to be considered; it serves as an introduction to the specifics presented later in this chapter for each of the passenger and freight modes. The layout and design process will be illustrated by an example of what is commonly done for a transit station or terminal.

Design Parameters and Guidelines

This would include factors necessary to create an environment suitable for processing passengers within the terminal. Passenger circulation requirements would be assessed to allow sizing of components. This encompasses (as applicable) the following: stairways, ramps, passageways; escalators and elevators; platforms; fare and exit control; moving walkways; bus and rail facilities; and parking facilities.

Of particular importance in the design of U.S. terminal facilities is the need for compliance with the Americans with Disabilities Act (ADA) of 1990. This law requires that all public facilities be accessible to persons with a variety of impairments, including vision, hearing, and mobility. ADA has fundamentally altered the approach to terminal design. While ADA requirements are not international standards, there is a recognition that accommodations for disabled individuals are a growing need; and their incorporation can improve the usefulness of terminals for all users.

Evacuation of transportation terminals in the event of a fire or other emergency must also be addressed during the design phase. For example, the National Fire Protection Association (NFPA) has developed the NFPA 130 Standard for Fixed Guideway Transit Systems, which specifies exit capacities, minimum widths for exit passageways, maximum evacuation times, and maximum distances for travel to an exit. Although the NFPA standards are widely accepted, local building codes may take precedence. Consequently, designers of intermodal passenger facilities must have extensive knowledge of applicable codes and standards for the jurisdiction in which each facility is located.

Design of the Station Environment

The station environment is a design objective that is as important as passenger flow and capacity, since this is a key determinant of passenger acceptance and usage. Points to consider are: lighting, ventilation, acoustics, and fire control;

passenger information and graphics; passenger security; commercial activities; and special provisions for the elderly and disabled. There are specific policies and guidelines developed by the Federal Transit Administration and Federal Aviation Administration on this last point that are of particular relevance for passenger terminals. They are focused on eliminating or reducing common concerns, such as: high curbs or steps, long stairways, inaccessible elevators, steep walks, gratings, difficult doors, narrow aisles, wheelchair accommodations, visual and nonvisual aids, and the like.

The Terminal Design Process

Station or terminal design involves the development and evaluation of alternative functional and physical configurations. The process of transit station design involves the testing and evaluation of alternative configurations. Included within the design stages are the following procedures: (1) define the constraints on station location; (2) develop passenger and vehicle flow data by origin, destination, access mode, line, and headway; (3) establish design objectives, criteria, standards, and requirements; (4) prepare alternative station design layouts; (5) evaluate the performance of each design; (6) select the design alternative that best meets the standards and criteria; and (7) iterate the process until an optimal design is determined. Transit station design proceeds after the transportation system plan is developed to the point that the terminal location has been established. A complete transit station design process is summarized in Figure 18–8.

This process is structured so that before transit station designs are investigated in terms of performance and cost, local policy must be established regarding the construction and operation of the facility. Furthermore, some station features may be restricted by their affect on the environment, usually as determined in environmental impact studies required for the transit systems. Other station aspects may be influenced by local Transportation Systems Management (TSM) plans that are directed at providing for short-range transportation needs of urbanized areas. For instance, TSM plans may call for widespread use of low-cost express bus stations or low-cost improvements to subway stations rather than major system changes.

After an acceptable design basis has been established with policy statements and the associated design concepts, detailed alternative designs are tested. At this point the analyst has the option to consider variations in the design relative to the physical environment, passenger orientation aids, safety, and security. Detailed station designs are evaluated in terms of performance and cost. It is in this phase that the available analytical techniques associated with pedestrian flows and orientation, the physical environment, safety, and security are applied to obtain measures of effectiveness. The performance and cost measures obtained are interpreted with an effectiveness model to select the "best" alternative. When the results of the evaluation indicate where design improvements are warranted and feasible, changes are made and new designs are developed. This process is repeated until a specific design is selected. The analytical stages in the design methodology of the transit interface facility are summarized in Figure 18–9.

Life-Cycle Planning[B]

In developing plans for new terminals or for major improvement of existing terminals, it is important to look beyond the initial construction and to consider operating, maintenance, and major capital rehabilitation needs during the projected life of the facility. Maintenance and rehabilitation needs are those economic and other analyses that would be considered for any major capital facility (e.g., structural integrity, design for simple and economical maintenance and cleaning operations, ability to carry out maintenance with minimal impact on facility users). Continuing operational considerations would include (1) security; (2) signing and other information

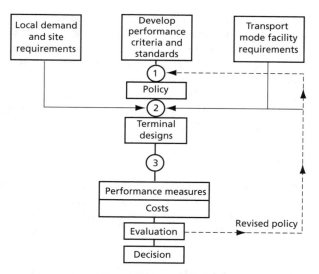

Figure 18–8   Transit Station Design Process

Source: Lester A. Hoel, "Elements of Terminal Design and Planning," Proceedings of the Conference on Multimodal Terminal Planning and Design, Irvine, Calif.: University of California, March 1981.

systems; (3) safety and maintainability of passenger or freight mechanical-assist systems; (4) sensitivity to long-term, day-to-day functional consequences of initial planning for "low first cost;" and (5) ancillary services.

Security

Terminals, particularly passenger terminals need to be planned so that they are well-lighted, inviting, and spacious with lines-of-sight as direct as possible. Even when supplemented by remote surveillance (e.g., television cameras), there should be no hidden corners and other possible real or perceived "trouble spots." This concern is not only related to potential criminal activity, but also to the growing presence of the homeless in terminals, regardless of whether or not any actual problems arise. The *perception* of a threatening or uncomfortable situation has a real effect on passenger usage of modes and their terminals.

Information Systems

Initial signing will need to be continuously reviewed and adjusted, in light of operating experience, to improve any lack of clarity or to reflect new or modified terminal operations. The signing, including electronic information systems, should be designed with this in mind. Flexibility, rather than impressive first impression, should be the watchword. In the BART rail transit system, for example, a major re-signing of all of the stations needed attention only ten years after the opening of the system.

Intelligent Transportation Systems (ITS) technology has led to the implementation of a variety of electronic information systems in terminals. Common devices include: television monitors displaying arrival and departure information; scrolling or stationary variable message signs using Light Emitting Diodes (LEDs), liquid crystal displays, and dot displays that use an array of two-colored dots that flip to form characters and graphics; "Solari" split-flap boards, which use hinged leaf signs that flip through a pre-printed list of message options; and flat screen plasma displays that can display full-motion, full color images. Other devices coming into use are interactive electronic kiosks, which use touch screen menus or audio input to allow users to choose from a library of information.

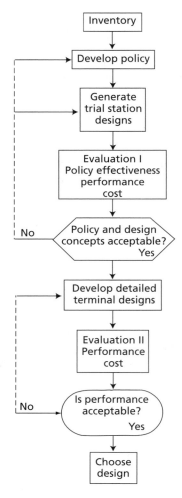

Figure 18–9   Stages in Transit Station Design Methodology

Source: Lester A. Hoel, "Elements of Terminal Design and Planning," Proceedings of the Conference on Multimodal Terminal Planning and Design, Irvine, Calif.: University of California, March 1981.

Terminal planners should consider a variety of factors in deciding on appropriate display devices. Some of these considerations are: locating devices to assure visibility; providing standing and queuing space for passengers to read or interact with devices without obstructing pedestrian flows; the need for protective enclosures for many devices; and the ability to easily change out devices as they become obsolete.

Safety and Maintenance Considerations

Major assist systems (e.g., escalators, elevators, moving sidewalks) need to be designed for minimal life-cycle costs and user impacts. A number of transit systems, for example, incorporate stairways and escalators that are not enclosed from inclement weather conditions. Aside from maintainability considerations, the concourse level of the stations in the landing areas have been found to be prime locations for slip-and-fall accidents during rainy weather.

Day-to-Day User Convenience and Costs

Lower construction costs have been used as justification for terminal systems that may not satisfactorily fulfill user needs. The tendency of planners to make only first cost comparisons in considering terminal design alternatives is a significant problem because human needs are very often subjective and not easily quantified in dollar terms. One such example can be seen in the advocacy of deep transit systems for the purpose of reducing tunneling costs, without considering that because of the deep stations every user may be required to spend several added minutes in the station complex for the life of the system. In the aggregate, the wasted time has a present worth of millions of dollars.

Ancillary Services

Transportation terminals have increasingly become important locations for the provision of ancillary services to commuters and travelers. Commuters face increasing pressures to combine other trip purposes into the daily work trip, especially as the number of workers per household increases. Consequently, commuter terminals are seen as good locations for retail establishments such as cleaners, take out food, banking, and convenience stores. Day care facilities and concierge-type services are also finding locations at or near major commuter terminals. International airports also have experienced an increase in retail sales. Airport shopping has become more prevalent as international business travelers and tourists spend more time at departure airports and enjoy the convenience of taking parcels directly on the plane or checking them through as baggage.

Environmental Impact Analyses[B]

The general principles and techniques for environmental analyses covered in Chapter 8, "Environmental and Energy Considerations," and in other technical literature are the basis for analyses for major terminals. Some typical environmental consideration for terminals are noted below. Environmental analysis needs to include the overall system of which the terminal is a part. The *net* environmental and socioeconomic effect is often beneficial, even though specific effects at the site may require mitigation efforts. Following are some of the key factors.

Legislative Basis

Virtually all new transit and airline terminals constructed in the United States fall within federal requirements of the 1969 National Environmental Protection Act, if federal funds are used in their planning, design, or construction. Legislated environmental requirements of states or of other countries need to be responded to, as appropriate. In most instances, construction or expansion of a transportation terminal will trigger the need for an environmental assessment or an environmental impact statement, either as part of an overall transportation system or as an independent project, depending upon the circumstances. The necessary environmental documentation should be based on a comprehensive program of environmental studies.

The Region and Community

Terminals have many types of regional and community effects. By performing the function of integrating the services of different kinds of regional transportation modes, they increase the utility and efficiency of the total system. The terminal acts as the coordinating and connecting node for the transportation system, maximizing the number of origin and destination trip pairs served by the network.

Land Use and Commercial Activity

Terminals may occupy large areas of land in the case of airports and strategically located urban core space in the case of transit stations and transportation centers. Land use control surrounding a terminal may become necessary to reserve space for terminal expansion or to mitigate community objections to terminal operations.

The potential for adverse effects on local businesses and jobs must be estimated. Land in downtown centers is often prized for commercial development, and its use for transportation should be coordinated with local land use goals and plans. In residential areas, careful attention must be paid to mitigation measures during the design stage. In downtowns, mitigation can include incorporation of commercial space in the terminal complex or provision for commercial air-rights development in the design. In residential areas, mitigation may include screening and incorporation of amenities that are valued by the local residents.

Socioeconomic Development

Socioeconomic benefits associated with transportation terminals include direct and indirect employment, improvement of transportation accessibility, and provision of a nucleus for some types of commercial development. The potential for generating substantial employment for the skilled and unskilled may be seen at large airports. Almost 40,000 persons, the population equivalent of a small city, are employed at New York's John F. Kennedy International Airport.

The mobility afforded by a good regional transportation network with well-planned interchange capabilities has many intangible economic benefits that are difficult to quantify. Public transit systems with wide route coverage and service provide many opportunities, including a wider selection of employment possibilities; access to cultural, educational, recreational, and entertainment facilities; increased retail and wholesale market exposure; and the better general health and community attitudes associated with a viable economy and environment.

Noise and Vibration

Noise of vehicle operations and other associated sources, such as public address systems and mechanical equipment, can constitute a significant environmental effect on proposed transportation terminals. Ambient noise measurements and modeling of future noise impacts are likely requirements for most proposed terminals. The location of existing noise and vibration in sensitive areas (e.g., residential areas, parks, hospitals, schools) must be mapped with respect to the "noise footprint" of the proposed facility. Increasing the distance to these sensitive receptors from sources is the simplest method of reducing the effects. Enclosures, mufflers, and noise barriers also can be used to mitigate noise impacts.

Transportation Systems Impact

Although terminals may have some detrimental site-specific environmental effects because of the nature of their operations, the efficiencies of consolidation can produce environmental benefits by reducing vehicle miles traveled (VMT). Additionally, strategic location of terminals can result in a beneficial restructuring of transport routes, improving system efficiency and shifting operations away from environmentally sensitive areas.

Regarding site-specific aspects, virtually all transportation terminals are generators of significant road traffic. Environmental impacts may be created when the traffic generated by the proposed terminal strains the capacity of the existing roadway system. Passenger transportation facilities that incorporate large parking areas and facilities that generate large numbers of truck trips will require special attention. A traffic impact study will be a requirement for most major terminal design projects.

Visual and Aesthetic Conditions

The size and scope of terminal activities must be continuously considered in the aesthetic evaluation of the site. Special care must be taken to ensure that existing views are preserved, and that the terminal design does not conflict with the scale and architectural character of the surrounding built environment. Screening and noise barriers should not be visually intrusive and should be in keeping with the existing environment.

Modal Ground Transportation Terminals

Streets and Highways

Within the street and highway system there are several classes of facilities (i.e., intersections, interchanges, parking) that provide terminal or interface functions, though they may not be explicitly called "terminals." *Intersections* and *interchanges* are the "nodes" that connect and interconnect all the individual street and highway segments of the system. The intersections and interchanges are usually the critical elements in assuring adequate capacity, minimizing delays, maximizing safety, and minimizing environmental impacts.

The degree to which intersections and interchanges will satisfactorily carry out their functions is related to their geometric design (in the first instance) and to their operational adequacy (on a continuing basis). Appropriate geometric and operational analyses are described in this handbook and in other transportation references.

Parking Facilities

On-street and off-street parking facilities provide the vehicle storage elements needed to allow the street and highway system to function efficiently and conveniently. Conceptually, parking elements (i.e., on-street spaces, off-street lots, multilevel garages) can be thought of as either "publicly available" or "associated." In the first case, any vehicle operator can use the facility, while in the second instance the parking is available only to those using an associated land use (e.g., a shopping center, a department store, an airport). Either type, "publicly available" or "associated parking," can be owned and operated by public agencies or by private companies. The principles of planning and designing the functional elements of parking facilities are covered in Chapter 14, "Parking," and in other references.

With the increasing use of and need for higher-occupancy modes, facilitation of transit and other ridesharing modes is an important technique. "Park-ride" parking (for rail and bus transit) and "pool-park" parking (for use by carpoolers and vanpoolers) need to be provided at well-located points in the street and highway system. These would be planned using some of the principles for transit park-rides (discussed later in this chapter) and general parking location and layout guidelines (discussed in Chapter 14, "Parking").

Commuter parking facilities can use a variety of payment systems, and they must be designed to accommodate appropriate systems. Because of the regularity with which they are used, some facilities can use prepaid permits that eliminate daily payment transactions and reduce operating costs. Such permit-payment lots can be designed with many access points and no barriers. Alternatively, as transportation systems are desired to become more "seamless," there is often a desire to use a single fare instrument for all modes of transportation, such as an electronic fare card. Access to such lots may require channeling all cars past a card reading device linked to a moveable gate or barrier. Access to controlled parking facilities can also use electronic transponders or "tags" mounted on the vehicles.

Commuter parking facilities also function in ways that may require special treatment from designers. Facilities that are served by rail transit systems may have surge loads of afternoon peak commuters alighting from trains at frequent intervals. Such loads may place large numbers of pedestrians in the lot coincident with large exiting volumes of vehicles. In addition, parking facility flows may conflict with "kiss-and-ride" pickup vehicle queues and flows. Coupled with the fact that in many locations, for most of the year, either one or both peak periods occur in darkness, surge loads of commuters rushing to and from trains require the designer to carefully consider safe movement of pedestrians through the facility.

Bus Terminals

The term "bus terminals" is interpreted broadly here, covering the simplest interface, a simple bus stop on a local street; and ranging through bus stops on freeways downtown, bus terminals, outlying off-street bus terminals, and park-and-ride facilities. It also includes downtown "bus streets" that can be an extended form of bus interface.

Bus Stops (On Streets)[C]

Planning of bus stops in a street system involves spacings and locations. As a compromise between shorter access to close stops and the higher operating speed of lines with sparse stops, the *spacings* of bus stops should be inversely related to the ratio of passenger origins and destinations to volume of passengers traveling through an area. Stop spacings should be such that, on the average, buses stop at distances of 400 to 600 m, in exceptional cases somewhat closer. In a number of U.S. cities, shorter spacings, as little as 150 m, are used in downtowns and other densely developed areas. This short spacing is not efficient and can degrade service quality (e.g., speed, comfort). The choice of stop spacings in many cases represents a blending of economic and technical factors and local policies and experiences.

There are three types of *locations* for bus stops along streets: near-side at an intersection before crossing the cross street; far-side at an intersection before crossing the cross street; and midblock, away from intersections. (Figure 18–10.) Since several different factors influence the choice of locations, variations among stop locations along a street, particularly near-side and far-side, can often bring considerable advantages in terms of higher bus speeds and passenger comfort. Major factors influencing the choice of stop locations are: traffic signal coordination, passenger access including transfers from other routes, vehicular and pedestrian traffic conditions at intersections, and geometry of bus turning and stopping. Each of the three bus stop location types has associated desired dimensions. Figure 18–11 shows each type of location and the associated dimensions.[4]

Bus Stops (On Freeways)[D]

Express buses often require intermediate stops on freeways to receive and discharge passengers. Although these stops may reduce bus operating speeds, they are essential to provide desired service levels and optimize bus patronage. Stops within interchange areas can be provided more easily and at lower cost if they are included in the original freeway design.

The location of freeway bus stops will be influenced by (1) density of population in the adjacent tributary area; (2) pedestrian, car, and bus access for potential transit users; (3) growth possibilities and estimates of prospective riders; (4) nearby generators such as hospitals and universities; (5) major intersecting transfer routes; and (6) major outlying parking areas. The stops can be developed at street level or at freeway level. Street level stops are generally more convenient for bus passengers since they do not have to change levels to access the bus. Freeway level stops are generally preferred by bus operators, because there is minimal time lost as a result of exiting and re-entering the freeway. Street level stops are usually preferable in urban areas, because they provide the most convenient access for passengers and require no special geometrics at freeway level; but there are specific circumstances where freeway level may work out better.

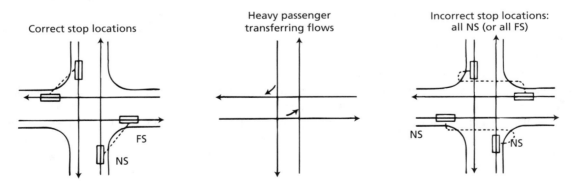

Figure 18–10   Impact of Bus Stop Locations on Convenience of Passenger Transfers Between Intersecting Routes

Source: Vukan R. Vuchic, *Urban Public Transportation Systems and Technology*, Prentice Hall, 1981.

---

[4] These bus stop dimensions are drawn from *Guidelines for the Location and Design of Bus Stops*, TCRP Report 19 (Washington, D.C.: Transportation Research Board, 1996).

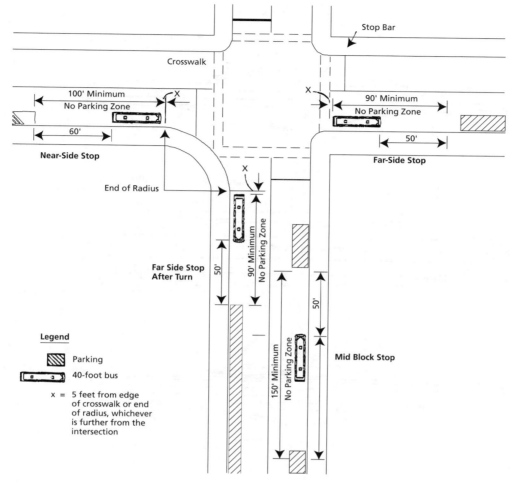

Notes:
1. Add 20 feet to bus stop zones for an articulated bus.

2. Increase bus stop zone by 50 feet for each additional standard 40-foot bus or 70 feet for each additional 60-foot articulated bus expected to be at the stop simultaneously.

Figure 18–11   Bus Stop Locations and Dimensions

Source: *Guidelines for the Location and Design of Bus Stops,* TCRP Report 19, Washington, D.C.: Transportation Research Board, 1996.

Street-level bus stops may be appropriate as a first stage of ultimate construction of more elaborate facilities at freeway level. Freeway-related bus stops should be located to minimize conflicts between buses, general traffic, and pedestrians. (Figure 18–12.) More specific planning and geometric guidelines are included in Chapter 5, "Transportation Planning Studies."

Off-Street Bus Terminals and Park-Ride Facilities[D]

Bus terminal and park-ride facilities serve at least two important functions: (1) They provide off-street downtown distribution for radial express bus operations, and (2) they help intercept motorists and local buses in outlying areas and facilitate passenger transfer to express transit lines. Terminals and park-rides can also be used to facilitate interchange among suburban-oriented bus and rail services and to aid in increasing usage of ridesharing modes (e.g., carpools, vanpools).

Terminal planning, location, and design embodies basic traffic circulation, transit operations, and site planning principles. Relevant factors include (1) line-haul transit routes (e.g., rail and bus); (2) passenger interchange needs; (3) passenger arrival and departure patterns; (4) bus distribution opportunities and constraints within the city center; and (5) land requirements, availability, impacts, and costs.

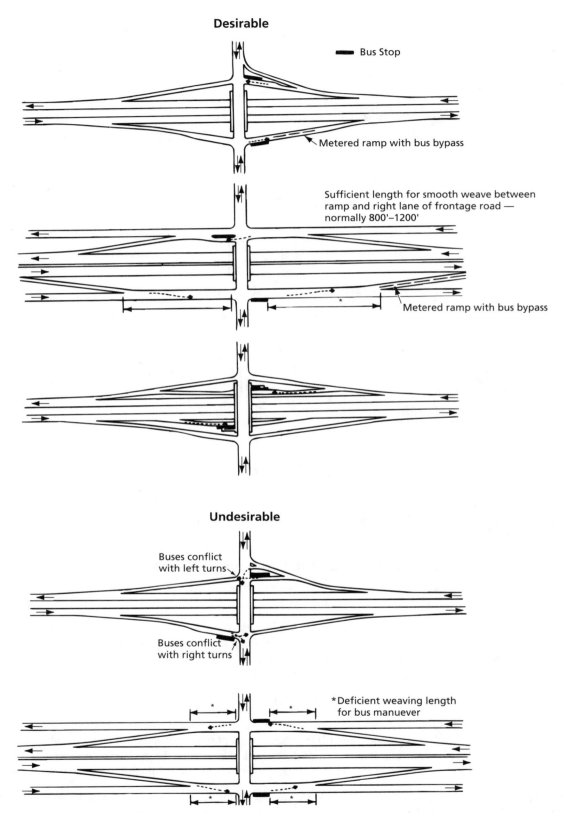

Figure 18–12   Freeway Bus Stop Concepts, Diamond Interchange

Source: *NCHRP Report #155,* "Bus Use of Highways," Washington, D.C.: Transportation Research Board, 1975.

Terminals in medium-sized communities will usually be part of "transportation centers" in which intercity bus services and parking facilities are the principal components, or they represent strategically located outlying parking lots serving express bus lines. Figure 18–13 shows plans for typical off-street bus stations suitable for bus terminals in most medium-sized transit service areas.

Central area terminals consolidate bus operations at a single location, facilitate passenger interchange between bus lines, reduce bus journey times, and improve general traffic flow. Terminals are essential to express bus operations where other bus priority measures are not feasible. They make it possible to achieve high bus volumes on expressways, across bridges, and in tunnels by providing off-street loading for large concentrations of buses. In conjunction with special bus ramps and bus roadways, they attain grade-separated bus operations in congested centers; and they provide an option to downtown busway development. One-point delivery in the downtown area usually requires secondary distribution by

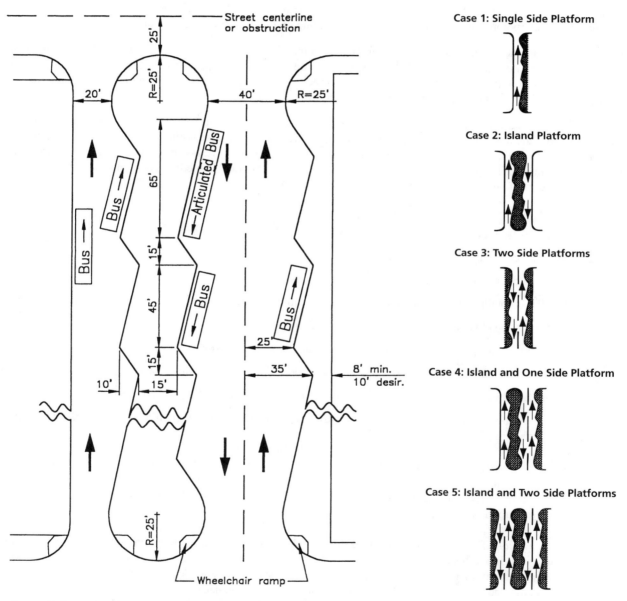

Figure 18–13   Typical Bus Station Plan, Medium-Sized Transit Service Area

Source: *Designing for Transit,* San Diego, Calif.: Metropolitan Transit Development Board, 1993.

local bus or rapid transit. Central terminals are often linked with successful freeway bus service, such as the Port Authority Bus Terminal (New York City), served by the Route 495 exclusive bus lane on the New Jersey approach to the Lincoln Tunnel; and the El Monte Bus Terminal (California), served by the bus/HOV lanes on the San Bernardino Freeway. The AC Transit Transbay Terminal in San Francisco is another major central area bus terminal.

Terminals range from single-level facilities that serve intercity buses and offer minimum passenger amenities, to large multilevel transportation centers that serve several modes and contain supporting land uses. Downtown off-street bus terminals should be considered wherever the attendant service improvements and development potentials exceed the costs involved. They are appropriate where (1) downtown curb loading capacity is limited; (2) large volumes of express buses aggregate; and (3) on-street bus routing is slow, unattractive, unreliable, and cannot be improved through bus priority measures.

Locations of existing and proposed central business district (CBD) bus terminals provide important locational guidelines. The terminals (1) provide direct connections to expressways, (2) are located between the expressways and the CBD core, (3) are removed from points of peak land value, and (4) are within a few blocks of major employment centers. These terminals may incorporate air rights developments, depending on the commercial potential of the location.

Terminal planning should include detailed estimates of demand, capacity, revenues, and costs. The design should allow for expansion of capacity, including adaptability to new bus sizes, types, and technologies. Revenues from ancillary land development and consumer services are especially important in conjunction with terminal facilities that mainly provide downtown distribution for urban express bus services.

Bus terminal type, size, and design should reflect specific passenger, bus service, and traffic access requirements. Relevant factors include: (1) passenger traffic volumes, arrival modes, and peaking patterns; (2) bus volumes and operating practices including fare collection, service frequency, loading patterns, layover times, reservoir requirements; and (3) access linkages to surrounding roads and streets. Desirable functional objectives are identified in Figure 18–14 for a "typical" central bus terminal. They include:

1. Grade separated bus entry and exit.

2. Direct pedestrian connections to other modes.

3. Separate commuter and intercity bus levels.

4. Separate commuter bus loading and unloading areas.

5. Parallel unloading areas with passing lanes for commuter buses.

6. Commuter bus loading areas in shallow sawtooth platforms.

7. Sawtooth loading-unloading platforms with passing lanes for intercity service.

8. Platform size adequate for accommodating the projected number of waiting passengers.

9. Air-rights development of commercial uses (including accessory parking), if commercially feasible.

Bus dimensions and maneuverability influence roadway widths, platform shapes, column spacing, ceiling heights, and other design aspects as follows:

1. *Bus lane widths.* Buses require additional clearance for mirrors, which can typically add 1.5 ft (0.46 m) to the total width required for the vehicle. Consequently, an 8.5 ft (2.6 m) wide bus can require 10.0 ft (3.1 m) of horizontal clearance. Eleven-foot lanes are preferable where ample terminal space is available and therefore are the minimum width for 8.5 ft wide buses.

2. *Runway width.* Double-width or two-lane runways should be provided wherever possible. They allow passing and overtaking of buses and provide temporary storage. Unloading bus roadways should be two lanes wide to enable empty or lightly loaded buses to proceed past a heavily loaded bus. This is essential where the unloading roadway is also the only terminal entrance road. Double-lane roadways should be at least 22 ft wide for overtaking buses parked close to the curb; a 24 ft width is preferable, especially where bus maneuvering distances are limited.

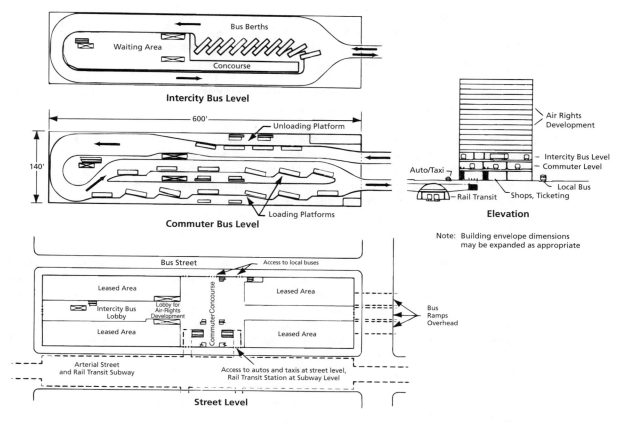

Figure 18–14   Typical CBD Bus Terminal Design, Large City

Source: *NCHRP Report #155*, "Bus Use of Highways," Washington, D.C.: Transportation Research Board, 1975.

3. *Additional clearances and widths.* Width and radii of driveway entrances and exits to runways should permit equipment to operate without extremely sharp turns.

4. *Ramping.* Ramp grades to and from street roadways (or busway connections) should be set to avoid rough treatment of equipment and passengers, particularly when buses are heavily loaded.

5. *Headroom and side clearance.* Adequate headroom and side clearance must be provided where buses enter terminal buildings and other structures. Minimum side clearance to all structures along the roadway should be at least 1 ft. Vertical clearance should be at least 12 ft for typical equipment. Special allowance should be made for use of terminals by deck-and-a-half or double-deck buses.

Design and arrangement of bus loading platforms should be scaled to specific capacity and operational requirements, as follows:

1. *Separate intercity and commuter services.* The two types of bus operation have differing service characteristics and platform design requirements, as follows:

  a. Intercity buses have long layover times to allow for passenger loading, unloading, baggage, and parcels. Closely stacked sawtooth platforms should be provided. They allow greater passenger amenity because they can be readily enclosed and climate controlled.

b.   Commuter buses need higher peak-hour capacities. Passenger unloading and loading areas should be clearly separated to minimize passenger conflicts and reduce dwell times. Accordingly, terminals should use linear or shallow sawtooth loading platforms that allow several buses to queue at the same platform and also allow pull-through bus movements.

2.   *Berth requirements.* Berth space requirements should use queuing theory and simulation analysis, taking into account projected passenger volumes and loading times.

3.   *Unloading platforms.* Unloading platform length should reflect (a) the number of berths required to accommodate peak unloading passenger volume and (b) bus pull-in, pull-out, and tail-out characteristics. Where a considerable number of empty buses enter a terminal with need to stop at the unloading platform, a separate lane protected from the unloading runway by a physical divider should be provided. Another important factor is whether or not buses are allowed to stand or layover empty at the unloading platform as a holding area in lieu of proceeding to (a) the loading platform, (b) a separate holding area, or (c) directly out of the terminal. Such layovers generally should not be permitted except for small-scale operations.

4.   *Loading platforms.* Loading platform space and arrangement is generally the most critical feature in terminal operation. Separate loading spaces for different main routes or destinations should be provided. Where several bus routes are involved the number of routes or different-types services assigned to one platform should be held to the lowest possible minimum—preferably not more than two or three. Loading platform widths for simple operations may be as narrow as 8 ft; however, platforms requiring substantial queuing of accumulated passengers and involving considerable circulation should be at least 12 ft wide. For sawtooth positions, loading platforms parallel to the bus door should be at least 5 ft wide. In layouts where passengers for different routes must circulate past each other, the platform space may need to be increased.

5.   *Loading queues.* Queuing is necessary for most rush-hour conditions to (1) avoid crowding and disorder and (2) minimize use of available space.

6.   *Passenger platforms.* Loading and unloading spaces and bus lanes may form one continuous flat surface for low-cost or temporary terminal layouts. For permanent installations, passenger loading platforms should be raised. Passengers should be protected from buses in multilane terminals by means of a guard railing fencing along the back edge adjacent to the next vehicle lane.

7.   *Platform shelters.* Canopy-type shelters over loading areas on open lots are important for patron convenience and protection. Canopies should extend over the roof of buses, for increased weather protection.

8.   *Vertical access.* Vertical access should be provided by stairways, ramps, and escalators in multilevel terminals. Elevator access should also be provided to accommodate wheel chair users. (Refer to the general ADA requirements described in another section of this chapter.) Location at one end of a platform usually minimizes obstruction, particularly if the platform is relatively narrow. Expanded circulation areas are needed at vertical access points to maintain passenger throughput.

9.   *Other facilities.* Intercity bus terminals and large commuter terminals should provide ancillary passenger and bus service facilities. Passenger concourses should be enclosed, well-lit, and climate-controlled. Restaurants, newsstands, stores, dispatchers' offices, and restrooms should be provided. Revenue from consumer services can be quite significant in helping to cover the capital and operating costs of the terminal.

Outlying mode transfer terminals form the interface between line-haul transit and neighborhood collection functions. They are usually found (1) along outlying rapid transit stations, (2) at ends of rapid transit lines, (3) at interchange points between major highway and rail lines, and (4) along express bus lines. They recognize the need for auto and local bus connection to express transit from areas where population densities are too low to rely on walk-in patronage. Parking at outlying express transit stations allows automobiles to serve areas in which it is not economical to operate local bus service. The proportions of park-and-ride and kiss-and-ride passengers increase with distance from the city center.

Outlying transfer facilities should be developed at a smaller scale than downtown terminals. Designs should be simple, ancillary facilities should be kept to a minimum, and relatively few bus bays should serve heavy peak-hour loads. Direct pedestrian access should be provided to major nearby generators such as office buildings, shops, and apartments. With the considerable variation of conditions for outlying transfer terminals it is not really possible to outline a "typical" layout. Application of appropriate transportation planning and engineering principles will produce the designs most suitable for a particular situation. The three designs described below will illustrate the application of these principles in several "outlying" transfer combinations. (Figures 18–15, 18–16, 18–17.)

1. *Arterial street bus-rail interchange.* (Figure 18–15.) The most common type of modal interchange involves bus turnouts on arterial streets that cross express transit lines. Turnouts are located adjacent to station entrance and exit points. A median island with a fence may be desirable to preclude midblock pedestrian crossings.

2. *Busway-local bus interchange.* (Figure 18–16.) Local buses circulate in a clockwise pattern crossing the busway at a signalized intersection. Direct platform access is provided to and from the major travel direction. The at-grade bus intersection provides opportunity for entry into the busway and direct expressway service to downtown.

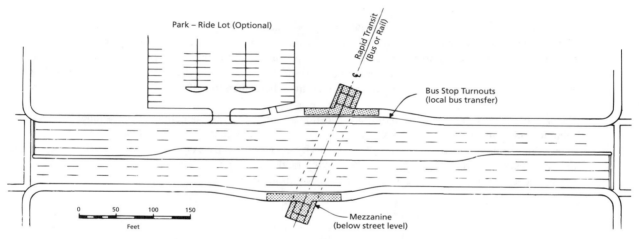

Figure 18–15   Typical Arterial Street Bus-Rail Interchange

Source: *NCHRP Report #155,* "Bus Use of Highways," Washington, D.C.: Transportation Research Board, 1975, p. 696.

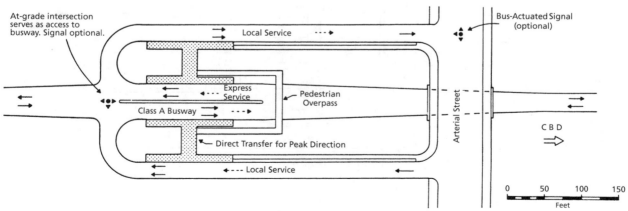

Figure 18–16   Typical Express-Local Bus Interchange

Source: *NCHRP Report #155,* "Bus Use of Highways," Washington, D.C.: Transportation Research Board, 1975.

3. *Typical bus terminal within freeway interchange.* (Figure 18–17.) A single bus bridge in conjunction with a pair of new bus runways adjacent to frontage roads alongside a depressed freeway provides direct access for arterial and freeway buses. Buses circulate clockwise around a central express transit station. Special bus-actuated traffic signals allow bus entry and exit from adjacent arterial streets. Where a secondary street bridge across the freeway is located within 500 ft of the arterial overcrossing, it may be used in lieu of the special bus bridge.

Park-and-ride facilities are part of a strategy designed to intercept automobiles at outlying locations along express transit lines and are also used as key elements of programs to encourage ridesharing. They are essential at all express transit stations in outlying areas, especially where population densities are too low to support suburban bus services. They permit principal portions of downtown trips to be made by public transport without reducing passenger convenience or increasing walking distances. Outlying parking facilities are provided in major cities with rail transit and along express bus routes. Individual facilities can range upward to 2,000 spaces with lots in the 100 to 300 space range common.

The optimum distance of intercept parking points from the city center depends on (1) locations of major topographic barriers as they relate to the center city, (2) street convergence patterns, (3) line-haul express transit system configuration, (4) land development intensities, (5) land availability and costs, and (6) parking costs. Other factors to be considered include:

1. *Road access.* Park-and-ride facilities should have good highway access and should intercept motorists prior to points of major route convergence and congestion. Facilities should be located as far from downtown as practical to remove the maximum number of VMT during the peak traffic period. It is clearly preferable, from an efficiency and environmental perspective, to have "farther-out" park-rides. It may be necessary, however, to locate them "closer-in" where there can be more frequent transit service and where, therefore, they may attract the greatest usage.

2. *Bus service.* Express bus travel from the park-and-ride station to the CBD or activity center should be quick and reliable, either in mixed traffic, in an exclusive lane, or on an exclusive bus roadway. The last stop of an express bus route inbound toward the CBD or activity center is usually a desirable location. Efficiency in bus operations is obtained by filling buses at the parking facility and running them nonstop to the terminal. At the same time, commuter travel times are minimized by eliminating intermediate stops.

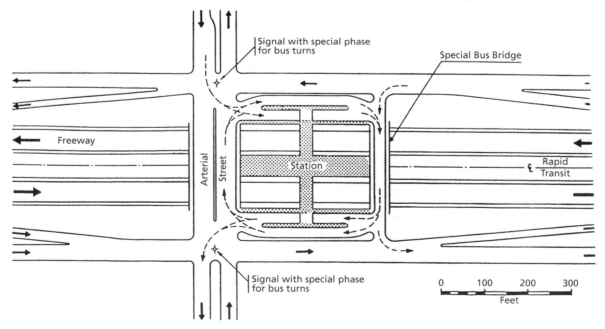

Figure 18–17 Typical Outlying Bus Terminal Within Freeway Right-of-Way

Source: *NCHRP Report #155*, "Bus Use of Highways," Washington, D.C.: Transportation Research Board, 1975.

3. *Land availability and use.* Sites should be compatible with adjacent land uses, should not adversely affect nearby environments, and should achieve a reasonable level of use relative to development costs. Development costs and environmental effects can sometimes be minimized by "joint use" (i.e., existing parking facilities in shopping or recreation centers) because peak use at these centers normally does not coincide with commuter peaks.

Outlying parking potentials should clearly recognize (1) CBD growth patterns, (2) constraints to increasing CBD parking supply, and (3) extension of express transit services into auto-oriented areas. Some factors requiring attention are:

1. *Demand estimates.* One approach involves estimating the patronage of express transit extensions (or service improvements). Multimodal choice models can be used to estimate parking demands related to major express transit service.

2. *Facility size.* Parking capacities should be scaled to approach roadway capacities as well as to parking demand and bus service potentials.

3. *Parking availability.* The design load factor at each park-and-ride facility (i.e., the number of autos simultaneously parked divided by the number of spaces) should not exceed 80 to 90 percent. This will assure commuters a reasonable chance of finding a parking space. If there is not an available community-acceptable "back up" space on nearby local streets, the design load factor should not exceed 70 to 80 percent.

Examples of park-and-ride lots at a rapid transit station (rail or bus) and at a highway interchange are shown in Figures 18–18 and 18–19.

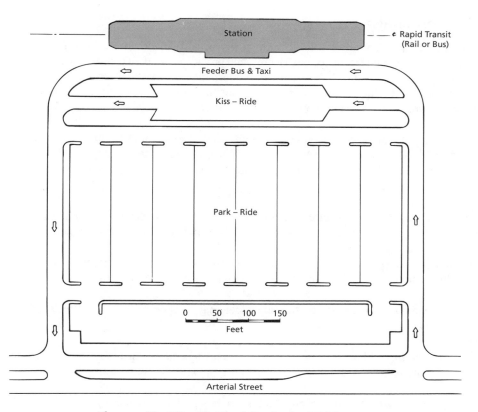

Figure 18–18 Typical Park-and-Ride Lot

Source: *NCHRP Report #155,* "Bus Use of Highways," Washington, D.C.: Transportation Research Board, 1975.

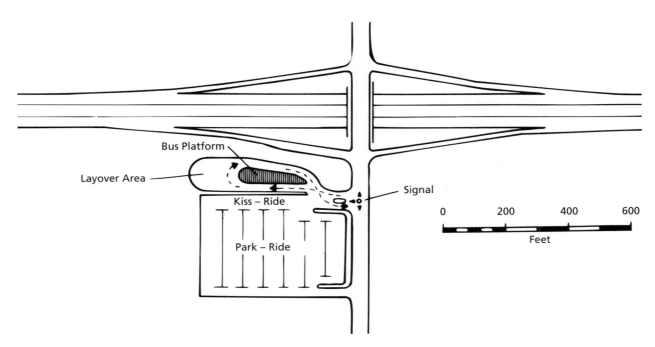

Figure 18–19   Typical Freeway Park-and-Ride Lot at Diamond Interchange

Source: *NCHRP Report #155,* "Bus Use of Highways," Washington, D.C.: Transportation Research Board, 1975.

On-Street Bus Terminals[D]

Bus streets represent a major commitment to downtown transit and development. They fully separate bus and car traffic, increase bus service reliability, enhance bus identity, and provide downtown distribution for regional express routes. For certain ranges of passenger volume, they can be an alternative to off-street terminals. In some cases, as noted below, they can be combined with off-street terminals. They enhance pedestrian access and, when accompanied by amenities, can improve the downtown environment.

Bus streets and auto-free zones incorporate environmental planning considerations combined with bus flow requirements. Examples include Nicollet Mall in downtown Minneapolis, Minnesota; the 16th Street Mall in Denver, Colorado; and the Fulton Street Mall in Brooklyn, New York. Short sections of bus streets are found also in several English and European cities.

Bus streets provide an early-action cost-effective downtown option for distribution to busways, freeways, bridges, tunnels, and transportation centers. Five typical applications are shown in Figure 18–20, namely:

1. *Terminal approach (bus street).* Exclusive bus access can be provided adjacent to a downtown bus terminal and on links connecting the terminal to express highways or busways.

2. *Bus loop.* A series of bus-only streets forming a loop may be appropriate where streets terminate and extended bus layovers are required.

3. *Short connector links.* Short sections of bus-only roadways may be desirable to achieve direct service where street continuity is limited and bus service over arterial streets is circuitous and slow.

4. *Bus-pedestrian mall.* Downtown bus streets (or bus malls)—as incorporated in urban redevelopment projects—provide direct bus access to major generators. They are designed to simultaneously improve pedestrian amenity and bus access. Bus malls could operate throughout the day or be limited to peak hours. Taxis and, during off-peak periods, service vehicles can use bus streets.

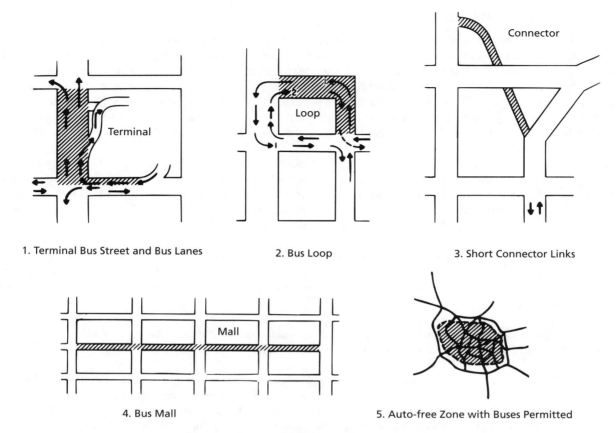

1. Terminal Bus Street and Bus Lanes

2. Bus Loop

3. Short Connector Links

4. Bus Mall

5. Auto-free Zone with Buses Permitted

Figure 18–20   Bus Street Concepts

Source: *NCHRP Report #155,* "Bus Use of Highways," Washington, D.C.: Transportation Research Board, 1975.

5. *Auto-free zone.* The elimination of automobiles from major portions of downtown areas is common in European cities with narrow, discontinuous, highly convergent street patterns. Buses are allowed to traverse the auto-free precincts to maintain route continuity and serve major activities.

Additional environmental considerations include:

* The nature, extent, and operating periods of bus streets should be adjusted to allow for essential services. One variant might be to allow local car access in bus lanes but prohibit through-traffic (as in some crosstown bus streets in New York City). Alternatively, midblock access bays could be provided for off-peak goods delivery.

* Traffic capacities of parallel streets should be increased to accommodate displaced traffic. This may entail additional one-way routings as well as further restriction of curb parking.

* Turns off of the bus street by buses, taxis, and service vehicles should be prohibited in the core area. This will permit conflict-free pedestrian crossings at intersections, and two-phase signal operations.

* Planting, kiosks, bus shelters and waiting areas should be located along the bus street. Consideration should be given to eliminating surface parking lots, especially where they can be served from other streets.

Summary (Bus Terminals)

The various types of bus terminals and interfaces described previously share a common objective, to provide an efficient, appropriate plan for the design volumes, consistent with community goals. Particularly for the more complex, higher volume situations there is no one "right" solution, even when anticipated passenger and vehicular volumes are relatively high. There are usually several potentially feasible schemes (i.e., on-street, off-street) or combinations of schemes. The planning *process* is very well illustrated by studies for a major express bus terminal in Phoenix, Arizona.[5] The Phoenix study, in the late 1980s, involved the planning of an interface between express buses on the proposed depressed I-10 Freeway and shuttle buses on the intersecting Central Avenue arterial. The two routes were to cross within a proposed 30-acre Deck Park.

The design of I-10 and the Deck Park created both opportunities and constraints. At the crossing of Central Avenue and I-10, the freeway was to be enclosed in a cut-and-cover tunnel, with the Deck Park extending one-fourth mile both to the east and to the west. Central Avenue would bridge the Deck Park to allow uninterrupted pedestrian movement in the park from one side to the other. This would place the shuttle buses on the bridge two levels above the express buses on the freeway, with an urban park between. Several alternatives were considered.

- *Bus mall on the freeway deck.* The first alternative was to build a busway across the top of the deck. Express bus passengers would ride escalators to the shuttle buses on the Central Avenue bridge. However bus operations through the Deck Park were deemed inconsistent with the purpose of the park. Consequently, this alternative was rejected.

- *A bus street north or south of the Deck Park.* A second option was to build a bus street north or south of the Park. No feasible location was found for an east to west bus street.

- *Bus on existing streets.* A bus loop could be established with buses exiting the freeway on the HOV ramps and traveling along local streets. Flexibility in operating buses would be attained, since buses could either continue around the loop and exit the way they came, turn north or south on Central Avenue, or continue back on the freeway in the direction they were headed. However, when bus operations exceed thirty buses per hour in each direction, buses would add significantly to congestion. In addition, buses lose the time advantage gained from HOV lanes on the freeway by operating on congested surface streets. Also, one-way bus loops are confusing to riders, who must board at a different location than they debark.

- *Median bus station.* A bus station could be placed in the median of I-10 under the Deck, as shown on Figure 18–21. Riders could walk through the deck park to nearby employment, or transfer onto buses on Central Avenue to reach other places in the corridor. Buses would enter and leave the station from separate bus-only ramps to the I-10 HOV lanes. The narrowness of the area posed a significant design challenge. Ventilation, noise, and security concerns would have to be overcome. On the other hand, the median bus transfer had greater

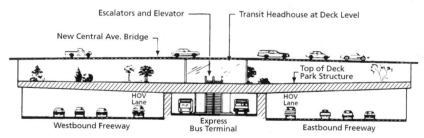

Figure 18–21   I-10 at Central Avenue: Cross-Section View Looking East

Source: Wulf Grote, Ben Martin, and Ken Howell, "I-10/Central Avenue Express Bus Terminal in Phoenix, Arizona," *Compendium of Technical Papers,* Washington, D.C.: ITE, 1987 Annual Meeting.

---

[5] Wulf Grote, Ben Martin, and Ken Howell, "I-10/Central Avenue Express Bus Terminal in Phoenix, Arizona," *Compendium of Technical Papers* (Washington, D.C.: ITE, 1987 Annual Meeting).

bus capacity than the other alternatives, avoided significant express bus operations on congested local streets, and avoided negative impact on the park. In fact, the presence of bus riders transferring in the middle of the park would contribute positively by bringing people into the "urban plaza" portion of the park. Consequently, this alternative was advanced into more detailed project planning.

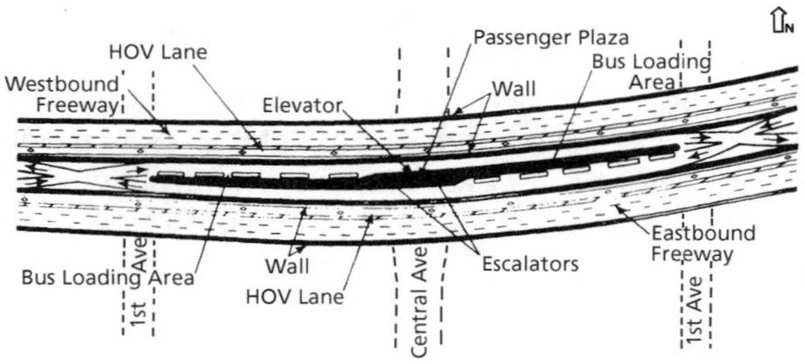

The Phoenix planning process resulted in the development of an innovative, unique design (Figure 18–22) adapted to the technical, social, environmental, and community characteristics of that particular situation.

Figure 18–22   I-10/Central Avenue Express Bus Terminal

Source: Wulf Grote, Ben Martin, and Ken Howell, "I-10/Central Avenue Express Bus Terminal in Phoenix, Arizona," *Compendium of Technical Papers,* Washington, D.C.: ITE, 1987 Annual Meeting.

Changing Technology

The planner of stops, stations, and terminals for buses needs to also recognize *newer "bus" developments* that are relatively recent and will become increasingly important in the coming years. Such developments include: the "tube" stations used as a key element of the surface bus transit system in Curitiba, Brazil; guided, dual-powered buses operating in urban transit systems in several countries; and the introduction of low-floor buses, which facilitate "stepless" boarding.

Curitiba's express bus system is designed as a single entity, rather than as disparate components of buses, stops, and roads. Most urban bus systems require passengers to pay as they board, slowing loading. Curitiba's raised-tube bus stops eliminate this step: passengers pay as they enter the tube, and so the bus spends more of its time actually moving people from place to place. (Figure 18–23.)

Similarly, the city installed wheelchair lifts at bus stops rather than on board buses (Figure 18–23), easing weight restrictions and simplifying maintenance—buses with built-in wheelchair lifts are notoriously trouble-prone, as are those that "kneel" to put their boarding steps within reach of the elderly. The tube-stop lifts also speed boarding by bringing disabled passengers to the proper height before the bus arrives.

Figure 18–23   "Tube" Bus Stop, Curitiba, Brazil

Source: Photo: Martha Welborne.

Guided bus systems have been put into operation in several urban areas, and additional applications are being planned. These systems use mechanical or electronic guidance and some are also dual-powered (e.g., internal combustion, diesel, CNG) or electric (e.g., overhead trolley wire). Examples include the O-Bahn in Essen, Germany and Adelaide, Australia; and other systems in England, France, and Japan.

Low-floor buses are available and have been put into service at a number of transit properties. Figure 18–24 shows an O-Bahn guided, dual-powered bus at a station stop located in a freeway median in Essen, Germany. The low-floor bus shown provides level, stepless entry for transit passengers there.

Truck Terminals[E]

Terminals of all sizes and shapes form key elements of the truck freight transportation systems. While their location and functions are closely related to the public street and highway system, the terminals are largely, if not exclusively, a private-sector function. They are usually owned and operated by the trucking company (carrier) providing the service.

The processes and facilities described in this section are derived from experience in North America. Decisions on the mission, location, and design of terminal facilities should not be made solely on the basis of a single terminal. The planning process should include:

- Developing a system operating plan.

- Defining the terminal's mission.

- Developing the terminal's design.

- Develop a site plan.

Figure 18–24   "O-Bahn" Guideway and Stop, Essen, Germany

Source: "O-Bahn in Theory and Practice," Mercedes-Benz brochure.

System Operating Plan

The system operating plan, based on the business plan, establishes the configuration of the terminals, their locations, and their missions. It also sets the policy on size and type of terminals and may include decision rules as to when a new terminal should be planned. There are relatively few basic concepts for terminal operations, as related to the system. The combinations, however, and the ways in which these concepts can be used are almost unlimited. (Figure 18–25.)

Considerable analysis is needed to quantify the service and cost effectiveness of alternative systems. The calculations may be entirely manual, partially done by computer, or done by constructing a model for computer simulation. Four of the most common system operation alternatives are outlined in Figure 18–25, including:

1. Conventional (major terminal) operation, Figure 18–25(a).

2. Satellite operation, Figure 18–25(b).

3. Cluster concept, Figure 18–25(c).

4. Stand-alone break-bulk, Figure 18–25(d).

Advantages of *conventional (major terminal) operation* include:

- Minimizes rehandling at intermediate break-bulk points.

- Provides direct, noncircuitous line-haul.

Depending upon the nature of the requirements, however, the conventional system has some severe disadvantages and limitations:

- Large terminals generally have higher handling costs than small ones.

- Additional rehandling is often required in setting up combination loads for drops at two or more smaller terminals.

- Small terminal operation is difficult. The systems lack flexibility to provide terminal facilities close to markets, often essential for customer service.

- Inflexibility for adding new areas or adapting to shifts in market demand locations.

- Difficulty in serving small stations contributes to inconsistent customer service.

The advantages of *satellite operation* include:

- Minimizes large terminal problems of productivity and labor. There are fewer people.

- Reduces pickup and delivery stem time. (Stem time is the travel required from the terminal to the general area of pickup and delivery for a defined route.)

- Provides consistent service.

- Is able to achieve market penetration because of proximity to customers.

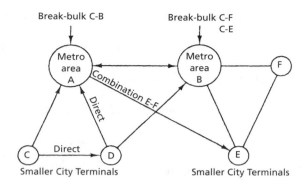

**(a) Major Terminal Operation —
Break-bulk concentrated in centers of the system.**

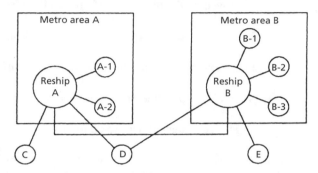

**(b) Satellite Operation —
Rehandle satellite traffic through reship terminal.**

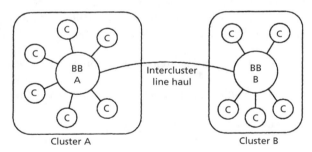

**(c) Cluster Concept — Terminal clusters.
Cluster terminal strip to break-bulk.
Flexibility for adding new areas.**

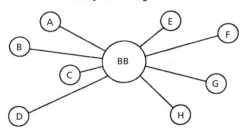

**(d) Stand-Alone Break-Bulk — All traffic, not direct move,
routed to break-bulk terminal.
No local operation at break-bulk terminal.**

**Figure 18–25(a)–(d)   Truck Terminals—
System Operation Alternatives**

Source: American Trucking Association.

- Has improved productivity because both dock and pickup and delivery functions are easier to manage.

- Has flexibility to service changing market demands and new areas.

The satellite concept, however, also has certain disadvantages including:

- Increase in volume of traffic rehandled.

- Additional (fixed) cost of facilities.

The *cluster* is similar to the satellite concept. In fact, the two terms are often used interchangeably. The cluster, however, is generally applicable to long-haul carriers serving a number of regions of the country. The advantages of this system include:

- Improved productivity in platform handling because stop-off loads are avoided.

- Improved load average because system is designed to move full loads on the longer intercluster line-haul.

- Provision for terminals close to markets; saving in stem time and support of customer service.

- Simplification of line-haul, reduction of premium cost of team drivers.

- Highly consistent service to all terminals.

The disadvantages include the need for rehandling and, possibly, some circuity in serving smaller stations through break-bulk. In practice, the carriers have found that there were few disadvantages as compared to the advantages.

The concept of a single *stand-alone break-bulk* terminal was developed by regional carriers, generally short-haul. The objective is to create a single break-bulk facility, central to the system, which will handle all the traffic not moved directly. The advantages of the stand-alone break-bulk include:

- Higher productivity than in conventional system. Specialization and simpler sorting at outbound stations.

- Ability to maintain schedules and consistent service.

- Improved load averages.

- Flexibility to support smaller terminals.

The disadvantages to the concept include:

- Possible difficulty in adding additional break-bulk stations as major acquisitions or expansions are made.

- Certain additional rehandling for local traffic formerly moved with break-bulk to the city terminal.

Terminal Mission (Planning Criteria)

The terminal mission is a definition of the workload that the terminal must accomplish in terms of volumes by type and source of traffic, the service standards that must be maintained, the workload availabilities and closeout times for activities, and information needed to plan the terminal.

Specific location requirements are defined, based on the system operations analysis. The objective is to relate, as specifically as possible, the market characteristics and conditions for the locations where a facility is needed to the overall plan. Finally, prepare an economic evaluation of the facility and its options, and then establish a statement of the detailed requirements for facility design. The steps include a marketing analysis, whose objective is to obtain information concerning the area, the trends in the area, growth or decline by industry, and the locations where industry and commerce are expanding.

Terminal Planning and Design

After developing the terminal mission, the next activity is to plan and design the physical terminal facilities.

1. *Establishing handling system requirements.* The first step is to establish a freight handling system.

    a. Use developed requirements. While developing the terminal mission, the four factors needed for establishing the best handling system have already been developed. These are:

        - The average and peak volume to be handled on both the inbound and outbound operations.

        - Arrival rates from other terminals as well as local pickups.

        - Closeout times by destination point.

        - The time standard established for the shipment cycle between pickup and delivery.

    b. Establish shipment profile. A fifth requirement is the characteristic of the freight to be handled.

    c. Determine number of doors. The last major requirement that significantly influences the handling system is the number of doors. The number of doors is based on the requirement for the peak volume shift, either inbound or outbound.

        - *Loading outbound.* A minimum of one door is required for each separate destination plus additional doors for points having a shipment volume greater than the amount that can be handled through a single door during the shift.

        - *Loading inbound.* The number of inbound loading doors is dependent on the number of destination delivery routes, plus the trucks or trailers used for interline freight or large customers.

        The general rule is that a minimum of one door is needed for each route or delivery location (i.e., large customer or interline).

2. *Evaluate handling system alternates.* The components of a typical handling system are divided into basic and support as follows:

    a. *Basic.* The basic system used in almost all truck terminals is a four-wheel platform cart. The platform is approximately 12 square ft (3 ft by 4 ft) and may be open or have one side on an end enclosed. The major difference is the system to move the cart. In smaller terminals of up to about 65 doors, the carts are manually pulled. In very large terminals (i.e., above 150 doors), a dragline that could be either overhead mounted or in-floor, and either switching or nonswitching, would probably be used.

    b. *Support.* The material handling system that typically supports a cart or dragline system is a fork truck and two-wheel hand trucks.

3. *Establish platform dimensions.* The third determination is to develop the specific dimensions of the terminal platform. This is done in two steps.

    a. Identify terminal operating plan. This plan, based on the handling system, identifies what activities will take place, when they will occur, and also their methods and procedures.

b. Calculate basic space requirements. Based on the basic length and width needs.

- *Length*—the primary determinant of length is the number of doors. Doors are generally set on 10 to 12 ft centers depending on the amount of operating space required at a door. Doors are almost always placed on the two sides of the terminal. Many carriers also place them on one or both ends as well, but leaving sufficient space for an office.

- Width—the width is based primarily on three factors:

    (1) Requirements for staging.

    (2) Requirements for aisles.

    (3) Requirements for operating space.

Typically, as terminal volume and complexity increase, the amount of freight that must be docked increases, but at a faster rate. Therefore, as the number of doors increases, the terminal width also increases.

The major requirement for operating space is in the area surrounding the doors. Space is required for several carts. The typical door-platform width relationship for terminals is shown in Table 18–6.

Terminal Site Planning

The site plan is determined from information developed in planning the terminal mission and is based on the terminal design. The first step is to establish the site specifications, including the general size and configuration of the plot. Next, the search area is defined, alternative sites are evaluated, and the best one is selected. When the specific plot is known, prepare a plan that will make the best use of space and provide for efficient flow.

1. *Prepare site specifications.* The objective is to determine the size of the plot and its minimal dimensions. The steps include:

    a. *Activities and buildings.* At this point the dimensions of the dock, its length, and its width are known. The plan should also include the requirements for office, shop, fuel lanes, and any fixed facilities.

    b. *Parking areas.* The major requirement is for parking of trailers. The facility must be able to accommodate the peak requirements, based on the operations plan.

    Parking of employee and visitor autos should also be planned for the peak. If line driver parking is required, this must also be included. As a general planning factor, 80 percent of the employees will require a parking space.

    c. *Plot size.* Depending upon growth projections, the land area required is generally a 25 to 35 multiple of the platform and office space. For a small terminal, such as 12 to 16 doors with a 40 ft width, the minimal width of the plot will be 280 ft. This dimension provides for a 120 ft apron area for spotting trailers on both sides of the dock. The depth, of course, will depend on the total area required for parking and expansion.

2. *Define search area.* The search area should be defined within about a five-mile radius. This should be an area that is well located to support present and future sources of business.

Table 18–6 Terminal Doors and Platform Width Relationships

Doors	Platform Width (feet)
Up to 20	40
20–30	50
30–50	60
Over 50	80

Source: American Trucking Association.

3. *Select site.* The site selection should be made by review of available properties of suitable size and configuration within the search area. Criteria for selection include:

   a. *Access.* Try to obtain a site within two miles of a state freeway or interstate highway, or with convenient access to another main traffic artery.

   b. *Site preparation cost.* Obtain estimates for site improvement and determine the length of time required to prepare the land for construction.

   c. *The area.* Check the zoning requirements and the building.

4. *Prepare a block site plan.* The first step in developing an efficient layout for the plot is to determine a general arrangement of buildings, parking spaces, and activity for the specific plot chosen. Next, prepare a flow chart of what happens in the terminal, including the sequence of steps that road drivers take from the time they enter the gate and park their equipment. Allow adequate space in the total employee parking area for the expanded design year, even though all this space may not be paved to begin with. An example of a block plan for a large facility shows how the flow should be traced and the general configuration of activities and facilities on the plot. (Figure 18–26.)

5. *Design a detailed plot plan.* The plan should show the details of the facility locations and paving and construction required. (Figure 18–27.)

The preceding material has dealt with the technical processes for developing efficient and well-functioning truck terminal sites. When integrating these technical factors with "real world" *community and environmental considerations,* there are issues that should be recognized to arrive at compatible solutions.

The location of truck terminals is a major issue and source of controversy. They generate considerable truck traffic on roads leading to the sites resulting in various types of actual and perceived adverse effects in their vicinity, which include traffic congestion, safety hazards, pavement deterioration, adverse visual and psychological consequences, noise, and air pollution. Further, they tend to attract other commercial activities and truck-oriented operations, such as truck repair shops and supply stores.

Truck terminals are not considered desirable "neighbors" of residential developments. In addition to the previously mentioned traffic-related effects, these terminals may have other types of physical and psychological effects on adjacent residential areas. For example, the high mast lighting used in terminals for work and security during night operation is not desirable for nearby residences; and the noise of trucks moving or idling inside terminals is also undesirable, especially at night.

Suitable locations for truck terminals can be identified through land use planning studies and engineering studies. Industrial parks are suitable sites for truck terminals. A transportation park may be developed to accommodate a cluster of terminals and, if it is located near a major truck route, then unnecessary travel of large trucks on internal local roads can be eliminated. A transportation park would provide an opportunity and justification for special design features and treatments such as exclusive access roads and buffer strips around the sites.

Truck Stops[F]

Truck stops are quite different from truck terminals. Whereas truck terminals involve the handling and transfer of freight and attract both large and small trucks, truck stops usually cater to large over-the-road trucks. Truck drivers utilize these stops for their own rest and for the refueling and servicing of trucks. These stops are located along major truck routes, such as the Interstate highways and near interchanges or major intersections. Thus, truck stops generate heavy movement of large trucks at these interchanges, intersections, and along roads leading to the sites. Truck stops also attract businesses like motels, fueling stations, and restaurants; although truck stops themselves may provide such services.

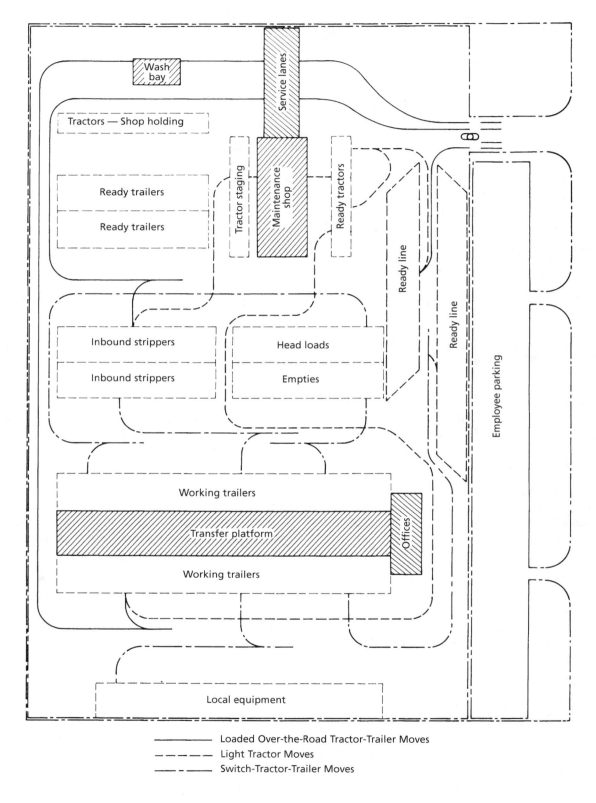

Figure 18–26 Block Site Plan

Source: American Trucking Association.

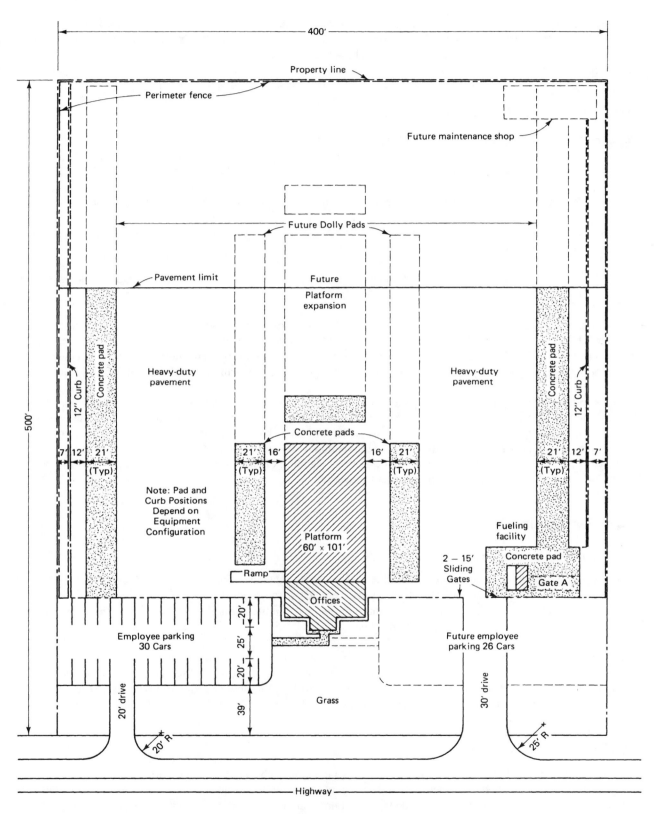

Figure 18–27 Typical Plot Plan—22-Door Terminal

Source: American Trucking Association.

The issues and problems related to truck stops are somewhat similar to those of truck terminals, and it involves the intermixing of large trucks with automobile traffic. The problems can be avoided by separating the truck stops, and the generated truck traffic, from sensitive areas. This can be achieved by providing facilities for trucks, separate from autos, and by buffering the areas around truck stop sites.

Rail Terminals (Passenger)

Passenger service is provided via several rail "submodes," including:

- Light rail (at-grade or grade-separated street cars, single or multiple-unit).

- Rapid rail (grade-separated, multiple-unit, usually serving central portions of the urban area).

- Commuter rail (at-grade or grade-separated, locomotive-hauled or multiple-unit, usually connecting outlying communities with the urban core area).

- Intercity rail (at-grade or grade-separated, usually locomotive-hauled, connecting urban core areas of cities in several states).

The interfaces for these varied types of rail services range from simple on-street stops (for streetcar and light rail); through at-grade, off-street light rail, and suburban commuter rail stops; through controlled access, grade-separated stations (for light rail and rapid rail); and on to major downtown rail terminals (for commuter rail and intercity rail). Some key planning guidelines and techniques are presented below for the stops, stations, and terminals of the various rail systems.

Stations and terminals are important components of rail systems, since they represent contact points of these systems with the surrounding areas and with other modes, such as walking, auto, or other transit services. Terminal operations strongly affect passenger convenience, comfort, and safety on the one hand; and service reliability, operating speed, and line capacity on the other. They also have a strong interaction with their surroundings and environment. Large stations often require considerable investment. Careful design and planning of station operations are therefore very important for optimal use of investment and efficient system operation.

Light Rail Stations[c]

Operational Considerations

Light rail operations should be considered in locating stations. Since light rail stations often have few obstacles to pedestrian circulation and most often have low level platforms, vehicle operators must have a clear view of pedestrians and waiting passengers as they approach stations. Sharp curves with limited visibility, steep grades, and sharp vertical curve crests should be avoided on station approaches.

Station platforms should be as close to level as possible, preferably with slopes limited to 1 or 2 percent. For new stations constructed in accordance with guidelines established pursuant to the ADA, the gap between the rail vehicle floor and the platform can be no more than 3 inches (76 mm) horizontally and 5/8ths of an inch (16 mm) vertically. Essentially, ADA requirements dictate that platform edges be tangent and parallel to the vehicle and have no vertical curvature.

Platform Access

Light rail platforms can be either center platforms, with a track on each side; or side platforms, with a track along one side only. (Figure 18–28.) Pedestrian access to light rail platforms may be at-grade in many instances. For side platforms with few obstructions, access may be provided at any appropriate location along the side of the platform opposite the track. For center platforms, at grade access is typically limited to the ends of the platform. Such "end-loaded" platforms require all passengers to walk to the end of the platform when exiting, and exiting flow capacity is limited by the width of the platform. Consequently, exit flow capacity must be calculated to permit platforms to be cleared of passenger crowding within the interval between arriving trains.

Waiting and Boarding Areas

Waiting areas for light rail stations generally include limited amenities. Most stations have canopies covering a portion of the platform, and most have some vertical surfaces that are usually transparent to maintain visibility and to provide limited protection from wind and wind-driven precipitation. On exposed platforms, especially in colder climates, more extensive passenger shelters are often used, with enclosures on all sides and in some instances heating provided. Limited seating and leaning areas are usually provided on platforms.

Fare Vending and Collection

As indicated in Chapter 13, almost all North American LRT systems use a self-service proof of payment (POP) fare system. To facilitate POP fare inspection, some LRT stations may have "free" areas and "paid" areas. All persons entering a "paid" area must possess, and display upon request, a valid ticket. This permits fare inspectors to check tickets in stations prior to passengers boarding vehicles. Ticket vending machines (TVMs) must be located in "free" areas. Free areas must have adequate space for TVMs and queuing, and good signage is needed to ensure passengers are aware of the limits and access requirements of "paid" areas.

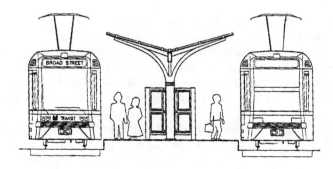

Platform Cross-Section—Center Platform

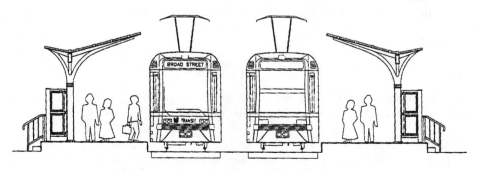

Platform Cross-Section—Side Platform

Figure 18–28   Typical Platform Cross-Sections for Light Rail Stations

Source: "Final Environmental Impact Statement 4(f) Statement for the Newark-Elizabeth Rail Link," Newark, N.J.: N.J. Transit and Federal Transit Administration, September 1998.

Platform and Vehicle Access

LRT stations must be designed to accommodate the needs of individuals with disabilities. TVMs and validators must be useable by individuals with vision and mobility impairments. Accessible paths of travel must be provided that are comparable with paths of travel provided for unimpaired riders. A 2 ft (61 cm) wide detectable warning strip is required along platform edges or other drop-offs not protected with railings or other barriers. Vertical level changes will require ramps or elevators.

To accommodate the needs of mobility-impaired passengers, all light rail systems include boarding and alighting provisions that accommodate wheelchairs. These accommodations depend on the height difference between the vehicle floor and the platform. Conventional light rail vehicles have floors approximately 1 m (30 in) above the top of the rail. Most of these vehicles require passengers to climb three to four steps to enter the vehicle. Mobility impaired passengers are accommodated by on-vehicle or wayside lifts, or by short platform sections constructed at the level of the vehicle floor. Such short high-level or "mini-high" level platforms are generally reached via ramps from the low level sections of the platforms, and they require deployment of portable or vehicle-mounted bridge plates to span the gap between the vehicle and the platform. Some LRT systems have stations with all high-level platforms, allowing all vehicle doors to be used by wheelchair users.

New low-floor light rail vehicles are being procured for many systems. Low floor light rail vehicles have all, or portions of, the vehicle's floor at a level approximately 14 inches (350 mm) above the top of the rail. Doors in the low floor portions of the vehicles may be boarded directly from platforms at floor height, or from platforms at a nominal 6–7 in (150–180 mm) curb height using short bridge plates deployed automatically from the vehicle.

Platform Dimensions

Platform lengths should be designed to accommodate the longest train normally used. Typically, LRT trains are from one to four cars long. Platform lengths will be dimensioned to accommodate a fixed number of car lengths, plus additional length at the ends of platforms to accommodate queuing at end doors, fare collection areas, and variations in stopping distances for vehicles. In many instances, LRT systems are constructed in stages. In those instances it is possible to reduce initial construction costs by constructing station platforms to accommodate train lengths required to support initial operations, while designing a station "footprint" that will allow future platform extensions to accommodate projected ridership.

Platform widths must be dimensioned to accommodate dynamic loads of waiting passengers and passengers exiting the trains. Such loads are usually determined by simulations of peak period conditions. End loaded center platforms, because of the obvious design constraints, require careful attention to peak loading conditions. Minimum platform widths must accommodate the detectable warning strip and unobstructed passage for wheelchairs and pedestrians of 6 ft adjacent to the warning strip. Consequently, side platforms must be no less than 8 ft (2.44 m) between platform edge and any obstruction, including structural members and platform furniture. However, the actual minimum platform width should be determined individually for each station according to local codes and standards for passenger queuing and evacuation.

Station Types

At grade LRT stations generally include four types: in street right of way, in reserved street median, side of street, and exclusive right of way. Typical LRT station configurations are shown in Figure 18–29 (a)–(e).

With the introduction of pedestrian areas with transit services in many cities in recent years, numerous LRT stops have been placed in the cores of such areas: malls, shopping streets, large pedestrian squares, and so on. In most cases, crossing the tracks is allowed everywhere, since LRT vehicles operate only at moderate speeds. The track consists of rails embedded in pavement with the tops of the rails either flush or slightly depressed and separated by low curbs.

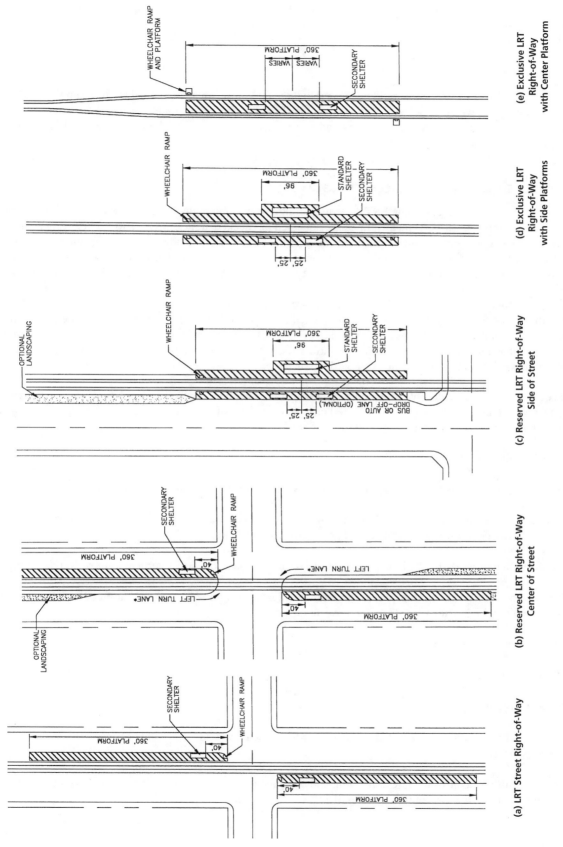

Figure 18–29 (a)–(e)   Typical LRT Station Configurations

(a) LRT Street Right-of-Way

(b) Reserved LRT Right-of-Way Center of Street

(c) Reserved LRT Right-of-Way Side of Street

(d) Exclusive LRT Right-of-Way with Side Platforms

(e) Exclusive LRT Right-of-Way with Center Platform

Source: *Designing for Transit*, San Diego, Calif.: Metropolitan Transit Development Board, 1993.

In addition to warning pedestrians, the curbs assist vehicle boarding at stops. An effective way of designating stop areas is the use of textured pavement, usually squares of two different colors.

At-Grade Transfer Stations

Major transfer stations for surface transit should be located in large pedestrian areas, separated from automobile traffic. Short walking distances between vehicles of different routes should be provided. Crossing tracks and roadways is usually unrestricted; controlled pedestrian crossings and overpasses or underpasses should be used only if vehicle speeds are high or pedestrian volumes are very heavy.

Rail Rapid Transit (Controlled-Access) Stations[c]

All rapid rail, some commuter rail, and some LRT systems use stations that are grade-separated from other facilities and have full control of passenger access. Typically, fares are collected or checked at the entrances to the boarding areas so that this process does not delay the vehicle boarding. This permits simultaneous loading on all doors along the train. In addition, fully controlled stations allow use of high-level platforms that make getting into and out of vehicles extremely easy and fast. Consequently, controlled-access stations represent by far the highest transit terminal capacity.

With long trains and many doors, it is possible to achieve boarding and alighting rates of 40 to 80 persons per sec. LRT vehicles with simultaneous loading of two 6-axle cars can achieve rates of 6 to 20 persons per sec., while LRT trains of three 8-axle cars and high-level platforms can reach rates of 15 to 30 persons per sec. These rates are one to two orders of magnitude greater than rates of passenger boarding of surface transit vehicles that involve fare collection at the entrance, stepping up into the vehicle, and only one or two boarding channels.

Controlled-access stations have a durable effect on both the operation of the transit system and on its interaction with the surrounding environment. Their design must be based on a very careful analysis of the requirements of the three major affected parties: passengers, operating agency, and the community.

Passengers utilizing the stations require:

- Minimum time and distance to the platform or between platforms for transferring between lines.

- Convenience, such as good information about service and orientation, adequate circulation patterns and capacity, easy boarding and alighting, and provisions for the disabled.

- Comfort, including aesthetically pleasing design, weather protection, small vertical climbs, and the like.

- Safety and security; maximum protection from accidents through safe surfaces; and good visibility and illumination, which deter vandalism and prevent crime.

Operating agency requires the following:

- Minimum operating costs.

- Adequate capacity of the transit system and pedestrian areas.

- Flexibility of operation, such as adaptability to different peaking conditions and changes in fare-collection methods.

- Good visibility of platforms, fare collection, and other areas to enable supervision of operations and ensure efficiency, safety, and prevention of vandalism.

- Good integration with surrounding areas and utilization of station space for various shops, displays, information booths, and so on.

The *community* is interested in having a well-used and efficiently operated transit system. It is therefore also concerned that the requirements of passengers and the operator be satisfied. The community considers these requirements, together with the investment costs, that are in many cases its obligation. In addition, however, the community is also interested in both the immediate and long-range effects of the station on its surroundings. The immediate effects include environmental impact, visual aspects, noise, and possible traffic congestion. Long-range effects include the type of development in the vicinity, which may be stimulated or discouraged by the station's presence.

Station Platforms

Rapid rail stations can have either lateral platforms, as shown in Figure 18–30(a); or a central platform, as depicted in Figure 18–30 (b). Since cars have doors on both sides, either of the two types can be used at a station along the line. Several older rapid rail systems used mostly central platforms to reduce operating personnel. However, with increasing and sometimes total automation and centralized supervision of stations, this difference has disappeared on some systems. The choice between the two types thus depends on many factors, such as fare collection, train departure procedure, and entrance locations.

Stations with multiple tracks and multiple platforms are provided in four different cases. First, when passenger interchange is heavy and the line operates at capacity, three platforms can be provided, so that each track has platforms on both sides. As Figure 18–30(c) shows, this design permits simultaneous boarding and alighting of passengers on the opposite sides of the trains, considerably reducing their standing times. This type of station exists in Barcelona and on the Munich S-Bahn system. The second case is on lines with local and express service. Common designs of local and express stations, found in New York and Philadelphia, are shown in Figure 18–30(d) and (e).

A third type of platform arrangement is used for stations where lines intersect and transfers are permitted. This type of station is seen in several locations on the Washington, D.C. Metro; on the Atlanta, Georgia MARTA system; and in Montreal, Canada. (Figure 18–31.) This type of station has rail lines crossing perpendicularly at different levels. Levels are connected by stairs, elevators, and escalators. Where possible, one level has side platforms and the other has a center platform. This configuration permits stairs and escalators to be parallel to the track on the center platform and perpendicular to the track on the side platforms. Where side platforms are not feasible, escalators and stairs from both track levels must connect with a third level mezzanine.

Platform length is usually determined as the length of the longest train plus a distance of 5 to 10 m. Although it requires additional construction cost, this extra distance actually reduces travel time since it requires a lower precision of braking. LRT stations are usually designed for simultaneous stopping of two to three cars or trains.

Platform heights have a major influence on station construction costs and space requirements, as well as on their operations. There are two categories of platforms heights:

1. Low-level platforms are at a ground level or one curb height above it. Used by all street cars, most light rail, and some commuter rail, these platforms require simple, low-cost arrangements; but they involve slower passenger boarding and alighting.

2. High-level platforms are even with, or slightly lower than, the car's floor (0.85 to 1.00 m above the top of the rails). Used on all rapid rail, most commuter rail, and some light rail systems, these platforms involve considerably higher construction costs and take more space; but they provide faster, safer, and easier boarding and alighting.

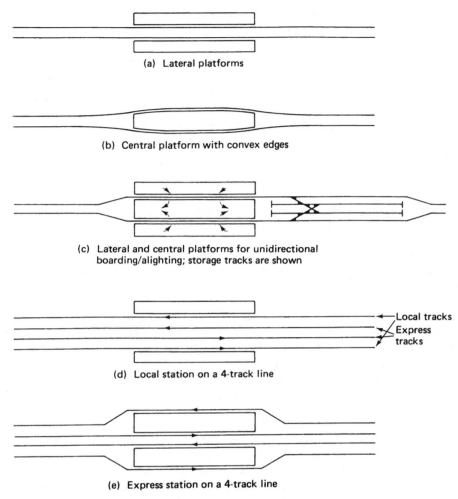

(a) Lateral platforms

(b) Central platform with convex edges

(c) Lateral and central platforms for unidirectional
boarding/alighting; storage tracks are shown

Local tracks
Express
tracks

(d) Local station on a 4-track line

(e) Express station on a 4-track line

Figure 18–30(a)–(e)   Single-Line Station Platform Types

Source: Vukan R. Vuchic, *Urban Public Transportation Systems and Technology*, Prentice Hall, 1981.

Most controlled stations (with access through fare-collection areas only) and some open stations have high-level platforms.

Station Levels

Controlled-access stations usually consist of three levels. Entrances and stairways are at the street level. The intermediate, mezzanine levels contain the fare-collection system, which divides it into a "free area" (part of a public street) and a "paid area" (the transit station proper). The third level is with platforms and tracks where train boarding takes place.

A great variety of designs of the three station levels is possible, but the most typical ones can be classified by their three basic characteristics: subway versus aerial stations, two versus three levels, and central versus lateral platforms. The differences between these designs can be seen clearly from their schematic cross sections in Figure 18–32.

Fare Collection

Virtually all rapid rail systems require passengers to pass through a barrier or turnstile where fares are collected. Gates or turnstiles are usually provided in a bank or several banks of parallel devices to accommodate anticipated peak passenger volumes and provide adequate queuing space. Older transit systems use tokens or coins as fare media. More recently, bill acceptors and magnetic stripe tickets (with stored value) have become typical fare media (for new systems and some older systems). To accommodate wheelchair-bound passengers, some gates have wider openings or are equipped with special release devices. On some systems, magnetic stripe cards must be inserted in turnstiles both on entry and exit, allowing the use of specific distance-based, station-to-station fares. Emerging technology is using "contactless" or "proximity" cards for fare payment. Such cards are not inserted in readers, but they can be placed on or near a designated area on the barrier and activate the gate using wireless communications.

In most systems, automatic ticket vending machines are located in "free" areas near station entrances to permit passengers to purchase fare media. Some systems with distance-based fares also locate "add-fare" machines in the "paid" areas near exits. In the event a passenger does not have a sufficient value stored on his or her card to exit at that station, the card is rejected and returned to the passenger by the turnstile and the passenger is directed to the "add-fare" machine, where additional fare value can be purchased and added to the card.

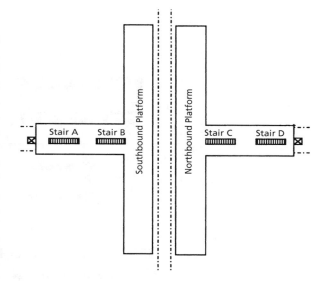

Upper Level Platform (North-South)

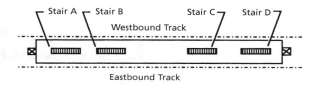

Lower Level Platform (East-West)

Figure 18–31 Typical Crossing Station with Transfer Between Two Rail Lines

Source: Jerome M. Lutin.

Entrances and Integration with Surroundings

The number of locations of station entrances directly influences passenger convenience and transit system integration with adjacent areas and buildings. Since passengers feel that they have reached the transit system when they come to station entrance, station layout should provide stairways at both ends of platform. Such a layout effectively results in an increased area coverage compared with single-entrance layout.

Direct connections between the station mezzanines and the basements of major stores or other buildings are also common. Well-designed and extensively used large underground plazas and malls with stores, restaurants, and connections with hotels, office buildings, rapid rail, and railroad stations exist in Frankfurt, Hamburg, London, Montreal (Place de la Marie complex), New York (World Trade Center), São Paolo, and many other cities.

Highway and Rail Transit Interface (Bus, Parking)

To achieve an interface between automobile travel in suburban areas and the transit network, stations must accommodate automobile access in two forms. Kiss-and-ride is the widely adopted term for the drop-off and pickup of passengers; park-and-ride is when transit passengers park their cars at the station. These access modes usually create high peak hour volumes, such that the station design must extensively utilize traffic engineering techniques. Because of traffic volumes and parking facilities, these stations require a very large area per passenger.

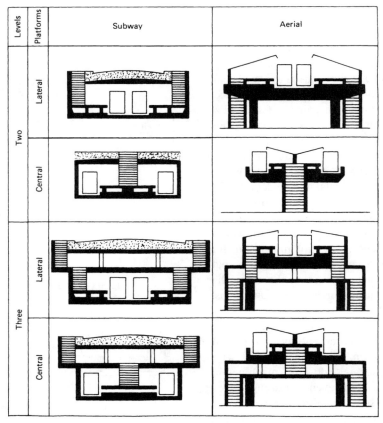

Figure 18–32 Rapid Transit Station Types

Source: Vukan R. Vuchic, *Urban Public Transportation Systems and Technology*, Prentice Hall, 1981.

The basic principles governing the design are:

- Priority in convenience of access should be given to modes in this sequence: pedestrians, feeder transit, bicyclists, taxis, kiss-and-ride, and park-and-ride.

- Maximum possible separation of all access modes is desirable.

- The pedestrian walk between access modes and the station platform should be safe, convenient, and as short as possible.

- Adequate capacity, easy orientation, and smooth traffic flow should be provided for each mode.

Typically, the station building is located in the middle of the station area. Feeder routes (usually buses) have stops close to station doors along curbs that may be straight or have a sawtooth pattern. Where conditions allow, bus ramps are built to provide direct, across-the-platform transfer to trains, eliminating the need for passengers to climb stairs. Pedestrian access from all streets and parking areas requires walkways that should be at least 1.50 m (two pedestrian lanes) wide. Lowered curbs, mild gradients, and convenient doors should allow access to stations by people in wheelchairs. Bicycle racks and, if bicycle volume is heavy (e.g., near schools and campuses), bicycle lanes should be provided.

The kiss-and-ride area should be easily reachable from all access streets. It should have a sheltered drop-off area and a parking area for waiting with good visibility of the station entrance. The remaining station area is used for parking. Its circulation roads should be remote from the station building to minimize auto and pedestrian conflicts. Aisles directed toward the building and right-angle parking are usually the best circulation and space utilization. Based on these principles, the design of a rapid rail station with major park-and-ride and kiss-and-ride facilities is shown in Figure 18–33.

Commuter Rail Stations

Commuter rail systems exist in a number of North American cities and are being developed in a number of additional corridors. Commuter rail is an attractive alternative in areas where existing freight rail lines parallel congested freeways. Most commuter rail stations have major termini in downtown business districts, often areas that were initially developed as commercial districts because of the presence of passenger railroads and terminals. Consequently, access to most of these termini will be on foot or by local mass transit service. Most commuter rail stations in suburban areas are accessed primarily by auto and have correspondingly sized park-and-ride lots.

Where new stations are developed along existing freight railroads, additional passing tracks may be required to permit simultaneous operation of freight and passenger service. Because freight railroads may need to accommodate high and wide loads, it is not desirable to operate freight on tracks adjacent to high level passenger platforms. Freight clearance dimensions would create a wide gap between the platform edge and typical commuter rail cars, which is an undesirable condition.

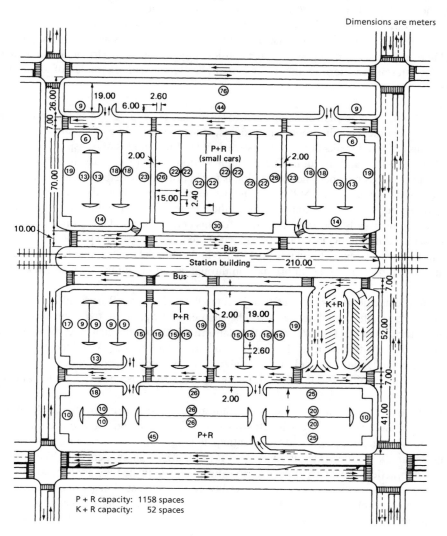

Figure 18–33   Outlying Station Design Utilizing Basic Principles

Source: Vukan R. Vuchic, *Urban Public Transportation Systems and Technology*, Englewood Cliffs, New Jersey, Prentice Hall, 1981.

If freight and passenger trains are permitted to operate simultaneously, grade-separated pedestrian access must be provided to commuter rail platforms. Similarly, grade-separated access is required for stations on lines that feature frequent, high-speed operations, have express trains bypassing stations, or have an electrified third rail. In areas where commuter trains are relatively short and operate at relatively low speeds, it is usually possible to permit pedestrians to cross commuter rail tracks at designated and suitably protected at-grade crossings, similar to light rail operations.

Most commuter rail stations have platforms at car floor level, which is approximately 4 ft (1.2 m) above the top of the rail. Standard railroad passenger cars are 85 ft (26 m) long and are seldom operated in trains less than two cars long. Typical trains include four to eight cars (ten to twelve cars in major metropolitan areas) and a locomotive.

Commuter rail systems generally feature on-board fare collection. High-volume stations may have ticket offices and automated ticket vending machines. Some commuter rail systems use proof of payment fare systems similar to light rail.

Intercity Rail Terminals[G]

Intercity rail travel in the United States, after a long period of declining traffic, is showing some growth. This is particularly true in the Northeast Corridor between Washington and Boston, which is the highest density intercity rail corridor in the country. During the late 1990s electrified operation on the Northeast Corridor was being extended from New Haven, Connecticut to Boston, Massachusetts; and new high-speed train sets were being acquired. In several states, including Florida, Ohio, and Texas, corridors were under consideration as candidates for high-speed rail operations. Some general principles for intercity rail terminals are presented here along with examples of some major existing rail terminals of this type.

A rail station complex will include platforms and platform tracks, concourse and other access ways, ticket sales, baggage and checkroom facilities, waiting rooms, rest rooms, other amenities like restaurants and sales booths, parking areas, and access through covered walks or tunnels to streets and to local modes of transport. Stations for rail transport are of two general types—stub and through. The through-station is, in effect, a way station with arriving trains continuing through to the stations beyond. The stub station is found primarily where the trains terminate their runs. Some stations have both stub and through-tracks. At the stub end the train is stopped, loaded or unloaded, and backed out; with electrified and diesel push-pull multipower unit equipment, the engineer shifts operations to the opposite end of the train. Stub-end terminal operations usually consume more time for this changeover and therefore usually require more tracks to accommodate the same hourly number of trains processed at the line stations. The problem of locomotive release and servicing arises with stub-end stations. This can be met by having additional track length beyond the stopping point and a crossover, so that the locomotive can be cut off and run through an adjoining track to the engine house.

At stations with light traffic, the platforms are usually adjacent to the main tracks. Where traffic is heavy, especially where many commuter trains operate, the main line tracks will be augmented by platform tracks out of or diverging from main tracks or terminal lead tracks. The tracks that connect the platform tracks to the principal leads or to the mains are termed "throat tracks." A general rule is to have a 2.5:1 to 3.0:1 ratio between a throat track and the number of platform tracks it serves. There must be enough platform tracks to serve all trains scheduled to arrive or depart at a particular time, plus a few additional to take care of off-schedule and extra trains. A track may also be reserved to park special equipment.

Minimum length of platform is based on the longest train anticipated (car length times the number of cars plus locomotive), plus two or three additional car lengths for emergency situations and to provide a factor of safety in stopping the train. Additional length may be added to anticipate longer trains of the future. Platform widths vary from 20 ft (6.1 m) if baggage trucks also use the platform to 13 ft (3.96 m) for passengers only. Wider platforms than these minimums are found in practice, especially if pedestrian flow studies indicate they are needed. Access to the platform gates is through a concourse from the street or through walkways from the station service area. When the waiting and service areas are on different levels, then ramps, stairways, escalators, and elevators are needed adjuncts. Pedestrian flow studies should also be done to size these facilities.

The usual intercity traveler moves slowly through the station area. The passenger may not be familiar with the routine; have baggage to handle and check or retrieve; have a long wait for connections or delayed trains; and may require information, food, and a comfortable place to sit. The commuter, on the contrary, is familiar with the route through the station, has little or no luggage, and is usually in a hurry. He or she wants direct access to or from local streets and transport. These two types of traffic should be kept separate to avoid conflict and confusion. In some large stations such as Grand Central Terminal in New York, commuter and intercity trains arrive and depart on different levels. In smaller stations, separate platforms should be used and traffic routed so that the two lines of movement do not cross. In some instances, separate stations are in use. In any event, clear, concise direction and routing signs and other means of channelization are desirable.

Rail Terminals (Freight)[G]

Terminals (facilities and systems) for rail freight in the United States have undergone major changes since World War II, particularly since the Staggers Act that deregulated the railroad industry. The terminal function has changed and will have to change even more as part of the intermodal revolution, which has involved international ocean shipping, domestic rail and truck transportation, and the aviation industry.

Prior to deregulation, rail freight movement had transitioned from break-bulk techniques into more use of "containerization" (i.e., Trailer-On-Flat-Car [TOFC] and Container-On-Flat-Car [COFC]). During this period, freight originally came to conventional rail yards from ships, by local truck, or via individual box cars at shippers' sidings. This changed when TOFC and COFC, more popularly referred to as "piggyback," allowed bringing "pre-packaged" freight in a trailer or a container for loading as a unit (rather than break-bulk loading) onto a flat car. The rail yards had to be relatively numerous so they could be located close to seaports, close to the shipper's loading dock, or close to warehouses.

Use of "conventional" break-bulk and TOFC and COFC continues; the material below describes the facilities and systems for those rail freight modes. Following this material, present and future conditions are discussed, such as unit trains, yard consolidations (hubs), Road Railers, and double-stack trains.

TOFC and COFC

"Piggyback" is the popular term used to describe a type of coordination in common use, especially on railroads. It is simply a form of ferry service that the transport unit of one carrier is moved by another. Highway motor freight trailers are loaded at the shipper's door or at a warehouse, brought by tractor to a railroad loading ramp or yard, placed on flatcars, and hauled in trains to a destination terminal. The trailers are then unloaded and terminal delivery is made to the consignee's door by tractor. TOFC line-haul service is potentially faster than highway haul, while the terminal times are practically equivalent. Much of the expense and nuisance of highway haul—traffic congestion, personnel problems, traffic violations, accident hazards, and restrictive limitations on weight and size—are avoided or markedly reduced.

Five systems of TOFC (with variations) are generally recognized:

- *Plan I.* Vehicles of common highway carriers are hauled by rail. The shipper deals with the highway carriers, which, in turn, deal with the railroad.

- *Plan II.* Only the railroad's highway trailers are carried. The public deals directly with the railroad or its highway subsidiary.

- *Plan III.* Anyone's trailer, including those of the individual or private trucker, is carried by rail.

- *Plan IV.* An intermediate or forwarding agency or broker secures the freight, loads it into its trailers and onto its own flatcars, and turns it over to the railroad to haul. The "third party" may be a company owned by one or more railroads, but the shipper deals with the third party.

- *Plan V.* Plan I plus joint rail-highway rates with the highway carrier. The shipper deals with either trucker or railroad.

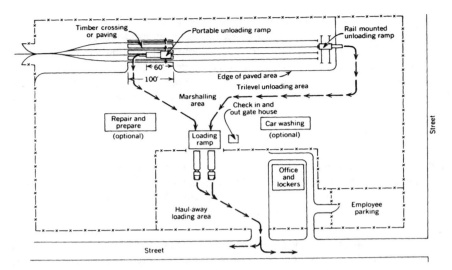

Figure 18–34(a)   Suggested Ramp Layout of a TOFC-COFC Terminal, Overhead Loading

Source: William W. Hay, *An Introduction to Transportation Engineering*, John Wiley and Sons, 1977.

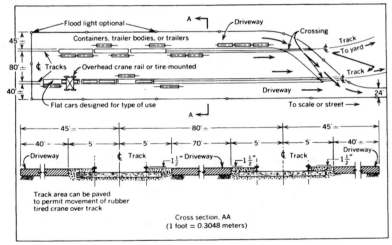

Figure 18–34(b)   Cross Section of a TOFC-COFC V Terminal

Source: William W. Hay, *An Introduction to Transportation Engineering*, John Wiley and Sons, 1977.

A variety of methods are available for loading and unloading. For small traffic volumes, end loading can be used; this enables trailers to be pushed or pulled on or off the rail car with tractors via fixed or portable ramps from pavement to car floor level. Eight trailer car lengths is about the limit for one track. Trailers can be unloaded only in the same (reversed) sequence as loaded. Trailers may also be handled by lift-on and lift-off devices, such as giant forklift trucks or by vertical-lift trucks with straddle yokes that fit over the tops of trailers and grasp underneath. Where large numbers of trailers and cars are involved, traveling gantry or straddle cranes are used that move up and down a line of cars on steerable rubber-tired wheels, straddling two tracks with an intermediate driveway.

TOFC has several techno-economic problems: (a) Full trailer capacity may be too great for some shippers so that their small shipments must still be consolidated across a freight-house platform—also the trailers are too large to place in an airplane or in other than specially designed ships; (b) the length of the car creates derailing tendencies, especially when coupled to a short car and under heavy draft on short curves; (c) the height of the trailer above the top of the rail, up to 17.5 ft, creates clearance problems that have led some railroads to make major changes in tunnels and bridge portal clearances, even to the extent of transforming tunnels into open cuts; (d) the high van with its undercarriage creates additional train resistance; and (e) TOFC decreases payload to an empty-weight ratio of 3 to 1 or, worse, from a possible 4 to 1.

A solution to these problems was the use of containers—boxes similar to trailers but without the undercarriage (COFC). During the 80s container sizes changed so that they became available with a width of 8.5 ft. and lengths greater than 40 ft. Containers may be simple boxes that are set on truck bodies, flat cars, gondola cars, ships holds, demountable truck bodies, or chassis for land movement. Only the largest aircraft can carry a standard container, but smaller units that fit the fuselage contour are in use (see Air Cargo section of this chapter). Individual freight items loaded in the container need not be rehandled from the time that the container is closed and sealed by the shipper until the seal is broken by the consignee.

A TOFC terminal, whether by itself or as part of a container port complex, is designed for the type of loading or unloading to be used. For end loading, tracks should not exceed 8 two-trailer rail cars. Figure 18–34 illustrates ramp layout and cross-section for a TOFC-COFC terminal.

Depressing the tracks below ground level assists by reducing the approach gradient, but drainage problems may be created. With moving straddle-type gantry operation, the crane should span at least two tracks and a 40 ft (12.9-m) driveway. Paths for the steerable rubber-tire wheels are usually painted on the pavement. Trailer parking is provided with spaces preferably slanted at a 45 to 60 degree angle for ease in parking. Truck scales should be long enough for a 48 ft trailer. There should be easy access to main highways and rail yards. Trailer parking space for both on-and off-loading should be provided.

Yards

Railroad yards serve the varied purposes of storage; holding reconsignment; public delivery; and supporting industrial, waterfront, and switching activity. The principal type of yard, and its function, is the classification yard, which also performs a concentration function by accumulating enough cars to fill out a train. Classification includes the receiving and breakup of trains and the sorting and classifying of the cars into new trains for road haul, transfer to other yards or railroads, or local delivery. These last two functions are distribution factors.

A large classification yard usually contains three yard units: the *receiving yard* into which trains are moved from the main line preparatory to sorting; *the classification yard* proper, where the sorting or classifying into blocks of common destinations takes place; and the *departure yard*, in which the sorted groups or blocks are made into trains and held pending main-line movement. Small yards consist of only one general yard, certain tracks within that one yard being assigned to receiving and departure purposes. (Figure 18–35.)

The track lengths of the receiving and departure yards are based on the number of cars in the average- and maximum-length trains (at 50 ft per car) plus length of locomotive (50 to 60 ft) per unit, and caboose (40 ft); 200 to 300 ft are added as a factor of safety in stopping. The number of tracks is based in part on the arrival rate of inbound trains but is governed fully as much by the rate of classifying, the rate at which cars can be taken from the receiving yard, sorted into groups or blocks, and assembled into trains in the departure yard.

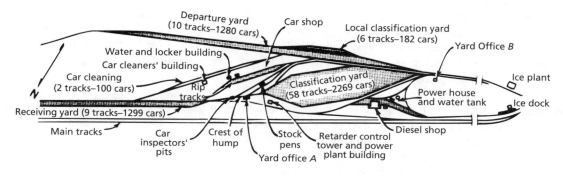

Figure 18–35 Plan of a Classification Yard

Source: William W. Hay, *An Introduction to Transportation Engineering*, John Wiley and Sons, 1977.

Semiautomatic yards have retarder units placed on leads to groups of tracks. The retarders control car speed by pressing brake shoes, electrically or electro pneumatically, against each side of the wheel as it moves through the retarder. Tower operators judge the cars' speeds and, by push-button arrangement, control the amount of braking pressure that will be applied. In this type of yard, classification rates vary from 100 to 180 cars per hour.

Completely automatic yards use electronic and radar devices to measure the weight and speed of each individual car and automatically apply the proper retardation. The most recent designs can feed the consists of a newly arrived train into a computer, possibly located hundreds of miles away; the computer automatically prepares and distributes a switch list complete with proper cuts and track designations. Classifying rates of 200 to 300 per hour can be obtained when there are no delays due to external causes.

An essential part of every yard is a comprehensive system of communication utilizing the latest Intelligent Transportation Systems (ITS) technology. The problem of the yard location in an urban area includes proximity of the yard to industrial, waterfront, and other traffic sources; and to other rail routes, land values and availability, taxation, and opportunities to expand. More significant to rail operation, however, is the location with respect to other yards on the system. The trend is for a few large strategically placed yards equipped with all modern car-handling devices and ITS technology.

The Present and the Future in Rail Freight (Intermodal Developments)[H,I,J]

One of the key rail freight strategies that developed as part of the containerization mode was the "land bridge" concept whereby traffic between the Far East and Europe or the East Coast of the United States is transferred from ship to rail to move COFC over a relatively short, rapid land route to Gulf or Atlantic Coast points rather than through the Panama Canal. Transit time for certain ships between Japan and the Atlantic Seaboard via the Canal is 32 days. By transshipping containers to rail cars at Western ports the transit time to the Eastern Seaboard can be reduced to 16 days. There are no technological problems with this, but there is the matter of returning empty containers and other administrative and regulatory concerns. With deregulation and increasing intermodal business entities and arrangements, ways have been found to overcome these problems. In fact, more and more use is now made of the "empty containers" for back hauls. This has led to increasing use of and focus on *domestic* containerization, particularly for high-density corridors over 500 miles long.

Another key development is the use of "double-stack" rail cars, usually in dedicated (i.e., single purpose, single-destination) trains. Industry analysts note three phases of double-stack development. *Phase One*, well underway by the late 80s, double-stack dedicated services by or for large trans-Pacific or trans-Atlantic container lines. *Phase Two*, which started in the late 80s, used domestic cargo in empty containers to balance the land transportation portion of the international container movement. *Phase Three*, the latest development, uses domestic only double-stack dedicated services. The increasing use of double-stack, with its increased per-train capacity, has had definite effects on right-of-way geometric planning and on the planning and design of the associated intermodal terminals.

Another technological innovation, the *Road Railer*, had some application by the late 80s and is being applied even more in the 90s. The concept—a freight vehicle capable of traveling over both railroads and highways—is not new. The Chesapeake & Ohio (C&O) introduced its Railvans in 1959, and for 10 years a fleet of 80 of the hybrids hauled mail and express in passenger-train consists. Subsequently, British Rail tested 50 road and rail vans adapted from the C&O design; but the project floundered in a sea of railroad-truck jurisdictional disputes. The Railvan of old has resurfaced in a technologically advanced version known as the Road Railer. (Figure 18–36.) It is believed that the Road Railer reduces intercity costs over 40 percent and fuel consumption 75 percent when compared to all highway operations. Road Railers may gradually replace conventional TOFC and COFC equipment.

Road Railer has some significant potential economic advantages in terminal operations. Because Road Railers are merely rolled in or out of trains, rather than being lifted on or off rail cars, the transfer operation is accomplished with low investment truck tractors rather than high investment cranes and without any rail cars to handle, and no switch engineers or car storage yards are required. Finally, each Road Railer's own simple mechanism performs the transfer between highway tires and rail wheels in less time than the lifting operation. The result is that Road Railer bimodal terminals require less land and an estimated 29 percent lower operating cost than TOFC intermodal terminals.

Figure 18–36   Road Railer

Source: ITE, *Transportation Planning Handbook,* 1992.

Related to the effects of dedicated-trains, unit trains, double-stacks, Road Railers, improved street and highway networks, and other factors, large railroads are making important savings by consolidating many intermodal ramps (yards) into a few strategically located, highly productive hubs. Burlington Northern, for example, in 1985 cut the number of intermodal ramps on its system from 144 to only 20. In 1986 that railroad had: five double-stack trains, 10 Expediter trains, three Road Railer trains, and 24 other intermodal trains of the more standard variety. By 1990 Road Railer usage expanded, with three railroads (Norfolk Southern, Burlington Northern, and Conrail) employing this "carless" technology.

All of these "intermodal" changes in the railroad industry will have profound effects on the interfaces. There will be many less "conventional" rail yards and many more interfaces at or close to the point of shipment. Planners need to remain constantly "in tune" with the latest market and industry developments.

Waterborne Transportation Terminals

Rivers, lakes, bays, and other bodies of water are often major obstacles to transportation; however, in some cases, they can also be used as transportation routes, offering more convenient and even faster travel than land-based systems. A variety of boat types used for different across-the-water connections can be classified in three basic technologies: ferryboats or ferries, hydrofoils, and hovercraft.

Ferries are by far the most common basic technology for transportation on water. Although they are rather slow, ferries offer low-cost, reliable, comfortable, and sometimes even faster service than any competing mode can offer among points served. Ferry systems can be planned for:

    a. Passengers only.

    b. Passengers and vehicles (e.g., autos, buses, trucks).

    c. Trains (i.e., lighterage).

System (c) is useful in only a few specialized situations.

Ferry Terminals (Passengers Only)[c]

System (a), passengers only, is in wide application around the world using "conventional" ferry vessels of various sizes and configurations. Notable examples include the Staten Island Ferry in New York City, the Golden Gate Ferry in the San Francisco area, and some services in the bays around Seattle.

A significant innovative concept in ferry services was introduced in 1977 in Vancouver. The Lions' Gate Bridge between Vancouver and North Vancouver became overloaded, and additional capacity for travel between the two areas was needed. The Provincial Government's Transit Services Division decided to introduce a ferry across the Burrard Inlet, called "SEA-BUS," which incorporated a number of new concepts and has many features of rapid transit operation. Acceptance of this service continues to be excellent.

The Sea-Bus vessels are fully symmetric bidirectional catamarans with the same dynamic performance in both directions. After embarkation, a boat immediately accelerates to 25 km/h (13.5 knots) and crosses the 3.2-km-long distance across the inlet in less than 10 min. Thus cycle times of 30 min. are easily achievable, resulting in a capacity of 1600 seats/h per direction by two boats.

Both ferry terminals, north and south, are focal points of several bus routes. The south (Vancouver) terminal is also connected by direct pedestrian passageway with the automated Advanced Light Rail Transit system, serving downtown Vancouver and some of the easterly suburbs. Schedules and fares of buses are integrated with those of the ferries. Each terminal has a floating structure with two docks to provide easy docking regardless of the tides, which fluctuate as much as 6 m. (Figure 18–37.) The ferries fit precisely in each dock and open six double doors on each side. Passengers embark from the central portion of the terminal, while those leaving the ferry disembark into its outer corridors, as the figure shows. This one-way passenger flow allows a complete exchange of 400 passengers (seating capacity of the boat) in 90 sec.

Ferry Terminals (Passengers and Vehicles)[K]

System (b), passengers and vehicles, serves geographical situations where highway transportation via fixed roadways and bridges is not feasible because of extreme circuity of available routes and economic or environmental infeasibility of providing fixed links. Ferries provide this service in many lakes, bays, sounds, and estuaries around the world. Examples include Delaware Bay, Puget Sound, and the Great Lakes (in the United States); Vancouver, Canada; and Scandinavia.

Design of these types of ferry terminals needs to be concerned with these functional elements:

- Marshaling yards and approach lanes.

- Passenger facilities.

- Ferry berths and ramps.

The base for the design of these elements is clearly the expected traffic. Both the total volume of the traffic and its distribution over time are important parameters, as well as the distribution of traffic over the different modes of land transport. The establishment of these parameters is a very delicate matter, as the accuracy is quite limited, and because once a new terminal is established it will itself influence the traffic pattern in ways that are difficult to predict. Fortunately, ferry routes are usually flexible systems, which within a year or two may be modified, relatively quickly, to cope with changes in the traffic volume and pattern. Traffic forecasts are prepared to provide information on:

1. Vehicles arriving at the terminals to board the ferry.

2. Vehicles to deliver passengers to the ferry.

3. Pedestrians to board the ferry.

Forecasting of the passenger traffic involves the evaluation of traffic generation and diversion, and the determination of yearly growth factors. A passenger traffic generation model can be used, if it is possible to establish sufficient calibration data. The basis for the forecasts of the future cargo traffic are the expected product movements between the regions connected by the ferry routes. It is essential to assess the competition with other modes of transport, such as conventional shipping and air freight.

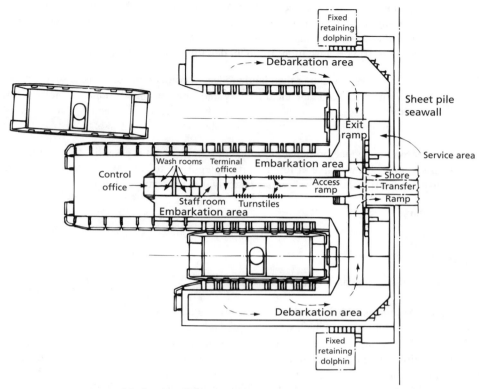

(a) Floating Terminal with Two Docks

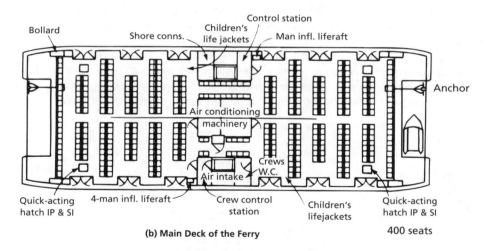

(b) Main Deck of the Ferry

400 seats

Figure 18–37   Burrard Inlet Ferry: Dock and Vessel Layout

Source: Vukan R. Vuchic, *Urban Public Transportation Systems and Technology,* Prentice Hall, 1981.

Having established the forecast of annual passenger and cargo vehicle peak traffic, volumes are projected, as direct design parameters for the functional elements of the ferry terminal. It is often practical to express the forecast traffic categories in equivalent passenger car units (pcus). One pcu may be considered to occupy 10 m of deck, including space around each one. Trucks are equivalent to 4 to 7 pcus, depending on their size, and buses to about 4 pcus. This is used for an estimate of the transfer capacity in terms of car deck area, as well as for marshaling yard requirements.

The turnaround time depends mainly on the geographical distance between the terminals, the cruising speed, and the loading and unloading time. Analysis of the operational economy will establish whether a few large ferries or more smaller ferries should be preferred, the desirable cruising speed, and the number of ferry berths. These options, however, will have different effects on the traffic because more frequent departures are likely to stimulate traffic.

Ferry operations are more sensitive to weather than land modes. In colder climates, where severe and extended freezing weather occurs, ice breakers may be needed to clear a navigable path. In some instances, thick ice formation can cause suspension of ferry operations. In addition, fog will reduce operating speeds. Consequently, planners must analyze seasonal variations in climate as an integral element of ferry service planning.

In order to speed up operations, reduce bottlenecks, and avoid accidents, it is essential to prepare the layout of the land areas *(marshaling areas)* in such a way that different traffic categories are not mixed. The departing traffic should never interfere with the arriving traffic. The latter should after arrival to the terminal be separated into:

a. Passenger cars.

b. Trucks and trailers.

c. Buses.

d. Vehicles that discharge passengers for crossing.

Further, lanes for waiting vehicles with and without reservation should be separated. Reservation possibilities will increase the required number of lanes for waiting vehicles, but they will reduce the required total length of the lanes because vehicles with reservations spend a shorter time waiting. A rough idea of the size of the marshaling area can be obtained under the assumption that waiting time during peak traffic of more than two to three hours would not be accepted. With trip frequencies of about 1 hour, this would indicate a marshaling area corresponding to two or three ferry departures. Figure 18–38 shows the layout of a terminal that has been designed according to the principles just outlined.

The required *passenger facilities* are mainly shelter for use while waiting for departure. In addition, provisions for refreshments, limited shopping, and toilet facilities should be considered. For safety reasons, special gangways for passengers should be provided.

In order to allow rapid *berthing*, a continuous fendering system with a smooth front panel is normally used. Movable ramps are installed ashore at the bottom of the ferry berth. As the ferries may not be equipped with ramps, the outer end of the shore ramp is connected to the bow or stern of the ferries directly. Ferries with two or more decks require more

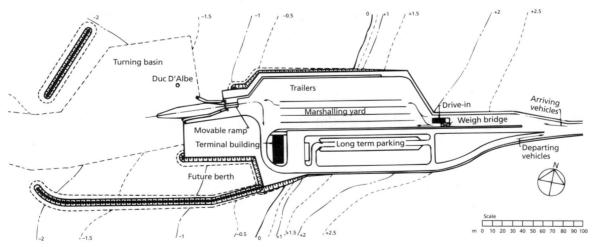

Figure 18–38   Ferry Terminal Layout

Source: Hans Agerschou, Helge Lundgren, and Torben Sorensen, *Planning and Design of Ports and Marine Terminals*, John Wiley and Sons, 1983.

than one shore ramp to provide access to the different decks. The approach road from the marshaling yard to the ramps must be designed in such a way that it is possible to divert cars to all the decks. Ramps are designed to sustain the traffic load and to be able to transfer the vehicles safely during extreme water levels. The length of the ramp may be determined on the basis of information on high- and low-water statistics and the maximum allowable steepness of the ramp (normally 1 in 10), together with specifications of the vehicles to be transported. The ramps must be able to allow small roll movements of the ferry at berth.

Multimodal Terminals

Terminals and interfaces related to "individual" passenger and freight transportation modes (i.e., highway, bus, truck, rail, water, and air) are discussed in other parts of this chapter. This section focuses on bringing together these elements and on how to best integrate multimodal considerations. Many "individual mode" terminals are multimodal to some degree. The terminals described here, however, are *designed* to incorporate more than one mode (e.g., a major rail station that incorporates a bus terminal within the facility, or vice-versa).

Passenger Multimodal Terminals[B,L,M]

Current thinking on the *functional planning* issues of multimodal passenger transportation terminals revolves around the concept of "seamless transportation." Truly seamless transportation is a one-seat, one-fare ride from origin to destination. However, virtually all journeys include an "access" trip to the boarding terminal, a "line haul" trip on the major mode of travel, possible transfers to other line haul modes, and an "egress" trip from the terminal to the final destination. To accommodate "seamless" travel, the terminal designer should strive to maximize passenger convenience for transfers between modes by: reducing distances between boarding and alighting points for transferring passengers in the terminal; providing clearly marked routes for transfers; minimizing level changes; and providing real time information on boarding locations, schedules, and delays.

Terminal planners should also examine market forecasts for travel demands and extract the demand for transfers. By studying the relative volumes of passengers transferring between modes, the planner can prioritize the importance of transfers between each pair of mode types served by the terminal facility and develop plans accordingly.

Frequently, there are some key *institutional issues* in the planning of intermodal passenger terminals. This applies when the terminal needs to accommodate systems operated by more than one operating authority or company. In some instances, transportation companies offer competing services at the same terminal or compete for terminal space or other resources. To provide convenient intermodal service, it may be necessary to overcome institutional barriers or incorporate behaviors that hinder cooperation. In such instances, terminal planners must develop a design process that includes strategies that clearly identify legitimate interests and requirements of all operators, foster open and nonthreatening communications among all involved parties, and forge a consensus on the allocation of terminal resources and interfaces. Among the issues that must be addressed are the integration of passenger information systems, fares, ticket vending and collection, and terminal management.

To illustrate integration of functional and institutional issues, a multimodal terminal for Fullerton, California is described next, along with several larger multimodal interfaces—including a complex urban rail, bus, and parking center in Jersey City, New Jersey; and a major renovation of the South Station multimodal passenger terminal in Boston, Massachusetts.

Fullerton had for some time been looking at a project that would become the entry point and the first phase in a total downtown redevelopment effort to upgrade and unify the downtown shopping area. A key element in this program was the idea of a transportation center that would tie together the local transit district bus operations, Amtrak service, Santa Fe Right-of-Way, park-and-ride, auto and taxi access in a multimodal terminal facility. This concept was then expanded to include the immediate surrounding blocks to see how such a transit facility could be developed into a possible transit mall, incorporating a nearby historic building and including commercial renovation and new construction. Figure 18–39, the master site plan, shows Commonwealth Avenue, a major east-west street; and Harbor Boulevard, the major north–south street, which together define the basic two-block area for the transportation center.

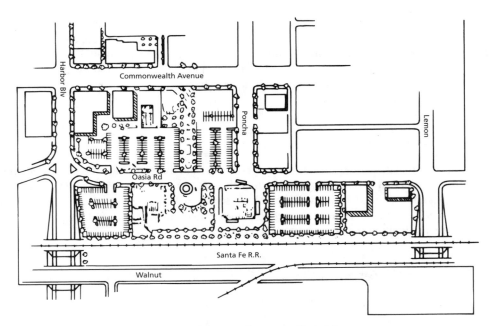

Figure 18–39   Fullerton Site Plan

Sources: Fullerton Transportation Center Feasibility Study, prepared by PDQ&P, Inc. and WMRT.

The proposed project consisted of: expanded retail parking, a public plaza from Commonwealth Avenue down to the Santa Fe Building, and an integrated transit and retail complex consisting of the existing Santa Fe Terminal (used by Amtrak), the renovated and expanded Union Pacific building (to be a restaurant), and a small courtyard and shelter structure for the transit district bus operations. Flanking this complex is parking for the restaurant and transit operations.

The final plans evolved from four previous alternatives that were studied in concert with local citizen groups, technical representatives of the transit operators, and the city redevelopment and planning agencies. The project required a very thorough traffic analysis, absolutely crucial in establishing the various bus routes to service the area and the best access patterns to the facility. A transfer facility must be located so as to serve bus routes with the least detour from their normal routing. The bus terminal consists of a 14 to 15 foot-wide perimeter of sheltered space for bus patrons around a landscaped square. The bus operations on the perimeter of this very direct design allow simple, easy transfers between buses and a short walk to the Amtrak station.

The Journal Square Transportation Center in Jersey City, N.J. (see Figure 18–40) is a multimodal transportation and commercial center located at a key station of the Port Authority Trans-Hudson (PATH) rail rapid system. It is a vertically-integrated interface among the rail, bus and auto parking modes, and incorporates a ten-story office tower and consumer service commercial space. Because of the high traffic volumes involved, a grade-separated bus terminal and structural parking for 600 cars are provided, tying in with the PATH rail service that operates every 3 min. during peak periods. The bus terminal serves over 20 bus routes. The bus terminal level and the parking level are directly accessible (by stairs, escalators, and elevators) to the underground rail platforms. The center provides off-street efficiency and convenience for bus and auto commuters, replacing former on-street locations for these feeder modes. The center, located in air rights above the PATH right-of-way, has been in operation since 1975. The total complex is basically owned and operated by a public agency (Port Authority of New York and New Jersey), so it is institutionally integrated as well as modally integrated. Subsequent to its completion an element of public-private ownership was introduced when sections of the office tower were sold to major tenants in an "office condominium" arrangement.

Boston's South Station is an example of a major intercity, commuter, and local transportation interface that has been upgraded and expanded. After major reconstruction, South Station has become a true intermodal transportation center. (Figure 18–41.)

Figure 18–40   Journal Square Transportation Center

Source: ITE, *Transportation Planning Handbook*, 1992.

In September 1989, passengers were able to transfer from the railroad into the city's existing subway system without braving the weather. Two more building phases complete the transformation concept: a bus depot built over the railroad tracks followed by a privately-developed commercial tower above the terminal. When the Massachusetts Bay Transportation Authority completed the second phase in 1992, South Station became one of the nation's largest mass transit centers.

In addition to physical integration of modes (in stations, terminals, and transportation centers), true multimodal coordination needs to include eliminating institutional barriers, such as different fare media, incompatible ticketing mechanisms, and conflicting fare policies. Examples from San Francisco and New York illustrate efforts in this direction.

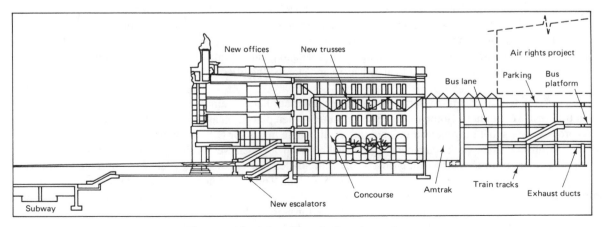

Figure 18–41   South Station, Boston

Source: *Engineering News-Record.*

A project was initiated in the 1980s to improve the integration of fares among the three largest public transit operators in the San Francisco Bay Area: the San Francisco Bay Area Rapid Transit District (BART), the Alameda-Contra Costa Transit District (AC), and the San Francisco Municipal Railway (Muni). AC-Muni and BART-Muni joint passes were introduced in 1981 and 1983, respectively. A new joint fare instrument for AC and BART was introduced in February 1987. For the first time, BART riders using a specially marked, high-value stored-fare ticket were able to use that ticket as flash pass for a boarding local AC buses. They would no longer need to stop at a transfer-issuing machine or carry exact change for the bus transfer payment. The added convenience and discounted fare were designed to be attractive to the regular riders and to induce them to purchase higher-valued BART tickets. Beyond the immediate goal of providing another two-agency fare instrument, the San Francisco project examined new ways to expand the use of stored-value tickets, including on-board bus equipment.

Large-scale introduction of a multimodal, multicompany stored value fare medium was realized in New York in the mid-1990s under the MetroCard program of the Metropolitan Transportation Authority (MTA). A magnetic "swipe" card, MetroCard provides a fare medium useable on all MTA transit modes (e.g., subways, New York City local buses, New York City express buses, suburban MTA buses), as well as on several privately-owned transit lines (e.g., local bus, express bus). System-wide introduction of MetroCard improved passenger convenience and reduced fare transaction times. This processing rate increase and fare medium integration has significant potential for improving interface functions of all of the rail and bus modes.

Freight Multimodal Terminals

The technical considerations for freight intermodal terminals are covered in this chapter's sections on the truck, rail, port and airport freight modes. Some of the environmental, regulatory, and institutional issues of the intermodal freight industry are discussed here. Intermodal freight movements have grown both in terms of volume and diversity. Virtually all intermodal interfaces currently occur in or abutting an urban area. Any examination of urban goods movement issues takes account of the influence and presence of intermodal facilities and movements. Intermodal freight movements usually involve the following combinations of different modes.:

- Truck and rail (e.g., piggyback, TOFC, COFC, Road Railer).

- Ship/barge and truck or rail (ports and containers).

- Pipeline/ship/barge and truck (petroleum distribution).

- Truck and air (air cargo at airports).

Intermodal terminals by nature are land intensive, and they generate movements of large and heavy trucks. Access roads leading to these facilities, and storage space for trucks inside the terminals, are important elements of the overall operation. Deficiencies in these elements would cause adverse effects on other road users by creating traffic congestion. The design of intermodal terminals, in many cases, failed to provide for the needs of all the modes involved. For example, the design of airports tends to emphasize the need for passenger access and may not adequately focus on air freight aspects. Seaports and rail terminals also need to consider adequate access and storage facilities for trucks.

A special issue related to intermodal terminals involves international containers referred to as International Standard Organization (ISO) containers. Some of the ISO containers when placed on appropriate chassis and pulled by tractors result in gross weights that may exceed the maximum allowable limits for U.S. highways. Truck drivers often have to accept overweight ocean-shipping containers at ports without knowing their weights because of the lack of scales to weigh either the containers prior to their loading on trucks or the loaded trucks before they leave the port area and travel on public highways. The size of containers may also be a problem. The height and length of international and domestic containers are increasing, and the routing of trucks carrying these containers through an urban area is becoming problematic in some cases because of restricted clearance through bridges, tunnels, and the like.

Airports

Terminal Planning (Landside)[N]

Introduction

The planning of an airport is such a complex process that the analysis of one activity without regard to the effect on other activities will not provide acceptable solutions. An airport encompasses a wide range of activities that have different and often conflicting requirements. Yet they are interdependent so that a single activity may limit the capacity of the entire complex. Airport planning efforts must be founded on the basis of a comprehensive airport system and master plans.

Elements of a large airport are shown in Figure 18–42. It is divided into two major components, the air side and the landside. The terminal buildings form the division between the two components. Within the system, the characteristics of the vehicles, both ground and air, have a large influence on planning. The passenger and the shipper of goods are interested in primarily the overall door-to-door travel time and not just in the duration of the air journey. For this reason access to airports is an essential consideration in planning.

In the early days of air transport, airports were located at a distance from the city, where inexpensive land and a limited number of obstructions permitted a maximum of flexibility in airport operations. Because of the nature of aircraft and the infrequency of flight, noise was not a problem to the community.

The phenomenal growth of air traffic has increased the probability of unfavorable community reaction, but developments in the aircraft themselves have had the most profound effect on airport–community relations. The greater size and speed of aircraft have resulted in increases in approach and runway requirements, while increases in the output of power plants have brought concern regarding noise. Modern passenger and cargo aircraft are considerably quieter than earlier jets, helping to reduce this as a factor in airport operations, though noise is still a major consideration. In addition, inappropriate land use planning and regulation has allowed residential areas to be developed in approach zones, further exacerbating the problem. Faced with these problems the airport must cope with the problems of securing sufficient airspace for access to the air, sufficient land for ground operations, and adequate ground access to the metropolitan area.

Forecasts[N]

In airport planning, the designer must view the entire airport system as well as the airport under immediate consideration. *Macro forecasts* are forecasts of the total aviation activity in a large region, such as a country, state, or metropolitan area. *Micro forecasts* deal with the activity at individual airports or on individual routes. Micro forecasts for airport planning determine such variables as the number of originations, the passenger origin-destination traffic, the number of enplaned passengers, and the number of aircraft operations by air-carrier and general aviation aircraft at an airport. Separate forecasts are usually made, depending upon the need in a particular study, for cargo movements, commuter service, and ground access vehicular traffic. These forecasts are normally prepared to indicate annual

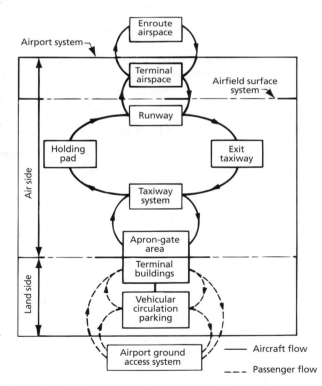

Figure 18–42   Components of the Airport Passenger System for a Large Airport

Source: Robert Horonjeff and Francis X. McKelvey, *Planning and Design of Airports*, Fourth Edition, McGraw-Hill, 1994.

levels of activity and are then desegregated for airport planning purposes to provide forecasts of the peaking characteristics of traffic during the hours of the day, days of the week, and months of the year.

A demand forecast is based on statistical analysis and historical data trends that are projected into the future. The procedure is not simply mathematical because there are so many variables to be considered. Demographic, economic, political, and geographic forces are just some of the other variables that must be reviewed. Past and future influences must be measured. This can be accomplished by using existing economic forecasting models and introducing the results as input for the forecast model. Factors to be considered include current carrier fleets, anticipated retirements, known and projected delivery schedules, and future aircraft development.

Deregulation in the United States accelerated the formation of transfer complexes. The volume of transfer passengers needs very intensive projection for each airport. This factor can have major effects on the design within the terminal complex as well as on the types, amounts, and peaking patterns of airport ground access transportation modes.

International Air Transport Association (IATA) member airlines use, as design days, selected busy days of the year. For instance the fortieth busiest day of the year or the second busiest day in a peak week of the year (the busiest week of normal airport traffic). Specifically excluded are weeks with large holiday traffic volumes. Initial results are always carefully evaluated, and adjustments are made if average peaks appear to be excessive.

U.S. scheduled airlines have concluded that facilities designed for the peak hour of the average day of the peak month of the selected design year will provide desired levels of service throughout the year and can be supported economically. For many airports in the United States, July or August is the peak month of the year. In this case, the average day of the peak month is 1/31 of the July or August traffic. Information on peak hour aircraft movements by category of seats is used to determine:

1. The number of aircraft gates by size.

2. The approximate gross size of the major terminal elements. U.S. carrier forecasts show passenger volumes as enplanements. The number of passengers in official publications are usually stated as total passengers, enplanements plus deplanements, which is approximately equal to two times the number of enplanements. Deplaning peak hour volumes may be different from enplaning peak hour volumes, and the two peaks often occur at different times of the day. Such information can be obtained by analysis of the historical data.

Passenger Terminal Flow and Function[o]

The way aircraft, passengers, baggage, and vehicles move at an airport can be best understood through graphic illustration. Flow diagrams identify sequences of functions for the preparation of schematic drawings in plan and cross section. A series of diagrams can be developed as graphic models, in order to test different arrangements of functions or subfunctions. Computer simulation programs can facilitate this testing.

Flow in an airport terminal complex takes place in the following three major areas' landside:

1. *Apron*—the area located between the runway-taxiway system and the terminal. Serves the flow of aircraft to and from gates and the flow of aircraft ground handling equipment.

2. *Terminal*—the area located between aircraft gate positions and the vehicular curb. Serves the flow of passengers and baggage.

3. *Ground transportation facility*—the area located between the terminal and airport points of ground access at the airport boundaries.

A distinction can be made between primary and secondary flow. Aircraft, passengers, and baggage constitute the *primary flow* in an airport terminal complex. The flow of arriving and departing aircraft is different for each terminal concept due to different aircraft gate configurations and different runway–taxiway arrangements. The flow of passengers and baggage, domestic and international, can be divided into four categories: originating, terminating, transfer, and transit.

1. *Originating*—departing or enplaning passengers, arriving at the terminal by ground transportation (outbound traffic).

2. *Terminating*—incoming or deplaning passengers arriving at the terminal by aircraft (inbound traffic).

It should be noted that originating and terminating passenger traffic generates visitor traffic—people escorting passengers. Visitor and passenger ratios vary by airport and must be established when the flow for a full day or for predetermined times of the day is calculated.

3. *Transfer*—passengers transferring from one flight to another, interline from one airline to another, or intraline, on the same airline. Baggage is handled by the airline, except for passengers transferring from an international flight to a domestic flight, in which case the passenger must claim his or her bag and pass through immigration and customs inspection.

4. *Transit or through-passengers*—passengers who do not change aircraft at an en route stop.

Figure 18–43 shows two diagrams of the primary flow of departing and arriving passengers, baggage, and vehicles between the airport point of entry and exit, and the aircraft gate position at the terminal. As can be seen in Figure 18–44, the processing of passengers, baggage, aircraft ground handling, and ground transportation operations are performed through a sequence of functional elements.

The vehicular curb and curb platform in front of the terminal building are used for the loading and off-loading of passengers and baggage. Curbside baggage check-in positions may be installed, with conveyors to move bags to the outbound baggage room. The length of the curb and the requirements for the platform are based on the size and the number of vehicles at the curb at a given time, but the length of the platform must relate to that of the building facade and entrances. Depth of curb frontage should also be determined (influenced by weather protection, number of pedestrians, curbside check-in facilities, and accumulation of passengers and baggage for commercial vehicles).

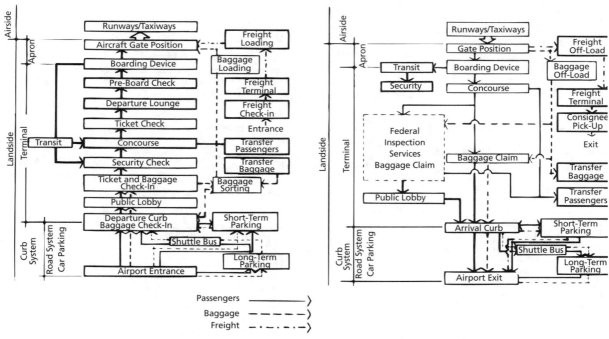

(a) Outbound U.S. Domestic and U.S. International Passenger and Baggage Flow (Federal Inspection Not Required)

(b) Inbound U.S. Domestic and U.S. International Passenger and Baggage Flow

Figure 18–43(a) and (b)   Airport Passenger and Baggage Flow

Source: Walter Hart, *The Airport Passenger Terminal,* Krieger Publishing Company, 1991.

Vehicles on fixed guideways need dedicated station stops with platforms, which can be installed on grade, below grade, or elevated. Vehicular parking may be on grade, below grade, or in a special structure; and they can be located close to the terminal or above or below the terminal, all in combination with remote areas.

Ticket check-in takes place at ticket counters with conveyor belts for the transportation of baggage to the outbound baggage room. The outbound baggage handling facility in a large terminal complex may be located in a place other than in the terminal building. Many larger airports are increasingly handling this function under the apron areas in centralized, automated facilities.

The terminal ticket lobby is the most prominent public space in an airport and has quite often invited a monumental design. The public area of the inbound baggage facilities interacts with the ground transportation facilities and the curbside. Therefore, this area is almost always a part of the terminal or is located adjacent to the terminal. (Figures 18–44 and 18–45.)

The *enplaning* flow through the concourse or corridors is a function of the rate at which passengers arrive at the terminal before scheduled departure time. The *deplaning* flow has surge characteristics because deplaning from each aircraft arrival takes place within a short span of time in one continuous flow. For instance, 300 passengers may deplane within 5 to 10 mins. The use of "flight bank" scheduling at hub airports intensifies the potential surge flows.

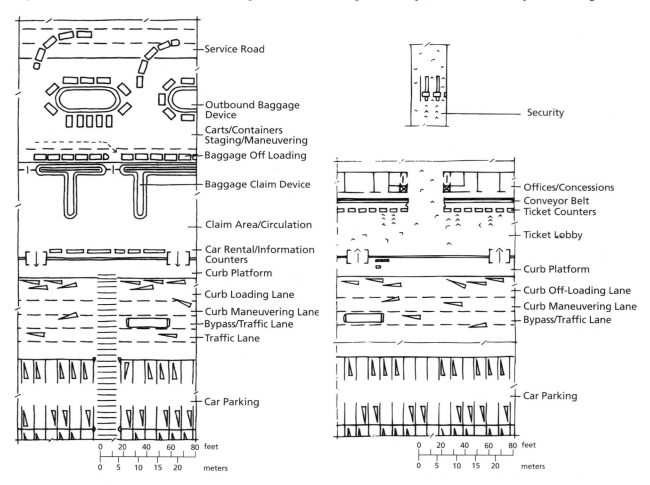

Figure 18–44   Arrivals, Baggage Claim, Ground Transportation, Outbound Baggage

Source: Walter Hart, *The Airport Passenger Terminal*, Krieger Publishing Company, 1991.

Figure 18–45   Departures, Ground Transportation, Ticket Security

Source: Walter Hart, *The Airport Passenger Terminal*, Krieger Publishing Company, 1991.

Departure lounges may be centralized in the terminal area, but as a rule they are decentralized and located in the concourse at each aircraft gate position.

Deplaning should take place through a dedicated area in order not to disturb enplaning passengers waiting or checking in. Most countries do not allow international passengers to mix with domestic passengers. United States domestic and international departing, and domestic arriving, passengers are allowed to mix because the arriving passengers passed through security before boarding at the originating airport. International departing passengers in the United States do not pass through immigration or customs and can mix with other passengers. In most countries, passengers departing for another country must pass through government controls, and visitors are not allowed beyond that point.

Departing passengers must pass *security checkpoints* before aircraft boarding. The locations of the checkpoints vary because of different terminal concepts and local regulations. The increasingly stringent security standards of the 1990s require intensive concentration on this aspect of terminal planning. Meeting these international, national, and local criteria basically requires a total rethinking of previous airport terminal flow and design.

At two-level terminals, *passenger-loading bridges* are attached to the building and are considered ramp equipment. The difference in height between the second level of the terminal boarding area, the aircraft door sills, and the maximum allowable slope determines the length of bridges.

Originating passengers can check *baggage* with the airline for carriage in the aircraft hold (outbound baggage). Terminating passengers can pick up their bags in the baggage claim area of the terminal after it is deposited there by the airline. The arrival rates of passengers, baggage ratios, and volumes of baggage require decisions on which type of system should be provided: stationary, mechanical, automatic, or semiautomatic sorting, and other such devices.

Terminal Concepts and Functions[o]

There are a number of ways in which the facilities of the passenger terminal system are physically arranged, and in which the various passenger-processing activities are performed. Centralized passenger processing means that all the facilities of the system are housed in one building and used for processing all passengers using the building. *Centralized processing facilities* offer economies of scale in that many of the common facilities may be used to service a large number of aircraft gate positions. *Decentralized processing*, on the other hand, means that the passenger facilities are arranged in smaller modular units and repeated in one or more buildings. Each unit is arranged around one or more aircraft gate positions.

There are four basic horizontal distribution concepts, as well as many variations or hybrids that include combinations of these basic concepts. Each can be used with varying degrees of centralization. These concepts are shown in Figure 18–46 and discussed in the following sections.

The following terminal concepts should be considered in the development of the terminal area plan. Many airports have combined one or more terminal types.

Pier or Finger Concept

The pier concept has an interface with aircraft along piers extending from the main terminal area. Aircraft are usually arranged around the axis of the pier in a parallel or nose-in parking alignment. Each pier has a row of aircraft gate positions on both sides, with a passenger concourse along the axis that serves as the departure lounge and circulation space for both enplaning and deplaning passengers.

The chief advantage of this concept is its ability to be expanded in incremental steps as the aircraft or passenger demands warrant. It is also relatively economical in terms of capital and operating costs. Its chief disadvantages are its relatively long walking distance from curb front to aircraft and the lack of a direct curb front relationship to aircraft gate positions.

Satellite Concept

The satellite concept consists of a building surrounded by aircraft, which is separated from the terminal and is usually reached by means of a surface, underground, or above-ground connector. The aircraft are normally parked in radial or parallel positions around the satellite. It often affords the opportunity for simple maneuvering and taxiing patterns for aircraft, but it requires more apron area than other concepts. It can have common or separate departure lounges. Since enplaning and deplaning from the aircraft are accomplished from a common and often remote area, mechanical systems may be employed to transport passengers and baggage between the terminal and satellite. Such systems might include automated guideway transit (AGT), popularly referred to as "people movers."

The main advantages of this concept lie in its adaptability to common departure lounge and check-in functions and the ease of aircraft maneuverability around the satellite structure. However, construction cost is relatively high because of the need to provide connecting concourses to the satellite. It lacks flexibility for expansion; and passenger walking distances are relatively long, unless mechanical assists are provided.

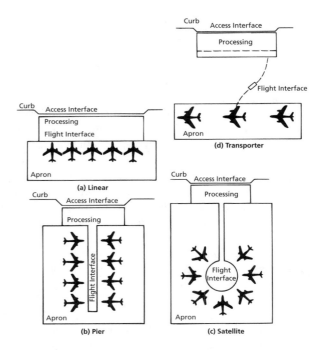

Figure 18–46 (a)–(d)   Horizontal Distribution Concepts, Passenger Terminals

Source: Robert Horonjeff and Francis X. McKelvey, *Planning and Design of Airports*, Fourth Edition, McGraw-Hill, 1994.

Linear, Frontal, or Gate Arrivals Concept

The simple linear terminal consists of a common waiting and ticketing area with exits leading to the aircraft parking apron. It is adaptable to airports with low airline activity that will usually have an apron providing close-in parking for three to six commercial passenger aircraft. The layout of the simple terminal should take into account the possibility of pier, satellite, or linear additions for terminal expansion. In the gate arrivals or frontal concept, aircraft are parked along the face of the terminal building. Concourses connect the various terminal functions with the aircraft gate positions. This concept offers ease of access and relatively short walking distances if passengers are delivered to a point near gate departure by vehicular circulation systems. Expansion may be accomplished by linear extension of an existing structure or by developing two or more terminal units with connectors.

These concepts provide direct access from curb to aircraft gate positions and afford a high degree of flexibility for expansion. They do not provide convenient opportunities for the use of common facilities and, as this concept is expanded into separate buildings, may lead to high operating costs.

Transporter, Open-Apron, or Mobile Conveyance Concept

Aircraft and aircraft-serving functions in the transporter concept are remotely located from the terminal. The connection to the terminal is provided by vehicular transport for enplaning and deplaning passengers. The characteristics of the transporter concept include flexibility in providing additional aircraft parking positions to accommodate increases in schedules or aircraft size, the capability to maneuver an aircraft in and out of a parking position under its own power, the separation of aircraft-servicing activities from the terminals, and reduced walking distances for the passenger.

This concept minimizes the level of capital costs since the building efficiently uses minimal departure lounge space and has gate positions for transporters rather than aircraft. It offers a high degree of flexibility in both operation and expansion.

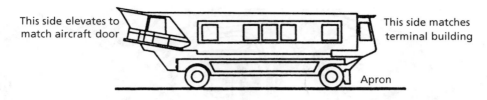

Figure 18–47   Typical Mobile Lounge

Source: Robert Horonjeff and Francis X. McKelvey, *Planning and Design of Airports*, Fourth Edition, McGraw-Hill, 1994.

Aircraft maneuverability is very high, and a separation between landside and air side is very obvious. The use of mobile lounges (Figure 18–47) to transport passengers to and from aircraft can increase passenger processing time; and, unless scheduling is carefully coordinated, unnecessary delays may result. Required security checks will also increase operating costs for this concept.

Concept Combinations and Variations

Combinations of concepts and variations are a result of changing conditions experienced from the initial conception of the airport throughout its life span. An airport may have many types of passenger activity, varying from originating and terminating passengers to passengers on commuter or connecting flights. Combined concepts acquire some of the advantages and disadvantages of each basic concept. A combination of concept types can be advantageous where more costly modifications would be necessary to maintain the original concept. Figure 18–48 illustrates a combination of three concepts at O'Hare International Airport in Chicago.

Many of the largest and busiest airports have not only combined concepts in a single terminal, but they have also been designed as multiterminal facilities. This provides the necessary air side and landside capacity, and it also affords the larger airlines the opportunity to operate from their own "unit" terminal. The multiterminal layout involves greater complexity and therefore needs special attention to assure a smoothly functioning total facility; and particular attention is needed in such matters as orientation and signing, ground access to and among the terminals, passenger movement among the terminals, separate or consolidated baggage facilities, centralized or decentralized vehicular access and parking, and equal access by ground transportation carriers.

Planning for *concessions* within the terminal buildings is an important consumer service and financial element of passenger terminal planning and design. It is important to carefully integrate several objectives that, at best, need intensive and detailed planning and may often actually conflict with each other. For example, the planner needs to maximize passenger convenience while also maximizing revenue potential from concession areas, which often means routing passengers through paths longer than function would indicate.

Airport shopping has become a major enterprise, especially at international airports. Increasingly, airport shopping at large airports has expanded into configurations similar to retail malls, with most of the retail area accessible without passing through security and customs checkpoints. Shops selling books, candy, clothing, electronics, gifts, jewelry and watches, luggage, music, shoes, spirits, specialty foods, and toys are all typically found in airport retail centers.

Centralized concepts such as the pier and finger concepts or satellite concepts are much better suited for efficient commercial activity. Like urban shopping centers, concessions perform better when grouped together and combined with a geometric focal point to provide a pleasing combination of form and function. The concept should be open with sufficient open space, which reduces congestion and increases visibility inside the terminal. The layout that serves this purpose best is the one with a central core or hub, with departure and arrival links serving the air side, and an entrance and exit corridor serving the land side.

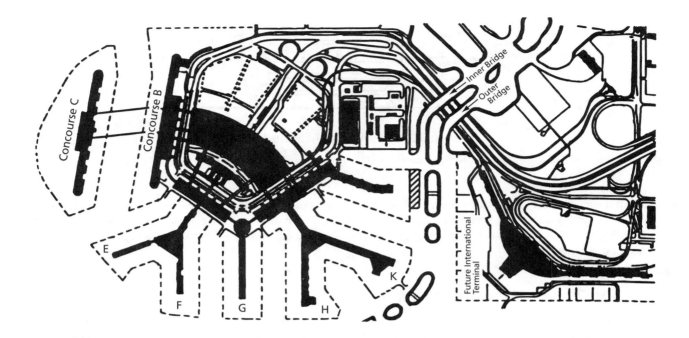

Figure 18–48　Linear, Satellite, and Pier Concepts, O'Hare International Airport, Chicago

Source: Robert Horonjeff and Francis X. McKelvey, *Planning and Design of Airports*, Fourth Edition, McGraw-Hill, 1994.

Terminal Circulation and Distribution

Whatever terminal concept is employed, an extensive amount of "people movement" is involved for circulation within the terminal(s) and for distribution to and from the terminals. Air passengers, airport employees, visitors, service and sales personnel, and others need convenient means to move, on foot, among the various airport elements. This includes moving:

- Between parking lots and garages and the terminal.

- Between curb frontage and gates.

- Within terminals (transfer passengers).

- Among several terminals and concourses.

Planning and design of the necessary walkways, corridors, stairways, and other fixed pedestrian facilities should be based on available pedestrian flow analysis techniques, as outlined earlier in this chapter and treated more fully in Chapter 16, "Bicycle and Pedestrian Facilities."

Mechanically-assisted pedestrian facilities (moving walks, escalators, elevators) and guideway "people mover" systems are covered later in this chapter, as well as in Chapter 16. Figure 18–49 is an example of the application of "people mover" technology for on-airport circulation and distribution. Tampa uses a radial arrangement, with the elevated guideways connecting a central "landside" building to "air side" satellites.

Orientation and Signing[O,P]

The planned flow of passengers and vehicles must be directed and supported by sign programs. Electronics, fast-resolve cathode ray tubes, LEDs, radio impulses, computer techniques, and lighting systems for the transfer and display of information have expanded the scope and capability of sign programs and, accordingly, influenced the concept development of terminals and ground transportation facilities. (Also see the Information Systems section of this chapter.)

Criteria must deal with the size, appearance, illumination, and type of construction of signs. Certain signs must have a capability for interchange and addition at reasonable costs. For example, road signs and facade or curb signs for new tenants should be easy to add or interchange.

Airport sign programs serve three main purposes:

1. *Direction and orientation*—for the direction and guidance of the flow of outbound and inbound traffic of:

   a. Passengers and visitors.

   b. Vehicles (e.g., private, public, and service).

   c. Ground transportation (e.g., highway, transit, taxis).

2. *Identification of locations*—such as those of airlines in ticket lobbies; in baggage claim areas; at gates or in concourses; telephones; restrooms; and concessions, such as car rentals, banks, shops, and newsstands.

3. *Information*—to be provided on:

   a. Aircraft arrivals and departures, originations, destinations, and gates.

   b. Baggage delivery by claim device, airline, flight number, and origination.

   c. Governmental regulations, such as security, immigration, and customs.

   d. Special services, such as public ground transportation, hotel and motel, rental car, and other courtesy vans.

   e. Matters of a general nature, such as tourism and conventions.

In a passenger terminal or on a road system, people must experience a seemingly effortless sequence of logical decisions. A terminal plan is correct when the decision-making process provides users with good orientation, enabling them to make quick decisions, one at a time, for the achievement of their objectives.

The sign programs of ground transportation systems surrounding the airport and entering an airport must be analyzed for acceptability and usefulness, even when their use is compulsory. Architects, planners, airport operators, and airlines all have a strong tendency to develop their own graphics and to exercise their own personal interpretation of the signs and symbols programs that have been established locally, nationally, or internationally. Such individual graphic design decisions should be avoided whenever possible.

Particularly for roadway signing on and near the airport, good traffic engineering practice should be followed based on the *Manual on Uniform Traffic Control Devices* and other relevant guides. The Institute of Transportation Engineers (ITE), for example, has developed the recommended practice *Airport Roadway Guide Signs*.[6] This report gives

---

[6] *Airport Roadway Guide Signs,* ITE Committee 50–1, Airport Guide Signing (Washington, D.C.: ITE, 1991).

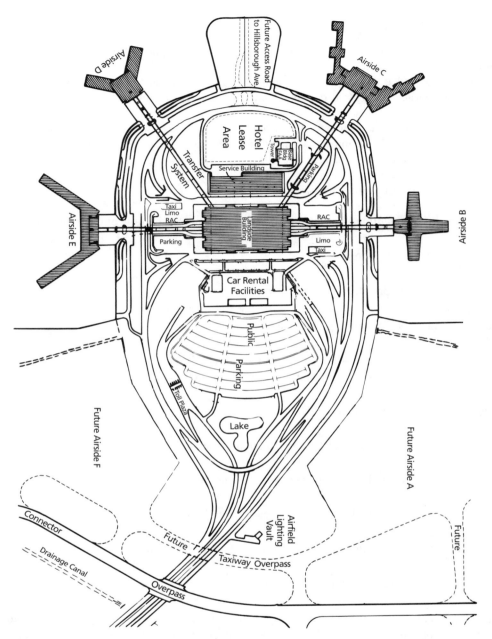

Figure 18–49 Example of the Satellite Concept, Tampa International Airport

Source: Robert Horonjeff and Francis X. McKelvey, *Planning and Design of Airports,* Fourth Edition, McGraw-Hill, 1994.

recommendations for both single terminal and multiterminal airports and considers practices in a wide range of airports in the United States and Canada. Some of its key recommendations are presented in the following paragraphs.

Particularly for larger airports, a good deal of judgment is required to determine where directional signs *to the airport* should be installed. An origin-destination flow map is useful in determining the major approaches that should receive the most visible signing. All of the major roads that intersect these feeders in the vicinity of the airport should carry the airport message as an integral part of their highway destination signs, including overhead signs. If there is only one airport in the area, the word "Airport" will suffice. If there is more than one airport, it is necessary to include its name: e.g., "Dulles Airport." If there is more than one entrance, it may be desirable to have variable message signs (VMS) operated from a transportation control center to direct motorists to the least congested entrance.

The overall design of signing for the *on-airport roadway system* differs for single and multiterminal airports; however, many individual design elements are the same. The recommended sequence is as follows:

1. Erect airport identification signs clearly indicating that the patron is on the airport grounds. For larger airports, indicate the distance to the terminal area so the driver is comfortable in passing ensuing exits to ancillary destinations.

2. Sign for all traffic not destined for the terminal but headed to other locations, such as hangars, industrial areas, air cargo facilities, airport services and deliveries, administration, hotel, air mail freight, and service roads.

3. Sign for rental cars if there is remote drop-off.

4. If there is a remote parking lot, provide a billboard indicating the various types of parking facilities at the airport and their relative rates—in simplified form.

5. Sign for the remote parking lot.

6. Sign for terminal(s).

7. Sign for the terminal—parking split.

8. Sign for the arrival—departure split. The choice of terminology depends largely on the airport terminal geometry and terminal function. The recommended signs are "Arrivals" and "Departures."

9. Sign *from* the terminal to parking and exit.

By using this signing sequence, the people who do not have to read the more difficult signs dealing with their terminals (airlines, parking, arrivals, and departures) are diverted before encountering them. Also, airline patrons continuing to the terminal are not interrupted.

Air Cargo[Q,R]

At airports where the cargo volume is high, cargo is usually processed at a terminal that is separate from the passenger terminal. However, the increase in large jet aircraft operations has led to a rise in the occurrence of mixed passenger and cargo operations. Large jet aircraft have a high cargo-carrying capacity in excess of what is needed to carry passengers and baggage. Therefore, it is essential when planning the apron-gate area to take cargo-handling considerations into account.

Cargo is composed of air freight and airmail. Airmail is usually conveyed by the carrier to a central airport airmail facility. Air freight is conveyed between the aircraft and the cargo terminal either by the carrier or by an air-freight forwarder. Incoming air freight carried on board a passenger-carrying aircraft usually has to be unloaded at the gate and transported to the cargo terminal. Outgoing air freight is conveyed from the cargo terminal before the scheduled departure and has to be stored in designated areas for expedient loading when the aircraft is ready. Small package express is becoming an increasing factor in air cargo planning, especially at the larger airports.

Another requirement related to cargo handling is for roadways that facilitate the movement of cargo trucks between the apron-gate area and the cargo terminal. Roadways are sometimes designated for cargo trucks to separate them from the movement of other aircraft service vehicles on the apron.

The use of efficient loading equipment is necessary for the loading and unloading of passenger aircraft carrying cargo. Most important are those that are loader-transporter combinations, which have the advantage of reducing the amount of equipment on the apron. Lift-type loaders are used to interface with a variety of aircraft with varying doorsill heights.

Another trend affecting the technology of air-cargo handling is the development of lower deck containers for different types of aircraft. Containers have the advantage that they can be loaded and prepared off the airport, transported directly to the aircraft, and easily loaded on and off the aircraft. As an example, Figure 18–50 shows LD-3 and LD-7 containers that are designed for a wide variety of jet aircraft.

The rapid rate of increase in air cargo traffic; the advent of very high-capacity aircraft capable of accommodating large size units as well as greatly increased quantities of cargo; and new developments in cargo handling methods, including the use of containers and automated equipment, all make flexibility and expandability overriding necessities. As is the case with passenger terminals, a single design concept cannot meet the varying needs of all carriers or all geographical areas.

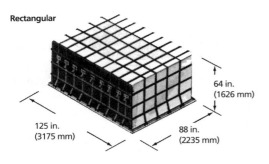

Rectangular

125 in.
(3175 mm)

88 in.
(2235 mm)

64 in.
(1626 mm)

Common Designation **LD-7**
IATA Rate Class 5
IATA ID Code . . . . .UA
Internal Volume . . . . .330 ft^3 (9.3 m^3) – 374 ft^3 (10.6 m^3)
AS 1825 Volume . . . . .Rectangular – 381 ft^3 (10.8 m^3)
Tare Weight . . . . .475 lb (215 kg) – 665 lb (302 kg)
Max. Gross Weight . . . . . .10,200 lb (4627 kg) – 13,300 lb (6033 kg)
Airplane Type . . . . .707, 727, 737, 757, main deck, 747 lower deck.
767 lower deck with large cargo door option.

Note: Rectangular-shaped LD-7 will not fit on main deck of 707, 727, 737, 757 due to interference with interior sidewall.

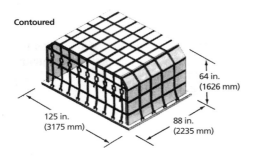

Contoured

125 in.
(3175 mm)

88 in.
(2235 mm)

64 in.
(1626 mm)

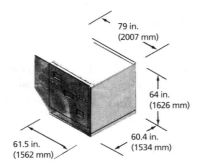

79 in.
(2007 mm)

64 in.
(1626 mm)

61.5 in.
(1562 mm)

60.4 in.
(1534 mm)

Common Designation **LD-3**
IATA Rate Class 8
IATA ID Code . . . . .AK
Internal Volume . . . . .118 ft^3 (3.3 m^3) – 158 ft^3 (4.5 m^3)
AS 1825 Volume . . . . .159 ft^3 (4.5 m^3)
Tare Weight . . . . .150 lb (68 kg) – 270 lb (168 kg)
Max. Gross Weight . . . . .3,500 lb (1588 kg)
Airplane Type . . . . .747, 767 lower deck.

Figure 18–50   LD-3 and LD-7 Cargo Containers

Source: Gerhardt Muller, *Intermodal Freight Transportation,* Eno Foundation for Transportation, Inc., 1995.

In *site planning* for cargo facilities, the site chosen should incorporate flexibility and expansibility to accommodate cargo growth over a period of 20 years. This includes new aircraft that may use the airport during the next 20 years, as well as enlarged cargo terminals and facilities required to handle increased volumes of cargo and, at the larger airports, to implement new cargo handling concepts.

The *planning, design, and layout of airport cargo facilities* should recognize the importance of basic cargo flow principles. Foremost among these are that all-cargo aircraft should be separated from combination (passenger and cargo) aircraft in the process of loading and unloading, preferably at a cargo terminal; and the flow of cargo to, from, and between aircraft should be as smooth as possible and should cover the shortest possible distance in the flow sequence. At the larger airports, adequate provision should be made for the handling of large containers and pallets between trucks and cargo terminals and between cargo terminals and aircraft.

The general principles described here apply to *cargo terminal buildings* of all sizes and all types of handling characteristics. However, the effect of these principles is less marked in very small and very large terminals. Generally, the criteria are best met by a square terminal configuration. However, the significance of truck dock frontage requirements may be such that a rectangle with longer landside and air side frontages than building depth is required. In the planning of *public road systems linked to the cargo terminal complex*, attention should be given to the following factors:

a) Present and future adequacy of the road system at peak periods, for the volume of pickup and delivery vehicles, in addition to other traffic.

b) Requirement for roadways to have sufficient bearing strength and height clearance.

c) The overall traffic road pattern should be engineered to permit easy access from the major road system external to the airport.

d) The need for a public road link between passenger and cargo terminals that is in addition to, and does not conflict with, any service road link.

Adequate *vehicle parking* space should be available on the land side of cargo terminals. Provision should be made for expansion of parking facilities in line with expected volumes of air cargo to be handled and the expansion of cargo terminals. Larger unit carriers (e.g., UPS, Federal Express) are requiring vehicle service areas as well. The parking requirements fall broadly into two categories—operational parking for vehicles for the pickup and delivery of air cargo; and personnel parking, which should be as close as possible to the working area.

The air freight community is realizing the wide and fundamental differences between traditional airport freight terminals and *small-package express hub airport terminals*. The following characteristics of small-package express hub airports illustrate the differences between them and traditional airport freight terminals:

1. They were initiated for the sole purpose of accommodating freight, not passengers.

2. They cater only to freight on freight airplanes, not to freight on combination passenger-freight airplanes.

3. They deal with traffic from only a single integrated company, not a collection of surface and air companies engaged in various aspects of air freight.

4. They deal only with high-priority, door-to-door, intermodal freight—not lower-value airport-to-airport shipments.

5. The number of shipments transferred is vast in relation to poundage.

6. No middlemen are involved because all intermodal transfers are performed from beginning to end by a single company that integrates all modes.

7. The hub principle brings together all the freight at one time.

8. The small-package express hub airport terminal may be located in a relatively rural location where there is inexpensive land and facilities and where a large pool of part-time labor can be obtained.

The differences between traditional airport freight terminals and small-package express hub airport terminals influence the type and uses of handling equipment for intermodal freight transfer at the respective locations. Since small-package express is the newest sector of the air transport business, intermodal handling equipment at hub airport terminals is advanced; but it is still in a developmental stage.

Ground Access

Introduction

Transit time from the point of origin to the ultimate destination for passengers and shippers of air freight is a matter of major concern. In many cases the ground time exceeds the air time by a considerable margin. For a journey of 400 miles between two large metropolitan areas, ground times can be as much as twice the air travel time. A primary concern, particularly for air passengers, is the *reliability* of the access time as well as the absolute travel time.

Surveys of ground transport to the airport indicate that in the United States the majority of passengers, visitors, and airport and airline employees travel by private automobile. Origins and destinations of travelers and shippers relative to airports are widely scattered throughout a metropolitan area. Because of the lack of concentration of origins and destinations of air passengers in a metropolitan area and the popularity of the automobile as a personal means of transportation, U.S. airports have not developed the relatively high use of public transportation that is achieved at airports in other countries, particularly in Europe. Airport operators are attempting to increase the use of the higher-occupancy ground access modes (e.g., regular and special transit services, shared-ride limousine services, taxis) through service improvements, combined with marketing programs. Service improvements include relatively high-capital programs (e.g., rail transit, light rail, busways) as well as new and improved ground services, such as park-ride satellite terminals; improved bus, limousine, taxi, and other shared-ride services; connections to rail transit services; remote terminals; and air passenger and employee public transportation promotion efforts.

In any event, the private automobile and other roadway-based modes will continue to provide the bulk of ground transportation services to the airport. Consequently the planning of streets and highways to the airport and parking at the airport are important factors that must be given consideration. Access to airports is required not only by air passengers but also by other users of the airport, such as employees, visitors, trucks hauling freight, and businesses dealing with the airport's tenants. All modes of access should be considered. The need for terminals in downtown areas or outer areas should also be examined. Although air cargo is growing rapidly, and its routing and geometric requirements must be considered, traffic volume of large trucks is not a major contributor to airport traffic. There is, however, a growing volume of small trucks and vans serving the increasingly important small package express business.

The starting point for estimating the ground traffic generated by air passengers is a forecast of future air travel. It is very desirable to have a forecast of the daily distribution of passenger demand in terms of enplaning and deplaning passengers, at least for the busy hours of the day. The next step is to estimate the modal split of ground transportation among the various alternatives, such as private automobiles, taxis, limousines, and transit. After estimating the modal split, it is necessary to estimate the occupancy in each mode. Using the modal split of airline passengers and the average occupancy by mode, the number of vehicles generated by airline passengers can be determined. From highway capacity calculations the number of lanes required to serve passengers can be estimated. In addition, an estimate is needed of the number of trips generated by sightseers and visitors. In some cases this may amount to 15 to 25 percent of the air passenger traffic. Another approach is to correlate air passenger activity hour by hour with corresponding ground activity by the use of statistical analysis. Such analyses may include the inherent assumption that the current ground-to-air traffic relationship will be maintained in the future, which may not be true if the modal choice split is altered significantly. Many of the larger airports have active "mode-split improvement" programs, so when planners make assumptions about future traffic volumes they need to assess the probable effects of these programs.

At some of the larger airports, traffic generated by employees during peak periods can exceed that generated by passengers and visitors. This makes it imperative to fully consider employee access requirements. Employees usually have a different origin and destination pattern, which may have some influence on access requirements. There does not appear to be a consistent relationship between the number of airport employees and the annual number of air passengers. While each airport needs to be analyzed based on its own individual characteristics, a "first approximation" of highway system requirements can be developed based on trip generation data gathered by organizations such as ITE.

Off-Airport vs. On-Airport

In dealing with ground access it has been convenient for airport planners to think in terms of off-airport and on-airport needs. While this facilitates planning (and often reflects the actual jurisdictional realities), it is important to recognize the close interrelationship between the off-airport access pattern and on-airport facility and service needs. Successful satellite park-rides or well-patronized suburban limousine or bus services can reduce on-airport parking needs. Also, some features that reduce "close-in" parking space needs, such as long-term parking located at the airport "edges," may actually increase vehicle trips on-airport (e.g., drive to drop-off at terminal frontage, drive from terminal to remote parking).

Data Needs for Ground Access Planning[S]

Airport ground access planning requires an understanding of present modal usage and projected patterns. These data should be as comprehensive as possible (e.g., covering all modes, times of day, days, months), and the future projections should be related as closely as possible to anticipated industry trends.

Projection of highway travel volumes uses historical trip generation data for air passengers and airport employees and is based on experience regarding other users (e.g., sightseers, well wishers, service vehicles). Use of public transportation modes cannot be projected using the various available techniques used for "regular" journey-to-work travel.

Planning for airport access by public transportation has particular data needs. These needs are addressed in an ITE committee report on this subject.[7] The following material, adapted from that report, summarizes the data needs and the type of surveys used. The ITE committee developed several working assumptions, including:

1. Public transit includes specialized forms of transit for the airport user (e.g., limousines, taxis, special employee shuttles, subscription buses) and the urban transit system for the region.

2. Potential airport users of public transit include airport employees and people doing business at the airport, as well as air passengers.

3. The base transit service, which is not at issue, is a service for the airport employees that meets the region's standards for transit service to employment centers of that size; and it also serves air travelers who wish to use it.

4. Data should be collected for use in determining what kinds of transit enhancement can be justified, to develop warrants for transit service, to analyze alternatives, and to consider the effects of transit changes.

The committee researched the literature and produced a variety of surveys, techniques, and proposals for collecting data. Examples follow, divided into the two general populations of airport users: (1) employees and (2) travelers and other visitors.

Employees represent the solid base for transit service. They come to the airport daily, on a regular schedule, without luggage or accompanying visitors, and with economic incentives to encourage shared rides. They do not all live in a central place, and they are not concentrated in the same residential neighborhoods air travelers come from. The information needed for planning employee transit, as in all employee travel surveys, is:

---

[7] *Data Needs for Planning Airport Access by Public Transportation* (Washington, D.C.: Institute of Transportation Engineers, October 1980).

1. *Origin*—home address, in sufficient detail to permit coding to travel zones, or zip codes.

2. *Destination*—where within the airport does the employee work?

3. *Hours of employment*—start time, end time, variability, and flexibility.

After this information is coded, it can be processed in a number of ways to determine a variety of high-occupancy mode opportunities, from carpools and vanpools to regularly scheduled transit. A survey conducted at work, with the cooperation of the employer, could obtain the information with a simple questionnaire.

Some airport authorities regularly conduct on-board *air passenger surveys* of a selected sample of arrivals and departures. These surveys are used for a variety of purposes. Planning of transit access can be one of them. There are many alternatives to an on-board survey, especially if the data needs are exclusively ground access related. They include roadside interviews, in-terminal surveys, and on-board surveys of the existing airport transit access. They may be less expensive than an on-board survey.

If such a data base already exists or can be made available, it can be used to determine the potential transit users—those people who fit into one or more of the following categories:

1. CBD oriented, out-of-town visitors.

2. Business travelers with minimal luggage.

3. Nonbusiness travelers of minimal budget.

4. People arriving or departing alone.

5. People whose value of time is, at the time of their arrival or departure, marginal.

6. Tour groups who are guided to public transit.

Other ground-access surveys or roadside interviews collect data for all airport users, including employees, travelers, cargo vehicles, and visitors. Special surveys may be desirable for taxis, limousines, buses, and rail transit (i.e., the present airport services).

Ground Access Modal Usage Patterns[Ta]

While each airport has its own particular access patterns (resulting from its location, market area, available transit services, or type of traffic), it is useful for the airport ground access planner to have a "feel" for typical patterns, generally and at the airport being analyzed. The rapid pace of changes in this deregulated industry must be recognized and planned for, as difficult as that may be. In-airport transfers, a major determinant of ground access needs can change very quickly, with examples of where a 5 percent air transfer proportion grew to 18 percent in only 6 years.

"Modal split" is obviously a key factor in ground access planning. Just *defining* the split needs careful attention as to what constitutes "private" transportation modes and what is meant by "public" transportation modes. "Private cars" and "car rental" are clear classifications. Bus and rail services available to the public (i.e., the common carriers) are certainly "public" transportation. Airport jurisdictions differ, however, in how they categorize taxis, airport limousines, hotel buses, "black cars," and vans. A few example modal splits from five U.S. airports in the mid-90s are shown in Table 18–7. These airports represent a reasonably high "modal split" level for high-occupancy vehicles, with many smaller airports and airports in smaller cities having a much lower public transportation use.

To provide further insight into access patterns and factors that need to be considered in planning airport access, following are some statistics in modal and peaking characteristics. Data on mode of access to airports were assembled from the most recent passenger surveys at over 35 airports. Figure 18–51 shows the minimum, maximum, and median percentages of passengers who gain access to differently sized airports via high-occupancy modes (e.g., rail, bus, van, limousine).

Table 18–7 Mode of Airport Access by Resident Status

Mode Split (Percent)	Los Angeles (LAX)		Baltimore/Washington (BWI)		Washington/Dulles (IAD)		Washington/National (DCA)		Boston/Logan (LGA)	
	Resident	Visitor	Resident	Visitor	Resident	Visitor	Resident	Visitor	Resident	Visitor
Private Vehicles	71	32	90	39	81	36	54	21	75	33
Rental Car	2	32	1	32	1	33	1	18	1	22
Taxi	4	6	3	11	14	13	31	39	13	27
Other On-Demand	7	4	—	—	—	—	—	—	3	7
Scheduled Bus/Van	7	8	—	—	—	—	—	—	8*	11*
Courtesy Vans	1	8	1	7	1	9	0	9	—	—
Rail	—	—	0	1	—	—	13	7	—	—
Other	8	10	5	10	3	9	1	6	—	—
Total	100	100	100	100	100	100	100	100	100	100

* Includes courtesy vans.

Source: Phillip S. Shapiro, et al., *Intermodal Ground Access to Airports: A Planning Guide,* Washington, D.C.: U.S. Department of Transportation, December 1996, p. 73.

Even though a clear-cut relationship cannot be identified from the available data, several observations about mode of access to airports can be made from Figure 18–51. The proportion of passengers who use high-occupancy ground access modes to reach an airport generally increases as originations increase. The median value for access by a high-occupancy mode at airports with less than 5 million annual originations is in the range of 11 percent to 15 percent, and the median for airports with over 5 million annual originations is 21 percent. The maximum high-occupancy mode use for airports with fewer than 2.5 million originations is 18 percent, while for airports with more than 2.5 million originations it is 35.6 percent.

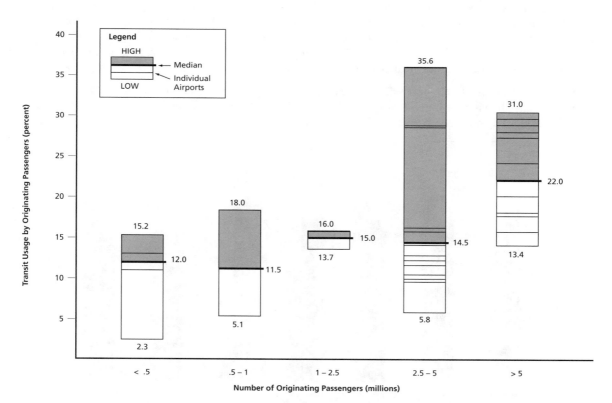

Figure 18–51 Use of High-Occupancy Modes at U.S. Airports

Source: Phillip S. Shapiro, et al., *Intermodal Ground Access to Airports: A Planning Guide,* Washington, D.C.: U.S. Department of Transportation, December 1996, p. 84.

Peaking Characteristics

To analyze demand for ground transportation facilities, such as roadways, parking lots, and curbsides, it is first necessary to determine the most representative "design period." Demand for a facility is usually represented as traffic volume using a roadway, the expected number of parked vehicles in lots or at the curbside, or the number of people using HOV service. The design period varies by the type of facility being planned. For example, roadway and curbside facilities are usually planned to accommodate traffic volumes during a peak one-hour period, called the design hour volume; however, some facilities may be designed to accommodate traffic volumes occurring over 15-min. periods. Parking lots intended for short-term use (i.e., less than a three-hour duration) are also sized to accommodate peak hourly volumes; but long-term and daily parking facilities are frequently sized to accommodate demand expected to occur on a given day of the week.

The level of demand accommodated by ground transportation facilities varies by season, day of the week, and hour of the day. Reasons for this variation, which are outlined in the following sections, should be considered when analyzing data to determine facility standards.

Seasonal Peaking[Tc]

Facility demands vary by month during the course of a year. For example, during peak holiday travel months, such as November and December, airport parking facility use and roadway congestion usually increase compared with off-peak periods. Airports usually experience relatively high facility demands during July and August, when vacation travel activity is high. At airports located in states with warm weather resort destinations, such as Florida and Arizona, the peak month may occur during April (the common spring break time for schools).

Daily Peaking[Td]

Facility demands vary by day of the week. For example, peak roadway traffic volumes may occur early or late in the week as business travelers begin or end their trips. Consequently, the demand for long-term parking facilities may be the greatest during the middle of the week when most business travelers are "on the road." At airports with a high number of nonbusiness or leisure travelers, peak demands may occur on weekend days. Figure 18–52 illustrates these kinds of differences by showing the daily variations in traffic entering the terminal areas, for three weeks in 1996, at a major domestic airport (Eppley Airfield in Omaha, Nebraska).

Daily traffic levels at the Omaha airport are fairly consistent from Sunday through Friday during the June and September periods, with Friday showing the highest volumes. However, during Thanksgiving week, the volumes are higher than during other weeks; and volumes are much higher on Tuesday, Wednesday, and Sunday.

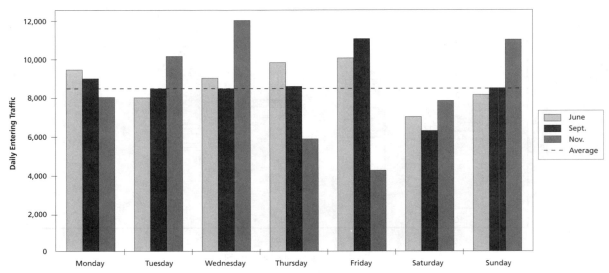

Figure 18–52   Daily Variations of Traffic Entering Eppley Airfield

Source: Phillip S. Shapiro, et al., *Intermodal Ground Access to Airports: A Planning Guide,* Washington, D.C.: U.S. Department of Transportation, December 1996, p. 86.

Hourly Peaking[Te]

Facility demands vary by time of day and type of traffic accommodated by the facility. At large airports, separate roadways and curbsides are often provided to accommodate different passenger activities (e.g., departing vs. arriving passengers, international vs. domestic passengers). Each of these facilities must be designed to accommodate the activity occurring at that facility during the design period. For example, roadways and curbsides serving the departures level or area of a terminal building should be related to the peak period of originating airline passenger activity. However, the curbside peak hour would actually occur before (i.e., "lead") the peak hour for originating passengers. Similarly, the arrivals level curbside peak hour would occur after (i.e., "lag") the peak hour for passengers terminating their trips at the airport. Figure 18–53 displays the 1995 peaking characteristics of a major international airport serving an east coast metropolitan airport (Dulles International Airport, serving Washington, D.C.).

Note that at Dulles Airport the peak period for traffic entering the airport is 4:00 P.M. to 6:00 P.M., and that the peak hour traffic is nearly double that which occurs during other times of the day. Contrast that with the temporal distribution for another airport serving the same metropolitan area displayed in Figure 18–54.

This airport primarily accommodates domestic flights serving areas within 1,000 miles (i.e., 1,200 km). Traffic entering this airport is consistent between 6:00 A.M. and 6:00 P.M., with only a slight peak between 3:00 P.M. and 6:00 P.M. The difference between these temporal distributions is a good example of why the planner should carefully examine the characteristics of the airport under study. The characteristics of access trips to each airport depend on the unique characteristics of that airport.

Along airport service roadways and nonpublic roadways, peak hour traffic volumes may be generated by airport employees, cargo-related vehicles, service vehicles, and other nonairline passenger traffic. Peak demands for the combination of these vehicles must be accommodated. Employee arrival times at the same international airport (Dulles Airport) for which total traffic is shown in Figure 18–53 are shown in Figure 18–55. Employee trips peak between 1:00 P.M. and 2:00 P.M., just before the peak for total airport traffic.

On-Airport Roadway Systems

There are many different operating patterns and geometric arrangements for *on-airport* roadway systems at airports. It is very important to develop the operating concepts along with the functional layout. How many air passenger vehicles will be going to the terminal first and then to parking? How many will go directly to parking? Where will employee vehicles be parked? Whatever the signed (or assumed) pattern, there needs to be flexibility to accommodate differences from the assumed pattern as well as to accommodate airline industry changes that may cause major changes in terminal roadway usage. The roadway system also needs to be integrated with other airport circulation systems (e.g., people mover systems) and with off-airport highway and public transportation systems.

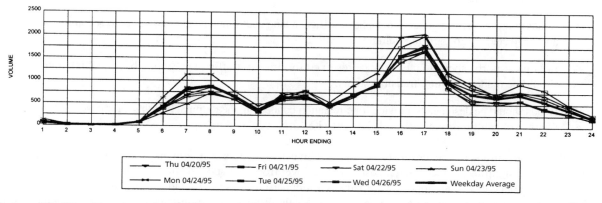

Figure 18–53   Temporal Distribution of Total Traffic Entering a Major International Airport

Source: Phillip S. Shapiro, et al., *Intermodal Ground Access to Airports: A Planning Guide,* Washington, D.C.: U.S. Department of Transportation, December 1996, p. 87.

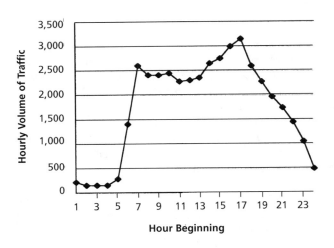

Figure 18–54   Temporal Distribution of Traffic Entering a Major Domestic Airport

Source: Phillip S. Shapiro, et al., *Intermodal Ground Access to Airports: A Planning Guide,* Washington, D.C.: U.S. Department of Transportation, December 1996, p. 87.

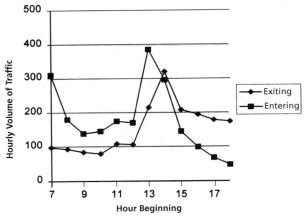

Figure 18–55   Employee Arrival Times at an International Airport

Source: Phillip S. Shapiro, et al., *Intermodal Ground Access to Airports: A Planning Guide,* Washington, D.C.: U.S. Department of Transportation, December 1996, p. 88.

Within this general framework, there are some guidelines for the planning of on-airport roadways. IATA's "Airport Terminals Reference Manual" offers the following suggestions:

1. Roads should be designed to accommodate peak traffic volumes and have adequate expansion capability.

2. The link between the external public road system and the nonpublic or service road system must be planned carefully to avoid congestion or lack of future expansion capability in either system.

3. Main through-roads should bypass the road running along the face of terminal building.

4. Roads running along the terminal building face should be wide enough to permit the passing of stopped vehicles and have a minimum of three lanes.

5. There must be no uncontrolled access to runways or taxiways from public roads.

6. The public road system accommodating service vehicles should connect with the terminals only for delivery of goods at designated locations.

7. Roads connecting to cargo areas must have sufficient lane widths and height clearances to accommodate existing and projected cargo-carrying vehicles.

8. In large airports, special lanes may be reserved for priority traffic (e.g., public buses, taxis); and provision should be made for future transit systems.

9. Roads should be designed to provide for circulation connecting the terminal buildings, for buses and the growing number of shuttle services provided by off-site, airport-related uses.

Also, while not a requirement, the terminal roadway system usually works best with one-way roadways. Other aspects, which can involve significant added capital costs, are two-level frontages and structures. Circulation is generally better with a two-level concept (i.e., an upper-level roadway for departing passengers and lower-level roadway for arriving passengers). Some newer terminals have three and four levels. Whether a single-level or multilevel scheme is used, adequate length of curb frontage is critical to efficient loading and unloading of passengers and luggage. Elimination of vehicular conflict points by overpass or underpass structures also has benefits.

Pedestrians usually access the terminals from the parking facilities by crossing the terminal roadways at-grade. The structural arrangement of the roadway levels, particularly at larger airports, can result in providing grade-separated pedestrian access; or "skywalks" can be used, a decided plus. *Off-airport* highway access and impacts also need thorough consideration. Although airports may be among the largest single-site travel generators in major metropolitan areas, they account for only a fraction (usually less than 2 percent) of the total travel within those areas, so their measurable traffic impacts are usually limited to those parts of the highway network within a radius of a few miles.

This is conceptually as true in the 90s as it was in earlier years, with traffic having gone up significantly on the off-airport connecting expressways and airport traffic also having increased significantly. While there is obviously an impact of airport traffic on adjacent roadways, it is rarely the major element even there. For example, at New York's Kennedy and LaGuardia airports or at Newark Airport, the "airport-related" vehicles approaching the airport boundary have been estimated at 10–25 percent of the total expressway or parkway peak hour traffic. This includes all airport traffic, particularly airport employees whose peak period vehicular volume on approach roads often exceeds air passenger vehicles. The relative timing of the air passenger flow peaks, airport employee peaks, and off-airport general traffic peaks needs careful study and analysis. Efforts to shift peak timing need to be considered, while recognizing market and institutional constraints.

If the airport is large enough to have more than one passenger and employee entrance, dynamically controlled variable message signs (VMSs) can be used to balance peak loads among the major approaches and to respond to on-airport real time traffic conditions.

Parking[U]

Even with increased promotion of other means of ground transportation to and from the airport, the use of the private automobile will continue to be substantial. A major goal for locating parking facilities for airline passengers is to minimize walking distances and therefore bring the automobile as close as possible to the aircraft. The volume and characteristics of users play a major role in planning parking facilities. Parking at an airport must be provided for airline passengers, visitors accompanying passengers, spectators, employees, and people having business with the airport tenants.

It may not be feasible to satisfy demand during the busiest hours of the year. This is a matter of policy that rests with airport management. In part it will be influenced by available space, the costs associated with providing parking, and the feasibility of increasing use of other access modes, possible only at the peak times of year. Special park-ride facilities or supplementary transit service might be provided during peak travel seasons. A separate parking area should be provided for employees, as close as possible to the facilities in which they work. In some situations, employee parking needs to be provided away from the work site with a connecting bus or van. For example, at passenger terminals, close in parking is generally reserved for air passengers. Consequently, terminal employee parking may be provided at some distance from the terminal, requiring employee shuttle or van service to connect the employee parking lot with the terminal work site.

Surveys at a number of airports in the United States have indicated that a large number of airline users, on the order of 80 percent, park 3 hours or less; and a very much smaller group park from 12 hours to several days or longer. The short-term parkers, however, represent only about 15 to 20 percent of the maximum vehicle accumulation in the parking facility. Therefore, many airports designate the most convenient spaces for short-term parkers who represent the highest number of users, and regulate these facilities by charging premium rates for parking. At large airports, parking may be provided outside the boundary of the airport by private concessionaires who provide transportation to the airport for their patrons.

At airports with less than 1,000,000 enplanements per year, long-and-short term parking occupy the same parking area in front of the terminals. Larger airports provide two or more distinct vehicular parking areas. Close-in parking is typically designed for short-term at prime rate. The majority of those parking here are visitors. Generally, the composition will be as follows:

1. Passengers returning the same day (a small percentage).

2. Passengers parking an average of 1 or 2 days.

3. Visitors (escorts) who deliver or pick up passengers.

4. Visitors (escorts) who use very short-term metered parking.

Remote parking at reduced rates is used by passengers who park for more than 1 to 3 days. Visitors typically do not use remote parking. A bus shuttle service with various stops in the parking lot may connect with the terminal complex. When long-and-short term parking lots are contiguous, distances over 600 ft from the terminal may require shuttle service. Such a service must be convenient. Otherwise a large percentage of the remote parkers will first drop baggage off at the curb before proceeding to the parking lot.

Projections of future public parking demand at an airport are generally made by correlation with projected growth in air traffic, usually airline passengers. At an existing airport, information on the hourly distribution of automobile traffic entering and leaving the parking facility daily is required. A plot of the hourly distribution of accumulated vehicles will yield the peak accumulation and when it occurs. An example of such a plot for determining the parking requirements at O'Hare International Airport is shown in Figure 18–56.

To project into the future, it is necessary to develop a relationship between the number of cars entering and leaving a parking facility in a specific period of time, usually one hour, and the total number of air passengers arriving and departing during the same period of time. The forecast of passengers and vehicle occupancy can be used to determine the size of the entrance and exit to the parking facility and the number of spaces required. The busy-hour vehicle flow into and out of the facility can be determined by dividing the forecast of busy-hour passenger demand by vehicle occupancy. The number of spaces that are needed can be determined in several ways. One way is to obtain a projection of the daily distribution of passengers entering or leaving the airport and converting the number of passengers to vehicles to find the peak accumulation of vehicles. Another way is to correlate the maximum accumulation of vehicles with busy-hour passenger demand during known years, and apply the correlation to projected future busy-hour demand.

Relatively simple methods based on parking experience at the airport may be sufficient for long-range master planning, but more sophisticated techniques may be required for more precise planning and design, especially when costly parking structures are involved.

The commonly recommended basic parking stall has been in the range of 8.5 ft to 9.0 ft wide by 18 ft long. For planning purposes (based on 8.5 ft × 18.0 ft stalls), about 420 sq ft is required per parking stall, including circulation. This translates to about 100 vehicles per acre for public and employee parking. It may be desirable to have wider stalls and angle parking for short-term metered parking or to use slightly smaller spaces for all-day employee parking. These are individual policy and design judgments for each airport management to consider.

Public Transportation

Airports, with their peripheral related development, are intense generators of travel activity. Most airports experience peak traffic periods that produce strains upon the roadway access systems and the parking facilities, which would be alleviated by a more intensive use of public transportation. There are, however, a number of factors that affect public transportation market potential, some positively and some negatively:

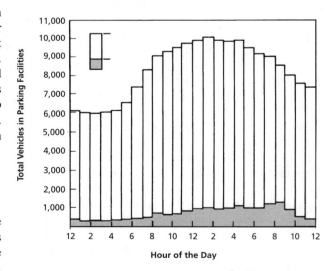

Figure 18–56   Total Accumulation of Vehicles in All Parking Facilities at O'Hare International Airport on a Typical Day in 1977

Source: Robert Horonjeff and Francis X. McKelvey, *Planning and Design of Airports*, Third Edition, McGraw-Hill, 1985.

- Many airport users use the facility infrequently.

- Many airport users are not residents of the area, and their own automobiles are not available.

- Airport usage tends to peak on weekdays, often (but not always) at the same time urban work trips peak.

- Airport employees work a variety of shifts.

- Airport workers and air travelers usually have differing local origins and destinations.

- Airport employment is often at dispersed locations in the airport.

- There is often airport-related employment dispersed around the periphery, including service employment, working a variety of shifts, and residing in areas of the city that do not generate much air traveler demand.

- Air travelers are often accompanied by "greeters and well wishers."

- Air travelers require dependable transportation to the airport—especially business travelers who often operate on tight schedules and require frequent or demand-responsive service.

- There are a variety of shared ride alternatives available at most airports.

Table 18–8   Ground Access Vehicle Trips Per Air Passenger Trip

Mode	VT/PT
Pickup/Drop-off	1.29
Taxi	1.09
Parking	.74
Rental Car	.69
Door-to-Door Shuttle	.33
Scheduled Bus	.10
Rapid Transit	0.00

Source: Phillip S. Shapiro, et al., *Intermodal Ground Access to Airports: A Planning Guide,* Washington, D.C.: U.S. Department of Transportation, December 1996, p. 41.

The net effect of all of these influences is that the absolute numbers of airport-related trips potential to public modes, particularly scheduled transit, is a challenge to capture. However, for large airports with heavy peak loads, public transit can play a major role in meeting peak period capacity needs cost-effectively and in an environmentally acceptable manner. Table 18–8 shows the vehicle trips per air passenger trip for Boston's Logan International Airport. Any strategy that can move a passenger (or an employee) to a lower ranking (higher-occupancy mode) in the table will have a positive effect on reducing airport traffic and roadway congestion.

Although most airport travel patterns tend to involve dispersed trip patterns at the nonairport end, where there is a major city or major concentrations of commercial development, rail access or other exclusive transit links to the airport may be feasible. In the United States there are nine airports with direct rail service: Atlanta, Chicago (both Midway and O'Hare), Baltimore-Washington, Cleveland, Michigan City, St. Louis, Philadelphia, and Washington National. At some other airports (e.g., Kennedy in New York and Logan in Boston) there is rail service to an airport boundary station, with a bus shuttle to the terminals. An airport busway is under construction to serve the Greater Pittsburgh International Airport. In addition, rail access is under construction at Newark International Airport and San Francisco International Airport and planned for several other airports.

In addition to regularly scheduled transit services, there are a variety of other alternatives to private auto access, including taxis, limousine (shared-ride), hotel buses, and buses from satellite terminals. Many airports are working intensively to develop "park-fly" services in conjunction with the operators of the connecting services, either bus or van operators. Waterborne transportation modes have also been suggested for airport access since many large airports are located on or near waterways. Some "public" waterborne access services have been implemented. Examples include the Delta Airlines water shuttle connecting Manhattan and LaGuardia Airport, and waterborne services for Logan Airport in Boston.

Projecting usage is a key question in the planning of the different types of airport-related public transportation. This is a highly specialized area of traffic forecasting, but a few general observations can be made:

1) Airport employees behave the same way nonairport employees do, and they are subject to the same decision process. Therefore the accepted regional mode split methodology will provide usable mode split data for employees.

2) Air travelers are a special case, subject to a variety of factors not generally found in mode split models, including:

   a. Lack of familiarity with the area.

   b. Luggage.

   c. Time constraints and dependability requirements.

   d. Accompanying visitors.

   e. Nature of travel (domestic and international).

Special mode split techniques are required, to account for these factors, based on empirical data. Data from Cleveland, Boston, London, Atlanta, and other cities with direct or "indirect" rail access to the airport, as well as numerous surveys in cities with bus transit access, can provide insights.

Once the public transportation services are operating, one of the keys to inducing greater use of those modes is the provision of complete, accurate, and readily available information. This can be done through "manual" techniques (e.g., the ground transportation counters at the Port Authority's New York-New Jersey area airports) and through computerized systems (e.g., Kiosks, the Internet).

Ports (Marine Terminals)

The functional aspects of port planning will be focused on here, particularly those elements of a "landside" nature, as compared with marine and vessel considerations. The emphasis is primarily on ocean ports, but some attention is also devoted to inland river ports. General principles and some specifics are presented regarding location, access, and modal connectivity; facilities requirements; berth and terminal design; cargo-handling systems; container terminals; and other, more specialized terminal types.

Ocean Ports

General Location, Access, and Modal Connectivity[K]

New ports or port extensions become necessary when traffic increases or when entirely new traffic has to be accommodated. In principle, new ports and also port extensions, if there is a choice, should be located where they will minimize the total sea and land transport costs to the economy for the cargo in question, considering its different origins and destinations. Obviously, this is not exclusively a matter of the geographical location for the port site (e.g., sheltered anchorage, minimum distance to sea) but also a matter of different port construction costs for different sites (e.g., water depth, dredging needs, siltation patterns).

Factors that are not quantifiable in economic terms, such as overall strategic planning for regional or demographic development, often play an important role in port site selection. With these general guidelines in mind, the following elements should be identified:

1. Linkages to the existing and planned highway network: Connectivity to the highway network in the area where the port is to be located is a key consideration. Ideally, the port should be located adjacent to an interstate highway or a major roadway with adequate capacity for high volumes of large trucks with heavy loads.

2. Linkages to the existing and planned rail network: The area's railroad system should be analyzed to determine the feasibility of providing rail connections between the port and rail lines serving the area.

3. Linkages to pipelines: If liquid commodities are to be transshipped through the port, the pipeline network should be evaluated to determine if connections to the port are feasible.

4. For inland waterways, commodities transported via the waterway: Waterway transportation consists primarily of relatively slow movement of commodities that have low unit value and high unit weight moved in massive quantities at relatively low cost.

5. Number and type of industries located within the port: Typically, an area establishes or upgrades a port to improve its economic development by taking advantage of the accessibility to the waterway transportation system.

Facilities Requirements[K]

Berth throughput capacity can be estimated empirically, based on experience from existing ports; or it can be developed from analytical methods, based on queuing theory. In some situations, computer simulation methods might be indicated. This section will provide an outline of the available analytical (and simulation) techniques and will also describe a simplified "modular" method, useful for general estimates of throughput.

General analytical solutions to queuing theory exist only for two cases, both of which have a Poisson distribution for the arrival rate (number of arrivals per time unit) and either an exponential distribution for service time or constant service time. For an exponential service time distribution, the ratios between average waiting time and average service time as functions of the berth utilization factor (utilized berth time divided by available berth time) and the number of berths are shown in Figure 18–57 (a). Actual arrival rate and service time distributions for many general cargo ports, in particular larger ports, often conform sufficiently well to the above distributions according to chi-square goodness of fit tests.

The other case for which a general analytical solution is available has constant service time. The solution includes the infinite series that are conveniently evaluated only by computer. It is shown in Figure 18–57(b).

Simulation is required when analytical solutions are not valid, which is typically when:

a. Arrival rates do not conform to a Poisson distribution.

b. The berth concept is replaced by the total length of quay concept.

c. All arriving ships cannot be accommodated at all berths.

d. Priority is given (e.g., at multipurpose berths) to ships that may only be accommodated at such berths.

e. Both alongside handling and lighterage of cargo take place.

f. Cargo-handling equipment and storage facilities need to be included in analyses of the whole port system.

A large number of computer simulation programs for alongside ports have been developed. They range from very simple and very useful programs to sophisticated, well-thought-out, and well-tested programs. In principle, it is possible to simulate any stochastic variable including the following:

a. Time between consecutive arrivals of ships.

b. Size of ship.

c. Cargo tonnage loaded or unloaded by ship.

d. Availability of quay cranes and other cargo-handling equipment with known handling rate distributions.

e. Working days and hours.

f. Time at berth before and after cargo handling.

g. Arrival of cargo in and removal of cargo from storage facilities.

h. Stoppages of cargo handling operations, partly or fully, for any reason such as strikes, repairs, and extreme weather conditions.

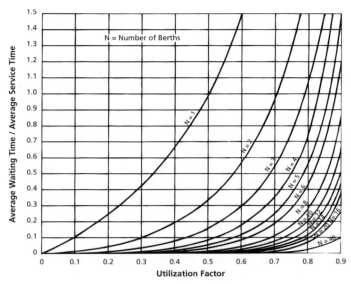

(a) Actual Arrival Rate and Service Time

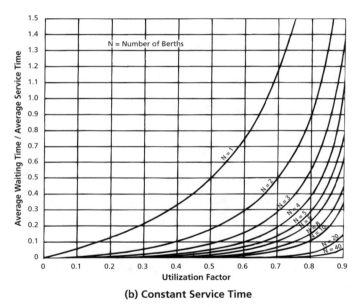

(b) Constant Service Time

Figure 18–57(a) and (b)   Queuing Analysis Solutions

Source: Hans Agerschou, Helge Lundgren, and Torben Sorensen, *Planning and Design of Ports and Marine Terminals*, John Wiley and Sons, 1983.

For applications where a "general estimate" is needed, the U.S. Maritime Administration has developed the Modular Method of estimating cargo throughput for ports and terminals in the United States. This method represents a simplified method of terminal capability estimating based on standardized berthing modules. Standard port planning modules are developed for each cargo transfer mode, such as break-bulk general cargo, containerized cargo, dry bulk cargo, and liquid bulk cargo. This method is designed to be used by administrators, engineers, planners, and designers without special skills in statistical analysis. Standardized berthing modules are particularly useful in master planning and port capacity evaluation.

To find the typical annual cargo throughput capability of the average marine cargo terminal in the United States, one would refer to Table 18–9, determine what cargo classification the terminal is, and then find the cargo throughput quantity in the table that corresponds to the cargo class. Port estimates are simply the sum of estimates of all terminals in the port. Multiple berth terminals are divided into equal single berth terminals for applying the throughput quantities.

Berth and Terminal Design[K]

Multipurpose usage should be aimed at layout and design of fixed facilities as well as in choice of equipment, except for clearly feasible specialized facilities. Storage facilities and cargo-handling systems should be as flexible as possible, and purchases of specialized equipment should only be made when future throughputs clearly justify the acquisition.

The general trend has for some time been towards more space, such as wider quay aprons and transit sheds as well as larger open storage areas. When the Port Authority of New York and New Jersey planned its Port Newark-Elizabeth marine terminal, which became the largest container terminal in the world, it was believed that a total land area of 5 hectares (12 acres), would be sufficient for a one-berth container terminal. This land area requirement estimate had, by 1979, increased by a factor of more than two.

Table 18–9   Typical Annual Cargo Throughput by Module

Single-Berth Terminal by Cargo Class	Cargo Throughput in Short Tons per Year
Break-bulk general cargo	66,000
Neo-bulk general cargo	
Low density (autos, lumber, etc.)	180,000
High density (steel)	400,000
Containerized general cargo	
Single berth	1,350,000
Two or more berths (per berth)	1,650,000
Dry bulk	
Silo storage	1,000,000
Open storage, low density	500,000
Open storage, high density	1,000,000
Liquid bulk, other than petroleum	80,000
Petroleum bulk	
Up to 50,000-dwt ships	1,500,000
50,000- to 200,000-dwt ships	6,000,000

Source: *Port Handbook for Estimating Marine Terminal Cargo Handling Capacity,* Washington, D.C.: U.S. Department of Administration, Maritime Administration, November 1986.

General cargo (break-bulk) berths require a continuous land-connected structure for berthing, mooring, and cargo handling. At the other end of the spectrum are tanker terminals. Cargo handling takes place only through one midship's manifold. Thus, only one loading platform of modest size is required for loading arms and hose-handling equipment.

For dry bulk terminals, compared with liquid bulk, the requirements are that loading and unloading has to take place through a number of hatches along the ship. Thus, more extensive loading platforms are required for the cargo-handling installations that have to cover a good part of the length of the ship.

Container terminal functional requirements are in principle similar to those for dry bulk terminals, when the containers are handled by portainer cranes. This is, of course, not the case when ship's gear or other short-reach handling equipment is used, making the requirements similar to those for general cargo berths. Roll-on/roll-off ships are similar to liquid bulk carriers by having one, or perhaps two (one in each end), well-defined loading/unloading points, requiring only one loading platform (ramp).

The apron width is the distance from the quay face to the transit shed or to the open storage area. The apron is no longer an alongside road-railway combination. It has become more of a short and wide road between ship and transit storage, serving a crisscross traffic of forklifts, tractor-trailer units, and the like, as well as a buffer storage area for cargo. The apron width is determined by considering:

- The distance between the hook of the ship's gear on the quay crane units extreme shoreward position and the transit shed should be as short as possible.

- There should be space for buffer storage or cargo.

- There should be space for lateral transport of cargo to and from open storage areas located behind and between transit sheds.

- There should be space for access of trucks for direct handling of inbound cargo.

When there is a need for warehouses, open storage and marshaling yards behind the transit storage facilities, the total width requirement increases considerably.

Cargo Handling Systems[K]

For handling between ship and apron, ships may be loaded and unloaded by means of portal cranes on rails, ship's gear, or mobile cranes on rubber wheels. Cargo-handling rates vary widely from less than 10 tons per crane (or gang) hour for mixed general cargo to more than 30 tons per crane hour for large consignments of preslung bagged cargo or other similar unitized cargo.

The choice of equipment between apron and transit storage depends largely upon cargo units, distance, stacking height, and consideration of equipment-intensive versus labor-intensive handling. If the distance does not exceed about 100 m, forklifts are normally preferred, unless more labor-intensive cargo handling is demonstrated to be more economical. For bagged cargo, manually loaded and unloaded tractor-drawn trailers are often economical, where labor costs are low, perhaps combined with the use of bag stackers (mobile conveyors) and gravity rollers. Tractor-drawn trailers are preferred over longer distances to and from transit storage yards. At least three trailers are needed for each tractor.

Container Terminals[K,R]

Containerization was developed in the United States during the 1950s by a combined sea and land transport organization, and at first it was intended for domestic traffic only. Door-to-door container traffic is ideally suited for a one-organization operation, without the involvement of separate terminal operators, shipping lines, trucking firms, and customs authorities. Its application in international traffic and with multiuser terminals is much more difficult.

Container terminals are, in principle, rapid transit facilities at the interface between land and sea transport. Inbound containers ought to continue their inland journey to the consignees soon after arriving in the terminal. Outbound cargo ought to arrive at the terminal as stuffed containers not long before the ship sails. These excellent intentions in regard to reduced storage duration and improved safety of cargo traffic have unfortunately only partly materialized.

Thus, both full and empty containers remain in storage much longer than intended; and the throughput capacity of terminals, which is inversely proportional to the average storage time for containers (commonly called dwell time), is greatly reduced. Figure 18–58 shows a typical layout of a container terminal that uses straddle carriers as yard equipment.

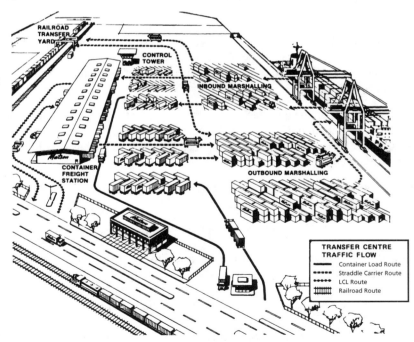

Figure 18–58   Container Terminal Layout

Source: ITE, *Transportation Planning Handbook*, 1992.

Table 18–10 Container Dimensions

Overall			Interior			Rear Swing Door		Cubic	Trailer
Length	Width	Height	Length	Width	Height[a]	Width	Height[b]	Feet	Weight (±3%)
40'	96"	12'6"	39'6"	92$\frac{1}{2}$"	94$\frac{1}{2}$"	92"	92"	2398	11,300 lb.
	96"	13'0"	39'6"	92$\frac{1}{2}$"	100$\frac{1}{2}$"	92"	98"	2550	11,400 lb.
	96"	13'6"	39'6"	92$\frac{1}{2}$"	106$\frac{1}{2}$"	92"	104"	2702	11,500 lb.
42'/43'	96"	12'6"	41'6"/42'6"	92$\frac{1}{2}$"	94$\frac{1}{2}$"	92"	92"	2549	11,800/12,000 lb.
	96"	13'0"	41'6"/42'6"	92$\frac{1}{2}$"	100$\frac{1}{2}$"	92"	98"	2711	11,900/12,100 lb.
	96"	13'6"	41'6"/42'6"	92$\frac{1}{2}$"	106$\frac{1}{2}$"	92"	104"	2873	12,000/12,200 lb.
45'	96"	12'6"	44'6"	92$\frac{1}{2}$"	94$\frac{1}{2}$"	92"	92"	2701	12,400 lb.
	96"	13'0"	44'6"	92$\frac{1}{2}$"	100$\frac{1}{2}$"	92"	98"	2873	12,500 lb.
	96"	13'6"	44'6"	92$\frac{1}{2}$"	106$\frac{1}{2}$"	92"	106"	3044	12,600 lb.
	102"	13'6"	44'6"	98$\frac{1}{2}$"	106$\frac{1}{2}$"	98"	106"	3242	12,950 lb.
48'	96"	13'6"	47'6"	92$\frac{1}{2}$"	106$\frac{1}{2}$"	92"	106$\frac{1}{2}$"	3250	13,200 lb.
	102"	13'6"	47'6"	98$\frac{1}{2}$"	106$\frac{5}{8}$"	98"	106$\frac{5}{8}$"	3464	13,500 lb.
	102"	13'6"	47'6"	98$\frac{1}{2}$"	108"	98"	108"	3509	13,500 lb.
53'[c]	102"	13'6"	47'6"	98$\frac{1}{2}$"	107$\frac{3}{8}$"	94"	102"	3489	14,400 lb.
48' Wedge	102"	13'6"	47'6"	98$\frac{1}{2}$"	Front 108" Rear 110"	98"	110"	3542	13,500 lb.
53' Wedge	102"	13'6"	52'6"	98$\frac{1}{2}$"	Front 108" Rear 110"	98"	110"	3914	14,400 lb.
45' Can	102"	13'6"	44'6"	98$\frac{1}{2}$"	110" Throughout	98"	110"	3348	13,100 lb.
48' Can	102"	13'6"	47'6"	98$\frac{1}{2}$"	110" Throughout	98"	110"	3574	13,500 lb.
53' Can	102"	13'6"	52'6"	98$\frac{1}{2}$"	110" Throughout	98"	110"	3950	14,200 lb.
57' Can	102"	13'6"	56'6"	98$\frac{1}{2}$"	110" Throughout	98"	110"	4251	14,950 lb.

[a] Based on 48" fifth wheel height. Also available with a 49" and 50" height which reduces inside height by 1" and 2", respectively.
[b] Deduct 5" on rear door height and 4" on rear door width for roll-up doors.
[c] Only available with roll-up rear door. Rear door width and height are as specified.
Specifications may vary by manufacturer.

Source: Gerhardt Muller, *Intermodal Freight Transportation*, Eno Foundation for Transportation, Inc., 1995.

The 8 × 8 × 20 ft dry cargo intermodal container is one of the simplest and most prominent intermodal containers in use. It is a basic measuring stick in many statistical comparisons. This container is referred to as a "TEU," meaning that it is a 20 ft equivalent unit. Consequently, an 8 × 8 × 40 ft container is equal to two TEUs, and a containership capable of accommodating 400, 40 ft containers is rated at 800 TEUs. The term "FEU" refers to 40 ft units. ISO international container standards are available in *Jane's Freight Containers (Yearbook)* and other publications.

The 1982 U.S. Surface Transportation Act allowed use of larger trailers, up to 8 ft, 6 in wide and 48 ft long. Influenced by this legislation and similar developments in other countries, container sizes increased from the 80s into the 90s. During the 1985–1995 period, for example, 40 ft containers were bought in numbers almost two-thirds those of the 20 ft or TEU size. At the same time, 45 ft, 48 ft, and 53 ft container types are rapidly displacing the 35 ft container. Table 18–10 shows dimensions of containers available from one of the leading supply companies in the mid-90s. Overall height represents the height of the mounted container above the pavement.

The apron elevation should, in principle, be the same as for general cargo berths. Container terminals, like general cargo berths normally have continuous aprons alongside the ships, although this is not strictly necessary in principle. If the apron is immediately adjacent to the ship, the apron width is governed by the distance between the legs of the gantry crane, which is typically 20 to 30 m for newer cranes and about 10 to 15 m for older cranes; plus the reach of the crane behind its inside rail, which is normally 10 to 20 m. Between the apron and the container storage yard, there may be a road for mobile equipment. The following yard equipment systems are in use at container terminals.

Cranes

Cranes of all types are used to transfer containers ship-to-shore and vice-versa. The most widely used is the rail-mounted gantry crane. It is built in the form of a bridge, supported by a trestle at each end. Its fixed horizontal boom projects over vessels being loaded or unloaded. The gantry crane usually has wheels so it can move along the edge of a pier from one ship to another. In recent years, many ports have had to raise the height of gantry cranes in order to stack and unstack containers higher on vessel docks. Until the mid-1990s, the largest cranes reached over 13 rows of containers (about 125 ft). They were big enough to work containerships that sailed through the Panama Canal. Carriers have ships much wider than the 105 ft limitation of the canal. Thus, some cranes now reach over 18 to 19 rows at a distance of about 145 ft. Cranes are also being designed to lift containers weighing 40 to 50 tons, compared to 30 to 40 tons in the past. This has become important as carriers begin to carry larger containers, up to 47 ft in length for international movements and 53 ft for domestic. The evolution of crane sizes is illustrated in Figure 18–59.

A hinged-boom crane is a flexible type of crane that can pivot on its base. Sometimes a hinged-boom crane is mounted on a gantry base. Shipboard cranes, operating from vessels being loaded or unloaded, are used mostly at ports without cranes. Some cranes, especially those used for lifting very heavy pieces, are based on heavy-lift barges or ships. Cranes on piers may be either fixed in place or mobile.

Straddle Carriers

Straddle carriers (Figure 18–60) lift heavy loads to a minimum height for short-distance travel. They transfer containers to and from cranes that are loading or unloading ships and trucks or rail cars. Straddle carriers illustrate the fact that intermodal handling equipment technology is constantly undergoing improvements. Container-handling straddle carriers have undergone changes in size, in carrying and stacking capabilities, and in numerous other areas. Computer control systems assist on-board computers for direction and control of the straddle carrier and identification of containers.

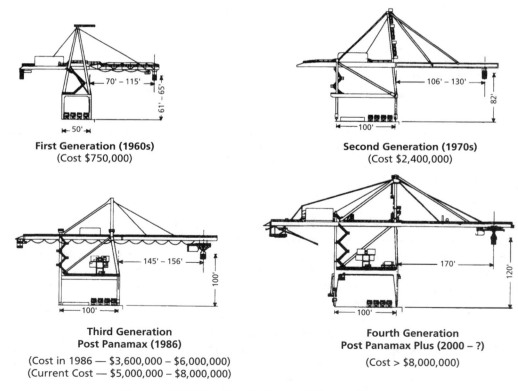

First Generation (1960s)
(Cost $750,000)

Second Generation (1970s)
(Cost $2,400,000)

Third Generation
Post Panamax (1986)

(Cost in 1986 — $3,600,000 – $6,000,000)
(Current Cost — $5,000,000 – $8,000,000)

Fourth Generation
Post Panamax Plus (2000 – ?)

(Cost > $8,000,000)

Figure 18–59   Evolution of Crane Sizes

Source: Gerhardt Muller, *Intermodal Freight Transportation*, Eno Foundation for Transportation, Inc., 1995.

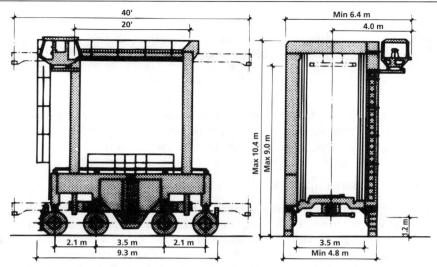

Turning Radius, Inside: 35 m.   Turning Radius, Outside: 9.4 m.   Wheel Load: 10 – 12 t.

Figure 18–60   Typical Straddle Carrier

Source: Hans Agerschou, Helge Lundgren, and Torben Sorensen, *Planning and Design of Ports and Marine Terminals*, John Wiley and Sons, 1983.

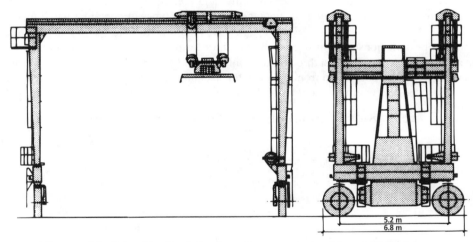

Figure 18–61   Typical Gantry Crane on Rubber Wheels

Source: Hans Agerschou, Helge Lundgren, and Torben Sorensen, *Planning and Design of Ports and Marine Terminals*, John Wiley and Sons, 1983.

Stacking Cranes or Rubber-Tired Gantry (RTG) Cranes

The stacking or RTG crane (Figure 18–61) is a hybrid, falling between the gantry crane and straddle carrier. It is fashioned after the ship-loading gantry, but it does not have the horizontal extended boom for ship loading and unloading. It stacks containers on the ground, just like the straddle carrier. Although it does not have the straddle carrier's darting mobility, it can usually stack containers higher and wider.

Forklift Trucks, Container Handlers, and Side Loaders

The many sizes and varieties of forklift trucks permit these machines to accomplish more than their originally intended tasks. Forklift trucks constitute a family of multipurpose cargo-handling machines rather than a single type. Roadstackers are making inroads at many terminals due to their ability to reach over obstacles such as chassis, tracks, and railcars. Container handlers move, stack, and load containers like forklift trucks; but they use an overhead boom rather than the underlift principle. Side loaders stack containers from relatively narrow aisles. There are many versions of side loaders to fit specific requirements.

Terminal Tractors

There is a variety of chassis-moving, container-handling equipment used at seaports and other terminals, sometimes referred to as yardhorses, hustlers, mules or terminal tractors. This type of motorized equipment is mostly confined to the seaport or terminal area, although it is a close relative of over-the-road truck tractors.

Container Chassis and Chassis Flippers

Chassis are marine and rail terminal equipment as well as over-the-road equipment. Some terminal applications make it necessary to have a large number of chassis at a terminal to receive containers coming off trains or vessels. Where different sizes of intermodal containers are handled, different sizes of chassis must be on hand. There also are extendable chassis (sliders), capable of accommodating several different sizes of intermodal containers.

The chassis flipper was designed to cope with terminal space problems. A chassis flipper elevates one end of the chassis to put the chassis into a vertical position. It then places the chassis in a specially designed rack. Chassis stored on end require only 10 percent of the land area otherwise needed if left in a horizontal position. In addition to saving space, the chassis flipper improves security, reduces search time, eliminates damage incurred in stacking chassis's on top of one another, increases speed of container handling, and consequently reduces loading and unloading times. Table 18–11 compares the advantages and disadvantages of different types of container handling equipment.

One of the most important questions in regard to container terminals is: How large must a yard be in order to accommodate a certain known or forecast throughput of inbound and outbound TEUs? The answer is intimately related to the equipment used for transport to and from the yard, for stacking, delivery, and receiving on the landside. Following are the important parameters governing the relationship between yard area and container throughput.

Table 18–11 Comparison of Container Handling Systems

Activity	Chasis System	Straddle Carrier	Yard Gantry Crane (RTG)	Reachstackers, Frontend Top-Pick Loader
Land area	70 TEUs per acre 173 per hectare	168 TEUs per acre 413 per hectare	325 TEUs per acre 802 per hectare	240 TEUs per acre 590 per hectare
Cost of Terminal Development	Low	Medium	High	Medium to high
Cost of Equipment[1]	Tractor $45,000 Chasis $7,000	$800,000	$ 1,000,000	$250,000 to $500,000
Support Equipment per Container Crane	4 to 5 tractors; 1 chasis per container	3 to 4	1 to 2 cranes, 5 tractors and chasis	2 such as RTG
Operating Labor	Low	Low	Medium to High	Medium
Equipment Maintenance	Low	High	Medium	Medium
Inventory Control	Good, but frequent yard checks required	Good, but frequent yard checks required	Very good	Good
Advantages	High accessibility, low cost	Versatility, less support equipment needed	Low maintenance, good control, expandable system	Versatility, low maintenance
Disadvantages	High land requirements, large chasis requirements	High damage and maintenance cost	Initial equipment and land preparation cost	Slower productivity compared to other equipment, i.e., RTG
Security	Excellent	Good	Poor	Good

[1] Approximate prices at U.S. 1994 levels.

Note: Use of different types of intermodal container-handling equipment offers a wide variety of advantages and disadvantages. The table illustrates these differences with the understanding that local conditions and work rules may cause considerable variations.

Source: Gerhardt Muller, *Intermodal Freight Transportation*, Eno Foundation for Transportation, Inc., 1995.

a. The average stacking height of containers and its statistical distribution. The maximum stacking height ranges from one to five, depending upon the yard equipment. The average stacking height as a fraction of the maximum height is governed by the traffic mixture and by the organization of the yard operations.

b. The open areas (ground slots) required for operation of equipment and for access to containers.

c. The number of calendar days or working days of period considered. The same category of days should be used for determination of average TEU storage time.

d. Average TEU storage time in days and its statistical distribution.

The relationship is often expressed in the equation:

$$C = \frac{L \times H \times W \times K}{D \times F} \qquad\qquad (18\text{--}10)$$

where

C = TEU throughput during the period of time

L = number of TEU ground slots

H = average stacking height in number of containers

W = average utilization factor for ground slots

K = number of days of the period of time

D = average TEU storage time in days

F = peaking factor for a combination of higher than average TEU throughput, less than average stacking height, and more than average storage time

For the four different yard parking layouts shown in Figure 18–62, area requirements (including roadways) have been determined. Different trailer sizes; different turning radii for tractor-trailer units; different numbers of slots per row; and for layouts 2 and 3, varying angles were investigated. Layout 4 is for an angle of 45 degrees only.

Specialized Marine Terminals[K]

Following is a list of several other, more specialized types of marine terminals; they are also sketched in Figures 18–63, 18–64, 18–65, and 18–66. More detail on these types, as well as on the more common types previously treated here, is available in the technical literature.

- Roll-on/roll-off (Ro-Ro).

- Lift-on/lift-off (Lo-Lo).

- Lighter-aboard-ship (LASH).

- Liquid bulk.

- Dry bulk.

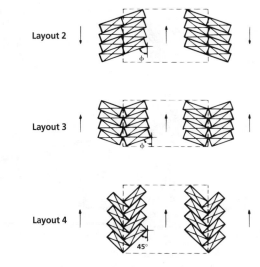

Figure 18–62   Semitrailer Parking Layouts

Source: Hans Agerschou, Helge Lundgren, and Torben Sorensen, *Planning and Design of Ports and Marine Terminals,* John Wiley and Sons, 1983.

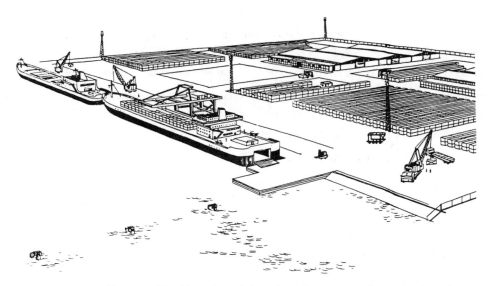

Figure 18–63   Combination Ro-Ro and Lo-Lo Berth

Source: Hans Agerschou, Helge Lundgren, and Torben Sorensen, *Planning and Design of Ports and Marine Terminals*, John Wiley and Sons, 1983.

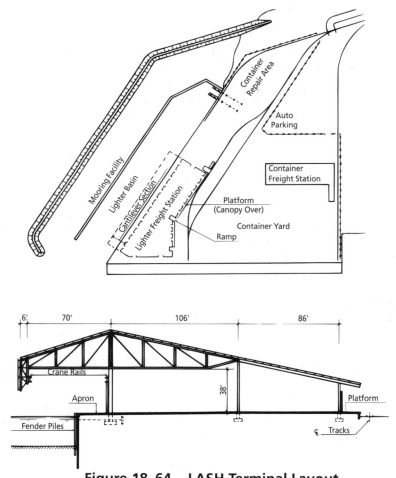

Figure 18–64   LASH Terminal Layout

Source: Hans Agerschou, Helge Lundgren, and Torben Sorensen, *Planning and Design of Ports and Marine Terminals*, John Wiley and Sons, 1983.

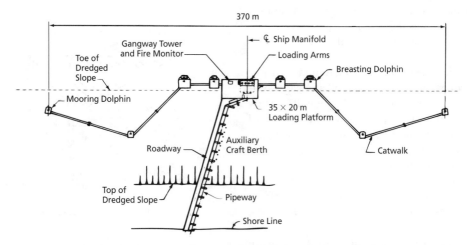

Figure 18–65   Typical Oil Tanker Berth Layout

Source: Hans Agerschou, Helge Lundgren, and Torben Sorensen, *Planning and Design of Ports and Marine Terminals*, John Wiley and Sons, 1983.

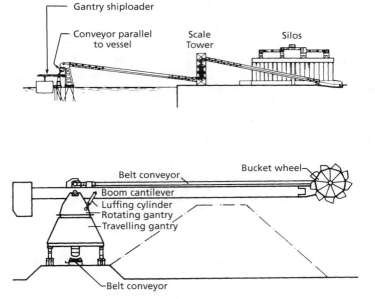

Figure 18–66   Stacker-Reclaimer Unit

Source: Hans Agerschou, Helge Lundgren, and Torben Sorensen, *Planning and Design of Ports and Marine Terminals*, John Wiley and Sons, 1983.

Inland River Ports[K]

The initial phase in the development of design principles for inland river ports consists of identifying and describing the transportation-related elements for specific sites. These elements will also form the basis for the detailed geometric designs. Two underlying principles should be considered.

1.   An inland river port should be viewed as an intermodal terminal and not solely as a location for loading and unloading goods from barges or other waterway vessels. One must consider the requirements of all

transportation modes, warehousing and storage needs, as well as the demands of the associated industries within the port itself.

2. The requirements of all transportation modes—rail pipeline and highway as well as waterway—should be given equal consideration. It is likely that within a given port, goods transfers will take place within a given mode (i.e., truck to truck) and between modes not including the waterway (i.e., rail to truck).

The types of terminals to be located along the waterfront will influence the design of the transportation facilities. Terminals can be of two types: (1) general purpose terminals and (2) special or industrial terminals. General purpose terminals are the essential link to industrial development both on nonriverfront lots within the port industrial complex and for industries generally up to 50 miles away. The general purpose terminals wharf a wide variety of barges carrying a range of commodities. They handle those commodities by crane from the wharf, warehouse some of the commodities within an adjacent transit shed, store some in open spaces, and transfer them to and from truck or rail. General purpose terminals should be at least 20 acres and may be much larger if additional storage space is required. Special purpose or industrial terminals are designed to handle a single commodity or type of commodity, with specialized loading and unloading and transfer equipment. They tend to be smaller than the general purpose terminals with lot sizes averaging 6 to 10 acres.

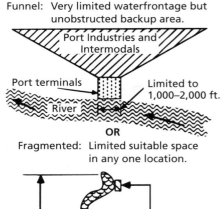

Special Situations

Funnel: Very limited waterfrontage but unobstructed backup area.

Port Industries and Intermodals

Port terminals — Limited to 1,000–2,000 ft.

River

OR

Fragmented: Limited suitable space in any one location.

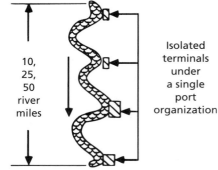

10, 25, 50 river miles

Isolated terminals under a single port organization

Figure 18–67　Special Port Situation, Navigable Inland Rivers

Source: Martin Lipinski and Marvin L. Jacobs, "Functional Design Principles for Goods Movement To and From Inland River Ports," *Compendium of Technical Papers,* ITE 1988 Annual Meeting.

After the waterway side of the port area has been fixed, the relationship of the water access points to industries within the port is determined. Figure 18–67 illustrates two special situations, funnel and fragmented forms, which are alternatives to the slack water harbor design and relate river and harbor access to the inland industries. Each of these forms requires transportation corridors between the waterfront and the industries.

Design of the elements to be included in the transportation system should begin by identifying how goods will be transferred among modes. Flexibility in design includes consideration of the types of handling systems and the capacity of these systems to carry the anticipated flow volumes. The symbolic flowchart in Figure 18–68 illustrates alternative methods for transfer of goods from barge to truck and truck to barge. Similar diagrams could be constructed for barge to rail or other required linkages.

Selection of the handling system or systems to be used is primarily an economic decision dictated by system costs and anticipated loadings. This evaluation should be comprehensive and consider the design of the handling system, its precise transfer points (i.e., the location where trucks are loaded or unloaded), and the supplemental requirements for each of the modes within the system. The design should provide for anticipated surges in commodity flows for all modes. Needed facilities include parking areas for trucks, marshaling yards for railcars, and fleeting areas in the waterway for barges. Input-output queuing models provide useful tools in determining the size of waiting areas.

The final phase in developing an overall inland port functional design consists of integrating the requirements for the terminals and industries and preparing the overall roadway, railway, and pipeline networks that will connect facilities within the port and provide linkage to the area's transportation system.

"Waterless" Inland Ports

Responding to ever-heightening competitive pressures, ocean port agencies throughout the United States have developed new ways to retain and to expand the cargo volumes moving through their ports. In the late 80s, the concept of an "inland intercept" for an ocean port (i.e., a "waterless" inland port) was analyzed and implemented in several locations in the southeast. The Virginia Inland Port (VIP) opened in May 1989, linked to the Port of Hampton Roads. This followed two earlier and somewhat similar inland port projects in the Carolinas, tied to the ports of Wilmington, North Carolina and Charleston, South Carolina.

The VIP facility, located more than 200 miles inland at Front Royal, Virginia, provides a rail-truck intermodal terminal linked to the Virginia Port Authority's Hampton Roads terminals by a dedicated Norfolk Southern rail haul. (Figure 18–69.) The inland port is positioned to intercept container traffic that is largely truck-hauled to rival mid-Atlantic ports. For VPA, the new inland port was intended to produce a significant increase in the volume of import-export container traffic moving through the authority's Hampton Roads terminals.

The potential time and cost savings provided by the combination of the inland port with a dedicated rail haul to Hampton Roads were based upon a unique combination of geographical factors. While Hampton Roads is only 18 miles from the open Atlantic, container ships destined for the Port of Baltimore have to steam an additional 200 miles up the Chesapeake Bay, which can take as much as 12 hours. The Hampton Roads-inland port rail route is able to move containers 200 miles inland in less time than needed to make the Chesapeake Bay transit alone.

The inland port location chosen, at Front Royal, is well situated for the "intercept" concept, located only five miles from the intersections of east-west (I-66) and north-south (I-81) Interstate highways. The authority's goal was to attract truck-hauled import-export container traffic from within a radius of 200 miles of the inland port, particularly from origins and destinations in western Maryland, Pennsylvania, West Virginia, and eastern Ohio.

In 1998, the VIP handled 11.2 million tons of general cargo (10.5 million tons via containers, and 0.7 million tons via breakbulk).

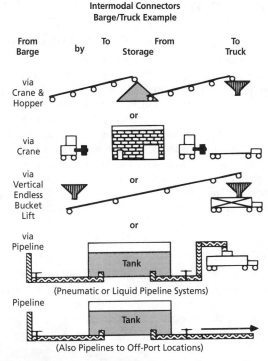

Figure 18–68   Intermodal Transfer Options, Inland River Port Plans

Source: Martin Lipinski and Marvin L. Jacobs, "Functional Design Principles for Goods Movement To and From Inland River Ports," *Compendium of Technical Papers*, ITE 1988 Annual Meeting.

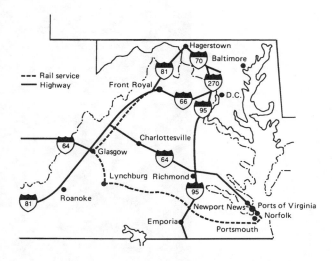

Figure 18–69   Virginia Inland Port

Source: Carlo J. Salzano, "Virginia Launches Inland Port in New Competitive Effort," *Traffic World Magazine*, May 29, 1989.

Distribution Systems

Passenger Moving and Distribution Systems

The effects and importance of short-haul transportation, particularly for CBDs, often are underestimated. In many cities inadequate short-haul service represents a major deterrent to transit use and creates pressures for provision of extensive parking in immediate vicinities of all major buildings. If, on the other hand, CBDs and other major activity centers are designed as unified areas with good internal mobility (i.e., easy travel among all points within them), these centers can be extremely efficient for conducting business as well as attractive for work, shopping, recreation, and other activities. Such mobility can be achieved only by careful planning and development of various short-haul transportation services, ranging from attractive pedestrian streets and routings to mechanically assisted pedestrian modes. Such systems should comply with local codes and national requirements, such as the ADA. Short-haul systems must be closely coordinated with regular transit services in the area and parking facilities located, preferably, along its periphery. Short-haul transportation can thus be a significant element in designing central cities and other activity centers that provide all the unique features of urban activities and environment.

Walking[B,C]

Walking is and will remain the basic mode of travel for short trips. It is always "instantly available," it involves no terminal times and its capacity is high. One of the most frequently undertaken and relatively easy methods of improving pedestrian circulation systems is the upgrading of aesthetics, as shown in Figure 18–70. A variety of types of partial and complete street pedestrianization schemes is shown in Figure 18–71 together with a description of each scheme.

Figure 18–70   Aesthetic Improvements to Pedestrian Circulation

Source: ITE, *Transportation Planning Handbook*, 1992.

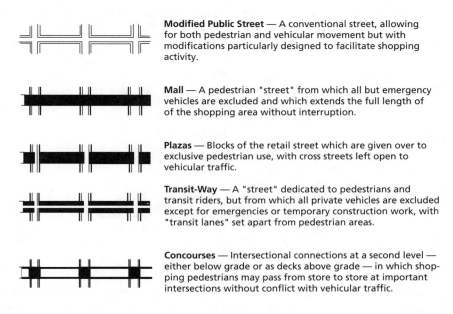

Modified Public Street — A conventional street, allowing for both pedestrian and vehicular movement but with modifications particularly designed to facilitate shopping activity.

Mall — A pedestrian "street" from which all but emergency vehicles are excluded and which extends the full length of of the shopping area without interruption.

Plazas — Blocks of the retail street which are given over to exclusive pedestrian use, with cross streets left open to vehicular traffic.

Transit-Way — A "street" dedicated to pedestrians and transit riders, but from which all private vehicles are excluded except for emergencies or temporary construction work, with "transit lanes" set apart from pedestrian areas.

Concourses — Intersectional connections at a second level — either below grade or as decks above grade — in which shopping pedestrians may pass from store to store at important intersections without conflict with vehicular traffic.

Figure 18–71   Types of Pedestrian Street Schemes

Source: ITE, *Transportation Planning Handbook*, 1992.

Walking distances, which are important because they are a factor in plan configuration and a measure of serviceability, are a subjective human variable. Distances of one mile or more are accepted by nonhandicapped pedestrians in the context of an amusement park or even a shopping center situation. But distances of more than 500 ft are sometimes considered unacceptable by auto parkers. Relatively long walking distances have been found at the Port Authority Bus Terminal in New York City, where the average distance for those who walk to their destinations from the terminal is 3,600 ft in favorable weather conditions. This rather long walking distance compares with the shorter, but severely criticized, maximum walking distances at major airports.

There are indications that the tolerable limit of human walking distance is more situation-related than energy-related. The maximum curb-to-plane walking distances represent a normal 5 to 7 minute walk for most persons; but the anxiety connected with meeting schedules, making the trip, and negotiating an unfamiliar building tend to make these distances appear to be much longer.

Average walking speed for pedestrians is approximately 250 ft (76 m) per minute. Speeds decline as age increases, when pedestrians are encumbered with baggage, and as crowding increases. Although bus and urban rail commuters can be expected to walk 5 to 10 minutes to reach a transit stop or terminal, walking distances for transfers inside terminals should be kept as short as possible.

Both walking distance and low speed can, of course, be addressed by mechanical systems for pedestrian movement, either continuously moving systems (e.g., escalators, moving walkways) or vehicle-based systems (e.g, elevators for vertical movement, automatic guideway, horizontal "people movers"). Before discussing these pedestrian assists, a brief mention of "entry" devices is in order, since these are the locations where pedestrians either enter, leave, or are processed relative to interfaces and terminals.

Doors, turnstiles, or other portal-like pedestrian facilities can be compared to walkway sections in which pedestrians have been channeled into lanes restricting movement. The pedestrian may also be required to perform some time-consuming function such as opening the door, depositing coins in a turnstile, or "swiping" a magnetic card through a reader. Pedestrians normally have a time and distance spacing or headway between each other in the traffic stream. This concept of a spacing between following pedestrians is useful in evaluating portal-like facilities. If the time-distance headway between pedestrians is too close, there may be insufficient time to allow pedestrians to perform the "portal" functions, thus interrupting uniform flow and causing a queue to develop. Table 18–12 summarizes observed time headways and equivalent pedestrian volumes for a number of portal situations.

Mechanical Pedestrian-Assist Systems[B]

Mechanical systems for pedestrian movement include escalators, moving walkways, and elevators. *Escalators* provide both horizontal and vertical movement at a 30-degree slope fixed by code. Moving walkways provide for horizontal movement and can be sloped for changes in grade up to a recommended maximum of 12 degrees. Elevators are used almost exclusively for vertical movement, but a sloped elevator called an inclinator is used in the subway in Stockholm, Sweden, for the disabled. The advantage of the inclinator is that it can be used in parallel with escalators, simplifying the design of transit station entrances and passenger control areas. Escalators have received more general application than elevators in transportation terminals because of their continuous service aspect and high capacity, but elevators should be applicable as an alternative to escalators in small-vehicle, people-mover systems, particularly where disabled needs require at least one unit to begin with.

The manufacturer's theoretical capacity of escalators is based on an assumed step occupancy and the number of steps delivered per minute; that is, the speed equivalent. Vacant step positions can be observed on even the most heavily used escalators. Photographic studies have shown that the vacant step positions are due to human reaction and boarding times that are slower than the step delivery rate or personal space preferences to avoid contact with others. Practical utilization rates can also vary according to the passenger arrival process, where there are intermittent gaps in the traffic stream. Typical observed values for maximum utilization of an escalator are about 60 percent of the manufacturer's theoretical capacity. A comparison of theoretical and practical capacities, at the 60 percent utilization rate, for a 120 feet per minute (fpm) slope speed escalator delivering 89 steps per minute is shown in Table 18–13.

Elevators have not been widely applied as primary vertical passenger movement systems in transportation terminals but, as previously stated, would be suitable for small-vehicle, people-mover systems where passenger demands could be matched to elevator capacity. Elevators have become more widely available for wheelchair users in terminals, and in some situations (e.g., deep transit stations), passengers prefer them to long escalator travel. The capacity of an elevator is determined by the platform area; its shaft time, including running time, acceleration deceleration, and door-opening times; the length of the shaft; and dwell times for boarding and exiting passengers. As with other mechanical systems the manufacturers' theoretical capacities, based on assumed area occupancies, tend to be high. Typical observed area occupancies on office elevators where workers are known to each other are 1.7 to 1.8 sq ft per person. Because of human preferences to avoid touching others, average area occupancies in other types of user populations are higher. The threshold for unavoidable touching contact in standing groups is 2.75 sq ft per person. Approximate calculations for elevator platform capacity can be developed using 2 sq ft per person. Approximate passenger boarding and exiting rates can also be developed using a one sec headway between passengers for each 27 to 30 in of clear door opening width. To accommodate wheelchairs, elevator doors must be a minimum of 36 in (915 mm) wide; and elevator cabs must be dimensioned to permit wheelchair-bound passengers to enter, maneuver to the controls, and exit.

Table 18–12   Observed Entrance Headways

Type of Device	Observed Average Headway (seconds)	Equivalent Pedestrian Volume (persons per minute)
Doors		
Free swinging	1.0–1.5	40–60
Revolving, one direction	1.7–2.4	25–35
Registering Turnstiles		
Free admission	1.0–1.5	40–60
With ticket collector	1.7–2.4	25–35
Coin-operated (low)		
Single slot	1.2–2.4	25–50
Double slot	2.5–4.0	15–25

Source: John J. Fruin, "Elements of Terminal Design and Planning," *Proceedings of the Conference on Multi-Modal Terminal Planning and Design,* Irvine, Cal.: University of California, March 1981.

Table 18–13   Escalator Capacity Comparison

Hip Width (inches)	Tread Width (inches)	Maximum Theoretical Pedestrians per Minute	Practical Observed Pedestrians per Minute	Additional Factors
32	24	111	67	5 pedestrians/4 steps
48	40	178	107	2 pedestrians/step

Source: John J. Fruin, "Elements of Terminal Design and Planning," *Proceedings of the Conference on Multi-Modal Terminal Planning and Design,* Irvine, Cal.: University of California, March 1981.

The manufacturer's theoretical capacity of *moving walkways* is based on the speed of the walkway and an assumed average spacing. Practical walkway capacity is also below the manufacturer's assumptions. Passenger boarding rates for a 48 in wide walkway are very close to that of the same width escalator. The maximum speed for moving walkways is 120 fpm in the United States, which is less than half of normal walking speed; although the ANSI-A17 code allows speeds up to 180 fpm on level runs. Walkway speeds are higher in Europe, commonly operating at 50 meters per minute or 164 fpm. Moving walkways are more widely used in transit systems and at airports in Europe, possibly because of the higher speeds.

There have been several innovative approaches suggested to improve the performance of moving walkways, some of which have been applied at theme parks and expositions. These include: lateral entry and exit at intermediate points using a short parallel belt, increasing speed by placing a higher speed belt longitudinally between slower speed belts at the entry and exit points, and an S-shaped walkway composed of plates that pivot horizontally to create effects of acceleration and deceleration. None of these approaches have found widespread use in terminals, but they may be subject to further development in the future.

The basic characteristics of the pedestrian-assisting systems include continuous service, high capacity and comfort, adequate safety, and the ability to carry people between different elevations. However, low speeds limit their applications to short distances (the longest moving sidewalks are about 200 to 300 m long, and the longest escalators negotiate vertical distances of some 25 to 30 m). Since they require a continuous, uninterrupted path, they cannot accommodate at-grade crossings. Other characteristics of pedestrian-assisting modes are their very high investment costs and their appreciable operating costs.

For distances greater than are considered desirable for walking, and beyond the practicable range of pedestrian-assisting systems, short-haul passenger distribution can be facilitated by use of existing regular transit, or preferably, special short-haul transit. The conditions for successful deployment of short-haul transit are that it offers high frequency of service, preferably a dense network with adequate information for passengers, and low fares. In large cities these requirements usually necessitate vehicle designs that allow rapid boarding and alighting (i.e., a high door and vehicle capacity ratio) to avoid excessive delays to through-passengers, rapid fare-collection methods, or even fare elimination within the core distribution area. The Times Square shuttle in New York, and Waterloo and City Line in London, are examples of transit services providing short-haul distribution. Seattle created a downtown zone within which fares on regular buses were eliminated for trips within the zone. Denver's 16th Street Mall, utilizing low-floor buses, is another example.

People Movers[X]

In most cases, however, this "beyond pedestrian assist" passenger distribution has been accomplished (or is proposed to be accomplished) via a class of Automated Guideway Transit (AGT), or "people movers." There has been considerable confusion in the professional community and the lay community over the classifications and technology applied to AGT and people movers. A great variety of terminology abounds, such as group rapid transit, monorails, light guideway transit, personal rapid transit, loop transit, shuttle transit, and shuttle-loop transit.

Because each AGT system and/or technology is a proprietary design, there exists a very wide range of features both in operation and applied technology. Specific types of applications are dependent upon certain features, whereas other features are not consequential. The subclasses of AGT systems are determined more by the types of applications than from the technologies employed. Technology becomes important only with regard to how the performance and functional features of a proprietary system design meet the requirements of a specific application.

Four basic subclasses of AGT are defined: line-haul AGT, people mover, group rapid transit, and personal rapid transit. People movers are one class of automated fixed-guideway transportation systems. People movers are applied only to move people within a restricted major activity center, such as an airport, an entertainment complex, a large retail or employment center, or a CBD. They are used to link "people places," transforming a closely arranged group of facilities having common purposes into a single functional unit. People movers are relatively small systems of short length (maximum of two or three miles) and a small number of stations and vehicles. A people mover may be configured as a shuttle, a loop, or a collapsed (or pinched) loop (Figure 18–72).

- *Shuttle People Mover Systems* have a single vehicle or train operating back and forth over a single-lane of guideway at 15 to 30 mph between on-line stations. Dual-lane shuttles simply have two lanes so equipped but may have the two separate vehicle and train movements coordinated to always travel in opposite directions. Shuttles are found to be practical applications for confined areas such as airports or in major activity centers for point-to-point service. Some systems will have an intermediate station. System length is governed by the maximum cruise speed because of the need to provide a reasonable frequency of service. Shuttle systems do not require traditional Automatic Train Protection systems for safety except to ensure safe stopping at the ends of the line. Several automated shuttles have been implemented using relatively low-cost, cable-propelled vehicles. Applications include a connection between a parking garage and a transit station, and a connection between a downtown business district and a commercial development on an island in Tampa, Florida.

- *Loop People Mover Systems* have been applied as circulators in downtowns (e.g., Miami and Detroit Downtown People Movers) and in major activity centers. The requirements for these two types of applications are somewhat different. Small to medium-size vehicles and trains circulate around either a single-lane loop in one direction or on two parallel loops for service in both directions. Usually, the loop is relatively short, about two miles or less in circumference. Stations are on-line and very close together, typically 0.25 mile. Therefore, there is little opportunity to utilize speeds as high as 30 mph. If satisfactory operating performance can be achieved with maximum speeds of 15 mph, switching is not required except to provide a means to place vehicles and trains into or out of service.

Vehicles may run on rubber tires or air cushions, or be magnetically levitated. Most designs have the vehicles riding over the guideway surface, but in some designs the vehicle is suspended from the guideway. Others may straddle a guideway beam. Monorails employ either the suspended or straddle-type configurations. Lateral control may be provided by a number of means such as side guidance rails, a center guidebeam, a center guide slot, or magnetic forces.

People movers are the simplest class of AGT system and consequently do not require the technological sophistication

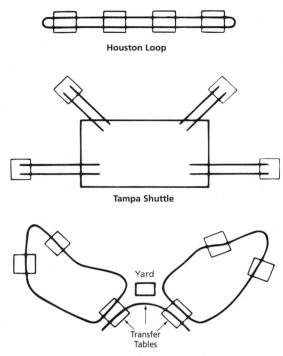

Houston Loop

Tampa Shuttle

Seattle-Tacoma Shuttle and Loop

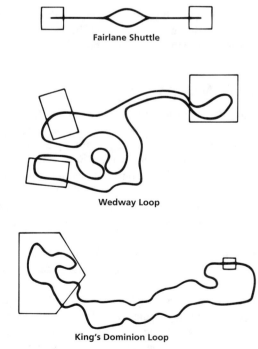

Fairlane Shuttle

Wedway Loop

King's Dominion Loop

Figure 18–72   Geometric Layouts of Six AGT Systems

Source: Charles P. Elms, "The Automated People Mover as One Class of AGT," ASCE Conference on Automated People Movers, Miami, Fla.: ASCE, March 1989. Reproduced by permission of ASCE.

found in line-haul and Group Rapid Transit systems, or proposed for Personal Rapid Transit. This simplification manifests itself as slower speed, lower capacity, simplified overall automatic control, simplified stations, very short distances, and the absence of operational switching. Stations are generally integrated into other buildings rather than being separate stand-alone facilities. Figure 18–73 shows some typical applications and technologies of people mover systems; some of these applications include:

- Airports.

- Circulation in an employment center.

- Linking an activity center with remote parking.

- Rapid transit station.

- Linking together various buildings of a hospital complex.

- Circulation on a university campus.

- Circulation in a downtown or large suburban retail and employment center.

- Circulation within an entertainment complex.

An additional advanced-technology "people mover" system is worthy of mention (e.g., the cableway, which has evolved from the commonplace ski lift). The "tramway" connecting Roosevelt Island with midtown Manhattan in New York City is an example of an urban application of this technology. (Figure 18–74.) Similar systems carry tourists to and from major amusement or recreation attractions.

Point-to-point shuttle of substantial numbers of people is the most significant service characteristic of such cableways. This technology may therefore be useful for passenger circulation in CBDs or activity centers, beyond the specialized, terrain-related applications it has been commonly used for.

Goods and Freight Distribution Systems[Y,Z]

There are many specialized forms of equipment and equipment systems that have been developed to move cargo between modes (e.g., truck-to-ship), from "shoreside" to ship (e.g., dock-to-ship), between terminals, within terminals and from point-of-origin to terminal (e.g., mine-to-seaport). Examples of some of these systems are provided in this section.

The simplest mechanical assists, beyond the obvious extremely limited capability of manual loading and unloading, involve a whole "family" of simple hand trucks,

Miami's Downtown People Mover AGT System

AIRTRANS GRT System at D/FW Airport

German Magnetic Levitated AGT System at Test Track

Simple Cable Power Shuttle People Mover System in Las Vegas

Figure 18–73   Typical AGT Systems

Source: Charles P. Elms, "The Automated People Mover as One Class of AGT," ASCE Conference on Automated People Movers, Miami, Fla.: ASCE, March 1989.

Figure 18–74   Large-Capacity Aerial Tramway in New York City

Sources: Graphic Gallery, photo by David I. Ozerkis. Appeared in *Urban Public Transportation Systems and Technology*, Prentice-Hall, 1981.

mechanized hand trucks, forklifts, and the like. An example of highly sophisticated equipment of this type is the "Ro-Ro forklift truck" used to load and unload Ro-Ro vessels. A Ro-Ro forklift truck has special design features that set it apart from others. The forklift has heavy-lift capacity, but it is short enough in height and length to work inside Ro-Ro vessels between decks. Working between decks, the Ro-Ro forklift's height constraint leads to two conflicting objectives: it has a very short mast to enter low-deck-height compartments, but a high-lift reach to raise and stack loads where greater deck height allows. Other design features of the Ro-Ro forklift truck are: exhaust emission and noise controls to permit tolerable working conditions between decks, ability to descend and climb access ramp inclines, spreading deck footprints through extra wheels and wide tires, and minimum turning radius for confined spaces.

Figure 18–75   Gyro-Truck

Source: ITE, *Transportation Planning Handbook*, 1992.

In Sweden, an innovative heavy-duty Ro-Ro forklift truck with lower fuel consumption has been developed. (Figure 18–75.) This truck is able to perform below-deck operations without emitting exhaust fumes, through the use of a unique gyro-power concept to drive the machine by kinetic energy stored in a high-speed flywheel.

Moving belts provide the key to moving packages between terminals and, most frequently, within terminals. The small-package express hub terminal, at airports, is an example of the latest industry where the moving belt is a key ingredient of the operation. The common denominator in handling equipment at all small-package express hub terminal systems is a moving belt combined with a manual sort for packages. Small-package operators deal with a fairly homogeneous collection of envelopes and small packages, making the hub sorting operation relatively easy. Freight is moved between airplanes and the sorting center in various types of small-package containers that also are carried in aircraft.

Whereas most hubs are engaged exclusively in the transfer of envelopes and small packages of limited size, there are some hubs that deal with shipments and pieces of unlimited sizes and have established separate sorting lines to cope with this situation. The moving belt systems have to be adaptable to this wide variety of package sizes. The hub system is said to improve reliability because the routing expert at the hub can efficiently make adjustments for problems, such as weather delays. This speeds intermodal transfer since it would be impossible for local employees at originating points to anticipate such problems.

Automatically controlled vehicles capable of operating in a mixed-traffic environment are used in some factories and office buildings for delivery of supplies, mail, and other items. The development of such robotic vehicles, capable of operating in several modes, is increasing in importance to the circulation requirements of many transportation interfaces.

Figure 18–76   Self-Unloading Ship

Source: ITE, *Transportation Planning Handbook*, 1992.

Figure 18–77   Rail-Mounted Ship Unloaders

Source: ITE, *Transportation Planning Handbook*, 1992.

For moving large quantities of bulk materials, *belt conveyors* are very often the optimum technique and, in some situations, are the only feasible method. They can be used in terminal functions (e.g., for short distance between modes, like dock-to-ship; or for longer, line-haul type of applications.

Belt conveyors have an important position in the transportation of bulk materials, owing to such inherent advantages as their economy and safety of operation, reliability, versatility, and a wide range of capacities. In addition, they are suitable for performing numerous processing functions, providing a continuous flow of material between operations. Belt conveyors can operate continuously—around the clock and around the calendar when required—without loss of time for loading and unloading. Operating labor costs differ little, regardless of capacity ratios. Costs per ton decrease as the annual tonnage handled increases.

Self-unloading ships (Figure 18–76) equipped with belt conveyors can be unloaded in all ports, even those that do not have dockside unloading equipment (Figure 18–77.) Unloading capacities of such systems are usually greater than those of several grab-bucket unloaders, requiring less turnaround time and lower labor and other operating costs.

In some longer-distance situations, the economic analysis may show that belt conveyors can be more than simply an interface facilitator between modes (i.e., between trucks or railroads and ships). The adaptability and economy of belt conveyors for transporting bulk materials over rugged terrain despite adverse weather conditions is illustrated by a system designed to deliver 1,300 tons/h of bauxite from ore dryers at the mine to a port facility in Jamaica. (Figure 18–78.)

Figure 18–78   Six-and-One-Half-Mile Conveyor System

Source: ITE, *Transportation Planning Handbook*, 1992.

Summary

This chapter has identified and reviewed the general principles and techniques for the planning and functional design of a wide variety of transportation terminals. It has also looked at specifics for the individual passenger and freight modes. Obviously, this material cannot possibly cover all situations or all modal combinations. This is left, as it should be, to individual planners and designers. They should be aiming to provide the safest, most efficient, most convenient, most environmentally compatible, and most imaginative interface for the particular planning objectives and traffic flows. They should also be alert to and seek out ways to integrate modes, to develop innovative combinations of public and private initiatives, and to apply the latest technological developments.

There are many examples of existing and proposed integrated plans, including: transportation centers combined with shopping and office development, ports and airports that incorporate industrial and commercial development, and ferry terminals directly connected with automated rail transit. No matter what specific interface or terminal is being planned, the central theme, the question that should always be kept in mind, is "how will users and other stakeholders perceive and use the facilities and services?" The market (i.e., the passengers, shippers, and communities) should be the key.

References

[A] Morlok, Edward K. *Introduction to Transportation Engineering and Planning,* McGraw-Hill, 1978.

[B] "Proceedings of the Conference on Multi-Modal Terminal Planning and Design," University of California, Irvine, March 1981.

[C] Vuchic, Vukan R. *Urban Public Transportation Systems and Technology,* Prentice-Hall, 1981.

[D] NCHRP Report #155, "Bus Use of Highways" (Planning and Design Guidelines), Transportation Research Board, Washington, D.C., 1975.

[E] "Effective Truck Terminal Planning and Operations," The Operations Council of American Trucking Associations, Inc., 1980.

[F] "Issues and Problems of Moving Goods in Urban Areas," ASCE Committee on Urban Goods movement, *ASCE Journal of Transportation Engineering,* January 1989.

[G] Hay, William W. *An Introduction to Transportation Engineering,* John Wiley & Sons, 1977.

[H] "The Inland Perspective of Intermodalism," by Paul Chilcote, PIANC Conference, October 1987.

[I] "Road-Railer: An Idea Whose Time Has Come?" Article in *Railway Age Magazine,* July 1977.

[J] "Rail Hubs: Meeting Shippers' Needs?" Article in *Intermodal Age Magazine,* May/June 1986.

[K] Agerschou, Hans, Helge Lundgren, and Torben Sorensen. *Planning and Design of Ports and Marine Terminals,* John Wiley and Sons, 1983.

[L] "Boston Revamps Old Railroad Station," *Engineering News-Record,* July 6, 1989.

[M] "AC-BART Joint Ticket," by Joel Markowitz, *Transportation Research Record #1144,* TRB 1987.

[N] Horonjeff, Robert and Francis X. McKelvey. *Planning and Design of Airports,* McGraw-Hill, Fourth Edition, 1994.

[O] Hart, Walter. *The Airport Passenger Terminal,* Krieger Publishing Company, 1991.

[P] "Airport Roadway Guide Signs," by ITE Technical Council Committee 50-1, 1991.

[Q] Airport Planning Manual, Part I, Master Planning, International Civil Aviation Organization, modified 1987.

[R] Muller, Gerhardt. *Intermodal Freight Transportation,* Eno Foundation for Transportation, Inc., 1995.

[S] "Data Needs for Planning Airport Access by Public Transportation," Information Report by ITE Technical Council Committee 6A19, *ITE Journal,* Washington, D.C., October 1980.

[T]

[Ta] Shapiro, Phillip S. et. al., *Intermodal Ground Access to Airports: A Planning Guide,* U.S. Department of Transportation, Washington, D.C, December 1966.

[Tb] op. cit. p. 83.

[Tc] op. cit. p. 85

[Td] op. cit. p. 85

[Te] op. cit. p. 85-88

[U] Horonjeff, Robert and Francis X. McKelvey. *Planning and Design of Airports,* McGraw-Hill, Third Edition, 1983.

[V] "Functional Design Principles for Goods Movement To and From Inland River Ports," by Martin E. Lipinski and Marvin L. Jacobs, Compendium, ITE 1988 Annual Meeting.

[W] "Virginia Launches Inland Port in New Competitive Effort," by Carlo J. Salzano, *Traffic World Magazine,* May 29, 1989 (and August 1999 Internet update from VIP Web site).

[X] "The Automated People Mover as One Class of AGT," by Charles P. Elms, ASCE Conference on Automated People Movers, March 1989, Miami, Florida.

[Y] Mahoney, John W. *Intermodal Freight Transportation,* Eno Foundation for Transportation, Inc., 1985.

[Z] *Transportation and Traffic Engineering Handbook,* Institute of Transportation Engineers, Prentice-Hall 2nd Edition, 1982.

CHAPTER 19
Transportation Operations and Management

Dennis C. Judycki
Director of Research, Development and Technology
Federal Highway Administration
U.S. Department of Transportation

Wayne Berman
Transportation Specialist
Federal Highway Administration
U.S. Department of Transportation

Background and Perspectives

Introduction

The movement of people, goods, and vehicles on the transportation system is now critically dependent on how effectively that system is operated and managed. While roadway system expansion is necessary in some key locations and corridors to facilitate this movement and in some cases economic development, the construction of new lanes will never alleviate the need for effective transportation operations and management of the system—on both existing and new segments. Well-planned, cost-effective transportation operations and management strategies can improve mobility, safety, and productivity of the system for transportation users in urban and rural areas.

This is particularly important considering the high cost of constructing new facility capacity and the current and projected increase in the rate of travel. It is estimated that new development, demographics, family composition, and trip-making trends will result in an annual average highway travel growth rate of 2.16 percent over the next twenty years.[1] Because of the burden on the transportation system, maximizing the usefulness and effectiveness of existing facilities and services to move people, goods, and vehicles is essential, even in those situations where new capacity is being added to the system.

Transportation operations and management is an umbrella term for the application of construction, operational and institutional actions, policies, and procedures to make the safest, most productive and cost-effective use of transportation facilities and services on both existing and new facilities in both metropolitan and rural areas. It is through the application of strategies such as transportation management changes and operational policies that an area is able to maintain mobility and safety in the face of growing demand for travel and limitations on system capacity growth.

Historical Context

Current transportation operations and management practices are the by-product of fundamental traffic engineering actions taken to improve the operation of the highway system beginning in the early 1930s. Decisions such as increasing or decreasing the parking supply, incorporating left-turn bays at intersections, or implementing progressively timed traffic

---

[1] U.S. Department of Transportation, Federal Highway Administration, and Federal Transit Administration, *Report to Congress: 1997 Status of the Nation's Surface Transportation System—Condition and Performance* (Washington, D.C.: U.S. DOT, FHWA, March 1998).

signals are also expected to become part of the overall concept of transportation operations and management. The application of advanced information technologies, known as intelligent transportation systems (ITS), to these concepts would profoundly change the way transportation professionals think about how the system is operated and managed.

Urban areas received a great deal of attention between the early 1960s and mid-1970s. In the United States, Congress recognized the importance of metropolitan planning in the Federal Aid Highway Act of 1962, which included the framework for an urban planning process. In the late 1960s, there was a great deal of pressure to establish a federally aided highway and public transportation program for larger cities. Recognition and support was given to urban operational planning and improvement needs with the creation of the Urban Area Traffic Operations Improvement Program in the Federal Aid Highway Act of 1968. This program became known as TOPICS (Traffic Operations Program to Improve Capacity and Safety). One of the problems identified by this program was that while earlier extensions of the freeway system into urban areas had relieved traffic congestion on many arterials, volumes had increased on other arterials and city streets on which local jurisdictions were unable to finance improvements. In establishing the TOPICS program, Congress also recognized that urban system traffic operational improvements were not receiving the full advantage of modern traffic engineering techniques. Recognition and support of local needs was provided by the Federal Aid Highway Act of 1970, which authorized a Federal Aid Urban System and a funding allocation for constructing exclusive bus lanes.

The concept of "Transportation System Management (TSM)" received formal recognition in the United States as part of the 1975 Joint FHWA/UMTA Urban Planning Regulations. In theory, TSM actions were intended to improve the operating efficiency of the existing transportation system (facilities, services, and modes). TSM actions consisted of both supply management elements (e.g., traffic engineering and signal improvements) and demand management elements (e.g., projects to increase the number of high-occupancy vehicles used for commuting). As reflected in the appendix to the regulations, TSM includes "operating, regulatory, and service policies so as to achieve maximum efficiency and productivity for the system as a whole."[2]

Continued Emphasis on Transportation Operations and Management

The Intermodal Surface Transportation Efficiency Act (ISTEA) of 1991 gave new emphasis and meaning to the concepts of transportation operations and management. This law emphasized the importance of transportation operations and management as a national policy. The law also gave credibility to the role that ITS will play in transportation policy at every level of government. As a result of ISTEA, transportation operations and management concepts are being re-thought and re-engineered with ITS. The Transportation Equity Act of the Twenty-First Century (TEA-21) renews and even strengthens that national emphasis on transportation operations and management.

The Goal of Integration

Throughout its evolution, there are some key overall goals regarding transportation operations and management that have remained over time. The first goal is to *continuously manage and improve* the operation of the transportation system. Because traffic congestion will always be a problem, actions must always be monitored, adjusted, or revised to be effective at providing relief and improvement over time. Systems need to be maintained and improved over time to be effective and responsive to demands.

The second goal is to have plans, policies, and operational actions be *integrated* with each other to support the overall long- and short-term mobility goals of a community. The transportation modes, services, policies, and programs must be designed to work together rather then compete. They also must be designed to "talk" to each other electronically through the application of information technologies. This is the essence of ITS. Regional and local plans must be developed to provide opportunities for integrating and applying a combination of policies, programs, and operational actions to

---

[2] U. S. Department of Transportation, Federal Highway Administration, and Urban Mass Transportation Administration, "Transportation Improvement Program," *Federal Register,* 23 CFR, Part 450, Subparts A and C (Washington, D.C.: U.S. DOT, FHWA, and Urban Mass Transportation Administration, September 17, 1975).

effectively meet mobility needs. In addition, transportation can no longer work in isolation. Both institutionally and technically, transportation services must be linked to other state and local agencies, such as public safety (police, fire, and emergency services) and intermodal (airports, harbors, and manufacturing centers). Today and in the future, integration is critical to the success and effectiveness of transportation operations and management.

The contemporary approach to transportation operations and management attempts to integrate services and functions across agency and jurisdictional lines. In addition, this contemporary approach tries to be more responsive to the traveling public by providing a variety of traveler information services. The integration of service and systems through the application of ITS technologies is a national goal that was articulated in January 1996 by then Secretary of Transportation Frederico Peña.

Today, transportation operations and management strategies attempt to integrate services and actions across traditional agency and jurisdictional lines. The private sector is also now playing a stronger role as a participant in system operations and management by developing products and services that help the public sector deliver vital transportation services demanded by the public.

Purpose of the Chapter

The primary purpose of this chapter is to present contemporary strategies, approaches, applications, and analyses of transportation operations and management concepts. The presentation is drawn from references, existing and ongoing programs and research, and current views of national organizations such as the Transportation Research Board, the Institute of Transportation Engineers, and the Association of Commuter Transportation. The chapter is structured as follows:

1. *Background and perspectives*—An overview of the evolution and contemporary philosophy of transportation operations and management.

2. *The need for transportation operations and management*—A presentation of the reasons for transportation operations and management from various perspectives.

3. *The spectrum of transportation operations and management strategies*—A summary of available actions, their general application and, where possible, expected benefits based upon experience.

4. *Planning for transportation operations and management*—A presentation on the role for planning transportation operations and management strategies and how it may be different from traditional planning for construction-related improvements.

5. *Design and implementation considerations*—A discussion of general techniques and contemporary tools used for designing, implementing, and evaluating the effectiveness of the strategies.

6. *Institutional considerations*—A discussion of the role that public and private institutions (and organizations) play in the development of integrated transportation operations and management strategies.

7. *Case studies and applications*—A presentation of strategies using selected case studies to demonstrate applications, perspectives (e.g., regional, local, state) issues, and lessons learned.

The Need for Transportation Operations and Management

The applications of transportation operations and management actions are intended to achieve one or more objectives for a city, county, region (either metropolitan or rural), or state. Implemented individually or in concert with one another, these actions can help to achieve one or more of ten clearly measurable goals. These objectives, which can also be considered as positive effects, are listed as follows:

1. Reducing the need to make a trip.

2. Reducing the length of a trip.

3. Promoting nonmotorized transport.

4. Promoting public transport.

5. Promoting ridesharing.

6. Shifting peak-hour travel.

7. Shifting travel from congested locations.

8. Reducing traffic delays.

9. Providing safety and efficiency for travelers during periods of construction, incidents, and weather-related road closures.

10. Obtaining and sharing travel information to help manage the system and to provide travelers an understanding of the current conditions of the facilities and services that they use.

While meeting these objectives has traditionally been thought to address the problems of traffic congestion, the contemporary perspective of transportation operations and management actions is that they must also address the broader and often more important issues facing cities, counties, states, and regions. These issues include public safety, quality of life, productivity, economic development, accessibility to jobs and services, and mobility for individuals who are not able to use an automobile. The contemporary view of transportation operations and management means that actions can no longer be applied from just the context of one city or agency. These actions can grow from a local application to a regional (or metropolitan) application through integration, information sharing, and coordination across agency and jurisdictional lines.

There are a number of reasons for this new perspective on the way local, regional, state, and the federal governments are viewing how the transportation system is operated and managed. These reasons include the technology of the information age; the demands on government for improved customer services; the need to use scarce government resources more efficiently; and the growing effects that congestion has on productivity, safety, economic development, and mobility.

The information age has provided the transportation system operators and managers with technologies that can link agency to agency, jurisdiction to jurisdiction, and government to its citizens easier and faster. The technologies applied to transportation are known as ITS, and they are reshaping the manner in which governments do business with each other and with the traveling public. In addition, ITS is enabling local governments to work together as a region to address problems that jump over city, county, and state boundary lines. Technology is allowing transportation system operators and managers to think of problems beyond just a local "stove-pipe" context; it is providing the opportunity for traffic, transit, and public safety systems operators and managers to also address their problems, together, in a regional context. (See Chapter 16 of the Institute of Transportation Engineer's *Traffic Engineering Handbook* for more information on ITS.)

The need for improved customer services is also reshaping the manner in which governments provide services. These demands, coupled with ITS, can provide system operators and managers with the ability to inform the traveling public of the condition of the systems that move people and goods. Information enables the public to make informed decisions about when, how, and where they travel. It also helps industry and shippers make informed decisions to efficiently move goods and commerce on the system.

Figure 19–1   An Example of Recurring Congestion

Source: Maryland Department of Transportation.

Information helps make travel on the transportation system more predictable for the users. A number of surveys of the general public (both in the United States and in Europe) have shown that the public is bothered more by nonrecurring congestion (such as an incident) than by recurring congestion due to routine delays. This customer perspective means that the system breaks down when it is no longer predictable to the users. Traveler information, customer service, as well as transportation operations and management actions can alter and improve the performance and predictability of the system locally and regionally.

Traffic congestion is everyone's problem; it affects lifestyle choice and travel behavior. It also influences capital and operational investment decisions made by the public and private sectors. In addition, studies have shown that traffic congestion significantly influences the availability and cost of providing goods and services to the consumer (i.e., the traveling public). Traffic congestion and its related costs contribute to the shift in jobs to the suburbs and the further decline of the economic base of the city-center. Freight carriers and shippers incur large economic costs from congestion and often have delivery schedules dictated by congestion avoidance.

Congestion is not simply an issue confined to corridors and activity centers of large cities or urban areas. Congestion affects work trips and the nonwork-related trips (Figure 19–1). It affects the movement of people and the flow of goods. Much work has also been done to show that traffic congestion significantly contributes to air quality problems, especially in our largest and most dense urban areas. In nonurban (rural) areas and intercity corridors, traffic is disrupted by incidents, maintenance operations, reconstruction, detours, congestion on tourist routes, and other factors.

From the road user's viewpoint, traffic delays are substantial and growing. Rush hour conditions in many urban areas often extend throughout the weekday and even on weekends. From the employer's viewpoint, congestion takes its toll in lost worker productivity and cost. Speed, reliability, and cost of urban, intercity, and international freight movements are increasingly affected by congestion. Traffic congestion becomes an especially critical factor to consider for industries and operations that depend on the "just-in-time" product delivery system in lieu of carrying a large inventory of goods.

The causes of traffic congestion can be categorized as either recurring or nonrecurring. Recurring congestion is predictable delay caused by high volumes of vehicles using the roadway during the same time periods (i.e., peak commute periods, holiday periods, or special events) and at the same locations (i.e., intersections, interchanges, or toll plaza areas). Major long-term roadway reconstruction projects also create significant, recurring, congestion during the construction period.

Nonrecurring congestion is unpredictable delay generally caused by spontaneous, unplanned occurrences (e.g., traffic accidents and incidents, road reconstruction, unforeseen special events, or emergency maintenance). Weather conditions can also create significant nonrecurring congestion problems. Unexpected traffic delays and accidents caused by snow, rain, and fog represent important considerations in the development of congestion reduction policies.

Increasing travel demands are placed on the roadway system, and the related traffic congestion problems continue, even in the face of substantial investment of public sector dollars. In 1995, the average number of vehicles owned per American household increased to 1.8, up from 1.7 in 1983, and 1.2 in 1969.[3] Nearly 20 percent of households own 3 or more vehicles.[4] Recently, the annual average number of miles driven per vehicle has shown stabilization at about 12,000 miles. The number of miles driven per vehicle increased from 10,300 miles in 1983 to 12,300 miles in 1995 and remained relatively stable in 1996 at 12,500 miles.[5] These numbers reflect the trend that people tend to keep their vehicles longer but drive them fewer miles annually as they age.

The growth in the number of person trips also indicates increasing system demands and reflects the related traffic congestion problems. The number of person trips increased 14 percent between 1990 and 1995.[6] The average trip length declined slightly by 3 percent over the same five-year period.[7] Commuting patterns have also changed, with suburb-to-suburb trips increasing nearly three times faster than trips from suburb to central cities. Between 1980 and 1990, commuter travel from suburb to central cities grew by 21 percent, trips from central cities to suburbs increased by 37 percent, and trips from suburb to suburb increased by 60 percent. The large growth in employment in the suburbs, particularly the high density centers (often referred to as "Edge Cities"), has contributed to this pattern.[8]

Despite numerous isolated success stories about increasing auto occupancy rates, especially at employment sites, the aggregate data from the 1990 census data paint a different picture. In nearly all of the 39 metropolitan areas with a population of one million or more, average vehicle occupancy levels for journey to work trips was less than 1.1 in 1990. Nationally, the share of workers driving to work alone increased from 64.4 percent in 1980 to 73.2 percent in 1990. Much of the increase in driving alone came at the expense of carpooling, and to a lesser degree from transit.[9]

Because of substantial increases in auto ownership, coupled with significant changes over the past decade in land-use, demographics, economics, and lifestyles, major public sector investments in infrastructure and operations have not kept pace with the congestion problems. Especially in light of the Clean Air Act Amendments of 1990 and ISTEA, it is widely understood that we cannot build our way out of traffic congestion. Further, congestion is a problem that must be efficiently managed, not necessarily solved.

[3] U.S. Department of Transportation, Federal Highway Administration, *Our Nation's Travel: 1995 Nationwide Personal Transportation Survey Early Results Report,* Publication Number FHWA-PL-97-028 (Washington, D.C.: U.S. DOT, FHWA, September 1997), Figure 2.

[4] U.S. Department of Transportation, Federal Highway Administration, *Our Nation's Travel: 1995 Nationwide Personal Transportation Survey Early Results Report*, Publication Number FHWA-PL-97-028 (Washington, D.C.: U.S. DOT, FHWA, September 1997), Figure 2.

[5] U.S. Department of Transportation, Federal Highway Administration, *Summary of Travel Trends: 1995 Nationwide Personal Transportation Survey,* Draft Report (Washington, D.C.: U.S. DOT, FHWA, December 1998), Table 21, p. 36.

[6] U.S. Department of Transportation, Federal Highway Administration, *Summary of Travel Trends: 1995 Nationwide Personal Transportation Survey,* Draft Report (Washington, D.C.: U.S. DOT, FHWA, December 1998), Table 21, p. 36.

[7] U.S. Department of Transportation, Federal Highway Administration, *Summary of Travel Trends: 1995 Nationwide Personal Transportation Survey*, Draft Report (Washington, D.C.: U.S. DOT, FHWA, December 1998), Table 21, p. 36.

[8] ENO Transportation Foundation, Inc., *Commuting in America II: The Second National Report on Commuting Patterns and Trends* (Washington, D.C.: Eno Transportation Foundation, 1996).

[9] U.S. Department of Transportation, Federal Highway Administration, *Journey-to-Work Trends in the United States and Its Major Metropolitan A' 1960–1990,* Publication Number FHWA-PL-94-012 (Washington, D.C.: U.S. DOT, FHWA, November 1993).

In summary, transportation operations and management actions must be applied strategically. They must be applied with an evolutionary vision. A vision that includes solutions that are integrated with actions of other agencies and jurisdictions. The vision then evolves from just a local approach to a regional coordinated action in which information can be shared for the benefit of all. Energy must be focused on providing improved public safety and customer services, including better information system conditions and performance. Applied in an integrated and coordinated manner, these actions can also help the government do its job better—that is serving the public.

The Spectrum of Transportation Operations and Management Strategies

Congestion is a major concern on roadways across the world. The most obvious solution for traffic congestion is adding lanes to increase the capacity of the roadway. In modern times, however, there is often no budget, or more practically no space, for such expansion. Transportation experts were forced to create an alternative. Today's communications and information technologies, known as ITS, have been key to solving such problems.

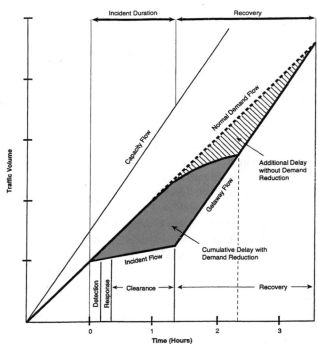

Figure 19–2   Impact of an Incident Traffic Flow

Source: Trucking Research Institute, ATA Foundation.

There are many facets of ITS, perhaps the most important being real-time information. For example, the faster an incident can be detected and cleared, the less congestion will occur as a result. This is where transportation operations and management enters the picture. In order to ensure accurate real-time information, the transportation system must be operated and managed to optimize its benefits. This chapter addresses the various strategies or methods of operating and managing effective transportation systems.

Capacity Enhancing (Including ITS Infrastructure)

The main objective of ITS is to bring communications, traffic, and management together to increase capacity and reduce delay. The following are methods of utilizing ITS to provide increased capacity without actually expanding the number of lanes in many congested roadway networks.

- *Incident management*—Incident management is an effective method of reducing incident clearance time. Incident management includes detection, verification, response, and clearance. The longer it takes to clear the results of an incident, the longer its effects will be felt in the form of added congestion. Traffic flowing at Levels of Service D or worse are particularly sensitive to even short disruptions caused by incidents. Therefore, the faster incidents can be detected and the more quickly they can be cleared, significantly less congestion can be expected to follow (Figure 19–2). Less congestion means more throughput and thus more capacity. For incident management to be an effective means of enhancing roadway capacity, efficient transportation operations and management of this program is essential.

- *Signal coordination*—The capacity of a local street and arterial network can be substantially increased with the deployment of a signal system. Congestion can be avoided when the timing of signals is coordinated to create a smooth, seamless flow of traffic. Another advantage of deploying a signal system is that priority can be given to emergency vehicles. Signals can be reset to provide green time to emergency medical services (EMS), fire trucks, and police cars. Furthermore, a signal system that is connected to a Traffic Management Center (TMC) can provide incident detection capabilities. Once an incident has been detected, priority can be given to some signals in order to reroute traffic through a network to avoid delays and congestion. This also allows for a faster incident clearance time, further reduction of congestion, and increased capacity of local streets.

- *High-occupancy vehicle (HOV) lanes*—HOV lanes provide a designated space for vehicles with typically more than two passengers. HOV lanes typically flow at a higher Level of Service than the rest of the mainline. This encourages people to use buses and to share rides because of the time-savings. Theoretically, for each person that decides to utilize HOV, there is one less vehicle on the mainline section of the freeway. The more people that choose this method, the significantly less number of vehicles place a demand on the roadway in both the HOV and single-occupancy vehicle lanes. Posting information on ridesharing may complement HOV effectiveness.

- *Electronic toll collection (ETC)*—Significant expansion of capacity can result from the implementation of an ETC system. It physically takes a long time for motorists to gather money, open their window, and pay a toll collector. This process also jeopardizes traffic patterns. Motorists tend to swerve and reduce speed when reaching for their money. These factors contribute to the low capacity of a toll collection facility. When ETC is introduced, these factors are eliminated. Drivers can safely pay attention to the roadway and efficiently pass through the toll. Data collected from the existing ETC system on the Tappan Zee Bridge reveals that the capacity has more than doubled from 450 to 1,000 vehicles per hour since the implementation of their ETC system.[10]

- *Ramp metering*—Ramp metering regulates the number of vehicles entering the freeway. The meters are equipped with detectors and signals to inform the motorist when he or she is permitted to enter the freeway after waiting on the ramp. Ramp meters help ensure that demand does not exceed capacity. The detectors determine where there is enough space for a vehicle to proceed and smoothly enter onto the main roadway with minimal effect on the flow of traffic. Ramp metering tends to maintain uninterrupted, noncongested flow on the freeway, utilizing the existing capacity of the freeway to its optimal extent.

- *Contra-flow lanes (on arterials)*—Contra-flow lanes can increase the capacity of the roadway in the peak direction. These lanes are operated reversibly. This technique can provide an additional lane in both directions, one at a time. Different barriers can be utilized to enforce this option, such as moveable barriers or electronic signing. This practice needs to be managed carefully to avoid head-on collisions.

Demand Reductions and Relocations (e.g., During Construction)

In addition to everyday capacity requirements, special circumstances frequently arise that may increase the demand on our nation's roadways. Incidents, construction, major maintenance, and special events all contribute to some of the worst traffic problems. ITS has also played a leading role in reducing their effects.

During construction, the capacity of a roadway is decreased. Options need to be analyzed for reducing the demand on construction zones. Planning appropriate staging and sequencing of construction schemes helps minimize interference with traffic flow and disruption to the local surrounding communities.

- *Construction coordination*—Construction coordination affects parallel or intersecting roadways. Motorists should ideally use these routes as alternates to roadways with construction. When construction activities are planned for two parallel roadways at the same time, the capacity of the network is reduced in two places and the demand remains the same. The effects of construction can be adverse with just one construction site. Therefore, an effort should be made to coordinate activities such that construction work on parallel or intersecting roadways can be avoided by communicating and coordinating with other agencies. It is important

---

[10] U.S. Department of Transportation, Federal Highway Administration and Federal Transit Administration, *Intelligent Transportation System Awareness Seminar*, CD-ROM (Washington, D.C.: U.S. DOT, FHWA, January 1999).

to recognize, however, that some construction cannot be delayed. A careful assessment should be performed to determine which activities should be planned at what times. Inter- and intra-agency coordination can prevent such unnecessary congestion.

- *Signal timing (to favor an alternate route)*—Street signal networks can be re-programmed to give priority to a particular route during construction. Motorists tend to follow the directions that are green. In this manner, vehicles can be rerouted around the construction site. It cannot be expected that all vehicles will follow the prioritized signals, but both motorists who do and do not follow them can benefit from this practice. Those who do follow the favored route avoid the congestion that results from a reduced capacity construction site. Motorists who do not follow the signal priority find that fewer vehicles are driving on their route, better suiting the smaller capacity of the construction site. Therefore, this method can reduce the demand on the construction site by increasing the demand on the alternate route.

- *Construction at off-peak hours*—Local, state, and federal DOTs have guidelines for the maintenance and protection of traffic (MPT) during construction. These guidelines are intended to ensure that the motorist receives the best possible roadway conditions during construction. There are many techniques to accomplish this. One common way of reducing congestion is performing the construction work during off-peak hours such as nighttime. However, nighttime construction is more expensive and is not appropriate for all types of construction activities. It is always recommended that an assessment of all anticipated construction activities be completed before any construction takes place. Some construction activities can be planned for the nighttime and some during the daytime, also at off-peak hours. So, the demand is smaller at off-peak times and the roadway can more easily handle the necessary volume, depending on the level of construction activity. The construction assessment should also be completed to coordinate such activities that can be carried out at the same time and to prioritize which activities are to be performed first.

- *Alternate routes*—Special routes can be formally designated and signed to take some of the demand off of the affected roadway. These diversions require clear signing, as many of the motorists will be unfamiliar with the new route. Variable message signs (VMS) or fixed panel signs are effective for marking alternate routes.

- *Alternate transit services*—Another way of reducing demand is to arrange alternate transit services to replace the service in the construction area. This encourages travelers to reduce the number of vehicles on the road by providing an alternate mode of transportation, such as a park-and-ride facility or transit service. Travelers may enjoy the convenience of using transit and continue to do so when the construction has been completed.

- *Closure(s) of entrance and exit ramps*—Closing entrance and exit ramps on a freeway that are within or adjacent to a construction site can provide a smoother Level of Service on the mainline. Additionally, because vehicles will have to travel farther in order to enter or exit the roadway, this may deter some motorists from taking short trips on the congested portion of the freeway. Both of these results can help reduce the demand on construction sites. (Figure 19–3.)

- *Service patrols and construction pull-off areas*—Special teams of service patrols and tow services can be positioned on the construction site to provide immediate emergency service for incidents in the construction area. This method of incident management expedites incident clearance in reduced capacity situations. A pull-off area can be cleared on the side of the road near the construction site to provide space for tow services and stalled vehicles. This furnishes space to clear an incident in its early stages. The pull-off area can be implemented with or without a service patrol team, depending on the particular needs of the area.

- *Use of shoulders*—To increase the capacity in a construction area, roadways that have shoulders can be restriped to temporarily utilize the shoulder lane as a regular lane. This should not be done on all roadways that have shoulders. It is important to determine if the shoulder lane is safe for regular usage.

- *Establish a command center*—During big construction projects, establishing a command center can prove to be effective. The command center works much like a TMC, managing the daily construction activities as well as providing incident management services.

Figure 19–3   An Example of Ramp Closure During Construction

Source: Maryland Department of Transportation.

- *Rerouting commercial traffic*—For some construction sites, the roadway requires temporary re-striping, making the lanes narrower. In these construction areas, it is important to consider trucks. Some commercial vehicles may no longer be safe to drive in very narrow lanes. In this case, commercial vehicles should be temporarily rerouted on alternate truck routes.

- *Ridesharing*—Signs with ridesharing information can also be used to help reduce the traffic demand during construction. Ridesharing services facilitate carpooling and vanpooling commuters. This method of demand reduction works well with companies that have a large number of commuting employees. Ridesharing services are especially effective in areas that have HOV lanes available.

- *Alternate work hours*—Alternating or rescheduling work hours can be effective in reducing roadway demand for peak hours during major construction projects. A temporary workday schedule can be set up to change traffic patterns during a big construction project. Employers would have to agree to change their work hours for the duration of the construction project. Some companies would work from 9 A.M. to 5 P.M., some from 10 A.M. to 6 P.M., and so on. This reduces the demand placed on the roadway during key peak hours.

Traveler Information Services (e.g., for Route and Mode Diversion)

History has shown that when travelers have pertinent information on incidents, construction, and planned events, they tend to change routes or modes accordingly. Significant improvements in traffic conditions are largely due to traveler information. Accurate and timely delivery of this information is key. Travelers can check a television news station for up-to-date traffic conditions before they depart on a trip. This may be very helpful in avoiding an incident that has occurred before that point in time. What happens if there is an accident about halfway through the trip? Travelers who do not know about this may then subsequently get stuck in traffic. On the other hand, if real-time information was available, travelers would be aware of any incidents as they occur. (See Chapter 16 of the Institute of Transportation Engineers' *Traffic Engineering Handbook,* 5th Ed. for more information.)

The following list illustrates the many methods of delivering traveler information to the public.

- *Fixed and portable VMS*—VMS is a great way to inform motorists of upcoming incidents, special events, alternate routes, and construction or congestion on freeways or surface streets. The number of vehicles that choose to take an alternate route reduces the demand on the roadway. These signs are especially effective because drivers do not have to do anything to obtain this valuable information. It's posted right there on the roadway for motorists to read. It is extremely important that the signs are maintained with appropriate up-to-date messages or drivers will stop trusting the signs and therefore stop utilizing them. Deploying fixed message signs can also be useful to inform motorists of long-term situations, such as road closures or upcoming projects.

- *Highway advisory radio (HAR)*—HAR is another method of reaching the users of a transportation system. This type of radio is designed to broadcast a prerecorded message only to motorists in a particular area who have immediate need of the information. The motorists are typically informed to tune in via a fixed freeway sign. Drivers have to tune in to a station typically on their A.M. radio. They have to perform a task to acquire the information. A significantly smaller number of drivers usually receive this message than the number of VMS readers. However, HAR is still effective in that it does relay pertinent traffic information to motorists who can then determine for themselves if they want to change routes. Another argument in favor of this method is that motorists who tune in to their radio and make the effort to obtain information are more likely to change their route than those passing by a VMS.

- *Commercial radio*—Numerous commuters tune in to their favorite radio station for a traffic update. Many stations have traffic air-watch or ground patrol units providing firsthand traffic condition information. Radio, especially if it is utilized by the motorist while driving, is quite effective in delivering real-time traveler information.

- *Print media*—Newspapers are another effective means for providing traffic information, particularly for reporting planned events, construction activities, and long-term incidents (such as a bridge collapse). Distributing brochures, pamphlets, and flyers to affected freeway users can also prove effective for this type of advance warning information.

- *Citizen band (CB) radios*—Many vehicles are currently equipped with CB radios. This type of radio is an effective means of providing traveler information in emergency situations, such as extraordinarily heavy rainfall and extensive flooding.

- *Cable television*—Some commuters check their favorite television news station before they depart on their trip. Television is a good method of reporting traffic and weather conditions before trip departure. Some TMCs broadcast real-time traffic conditions on a local cable television station. However, roadway conditions fluctuate and are likely to change while the motorist is on the roadway.

- *Cellular telephone*—A dedicated cellular number, such as *123 in Chicago, can provide prerecorded or computer-generated voice broadcasts of traveler information. Many motorists today have vehicles that are equipped with cellular telephones. Cellular phones are also effective in making 911 calls to report incidents.

- *Alphanumeric pager and Internet/fax-back capabilities*—Traveler information can be transmitted via alpha-numeric pager. This can have two main functions. The TRANSCOM program in the New York metropolitan area uses such pagers to inform other agencies of incidents and other traffic-related information. Pagers are effective in transmitting internal transportation conditions. Studies are being conducted now in the TRANSCOM area under the Federal Highway Administration's (FHWA's) Model Deployment Initiative (MDI) to provide a paging service for the traveling public. It will be a fee-based service that will page a customer when an incident has occurred in their normal commute route. Under the NY/NJ/CT MDI project, a relatively new method of providing traveler information is being investigated. Personal Traveler Service (PTS) will soon be available in the New York metropolitan area. For a fee, PTS will input customer profiles consisting of where and when, for example, a commuter drives to and from each day. If an incident occurs in the motorist's route, that customer will be notified via fax, e-mail, pager, or whatever the traveler has chosen as the method of communication.

- *Kiosks*—Another effective means of traveler information services are kiosks. Kiosks can be set up in transportation terminals, tourist attractions, rental car garages, and hotels. There are many different types of kiosks ranging from static to real-time information. Some kiosks have printers to provide users with written directions or other traveler information. These are particularly effective in tourist areas such as hotels and rental car locations. Others are directly connected to the Internet and perform the same functions with a touch-screen. A good example that demonstrates the practical use of kiosks is the Atlanta Olympics Showcase. Many travelers who were unfamiliar with the Atlanta area utilized kiosks throughout the city to find information about and directions to attractions, restaurants, and Olympic games in the area.

- *In-vehicle navigation systems*—Also effectively utilized in the Atlanta Olympic games were in-vehicle navigation systems. These are little computer screens that are mounted in a vehicle. Some types of these systems include a voice (either prerecorded or computer generated) and a global positioning system-based map with vehicle tracking. These systems are especially effective for motorists who are unfamiliar with the area in which they are driving. Many rental car services offer their customers in-vehicle navigation systems to that recommend restaurants and tourist attractions based upon how far the user wishes to travel.

Integrated and Coordinated Services

The condition of any transit or roadway system has a direct effect on many other modes and roadways in the same transportation network. For example, if a train incident occurs on a commuter railroad and major delays result, a greater demand is placed upon roadways and other alternative means. Interagency coordination is key for accommodating the needs of an entire network. The following sections are all areas where integration and coordinated services provide advantages to the agencies as well as the traveling public.

- *Traffic information center (TIC)*—History has proven that travelers find it difficult to plan trips using more than one mode of transportation. They have to acquire scheduling information, make reservations, and purchase tickets at separate locations for each mode. These inconveniences tend to set back the number of travelers willing to use mass transit facilities. A regional TIC serves to coordinate all agencies' traveler information together. This can benefit both the traveling public as well as the agencies involved in the program. The TIC provides a seamless transportation information system for an entire region or state by supplying traveler information on all modes of transit. This makes learning how to use the many components of a complicated transportation system much easier. A traveler can contact one location (e.g., via phone, fax, Internet) and find out when, where, and how to take each mode of transportation, including transfers. This can make a complicated transportation system seem a whole lot friendlier to travelers, thereby encouraging the use of transit and helping increase ridership. A regional TIC can also benefit the agencies that participate in the program by sharing information. One agency or mode can provide extra service when another agency or mode is out of service. Interagency coordination and a solid communication system are keys to a successful regional TIC.

- *TMC integration and resource sharing*—Another important place for information sharing is traffic management systems. Often, a freeway management system will have a TMC operated and managed by the state, for instance. Local governments may decide to build a signal system and their own TMC to manage that process. It would make sense if these two TMCs shared their information to better coordinate traveler information. An integrated TMC can also share resources and cut operation and management costs. Complying with standards, such as the National Transportation Communications for ITS Protocol, facilitate the sharing of information and equipment.

  Another area where integration would be beneficial is electronic toll collection. Travelers would find it convenient if they could use their in-vehicle transponder in more places than their home state. Ideally, the same tag should be accepted worldwide.

- *Transit coordination*—Transit coordination is where agencies adjust schedules to enable and simplify transfers among transit modes and agencies. When a transfer is simplified or expedited, both agencies tend to reap the benefits. A prime example of this is the Metrocard program, sponsored by the Metropolitan Transportation Authority, which enables free transfers between buses and subways within the New York City metropolitan area. With the implementation of this program, ridership jumped for both subways and buses.

- *Smart Cards*—Smart Cards can be effective in connecting all modes of transit, from subway to bus to train, and so on. Using the same card for many modes of transit is convenient for travelers and therefore encourages the use of multimodes. Smart Cards make a complicated transportation system seem smaller and easier to use.

- *Mutual aid*—Mutual aid allows the vehicles of one jurisdiction to operate in another zone. If an out-of-state emergency vehicle can arrive more quickly at the site of an incident, the jurisdictional boundary should be "blurred" to a certain extent. For example, Maryland and Virginia have implemented the "blurring" of their traditional state boundaries to better respond to incidents close to their borders.

Planning for Transportation Operations and Management

Suppose you and a group of friends decide to take a vacation trip together. None of you are sure exactly where to go, but the general idea is acceptable. To make the trip happen, you and your friends would go through a planning and consensus-building process that roughly goes as follows:

- *Agree on what to do*—will the group go to the beach, snow skiing, or sightseeing? Ideas would be suggested and discussed. Some may have concerns about certain ideas, such as the ability to afford such a vacation or the time it takes. The group may not know all the details at this point, but they will know enough to agree on the type of trip to take so they can move on to the next step.

- *Agree on expectations*—suppose the group decides to go snow skiing. Members must now consider which ski resort to go to and how to get there. In order to make the decision, the group must agree on a budget, how much time they have for the trip, and other factors (e.g., whether some members have an aversion to flying).

At this point, the group should contact a travel agent to get accurate information. The travel agent will tell the group how much the ski resorts cost and how long it will take to and from resorts.

- *Agree on a plan of action*—once the group agrees on expectations, details of the trip are worked out. They may want to evaluate several destinations or they may agree on one destination right off the bat. Once they agree on a destination and a date, they can prepare an itinerary and make airline, hotel, and rental car reservations. Again, a travel agent is extremely helpful with these details.

- *Take the trip*—the members follow the travel itinerary and have a wonderful vacation. Almost everything goes as planned and the group stays within its budget.

Of course, the trip can be made without any planning, but think about how difficult such a trip would be. What if the group made its way to the ski slope and found no rooms at the lodge? Not only would the group have to find another place to stay, members would have to agree on another place—in relatively short order—something that will likely disgruntle one or two. String along several of these misfortunes and some of the members may vow never to see each other again.

The need for and approach to planning for transportation operations and management are similar to vacation planning. A group of decision-makers must generally agree on what to do, then on the details as they move towards action. While there is no one right way of getting through an operations and management planning process, the steps in the above vacation-planning example provide a reasonable structure:

- *Agree on what to do*—The process begins by convening stakeholders to discuss and agree on what transportation system operations and management will do. Their agreement is documented in a vision statement or by a set of goals and objectives.

- *Agree on expectations*—With a vision statement, attention shifts to agreeing on expectations. For this step, decision-makers rely on operators and managers to provide information. The end result is a list of operational objectives and functional requirements that specify implementation parameters.

- *Agree on a plan of action*—Like preparing a travel itinerary, a detailed plan of what, when, and how is developed. This can be done in any number of ways. The end product is a regional operational strategy, or architecture, and it should provide enough detail for operators and managers to define and agree on operational procedures and to buy, implement, and use needed equipment.

- *Make it happen*—With a regional operational strategy, the system is operated and managed within budget and to everyone's satisfaction.

This section follows these planning steps, providing examples from regions and states throughout the country.

Agree on What To Do (Creating a Vision)

A vision is a high level, nontechnical statement of where the region or state is going and what end results are expected. It is the first building block in consensus building and, if properly created, it makes later decisions easier. Before everything else, consideration needs to be given to much broader issues, such as improved customer services, the need to use scare government resources more effectively, and the growing effects the congestion has on productivity, safety, economic development and mobility.

Vision statements are typically associated with long-range planning efforts, not with transportation operations and management. Yet, decisions made in the short-term are cumulative and lead to an end state. Furthermore, an orchestrated set of decisions has much more resonance and influence than a collection of uncoordinated decisions. By making decisions within a unified context, operators and managers are able to work together to provide more understandable and predictable services to users.

Visioning Process

There is no one right way to create a vision statement; however, there are several rules of thumb that may be helpful.

The process should be open, and it should include decision-makers. A common remark from transportation system operators and managers is the lack of support from upper level management and elected officials. One way of gaining support is to involve these stakeholders in creating the vision. In fact, they should take the lead, with support from mid-level managers.

The process should include certain stakeholders not normally involved in the traditional transportation planning process, such as private communications companies, local management information system departments, private traveler information providers, and local or state emergency management services. By involving these other interests, opportunities are identified that would not be otherwise.

The process must not get bogged down in technical details. While there is a temptation to answer detailed technical questions during the visioning process, the process will struggle towards completion if it attempts to deal with all levels of detail at once. There is nothing wrong with not having all of the answers because there will be opportunities to revisit the vision statement as more is learned. Furthermore, details can limit the possibilities, which is not the intent of the vision statement. There may be an institutional arrangement or a technology on the horizon that can make the vision a reality.

Relationship with the Metropolitan Planning Organization and Statewide Planning Processes

TEA-21 strongly encourages Metropolitan Planning Organizations (MPOs) and states to incorporate transportation operations and management into their planning processes. To receive federal funding, TEA-21 requires that MPOs prepare financially constrained transportation plans that account for all costs (operations, management, and capital). The intent is to make decision-makers aware of the investment choices they have, not only for construction but also for operations and management.

In part, this policy directive is due to the deployment of ITS. ITS has significantly increased the effects of transportation system operations and management because it enables agencies and equipment to work together in real-time to respond to system changes. For example, prior to ITS, agencies could do little to manage traffic delays caused by major incidents. With ITS, agencies can detect and respond to incidents faster, instantaneously informing travelers of what happened and of travel alternatives, and changing system operations, such as re-timing traffic signals on a parallel route.

While there is a regulatory reason to connect transportation operations and management planning with the MPO and statewide transportation planning processes, there is also a very practical reason—to gain the support of decision-makers. Transportation plans have vision statements or goals that have already been blessed by decision-makers. As such, these plans are a starting point for the visioning process.

The Vision Statement

Just as there is no one right way to go through the visioning process, there is no one right vision statement, with each tailored to the needs, goals, and opportunities of the region.

The vision statement for Minnesota's Guidestar program is:

> Minnesota's citizens, businesses and visitors will benefit from the application of ITS to the state's transportation system. ITS will be fully integrated into the transportation strategies for the enhancement of safety, mobility and economic vitality, for the protection of the environment, and for the development of sustainable communities.[11]

This vision statement clearly conveys a direction—it describes who will benefit from the program, how the program will be implemented, and what the program will accomplish.

Decisions made after this vision statement was adopted should further the vision. For example, in order to benefit visitors, state and local tourism agencies and private tourist destinations should be active stakeholders in the program. All project evaluations should measure the extent to which the statement is fulfilled. If an expensive, high-tech ITS solution does less to improve safety on a corridor than a lower cost, low-tech solution, then it should not be advanced. The vision statement promotes safety, not the use of high-tech solutions.

Agree on Expectations (Operational Objectives)

Operational objectives (sometimes referred to as operational or functional requirements) translate the vision statement into expectations. Like the vision statement, operational objectives should be simple statements, lacking technical jargon, which are collectively understood and accepted.

---

[11] Minnesota Department of Transportation, "Message from the Director," *Minnesota Guidestar* (St. Paul, Minn.: Minnesota Department of Transportation, Summer 1997).

Operational objectives are guiding the planning, design, deployment, and operations of the TransGuide program in San Antonio, Texas. The region developed goals, which served as the vision statement, and related operational objectives to define performance expectations. One of the program's key operational objectives is:

> … incident detection within two minutes and alteration of the traffic management systems to the correct response within 15 seconds over the entire South Texas region.[12]

According to those involved with the TransGuide program, this simple statement, understandable by technicians and nontechnicians, provided invaluable guidance to planning, design, and deployment.

As noted in the vacation trip example, those who understand the technical details of transportation operations and management are consulted during this step. It makes no sense to define expectations that cannot be met. Unlike the vision statement, operational objectives should be grounded on what is currently possible. Therefore, before agreeing on the incident response objective, the TransGuide team went through reality checks, such as:

- How fast can the technology detect and respond to incidents?

- Can agencies work together to respond, and how fast can they respond?

- Can the region afford to meet this expectation?

Obviously, more detailed information was needed to answer these questions, but the questions required a simple yes or no answer. Therefore, a detailed plan was not needed to adopt this objective.

Agreeing on a Detailed Plan (Creating an Operations Strategy)

The final phase in the planning process is creating an operations strategy (sometimes referred to as a framework or architecture). During this phase, technical details are worked out by the system operators and managers, just like travel agents prepare the itinerary. Again, there is no one right way to create an operations strategy, but the following steps illustrate a possible approach:

- Step 1—establish partnerships.

- Step 2—inventory existing functions and equipment.

- Step 3—organize and coordinate functions (operating agreements).

- Step 4—develop the strategy.

- Step 5—prioritize projects and programs.

The process should connect with the transportation planning process as much as possible. Furthermore, the ITS National Architecture is available as a planning tool.

Integrating with MPO and Statewide Plans

It was noted previously that any programs or projects identified by the operations strategy must eventually integrate into the MPO's or state's transportation plan to receive federal funding. The operations strategy could be developed outside

---

[12] Texas Department of Transportation, *TRANSGUIDE—Technology in Motion,* promotional brochure (San Antonio, Texas: Texas Department of Transportation, 1997).

the MPO or state planning process, with recommendations submitted for consideration. However, this approach is not an effective way to get buy-in from upper level management and decision-makers. Therefore, it is best to take advantage of any logical connections with the MPO and statewide planning processes, such as:

- Making sure the operations and management vision statement (or goals) supports the regional transportation vision, noted previously.

- Using the financial projections and long-range funding commitments in the transportation plan to check the feasibility of operational objectives.

- Reviewing the projects listed in the plan to identify opportunities for deploying needed communications links or equipment. For example, a major roadway construction project could provide an opportunity to fund and install a communications conduit.

Applying the National ITS Architecture

Before describing the role of the National ITS Architecture (NA) in transportation operations and management planning, it may be helpful to describe the relationship between ITS and transportation operations and management. As noted above, ITS enables real-time operations and management, which is redefining transportation operating and management functions. For example, prior to ITS, TransGuide's operational requirement of detecting incidents within two minutes was not possible. Furthermore, ITS is redefining institutional coordination. TransGuide's objective of altering the traffic management system within 15 seconds of verifying an incident requires a seamless operation between those agencies that manage traffic in San Antonio.[13] The willingness of agencies to work together may be more of an issue in transportation operations and management than the capabilities of technology—thus the need to address these issues in the planning process.

The NA is an ITS planning and deployment tool, developed by the U.S. Department of Transportation (DOT) and a consortium of private industries. The NA defines:

- A common *structure* for collecting, processing, sharing, and managing ITS data.

- Key *component*s of ITS, including specification of the scope, boundaries, and relationships among the components.

- The *standards* for connecting and integrating ITS.

The NA does not prescribe specific technologies or designs; rather, it offers a global framework for the deployment of mutually compatible technologies. It enables ITS stakeholders everywhere to speak the "same language"—thereby avoiding confusion and allowing for rigorous technical discussion and planning. It ensures that ITS components developed and deployed according to the architecture are compatible. It also encourages information exchange among the communities in a region and the joint deployment and operation of regional systems.[14]

The NA provides a list of thirty User Services that describe the capabilities of ITS. These User Services help connect the NA with the regional vision statement and operational objectives. For example, the *incident management* User Service in the NA addresses TransGuide's operational objective of incident detection and response. The NA provides a list of functional requirements for incident management, and the logical architecture in the NA illustrates how these functions

---

[13] U.S. Department of Transportation, Federal Highway Administration, and Federal Transit Administration, "ITS Fact Sheet 2—The National ITS Architecture: A Framework for Intelligent Transportation Systems," Prepared for use by members of the National Associations Working Group for ITS, Publication No. FHWA-SA-98-056 (Washington, D.C.: U.S. DOT, FHWA, FTA, 1998).

[14] U.S. Department of Transportation, Federal Highway Administration, Federal Transit Administration, "ITS Fact Sheet 2—The National Architecture: A Framework for Intelligent Transportation Systems," Publication No. FHWA-SA-98-056 (Washington, D.C.: U.S. DOT, FHWA, FTA, 1998).

can connect with others. The NA provides even more detail as stakeholders explore lower levels, down to identifying the specifications for needed equipment and software.

Step 1—Establishing Partnerships

ITS allows agencies to forge new transportation operation and management partnerships among public agencies and between agencies and private companies. The Omaha, Nebraska/Council Bluffs, Iowa, region took advantage of the opportunity to involve a local communications company and a local travel information provider in the preparation of its Early Deployment Plan (EDP). The region also invited local emergency service agencies and the state police into the process. The EDP has been completed, yet each of these stakeholders remains actively involved in regional transportation operations and management. These partnerships enable the region to continually identify opportunities to work together, such as the communications company providing fiber optics access in exchange for the ability to use roadway right-of-way.

The key to effective partnering is strategically including partners in the planning process. Buy-in is needed from potential partners, which is best attained by involving partners from the beginning, as was the case in the Omaha/Council Bluffs region. Involving partners after key decisions are made can alienate some. It can also limit the potential of the regional strategy because partners have not communicated well enough to identify mutually beneficial opportunities.

Of course, involving partners unnecessarily can also negatively affect partnerships. Inviting stakeholders to meetings that do not require their specific participation wastes time and decreases the likelihood that they will attend future meetings.

There are several rules of thumb that are helpful in determining how and when to involve stakeholders:

- Take the time to list the steps in the planning process before beginning and distribute the list to all potential stakeholders. It is helpful to have stakeholders tell you when they would like to be involved.

- Ask stakeholders very early in the process to suggest others to add. The suggestions should be accompanied with a convincing explanation of what the stakeholder will add to the process.

- Take the time to prepare and distribute an agenda for each stakeholder meeting. Make sure the agenda clearly identifies the decisions (action items) to be made. Stakeholders can then decide if the meeting is relevant.

- Take the time to record and distribute all comments made at each stakeholder meeting. Keep the minutes short and simple, with a focus on the decisions made. This allows those who did not attend meetings to stay in touch with the process.

- Allow stakeholders an opportunity to comment on decisions made, either by mail or at the following meeting.

The NA provides help with identifying potential stakeholders. As noted above, it includes a Logical Architecture, which identifies all possible connections between desired functions and others. The Logical Architecture illustrates possible connections with the ITS planning function. It is obvious that transportation planners should be involved—what may not be so obvious is the need to include those who prepare and update maps.

ITS is causing new partnerships to form. As illustrated by the incident management example above, emergency management agencies, traffic information providers and others who have not been part of the traditional transportation planning process are now key partners. Some of the issues in public agency and private company partnerships are:

- *Public agency partnerships*—Partnering among public agencies requires an understanding of the functions of partner agencies. As described in the next section ("Step 2 …"), an inventory is one way for agencies to learn what others are doing. Some agencies may have a concern about how partnering will affect their functions and staffing. For example, the inventory may identify overlapping functions, which may require one of the overlapping agencies to drop a function and reassign or dismiss staff. There may be no way to avoid such concerns other than to identify new opportunities for those affected. For example, some Montana DOT staff were concerned about the effect of ITS snow sensors on snow-plowing crews. The sensors would pinpoint where snow accumulations made roads impassable, thereby improving the ability to deploy crews to the right locations and possibly reduce the need for as many crews. Others in the department thought this was an opportunity to deploy the current crews to additional locations, thereby improving the department's service to travelers.

- *Public–private partnerships*—Public company and private agency partnerships present their own set of challenges. The adage "time is money" is certainly true for private companies, who become frustrated with the slower pace of government. Furthermore, private companies are motivated by return on investments, not on serving broader constituencies, as is the case with public agencies. In addition, private companies are more likely to investigate new opportunities as a way of increasing their competitive edge, while public agencies are more prudent. One key to effective public–private partnerships is understanding and accepting these differences in philosophy and approach. Another is maintaining continuing communications that enable private companies and public agencies to identify opportunities for cooperating. For example, the Colorado DOT allowed a private television station in Denver to install a closed circuit television camera on an interstate west of Denver in exchange for a video feed and control of the camera. A slightly different agreement was reached in Omaha, Nebraska—the only difference being the television station reserved the right to control the camera. In both cases, the partnerships would not have occurred if the private companies and public agencies did not recognize the opportunities.

Step 2—Transportation Operations and Management Inventory

The second step is to inventory who is doing what and how they make it happen. In many cases, agencies are aware of their own operations, but not of what others are doing. The inventory helps identify redundancies among agencies or private firms and opportunities for cooperation. The inventory should include the following:

- List of transportation operations and management staffing and organizational structures.

- List of normal agency operations.

- List of equipment used for operations and management functions.

- Map of equipment locations (including communications links).

Operational matrices may be helpful to summarize and evaluate the inventory. The first matrix would identify transportation operations and management gaps by listing the current functions and equipment as rows and the operational objectives as columns. The second matrix would identify agency redundancies or gaps by listing the current functions and equipment as rows and the agencies and private firms as columns. Together, these matrices should provide a common and complete understanding of the current state of transportation operations and management across the region.

Step 3—Organizing and Coordinating (Operating Agreements)

There are several dimensions to partnerships, with each requiring different levels of agreement and commitment. The dimensions, from the easiest to the most difficult to agree on and commit to, are:

- Communication (what information to share and how it will be shared).

- Decision making (what actions to take with shared information).

- Responsibilities (who is responsible and when).

- Internal operations (what changes are needed to respond to information).

As noted previously, the logical architecture in the NA identifies possible connections between ITS functions. It also describes the information that should be shared between functions. While the NA can help identify partnerships, it does not establish the ground rules for how agencies and companies are to work together.

Funding, staffing, and liability issues must be addressed before agreements can be reached, and the planning process can help resolve these issues. The visioning phase helps partners understand the need for, and value of, working together—particularly those in upper management and local and state officials. The inventory identifies existing relationships among agencies, and the NA provides details on what information needs to be shared and how it can be shared. The process itself will likely foster communication among agencies and, if handled properly, it will improve trust among agencies.

With the help of the planning process, agencies can assess the effects of sharing information or responsibilities on their current operations. Each agency must answer questions, such as:

- What new functions and equipment are needed?

- Is new staff needed to perform this function?

- Is staff training needed to perform this function?

- What sort of liability is transferred to this agency?

- Can we still provide the same service to our customers?

A locality and transit agency in the San Francisco Bay Area worked through such an exercise. The locality, responsible for traffic signals, was approached by the transit agency to allow its buses to have priority at traffic signals in order to improve schedule adherence. The local traffic engineer was concerned about how signal priorities would affect signal timing and agreed to only allow buses to over-ride normal timing patterns when they were significantly behind schedule. To make the determination, the transit agency agreed to purchase and install automatic vehicle location equipment on its buses and to install a communications link with the local traffic engineer that provided real-time bus locations. The agreement was not easy to reach, but it enabled the agencies to meet their own operational objectives without compromising the other's objectives.

The level of detail needed at this stage is critical. Enough needs to be known to come to an agreement about cooperation. However, too much detail can slow or even stop a process.

Step 4—Developing the Strategy

Developing an operations strategy presents a unique challenge because, as noted above, ITS influences the way agencies operate and manage the system; and technologies change rapidly. In many ways, the regional strategy attempts to identify a desired end state for an unpredictable future.

Despite this dilemma, there are a few certainties that make the operations strategy useful, such as:

- The vision statement provides a direction that guides the deployment and use of ITS. This reduces the problem of a "technology searching for a solution."

- The effort identifies who does what, when, and how—which should help agencies coordinate in the near- and long-term.

- There are functions that are required regardless of the technology, such as the need to communicate among agencies.

- The regional strategy lets others know what is anticipated, which provides opportunities to deploy and implement ITS as part of other system improvements.

- When integrated into the overall MPO or statewide planning process, the operations strategy creates a "place holder" in the plan for funding, which allocates federal funding for transportation operations and management, including needed ITS equipment.

With regard to this last point, a very practical way to simplify the inclusion of transportation operations and management in the transportation plan and the Transportation Improvement Program (TIP) is to prepare a list of projects and programs that identify the costs and a brief justification statement for each. If the process has made connections with the transportation planning process so that everyone is aware of the need and justification for projects and programs, decision makers can easily insert projects and programs from such a list into the transportation plan.

Estimating the costs of ITS projects and programs requires considerations that are not typical in most highway planning efforts. Unlike highways, ITS requires continual attention, which requires an estimate and projection of transportation operating and management costs. For a number of ITS applications, these costs can be higher than the cost of purchasing and installing the equipment. In Southern California, CALTRANS evaluated both the capital and operating costs of various VMSs and found that, because of lower operating costs, the more expensive signs were actually cheaper over the expected life of the signs.

The human element cannot be overlooked either. New technologies and equipment may require specialized service that may not be available from current staff. If this is the case, then current staff will need training or contract service will be needed, and costs must be factored into the evaluation.

Furthermore, most ITS equipment quickly becomes obsolete because of new technology and failures. An obvious example is computers, which become outdated in a matter of years. Software and hardware upgrades must be factored into cost estimates.

As noted above, technologies are changing rapidly, which makes it difficult to estimate costs with any precision. However, as technologies change, the cost per unit of productivity decreases. This is certainly evident in the computer industry, where faster machines cost roughly the same as slower ones bought several years previously. Therefore, agencies can reasonably assume that today's prices will buy at least the same, if not more, productivity.

Step 5—Prioritizing Projects and Programs

Given the many demands for transportation funding, it is doubtful whether the entire operational strategy can be implemented in the short-term. Thus, there is a need to develop a phasing plan. The following rules of thumb offer some guidance about how to prioritize projects and programs:

- Identify those functions and related equipment packages that must be in place first, such as communications links. The NA provides guidance.

- Identify those functions and equipment packages that best address the vision statement and operational objectives. For example, deploy incident management equipment on freeways with the highest number of incidents.

- Identify and work with funding partners. Take advantage of local or state agencies and private interests willing to pay a portion of the costs.

For regions without much experience with ITS, start with functions and equipment packages that have proven track records and have high visibility. This helps ensure continued support for future endeavors.

Funding limitations may not be the only reason for program and project phasing. The freeway management system in San Antonio was deliberately phased so that operators could refine the system with the lessons learned from the initial phases.

Analysis Tools and Applications

State and MPO planners rely on analysis methods and tools to justify transportation improvement options. Because the planning process has historically focused on roadway construction and transit expansion projects, these methods and tools are not able to evaluate other types of improvements, such as ITS. This inability to quantify the benefits of these "other" projects reduces their consideration in the planning process.

As of 1998, the U.S. DOT had several major initiatives underway to address this problem, such as the MDI program. One of the objectives of MDI is to better understand the benefits and effects of a regionally integrated ITS. The U.S. DOT will use the empirical data from MDIs to inform states and regions about what to expect from ITS deployments and as inputs to a new generation of planning analysis tools.

For the near-term, the U.S. DOT is developing a set of tools that complement existing planning tools, principally travel demand models. The program is known as ITS Deployment Analysis System, and the tools should be available by the year 2000. For the long-term, the U.S. DOT is developing a travel demand forecasting model capable of detailed simulation. The program is known as TRANSIMS, and it should be available by the year 2005.

In the meantime, there are tools and methods available to assist planners, such as:

- Traffic simulation models (e.g., NETSIM and CORESIM)—these models can evaluate the effects of certain types of improvements, such as ramp metering or signal coordination.

- Refined travel demand models—refinements such as peak-period modeling or integrating the models with simulation models have been made.

- Applying the results of other applications—the U.S. DOT has evaluated a number of ITS deployments, such as the TRAVTEK program in Orlando, which provide reasonable estimates of effects in similar situations.

Summary

Like planning for a vacation, transportation operations and management planning provides an opportunity for stakeholders to collectively agree on what they will do, what their expectations are, and how they will get it done. This section presents a very general process that states and regions can use as a guide. It begins with a visioning phase, which defines transportation operations and management goals and the desired end-state. The next phase is developing realistic expectations, or operational objectives, that are based on the vision statement and that help operators and managers plan in more detail. The third phase is developing an operations strategy, which details how operations and management will happen in the region or state. The following steps are a possible approach to this phase:

- Step 1—establish partnerships.

- Step 2—inventory existing functions and equipment.

- Step 3—organize and coordinate functions (operating agreements).

- Step 4—develop the strategy.

- Step 5—prioritize projects and programs.

The process presented in this section is a general approach. There are a number of variations that each region and state can use to tailor the approach.

Transportation operations and management planning should take advantage of the many opportunities available to connect with the transportation planning process. ISTEA requires a connection if federal funding for transportation operations and management is sought. However, it should be emphasized that these connections help make upper-level management and local and state officials aware of the need for transportation operations and management. This awareness will improve the chances for project and program acceptance and funding.

The NA is a tool that can be used during the transportation operations and management planning process. It identifies the many institutional coordination and technical integration opportunities available, plus it simplifies the effort.

Traditional planning analysis tools can be used to evaluate proposed projects and programs, but there is room for improvement. The U.S. DOT is currently developing a new generation of tools to address this issue.

In sum, transportation operations and management planning provides a state or region with an opportunity to get buy-in from upper-level management and decision makers and for public and private stakeholders to work together to improve the performance of the transportation system and service to users.

Design and Implementation Considerations

NA for Systems Integration and Information Sharing

Currently, "islands" of ITS deployment are found throughout the United States. In other words, today's individual ITS systems are for the most part incompatible with neighboring systems. Stakeholders for each system should continue to focus on area-specific needs, but they should also be concentrating on how their system can benefit from being compatible with neighboring systems. Ideally, all ITS deployments should be integrated to provide a seamless transportation system across the country, while still allowing for innovative area-specific design solutions. Systems should be integrated based on the need to share information among agencies in order to improve the operational efficiency of one system or a particular agency. Because current systems may not follow a common architecture, integrating systems and sharing valuable information may not be a simple task. The NA is an open system framework that all new systems should use in order to facilitate the integration of systems and information sharing.

Where appropriate, sharing data, providing integrated operations, and supporting interoperable equipment and services can all maximize the benefits of ITS technology. In order for these functions to work, system design solutions must be compatible at the system interface level. The NA provides a common structure that ensures system, product, and service compatibility, without limiting design options. It creates the opportunity for interoperability across diverse ITS deployments while preserving flexibility and choice for system designers. In order for the NA to work, it must be scalable to accommodate the needs of different size systems and technology independent to support the various current and future technologies. The following are explanations of the basic aspects of the NA:

- *Logical Architecture*—The Logical Architecture is the part of the NA that focuses on a functional view of the ITS user services. The Logical Architecture defines the functions that are required to perform user services as well as the data flows that need to be exchanged between these functions. The first step in the functional decomposition process is to define the elements that are included as being "inside" the architecture. For example, the equipment that travelers use to obtain information or provide input to the system is inside the architecture, while the travelers themselves are external. The next step is to organize the ITS functions into a data flow diagram.

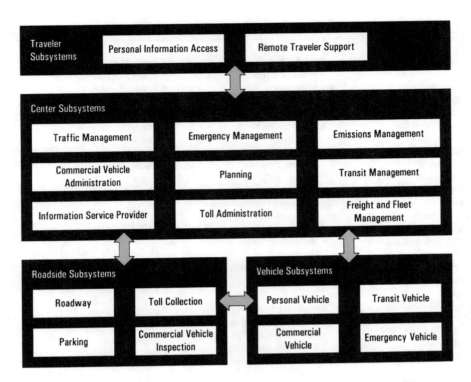

Figure 19–4   A Diagram of Architecture Systems and Subsystems

Source: U.S. Department of Transportation.

- *Physical Architecture*—The Physical Architecture further separates the functions defined in the Logical Architecture into systems and subsystems, based on the functional similarity of the process specifications and the location where the functions take place. There are four systems defined by the Physical Architecture: Traveler, Center, Roadside, and Vehicle. There are a total of nineteen subsystems that are intended to include all anticipated functions for the present and 220 years into the future. The subsystems are composed of equipment packages, the smallest units within a subsystem that might be purchased. Figure 19–4 depicts the top level diagram of the Physical Architecture.

Beyond the fundamentals of the NA, it is important to discuss its application, or implementation strategy. The following steps should be used as a guide for implementing the architecture:

- *Identify ITS building blocks*—There are many service options for a system designer to consider. These options have been developed into a set of Market Packages that are tailored to fit transportation problems and needs. The market packages represent the "building blocks" that can be deployed over time to create ITS services. There are 56 market packages partitioned under the following seven categories: Traffic Management, Emergency Management, Traveler Information, Commercial Vehicles, Transit Management, Advanced Vehicles, and ITS Planning. Several market packages are identified for each major application area to provide an array of services at different costs. The Market Packages were also developed to be incremental, allowing more advanced packages to be efficiently implemented after the deployment of more basic packages. A list of these Market Packages is provided in Table 19–1.

- *Recommend early deployments*—It is important to initiate ITS deployment with basic Market Packages that are not dependent on technology advances or institutional change and that enable the implementation of a range of more advanced packages over time. There are ten packages that have been classified as early Market Packages; they are underlined in Table 19–1.

Table 19–1 Market Packages

Traffic Management
- Network Surveillance
- Probe Surveillance
- Surface Street Control
- Freeway Control
- HOV and Reversible Lane Management
- Traffic Information Dissemination
- Regional Traffic Control
- Incident Management System
- Traffic Network Performance Evaluation
- Dynamic Toll/Parking Fee Management
- Emissions and Environmental Hazards Sensing
- Virtual TMC and Smart Probe
- Standard Railroad Grade Crossing
- Advanced Railroad Grade Crossing
- Railroad Operations Coordination

Emergency Management
- Emergency Response
- Emergency Routing
- Mayday Support

Traveler Information
- Broadcast Traveler Information
- Interactive Traveler Information
- Autonomous Route Guidance
- Dynamic Route Guidance
- ISP-Based Route Guidance
- Integrated Transportation Management/Route Guidance
- Yellow Pages and Reservation
- Dynamic Ridesharing
- In-Vehicle Signing

Commercial Vehicles
- Fleet Administration
- Freight Administration
- Electronic Clearance
- Electronic Clearance Enrollment
- International Border Electronic Clearance
- Weigh-In-Motion
- Roadside CVO Safety
- On-board CVO Safety
- CVO Fleet Maintenance
- HAZMAT Management

Transit Management
- Transit Vehicle Tracking
- Transit Fixed-Route Operations
- Demand Response Transit Operations
- Transit Passenger and Fare Management
- Transit Security
- Transit Maintenance
- Multi-modal Coordination

Advanced Vehicles
- Vehicle Safety Monitoring
- Driver Safety Monitoring
- Longitudinal Safety Warning
- Lateral Safety Warning
- Pre-Crash Restraint Deployment
- Driver Visibility Improvement
- Advanced Vehicle Longitudinal Control
- Advanced Vehicle Lateral Control
- Intersection Collision Avoidance
- Automated Highway System

ITS Planning
- ITS Planning

Source: U.S. Department of Transportation, Federal Highway Administration.

- *Encourage private-sector participation*—Government officials are increasingly being challenged to provide a successful ITS program despite limited financial resources. According to ITS America's Strategic Plan, it is assumed that 80 percent of the eventual cost of ITS deployment will be covered by the private sector and their customers. The remaining 20 percent invested by the government will be integral to the beginning of ITS deployment, to properly instrument the roadway and transit network. There are not enough public resources to support full deployment of ITS systems nationally. With significant presence of the private sector, the nation can realize the full potential of these technologies. In addition to the financial constraints, private-sector participation can be beneficial due to competitive forces and the desire to improve efficiency. Therefore, public-private partnerships should be encouraged.

- *Enable service integration and extend interoperability*—As mentioned earlier, today's ITS deployments are "islands" of basic ITS services that have been implemented in response to local needs. These islands can be linked together to form a more effective and comprehensive system if each system complies with current standards. Promoting the development of new ITS standards that enable service integration and interoperability should also be encouraged.

- *Progressive implementation of more advanced services*—Initiating ITS deployment with Early Market Packages sets the stage for progressive, more advanced Market Packages to follow. Progressive implementation of more advanced services follows the same basic principle with each step. A good example of this would be the early deployment of basic toll collection capabilities. This package enables the natural progression to more advanced services such as vehicle probe data collection, which in turn can enhance traveler information packages and more advanced, area-wide traffic control strategies.

- *Integration into state and local planning and programming*—The transportation professional has many available implementation options. When determining which ITS services to provide and which Market Packages to implement, emphasis should be placed on decisions that benefit the region, not just those that satisfy local needs. NA deployment should be integrated with state and metropolitan transportation planning, programming, and maintenance decisions. This way, the options can be selected to achieve tailored implementations best suited to regional needs.

- *Recommend DOT strategic actions*—Implementing ITS is for the most part dependent on decisions made by state and local governments as well as the private sector. However, U.S. DOT also has several important roles in the implementation of ITS technologies. These responsibilities include:

  ◆ *Facilitating compatibility on a national level*—National compatibility can benefit the consumer by providing a seamless transportation system that is convenient for the user. From the producer's standpoint, standardization can assist in consolidating markets and developing economies of scale, which can therefore increase the likelihood for early deployment.

  ◆ *Providing policy and guidance*—Providing policy and guidance equips the implementor with sufficient education and training to make appropriate ITS architecture decisions.

  ◆ *Strategic investing in research and testing*—Strategic investing is important because it facilitates early and sustainable deployments of ITS.

Standards

The interconnections identified in the NA require standardization in order for ITS to be nationally compatible and interoperable. Standards provide a consistent, documented way of implementing a particular function, service, or information flow. This grants system designers the freedom to choose various pieces of equipment that meet the standard specification with the certainty that these pieces will work together and that individual parts can be upgraded without having to replace the whole system. Standards also entitle manufacturers to design components that will work with components from other manufacturers. Furthermore, standards allow local jurisdictions to easily interface with the systems in other jurisdictions.

There are many standards development organizations (SDOs) who have established such standards and are currently continuing their efforts today. These SDOs include expertise from all the various disciplines of ITS. The Jet Propulsion Laboratory, a division of the U.S. DOT, has created a comprehensive listing of the status of all the ITS standards currently published or proposed. This listing is current as of January 7, 1998, and is provided in Table 19–2.

U.S. DOT's Joint Program Office is supporting an extensive program that supports, guides, and accelerates the existing ITS consensus-based volunteer standards processes already underway by providing funding to five SDOs. In order to ensure that the standards developed have consensus support and benefit as much as possible from the expertise of the entire ITS community, the U.S. DOT has decided not to impose the standards, but rather to reinforce the existing efforts. The organizations chosen for funding are the Society of Automotive Engineers, the American Society of Testing and Materials, the Institute of Electrical and Electronics Engineers, the American Association of State Highway Transportation Officials, and the Institute of Transportation Engineers.

The standards chosen for funding were based on a survey that was distributed at the ITS America 1995 Annual Meeting and by mail to over 4,000 representatives of the ITS community. This survey resulted in a list of 44 standards requirements, listed in order of priority. Those standards that were highest priority (i.e., that were urgently needed and key to deployment) were funded by the U.S. DOT.

Table 19–2   Standards Development Milestones—Proposed Dates

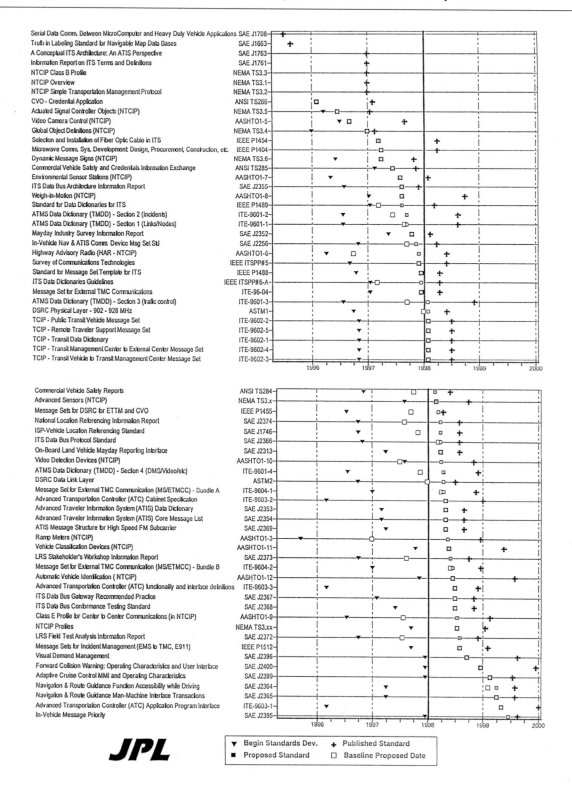

Source: U.S. Department of Transportation, Federal Highway Administration.

Specifications and Procurement Factors

Procurement plays a key role in ITS deployment, particularly for achieving proper transportation operations and management. ITS professionals need to think about procurement issues throughout all phases of the project. They should consider including provisions for training, spares, warranties, property rights, equipment, and tools. Agencies should also incorporate performance measures in the procurement process. These measures can include staffing response times, staffing levels, preventative upkeep work orders, signal timing adjustments, transit vehicle progression, and others. For all of these procurement issues, there are many options to consider. These include:

- *Engineer/contractor (design/bid/build)*—This is the traditional approach that typically involves the engineer/agency/contractor for design/bid/build. It is well-suited for highway construction, and the agency is the responsible entity.

- *System manager*—In this option, the manager is the responsible entity. The manager does all work with the exception of construction. Partnerships and shared responsibilities are required. This option is suitable for ITS projects.

- *System integrator*—This procurement option is similar to the system manager with the exception that the responsible agency may direct bid work and perform construction.

- *Design/build*—This approach is rather new and emerging. The design/build team is the responsible entity. This option is advantageous because it allows for rapid project completion and a streamlined procurement process. Typically, the agency provides 15–30 percent of the design plans. There are many variations of design/build. They include design/build/operate/maintain; design/build/lease; build, own, operate, transfer; franchise/lease; and design to budget.

- *Shared resources*—shared resources is a bartered relationship usually among a public–private partnership.

- *Variations on a theme*—This option uses approved vendor lists. It is an extension of the "government-furnished equipment" concept.

- *Operations and management*—This option can be either in-house or outsourced.

In order to determine which one of these procurement options is best suited for a particular system, certain issues should be considered. It is critical to begin by setting a strategy or goal that your procurement process is trying to achieve. Starting with desired outcomes can help keep this process on track. It is also important to involve several persons in the procurement decision-making process to gain the advantage of different perspectives. With a specific goal and a diverse procurement team, the next step is to consider the following issues:

- Providing ongoing transportation operations and management.

- Funding sources.

- Integration requirements.

- Legal constraints.

- Project and program relationships to others.

- Completion date.

- Available skills and resources.

- Project risks.

- Administrative burden.

- Need for flexibility.

The large number of procurement options and issues makes procurement a major element that needs to specifically reflect local conditions and needs. Keeping procurement in mind throughout all phases of ITS deployment is key to successful ITS projects.

Funding and Life-Cycle Costing Considerations

The ability to effectively operate and manage ITS projects is vital to the success of traffic management systems. It is therefore important for agencies to develop a strategy for estimating and funding the recurring costs in the early stages of ITS deployment to ensure proper funding and budget. This effort should be updated throughout the life of the system. Innovative funding sources should be explored such as public–private partnerships, resource sharing within and external to the agency, and revenue opportunities.

Human Factors Aspects

Human factors engineering analyzes data on the physical and mental characteristics, capabilities, limitations, and propensities of people. This information is then used to design and evaluate tools, workplaces, and other things that people use with the goal of increasing their efficiency, comfort, and safety. Human factors practices and standards have become a major consideration in many design areas, particularly those in which the human and system interface is critical to overall system effectiveness, safety and convenience. Human factors are significant elements to consider in the early stages of designing ITS, especially the TMC. Proper functioning of the system depends on the design team recognizing the roles of humans and machines.

- *Human requirements*—It is important for the design team to apply human factors design at the appropriate points in the design process. User-Centered Design is an iterative system design process that accommodates the capabilities and limitations of humans in a system. This process allows system elements and procedures to be defined, refined, and evaluated in a series of cycles. Some of the major steps include:

  - Conducting a missions analysis.

  - Preparing a design concept.

  - Conducting a functional analysis and allocation procedures.

  - Conducting an operator task analysis.

  - Identifying sources of human operator error.

  - Identifying human performance constraints.

  - Designing jobs.

  - Designing the physical work environment.

  - Designing and specifying workstations.

  - Designing and specifying controls, displays, and user interfaces.

  User-Centered Design can also help avoid costly design mistakes as some design teams tend to seek state-of-the-art technology without or before considering human factors.

- *Functions, tasks, and human/machine systems*—The functional requirements of the TMC should be analyzed with particular emphasis placed on the user. The design team should examine how functions are allocated to human and machine, how human tasks are analyzed and described, and on how to plan the TMC to enhance human and system performance. Performing these analyses is critical in the design stage of a system because subtle repairs and workarounds can never quite overcome the damage done by faulty design.

- *Human error*—Error is a normal component of human behavior. Due to this fact, it is important to understand human error and to plan for it when designing systems. Many of the mistakes appearing in the human part of the system are originated from design flaws. The design team should always keep human error in mind and focus on designing the system to minimize human error. Classifying human errors into categories (i.e., intended and unintended actions) can help pinpoint problems and therefore lead to reducing probability of error.

- *Support human performance*—The design team should make decisions that enhance human performance. The nature of attention, fatigue, memory, stress, and decision making should all be taken into consideration as these human factors largely influence successful system operation. The probability of operators making correct decisions and maintaining appropriate human control over the system increases when the TMC is designed to enhance human performance.

- *Job design*—Applying human factors engineering to job design can also improve the operations of a TMC. This area concentrates on assigning appropriate job responsibilities to the staff in terms of integrating tasks, reducing errors, motivation, workload and work pacing, scheduling, task allocations, and individual differences such as a handicap. Effective job design reduces errors and their consequences, provides motivation to operators, paces work appropriately, and divides work evenly across teams that operate together.

- *Anthropometry*—Anthropometry is the science concerned with measuring humans' physical characteristics and understanding their implications in the design of human/machine systems. This includes static measures such as height and dynamic measures such as strength. Designing a system without recognizing anthropometry might include work-related injuries or conditions such as carpal tunnel syndrome. Understanding the principles of anthropometry and applying them to designing a TMC may prevent employee health problems, lost work time, and litigation. The application of anthropometric data for such things as workplace design is part of ergonomics.

- *Displays and controls*—Effective displays and controls are vital in the successful and accurate operation of a system. Displays and controls need to be designed properly to avoid operator errors, poor communication and inaccurate output. User interfaces are designed to manipulate raw data in order to provide useful sets of information to the user. The design team should concentrate on maximizing the usability of this information through displays and controls.

- *Workplace design, user interfaces with information systems, user aids, and data presentation*—The design team should comply with standards for workspace conditions such as illumination, physical arrangement, furniture selection, temperature, noise levels, and workstations. Applying the principles and standards are equally important for user interfaces with information systems. Good designs that channel and display information can promote operator understanding and confidence as well as reduce the probability of error. User aids are another area that should comply with principles and standards. User aids are user manuals, online help, quick reference guides, and mnemonic devices designed to promote accuracy, and make the operators confident of their ability to intervene appropriately when human decisions and reactions are required. Data presentation is also an important consideration as the presentation of data is critical to the operator understanding the status of the system. For all of these areas, compliance with all principles and standards are crucial for the proper operation of the system.

Institutional Considerations

As noted above, the key to effective regional transportation operations and management is public agencies and private interests working together to provide seamless transportation services and useful information to the public. This presents both technical and institutional challenges. The technical challenges focus on communications and equipment interoperability. The institutional challenges focus on establishing working relationships that, for the most part, have not existed. This section identifies the issues that will arise as agencies establish relationships and ways in which to address those issues.

Applying the NA

The NA provides a number of helpful insights into institutional relationships. The logical architecture identifies all possible transportation operations and management functions and the relationships between these functions. Agencies can match existing and proposed functions to those in the logical architecture to identify potential partners. The NA also includes an institutional layer in the physical architecture that documents those institutional structures, policies, and strategies needed for implementation. The NA can be used to help define the roles and responsibilities of partners, which are needed to reach binding agreements.

Information Sharing Versus Control

Operations and management relationships occur at several levels, ranging from sharing information to sharing responsibilities and control. Underlying any relationship is a level of trust on all sides. Trust begins with open and honest communications, and with a common understanding of expectations. The transportation operations and management planning section of this chapter suggests ways in which agencies can begin a dialogue. It also presents ways in which partners can reach a common understanding through operational objectives and a regional strategy.

Information sharing can be a relatively simple and straightforward way for agencies to work together. ITS takes information sharing to new levels because it provides the capability to communicate instantaneously. This real-time capability does not require high-tech communications equipment, it can be done with readily available technology. For example, in one region, the location and type of incident is written on a piece of paper and simultaneously distributed to several agencies via a speed dial button on a fax machine.

Of course, agencies may decide that operations can be improved considerably by using communications technologies other than telephones and fax machines. The most obvious example is video feeds from closed circuit television cameras. With video, agencies can see and more accurately size up conditions, such as an incident, which improves the response time (improves service to customers) and reduces response costs (improves operational effectiveness). In order to transmit the video feed with some clarity, the communications links must have more capacity than is currently available with telephone lines, and the cost of these links can be significant. So agencies weigh the costs and benefits of communicating via video.

Stakeholders in San Antonio decided that the benefits of video outweighed its costs, so the region installed closed circuit television cameras and a fiber optic communication backbone that connect the cameras with the TransGuide transportation operations center. Emergency room doctors, who were actively involved in the planning and design of the system, thought that video feeds from the incident site and ambulances would improve their effectiveness because they could see the nature of injuries and provide medical advice to emergency management personnel. This required another type of communications technology, the wireless transmission of video feeds from the ambulances to roadside antennas, which then relayed the feeds via wireline to hospitals. The region weighed the costs and benefits of this level of information sharing and agreed to proceed.

Thus, information sharing can range from being technically simple and straightforward to being highly complicated. Obviously, as the level of complication increases, funding commitments for the needed technology becomes an issue. The stakeholders must agree on who pays for the equipment and the operation costs of the equipment.

Responsibility sharing takes relationships to an increased level of complexity. Agencies and other partners must agree on who takes control, when, and how. Liability becomes an issue as agencies assume, or transfer, control. Agencies assuming control have to determine whether they are willing to take on the liability. Agencies transferring control do not necessarily transfer liability, so they must be comfortable with the ability of the partner to assume control in a way that does not increase their liability.

While some types of information sharing may not need documented agreements, nearly all types of responsibility sharing do. These agreements may be as simple as memoranda of understanding or as binding as legal contracts. Documenting the agreement ensures that all sides understand their obligations. After reaching an agreement, it can be referred to should a partner question obligations of the agreement, which often occurs with a change in staff.

Despite the complexities of responsibility sharing, there are times when the benefits outweigh the complexities. For instance, transportation operations and management of a system can be a 24-hour, seven days per week endeavor. Many local governments do not have the ability to fund around-the-clock operations and are willing to transfer responsibility to larger agencies that have the resources. This is the case in Atlanta, where Clayton County, a fast growing county on the fringe of the urban area, asked the Georgia DOT to assume control of its traffic operations center at night and during the weekends.

Roles and Responsibilities

Whether agencies and other partners agree to share information and control, there should be a common understanding of the roles and responsibilities of the partners. As noted above, such an understanding should be agreed to early by all partners and documented.

Each step of the transportation operations and management planning process, presented above, provides an opportunity for agencies to define and refine roles and responsibilities in increasing detail. During the development of operational objectives, stakeholders identify what they want. Each agency should somewhat temper its expectations with the willingness to commit staffing, equipment, or funding. The inventory of functions and equipment identifies who is currently doing what and how. Once agencies know where they are and collectively agree to where they are going, they can begin defining roles and responsibilities. These should be in the form of operating agreements (as described above).

The level of detail about roles and responsibilities will increase as agencies proceed through the planning process. It is recommended that the level of detail be dictated by what is needed to reach an agreement at each step of the process to avoid getting bogged down in details during the early steps.

The Baton Rouge Metropolitan Planning Organization, which is part of the Capital Region Planning Commission (CRPC), has recognized, through its planning process, the benefits of regional transportation system operations and management. The CRPC also recognized opportunities to partner with others in this endeavor, particularly the Louisiana DOT and Development (LADOTD) and the regional EMS agency.

The EDP prepared by CRPC used roughly the same process described earlier in this chapter. The CRPC convened stakeholders, identified regional operational strategies, and conducted an inventory of functions and equipment before developing the regional strategy.

The inventory identified several significant opportunities for coordination. First, it revealed overlaps between transportation agency and EMS/police functions. EMS was continuously monitoring roads in flood-prone areas and providing information about road closures due to floods. In addition, EMS/police dispatch had assembled an extensive roadway data base with up-to-date addresses and was receiving and responding to information about incidents on the roadway system. More revealing was the magnitude of fiber optic backbone already installed by EMS and others that could be used for ITS. The inventory also revealed that EMS was planning to move its operations and police dispatch functions into a new operations center.

Recognizing these opportunities, the CRPC and its partners began to merge the ITS regional architecture and the EMS architecture. Communications and information needs of all partner agencies were coordinated. Just as important, agencies worked out agreements that defined the roles and responsibilities of partner agencies, as well as funding and staffing commitments. For example, the EMS would continue to monitor flood-prone areas and pass that information to the LADOTD and local traffic departments who will disseminate the information to the public and modify system operations accordingly. Local police dispatch will continue to receive incident management calls, but will now pass that information on to LADOTD and local traffic departments. While implementation will present new challenges, CRPC's EDP process succeeded at recognizing opportunities and defining roles and responsibilities among partners in enough detail to make critical strategy and funding decisions.

There are differing perspectives about where the day-to-day coordination of operations and management should occur. In Houston, most of the regional transportation and emergency management functions are done in a single room of the TranStar building. Local traffic engineers, local police, state police, incident management staff, and local traffic information providers sit side by side in the building. TranStar management has concluded that this colocation has improved cooperation among agencies.

In Atlanta, the Georgia DOT operates a regional traffic management center that shares information with traffic operations centers in other parts of the region. Operators in the region like this approach because they have ITS information available at the place where most traffic engineering and other local functions occur.

In sum, agencies must reach agreements about who is responsible for what functions and equipment packages and where those functions will take place. These agreements should include realistic assessments of funding and staffing needs for both the short and long-term.

Public–Private Partnerships

Public-private partnerships are not common, yet there are a number of emerging transportation operations and management functions that can benefit from such partnerships. The key to success is understanding expectations. The private sector is motivated by profit, or return on investment. Of significance to public agencies is the practice of private companies protecting their market share with proprietary equipment, software, or information. Public agencies are charged with furthering societal goals, such as providing mobility. To accomplish their mission, agencies provide unlimited access to equipment, software, and information.

Although the expectations of the private and public sector differ, there are reasons for partnering. One of the most important reasons is the ability to provide additional public services through private funding or, more typically, through an exchange of services or equipment. For example, the Missouri DOT allowed private communications companies to lay fiber optics backbone in its roadway right-of-way in exchange for access to fiber optic strands in the backbone.

The public sector has partnered with private companies in several ways, including:

- *Suppliers of needed services, equipment, or software*—most of the ITS equipment used, such as traffic signals and VMSs, is purchased from private vendors. Increasingly, ITS software developers are customizing off-the-shelf software from private vendors (such as operating systems and data base packages) as a way to hold down software development costs. Increasingly, ITS equipment and software is becoming available in consumer items, such as in-vehicle navigation devices.

- *Franchisees*—Public agencies are increasingly using private companies to operate and manage systems. Examples include the INFORM freeway management system on Long Island, New York; toll operations for the Massachusetts Turnpike Authority; and incident management operations in Southern California.

- *Information service providers*—Many private companies are collecting travel information from public agencies and other sources and repackaging the information for the public. The companies are reimbursed through advertisements.

As public and private interests enter into partnerships, both sides must understand the expectations of each other and realistically assess whether the partnership makes sense. The most important issues to resolve are the ability of both sides to meet both short-term and long-term commitments; how the public sector will procure private services; and the public's access to the proprietary equipment, software, and information.

Since private companies can decide to go out of business or drop a business line at any time, public agencies must clearly understand their options before entering into relationships. Questions to answer include:

- How would the loss of the private service affect operations?

- Are there other companies that can provide the service and, if so, what is the quality of their service?

- How much would it cost to take on the service?

One way to ensure that companies live up to agreements is requiring product and service warranties. Most companies are willing to provide short-term warranties. Extended warranties are available for an additional cost or, more commonly, maintenance agreements are available for an additional cost.

Procurement is another major issue with public-private partnerships. Agencies and companies are finding that the traditional engineer-contractor procurement method, commonly used for roadway construction procurements, does not work well for ITS procurements. Much of the problem is due to software specifications in procurement documents. Without precise definitions of software capabilities, expectations on both sides can differ; yet the software developer is expected to estimate one price. This has resulted in dissatisfaction on both sides. Other procurement options, such as system integrator, design-build, and franchises are being increasingly used.

The proprietary issue can also be resolved to each side's satisfaction, and the NA provides help with this issue. Public agencies can use the NA to define the functionality of equipment and software, and private vendors can then provide existing equipment and software that deliver the required functionality. Public agencies can also require private vendors to comply with the standards in the NA to ensure interoperability among components. In recognition of this, many private companies are developing products and software that conform to the NA.

Operational Implications of Information and Responsibility Sharing

Integrating transportation operations and management and the deployment of ITS will often change the way agencies operate. Agencies and other partners need to understand the operating and cost implications of information or responsibility sharing before entering into agreements.

In Houston, the Houston-Galveston Area Council (HGAC) needed travel time and turning movement count information for its planning process. Much of the needed information was routinely collected by TranStar, a division of Houston County Metro that is responsible for regional ITS functions. While TranStar management was willing to provide data, the agency did not have the resources to reformat and summarize the data as needed by HGAC. Furthermore, as part of its traffic signal upgrade project, TranStar was able to enhance its intersection detectors in order to provide more accurate turning movement counts to HGAC but, again, would not take on the added expense. HGAC had to decide whether or not to add or pay for these functional capabilities or to continue to collect the data with other sources.

Agencies should also be aware of the long-term implications of operations and management functions before entering into agreements. Without constant attention, the benefits of ITS will not only diminish quickly—they may turn into liabilities. A relevant example is VMSs that provide either no information or the wrong information. In one area, the signs displayed only time and the public quickly referred to the signs as expensive roadside clocks. To make matters worse, the signs often displayed the wrong time, which created a credibility problem.

Interjurisdictional Issues

The jurisdiction of public agencies differs by geographic areas of responsibility (i.e., national, state, regional, and local governments), by functional areas of responsibility (e.g., transportation, land use, environmental regulation) or both. Coordination issues will differ along each of these dimensions.

Agencies with dissimilar geographic areas and like functions, such as FHWA and state DOTs, tend to coordinate frequently. The coordination focuses on how best to further the unique objectives of each agency and on who is responsible for doing what.

Thus, a significant coordination challenge among transportation agencies is agreeing on a regional transportation operations and management program that collectively meets the specific objectives of each agency. Problems arise when a partner agency does not see the value of proposed transportation operations and management strategies and refuses to buy-in to the program. Without a buy-in, the transportation funding pie is re-sliced and money is allocated elsewhere.

If all agencies agree to the program, the second challenge is defining the roles and responsibilities. Ways in which to do this were presented in a preceding section.

Agencies with similar geographic areas and dissimilar functions, such as local police and water departments, tend to coordinate less frequently. The coordination usually focuses on how to share resources in order to improve the functional capabilities of each department. For example, the fire department coordinates with the water department for its water supply.

Because agencies and departments with dissimilar functions do not communicate often, a significant challenge to cross-functional coordination is recognizing the opportunities for coordination. The NA identifies potential nontransportation partners that should be involved. The key is identifying and involving these potential partners early.

Once the nontransportation partners are identified and invited to participate, the next challenge is to learn how to communicate. Again, the NA can help improve the communications. Misunderstandings are likely during the first meetings, but if all parties stick with it, the stakeholders will begin to understand each other.

One of the biggest opportunities of interjurisdictional partnering is the ability to rely on the resources and funding of other departments and agencies, which can increase the size of the funding pie. This is especially true at the local level, where a relatively small portion of total funding is devoted to transportation.

Opportunities have been identified in those regions where transportation agencies have involved nontransportation departments and agencies to participate in operations and management. The examples from Omaha, Nebraska, and Baton Rouge, Louisiana, clearly illustrate how other partners can increase the capabilities of transportation agencies.

Interagency Issues

There are differences within agencies that are similar to those between agencies. This is certainly the case within transportation agencies, with most subdivided by travel modes (roadway, transit, air) and function (planning, project development, design and operations and maintenance).

Integrated transportation operations and management cuts across modes and functions in a number of ways. Because of the increased flexibility in transportation funding, planners must now understand and consider transportation operations and management costs as they allocate anticipated resources. In order to reach agreements about roles and responsibilities, operators must coordinate with each other and with planners during the planning process. Project development and design staff should know about the regional transportation operations and management strategy so that they can integrate transportation operations and management into their projects. Planners and operators should be involved in project development and design efforts so that they can integrate transportation operations and management strategies into projects.

If the transportation system is to operate seamlessly, then agencies must integrate the transportation operations and management of different modes. The most common example is the use of traffic signal priorities in order to improve the schedule performance of transit. Atlanta is embarking on an even more ambitious program, integrating real-time information from both the highway and transit systems so that commuters can make informed decisions about the best travel option. A continuing difficulty in Atlanta is participation by the airport, a major transportation hub for the region, in regional transportation operations and management.

Role of MPOs

MPOs are in a unique position because they are, in most regions, the only regional political body with funding authority. MPOs are required by federal legislation to develop financially feasible Long-Range Transportation Plans and TIPs, which identify those transportation projects and strategies that will be funded during the next 20 years.

MPOs, by nature, are consensus-building agencies. They must not only reach consensus among localities within the urban area, they must also work cooperatively with state DOTs. In the past, MPOs have focused on planning and programming large capital improvement projects, not on transportation operations and management. With the federal initiative of regionally integrated transportation operations and management, using ITS, MPOs are in a logical position to provide regional facilitation, coordination, and consensus building. For most MPOs, this will mean a better understanding of transportation operations and management and of ITS capabilities.

There are several options for MPOs to consider as they take on regional transportation operations and management responsibilities. One option is for MPOs to assume regional transportation operations and management functions, similar to TranStar in Houston (which is run by Houston Metro, not the Houston MPO). This option is unlikely for most MPOs because of their lack of transportation operations and management expertise. Furthermore, such an option would either create an overlap between the MPO and other transportation operating and managing agencies or, to avoid the overlap, require that functions shift from operating agencies to the MPO.

A more likely option is for MPOs to become regional transportation operations and management planners and facilitators. In this scenario, the MPO identifies and convenes the stakeholders, including operating agencies, in order to develop a regional strategy and ITS architecture. The MPO then integrates the strategy and architecture into the Long-Range Transportation Plan and the TIP to ensure funding support for the program. Once the strategy and architecture are approved, the MPO provides ongoing facilitation support for regional operations and management.

Many MPOs in the country have chosen this second option, such as Chicago, Illinois; Baltimore, Maryland; Washington, D.C.; Omaha, Nebraska; and Baton Rouge, Louisiana.

Federal Issues

The role of FHWA and the Federal Transit Administration (FTA) is changing along with federal transportation policy. With the completion of the interstate highway system, FHWA's technical oversight role is diminishing. With the increased policy emphasis on efficient, multimodal transportation systems, FHWA's technical advisory role is increasing.

The TEA-21 legislation includes new requirements and funding flexibility for regional transportation operations and management. The legislation requires regions to integrate ITS in a way that is consistent with the NA. If this is not done, federal funding cannot be used for ITS projects. Furthermore, the legislation allows the use of Surface Transportation Program and Congestion Mitigation, Air Quality funds for operations and management.

The immediate challenge for FHWA and FTA is further defining the consistency requirement. FHWA and FTA also face the challenge of providing policy direction and technical insight to states and regions. This continues the current efforts of both agencies.

State Issues

State DOTs have primary responsibilities for rural transportation operations and management, such as commercial vehicle operations. Many states have begun to coordinate with the freight and goods movement industry and others to provide seamless operations to commercial vehicles. The Advantage I-75 program that extends along I-75 from Indiana to Florida, is an example of a interstate, public-private coordination effort led by state DOTs.

Some state DOTs have also assumed leadership of metropolitan area coordination efforts. An example is the Georgia DOT, which was the lead agency in the planning, design, and deployment of the regional ITS for Atlanta. GDOT is now leading regional ITS efforts in the other urban areas of the state.

The leadership and funding commitments from GDOT have jump-started regional ITS deployment in Georgia. A new challenge for the agency is improving how the ITS infrastructure can meet regional and local transportation operations and management needs. Now that the 1996 Olympics are over, the Atlanta region is undergoing another planning process, with the focus this time on how to improve interagency operations and management using the equipment and communications links in place, with enhancements as needed.

Further Reading

Dolan, Frank. Funding and budget presentation prepared for session 8 of the "Operating and Managing ITS Course." Presented at the Institute of Transportation Engineers (ITE) seminar, February 28 to March 1, 1998.

Georgia Tech Research Institute. *Human Factors Handbook for Advanced Traffic Management Center Design.* Washington, D.C.: U.S. DOT, October 1995.

Kraft, Walter H. Procurement presentation prepared for session 13 of the "Operating and Managing ITS Course." Presented at the Institute of Transportation Engineers (ITE) seminar, February 28 to March 1, 1998.

Parsons Brinckerhoff Quade & Douglas/PB Farradyne Inc., in association with Dunn Engineering Associates, Eng-Wong, Taub & Associates, and JAC Planning Corporation. *Public-Private Partnership Opportunities for Long Island ITS, Technical Memorandum Number 40.* Feasibility Study for the Expansion of the INFORM, Southern State Parkway, P.I.N. 0534.46. New York: New York State Department of Transportation. September 1996.

Schagrin, Michael, and Susan Scott. "Accelerating ITS Deployment Through Consensus Standards," *Proceedings of the ITS America Seventh Annual Meeting.* Washington, D.C.: U.S. Department of Transportation Joint Program Office Standards Program, 1997.

U.S. Department of Transportation, Federal Highway Administration. *Freeway Incident Management Handbook,* Report No. FHWA-SA-91-056. Washington, D.C.: U.S. DOT, FHWA, July 1991.

U.S. Department of Transportation, Federal Highway Administration, and Federal Transit Administration. "Intelligent Transportation Systems Awareness Seminar," CD-ROM. Washington, D.C.: U.S. DOT, FHWA, 1999.

U.S. Department of Transportation, Federal Highway Administration, and Federal Transit Administration. *The National Architecture for ITS, A Framework for Integrated Transportation into the 21st Century,* CD-ROM. Washington, D.C.: U.S. DOT, FHWA, 1998.

U.S. Department of Transportation, Federal Highway Administration. *Traffic Control Systems Handbook,* Publication No. FHWA-SA-95-032. Washington, D.C.: U.S. DOT, FHWA, February 1996.

CHAPTER 20
Regulatory and Legal Issues

George L. Reed, J.D., P.E.
Vice President
The TransTech Group, Inc.

Introduction

This chapter presents an overview of the myriad federal, state, regional, and local laws, ordinances, regulations, and policies that affect the planning, design, and administration of transportation facilities. The subject area is extensive and varies significantly by geographic location and agency jurisdiction. Although a complete compilation is not possible, this chapter presents a broad survey of the different types of laws and regulations applicable primarily to transportation planning. The emphasis is upon the United States, but a brief overview of Canadian transportation law is also presented.

Most transportation professionals seek legal information and knowledge of how various laws and regulations affect their areas of practice, but not to the degree necessary for the practice of law. Words, phrases, or laws may have unintended legal consequences. Thus, although the transportation professional is encouraged to take advantage of the rapidly increasing legal information and knowledge base, he or she should use it with proper care and legal assistance when needed.

Regulatory Transportation Law

Governmental transportation agencies are administrative in nature. This means that while they can make and carry out regulations, they do not have the power of courts or legislative bodies. *Administrative law* is the subject area dealing with the regulatory procedures and decision-making powers of these agencies.

Agency Legal Controls

Agency direction originates at the legislative level through laws, statutes and ordinances, legislative controls, and court decisions. Statutes are acts of a legislature (federal or state) that establish the agency and define its functional responsibility. Legislative controls exist as part of the execution of these statutes, with revisions to the original legislation and apportionment of funding being two key elements. Local laws and ordinances provide direction to local agencies, but they may be subordinate to federal and state legislation. Court decisions influence the interpretation and application of all types of enactments and may result in their being declared invalid or void.

How Agencies Make Rules

In the conduct of its business, an agency establishes rules and procedures through both informal and formal processes. Informal processes can include written policies and procedures, which are usually flexible in application and subject to negotiation and agreement. Appeals from informal processes are in turn informal, and they are normally resolved without court-like hearings or procedures. How much reliance can be placed upon informal agency decisions to cover future events or changes in agency personnel is an important issue. Nevertheless, informal processes simplify the work of transportation agencies and those affected by their rules.

Formal administrative processes include rulemaking and adjudication through the courts or court-like administrative hearings. Rulemaking is generally preferred to adjudication, because it guides future events, results from agencies making choices among alternative policies, and includes notice to and response from affected parties. Rulemaking results in written policy and procedures that have undergone a more formal review and adoption process. On the other hand, adjudication determines the legal consequences of past events and is primarily retrospective.

Current Sources of Legal Information

There are two basic formats for legal and regulatory information: printed or electronic. Both have advantages and disadvantages. For example, printed documents provide ease of use and formality of presentation of materials but often require bulky and inconvenient storage. Trips to a library or central location may be necessary to access the desired volume. Electronic documents, in various formats, can also result in greater convenience, portability, and ease of use. A major advantage resulting from the use of electronic documents is the ability to transcribe portions without having to retype or reenter the data. However, the singular major advantage resulting from the use of electronic documents is the capability to accomplish automated searches for words, phrases, or ideas.

Since the first edition of this handbook, the continued explosion of information distribution via the Internet has had a significant effect upon the availability, convenience, and cost of obtaining legal and regulatory information. A large amount of regulatory information is available to the transportation professional via the Internet and its associated component, the World Wide Web (referred to as the "Web"), including multimedia and hyperlinked usage of interconnected sites.[1]

While some electronic data bases or sites are proprietary and have an associated user fee, many are free. For example, most professional organizations, companies, universities, federal and state governmental agencies, and similar entities now have Web sites (also referred to as "home pages" or "Internet sites") with varying degrees of available information. Electronic mail (referred to as "email") also enhances communication between individuals and allows the transfer of information electronically.

Whatever the source consulted, the transportation professional should be familiar with the various laws and regulations underlying the programs within their area of responsibility.

U.S. Federal Law and Sources

Basic federal law in the United States is contained in the *United States Code* (U.S.C.), which is a lengthy and intimidating 50-title compilation of federal law. While the U.S.C. is available in printed format, it is also available in searchable, electronic format from several online sites, some of which are noted below. For the occasional user, use of automated, electronic searches will save considerable time.

The *Code of Federal Regulations* (C.F.R.) is a compilation of the general and permanent rules published by the executive department and agencies of the federal government. The C.F.R. is a source of authority for each federal program and is available online from several sources. The *Federal Register* contains proposed rules, notices, regulations and other similar documents. Information concerning pending federal legislation or recently published statutes can usually be obtained in printed copy by request from congressional offices or from the originating agency.

The federal General Services Administration maintains the FedLaw site at www.legal.gsa.gov/ containing U.S.C., the C.F.R., and other federal and state legislation. The U.S. House of Representatives' Internet Law Library at http://law.house.gov has extensive legal resources, including links to many other sites. The C.F.R. is also available from the National Archives and Records Administration at www.access.gpo.gov/nara/. The Legal Information Institute of the Cornell Law School is one such source providing extensive federal and state legal information including U.S.C., the

---

[1] For further information, see *Internet Starter Kit Update 1997* (Washington, D.C.: U.S. DOT, Bureau of Transportation Statistics, 1997) or any of the numerous proprietary Internet usage guides.

Federal Rules of Evidence, the *Federal Rules of Civil Procedure*, and other information at www.law.cornell.edu/. The Internet Legal Resource Guide at http://www.ilrg.com provides an extensive list of other legal information sites.

The U.S. Department of Transportation (DOT), Bureau of Transportation Statistics (BTS) is a leader in providing transportation information via the Internet, including transportation statistics and many links or addresses of other transportation-related agencies. The Internet address for the BTS is http://www.bts.gov. The U.S. DOT is committed to online information, including news releases, rulemaking, and other legal documents; and it maintains a Document Management System home page at http://dms.dot.gov. Individual U.S. DOT administrative agency sites are given later in this chapter.

Written publications are also available for federal agencies and their regulations. The *United States Government Manual,* published annually, provides a printed overview of each department and agency of the federal government, including current agency addresses and telephone numbers and some citations to authorizing statutes.[2] The FHWA's *Glossary of Transportation Terms* provides many definitions and explanations that are useful in interpreting transportation-related documents.[3]

Canadian Federal and Provincial Law and Sources

Transport Canada is the governmental department responsible for most of the transportation policies, programs, and goals set by the government of Canada. The department consists of programs and support groups working at headquarters in Ottawa and other locations across Canada. The headquarters organization is made up of several groups: Policy, Safety and Security, Programs and Divestiture, and Corporate Services. Transport Canada also has five regions responsible for the delivery of transportation programs and service in their respective areas. In addition, Canada's ten provinces and the Yukon Territory also have transportation agencies, similar in nature to the individual state DOTs in the United States.

Transport Canada's mission is "to develop and administer policies, regulations, and services for the best possible transportation system." In the words of the agency:

> Transport Canada is modernizing to respond to the needs of Canadian society. The department is commercial-izing many of its operational activities, overhauling transportation policy, streamlining regulations, reducing sub-sidies, and cutting overhead. No longer will the department own, operate or subsidize large parts of the transportation system. The role of new Transport Canada will be to develop up-to-date, relevant transportation policies and legislation and to maintain a high level of safety and security. This process of modernization will ensure that Canada's transportation system can support trade, tourism, and job creation by bolstering Canadian competitiveness.[4]

The Canada Transport Act of 1996 is the current law for the major policies noted above. Regulatory information for individual provinces and the 1996 Act may be found at the Web sites listed in the main Transport Canada site.

U.S. State and Local Law

At the time of this writing, most state transportation agencies and many local agencies have Web sites, with varying degrees of regulatory data available. State sites often provide access to transportation regulations, publications, and other information. An index to these sites is maintained at the FHWA Web site. A good city index can be found at http://www/city.net/. Some agencies maintain news release programs via their Web site or through automated email subscription services.

---

[2] *The United States Government Manual* (Washington, D.C.: U.S. Government Printing Office).

[3] *Glossary of Transportation Terms* (Washington, D.C.: U.S. DOT, FHWA, 1994).

[4] Transport Canada's Web site, http://www.tc.gc.ca

State laws and regulations are documented in various formats by individual states. State statute volumes contain the full text of laws and serve as a primary reference. These are always available in printed format but may also be available on CD-ROM at a lower price. They may also be available through the Internet. Annotated statute volumes give the history, dates of change, and case citations for pertinent statute sections. Each state will also have a publication for notice of agency rulemaking activities and decisions. The state administrative code will publish agency rules along with appropriate background information.

Local laws and regulations are contained in various municipal and county codes and ordinances. These are normally published in loose-leaf format for ease of updating. In addition, the more frequently used rules such as subdivision regulations may be compiled into guides and handbooks. Obviously, these can be obtained from the pertinent agencies.

Other Sources

Private reporting services also publish compilations of federal and state law, regulations, and administrative actions. These services collect and distribute up-to-date information about a specific agency or administrative function and are available by subscription in printed or electronic format. For those involved heavily in transportation law and research, these services are worthwhile.

Many transportation-related organizations maintain Web sites. Proposed changes in legislation or regulatory policy, along with comments and responses from the organization and its membership, are a valuable benefit provided by these sites. Following are a few examples.

- Air Transport Association—http://www.air-transport.org/

- American Association of State Highway and Transportation Officials—http://www. aashto.org

- American Public Transit Association—http://www.apta.com/

- American Road and Transportation Builder's Association—http://www.artba.org

- American Trucking Associations—http://www.trucking.org

- Association of American Railroads—http://www.aar.org

- Institute of Transportation Engineers—http://www.ite.org.

- Intelligent Transportation Society of America—http://www.itsa.org

- International Bridge, Tunnel and Turnpike Association—http://www.ibtta.org

- Transportation Research Board—http://www.nas.edu/trb

The frequent changes in legislation, agency rules, and procedures make it imperative to be sure that the latest version of an electronic or written document is being used. Monitoring rulemaking via electronic or printed means is important for practitioners. Periodic and timely reference to the agency in question can also help to ensure that the latest version is used. By any comparison, use of the Internet and the availability of the personal computer will continue to revolutionize the way information is stored and distributed.

Jurisdiction of Transportation Agencies

Within the hierarchy of laws and ordinances, jurisdiction on a geographic or subject area basis establishes the span of control of an agency. In addition, within the United States, there is an important precedence for laws, extending from the U.S. Constitution through federal and state law, and ultimately to local law. While U.S. federal law has precedence over many subject areas, understanding the span of each law is important for each subject area, modal system, geographic area, or funding basis.

State statutory law establishes authority and responsibility for state, regional, or local transportation matters. A state's transportation legislation designates jurisdictional responsibility for each element of its transportation system. State legislation normally requires development of system design and operational standards. State statutes also contain a motor vehicle code; a state uniform traffic control code; and other regulations related to motor vehicle operation, licensing, and titling.

Transportation regulations for counties and municipalities designate responsibility for elements of the transportation system. Responsibility for specific elements may also be transferred among agencies by formal agreement.

U.S. Federal and State Transportation Legislation

The Intermodal Surface Transportation Efficiency Act of 1991 (ISTEA)[5] is one of the predominant federal laws guiding surface transportation planning and development. Signed into law in December 1991, ISTEA with its eight titles for highways, mass transit, and safety programs continues to direct the nation's transportation policy. Funding authorization under ISTEA expired on September 30, 1997 but was extended for six months. Reauthorization bills, known in various forms as BESTEA, ISTEA II, or NEXTEA were debated by the Congress during the time this chapter was being prepared. The Transportation Equity Act for the 21st Century (TEA-21),[6] which was enacted during May 1998, continued many of the ISTEA provisions but with increased funding.

ISTEA increased citizen and local involvement in programming transportation improvements as major effort to address some social and physical issues that many think has eluded previous transportation enactments. The Act provided great flexibility on funding and expenditures. Statewide and local transportation planning requirements were strengthened and several new management programs were set to encourage more efficient use of existing and planned resources.

Basic Provisions of ISTEA

Title 1, Surface Transportation, established a requirement for a 159,000-mile National Highway System (NHS) composed predominantly of interstate, arterial, and other strategic highways. The NHS accounts for less than five percent of all roadway mileage, but it is estimated to carry as much as eighty percent of all roadway travel. The NHS was legislatively established by the National Highway System Designation Act of 1994, modifying pertinent sections of 23 U.S.C.

Title 1 also contained the Surface Transportation Program (STP), which provides flexibility between highway, mass transit, and several other transportation programs. ISTEA gave local transportation officials, through the individual Metropolitan Planning Organizations (MPOs), a greater say in transportation destiny and funding. For example, the following generally applies to selection of projects using federal funds under ISTEA:

- Areas with populations less than 200,000 persons or otherwise not designated as Transportation Management Areas (TMAs)—in these areas projects are to be selected by the state DOT and the transit operator, in cooperation with the MPOs.

- Areas with populations of 200,000 persons or more are designated TMAs—in these areas the MPO has selection power in consultation with the state DOT and the transit operator.

---

[5] 23 U.S.C. 101 *et seq.*

[6] HR 2400 as enrolled (23 U.S.C. 101 *et seq.*).

- Projects on the NHS or under the bridge and interstate system maintenance programs are selected by the state in cooperation with MPOs in areas with populations of over 50,000 persons and in consultation with local officials in all other areas.

ISTEA particularly expanded the role of the MPO and added requirements for local transportation planning. TMAs have increased planning requirements, particularly for congestion management. In areas of nonattainment of air quality standards, development of the long-range plan must contain transportation control measures and be coordinated with the state air quality implementation plan. ISTEA has further emphasized the needed coordination with land use development and the use of intelligent transportation system elements.[7]

ISTEA Management Systems

ISTEA initially mandated six management systems for transportation, including:

1. highway pavements,

2. bridges,

3. highway safety,

4. traffic congestion,

5. public transportation,

6. intermodal transportation.

Although The National Highway System Designation Act of 1994 rendered some management systems optional, ISTEA encouraged transportation efficiency through various programs and techniques. These continue to include promotion of high-occupancy vehicles, increased use of public transportation, travel demand management, encouragement of walking and bicycling, and similar techniques to reduce single-occupant vehicle travel.

ISTEA also promoted nontraditional transportation programs through transportation enhancements. This portion of ISTEA's STP provided funding for programs such as facilities for bicycles and pedestrians, scenic roadways, historic preservation, and reuse of abandoned railway corridors. Local input is even more important for the ISTEA Enhancement Programs, intended to build elements of the transportation system providing more human appeal. See Figure 20–1 for a typical enhancement project.

Transportation Equity Act for the 21st Century

The TEA-21[8] is the successor to ISTEA. TEA-21 was passed by Congress in May 1998 and signed into law on June 9, 1998. TEA-21 is primarily a funding bill, leaving most of the ISTEA provisions intact. One of the main provisions of TEA-21 includes an increase in transportation funding to an estimated 6-year total of about $215 billion, or nearly a forty-percent increase from ISTEA's $155 billion.

Important provisions of TEA-21 include reauthorization of the core federal highway, transit, safety, research, and motor carrier programs for the six-year period. This includes $175 billion for highways, $41.4 billion for transit, $2.2 billion for highway safety programs. TEA-21 also ensures that on an annual basis, tax revenues deposited into the Highway Trust Fund are spent on transportation improvements, and it provides a guaranteed return to donor states of

---

[7] *Metropolitan Transportation Planning Under ISTEA, The Shape of Things to Come* (Washington, D.C.: U.S. DOT, FHWA).

[8] H.R. 2400 as enrolled (23 U.S.C.).

**Figure 20–1   Typical TEA-21 Enhancement Project—
Cartersville, Ga., Railroad Depot Rehabilitation**

Source: Cartersville Downtown Development Authority.

90.5 percent of funds they contribute to the Highway Trust Fund. Important aspects of TEA-21's transit program include over $41 billion for the transit program; and a new Clean Fuels Program funded at $1.2 billion, which gives transit agencies increased flexibility to use their funds and reforms the "new starts" criteria to ensure projects with national and regional significance are built. TEA-21 also contains nearly 1,900 specific projects added during the negotiation process. The TEA-21 text and many program summaries can be found at http://www.fhwa.dot.gov/tea21/summary.

Federal and State Transportation Agencies

The predominant federal agency for transportation is, of course, the U.S. DOT. Established in 1966, the U.S. DOT is a cabinet-level federal agency responsible for the planning, safety, and system and technology development of national transportation, including highways, mass transit, aircraft, and ports. The U.S. DOT contains nine operating administrations, including the Federal Highway Administration (FHWA), Federal Transit Administration (FTA), Federal Aviation Administration, Federal Railroad Administration, and the Maritime Administration among others. These agencies, along with their state counterparts, are discussed briefly in the following sections.

Federal Highway Administration

The FHWA was established to ensure development of an effective national road and highway transportation system. FHWA became a component of the U.S. DOT in 1967. The FHWA assists the states in construction of highways and administers the federal-aid financial assistance program for highway construction and improvement of efficiency and safety in highway and traffic operations. The agency delegates responsibility for the planning, design, construction, and administration of all federal-aid highway projects to the various states:

> The Administrator shall cooperate with the States, through their respective State highway departments in the construction of Federal-aid highways. Each State Highway Department . . . shall be authorized, by the laws of the

State, to make final decisions for the State in all matters relating to, and to enter into, on behalf of the State, all contracts and agreements for projects and to take such other actions on behalf of the State as may be necessary to comply with the Federal laws and the regulations in this part.[9]

In the United States, the federal-aid highway programs are authorized under specific federal-aid highway act provisions, which are passed and authorized periodically by the U.S. Congress. A highway act establishes the ground rules under which funds may be used. The highway acts are "authorization acts" in that they empower the FHWA to carry out a particular program, while establishing the upper limit on the amount of funds available for a specific program. Corresponding appropriations acts make the necessary funds available for expenditures. However, funds apportioned (based on prescribed formulas) and financed from the Highway Trust Fund do not need an appropriation. This latter method, which encompasses the largest portion of federal-aid funds, is known as "contract authority." Finally, the federal-aid highway program is a reimbursable program in which the federal government reimburses states only for costs incurred.[10]

Over the years, FHWA has published many policies and directives regarding their programs. Current practice is to publish the federal highway regulations in the *Code of Federal Regulations* or the *Federal Register*. Preliminary versions are published as Notice(s) of Proposed Rule Making (NPRMs), and with the Final Rules, responses to comments on proposed regulations are helpful. The FHWA also operates several Web sites, presenting information on its basic legislation including 23 C.F.R., 49 C.F.R., ISTEA, TEA-21, The National Highway System Designation Act of 1995, and NPRMs from the *Federal Register*. Basic access is through http://www.fhwa.dot.gov/.

Policies and procedures developed by other agencies may be incorporated into federal regulations by reference. Some of these remain as guides or suggested practice, while others are formally adopted through administrative rulemaking as mandatory standards. Such issues become important in matters of litigation. Few formal standards relate strictly to transportation planning, but several relate indirectly. A particular example is the *Manual on Uniform Traffic Control Devices for Streets and Highways* (MUTCD).[11] The MUTCD is the standard for all traffic control devices installed on any street, highway, or bicycle trail open to public travel and represents a legal standard applying to all jurisdictions. Updates to the MUTCD may be obtained electronically through the FHWA Web site.

The American Association of State Highway and Transportation Officials (AASHTO) also develops numerous highway planning and engineering guidelines. AASHTO is composed of representatives from various state transportation agencies and adopts its recommendations by vote of member departments. Resulting documents, such as the *Policy on Geometric Design of Highways and Streets*, have officially been adopted the FHWA.[12] AASHTO maintains a Web site as previously noted.

State Highway and Transportation Agencies

Each state has a department of transportation extending jurisdiction to its transportation facilities. While exact organizations and forms of these agencies vary by state, each generally covers all modes of transportation. For example, as related to the highway mode, a state's DOT will have responsibility for projects to be undertaken with federal-aid highway funds. Each state's legislation for transportation (normally the State Transportation Code) establishes operational and jurisdictional responsibility for all roads throughout the state. Such a designation is most important not only for program administration but also for tort liability issues.

The State Transportation Code normally contains many provisions for the planning, design, construction, and operation of the state highway system. General topics related to planning include:

- functional classification,

---

[9] 23 C.F.R. 1.3.

[10] *Financing Federal-Aid Highways* (Washington, D.C.: U.S. DOT, FHWA, Nov. 1987).

[11] *Manual on Uniform Traffic Control Devices for Streets and Highways* (Washington, D.C.: U.S. DOT, FHWA, 1988 ed., as periodically updated).

[12] *A Policy on Geometric Design of Highways and Streets* (Washington, D.C.: American Association of State Highway and Transportation Officials, 1990, S.I.; 1994, metric). Also see 23 C.F.R. 625.4(a) for federal adoption.

- sufficiency ratings and safety inspection,

- a uniform system of traffic control devices,

- access regulation and permitting,

- statewide and urban area transportation system planning.

A State Transportation Code also generally requires development of a statewide transportation plan and a financial work program, designating planned use of both federal-aid and state funds. A typical work program will set forth planned expenditures classified by major programs for a multiyear period. Specific projects are listed and expenditures are balanced to estimated revenues. When legislatively adopted, the work program establishes the resulting year's budget.

Several other requirements may direct a state's transportation system administration. Examples include the urban area transportation planning process; transportation issues of growth management, development, and access permitting; emergency access issues; and transportation statistics. Other important functions include the administration of the design, construction, maintenance, operational, and safety aspects of the system; and establishment and adoption of uniform minimum design and construction standards and criteria.

Mass Transit

The FTA is a component of the U.S. DOT and administers the federal transit program. FTA's predecessor agency, the Urban Mass Transportation Administration, was absorbed as a division of the U.S. DOT in 1968 with its mission originally established in the Urban Mass Transportation Act of 1964.

FTA was created under ISTEA in 1991. The FTA assists in the development of improved public and private mass transportation facilities and encourages the planning and establishment of area-wide urban mass transportation systems. As presented on its Web site, FTA's mission statement is "to ensure personal mobility and America's economic and community vitality by supporting high quality public transportation through leadership, technical assistance and financial resources." As authorized under several parts of 49 U.S.C., FTA provides considerable assistance to state and local governments for public and private mass transportation operations.

FTA's role includes urban and rural transit; capital and operational grants; implementation of the Americans with Disabilities Act of 1990 (49 C.F.R. 37), particularly as related to transportation of the elderly and disabled individuals; and transportation planning responsibilities for Transportation Improvement Programs (TIPs) and TMAs as defined in 49 U.S.C. 53. FTA maintains a Web site at http://www.fta.dot.gov/.

States and local agencies have an important role in public transportation. While transit systems are usually operated by local authorities, many states provide technical and financial assistance through special provisions embodied in their State Transportation Code. Systems range from conventional public mass transit to new methodologies, such as high speed rail.

The state public transportation authorities are charged with activities similar to the following:

- Maintain a statewide public transit needs plan, including specific programs and project financing proposals.

- Maintain state management and performance standards for government-owned public transit systems and privately owned or operated systems financed wholly or in part by state funding.

- Provide technical and financial assistance to units of local government to help in establishing and implementing effective transit systems and related support programs.

- Provide transit demonstration projects to assist in the development of new systems.

The authorizing statute will normally specify transit project eligibility and availability of funding. This may be limited to capital assistance, or may include operating assistance.

A state may also authorize other types of transportation systems, such as a regional or high-speed rail. The legislative intent for such a system in Florida, for example, is to establish a centralized and coordinated permitting and planning process to develop high-speed rail lines. A combination of public and private sector involvement is being encouraged, with significant benefits for the developers of such facilities.

Aviation and Airports

With the interstate and international aspects of air transportation, the federal government provides the predominant regulatory function for airports, use of airspace, safety, and equipment certification. Regulation of air transportation began with the Federal Air Commerce Act of 1926, under the U.S. Department of Commerce. In 1938, the federal role in aviation was transferred to the Civil Aeronautics Authority. Following several revisions to responsibility and authority, the Federal Aviation Authority was created by the Federal Aviation Act of 1958. In 1967, the Federal Aviation Authority became the Federal Aviation Administration (FAA) and a component of the U.S. DOT.

The FAA maintains a Web site at http://www.tc.faa.gov. Its mission is to provide "safe, secure, and efficient global aerospace system that contributes to national security and the promotion of U.S. aerospace." Its major responsibilities include:

- Planning and development of airports.

- Regulation of airspace, including policies and equipment.

- Promotion and regulation of the air transport industry.

- Development and accomplishment of aviation safety standards.

- Research and development of aviation facilities.

State DOTs normally include an aviation division with the responsibility to administer federal aviation programs and financial assistance, to help local agencies in developing and operating airports, and to develop statewide aviation programs. Individual airports may be operated by regional authorities authorized by state statute, local governments, or private enterprise.

Railroads

The Federal Railroad Administration (FRA), a component of the U.S. DOT, was established in 1966 and derives its authority from 49 U.S.C. The FRA coordinates federal activities related to the railroad industry. One of FRA's major responsibilities is the promotion of safety for rail operations, particularly for the at-grade intersections of highways and railroads. FRA, with assistance from the individual states, is responsible for the national highway-railroad grade crossing inventory and compilation of vehicle crash (accident) statistics at these intersections. The FRA maintains a Web site at http:// www.fra.dot.gov.

Ports and Waterways

Federal law governing ships and shipping falls under the topic of admiralty law, and generally extends to any navigable waters within the United States for interstate or foreign commerce. Administration of regulations relating to admiralty law is divided among several federal agencies, including the U.S. Maritime Administration (MARAD), the U.S. Coast Guard, and occasionally the U.S. Navy. Important federal statutes include 14, 28, 33, and 46 U.S.C.

MARAD is a component of the U.S. DOT and has "primary federal responsibility for ensuring the availability of efficient water transportation service to American shippers and consumers." MARAD also has responsibility for ports and effective intermodal water and land transportation systems. MARAD's Web site is http://marad.dot.gov/.

Operation of the nation's port facilities is also an important state or local function. States may have port authorities for all state ports or a separately-authorized authority for a single port. Consult state laws for matters relating to port operations.

Other Federal Transportation-Related Regulations

Several other federal agencies promulgate regulations or offer resources affecting the provision or operation of transportation facilities. The U.S. Environmental Protection Agency (EPA) is an independent federal agency in the executive branch with responsibilities that include development and enforcement of national air quality emission standards and support of antipollution activities by state and local governments. EPA's Web site is http://www.epa.gov. A key enactment is the National Environmental Policy Act of 1969 (NEPA) and the Clean Air Act Amendment of 1990. See Chapter 8 for more details.

The federal ADA grants civil rights protection to persons with disabilities in employment, public accommodations, access to state and local government facilities, and public transportation. The ADA has important requirements for public transportation, which for transit operations are administered by the FTA. The Department of Labor may become involved with certain labor disputes, which in turn may affect program funding.

Finally, but not exclusively, the U.S. Army Corps of Engineers administers environmental regulations for such matters as wetlands, flood control, and related structural matters. The Corps publication data base can be found at http://www.usace.army.mil/inet/usace-docs/.

The Urban Transportation Planning Process

The 1962 Federal-Aid Highway Act established special requirements for "continuing, comprehensive, and cooperative" (the "3-C" process) transportation planning in all urbanized areas with populations of 50,000 persons or more as a prerequisite to receiving federal highway funding. The Urban Mass Transportation Act of 1964 brought planning for public transit facilities into this arena. These two acts, as amended particularly by ISTEA and covered in the federal Metropolitan Planning Regulations,[13] provide the basis for urban area transportation planning of today.[14]

Each area with a 3-C planning process is required to have a MPO.[15] Normally, a section of the State Transportation Code establishes the creation, composition, role, and responsibility of an MPO. The MPO, composed of elected or appointed representatives, serves as an area's transportation decision-making body. Each MPO must establish a Technical Coordinating Committee to provide technical and administrative support. Citizen input and involvement are also mandated. An interlocal agreement between the local area and the state DOT facilitates the MPO process.

Each MPO Produces a Long-Range Transportation Plan, a TIP, and a Unified Planning Work Program. Other products may include a Transit Development Program, a Transportation Disadvantaged Plan, a State Implementation Plan for air quality improvements, or Transportation Systems Management (TSM) elements. See Chapters 9 and 12 for more detail and additional legislation on these requirements and the urban transportation planning process.

---

[13] Final Rule: Statewide and Metropolitan Planning, *Federal Register*, joint regulations (Washington, D.C.: U.S. DOT, FHWA/FTA, Oct. 28, 1993).

[14] Edward Wiener, *Urban Transportation Planning in the United States—An Historical Overview*, revised ed. (Washington, D.C.: U.S. DOT, Office of Asst. Secretary for Policy and International Affairs, Nov. 1992).

[15] The MPO transportation planning process is described in 23 C.F.R. 450.

Public Involvement

Public involvement in nearly all types of transportation projects is mandated in many federal and state transportation regulations. It is also a common sense requirement for most transportation proposals. The 1962 Federal-Aid Highway Act established the requirement for public involvement in transportation planning. Through the years, this requirement has been strengthened, and in development of long-range plans ISTEA requires each state to "provide citizens, affected public agencies, representatives of transportation agency employees, other affected employee representatives, private providers of transportation, and other interested parties with a reasonable opportunity to comment on the proposed plan."[16]

States have generally embodied federal requirements in their transportation codes. For example, Florida has incorporated the provisions of ISTEA in its statutes and generally requires a public hearing during:

> development of major transportation improvements, such as those increasing the capacity of a facility through the addition of new lanes or providing new access to a limited or controlled access facility or construction of a facility in a new location . . . . Such public hearings shall be conducted so as to provide an opportunity for effective participation by interested persons in the process of transportation planning and site and route selection and in the specific location and design of transportation facilities.[17]

Citizen committees and the public do not have the authority to adopt or change official government plans. Local, state, and federal agencies are empowered to adopt and carry out such plans. However, the public must be permitted the opportunity to voice their opinions and recommendations. The public also has the recourse of legal action through the courts and political action through the vote for government offices.

Public involvement, as it has evolved to today, is not merely a mechanism for the public to review previously-made decisions, but it is to be ongoing throughout the planning and design process to explain public agency decisions and to receive public opinion before reaching a binding decision. The process is to be prospective, meaning that public opinion is to be received at a time when it can be considered and will contribute to the public processes. Many agencies have formal processes to encompass various forms of required public involvement. These include informal meetings and formal hearings. Nevertheless, many go the extra mile to inform the public and to solicit their opinions even when not required.[18]

Environmental Justice

Environmental justice is an important element of transportation planning, involving both federal and state requirements for public involvement. The subject is emphasized by ISTEA and a 1994 Presidential Executive Order.[19] Environmental justice involves identifying disproportionately high effects of proposed transportation decisions on minority and low-income populations; equity issues in the provision of transportation services; and the social, environmental, and economic issues in siting transportation facilities.

To date, no new federal regulations have been issued regarding environmental justice, and debate continues over the need for them. The U.S. DOT has issued a Final Environmental Justice Strategy.[20] The U.S. DOT said it would not issue new regulations; but it expects any disproportionate effects, mitigation and enhancement measures, or offsetting benefits to be identified through existing regulations.

---

[16] 23 U.S.C.135 (e).

[17] ' 339.155(6), F.S.

[18] Several important guides exist for public involvement programs and indirectly address legal issues. Among these are: *Public Involvement Techniques for Transportation Decisionmaking* (Washington, D.C.: U.S. DOT, FHWA/FTA, September 1996), available via the Internet at http://www.fhwa.dot.gov; *Guidelines on Citizen Participation in Transportation Planning*, (Washington, D.C.: AASHTO, 1978); *Public Outreach Handbook for Departments of Transportation, NCHRP Report 364* (Washington, D.C.: Transportation Research Board, National Research Council, 1994); *Project Development and Environmental Handbook*, (Tallahassee, FL: Florida Department of Transportation, first published in July 1988, updated in December 1998); and *Effective Communications for the Transportation Professional*, (Washington, D.C.: Institute of Transportation Engineers, 1984).

[19] *Federal Actions to Address Environmental Justice in Minority Populations and Low-Income Populations*, Executive Order 12898 (Feb. 11, 1994).

[20] *Federal Register*, Vol. 60, No. 125 (Washington, D.C.: U.S. DOT, FHWA, June 29, 1995).

State Regulation of Land Development

Regulation of land development through traffic and other infrastructure requirements has become an important activity for state governments in many high-growth states. Land development in these areas has outstripped the ability to provide the necessary public facilities or infrastructure. This, along with an increasing concern for the environment and the overall quality of life, has led to increased state regulation.

State regulation of land development may range from requirements for permits for access to the state highway system to regulations governing the type and amount of development that may be allowed. State land development controls are obviously shared with local governments, but they may override or otherwise influence local regulations. Both state and local regulations also reflect a desire to tax or surcharge growth, with local regulations often being directly related to infrastructure funding.

State Land Planning Regulation

Florida has extensive state land planning and development regulations, in particular, for transportation planning and administration. While these regulations may not exactly parallel those of other states or necessarily serve as a model, they provide a comprehensive example of a regulatory scheme enacted for a high-growth state. The regulations begin with overall land development planning and extend into a highly technical level of service analysis for most infrastructure elements.

Land planning in Florida is administered by local governments, with review oversight through the state's Department of Community Affairs (DCA), including close coordination with the DOT; the Department of Environmental Protection; and several other specialized agencies, such as the Regional Planning Commissions and Water Management Districts. In 1972, Florida enacted its regulatory process for Developments of Regional Impact (DRIs). A DRI is "any development that, because of its character, magnitude, or location, would have a substantial effect upon the health, safety, or welfare of citizens of more than one county."[21] The state planning agency prepares numerical threshold guidelines to define projects that must be treated as DRIs, which vary throughout the state.

Elements of the DRI include an extensive list of development- and effect-related questions, public hearings, and negotiations. From a transportation planning standpoint, a DRI requires extensive analysis to determine the potential effects of the development's traffic on the area's street system and the required mitigation or fees. Typical traffic analyses require determination of the existing and future capacity of the surrounding street system, existing and future project and nonproject traffic, internal trip capture ratios, and necessary highway (or transit) improvements to maintain a specific level of service. The process requires a preapplication conference to establish the necessary analyses and results in several meetings held throughout the project's review and approval phase. The analysis process also involves a determination of who will pay for the needed improvements. Following agreement among all parties and approval by the public agencies, conditions under which the project may be developed are described in a Development Order.

While there are no statutory mitigation or approval fees within the DRI process, a proportionate share formula is included. Thus, the focus is often on the estimate of project effects. Considerable discussion normally results. The transportation engineer will be called upon to analyze "what if" questions involving alternative schemes of development and potential effect. Negotiations can involve the type and quantity of development that may be approved and the need for additional transportation facilities or traffic management strategies.

In 1985, Florida adopted further land planning regulations requiring every local government to develop and adopt a local comprehensive plan.[22] Control of urban sprawl is a major goal, but the plans must also address critical areas of public works infrastructure. Transportation obviously has a key role. Following a critical review at the state level and local adoption of the overall plan, a series of Land Development Regulations must be adopted. These are "specific and detailed provisions necessary . . . to implement the adopted comprehensive plan . . . ."[23]

---

[21] ' 380.06(1), F.S.

[22] By 1993, this had evolved into the *Local Government Comprehensive Planning and Land Development Regulation Act,* ' 163.3161, F.S., *et seq.*

[23] ' 163.3202(2), F.S.

The needed public facilities required by the growth must be in place or provided concurrently to serve the desired development:

> A local government shall not issue a development order or permit which results in a reduction in the level of services for the affected public facilities below the level of services provided in the comprehensive plan of the local government.[24]

This provision clearly establishes the requirement of *concurrency* for the infrastructure necessary to support development, which involves several additional issues. These include level of service, concurrency management systems, development and monitoring strategies, and other legal and interpretative issues regarding the law.[25] The Growth Management Act also places extensive financial and administrative burdens on local governments and provides sanctions for noncompliance.

Level of service for each infrastructure element, including transportation, is a critical issue and is closely related to local financing abilities. A local government may set a high level of service that will curb growth, or it may set a lower level to encourage growth. An adjacent jurisdiction may have a lower level of service, which will influence development in that area as compared with the area with the higher standard. Level of service affects the need for improvements, which increasingly have to be met at the local level.

For the state highway system, level of service has become a critical issue:

> For facilities on the Florida Intrastate Highway System,[26] the local governments shall adopt the level of service standards established by the Department of Transportation by rule. For all other facilities on the future traffic circulation map or the future transportation map, local governments shall adopt adequate level of service standards. These level of service standards shall be adopted to ensure that adequate facility capacity will be provided to serve the existing and future land uses . . . .[27]

Florida has developed its own level of service definitions and analysis procedures, although these follow national methodologies.[28] Depending on type of roadway and degree of urbanization, Florida's permitted levels of service range from "B" to "E," and represent the "lowest acceptable quality peak hour operating conditions . . . through a 20-year planning horizon." Two special categories are provided: (1) constrained roads, which are those that cannot be widened; and (2) backlogged roads, which are those not scheduled for widening or other improvements. Both may continue to operate in deficits if the proposed development does not deteriorate their level of service by more than ten percent below existing conditions (five percent in rural areas).[29]

Level of service and similar requirements can be anticipated in other high-growth states. They will have a major effect upon growth, development, and the entire transportation system.

Access Management

An important governmental function involves regulation of access to its transportation facilities as applied to both state highways and local arterial roads. This function evolves from requirements of safety and efficiency. A balance is normally sought between public and private interests. Efforts in two states are briefly examined and illustrate the general rule regarding land service access.

---

[24] ' 163.3202(2)(g), F.S.

[25] *Minimum Criteria for Review of Local Government Comprehensive Plans and Plan Amendments and Determination of Compliance,* Rule Chapter 9J-5, Florida Administrative Code (Tallahassee,Fla.: Florida Department of Community Affairs, 1994).

[26] The FIHS is composed of about 4,200 miles of major roadways of the total 11,000-mile State Highway System.

[27] Rule Chapter 9J-5.007(3)(c)1, F.A.C.

[28] *Level of Service Standards and Guidelines Manual* (Tallahassee, Fla.: Florida Department of Transportation, 1995); see also *Highway Capacity Manual, Special Report 209,* 3rd Ed. (Washington, D.C.: Transportation Research Board, National Research Council 1994).

[29] *Level of Service Standards and Guidelines Manual* (Tallahassee, Fla.: Florida Department of Transportation, 1995).

Colorado is considered a leader in highway access management. Colorado first adopted its State Highway Access Code in 1979 and has amended it several times.[30] Based partly upon an extensive demonstration project and broadened and refined through court decisions and practical application, Colorado's access law gave its governmental units more power to regulate access to and from the roadways under their jurisdiction. The code followed then-current principles of access law: landowners are permitted reasonable but not unlimited or indiscriminate access to public roads.

Reasonable access is an issue that must be decided for each case in question, and it is normally a jury question. Thus, when considering access restrictions, public authorities must examine each parcel and conclude whether or not the remaining access is reasonable or if there are fewer intrusive ways to accomplish the same traffic objectives.

Florida has also provided extensive legislation regulating access to the state highway system. Its State Highway System Access Management Act provides that a property owner has:

> a right to reasonable access to the abutting state highway but does not have the right of unregulated access to such highways. The operational capabilities of an access connection may be restricted by the department. However, a means of reasonable access to an abutting state highway may not be denied by the department, except on the basis of safety or operational concerns. . . . . [31]

The statute goes on to note that access shall be allowed "unless the permitting of such access would jeopardize the safety of the public or have a negative impact upon the operational characteristics of the highway."[32] The access management procedure is adopted by rule and defines the necessary supporting studies, appeals, and contains design standards and procedures for permit applications. Permits are required for all new connections, alterations of existing connections, median openings and acceleration and deceleration lanes. Access management classifications, median opening standards for controlled-access facilities, and interchange spacing for limited-access facilities are defined.[33]

Language of the Florida Access Management Act also serves to illustrate how modification of a statutory requirement that is determined to be too restrictive may result in modification. Initially, the statute language provided that a landowner had a right of reasonable access, but not a right of particular access. This language resulted in numerous challenges involving differences in opinion as to the exact meanings of the terms and complaints from landowners and developers. The language was changed in 1992 to the current version by legislative action as noted above to restrict a landowner only from unregulated access. Moreover, in the initial version, the department could deny direct access if "reasonable access may be provided pursuant to local regulations to another public road that abuts the property."[34]

The department has developed extensive documentation on access management.[35] Florida's access regulations and policies encompass interstate and other freeway interchange justification and location procedures.[36] The issue of access management also involves local land development regulations, as discussed in the next section of this chapter.

Local Regulation of Land Use

The focus of much of the regulation of land development and related transportation issues is at the local level. Local regulations shape the provision of private facilities and represent an arena of conflict and resolution for the transportation

---

[30] *Colorado Access Control Demonstration Project* and the *State Highway Access Code*, 2 CCR 601-1, as amended (Denver, Colo.: Colorado State Department of Highways, 1985).

[31] ' 335.181(2)(a), F.S.

[32] ' 335.184(3), F.S.

[33] *State Highway System Connection Permits, Administrative Process*, Rule Chapter 14-96, Florida Administrative Code; *Access Management Standards*, Rule Chapter 14-97, Florida Administrative Code.

[34] ' 335.181(2)(a) 1989 (emphasis added).

[35] *Median Handbook* (Tallahassee, Fla.: Florida Department of Transportation, 1997); *Interchange Request Development and Review Manual*, 2nd Ed., draft (Tallahassee, Fla.: Florida Department of Transportation, Nov. 1997).

[36] George L. Reed, "Revised Policies for Interstate Interchanges," *Technical Papers from ITE's 1990, 1989 and 1988 Conferences* (Washington, D.C.: ITE, 1990); also available through the *ITE Digital Library*, CD-ROM (Washington, D.C.: ITE, 1997).

professional. Local regulations take the form of zoning ordinances, subdivision regulations, and land development impact fees. In addition, other regulations may cover such subjects as parking standards or tree ordinances.

Governmental Authority to Regulate Land Development

Local authority to regulate land development within its jurisdictional area is well settled in law. However, the extent of this authority is not as clear and has continued as an evolving area of the law, with court actions and decisions shaping many interpretations and conclusions. The basis and current direction of local land use regulatory law is thus of more than just an academic interest.

Land use regulation has its roots in the conflict between public goals for the character and development of an area and individual rights to use their property in an unrestricted manner. Originally, public control was vested in court proceedings; but as issues became more frequent, governmental regulations became a more efficient control mechanism. In 1926, the landmark case of *Euclid v. Ambler Realty Company,* 272 U.S. 365 was decided by the U.S. Supreme Court, which held that land use laws and regulations were permissible because they were rationally related to the protection of public health, safety, and welfare. *Euclid* set the pace for zoning regulations; and if a public entity acts in a reasonable way, its principles still apply.

Zoning Ordinances

Zoning ordinances, regulations, and maps designate the overall type and balance of land use allowed within a particular area. Subdivision regulations, on the other hand, deal with development of specific sites or areas, the provision of infrastructure, design standards, and similar matters. Overall administration of both is normally vested in an area's planning commission or board. These are composed of elected, appointed, or part-time officials. Depending on the complexity of the area, several other entities may include:

1. Planning agencies—provide technical and administrative staff and services for the planning commissions.

2. Boards of zoning appeal—hear requests for variations and are normally separate from the planning commission, board, or agency.

3. Engineering departments—oversee design and construction of public facilities.

4. Building departments or permit agencies—administer the permitting and inspection process for construction or other regulated activities.

Zoning and land development regulations relate to growth management through density regulations (land use) and public facility requirements. The relationship of development approvals to any required comprehensive plan and the quantity and timing issues of development to traffic generation, loading, and street capacity are important.

Subdivision Regulations

Subdivision regulations normally apply when land is divided into two or more parcels for ownership transfer or creation of building lots. When land is subdivided or developed, many transportation requirements arise, including issues of access management. Lot size (density), land access design (driveway spacing and connection to the local or state street system), overall street and roadway classification schemes (arterial, collector, or land access roadways), and interchange spacing are examples.[37]

---

[37] K. Williams and J. Forester, *Land Development Regulations that Promote Access Management, NCHRP Synthesis 233* (Washington, D.C.: Transportation Research Board, 1996).

Subdivision regulations vary considerably by jurisdiction. An initial issue is whether the proposed land subdivision falls into an exempt category. Exemptions may relate to timing, number of lots created, need for public streets, size of lots created, and similar provisions.

Subdivision ordinances specify the procedural steps that must be followed. These normally include:

1. Preliminary conferences—submittal of a sketch plan of proposed subdivision and correlation with planning officials.

2. Formal application—submittal of a detailed plat, area map, preliminary engineering design, and application fees.

3. Public notification—may include formal reviews, hearings, and preliminary approval of the scheme of development.

4. Final submittals—to include final plat and engineering design, approval of construction plans and specifications, required fees or dedications, and formal acceptance by the public body.

During the entire process, there will be considerable interaction with various public agencies and departments. Being aware of all pertinent environmental, mitigation, and permitting requirements is very important as the project advances.

From a transportation standpoint, subdivision design standards normally encompass street geometric design, traffic and access control, location of public driveways, sidewalks, and other similar matters. Agencies normally publish their own standards, or may incorporate those of adjacent or state jurisdictions. These standards must be met, or variances must be received. A key to prompt resolution of differences is communication with the agency reviewers early in the design process to discuss any necessary variances or required changes.

Frequently, ancillary studies supporting the requested change or variance will be required These may include traffic impact studies, designs of special traffic control devices or other similar activities. Occasionally, jurisdictions may overlap and several sets of requirements or agencies will be involved. In these cases, extra coordination is required, and usually the more rigid standard must be met.

All fees, land dedications, construction commitments, permits, and other similar requirements usually must be presented at the time acceptance of the subdivision is requested, or otherwise must be secured by bond or cash deposit. Acceptance is through formal action of the appropriate governing body. Negotiations for the amount of the bond, or later bond reductions, can be intensive.

Subdivision Construction Ordinances

Special rules usually apply to the construction of subdivision improvements. Because the resulting construction will be accepted by the public agency for operation and maintenance, the agency will normally inspect the ongoing construction.

Two alternative procedures from the Memphis and Shelby County, Tennessee regulations illustrate subdivision construction options open to a developer:

1. If a developer wants to sell individual lots before construction of the public elements of the subdivision is completed, the required improvements must be secured by performance bonds (or alternatively, by letters of credit or cash deposits).

2. If the developer intends to complete construction before selling lots, a bond is not required.[38]

---

[38] *Subdivision Regulations* (Memphis and Shelby County, Tenn.: Office of Planning and Development, first published in 1985).

The land developer is usually responsible for construction of all land service streets (and other infrastructure elements as well) Responsibility for construction or improvement of major traffic service streets may vary depending upon the jurisdiction.

The regulations cited above also provide an example of how dedication and construction requirements vary by time and street function. In that jurisdiction, a subdivider must contribute to the improvement of all major roads and streets adjacent to the subdivision according to the roadway construction priority contained in the adopted urban area major road plan:

1. Road construction priorities of five years or less—the subdivider either constructs the roadway (all but final paving) or alternatively, contributes the construction funding and dedicates both right-of-way and right-of-access, as appropriate, for most major arterial and collector streets.

2. Priorities of five to fifteen years and all limited access facilities—the subdivider must dedicate right-of-way and right-of-access only.

3. Priorities more than fifteen years—dedication (at the option of the subdivider) or corridor reservation is required.[39]

Payments and dedications are made at the time of approval of the subdivision for construction. This process is triggered only when land is brought forward for development. Direct contribution of right-of-way in this manner is more efficient than later purchase through an impact fee, because the escalation of right-of-way cost is stopped as of the time of dedication. Proper corridors for necessary future streets are automatically reserved as land is developed.

Administrative Site Review

A special condition arises when land is to be developed but when subdivision regulations do not apply. The jurisdictional agency may only have administrative site review with no statutory rights to obtain needed right-of-way or other public improvements. In these cases, the agency may seek to convince the developer to contribute the necessary street rights-of-way or make other improvements, possibly as a credit against other project requirements. The developer may feel unduly influenced by this so-called "velvet fist" approach to provide dedications or other improvements without a specific statutory requirement. To complicate the issue, mounting a legal challenge against the government action is usually difficult because no formal request may be in existence. Moreover, another reason to oppose or delay the project may suddenly surface.

In such cases, both the developer and the public agency must proceed carefully. The private development may be unsuccessful without certain improvements, for which there may be no public funds. The public may suffer if the development occurs without some needed public facility. Thus, it may behoove the developer to provide extra improvements to ensure the success of the project. The public agency must be careful not to overreach minimal but necessary improvements.

Impact Fees

Impact fees are one-time charges, imposed upon development to provide some of the capital cost of public facilities made necessary by the development. From a transportation standpoint, impact fees are often based upon the size of the development and the traffic it generates.

Impact fees are usually payable at the time of development approval, or they may be secured (bond, a letter of credit, etc.) for later payment. Impact fees can be distinguished from impact taxes, which normally flow into the state's general fund and do not have the use-relationship restrictions of impact fees. A final comparison can be made between

---

[39] *Subdivision Regulations* (Memphis and Shelby County, Tenn.: Office of Planning and Development, first published in 1985).

impact and mitigation fees. Mitigation fees are assessed against development but can be used for infrastructure improvements throughout the urban area, where impact fees must relate to the development's specific impacts.

Impact fees are often characterized as an element of growth control. However, impact fees per se provide little influence upon location but address costs arising from the growth. Impact fees minimally affect the timing of growth and pay only some of the growth-induced cost. They surcharge new growth and ignore the problems created by existing growth. In addition, they are not "amenable to bonding; first, because they are volatile revenue streams tied to fluctuations in the business cycle and to rates of growth; and second, because they must be earmarked and expended carefully to avoid challenges to validity."[40] Nevertheless, impact fees are well established, and their use is expanding.

Evolution of Impact Fees

Impact fees originated in the 1960s as fees instead of land dedications. Court challenges during the 1970s focused upon statutory authority and the amount and use planned for such fees. A "rational nexus" test was established, which examines the relationship of the proposed fee to the development and how the funds will be spent.

Before the mid-1970s, Florida law did not allow impact fees. Since then, the state has become a leader in the use of impact fees placed upon development. In 1976, the Florida Supreme Court upheld the use of water and sewer facility fees in *Contractors and Builders Association of Pinellas County v. City of Dunedin*, 329 So.2d 314 (Fla. 1976). The court noted that such a fee should be limited to a *pro rata* share of reasonable costs to accommodate the development. Additional cases upheld this position, establishing the requirement that the fees be spent for the "substantial benefit" of the development, with a reasonable relationship between the need for additional facilities and the needs generated by the development, *Hollywood, Inc. v. Broward County*, 431 So.2d 606 (Fla. 4th DCA 1983).

Another Florida case, *Home Builders and Contractors Association v. Palm Beach County*, 446 So. 2d 140 (Fla. 4th DCA 1983) clearly established the validity of transportation impact fees. *Home Builders* followed national standards in requiring impacts from development to be distinguished from existing need, credits to be allowed for other fees, and earmarking of fees to benefit the development in question.

Impact fees have statutory recognition in Florida. With the requirement of comprehensive planning for all counties and municipalities, the Legislature encourages "innovative land development regulations that include provisions such as . . . impact fees."[41] Legislation codifies case law on impact fees, noting that they must have "a rational nexus to the proposed development, and the need to construct new facilities . . . must be reasonably attributable to the proposed development."[42]

Conditional Zoning, Developer Agreements, and Proffers

Although the entire development approval process is usually covered by regulations, negotiations can occur at any point. Frequently governmental approval will be based upon agreements with the land developer.

Conditional zoning (or rezoning) is approval of a scheme of development with particular conditions attached. These conditions normally remain with the land through subsequent transfer of title, and at times, may be made enforceable through a performance bond or another form of security. The conditions may include land dedication, a particular fee, or construction of a particular type of improvement.

A proffer is a similar form of conditional zoning and development approval that is a derivative if indirect form of an impact fee. A proffer is a voluntary offer of public improvements along with a rezoning request and may include

---

[40] *Impact Fees in Florida* (Tallahassee, Fla.: Florida Advisory Council on Intergovernmental Relations, Nov. 1986).

[41] ' 163.3202, F.S.

[42] ' 380.06(15)(e)1, F.S.

specific transportation improvements. For example, a developer may commit to a maximum site trip generation level, with project phasing and future development controlled by the success of the TSM program.

In contrast to impact fees, proffers can offer more flexibility in improvement funding, ease of administration, and reduction of the potential for litigation. On the other hand, they apply only to a particular issue and may result in complex negotiations. Proffers, when allowed, provide flexibility in addressing growth issues.

Transportation Management Associations

Transportation Management Associations (TMAs)[43] are the subject of special development agreements. TMAs and Trip Reduction Ordinances are both voluntary by nature. They form the basis to reduce peak-period traffic through private agreements. Techniques involve ridesharing, increased transit usage, variable work hours, parking management, and other similar strategies.

If an agreement can be reached upon strategies for trip reduction that will not detract from the function of a particular development, economies can result in the development that will be allowed, or in the overall impact fee that will result. The transportation planner will have a key role in determining reduction strategies and the potential transportation effect upon the function of a particular development.

Negotiation of Land Development Appeals, Variances, and Fees

An important area involving land development regulation is the negotiation of appeals, variances, and impact fees. Frequently, the transportation professional will be involved with requested changes from specific regulations, or negotiations of decisions and fees. These may be formal or informal, with the formal process encompassing a petition for rehearing, public notice, hearing, and formal decision.

The need for variances from engineering or planning standards frequently arises from development hardships of a particular site or surrounding area conditions, or a desire to provide a different type of development than may be allowed under the governing regulations. The Charlotte, North Carolina subdivision ordinance concisely summarizes the rationale for a variance:

1. The hardship results only from the application of the regulations.

2. The hardship is peculiar to the property in question.

3. The hardship prevents the owner from making a reasonable use of the property. (Greater profit is not considered grounds for a variance.)

4. The relationship of the property to natural topography or adjacent properties warrants relief.

5. A variance would preserve a historic structure or site.[44]

Negotiations can be extensive and can involve any element of the development approval process. For example, where a developer must preserve a level of service, negotiations can involve determination of street capacity; an internal trip capture ratio (amount of travel remaining within the project); trip generation for particular land uses; timing, extent, or financing of construction and many other similar facets. Most of these negotiations focus upon the amount of an impact fee or the timing of the payment based upon project phasing.

---

[43] Transportation Management *Associations* should not be confused with ISTEA's Transportation Management *Areas*.

[44] *Subdivision Ordinance*, as amended (City of Charlotte, N.C.: first published in 1985).

Negotiations can cover several topics:

1. If an impact fee is based strictly upon the number of units of development, flexibility in negotiation may be limited to project phasing or timing issues.

2. If the fee is based upon the number of trips or a trip generation rate, a different rate or fee may be negotiated through better data, the particular land use, or other similar components of the fee calculation.

3. Frequently, the internal trip capture ratio is an issue based upon the particular mix of land uses.

4. For capacity or service volume calculations, specific, timely, or otherwise better data may allow negotiation of established or default values.

5. Fee payments may vary by project phasing or timing, reductions due for transportation management considerations, or other similar elements.

6. Impact fee credits for contributions such as right-of-way contributions should always be included.

Formal, hostile, or adversarial challenges of agency decisions have the potential to polarize and publicize issues and establish positions from which retreat may be difficult. An open discussion of the needs of all parties, including equitable and reasonable solutions, has a much better chance of mutual success and agreement.

Traffic Calming and Neighborhood Street Ordinances

A recent development involves the use of "traffic calming" techniques, or those oriented to making urban streets more "pedestrian friendly" or less intrusive into neighborhood areas. Techniques such as lane narrowing, wider sidewalks, angle parking, curb extensions, roundabouts, or similar features are often requested to slow vehicular travel while providing an improved or more human-scaled environment. See Chapter 17 for more details.

A recent FHWA publication notes:

> One of the greatest challenges the highway community faces is providing safe, efficient transportation service that conserves, and even enhances the environment, scenic, historic, and community resources that are so vital to our way of life.[45]

The FHWA document stresses flexibility in design and does not establish new regulations or design procedures. However, requests involving these types of techniques sometimes conflict with traditional highway design and traffic engineering principles, and they may impinge upon safety practices. Inadequate attention to the conflict between aesthetics and safety can result in increased liability for the transportation agency. Regulations for these and similar roadway features should be closely monitored by the highway system planner and designer.

Other Local Ordinances

In the provision of transportation facilities, there are other regulations that must be observed. Two frequently encountered examples are tree or landscape ordinances and parking regulations.

Tree preservation, placement of new trees, and other landscaping features with development or the construction or reconstruction of roadway facilities has become an increasingly important issue for many jurisdictions. One typical tree ordinance requires a permit for the removal of any trees having a trunk diameter of six inches or more, measured

---

[45] *Flexibility in Highway Design* (Washington, D.C.: U.S. DOT, FHWA, 1997).

4-$\frac{1}{2}$ feet above ground level. The permit application requires a site plan and an explanation of the need for removal. The ordinance includes tree planting requirements and protection of existing trees during construction. Visibility standards are also set for intersections interior to a development, as well as connections to the urban street system.[46]

Provisions for automobile parking are found in zoning ordinances or separately in parking ordinances. These may specify the number (maximum or minimum) of parking spaces that must be provided for a particular type of land use and development, or by specific area within a city such as the central business district. Such regulations may also allow a reduced number of parking spaces with development of rail transit or land redevelopment proposals.

Parking ordinances, along with the State Transportation Code, also regulate the use of public streets for parking (curb parking), and the use of off-street parking facilities. Special provisions may relate to the right of a local area to establish a separate parking authority, to restrict parking within specific areas to certain user groups, or the right to issue bonds to finance the construction of parking facilities.

Government Acquisition of Land

The transportation planner or engineer may also be involved with land acquisition for construction projects or maintenance purposes. There are many laws and procedures involved in this function. The subject is well documented.[47]

State and local governments have several processes for acquisition of private lands for public purposes. The federal and state constitutions that grant the necessary acquisition powers also provide significant protection for the private landowner. The basic powers have also been shaped through court decisions and statutory provisions. Acquisition can be by donation, direct purchase, or condemnation.

Acquisition of right-of-way by donation is common. This will facilitate a project and often offers tax benefits or impact fee credits to a private party. Agreeable sale and purchase, with good faith negotiation, is a second method of property acquisition. A willing seller, coupled with a fair offer from the public entity, can facilitate a speedy transfer of ownership. This method of acquisition is usually covered by statute or rule. Should negotiations fail, the discussions of the parties probably will not be admissible as later evidence.

A more common method for public acquisition involves condemnation through the power of eminent domain. This process allows the public entity to condemn and purchase private property for public use. Payment is due when the land is acquired. Usually, each state or local agency will have a statutory scheme for eminent domain. These statutes cover the procedures and protection due to the private party. The eminent domain powers of the public agency are not limitless. Just or full-and-fair compensation is required, and if the amount becomes an issue, it usually requires a jury determination. The public agency may also be responsible for all costs of the resulting court proceeding for both sides, certain relocation expenses, and other purchase costs.

Land acquisition involving federal-aid funds has additional requirements for nondiscrimination, relocation assistance and other individual protection.[48] An important consideration for state and local government is that no matter how the land is acquired, federal regulations must be met if federal-aid is to be received.

Inverse Condemnation

Of greater interest are public actions that result in only a partial taking, or that deprives a private owner of substantial, economic use of the property without compensation. These results frequently occur from an application of a regulation in a manner to result in a "taking" of a substantial interest in the property, but without a direct invasion or condemnation.

---

[46] *Tree Protection and Landscape Regulations* (Jacksonville, Fla.: Florida Ordinance Code 656.12, 1990).

[47] J. Maiorana, *Corridor Preservation, NCHRP Synthesis 197* (Washington, D.C.: Transportation Research Board, 1994).

[48] 23 C.F.R. 710–712.

Like the corridor preservation issues discussed below, such an action is an "inverse condemnation." Inverse condemnation results when private property is indirectly taken for public use, without compensation as in a regular condemnation proceeding. It is a legal theory allowing private landowners to recover damages for depletion of their property rights.

Transportation Corridor Preservation

A major issue involves preservation of transportation corridors for future development. Rapid land development may result in prohibitive later costs of transportation right-of-way or extensive disruption to adjacent development. Nevertheless, other than actual purchase, there are few methods available to preserve lands for transportation corridors without triggering claims for condemnation or running aground on the federal land acquisition procedures. Although there are a few procedures for advanced acquisition, these have been used infrequently.

Transportation location decisions have traditionally been based upon priority and demonstrated need. By the time a need develops, many land use decisions will have been made that affect the timing, cost, environmental impact and feasibility of the proposed transportation improvements to existing facilities. Further development and higher cost may have occurred by the time actual construction begins. Increased right-of-way costs result.

States cannot normally act unilaterally in transportation corridor preservation issues because federal aid is frequently involved. In simple terms, federal funds cannot be used for transportation land purchase before receipt of location approval from FHWA for the project. In turn, this requires examination of the environmental effect of the project under the NEPA requirements. This is achieved through either a basic environmental assessment or a detailed environmental impact statement for projects that will significantly affect the environment.

Considering that funds may not be available for immediate purchase, states have attempted to preserve lands for transportation by legislation that precludes private development within the corridor. States are allowed considerable leeway in transportation facility planning, design, land appraisals, or negotiations without triggering inverse condemnation recoveries. However, once a state acts to preclude development or use of private lands, such as denying development permits or other legal interference without payment, inverse condemnation claims may result.[49]

Recent case law in "takings" issues turn on deprivation of "substantial economic rights," and the issues involved have reached both the U.S. and state supreme courts. Several U.S. Supreme Court decisions illustrate how this trend in the law continues to develop.

In *Agins v. City of Tiburon*, 447 U.S. 255 (1980), the issues of a land downzoning as a taking reached the U.S. Supreme Court, but they were not clearly resolved. In 1987, *First Evangelical Lutheran Church of Glendale v. County of Los Angeles*, 482 U.S. 304 (1987), the Court held that a taking through a land use regulation would require compensation. It was further pointed out that should the government later change its mind about the regulation, compensation would still be due for the time the taking affected the value of the property. Then, in *Nollan v. California Coastal Commission*, 483 U.S. 825 (1987), the Court further limited uncompensated takings by holding that a land dedication exaction must substantially advance a legitimate governmental interest, and underlined a government's duty to pay for land it condemns for public purposes. *Dolan v. City of Tigard*, 512 U.S. 374 (1994) provided another step in dimensioning a public agency's rights to condition development approval upon a land exaction. In *Dolan* the Court required a "rough proportionality" of the exaction to the issue at hand. Thus, the requirement of a legitimate government interest established in *Nollan* was developed further in *Dolan*, establishing that the exaction must be proportional to the proposed development.

States have also acted in issues of land exactions and takings. In 1995, Florida comprehensively increased the protection for private property against unjust governmental takings of land:

---

[49] A.B. Kolis and D.R. Mandelker, "Legal Techniques for Reserving Right-of-Way for Future Projects Including Corridor Protection," *Research Results Digest 165* (Washington, D.C.: Transportation Research Board, Nov. 1987); Also in *Selected Studies in Highway Law 2* (Washington, D.C.: Transportation Research Board, June 1988).

some laws, regulations, and ordinances of the state and political entities . . . may inordinately burden, restrict, or limit private property rights without amounting to a taking under the State Constitution or the United States Constitution. The Legislature determines that there is an important state interest in protecting the interests of private property owners from such inordinate burdens. Therefore, it is the intent of the Legislature that, as a separate and distinct cause of action from the law of takings, the Legislature herein provides for relief, or payment of compensation, when a new law, rule, regulation, or ordinance of the state or a political entity in the state, as applied, unfairly affects real property.[50]

This law creates a new cause of action for landowners against any jurisdiction within the state, protects landowners against actual takings, and includes regulatory actions that do not result in a taking.

Beyond questions of constitutionality, land taking issues usually result in a duel of expert witnesses in an attempt to prove or disprove damages. If a substantial economic deprivation is found to have occurred, damages to the owner will usually result.

Transportation Funding

An important regulatory topic involves funding transportation improvements. Traditional funding methods, including federal programs, are well established in law and have been covered briefly in preceding sections of this chapter. Innovative methods seek to overcome the traditional limits of tax-based funding by deriving funds from specific developments.

As noted earlier, impact fees provide additional funds but have shortcomings. Impact fees tend to lag development and do not directly aid the concurrency requirement. When "pipelining" (or concentrating funds on specific facilities) is allowed, flexibility results. When funds are pipelined, all needed facilities may not be improved. Moreover, impact fees are applied to development and do not cover existing deficiencies caused by earlier growth and development.

Special taxing districts hold some, if limited, promise. These allow receipt of special taxes or other funds to cover transportation improvements within a specific area. Bonding allows advanced construction. Like many other localized taxes, these could result in shifts of development, could affect the provision of economic facilities, and cannot normally be used for public facilities outside the special taxing district.

If allowed by state statute, transportation corporations are possibilities. These are different from taxing districts in that more powers are provided for construction of specific facilities, providing a means to concentrate emphasis on specific facilities or within a specific area. They allow receipt of right-of-way contributions, funding, and other concentrated efforts. The corporation may terminate after completion of the improvements, or it may continue to operate the facility. Some states may allow a general form of a transportation corporation but restrict some powers such as limiting the issuance of bonds, contracts, or prohibiting the actual construction of facilities.[51]

Community development districts (CDDs) are another special entity. Within a CDD, special governmental planning, environmental, and land development regulations apply. Depending on state law, a CDD may acquire and hold land, borrow money, issue bonds, levy and collect taxes and other assessments, or execute other powers. CDDs can often acquire, construct, and operate all types of infrastructure facilities, including streets and roads of every type.[52]

All property owners within a proposed CDD must normally agree to its formation. The CDD offers an attractive way to finance and construct needed infrastructure improvements to serve large developments. The idea offers a way to meet the concurrency requirement regarding infrastructure and development. It also allows pre-development funding available without avoiding existing laws, which can be a major problem of the more traditional forms of financing.

---

[50] *Bert J. Harris, Jr., Private Property Rights Protection Act,* ' 70.001(1), F.S.

[51] *Florida Transportation Corporation Act,* ' 339.412, F.S.

[52] *Uniform Community Development District Act of 1980,* ' 190.03, F.S.

Finally, while toll roads and bridges are an old concept, the use of this technique has enjoyed a revitalization. For example, Florida has undertaken a statewide expansion of its toll road system based, in part, with income formerly used to pay for now-retired Turnpike bonds.[53] Other areas are considering establishment of new toll roads and bridges as well. A special form is the public–private partnership where private funding covers a part or all of the construction of a facility and is recouped through tolls. Several forms of partnerships are possible.[54]

Regulation of Professionals

A final area involves the regulation of professional practice for transportation engineers and planners. In the United States, the individual states have the authority to regulate certain professional activities to protect the public from undesirable or unsafe actions. Regulation of professionals covers a broad spectrum, ranging from actions required by legal dictate, to those emphasized by professional canons of ethics, honesty, and common sense. The professional will achieve greater credibility and acceptance of his or her opinions and recommendations when those pronouncements are considered honest.

Usually, professionals licensed by a state will be regulated by licensing statues and rules of a state regulatory agency. For example, the practice of engineering is regulated by the individual states and provinces based on public welfare or safeguarding of life, health, and property. Engineers must pass examinations of academic and applied subjects, and they must normally complete a period of service as engineers-in-training. Individuals licensed as engineers must then follow the rules of their regulatory board, or face discipline for violations. Among other things, the regulations require that engineers only offer services in their areas of expertise and prohibit unlicensed practitioners from offering such services. Many states now require evidence of continued professional competency (continuing education) for license renewal.

A second level of guidance is contained in the Canons of Ethics of professional societies and organizations. While these may not carry the force of law, they provide appropriate guidance for professional activities. A logical example is the Canon of Ethics of the Institute of Transportation Engineers (ITE), which, among other things, notes that an ITE member will:

1. Use professional knowledge and skill for the advancement of human welfare.

2. Be honest and impartial in dealing with employer, clients, and the public.

3. Strive to increase the competence and prestige of the profession.

While these three principles are idealized, the Canon goes on to provide nearly two dozen specific guidance statements covering many areas of practice.[55] Other professional associations have similar guidance for members.

A final subject area involves consistency and credibility for professional statements, findings, and recommendations. Professional opinions may often differ, particularly in certain areas such as traffic impact studies or expert witness areas. However, underlying studies should be honestly done, based on correct and complete facts and data, and use reasonable assumptions and credible methodologies. A special report of an ITE Coordinating Council addressed this subject, noting that despite the individual or professional role, "credibility is necessary in order . . . to convince decision-makers to make what we think are the correct decisions."[56]

---

[53] *Florida's Turnpike Futures Report* (Turnpike District, Tallahasse, Fla.: FDOT, 1997).

[54] *Transportation Finance for the 21st Century*, Conference Proceedings 15 (Washington, D.C.: Transportation Research Board, 1997). For a discussion of public transportation funding methodologies, see *Funding Strategies for Public Transportation*, Vol. 1, *Final Report*; and Vol. 2, *Casebook*, Transit Cooperative Research Program Report 31 (Washington, D.C.: Transportation Research Board 1998).

[55] *Canons of Ethics*, adopted 1970 and amended through 1996 (Washington, D.C.: ITE).

[56] ITE Coordinating Council, "How to Avoid Technical Inconsistency and Maintain Credibility," *ITE Journal* (Washington, D.C.: ITE, April 1997).

Summary

The intent of this chapter has been to provide a brief overview of the extensive and rapidly changing regulatory environment for transportation. Yet it has been possible to only provide examples of typical statutes, ordinances, and policies from diverse jurisdictions.

There are several other important subject areas having legal or regulatory implications. They include environmental regulations, transportation facility negligence, and contractual matters. Environmental law has been briefly covered in a preceding chapter. Transportation facility negligence falls within the legal area of torts (civil wrongs), is extensive, evolving, often unique to a particular jurisdiction, and beyond the scope of this chapter. The transportation engineer or planner involved in this area of the law will be interested in jurisdictional issues and questions involving design standards or safety issues. Contract law involves the acquisition or provision of professional services and is also an extensive area of law. Many references may be found covering all these subject areas.

Finally, it is hoped that each transportation professional would have a working understanding of the basic regulatory framework covering his or her area of responsibility. This understanding can be formed by a reasonable investigation into the laws, ordinances, and regulations underlying a particular set of policies and procedures. With this basic understanding, although complicated issues remain the province of an attorney, transportation professionals can proceed with confidence, knowing their work meets the objectives of their clients, the government entity, and the public.

INDEX

A

Access relationships 456, 458

Activity centers 98–99, 102, 104, 431–432, 554, 560–562, 573
academic complexes 560
central business districts 562, 565
characteristics of downtowns 564
downtown travel 567
CBD work trips by transit 567
midday trip making 567
parking principles, pedestrian circulation principles 569
planning concepts and principles 568
traffic circulation principles 569
transit principles 569
employment trends 563
population trends 563, 564
real estate market trends 562
travel characteristics 565, 568
colleges, universities, and medical centers 570
medical center operations 572
transportation planning principles 569, 573
bicycles, emergency access (medical centers), goods and services, parking, pedestrian circulation, transit 571
implementation of transportation plans 597
institutional instruments 597
industrial users 560
medical centers 560, 562, 570
office parks 560, 575
regional shopping centers 560, 582
significant traffic generators 560
suburban activity centers 560, 573–574
origins and development 574
activity center characteristics 575
transportation planning 584

transportation planning principles 585
parking 586
roadway system and traffic circulation 586
transit 586
transportation-related issues 585
general roadway system characteristic, internal circulation, parking, property access, regional access, service, through traffic, transportation improvements, travel projections 585
transportation planning methodology 587
activity center analyses 595
facility traffic or transit volume, land use and demographic projections, parking, system capacity analysis, traffic signal system, transit ridership, travel patterns, trip generation 595
building for the pedestrian 588
managing demand 591
parking 594
planning scope 587
streets and highways 593
transit 588, 590
transportation terminals 560
travel characteristics at suburban centers 578
parking characteristics 583
residential 576–577, 582–583
retail center trips 580–581
internal trips to major retail centers 581
office employee trips 581
suburban center commute 578
types of activity centers 560, 562
colleges and universities 560, 570
downtowns 560–564, 568
institutional complexes 560–561
major government centers 560
medical centers 560

Aerial tramway 430, 784

Airports and ports 4

American Public Transit Association 284, 427, 498, 828

Articulated bus 231, 430, 449, 697

Associated vehicle stock 4

Automated guideway 439, 453

Automated guideway transit 232, 430, 454, 746, 781

Automated highways 10

Automated systems 298, 438, 446, 453

B

Bangladesh 19

Bicycle and Pedestrian Facilities 599, 602, 610, 612
bicycle facility design 617
appropriate bicycle facility type 619
bicycle storage and parking 629
bicycle parking types 629
bike lane striping 620
bikeway types 621
bike lanes 623
bike routes (signed shared roadways) 621
paved shoulders 625
shared roadways 621
wide outside lane 623
Guide for the Development of Bicycle Facilities 617
multi-use trails 627
selecting roadway design treatments to accommodate bicyclists 617
spot improvements 626
at-grade railroad crossings, bicycle-safe drainage grates, bridge crossings, manholes and utility covers, street maintenance work 626
The Americans with Disabilities Act Accessibility Guidelines 617
The Manual on Uniform Traffic Control Devices 617
global perspective 600